List of Minicases

www.mcgrawhill.ca/edumarketinsight

Check out your textbook's Web site for details on how this special offer enhances the value of your purchase!

Welcome to the Educational Version of Market Insight!

1. To get started, use your Web browser to go to **www.mcgrawhill.ca/edumarketinsight.**

2. Enter your site ID exactly as it appears below.

3. You may be prompted to enter the site ID for future use—please keep this card.

Your site ID is:

am17a425

*If you purchased a used book, this site ID may have expired. For new password purchase, please go to **www.mcgrawhill.ca/edumarketinsight**. Password activation is good for a 6-month duration.

CORPORATE FINANCE

FIFTH CANADIAN EDITION

Stephen A. Ross

Sloan School of Management
Massachusetts Institute of Technology

Randolph W. Westerfield

Marshall School of Business
University of Southern California

Jeffrey F. Jaffe

Wharton School of Business
University of Pennsylvania

Gordon S. Roberts

Schulich School of Business
York University

McGraw-Hill Ryerson

Toronto Montréal Boston Burr Ridge, IL Dubuque, IA Madison, WI New York
San Francisco St. Louis Bangkok Bogotá Caracas Kuala Lumpur Lisbon London
Madrid Mexico City Milan New Delhi Santiago Seoul Singapore Sydney Taipei

To our parents, family, and friends with love and gratitude.
S.A.R.
R.W.W.
J.F.J.

To the memory of my parents, who encouraged me to write.
G.S.R.

McGraw-Hill Ryerson

Corporate Finance
Fifth Canadian Edition

Copyright © 2008, 2005, 2003, 1999, 1995 by McGraw-Hill Ryerson Limited, a Subsidiary of The McGraw-Hill Companies. All rights reserved. No part of this publication may be reproduced or transmitted in any form or by any means, or stored in a data base or retrieval system, without the prior written permission of McGraw-Hill Ryerson Limited, or in the case of photocopying or other reprographic copying, a licence from The Canadian Copyright Licensing Agency (Access Copyright). For an Access Copyright licence, visit www. accesscopyright.ca or call toll free to 1-800-893-5777.

ISBN-13: 978-0-07-096531-7
ISBN-10: 0-07-096531-5

3 4 5 6 7 8 9 10 TCP 0 9

Printed and bound in Canada.

Care has been taken to trace ownership of copyright material contained in this text; however, the publisher will welcome any information that enables them to rectify any reference or credit for subsequent editions.

Editorial Director: Joanna Cotton
Senior Sponsoring Editor: Rhondda McNabb
Sponsoring Editor: Kimberley Redhead
Senior Marketing Manager: Joy Armitage Taylor
Senior Developmental Editor: Maria Chu
Editorial Associate: Stephanie Hess
Supervising Editor: Joanne Limebeer
Copy Editor: Evan Turner
Senior Production Coordinator: Madeleine Harrington
Cover Design: Sharon Lucas
Cover Image: © FirstLight
Interior Design: Sharon Lucas
Page Layout: Laserwords Private Limited
Printer: Transcontinental Printing Group

Library and Archives Canada Cataloguing in Publication Data

Corporate finance / Stephen A. Ross . . . [et al.].—5th Canadian ed.

Includes Bibliographical references and index.
ISBN 978-0-07-096531-7

    1. Corporations—Finance—Textbooks. 2. Corporations—Canada—Finance—Textbooks. I. Ross, Stephen A

HG4026.C64 2008   658.15   C2007-905149-9

About the Authors

STEPHEN A. ROSS *Sloan School of Management, Massachusetts Institute of Technology* Stephen Ross is presently the Franco Modigliani Professor of Financial Economics at the Sloan School of Management, Massachusetts Institute of Technology. One of the most widely published authors in finance and economics, Professor Ross is recognized for his work in developing the Arbitrage Pricing Theory, as well as for having made substantial contributions to the discipline through his research in signalling, agency theory, option pricing, and the theory of the term structure of interest rates, among other topics. A past president of the American Finance Association, he currently serves as an associate editor of several academic and practitioner journals. He is a trustee of CalTech, and a director of the College Retirement Equity Fund (CREF), Freddie Mac, and Algorithmics Inc. He is also the co-chairman of Roll and Ross Asset Management Corporation.

RANDOLPH W. WESTERFIELD *Marshall School of Business, University of Southern California* Randolph W. Westerfield is Dean of the University of Southern California's Marshall School of Business and holder of the Robert R. Dockson Dean's Chair of Business Administration.

He came to USC from the Wharton School, University of Pennsylvania, where he was the chairman of the finance department and a member of the finance faculty for 20 years. He is a member of several public company boards of directors including Health Management Associates Inc., William Lyon Homes, and the Nicholas Applegate growth fund. His areas of expertise include corporate financial policy, investment management, and stock market price behaviour.

JEFFREY F. JAFFE *Wharton School of Business, University of Pennsylvania* Jeffrey F. Jaffe has been a frequent contributor to finance and economic literature in such journals as the *Quarterly Economic Journal, The Journal of Finance, The Journal of Financial and Quantitative Analysis, The Journal of Financial Economics,* and *The Financial Analysts Journal.* His best known work concerns insider trading, where he showed both that corporate insiders earn abnormal profits from their trades and that regulation has little effect on these profits. He has also made contributions concerning initial public offerings, regulation of utilities, the behaviour of marketmakers, the fluctuation of gold prices, the theoretical effect of inflation on the interest rate, the empirical effect of inflation on capital asset prices, the relationship between small capitalization stocks and the January effect, and the capital structure decision.

GORDON S. ROBERTS *Schulich School of Business, York University* Gordon Roberts is Canadian Imperial Bank of Commerce Professor of Financial Services at the Schulich School of Business, York University. A winner of numerous teaching awards, his extensive experience includes finance classes for undergraduate and MBA students, managers, and bankers. Professor Roberts conducts research in corporate finance and banking. He serves on the editorial boards of several Canadian and international academic journals. Professor Roberts has been a consultant to a number of organizations, including the Office of the Superintendent of Financial Institutions, the Canada Deposit Insurance Corporation, and Canada Investment and Savings, as well as the Debt Management Office of New Zealand. He has appeared as an expert witness on utility rates of return and capital structures in regulatory hearings in Nova Scotia, Quebec, Ontario, and Alberta.

Brief Contents

Table of Contents

Chapter 5

The Time Value of Money   95

Chapter 6

How to Value Bonds and Stocks   132

Chapter 7

Net Present Value and Other Investment Rules   171

Chapter 8

Net Present Value and Capital Budgeting   204

Chapter 9

Risk Analysis, Real Options, and Capital Budgeting 240

Part 3

Risk 266

Chapter 10

Risk and Return: Lessons from Market History 266

Chapter 11

Risk and Return: The Capital Asset Pricing Model (CAPM) 288

Chapter 12

**An Alternative View of Risk and Return:
The Arbitrage Pricing Theory   329**

Chapter 13

Risk, Return, and Capital Budgeting   352

Part 4

Capital Structure and Dividend Policy   385

Chapter 14

**Corporate Financing Decisions and
Efficient Capital Markets   385**

Chapter 18

Valuation and Capital Budgeting for the Levered Firm   511

Chapter 19

Dividends and Other Payouts   533

Part 5

Long-Term Financing   569

Chapter 20

Issuing Equity Securities to the Public   569

Chapter 21

Long-Term Debt 596

Chapter 22

Leasing 623

Part 6

Options, Futures, and Corporate Finance 648

Chapter 23

Options and Corporate Finance: Basic Concepts 648

Preface

The teaching and the practice of corporate finance in Canada is more challenging and exciting than ever before. The last decade has seen fundamental changes in financial markets and financial instruments. In the early years of the 21st century, we still see announcements in the financial press about such matters as takeovers, junk bonds, financial restructuring, initial public offerings, bankruptcy, and derivatives. In addition, there is the new recognition of "real" options (Chapters 21 and 22), private equity and venture capital (Chapter 19), and the reappearing dividend (Chapter 18). The world's financial markets are more integrated than ever before. Both the theory and practice of corporate finance have been moving ahead with uncommon speed, and our teaching must keep pace.

These developments place new burdens on the teaching of corporate finance. On one hand, the changing world of finance makes it more difficult to keep materials up to date. On the other hand, the teacher must distinguish the permanent from the temporary and avoid the temptation to follow fads. Our solution to this problem is to emphasize the modern fundamentals of the theory of finance and make the theory come to life with contemporary examples. All too often, the beginning student views corporate finance as a collection of unrelated topics that are unified largely because they are bound together between the covers of one book. As in the previous editions, our aim is to present corporate finance as the working of a small number of integrated and powerful institutions.

The Intended Audience of This Book

This book has been written for the introductory courses in corporate finance at the MBA level and for the intermediate courses in many undergraduate programs. Some instructors will find our text appropriate for the introductory course at the undergraduate level as well.

We assume that most students either will have taken, or will be concurrently enrolled in, courses in accounting, statistics, and economics. This exposure will help students understand some of the more difficult material. However, the book is self-contained, and a prior knowledge of these areas is not essential. The only mathematics prerequisite is basic algebra.

New to the Fifth Canadian Edition

Following are key revisions and updates to this edition:

- Expanded discussion of **corporate social responsibility**, **taxation of income trusts**, and *Sarbanes-Oxley* in Chapter 1.
- Updates of **capital market data** through 2006 in Chapter 10. More details added on the **geometric vs. arithmetic mean**.
- Updated discussion of **best practices in computing the weighted average cost of capital** with a new detailed example based on Rogers Communications Inc.
- New discussion of **research results on IPOs** in Chapter 20.
- Amplified coverage of **leasing and taxes** in Chapter 22.

• **Minicases** added to most chapters.
• **New problems** added in most chapters.

Below are the new and updated fifth edition features.

Learning Solutions

Keeping the theory and concepts current and up-to-date is only one phase of developing a corporate finance text. To be an effective teaching tool, the text must present the theory and concepts in a coherent way that can be easily learned. With this in mind, we have included several study features:

Executive Summary

Each chapter begins with a "roadmap" that describes the objectives of the chapter and how it connects with concepts already learned in previous chapters. Real company examples that will be discussed are highlighted in this section.

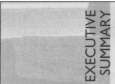

EXECUTIVE SUMMARY

Chapter 2 describes the basic accounting statements used for reporting corporate activity. It focuses on practical details of cash flow. It will become clear in the next several chapters that knowing how to determine cash flow helps the financial manager make better decisions. The increasing number of corporate accounting scandals involving companies such as Hollinger, Tyco, and Adelphia has highlighted the importance of accurate financial reporting. Students who have had accounting courses will not find the material new and can think of it as a review with an emphasis on finance. We discuss cash flow further in later chapters.

In Their Own Words Boxes

Located throughout the chapters, this unique series consists of articles written by distinguished scholars or practitioners on key topics in the text.

IN THEIR OWN WORDS

B. Espen Eckbo on Corporate Governance

Voluntary shareholder absenteeism and a powerful culture of "corporate insiders" have led to a crisis in corporate governance. Without a fundamental shift in the balance of power, the problems will only worsen. Recent corporate scandals have resurrected public suspicion that there is plenty of potential for mischief inside large public companies.

governance crisis. The important historical lesson is that the absentee shareholder system breeds arrogance on the part of corporate insiders. A vigorous corporate governance system is thus required to prevent shareholder rights being expropriated by insiders.

A major task of the board is to hire and fire top managers, and to set their compensation. Therefore, corpo-

Concept Questions

Included after each major section in a chapter, Concept Questions point to essential material and allow students to test their recall and comprehension before moving forward.

Figures and Tables

This text makes extensive use of real data and presents them in various figures and tables. Explanations in the narrative, examples, and end-of-chapter problems will refer to many of these exhibits.

Examples

Separate called-out examples are integrated throughout the chapters. Each example illustrates an intuitive or mathematical application in a step-by-step format. There is enough detail in the explanations that the student doesn't have to look elsewhere for additional information.

EXAMPLE 6.1

Selected bond trading figures for November 16, 2006 appear in Figure 6.2. Suppose an investor was interested in the EDC 5.000 Feb 09/09. This is jargon that means the bond was issued by Export Development Canada, a federal Crown corporation, and the annual coupon rate is 5.00 percent.[i] The face value is $1,000, implying that the yearly coupon is $50.00 (5% × $1,000). Interest is paid each February and August implying that the coupon every six months is $25 ($50/2). The face value will be paid out in February 2009, two years later. By this we mean that the purchaser obtains claims to the following cash flows:

Feb-07	Aug-07	Feb-08	Aug-08	Feb-09
$25	$25	$25	$25	$25 + $1,000

Equations

Key equations are numbered and highlighted for easy reference.

Highlighted Concepts

Throughout the text, important ideas are pulled out and presented in a box—signalling to students that this material is particularly relevant and critical to their understanding.

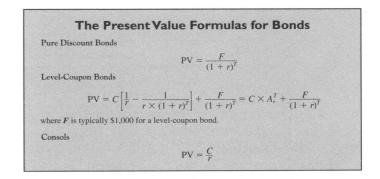

The Present Value Formulas for Bonds

Pure Discount Bonds

$$PV = \frac{F}{(1 + r)^T}$$

Level-Coupon Bonds

$$PV = C\left[\frac{1}{r} - \frac{1}{r \times (1 + r)^T}\right] + \frac{F}{(1 + r)^T} = C \times A_r^T + \frac{F}{(1 + r)^T}$$

where F is typically $1,000 for a level-coupon bond.

Consols

$$PV = \frac{C}{r}$$

End-of-Chapter Material

The end-of-chapter material reflects and builds upon the concepts learned from the chapter and study features.

Summary and Conclusions

The numbered summary provides a quick review of key concepts in the chapter.

5.6 SUMMARY AND CONCLUSIONS

1. Two basic concepts, *future value* and *present value*, were introduced in the beginning of this chapter. With a 10 percent interest rate, an investor with $1 today can generate a future value of $1.10 in a year, $1.21 [$1 × (1.10)²] in two years, and so on. Conversely, present value analysis places a current value on a later cash flow. With the same 10 percent interest rate, a dollar to be received in one year has a present value of $0.909($1/1.10) in year 0. A dollar to be received in two years has a present value of $0.826 [$1/(1.10)²].

2. One commonly expresses the interest rate as, say, 12 percent per year. However, one can speak of the interest rate as 3 percent per quarter. Although the stated annual interest rate remains 12 percent (3 percent × 4), the effective annual interest rate is 12.55 percent [(1.03)⁴ − 1]. In other words, the compounding process increases the future value of an investment. The limiting case is continuous compounding, where funds are assumed to be reinvested every infinitesimal instant.

List of Key Terms

A list of the boldfaced key terms in the text with page numbers is included for easy reference.

Suggested Readings

Each chapter is followed by a short, annotated list of books, articles, and websites to which interested students can refer for additional information on key topics.

Questions and Problems

Because solving problems is so critical to a student's learning, new questions and problems have been added, and existing questions and problems have been revised. All problems have also been thoroughly reviewed and accuracy-checked.

Problems have been grouped according to the concepts they test on, with the concept headings listed at the beginning of each group.

Additionally, we have tried to make the problems in the critical "concept" chapters, such as those on value, risk, and capital structure, especially challenging and interesting.

We provide answers to selected problems in Appendix B, located on the OLC at *www.mcgrawhill.ca/olc/ross*.

S&P Problems

Now included in the end-of-chapter material are problems directly incorporating the Educational Version of Market Insight, a service based on Standard & Poor's renowned Compustat database. These problems provide you with an easy method of including current real-world data into the finance course. This Web-based resource is available with each new copy of the text.

STANDARD &POOR'S	11.35 Go to the "Excel Analytics" link for Nexen Inc. (NXY) and Thomson Corp. (TOC) and download the monthly adjusted stock prices. Copy the monthly returns for each stock into a new spreadsheet. Calculate the covariance and correlation between the two stock returns. Would you expect a higher or lower correlation if you had chosen Petro-Canada (PCA) instead of Thomson Corp.? What is the standard deviation of a portfolio 75 percent invested in NXY and 25 percent in TOC? What about a portfolio equally invested in the two stocks? What about a portfolio 25 percent in NXY and 75 percent in TOC?

EXCEL

Excel Problems

Indicated by the Excel icon in the margin, these problems can be found at the end of almost all chapters. Located on the book's website, Excel templates have been created for each of these problems, where students can use the data in the problem to work out the solution using Excel skills.

Minicase

This end-of-chapter feature, located in most chapters, parallels the Case Study feature found in various chapters. These Minicases apply what is learned in a number of chapters to a real-world type of scenario. After presenting the facts, the student is given guidance in rationalizing a sound business decision.

MINICASE: I.Q. Inc.

In order to maintain its leadership position in the computer peripherals industry, particularly inkjet printers and accessories, I.Q. has begun to develop a new ink for its 8xx line of inkjet printers. As a marketing manager of the 8xx line of inkjet printers and accessories, you are in the position to make a decision whether or not to continue the development. The project is codenamed IQ8Ink.

Research efforts for the IQ8Ink have cost I.Q. Inc. $2 million so far, in addition to a positive test marketing effort costing $0.75 million. However, these are sunk costs and will not impact your decision making. What should be considered are the new investment and future cash inflows. From your observation, you know that you

As for the potential customers, there are two distinct segments:

1. New 8xx printers—For every new 8xx printer, one unit of this new ink will be used. (Assume complete retirement of old ink models with no costs associated.) Internal transfer price is at $1.75 now. The variable cost to produce per unit is $0.50.

2. Existing 8xx printers—While competitors exist, offering generic ink, IQ8Ink is superior and will take a large percentage of market share. Wholesale price is at $11 now. The variable cost to produce per unit is the same as above.

Technology Solutions

LYRYX LEARNING INC
Online Learning and Assessment
lyryx.com

Lyryx for Finance

Lyryx Assessment for Finance is a leading-edge online assessment system, designed to support both students and instructors. The assessment takes the form of a homework assignment called a Lab. The assessments are algorithmically generated and automatically graded so that students get instant grades and feedback. New Labs are randomly generated each time, providing the student with unlimited opportunities to try a type of question. After they submit a Lab for marking, students receive extensive feedback on their work, thus promoting their learning experience.

Lyryx for the student offers algorithmically generated and automatically graded assignments. Students get instant grades and instant feedback—no need to wait until the next class to find out how well they did! Grades are instantly recorded in a grade book that the student can view.

Students are motivated to do their Labs for two reasons: first because the results can be tied to assessment, and second, because they can try the Lab as many times as they wish prior to the due date, with only their best grade being recorded.

Instructors know from experience that if students do their finance homework, they will be successful in the course. Recent research regarding the use of Lyryx has shown that when Labs are tied to assessment, even if worth only a small percentage of the total grade of the course, students WILL do their homework—and MORE THAN ONCE!

Please contact your *i*Learning Sales Specialist for additional information on the Lyryx Assessment Finance system. Visit **http://lyryx.com**.

Fingame Online 5.0

By Leroy Brooks

In this comprehensive simulation game, students control a hypothetical company over numerous periods of operation. As students make major financial and operating decisions for their company, they will develop and enhance skills in financial management and financial accounting statement analysis. Please contact your *i*Learning Sales Specialist for additional information regarding packaging access to *FinGame* with the student text.

Financial Analysis With an Electronic Calculator, Sixth Edition

By Mark A. White

This helpful guide provides you with information and procedures to master financial calculators and gain a deeper understanding of financial mathematics. Complete instructions are included for solving all major problem types on three popular models of financial calculators: Hewlett-Packard's HP-10B II, Sharp Electronics' EL-733A, and Texas Instruments' BA II Plus. Sixty hands-on problems with detailed solutions will allow you to practice the skills outlined in the book and obtain instant reinforcement. Please contact your *i*Learning Sales Specialist for additional information.

Online LearningCentre

Student Online Learning Centre (OLC)

www.mcgrawhill.ca/olc/ross

Prepared by Ian Rakita, Concordia University, the OLC offers aids such as Online Quizzes, Problems, Essay Questions, Annotated Web Links, Excel Templates, S&P Problems, Appendix B (Answers to selected End-of-Chapter Problems) and a link to the S&P site. The Corporate Finance OLC is located at www.mcgrawhill.ca/olc/ross.

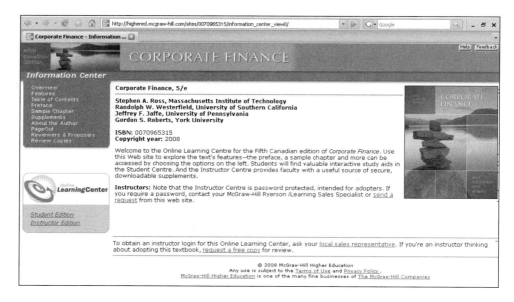

Standard & Poor's Educational Version of Market Insight

McGraw-Hill Ryerson and the Institutional Market Services division of Standard & Poor's is pleased to announce an exclusive partnership that offers instructors and students FREE access to the educational version of Standard & Poor's Market Insight with each new textbook. The Educational Version of Market Insight is a rich online resource that provides six years of fundamental financial data for over 1000 companies in the database. S&P-specific problems can be found at the end of almost all chapters in this text. For more details, please see the bound-in card inside the front cover of this text, or visit *www.mcgrawhill.ca/edumarketinsight.*

Support For the Instructor

Service takes on a whole new meaning with McGraw-Hill Ryerson and *Corporate Finance.* More than just bringing you the textbook, we have consistently raised the bar in terms of innovation and educational research—both in finance and in education in general. These investments in learning and the education community have helped us to understand the needs of students and educators across the country, and allowed us to foster the growth of truly innovative, integrated learning.

Instructor's Online Learning Centre (www.mcgrawhill.ca/olc/ross)

The Online Learning Centre includes a password-protected website for instructors. The site offers downloadable supplements, solutions to the Excel spreadsheets found on the student site, and PageOut, the McGraw-Hill Ryerson course website and development centre.

Instructor's CD-ROM

This CD-ROM includes the following Instructors Supplements:

Instructor's Manual
Prepared by Larbi Hammami, McGill University. Part I of the Instructor's Manual contains, by chapter, a brief chapter outline, an introduction, and an annotated outline. This outline provides additional explanations, examples, and teaching tips. Part II consists of answers to all Concept Check questions. Part III of the Instructor's Manual consists of solutions for all end-of-chapter problems and has been thoroughly reviewed for accuracy.

PowerPoint Presentation System
Prepared by Gady Jacoby, University of Manitoba, these slides contain useful outlines, summaries, and exhibits from the text.

Test Bank
Prepared by Sujata Madan, McGill University, the test bank provides a variety of question formats, multiple-choice questions, problems, and essay questions and levels of difficulty to meet any instructor's testing needs.

Image Bank
All figures and tables are available in digital format on the Instructor's CD.

Excel Templates (with solutions)
Prepared by Ian Rakita, Concordia University, Excel templates are included with solutions for end-of-chapter problems indicated by an Excel icon in the margin of the text.

Course Management

PAGEOUT　McGraw-Hill Ryerson's course management system, PageOut, www.mhhe.com/pageout, is the easiest way to create a website for your corporate finance course. There is no need for HTML coding, graphic design, or a thick how-to book. Just fill in a series of boxes in plain English and click on one of our professional designs. In no time, your course is online!

For the integrated instructor, we offer *Corporate Finance* content for complete online courses. Whatever your needs, you can customize the *Corporate Finance* Online Learning Centre content and author your own online course materials. It is entirely up to you. You can offer online discussion and message boards that will complement your office hours, and reduce the lines outside your door. Content cartridges are also available for course management systems, such as **WebCT** and **Blackboard.** Ask your *i*Learning Sales Specialist for details.

INTEGRATED LEARNING　Your Integrated Learning Sales Specialist is a McGraw-Hill Ryerson representative who has the experience, product knowledge, training, and support to help you assess and integrate any of our products, technology, and services into your course for optimum teaching and learning performance. Whether it's helping your students improve their grades, or putting your entire course online, your *i*Learning Sales Specialist is there to help you do it. Contact your *i*Learning Sales Specialist today to learn how to maximize all of McGraw-Hill Ryerson's resources!

iLEARNING SERVICES　McGraw-Hill Ryerson offers a unique *i*Service package designed for Canadian faculty. Our mission is to equip providers of higher education with superior tools and resources required for excellence in teaching. For additional information, visit *www.mcgrawhill.ca/highereducation/iservices.*

TEACHING, TECHNOLOGY & LEARNING CONFERENCE SERIES　The educational environment has changed tremendously in recent years, and McGraw-Hill Ryerson continues to be committed to helping you acquire the skills you need to succeed in this new milieu. Our innovative Teaching, Technology & Learning Conference Series brings faculty together from across Canada with 3M Teaching Excellence award winners to share teaching and learning best practices in a collaborative and stimulating environment. Preconference workshops on general topics, such as teaching large classes and technology integration, will also be offered. We will also work with you at your own institution to customize workshops that best suit the needs of your faculty.

RESEARCH REPORTS INTO MOBILE LEARNING AND STUDENT SUCCESS
These landmark reports, undertaken in conjunction with academic and private sector advisory boards, are the result of research studies into the challenges professors face in helping students succeed and the opportunities that new technology presents to impact teaching and learning.

Acknowledgments

Many people have contributed their time and expertise to the development and writing of this text. We extend our thanks once again for their assistance and countless insights.

For the Fifth Canadian Edition, we thank the following reviewers:

Ben Amoako-Adu, *Wilfrid Laurier University*
Francois Derrien, *University of Toronto*
Asher Drory, *University of Toronto*
Alex Faseruk, *Memorial University of Newfoundland*
Keith Freeland, *University of Waterloo*
Larbi Hammami, *McGill University*
Lew Johnson, *Queen's University*
Mary Kelly, *Wilfrid Laurier University*
Kaouthar Lajili, *University of Ottawa*
Sujata Madan, *McGill University*
Richard Nason, *Dalhousie University*
David Saunders, *University of Waterloo*
Bob Scott, *University of Manitoba*
David Stangeland, *University of Manitoba*

A special thank you must be given to Jacques Schnabel, Wilfrid Laurier University, and Keke Song, York University for their vigilant efforts as the technical reviewers for the text. Their keen eyes and attention to detail have contributed greatly to the quality of the final product.

In addition, further thanks must be extended to Keke Song for providing technical reviews of the solutions and answers.

While completing the last year of his BBA at the Schulich School of Business, Joseph Gareri worked as the research assistant on the Fifth Canadian Edition researching updates, drafting revisions, and responding to editorial queries. We will miss his capable assistance as he moves on to a career on Bay Street.

Much credit must go to a first-class group of people at McGraw-Hill Ryerson who worked on the Fifth Canadian Edition and the support package. Especially important were Lynn Fisher, Publisher, and Maria Chu, Senior Developmental Editor. Lynn Fisher championed the project, ensuring that it was well launched. Maria Chu had hands-on responsibility for the revision, fielding queries, and juggling deadlines with aplomb. Copy editing of the manuscript was handled ably by Evan Turner with the in-house supervision of Joanne Limebeer.

Through the development of this edition, we have taken great care to discover and eliminate errors. Our goal is to provide the best Canadian textbook available on this subject. Please write and tell us how to make this a better text. Forward your comments to:

Professor Gordon S. Roberts
Schulich School of Business
4700 Keele Street
York University
North York, Ontario
M3J 1P3

Or, e-mail your comments to *groberts@schulich.yorku.ca*

Stephen A. Ross   **Jeffrey F. Jaffe**
Randolph W. Westerfield   **Gordon S. Roberts**

PART I

Chapter 1

Introduction to Corporate Finance

EXECUTIVE SUMMARY

Air Canada has long been the nation's largest airline. As a result of numerous setbacks in the travel industry, the company entered bankruptcy protection in 2003, with cash flows falling significantly short of the $12 billion owing to creditors. As of April 2004, the company had $900 million in available cash, despite suffering a loss of $1.9 billion in the previous year.[1] In the face of insolvency, Air Canada's unions agreed to take $850 million in job and pay cuts in an attempt to alleviate cash flow pressures on the company in 2004. Air Canada's restructuring plan has been very successful. In August 2006, Air Canada posted net income of $236 million and in October 2006 the company received court approval for a special distribution of $2 billion in cash and securities to shareholders. At the time of writing, ACE Aviation's (Air Canada's parent company) stock price was trading at $35 per share. Air Canada's experience illustrates the basic concerns of corporate finance (discussed in Section 1.1):

1. What long-term investment strategy should a company take on?
2. How can cash be raised?
3. How much short-term cash flow does a company need to pay its bills?

These are not the only questions of corporate finance. For example, another important question covered in this text is, how should a company divide earnings between payouts to shareholders (dividends) and reinvestment? The three on our list are, however, among the most important questions and, taken in order, they provide a rough outline of our book.

One way that companies raise cash to finance their investment activities is by selling or "issuing" securities. The securities, sometimes called *financial instruments* or *claims,* may be roughly classified as *equity* or *debt,* loosely called *stocks* or *bonds.* The difference between equity and debt is a basic distinction in the modern theory of finance. All securities of a firm are claims that depend on or are contingent on the value of the firm.[2] In Section 1.2 we show how debt and equity securities depend on the firm's value, and we describe them as different contingent claims.

In Section 1.3 we discuss different organizational forms and the pros and cons of the decision to become a corporation.

In Section 1.4 we take a close look at the goals of the corporation and discuss why maximizing shareholder wealth is likely to be its primary goal. Throughout the rest of the book, we assume that the firm's performance depends on the value it creates for its shareholders. Shareholders are made better off when the value of their shares is increased by the firm's decisions.

A company raises cash by issuing securities in the financial markets. In Section 1.5 we describe some of the basic features of the financial markets. Roughly speaking, there are two types of financial markets: money markets and capital markets.

Section 1.6 covers trends in financial markets and management, and the last section of this chapter (1.7) outlines the rest of the book.

---

[1] "Air Canada Unions Dig In As Rescue Falters," *Airwise News,* April 19, 2004.

[2] We tend to use the words *firm, company,* and *business* interchangeably. However, there is a difference between these and a corporation. We discuss this difference in Section 1.3.

1.1 What Is Corporate Finance?

Suppose you decide to start a firm to make tennis balls. To do this, you hire managers to buy raw materials, and you assemble a workforce that will produce and sell finished tennis balls. In the language of finance, you make an investment in assets such as inventory, machinery, land, and labour. The amount of cash you invest in assets must be matched by an equal amount of cash raised by financing. When you begin to sell tennis balls, your firm will generate cash. This is the basis of value creation. The purpose of the firm is to create value for you, the owner (shareholder). In other words, the goal of the firm and its managers should be to maximize the value of the shareholders' wealth. The value is reflected in the framework of the simple balance-sheet model of the firm.

The Balance-Sheet Model of the Firm

Suppose we take a financial snapshot of the firm and its activities at a single point in time. Figure 1.1, a graphic conceptualization of the balance sheet, will help introduce you to corporate finance.

The assets of the firm are on the left side of the balance sheet. These assets can be thought of as current and fixed. *Fixed assets* are those that will last a long time, such as a building. Some fixed assets are tangible, such as machinery and equipment. Other fixed assets are intangible, such as patents, trademarks, and the quality of management. The other category of assets, *current assets,* comprises those that have short lives, such as inventory. The tennis balls that your firm has made but has not yet sold are part of its inventory. Unless you have overproduced, they will leave the firm shortly.

Before a company can invest in an asset, it must obtain financing, which means that it must raise the money to pay for the investment. The forms of financing are represented on

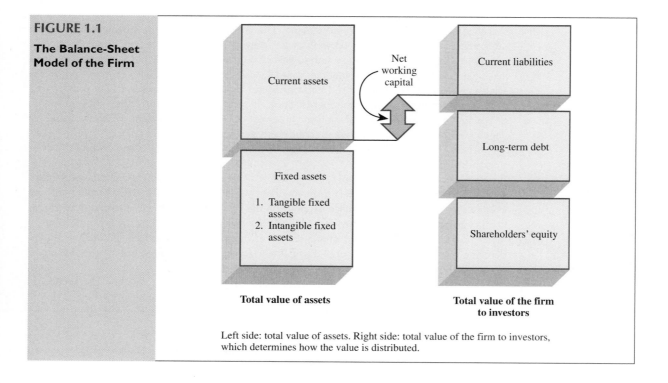

FIGURE 1.1

The Balance-Sheet Model of the Firm

Left side: total value of assets. Right side: total value of the firm to investors, which determines how the value is distributed.

the right side of the balance sheet. A firm will issue (sell) pieces of paper called *debt* (loan agreements) or *equity shares* (share certificates). Just as assets are classified as long-lived or short-lived, so too are liabilities. A short-term debt is called a *current liability*. Short-term debt represents loans and other obligations that must be repaid within one year. Long-term debt is debt that does not have to be repaid within one year. Shareholders' equity represents the difference between the value of the assets and the debt of the firm. In this sense it is a residual claim on the firm's assets.

From the balance-sheet model of the firm it is easy to see why finance can be thought of as the study of the following three questions:

1. In what long-lived assets should the firm invest? This question concerns the left side of the balance sheet. Of course, the type and proportions of assets the firm needs tend to be set by the nature of the business. We use the terms **capital budgeting** and *capital expenditure* to describe the process of making and managing expenditures on long-lived assets.

2. How can the firm raise cash for required capital expenditures? This question concerns the right side of the balance sheet. The answer involves the firm's **capital structure,** which represents the proportions of the firm's financing from current and long-term debt and equity.

3. How should short-term operating cash flows be managed? This question concerns the upper portion of the balance sheet. There is a mismatch between the timing of cash inflows and cash outflows during operating activities. Furthermore, the amount and timing of operating cash flows are not known with certainty. The financial managers must attempt to manage the gaps in cash flow. From an accounting perspective, short-term management of cash flow is associated with a firm's **net working capital.** Net working capital is defined as current assets minus current liabilities. From a financial perspective, the short-term cash flow problem comes from the mismatching of cash inflows and outflows. It is the subject of short-term finance.

Capital Structure

Financing arrangements determine how the value of the firm is sliced up like a pie. The persons or institutions that buy debt from the firm are called *creditors*.[3] The holders of equity shares are called *shareholders*.

Sometimes it is useful to think of the firm as a pie. Initially, the size of the pie will depend on how well the firm has made its investment decisions. After a firm has made its investment decisions, financial markets determine the value of its assets (e.g., its buildings, land, and inventories).

The firm can then determine its capital structure. It might initially have raised the cash to invest in its assets by issuing more debt than equity; now it can consider changing that mix by issuing more equity and using the proceeds to buy back some of its debt. Financing decisions like this can be made independently of the original investment decisions. The decisions to issue debt and equity affect how the pie is sliced.

The pie we are thinking of is depicted in Figure 1.2. The size of the pie is the value of the firm in the financial markets. We can write the value of the firm, *V,* as

$$V = B + S$$

where *B* is the value of the debt (bonds) and *S* is the value of the equity (shares). The pie diagram considers two ways of slicing the pie: 50 percent debt and 50 percent equity, and

---

[3]We tend to use the words *creditors, debtholders,* and *bondholders* interchangeably. In later chapters we examine the differences among the kinds of creditors.

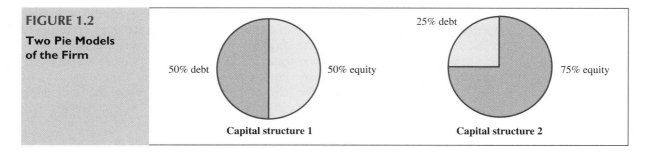

FIGURE 1.2

Two Pie Models of the Firm

50% debt　50% equity

Capital structure 1

25% debt　75% equity

Capital structure 2

25 percent debt and 75 percent equity. The way the pie is sliced could affect its value. If so, the goal of the financial manager will be to choose the ratio of debt to equity that makes the value of the pie—that is, the value of the firm, V—as large as it can be.

The Financial Manager

In large firms the finance activity is usually associated with a senior officer of the firm (such as a vice-president of finance) and some lesser officers. Figure 1.3 depicts one example of a general organizational structure emphasizing the finance activity within the firm. Reporting to the vice-president of finance are the treasurer and controller. The treasurer is responsible for handling cash flows, analyzing capital expenditures, and making financing plans. The controller handles the accounting function, which includes taxes, cost and financial accounting, and information systems. Our discussion of corporate finance is much more relevant to the treasurer's function.

As Figure 1.3 shows, there are four general position categories under the treasurer. Corporations usually hire undergraduate or MBA graduates with a finance background for these positions. In contrast, the positions under the controller are geared more towards accounting majors.

We think that a financial manager's most important job is to create value from the firm's capital budgeting, financing, and liquidity activities. How do financial managers create value?

1. The firm should try to buy assets that generate more cash than they cost.
2. The firm should sell bonds, shares, and other financial instruments that raise more cash than they cost.

Thus, the firm must create more cash flow than it uses. The cash flow paid to bondholders and shareholders of the firm should be higher than the cash flows put into the firm by the bondholders and shareholders. To see how this is done, we can trace the cash flows from the firm to the financial markets and back again.

The interplay of the firm's finance with the financial markets is illustrated in Figure 1.4. To finance its planned investment the firm sells debt and equity shares to participants in the financial markets. The resulting cash flows from the financial markets to the firm (A). This cash is invested in the investment activities of the firm (B) by the firm's management. The cash generated by the firm (C) is paid to shareholders and bondholders (F). Shareholders receive cash from the firm in the form of dividends or as share repurchases; bondholders who lent funds to the firm receive interest and, when the initial loan is repaid, principal. Not all of the firm's cash is paid out to shareholders and bondholders. Some is retained (D), and some is paid to governments as taxes (E).

Over time, if the cash paid to shareholders and bondholders (F) is greater than the cash raised in the financial markets (A), value will be created.

FIGURE 1.3

**Hypothetical
Organization Chart**

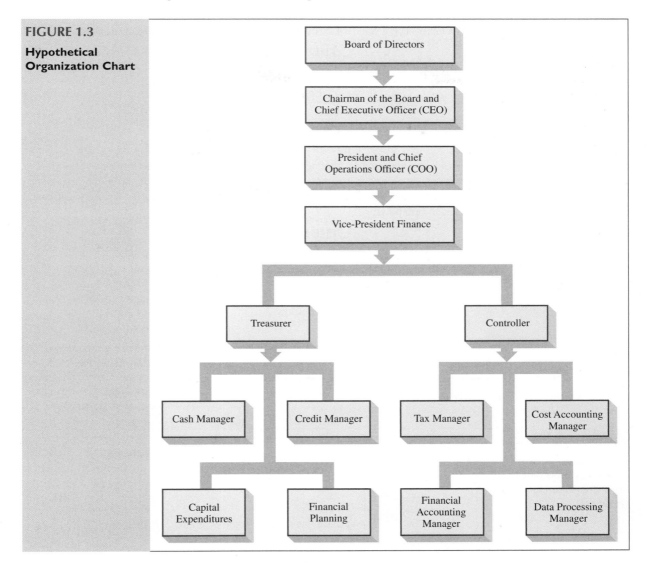

Identification of Cash Flows

Unfortunately, it is not all that easy to observe cash flows directly. Much of the information we obtain is in the form of accounting statements, and much of the work of financial analysis is to extract cash flow information from accounting statements. Example 1.1 illustrates how this is done.

EXAMPLE 1.1

The Midland Company refines and trades gold. At the end of the year it sold some gold for $1 million. The company had acquired the gold for $900,000 at the beginning of the year. The company paid cash for the gold when it was purchased. Unfortunately, it has yet to collect from the customer to whom the gold was sold.

The following is a standard accounting of Midland's financial circumstances at year-end:

THE MIDLAND COMPANY
Accounting View
Income Statement
Year Ended December 31

Sales	$1,000,000
Costs	− 900,000
Profit	$ 100,000

By generally accepted accounting principles (GAAP), the sale is recorded even though the customer has yet to pay. It is assumed that the customer will pay soon. From the accounting perspective, Midland seems to be profitable. The perspective of corporate finance is different. It focuses on cash flows:

THE MIDLAND COMPANY
Corporate Finance View
Income Statement
Year Ended December 31

Cash inflow	0
Cash outflow	−$900,000
	−$900,000

The perspective of corporate finance examines whether cash flows are being created by the gold trading operations of Midland. Value creation depends on cash flows. For Midland, value creation depends on whether and when it actually receives $1 million.

FIGURE 1.4

Cash Flows Between the Firm and the Financial Markets

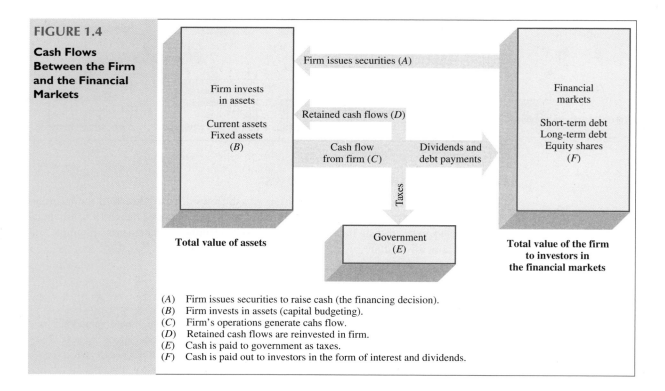

(A)   Firm issues securities to raise cash (the financing decision).
(B)   Firm invests in assets (capital budgeting).
(C)   Firm's operations generate cahs flow.
(D)   Retained cash flows are reinvested in firm.
(E)   Cash is paid to government as taxes.
(F)   Cash is paid out to investors in the form of interest and dividends.

Timing of Cash Flows

The value of an investment made by the firm depends on the timing of cash flows. One of the most important principles of finance is that individuals prefer to receive cash flows earlier rather than later. One dollar received today is worth more than one dollar received next year because today's dollar can be invested to earn interest. This time preference plays a role in stock and bond prices.

EXAMPLE 1.2

The Midland Company is attempting to choose between two proposals for new products. Both proposals will provide cash flows over a four-year period and will initially cost $10,000. The cash flows from the proposals are as follows:

Year	New Product A	New Product B
1	0	$ 4,000
2	0	4,000
3	0	4,000
4	$20,000	4,000
Total	$20,000	$16,000

At first it appears that new product A would be better. However, the cash flows from proposal B come earlier than those of A. Without more information we cannot decide which set of cash flows would create greater value. It depends on whether the value of getting cash from B up front outweighs the extra total cash from A. Bond and stock prices reflect this preference for earlier cash, and we will see how to use them to decide between A and B.

Risk of Cash Flows

The firm must consider risk. The amount and timing of cash flows are not usually known with certainty. Most investors have an aversion to risk.

EXAMPLE 1.3

The Midland Company is considering expanding operations overseas. It is evaluating Europe and Japan as possible sites. Europe is considered to be relatively safe, whereas Japan is seen as very risky. In both cases the company would close down operations after one year.

After doing a complete financial analysis, Midland has come up with the following cash flows of the alternative plans for expansion under three equally likely scenarios: pessimistic, most likely, and optimistic:

	Pessimistic	Most Likely	Optimistic
Europe	$75,000	$100,000	$125,000
Japan	0	150,000	200,000

If we ignore the pessimistic scenario, perhaps Japan is the better alternative. When we take the pessimistic scenario into account, the choice is unclear. Japan appears to be riskier, but it may also offer a higher expected level of cash flow. What is risk and how can it be defined? We must try to answer this important question. Corporate finance cannot avoid coping with risky alternatives, and much of our book is devoted to developing methods for evaluating risky opportunities.

- **What are three basic questions of corporate finance?**
- **Describe capital structure.**
- **List three reasons why value creation is difficult.**

1.2 Corporate Securities as Contingent Claims on Total Firm Value

What is the essential difference between debt and equity? The answer can be found by thinking about what happens to the payoffs to debt and equity when the value of the firm changes.

The basic feature of debt is that it is a promise by the borrowing firm to repay a fixed dollar amount by a certain date.

EXAMPLE 1.4

The Canadian Corporation promises to pay $100 to the True North Insurance Company at the end of one year. This is a debt of the Canadian Corporation. Holders of the Canadian Corporation's debt will receive $100 if the value of the Canadian Corporation's assets equals $100 or more at the end of the year.

Formally, the debtholders have been promised an amount F at the end of the year. If the value of the firm, X, is equal to or greater than F at year-end, debtholders will get F. Of course, if the firm does not have enough to pay off the promised amount, the firm will be "broke." It may be forced to liquidate its assets for whatever they are worth, and bondholders will receive X. Mathematically this means that the debtholders have a claim to X or F, whichever is smaller. Figure 1.5 illustrates the general nature of the payoff structure to debtholders.

FIGURE 1.5

Debt and Equity as Contingent Claims

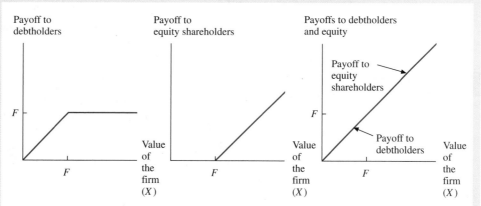

F is the promised payoff to debtholders. $X - F$ is the payoff to equity shareholders if $X - F > 0$. Otherwise the payoff is 0.

Suppose at year-end the Canadian Corporation's value is $100. The firm has promised to pay the True North Insurance Company $100, so the debtholders will get $100.

Now suppose the Canadian Corporation's value is $200 at year-end and the debtholders are promised $100. How much will the debtholders receive? It should be clear that they will receive the same amount as when the Canadian Corporation was worth $100.

Suppose the firm's value is $75 at year-end and debtholders are promised $100. How much will the debtholders receive? In this case the debtholders will get $75.

The shareholders' claim on firm value at the end of the period is the amount that remains after the debtholders are paid. Of course, shareholders get nothing if the firm's value is equal to or less than the amount promised to the debtholders.

EXAMPLE 1.5

The Canadian Corporation will sell its assets for $200 at year-end. The firm has promised to pay the insurance company $100 at that time. The shareholders will get the residual value of $100.

Algebraically, the shareholders' claim is $X - F$ if $X > F$ and zero if $X \leq F$. This is depicted in Figure 1.5. The sum of the debtholders' claim and the shareholders' claim is always the value of the firm at the end of the period.

The debt and equity securities issued by a firm derive their value from the total value of the firm. In the words of finance theory, debt and equity securities are **contingent claims** on the total firm value.

When the value of the firm exceeds the amount promised to debtholders, the shareholders obtain the residual of the firm's value over the amount promised the debtholders, and the debtholders obtain the amount promised. When the value of the firm is less than the amount promised to the bondholders, the shareholders receive nothing and the debtholders get the value of the firm.

? Concept Questions

- **What is a contingent claim?**
- **Describe equity and debt as contingent claims.**

1.3 The Corporate Firm

The firm is a way of organizing the economic activity of many individuals. There are many reasons why so much economic activity is carried out by firms and not by individuals. The theory of firms, however, does not tell us much about why most large firms are corporations rather than any of the other legal forms that firms can assume.

A basic problem of the firm is how to raise cash. The corporate form of business (that is, organizing the firm as a corporation) is the standard method for solving problems encountered in raising large amounts of cash. However, business can take other forms. In this section we consider the three basic legal forms of organizing firms (sole proprietorship, partnership, and corporation) and we see how firms go about the task of raising large amounts of money under each form. We also introduce the income trust, a new noncorporate form of business organization.

The Sole Proprietorship

A **sole proprietorship** is a business owned by one person. Suppose you decide to start a business to produce mousetraps. Going into business is simple: You announce to all who will listen, "Today I am going to build a better mousetrap."

Most large cities require that you obtain a business licence. Afterward, you can try to hire as many people as you need and borrow whatever money you need. At year-end all the profits and the losses will be yours.

Here are some important factors in considering a sole proprietorship:

1. The sole proprietorship is the cheapest type of business to form. No formal charter is required, and few government regulations must be satisfied.

2. A sole proprietorship pays no corporate income taxes. All profits of the business are taxed as individual income.

3. The sole proprietorship has unlimited liability for business debts and obligations. No distinction is made between personal and business assets.

4. The life of the sole proprietorship is limited by the life of the sole proprietor.

5. Because the only money invested in the firm is the proprietor's, the equity money that can be raised by the sole proprietor is limited to the proprietor's personal wealth.

The Partnership

Any two or more persons can get together and form a **partnership.** Partnerships fall into two categories: general partnerships and limited partnerships.

In a *general partnership* all partners agree to provide some fraction of the work and cash and to share the profits and losses. Each partner is liable for the debts of the partnership. A partnership agreement specifies the nature of the arrangement. The partnership agreement may be an oral agreement or a formal document setting forth the understanding.

Limited partnerships permit the liability of some of the partners to be limited to the amount of cash each has contributed to the partnership. Limited partnerships usually require that (1) at least one partner be a general partner and (2) the limited partners do not participate in managing the business.

Here are some points that are important when considering a partnership:

1. Partnerships are usually inexpensive and easy to form. In complicated arrangements, including general and limited partnerships, written documents are required. Business licences and filing fees may be necessary.

2. General partners have unlimited liability for all debts. The liability of limited partners is usually limited to the contribution each has made to the partnership. If one general partner is unable to meet his or her commitment, the shortfall must be made up by the other general partners.

3. The general partnership is terminated when a general partner dies or withdraws (but this is not so for a limited partner). It is difficult for a partnership to transfer ownership without dissolving. Usually, all general partners must agree. However, limited partners may sell their interest in a business.

4. It is difficult for a partnership to raise large amounts of cash. Equity contributions are limited to a partner's ability and desire to contribute to the partnership. Sometimes the partners have no choice about contributing. For example, in 2001, a major global management consulting firm, McKinsey & Company, called on its partners to contribute up to $300,000 each to finance growing accounts receivable. Many companies, such as Apple Computer, start life as a proprietorship or partnership, but at some point they need to convert to corporate form.

5. Income from a partnership is taxed as personal income to the partners.

6. Management control resides with the general partners. Usually a majority vote is required on important matters, such as the amount of profit to be retained in the business.

It is very difficult for large business organizations to exist as sole proprietorships or partnerships. The main advantage is the cost of getting started. Afterward, the disadvantages, which may become severe, are (1) unlimited liability, (2) limited life of the enterprise, and (3) difficulty of transferring ownership. These three disadvantages lead to (4) the difficulty of raising cash.

The Corporation

Of the many forms of business enterprise, the **corporation** is by far the most important. Most large Canadian firms, such as Bank of Montreal and Bombardier, are organized as corporations. As a distinct legal entity, a corporation can have a name and enjoy many of the legal powers of natural persons. For example, corporations can acquire and exchange property. Corporations may enter into contracts and may sue and be sued. For jurisdictional purposes, the corporation is a citizen of its province of incorporation. (It cannot vote, however.)

Starting a corporation is more complicated than starting a proprietorship or partnership. The incorporators must prepare articles of incorporation and a set of bylaws. The articles of incorporation must include:

1. Name of the corporation
2. Business purpose
3. Number of shares that the corporation is authorized to issue, with a statement of limitations and rights of different classes of shares
4. Nature of the rights granted to shareholders
5. Number of members of the initial board of directors.

A Comparison of Partnerships and Corporations

	Corporation	Partnership
Liquidity and marketability	Common stock can be listed on stock exchange.	Units are subject to substantial restrictions on transferability. There is no established trading market for partnership units.
Voting rights	Usually each share of common stock entitles each holder to one vote per share on matters requiring a vote and on the election of the directors. Directors determine top management.	Some voting rights by limited partners. However, general partner has exclusive control and management of operations.
Taxation	Corporate income is taxable. Dividends to shareholders are also taxable with partial integration through use of the dividend tax credit.	Partnership income is taxable.
Reinvestment and dividend payout	Corporations have broad latitude on dividend payout decisions.	Partnerships are generally prohibited from reinvesting partnership cash flow. All net cash flow is distributed to partners.
Liability	Shareholders are not personally liable for obligations of the corporation.	Limited partners are not liable for obligations of partnerships. General partners may have unlimited liability.
Continuity of existence	Corporations have perpetual life.	Partnerships have a limited life.

The bylaws (the rules to be used by the corporation to regulate its own existence) concern its shareholders, directors, and officers. Bylaws range from the briefest possible statement of rules for the corporation's management to hundreds of pages of text.

In its simplest form, the corporation comprises three sets of distinct interests: the shareholders (the owners), the directors, and the corporation officers (the top management). Traditionally, the shareholders control the corporation's direction, policies, and activities. The shareholders elect a board of directors, who in turn select top management who serve as corporate officers.

The separation of ownership from management gives the corporation several advantages over proprietorships and partnerships:

1. Because ownership in a corporation is represented by shares, ownership can be readily transferred to new owners. Because the corporation exists independently of those who own its shares, there is no limit to the transferability of shares as there is in partnerships.

2. The corporation has unlimited life. Because the corporation is separate from its owners, the death or withdrawal of an owner does not affect its existence. The corporation can continue on after the original owners have withdrawn.

3. The shareholders' liability is limited to the amount invested in the ownership shares. For example, if a shareholder purchased $1,000 in shares of a corporation, the potential loss would be $1,000. In a partnership, a general partner with a $1,000 contribution could lose the $1,000 plus any other indebtedness of the partnership.

Limited liability, ease of ownership transfer, and perpetual succession are the major advantages of the corporate form of business organization. These give the corporation an enhanced ability to raise cash.

There is, however, one great disadvantage to incorporation. Federal and provincial governments tax corporate income. Corporate dividends received by shareholders are also taxable. The dividend tax credit for individual shareholders and a corporate dividend exclusion provide a degree of tax integration for Canadian corporations. These tax provisions are discussed in Appendix 1A.

The Income Trust

The income trust, a non-corporate form of business organization, grew in importance in Canada after 2001. As of June 2006, there were 247 income trusts listed on the TSX, with a sector market capitalization of $195.4 billion.[4] Within this sector, the fastest-growing component of this form of business organization was business income trusts, especially in real estate and oil and gas. Businesses like telephone listings, container ports, restaurant chains, and other businesses usually organized as corporations were also included in this component. In response to the growing importance of this sector, provincial legislation extended limited liability protection—previously limited to corporate shareholders—to trust unitholders. Along the same lines, at the end of 2005, the TSX began to include trusts in its benchmark S&P / TSX composite index.

Business income trusts (also called income funds) hold the debt and equity of an underlying business and distribute the income generated to unitholders. Because income trusts are not corporations, they are not subject to corporate income tax and their income is typically taxed only in the hands of unitholders. As a result, investors saw trusts as tax-efficient and were generally willing to pay more for a company after it converted from a

---

[4]For more on income trusts see J. Fenwick and B. Kalymon, "A Note on Income Trusts," Ivey Publishing, 2004 and F. Aguerrevere, F. Pazzaglia and R. Ravi, "Income Trusts," *Canadian Investment Review,* Winter 2005.

corporation to a trust. This tax advantage largely disappeared in 2006 when the government announced plans to tax income trusts as corporations, prompting Bell Canada Enterprises (BCE) to reverse its mid-October 2006 announcement to convert into an income trust. As a result, the company quickly became a target for private equity.

- **Define a proprietorship, a partnership, a corporation, and an income trust.**
- **What are the advantages of the corporate form of business organization?**

1.4 Goals of the Corporate Firm

What is the primary goal of the corporation? The traditional answer is that managers in a corporation make decisions for the shareholders because the shareholders own and control the corporation. If so, the goal of the corporation is to add value for the shareholders. This goal is a little vague and so we will try to come up with a precise formulation. It is also impossible to give a definitive answer to this important question because the corporation is an artificial being, not a natural person. It exists in the "contemplation of the law."[5]

It is necessary to precisely identify who controls the corporation. We shall consider the **set-of-contracts viewpoint.** This viewpoint suggests the corporate firm will attempt to maximize the shareholders' wealth by taking actions that increase the current value per share of existing stock of the firm.

Agency Costs and the Set-of-Contracts Perspective

The set-of-contracts theory of the firm states that the firm can be viewed as nothing more than a set of contracts.[6] One of the contract claims is a residual claim (equity) on the firm's assets and cash flows. The equity contract can be defined as a principal–agent relationship. The members of the management team are the agents hired to act on behalf of the equity investors (shareholders), who are the principals. This discussion focuses on conflict between shareholders and managers. It is assumed that each of the two groups, left alone, will attempt to act in its own self-interest. We also assume that shareholders are unanimous in defining their self-interest; we explain how perfect markets make this happen in Chapter 4.

The shareholders, however, can discourage the managers from diverging from the shareholders' interests by devising appropriate incentives for managers and then monitoring their behaviour. Doing so, unfortunately, is complicated and costly. The costs of resolving the conflicts of interest between managers and shareholders are special types of costs called **agency costs.** These costs include the monitoring costs of the shareholders and the incentive fee paid to the managers. It can be expected that contracts will be devised that will provide the managers with appropriate incentives to maximize the shareholders' wealth. Thus, agency problems do not mean that the corporate firm will not act in the best interests of shareholders, only that it is costly to make it do so. However, agency problems can never be perfectly solved, and managers may not always act in the best interests of shareholders. *Residual losses* are the lost wealth of the shareholders due to divergent behaviour of the managers.

---

[5]These are the words of U.S. Chief Justice John Marshall from *The Trustees of Dartmouth College v. Woodward,* 4, Wheaton 636 (1819).

[6]M. C. Jensen and W. Meckling, "Theory of the Firm: Managerial Behavior, Agency Costs and Ownership Structure," *Journal of Financial Economics* 3 (1976).

Managerial Goals

Managerial goals are different from those of shareholders. What will managers maximize if they are left to pursue their own goals rather than shareholders' goals?

Williamson proposes the notion of *expense preference*.[7] He argues that managers obtain value from certain kinds of expenses. In particular, company cars, office furniture, office location, and funds for discretionary investment have value to managers beyond that which comes from their productivity.

Donaldson conducted a series of interviews with chief executives of several large companies.[8] He concluded that managers are influenced by three underlying motivations in defining the corporate mission:

1. *Survival.* Organizational survival means that management must always command sufficient resources to support the firm's activities.
2. *Independence.* This is the freedom to make decisions and take action without encountering external parties or depending on outside financial markets.
3. *Self-sufficiency.* Managers do not want to depend on external parties.

These motivations lead to what Donaldson concludes is the basic financial objective of managers: the maximization of corporate wealth. Corporate wealth is that wealth over which management has effective control; it is closely associated with corporate growth and corporate size. Corporate wealth is not necessarily shareholder wealth. Corporate wealth tends to lead to increased growth by providing funds for growth and limiting the extent to which equity is raised. Increased growth and size are not necessarily the same thing as increased shareholder wealth.

Separation of Ownership and Control

Some people argue that shareholders do not control the corporation. They argue that shareholder ownership is too diffuse and fragmented for effective control of management. A striking feature of the modern large corporation is the diffusion of ownership among thousands of investors. For example, Table 1.1 shows that the largest corporations in Canada are widely held with no shareholder owning 10 percent or more of the shares. While this argument is certainly worth considering, it is less true in Canada than in the United States. Over 70 percent of U.S. corporations were widely held compared to only 15 percent in

TABLE 1.1
The Largest Canadian Corporations, October 2006

	Number of Shares Outstanding	Market Value (in $ millions)	Ownership
Royal Bank of Canada	1,281,028,553	63,833.7	Widely held
Manulife Financial Corporation	1,549,519,024	56,247.5	Widely held
Bank of Nova Scotia	989,085,934	48,059.7	Widely held
Toronto-Dominion Bank	721,682,082	47,912.5	Widely held
EnCana Corporation	812,166,902	41,989.0	Widely held

Source: www.tsx.com.

---

[7] O. Williamson, "Managerial Discretion and Business Behavior," *American Economic Review* 53 (1963).

[8] G. Donaldson, *Managing Corporate Wealth: The Operations of a Comprehensive Financial Goals System* (New York: Praeger, 1984).

Canada. Many domestically owned Canadian corporations have controlling shareholders.[9] Still, controlling agency costs through re-examining the rules of corporate governance is of considerable interest in corporate Canada.

As we discussed earlier, one of the most important advantages of the corporate form of business organization is that it allows ownership of shares to be transferred. The resulting diffuse ownership, however, brings with it the separation of ownership and control of the large corporation. The possible separation of ownership and control raises an important question: Who controls the firm?

Do Shareholders Control Managerial Behaviour?   The claim that managers can ignore the interests of shareholders is deduced from the fact that ownership in large corporations is widely dispersed. As a consequence, it is often claimed that individual shareholders cannot control management. There is some merit in this argument, but it is too simplistic.

The extent to which shareholders can control managers depends on (1) the costs of monitoring management, (2) the costs of implementing the control devices, and (3) the benefits of control.

When a conflict of interest exists between management and shareholders, who wins? Do managers or shareholders control the firm? Ownership in large corporations is diffuse compared to the closely held corporation. However, shareholders have several control devices (some more effective than others) to bond management to the self-interest of shareholders.

1. Shareholders determine the membership of the board of directors by voting. Thus, shareholders control the directors, who in turn select the management team.

2. Contracts with management and arrangements for compensation, such as stock option plans, can be made so that management has an incentive to pursue shareholders' goals. Similarly, management may be given loans to buy the firm's shares.

3. If the price of a firm's stock drops too low because of poor management, the firm may be acquired by a group of shareholders, by another firm, or by an individual. This is called a takeover. In a takeover, top management of the acquired firm may find itself out of a job. For example, the CEO of Chapters Inc. lost his job when the bookseller was taken over by Indigo in 2001. This pressures management to make decisions in the shareholders' interests. Fear of a takeover gives managers an incentive to take actions that will maximize stock prices.

4. Competition in the managerial labour market may force managers to perform in the best interest of shareholders. Otherwise they will be replaced. Firms willing to pay the most will lure good managers. These are likely to be firms that compensate managers based on the value they create. Compensation design is far from perfect, however, and many firms have come under intense criticism for having high rates of executive compensation amid corporate governance scandals at such companies as Enron and Hollinger.

The available evidence and theory are consistent with the idea of shareholder control. However, there can be no doubt that, at times, corporations pursue managerial goals at the expense of shareholders. In addition to the issue of excessive executive compensation already discussed, management may change the firm's corporate governance rules by removing independent directors who might challenge management. Major pension funds

---

[9]Important exceptions are chartered banks. The *Bank Act* prohibits any one interest from owning more than 20 percent of the shares.

B. Espen Eckbo on Corporate Governance

Voluntary shareholder absenteeism and a powerful culture of "corporate insiders" have led to a crisis in corporate governance. Without a fundamental shift in the balance of power, the problems will only worsen. Recent corporate scandals have resurrected public suspicion that there is plenty of potential for mischief inside large public companies.

In countries with highly developed financial systems, much of the governance debate focuses on the balance of power between shareholders, boards, and top executives in widely held public companies. This balance is the result of three main influences, which differ substantially across countries: legal precedent (case law); the cost of shareholder activism; and the political strength of employee unions. When a company is founded, this balance of power is hardly an issue. However, as the company grows and prospers, attitudes start to change. With growth comes the need for additional capital. Naturally, with limited wealth, the founding shareholders relinquish control, preferring instead to diversify personal holdings. New investors are brought in and the shareholder base becomes dispersed. Corporate insiders increasingly view shareholders as a remote constituency and as largely irrelevant for the company on a daily basis. By choosing to diversify, shareholders for their part agree to play a diminished role in the company's affairs. The cost of actively monitoring the performance of management swamps investment returns, so they no longer show up to annual meetings and either vote with management or throw the proxy in the wastebasket. The combination of voluntary shareholder absenteeism and strong corporate insiders creates a problem that lies at the heart of today's

governance crisis. The important historical lesson is that the absentee shareholder system breeds arrogance on the part of corporate insiders. A vigorous corporate governance system is thus required to prevent shareholder rights being expropriated by insiders.

A major task of the board is to hire and fire top managers, and to set their compensation. Therefore, corporate insiders come with an inherent conflict of interest when they sit on boards. Nevertheless, corporate insiders sit on boards in all major developed countries. In the U.S., it is common for the CEO also to occupy the post of board chairman. For the first time, the governance debate is openly questioning this tradition. Institutional shareholders and other governance activists recommend separation of the roles. In Europe, the tradition has been not to place the CEO in the chair, in some countries by statute. However, while non-executive members make up a clear majority of directors in the U.S., there is a tradition in Europe for placing a greater portion of employees on boards. The typical defence of having insiders on boards is one of efficiency: the board requires CEO and other management input to make proper decisions. What is not explained, however, is why the CEO needs a vote on the board—let alone the chairmanship—in order to supply the board with his or her input. It takes strong-willed character to resist the will of the CEO-chairman, even for directors that meet technical criteria for independence. In today's system, the vast majority of directors sit on boards because the CEO recommended their appointment, so a certain loyalty can be expected.

Research shows more generally that countries with a French civil law tradition—as opposed to British

such as the Alberta Teachers' Retirement Fund Board and the Ontario Teachers' Pension Plan Board have joined with professional money managers to form the Canadian Coalition for Good Governance. The Coalition has set up detailed governance guidelines backed by action in voting its shares at annual meetings.[10]

Stakeholders In addition to shareholders and management, employees, customers, suppliers, and the public all have a financial interest in the firm and its decisions. This enlarged stakeholder group may introduce alternative goals such as preserving the environment or avoiding alcohol, tobacco, gambling, nuclear power, and military weapons. Stakeholder concerns are attaining additional clout through the growth of interest in ethical or **socially responsible investing.** Such funds screen and select securities based

[10]www.ccgg.ca.

common law—rely primarily on banks to finance corporate growth. With poorly developed stock markets, and with creditors and employees having a major influence on boards, risk-taking is muted. In addition to Germany, civil law countries with historically small stock markets but broad-based banking systems include France, the countries of Scandinavia, Italy, Spain, Japan, South Korea, and China. These economies are also characterised by insider-controlled companies, corporate cross-holdings of voting stock and pyramidal ownership structures allowing founding families to maintain control.

In contrast, countries with a common law tradition, such as the U.K., U.S., English Canada, Australia, and India, have developed a greater reliance on external equity markets, resulting in a more pronounced dispersion of share ownership and a more specialized role for banks. Ultimately, international trade and the global competition for capital force a Darwinian convergence of both civil law and common law countries towards a system of corporate governance and finance that promotes maximum economic efficiency. Countries with small stock markets today must prepare these markets for the influx of future pension savings. In western countries, pension funds increasingly prefer to use broadly diversified, international stock and bond portfolios.

In his best-selling book *Economics,* Nobel laureate Paul Samuelson explains that "Takeovers, like bankruptcy, represent one of Nature's methods of eliminating deadwood." In the case of a hostile takeover bid designed to replace inefficient executives (presumably one form of "deadwood"), those very same executives sit on a board vested with powers to thwart the takeover. Are they likely to put the interests of shareholders ahead of their own? Insiders have largely succeeded in blocking the right of small shareholders to even sell their shares to someone who wants to accumulate a controlling block of stock.

A particularly effective defence is the so-called "poison pill." This is typically triggered if an investor accumulates a 15 percent shareholding in the target company. When this happens, all shareholders except the 15 percent blockholder get to purchase new shares for, say, half their market value. It is equivalent to asking the blockholder to pay a dividend to all the other shareholders, financed out of the blockholder's private wealth. Boards can issue such pills without consulting shareholders, even right after receiving a hostile bid (a so-called "morning after pill").

The poison pill has proven extremely effective. Hostile takeovers, which in the period 1975–85 resulted in numerous restructurings of inefficiently run companies, have come to a virtual standstill in the U.S. The poison pill stands as a symbol of state-sanctioned expropriation of the fundamental shareholder right to sell shares to the highest bid. Today, no takeover can go ahead unless corporate insiders agree to remove the pill. Some boards refuse to remove the pill because it means they will lose their positions in the company. It is no accident that this legal precedent has precipitated an era of governance decline in corporate America.

B. Espen Eckbo is the Tuck Centennial Professor of Finance and founding director of the Center for Corporate Governance at the Tuck School of Business at Dartmouth College. b.espen.eckbo@dartmouth.edu. This material is excerpted with permission from B. Espen Eckbo.

on social or environmental criteria. For example, ethical investors like Canadian Hydro, a small electric utility in Alberta, B.C., and Ontario, is noted for its green power projects with renewable energy sources and low emissions.[11] Another example is Aber Diamond Corporation, a diamond mining company operating in the Northwest Territories. The company is noted for its partnership with local indigenous communities, and its community involvement policy, which considers the issues, concerns, and suggestions put forth by the local communities regarding all exploration, development, operation, and closure.[12] While some studies find that socially responsible investment practices do not impact portfolio returns and risk consistently, the most recent study supports the

---

[11]J. Schreiner, "Ethics team applauds Canadian Hydro," *National Post* (February 2, 2001), D3.

[12]Discussion on Aber Diamond Corporation is drawn from Jantzi Research's report on the corporation, which can be found in their Canadian Social Investment Database.

critics.[13] Given the mixed evidence, major Canadian institutional investors like the Ontario Teachers' Pension Plan and the Ontario Municipal Employees' Retirement System pay careful attention to corporate social responsibility in selecting investments, but do not eliminate companies from their portfolios based solely on environmental and other social issues.

? Concept Questions

- What are two types of agency costs?
- How are managers bonded to shareholders?
- Can you recall some managerial goals?
- What is the set-of-contracts perspective?
- What is socially responsible investing?

1.5 Financial Institutions, Financial Markets, and the Corporation

We have seen that the primary advantages of the corporate form of organization are that (1) ownership can be transferred more quickly and easily than with other forms and (2) money can be raised more readily. Both advantages are significantly enhanced by the existence of financial institutions and markets. Financial markets play an extremely important role in corporate finance.

Financial Institutions

Financial institutions act as intermediaries between investors (funds suppliers) and firms raising funds. (Federal and provincial governments and individuals also raise funds in financial markets but our examples will focus on firms.) Financial institutions justify their existence by providing a variety of services that promote efficient allocation of funds. Canadian financial institutions include chartered banks and other depository institutions (trust companies and credit unions) as well as non-depository institutions (investment dealers, insurance companies, pension funds, and mutual funds).[14]

Table 1.2 ranks Canada's top 10 financial institutions by total assets. They include the "Big Six" domestically owned chartered banks, one credit union (Caisses Desjardins), a pension fund (Caisse de dépôt), one financial holding companies (Power Financial) and one mortgage company (Canada Mortgage and Housing Corp.).

Because they are allowed to diversify by operating in all provinces, Canada's chartered banks are good-sized on an international scale. Table 1.2 shows that the chartered banks also held the top slots domestically in 2006. Over time, pension funds and financial holding companies offering one-stop financial shopping are gaining on the banks.

Chartered banks operate under federal regulation, accepting deposits from suppliers of funds and making commercial loans to mid-sized businesses, corporate loans to large

---

[13]A Canadian study supporting the view that socially responsible investing does not harm returns is P. Amundson and S. R. Foerster, "Socially Responsible Investing: Better for Your Soul or Your Bottom Line?" *Canadian Investment Review,* Winter 2001, pp. 26–34. A contrary U.S. study is C. Geczy, R. F. Stambaugh, and D. Levin, "Investing in Socially Responsible Mutual Funds," October 2005, available at SSRN: http://ssrn.com/abstract=416380.

[14]Our discussion of Canadian financial institutions draws on L. Kryzanowski and G. S. Roberts, "Bank Structure in Canada," in *Banking Structure in Major Countries,* ed. G. G. Kaufman (Boston: Kluwer, 1992).

TABLE 1.2
The Largest Financial Institutions in Canada, 2006

	Rank by Total Assets	Assets (in $ millions)
Royal Bank of Canada	1	469,521
Toronto-Dominion Bank	2	365,210
The Bank of Nova Scotia	3	314,025
Bank of Montreal	4	297,532
Canadian Imperial Bank of Commerce	5	280,370
Caisse de dépôt et placement du Québec	6	179,739
Mouvement des caisses Desjardins	7	118,068
Power Financial Corp.	8	110,896
National Bank of Canada	9	107,598
Canada Mortgage and Housing Corp.	10	101,093

Source: *National Post BUSINESS,* June 2006 edition.

companies, and personal loans and mortgages to individuals. Banks make the majority of their income from the spread between the interest paid on deposits and the higher rate earned on loans. This process is called indirect finance because banks receive funds in the form of deposits and engage in a separate lending contract with funds demanders. Figure 1.6's top panel illustrates indirect finance.

Chartered banks also provide other services that generate fees instead of spreading income. For example, a large corporate customer seeking short-term debt funding can borrow directly from another large corporation with funds to supply through a banker's acceptance. This is an interest-bearing IOU that is stamped by a bank guaranteeing the borrower's credit. Instead of spread income, the bank receives a stamping fee. Banker's acceptances are an example of direct finance as illustrated in Figure 1.6's lower panel. Notice that in this case, funds do not pass through the bank's balance sheet in the form of a deposit and loan. This is often called securitization because a security (the banker's acceptance) is created.

Trust companies also accept deposits and make loans. In addition, trust companies engage in fiduciary activities—managing assets for estates, registered retirement savings plans, and so on. Banks own all the major trust companies. Like trust companies, credit unions also accept deposits and make loans.

Investment dealers are non-depository institutions that assist firms in issuing new securities in exchange for fee income. Investment dealers also aid investors in buying and selling securities. Chartered banks own majority stakes in Canada's top investment dealers.

Insurance companies include property and casualty insurance and health and life insurance companies. Life insurance companies accept funds in a form similar to deposits and make loans.

FIGURE 1.6
Two Types of Finance

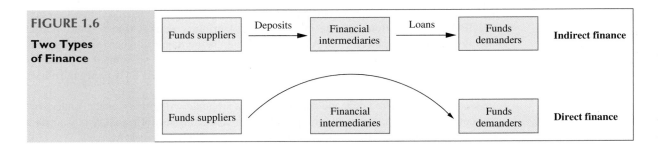

Pension funds invest contributions from employers and employees in securities offered by financial markets. Mutual funds pool individual investments to purchase a diversified portfolio of securities.

We base this survey of the principal activities of financial institutions on their main activities today. Recent deregulation now allows chartered banks, insurance companies, and investment dealers to engage in most activities of the others with one exception: Chartered banks are not allowed to sell life insurance through their branch networks. Although not every institution plans to become a one-stop financial supermarket, the different types of institutions will likely continue to become more alike.

Like financial institutions, financial markets differ. Principal differences concern the types of securities that are traded, how trading is conducted, and who the buyers and sellers are. Some of these differences are discussed next.

Money Versus Capital Markets

Financial markets can be classified as either money markets or capital markets. Short-term debt securities of many varieties are bought and sold in **money markets.** These short-term debt securities are often called money-market instruments. For example, a banker's acceptance represents short-term borrowing by large corporations and is a money-market instrument. Treasury bills are promissory notes of the Government of Canada. **Capital markets** are the markets for long-term debt and shares of stock, so the Toronto Stock Exchange, for example, is a capital market.

The money market is a dealer market. Generally speaking, dealers buy and sell something for themselves at their own risk. A car dealer, for example, buys and sells automobiles. In contrast, brokers and agents match buyers and sellers, but they do not actually own the commodity. A real estate agent or broker, for example, does not normally buy and sell houses.

The largest money-market dealers are chartered banks and investment dealers. Their trading facilities, along with other market participants, are connected electronically via telephone and computer so the money market has no actual physical location.

Primary Versus Secondary Markets

Financial markets function as both primary and secondary markets for debt and equity securities. The term *primary market* refers to the original sale of securities by governments and corporations. The secondary markets are where these securities are bought and sold after the original sale. Equities are, of course, issued solely by corporations. Debt securities are issued by both governments and corporations. The following discussion focuses on corporate securities only.

Primary Markets   In a primary market transaction, the corporation is the seller and raises money through the transaction. For example, in 1999 and early 2000, many untested dot-com companies issued public shares for the first time in initial public offerings (IPOs). Corporations engage in two types of primary market transactions: public offerings and private placements. A public offering, as the name suggests, involves selling securities to the general public, while a private placement is a negotiated sale involving a specific buyer. These topics are detailed in Chapters 20 and 21 so we only introduce the bare essentials here.

Most publicly offered debt and equity securities are underwritten. In Canada, underwriting is conducted by investment dealers specializing in marketing securities. Three of Canada's largest underwriters are RBC Dominion, Merrill Lynch, and CIBC World Markets.

When a public offering is underwritten, an investment dealer or a group of investment dealers (called a *syndicate*) typically purchases the securities from the firm and markets them to the public. The underwriters hope to profit by reselling the securities to investors at a higher price than they paid the firm for them.

By law, public offerings of debt and equity must be registered with provincial authorities, the most important being the Ontario Securities Commission (OSC). Registration requires the firm to disclose a great deal of information before selling any securities. The accounting, legal, and underwriting costs of public offerings can be considerable.

Partly to avoid the various regulatory requirements and the expense of public offerings, debt and equity are often sold privately to large financial institutions such as life insurance companies or pension funds. Such private placements do not have to be registered with the OSC and do not require the involvement of underwriters.

Secondary Markets   A secondary market transaction involves one owner or creditor selling to another. It is therefore the secondary markets that provide the means for transferring ownership of corporate securities. There are two kinds of secondary markets: auction markets and dealer markets.

Dealer markets in stocks and long-term debt are called over-the-counter (OTC) markets. Today, like the money market, a significant fraction of the market for stocks and all of the market for long-term debt has no central location; the many dealers are connected electronically. Nasdaq in the U.S. is a well-known over-the-counter market. As Table 1.3 shows, it is the third-largest stock market in the world. The name comes from the National Association of Securities Dealers (NASD), which sets up the automated quotation (AQ) system. Many smaller technology stocks are listed on Nasdaq, and the Nasdaq 100 index reflects the rise and fall of tech stocks.

The equity shares of most large firms in Canada trade in organized auction and dealer markets. The largest stock market in Canada is the Toronto Stock Exchange (TSX). Table 1.3 shows the top 10 stock exchanges in the world in 2005. The TSX ranked sixth. Smaller exchanges in Canada include the Montreal Exchange and the TSX Venture, which consists primarily of small oil and gas, mining, IT, and biotechnology companies that do not have the market capitalization to list on the TSX.

Auction markets differ from dealer markets in two ways. First, an auction market or exchange, unlike a dealer market, has a physical location (like Bay Street or Wall Street). Second, in a dealer market, most buying and selling is done by the dealer. The primary purpose of an auction market, on the other hand, is to match those who wish to sell with

TABLE 1.3
The Largest Stock Markets in the World By Market Capitalization in 2005

	Market Value (in U.S. $ billions)	Rank in 2005
New York	13,310.6	1
Tokyo	4,572.9	2
Nasdaq	3,604.0	3
London	3,058.2	4
Euronext	2,706.8	5
TSX Group	1,482.2	6
Deutsche Borse	1,221.1	7
Hong Kong Exchanges	1,055.0	8
BME Spanish Exchanges	959.9	9
Swiss Exchange	935.4	10

Source: World Federation of Exchanges at http://www.world-exchanges.org/publications/EQUITY105.XLS.

those who wish to buy. Dealers play a limited role. For example, the TSX has computerized its floor trading, replacing the trading floor with a wide-area computer network. This technological shift makes the TSX a hybrid of auction and dealer markets.

Listing

Stocks that trade on an organized exchange are said to be *listed* on that exchange. Companies seek exchange listing in order to enhance the liquidity of their shares, making them more attractive to investors by facilitating raising equity.[15] To be listed, firms must meet certain minimum criteria concerning, for example, the number of shares and shareholders and the market value. These criteria differ for different exchanges. To be listed on the TSX, a company must have at least one million shares trading, at least 300 public shareholders, and a market value of $4 million. There are additional requirements for earnings and assets that depend on the industry and whether the company is established and profitable or a junior firm. For example, profitable industrial firms must have earnings before tax of at least $200,000 in the year before listing and net tangible assets of $2 million. In contrast, technology firms with no earnings are allowed to list provided they have $10 million in the treasury and a market value of at least $50 million.

Listed companies face significant disclosure requirements. Particularly relevant for Canadian companies listing in the U.S. is the *Sarbanes-Oxley Act* of 2002. The act, better known as "Sarbox" or "SOX," is intended to protect investors from corporate abuses. For example, one section of Sarbox prohibits personal loans from a company to its officers, such as the ones that were received by WorldCom CEO Bernie Ebbers.

Section 404 of Sarbox requires, among other things, that each company's annual report must have an assessment of the company's internal control structure and financial reporting. The auditor must then evaluate and attest to management's assessment of these issues.

Sarbox contains other key requirements. For example, the officers of the corporation must review and sign the annual reports. They must explicitly declare that the annual report does not contain any false statements or material omissions; that the financial statements fairly represent the financial results; and that they are responsible for all internal controls. Finally, the annual report must list any deficiencies in internal controls. In essence, Sarbox makes company management responsible for the accuracy of the company's financial statements.

Of course, as with any law, there are compliance costs, and Sarbox has increased the cost of corporate audits, sometimes dramatically. Estimates of the increase in company audit costs to comply with Sarbox range from US$500,000 to over US$5 million, which has led to some unintended consequences. For example, in 2004, 134 firms delisted their shares from exchanges, or "went dark." This was up from 30 delistings in 1999. Most of the companies that delisted stated that their reason was to avoid the cost of compliance with Sarbox.

Foreign Exchange Market

The **foreign exchange market** is undoubtedly the world's largest financial market. It is the market where one country's currency is traded for another's. Most of the trading takes place in a few currencies: the U.S. dollar ($), the euro (€), British pound sterling (£), Japanese yen (¥), and Swiss franc (SF).

---

[15]Two relevant studies of Canadian companies listing in the U.S. are S. R. Foerster and G. A. Karolyi, "The Effects of Market Segmentation and Investor Recognition on Asset Prices: Evidence from Foreign Listings in the U.S.," *Journal of Finance* 54 (June 1999), pp. 981–1013 and U. R. Mittoo, "The Winners and Losers of Listings in the U.S.," *Canadian Investment Review* (Fall 1998), pp. 13–17.

The foreign exchange market is an over-the-counter market. There is no single location where traders get together. Instead, traders are located in the major commercial and investment banks around the world. They communicate using computer terminals, telephones, and other telecommunication devices. One element in the communications network for foreign transactions is the *Society for Worldwide Interbank Financial Telecommunications* (SWIFT). It is a Belgian not-for-profit cooperative. A bank in Toronto can send messages to a bank in London via SWIFT's regional processing centres. The connections are through data-transmission lines.

The many different types of participants in the foreign exchange market include the following:

1. Importers who convert their domestic currency to foreign currency to pay for goods from foreign countries
2. Exporters who receive foreign currency and may want to convert to the domestic currency
3. Portfolio managers who buy and sell foreign stocks and bonds
4. Foreign exchange brokers who match buy and sell orders
5. Traders who make the market in foreign exchange.

? Concept Questions
- **Distinguish between money markets and capital markets.**
- **What is listing?**
- **What is the difference between a primary market and a secondary market?**
- **What are the principal financial institutions in Canada? What is the principal role of each?**
- **What are direct and indirect finance? How do they differ?**
- **What is a dealer market? How do dealer and auction markets differ?**
- **What is the largest auction market in Canada?**

1.6 Trends in Financial Markets and Management

Like all markets, financial markets are experiencing rapid globalization. At the same time, interest rates, foreign exchange rates, and other macroeconomic variables have become more volatile. The toolkit of available financial management techniques has expanded rapidly in response to a need to control increased risk from volatility and to track complexities arising from dealings in many countries. Improved computer technology makes new financial engineering applications practical.

When financial managers or investment dealers design new securities or financial processes, their efforts are referred to as financial engineering. Successful financial engineering reduces and controls risk and minimizes taxes. Financial engineering creates a variety of debt securities and reinforces the trend toward securitization of credit introduced earlier. In addition, options and optionlike securities are becoming important in risk management.

Financial engineering also seeks to reduce financing costs of issuing securities as well as the costs of complying with rules laid down by regulatory authorities. An example is the Short Form Prospectus Distribution (SFPD) system, which allows firms that frequently issue new equity to bypass repetitive OSC registration requirements.

In addition to financial engineering, advances in computer technology also create opportunities to combine different types of financial institutions to take advantage of economies of scale and scope. Large institutions operate in all provinces and internationally, enjoying more lax regulations in some jurisdictions than in others. Financial institutions pressure authorities to deregulate in a push–pull process called the regulatory dialectic.

Deregulation is opening the possibility for further changes. For example, in 2001, financial services legislation reopened discussion on bank mergers. Two pairs of banks had been unsuccessful in their plans to merge several years earlier, and the industry revived this issue to pressure for government approval for future mergers. Starting in January 2002, life insurance company mergers were allowed. This means that large Canadian life insurers such as Manulife can acquire smaller companies, leading to industry consolidation.

These trends have made financial management a much more complex and technical activity. For this reason, many business students find introductory finance one of their most challenging subjects. The trends we reviewed have also increased the stakes. In the face of increased competition globally, the payoff for good financial management is great. The finance function is also becoming important in corporate strategic planning. The good news is that career opportunities (and compensation) in financial positions are highly competitive.

? Concept Questions

• **How do key trends in financial markets affect Canadian financial institutions?**

1.7 Outline of the Text

Now that we have taken the quick tour through all of corporate finance, we can take a closer look at this book. The book is divided into eight parts. The long-term investment decision is covered first. Financing decisions and working capital are covered next. Finally, a series of special topics is covered. Here are the eight parts:

Part I:	Overview
Part II:	Value and Capital Budgeting
Part III:	Risk
Part IV:	Capital Structure and Dividend Policy
Part V:	Long-Term Financing
Part VI:	Options, Futures, and Corporate Finance
Part VII:	Short-Term Finance
Part VIII:	Special Topics

Part II describes how investment opportunities are valued in financial markets. This part contains the basic theory. Because finance is a subject that builds understanding from the ground up, the material is very important. The most important concept in Part II is net present value. We develop the net present value rule into a tool for valuing investment alternatives. We discuss general formulas and apply them to a variety of different financial instruments.

Part III introduces basic measures of risk. The capital asset pricing model (CAPM) and the arbitrage pricing theory (APT) are used to devise methods for incorporating risk in valuation. As part of this discussion, we describe the famous beta coefficient. Finally, we use the preceding pricing models to handle capital budgeting under risk.

Part IV examines two interrelated topics: capital structure and dividend policy. Capital structure is the extent to which the firm relies on debt. It cannot be separated from the amount of cash dividends the firm decides to pay out to its equity shareholders.

Part V concerns long-term financing. We describe the securities that corporations issue to raise cash as well as the mechanics of offering securities for public sale. Here we discuss call provisions and leasing.

Part VI covers options and futures and their use in risk management. We introduce these derivatives and show how understanding the underlying concepts opens up new insights into corporate finance. Next we focus on warrants and convertibles—two important kinds of corporate securities with options embedded in them. In the final chapter in this section, we introduce the important topic of risk management.

Part VII is devoted to short-term finance. We focus on managing the firm's current assets and current liabilities. We describe aspects of the firm's short-term financial management. Separate chapters on cash management and credit management are included.

Part VIII covers two important special topics: mergers and international corporate finance.

KEY TERMS

Agency costs 13
Capital budgeting 3
Capital gains 27
Capital markets 20
Capital structure 3

Contingent claims 9
Corporation 11
Foreign exchange market 22
Money markets 20
Net working capital 3

Partnership 10
Set-of-contracts viewpoint 13
Socially responsible investing 16
Sole proprietorship 9

SUGGESTED READING

A survey of trends affecting chartered banks and other Canadian financial institutions is found in:
A. Saunders, H. Thomas, and P. McGraw. *Financial Institutions Management.* 3rd Canadian ed., Toronto: McGraw-Hill Ryerson, 2006.

A current survey of theory and evidence on socially responsible investing is:
J. Hudson. *The Social Responsibility of the Investment Profession.* Research Foundation of the CFA Institute, 2006.

Evidence is provided on the tax factor in choosing to incorporate in:
J. K. Mackie-Mason and R. H. Gordon. "How Much Do Taxes Discourage Incorporation?" *Journal of Finance* (June 1997).

What are the patterns of corporate ownership around the world? This is the question posed by:
R. La Porta, F. Lopez-De-Silanes, and A. Shleifer. "Corporate Ownership Around the World." *Journal of Finance* 54 (1999).

A survey of international corporate governance can be found in:
D. K. Denis and J. S. McConnell. "International Corporate Governance." *Journal of Financial and Quantitative Analysis* 38 (March 2003).

QUESTIONS & PROBLEMS

1.1 Can our goal of maximizing the value of the shareholders' wealth conflict with other goals such as avoiding unethical or illegal behaviour? In particular, do you think that topics such as customer and employee safety, the environment, and the general good of society fit into this framework? Think of some specific scenarios to illustrate your answer.

1.2 Who owns a corporation? Describe the process whereby the owners control the firm's management. What is the main reason that an agency relationship exists in the corporate form of organization? In this context, what kinds of problems can arise?

1.3   Corporate ownership varies around the world. Historically, individuals have owned the majority of shares in public corporations in the United States. In Canada this is also the case, but ownership is more often concentrated in the hands of a majority shareholder. In Germany and Japan, banks, other financial institutions, and large companies own most of the shares in public corporations. How do you think these ownership differences affect the severity of agency costs in different countries?

1.4   What are the major types of financial institutions and financial markets in Canada?

1.5   What are some major trends in Canadian financial markets? Explain how these trends affect the practice of financial management in Canada.

1.6   On the Market Insight Home Page, follow the "industry" link. From the pull-down menu, you can select various industries. Answer the following questions for these industries: Aerospace & Defense, Application Software, Diversified Capital Markets, Homebuilding, Personal Products, Restaurants, and Precious Metals & Minerals.
a.   How many companies are in each industry?
b.   What are the total sales of each industry?
c.   Does the industry with the largest total sales have the largest number of competitors? What does this tell you about the competition in each industry?

Appendix 1A   Taxes

Taxes are very important since cash flows are measured after taxes. In this section, we examine corporate and personal tax rates and how taxes are calculated. We apply this knowledge to see how different types of income are taxed in the hands of individuals and corporations.

The size of the tax bill is determined through tax laws and regulations in the annual budgets of the federal government (administered by the Canada Revenue Agency) and provincial governments. If the various rules of taxation seem a little bizarre or convoluted to you, keep in mind that tax law is the result of political forces as well as economic forces. The tax law is continually evolving, so our discussion cannot make you a tax expert. Rather, it will give you an understanding of the tax principles important for financial management along with the ability to ask the right questions when consulting a tax expert.

Individual Tax Rates

Individual tax rates in effect for federal and selected provincial taxes for 2006 are shown in Table 1A.1. These rates apply to income from employment (wages and salary) and from unincorporated businesses. Investment income is also taxable. Interest income is taxed at the same rates as employment income, but special provisions reduce the taxes payable on dividends and capital gains. We discuss these in detail later in the appendix.

In making financial decisions it is frequently important to distinguish between average and marginal tax rates. The percentage rates shown in Table 1A.1 are all marginal rates.

To illustrate, suppose you live in Ontario and have a taxable income of $120,000. Your tax on the next dollar is:[16]

$$40.16\% = \text{Federal tax rate} + \text{Provincial tax rate} = 29\% + 11.16\%$$

Tax rates vary somewhat across provinces. For example, in Quebec the same taxable income faces tax on the next dollar at 53 percent.

---

[16]Actual rates for 2006 are somewhat higher as we ignore surtaxes that apply in higher brackets.

TABLE 1A.1

Individual Income Tax Rates, 2006

	Taxable Income	Tax Rate
Federal Taxes	$0–36,378	15.25%
	$36,379–72,756	22.00
	$72,757–118,285	26.00
	$118,286 and over	29.00
British Columbia	$0–33,755	6.05%
	$33,756–67,511	9.15
	$67,512–77,511	11.70
	$77,512–94,121	13.70
	$94,122 and over	14.70
Alberta	All income	10.00%
Ontario	$0–34,758	6.05%
	$34,759–69,516	9.15
	$69,517 and over	11.16
Quebec	$0–28,710	16.00%
	$28,711–57,430	20.00
	$57,431 and over	24.00
Nova Scotia	$0–29,590	8.79%
	$29,591–59,180	14.95
	$59,181–93,000	16.67
	$93,001 and over	17.50

Source: Canada Revenue Agency, www.cra-arc.gc.ca/tax.

With the exception of Quebec residents, taxpayers file one tax return. In computing your tax, you first find the federal tax and then calculate the provincial tax as a percentage of the federal tax.

Taxes on Investment Income

A dividend tax credit provides a degree of integration between corporate and individual taxation. This credit applies only to dividends paid by Canadian corporations. The result is to encourage Canadian investors to invest in Canadian companies as opposed to foreign ones.[17]

To see how dividends are taxed we start with common shares held by individual investors. Table 1A.2 shows how the dividend tax credit reduces the effective tax rate on dividends for investors in the top federal tax bracket. The steps follow the instructions on federal tax returns. Actual dividends are grossed up by 45 percent and federal tax is calculated on the grossed-up figure. A dividend tax credit of 19 percent of the actual dividend is subtracted from the federal tax to get the federal tax payable. The provincial tax (for Ontario in this example) is calculated and added. Note that each province has its own dividend tax credit.

Individual Canadian investors also benefit from a tax reduction for **capital gains.** Capital gains arise when an investment increases in value above its purchase price. Only half of capital gains are taxable.

---

[17]Evidence that the dividend tax credit causes investors to favour Canadian stocks is provided in L. Booth, "The Dividend Tax Credit and Canadian Ownership Objectives," *Canadian Journal of Economics* 20 (May 1987).

TABLE 1A.2

Investment Income Tax Treatment for Ontario Residents in Top Bracket (over $118,826) for 2006

Interest Tax Treatment	
Interest	$ 1,000.00
Federal tax at 29%	290.00
Provincial tax at 11.16%	111.60
Total tax	$ 401.60
Capital Gains Tax Treatment	
Capital gains	$ 1,000.00
Taxable capital gains (50% × $1,000)	500.00
Federal tax at 29%	145.00
Provincial tax at 11.16%	55.80
Total tax	$ 200.80
Dividend Tax Treatment	
Dividends	$ 1,000.00
Gross up at 45%	450.00
Grossed up dividend	1450.00
Federal tax at 29%	420.50
Less dividend tax credit (19% × $1,450)	275.50
Federal tax payable	$ 145.00
Provincial tax at 11.16% (11.16% × $1,450)	$ 161.82
Less dividend tax credit (7.16% × $1,450)	103.82
Provincial tax payable	$ 58.00
Total tax	$ 203.00

Source: Adapted from 2006 KPMG Tax Rate Publication.

Additionally, capital gains are lightly taxed since individuals only pay taxes on realized capital gains when shares are sold. Since many individuals hold shares for a long time (have unrealized capital gains), the time value of money dramatically reduces the effective tax rate on capital gains.

Corporate Taxes

Canadian corporations, like individuals, are subject to corporate taxes levied by the federal and provincial governments. Table 1A.3 shows corporate tax rates using Ontario as an example. You can see from the table that small corporations (income under $300,000) and, to a lesser degree, manufacturing and processing companies, pay tax at lower rates.

Comparing the rates in Table 1A.3 with the personal tax rates in Table 1A.1 appears to reveal a tax advantage for small businesses and professionals in forming a corporation. The tax rate on corporate income of, say, $150,000 is less than the personal tax rate assessed on income of unincorporated businesses. But this is oversimplified because dividends paid to the owners are also taxed, as we saw earlier.

TABLE 1A.3

Corporate Tax Rates in Percentages, 2006

	Federal	Ontario	Combined
Basic Corporations	22.10%	14.01%	36.10%
All small corporations with a taxable income less than $300,000	13.10%	5.50%	18.60%

Source: Adapted from 2006 tax rate publication.

Taxable Income

Interest and dividends are treated differently in calculating corporate tax. Interest paid is deducted from EDIT (earnings before interest and taxes) in calculating taxable income, but dividends paid are not. Because interest is a tax-deductible expense, debt financing has a tax advantage over financing with common stock.

The tables are turned when we contrast interest and dividends earned by the firm. Interest earned is fully taxable just like any other form of ordinary income. Dividends on common and preferred shares received from other Canadian corporations qualify for a 100 percent exemption and are received tax-free.[18]

Capital Gains, Carryforward, and Carryback

If a firm disposes of an asset for more than it paid originally, the difference is a capital gain. As with individuals, firms' capital gains are taxed at 50 percent of the tax rate.

When calculating capital gains for tax purposes, a firm nets out all capital losses in the same year. If capital losses exceed capital gains, the net capital loss may be carried back to reduce taxable income in the three prior years. Any capital losses remaining may be carried forward indefinitely. Under the carryback feature, a firm files a revised tax return and receives a refund of prior years' taxes.

A similar carryback and carryforward provision applies to operating losses. In this case, the carryback period is three years and carryforward is allowed for up to seven years.

Investment Tax Credits

An investment tax credit applies in certain regions of the country—presently Atlantic Canada but applied more broadly in past years. An investment tax credit allows a qualified firm to subtract a set percentage of an investment directly from taxes payable.

Appendix Questions and Problems

1.A1   Distinguish between an average tax rate and a marginal tax rate.

1.A2   How does tax treatment of investment income differ among interest, dividends, and capital gains?

1.A3   Explain how carryback/carryforward provisions and investment tax credits reduce corporate taxes.

Marginal Versus Average Tax Rates

1.A4   (Refer to Table 1A.3.) Corporation X has $100,000 in taxable income, and Corporation Y, a manufacturer, has $1 million in taxable income.
   a. What is the tax bill for each firm in Ontario?
   b. Suppose both firms have identified a new project that will increase taxable income by $10,000. How much in additional taxes will each firm pay? Why aren't these amounts the same?

Taxes on Investment Income

1.A5   Mary Song, a Toronto investor, receives $10,000 in dividends from B.C. Forest Products shares, $10,000 in interest from a deposit in a chartered bank, and a $10,000 capital gain from selling Central B.C. Mines shares. Use the information in Table 1A.2 to calculate the after-tax cash flow from each investment. Ms. Song's taxable income is $60,000.

---

[18]We ignore refundable taxes on dividends here and discuss them in Chapter 19.

Chapter **2**

Accounting Statements and Cash Flow

EXECUTIVE SUMMARY

Chapter 2 describes the basic accounting statements used for reporting corporate activity. It focuses on practical details of cash flow. It will become clear in the next several chapters that knowing how to determine cash flow helps the financial manager make better decisions. The increasing number of corporate accounting scandals involving companies such as Hollinger, Tyco, and Adelphia has highlighted the importance of accurate financial reporting. Students who have had accounting courses will not find the material new and can think of it as a review with an emphasis on finance. We discuss cash flow further in later chapters.

2.1 The Balance Sheet

The **balance sheet** is an accountant's snapshot of the firm's accounting value on a particular date, as though the firm momentarily stood still. The balance sheet has two sides: On the left are the *assets* and on the right the *liabilities* and *shareholders' equity*. The balance sheet states what the firm owns and how it is financed. The accounting definition that underlies the balance sheet and describes the balance is:

$$\text{Assets} \equiv \text{Liabilities} + \text{Shareholders' equity}$$

We have put a three-line equality in the balance sheet equation to indicate that it must always hold, by definition. In fact, the shareholders' equity is defined to be the difference between the assets and the liabilities of the firm. In principle, equity is what the shareholders would have remaining after the firm discharged its obligations.

Table 2.1 gives the 20X7 and 20X6 balance sheet for the fictitious Canadian Composite Corporation. The assets in the balance sheet are listed in order by the length of time it normally takes a going concern to convert them to cash. The asset side depends on the nature of the business and how management chooses to conduct it. Management must make decisions about cash versus marketable securities, credit versus cash sales, whether to make or buy commodities, whether to lease or purchase items, the types of business in which to engage, and so on. The liabilities and the shareholders' equity are listed in the order in which they must be paid.

The liabilities and shareholders' equity side reflects the types and proportions of financing, which depend on management's choice of capital structure, as between debt and equity and between current debt and long-term debt.

When analyzing a balance sheet, the financial manager should be aware of three concerns: accounting measures of liquidity, debt versus equity, and value versus cost.

TABLE 2.1   Balance Sheet of the Canadian Composite Corporation

			Liabilities (debt)		
CANADIAN COMPOSITE CORPORATION Balance Sheet 20X7 and 20X6 (in $ millions)					
Assets	20X7	20X6	and Shareholders' Equity	20X7	20X6
Current assets:			Current liabilities:		
Cash and equivalents	$ 140	$ 107	Accounts payable	$ 213	$ 197
Accounts receivable	294	270	Notes payable	50	53
Inventories	269	280	Accrued expenses	223	205
Other	58	50	Total current liabilities	486	455
Total current assets	761	707			
Long-term assets:			Long-term liabilities:		
Property, plant, and equipment	1,423	1,274	Deferred taxes	117	104
Less accumulated depreciation	(550)	(460)	Long-term debt	471	458
Net property, plant, and equipment	873	814	Total long-term liabilities	588	562
Intangible assets and others	245	221	Shareholders' equity:		
			Preferred shares	39	39
			Common shares	376	339
Total long-term assets	1,118	1,035	Accumulated retained earnings	390	347
			Total equity	805	725
Total assets	$1,879	$1,742	Total liabilities and shareholders' equity	$1,879	$1,742

Liquidity

Liquidity refers to the ease and speed with which assets can be converted to cash. Current assets are the most liquid and include cash and those assets that can reasonably be expected to be turned into cash within a year from the date of the balance sheet. Accounts receivable are the amount not yet collected from customers for goods or services sold to them (after adjustment for potential bad debts). Inventory is composed of raw materials to be used in production, work in process, and finished goods. Fixed assets are the least liquid kind of asset. Tangible fixed assets include property, plant, and equipment. These assets do not convert to cash from normal business activity, and they are not usually used to pay expenses, such as payroll.

Some fixed assets are not tangible. Intangible assets have no physical existence but can be very valuable. Examples of intangible assets are the value of a trademark, the value of a patent, and the value of customer recognition. The more liquid a firm's assets, the less likely the firm is to experience problems meeting short-term obligations. Thus, the probability that a firm will avoid financial distress can be linked to its liquidity. Unfortunately, liquid assets frequently have lower rates of return than fixed assets; for example, cash generates no investment income. To the extent a firm invests in liquid assets, it sacrifices an opportunity to invest in more profitable investment vehicles.

Debt Versus Equity

Liabilities are obligations of the firm that require a payout of cash within a stipulated time period. Many liabilities involve contractual obligations to repay a stated amount with interest over a period. Thus, liabilities are debts and are frequently associated with nominally fixed cash burdens, called *debt service,* that put the firm in default of a contract if they are not paid. *Shareholders' equity* is a claim against the firm's assets that is residual and not fixed. In general terms, when the firm borrows, it gives the bondholders first claim on the firm's cash flow.[1] Bondholders can sue if the firm defaults on its bond contracts. This may lead the firm to declare itself bankrupt. Shareholders' equity is the residual difference between assets and liabilities:

$$\text{Assets} - \text{Liabilities} \equiv \text{Shareholders' equity}$$

This is the shareholders' share in the firm stated in accounting terms. The accounting value of shareholders' equity increases when retained earnings are added. This occurs when the firm retains part of its earnings instead of paying them out as dividends.

Value Versus Cost

The accounting value of a firm's assets is frequently referred to as the *carrying value* or the *book value* of the assets.[2] Under **generally accepted accounting principles (GAAP),** audited financial statements of firms in Canada carry the assets at historical cost adjusted for depreciation. Thus the terms *carrying value* and *book value* are unfortunate. They specifically say "value," when in fact the accounting numbers are based on cost. This misleads many readers of financial statements into thinking that the firm's assets are recorded at true market values. *Market value* is the price at which willing buyers and sellers trade the assets. It would be only a coincidence if accounting value and market value were the same. In fact, management's job is to create a value for the firm that is higher than its cost. When market values are considerably below book values, it is customary accounting practice to write down assets. For example, in March 2003, the Ontario Municipal Employees' Retirement System (OMERS), a large pension fund, announced $600 million in write-downs as a result of changes in the value of real estate holdings, private equity, and infrastructure projects.[3] Sometimes, huge write-offs are also indicative of overstated profits in previous years, as assets were not expensed properly.

There are many users of a firm's balance sheet and each may seek different information from it. A banker may look at a balance sheet for evidence of liquidity and working capital. A supplier may also note the size of accounts payable, which reflects the general promptness of payments. Many users of financial statements, including managers and investors, want to know the value of the firm, not its cost. This is not found on the balance sheet. In fact, many of a firm's true resources (good management, proprietary assets, and so on) do not appear on the balance sheet. Henceforth, whenever we speak of the value of an asset or the value of the firm, we will normally mean its market value. So, for example, when we say the goal of the financial manager is to increase the value of the stock, we mean the market value of the stock.

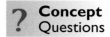

Concept Questions

- **What is the balance sheet equation?**
- **What three things should be kept in mind when looking at a balance sheet?**

---

[1]Bondholders are investors in the firm's debt. They are creditors of the firm. In this discussion, the term *bondholder* means the same thing as *creditor.*

[2]Confusion often arises because many financial accounting terms have the same meaning. This presents a problem with jargon for the reader of financial statements. For example, the following terms usually refer to the same thing: *assets minus liabilities, net worth, shareholders' equity, owner's equity,* and *equity capitalization.*

[3]E. Church, "OMERS Taking Huge Writedown," globeinvestor.com, March 31, 2004. This process does not work the other way—accounting principles are conservative and carry assets at adjusted cost when market values are higher.

TABLE 2.2
Income Statement of the Canadian Composite Corporation

CANADIAN COMPOSITE CORPORATION Income Statement 20X7 (in $ millions)	
Total operating revenues	$ 2,262
Cost of goods sold	(1,655)
Selling, general, and administrative expenses	(327)
Depreciation	(90)
Operating income	190
Other income	29
Earnings before interest and taxes	219
Interest expense	(49)
Pre-tax income	170
Taxes	(84)
Current: $71	
Deferred: $13	
Net income	$ 86
Retained earnings: $43	
Dividends: $43	

2.2 The Income Statement

The **income statement**[4] measures performance over a specific period of time (say, a year). The accounting definition of income is:

$$\text{Revenue} - \text{Expenses} \equiv \text{Income}$$

If the balance sheet is like a snapshot, the income statement is like a video recording of what happened between two snapshots. Table 2.2 gives the income statement for the Canadian Composite Corporation for 20X7.

The income statement usually includes several sections. The operations section reports the firm's revenues and expenses from principal operations. Among other things, the non-operating section of the income statement includes all financing costs, such as interest expense. Usually a second section reports as a separate item the amount of taxes levied on income. The last item on the income statement is the bottom line, or net income. Net income is frequently expressed per share of common stock, that is, earnings per share.

When analyzing an income statement, the financial manager should keep in mind GAAP, non-cash items, time, and costs.

Generally Accepted Accounting Principles (GAAP)

As pointed out earlier, the focus in financial decisions is on market value, which depends on cash flow. However, like the balance sheet, the income statement has many different users and the accounting profession has developed GAAP to provide information for a broad audience not necessarily concerned with cash flow. For this reason, it is necessary to make adjustments to information on income statements to obtain cash flow.

---

[4]The CICA is encouraging replacement of the term "Income Statement" with "Statement of Earnings." However, as the term "Income Statement" is still widely accepted, it will be used throughout this textbook.

For example, revenue is recognized on an income statement when the earnings process is virtually completed and an exchange of goods or services has occurred. Therefore, the unrealized appreciation in owning property will not be recognized as income. This provides a device for smoothing income by selling appreciated property at convenient times. For example, if the firm owns a tree farm that has doubled in value, then in a year when its earnings from other businesses are down, it can raise overall earnings by selling some trees. The matching principle of GAAP dictates that revenues be matched with expenses. Thus, income is reported when it is earned or accrued, even though no cash flow has necessarily occurred. (For example, when goods are sold for credit, sales and profits are reported.)

Non-cash Items

The economic value of assets is intimately connected to their future incremental cash flows. However, cash flow does not appear on an income statement. There are several **non-cash items** that are expenses against revenues, but do not affect cash flow directly.[5] The most important of these is *depreciation*. Depreciation reflects the accountant's estimate of the cost of equipment used up in the production process.[6] For example, suppose an asset with a five-year life and no resale value is purchased for $1,000. According to accountants, the $1,000 cost must be expensed over the useful life of the asset. If straight-line depreciation is used, there will be five equal installments and $200 of depreciation expense will be incurred each year. From a finance perspective, the cost of the asset is the actual negative cash flow incurred when the asset is acquired (that is, $1,000, not the accountant's smoothed $200-per-year depreciation expense).

Another non-cash expense is *deferred taxes*. Deferred taxes result from differences between accounting income and true taxable income.[7] Notice that the accounting tax shown on the income statement for the Canadian Composite Corporation is $84 million. It can be broken down as current taxes and deferred taxes. The current tax portion is actually sent to the tax authorities (for example, Canada Revenue Agency). The deferred tax portion is not. However, the theory is that if taxable income is less than accounting income in the current year, it will be more than accounting income later. Consequently, taxes that are not paid today will have to be paid in the future, and they represent a liability of the firm. It shows up on the balance sheet as deferred tax liability. From the cash flow perspective, though, deferred tax is not a cash outflow.

Time and Costs

It is often useful to think of the future as having two distinct parts: the *short run* and the *long run*. The short run is that period in which certain equipment, resources, and commitments of the firm are fixed; but it is long enough for the firm to vary its output by using more labour and raw materials. The short run is not a precise period of time that will be the same for all industries. However, all firms making decisions in the short run have some fixed costs, that is, costs that will not change because of the fixed commitments. In real business activity, examples of fixed costs are bond interest, overhead, and property taxes. Costs that are not fixed are variable. Variable costs change as the output of the

---

[5]Although it is a non-cash expense, depreciation has tax implications (discussed later) that affect cash flow.

[6]Depreciation is the form of amortization that applies to capital assets.

[7]One situation in which taxable income may be lower than accounting income is when the firm uses capital cost allowance (CCA) depreciation expense procedures for calculating taxes but uses straight-line procedures allowed by GAAP for reporting purposes. We discuss CCA in Chapter 8. Accountants refer to deferred taxes as a future income tax liability.

firm changes; some examples are raw materials and wages for production line workers. In the long run, all costs are variable.[8]

Financial accountants do not distinguish between variable costs and fixed costs. Instead, accounting costs usually fit into a classification that distinguishes product costs from period costs. Product costs are the total production costs (raw materials, direct labour, and manufacturing overhead) incurred during a period and are reported on the income statement as the cost of goods sold. Both variable and fixed costs are included in product costs. Period costs are costs that are allocated to a time period; they are called *selling, general,* and *administrative expenses.* One period cost would be the company president's salary.

? Concept Questions

- **What is the income statement equation?**
- **What are three things to keep in mind when looking at an income statement?**
- **What are non-cash expenses?**

2.3 Net Working Capital

Net working capital is current assets minus current liabilities. Net working capital is positive when current assets are greater than current liabilities. This means the cash that will become available over the next 12 months is greater than the cash that must be paid out. The net working capital of the Canadian Composite Corporation is $275 million in 20X7 and $252 million in 20X6:

	Current assets ($ millions)	−	Current liabilities ($ millions)	=	Net working capital ($ millions)
20X7	$761	−	$486	=	$275
20X6	$707	−	$455	=	$252

In addition to investing in fixed assets (capital spending), a firm can invest in net working capital—called the *change in net working capital.* The **change in net working capital** in 20X7 is the difference between the net working capital in 20X7 and 20X6; that is, $275 million − $252 million = $23 million. The change in net working capital is usually positive in a growing firm because higher levels of net working capital are necessary for increased sales.

Investment in net working capital occurs when raw materials and other inventory are purchased and stored. Keeping all raw material and other inventory purchases constant, the investment in net working capital will decrease when the raw materials are consumed for the manufacture of finished goods. Working capital also increases when cash is kept in a particular project as a buffer against unexpected expenditures or when credit sales are made, increasing accounts receivable instead of cash. Positive increases in current assets lead to greater investment in net working capital. However, investments in net working capital can be offset by any purchases made by the company on credit. Net working capital will be discussed in more depth in Chapter 8 where the concept of net working capital will be applied in forecasting for capital budgeting and helping to calculate the net present value.

? Concept Questions

- **What is net working capital?**
- **What is the change in net working capital?**

---

[8]When one famous economist was asked about the difference between the long run and the short run, he said, "In the long run we are all dead."

2.4 Financial Cash Flow

Perhaps the most important item that can be extracted from financial statements is the actual **cash flow.** There is an accounting statement called the *statement of changes in financial position.* This statement helps to explain the change in accounting cash and equivalents, which for Canadian Composite is $33 million in 20X7. (See Appendix 2B.) Notice in Table 2.1 that cash and equivalents increases from $107 million in 20X6 to $140 million in 20X7. However, we will look at cash flow from a different perspective, the perspective of finance. In finance, the value of the firm is its ability to generate financial cash flow. (We will talk more about financial cash flow in Chapter 8.)

The first point we should mention is that cash flow is not the same as net working capital. For example, increasing inventory requires using cash. Because both inventories and cash are current assets, this does not affect net working capital. In this case, an increase in a particular net working capital account, such as inventory, is associated with decreasing cash flow.

Just as we established that the value of a firm's assets is always equal to the value of the liabilities plus the value of the equity, the cash flows from the firm's assets generated by its operating activities, CF(A), must equal the cash flows to the firm's creditors, CF(B), and equity investors, CF(S):

$$CF(A) = CF(B) + CF(S)$$

The first step in determining a firm's cash flows is to figure out the *cash flow from operations.* Table 2.3 shows that operating cash flow is the cash flow generated by business activities, including sales of goods and services. Operating cash flow reflects tax payments, but not financing, capital spending, or changes in net working capital.

TABLE 2.3
Financial Cash Flow of the Canadian Composite Corporation

CANADIAN COMPOSITE CORPORATION Financial Cash Flow 20X7 (in $ millions)	
Cash Flow of the Firm	
Operating cash flow (Earnings before interest and taxes plus depreciation minus taxes)	$ 238
Capital spending (Acquisitions of long-term assets minus sales of long-term assets)	(173)
Additions to net working capital	(23)
Total	$ 42
Cash Flow to Investors in the Firm	
Debt (Interest plus retirement of debt minus long-term debt financing)	$ 36
Equity (Dividends plus repurchase of equity minus new equity financing)	6
Total	$ 42

	(in \$ millions)
Earnings before interest and taxes	\$219
Depreciation[9]	90
Current taxes	(71)
Operating cash flow	\$238

Another important component of cash flow involves *changes in long-term assets*. For example, when Canadian Composite sold its power systems subsidiary in 20X7 it generated \$25 in cash flow. The net change in long-term assets equals sales of long-term assets minus the acquisition of long-term assets. The result is the cash flow used for capital spending:

Acquisition of long-term assets	\$198
Sales of fixed assets	(25)
Capital spending	\$173

We can arrive at the same number by adding the increase in property, plant, and equipment (\$149) to the increase in intangible assets (\$24).

Cash flows are also used for making investments in net working capital. In the Canadian Composite Corporation in 20X7, *additions to net working capital* are

Additions to net working capital	\$ 23

Total cash flows generated by the firm's assets are the sum of

Operating cash flow	\$ 238
Capital spending	(173)
Additions to net working capital	(23)
Total cash flow of the firm	\$ 42

The total outgoing cash flow of the firm can be separated into cash flows paid to creditors and cash flows paid to shareholders. The cash flow paid to creditors represents a regrouping of the data in Table 2.3 and an explicit recording of interest expense from Table 2.2. An important source of cash flow comes from selling new debt. Thus, an increase in long-term debt is the net effect of new borrowing and repayment of maturing obligations plus interest expense.

Cash Flow Paid to Creditors
(\$ millions)

Interest	\$ 49
Net proceeds from long-term debt sales	(13)
Total	\$ 36

Cash flow of the firm also is paid to the shareholders. It is the sum of dividends plus net new equity from repurchasing outstanding shares of stock and issuing new shares of stock.

[9]The accounting profession is moving toward using the term "amortization" instead of "depreciation." Since "depreciation" is widely used in finance, we retain its usage here and throughout this book.

<table>
<thead>
<tr><th colspan="2">Cash Flow to Shareholders
($ millions)</th></tr>
</thead>
<tbody>
<tr><td>Dividends</td><td>$ 43</td></tr>
<tr><td>Net new equity</td><td>(37)</td></tr>
<tr><td>Total</td><td>$ 6</td></tr>
</tbody>
</table>

In general, cash flow to shareholders can be determined as:

$$\text{Cash flow to shareholders} = \text{Dividends paid} - \text{Net new equity raised}$$
$$= \text{Dividends paid} - (\text{Stock sold} - \text{Stock repurchased})$$

To determine stock sold, notice that the common stock and capital surplus accounts went up by a combined $23 + 20 = $43, which implies that the company sold $43 million worth of stock. Second, treasury stock went up by $6, indicating that the company bought back $6 million worth of stock. Net new equity is thus $43 − 6 = $37. Dividends paid were $43 million, so the cash flow to shareholders was:

$$\text{Cash flow to shareholders} = \$43 - (43 - 6) = \$6,$$

which is what we previously calculated.

Some important observations can be drawn from our discussion of cash flow:

1. Several types of cash flow are relevant to understanding the financial situation of the firm. **Cash flow from operations,** defined as earnings before interest and depreciation minus taxes, measures the cash generated from operations not counting capital spending or working capital requirements. It should usually be positive; a firm is in trouble if operating cash flow is negative for a long time because the firm is not generating enough cash to pay operating costs.

Total cash flow of the firm includes adjustments for capital spending and additions to net working capital. It will frequently be negative. When a firm is growing at a rapid rate, spending on inventory and fixed assets can be higher than cash flow from sales. On the other hand, positive total cash flow is not always a sign of financial health. An unprofitable firm with negative cash flow from operations could show positive total cash flow temporarily by selling assets. This was a common occurrence in the airline industry in the early 1990s.

2. Net income is not cash flow. The net income of the Canadian Composite Corporation in 20X7 was $86 million, whereas cash flow was $42 million. The two numbers are not usually the same. In determining the economic and financial condition of a firm, cash flow is more revealing.

3. Cash flow from assets sometimes goes by a different name, **free cash flow.** The term refers to cash that the firm is free to distribute to creditors and shareholders because it is not needed for working capital or fixed asset investment. (We return to free cash flow in Chapter 17.)

? Concept Questions

- How is cash flow different from changes in net working capital?
- What is the difference between operating cash flow and total cash flow of the firm?
- What is free cash flow?

2.5 SUMMARY AND CONCLUSIONS

Besides introducing you to corporate accounting, the purpose of this chapter has been to teach you how to determine cash flow from the accounting statements of a typical company.

1. Cash flow is generated by the firm and paid to creditors and shareholders. It can be classified as
   a. Cash flow from operations.
   b. Cash flow from changes in fixed assets.
   c. Cash flow from changes in working capital.
2. There is a cash flow identity that says that cash flow from assets equals cash flow to bondholders and shareholders.
3. Calculations of cash flow are not difficult, but they require care and particular attention to detail in properly accounting for noncash expenses such as depreciation and deferred taxes. It is especially important that you do not confuse cash flow with changes in net working capital and net income.

KEY TERMS

Balance sheet 30
Cash flow 36
Cash flow from operations 38
Change in net working capital 35

Free cash flow 38
Generally accepted accounting principles (GAAP) 32
Income statement 33

Non-cash items 34
Total cash flow of the firm 38

SUGGESTED READING

There are many excellent textbooks on accounting. One that we have found helpful is:
R. H. Garrison, E. Noreen, G. R. Chesley, and R. F. Carroll. *Managerial Accounting.*
   7th Canadian ed. McGraw-Hill Ryerson, 2006.

QUESTIONS & PROBLEMS

The Balance Sheet

2.1   Prepare a 2007 balance sheet for Barney Corp. based on the following data.

Cash	$ 175,000
Patents and copyrights	720,000
Accounts payable	430,000
Accounts receivable	140,000
Tangible net fixed assets	2,900,000
Inventory	265,000
Notes payable	180,000
Retained earnings	1,240,000
Long-term debt	1,430,000

2.2   The following table presents the long-term liabilities and shareholders' equity of Information Control Corp. one year ago.

Long-term debt	$ 60,000,000
Preferred stock	18,000,000
Common shares ($1 par value)	25,000,000
Retained earnings	138,000,000

Visit us at www.mcgrawhill.ca/olc/ross

During the past year, Information Control issued 10 million shares of new stock at a total price of $26 million, and issued $8 million in new long-term debt. The company generated $7 million in net income and paid $4 million in dividends. Construct the current balance sheet reflecting the changes that occurred at Information Control Corp. during the year.

The Income Statement

2.3   During the year, the Senbet Discount Tire Company had gross sales of $1 million. The firm's cost of goods sold and selling expenses were $300,000 and $200,000, respectively. Senbet also had notes payable of $1 million. These notes carried an interest rate of 10 percent. Depreciation was $100,000. Senbet's tax rate was 35 percent.

a. What was Senbet's net income?
b. What was Senbet's operating cash flow?

Financial Cash Flow

EXCEL

2.4   Schwert Corp. shows the following information on its 2007 income statement:

Sales	$145,000
Costs	86,000
Other expenses	4,900
Depreciation expense	7,000
Interest expense	15,000
Taxes	12,840
Dividends	8,700

In addition, you're told that the firm issued $6,450 in new equity during 2007 and redeemed $6,500 in outstanding long-term debt.

a. What is the 2007 operating cash flow?
b. What is the 2007 cash flow to creditors?
c. What is the 2007 cash flow to shareholders?
d. If net fixed assets increased by $5,000 during the year, what was the addition to net working capital (NWC)?

2.5   The Stancil Corporation provided the following current information:

Proceeds from short-term borrowing	$ 7,000
Proceeds from long-term borrowing	18,000
Proceeds from the sale of common stock	2,000
Purchases of fixed assets	3,000
Purchases of inventories	1,000
Payment of dividends	23,000

Determine the cash flows from the firm and the cash flows to investors of the firm.

2.6   Cusic Industries had the following operating results for 2007:

Sales	$12,800
Cost of goods sold	10,400
Depreciation expense	1,900
Interest expense	450
Dividends paid	500

At the beginning of the year, net fixed assets were $9,100, current assets were $3,200, and current liabilities were $1,800. At the end of the year, net fixed assets were $9,700, current assets were $3,850, and current liabilities were $2,100. The tax rate for 2007 was 34 percent.

a. What is net income for 2007?
b. What is the operating cash flow for 2007?
c. What is the cash flow from assets for 2007? Is this possible? Explain.
d. If no new debt was issued during the year, what is the cash flow to creditors? What is the cash flow to shareholders? Explain and interpret the positive and negative signs of your answers in (a) through (d).

EXCEL

2.7   During 2007, Raines Umbrella Corp. had sales of $850,000. Cost of goods sold, administrative and selling expenses, and depreciation expenses were $630,000, $120,000, and $130,000, respectively. In addition, the company had an interest expense of $85,000 and a tax rate of 35 percent. (Ignore any tax loss carryback or carryforward provisions.)

a. What is Raines's net income for 2007?
b. What is its operating cash flow?
c. Explain your results in (a) and (b).

2.8   Ritter Corporation's accountants prepared the following financial statements for year-end 20X8.

RITTER CORPORATION
Income Statement
20X8

Revenue	$ 500
Expenses	300
Depreciation	75
Net income	$ 125
Dividends	$ 65

RITTER CORPORATION
Balance Sheets
December 31

Assets	20X7	20X8
Cash	$ 45	$ 10
Other current assets	145	120
Net fixed assets	250	150
Total assets	$440	$280
Liabilities and Equity		
Current liabilities	$ 70	$ 60
Long-term debt	90	0
Shareholders' equity	280	220
Total liabilities and equity	$440	$280

a. Explain the change in cash during the year 20X7.
b. Determine the change in net working capital in 20X7.
c. Determine the cash flow of the firm during the year 20X7.

MINICASE: Cash Flows at Warf Computers Inc.

Warf Computers Inc. was founded 15 years ago by Nick Warf, a computer programmer. The small initial investment to start the company was made by Nick and his friends. Over the years, this same group has supplied the limited additional investment needed by the company in the form of both equity and short- and long-term debt. Recently the company has developed a virtual keyboard (VK). The VK uses sophisticated artificial intelligence algorithms that allow the user to speak naturally and have the computer input the text, correct spelling and grammatical errors, and format the document according to preset user guidelines. The VK even suggests alternative phrasing and sentence structure, and it provides detailed stylistic diagnostics. Based on a proprietary, very advanced software/hardware hybrid technology, the system is a full generation beyond what is currently on the market. To introduce the VK, the company will require significant outside investment.

Nick has made the decision to seek this outside financing in the form of new equity investments and bank loans. Naturally, new investors and the banks will require a detailed financial analysis. Your employer, Angus Jones & Partners, LLC, has asked you to examine the financial statements provided by Nick. Here are the balance sheet for the two most recent years and the most recent income statement:

WARF COMPUTERS
Balance Sheet
($ in thousands)

	2007	2006		2007	2006
Current assets:			Current liabilities:		
Cash and equivalents	$ 232	$ 201	Accounts payable	$ 263	$ 197
Accounts receivable	367	342	Notes payable	68	53
Inventories	329	340	Accrued expenses	126	205
			Total current		
Other	47	40	liabilities	$ 457	$ 455
Total current assets	$ 975	$ 923			
Fixed assets:			Long-term liabilities:		
Property, plant, and					
equipment	$2,105	$1,630	Deferred taxes	$ 143	$ 82
			Long-term debt	629	589
Less accumulated			Total long-term		
depreciation	687	560	liabilities	$ 772	$ 671
Net property, plant, and					
equipment	$1,418	$1,070			
			Shareholders' equity:		
Intangible assets and others	406	363	Preferred stock	$ 10	$ 10
Total fixed assets	$1,824	$1,433	Common stock	72	64
			Retained Earnings	1585	1221
			Less treasury stock	−97	−65
			Total equity	$1,570	$1,230
			Total liabilities and		
Total assets	$2,799	$2,356	shareholders' equity	$2,799	$2,356

WARF COMPUTERS Income Statement ($ in thousands)	
Sales	$3,875
Cost of goods sold	2,286
Selling, general, and administrative expense	434
Depreciation	127
Operating income	$1,028
Other income	38
Earnings before interest and taxes (EBIT)	$1,066
Interest expense	76
Pre-tax income	$ 990
Taxes	347
Current: $286	
Deferred: 61	
Net income	$ 643
Addition to retained earnings	$ 325
Dividends	$ 318

Nick has also provided the following information: During the year the company raised $94,000 in new long-term debt and retired $54,000 in long-term debt. The company also sold $47,000 in new stock and repurchased $32,000 in stock. The company purchased $629,000 in fixed assets and sold $111,000 in fixed assets.

Angus has asked you to prepare the financial statement of cash flows and the accounting statement of cash flows. He has also asked you to answer the following questions:

1. How would you describe Warf Computers' cash flows?
2. Which cash flow statement more accurately describes the cash flows at the company?
3. In light of your previous answers, comment on Nick's expansion plans.

Appendix 2A   Financial Statement Analysis

This appendix shows how to rearrange data from financial statements into financial ratios that provide information about five areas of financial performance:

1. *Short-term solvency*—the firm's ability to meet its short-run obligations.
2. *Activity*—the firm's ability to control its investment in assets.
3. *Financial leverage*—the extent to which a firm relies on debt financing.
4. *Profitability*—the extent to which a firm is profitable.
5. *Value*—the value of the firm.

This appendix also discusses the interpretation, uses, and shortcomings of financial ratios.

Our discussion covers a representative sampling of ratios chosen to be consistent with the practice of experienced financial analysts and the output of commercially available financial analysis software.

For each of the ratios discussed, several questions are important:

1. How is the ratio calculated?
2. What is it intended to measure, and why might we be interested?
3. What might a high or low value be telling us? How might such values be misleading?
4. How could this measure be improved?

We consider each question in turn. The Canadian Composite Corporation financial statements in Tables 2.1, 2.2, and 2.3 provide inputs for the examples that follow. (Monetary values are given in millions of dollars.)

Short-Term Solvency

Ratios of short-term solvency measure the firm's ability to meet recurring financial obligations (that is, to pay its bills). To the extent that a firm has sufficient cash flow, it can avoid defaulting on its financial obligations and thus avoid financial distress. Liquidity measures short-term solvency and is often associated with net working capital, the difference between current assets and current liabilities. Recall that current liabilities are debts due within one year from the date of the balance sheet. One source from which to pay these debts is current assets.

The most widely used measures of liquidity are the current ratio and the quick ratio.

Current Ratio To find the current ratio, divide current assets by current liabilities. For the Canadian Composite Corporation, the figure for 20X7 is

$$\text{Current ratio} = \frac{\text{Total current assets}}{\text{Total current liabilities}} = \frac{761}{486} = 1.57$$

If a firm is having financial difficulty, it may not be able to pay its bills (accounts payable) on time or it may need to extend its bank credit (notes payable). As a consequence, current liabilities may rise faster than current assets and the current ratio may fall. This could be the first sign of financial trouble. Of course, a firm's current ratio should be calculated over several years for historical perspective, and it should be compared to the current ratios of other firms with similar operating activities.

While a higher current ratio generally indicates greater liquidity, it is possible for the current ratio to be too high. A current ratio far above the industry average could indicate excessive inventory or difficulty in collecting accounts receivable.

Quick Ratio The quick ratio is computed by subtracting inventories from current assets and dividing the difference (called *quick assets*) by current liabilities:

$$\text{Quick ratio} = \frac{\text{Quick assets}}{\text{Total current liabilities}} = \frac{492}{486} = 1.01$$

Quick assets are those current assets that are quickly convertible into cash. Inventories are the least liquid current assets. Many financial analysts believe it is important to determine a firm's ability to pay off current liabilities without relying on the sale of inventories. Comparing the quick ratio to the industry average may help to detect cases in which a high current ratio reflects excessive inventory.

Activity

Activity ratios are constructed to measure how effectively the firm's assets are being managed. The level of a firm's investment in assets depends on many factors. For example, The Bay might have a large stock of toys at the peak of the Christmas season; yet that same inventory in January would be undesirable. How can the appropriate level of investment in assets be measured? One logical starting point is to compare assets with sales for the year to arrive at turnover. The idea is to find out how quickly assets are used to generate sales and we come back to these ideas in Chapter 27.

Total Asset Turnover The total asset turnover ratio is determined by dividing total operating revenues for the accounting period by the average of total assets. The total asset turnover ratio for the Canadian Composite Corporation for 20X7 is:

$$\text{Total asset turnover} = \frac{\text{Total operating revenues}}{\text{Average total assets}} = \frac{2{,}262}{1{,}810.5} = 1.25$$

$$\text{Average total assets} = \frac{1{,}879 + 1{,}742}{2} = 1{,}810.5$$

This ratio is intended to indicate how effectively a firm is using its assets. If the asset turnover ratio is high, the firm is presumably using its assets effectively in generating sales. If the ratio is low, the firm is not using its assets up to their capacity and must either increase sales or dispose of some of the assets. Total asset turnover differs across industries. Firms with relatively small investments in fixed assets, such as retail and wholesale trade firms, tend to have high ratios of total asset turnover when compared with firms that require a large investment in fixed assets, such as manufacturing firms. One problem in interpreting this ratio is that it is maximized by using older assets because their accounting value is lower than newer assets.

Receivables Turnover The receivables turnover ratio is calculated by dividing sales by average receivables during the accounting period. If the number of days in the year (365) is divided by the receivables turnover ratio, the average collection period can be determined. Net receivables are used for these calculations.[10] The average receivables, receivables turnover ratio, and average collection period for the Canadian Composite Corporation are:

$$\text{Average receivables} = \frac{294 + 270}{2} = 282$$

$$\text{Receivables turnover} = \frac{\text{Total operating revenues}}{\text{Average receivables}} = \frac{2{,}262}{282} = 8.02$$

$$\text{Average collection period} = \frac{\text{Days in period}}{\text{Receivables turnover}} = \frac{365}{8.02} = 45.5 \text{ days}$$

The receivables turnover ratio and the average collection period provide some information on the success of the firm in managing its investment in accounts receivable. The actual value of these ratios reflects the firm's credit policy. If a firm has a liberal credit policy, the amount of its receivables will be higher than under a restrictive credit policy. One common rule of thumb that financial analysts use is that the average collection period of a firm should not exceed the time allowed for payment in the credit terms by more than 10 days.

Inventory Turnover The ratio of inventory turnover is calculated by dividing the cost of goods sold by average inventory. Because inventory is always stated in terms of historical cost, it must be divided by cost of goods sold instead of sales. (Sales include a margin for profit and are not commensurate with inventory.) The number of days in the year divided by the inventory turnover ratio yields the *days in inventory ratio* (the number of days it

---

[10]Net receivables are determined after an allowance for potential bad debts.

takes to get goods produced and sold). It is called *shelf life* for retail and wholesale trade firms. The inventory ratios for the Canadian Composite Corporation are

$$\text{Average inventory} = \frac{269 + 280}{2} = 274.5$$

$$\text{Inventory turnover} = \frac{\text{Cost of goods sold}}{\text{Average inventory}} = \frac{1,655}{274.5} = 6.03$$

$$\text{Days in inventory} = \frac{\text{Days in period}}{\text{Inventory turnover}} = \frac{365}{6.03} = 60.5 \text{ days}$$

The inventory ratios measure how quickly inventory is produced and sold. They are significantly affected by the production technology of goods being manufactured. It takes longer to produce a gas turbine engine than a loaf of bread. The ratios are also affected by the perishability of the finished goods. A large increase in the ratio of days in inventory could suggest either an ominously high inventory of unsold finished goods or a change in the firm's product mix to goods with longer production periods.

The method of inventory valuation can materially affect the computed inventory ratios. Thus, financial analysts should be aware of the different inventory valuation methods and how they might affect the ratios.

Financial Leverage

Financial leverage measures the extent to which a firm relies on debt financing rather than equity. Measures of financial leverage are tools in determining the probability that the firm will default on its debt contracts. The more debt a firm has, the more likely it is that the firm will become unable to fulfill its contractual obligations. In other words, too much debt can lead to a higher probability of insolvency and financial distress.

On the positive side, debt is an important form of financing, and provides a significant tax advantage because interest payments are tax deductible. If a firm uses debt, creditors and equity investors may have conflicts of interest. Creditors may want the firm to invest in less risky ventures than those the equity investors prefer.

We discuss the advantages and disadvantages of debt in depth in Chapters 16 and 17.

Debt Ratio The debt ratio is calculated by dividing total debt by total assets. We can also use several other ways to express the extent to which a firm uses debt, such as the debt–equity ratio and the equity multiplier (that is, total assets divided by equity). The debt ratios for the Canadian Composite Corporation for 20X7 are:

$$\text{Debt ratio} = \frac{\text{Total debt}}{\text{Total assets}} = \frac{1,074}{1,879} = 0.57$$

$$\text{Debt-equity ratio} = \frac{\text{Total debt}}{\text{Total equity}} = \frac{1,074}{805} = 1.33$$

$$\text{Equity multiplier} = \frac{\text{Total assets}}{\text{Total equity}} = \frac{1,879}{805} = 2.33$$

Debt ratios provide information about protection of creditors from insolvency and the ability of firms to obtain additional financing for potentially attractive investment opportunities. However, debt is carried on the balance sheet simply as the unpaid balance. Consequently, no adjustment is made for the current level of interest rates (which may be higher or lower than when the debt was originally issued) or risk. Thus, the accounting value of debt may differ substantially from its market value. Some forms of debt, such as pension liabilities or lease obligations, may not appear on the balance sheet at all.

Interest Coverage The interest coverage ratio is calculated by dividing earnings (before interest and taxes) by interest. This ratio emphasizes the ability of the firm to generate enough income to cover interest expense. For the Canadian Composite Corporation, this ratio is

$$\text{Interest coverage} = \frac{\text{Earnings before interest and taxes}}{\text{Interest expense}} = \frac{219}{49} = 4.5$$

Interest expense is an obstacle that a firm must surmount if it is to avoid default. The interest coverage ratio is directly connected to the firm's ability to pay interest. However, since interest is paid in cash, it would probably make sense to add back depreciation (a noncash expense) to income in computing this ratio and to include other financing expenses paid in cash, such as payments of principal and lease payments.

A large debt burden is a problem only if the firm's cash flow is insufficient to make the required debt service payments. This is related to the uncertainty of future cash flows. Firms with predictable cash flows are frequently said to have more *debt capacity* than firms with highly uncertain cash flows. Therefore, it makes sense to compute the variability of the firm's cash flows. One possible way to do this is to calculate the standard deviation of cash flows relative to the average cash flow.

Profitability

One of the most difficult attributes of a firm to conceptualize and to measure is profitability. In a general sense, accounting profits are the difference between revenues and costs. Unfortunately, there is no completely unambiguous way to know when a firm is profitable. At best, a financial analyst can measure current or past accounting profitability. Many business opportunities, however, involve sacrificing current profits for future profits. For example, all new products require large start-up costs and, as a consequence, produce low initial profits. Thus, current profits can be a poor reflection of true future profitability.

Different industries employ different amounts of capital and differ in risk. For this reason, benchmark measures of profitability differ among industries.

Profit Margin Profit margins are computed by dividing profits by total operating revenue. Thus, they express profits as a percentage of total operating revenue. The most important margin is the net profit margin. The net profit margin for the Canadian Composite Corporation is

$$\text{Net profit margin} = \frac{\text{Net income}}{\text{Total operating revenue}} = \frac{86}{2,262} = 0.038 \ (3.8\%)$$

In general, profit margins reflect the firm's ability to produce a product or service at a low cost or to sell it at a high price. Profit margins are not direct measures of profitability because they are based on total operating revenue, not on the investment made in assets by the firm or the equity investors. Trade firms tend to have low margins and service firms tend to have high margins.

Return on Assets One common measure of managerial performance is the ratio of income to average total assets, both before tax and after tax. These ratios for the Canadian Composite Corporation for 20X7 are:

$$\text{Net return on assets} = \frac{\text{Net income}}{\text{Average total assets}} = \frac{86}{1,810.5} = 0.0475 \ (4.75\%)$$

$$\text{Gross return on assets} = \frac{\text{Earnings before interest and taxes}}{\text{Average total assets}} = \frac{219}{1,810.5} = 0.121 \ (12.1\%)$$

One of the most interesting aspects of return on assets (ROA) is how some financial ratios can be linked together to compute ROA in the *DuPont system of financial control.* This system expresses ROA in terms of the profit margin and asset turnover. The basic components of the system are as follows:

$$\text{ROA} = \text{Profit margin} \times \text{Asset turnover}$$

$$\text{ROA (net)} = \frac{\text{Net income}}{\text{Total operating revenue}} \times \frac{\text{Total operating revenue}}{\text{Average total assets}}$$

$$0.0475 = 0.038 \times 1.25$$

$$\text{ROA (gross)} = \frac{\text{Earnings before interest and taxes}}{\text{Total operating revenue}} \times \frac{\text{Total operating revenue}}{\text{Average total assets}}$$

$$0.121 = 0.097 \times 1.25$$

Firms can increase ROA by increasing profit margins or asset turnover. Of course, competition limits their ability to do so simultaneously. Thus, firms tend to face a trade-off between turnover and margin. In retail trade, for example, mail-order companies have low margins and high turnover whereas high-quality jewellery stores have high margins and low turnover.

It is often useful to describe financial strategies in terms of margins and turnover. Suppose a firm selling pneumatic equipment is thinking about providing customers with more liberal credit terms. This will probably decrease asset turnover (because receivables would increase more than sales). Thus, the margins will have to go up to keep ROA from falling.

Return on Equity This ratio (ROE) is defined as net income after interest and taxes divided by average common shareholders' equity, which for the Canadian Composite Corporation is

$$\text{ROE} = \frac{\text{Net income}}{\text{Average shareholders' equity}} = \frac{86}{765} = 0.112 \ (11.2\%)$$

$$\text{Average shareholders' equity} = \frac{805 + 725}{2} = 765$$

The difference between ROA and ROE is due to financial leverage. To see this, consider the following breakdown of ROE expanding the DuPont equation:

$$\text{ROE} = \text{Profit margin} \times \text{Asset turnover} \times \text{Equity multiplier}$$

$$= \frac{\text{Net income}}{\text{Total operating revenue}} \times \frac{\text{Total operating revenue}}{\text{Average total assets}} \times \frac{\text{Average total assets}}{\text{Average shareholders' equity}}$$

$$0.112 = 0.038 \times 1.25 \times 2.36$$

From the preceding numbers, it would appear that financial leverage always magnifies ROE. Actually, this occurs only when ROA (gross) is greater than the interest rate on debt.

Payout Ratio The *payout ratio* is the proportion of net income paid out in cash dividends. For the Canadian Composite Corporation:

$$\text{Payout ratio} = \frac{\text{Cash dividends}}{\text{Net income}} = \frac{43}{86} = 0.5$$

The *retention ratio* is the proportion of net income added to annual retained earnings. For the Canadian Composite Corporation this ratio is:

$$\text{Retention ratio} = \frac{\text{Annual retained earnings}}{\text{Net income}} = \frac{43}{86} = 0.5$$

$$\text{Retained earnings} = \text{Net income} - \text{Dividends}$$

The Sustainable Growth Rate

One ratio that is very helpful in financial analysis is called the sustainable growth rate. It is the maximum rate of growth a firm can sustain by self-generated financing. The precise value of sustainable growth can be calculated as

$$\text{Sustainable growth rate} = \text{ROE} \times \text{Retention ratio}$$

For the Canadian Composite Corporation, ROE is 11.2 percent. The retention ratio is 1/2, so we can calculate the sustainable growth rate as

$$\text{Sustainable growth rate} = 11.2 \times (1/2) = 5.6\%$$

The Canadian Composite Corporation can expand at a maximum rate of 5.6 percent per year with no external equity financing or without increasing financial leverage. (We discuss sustainable growth in Chapters 3 and 6.)

Market Value Ratios

We can learn many things from a close examination of balance sheets and income statements. However, one very important characteristic of a firm that cannot be found on an accounting statement is its market value.

Market Price The market price of a share of common stock is the price that buyers and sellers establish when they trade the stock. The market value of the common equity of a firm is the market price of a share of common stock multiplied by the number of shares outstanding.

Sometimes the words *fair market value* are used to describe market prices. Fair market value is the price at which common stock would change hands between a willing buyer and a willing seller, both having knowledge of the relevant facts. Thus, market prices give guesses about the true worth of the assets of a firm. In an efficient stock market, market prices reflect all relevant facts about firms, and thus reveal the true value of the firm's underlying assets.

The market value of Imperial Oil is many times greater than that of Rio Alta. This may suggest nothing more than the fact that Imperial Oil is a bigger firm than Rio Alta (hardly a surprising revelation). Financial analysts construct ratios to extract information that is independent of a firm's size.

Price–Earnings (P/E) Ratio The price–earnings (P/E) ratio is the ratio of market price for a stock to its current annual earnings per share. The following table shows average P/Es for three selected companies on the TSX on January 23, 2007.

	P/E	Div. Yield
Research in Motion (RIM-T)	56.84	0.00
Royal Bank of Canada (RY-T)	14.96	2.93
Suncor (SU-T)	11.70	0.37

Visit us at www.mcgrawhill.ca/olc/ross

The P/E ratio shows how much investors are willing to pay for $1 of earnings per share. Looking at our example, Research in Motion had a greater P/E than Suncor and Royal Bank.

The price–earnings ratio reflects investors' views of the growth potential of different sectors. The reason an investor would pay $56.84 for a dollar of earnings in a tech stock like RIM is that the investor expects large earnings growth. If this expectation is realized, higher P/E stocks will have higher returns. If earnings do not grow to meet expectations, these stocks will be very risky. We return to P/E ratios in Chapter 6.

Dividend Yield The dividend yield is calculated by annualizing the last observed dividend payment of a firm and dividing by the current market price:

$$\text{Dividend yield} = \frac{\text{Dividend per share}}{\text{Market price per share}}$$

The table above shows dividend yields for selected indexes. Like P/E ratios, dividend yields are related to the market's perception of future growth prospects for firms. Firms with high growth prospects will generally have lower dividend yields.

Market-to-Book (M/B) Value and the Q Ratio The market-to-book value ratio is calculated by dividing the market price per share by the book value per share. Since book value per share is an accounting number, it reflects historical costs. In a loose sense, the market-to-book ratio therefore compares the market value of the firm's assets to their cost. A value less than 1 could mean that the firm has not been successful overall in creating value for its shareholders.

There is another ratio, called Tobin's Q, that is very much like the M/B ratio. Tobin's Q ratio divides the market value of all of the firm's debt plus equity by the replacement value of the firm's assets. The Q ratios for several firms in the past were:[11]

High Qs	
Coca-Cola	4.20
IBM	4.20
Low Qs	
National Steel	0.53
U.S. Steel	0.61

The Q ratio differs from the M/B ratio in that the Q ratio uses market value of the debt plus equity. It also uses the replacement value of all assets and not the historical cost value.

If a firm has a Q ratio above 1 it provides an incentive to invest that is probably greater than for a firm with a Q ratio below 1. Firms with high Q ratios tend to be those firms with attractive investment opportunities or a significant competitive advantage.

Using Financial Ratios

Financial ratios have a variety of uses within a firm. Among the most important is performance evaluation. For example, managers are frequently evaluated and compensated on the basis of accounting measures of performance such as profit margin and return on equity. Also, firms with multiple divisions frequently compare their performance using financial statement information. Another important internal use is planning for the future. Historical financial statement information is very useful for generating projections about the future and for checking the realism of assumptions made in those projections.

---

[11]E. B. Lindberg and S. Ross, "Tobin's Q and Industrial Organization," *Journal of Business* 54 (January 1981).

TABLE 2A.1

Selected Ratios for Canadian Composite Corporation

	20X7	Industry	Rating
Short-Term Solvency			
Current ratio	1.57	1.52	OK
Quick ratio	1.01	1.10	OK
Activity			
Total asset turnover	1.25	1.31	OK
Receivables turnover	8.02	7.80	OK
Average collection period (days)	45.5	46.79	OK
Inventory turnover	6.03	7.12	–
Days in inventory	60.5	51.26	–
Financial Leverage			
Debt ratio	0.57	0.60	OK
Debt–equity ratio	1.33	1.33	OK
Equity multiplier	2.33	2.33	OK
Interest coverage	4.5	4.0	OK
Profitability			
Profit margin	3.8%	2.3%	+
Net return on assets	4.8%	3.0%	+
Return on equity	11.2%	7.0%	+
Payout ratio	0.5	0.3	
Retention ratio	0.5	0.7	
Sustainable growth rate	5.6%	4.9%	+

Financial statements are useful to parties outside the firm, including short-term and long-term creditors and potential investors. For example, such information is quite useful in deciding whether or not to grant credit to a new customer.[12] When firms borrow from chartered banks, loan agreements almost always require that financial statements be submitted periodically. Most bankers use computer software to prepare common-size statements expressing income statement items as percentages of sales and balance sheet items as percentages of total assets. They also calculate ratios for their accounts. More advanced software uses expert system technology to generate a preliminary diagnosis of the borrower by comparing the company's ratios against benchmark parameters selected by the banker.

Table 2A.1 shows such a table prepared for the financial statement ratios for our example, the Canadian Composite Corporation.

Choosing a Benchmark

The firm's historical ratios are standard benchmarks for financial ratio analysis. Historical benchmarks are used to establish a trend. Another means of establishing a benchmark is to identify firms that are similar in the sense that they compete in the same markets, have similar assets, and operate in similar ways. In practice, establishing such a peer group involves judgment on the part of the analyst since no two companies are identical.

---

[12]Chapter 31 shows how statistical models based on ratios are used to predict insolvency.

Various benchmarks are available.[13] Statistics Canada publications include typical balance sheets, income statements, and selected ratios for firms in around 180 industries. Statistics Canada also provides *Financial Performance Indicators,* which is a datafile containing key financial ratios by industry, some of which include net profit margin, pre-tax profit margin, return on equity, and liabilities to assets. *Dun & Bradstreet Industry Norms and Key Business Ratios* provides key business ratios for Canadian companies. Other sources of financial data are *Financial Post Advisor,* Bloomberg, and *Standard & Poor's Industry Surveys.*[14] Several financial institutions gather their own financial ratio databases by compiling information on their loan customers. In this way, they seek to obtain more current, industry-specific information than is available from services like Statistics Canada and Dun & Bradstreet.

Obtaining current information is not the only challenge facing the financial analyst. Most large Canadian corporations do business in several industries, so the analyst often compares the company against several industry averages. Further, it is necessary to recognize that the industry average is not necessarily optimal. For example, agricultural analysts know that farmers are suffering with painfully low average profitability coupled with excessive debt. Despite these shortcomings, the industry average is a useful benchmark for ratio analysis.

Potential Pitfalls of Financial Ratio Analysis

Financial ratio analysis is not based on any underlying theory to help identify which quantities to examine and to guide in establishing benchmarks. For this reason, individual judgment guided by experience plays an important role. Recognizing this, chartered banks are investing in expert system technology to pool the experience of many individual lenders and to standardize judgment.

Several other general problems frequently crop up. Different firms end their fiscal years at different times. For firms in seasonal businesses (such as a retailer with a large Christmas season), this can lead to difficulties in comparing balance sheets because of fluctuations in accounts during the year. For any particular firm, unusual or transient events, such as a one-time profit from an asset sale, may affect financial performance. In comparing firms, such events can give misleading signals.

SUMMARY AND CONCLUSIONS

Much research indicates that accounting statements provide important information about the value of the firm. Financial analysts and managers learn how to rearrange financial statements to squeeze out the maximum amount of information. In particular, analysts and managers use financial ratios to summarize the firm's liquidity, activity, financial leverage, and profitability. When possible, they also use market values. This appendix describes the most popular financial ratios. The following points should be kept in mind when trying to interpret financial statements:

1. Measures of profitability such as return on equity suffer from several potential deficiencies as indicators of performance. They do not take into account the risk or timing of cash flows.

---

[13]This discussion draws on L. Kryzanowski, M. To, and R. Seguin, *Business Solvency Risk Analysis* (Institute of Canadian Bankers, 1990), Chapter 3.

[14]Analysts examining U.S. companies will find comparable information available from Robert Morris Associates, Bloomberg, EDGAR, and Marketline.

2. Financial ratios are linked to one another. For example, return on equity is determined from the profit margins, the asset turnover ratio, and the financial leverage.

3. Financial ratio analysis seldom looks at ratios in isolation. As we have illustrated, financial analysts compare a firm's present ratios against historical ratios and industry averages.

4. Because ratio analysis is based on experience rather than on theory, special care must be taken to achieve consistent interpretations. Since financial ratios are based on accounting numbers, ratios may be misleading if management engages in accounting window dressing to improve reported performance. The hardest performance measures for management to manipulate are those based on market values because the market can usually see through attempts to manipulate accounting numbers.

Appendix 2B   Statement of Cash Flows

There is an official accounting statement called the statement of cash flows. This statement helps explain the change in accounting cash, which for Canadian Composite is $33 million in 20X7. It is very useful in understanding financial cash flow. Notice in Table 2.1 that cash increases from $107 million in 20X6 to $140 million in 20X7.

The first step in determining the change in cash is to figure out cash flow from operating activities. This is the cash flow that results from the firm's normal activities producing and selling goods and services. The second step is to make an adjustment for cash flow from investing activities. The final step is to make an adjustment for cash flow from financing activities. Financing activities are the net payments to creditors and owners (excluding interest expense) made during the year.

The three components of the statement of cash flows are determined below.

Cash Flow from Operating Activities

To calculate cash flow from operating activities we start with net income. Net income can be found on the income statement and is equal to $86. We now need to add back non-cash expenses and adjust for changes in current assets and liabilities (other than cash). The result is cash flow from operating activities.

CANADIAN COMPOSITE CORPORATION
Cash Flow from Operating Activities
20X7
(in $ millions)

Net income	$ 86
Depreciation	90
Deferred taxes	13
Change in assets and liabilities	
Accounts receivable	(24)
Inventories	11
Accounts payable	16
Accrued expense	18
Notes payable	(3)
Other	(8)
Cash flow from operating activities	$199

Visit us at www.mcgrawhill.ca/olc/ross

Cash Flow from Investing Activities

Cash flow from investing activities involves changes in capital assets: acquisition of fixed assets and sales of fixed assets (i.e., net capital expenditures). The result for Canadian Composite follows.

CANADIAN COMPOSITE CORPORATION
Cash Flow from Investing Activities
20X7
(in $ millions)

Acquisition of fixed assets	$(198)
Sales of fixed assets	25
Cash flow from investing activities	**$(173)**

Cash Flow from Financing Activities

Cash flows to and from creditors and owners include changes in equity and debt.

CANADIAN COMPOSITE CORPORATION
Cash Flow from Financing Activities
20X7
(in $ millions)

Retirement of debt (includes notes)	$(73)
Proceeds from long-term debt sales	86
Dividends	(43)
Repurchase of stock	(6)
Proceeds from new stock issue	43
Cash flow from financing activities	**$ 7**

The statement of cash flows is the addition of cash flows from operations, cash flows from investing activities, and cash flows from financing activities, and is produced in Table 2B.1.

Appendix Questions and Problems

2.A1   What effect would the following actions have on a firm's current ratio? Assume that net working capital is positive.
  a. Inventory is purchased for cash.
  b. A supplier is paid.
  c. A bank loan is repaid.
  d. A long-term debt matures and is paid.
  e. A customer pays off an account.
  f. Inventory is sold.

2.A2   If a company reports a 7 percent profit margin, a total asset turnover of 1.8, and a total debt ratio of 0.72, what are its ROA and ROE?

TABLE 2B.1

Statement of Consolidated Cash Flows of the Canadian Composite Corporation

CANADIAN COMPOSITE CORPORATION Statement of Cash Flows 20X7 (in $ millions)	
Operations	
Net income	$ 86
Depreciation	90
Deferred taxes	13
Changes in assets and liabilities	
Accounts receivable	(24)
Inventories	11
Accounts payable	16
Accrued expenses	18
Notes payable	(3)
Other	(8)
Total cash flow from operations	$ 199
Investing activities	
Acquisition of fixed assets	$(198)
Sales of fixed assets	25
Total cash flow from investing activities	$(173)
Financing activities	
Retirement of debt (including notes)	$ (73)
Proceeds of long-term debt	86
Dividends	(43)
Repurchase of stock	(6)
Proceeds from new stock issues	43
Total cash flow from financing activities	$ 7
Change in cash (on the balance sheet)	$ 33

2.A3   Consider the following information for the PVI Corporation:

Credit sales	$18,365
Cost of goods sold	13,821
Accounts receivable	2,911
Accounts payable	2,073

How long does it take PVI to collect on its sales? How long does PVI take to pay its suppliers?

Use the following financial statement information for Stowe Enterprises to work Problems 2.A4 through 2.A7.

STOWE ENTERPRISES
2007 Statement of Earnings

Sales	$4,200
Cost of goods sold	2,100
Depreciation	600
Earnings before interest and taxes	$1,500
Interest paid	450
Taxable income	$1,050
Taxes	357
Net income	$ 693
Addition to retained earnings	$ 186
Dividends	$ 507

STOWE ENTERPRISES
Abbreviated Balance Sheet, 2006–2007

Assets	2006	2007	Liabilities and Owners' Equity	2006	2007
Current assets			Current liabilities		
Cash	$ 600	$ 1,695	Accounts payable	$ 1,500	$ 1,590
Accounts receivable	1,950	2,064	Notes payable	1,629	1,380
Inventory	3,135	2,100	Other	642	549
Fixed assets			Long-term debt	3,291	3,552
Net plant and			Owners' equity		
equipment	4,470	5,067	Common stock	570	1,146
			Accumulated retained earnings	2,523	2,709
			Total liabilities and		
Total assets	$10,155	$10,926	**owners' equity**	$10,155	$10,920

2.A4 Compute the following ratios for Stowe Enterprises for 2006 and 2007:

Short-Term Solvency Ratios	Asset Management Ratios	Long-Term Solvency Ratios	Profitability Ratios
Current ratio	Total asset turnover	Debt ratio	Profit margin
Quick ratio	Inventory turnover	Debt–equity ratio	Return on assets
Cash ratio	Receivables turnover	Equity multiplier	Return on equity
		Times interest earned	
		Cash coverage ratio	

2.A5 Prepare a statement of cash flows for Stowe.

2.A6 For how many days in 2007 could Stowe continue to operate if its production were suspended?

2.A7 Stowe has 80 shares outstanding in 2007. The price per share is $45. What are the P/E ratio and market-to-book ratio?

2.A8 Select an industry featured in recent financial news. Then obtain annual reports on two companies in that industry and conduct a ratio analysis for the most recent two years. Make the relevant comparisons between the companies and against industry norms. Based on your ratio analysis, how do the two companies differ? Compare your comments against recent newspaper articles on the industry. (Note: This question is much easier to answer using ratio analysis software.)

2.A9 Enter the ticker symbol "IPS" for IPSCO Inc. and follow the "Excel Analytics" link. You will find the annual balance sheets for IPS for each of the past five years. Calculate the change in the net working capital for each year. How has net working capital changed over this entire period?

2.A10 Under the "Excel Analytics" link for Alcan, download the annual income statements and balance sheets for Alcan Inc. (AL). Calculate the operating cash flow, cash flow to creditors, and cash flow to shareholders for the most recent year. After you have completed your calculations, download the annual cash flow report and compare the given numbers to your calculations.

Chapter 3

Financial Planning and Growth

EXECUTIVE SUMMARY

Corporate financial planning establishes guidelines for change in the firm. These guidelines should include (1) an identification of the firm's financial goals, (2) an analysis of the differences between these goals and the current financial status of the firm, and (3) a statement of the actions needed for the firm to achieve its financial goals. In other words, as one member of GM's board was heard to say, "Planning is a process that at best helps the firm avoid stumbling into the future backwards."

The basic elements of financial planning comprise (1) the investment opportunities the firm elects to take advantage of, (2) the amount of debt the firm chooses to employ, and (3) the amount of cash the firm thinks is necessary and appropriate to pay shareholders. These are the financial policies that the firm must decide upon for its growth, profitability, and shareholder value. For example, at Procter & Gamble, capital budgeting analysts screen project proposals submitted by division managers promoting new product ideas. Each proposal must contain a detailed financial plan for the suggested product showing how it will impact cash flow.

Almost all firms identify a companywide growth rate as a major component of their financial planning.[1] In one famous case, International Business Machines' stated growth goal was simple but typical: to match the growth of the computer industry, which was projected to be 15 percent per year through the end of the 1990s. Though we may have had some doubts about IBM's ability to sustain a 15 percent growth rate, we are certain there are important financial implications of the strategies that IBM will adopt to achieve that rate. There are direct connections between the growth that a company can achieve and its financial policy. One purpose of this chapter is to look at the financial aspects of how fast a firm can grow.

The chapter first describes what is usually meant by financial planning. This enables us to make an important point: Investment and financing decisions frequently interact. The different interactions of investment and financing decisions can be analyzed in the financial statements. We show how financial statements can be used to better understand how growth is achieved.

3.1 What Is Financial Planning?

Financial planning formulates the method by which financial goals are to be achieved. It has two dimensions: a time frame and a level of aggregation.

A financial plan is a statement of what is to be done in a future time. The GM board member was right on target when he explained the virtues of financial planning. Most decisions have long lead times, which means they take a long time to implement. In an uncertain world, this requires that decisions be made far in advance of their implementation. If a firm

---

[1] We think that a firm's growth should be a consequence of its trying to achieve maximum shareholder value.

wants to build a factory in 2008, it may need to line up contractors in 2006. It is sometimes useful to think of the future as having a short run and a long run. The short run, in practice, is usually the coming 12 months. We focus our attention on financial planning over the long run, which is usually taken to be a two-year to five-year period of time.

Financial plans are compiled from the capital-budgeting analyses of each of a firm's projects. In effect, the smaller investment proposals of each operational unit are added up and treated as a big project. This process is called **aggregation.**

Financial plans always entail alternative sets of assumptions. For example, suppose a company has two separate divisions: one for consumer products and one for gas turbine engines. The financial planning process might require each division to prepare three alternative business plans for the next three years.

1. *A Worst Case.* This plan would require making the worst possible assumptions about the company's products and the state of the economy. It could mean divestiture and liquidation.
2. *A Normal Case.* This plan would require making the most likely assumptions about the company and the economy.
3. *A Best Case.* Each division would be required to work out a case based on the most optimistic assumptions. It could involve new products and expansion.

Because the company is likely to spend a lot of time preparing proposals on different scenarios that will become the basis for the company's financial plan, it seems reasonable to ask what the planning process will accomplish.

1. *Interactions.* The financial plan must make the linkages between investment proposals for the different operating activities of the firm and the financing choices available to the firm explicit. IBM's 15 percent growth target goes hand in hand with its financing program.
2. *Options.* The financial plan provides the opportunity for the firm to work through various investment and financing options. The firm addresses questions of what financing arrangements are optimal and evaluates options of closing plants or marketing new products.
3. *Feasibility.* The different plans must fit into the overall corporate objective of maximizing shareholder wealth.
4. *Avoiding Surprises.* Financial planning should identify what may happen in the future if certain events take place. Thus, one of the purposes of financial planning is to avoid surprises.

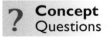

Concept Questions

- **What are the two dimensions of the financial planning process?**
- **Why should firms draw up financial plans?**

3.2 A Financial Planning Model: The Ingredients

Just as companies differ in size and products, financial plans are not the same for all companies. However, there are some common elements:

1. **Sales forecast.** All financial plans require a sales forecast. Perfectly accurate sales forecasts are not possible, because sales depend on the uncertain future state of the economy. Firms can get help from businesses specializing in macroeconomic and

industry projections. A good sales forecast should be the consequence of having identified all valuable investment opportunities.

2. **Pro forma statements.** The financial plan will have a forecast balance sheet, an income statement, and a sources-and-uses statement. These are called *pro forma statements,* or *pro formas.*[2]

3. **Asset requirements.** The plan will describe projected capital spending. In addition, it will discuss the proposed uses of net working capital.

4. **Financial requirements.** The plan will include a section on financing arrangements. This part of the plan should discuss dividend policy and debt policy. Sometimes firms will expect to raise equity by selling new shares of stock. In this case the plan must consider what kinds of securities must be sold and what methods of issuance are most appropriate.

5. **Plug.** Suppose a financial planner assumes that sales, costs, and net income will rise at a particular rate, g_1. Further suppose that the planner wants assets and liabilities to grow at a different rate, g_2. These two different growth rates may be incompatible unless a third variable is also adjusted. For example, compatibility may only be reached if outstanding stock grows at a different rate, g_3. In this example, we treat the growth in outstanding stock as the *plug* variable. That is, the growth rate in outstanding stock is chosen to make the growth rate in income statement items consistent with the growth rate in balance sheet items. Surprisingly, even if the income statement items grow at the *same* rate as the balance sheet items, consistency might be achieved only if outstanding stock grows at a different rate.

   Of course, the growth rate in outstanding stock need not be the plug variable. One could have income statement items grow at g_1, and assets, long-term debt, and outstanding stock grow at g_2. In this case, compatibility between g_1 and g_2 might be achieved by letting short-term debt grow at a rate of g_3.

6. **Economic assumptions.** The plan must explicitly state the economic environment in which the firm expects to reside over the life of the plan. Among the economic assumptions that must be made is the level of interest rates.

3.3 The Percentage of Sales Method

In the previous section, we described a simple planning model in which every item increased at the same rate as sales. This may be a reasonable assumption for some elements. For others, such as long-term borrowing, it probably is not, because the amount of long-term borrowing is something set by management, and it does not necessarily relate directly to the level of sales. We return to this in detail in Chapters 16 and 17.

In this section, we describe an extended version of our simple model. The basic idea is to separate the income statement and balance sheet accounts into two groups: those that do vary directly with sales, and those that do not. Given a sales forecast, we will then be able to calculate how much financing the firm will need to support the predicted sales level.

---

[2]Microsoft Excel is one of the most widely used software programs in the business world when it comes to financial modelling. The program is sophisticated and provides the ability to do tasks much quicker than by hand. For more information on the use of Microsoft Excel as a tool for modelling, see Simon Benninga, *Principles of Finance with Excel,* Oxford, 2006.

EXAMPLE 3.1

The Computerfield Corporation's 20X5 financial statements are as follows:

Income Statement 20X5			Balance Sheet Year-End 20X5			
Sales	$1,000		Assets	$500	Debt	$250
Costs	800				Equity	250
Net income	$ 200		Total	$500	Total	$500

In 20X5, Computerfield's profit margin is 20 percent, and it has never paid a dividend. Its debt–equity ratio is 1. This is also the firm's *target* debt–equity ratio. Unless otherwise stated, the financial planners at Computerfield assume that all variables are tied directly to sales and that current relationships are optimal.

Suppose that sales increase by 20 percent from 20X5 to 20X6. Because the planners would then also forecast a 20 percent increase in costs, the pro forma income statement would be:

Income Statement 20X6	
Sales	$1,200
Costs	960
Net income	$ 240

The assumption that all variables will grow by 20 percent will enable us to construct the pro forma balance sheet as well:

Balance Sheet Year-End 20X6			
Assets	$600	Debt	$300
		Equity	300
Total	$600	Total	$600

Now we must reconcile these two pro formas. How, for example, can net income be equal to $240 and equity increase by only $50? The answer is that Computerfield must have paid a dividend or repurchased stock equal to $190. In this case dividends are the plug variable.

Suppose Computerfield does not pay a dividend and does not repurchase its own stock. With these assumptions, Computerfield's equity will grow to $490, and debt must be retired to keep total assets equal to $600. In this case the debt-to-equity ratio is the plug variable; with $600 in total assets and $490 in equity, debt will have to be $600 − $490, or $110. Since we started with $250 in debt, Computerfield will have to retire $250 − $110, or $140 of debt. The resulting balance sheet would look like this:

Balance Sheet Year-End 20X6			
Assets	$600	Debt	$110
		Equity	490
Total	$600	Total	$600

The thing to notice in our simple example is the way the change in liabilities and equity depends on the firm's financing policy and the firm's dividend policy. The firm ensures growth in assets by having a plan in place to finance such growth.

This example shows the interaction of sales growth and financial policy. The next section focuses on the need for external funds. It identifies a six-step procedure for constructing the pro forma balance sheet.

The financial planning model we describe next is based on the **percentage of sales approach.** Our goal here is to develop a quick and practical way of generating pro forma statements. We defer discussion of some possible extensions to a later section.

The Income Statement

We start out with the most recent income statement for the Rosengarten Corporation, as shown in Table 3.1. Notice we have still simplified things by including costs, depreciation, and interest in a single cost figure. We separate these out in a later section.

Rosengarten has projected a 10 percent increase in sales for the coming year, so we are anticipating sales of $20 million $\times$ 1.1 = $22 million. To generate a pro forma income statement, we assume that total costs will continue to run at $16.9697 million/$20 million = 84.85% of sales. With this assumption, Rosengarten's pro forma income statement is as shown in Table 3.2. The effect here of assuming that costs are a constant percentage of sales is to assume that the profit margin is constant. To check this, notice that the profit margin was $2 million/$20 million = 10%. In our pro forma, the profit margin is $2.2 million/ $22 million = 10%; so it is unchanged.

Next, we need to project the dividend payment. This amount is up to Rosengarten's management. We will assume Rosengarten has a policy of paying out a constant fraction of net income in the form of a cash dividend. For the most recent year, the **dividend payout ratio** was:

$$\text{Dividend payout ratio} = \frac{\text{Cash dividends}}{\text{Net income}}$$

$$= \frac{\$1 \text{ million}}{\$2 \text{ million}} = 50\% \tag{3.1}$$

We can also calculate the ratio of the addition to retained earnings to net income as:

$$\frac{\text{Addition to retained earnings}}{\text{Net income}} = \frac{\$1 \text{ million}}{\$2 \text{ million}}$$

This ratio is called the **retention ratio** or **plowback ratio,** and it is equal to 1 minus the dividend payout ratio because everything not paid out is retained. Assuming that the payout ratio is constant, the projected dividends and addition to retained earnings will be:

TABLE 3.1
Rosengarten Corporation Income Statement

ROSENGARTEN CORPORATION Income Statement ($ in thousands)		
Sales		$20,000.00
Costs		16,969.70
Taxable income		$ 3,030.30
Taxes (34%)		1,030.30
Net income		$ 2,000.00
Dividends	$1,000.00	
Addition to retained earnings	1,000.00	

TABLE 3.2
Rosengarten Corporation Pro Forma Income Statement

ROSENGARTEN CORPORATION Pro Forma Income Statement ($ in thousands)	
Sales (projected)	$22,000.00
Costs (84.85% of sales)	18,666.00
Taxable income	$ 3,334.00
Taxes (34%)	1,134.00
Net income	$ 2,200.00

Projected dividends paid to shareholders = $1.1 million $\times \frac{1}{2}$ = $ 550 thousand

Projected addition to retained earnings = $1.1 million $\times \frac{1}{2}$ =   550 thousand

$1,100 thousand

The Balance Sheet

To generate a pro forma balance sheet, we start with the most recent statement, as shown in the table below.

On our balance sheet, we assume that most of the items vary directly with sales. Only common stock does not. For those items that do vary with sales, we express each as a percentage of sales for the year just completed. When an item does not vary directly with sales, we write "constant."

For example, on the asset side, fixed assets are equal to 120 percent of sales ($24 million/ $20 million) for the year just ended. We assume this percentage applies to the coming year, so for each $1 increase in sales, fixed assets will rise by $1.20.

Current Balance Sheet($ in thousands)		Pro Forma Balance Sheet ($ in thousands)	
			Explanation
Current assets	$ 6,000	$ 6,600	30% of sales
Fixed assets	24,000	26,400	120% of sales
Total assets	$30,000	$33,000	150% of sales
Short-term debt	$10,000	$11,000	50% of sales
Long-term debt	6,000	6,600	30% of sales
Common stock	4,000	4,000	Constant
Retained earnings	10,000	11,100	Net income
Total financing	$30,000	$32,700	
		$ 300	Funds needed (the difference between total assets and total financing)

From this information we can determine the pro forma balance sheet, which is on the right-hand side. The change in retained earnings will be

Net income   −   Dividends   = Change in retained earnings

$(0.10 \times \$22 \text{ million}) - (0.5 \times 0.10 \times \$22 \text{ million}) = \$1.1 \text{ million}$

In this example the plug variable is new shares of stock. The company must issue $300,000 of new stock. The equation that can be used to determine if external funds are needed is

External Funds Needed (EFN):

$$\left(\frac{\text{Assets}}{\text{Sales}}\right) \times \Delta\text{Sales} - \frac{\text{Debt}}{\text{Sales}} \times \Delta\text{Sales} - (p \times \text{Projected sales}) \times (1 - d)$$

$$= (1.5 \times \$2 \text{ million}) - (0.80 \times \$2 \text{ million}) - (0.10 \times \$22 \text{ million} \times 0.5)$$

$$= \$1.4 \text{ million} \qquad\qquad - \$1.1 \text{ million}$$

$$= \$0.3 \text{ million}$$

where

$$\frac{\text{Assets}}{\text{Sales}} = 1.5$$

$$\frac{\text{Debt}}{\text{Sales}} = 0.8$$

$$p = \text{Net profit margin} = 0.10$$

$$d = \text{Dividend payout ratio} = 0.5$$

$$\Delta\text{Sales} = \text{Projected change in sales}$$

The steps in the estimation of the pro forma sheet for the Rosengarten Corporation and the external funds needed (EFN) are as follows:

1. Express balance sheet items that vary with sales as a percentage of sales.
2. Multiply the percentages determined in step 1 by projected sales to obtain the amount for the future period.
3. Where no percentage applies, simply insert the previous balance sheet figure in the future period.
4. Compute projected retained earnings as follows:

$$\text{Projected retained earnings} = \text{Present retained earnings}$$
$$+ \text{Projected net income} - \text{Cash dividends}$$

5. Add the asset accounts to determine projected assets. Next, add the liabilities and equity accounts to determine the total financing; any difference is the *shortfall*. This equals external funds needed (EFN).
6. Use the plug to fill EFN. In this example, new shares are the plug but debt could also be used. The choice depends on the firm's optimal capital structure as we discuss in chapters 16 and 17.

Table 3.3 computes EFN for several different growth rates. For low growth rates, Rosengarten will run a surplus, and for high growth rates, it will run a deficit. The "break-even" growth rate is 7.7 percent. Figure 3.1 illustrates the relation between projected sales growth and EFN. As can be seen, the need for new assets from projected sales growth grows much faster than the additions to retained earnings plus new debt. Eventually, a deficit is created and a need for external financing becomes evident.

TABLE 3.3
Projected Sales Growth and EFN for the Rosengarten Corporation

Projected Sales Growth	Increase in Assets Required	Addition to Retained Earnings	External Financing Needed (EFN)
0 %	$ 0	$1,000,000	− $1,000,000
5	1,500,000	1,050,000	−350,000
7.7	2,310,000	1,077,000	—
10	3,000,000	1,100,000	300,000
20	6,000,000	1,200,000	1,600,000

3.4 What Determines Growth?

This section furthers our discussion of a firm's growth and its accounting statements. It is obvious that the need for external financing and growth are related. All other factors remaining equal, the higher the rate of growth in sales or assets, the greater will be the need for external financing. This text places a strong emphasis and focus on growth not because growth is an appropriate goal, but because growth is simply a convenient means of examining the interactions between investment and financing decisions.

Firms frequently make growth forecasts an explicit part of financial planning. Donaldson reports on the pervasiveness of stating corporate goals in terms of growth rates.[3] This may seem puzzling in the light of our previous emphasis on maximizing the shareholder's value as the central goal of management. One way to reconcile the difference is to think of growth as an intermediate goal that leads to higher value. Rappaport correctly points out that, in applying the shareholder value approach, growth should not be a goal but must be a consequence of decisions that maximize shareholder value.[4] In fact, if the firm is willing to accept any project just to grow in size, growth will probably make the shareholders worse off.

FIGURE 3.1

Growth and EFN for the Rosengarten Corporation

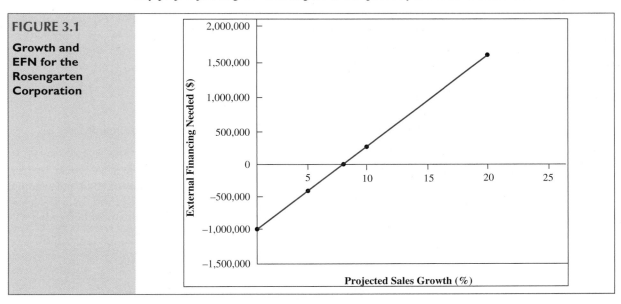

[3]G. Donaldson, *Managing Corporation Wealth: The Operations of a Comprehensive Financial Goals System* (New York: Praeger, 1984).

[4]A. Rappaport, *Creating Shareholder Value: The New Standard for Business Performance* (New York: Free Press, 1986).

Donaldson also concludes that most major industrial companies are very reluctant to use external equity as a regular part of their financial planning. To illustrate the linkages between the ability of a firm to grow and its accounting statements when the firm does not issue equity, we can make some planning assumptions.

1. The firm's assets will grow in proportion to its sales.
2. Net income is a constant proportion of its sales.
3. The firm has a given dividend-payout policy and a given debt–equity ratio.
4. The firm will not change the number of outstanding shares of stock.

There is only one growth rate that is consistent with the preceding assumptions. In effect, with these assumptions, growth has been made a plug variable. To see this, recall that a change in assets must always be equal to a change in debt plus a change in equity:

$$\boxed{\text{Change in assets}} \quad = \quad \boxed{\begin{array}{c}\text{Change in debt} \\ + \\ \text{Change in equity}\end{array}}$$

Now we can write the conditions that ensure this equality and solve for the growth rate that will give it to us.

The variables used in this demonstration are the following:

T = The ratio of total assets to sales
p = The net profit margin on sales
d = The dividend-payout ratio
L = The debt–equity ratio
S_0 = Sales this year
ΔS = The change in sales ($S_1 - S_0 = \Delta S$)
S_1 = Next year's projected sales
RE = Retained earnings = Net income × Retention ratio = $S_1 \times p \times (1 - d)$
NI = Net income = $S_1 \times p$

If the firm is to increase sales by ΔS during the year, it must increase assets by $T\Delta S$. The firm is assumed not to be able to change the number of shares of stock outstanding, so the equity financing must come from retained earnings. Retained earnings will depend on next year's sales, the payout ratio, and the profit margin. The amount of borrowing will depend on the amount of retained earnings and the debt–equity ratio.

New equity: plus	$S_1 \times p \times (1 - d)$
Borrowing: equals	$[S_1 \times p \times (1 - d)] \times L$
Capital spending:	$T\Delta S$

Moving things around a little gives the following:

$$T\Delta S = [S_1 \times p \times (1 - d)] + [S_1 \times p \times (1 - d) \times L]$$

TABLE 3.4
Current Financial Statements: The Hoffman Corporation (in thousands)

THE HOFFMAN CORPORATION	
Income Statement	
	This Year
Net sales (*S*)	$10,000
Cost of sales	7,000
Earnings before taxes and interest	3,000
Interest expense	500
Earnings before taxes	2,500
Taxes	850
Net income (NI)	$ 1,650

Sources and Uses of Cash	
	This Year
Sources:	
Net income (NI)	$ 1,650
Depreciation	500
Operating cash flow	2,150
Borrowing	455
New stock issue	0
Total sources	$ 2,605
Uses:	
Increase in net working capital	455
Capital spending	955
Dividends	1,195
Total uses	$ 2,605

Balance Sheet			
	This Year	*Last Year*	*Change*
Assets			
Net working capital	$ 5,000	$4,545	$455
Fixed assets	5,000	4,545	455
Total assets	$10,000	$9,090	$910
Liabilities and Shareholders' Equity			
Debt	$ 5,000	$4,545	$455
Equity	5,000	4,545	455
Total liabilities and shareholders' equity	$10,000	$9,090	$910

and

$$\frac{\Delta S}{S_0} = \frac{p \times (1 - d) \times (1 + L)}{T - [p \times (1 - d) \times (1 + L)]} = \text{Growth rate in sales} \quad (3.2)$$

This is the growth-rate equation. Given the profit margin (*p*), the payout ratio (*d*), the debt–equity ratio (*L*), and the asset-requirement ratio (*T*), the growth rate can be determined. It is the only growth possible with the preset values for the four variables. Higgins has referred to this growth rate as the firm's **sustainable growth rate.**[5]

---

[5]R. C. Higgins, "Sustainable Growth Under Inflation," *Financial Management* (Autumn 1981). The definition of sustainable growth was popularized by the Boston Consulting Group and others.

Robert C. Higgins on Sustainable Growth

Most financial officers know intuitively that it takes money to make money. Rapid sales growth requires increased assets in the form of accounts receivable, inventory, and fixed plant, which, in turn, require money to pay for assets. They also know that if their company does not have the money when needed, it can literally "grow broke." The sustainable growth equation states these intuitive truths explicitly.

Sustainable growth is often used by bankers and other external analysts to assess a company's credit-worthiness. They are aided in this exercise by several sophisticated computer software packages that provide detailed analyses of the company's past financial performance, including its annual sustainable growth rate.

Bankers use this information in several ways. Quick comparison of a company's actual growth rate to its sustainable rate tells the banker what issues will be at the top of management's financial agenda. If actual growth consistently exceeds sustainable growth, management's problem will be where to get the cash to finance growth. The banker thus can anticipate interest in loan products. Conversely, if sustainable growth consistently exceeds actual, the banker had best be prepared to talk about

investment products, because management's problem will be what to do with all the cash that keeps piling up in the till.

Bankers also find the sustainable growth equation useful for explaining to financially inexperienced small business owners and overly optimistic entrepreneurs that, for the long-run viability of their business, it is necessary to keep growth and profitability in proper balance.

Finally, comparison of actual to sustainable growth rates helps a banker understand why a loan applicant needs money and for how long the need might continue. In one instance, a loan applicant requested $100,000 to pay off several insistent suppliers and promised to repay in a few months when he collected some accounts receivable that were coming due. A sustainable growth analysis revealed that the firm had been growing at four to six times its sustainable growth rate and that this pattern was likely to continue in the foreseeable future. This alerted the banker that impatient suppliers were only a symptom of the much more fundamental disease of overly rapid growth, and that a $100,000 loan would likely prove to be only the down payment on a much larger, multiyear commitment.

Robert C. Higgins is Professor of Finance at the University of Washington. He pioneered the use of sustainable growth as a tool for financial analysis.

EXAMPLE 3.2

Table 3.4 shows the current income statement, the sources-and-uses-of-cash statement, and the balance sheet for the Hoffman Corporation. Net income for the corporation was 16.5 percent ($1,650/$10,000) of sales revenue. The company paid out 72.4 percent ($1,195/$1,650) of its net income in dividends. The interest rate on debt was 10 percent, and the long-term debt was 50 percent ($5,000/$10,000) of assets. (Notice that, for simplicity, we use the single term *net working capital*, in Table 3.4, instead of separating current assets from current liabilities.) Hoffman's assets grew at the rate of 10 percent ($910/$9,090). In addition, sales grew at 10 percent, though this increase is not shown in Table 3.4.

The cash flow generated by Hoffman was enough not only to pay a dividend but also to increase net working capital and fixed assets by $455 each. The company did not issue any shares of stock during the year. Its debt–equity ratio and dividend-payout ratio remained constant throughout the year.

The sustainable growth rate for the Hoffman Corporation is 10 percent, or[6]

$$\frac{0.165 \times 0.276 \times 2}{1 - (0.165 \times 0.276 \times 2)} = 0.1$$

---

[6]This expression is exactly equal to the rate of return on equity (ROE) multiplied by the retention rate (RR): ROE × RR if by ROE we mean net income this year divided by equity *last year,* i.e., $1,650/$4,545 = 36.3%. In this case ROE × RR = 36.3% × 27.6% = 10% = sustainable growth in sales. On the other hand, if by ROE we mean net income this year divided by equity *this year,* i.e., $1,650/$5,000 = 33%, the sustainable growth rate in sales = ROE × RR/(1 − ROE × RR).

However, suppose its desired growth rate was to be 20 percent. It is possible for Hoffman's desired growth to exceed its sustainable growth because Hoffman is able to issue new shares of stock. A firm can do several things to increase its sustainable growth rate as seen from the Hoffman example:

1. Sell new shares of stock.
2. Increase its reliance on debt.
3. Reduce its dividend-payout ratio.
4. Increase profit margins.
5. Decrease its asset-requirement ratio.

Now we can see the use of a financial planning model to test the feasibility of the planned growth rate. If sales are to grow at a rate higher than the sustainable growth rate, the firm must improve operating performance, increase financial leverage, decrease dividends, or sell new shares. At the other extreme, suppose the firm is losing money (has a negative profit margin) or is paying out more than 100 percent of earnings in dividends so that the retention rate $(1 - d)$ is negative. In each of these cases, the negative sustainable growth rate signals the rate at which sales and assets must shrink. Firms can achieve negative growth by selling off assets and laying off employees. Nortel is an example of a Canadian firm that has had to undergo this painful downsizing process.

Of course, either way the planned rates of growth should be the result of a complete maximization of shareholder value-based planning process.

? **Concept** Questions
- **When might the goals of growth and value maximization be in conflict, and when would they be aligned?**
- **What are the determinants of growth?**

Some Caveats on Financial Planning Models

Financial planning models such as sustainable growth suffer from a great deal of criticism. We present two commonly voiced attacks below.

First, financial planning models do not indicate which financial policies are the best. For example, our model could not tell us whether Hoffman's decision to issue new equity to achieve a higher growth rate raises the shareholder value of the firm.

Second, financial planning models are too simple. In reality, costs are not always proportional to sales, assets need not be a fixed percentage of sales, and capital budgeting involves a sequence of decisions over time. These assumptions are generally not incorporated into financial plans.

Financial planning models are necessary to assist in planning the future investment and financial decisions of the firm. Without some sort of long-term financial plan, the firm may find itself adrift in a sea of change without a rudder for guidance. But, because of the assumptions and the abstractions from reality necessary in the construction of the financial plan, we also think that they should carry the label: Let the user beware!

3.5 SUMMARY AND CONCLUSIONS

Financial planning forces the firm to think about and forecast the future. It involves the following:

1. Building a corporate financial model.
2. Describing different scenarios of future development from worst to best cases.
3. Using the models to construct pro forma financial statements.
4. Running the model under different scenarios (conducting sensitivity analysis).
5. Examining the financial implications of ultimate strategic plans.

Corporate financial planning should not become a purely mechanical activity. If it does, it will probably focus on the wrong things. In particular, plans are formulated all too often in terms of a growth target with an explicit linkage to creation of value. We talk about a particular financial planning model called sustainable growth. It is a very simple model. Nonetheless, the alternative to financial planning is stumbling into the future.

KEY TERMS

Aggregation 59	Financial requirements 60	Retention ratio (plowback
Asset requirements 60	Percentage of sales approach 62	ratio) 62
Dividend payout ratio 62	Plug 60	Sales forecast 59
Economic assumptions 60	Pro forma statements 60	Sustainable growth rate 67

SUGGESTED READING

Some aspects of economic growth and stock market returns are covered in:

Jay Ritter. "Economic Growth—Equity Returns." Unpublished working paper. University of Florida, March 1, 2003.

We also recommend:

John K. Campbell and Robert Shiller. "Valuation Ratios and the Long Run Stock Market Outlook: An Update." Cowles Foundation Discussion Paper, no. 1295.

Phillippe Jorion and William Coetzmann. "Global Stock Markets in the Twentieth Century." *Journal of Finance* (1995).

Lamont Owen. "Earnings and Expect Returns." *Journal of Finance* 53 (1998).

QUESTIONS & PROBLEMS

Financial Planning Models: The Ingredients

3.1   After examining patterns from recent years, management found the following regression-estimated relationships between some company balance sheets and income statement accounts and sales.

$$CA = 0.7 \text{ million} + 0.20S$$
$$FA = 1.0 \text{ million} + 0.45S$$
$$CL = 0.1 \text{ million} + 0.25S$$
$$NP = 0.0 \text{ milion} + 0.04S$$

where
  CA = Current assets
  FA = Fixed assets
  CL = Current liabilities
  NP = Net profit after taxes
   S = Sales

The company's sales for last year were $10 million. The year-end balance sheet is reproduced below.

Current assets	$ 3,500,000	Current liabilities	$ 1,600,000
Fixed assets	7,000,000	Bonds	2,500,000
		Common stock	2,600,000
		Retained earnings	3,800,000
Total	$10,500,000	Total	$10,500,000

Management further found that the company's sales bear a relationship to GNP. That relationship is:

$$S = 0.00001 \times GNP$$

The forecast of GNP for next year is $2.1 trillion. The firm pays out 40 percent of net profits after taxes in dividends.

Create a pro forma balance sheet for this firm.

3.2   Cheryl Colby, CFO of Charming Florist Ltd., has created the firm's pro forma balance sheet for the next fiscal year. Sales are projected to grow by 10 percent to $440 million. Current assets, fixed assets, and short-term debt are 20 percent, 140 percent, and 15 percent of sales, respectively. Charming Florist pays out 40 percent of its net income in dividends. The company currently has $145 million of long-term debt and $50 million in common stock par value. The profit margin is 12 percent.

a. Construct the current balance sheet for the firm using the projected sales figure.
b. Based on Ms. Colby's sales growth forecast, how much does Charming Florist need in external funds for the upcoming fiscal year?
c. Construct the firm's pro forma balance sheet for the next fiscal year and confirm the external funds needed you calculated in part (b).

What Determines Growth?

3.3   The Steiben Company has a ROE of 8.5 percent and a payout ratio of 35 percent.

a. What is the company's sustainable growth rate?
b. Can the company's actual growth rate be different from its sustainable growth rate? Why or why not?
c. How can the company change its sustainable growth rate?

X

EXCEL

3.4   The Optical Scam Company has forecast a 20 percent sales growth rate for next year. The current financial statements are shown here:

Income Statement

Sales	$38,000,000
Costs	33,400,000
Taxable income	$ 4,600,000
Taxes	1,610,000
Net income	$ 2,990,000
Dividends	$ 1,196,000
Additions to retained earnings	$ 1,794,000

Assets, Liabilities and Equity

Current assets	$ 9,000,000	Short-term debt	$ 8,000,000
		Long-term debt	6,000,000
Fixed assets	22,000,000		
		Common stock	$ 4,000,000
		Accumulated retained earnings	13,000,000
		Total equity	$ 17,000,000
Total assets	$31,000,000	Total liabilities and equity	$ 31,000,000

a. Using the equation from the chapter, calculate the external funds needed for next year.
b. Construct the firm's pro forma balance sheet for next year and confirm the external funds needed that you calculated in part (a).

c. Calculate the sustainable growth rate for the company.

d. Can Optical Scam eliminate the need for external funds by changing its dividend policy? What other options are available to the company to meet its growth objectives?

EXCEL

3.5   The CCD Company does not want to grow. The company's financial management believes it has no positive NPV projects. The company's operating financial characteristics are:

Profit margin $= 11\%$

Asset–sales ratio $= 150\%$

Debt–equity ratio $= 100\%$

Dividend payout ratio $= 50\%$

a. Calculate the sustainable growth rate for the company.

b. How can the company achieve its stated growth goal?

3.6   Starting in Chapter 1, we argue that financial managers should select positive shareholder value projects. How does this project selection criterion relate to financial planning models?

3.7   Your firm recently hired a new MBA. She insists that your firm is incorrectly computing its sustainable growth rate. Your firm computes the sustainable growth rate using the following formula:

$$\frac{P \times (1 - d) \times (1 + L)}{T - P \times (1 - d) \times (1 + L)}$$

P = Net profit margin on sales

d = Dividend-payout ratio

L = Debt–equity ratio

T = Ratio of total assets to sales

Your new employee claims that the correct formula is ROE $\times$ $(1 - d)$ where ROE is net profit divided by net worth and d is dividends divided by net profit. Is your new employee correct?

3.8   Atlantic Transportation Co. has a payout ratio of 55 percent, debt–equity ratio of 30 percent, return on equity of 18 percent, and an assets–sales ratio of 195 percent.

a. What is its sustainable growth rate?

b. What must its profit margin be in order to achieve its sustainable growth rate?

3.9   A firm wishes to maintain a growth rate of 12 percent per year and a debt–equity ratio of 0.60. Its profit margin is 6 percent and the ratio of total assets to sales is constant at 2.15. Is this growth rate possible? To answer, determine what the dividend payout must be and interpret the result.

3.10   Bulla Recording Inc. wishes to maintain a growth rate of 14 percent per year and a debt–equity ratio of 0.30. Profit margin is 6.2 percent, and the ratio of total assets to sales is constant at 1.55. Is this growth rate possible? To answer, determine what the dividend-payout ratio must be. How do you interpret the result?

Some Caveats of Financial Planning Models

3.11   What are the shortcomings of financial planning models that we should be aware of?

3.12   Use the annual income statements and balance sheets under the "Excel Analytics" link to calculate the sustainable growth rate for Molson Coors Brewing Company (TAP) each year for the past four years. Is the sustainable growth rate the same every year? What are possible reasons the sustainable growth rate may vary from year to year?

3.13   Hilton Hotels Inc. (HLT) operates over 60 hotels in 29 countries. Under the "Financial Highlights" link you can find a five-year growth rate for sales. Using this growth rate and the most recent income statement and balance sheet, compute the external funds needed for ESA next year.

MINICASE: Ratios and Financial Planning at East Coast Yachts

Dan Ervin was recently hired by East Coast Yachts to assist the company with its short-term financial planning and also to evaluate the company's financial performance. Dan graduated from college five years ago with a finance degree, and he has been employed in the treasury department of a *Fortune* 500 company since then.

East Coast Yachts was founded 10 years ago by Larisa Warren. The company's operations are located near Luneburg, Nova Scotia, and the company is structured as an LLC. The company has manufactured custom mid-size, high-performance yachts for clients over this period, and its products have received high reviews for safety and reliability. The company's yachts have also recently received the highest award for customer satisfaction. The yachts are primarily purchased by wealthy individuals for pleasure use. Occasionally, a yacht is manufactured for purchase by a company for business purposes.

The custom yacht industry is fragmented, with a number of manufacturers. As with any industry, there are market leaders, but the diverse nature of the industry ensures that no manufacturer dominates the market. The competition in the market, as well as the product cost, ensures that attention to detail is a necessity. For instance, East Coast Yachts will spend 80 to 100 hours on hand-buffing the stainless steel stem-iron, which is the metal cap on the yacht's bow that conceivably could collide with a dock or another boat.

To get Dan started with his analyses, Larisa has provided the following financial statements. Dan has gathered the industry ratios for the yacht manufacturing industry.

EAST COAST YACHTS
20X6 Income Statement

Sales	$128,700,000
Cost of goods sold	90,700,000
Other expenses	15,380,000
Depreciation	4,200,000
Earnings before interest and taxes (EBIT)	$ 18,420,000
Interest	2,315,000
Taxable income	$ 16,105,000
Taxes (40%)	6,442,000
Net income	$ 9,663,000
Dividends	$5,797,800
Addition to retained earnings	3,865,200

EAST COAST YACHTS
Balance Sheet as of December 31, 20X6

Assets		Liabilities & Equity	
Current assets		Current liabilities	
Cash	$ 2,340,000	Accounts payable	$ 4,970,000
Accounts receivable	4,210,000	Notes payable	10,060,000
Inventory	4,720,000		
Total	$11,270,000	Total	$15,030,000
Fixed assets		Long-term debt	$25,950,000
Net plant and equipment	$72,280,000		
		Shareholders' equity	
		Common stock	$ 4,000,000
		Retained earnings	38,570,000
		Total equity	$42,570,000
Total assets	$83,550,000	Total liabilities and equity	$83,550,000

Visit us at www.mcgrawhill.ca/olc/ross

Yacht Industry Ratios			
	Lower Quartile	Median	Upper Quartile
Current ratio	0.50	1.43	1.89
Quick ratio	0.21	0.38	0.62
Total asset turnover	0.68	0.85	1.38
Inventory turnover	4.89	6.15	10.89
Receivables turnover	6.27	9.82	14.11
Debt ratio	0.44	0.52	0.61
Debt–equity ratio	0.79	1.08	1.56
Equity multiplier	1.79	2.08	2.56
Interest coverage	5.18	8.06	9.83
Profit margin	4.05%	6.98%	9.87%
Return on assets	6.05%	10.53%	13.21%
Return on equity	9.93%	16.54%	26.15%

1. Calculate all of the ratios listed in the industry table for East Coast Yachts.
2. Compare the performance of East Coast Yachts to the industry as a whole. For each ratio, comment on why it might be viewed as positive or negative relative to the industry. Suppose you create an inventory ratio calculated as inventory divided by current liabilities. How do you interpret this ratio? How does East Coast Yachts compare to the industry average?
3. Calculate the sustainable growth rate of East Coast Yachts. Calculate external funds needed (EFN) and prepare pro forma income statements and balance sheets assuming growth at precisely this rate. Recalculate the ratios in the previous question. What do you observe?
4. As a practical matter, East Coast Yachts is unlikely to be willing to raise external equity capital, in part because the owners don't want to dilute their existing ownership and control positions. However, East Coast Yachts is planning for a growth rate of 20 percent next year. What are your conclusions and recommendations about the feasibility of East Coast's expansion plans?
5. Most assets can be increased as a percentage of sales. For instance, cash can be increased by any amount. However, fixed assets often must be increased in specific amounts because it is impossible, as a practical matter, to buy part of a new plant or machine. In this case a company has a "staircase" or "lumpy" fixed cost structure. Assume that East Coast Yachts is currently producing at 100 percent of capacity. As a result, to expand production, the company must set up an entirely new line at a cost of $25,000,000. Calculate the new EFN with this assumption. What does this imply about capacity utilization for East Coast Yachts next year?

PART 2

Chapter 4

Financial Markets and Net Present Value: First Principles of Finance

EXECUTIVE SUMMARY

Finance refers to the process by which special markets deal with cash flows over time. These markets are called *financial markets*. Making investment and financing decisions requires an understanding of the basic economic principles of financial markets. This introductory chapter describes a financial market as one that makes it possible for individuals and corporations to borrow and lend. As a consequence, financial markets can be used by individuals to adjust their patterns of consumption over time and by corporations to adjust their patterns of investment spending over time. The main point of this chapter is that individuals and corporations can use the financial markets to help them make investment decisions. We introduce one of the most important ideas in finance: net present value.

By far the most important economic decisions are those that involve investments in real assets. We don't mean savings decisions, which are decisions not to consume some of this year's income, but decisions regarding actual investments: building a machine or a whole factory or a Tim Hortons, for example. These decisions determine the economic future for a society. Economists use the word *capital* to describe the total stock of machines and equipment that a society possesses and uses to produce goods and services. Investment decisions are decisions about whether or not to increase this stock of capital.

The investment decisions made today determine how much additional capital society will add to its current stock of capital. That capital then can be used in the future to produce goods and services for the society. Some of the forms that capital takes are obvious, like steel mills and computers. But many kinds of capital are things that you probably never would have considered as part of a country's capital stock. Public roads, for example, are a form of capital, and the decisions to build them are investment decisions. Perhaps most important, the decision you are making to invest in an education is no different in principle from these other investment decisions. Your decision to invest in education is a decision to build your human capital, just as a company's decision to build a new factory is a decision to invest in physical capital.[1] The total of all the capital possessed by a society is a measure of its wealth. The purpose of this chapter is to develop the basic principles that guide rational investment decision making. We show that a particular investment decision should be made if it is superior to available alternatives in the financial markets.

---

[1] If you have any doubt about the importance of human capital as part of a country's wealth, think about the conditions of Germany and Japan at the end of World War II. The physical capital of these countries had been destroyed, and even the basic social capital like roads, sewer systems, and factories was in rubble. Even though these countries might have appeared to be economically crippled beyond repair, a look below the surface would have revealed a different picture. A huge part of the wealth of these countries consisted of the human capital inherent in their literate and skilled populations. Building on this substantial base of capital by a long-term policy of investment has brought Germany and Japan to a very high standard of living.

4.1 The Financial Market Economy

Financial markets develop to facilitate borrowing and lending between individuals. Here we talk about how this happens. Suppose we describe the economic circumstances of two people: Tom and Leslie. Both Tom and Leslie have current income of $100,000. Tom is a very patient person, and some people call him a miser. He wants to consume only $50,000 of current income and save the rest. Leslie is a very impatient person, and some people call her extravagant. She wants to consume $150,000 this year. Tom and Leslie have different intertemporal consumption preferences.

Such preferences are personal matters and have more to do with psychology than with finance. However, it seems that Tom and Leslie could strike a deal: Tom could give up some of his income this year in exchange for future income that Leslie can promise to give him. Tom can *lend* $50,000 to Leslie, and Leslie can *borrow* $50,000 from Tom. This deal illustrates the useful role of financial markets in allowing borrowing and lending.

Suppose that they do strike this deal, with Tom giving up $50,000 this year in exchange for $55,000 next year. This is illustrated in Figure 4.1 with the basic cash flow time chart, a representation of the timing and amount of the cash flows. The cash flows that are received are represented by an arrow pointing up from the point on the time line at which the cash flow occurs. The cash flows paid out are represented by an arrow pointing down. In other words, for each dollar Tom trades away or lends, he gets a commitment to get it back as well as to receive 10 percent more.

In the language of finance, 10 percent is the annual rate of interest on the loan. When a dollar is lent out, the repayment of $1.10 can be thought of as being made up of two parts. First, the lender gets the dollar back; that is the *principal repayment.* Second, the lender receives an *interest payment,* which is $0.10 in this example.

Now, not only have Tom and Leslie struck a deal, but as a by-product of their bargain they have created a financial instrument, the IOU. This piece of paper entitles whoever receives it to present it to Leslie next year and redeem it for $55,000. Financial instruments that entitle whoever possesses them to receive payment are called *bearer instruments* because whoever bears them can use them. Presumably there could be more such IOUs in the economy written by many different lenders and borrowers like Tom and Leslie.

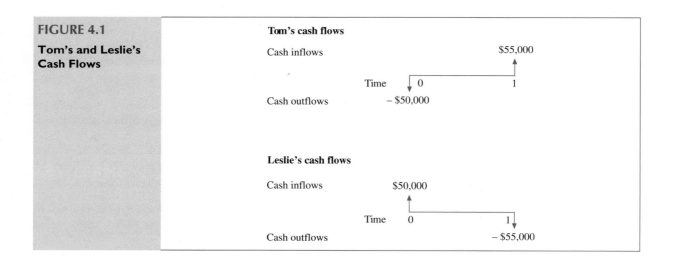

FIGURE 4.1

Tom's and Leslie's Cash Flows

The Anonymous Market

If the borrower does not care whom she has to pay back, and if the lender does not care whose IOUs he is holding, we could just as well drop Tom's and Leslie's names from their contract. All we need is a record book, in which we could record the fact that Tom has lent $50,000 and Leslie has borrowed $50,000 and that the terms of the loan, the interest rate, are 10 percent. Perhaps another person could keep the records for borrowers and lenders—for a fee, of course. In fact—and this is one of the virtues of such an arrangement—Tom and Leslie wouldn't even need to meet. Instead of needing to find and trade with each other, they could each trade with the recordkeeper. The recordkeeper could deal with thousands of such borrowers and lenders, none of whom would need to meet the other.

Institutions that perform this sort of market function, matching borrowers and lenders or traders, are called **financial intermediaries.** Chartered banks are modern examples of financial intermediaries. A bank's depositors lend the bank money, and the bank makes loans from the funds it has on deposit. In essence, the bank is an intermediary between the depositors and the ultimate borrowers. To make the market work, we must be certain that the market clears. By *market clearing* we mean that the total amount that people like Tom wish to lend to the market, say $11 million, equals the total amount that people like Leslie wish to borrow.

Market Clearing

If the lenders wish to lend more than the borrowers want to borrow, then presumably the interest rate is too high. Because there would not be enough borrowing for all of the lenders at, say, 15 percent, there are really only two ways that the market could be made to clear. One is to ration the lenders. For example, if the lenders wish to lend $20 million when interest rates are at 15 percent and the borrowers wish to borrow only $8 million, the market could take, say, 8/20 of each dollar, or $0.40, from each of the lenders and distribute it to the borrowers. This is one possible scheme for making the market clear, but it is not one that would be sustainable in a free and competitive marketplace. Why not?

To answer this important question, we return to our lender, Tom. Tom sees that interest rates are 15 percent and, not surprisingly, rather than simply lending the $50,000 that he was willing to lend when rates were 10 percent, Tom decides that at the higher rates he would like to lend more, say, $80,000. But since the lenders want to lend more money than the borrowers want to borrow, the recordkeepers tell Tom that they won't be able to take all of his $80,000; rather, they will take only 40 percent of it, or $32,000. With the interest rate at 15 percent, people are not willing to borrow enough to match up with all of the loans that are available at that rate.

Tom is not very pleased with that state of affairs, but he can do something to improve his situation. Suppose that he knows that Leslie is borrowing $20,000 in the market at the 15 percent interest rate. That means that Leslie must repay $20,000 on her loan next year plus the interest of 15 percent of $20,000, or $0.15 \times \$20,000 = \$3,000$. Suppose that Tom goes to Leslie and offers to lend her the $20,000 for 14 percent. Leslie is happy because she will save 1 percent on the deal and will need to pay back only $2,800 in interest next year. This is $200 less than if she had borrowed from the recordkeepers. Tom is happy, too, because he has found a way to lend some of the money that the recordkeepers would not take. The net result of this transaction is that the recordkeepers have lost Leslie as a customer. Why should she borrow from them when Tom will lend her the money at a lower interest rate?

Tom and Leslie are not the only ones cutting side deals in the marketplace, and it is clear that the recordkeepers will not be able to maintain the 15 percent rate. The interest rate must fall if they are to stay in business.

Suppose, then, that the market clears at the rate of 10 percent. At this rate the amount of money that the lenders wish to lend, $11 million, is exactly equal to the amount that the borrowers desire. We refer to the interest rate that clears the market, 10 percent in our example, as the **equilibrium rate of interest.**

In this section we have shown that, in the market for loans, bonds or IOUs are traded. These are *financial instruments*. The interest rate on these loans is such that the total demand for such loans by borrowers equals the total supply of loans by lenders. At a higher interest rate, lenders wish to supply more loans than are demanded, and if the interest rate is lower than this equilibrium level, borrowers demand more loans than lenders are willing to supply.

? **Concept Questions**
- **What is an interest rate?**
- **What do we mean when we say a market clears?**
- **What is an equilibrium rate of interest?**

4.2 Making Consumption Choices Over Time

Figure 4.2 illustrates the situation faced by an individual in the financial market. This person is assumed to have an income of $50,000 this year and an income of $60,000 next year. The market allows him not only to consume $50,000 worth of goods this year and $60,000 next year, but also to borrow and lend at the equilibrium interest rate. The line *AB* in Figure 4.2 shows all of the consumption possibilities open to the person through borrowing or lending, and the shaded area contains all of the feasible choices. Notice that the lender chooses to consume less than $50,000 and the borrower more than this amount.

We will use the letter *r* to denote the interest rate—the equilibrium rate—in this market. The rate is risk-free because we assume that no default can take place. Look at point *A* on the vertical axis of Figure 4.2. Point *A* represents consumption next year (on the vertical axis) of:

$$A = \$60,000 + \$50,000 \times (1 + r)$$

FIGURE 4.2

Intertemporal Consumption Opportunities

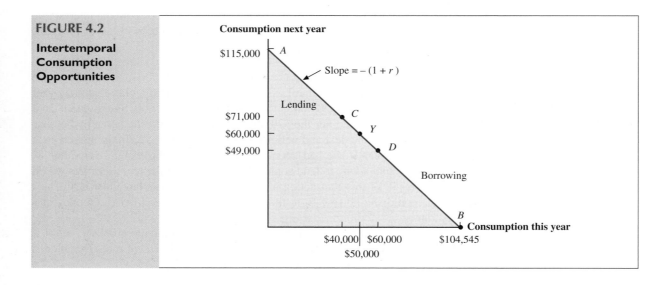

For example, if the rate of interest is 10 percent, then point A is

$$A = \$60{,}000 + \$50{,}000 \times (1 + 0.1)$$

$$= \$60{,}000 + \$55{,}000$$

$$= \$115{,}000$$

Point A is the maximum amount of wealth that this person can spend in the second year. He gets to point A by lending the full income that is available this year, $50,000, and consuming none of it. In the second year, then, he will have the second year's income of $60,000 plus the proceeds from the loan that he made in the first year, $55,000, for a total of $115,000.

Following the same logic, point B is a distance of

$$B = \$50{,}000 + \$60{,}000/(1 + r)$$

along the horizontal axis. If the interest rate is 10 percent, point B will be

$$B = \$50{,}000 + \$60{,}000/(1 + 0.1)$$

$$= \$50{,}000 + \$54{,}545$$

$$= \$104{,}545 \text{ (rounded off to the nearest dollar)}$$

Why do we divide next year's income of $60,000 by $(1 + r)$ or 1.1 in the preceding computation? Point B represents the maximum amount available for this person to consume this year. To achieve that maximum he would borrow as much as possible and repay the loan from the income, $60,000, that he was going to receive next year. Because $60,000 will be available to repay the loan next year, we are asking how much he could borrow this year at an interest rate of r and still be able to repay the loan. The answer is

$$\$60{,}000/(1 + r)$$

because if he borrows this amount, he must repay it next year with interest. Thus, next year he must repay

$$[\$60{,}000/(1 + r)] \times (1 + r) = \$60{,}000$$

no matter what the interest rate, r, is. In our example we found that he could borrow $54,545 and, sure enough,

$$\$54{,}545 \times 1.1 = \$60{,}000$$

(after rounding off to the nearest dollar).

Furthermore, by borrowing and lending different amounts, the person can achieve any point on the line AB. For example, at point C he has chosen to lend $10,000 of today's income. This means that at point C he will have

$$\text{Consumption this year at point } C = \$50{,}000 - \$10{,}000 = \$40{,}000$$

and

$$\text{Consumption next year at point } C = \$60{,}000 + \$10{,}000 \times (1 + r) = \$71{,}000$$

when the interest rate is 10 percent.

Similarly, at point D, the individual has decided to borrow $10,000 and repay the loan next year. At point D, then,

$$\text{Consumption this year at point } C = \$50{,}000 + \$10{,}000 = \$60{,}000$$

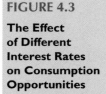

FIGURE 4.3

The Effect
of Different
Interest Rates
on Consumption
Opportunities

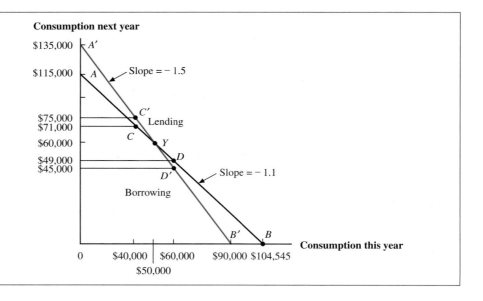

and

$$\text{Consumption next year at point } D = \$60,000 - \$10,000 \times (1 + r) = \$49,000$$

at an interest rate of 10 percent.

In fact, this person can consume at any point on the line *AB*. This line has a slope of $-(1 + r)$, which means that, for each dollar that is added to the *x*-coordinate along the line, $(1 + r)$ dollars are subtracted from the *y*-coordinate. Moving along the line from point *A*, the initial point of $50,000 this year and $60,000 next year, toward point *B* gives the person more consumption today and less next year. In other words, moving toward point *B* is borrowing. Similarly, moving up toward point *A,* he is consuming less today and more next year and he is lending. The line is a straight line because the individual has no effect on the interest rate. This is one of the assumptions of perfectly competitive financial markets.

Where in Figure 4.2 will the person actually be? The answer to that question depends on the individual's tastes and personal situation, just as it did before there was a market. If the person is impatient, he might wish to borrow money at a point such as *D,* and if he is patient, he might wish to lend some of this year's income and enjoy more consumption next year at, for example, a point such as *C.*

Notice that whether we think of someone as patient or impatient depends on the interest rate he or she faces in the market. Suppose that our individual was impatient and chose to borrow $10,000 and move to point *D.* Now suppose that we raise the interest rate to 20 percent or even 50 percent. Suddenly our impatient person may become very patient and might prefer to lend some of this year's income to take advantage of the very high interest rate. The general result is depicted in Figure 4.3. We can see that lending at point *C'* yields much greater future income and consumption possibilities than before.[2]

? Concept Questions

• **How does an individual change consumption across periods through borrowing and lending?**
• **How do interest rate changes affect one's degree of impatience?**

<hr/>

[2]Those familiar with consumer theory might be aware of the surprising case where raising the interest rate actually makes people borrow more or lowering the rate makes them lend more. The latter case might occur, for example, if the decline in the interest rate made the lenders have so little consumption next year that they have no choice but to lend out even more than they did before, just to subsist. Nothing we do depends on excluding such cases, but it is much easier to ignore them, and the resulting analysis fits the real markets much more closely.

4.3 The Competitive Market

In the previous analysis we assumed the individual moves freely along the line *AB,* and we ignored—and assumed that the individual ignores—any effect his borrowing or lending decisions might have on the equilibrium interest rate itself. What would happen, though, if the total amount of loans outstanding in the market when the person was doing no borrowing or lending was $10 million, and if our person then decided to lend, say, $5 million? His lending would be half as much as the rest of the market put together, and it would not be unreasonable to think that the equilibrium interest rate would fall to induce more borrowers into the market to take his additional loans. In such a situation the person has some power in the market to influence the equilibrium rate significantly, and he would take this power into consideration in making his decisions.

In modern financial markets, however, the total amount of borrowing and lending is not $10 million; rather, as we say in Chapter 1, it is far higher. In such a huge market no one investor or even any single company can have a significant effect (although a government might). We assume, then, in all of our subsequent discussions and analyses that the financial market is perfectly competitive. By that we mean no individuals or firms think they have any effect whatsoever on the interest rates that they face no matter how much borrowing, lending, or investing they do. In the language of economics, individuals who respond to rates and prices by acting as though they have no influence on them are called *price takers,* and this assumption is sometimes called the *price-taking assumption*. It is the condition of **perfectly competitive financial markets** (or, more simply, *perfect markets*). The following conditions characterize perfect financial markets:

1. Trading is costless. Access to the financial markets is free.
2. Information about borrowing and lending opportunities is readily available.
3. There are many traders, and no single trader can have a significant impact on market prices.

In Chapter 14 we introduce the concept of efficient markets. Although efficient markets are less than perfectly competitive, available evidence suggests that most of the time, the three conditions above are a good approximation for financial markets.

How Many Interest Rates Are There in a Competitive Market?

An important point about this one-year market where no defaults can take place is that only one interest rate can be quoted in the market at any one time. Suppose that some competing recordkeepers decide to set up a rival market. To attract customers, their business plan is to offer lower interest rates, say, 9 percent, to attract borrowers away from the first market and soon have all of the business.

Their business plan will work, but it will do so beyond their wildest expectations. They will indeed attract the borrowers, all $11 million worth of them! But the matter doesn't stop there. By offering to borrow and lend at 9 percent when another market is offering 10 percent, they have created the proverbial money machine.

The world of finance is populated by sharp-eyed inhabitants who would not let this opportunity slip by them. Any one of these, whether a borrower or a lender, would go to the new market and borrow everything he could at the 9 percent rate. At the same time he was borrowing in the new market, he would also be striking a deal to lend in the old market at

82 Part 2   Value and Capital Budgeting

the 10 percent rate. If he could borrow $100 million at 9 percent and lend it at 10 percent, he could net 1 percent, or $1 million, next year. He would repay the $109 million he owed to the new market from the $110 million he would receive when the 10 percent loan he had made in the original market was repaid, pocketing $1 million.

This process of striking a deal in one market and an offsetting deal in another simultaneously and at more favourable terms is called *arbitrage*; the individuals who do it are called *arbitrageurs*. Of course, someone must be paying for all of this free money, and it must be the recordkeepers because the borrowers and the lenders are all making money. Our intrepid, entrepreneurial recordkeepers will lose their proverbial shirts and go out of business. The moral of this is clear: As soon as different interest rates are offered for essentially the same risk-free loans, arbitrageurs will take advantage of the situation by borrowing at the low rate and lending at the high rate. The gap between the two rates will be closed quickly, and for all practical purposes there will be only one rate available in the market.

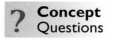 **Concept Questions**

- **What is the most important feature of a competitive financial market?**
- **What conditions are likely to lead to this?**
- **What is arbitrage and why does it result in one rate for riskless loans?**

4.4 The Basic Principle

We have already shown how people use the financial markets to adjust their patterns of consumption over time to fit their particular preferences. By borrowing and lending, they can greatly expand their range of choices. They need only to have access to a market with an interest rate at which they can borrow and lend.

In the previous section we saw how these savings and consumption decisions depend on the interest rate. The financial markets also provide a benchmark against which proposed investments can be compared, and the interest rate is the basis for a test that any proposed investment must pass. The financial markets give the individual, the corporation, or even the government a standard of comparison for economic decisions. This benchmark is critical when investment decisions are being made.

The way we use the financial markets to aid us in making investment decisions is a direct consequence of our basic assumption that individuals can never be made worse off by increasing the range of choices open to them. People always can make use of the financial markets to adjust their savings and consumption by borrowing or lending. An investment project is worth undertaking only if it increases the range of choices in the financial markets. To do this, the project must be at least as desirable as what is available in the financial markets.[3] If it were not as desirable as what the financial markets have to offer, people could simply use the financial markets instead of undertaking the investment. This point will govern us in all of our investment decisions. It is the *first principle of investment decision making,* and it is the foundation on which all of our rules are built.

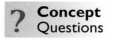 **Concept Questions**

- **Describe the basic financial principle of investment decision making.**

---

[3]You might wonder what to do if an investment is exactly as desirable as an alternative in the financial markets. In principle, if there is a tie, it doesn't matter whether or not we take on the investment. In practice, we've never seen an exact tie.

4.5 Practising the Principle

Let us apply the basic principle of investment decision making to some concrete situations.

A Lending Example

Consider a person who is concerned only about this year and next. She has an income of $100,000 this year and expects to make the same amount next year. The interest rate is 10 percent. This individual is thinking about investing in a piece of land that costs $70,000. She is certain that next year the land will be worth $75,000, a sure $5,000 gain. Should she undertake the investment? This situation is described in Figure 4.4 with the cash flow time chart.

A moment's thought should be all it takes to convince her that this is not an attractive business deal. By investing $70,000 in the land, she will have $75,000 available next year. Suppose, instead, that she puts the same $70,000 into a loan in the financial market. At the 10 percent rate of interest, this $70,000 would grow to

$$(1 + 0.1) \times \$70{,}000 = \$77{,}000$$

next year.

It would be foolish to buy the land when the same $70,000 investment in the financial market would beat it by $2,000 (that is, $77,000 from the loan minus $75,000 from the land investment).

Figure 4.5 illustrates this situation. Notice that the $70,000 loan gives no less income today and $2,000 more next year. This example illustrates some amazing features of the financial markets. It is remarkable to consider all of the information that we did *not* use when arriving at the decision not to invest in the land. We did not need to know how much income the person has this year or next year. We also did not need to know whether the person preferred more income this year or next.

We did not need to know any of these other facts, and, more importantly, the person making the decision did not need to know them either. She only needed to be able to compare the investment with a relevant alternative available in the financial market. When the proposed investment fell short of that standard—by $2,000 in the previous example—regardless of what the individual wanted to do, she knew that she should not buy the land.

A Borrowing Example

Let us sweeten the deal a bit. Suppose that instead of being worth $75,000 next year, the land will be worth $80,000. What should our investor do now? This case is a bit more difficult. After all, even if the land seems like a good deal, this person's income this year is $100,000. Does she really want to make a $70,000 investment this year? Won't that leave only $30,000 for consumption?

The answers to these questions are yes, the individual should buy the land; yes, she does want to make a $70,000 investment this year; and, most surprising of all, even though

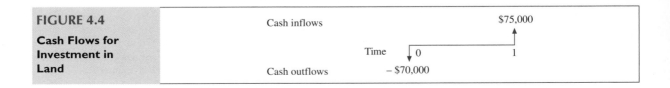

FIGURE 4.4

Cash Flows for Investment in Land

Cash inflows $75,000

Time   0   1

Cash outflows   − $70,000

FIGURE 4.5

Consumption Opportunities with Borrowing and Lending

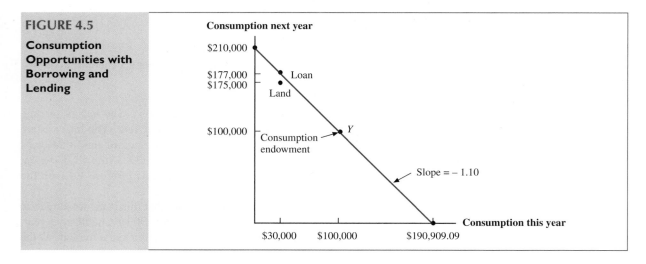

Consumption next year

$210,000

$177,000 ● Loan
$175,000 ●
Land

$100,000 ● *Y*
Consumption
endowment

Slope = – 1.10

Consumption this year

$30,000 $100,000 $190,909.09

her income is $100,000, making the $70,000 investment will not leave her with $30,000 to consume this year! Now let us see how finance lets us get around the basic laws of arithmetic.

The financial markets are the key to solving our problem. First, the financial markets can be used as a standard of comparison against which any investment project must measure up. Second, they can be used as a tool to help the individual actually undertake investments. These twin features of the financial markets enable us to make the right investment decision.

Suppose that the person borrows the $70,000 initial investment that is needed to purchase the land. Next year she must repay this loan. Because the interest rate is 10 percent, she will owe the financial market $77,000 next year. This is depicted in Figure 4.6. Because

FIGURE 4.6

Cash Flows of Borrowing to Purchase the Land

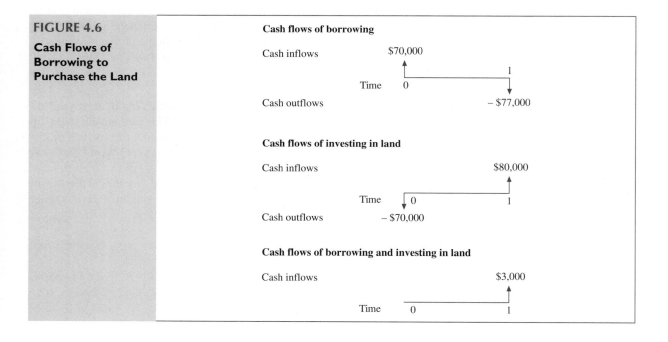

Cash flows of borrowing

Cash inflows $70,000

Time   0   1

Cash outflows   – $77,000

Cash flows of investing in land

Cash inflows $80,000

Time   0   1

Cash outflows   – $70,000

Cash flows of borrowing and investing in land

Cash inflows $3,000

Time   0   1

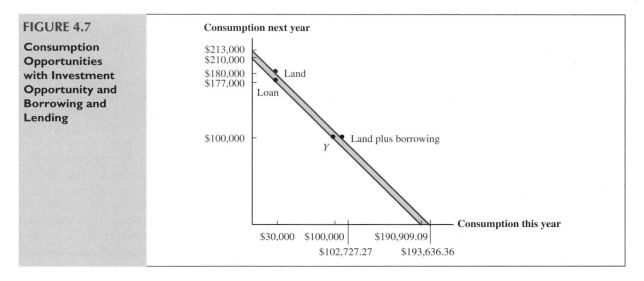

FIGURE 4.7

Consumption Opportunities with Investment Opportunity and Borrowing and Lending

the land will be worth $80,000 next year, she will be able to sell it, pay off her debt of $77,000, and have $3,000 extra cash.

If she wishes, this person can now consume an extra $3,000 worth of goods and services next year. This possibility is illustrated in Figure 4.7. In fact, even if she wants to do all of her consuming this year, she is still better off taking the investment. All she must do is take out a loan this year and repay it from the proceeds of the land next year and profit by $3,000.

Furthermore, instead of borrowing just the $70,000 that she needed to purchase the land, she could have borrowed $72,727.27. She could have used $70,000 to buy the land and consumed the remaining $2,727.27. We will call $2,727.27 the net present value of the transaction. Notice that it is equal to $3,000 × 1/1.1. How did we figure out that this was the exact amount that she could borrow? It was easy: If $72,727.27 is the amount that she borrows, then, because the interest rate is 10 percent, she must repay

$$\$72,727.27 \times (1 + 0.1) = \$80,000$$

next year, and that is exactly what the land will be worth. The line through the investment position in Figure 4.7 illustrates this borrowing possibility.

The amazing thing about both of these cases, one where the land is worth $75,000 next year and the other where it is worth $80,000 next year, is that we needed only to compare the investment with the financial markets to decide whether it was worth undertaking or not. This is one of the more important points in all of finance. It is true regardless of the consumption preferences of the individual. This is one of a number of *separation theorems* in finance. It states that the value of an investment to an individual is not dependent on consumption preferences. In our examples we showed that the person's decision to invest in land was not affected by consumption preferences. However, these preferences dictated whether the person borrowed or lent.

? Concept Questions

- Describe how the financial markets can be used to evaluate investment alternatives.
- What is the separation theorem? Why is it important?

4.6 Illustrating the Investment Decision

Figure 4.2, discussed earlier, describes the possibilities open to a person who has an income of $50,000 this year and $60,000 next year and faces a financial market in which the interest rate is 10 percent. But at that moment, the person has no investment possibilities beyond the 10 percent borrowing and lending that is available in the financial market.

Suppose that we give this person the chance to undertake an investment project that will require a $30,000 outlay of cash this year and that will return $40,000 to the investor next year. Refer to Figure 4.2 and determine how you could include this new possibility in that figure and how you could use the figure to help you decide whether to undertake the investment.

Now look at Figure 4.8. In Figure 4.8 we have labelled the original point with $50,000 this year and $60,000 next year as point *A*. We have also added a new point *B*, with $20,000 available for consumption this year and $100,000 next year. The difference between point *A* and point *B* is that at point *A* the person is just where we started him off, and at point *B* the person has also decided to undertake the investment project. As a result of this decision, the person at point *B* has

$$\$50,000 - \$30,000 = \$20,000$$

left for consumption this year, and

$$\$60,000 + \$40,000 = \$100,000$$

available next year. These are the coordinates of point *B*.

We must use our knowledge of the individual's borrowing and lending opportunities in order to decide whether to accept or reject the investment. This is illustrated in Figure 4.9. Figure 4.9 is similar to Figure 4.8, but in it we have drawn a line through point *A* that shows the possibilities open to the person if he stays at point *A* and does not take the investment. This line is exactly the same as the one in Figure 4.2. We have also drawn a parallel line through point *B* that shows the new possibilities that are available to the person if he undertakes the investment. The two lines are parallel because the slope of each is determined by the same interest rate, 10 percent. It does not matter whether the person takes the investment and goes to point *B* or does not and stays at point *A;* in the financial market, each dollar of lending is a dollar less available for consumption this year and moves him to the left by a dollar along the *x*-axis. Because the interest rate is 10 percent, the $1 loan repays $1.10 and it moves him up by $1.10 along the *y*-axis.

FIGURE 4.8

Consumption Choices with Investment Opportunities but No Financial Markets

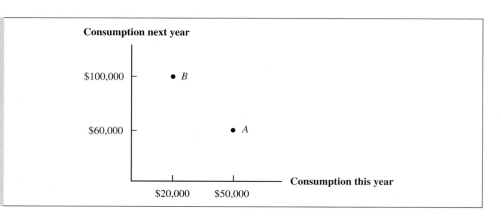

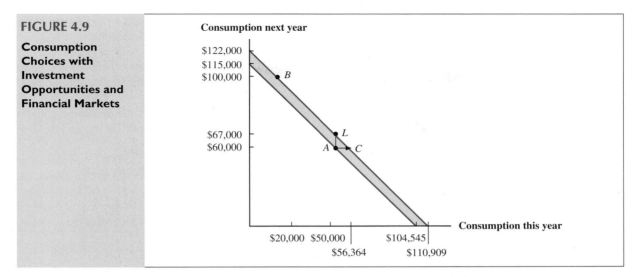

FIGURE 4.9

Consumption Choices with Investment Opportunities and Financial Markets

It is easy to see from Figure 4.9 that the investment has made the person better off. The line through point *B* is higher than the line through point *A*. Thus, no matter what pattern of consumption this person wanted this year and next, he could have more in each year if he undertook the investment.

For example, suppose that our individual wanted to consume everything this year. If he did not take the investment, the point where the line through point *A* intersected the *x*-axis would give the maximum amount of consumption he could enjoy this year—$104,545. To recall how we found this figure, review the analysis of Figure 4.2. But in Figure 4.9 the line that goes through point *B* intersects the *x*-axis at a higher point than the line that goes through point *A*. Along this line the person can have the $20,000 that is left after investing $30,000, plus all that he can borrow and repay with both next year's income and the proceeds from the investment. The total amount available to consume today is therefore

$$\$50{,}000 - \$30{,}000 + (\$60{,}000 + \$40{,}000)/(1 + 0.1)$$

$$= \$20{,}000 + \$100{,}000/(1.1)$$

$$= \$110{,}909$$

The additional consumption available this year from undertaking the investment and using the financial market is the difference on the *x*-axis between the points where these two lines intersect:

$$\$110{,}909 - \$104{,}545 = \$6{,}364$$

This difference is an important measure of what the investment is worth to the person. It answers a variety of questions. For example, it is the answer to the question: How much money would we need to give the investor this year to make him just as well off as he is with the investment?

Because the line through point *B* is parallel to the line through point *A* but has been moved over by $6,364, we know that if we were to add this amount to the investor's current income this year at point *A* and take away the investment, he would wind up on the line through point *B* and with the same possibilities. If we do this, the person will have $56,364 this year and $60,000 next year, which is the situation of the point on the line through point *B* that lies to the right of point *A* in Figure 4.9. This is point *C*.

We could also ask a different question: How much money would we need to give the investor next year to make him just as well off as he is with the investment?

This is the same as asking how much higher the line through point *B* is than the line through point *A*. In other words, what is the difference in Figure 4.9 between the point where the line through *A* intercepts the *y*-axis and the point where the line through *B* intercepts the *y*-axis?

The point where the line through *A* intercepts the *y*-axis shows the maximum amount the person could consume next year if all of his current income were lent out and the proceeds of the loan were consumed along with next year's income.

As we showed in our analysis of Figure 4.2, this amount is $115,000. How does this compare with what the person can have next year if he takes the investment? By taking the investment we saw that the person would be at point *B,* where he has $20,000 left this year and would have $100,000 next year. By lending the $20,000 that is left this year and adding the proceeds of this loan to the $100,000, we find the line through *B* intercepts the *y*-axis at

$$\$20,000 \times (1.1) + \$100,000 = \$122,000$$

The difference between this amount and $115,000 is

$$\$122,000 - \$115,000 = \$7,000$$

which is the answer to the question of how much we would need to give the person next year to make him as well off as he is with the investment.

There is a simple relationship between these two numbers. If we multiply $6,364 by 1.1 we get $7,000! Consider why this must be so. The $6,364 is the amount of extra cash we must give the person this year to substitute for having the investment. In a financial market with a 10 percent rate of interest, however, $1 this year is worth exactly the same as $1.10 next year. Thus, $6,364 this year is the same as $6,364 $\times$ 1.1 next year. In other words, the person does not care whether he has the investment, $6,364, this year or $6,364 $\times$ 1.1 next year. But we already showed that the investor is equally willing to have the investment and to have $7,000 next year. This must mean that

$$\$6,364 \times 1.1 = \$7,000$$

You can also verify this relationship between these two variables by using Figure 4.9. Because the lines through *A* and *B* have the same slope of -1.1, the difference of $7,000 between where they intersect on the *y*-axis and $6,364 between where they intersect on the *x*-axis must be in the ratio of 1.1 to 1.

Now we can show you how to evaluate the investment opportunity on a stand-alone basis. Here are the relevant facts: The individual must give up $30,000 this year to get $40,000 next year. These cash flows are illustrated in Figure 4.10.

The investment rule that follows from the previous analysis is the net present value (NPV) rule. Here we convert all consumption values to the present and add them up:

$$\text{Net present value} = -\$30,000 + \$40,000 \times (1/1.1)$$

$$= -\$30,000 + \$36,364$$

$$= \$6,364$$

The future amount, $40,000, is called the *future value (FV)*.

The net present value of an investment is a simple criterion for deciding whether or not to undertake it. NPV answers the question of how much cash an investor would need to have today as a substitute for making the investment. If the net present value is positive, the investment is worth taking on because doing so is essentially the same as receiving a

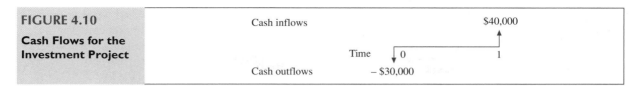

FIGURE 4.10

Cash Flows for the Investment Project

Cash inflows

$40,000

Time   0   1

Cash outflows   − $30,000

cash payment equal to the net present value. If the net present value is negative, taking on the investment today is equivalent to giving up some cash today, and the investment should be rejected.

We use the term *net present value* to emphasize that we are already including the current cost of the investment in determining its value and not simply measuring what it will return. For example, if the interest rate is 10 percent and an investment of $30,000 today will produce a total cash return of $40,000 in one year's time, the *present value* of the $40,000 by itself is

$$\$40,000/1.1 = \$36,364$$

but the *net present value* of the investment is $36,364 minus the original investment:

$$\text{Net present value} = \$36,364 - \$30,000 = \$6,364$$

The present value of a future cash flow is the value of that cash flow after considering the appropriate market interest rate. The net present value of an investment is the present value of the investment's future cash flows, minus the initial cost of the investment. We have just decided that our investment is a good opportunity. It has a positive net present value because it is worth more than it costs.

In general, the above can be stated in terms of the **net present value rule:**

An investment is worth making if it has a positive NPV. If an investment's NPV is negative, it should be rejected.

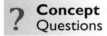 **Concept Questions**

- **Give the definitions of net present value, future value, and present value.**
- **What information does a person need to compute an investment's net present value?**

4.7 Corporate Investment Decision Making

Up to now, everything we have done has been from the perspective of the individual investor. How do corporations and firms make investment decisions? Are their decisions governed by a much more complicated set of rules and principles than the simple NPV rule that we have developed for individuals?

We discussed corporate decision making, corporate governance, and stakeholder issues in Chapter 1 and will return to these issues later in the book. Still, it is remarkable how well our central ideas and the NPV rule hold up even when applied to corporations.

We may view firms as means by which many investors can pool their resources to make large-scale business decisions. Suppose, for example, that you own 1 percent of some firm. Now suppose further that this firm is considering whether or not to undertake some investment. If that investment passes the NPV rule, that is, if it has a positive NPV, then 1 percent of the NPV belongs to you. If the firm takes on this investment, the value of the whole firm will rise by the NPV and your investment in the firm will rise by 1 percent of the NPV of the investment. Similarly, the other shareholders in the firm will profit by having the firm take on the positive NPV project because the value of their shares in the firm will also

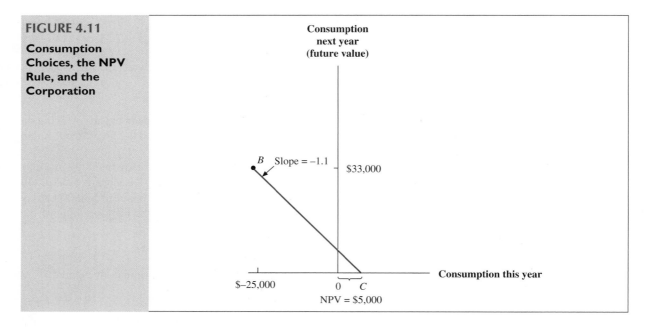

FIGURE 4.11

Consumption Choices, the NPV Rule, and the Corporation

increase. This means that the shareholders in the firm will be unanimous in wanting the firm to increase its value by taking on the positive NPV project. If you follow this line of reasoning, you will also be able to see why the shareholders would oppose the firm's taking on any projects with a negative NPV because this would lower the value of their shares.

One difference between the firm and the individual is that the firm has no consumption endowment. In terms of our one-period consumption diagram, the firm starts at the origin. Figure 4.11 illustrates the situation of a firm with investment opportunity *B*. *B* is an investment that has a future value of $33,000 and will cost $25,000 now. If the interest rate is 10 percent, the NPV of *B* can be determined using the NPV rule. This is marked as point *C* in Figure 4.11. The cash flows of this investment are depicted in Figure 4.12.

One common objection to this line of reasoning is that people differ in their tastes and that they won't necessarily agree to take on or reject investments by the NPV rule. For instance, suppose that you and we each own some shares in a company. Further suppose that we are older than you and might be anxious to spend our money. Being younger, you might be more patient than we are and more willing to wait for a good long-term investment to pay off.

Because of the financial markets we all agree that the company should take on investments with positive NPVs and reject those with negative NPVs. If there were no financial markets, then, being impatient, we might want the company to do little or no investing so that we could have as much money as possible to consume now, and, being patient, you might prefer the company to make some investments. With financial markets, we are both satisfied by having the company follow the NPV rule.

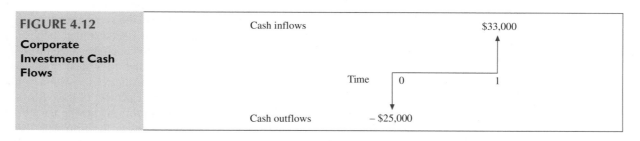

FIGURE 4.12

Corporate Investment Cash Flows

To see why this is so, suppose that the company takes on a positive NPV investment. Let us assume that this investment has a net payoff of $1 million next year. That means that the value of the company will increase by $1 million next year; consequently, if you own 1 percent of the company's shares, the value of your shares will increase by 1 percent of $1 million, or $10,000, next year. Because you are patient, you might be prepared to wait for your $10,000 until next year. Being impatient, we do not want to wait—and with financial markets, we do not need to wait. We can simply borrow against the extra $10,000 we will have tomorrow and use the loan to consume more today.

In fact, if there is also a market for the firm's shares, we do not even need to borrow. After the company takes on a positive NPV investment, our shares in the company increase in value today. This is because owning the shares today entitles investors to their portion of the extra $1 million the company will have next year. This means that the shares would rise in value today by the present value of $1 million. Because you want to delay your consumption, you could wait until next year and sell your shares then to have extra consumption next year. Being impatient, we might sell our shares now and use the money to consume more today. If we owned 1 percent of the company's shares, we could sell our shares for an extra amount equal to the present value of $10,000.

In reality, shareholders in big companies do not vote on every investment decision, and their managers must have rules to follow. We have seen that all shareholders in a company will be made better off—no matter what their levels of patience or impatience—if managers follow the NPV rule. This is a marvellous result because it makes it possible for many different owners to delegate decision-making powers to the managers. They need only to tell the managers to follow the NPV rule, and if the managers do so, they will be doing exactly what the shareholders want them to do. Sometimes this form of the NPV rule is stated as having the managers maximize the value of the company. As we argued, the current value of the shares of the company will increase by the NPV of any investments that the company undertakes. This means that the managers of the company can make the shareholders as well off as possible by taking on all positive NPV projects and rejecting projects with negative NPVs.

Separating investment decision making from the owners is a basic requirement of the modern large firm. An important **separation theorem** in financial markets says that all investors will want to accept or reject the same investment projects by using the NPV rule, regardless of their personal preferences. Investors can delegate the operations of the firm and require that managers use the NPV rule. Of course, much remains for us to discuss about this topic. For example, what ensures that managers will actually do what is best for their shareholders?

We discussed this interesting topic in Chapter 1, and we take it up again later in the book. For now, though, we will no longer consider our perspective to be that of the lone investor. Instead, thanks to the separation theorem, we will use the NPV rule for companies as well as for investors. Our justification of the NPV rule depends on the conditions necessary to derive the separation theorem. These conditions are the ones that result in competitive financial markets. The analysis we have presented has been restricted to risk-free cash flows in one time period. However, the separation theorem also can be derived for risky cash flows that extend beyond one period.

For the reader interested in studying further about the separation theorem, we include several suggested readings at the end of this chapter that build on the material we have presented.

? Concept Questions

- **In terms of the net present value rule, what is the essential difference between the individual and the corporation?**

4.8 SUMMARY AND CONCLUSIONS

Finance is a subject that builds understanding from the ground up. Whenever you encounter a new problem or issue in finance, you can always return to the basic principles of this chapter for guidance.

1. Financial markets exist because people want to adjust their consumption over time. They do so by borrowing and lending.

2. Financial markets provide the key test for investment decision making. Whether a particular investment decision should or should not be taken depends only on this test: If there is a superior alternative in the financial markets, the investment should be rejected; if not, the investment is worth taking. The most important thing about this principle is that the investor need not use his preferences to decide whether the investment should be taken. Regardless of the individual's preference for consumption this year versus next, regardless of how patient or impatient the individual is, making the proper investment decision depends only on comparing it with the alternatives in the financial markets.

3. The net present value of an investment helps us make the comparison between the investment and the financial market. If the NPV is positive, our rule tells us to undertake the investment. This illustrates the second major feature of the financial markets and investment. Not only does the NPV rule tell us which investments to accept and which to reject, but the financial markets also provide us with the tools for acquiring the funds to make the investments. In short, we use the financial markets to decide both what to do and how to do it.

4. The NPV rule can be applied to corporations as well as to individuals. The separation theorem developed in this chapter says that all of the owners of the firm would agree that the firm should use the NPV rule even though each might differ in personal tastes for consumption and savings.

In the next chapter we learn more about the NPV rule by using it to examine a wide array of problems in finance.

KEY TERMS

Equilibrium rate of interest 78	Net present value rule 89	Separation theorem 91
Financial intermediaries 77	Perfectly competitive financial market 81	

SUGGESTED READING

Two books that have good discussions of the consumption and savings decisions of individuals and the beginnings of financial markets are:

E. F. Fama and M. H. Miller. *The Theory of Finance.* Ch. 1. New York: Holt, Rinehart & Winston, 1971.

J. Hirshleifer. *Investment, Interest and Capital.* Ch. 1. Englewood Cliffs, N.J.: Prentice Hall, 1970.

The seminal work on the net present value rule is:

J. G. Fisher. *The Theory of Interest.* New York: Augustus M. Kelly, 1965. (This is a reprint of the 1930 edition.)

A rigorous treatment of the net present value rule along the lines of Irving Fisher can be found in:

J. Hirshleifer. "On the Theory of Optimal Investment Decision." *Journal of Political Economy* 66 (August 1958).

QUESTIONS & PROBLEMS

Making Consumption Choices

4.1   Currently, Jack Morris makes $85,000 per annum. Next year his income will be $108,000. Jack is a big spender and he wants to consume $135,000 a year. The equilibrium interest rate is 7 percent. What will be Jack's consumption potential next year if he consumes $135,000 this year?

4.2   Rich Pettit is a miser. His current income is $55,000; next year he will earn $38,000. He plans to consume only $20,000 this year. The current interest rate is 9 percent. What will Rich's consumption potential be next year?

The Competitive Market

4.3   What is the basic reason that financial markets develop?

4.4   Suppose that the equilibrium interest rate is 5.5 percent. What would happen in the market if a group of financial intermediaries attempted to control interest rates at 4 percent?

Illustrating the Investment Decision

4.5   The following figure depicts the financial situation of Ms. J. Fawn. In period 0 her labour income and current consumption are $50; later, in period 1, her labour income and consumption will be $44. She has an opportunity to make the investment represented by point *D.* By borrowing and lending, she will be able to reach any point along the line *FDE.*
   a.   What is the market rate of interest? (Hint: The new market interest rate line *EF* is parallel to *AH.*)
   b.   What is the NPV of point *D?*
   c.   If Ms. Fawn wishes to consume the same quantity in each period, how much should she consume in period 0?

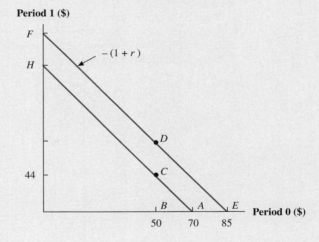

4.6   Enrique Rodrigues has $65,000 this year. He faces the investment opportunities represented by point *B* in the following figure. He wants to consume $22,000 this year and $69,000 next year. This pattern of consumption is represented by point *F.*
   a.   What is the market interest rate?
   b.   How much must Enrique invest in financial assets and productive assets today if he follows an optimum strategy?
   c.   What is the NPV of his investment in nonfinancial assets?

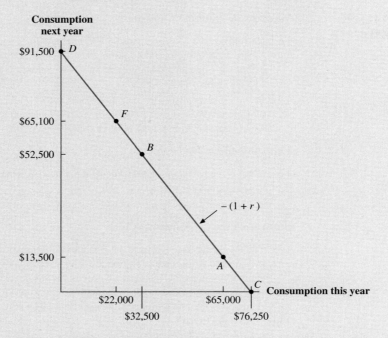

4.7   To answer this question, refer to the figure below. The Badvest Corporation is an all-
      equity firm with *BD* in cash on hand. It has an investment opportunity at point *C,* and it
      plans to invest *AD* in real assets today. Thus, the firm will need to raise *AB* by a new issue
      of equity.
      a. What is the present value of the investment?
      b. What is the rate of return on the old equity? Measure this rate of return from before the
           investment plans are announced to afterwards.
      c. What is the rate of return on the new equity?

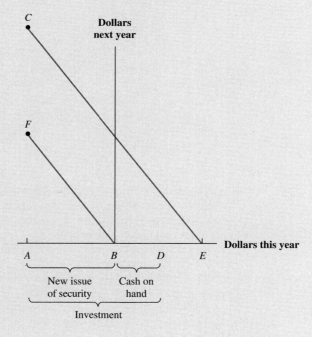

Chapter 5

The Time Value of Money

EXECUTIVE SUMMARY

We now examine one of the most important concepts in all of corporate finance: the relationship between $1 today and $1 in the future. Consider the following example: A firm is contemplating investing $1 million in a project that is expected to pay out $200,000 per year for nine years. Should the firm accept the project? One might say yes at first glance, since the total inflows of $1.8 million (= $200,000 × 9) are greater than the $1 million outflow. However, the $1 million is paid out *immediately*, whereas the $200,000 per year is received in the future. Also, the immediate payment is known with certainty, whereas the later inflows can only be estimated. Thus, we need to know the relationship between a dollar today and a (possibly uncertain) dollar in the future before deciding on the project.

This relationship is called the *time value of money concept.* It is important in such areas as capital budgeting, lease-versus-buy decisions, accounts receivable analysis, financing arrangements, mergers, and pension funding.

The basics are presented in this chapter. We begin by discussing two fundamental concepts: future value and present value. Next, we treat simplifying formulas such as perpetuities and annuities.

5.1 The One-Period Case

EXAMPLE 5.1

Antony Robart is trying to sell a piece of raw land in Saskatchewan. Yesterday, he was offered $10,000 for the property. He was ready to accept the offer when another individual offered him $11,424. However, the second offer was to be paid a year from now. Antony has satisfied himself that both buyers are honest, so he has no fear that the offer he selects will fall through. These two offers are pictured as cash flows in Figure 5.1. Which offer should Mr. Robart choose?

FIGURE 5.1

Cash Flow for Mr. Robart's Sale

	$10,000	$11,424
Alternative sale prices	↑	↑
Year:	0	1

Cynthia Titos, Antony's financial adviser, points out that if Antony takes the first offer, he could invest the $10,000 in the bank at 12 percent. At the end of one year, he would have:

$$\underset{\substack{\text{Return of} \\ \text{principal}}}{\$10,000} + \underset{\text{Interest}}{(0.12 \times \$10,000)} = \$10,000 \times 1.12 = \$11,200$$

Because this is less than the $11,424 Antony could receive from the second offer, Ms. Titos recommends that he take the latter. This analysis uses the concept of **future value** or **compound value,** which is the value of a sum after investing over one or more periods. Here the compound or future value of $10,000 is $11,200.

An alternative method employs the concept of **present value (PV).** One can determine present value by asking the following question: How much money must Antony put in the bank today so that he will have $11,424 next year? We can write this algebraically as:

$$\text{PV} \times 1.12 = \$11,424 \qquad\qquad (5.1)$$

We want to solve for present value (PV), the amount of money that yields $11,424 if invested at 12 percent today. Solving for PV, we have

$$\text{PV} = \frac{\$11,424}{1.12} = \$10,200$$

The formula for PV can be written as

Present Value of Investment:

$$\text{PV} = \frac{C_1}{1 + r}$$

where C_1 is cash flow at date 1 and r is the interest rate.

Present value analysis tells us that a payment of $11,424 to be received next year has a present value of $10,200 today. In other words, at a 12 percent interest rate, Mr. Robart should be indifferent to whether you give him $10,200 today or $11,424 next year. If you give him $10,200 today, he can put it in the bank and receive $11,424 next year.

Because the second offer has a present value of $10,200, whereas the first offer is for only $10,000, present value analysis also indicates that Mr. Robart should take the second offer. In other words, both future value analysis and present value analysis lead to the same decision. As it turns out, present value analysis and future value analysis must always lead to the same decision.

As simple as this example is, it contains the basic principles that we will be working with over the next few chapters. We now use Example 5.2 to develop the concept of net present value.

EXAMPLE 5.2

Geneviève Gagnon is thinking about investing in a piece of land that costs $85,000. She is certain that next year the land will be worth $91,000, a sure $6,000 gain. Given that the interest rate in the bank is 10 percent, should she undertake the investment in land? Ms. Gagnon's choice is described in Figure 5.2 with the cash flow time chart.

FIGURE 5.2

Cash Flows for Land Investment

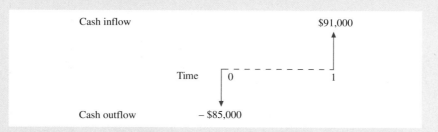

A moment's thought should be all it takes to convince her that this is not an attractive business deal. By investing $85,000 in the land, she will have $91,000 available next year. Suppose, instead, that she puts the same $85,000 into the bank. At the interest rate of 10 percent, this $85,000 would grow to

$$(1 + 0.10) \times \$85,000 = \$93,500$$

next year.

It would be foolish to buy the land when investing the same $85,000 in the financial market would produce an extra $2,500 (that is, $93,500 from the bank minus $91,000 from the land investment). This is a future-value calculation. Alternatively, she could calculate the present value of the sale price next year as

$$\text{Present value} = \frac{\$91,000}{1.10} = \$82,727.27$$

Since the present value of next year's sale price is less than this year's purchase price of $85,000, present value analysis also indicates that she should not purchase the property.

Frequently, businesspeople want to determine the exact *cost* or *benefit* of a decision. The decision to buy this year and sell next year can be evaluated as

Net Present Value of Investment:

$$-\$2,273 = -\$85,000 + \frac{\$91,000}{1.10} \qquad (5.2)$$

Cost of   Present value of
land today   next year's sales price

Equation (5.2) says that the value of the investment is −$2,273, after stating all the benefits and all the costs as of date 0. We say that −$2,273 is the **net present value (NPV)** of the investment. That is, NPV is the present value of future cash flows minus the present value of the cost of the investment. Because the net present value is negative, Geneviève Gagnon should not purchase the land.

Both the Robart and the Gagnon examples deal with perfect certainty. That is, Antony Robart knows with perfect certainty that he could sell his land for $11,424 next year. Similarly, Geneviève Gagnon knows with perfect certainty that she could receive $91,000 for selling her land. Unfortunately, businesspeople frequently do not know future cash flows. This uncertainty is treated in Example 5.3.

EXAMPLE 5.3

Atkinson Art Inc. is a firm that speculates in modern paintings. The manager is thinking of buying an original Picasso for $400,000 with the intention of selling it at the end of one year. The manager *expects* that the painting will be worth $480,000 in one year. The relevant cash flows are depicted in Figure 5.3.

FIGURE 5.3

Cash Flows for Investment in Painting

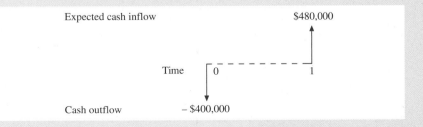

> Of course, this is only an expectation—the painting could be worth more or less than $480,000. Suppose the interest rate granted by banks is 10 percent. Should the firm purchase the piece of art?
>
> Our first thought might be to discount at the interest rate, yielding
>
> $$\frac{\$480,000}{1.10} = \$436,364$$
>
> Because $436,364 is greater than $400,000, it looks at first glance as if the painting should be purchased. However, 10 percent is the return one can earn on a riskless investment. Because the painting is quite risky, a higher *discount rate* is called for. The manager chooses a rate of 25 percent to reflect this risk. In other words, he argues that a 25 percent expected return is fair compensation for an investment as risky as this painting.
>
> The present value of the painting becomes
>
> $$\frac{\$480,000}{1.25} = \$384,000$$
>
> Thus, the manager believes that the painting is currently overpriced at $400,000 and does not make the purchase.

The above analysis is typical of decision making in today's corporations, though real-world examples are, of course, much more complex. Unfortunately, any example with risk poses a problem not faced by a riskless example. In an example with riskless cash flows, the appropriate interest rate can be determined by simply checking with a few banks.[1] The selection of the discount rate for a risky investment is quite a difficult task. We simply do not know at this point whether the discount rate on the painting should be 11 percent, 25 percent, 52 percent, or some other percentage.

Because the choice of a discount rate is so difficult, we merely wanted to broach the subject here. The rest of the chapter will revert back to examples under perfect certainty. We must wait until the specific material on risk and return is covered in later chapters before a risk-adjusted analysis can be presented.

? Concept Questions
- **Define future value and present value.**
- **How does one use net present value when making an investment decision?**

5.2 The Multiperiod Case

The previous section presented the calculation of future value and present value for one period only. We will now perform the calculations for the multiperiod case.

Future Value and Compounding

Suppose an individual were to make a loan of $1. At the end of the first year, the borrower would owe the lender the principal amount of $1 plus the interest on the loan at the interest rate of r. For the specific case where the interest rate is, say, 9 percent, the borrower owes the lender

$$\$1 \times (1 + r) = \$1 \times 1.09 = \$1.09$$

At the end of the year, though, the lender has two choices. He or she can either take the $1.09—or, more generally, $(1 + r)$—out of the capital market, or leave it in and lend it

---

[1] In Chapter 9, we discuss estimation of the riskless rate in more detail.

again for a second year as shown in Figure 5.4. The process of leaving the money in the capital market and lending it for another year is called **compounding.**

Suppose that the lender decides to compound the loan for another year by taking the proceeds from the first one-year loan, $1.09, and lending this amount for the next year. At the end of next year, then, the borrower will owe

$$\$1 \times (1 + r) \times (1 + r) = \$1 \times (1 + r)^2 = 1 + 2r + r^2$$
$$\$1 \times (1.09) \times (1.09) = \$1 + \$0.18 + \$0.0081 = \$1.1881$$

This is the total the lender will receive two years from now by compounding the loan.

In other words, by providing a ready opportunity for lending, the capital market enables the investor to transform $1 today into $1.1881 at the end of two years. At the end of three years, the cash will be $1 \times (1.09)^3 = \$1.2950$. The shaded area indicates the difference between compound and simple interest. The difference is substantial over a period of many years or decades, as shown in Figure 5.4.

The most important point to notice is that the total amount that the lender receives is not just the $1 lent out plus two years' worth of interest on $1:

$$2 \times r = 2 \times \$0.09 = \$0.18$$

The lender also gets back an amount r^2, which is the interest in the second year on the interest that was earned in the first year. The term, $2 \times r$, represents **simple interest** over the two years, and the term, r^2, is referred to as the *interest on interest*. In our example this latter amount is exactly

$$r^2 = (\$0.09)^2 = \$0.0081$$

When cash is invested at **compound interest,** each interest payment is reinvested. With simple interest, the interest is not reinvested. Benjamin Franklin's statement, "Money makes money and the money that money makes makes more money," is a colourful way of explaining compound interest. The difference between compound interest and simple interest is also illustrated in Figure 5.4. In this example the difference does not amount to much because the loan is for $1. If the loan were for $1 million, the lender would receive $1,188,100 in two years' time. Of this amount, $8,100 is interest on interest. The lesson is that those small numbers beyond the decimal point can add up to significant dollar

FIGURE 5.4

Simple and Compound Interest

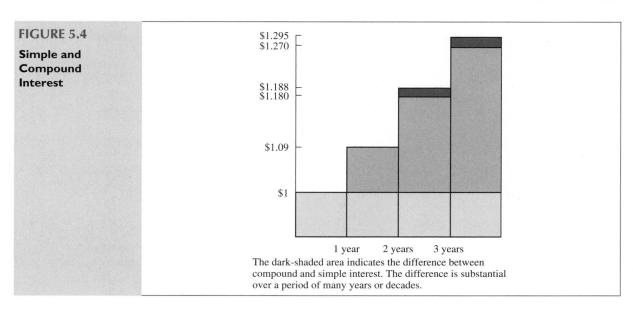

The dark-shaded area indicates the difference between compound and simple interest. The difference is substantial over a period of many years or decades.

amounts when the transactions are for large amounts. In addition, the longer-lasting the loan, the more important interest on interest becomes.

The general formula for an investment over many periods can be written as

Future Value of an Investment:

$$FV = C_0 \times (1 + r)^T$$

where C_0 is the cash to be invested at date 0, r is the interest rate, and T is the number of periods over which the cash is invested.

EXAMPLE 5.4

Irene Lau has put $500 in a savings account at the Home Bank of Canada. The account earns 7 percent, compounded annually. How much will Ms. Lau have at the end of three years?

$$\$500 \times 1.07 \times 1.07 \times 1.07 = \$500 \times (1.07)^3 = \$612.52$$

Figure 5.5 illustrates the growth of Ms. Lau's account.

FIGURE 5.5

Ms. Lau's Savings Account

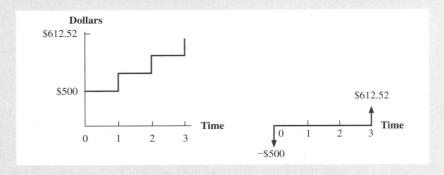

EXAMPLE 5.5

Heather Courtney invested $1,000 in the stock of the BMH Company. The company pays a current dividend of $2 per share, which is expected to grow by 20 percent per year for the next two years. What will the dividend of the BMH Company be after two years?

$$\$2 \times (1.20)^2 = \$2.88$$

Figure 5.6 illustrates the increasing value of BMH's dividends.

FIGURE 5.6

The Growth of Dividends

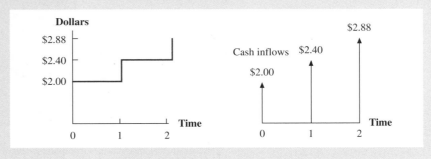

Examples 5.4 and 5.5 can be calculated in any one of three ways: by hand, by calculator, or with the help of a table.[2] The appropriate table is Table A.3, which appears in Appendix A. This table presents *future values of $1 at the end of* T *periods*. The table is used by locating the appropriate interest rate on the horizontal and the appropriate number of periods on the vertical.

For example, Irene Lau would look at the following portion of Table A.3:

| | Interest Rate | | |
Period	6%	7%	8%
1	1.0600	1.0700	1.0800
2	1.1236	1.1449	1.1664
3	1.1910	1.2250	1.2597
4	1.2625	1.3108	1.3605

She could calculate the future value of her $500 as

$$\underset{\substack{\text{Initial} \\ \text{investment}}}{\$500} \quad \times \quad \underset{\substack{\text{Future value} \\ \text{of }\$1}}{1.2250} \quad = \quad \$612.50$$

In Example 5.4 concerning Irene Lau, we gave you both the initial investment and the interest rate and then asked you to calculate the future value. Alternatively, the interest rate could have been unknown, as shown in Example 5.6.

EXAMPLE 5.6

Raghu Venugopal, who recently won $10,000 in a lottery, wants to buy a car in five years. Raghu estimates that the car will cost $16,105 at that time. His cash flows are displayed in Figure 5.7.

What interest rate must he earn to be able to afford the car? The ratio of purchase price to initial cash is

$$\frac{\$16,105}{\$10,000} = 1.6105$$

FIGURE 5.7

Cash Flows for Future Purchase of a Car

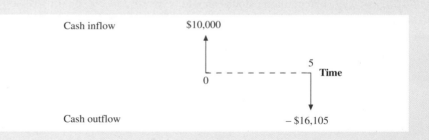

---

[2] To solve this problem on a financial calculator:
1. Make sure to clear the calculator.
2. Enter the number of periods as 2 and press *n*.
3. Enter the interest rate of 20 percent as 20 (not 0.20) and press *I* or *r* depending on device.
4. Enter the present value of −2.00 and press *PV*.
5. Calculate the future value by pressing the compute button and *FV*.

Thus, he must earn an interest rate that allows $1 to become $1.6105 in five years. Table A.3 tells us that an interest rate of 10 percent will allow him to purchase the car. One can express the problem algebraically as

$$\$10,000 \times (1 + r)^5 = \$16,105$$

where r is the interest rate needed to purchase the car. Because $16,105/$10,000 = 1.6105, we have

$$(1 + r)^5 = 1.6105$$

Either the table or any sophisticated hand calculator solves[3] for r = 10%.

The Power of Compounding: A Digression

Most people who have had any experience with compounding are impressed with its power over long periods of time. Take the stock market, for example. In Chapter 10, we use historical data to calculate that the average Canadian common stock averaged approximately an 11 percent rate of return per year from 1957 through 2006. A return of this magnitude may not appear to be anything special over, say, a one-year period. However, $1 placed in these stocks at the beginning of 1957 would have been worth $107.66 at the end of 2006. Figure 10.4 shows the return of $1 from 1957 to 2006.

The example illustrates the great difference between compound and simple interest. At 11 percent, simple interest on $1 is 11 cents a year. Simple interest over 50 years is $5.50 (50 × $0.11). That is, an individual withdrawing 11 cents every year would have withdrawn $5.50 over 50 years. This is quite a bit below the $107.66 that was obtained by reinvestment of all principal and interest.

The results are more impressive over even longer periods of time. A person with no experience in compounding might think that the value of $1 at the end of 100 years would be twice the value of $1 at the end of 50 years, if the yearly rate of return stayed the same. Actually the value of $1 at the end of 100 years would be the *square* of the value of $1 at the end of 50 years. That is, if the annual rate of return remained the same, a $1 investment in common stocks should be worth $11,590.68 (or $107.66 × 107.66).

A few years ago an archaeologist unearthed a relic stating that Julius Caesar lent the Roman equivalent of one penny to someone. Since there was no record of the penny ever being repaid, the archaeologist wondered what the interest and principal would be if a descendant of Caesar tried to collect from a descendant of the borrower in the twentieth century. The archaeologist felt that a rate of 6 percent might be appropriate. To his surprise, the principal and interest due after more than 2000 years was far greater than the entire wealth on Earth.

---

[3]Conceptually, we are taking the fifth roots of both sides of the equation. That is,

$$r = \sqrt[5]{1.6105} - 1$$

To solve this problem on a financial calculator:

1. Clear the calculator.
2. Enter the number of periods as 5 and press *n*.
3. Enter the present value of −10,000 and press *PV*.
4. Enter the future value of $16,105 and press *FV*.
5. Ask the calculator for the interest rate by pressing the compute button and *I*.

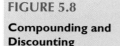

FIGURE 5.8

Compounding and Discounting

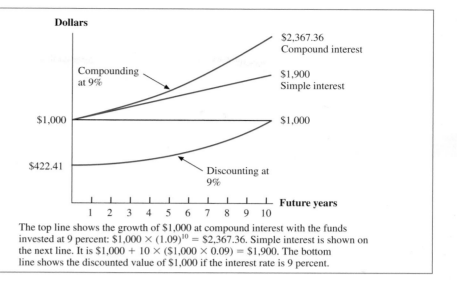

The top line shows the growth of $1,000 at compound interest with the funds invested at 9 percent: $1,000 × (1.09)^{10} = $2,367.36. Simple interest is shown on the next line. It is $1,000 + 10 × ($1,000 × 0.09) = $1,900. The bottom line shows the discounted value of $1,000 if the interest rate is 9 percent.

The power of compounding can explain one reason why the parents of well-to-do families frequently bequeath wealth to their grandchildren rather than to their children. That is, they skip a generation. The parents would rather make the grandchildren very rich than make the children moderately rich. We have found that in these families the grandchildren have a more positive view of the power of compounding than do the children.

Present Value and Discounting

We now know that an annual interest rate of 9 percent enables the investor to transform $1 today into $1.1881 two years from now. In addition, we would like to know:

> How much would an investor need to lend today to make it possible to receive $1 two years from today?

Algebraically, we can write this as

$$PV \times (1.09)^2 = \$1 \qquad (5.3)$$

In (5.3), PV stands for present value, the amount of money we must lend today in order to receive $1 in two years' time. Solving for PV in (5.3), we have

$$PV = \frac{\$1}{1.1881} = \$0.84$$

This process of calculating the present value of a future cash flow is called **discounting**.[4] It is the opposite of compounding. The difference between compounding and discounting is illustrated in Figure 5.8.

To be certain that $0.84 is in fact the present value of $1 to be received in two years, we must check whether or not, if we lent out $0.84 and rolled the loan over for two years, we would get exactly $1 back. If this were the case, the capital markets would be saying that $1 received in two years' time is equivalent to having $0.84 today. Checking with the exact numbers, we get

$$\$0.84168 \times 1.09 \times 1.09 = \$1$$

---

[4]The discount rate, *r*, is defined as the rate used to calculate the present value of future cash flows.

In other words, when we have capital markets with a sure interest rate of 9 percent, we are indifferent between receiving $0.84 today or $1 in two years. We have no reason to treat these two choices differently from each other, because if we had $0.84 today and lent it out for two years, it would return $1 to us at the end of that time. The value 0.84 $[1/(1.09)^2]$ is called the **present value factor.** It is the factor used to calculate the present value of a future cash flow.

EXAMPLE 5.7

Pat Song will receive $10,000 three years from now. Pat can earn 8 percent on his investments. What is the present value of his future cash flow?

$$PV = \$10,000 \times (1/1.08)^3$$
$$= \$10,000 \times 0.7938$$
$$= \$7,938$$

Figure 5.9 illustrates the application of the present value factor to Pat's investment.

FIGURE 5.9

Discounting Pat Song's Opportunity

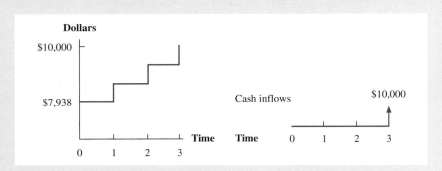

When his investments grow at an 8 percent rate of interest, Pat Song is equally inclined toward receiving $7,938 now or receiving $10,000 in three years' time. After all, he could convert the $7,938 he receives today into $10,000 in three years by lending it at an interest rate of 8 percent.

Pat Song could have reached his present value calculation in one of three ways. The computation could have been done by hand, by calculator, or with the help of Table A.1 in Appendix A. This table presents *present value of $1 to be received after* T *periods.* The table is used by locating the appropriate interest rate on the horizontal and the appropriate number of periods on the vertical. For example, Pat Song would look at the following portion of Table A.1:

	Interest Rate		
Period	7%	8%	9%
1	0.9346	0.9259	0.9174
2	0.8734	0.8573	0.8417
3	0.8163	0.7938	0.7722
4	0.7629	0.7350	0.7084

The appropriate present value factor is 0.7938.

In Example 5.7, we gave both the interest rate and the future cash flow. Alternatively, the interest rate could have been unknown.

EXAMPLE 5.8

A customer of the Cristall Corp. wants to buy a tugboat today. Rather than paying immediately, he will pay $50,000 in three years. It will cost the Cristall Corp. $38,610 to build the tugboat immediately. The relevant cash flows to Cristall Corp. are displayed in Figure 5.10. By charging what interest rate would the Cristall Corp. neither gain nor lose on the sale?

FIGURE 5.10

Cash Flows for Tugboat

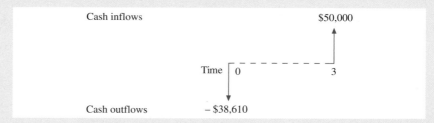

The ratio of construction cost to sale price is

$$\frac{\$36,810}{\$50,000} = 0.7722$$

We must determine the interest rate that allows $1 to be received in three years to have a present value of $0.7722. Table A.1 tells us that 9 percent is that interest rate.[5]

Frequently, an investor or a business will receive more than one cash flow. The present value of the set of cash flows is simply the sum of the present values of the individual cash flows. This is illustrated in Example 5.9.

EXAMPLE 5.9

While on vacation in the U.S., Terence Chiu won a lottery and will receive the following set of cash flows over the next two years:

Year	Cash Flow
1	$2,000
2	$5,000

Terence can currently earn 6 percent in his savings account. The present value of the cash flows is

Year	Cash flow	× Present value factor	= Present value
1	$2,000	× 1/1.06 = 0.943	= $1,887
2	$5,000	× 1/(1.06)² = 0.890	= $4,450
		Total	$6,337

In other words, Terence is equally inclined toward receiving $6,337 today and receiving $2,000 and $5,000 over the next two years.

---

[5]Algebraically, we are solving for r in the equation

$$\frac{\$50,000}{(1 + r)^3} = \$38,610$$

or, equivalently,

$$\frac{\$1}{(1 + r)^3} = \$0.7722$$

EXAMPLE 5.10

Finance.com has an opportunity to invest in a new high-speed computer that costs $50,000. The computer will generate cash flows (from cost savings) of $25,000 one year from now, $20,000 two years from now, and $15,000 three years from now. The computer will be worthless after three years, and no additional cash flows will occur. Finance.com has determined that the appropriate discount rate is 7 percent for this investment. Should Finance.com make this investment in a new high-speed computer? What is the present value of the investment?

The cash flows and present value factors of the proposed computer are as follows.

	Cash Flows	Present Value Factor	
Year 0	−$50,000	1	$= 1$
1	$25,000	$\dfrac{1}{1.07}$	$= 0.9346$
2	$20,000	$\left(\dfrac{1}{1.07}\right)^2$	$= 0.8734$
3	$15,000	$\left(\dfrac{1}{1.07}\right)^3$	$= 0.8163$

The present values of the cash flows are:

$$\text{Cash flows} \times \text{Present value factor} = \text{Present value}$$

$$
\begin{array}{llll}
\text{Year 0} & -\$50,\!000 \times 1 & = & -\$50,\!000 \\
1 & \$25,\!000 \times 0.9346 & = & \$23,\!365 \\
2 & \$20,\!000 \times 0.8734 & = & \$17,\!468 \\
3 & \$15,\!000 \times 0.8163 & = & \underline{\$12,\!244.5} \\
& & \text{Total:} & \$\ 3,\!077.5
\end{array}
$$

Finance.com should invest in a new high-speed computer because the present value of its future cash flows is greater than its cost. The NPV is $3,077.5.

The Algebraic Formula

To derive an algebraic formula for net present value of a cash flow, recall that the PV of receiving a cash flow one year from now is

$$PV = C_1/(1 + r)$$

and the PV of receiving a cash flow two years from now is

$$PV = C_2/(1 + r)^2$$

We can write the NPV of a T-period project as

$$NPV = -C_0 + \frac{C_1}{1 + r} + \frac{C_2}{(1 + r)^2} + \ldots + \frac{C_T}{(1 + r)^T} = -C_0 + \sum_{t=1}^{T} \frac{C_t}{(1 + r)^t}$$

The initial flow, $-C_0$, is assumed to be negative because it represents an investment. The term Σ is shorthand for the sum of the series.[6]

? Concept Questions
- **What is the difference between simple interest and compound interest?**
- **What is the formula for the net present value of a project?**

---

[6]In Chapter 6 we apply the NPV formula to investments that have a cash inflow in year 0 and outflows in later years. For these investments, the term $-C_0$ is replaced by $-PV$ (outflows).

5.3 Compounding Periods

So far we have assumed that compounding and discounting occur yearly. Sometimes compounding may occur more frequently than just once a year. For example, imagine that a bank pays a 10 percent interest rate "compounded semiannually." This means that a $1,000 deposit in the bank would be worth $1,000 × 1.05 = $1,050 after six months, and $1,050 × 1.05 = $1,102.50 at the end of the year. The end-of-the-year wealth can be written as[7]

$$\$1,000\,(1 + 0.10/2)^2 = \$1,000 \times (1.05)^2 = \$1,102.50$$

Of course, a $1,000 deposit would be worth $1,100 (or $1,000 × 1.10) with yearly compounding. Note that the future value at the end of one year is greater with semiannual compounding than with yearly compounding. With yearly compounding, the original $1,000 remains the investment base for the full year. The original $1,000 is the investment base only for the first six months with semiannual compounding. The base over the second six months is $1,050. Hence, one gets *interest on interest* with semiannual compounding.

Because $1,000 × 1.1025 = $1,102.50, 10 percent compounded semiannually is the same as 10.25 percent compounded annually. In other words, a rational investor will be indifferent between a rate of 10 percent compounded semiannually, or a rate of 10.25 percent compounded annually.

Quarterly compounding at 10 percent yields wealth at the end of one year of

$$\$1,000\,(1 + 0.10/4)^4 = \$1,103.81$$

More generally, compounding an investment *m* times a year provides end-of-year wealth of

$$C_0(1 + r/m)^m \tag{5.4}$$

where C_0 is one's initial investment and *r* is the **stated annual interest rate.** The stated annual interest rate is the annual interest rate without consideration of compounding. Banks and other financial institutions may use other names for the stated annual interest rate. **Annual percentage rate** is perhaps the most common synonym.

EXAMPLE 5.11

What is the end-of-year wealth if Julie Andrew receives a 24 percent rate of interest compounded monthly on a $1 investment? Using (5.4), her wealth is

$$\$1(1 + 0.24/12)^{12} = \$1 \times (1.02)^{12}$$
$$= \$1.2682$$

The annual rate of return is 26.82 percent. This annual rate of return is called the **effective annual interest rate.** Due to compounding, the effective annual interest rate is greater than the stated annual interest rate of 24 percent. Algebraically, we can rewrite the effective annual interest rate as

Effective Annual Interest Rate:
$$(1 + r/m)^m - 1 \tag{5.5}$$

Students are often bothered by the subtraction of 1 in (5.5). Note that end-of-year wealth is composed of both the interest earned over the year and the original principal. We remove the original principal by subtracting 1 in (5.5).

---

[7]In addition to using a calculator, one can still use Table A.3 when the compounding period is less than a year. Here, one sets the interest rate at 5 percent and the number of periods at two.

EXAMPLE 5.12

If the stated annual rate of interest, 8 percent, is compounded quarterly, what is the effective annual rate of interest? Using (5.5), we have

$$(1 + r/m)^m - 1 = (1 + 0.08/4)^4 - 1 = 0.0824 = 8.24\%$$

Referring back to our original example where $C_0 = \$1,000$ and $r = 10\%$, we can generate the following table:

C_0	Compounding Frequency (m)	C_1	Effective Annual Interest Rate = $(1 + r/m)^m - 1$
$1,000	Yearly ($m = 1$)	$1,100.00	0.10
1,000	Semiannually ($m = 2$)	1,102.50	0.1025
1,000	Quarterly ($m = 4$)	1,103.81	0.10381
1,000	Daily ($m = 365$)	1,105.16	0.10516

As Example 5.12 shows, the formula converts any stated annual rate into an effective annual rate.

Compounding Over Many Years

Equation (5.4) applies for an investment over one year. For an investment over one or more (T) years, the formula becomes

Future Value with Compounding:
$$\text{FV} = C_0 (1 + r/m)^{mT} \tag{5.6}$$

EXAMPLE 5.13

Margaret Cortes is investing $5,000 at 4 percent per year, compounded quarterly for five years. What is her wealth at the end of five years? Using (5.6), her wealth is

$$\$5,000 \times (1 + 0.04/4)^{4 \times 5} = \$5,000 \times (1.01)^{20}$$
$$= \$5,000 \times 1.2202 = \$6,101.00$$

Cost of Borrowing Disclosure regulations (part of the *Bank Act*) in Canada require that lenders disclose an annual percentage rate on virtually all consumer loans. This rate must be displayed on a loan document in a prominent and unambiguous way. Unfortunately, this does not tell the borrower the effective annual rate on the loan.

EXAMPLE 5.14

Suppose that a credit card agreement quotes an annual percentage rate of 18 percent. Monthly payments are required. Based on our discussion, an annual percentage rate of 18 percent with monthly payments is really $0.18/12 = 0.015$ or 1.5 percent per month. The effective annual rate is thus

$$\text{Effective annual rate} = [1 + 0.18/12]^{12} - 1$$
$$= 1.015^{12} - 1$$
$$= 1.1956 - 1$$
$$= 19.56\%$$

The difference between an annual percentage rate and an effective annual rate probably will not be great, but it is somewhat ironic that cost-of-borrowing disclosure regulations sometimes require lenders to be a little misleading about the actual rate on a loan.

The distinction between the annual percentage rate or APR, and the effective annual rate (EAR) is frequently troubling to students. We can reduce the confusion by noting that the APR becomes meaningful only if the compounding interval is given. For example, for an APR of 10 percent, the future value at the end of one year with semiannual compounding is $[1 + (.10/2)]^2 = 1.1025$. The future value with quarterly compounding is $[1 + (.10/4)]^4 = 1.1038$. If the APR is 10 percent but no compounding interval is given, we cannot calculate future value. In other words, we do not know whether to compound semiannually, quarterly, or over some other interval.

By contrast, the EAR is meaningful *without* a compounding interval. For example, an EAR of 10.25 percent means that a $1 investment will be worth $1.1025 in one year. We can think of this as an APR of 10 percent with semiannual compounding or an APR of 10.25 percent with annual compounding, or some other possibility.

EXAMPLE 5.15

The Alberta Treasury Branch offers one-year Guaranteed Investment Certificates (GICs) at 4 percent per year compounded semiannually. TD Canada Trust offers one-year GICs at 4.25 percent compounded annually. Which would you prefer?

The effective annual rate at TD Canada Trust is 4.25 percent since the compounding is annual. To find the effective annual rate offered by the Alberta Treasury Branch, use Equation 5.5:

$$\text{Effective annual interest rate} = (1 + r/m)^m - 1$$
$$= (1 + 0.04/2)^2 - 1$$
$$= 4.04\%$$

You would prefer the TD Canada Trust GIC since it offers a higher effective annual rate.

? Concept Questions

- **What is a stated annual interest rate?**
- **What is an effective annual interest rate?**
- **What is the relationship between the stated annual interest rate and the effective annual interest rate?**

Continuous Compounding (Advanced)

The previous discussion shows that one can compound much more frequently than once a year. One could compound semiannually, quarterly, monthly, daily, hourly, each minute, or even more often. The limiting case would be to compound every infinitesimal instant, which is commonly called **continuous compounding.**

Though the idea of compounding this rapidly may boggle the mind, a simple formula is involved.[8] With continuous compounding, the value at the end of T years is expressed as

$$C_0 \times e^{rT} \tag{5.7}$$

where C_0 is the initial investment, r is the stated annual interest rate, and T is the number of years over which the investment runs. The number e is a constant and is approximately equal to 2.718. It is not an unknown like C_0, r, and T.

---
[8]Readers familiar with introductory calculus will recognize the expression:
$$\lim_{m \to \infty} (1 + r/m)^m = e^r$$

EXAMPLE 5.16

John MacDonald invested $1,000 at a continuously compounded rate of 10 percent for one year. What is the value of his wealth at the end of one year?
From Equation (5.7) we have

$$\$1,000 \times e^{0.10} = \$1,000 \times 1.1052 = \$1,105.20$$

This number can easily be read from our Table A.5 in Appendix A. One merely sets r, the value on the horizontal dimension, to 10 percent and sets T, the value on the vertical dimension, to 1. For this problem, the relevant portion of the table is

	Continuously Compounded Rate (r)		
Period	9%	10%	11%
1	1.0942	1.1052	1.1163
2	1.1972	1.2214	1.2461
3	1.3100	1.3499	1.3910

Note that a continuously compounded rate of 10 percent is equivalent to an annually compounded rate of 10.52 percent. In other words, John MacDonald would not care whether his bank quoted a continuously compounded rate of 10 percent or a 10.52 percent rate, compounded annually.

EXAMPLE 5.17

John MacDonald's brother, Robert, invested $1,000 at a continuously compounded rate of 10 percent for two years.
The appropriate formula here is

$$\$1,000 \times e^{0.10 \times 2} = \$1,000 \times e^{0.20} = \$1,221.40$$

Using the portion of the table of continuously compounded rates reproduced above, we find the value to be 1.2214.

Figure 5.11 illustrates the relationship among annual, semiannual, and continuous compounding. Semiannual compounding gives rise to both a smoother curve and a higher ending value than does annual compounding. Continuous compounding has both the smoothest curve and the highest ending value of all.

EXAMPLE 5.18

An investment is going to pay you $1,000 at the end of four years. If the annual continuously compounded rate of interest is 8 percent, what is the present value of this payment?

$$\$1,000 \times \frac{1}{e^{0.08 \times 4}} = \$1,000 \times \frac{1}{1.3771} = \$726.16$$

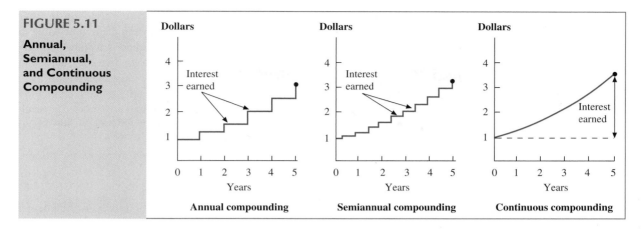

FIGURE 5.11

Annual, Semiannual, and Continuous Compounding

Annual compounding   Semiannual compounding   Continuous compounding

5.4 Simplifications

The first part of this chapter has examined the concepts of future value and present value. Although these concepts allow one to answer a host of problems concerning the time value of money, the human effort involved can frequently be excessive. For example, consider a bank calculating the present value on a 20-year mortgage with monthly payments. Because this mortgage has 240 (or 20 × 12) payments, a lot of time is needed to perform a conceptually simple task.

Because many basic finance problems are potentially so time-consuming, we search out simplifications in this section. We provide simplifying formulas for four classes of cash flow streams:

- Perpetuity
- Growing perpetuity
- Annuity
- Growing annuity

Perpetuity

A **perpetuity** is a constant stream of cash flows without end. If you are thinking that perpetuities have no relevance to reality, it will surprise you that there is a well-known case of an unending cash flow stream: the British bonds called *consols*. An investor purchasing a consol is entitled to receive yearly interest from the British government forever.

How can the price of a consol be determined? Consider a consol that pays a coupon of *C* dollars each year and will do so forever. Simply applying the PV formula gives us

$$PV = \frac{C}{1 + r} + \frac{C}{(1 + r)^2} + \frac{C}{(1 + r)^3} + \ldots$$

where the dots at the end of the formula stand for the infinite string of terms that continues the formula. Series like the preceding one are called *geometric series*. It is well known that even though they have an infinite number of terms, the whole series has a finite sum because each term is only a fraction of the preceding term. Before turning to a calculus book, though, it is worth going back to our original principles to see if a bit of financial intuition can help us find the PV.

The present value of the consol is the present value of all of its future coupons. In other words, it is an amount of money that, if an investor had it today, would make it possible to achieve the same pattern of expenditures that the consol and its coupons would. Suppose that an investor wanted to spend exactly C dollars each year. If our investor owned the consol, this spending pattern would be possible. How much money must the investor have today to spend the same amount? Clearly the amount needed is exactly enough so that the interest on the money would be C dollars per year. If the investor had any more, spending could be more than C dollars each year. If the amount were any less, the investor would eventually run out of money spending C dollars per year.

The amount that will give the investor C dollars each year, and therefore the present value of the consol, is simply

$$PV = \frac{C}{r} \qquad (5.8)$$

To confirm that this is the right answer, notice that if we lend the amount C/r, the interest it earns each year will be

$$Interest = \frac{C}{r} \times r = C$$

which is exactly the consol payment.[9] To sum up, we have shown that for a consol

Formula for Present Value of Perpetuity:
$$PV = \frac{C}{1+r} + \frac{C}{(1+r)^2} + \frac{C}{(1+r)^3} + \ldots$$
$$= C/r$$

It is comforting to know how easily we can use a bit of financial intuition to solve this mathematical problem.

EXAMPLE 5.19

Consider a perpetuity paying $100 a year. If the interest rate is 8 percent, what is the value of the consol? Using (5.8), we have

$$PV = \frac{\$100}{0.08} = \$1,250$$

Now suppose that the interest rate falls to 6 percent. Using (5.8), the value of the perpetuity is

$$PV = \frac{\$100}{0.06} = \$1,666.67$$

Note that the value of the perpetuity rises with a drop in the interest rate. Conversely, the value of the perpetuity falls with a rise in the interest rate.

Growing Perpetuity

Imagine an apartment building where cash flows to the landlord after expenses will be $100,000 next year. These cash flows are expected to rise at 5 percent per year. If one

---

[9]We can prove this by looking at the PV equation:
$$PV = C/(1+r) + C/(1+r)^2 + \ldots$$
Let $C/(1+r) = a$ and $1/(1+r) = x$. We now have
$$PV = a(1 + x + x^2 + \ldots) \qquad (1)$$
Next we can multiply by x:
$$xPV = ax + ax^2 + \ldots \qquad (2)$$
Subtracting (2) from (1) gives
$$PV(1 - x) = a$$
Now we substitute for a and x and rearrange:
$$PV = C/r$$

assumes that this rise will continue indefinitely, the cash flow stream is termed a **growing perpetuity.** Positing an 11 percent discount rate, the present value of the cash flows can be represented as

$$PV = \frac{\$100,000}{1.11} + \frac{\$100,000(1.05)}{(1.11)^2} + \frac{\$100,000(1.05)^2}{(1.11)^3} + \cdots + \frac{\$100,000(1.05)^{N-1}}{(1.11)^N} + \cdots$$

Algebraically, we can write the formula as

$$PV = \frac{C}{1+r} + \frac{C \times (1+g)}{(1+r)^2} + \frac{C \times (1+g)^2}{(1+r)^3} + \cdots + \frac{C \times (1+g)^{N-1}}{(1+r)^N} + \cdots \quad (5.9)$$

where C is the cash flow to be received one period hence, g is the rate of growth per period, expressed as a percentage, and r is the interest rate.

Fortunately, (5.9) reduces to the following simplification:[10]

Formula for Present Value of Growing Perpetuity:

$$PV = \frac{C}{r-g} \quad (5.10)$$

From (5.10), the present value of the cash flows from the apartment building is

$$\frac{\$100,000}{0.11 - 0.05} = \$1,666,667$$

There are three important points concerning the growing perpetuity formula:

1. *The Numerator.* The numerator in (5.10) is the cash flow one period hence, not at date 0. Consider Example 5.20.

EXAMPLE 5.20

Hoffstein Corporation paid a dividend of $3.00 per share last year. Investors anticipate that the annual dividend will rise by 6 percent a year forever. The applicable interest rate is 11 percent. What is the price of the stock today?

The numerator in Equation (5.10) is the cash flow to be received next period. Since the growth rate is 6 percent, the dividend next year is $3.18 (or $3.00 × 1.06). The price of the stock today is

$$\$63.60 = \frac{\$3.18}{0.11 - 0.06}$$

Present value
of all dividends
beginning a year
from now

The price of $63.60 represents the present value of all dividends beginning a year from now. Equation (5.10) only makes it possible to calculate the present value of all dividends beginning a year from now. Be sure you understand this example; test questions on this subject always seem to trip up a few of our students.

----

[10]PV is the sum of an infinite geometric series:

$$PV = a(1 + x + x^2 + \cdots)$$

where $a = C/(1+r)$ and $x = (1+g)/(1+r)$. Previously we showed that the sum of an infinite geometric series is $a/(1-x)$. Using this result and substituting for a and x, we find

$$PV = C/(r-g)$$

Note that this geometric series converges to a finite sum only when x is less than 1. This implies that the growth rate, g, must be less than the interest rate, r.

2. *The Interest Rate and the Growth Rate.* The interest rate r must be greater than the growth rate g for the growing perpetuity formula to work. Consider the case in which the growth rate approaches the interest rate in magnitude. Then the denominator in the growing perpetuity formula gets infinitesimally small and the present value grows infinitely large. The present value is in fact undefined when r is less than g.[11]

3. *The Timing Assumption.* Cash generally flows into and out of real-world firms both randomly and nearly continuously. However, Equation (5.10) assumes that cash flows are received and disbursed at regular and discrete points in time. In the example of the apartment, we assumed that the net cash flows of $100,000 only occurred once a year. In reality, rent cheques are commonly received every month. Payments for maintenance and other expenses may occur anytime within the year.

The growing perpetuity formula of (5.10) can be applied only by assuming a regular and discrete pattern of cash flow. Although this assumption is sensible because the formula saves so much time, the user should never forget that it is an assumption. This point will be mentioned again in the chapters ahead.

A few words should be said about terminology. Authors of financial textbooks generally use one of two conventions to refer to time. A minority of financial writers treat cash flows as being received on exact *dates*, for example date 0, date 1, and so forth. Under this convention, date 0 represents the present time. However, because a year is an interval, not a specific moment in time, the great majority of authors refer to cash flows that occur at the end of a year (or, alternatively, at the end of a period). Under this *end-of-the-year* convention, the end of year 0 is the present, the end of year 1 occurs one period hence, and so on.[12] (The beginning of year 0 has already passed and is not generally referred to.)

The interchangability of the two conventions can be seen from the following chart:

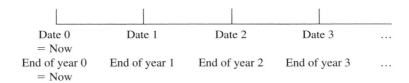

Date 0	Date 1	Date 2	Date 3	...
= Now				
End of year 0	End of year 1	End of year 2	End of year 3	...
= Now				

We strongly believe that the *dates convention* reduces ambiguity. However, we use both conventions because you are likely to see the *end-of-year convention* in later courses. In fact, both conventions may appear in the same example for the sake of practice.

Annuity

An **annuity** is a level stream of regular payments that lasts for a fixed number of periods. Not surprisingly, annuities are among the most common kinds of financial instruments. The pensions that people receive when they retire are often in the form of an annuity. Leases, mortgages, and pension plans are also annuities.

---

[11]In Chapter 6, we will discuss how to handle the situation when $r = g$.

[12]Sometimes financial writers merely speak of a cash flow in year x. Although this terminology is ambiguous, such writers generally mean the *end of year x.*

To figure out the present value of an annuity we need to evaluate the following equation:

$$\frac{C}{1 + r} + \frac{C}{(1 + r)^2} + \frac{C}{(1 + r)^3} + \ldots + \frac{C}{(1 + r)^T}$$

The present value of receiving only the coupons for T periods must be less than the present value of a consol, but how much less? To answer this we have to look at consols a bit more closely. Consider the following time chart:

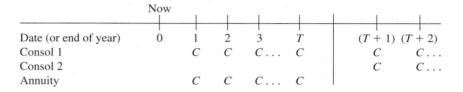

Consol 1 is a normal consol with its first payment at date 1. The first payment of consol 2 occurs at date $T + 1$.

The present value of having a cash flow of C at each of T dates is equal to the present value of consol 1 minus the present value of consol 2. The present value of consol 1 is given by

$$PV = \frac{C}{r} \tag{5.11}$$

Consol 2 is just a consol with its first payment at date $T + 1$. From the perpetuity formula, this consol will be worth C/r at date T.[13] However, we do not want the value at date T. We want the value now (in other words, the present value at date 0). We must discount C/r back by T periods. Therefore, the present value of consol 2 is

$$PV = C/r \times 1/(1 + r)^T \tag{5.12}$$

The present value of having cash flows for T years is the present value of a consol with its first payment at date 1 minus the present value of a consol with its first payment at date $T + 1$. Thus, the present value of an annuity is Equation (5.11) minus Equation (5.12). This can be written as

$$C/r - C/r[1/(1 + r)^T]$$

This simplifies to

Formula for Present Value of Annuity:[14,15]

$$PV = C\left[\frac{1}{r} - \frac{1}{r(1 + r)^T}\right] \tag{5.13}$$

---

[13]Students frequently think that C/r is the present value at date $T + 1$ because the consol's first payment is at date $T + 1$. However, the formula values the annuity as of one period prior to the first payment.

[14]This can also be written as $C[1 - 1/(1 + r)^T]/r$.

[15]We can also provide a formula for the future value of an annuity:

$$FV = C[(1 + r)^T/r - 1/r]$$

EXAMPLE 5.21

Andrea Mullings has just won a lottery in the U.S., paying $50,000 a year for 20 years. She is to receive her first payment a year from now. The lottery advertisements bill this as the Million Dollar Lottery because $1,000,000 = $50,000 × 20. If the interest rate is 8 percent, what is the true value of the prize?

Equation (5.13) yields

$$\text{Present value of Million Dollar Lottery} = \$50,000 \times [1/0.08 - 1/0.08(1.08)^{20}]$$

$$\underset{\text{Periodic payment}}{} \underset{\text{Annuity factor}}{}$$

$$= \$ \ 50,000 \ \times \ 9.8181$$

$$= \$490,905$$

Rather than being overjoyed at winning, Ms. Mullings sues the lottery authorities for misrepresentation and fraud. Her legal brief states that she was promised $1 million but received only $490,905.[16]

The term we use to compute the value of the stream of level payments, C, for T years is called an **annuity factor.** The annuity factor in the current example is 9.8181. Because the annuity factor is used so often in PV calculations, we have included it in Table A.2 in Appendix A. The table gives the values of these factors for a range of interest rates, r, and maturity dates, T.

The annuity factor as expressed in the brackets of (5.13) is a complex formula. For simplification, we may from time to time refer to the annuity factor as

$$A_r^T \tag{5.14}$$

that is, expression (5.14) stands for the present value of $1 a year for T years at an interest rate of r.

Mortgages

Mortgages are a common example of an annuity with monthly payments. To understand mortgage calculations, you need to keep in mind two institutional arrangements. First, although payments are monthly, regulations for Canadian financial institutions require that mortgage rates be quoted with semiannual compounding. Further, payments on conventional mortgages are calculated to maturity (usually after 25 years) although rate adjustments after the initial locked-in period will cause payments to change subsequently.

---

[16]To solve this problem on a common financial calculator, you should do the following:

1. Make sure *FV* is set to zero.
2. Enter the payment 50,000 and press *PMT*.
3. Enter the interest rate 8 and press *I% YR*.
4. Enter the number of periods 20 and press *N*.
5. Finally, solve for *PV*.

Notice your answer is $490,907.370372. The calculator uses 11 digits for the annuity factor and the answer, whereas the example uses only four digits in the annuity factor and rounds the final answer to the nearest dollar. That is why the answer in the text example differs from the one using the calculator. In practice, the answer using the calculator is the best because it is more precise.

EXAMPLE 5.22

A financial institution is offering a $100,000 mortgage at a stated rate of 6 percent. To find the payments we first need to find the effective *monthly* rate. To do this we convert the stated semi-annual rate to an equivalent annual rate.[17]

$$\text{Effective annual interest rate} = [1 + r/m]^m - 1$$
$$= [1 + 0.06/2]^2 - 1$$
$$= 1.0609 - 1$$
$$= 6.09\%$$

Then we find the effective monthly rate used to calculate the payments.

$$\text{Stated rate} / m = (\text{Effective annual rate} + 1)^{1/m} - 1$$
$$\text{Stated rate} / 12 = (1.0609)^{1/12} - 1$$
$$= 1.0049 - 1 = 0.49\%$$

The effective monthly rate is 0.49 percent and there are $12 \times 25 = 300$ payments so we need to find $A_{0.0049}^{300}$. Since this in not in Table A.2, we use (5.13) as rearranged in footnote 13 to solve for C, the monthly payment.

$$\text{PV} = \$100,000 = C \times (1 - \text{Present value factor})/r$$
$$\$100,000 = C \times (1 - 1/1.0049^{300})/0.0049$$
$$C = \$636.99$$

The monthly mortgage payments will be **$636.99**.

EXAMPLE 5.23

Earlier, we pointed out that, while mortgages are amortized over 300 months, the rate is fixed for a shorter period usually no longer than five years. Suppose the rate of 6 percent in the previous example is fixed for five years and you are wondering whether to lock in this rate or to take a lower rate of 5 percent fixed for only one year. If you choose the one-year rate, how much lower will your payments be for the first year?

The payments at 5 percent are $579.94, a reduction of $57.05 per month. If you choose to take the shorter-term mortgage with lower payments, you are betting that rates will not take a big jump over the next year leaving you with a new rate after one year much higher than 6 percent. While the mortgage formula cannot make this decision for you (it depends on risk and return discussed in Chapter 9), it does give you the risk you are facing in terms of higher monthly payments. In 1981, mortgage rates were around 20 percent!

Using Annuity Formulas

Our experience is that annuity formulas are not hard, but can be tricky for the beginning student. Here we present four tricks.

Trick 1: A Delayed Annuity.   One of the tricks in working with annuities or perpetuities is getting the timing exactly right. This is particularly useful when an annuity or perpetuity begins at a date many periods in the future. Consider Example 5.24.

---

[17]Chartered banks use 10 decimal places for all calculations. This may result in some rounding error in using this formula to check the payments on an outstanding mortgage.

EXAMPLE 5.24

Fauzia Mohammed will receive a four-year annuity of $500 per year beginning at date 6. If the interest rate is 10 percent, what is the present value of her annuity?

This situation can be graphed as

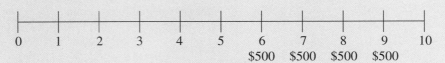

The analysis involves two steps:

1. Calculate the present value of the annuity using (5.13). This is

Present Value of Annuity at Date 5:

$$\$500\left[\frac{1}{0.10} - \frac{1}{0.10(1.10)^4}\right] = \$500 \times A_{0.10}^4$$

$$= \$500 \times 3.1699$$

$$= \$1,584.95$$

Note that $1,584.95 represents the present value at date 5.

Students frequently think that $1,584.95 is the present value at date 6, because the annuity begins at date 6. However, our formula values the annuity as of one period prior to the first payment. This can be seen in the most typical case where the first payment occurs at date 1. The formula values the annuity as of date 0 here.

2. Discount the present value of the annuity back to date 0. That is

Present Value at Date 0:

$$\frac{\$1,584.95}{(1.10)^5} = \$984.13$$

Again, it is worthwhile mentioning that, because the annuity formula brings Fauzia's annuity back to date 5, the second calculation must discount over the remaining five periods. The two-step procedure is graphed in Figure 5.12.

FIGURE 5.12

Discounting Fauzia Mohammed's Annuity

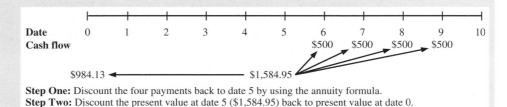

Step One: Discount the four payments back to date 5 by using the annuity formula.
Step Two: Discount the present value at date 5 ($1,584.95) back to present value at date 0.

Trick 2: Annuity in Advance.   The annuity formula of (5.12) assumes that the first annuity payment begins a full period hence. This type of annuity is frequently called an *annuity in arrears*. What happens if the annuity begins today, in other words, at date 0?

EXAMPLE 5.25

In Example 5.21, Andrea Mullings received $50,000 a year for 20 years as a prize in a U.S. lottery. In that example, she was to receive the first payment a year from the winning date. Let us now assume that the first payment occurs immediately. The total number of payments remains 20. Under this new assumption, we have a 19-date annuity with the first payment occurring at date 1—plus an extra payment at date 0. The present value is

$$\underset{\text{Payment at date 0}}{\$50,000} + \underset{\text{19-year annuity}}{\$50,000 \times A_{0.08}^{19}}$$
$$= \$50,000 + \$50,000 \times 9.6036$$
$$= \$530,180$$

The present value in this example is greater than $490,905, the present value in the earlier lottery example. This is to be expected because the annuity of the current example begins earlier. An annuity with an immediate initial payment is called an *annuity in advance*. Always remember that both Equation (5.13) and Table A.2 refer to an *annuity in arrears*.[18]

A second way to find the present value of our annuity in advance is to compute the present value of a 20-year annuity in arrears and compound the result for one period. This gives the same present value (except for a small rounding error):

$$\$50,000 \times A_{0.08}^{20} = \$50,000 \times 9.8181 = \$490,905$$
$$\$490,905 (1.08) = \$530,177$$

Trick 3: The Infrequent Annuity.   Example 5.26 deals with an annuity with payments occurring less frequently than once a year.

EXAMPLE 5.26

Alex Bourne receives an annuity of $450 payable once every two years. The annuity stretches out over 20 years. The first payment occurs at date 2, that is, two years from today. The annual interest rate is 6 percent.

The trick is to determine the interest rate over a two-year period. The interest rate over two years is

$$1.06 \times 1.06 - 1 = 12.36\%$$

That is, $100 invested over two years will yield $112.36.

What we want is the present value of a $450 annuity over 10 periods, with an interest rate of 12.36 percent per period. This is

$$\$450\left[\frac{1}{0.1236} - \frac{1}{0.1236 \times (1.1236)^{10}}\right] = \$450 \times A_{0.1236}^{10} = \$2,505.57$$

---

[18]To solve this problem on a financial calculator:

1. Clear the calculator.
2. Set the calculator for an annuity in advance.
3. Enter the number of periods as 19 and press *N*.
4. Enter the payment as 50,000 and press *PMT*.
5. Enter the interest rate of 8 percent and press *i*.
6. Ask the calculator for the present value by pressing the compute button and *PV*.

Trick 4: **Equating Present Value of Two Annuities.**   Example 5.27 equates the present value of inflows with the present value of outflows.

EXAMPLE 5.27

Jon Rabinowitz and Gila Messeri are saving for the university education of their newborn daughter, Gabrielle. They estimate that expenses will run $30,000 per year when their daughter enters university in 18 years. The annual return on their university investment account over the next few decades will be 14 percent. How much money must they deposit in the bank each year so that their daughter will be completely supported through four years of university?

To simplify the calculations, we assume that Gabrielle is born today. Her parents will make the first of her four annual tuition payments on her 18th birthday. They will make equal deposits on each of her first 17 birthdays, but no deposit at date 0. This is illustrated as

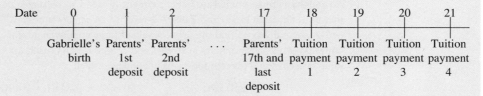

Date	0	1	2		17	18	19	20	21
	Gabrielle's birth	Parents' 1st deposit	Parents' 2nd deposit	. . .	Parents' 17th and last deposit	Tuition payment 1	Tuition payment 2	Tuition payment 3	Tuition payment 4

Jon and Gila will be making deposits over the next 17 years. They will be withdrawing $30,000 per year over the following four years. We can be sure they will be able to withdraw fully $30,000 per year if the present value of the deposits equals the present value of the four $30,000 withdrawals.

This calculation requires three steps. The first two determine the present value of the withdrawals. The final step determines yearly deposits that will have a present value equal to that of the withdrawals.

1. We calculate the present value of the four years at university using the annuity formula:

$$\$30,000 \times \left[\frac{1}{0.14} - \frac{1}{0.14 \times (1.14)^4} \right] = \$30,000 \times A_{0.14}^4$$
$$= \$30,000 \times 2.9137 = \$87,411$$

We assume that Gabrielle enters university on her 18th birthday.
Given our discussion in trick 1 above, $87,411 represents the present value at date 17.

2. We calculate the present value of a university education at date 0 as

$$\frac{\$87,411}{(1.14)^{17}} = \$9,422.91$$

3. Assuming that Gila Messeri and Jon Rabinowitz make deposits to the bank at the end of each of the 17 years, we calculate the annual deposit that will yield a present value of all deposits of $9,422.91 as

$$C \times A_{0.14}^{17} = \$9,422.91$$

Since

$$A_{0.14}^{17} = 6.3729$$

we find that

$$C = \frac{\$9,422.91}{6.3729} = \$1,478.59$$

Thus, deposits of $1,478.59 made at the end of each of the first 17 years and invested at 14 percent will provide enough money to make tuition payments of $30,000 over the following four years.

An alternative method would be: (1) calculate the present value of the tuition payments at Gabrielle's 18th birthday and (2) calculate annual deposits such that the future value of the deposits at her 18th birthday equals the present value of the tuition payments at that date. Although this technique can also provide the right answer, we have found that it is more likely to lead to errors. Therefore, we only equate present values in our presentation.

Growing Annuity

Cash flows in business are very likely to grow over time, due either to real growth or to inflation. The growing perpetuity, which assumes an infinite number of cash flows, provides one formula to handle this growth. We now consider a **growing annuity,** which is a *finite* number of growing cash flows. Because perpetuities of any kind are rare, a formula for a growing annuity would be useful indeed. The formula is[19]

Formula for Present Value of Growing Annuity:

$$\text{PV} = C\left[\frac{1}{r-g} - \frac{1}{r-g} \times \left(\frac{1+g}{1+r}\right)^T\right] \qquad (5.15)$$

where, as before, C is the payment to occur at the end of the first period, r is the interest rate, g is the rate of growth per period, expressed as a percentage, and T is the number of periods for the annuity. It should be noted that for Equation (5.15) the growth rate cannot equal the interest rate. If these two are equal, then $r - g$ is 0 and Equation (5.15) becomes mathematically undefined.

---

[19]This can be proved as follows. A growing annuity can be viewed as the difference between two growing perpetuities. Consider a growing perpetuity *A,* where the first payment of C occurs at date 1. Next, consider growing perpetuity *B,* where the first payment of $C(1 + g)^T$ is made at date $T + 1$. Both perpetuities grow at rate g. The growing annuity over T periods is the difference between annuity *A* and annuity *B*. This can be represented as:

Date	0	1	2	3	...	T	T + 1	T + 2	T + 3
Perpetuity A		C	$C \times (1+g)$	$C \times (1+g)^2$	...	$C \times (1+g)^{T-1}$	$C \times (1+g)^T$	$C \times (1+g)^{T+1}$	$C \times (1+g)^{T+2}\ldots$
Perpetuity B							$C \times (1+g)^T$	$C \times (1+g)^{T+1}$	$C \times (1+g)^{T+2}\ldots$
Annuity		C	$C \times (1+g)$	$C \times (1+g)^2$	...	$C \times (1+g)^{T-1}$			

The value of perpetuity *A* is $\frac{C}{r-g}$.

The value of perpetuity *B* is $\frac{C \times (1+g)^T}{r-g} \times \frac{1}{(1+r)^T}$.

The difference between the two perpetuities is given by (5.15).

EXAMPLE 5.28

Gilles Lebouder, a second-year MBA student, has just been offered a job at $50,000 a year. He anticipates his salary increasing by 9 percent a year until his retirement in 40 years. Given an interest rate of 20 percent, what is the present value of his lifetime salary?

We simplify by assuming he will be paid his $50,000 salary exactly one year from now, and that his salary will continue to be paid in annual installments. From (5.15), the calculation is

Present value
of Gilles' $= \$50,000 \times \{[1/(0.20 - 0.09)] - [1/(0.20 - 0.09)\,(1.09/1.20)^{40}]\}$
lifetime salary

$= \$444,832$

EXAMPLE 5.29

In Example 5.27, Jon Rabinowitz and Gila Messeri planned to make 17 identical payments to fund the university education of their daughter, Gabrielle. Alternatively, imagine that they planned to increase their payments at 4 percent per year. What would their first payment be?

The first two steps of the previous Messeri–Rabinowitz example showed that the present value of the university costs was $9,422.91. These two steps would be the same here. However, the third step must be altered. Now we must ask, How much should their first payment be so that, if payments increase by 4 percent per year, the present value of all payments will be $9,422.91?

We set the growing annuity formula equal to $9,422.91 and solve for C:

$$C[1/r - g - (1/r - g)\,(1 + g/1 + r)^T]$$
$$= C[1/0.14 - 0.04 - (1/0.14 - 0.04)\,(1.04/1.14)^{17}]$$
$$= \$9,422.91$$

Here, $C = \$1,192.78$. Thus, the deposit on their daughter's first birthday is $1,192.78, the deposit on the second birthday is $1,240.49 (or $1.04 \times \$1,192.78$), and so on.

? Concept Questions

- What are the formulas for a perpetuity, growing perpetuity, annuity, and growing annuity?
- What are three important points concerning the growing perpetuity formula?
- What are four tricks concerning annuities?

5.5 What Is a Firm Worth?

Suppose you are a business appraiser who determines the value of small companies. The lesson you learn from this chapter is that the present value of a firm depends upon its future cash flows.

Let us consider the example of a firm that is expected to generate net cash flows (cash inflows minus cash outflows) of $5,000 in the first year and $2,000 for each of the next five years. The firm can be sold for $10,000 seven years from now. The owners of the firm would like to be able to make 10 percent on their investment.

The value of the firm is found by multiplying the net cash flow by the appropriate present value factor. The value of the firm is simply the sum of the present values of the individual net cash flows.

The present value of the net cash flows is given below:

End of Year	Net Cash Flow of the Firm	Present Value Factor (10%)	Present Value of Net Cash Flows
	The Present Value of the Firm		
1	$ 5,000	0.90909	$ 4,545.45
2	2,000	0.82645	1,652.90
3	2,000	0.75131	1,502.62
4	2,000	0.68301	1,366.02
5	2,000	0.62092	1,241.84
6	2,000	0.56447	1,128.94
7	10,000	0.51315	5,131.58
	Present value of firm		$16,569.35

We can also use the simplifying formula for an annuity to give us

$$\frac{\$5,000}{1.1} + \frac{\$2,000}{1.1} \times A_{0.10}^5 + \frac{\$10,000}{(1.1)^7} = \$16,569.35$$

Suppose you have the opportunity to acquire the firm for $12,000. Should you make this investment? The answer is yes because the NPV is positive.

$$\text{NPV} = \text{PV} - \text{Cost}$$
$$\$4,569.35 = \$16,569.35 - \$12,000$$

The incremental value (NPV) of acquiring the firm is $4,569.35.

EXAMPLE 5.30

The Napoli Pizza Company is contemplating investing $1 million in four new outlets in Calgary. Matthew Lee, the firm's chief financial officer (CFO), has estimated that the investments will pay out cash flows of $200,000 per year for nine years and nothing thereafter. (The cash flows will occur at the end of each year and there will be no cash flow after year 9.) Mr. Lee has determined that the relevant discount rate for this investment is 15 percent. This is the rate of return that the firm can earn for comparable projects. Should the Napoli Pizza Company make the investments in the new outlets?

The decision can be evaluated as:

$$\text{NPV} = -\$1,000,000 + \frac{\$200,000}{1.15} + \frac{\$200,000}{(1.15)^2} + \ldots + \frac{\$200,000}{(1.15)^9}$$
$$= -\$1,000,000 + \$200,000 \times A_{0.15}^9$$
$$= -\$1,000,000 + \$954,316.78$$
$$= -\$45,683.22$$

The present value of the four new outlets is only $954,316.78. The outlets are worth less than they cost. The Napoli Pizza Company should not make the investment because the NPV is −$45,683.22. If the Napoli Pizza Company requires a 15 percent rate of return, the new outlets are not a good investment.

5.6 SUMMARY AND CONCLUSIONS

1. Two basic concepts, *future value* and *present value,* were introduced at the beginning of this chapter. With a 10 percent interest rate, an investor with $1 today can generate a future value of $1.10 in a year, $1.21 [$1 × (1.10)²] in two years, and so on. Conversely, present value analysis places a current value on a later cash flow. With the same 10 percent interest rate, a dollar to be received in one year has a present value of $0.909($1/1.10) in year 0. A dollar to be received in two years has a present value of $0.826 [$1/(1.10)²].

2. One commonly expresses the interest rate as, say, 12 percent per year. However, one can speak of the interest rate as 3 percent per quarter. Although the stated annual interest rate remains 12 percent (3 percent × 4), the effective annual interest rate is 12.55 percent [(1.03)⁴ − 1]. In other words, the compounding process increases the future value of an investment. The limiting case is continuous compounding, where funds are assumed to be reinvested every infinitesimal instant.

3. A basic quantitative technique for financial decision making is net present value analysis. The net present value formula for an investment that generates cash flows (C_t) in future periods is

$$NPV = -C_0 + \frac{C_1}{1+r} + \frac{C_2}{(1+r)^2} + \ldots + \frac{C_T}{(1+r)^T} = -C_0 + \sum_{t=1}^{T} \frac{C_t}{(1+r)^t}$$

The formula assumes that the cash flow at date 0 is the initial investment (a cash outflow).

4. Frequently, the actual calculation of present value is long and tedious. The computation of the present value of a long-term mortgage with monthly payments is a good example of this. We presented four simplifying formulas:

$$\text{Perpetuity: PV} = \frac{C}{r}$$

$$\text{Growing perpetuity: PV} = \frac{C}{r-g}$$

$$\text{Annuity: PV} = C\left[\frac{1}{r} - \frac{1}{r(1+r)^T}\right]$$

$$\text{Growing annuity: PV} = C\left[\frac{1}{r-g} - \frac{1}{r-g} \times \left(\frac{1+g}{1+r}\right)^T\right]$$

5. We stressed a few practical considerations in the application of these formulas:

   a. The numerator in each of the formulas, *C,* is the cash flow to be received *one full period hence.*

   b. Cash flows are generally irregular in practice. To avoid unwieldy problems, assumptions to create more regular cash flows are made both in this textbook and in practice.

   c. A number of present value problems involve annuities (or perpetuities) beginning a few periods hence. Students should practise combining the annuity (or perpetuity) formula with the discounting formula to solve these problems.

   d. Annuities and perpetuities may have periods of every two or every *n* years, rather than once a year. They may also have shorter periods like one month or one quarter. The annuity and perpetuity formulas can easily handle such circumstances.

   e. One frequently encounters problems where the present value of one annuity must be equated with the present value of another annuity.

KEY TERMS

Annual percentage rate 107	Discounting 103	Perpetuity 111
Annuity 114	Effective annual interest	Present value (PV) 96
Annuity factor 116	rate 107	Present value factor 104
Compounding 99	Future value 96	Simple interest 99
Compound interest 99	Growing annuity 121	Stated annual interest rate 107
Compound value 96	Growing perpetuity 113	
Continuous compounding 109	Net present value (NPV) 97	

SUGGESTED READING

To learn how to perform the mathematics of present value, we encourage you to see the handbooks that come with your calculator.

We also recommend:

M. White. *Financial Analysis with a Calculator.* 5th ed. Burr Ridge, Ill.: McGraw-Hill/Irwin, 2004.

QUESTIONS & PROBLEMS[20]

Annual Compounding

5.1 Manitoba Bank pays 7 percent simple interest on its savings account balances, whereas Saskatchewan Bank pays 7 percent interest compounded annually. If you made a $5,000 deposit in each bank, how much more money would you earn from your Saskatchewan Bank account at the end of 10 years?

5.2 Compute the future value of $1,000 compounded annually for:
   a. 10 years at 5 percent
   b. 10 years at 7 percent
   c. 20 years at 5 percent
   d. Why is the interest earned in part (c) not twice the amount earned in part (a)?

5.3 For each of the following, compute the present value:

Years	Interest Rate	Future Value
6	5%	$ 15,451
9	11	51,557
18	16	886,073
23	19	550,164

EXCEL

5.4 Compute the future value of $1,000 continuously compounded for:
   a. 5 years at a stated annual interest rate of 12 percent
   b. 3 years at a stated annual interest rate of 10 percent
   c. 10 years at a stated annual interest rate of 5 percent
   d. 8 years at a stated annual interest rate of 7 percent

5.5 Find the EAR in each of the following cases:

Stated Rate (APR)	Number of Times Compounded	Effective Rate (EAR)
11%	Quarterly	
7	Monthly	
9	Daily	
17	Infinite	

5.6 Find the APR, or state rate, in each of the following cases:

Stated Rate (APR)	Number of Times Compounded	Effective Rate (EAR)
	Semiannually	8.1%
	Monthly	7.6
	Weekly	16.8
	Infinite	26.2

---

[20]The following conventions are used in the questions and problems for this chapter.

   If more frequent compounding than once a year is indicated, the problem will either state: (1) both a stated annual interest rate and a compounding period, or (2) an effective annual interest rate.

   If annual compounding is indicated, the problem will provide an annual interest rate. Since the stated annual interest rate and the effective annual interest rate are the same here, we use the simpler annual interest rate.

5.7   The IntraCanada Bank charges 12.2 percent compounded monthly on its business loans. Bank Depot charges 12.4 percent compounded semiannually. As a potential borrower, to which bank would you go for a new loan?

5.8   Friendly's Quick Loans Inc. offers you "three for four or I knock on your door." This means you get $3 today and repay $4 when you get your paycheque in one week (or else). What's the effective annual return Friendly's earns on this lending business? If you were brave enough to ask, what APR would Friendly's say you were paying? If the maximum interest rate that a financial institution can legally charge is 60 percent per annum, are Friendly's operations legal?

5.9   Well-known financial writer Andrew Tobias argues that he can earn 177 percent per year buying wine by the case. Specifically, he assumes that he will consume one $50 bottle of fine Bordeaux per week for the next 12 weeks. He can either pay $50 per week or buy a case of 12 bottles today. If he buys the case, he receives a 10 percent discount and, by doing so, earns the 177 percent. Assume he buys the wine and consumes the first bottle today. Do you agree with his analysis? Do you see a problem with his numbers?

5.10 You are planning to save for retirement over the next 30 years. To do this, you will invest $700 a month in a stock account and $300 a month in a bond account. The return of the stock account is expected to be 11 percent, and the bond account will pay 7 percent. When you retire, you will combine your money into an account with a 9 percent return. How much can you withdraw each month from your account assuming a 25-year withdrawal period?

5.11 Suppose an investment offers to triple your money in 12 months (don't believe it). What rate of return per quarter are you being offered?

5.12 You're trying to choose between two different investments, both of which have upfront costs of $50,000. Investment G returns $85,000 in five years. Investment H returns $175,000 in 11 years. Which of these investments has the higher return?

5.13 What is the value today of a 15-year annuity that pays $500 a year? The annuity's first payment occurs at the end of year 6. The annual interest rate is 12 percent for years 1 through 5, and 15 percent thereafter.

5.14 You receive a credit card application from Shady Bank Savings and Loan offering an introductory rate of 1.90 percent per year, compounded monthly for the first six months, increasing thereafter to 16 percent compounded monthly. Assuming you transfer the $4,000 balance from your existing credit card and make no subsequent payments, how much interest will you owe at the end of the first year?

5.15 You want to borrow $45,000 from your local bank to buy a new sailboat. You can afford to make monthly payments of $950, but no more. Assuming monthly compounding, what is the highest APR you can afford on a 60-month loan?

5.16 You need a 30-year, fixed-rate mortgage to buy a new home for $200,000. Your mortgage bank will lend you the money at a 6.8 percent APR for this 360-month loan. However, you can only afford monthly payments of $1,000, so you offer to pay off any remaining loan balance at the end of the loan in the form of a single balloon payment. How large will this balloon payment have to be for you to keep your monthly payments at $1,000?

5.17 The present value of the following cash flow stream is $5,979 when discounted at 10 percent annually. What is the value of the missing cash flow?

Year	Cash Flow
1	$1,000
2	?
3	2,000
4	2,000

5.18 You have just purchased a new warehouse. To finance the purchase, you've arranged for a 30-year mortgage for 80 percent of the $1,600,000 purchase price. The monthly payment on this loan will be $10,000. What is the APR on this loan? The EAR?

5.19 What is the present value of $2,000 per year, at a discount rate of 12 percent, if the first payment is received 9 years from now and the last payment is received 25 years from now?

5.20 A 15-year annuity pays $1,500 per month, and payments are made at the end of each month. If the interest rate is 15 percent compounded monthly for the first seven years, and 12 percent compounded monthly thereafter, what is the present value of the annuity?

5.21 You have your choice of two investment accounts. Investment A is a 15-year annuity that features end-of-month $1,000 payments and has an interest rate of 10.5 percent compounded monthly. Investment B is a 9 percent continuously compounded lump-sum investment, also good for 15 years. How much money would you need to invest in B today for it to be worth as much as Investment A 15 years from now?

5.22 A 5-year annuity of ten $6,000 semiannual payments will begin 9 years from now, with the first payment coming 9.5 years from now. If the discount rate is 12 percent compounded monthly, what is the value of this annuity five years from now? What is the value three years from now? What is the current value of the annuity?

5.23 You want to buy a new sports car from Muscle Motors for $56,000. The contract is in the form of a 48-month annuity due at an 8.15 percent APR. What will your monthly payment be?

5.24 You are saving for the university education of your two children. They are two years apart in age; one will begin university 15 years from today and the other will begin 17 years from today. You estimate your children's university expenses to be $23,000 per year per child, payable at the beginning of each school year. The annual interest rate is 6.5 percent. How much money must you deposit in an account each year to fund your children's education? Your deposits begin one year from today. You will make your last deposit when your oldest child enters college. Assume four years of university.

5.25 Bilbo Baggins wants to save money to meet three objectives. First, he would like to be able to retire 30 years from now with a retirement income of $25,000 per month for 20 years, with the first payment received 30 years and 1 month from now. Second, he would like to purchase a cabin in Rivendell in 10 years at an estimated cost of $350,000. Third, after he passes on at the end of the 20 years of withdrawals, he would like to leave an inheritance of $750,000 to his nephew Frodo. He can afford to save $2,100 per month for the next 10 years. If he can earn an 11 percent EAR before he retires and an 8 percent EAR after he retires, how much will he have to save each month in years 11 through 30?

5.26 After deciding to buy a new car, you can either lease the car or purchase it with a three-year loan. The car you wish to buy costs $35,000. The dealer has a special leasing arrangement where you pay $1 today and $450 per month for the next three years. If you purchase the car, you will pay it off in monthly payments over the next three years at an 8 percent APR. You believe that you will be able to sell the car for $23,000 in three years. Should you buy or lease the car? What break-even resale price in three years would make you indifferent between buying and leasing?

5.27 Two banks in the area offer 30-year, $200,000 mortgages at 7.5 percent and charge a $1,500 loan application fee. However, the application fee charged by Insecurity Bank and Trust is refundable if the loan application is denied, whereas that charged by I. M. Greedy and Sons Mortgage Bank is not. The current disclosure law requires that any fees that will be refunded if the applicant is rejected be included in calculating the APR, but this is not required with nonrefundable fees (presumably because refundable fees are part of the loan rather than a fee). What are the EARs on these two loans? What are the APRs?

5.28 This is a classic retirement problem. A time line will help in solving it. Your friend is celebrating her 35th birthday today and wants to start saving for her anticipated retirement at age 65. She wants to be able to withdraw $90,000 from her savings account on each birthday for 15 years following her retirement; the first withdrawal will be on her 66th birthday. Your friend intends to invest her money in the local credit union, which offers 8 percent interest per year. She wants to make equal annual payments on each birthday into the account established at the credit union for her retirement fund.

    a. If she starts making these deposits on her 36th birthday and continues to make deposits until she is 65 (the last deposit will be on her 65th birthday), what amount must she deposit annually to be able to make the desired withdrawals at retirement?

    b. Suppose your friend has just inherited a large sum of money. Rather than making equal annual payments, she has decided to make one lump-sum payment on her 35th birthday to cover her retirement needs. What amount does she have to deposit?

    c. Suppose your friend's employer will contribute $1,500 to the account every year as part of the company's profit-sharing plan. In addition, your friend expects a $25,000 distribution from a family trust fund on her 55th birthday, which she will also put into the retirement account. What amount must she deposit annually now to be able to make the desired withdrawals at retirement?

5.29 You have just won the lottery. You will receive $1,000,000 today, and then receive 40 payments of $500,000. These payments will start one year from now and will be paid every six months. A representative from Greenleaf Investments has offered to purchase all the payments from you for $10 million. If the appropriate interest rate is a 9 percent APR compounded daily, should you take the offer? Assume there are 12 months in a year, each with 30 days.

5.30 A financial planning service offers a university savings program. The plan calls for you to make six annual payments of $8,000 each, with the first payment occurring today, your child's 12th birthday. Beginning on your child's 18th birthday, the plan will provide $20,000 per year for four years. What return is this investment offering?

Compounding Periods

5.31 Solve for the unknown number of years in each of the following:

Present Value	Years	Interest Rate	Future Value
$ 625		8%	$ 1,284
810		7	4,341
18,400		21	402,662
21,500		29	173,439

5.32 One of your customers is delinquent on his accounts payable balance. You've mutually agreed to a repayment schedule of $500 per month. You will charge .9 percent per month interest on the overdue balance. If the current balance is $16,500, how long will it take for the account to be paid off?

5.33 You're prepared to make monthly payments of $125, beginning at the end of this month, into an account that pays 10 percent interest compounded monthly. How many payments will you have made when your account balance reaches $20,000?

5.34 What is the future value in three years of $1,000 invested in an account with a stated annual interest rate of 8 percent,

    a. Compounded annually?

    b. Compounded semiannually?

    c. Compounded monthly?

    d. Compounded continuously?

    e. Why does the future value increase as the compounding period shortens?

5.35 Calculate the present value of $9,543 received 13 years from today. Assume a stated annual interest rate of 11.3 percent, compounded daily.

5.36 On August 1, 2007, Johnny Rocket bought a motorcycle for $9,000. He paid $1,500 down and financed the balance with a five-year loan at a stated annual interest rate of 7.5 percent, compounded monthly. He started the monthly payments exactly one month after the purchase. Two years later, at the end of September, 2009, Johnny got a new job and decided to pay off the loan. If the bank charges him a 1.2 percent prepayment penalty based on the loan balance, how much must she pay the bank on October 1, 2009?

5.37 In November 2005, the Toronto Blue Jays signed closer B. J. Ryan to a five-year contract paying him a total of $47 million. His contract pays him $4 million in the first year, $7 million in the second year, and $12 million each year for the final three years. If the annual interest rate is 8 percent and all payments are made on November 1 of each year, what would the present value of these payments be on November 1, 2005? If he were to receive an equal annual salary at the end of each of the five years of his contract, what would be the present value of B. J. Ryan's equivalent annual salary?

Perpetuities, Growing Perpetuities, Annuities and Growing Annuities

5.38 An investor purchasing a British consol is entitled to receive annual payments from the British government forever. What is the price of a consol that pays $120 annually if the next payment occurs one year from today? The market interest rate is 15 percent.

5.39 The Perpetual Life Insurance Co. is trying to sell you an investment policy that will pay you and your heirs $15,000 per year forever. If the required return on this investment is 8 percent, how much will you pay for the policy? Suppose the Perpetual Life Insurance Co. told you the policy costs $195,000. At what interest rate would this be a fair deal?

EXCEL

5.40 Robert Weinstein has been working on an advanced technology in laser eye surgery. His technology will be available in the near term. He anticipates his first annual cash flow from the technology to be $200,000, received two years from today. Subsequent annual cash flows will grow at 5 percent in perpetuity. What is the present value of the technology if the discount rate is 10 percent?

5.41 A prestigious investment bank designed a new security that pays a quarterly dividend of $10 in perpetuity. The first dividend occurs one quarter from today. What is the price of the security if the stated annual interest rate is 12 percent, compounded quarterly?

5.42 Barrett Pharmaceuticals is considering a drug project that costs $240,000 today and is expected to generate end-of-year annual cash flows of $21,000, forever. At what discount rate would Barrett be indifferent between accepting or rejecting the project?

5.43 Southern Ontario Publishing Company is trying to decide whether to revise its popular textbook, *Financial Psychoanalysis For Dummies.* The company has estimated that the revision will cost $50,000. Cash flows from increased sales will be $12,000 the first year. These cash flows will increase by 6 percent per year. The book will go out of print five years from now. Assume that the initial cost is paid now and revenues are received at the end of each year. If the company requires an 11 percent return for such an investment, should it undertake the revision?

EXCEL

5.44 Your job pays you only once a year for all the work you did over the previous 12 months. Today, December 31, you just received your salary of $50,000, and you plan to spend all of it. However, you want to start saving for retirement beginning next year. You have decided that one year from today you will begin depositing 2 percent of your annual salary

MINICASE: The MBA Decision

Ben Bates graduated from college six years ago with a finance undergraduate degree. Although he is satisfied with his current job, his goal is to become an investment banker. He feels that an MBA degree would allow him to achieve this goal. After examining schools, he has narrowed his choice to either Red River University or University of Upper Canada. Although internships are encouraged by both schools, to get class credit for the internship, no salary can be paid. Other than internships, neither school will allow its students to work while enrolled in its MBA program.

Ben currently works at the money management firm of Dewey and Louis. His annual salary at the firm is $50,000 per year, and his salary is expected to increase at 3 percent per year until retirement. He is currently 28 years old and expects to work for 35 more years. His current job includes a fully paid health insurance plan, and his current average tax rate is 26 percent. Ben has a savings account with enough money to cover the entire cost of his MBA program.

The Ritter College of Business at Red River University is one of the top MBA programs in the country. The MBA degree requires two years of full-time enrollment at the university. The annual tuition is $60,000, payable at the beginning of each school year. Books and other supplies are estimated to cost $2,500 per year. Ben expects that after graduation from Red River, he will receive a job offer for about $95,000 per year, with a $15,000 signing bonus. The salary at this job will increase at 4 percent per year. Because of the higher salary, his average income tax rate will increase to 31 percent.

The Bradley School of Business at University of Upper Canada began its MBA program 16 years ago.

The Bradley School is smaller and less well known than the Ritter. Bradley offers an accelerated, one-year program, with a tuition cost of $75,000 to be paid upon matriculation. Books and other supplies for the program are expected to cost $3,500. Ben thinks that he will receive an offer of $78,000 per year upon graduation, with a $10,000 signing bonus. The salary at this job will increase at 3.5 percent per year. His average tax rate at this level of income will be 29 percent.

Both schools offer a health insurance plan that will cost $3,000 per year, payable at the beginning of the year. Ben also estimates that room and board expenses will cost $20,000 per year at either school. The appropriate discount rate is 6.5 percent.

1. How does Ben's age affect his decision to get an MBA?
2. What other, perhaps nonquantifiable factors affect Ben's decision to get an MBA?
3. Assuming all salaries are paid at the end of each year, what is the best option for Ben— from a strictly financial standpoint?
4. Ben believes that the appropriate analysis is to calculate the future value of each option. How would you evaluate this statement?
5. What initial salary would Ben need to receive to make him indifferent between attending Wilton University and staying in his current position?
6. Suppose, instead of being able to pay cash for his MBA, Ben must borrow the money. The current borrowing rate is 5.4 percent. How would this affect his decision?

in an account that will earn 8 percent per year. Your salary will increase at 4 percent per year throughout your career. How much money will you have on the date of your retirement 40 years from today?

5.45 Tom Adams has received a job offer from a large investment bank as a clerk to an associate banker. His base salary will be $35,000. He will receive his first annual salary payment one year from the day he begins to work. In addition, he will get an immediate $10,000 bonus for joining the company. His salary will grow at 4 percent each year. Each year he will receive a bonus equal to 10 percent of his salary. Mr. Adams is expected to work for 25 years. What is the present value of the offer if the discount rate is 12 percent?

5.46 You have 30 years left until retirement and want to retire with $1 million. Your salary is paid annually, and you will receive $55,000 at the end of the current year. Your salary will increase at 3 percent per year, and you can earn a 10 percent return on the money you invest. If you save a constant percentage of your salary, what percentage of your salary must you save each year?

5.47 What is the value of an investment that pays $6,700 every *other* year forever, if the first payment occurs one year from today and the discount rate is 13 percent compounded daily? What is the value today if the first payment occurs four years from today?

5.48 What is the equation for the present value of a growing perpetuity with a payment of C one period from today if the payments grow by C each period?

Chapter 6

How to Value Bonds and Stocks

EXECUTIVE SUMMARY

The previous chapter discussed the mathematics of compounding, discounting, and present value. We now use the mathematics of compounding and discounting to determine the present values of financial instruments, beginning with a discussion of how bonds are valued. Since the future cash flows of bonds are known (at least for government bonds and issues of high-quality corporations with minimal default risk), application of net present value techniques is fairly straightforward. The uncertainty of future cash flows makes the pricing of stocks more difficult.

6.1 Definition and Example of a Bond

A *bond* is a certificate showing that a borrower owes a specified sum. In order to repay the money, the borrower has agreed to make interest and principal payments on designated dates. For example, imagine that Kreuger Enterprises just issued 100,000 bonds for $1,000 each carrying a coupon rate of 5 percent and a maturity of two years. Interest on the bonds is to be paid yearly. This means that

1. $100 million (or 100,000 × $1,000) has been borrowed by the firm.
2. The firm must pay interest of $5 million (or 5% × $100 million) at the end of one year.
3. The firm must pay both $5 million of interest and $100 million of principal at the end of two years.

We now consider how to value a few different types of bonds.

6.2 How to Value Bonds

Pure Discount Bonds

The **pure discount bond** is perhaps the simplest kind of bond. It promises a single payment, say $1, at a fixed future date. If the payment is one year from now, it is called a *one-year discount bond;* if it is two years from now, it is called a *two-year discount bond,* and so on. The date when the issuer of the bond makes the last payment is called the **maturity date** of the bond, or just its *maturity* for short. The bond is said to mature or *expire* on the date of its final payment. The payment at maturity ($1 in this example) is termed the bond's **face value.**

Pure discount bonds are often called *zero-coupon bonds* or *zeros* to emphasize the fact that the holder receives no cash payments until maturity. We will use the terms *zero, bullet,* and *discount* interchangeably to refer to bonds that pay no coupons.

The first row of Figure 6.1 shows the pattern of cash flows from a four-year pure discount bond. Note that the face value, *F,* is paid when the bond expires in the 48th month. There are no payments of either interest or principal prior to this date.

In Chapter 5, we indicated that one discounts a future cash flow to determine its present value. The present value of a pure discount bond can easily be determined by the techniques of the previous chapter. For short, we sometimes speak of the *value* of a bond instead of its present value.

Consider a pure discount bond that pays a face value of *F* in *T* years, where the interest rate is *r* in each of the *T* years. (We also refer to this rate as the *market interest rate.*) Because the face value is the only cash flow that the bond pays, the present value of this face amount is

Value of a Pure Discount Bond:

$$PV = \frac{F}{(1 + r)^T}$$

The present value formula can produce some surprising results. Suppose that the interest rate is 10 percent. Consider a bond with a face value of $1 million that matures in 20 years. Applying the formula to this bond, its PV is given by

$$PV = \frac{\$1 \text{ million}}{(1.1)^{20}}$$
$$= 148,644$$

or only about 15 percent of the face value.

Level-Coupon Bonds

Many bonds, however, are not of the simple, pure discount variety. Typical bonds issued by either governments or corporations offer cash payments not just at maturity, but also at regular times in between. For example, payments on Canadian government issues and Canadian corporate bonds are made every six months until the bond matures. These payments are called the **coupons** of the bond. The middle row of Figure 6.1 illustrates the case of a four-year, *level-coupon* bond: The coupon, *C,* is paid every six months and is the same throughout the life of the bond.

Note that the face value of the bond, *F,* is paid at maturity (end of year 4). *F* is sometimes called the *principal* or the *denomination.* Bonds issued in Canada typically have face values of $1,000, though this can vary with the type of bond.

FIGURE 6.1

Different Types of Bonds: *C,* Coupon Paid Every Six Months; *F,* Face Value at Year 4 (maturity for pure discount and coupon bonds)

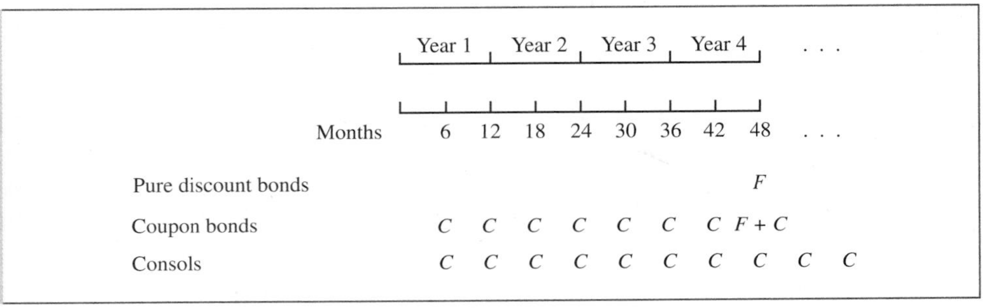

			Year 1	Year 2	Year 3	Year 4	. . .
Months			6 12	18 24	30 36	42 48	. . .
Pure discount bonds						*F*	
Coupon bonds			*C* *C*	*C* *C*	*C* *C*	*C* *F* + *C*	
Consols			*C* *C*	*C* *C*	*C* *C*	*C* *C*	*C* *C*

As we mentioned above, the value of a bond is simply the present value of its cash flows. Therefore, the value of a level-coupon bond is merely the present value of its stream of coupon payments plus the present value of its repayment of principal. Because a level-coupon bond is just an annuity of C each period, together with a payment at maturity of $1,000, the value of a level-coupon bond is

Value of a Level-Coupon Bond:

$$PV = \frac{C}{1+r} + \frac{C}{(1+r)^2} + \ldots + \frac{C}{(1+r)^T} + \frac{\$1,000}{(1+r)^T}$$

where C is the coupon and the face value, F, is $1,000. The value of the bond can be rewritten as

Value of a Level-Coupon Bond:

$$PV = C \times A_r^T + \frac{\$1,000}{(1+r)^T}$$

As mentioned in the previous chapter, A_r^T is the present value of an annuity of $1 per period for T periods at an interest rate per period of r.

EXAMPLE 6.1

Selected bond trading figures for November 16, 2006 appear in Figure 6.2. Suppose an investor was interested in the EDC 5.000 Feb 09/09. This is jargon that means the bond was issued by Export Development Canada, a federal Crown corporation, and the annual coupon rate is 5.00 percent.[1] The face value is $1,000, implying that the yearly coupon is $50.00 (5% × $1,000). Interest is paid each February and August, implying that the coupon every six months is $25 ($50/2). The face value will be paid out in February 2009, two years later. By this we mean that the purchaser obtains claims to the following cash flows:

Feb-07	Aug-07	Feb-08	Aug-08	Feb-09
$25	$25	$25	$25	$25 + $1,000

If the stated annual interest rate in the market is 4.11 percent per year, what is the present value of the bond?

The standard North American method of expressing both bond coupons and bond yields is as a stated rate per year, compounded semiannually. Our work on compounding in the previous chapter showed that the interest rate over any six-month interval is one-half of the stated annual interest rate. In the current example, this semiannual rate is 2.055 percent (4.11%/2). Since the coupon payment in each period is $25, and there are five of these payment dates, the present value of the bond is

$$PV = \frac{\$25}{(1.02055)} + \frac{\$25}{(1.02055)^2} + \ldots + \frac{\$25}{(1.02055)^5} + \frac{\$1,000}{(1.02055)^5}$$

$$= \$25 \times A_{0.02055}^5 + \$1,000/(1.02055)^5$$

$$= \$117.65 + \$903.29$$

$$= 1020.94$$

Traders will generally quote the bond as 102.09, indicating that it is selling at 102.09 percent of the face value of $1,000. This can be seen in Figure 6.2 in the "Bid $" column of our bond. (The small difference in price ($0.23) between our price calculations and the newspaper listing reflects accrued interest arising from the 99 days between August 9 and November 16 and rounding differences.)

---

[1]The coupon rate is specific to the bond and indicates what cash flow should appear in the numerator of the NPV equation. The coupon rate does not appear in the denominator of the NPV equation.

FIGURE 6.2

Sample of a Bond Quotation

				Bonds							
Federal				**Provincial**				**Corporate**			
	Coupon	Mat. Date	Bid $ Yid %		Coupon	Mat. Date	Bid $ Yid %		Coupon	Mat. Date	Bid $ Yid %
Canada	2.750	01/07	98.65 4.10	B C	6.000	Jun 09/08	102.77 4.13	AGT Lt	8.800	Sep 22/25	143.05 5.19
Canada	12.750	01/08	110.69 4.07	B C	6.375	Aug 23/10	107.90 4.08	Bell	6.550	01/29	110.07 5.75
Canada	3.750	Jun 01/08	99.58 4.04	B C	8.500	Aug 23/13	125.40 4.15	BellAlt	4.720	Sep 26/11	100.12 4.69
Canada	6.000	Jun 01/08	102.89 4.03	B C	5.700	Jun 18/29	118.09 4.42	BMO	6.903	Jun 30/10	108.29 4.39
Canada	4.250	01/08	100.51 3.99	B C MF	5.500	Mar 24/08	101.71 4.17	BMO	6.647	Dec 31/10	108.31 4.41
Canada	5.500	Jun 01/09	103.69 3.95	B C MF	5.900	Jun 01/11	107.29 4.12	BMO	6.685	Dec 31/11	109.92 4.49
Canada	11.000	Jun 01/09	116.88 3.93	HydQue	6.500	Feb 15/11	109.10 4.13	BNS	3.470	Sep 02/08	98.66 4.25
Canada	4.250	01/09	100.74 3.96	HydQue	6.000	Aug 15/31	119.52 4.66	BNS	4.515	Nov 19/08	100.49 4.25
Canada	10.750	Oct 01/09	118.17 3.97	HydQue	6.500	Feb 15/35	128.88 4.65	BNS	3.930	Feb 18/10	99.00 4.26
Canada	5.500	Jun 01/10	105.05 3.95	HydQue	6.000	Feb 15/40	123.07 4.63	BNS	7.310	Dec 31/10	110.82 4.40
Canada	4.000	01/10	100.17 3.95	Manit	5.750	Jun 02/08	102.36 4.14	CardTr2	3.869	Oct 15/10	98.50 4.29
Canada	9.000	01/11	119.71 3.94	Manit	7.750	Dec 22/25	141.25 4.50	CDP	4.200	Oct 14/08	99.97 4.21
Canada	6.000	Jun 01/11	108.42 3.95	NewBr	5.700	Jun 02/08	102.28 4.14	CIBC	3.750	Sep 09/10	97.98 4.33
Canada	3.750	01/11	99.13 3.95	NewBr	6.000	Dec 27/17	114.24 4.37	CIBC	4.550	Mar 28/11	100.66 4.38
Canada	5.250	Jun 01/12	106.31 3.97	Newfld	6.150	Apr 17/28	121.51 4.56	Domtar	10.000	Apr 15/11	107.47 7.95
Canada	5.250	Jun 01/13	107.21 3.98	NovaSc	6.600	Jun 01/27	127.68 4.52	GE CAP	5.000	Apr 23/08	101.00 4.26
Canada	10.250	15/14	139.24 4.01	Ontario	6.125	Sep 12/07	101.48 4.23	GE CAP	5.100	Jun 01/16	104.07 4.57
Canada	5.000	Jun 01/14	106.37 4.01	Ontario	3.875	Mar 08/08	99.64 4.16	Genss	4.002	Mar 15/10	99.19 4.26
Canada	11.250	Jun 01/15	151.82 4.01	Ontario	5.700	Dec 01/08	103.09 4.09	Genss	4.245	Sep 15/11	99.84 4.28
Canada	4.500	Jun 01/15	103.41 4.02	Ontario	6.200	Nov 19/09	105.89 4.09	GldCrd	4.159	Oct 15/08	99.79 4.27
Canada	4.000	Jun 01/16	99.70 4.04	Ontario	4.000	19/10	99.70 4.09	GrTAA	5.950	Dec 03/07	101.60 4.35
Canada	4.000	Jun 01/17	99.43 4.07	Ontario	6.100	Nov 19/10	107.31 4.10	GrTAA	6.450	Dec 03/27	115.23 5.25
Canada	10.500	15/21	168.55 4.11	Ontario	6.100	Dec 02/11	109.01 4.10	GTC Tr	6.200	Jun 01/07	100.79 4.67
Canada	9.750	Jun 01/21	161.12 4.12	Ontario	5.375	Dec 02/12	106.58 4.13	Gulf C	6.450	Oct 01/07	106.75 4.39
Canada	9.250	Jun 01/22	158.29 4.13	Ontario	4.750	Jun 02/13	103.43 4.15	GWLife	6.750	Aug 10/10	108.36 4.29
Canada	8.000	Jun 01/23	145.88 4.14	Ontario	5.000	Mar 08/14	105.06 4.19	GWLife	6.140	Mar 21/18	112.04 4.75
Canada	9.000	Jun 01/25	162.22 4.15	Ontario	4.500	Mar 08/15	101.81 4.24	GWLife	6.740	Nov 24/31	122.61 5.13
Canada	8.000	Jun 01/27	152.78 4.15	Ontario	4.400	Mar 08/16	100.81 4.29	HSBC	7.780	Dec 31/10	112.09 4.52
Canada	5.750	Jun 01/29	123.34 4.15	Ontario	6.200	Jun 02/31	124.67 4.52	HydOne	7.150	Jun 03/10	109.58 4.20
Canada	5.750	Jun 01/33	126.31 4.11	Ontario	4.700	Jun 02/37	103.07 4.51	HydOne	6.930	Jun 01/32	129.29 4.91
Canada	5.000	Jun 01/37	116.02 4.08	OntHyd	5.600	Jun 02/08	102.13 4.14	IPL	8.200	Feb 15/24	136.81 4.99
CHT	4.750	15/07	100.17 4.23	Quebec	6.500	Oct 01/07	101.89 4.23	Loblaw	6.650	Nov 08/27	113.21 5.57
CHT	5.100	15/07	100.70 4.21	Quebec	5.500	Jun 01/09	103.28 4.12	MLI	6.240	Feb 16/11	107.23 4.35
CHT	3.550	15/09	98.85 4.07	Quebec	6.250	Dec 01/10	107.76 4.14	MLI	6.700	Jun 30/12	110.86 4.49
CHT	4.650	15/09	101.55 4.06	Quebec	6.000	Oct 01/12	109.29 4.19	MolsonC	5.000	Sep 22/15	98.92 5.15
CHT	3.750	15/10	99.07 4.05	Quebec	5.500	Dec 01/14	107.98 4.31	MstrCr	4.444	Nov 21/11	100.77 4.27
CHT	3.550	15/10	98.22 4.06	Quebec	5.000	Dec 01/15	104.62 4.38	Nexen	6.300	Jun 02/08	102.87 4.34
CMHC	5.250	01/06	100.02 4.14	Quebec	4.500	Dec 01/16	100.50 4.44	Renais	6.850	Feb 06/07	100.47 4.39
CMHC	5.300	03/07	101.23 4.08	Quebec	9.375	Jan 16/23	153.50 4.63	RoyBnk	4.180	Jun 01/09	99.76 4.28
CMHC	5.500	Jun 01/12	106.93 4.09	Quebec	6.000	Oct 01/29	118.93 4.65	RoyBnk	3.700	Jun 24/10	98.02 4.30
EDC	5.000	Feb 09/09	101.86 4.11	Quebec	6.250	Jun 01/32	123.60 4.66	RoyBnk	7.288	Jun 30/10	109.56 4.39
EDC	5.100	Jun 02/14	106.18 4.14	Quebec	5.750	Dec 01/36	117.86 4.64	RoyBnk	7.183	Jun 30/11	111.23 4.46

Source: www.canada.com/nationalpost, November 16, 2006. Used with permission.

One final note concerning level-coupon bonds: Although our example uses government bonds, corporate bonds are identical in form. For example, BMO has a 6.903 percent bond maturing in 2010. This means that BMO will make semiannual payments of $34.52 (6.903%/2 × $1000) between now and 2010 for each face value of $1,000.[2]

A Note on Bond Price Quotes

As the EDC example showed, when buying a bond between coupon payment dates, the price paid is usually more than the price quoted. The reason is that standard convention in the bond market is to quote prices net of "accrued interest," which means that accrued interest is deducted to arrive at the quoted price. This quoted price is called the **clean price.** The price actually paid, however, includes the accrued interest. This is the **dirty price,** also know as the "full" or "invoice" price.

For example, suppose a bond is bought with a 12 percent annual coupon, payable semiannually. The actual price paid or the dirty price is $1,080. The next coupon is due four months from the date the bond is purchased. The next coupon will be $60. The accrued interest on a bond is calculated by taking the fraction of the coupon period that has passed, in this case two months out of six, and multiplying this fraction by the next coupon. Thus, accrued interest in this example would be 2/6 × $60 = $20. The bond's clean price would be $1,080 − $20 = $1,060.

---

[2]Corporate bonds have a number of features that affect their risk and cash flows and these features will be discussed in Chapter 21.

Consols

Not all bonds have a final maturity date. As we mentioned in the previous chapter, consols are bonds that never stop paying a coupon, have no final maturity date, and therefore never mature. Thus, a consol is a perpetuity. In the eighteenth century the Bank of England issued such bonds, called *English consols.* These were bonds that the Bank of England guaranteed would pay the holder a cash flow forever! Through wars and depressions, the Bank of England continued to honour this commitment, and you can still buy such bonds in London today. The Government of Canada also once sold consols. Even though these Canadian bonds were supposed to last forever and to pay their coupons forever, don't go looking for any. There was a special clause in the bond contract that gave the government the right to buy them back from the holders, and that is what the government did. Clauses like that are *call provisions;* we'll study them later.

An important current Canadian example of a consol is fixed-rate preferred stock that provides the holder a fixed dividend in perpetuity. If there were never any question that the firm would actually pay the dividend on the preferred stock, such stock would in fact be a consol.

These instruments can be valued by the perpetuity formula of the previous chapter. For example, if the marketwide interest rate is 10 percent, a consol with a yearly interest payment of $50 is valued at

$$\frac{\$50}{0.10} = \$500$$

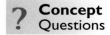 **Concept Questions**
- Define pure discount bonds, level-coupon bonds, and consols.
- Contrast the stated interest rate and the effective annual interest rate for bonds paying semiannual interest.

6.3 Bond Concepts

We complete our discussion on bonds by considering three important concepts: the relationship between interest rates and bond prices, the concept of yield to maturity, and the idea of holding-period return.

Interest Rates and Bond Prices

The above discussion on level-coupon bonds allows us to relate bond prices to interest rates. Consider Example 6.2.

EXAMPLE 6.2

The interest rate is 10 percent. A two-year bond with a 10 percent coupon pays interest of $100 (or $1,000 × 10%). For simplicity, we assume that the interest is paid annually. The bond is priced at its face value of $1,000:

$$\$1,000 = \frac{\$100}{1.1} + \frac{\$1,000 + \$100}{(1.1)^2}$$

If the interest rate unexpectedly rises to 12 percent, the bond sells at

$$\$966.20 = \frac{\$100}{1.12} + \frac{\$1,000 + \$100}{(1.12)^2}$$

Because $966.20 is below $1,000, the bond is said to sell at a **discount.** This is a sensible result. Now that the interest rate is 12 percent, a newly issued bond with a 12 percent coupon rate will sell at $1,000. This newly issued bond will have coupon payments of $120 (or 0.12 × $1,000). Because our bond has interest payments of only $100, investors will pay less than $1,000 for it. If the interest rate fell to 8 percent, the bond would sell at

$$\$1.035.67 = \frac{\$100}{1.08} + \frac{\$1,000 + \$100}{(1.08)^2}$$

Because $1,035.67 is above $1,000, the bond is said to sell at a **premium.**

Thus, we find that bond prices fall with a rise in interest rates and rise with a fall in interest rates. Furthermore, the general principle is that a level-coupon bond trades in the following ways:

1. At the face value of $1,000 if the coupon rate is equal to the marketwide interest rate.
2. At a discount if the coupon rate is below the marketwide interest rate.
3. At a premium if the coupon rate is above the marketwide interest rate.

Yield to Maturity

Let us now consider the previous example in reverse. If our bond is selling at $1,035.67, what return is a bondholder receiving? This can be answered by considering the following equation:

$$\$1,035.67 = \frac{\$100}{1 + y} + \frac{\$1,000 + \$100}{(1 + y)^2}$$

The unknown, y, is the rate of return that the holder is earning on the bond.[3] Our earlier work implies that $y = 8\%$. Thus, traders state that the bond is yielding an 8 percent return. Equivalently, they say that the bond has a **yield to maturity** of 8 percent. The yield to maturity is frequently called the bond's yield for short. So we would say the bond with its 10 percent coupon is priced to yield 8 percent at $1,035.67.

Holding-Period Return

Our example of interest rates and bond prices showed how the price of a two-year bond with a 10 percent coupon varied as market yields changed. Suppose that a bond trader bought the bond when its market yield was 12 percent and sold a month later when the yield was 8 percent. This means that the trader succeeded in buying low ($966.20) and selling high ($1,035.67). In this example the trader earned a **holding-period return** of 7.19 percent:

Holding-period return = (Ending price − Beginning price)/Beginning price

= ($1,035.67 − $966.20)/$966.20 = 7.19%

This annualizes to an effective rate of $(1.0719)^{11} - 1 = 2.1463$ or 215 percent! While this is a bit extreme it does illustrate how a bond trader who could correctly anticipate shifts in market yields could make large profits. By working the example backwards we can also see how such a strategy has potentially large risks.

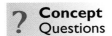

Concept Questions

• **What is the relationship between interest rates and bond prices?**
• **How does one calculate the yield to maturity on a bond?**

---

[3]Technically, the yield to maturity calculation assumes that the bond is held to maturity and all coupons are reinvested at y.

The Present Value Formulas for Bonds

Pure Discount Bonds

$$PV = \frac{F}{(1 + r)^T}$$

Level-Coupon Bonds

$$PV = C\left[\frac{1}{r} - \frac{1}{r \times (1 + r)^T}\right] + \frac{F}{(1 + r)^T} = C \times A_r^T + \frac{F}{(1 + r)^T}$$

where F is typically $1,000 for a level-coupon bond.

Consols

$$PV = \frac{C}{r}$$

6.4 The Present Value of Common Stocks

Dividends Versus Capital Gains

Our goal in this section is to value common stocks. We learned in the previous chapter that an asset's value is determined by the present value of its future cash flows. A stock provides two kinds of cash flows. First, most stocks pay dividends on a regular basis. Second, the shareholder receives the sale price when the stock is sold. Thus, in order to value common stocks, we need to answer an interesting question: Is the value of a stock equal to

1. The discounted present value of the sum of next period's dividend plus next period's stock price, or
2. The discounted present value of all future dividends?

This is the kind of question that students would love to see on a multiple-choice exam because both (1) and (2) are correct.

To see that (1) and (2) are the same, we start with an individual who will buy the stock and hold it for one year. In other words, this investor has a one-year *holding period.* In addition, the investor is willing to pay P_0 for the stock today.

$$P_0 = \frac{\text{Div}_1}{1 + r} + \frac{P_1}{1 + r} \tag{6.1}$$

Div_1 is the dividend paid at year-end and P_1 is the price at year-end. P_0 is the PV of the common stock investment. The term r in the denominator is the discount rate for the stock. It is the required rate of return for investments of similar risk.

That seems easy enough, but where does P_1 come from? P_1 is not pulled out of thin air. Rather, there must be a buyer at the end of year 1 who is willing to purchase the stock for P_1. This buyer determines price by

$$P_1 = \frac{\text{Div}_2}{1 + r} + \frac{P_2}{1 + r} \tag{6.2}$$

Substituting the value of P_1 from (6.2) into Equation (6.1) yields

$$P_0 = \frac{1}{1+r}\left[\text{Div}_1 + \left(\frac{\text{Div}_2 + P_2}{1+r}\right)\right] \tag{6.3}$$

We can ask a similar question for (6.3): Where does P_2 come from? An investor at the end of year 2 is willing to pay P_2 because of the dividend and stock price at year 3. This process can be repeated ad nauseam.[4] At the end, we are left with

$$P_0 = \frac{\text{Div}_1}{1+r} + \frac{\text{Div}_2}{(1+r)^2} + \frac{\text{Div}_3}{(1+r)^3} + \cdots = \sum_{t=1}^{\infty} \frac{\text{Div}_t}{(1+r)^t} \tag{6.4}$$

Thus, the value of a firm's common stock to the investor is equal to the present value of all of the expected future dividends.[5]

This is a very useful result. A common objection to applying present value analysis to stocks is that investors are too shortsighted to care about the long-run stream of dividends. Critics argue that an investor will generally not look past his or her time horizon. Thus, prices in a market dominated by short-term investors will reflect only near-term dividends. However, our discussion shows that a long-run dividend discount model holds even when investors have short-term time horizons. Although an investor may want to cash out early, he or she must find another investor who is willing to buy. The price this second investor pays is dependent on dividends *after* the date of purchase.

Valuation of Different Types of Stocks

The discussion to this point shows that the value of the firm is the present value of its future dividends. How do we apply this idea in practice? Equation (6.4) represents a very general model and is applicable regardless of whether the level of expected dividends is growing, fluctuating, or constant. The general model can be simplified if the firm's dividends are expected to follow any of three basic patterns: (1) zero growth, (2) constant growth, and (3) differential growth. These cases are illustrated in Figure 6.3.

Case 1 (Zero Growth)   The value of a stock with a constant dividend is given by

$$P_0 = \frac{\text{Div}_1}{1+r} + \frac{\text{Div}_2}{(1+r)^2} + \cdots = \frac{\text{Div}}{r}$$

Here it is assumed that $\text{Div}_1 = \text{Div}_2 = \cdots = \text{Div}$. This is just an application of the perpetuity formula of the previous chapter.

Case 2 (Constant Growth)   Dividends grow at rate g, as follows:

End of Year	1	2	3	4	...
Dividend	Div	Div$(1+g)$	Div$(1+g)^2$	Div$(1+g)^3$	

Note that Div is the dividend at the end of the first period.

---

[4]This procedure reminds us of the physicist lecturing on the origins of the universe. He was approached by an elderly gentleman in the audience who disagreed with the lecture. The attendee said that the universe rests on the back of a huge turtle. When the physicist asked what the turtle rested on, the gentleman said another turtle. Anticipating the physicist's objections, the attendee said, "Don't tire yourself out, young fellow. It's turtles all the way down."

[5]The dividend valuation model is often called the Gordon model in honour of Professor Myron Gordon of the University of Toronto, its best-known developer.

FIGURE 6.3

Zero-Growth, Constant-Growth, and Differential-Growth Patterns

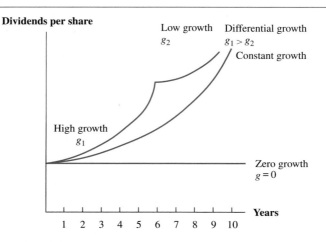

Dividends per share

Low growth g_2 Differential growth $g_1 > g_2$

Constant growth

High growth g_1

Zero growth $g = 0$

Years

1 2 3 4 5 6 7 8 9 10

Dividend-growth models

Zero growth: $P_0 = \dfrac{\text{Div}}{r}$

Constant growth: $P_0 = \dfrac{\text{Div}}{r - g}$

Differential growth: $P_0 = \displaystyle\sum_{t=1}^{T} \dfrac{\text{Div}\,(1 + g_1)^t}{(1 + r)^t} + \dfrac{\dfrac{\text{Div}_{T+1}}{r - g_2}}{(1 + r)^T}$

EXAMPLE 6.3

Canadian Products will pay a dividend of $4 per share a year from now. Financial analysts believe that dividends will rise at 6 percent per year for the foreseeable future. What is the dividend per share at the end of each of the first five yars?

End of Year	1	2	3	4	5
Dividend	$4.00	$4 × (1.06)$ = $4.24	$4 × (1.06)^2$ = $4.4944	$4 × (1.06)^3$ = $4.7641	$4 × (1.06)^4$ = $5.0499

The value of a common stock with dividends growing at a constant rate is

$$P_0 = \frac{\text{Div}}{1 + r} + \frac{\text{Div}(1 + g)}{(1 + r)^2} + \frac{\text{Div}(1 + g)^2}{(1 + r)^3} + \frac{\text{Div}(1 + g)^3}{(1 + r)^4} + \ldots = \frac{\text{Div}}{r - g}$$

where g is the growth rate. Div is the dividend on the stock at the end of the first period. This is the formula for the present value of a growing perpetuity, which we derived in the previous chapter.

EXAMPLE 6.4

Suppose an investor is considering the purchase of a share of the Saskatchewan Mining Company. The stock will pay a $3 dividend a year from today. This dividend is expected to grow at 10 percent per year ($g = 10\%$) for the foreseeable future. The investor thinks that the required return (r) on this stock is 15 percent, given her assessment of Saskatchewan Mining's risk. (We also refer to r as the discount rate of the stock.) What is the value of a share of Saskatchewan Mining Company's stock?

Using the constant growth formula of case 2, we assess the value to be $60:

$$\$60 = \frac{\$3}{0.15 - 0.10}$$

P_0 is quite dependent on the value of g. If g had been estimated to be 12½ percent, the value of the share would have been

$$\$120 = \frac{\$3}{0.15 - 0.125}$$

The stock price doubles (from $60 to $120) when g increases only 25 percent (from 10 percent to 12.5 percent). Because of P_0's dependency on g, one must maintain a healthy sense of skepticism when using this constant growth version of the dividend valuation model.

Furthermore, note that P_0 is equal to infinity when the growth rate, g, equals or exceeds the discount rate, r. Because stock prices do not grow infinitely, an estimate of g greater than r implies an error in estimation. More will be said about this later.

Case 3 (Differential Growth)   In this case, an algebraic formula would be too unwieldy. Instead, we present examples.

EXAMPLE 6.5

Consider the stock of Elixir Drug Company, which has a new back-rub ointment and is enjoying rapid growth. The dividend a year from today will be $1.15. During the next four years, the dividend will grow at 15 percent per year ($g_1 = 15\%$). After that, growth (g_2) will be equal to 10 percent per year. What is the present value of the stock if the required return (r) is 15 percent?

Figure 6.4 displays the growth in the dividends. We need to apply a two-step process to discount these dividends. We first calculate the net present value of the dividends growing at

FIGURE 6.4

Growth in Dividends for Elixir Drug Company

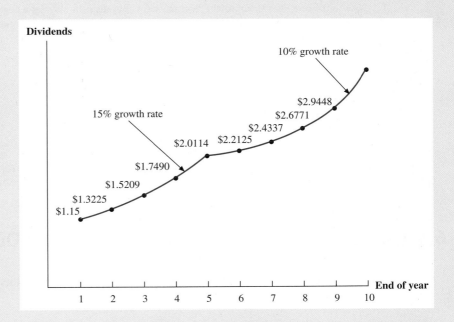

15 percent per annum. That is, we first calculate the present value of the dividends at the end of each of the first five years. Second, we calculate the present value of the dividends beginning at the end of year 6.

Calculate Present Value of First Five Dividends   The present values of dividend payments in years 1 through 5 are

Future Year	Growth Rate (g_1)	Expected Dividend	Present Value
1	0.15	$ 1.15	$1
2	0.15	1.3225	$1
3	0.15	1.5209	$1
4	0.15	1.7490	$1
5	0.15	2.0114	$1
Years 1–5		The present value of dividends =	$5

The growing-annuity formula of the previous chapter could normally be used in this step. However, note that dividends grow at 15 percent, which is also the discount rate. Since $g = r$, the growing-annuity formula cannot be used in this example.

Calculate Present Value of Dividends Beginning at End of Year 6   This is the procedure for deferred perpetuities and deferred annuities that we mentioned in the previous chapter. The dividends beginning at the end of year 6 are

End of Year	6	7	8	9
Dividend	$\text{Div}_5 \times (1 + g_2)$	$\text{Div}_5 \times (1 + g_2)^2$	$\text{Div}_5 \times (1 + g_2)^3$	$\text{Div}_5 \times (1 + g_2)^4$
	$\$2.0114 \times 1.10$	$2.0114 \times (1.10)^2$	$2.0114 \times (1.10)^3$	$2.0114 \times (1.10)^4$
	$= \$2.2125$	$= \$2.4337$	$= \$2.6771$	$= \$2.9448$

As stated in the previous chapter, the growing-perpetuity formula calculates present value as of one year prior to the first payment. Because the payment begins at the end of year 6, the present value formula calculates present value as of the end of year 5. The price at the end of year 5 is given by

$$P_5 = \frac{\text{Div}_6}{r - g_2} = \frac{\$2.2125}{0.15 - 0.10}$$

$$= \$44.25$$

The present value of P_5 at the end of year 0 is

$$\frac{P_5}{(1 + r)^5} = \frac{\$44.25}{(1.15)^5} = \$22$$

The present value of all dividends as of the end of year 0 is $27 (or $22 + $5).

6.5 Estimates of Parameters in the Dividend Discount Model

The value of the firm is a function of its growth rate, g, and its discount rate, r. How does one estimate these variables?

Where Does g Come From?

The previous discussion on stocks assumed that dividends grow at the rate g. We now want to estimate this rate of growth. Consider a business whose earnings next year are expected to be the same as earnings this year unless a *net investment* is made. This situation is likely to occur, because net investment is equal to gross, or total, investment less depreciation. A net investment of zero occurs when *total investment* equals depreciation. If total investment is equal to depreciation, the firm's physical plant is maintained, consistent with no growth in earnings.

Net investment will be positive only if some earnings are not paid out as dividends, that is, only if some earnings are retained.[6] This leads to the following equation:

$$
\underset{\text{Increase in earnings}}{\begin{array}{ccccc}
\begin{array}{c}\text{Earnings}\\\text{next}\\\text{year}\end{array} & = & \begin{array}{c}\text{Earnings}\\\text{this}\\\text{year}\end{array} & + & \underbrace{\begin{array}{c}\text{Retained}\\\text{earnings}\\\text{this year}\end{array} \times \begin{array}{c}\text{Return on}\\\text{retained}\\\text{earnings}\end{array}}
\end{array}} \quad \textbf{(6.5)}
$$

As explained in Chapter 3, the increase in earnings is a function of both the *retained earnings* and the return on the retained earnings.

We now divide both sides of (6.5) by earnings this year, yielding

$$
\frac{\text{Earnings next year}}{\text{Earnings this year}} = \frac{\text{Earnings this year}}{\text{Earnings this year}} + \left(\frac{\begin{array}{c}\text{Retained earings}\\\text{this year}\end{array}}{\text{Earnings this year}} \right) \times \begin{array}{c}\text{Return on}\\\text{retained}\\\text{earnings}\end{array} \quad \textbf{(6.6)}
$$

The left-hand side of (6.6) is simply 1 plus the growth rate in earnings, which we write as $1 + g$.[7] The ratio of retained earnings to earnings is called the retention ratio. Thus, we can write

$$
1 + g = 1 + \text{Retention ratio} \times \text{Return on retained earnings} \quad \textbf{(6.7)}
$$

It is difficult for a financial analyst to determine the return to be expected on currently retained earnings, because the details on forthcoming projects are not generally public information. However, it is frequently assumed that the projects selected in the current year have an anticipated return equal to returns from projects in other years. Here, we can estimate the anticipated return on current retained earnings by the historical **return on equity (ROE)**. After all, ROE is simply the return on the firm's entire equity, which is the return on the cumulation of all the firm's past projects.[8]

From (6.7), we have a simple way to estimate growth:

Formula for Firm's Growth Rate:

$$
g = \text{Retention ratio} \times \text{Return on retained earnings} \quad \textbf{(6.8)}
$$

---

[6]We ignore the possibility of the issuance of stocks or bonds in order to raise capital. These possibilities are considered in later chapters.

[7]Previously g referred to growth in dividends. However, the growth rate in earnings is equal to the growth rate in dividends in this context because, as we will presently see, the ratio of dividends to earnings is held constant.

[8]Students frequently wonder whether return on equity (ROE) or return on assets (ROA) should be used here. ROA and ROE are identical in our model because debt financing is ignored. However, most real-world firms have debt. Because debt is treated in later chapters, we are not yet able to treat this issue in depth now. Suffice it to say that ROE is the appropriate rate, because both ROE for the firm as a whole and the return to equityholders from a future project are calculated after interest has been deducted.

EXAMPLE 6.6

Trent Enterprises just reported earnings of $2 million. It plans to retain 40 percent of its earnings. The historical return on equity (ROE) was 0.16, a figure that is expected to continue into the future. How much will earnings grow over the coming year?

We first perform the calculation without reference to (6.8). Then we use (6.8) as a check.

Calculation Without Reference to Equation (6.8)   The firm will retain $800,000 (or 40% × $2 million). Assuming that historical ROE is an appropriate estimate for future returns, the anticipated increase in earnings is

$$\$800,000 \times 0.16 = \$128,000$$

The percentage growth in earnings is

$$\frac{\text{Change in earnings}}{\text{Total earnings}} = \frac{\$128,000}{\$2 \text{ million}} = 0.064$$

This implies that earnings in one year will be $2,128,000 (or $2,000,000 × 1.064).

Check Using Equation (6.8)   We use g = Retention ratio × ROE. We have

$$g = 0.4 \times 0.16 = 0.064$$

Where Does r Come From?

In this section, we want to estimate r, the rate used to discount the cash flows of a particular stock. There are two methods developed by academics. We present one method below but must defer the second until we give it extensive treatment in later chapters.

The first method begins with the concept that the value of a growing perpetuity is

$$P_0 = \frac{\text{Div}}{r - g}$$

Solving for r, we have

$$r = \frac{\text{Div}}{P_0} + g \tag{6.9}$$

As stated earlier, Div refers to the dividend to be received one year hence.

Thus, the discount rate can be broken into two parts. The ratio, Div/P_0, places the dividend return on a percentage basis, frequently called the *dividend yield*. The second term, g, is the growth rate of dividends.

Because information on both dividends and stock price is publicly available, the first term on the right-hand side of (6.9) can be easily calculated. The second term on the right-hand side, g, can be estimated from (6.8).

EXAMPLE 6.7

Trent Enterprises, the company examined in the previous example, has 1,000,000 shares of stock outstanding. The stock is selling at $10. What is the required return on the stock?

Because the retention ratio is 40 percent, the payout ratio is 60 percent (1 − Retention ratio). The **payout ratio** is the ratio of dividends/earnings. Because earnings one year from now will be $2,128,000 (or $2,000,000 × 1.064), dividends will be $1,276,800 (or 0.60 × $2,128,000). Dividends per share will be $1.28 (or $1,276,800/1,000,000). Given our previous result that $g = 0.064$, we calculate r from (6.9) as follows:

$$0.192 = \frac{\$1.28}{\$10.00} + 0.064$$

A Healthy Sense of Skepticism

It is important to emphasize that our approach merely *estimates g;* it does not determine *g* precisely. We mentioned earlier that our estimate of *g* is based on a number of assumptions. For example, we assume that the return on reinvestment of future retained earnings is equal to the firm's past ROE. We assume that the future retention ratio is equal to the past retention ratio. Our estimate for *g* will be off if these assumptions prove to be wrong.

Unfortunately, the determination of *r* is highly dependent on *g*. In our example, if *g* is estimated to be 0, *r* equals 12.8 percent ($1.28/$10.00). If *g* is estimated to be 12 percent, *r* equals 24.8 percent ($1.28/$10.00 + 12%). Thus, one should view estimates of *r* with a healthy sense of skepticism.

For this reason, some financial economists generally argue that the estimation error for *r* for a single security is too large to be practical. Therefore, they suggest calculating the average *r* for an entire industry. This *r* would then be used to discount the dividends of a particular stock in the same industry.

One should be particularly skeptical of two polar cases when estimating *r* for individual securities. First, consider a firm currently paying no dividend. The stock price will be above zero because investors believe that the firm may initiate a dividend at some point or the firm may be acquired at some point. However, when a firm goes from no dividend to a positive number of dividends, the implied growth rate is *infinite*. Thus, Equation (6.9) must be used with extreme caution here, if at all—a point we emphasize later in this chapter.

Second, we mentioned earlier that the value of the firm is infinite when *g* is equal to *r*. Because prices for stocks do not grow infinitely, an analyst whose estimate of *g* for a particular firm is equal to or above *r* must have made a mistake. Most likely, the analyst's high estimate for *g* is correct for the next few years. However, firms simply cannot maintain an abnormally high growth rate *forever*. The analyst's error was to use a short-run estimate of *g* in a model requiring a perpetual growth rate.

In brief, there are a number of difficulties with using the dividend discount model to determine *r*. In practice, analysts use a number of models including the capital asset pricing model, which we present in Chapters 11 and 13.

6.6 Growth Opportunities

We previously spoke of the growth rate of dividends. We now want to address the related concept of growth opportunities. Imagine a company with a level stream of earnings per share in perpetuity. The company pays all of these earnings out to shareholders as dividends. Hence,

$$EPS = Div$$

where EPS is *earnings per share* and Div is dividend per share. A company of this type is frequently called a *cash cow*.

From the perpetuity formula of the previous chapter, the value of a share of stock is

Value of a Share of Stock When Firm Acts as a Cash Cow:

$$\frac{EPS}{r} = \frac{Div}{r}$$

where *r* is the discount rate on the firm's stock.

The above policy of paying out all earnings as dividends may not be the optimal one. Many firms have *growth* opportunities, that is, opportunities to invest in profitable projects. Because these projects can represent a significant fraction of the firm's value, it would be foolish to forgo them in order to pay out all earnings as dividends.

While firms frequently think in terms of a *set* of growth opportunities, we focus here on only one opportunity, that is, the opportunity to invest in a single project. Suppose the firm retains the entire dividend at date 1 in order to invest in a particular capital budgeting project. The net present value *per share* of the project as of date 0 is *NPVGO*, which stands for the *net present value (per share) of the growth opportunity*.

What is the price of a share of stock at date 0 if the firm decides to take on the project at date 1? Because the per share value of the project is added to the original stock price, the stock price must now be

Stock Price After Firm Commits to New Project:

$$\frac{EPS}{r} + NPVGO \qquad\qquad (6.10)$$

Equation (6.10) indicates that the price of a share of stock can be viewed as the sum of two different items. The first term (EPS/r) is the value of the firm if it rested on its laurels, that is, if it simply distributed all earnings to the shareholders. The second term is the *additional* value if the firm retains earnings in order to fund new projects.

EXAMPLE 6.8

Nova Scotia Shipping Ltd. expects to earn $1 million per year in perpetuity if it undertakes no new investment opportunities. There are 100,000 shares outstanding, so earnings per share equal $10 (or $1,000,000/100,000). The firm will have an opportunity at date 1 to spend $1,000,000 in a new marketing campaign. The new campaign will increase earnings in every subsequent period by $210,000 (or $2.10 per share). This is a 21 percent return per year on the project. The firm's discount rate is 10 percent. What is the value per share before and after deciding to accept the marketing campaign?

The value of a share of Nova Scotia Shipping before the campaign is

Value of a Share of Nova Scotia Shipping When Firm Acts as a Cash Cow:

$$\frac{EPS}{r} = \frac{\$10}{0.1} = \$100$$

The value of the marketing campaign as of date 1 is

Value of Marketing Campaign at Date 1:

$$-\$1,000,000 + \frac{\$210,000}{0.1} = \$1,100,000 \qquad\qquad (6.11)$$

Because the investment is made at date 1 and the first cash inflow occurs at date 2, Equation (6.11) represents the value of the marketing campaign as of date 1. We determine the value at date 0 by discounting back one period as follows:

Value of Marketing Campaign at Date 0:

$$\frac{\$1,100,000}{1.1} = \$1,000,000$$

Thus, NPVGO per share is $10 (or $1,000,000/100,000).

The price per share is

$$EPS/r + NPVGO = \$100 + \$10 = \$110$$

The calculation can also be made on a straight net present value basis. Because all the earnings at date 1 are spent on the marketing effort, no dividends are paid to shareholders at that date. Dividends in all subsequent periods are $1,210,000 (or $1,000,000 + $210,000). In this case, $1,000,000 is the annual dividend when Nova Scotia Shipping is a cash cow. The additional contribution to the dividend from the marketing effort is $210,000. Dividends per share are $12.10 (or $1,210,000/100,000). Because these dividends start at date 2, the price per share at date 1 is $121 (or $12.10/0.1). The price per share at date 0 is $110 (or $121/1.1).

Note that value is created in this example because the project earned a 21 percent rate of return when the discount rate was only 10 percent. No value would have been created had the project earned a 10 percent rate of return—the NPVGO would have been zero. Value would have been negative had the project earned a percentage return below 10 percent—the NPVGO would be negative in that case.

Two conditions must be met in order to increase value:

1. Earnings must be retained so that projects can be funded.[9]
2. The projects must have positive net present value.

Surprisingly, a number of companies seem to invest in projects known to have *negative* net present values. For example, Jensen has pointed out that, in the late 1970s, oil companies and tobacco companies were flush with cash.[10] Due to declining markets in both industries, high dividends and low investment would have been the rational action. Unfortunately, a number of companies in both industries reinvested heavily in what were widely perceived to be negative-NPVGO projects. A study by McConnell and Muscarella documents this perception.[11] They find that, during the 1970s, the stock prices of oil companies generally decreased on the days that announcements of increases in exploration and development were made.

Canada is not immune to the practice of investing in negative-NPV projects. For example, Nortel lost money for investors large and small. Many technology companies have made acquisitions that have subsequently been written down or written off, and therefore have lowered the value of the companies.

Given that NPV analysis (such as that presented in the previous chapter) is common knowledge in business, why would managers choose projects with negative NPVs? Bad judgment and bad luck are two reasons. Another is that some managers enjoy controlling a large company. Because paying dividends in lieu of reinvesting earnings reduces the size of the firm, some managers find it emotionally difficult to pay high dividends.

Growth in Earnings and Dividends Versus Growth Opportunities

As mentioned earlier, a firm's value increases when it invests in growth opportunities with positive NPVGOs. A firm's value falls when it selects opportunities with negative NPVGOs. However, dividends grow whether projects with positive NPVs or negative NPVs are selected. This surprising result can be explained by Example 6.9.

---

[9]Later in the text we discuss issuing stock or debt in order to fund projects.

[10]M. C. Jensen, "Agency Costs of Free Cash Flows, Corporate Finance and Takeovers," *American Economic Review* (May 1986).

[11]J. J. McConnell and C. J. Muscarella, "Corporate Capital Expenditure Decisions and the Market Value of the Firm," *Journal of Financial Economics* 14 (1985).

EXAMPLE 6.9

Lane Supermarkets, a new firm, will earn $100,000 a year in perpetuity if it pays out all its earnings as dividends. However, the firm plans to invest 20 percent of its earnings in projects that earn 10 percent per year. The discount rate is 18 percent. An earlier formula tells us that the growth rate of dividends is

$$g = \text{Retention ratio} \times \text{Return on retained earnings} = 0.2 \times 0.10 = 2\%$$

For example, in this first year of the new policy, dividends are $80,000, calculated from $(1 - 0.2) \times \$100,000$. Dividends next year are $81,600 (or $80,000 × 1.02). Dividends the following year are $83,232 or $80,000 \times (1.02)^2$ and so on. Because dividends represent a fixed percentage of earnings, earnings must grow at 2 percent a year as well.

However, note that the policy reduces value because the rate of return on the projects of 10 percent is less than the discount rate of 18 percent. That is, the firm would have had a higher value at date 0 if it had a policy of paying all its earnings out as dividends. Thus, a policy of investing in projects with negative NPVs rather than paying out earnings as dividends will lead to growth in dividends and earnings, but will reduce value.

Dividends or Earnings: Which to Discount?

As mentioned earlier, this chapter applied the growing-perpetuity formula to the valuation of stocks. In our application, we discounted dividends, not earnings. This is sensible since investors select a stock for the cash flows they can get out of it. They only get two things out of a stock: dividends and the ultimate sales price, which is determined by what future investors expect to receive in dividends.

The calculated stock price would be too high were earnings to be discounted instead of dividends. As we saw in our estimation of a firm's growth rate, only a portion of earnings goes to the shareholders as dividends. The remainder is retained to generate future dividends. In our model, retained earnings are equal to the firm's investment. To discount earnings instead of dividends would be to ignore the investment that a firm must make today in order to generate future returns.

The No-Dividend Firm

Students frequently ask the following question: If the dividend discount model is correct, why are no-dividend stocks not selling at zero? This is a good question that addresses the goals of the firm. A firm with many growth opportunities is faced with a dilemma: The firm can pay out dividends now, or it can forgo current dividends in order to make investments that will generate even greater dividends in the future.[12] This is often a painful choice, because a strategy of dividend deferment may be optimal yet unpopular among certain shareholders.

Many firms choose to pay no dividends—and these firms sell at positive prices.[13] Rational shareholders believe that they will either receive dividends at some point or they will receive something just as good. That is, the firm will be acquired in a merger, with the shareholders receiving either cash or shares in the acquiring firm.

---

[12]A third alternative is to issue stock so that the firm has enough cash both to pay dividends and to invest. This possibility is explored in a later chapter.

[13]For example, tech stocks like Amazon.com and Research in Motion pay no dividends.

Of course, the actual application of the dividend discount model is difficult for firms of this type. Clearly, the model for constant growth of dividends does not apply. Though the differential growth model can work in theory, the difficulties of estimating the date of first dividend, the growth rate of dividends after that date, and the ultimate merger price make application of the model quite difficult in reality.

Empirical evidence suggests that firms with high growth rates are likely to pay lower dividends, a result consistent with the above analysis. For example, consider Rogers Communications Inc. The company started in the 1960s and grew rapidly throughout the decades thereafter. It paid its first dividend in history in July of 2003, though it was a multimillion dollar company prior to that date. Why did it wait so long to pay a dividend? It likely waited because it had so many positive growth opportunities, largely in the form of acquisitions.

Utilities are an interesting contrast because, as a group, historically they have had few growth opportunities. As a result, they pay out a large fraction of their earnings in dividends. For example, Canadian Utilities Limited, Utilicorp United, and Nova Scotia Power have had payout ratios of over 70 percent in many recent years. Today, the utility business is getting more exciting as deregulation allows companies to diversify into new businesses. This suggests utility payout ratios may fall.

6.7 The Dividend Growth Model and the NPVGO Model (Advanced)

This chapter has revealed that the price of a share of stock is the sum of its price as a cash cow plus the per share value of its growth opportunities. The Nova Scotia Shipping example illustrated this formula using only one growth opportunity. We also used the growing perpetuity formula to price a stock with a steady growth in dividends. When the formula is applied to stocks, it is typically called the *dividend growth model*. A steady growth in dividends results from a continual investment in growth opportunities, not just investment in a single opportunity. Therefore, it is worthwhile to compare the dividend growth model with the *NPVGO model* when growth occurs through continual investing.

EXAMPLE 6.10

Prairie Book Publishers has EPS of $10 at the end of the first year, a dividend payout ratio of 40 percent, a discount rate of 16 percent, and a return on its retained earnings of 20 percent. Because the firm retains some of its earnings each year, it is selecting growth opportunities each year. This is different from Nova Scotia Shipping, which had a growth opportunity in only one year. We wish to calculate the price per share using both the dividend growth model and the NPVGO model.

The Dividend Growth Model

The dividends at date 1 are $0.40 \times \$10 = \$4$ per share. The retention ratio is 0.60 (or $1 - 0.40$), implying a growth rate in dividends of 0.12 (or 0.60×0.20).

From the dividend growth model, the price of a share of stock is

$$\frac{\text{Div}}{r - g} = \frac{\$4}{0.16 - 0.12} = \$100$$

The NPVGO Model

Using the NPVGO model, it is more difficult to value a firm with growth opportunities each year (like Prairie) than a firm with growth opportunities in only one year (like Nova Scotia Shipping). In order to value according to the NPVGO model, we need to calculate on a per share basis (1) the net present value of a single growth opportunity, (2) the net present value of all growth opportunities, and (3) the stock price if the firm acts as a cash cow, that is, the value of the firm without these growth opportunities. The value of the firm is the sum of (2) + (3).

1. *Value Per Share of a Single Growth Opportunity.* Out of the earnings per share of $10 at date 1, the firm retains $6 (or $0.6 \times \$10$) at that date. The firm earns $1.20 (or $\$6 \times 0.20$) per year in perpetuity on that $6 investment. The NPV from the investment is

Per Share NPV Generated from Investment at Date 1:

$$-\$6 + \frac{\$1.20}{0.16} = \$1.50 \tag{6.12}$$

That is, the firm invests $6 in order to reap $1.20 per year on the investment. The earnings are discounted at 0.16, implying a value per share from the project of $1.50. Because the investment occurs at date 1 and the first cash flow occurs at date 2, $1.50 is the value of the investment at *date 1*. In other words, the NPV from the date 1 investment has *not* yet been brought back to date 0.

2. *Value Per Share of All Opportunities.* As pointed out earlier, the growth rate of earnings and dividends is 12 percent. Because retained earnings are a fixed percentage of total earnings, retained earnings must also grow at 12 percent a year. That is, retained earnings at date 2 are $6.72 (or $\$6 \times 1.12$), retained earnings at date 3 are $7.5264 [or $\$6 \times (1.12)^2$], and so on.

Let's analyze the retained earnings at date 2 in more detail. Because projects will always earn 20 percent per year, the firm earns $1.344 (or $\$6.72 \times 0.20$) in each future year on the $6.72 investment at date 2.

The NPV from the investment is

NPV Per Share Generated from Investment at Date 2:

$$-\$6.72 + \frac{\$1.344}{0.16} = \$1.68 \tag{6.13}$$

$1.68 is the NPV as of date 2 of the investment made at date 2. The NPV from the date 2 investment has *not* yet been brought back to date 0.

Now consider the retained earnings at date 3 in more detail. The firm earns $1.5053 (or $\$7.5264 \times 0.20$) per year on the investment of $7.5264 at date 3. The NPV from the investment is

NPV Per Share Generated from Investment at Date 3:

$$-\$7.5264 + \frac{\$1.5053}{0.16} = \$1.882 \tag{6.14}$$

From (6.12), (6.13), and (6.14), the NPV per share of all of the growth opportunities, discounted back to date 0, is

$$\frac{\$1.50}{1.16} + \frac{\$1.68}{(1.16)^2} + \frac{\$1.882}{(1.16)^3} + \cdots \tag{6.15}$$

Because it has an infinite number of terms, this expression looks quite difficult to compute. However, there is an easy simplification. Note that retained earnings are growing at 12 percent per year. Because all projects earn the same rate of return per year, the NPVs in (6.12), (6.13), and (6.14) are also growing at 12 percent per year. Hence, we can rewrite (6.15) as

$$\frac{\$1.50}{1.16} + \frac{\$1.50 \times 1.12}{(1.16)^2} + \frac{\$1.50 \times (1.12)^2}{(1.16)^3} + \ldots$$

This is a growing perpetuity whose value is

$$\text{NPVGO} = \frac{\$1.50}{0.16 - 0.12} = \$37.50$$

Because the first NPV of $1.50 occurs at date 1, the NPVGO is $37.50 as of date 0. In other words, the firm's policy of investing in new projects from retained earnings has an NPV of $37.50.

3. *Value Per Share If Firm Is a Cash Cow.* We now assume that the firm pays out all of its earnings as dividends. The dividends would be $10 per year in this case. Since there would be no growth, the value per share would be evaluated by the perpetuity formula:

$$\frac{\text{Div}}{r} = \frac{\$10}{0.16} = \$62.50$$

Summation

Equation (6.10) states that value per share is the value of a cash cow plus the value of the growth opportunities. This is

$$\$100 = \$62.50 + \$37.50$$

Hence, value is the same whether calculated by a discounted-dividend approach or a growth opportunities approach. The share prices from the two approaches must be equal, because the approaches are different yet equivalent methods of applying concepts of present value.

6.8 Price–Earnings Ratio

We argued earlier that one should not discount earnings in order to determine price per share. Nevertheless, financial analysts frequently relate earnings and price per share, as made evident by their heavy reliance on the price–earnings (or P/E) ratio. Their logic is that earnings provide the basis for dividends and capital gains.

Our previous discussion stated that

$$\text{Price per share} = \frac{\text{EPS}}{r} + \text{NPVGO}$$

Dividing by EPS yields

$$\frac{\text{Price per share}}{\text{EPS}} = \frac{1}{r} + \frac{\text{NPVGO}}{\text{EPS}}$$

The left-hand side is the formula for the price–earnings ratio. The equation shows that the P/E ratio is related to the net present value of growth opportunities. As an example, consider two firms, each having just reported earnings per share of $1. However, one firm has many valuable growth opportunities while the other firm has no growth opportunities at all. The firm with growth opportunities should sell at a higher price, because an investor is buying both current income of $1 and growth opportunities. Suppose that the firm with growth opportunities sells for $16 and the other firm sells for $8. The $1 earnings per share number appears in the denominator of the P/E ratio for both firms. Thus, the P/E ratio is 16 for the firm with growth opportunities, but only 8 for the firm without the opportunities.

This explanation seems to hold fairly well in the real world. Biotech and other high-tech stocks generally sell at very high P/E ratios (or *multiples,* as they are often called) because they are perceived to have high growth rates. For example, in November 2006, Research in Motion traded at a P/E of 56. In fact, some technology stocks sell at high prices even though the companies have never earned a profit. The P/E ratios of these companies are infinite. Conversely, utilities and financial services companies sell at lower multiples because of the prospects of lower growth.

Of course, the market is merely pricing *perceptions* of the future, not the future itself. We will argue later in the text that the stock market generally has realistic perceptions of a firm's prospects. However, this is not always true. In the late 1960s, many electronics firms were selling at multiples of 200 times earnings. The high perceived growth rates did not materialize, causing great declines in stock prices during the early 1970s. In earlier decades, fortunes were made in stocks like IBM and Xerox because the high growth rates were not anticipated by investors.

There are two additional factors explaining the P/E ratio. The first is the discount rate, *r.* The above formula shows that the P/E ratio is *negatively* related to the firm's discount rate. We have already suggested that the discount rate is positively linked to the stock's risk or variability. Thus, the P/E ratio is negatively related to the stock's risk. To see that this is a sensible result, consider two firms, *A* and *B,* behaving as cash cows. The stock market *expects* both firms to have annual earnings of $1 per share forever. However, the earnings of firm *A* are known with certainty while the earnings of firm *B* are quite variable. A rational shareholder is likely to pay more for a share of firm *A* because of the absence of risk. If a share of firm *A* sells at a higher price and both firms have the same EPS, the P/E ratio of firm *A* must be higher.

The second additional factor concerns the firm's choice of accounting methods. Under current accounting rules, companies are given a fair amount of leeway. For example, consider depreciation accounting where many different methods may be used. A firm's choice of depreciation method can increase or decrease its earnings in different years. Similar accounting leeway exists for construction costs (completed-contracts versus percentage-of-completion methods).

As an example, consider two identical firms: *C* and *D*. Firm *C* uses straight-line depreciation and reports earnings of $2 per share. Firm *D* uses declining-balance depreciation and reports earnings of $3 per share. The market knows that the two firms are identical and prices both at $18 per share. This price–earnings ratio is 9 (or $18/$2) for firm *C* and 6 (or $18/$3) for firm *D*. Thus, the firm with the more conservative principles has a higher P/E ratio.

This last example depends on the assumption that the market sees through differences in accounting treatments. A significant portion of the academic community believes this, adhering to the hypothesis of *efficient capital markets,* a theory that we explore in great detail later in the text. Though many financial people might be more moderate in their beliefs regarding this issue, the consensus view is certainly that many of the accounting differences are seen through. Thus, the proposition that firms with conservative accountants have high P/E ratios is widely accepted.

In summary, our discussion argued that the P/E ratio is a function of three different factors. A company's ratio or multiple is likely to be high if (1) it has many growth opportunities, (2) it has low risk (reflected in a low discount rate), and (3) its accounting is conservative. While each of the three factors is important, it is our opinion that the first factor is the most important. Thus, our discussion of growth is quite relevant in understanding price–earnings multiples.

During the tech "bubble" of 1999 and early 2000, Internet stocks like Yahoo and Research in Motion were trading at P/Es over 1000! Clearly the P/E analysis we present could never explain these prices in terms of growth opportunities. Some analysts who recommended buying these stocks developed new measures to justify their recommendation. On the other side, many analysts believed that the market had lost touch with reality. To these analysts, Internet stock prices were the result of speculative fever.

By 2001, it was clear the pessimists were correct that tech stocks were overvalued. Investment dealers on Wall Street and Bay Street were establishing rules to curb possible conflicts of interest on the part of overenthusiastic analysts. Around the same time, a New

York investor brought a lawsuit against Merrill Lynch and its star Internet analyst. Merrill Lynch settled out of court without admitting any wrongdoing. The claim criticized "newly minted 'valuation criteria' [that] justify widely inflated price targets and 'buy' recommendations for Internet and technology companies with no profits expected for years."

? **Concept Questions**
- **What are the three factors determining a firm's P/E ratio?**
- **How does each affect the P/E and why?**

6.9 Stock Market Reporting

Financial newspapers publish information on a large number of stocks in several different markets. Figure 6.5 produces sample stock listings for the Toronto Stock Exchange (TSX) for November 16, 2006. In Figure 6.5, locate the line for Telus Corporation (TELUS). The first two numbers, 65.60 and 42.62, are the high and low prices for the last 52 weeks. Stock prices are quoted in decimals.

The number $1.50 is the annual dividend rate. Since Telus, like most companies, pays dividends quarterly, this $1.50 is actually the last quarterly dividend multiplied by 4. So the last cash dividend was $1.50/4 = $0.375. Jumping ahead a bit, the column labelled "Yld %" gives the dividend yield based on the current dividend and the closing price. For Telus this is $1.50/57.10 = 2.6% as shown.

FIGURE 6.5

Sample Stock Market Quotation

52 Week High	52 Week Low	Company	Ticker	Div	Yld %	P/E	Volume	High	Low	Close	Net Chg
104.30	100.00	TD Mortgage Invt Corp	TDB.M	$64.60	64.3	–	120	100.40	100.40	100.40	–1
65.60	42.62	TELUS Corp	T	$1.50	2.6	20.5	737,884	57.59	56.65	57.10	–0.07
54.50	36.65	TSX Group Inc	X	$1.32	2.9	25.1	218,389	46.24	45.42	45.64	–0.17
5.25	2.50	TUSK Energy Corp	TSK	–	–	–	537,900	2.85	2.55	2.55	0.04
105.00	98.75	Taiga Building Prods Ltd	TBL.NT	–	–	–	1,250	99.00	99.00	99.00	21
24.84	16.12	Talisman Energy Inc	TLM	$0.15	0.8	11.2	6,670,658	18.61	17.90	17.99	20.32
4.66	1.85	Taseko Mines Ltd	TKO	–	–	9	467,304	2.80	2.59	2.60	20.09
16.61	8.30	Tenke Mining Corp	TNK	–	–	–	122,626	13.09	12.72	12.99	0.17
11.05	7.71	Teranet Income Fund	TF.UN	$0.75	8.3	–	1,689,841	9.25	8.91	9.00	0.01
3.34	0.95	Theratechnologies Inc	TH	–	–	–	76,985	3.00	2.86	2.99	20.01
47.91	39.40	Thomson Corp	TOC	0.88	2.1	27.3	482,790	47.91	47.45	47.63	0.06
12.75	5.04	Thunder Energy Trust	THY.UN	$1.44	27.1	75.9	579,200	5.93	5.31	5.31	20.21
0.20	0.07	Thundermin Resources Inc	THR	–	–	–	21,041	0.08	0.08	0.08	0
37.99	26.67	Tim Hortons Inc	THI	$0.28	0.8	24.1	327,657	34.18	33.38	33.70	20.27
0.50	0.20	Timminco Ltd	TIM	–	–	–	2,000	0.27	0.27	0.27	20.02
0.56	0.16	Tiomin Resources Inc	TIO	–	–	–	460,525	0.24	0.23	0.23	0
0.09	0.03	Tiomin Resources Inc	TIO.WT	–	–	–	100,000	0.05	0.05	0.05	0.01
7.55	4.00	Titan Exploration Ltd	TTN.A	–	–	22.4	684,825	4.55	4.25	4.25	20.34
2.20	0.57	Tm Bioscience Corp	TMC	–	–	–	55,320	0.89	0.81	0.81	20.06
27.15	20.08	Toromont Industries Ltd	TIH	$0.40	1.7	16.6	84,569	23.24	22.45	23.24	0.68
67.94	55.62	TD Bank	TD	$1.92	2.8	11	1,401,128	67.94	67.21	67.75	0.46
28.50	26.90	TD Bank	TD.PR.N	$1.15	4.2	–	314	27.58	27.50	27.50	0.18
26.39	25.00	TD Bank	TD.PR.O	$1.21	4.6	–	35,990	26.25	26.15	26.18	0.07
4.60	3.27	Trafalgar Energy Ltd	TFL	–	–	–	27,626	4.15	4.05	4.15	0.1
26.91	21.88	TransAlta Corp	TA	$1.00	4.2	18.7	639,789	23.66	23.34	23.54	0.03
26.28	24.96	TransAlta Corp	TA.PR.C	$1.94	7.7	–	5,300	25.34	25.25	25.30	20.05
10.10	6.05	TransAlta Power LP	TPW.UN	$0.80	11.1	–	204,494	7.23	7.10	7.16	20.04
28.60	17.30	Transat AT Inc	TRZ.B	$0.28	1	14.7	104,664	28.50	28.25	28.49	0.05
39.12	30.77	TransCanada Corp	TRP	$1.28	3.3	16.7	1,964,450	39.12	38.19	38.83	0.62
55.50	51.10	TransCanada PipeLines Ltd	TCA.PR.X	$2.80	5.1	–	1,000	54.84	54.70	54.84	0.04
55.40	51.25	TransCanada PipeLines Ltd	TCA.PR.Y	$2.80	5.1	–	3,450	54.91	54.80	54.80	20.07
19.85	12.50	TransForce Income Fund	TIF.UN	$1.53	11	8.6	243,818	13.95	13.35	13.89	0.63
7.35	4.50	TransGlobe Energy Corp	TGL	–	–	11	28,700	5.80	5.55	5.55	20.1
1.09	0.40	Transition Therapeutics	TTH	–	–	–	2,055,553	1.00	0.96	1.00	0.03
11.55	9.94	Tremont Capital Opport Tr	TT.UN	–	–	14.5	500	10.26	10.26	10.26	0.01
3.75	2.25	Trimin Capital Corp	TMN	–	–	–	7,300	3.12	3.11	3.11	0.01
19.34	11.03	Trinidad Energy Svcs Incm	TDG.UN	$1.38	11.1	8.8	1,067,264	13.10	12.23	12.45	20.21
9.88	4.86	TriStar Oil & Gas Ltd	TOG	–	–	–	98,224	6.19	5.81	5.83	20.18
21.85	7.50	True Energy Trust	TUI.UN	$2.16	26.7	15.8	904,050	8.50	8.02	8.08	20.12
103.00	92.00	True Energy Trust	TUI.DB	–	–	–	570	93.75	92.00	92.00	22
1.22	0.80	Tucows Inc	TC	–	–	21	20,051	0.96	0.96	0.96	20.02
18.80	11.15	Tundra Semiconductor Corp	TUN	–	–	27.9	15,475	13.40	13.10	13.10	20.22

Source: www.canada.com/nationalpost, November 16, 2006. Used with permission.

The High, Low, and Close figures are the high, low, and closing prices during the day. The "Net Chg" of −0.07 tells us that the closing price of $57.10 per share is $0.07 lower than the closing price the day before.

The column labelled P/E (short for price/earnings or P/E ratio), is the closing price of $57.10 divided by annual earnings per share (based on the most recent full fiscal year). In the jargon of Bay Street, we might say that Telus "sells for 20.5 times earnings."

The remaining column, "Volume," tells how many shares traded during the reported day. For example, 737,884 shares changed hands. The dollar volume of transactions was on the order of $57.10 × 737,884 = $42,133,176 worth of Telus stock.

6.10 SUMMARY AND CONCLUSIONS

In this chapter we use general present-value formulas from the previous chapter to price bonds and stock.

1. Pure discount bonds and perpetuities are the polar cases of bonds. The value of a pure discount bond (also called a *zero-coupon bond* or simply a *zero*) is

$$PV = \frac{F}{(1+r)^T}$$

The value of a perpetuity (also called a *consol*) is

$$PV = \frac{C}{r}$$

2. Level-payment bonds represent an intermediate case. The coupon payments form an annuity and the principal repayment is a lump sum. The value of this type of bond is simply the sum of the values of its two parts.

3. The yield to maturity on a bond is that single rate that discounts the payments on the bond to its purchase price.

4. A stock can be valued by discounting its dividends. We mention three types of situations:
   a. The case of zero growth of dividends.
   b. The case of constant growth of dividends.
   c. The case of differential growth.

5. An estimate of the growth rate of a stock is needed for cases (4b) or (4c) above. A useful estimate of the growth rate is

$$g = \text{Retention ratio} \times \text{Return on retained earnings}$$

6. It is worthwhile to view a share of stock as the sum of its worth if the company behaves as a cash cow (the company does no investing) and the value per share of its growth opportunities. We write the value of a share as

$$\frac{EPS}{r} + NPVGO$$

We show that, in theory, share price must be the same whether the dividend growth model or the above formula is used.

7. From accounting, we know that earnings are divided into two parts: dividends and retained earnings. Most firms continually retain earnings in order to create future dividends. One should not discount earnings to obtain price per share since part of earnings must be reinvested. Only dividends reach the shareholders and only they should be discounted to obtain share price.

8. We suggested that a firm's price–earnings ratio is a function of three factors:

  a. The per share amount of the firm's valuable growth opportunities.

  b. The risk of the stock.

  c. The conservatism of the accounting methods used by the firm.

KEY TERMS

Clean price 135
Coupons 133
Dirty price 135
Discount 136
Face value 133

Holding-period
  return 137
Maturity date 132
Payout ratio 144

Premium 137
Pure discount bond 132
Return on equity (ROE) 143
Yield to maturity 137

SUGGESTED READING

The best place to look for additional information is in investment textbooks. Some good ones are:

Z. Bodie, A. Kane, A. Marcus, S. Perrakis, and P. J. Ryan. *Investments.* 5th Canadian ed. Whitby, Ontario: McGraw-Hill Ryerson, 2005.

W. F. Sharpe, G. J. Alexander, J. W. Bailey, D. J. Fowler and D. Domian. *Investments.* 3rd Canadian ed. Scarborough, Ont.: Prentice-Hall, 2000.

For more on tech stocks, see:

G. Athanassakos. "Valuation of Internet Stocks." *Canadian Investment Review* (Summer 2000).

QUESTIONS & PROBLEMS

Valuing Bonds

6.1   What is the price of a 10-year, pure discount bond paying $1,000 at maturity if the YTM is
  a. 5 percent
  b. 10 percent
  c. 15 percent

6.2   Microhard has issued a bond with the following characteristics:

  Par: $1,000

  Time to maturity: 20 years

  Coupon rate: 8 percent

  Semiannual payments

  Calculate the price of this bond if the YTM is
  a. 8 percent
  b. 10 percent
  c. 6 percent

6.3   Raines Umbrella Corp. issued 12-year bonds two years ago at a coupon rate of 8.6 percent. The bonds make semiannual payments. If these bonds currently sell for 97 percent of par value, what is the YTM?

6.4   Miller Corporation has a premium bond making semiannual payments. The bond pays an 8 percent coupon, has a YTM of 6 percent, and has 13 years to maturity. The Modigliani Company has a discount bond making semiannual payments. This bond pays a 6 percent coupon, has a YTM of 8 percent, and also has 13 years to maturity. If interest rates remain unchanged, what do you expect the price of these bonds to be one year from now? In 3 years? In 8 years? In 12 years? In 13 years? What's going on here? Illustrate your answers by graphing bond prices versus time to maturity.

6.5   Petty Co. wants to issue new 20-year bonds for some much-needed expansion projects. The company currently has 8 percent coupon bonds on the market that sell for $1,095, make semiannual payments, and mature in 20 years. What coupon rate should the company set on its new bonds if it wants them to sell at par?

Visit us at www.mcgrawhill.ca/olc/ross

6.6   The East Winnipeg Mining Corporation has two different bonds currently outstanding. Bond M has a face value of $20,000 and matures in 20 years. The bond makes no payments for the first six years, then pays $1,200 every six months over the subsequent eight years, and finally pays $1,500 every six months over the last six years. Bond N also has a face value of $20,000 and a maturity of 20 years; it makes no coupon payments over the life of the bond. If the required return on both these bonds is 10 percent compounded semiannually, what is the current price of Bond M? Of Bond N?

Bond Concepts

6.7   Bond P is a premium bond with a 10 percent coupon. Bond D is a 6 percent coupon bond currently selling at a discount. Both bonds make annual payments, have a YTM of 8 percent, and have five years to maturity. What is the current yield for Bond P? For Bond D? If interest rates remain unchanged, what is the expected capital gains yield over the next year for Bond P? For Bond D? Explain your answers and the interrelationship among the various types of yields.

EXCEL

6.8   The YTM on a bond is the interest rate you earn on your investment if interest rates don't change. If you actually sell the bond before it matures, your realized return is known as the holding period yield (HPY).
  a.   Suppose that today you buy an 8 percent annual coupon bond for $1,150. The bond has 10 years to maturity. What rate of return do you expect to earn on your investment?
  b.   Two years from now, the YTM on your bond has declined by 1 percent, and you decide to sell. What price will your bond sell for? What is the HPY on your investment? Compare this yield to the YTM when you first bought the bond. Why are they different?

6.9   BetterSoft Software has 8.4 percent coupon bonds on the market with nine years to maturity. The bonds make semiannual payments and currently sell for 104 percent of par. What is the current yield on the bonds? The YTM? The effective annual yield?

6.10   Consider 2 bonds, A and B. The coupon rates are 10 percent and the face values are $1,000 for both bonds. Both bonds have annual coupons. Bond A has 15 years to maturity while bond B has 25 years to maturity.
  a.   What are the prices of the two bonds if the relevant market interest rate for both bonds is 11 percent?
  b.   If the market interest rate increases 12.9 percent, what will be the prices of the two bonds?
  c.   If the market interest rate decreases to 7.6 percent, what will be the prices of the two bonds?

6.11   Company Gold Inc. has two different bonds currently outstanding. Bond A has a face value of $40,000 and matures in five years. The bond makes no payments for the first three years, and pays $3,500 semiannually for the last two years. Bond B also has a face value of $40,000 and matures in 10 years. However, it makes no payments over the life of the bond. If the stated annual interest rate is 12 percent, compounded semiannually,
  a.   What is the current price of Bond A?
  b.   What is the current price of Bond B? What would be the price of Bond B if it matures in 5 years?

The Value of Common Stocks

6.12   The Brenner Co. just paid a dividend of $1.40 per share on its stock. The dividends are expected to grow at a constant rate of 6 percent per year indefinitely. If investors require a 12 percent return on the Brenner Co. stock, what is the current price? What will the price be in three years? In 15 years?

6.13   The next dividend payment by PUG Inc. will be $3.10 per share. The dividends are anticipated to maintain a 5 percent growth rate forever. If PUG stock currently sells for $48.00 per share, what is the required return?

6.14   The Warn Buffet Corporation will pay a $3.60 per share dividend next year. The company pledges to increase its dividend by 4.5 percent per year indefinitely. If you require a 13 percent return on your investment, how much will you pay for the company's stock today?

6.15   Consider the stock of H. David & Son, which will pay an annual dividend of $2 on year from today. The dividend will grow at a constant rate of 6.3 percent, forever. The market requires a 14 percent return on the company's stock.
a. What is the current price of a share of the stock?
b. What will be the stock price be 10 years from today?

6.16   Supposed Amsterdam Farms Inc. has just paid a dividend of $1.25 per share. Its dividend is expected to grow at 5 percent per year for the next seven years and 2 percent per annum every year after that. If the required return is 13.5 percent, what is the expected value of Amsterdam Farms?

6.17   In order to buy back its own shares, Pennzoil Co. has decided to suspend dividends for the next four years. It will resume its annual cash dividend of $2.80 in year 5 and 6. Thereafter, its dividend payments will grow at an annual growth rate of 6 percent, forever. The required rate of return on Pennzoil's stock is 21 percent. According to the discount dividend model, what should Pennzoil's current share price be?

6.18   The Gordon Corporation has just paid a dividend of $6.90 a share. The company will increase its dividend by 8 percent next year. The company will then reduce its dividend growth rate by 1.5 percent each year until the dividend reaches the industry average of 5 percent growth. The company will maintain that dividend growth rate, forever. The required rate of return for the Gordon Corporation is 17 percent. What is the price of the stock?

Estimates of Parameters in the Dividend Discount Model

6.19   Suppose you know that a company's stock currently sells for $70 per share and the required return on the stock is 12 percent. You also know that the total return on the stock is evenly divided between a capital gains yield and a dividend yield. If it's the company's policy to always maintain a constant growth rate in its dividends, what is the current dividend per share?

6.20   Corn Inc. has an odd dividend policy. The company has just paid a dividend of $9 per share and has announced that it will increase the dividend by $3 per share for each of the next four years, and then never pay another dividend. If you require an 11 percent return on the company's stock, how much will you pay for a share today?

6.21   South Side Corporation is expected to pay the following dividends over the next four years: $8, $6, $3, and $2. Afterward the company pledges to maintain a constant 5 percent growth rate in dividends forever. If the required return on the stock is 13 percent, what is the current share price?

6.22   Hollin Corporation stock currently sells for $50 per share. The market requires a 14 percent return on the firm's stock. If the company maintains a constant 8 percent growth rate in dividends, what was the most recent dividend per share paid on the stock?

6.23   ExCo Inc. is expected to pay equal dividends at the end of each of the next two years. Thereafter, the dividend will grow at a constant annual rate of 4 percent forever. The current stock price is $30. What is next year's dividend payment if the required rate of return is 12 percent?

6.24   Most corporations pay quarterly rather than annual dividends on their common stock. Barring any unusual circumstances during the year, the board raises, lowers, or maintains the current dividend once a year and then pays this dividend out in equal quarterly installments to its shareholders.

a. Suppose a company currently pays a $3.00 annual dividend on its common stock in a single annual installment, and management plans on raising this dividend by 6 percent per year indefinitely. If the required return on this stock is 14 percent, what is the current share price?

b. Now suppose that the company in (a) actually pays its annual dividend in equal quarterly installments; thus this company has just paid a $.75 dividend per share, as it has for the previous three quarters. What is your value for the current share price now? (*Hint:* Find the equivalent annual end-of-year dividend for each year.) Comment on whether you think that this model of stock valuation is appropriate.

6.25 Juggernaut Satellite Corporation earned $10 million for the fiscal year ending yesterday. The firm also paid out 25 percent of its earnings as dividends yesterday. The firm will continue to pay out 25 percent of its earnings as annual, end-of-year dividends. The remaining 75 percent of earnings is retained by the company for use in projects. The company has 1.25 million shares of common stock outstanding. The current stock price is $40. The historical return on equity (ROE) of 11 percent is expected to continue in the future. What is the required rate of return on the stock?

EXCEL

6.26 Four years ago, Bling Diamond Inc. paid a dividend of $.90 per share. Bling paid a dividend of $1.66 per share yesterday. Dividends will grow over the next five years at the same rate they grew over the last four years. Thereafter dividends will grow at 8 percent per year. The required return on the stock is 18 percent. What will Bling Diamond's cash dividend be in seven years?

Growth Opportunities

6.27 Rite Bite Enterprises sells toothpicks. Gross revenues last year were $3 million, and total costs were $1.5 million. Rite Bite has 1 million shares of common stock outstanding. Gross revenues and costs are expected to grow at 5 percent per year. Rite Bite pays no income taxes. All earnings are paid out as dividends.

a. If the appropriate discount rate is 15 percent and all cash flows are received at year's end, what is the price per share of Rite Bite stock?

b. Rite Bite has decided to produce toothbrushes. The project requires an immediate outlay of $15 million. In one year, another outlay of $5 million will be needed. The year after that, earnings will increase by $6 million. That profit level will be maintained in perpetuity. What effect will undertaking this project have on the price per share of the stock?

6.28 The Stambaugh Corporation currently has earnings per share of $7.00. The company has no growth and pays out all earnings as dividends. It has a new project that will require an investment of $1.75 per share in one year. The project will only last two years and will increase earnings in the two years following the investment by $1.90 and $2.10, respectively. Investors require a 12 percent return on Stambaugh stock.

a. What is the value per share of the company's stock assuming the firm does not undertake the investment opportunity?

b. If the company does undertake the investment, what is the value per share now?

c. Again assume the company undertakes the investment. What will the price per share be four years from today?

6.29 Newfoundland Real Estate Inc. expects to earn $110 million per year in perpetuity if it does not undertake any new projects. The firm has an opportunity to invest $12 million today and $7 million in one year in real estate. The new investment will generate annual earnings of $10 million in perpetuity, beginning two years from today. The firm has 20 million shares of common stock outstanding, and the required rate of return on the stock is 15 percent. Land investments are not depreciable. Ignore taxes.

a. What is the price of a share of stock if the firm does not undertake the new investment?

b. What is the value of the investment?

c. What is the per-share stock price if the firm undertakes the investment?

6.30 The annual earnings of Avalanche Skis Inc. will be $5 per share in perpetuity if the firm makes no new investments. Under such a situation the firm would pay out all of its earnings as dividends. Assume the first dividend will be received exactly one year from now. Alternatively, assume that three years from now, and in every subsequent year in perpetuity, the company can invest 25 percent of its earnings in new projects. Each project will earn 40 percent at year-end in perpetuity. The firm's discount rate is 14 percent.

    a. What is the price per share of Avalanche Skis Inc. stock today without the company making the new investment?

    b. If Avalanche announces that the new investment will be made, what will the per-share stock price be today?

6.31 Shane Inc. has earnings of $10 million and is projected to grow at a constant rate of 5 percent forever because of the benefits gained from the learning curve. Currently all earnings are paid out as dividends. The company plans to launch a new project two years from now that would be completely internally funded and require 20 percent of the earnings that year. The project would start generating revenues one year after the launch of the project, and the earnings from the new project in any year are estimated to be constant at $5 million. The company has 10 million shares of stock outstanding. Estimate the value of Shane stock. The discount rate is 10 percent.

Price–Earnings Ratio

6.32 Lewin Skis Inc. (today) expects to earn $6 per share for each of the future operating periods (beginning at time 1) if the firm makes no new investments and returns the earnings as dividends to the shareholders. However, Clint Williams, president and CEO, has discovered an opportunity to retain and invest 30 percent of the earnings beginning three years from today. This opportunity to invest will continue for each period indefinitely. He expects to earn 12 percent on this new equity investment, the return beginning one year after each investment is made. The firm's equity discount rate is 14 percent throughout.

    a. What is the price per share of Lewin Skis Inc. stock without making the new investment?

    b. If the new investment is expected to be made, per the preceding information, what would the price of the stock be now?

    c. Suppose the company could increase the investment in the project by whatever amount it chose. What would the retention ratio need to be to make this project attractive?

6.33 Consider Pacific Energy Company and U.S. Bluechips Inc. both of which reported earnings of $800,000. Without new projects, both firms will continue to generate earnings of $800,000 in perpetuity. Assume that all earnings are paid as dividends and that both firms require a 15 percent rate of return.

    a. What is the current PE ratio for each company?

    b. Pacific Energy Company has a new project that will generate additional earnings of $100,000 each year in perpetuity. Calculate the new PE ratio of the company.

    c. U.S. Bluechips has a new project that will increase by $200,000 in perpetuity. Calculate the new PE ratio of the firm.

Valuation of Stocks

6.34 Enter the ticker symbol "FD" for Federal Department Stores. Using the most recent balance sheet and income statement under the "Excel Analytics" link, calculate the sustainable growth rate for Sears. Now download the "Mthly. Adj. Price" and find the closing stock price for the same month as the balance sheet and income statement you used. What is the implied return on Sears according to the dividend growth model? Does this number make sense? Why or why not?

MINICASE: Stock Valuation at Ragan Thermal Systems

Ragan Thermal Systems Inc. was founded nine years ago by brother and sister Carrington and Genevieve Ragan. The company manufactures and installs commercial heating, ventilation, and air conditioning (HVAC) units. Ragan has experienced rapid growth because of a proprietary technology that increases the energy efficiency of its systems. The company is equally owned by Carrington and Genevieve. The original agreement between the siblings gave each 50,000 shares of stock.

In the event either wished to sell the stock, the shares first had to be offered to the other at a discounted price. Although neither sibling wants to sell any shares at this time, they have decided they should value their holdings in the company for financial planning purposes. To accomplish this, they have gathered the following information about their main competitors.

Expert HVAC Corp.'s negative earnings per share (EPS) were the result of an accounting write-off last

technological advantage, Josh's research indicates that Ragan's competitors are investigating other methods to improve efficiency. Given this, Josh believes that Ragan's technological advantage will last for only the next five years. After that period, the company's growth will likely slow to the industry average. Additionally, Josh believes that the required return the company uses is too high. He believes the industry average required return is more appropriate. Under Josh's assumptions, what is the estimated stock price?

3. What is the industry average price–earnings ratio? What is Ragan's price–earnings ratio? Comment on any differences and explain why they may exist.

4. Assume the company's growth rate declines to the industry average after five years. What percentage of the stock's value is attributable to growth opportunities?

	EPS	DPS	Stock Price	ROE	r
Ragan Thermal Systems Inc. Competitors					
Arctic Cooling Inc.	$ .82	$ .16	$ 15.19	11%	10%
National Heating & Cooling	1.32	.52	12.49	14	13
Expert HVAC Corp.	−.47	.54	48.60	14	12
Industry Average	$ 0.56	$ 0.41	$ 25.43	13%	11.67%

year. Without the write-off, EPS for the company would have been $2.34. Last year, Ragan had an EPS of $4.32 and paid a dividend to Carrington and Genevieve of $54,000 each. The company also had a return on equity of 25 percent. The siblings believe a required return for the company of 20 percent is appropriate.

1. Assuming the company continues its current growth rate, what is the value per share of the company's stock?

2. To verify their calculations, Carrington and Genevieve have hired Josh Schlessman as a consultant. Josh was previously an equity analyst, and he has covered the HVAC industry. Josh has examined the company's financial statements as well as those of its competitors. Although Ragan currently has a

5. Assume the company's growth rate slows to the industry average in five years. What future return on equity does this imply?

6. After discussions with Josh, Carrington and Genevieve agree that they would like to try to increase the value of the company stock. Like many small business owners, they want to retain control of the company and do not want to sell stock to outside investors. They also feel that the company's debt is at a manageable level and do not want to borrow more money. What steps can they take to increase the price of the stock? Are there any conditions under which this strategy would not increase the stock price?

Appendix 6A   The Term Structure of Interest Rates

Spot Rates and Yield to Maturity

In the main body of this chapter, we have assumed that the interest rate is constant over all future periods. In reality, interest rates vary through time. This occurs primarily because inflation rates are expected to differ through time.

To illustrate, we consider two zero-coupon bonds. Bond A is a one-year bond and bond B is a two-year bond. Both have face values of $1,000. The one-year interest rate, r_1, is 8 percent. The two-year interest rate, r_2, is 10 percent. These two rates of interest are examples of spot rates. Perhaps this inequality in interest rates occurs because inflation is expected to be higher over the second year than over the first year. The two bonds are depicted in the following time chart:

$$
\begin{array}{c|c|c}
0 & \text{Year 1} & 1 \quad \text{Year 2} \quad 2 \\
\end{array}
$$

Bond A ◄——— 8% ———► $1,000

Bond B ◄————————— 10% —————————► $1,000

We can easily calculate the present values for bond A and bond B as

$$PV_A = \$925.93 = \frac{\$1,000}{1.08}$$

and

$$PV_B = \$826.45 = \frac{\$1,000}{(1.10)^2}$$

Of course, if PV_A and PV_B were observable and the spot rates were not, we could determine the spot rates using the PV formula, because

$$PV_A = \$925.93 = \frac{\$1,000}{(1 + r_1)} \rightarrow r_1 = 8\%$$

and

$$PV_B = \$826.45 = \frac{\$1,000}{(1 + r_2)^2} \rightarrow r_2 = 10\%$$

Now we can see how the prices of more complicated bonds are determined. Try to do Example 6A.1. It illustrates the difference between spot rates and yields to maturity.

EXAMPLE 6A.1

Given the spot rates, r_1 equals 8 percent and r_2 equals 10 percent, what should a 5 percent coupon, two-year bond cost? The cash flows C_1 and C_2 are illustrated in the following time chart:

$$
\begin{array}{c|c|c}
0 & \text{Year 1} & 1 \quad \text{Year 2} \quad 2 \\
\end{array}
$$

◄——— 8% ———► $50

◄————————— 10% —————————► $1,050

The bond can be viewed as a portfolio of zero-coupon bonds with one- and two-year maturities. Therefore

$$PV = \frac{\$50}{1 + 0.08} + \frac{\$1,050}{(1 + 0.10)^2} = \$914.06 \qquad \text{(6A.1)}$$

Visit us at www.mcgrawhill.ca/olc/ross

We now want to calculate a single rate for the bond. We do this by solving for y in the following equation:

$$\$914.06 = \frac{\$50}{1 + y} + \frac{\$1{,}050}{(1 + y)^2} \tag{6A.2}$$

In (6A.2), y equals 9.95 percent. As mentioned in the chapter, we call y the *yield to maturity* on the bond. Solving for y for a multiyear bond is generally done by means of trial and error.[14] While this can take much time with paper and pencil, it is virtually instantaneous on a hand-held calculator.

It is worthwhile to contrast Equation (6A.1) and Equation (6A.2). In (6A.1), we use the marketwide spot rates to determine the price of the bond. Once we get the bond price, we use (6A.2) to calculate its yield to maturity. Because Equation (6A.1) employs two spot rates whereas only one appears in (6A.2), we can think of yield to maturity as some sort of average of the two spot rates.[15]

Using the above spot rates, the yield to maturity of a two-year coupon bond whose coupon rate is 12 percent and PV equals \$1,036.73 can be determined by

$$\$1{,}036.73 = \frac{\$120}{1 + r} + \frac{\$1{,}120}{(1 + r)^2} \rightarrow r = 9.89\%$$

As these calculations show, two bonds with the same maturity will usually have different yields to maturity if the coupons differ.

Graphing the Term Structure

The *term structure* describes the relationship of spot rates with different maturities. Figure 6A.1 graphs a particular term structure. In Figure 6A.1 the spot rates are increasing with longer maturities, that is, $r_3 > r_2 > r_1$. Graphing the term structure is easy if we can observe spot rates. Unfortunately, this can be done only if there are enough zero-coupon government bonds.

A given term structure, such as that in Figure 6A.1, exists for only a moment in time, say, 10:00 AM, July 30, 2005. Interest rates are likely to change in the next minute, so that a different (though quite similar) term structure would exist at 10:01.

? Concept Questions

• What is the difference between a spot interest rate and the yield to maturity?

FIGURE 6A.1

The Term Structure of Interest Rates

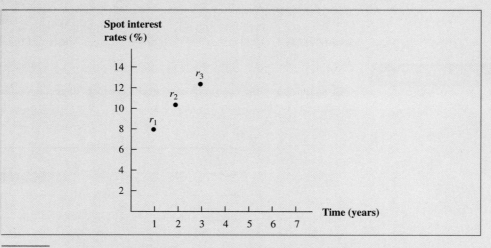

---

[14]The quadratic formula may be used to solve for y for a two-year bond. However, formulas generally do not apply for longer-term bonds.

[15]Yield to maturity is not a simple average of r_1, and r_2. Rather, financial economists speak of it as a time-weighted average of r_1, and r_2.

Explanations of the Term Structure

Figure 6A.1 showed one of many possible relationships between the spot rate and maturity. We now want to explore the relationship in more detail. We begin by defining a new term, the *forward rate,* and relate it to future interest rates. We also consider alternative theories of the term structure.

Definition of Forward Rate

Earlier in this appendix, we developed a two-year example where the spot rate over the first year is 8 percent and the spot rate over the two years is 10 percent. Here, an individual investing \$1 in a two-year zero-coupon bond would have \$1 $\times (1.10)^2$ in two years.

In order to pursue our discussion, it is worthwhile to rewrite[16]

$$\$1 \times (1.10)^2 = \$1 \times 1.08 \times 1.1204 \qquad (6A.3)$$

Equation (6A.3) tells us something important about the relationship between one- and two-year rates. When an individual invests in a two-year zero-coupon bond yielding 10 percent, his wealth at the end of two years is the same as if he received an 8 percent return over the first year and a 12.04 percent return over the second year. This hypothetical rate over the second year, 12.04 percent, is called the *forward rate.* Thus, we can think of an investor with a two-year zero-coupon bond as getting the one-year spot rate of 8 percent and locking in 12.04 percent over the second year. This relationship is presented in Figure 6A.2.

More generally, if we are given spot rates r_1 and r_2, we can always determine the forward rate, f_2, such that

$$(1 + r_2)^2 = (1 + r_1) \times (1 + f_2) \qquad (6A.4)$$

We solve for f_2, yielding

$$f_2 = \frac{(1 + r_2)^2}{1 + r_1} - 1 \qquad (6A.5)$$

EXAMPLE 6A.2

If the one-year spot rate is 7 percent and the two-year spot rate is 12 percent, what is f_2?
We plug in (6A.5), yielding

$$f_2 = \frac{(1.12)^2}{1.07} - 1 = 17.23\%$$

Consider an individual investing in a two-year zero-coupon bond yielding 12 percent. We say it is as if he receives 7 percent over the first year and simultaneously locks in 17.23 percent over the second year. Note that both the one-year spot rate and the two-year spot rate are known at date 0. Because the forward rate is calculated from the one-year and two-year spot rates, it can be calculated at date 0 as well.

Forward rates can be calculated over later years as well. The general formula is

$$f_n = \frac{(1 + r_n)^n}{(1 + r_{n-1})^{n-1}} - 1 \qquad (6A.6)$$

where f_n is the forward rate over the nth year, r_n is the n-year spot rate, and r_{n-1} is the spot rate for $n - 1$ years.

---

[16]12.04 percent is equal to

$$\frac{(1.10)^2}{1.08} - 1$$

when rounding is performed after four digits.

Visit us at www.mcgrawhill.ca/olc/ross

FIGURE 6A.2

Breakdown of a Two-Year Spot Rate Into a One-Year Spot Rate and Forward Rate Over the Second Year

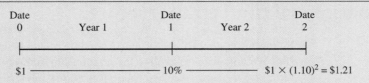

With a two-year spot rate of 10 percent, investor in two-year bond receives $1.21 at date 2.

This is the same return *as if* investor received the spot rate of 8 percent over the first year and 12.04 percent return over the second year.

$1———8%———— $1.08 —— 12.04% —— $1 × 1.08 × 1.1204 = $1.21

Because both the one-year spot rate and the two-year spot rate are known at date 0, the forward rate over the second year can be calculated at date 0.

EXAMPLE 6A.3

Assume the following set of rates:

Year	Spot Rate
1	5%
2	6%
3	7%
4	6%

What are the forward rates over each of the four years?

The forward rate over the first year is, by definition, equal to the one-year spot rate. Thus, we do not generally speak of the forward rate over the first year. The forward rates over the later years are

$$f_2 = \frac{(1.06)^2}{1.05} - 1 = 7.01\%$$

$$f_3 = \frac{(1.07)^3}{(1.06)^2} - 1 = 9.03\%$$

$$f_4 = \frac{(1.06)^4}{(1.07)^3} - 1 = 3.06\%$$

An individual investing $1 in the two-year zero-coupon bond receives $1.1236 [or $1 × (1.06)²] at date 2. He can be viewed as receiving the one-year spot rate of 5 percent over the first year and receiving the forward rate of 7.01 percent over the second year. Another individual investing $1 in a three-year zero-coupon bond receives $1.2250 [or $1 × (1.07)³] at date 3. She can be viewed as receiving the two-year spot rate of 6 percent over the first two years and receiving the forward rate of 9.03 percent over the third year. An individual investing $1 in a four-year zero-coupon bond receives $1.2625 [or $1 × (1.06)⁴] at date 4. He can be viewed as receiving the three-year spot rate of 7 percent over the first three years and receiving the forward rate of 3.06 percent over the fourth year.

Note that all of the four spot rates in this problem are known at date 0. Because the forward rates are calculated from the spot rates, they can be determined at date 0 as well.

The material in this appendix is likely to be difficult for a student exposed to term structure for the first time. In brief, here is what the student should know at this point. Given Equations (6A.5) and (6A.6), a student should be able to calculate a set of forward rates given a set of spot rates. This can simply be viewed as a mechanical computation. In addition to the calculations, a student should understand the intuition of Figure 6A.2.

We now turn to the relationship between the forward rate and the expected spot rates in the future.

Estimating the Price of a Bond at a Future Date

In the example from the body of this chapter, we considered zero-coupon bonds paying $1,000 at maturity and selling at a discount prior to maturity. We now wish to change the example slightly. Now, each bond initially sells for $1,000 so that its payment at maturity is above $1,000.[17] Keeping the spot rates at 8 percent and 10 percent, we have

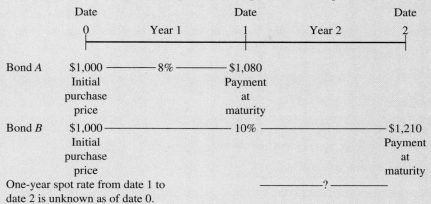

One-year spot rate from date 1 to date 2 is unknown as of date 0.

The payments at maturity are $1,080 and $1,210 for the one- and two-year zero-coupon bonds, respectively. The initial purchase price of $1,000 for each bond is determined as

$$\$1,000 = \frac{\$1,080}{1.08}$$

$$\$1,000 = \frac{\$1,210}{(1.10)^2}$$

We refer to the one-year bond as bond A and the two-year bond as bond B.

There will be a different one-year spot rate when date 1 arrives. This will be the spot rate from date 1 to date 2. We can also call it the spot rate over year 2. This spot rate is not known as of date 0. For example, should the rate of inflation rise between date 0 and date 1, the spot rate over year 2 would likely be high. Should the rate of inflation fall between date 0 and date 1, the spot rate over year 2 would likely be low.

Now that we have determined the price of each bond at date 0, we want to determine what the price of each bond will be at date 1. The price of the one-year bond (bond A) must be $1,080 at date 1, because the payment at maturity is made then. The hard part is determining what the price of the two-year bond (bond B) will be at that time.

Suppose we find that, on date 1, the one-year spot rate from date 1 to date 2 is 6 percent. We state that this is the one-year spot rate over year 2. This means that one can invest $1,000 at date 1 and receive $1,060 (or $1,000 × 1.06) at date 2. Because one year has already passed for bond B, the bond has only one year left. Because bond B pays $1,210 at date 2, its value at date 1 is

$$\$1,141.51 = \frac{\$1,210}{1.06} \tag{6A.7}$$

Note that no one knew ahead of time the price that bond B would sell for on date 1, because no one knew that the one-year spot rate over year 2 would be 6 percent.

Suppose the one-year spot rate beginning at date 1 turned out not to be 6 percent, but to be 7 percent instead. This means that one can invest $1,000 at date 1 and receive $1,070 (or $1,000 × 1.07) at date 2. In this case, the value of bond B at date 1 would be

$$\$1,130.84 = \frac{\$1,210}{1.07} \tag{6A.8}$$

---

[17]This change in assumptions simplifies our presentation but does not alter any of our conclusions.

Finally, suppose that the one-year spot rate at date 1 turned out to be neither 6 percent nor 7 percent, but 14 percent instead. This means that one can invest $1,000 at date 1 and receive $1,140 (or $1,000 × 1.14) at date 2. In this case, the value of bond B at date 1 would be

$$\$1,061.40 = \frac{\$1,210}{1.14}$$

The above possible bond prices are represented in Table 6A.1. The price that bond B will sell for on date 1 is not known before date 1 since the one-year spot rate prevailing over year 2 is not known until date 1.

TABLE 6A.1

Price of Bond B at Date 1 as a Function of Spot Rate Over Year 2

Price of Bond B at Date 1	Spot Rate Over Year 2
$\$1,141.51 = \dfrac{\$1,210}{1.06}$	6%
$\$1,130.84 = \dfrac{\$1,210}{1.07}$	7%
$\$1,061.40 = \dfrac{\$1,210}{1.14}$	14%

It is important to re-emphasize that, although the forward rate is known at date 0, the one-year spot rate beginning at date 1 is *unknown* ahead of time. Thus, the price of bond B at date 1 is unknown ahead of time. Prior to date 1, we can speak only of the amount that bond B is *expected* to sell for on date 1. We write this as[18]

The Amount That Bond B Is Expected to Sell for on Date 1:

$$\frac{\$1,210}{1 + \text{Spot rate expected over year 2}} \tag{6A.9}$$

Making two points is worthwhile now. First, because all individuals are different, the expected value of bond B differs across individuals. Later we will speak of a consensus expected value across investors. Second, Equation (6A.9) represents one's forecast of the price that the bond will be selling for on date 1. The forecast is made ahead of time, that is, on date 0.

The Relationship Between Forward Rate over Second Year and Spot Rate Expected Over Second Year

Given a forecast of bond B's price, an investor can choose one of two strategies at date 0:

1. Buy a one-year bond. Proceeds at date 1 would be

$$\$1,080 = \$1,000 \times 1.08 \tag{6A.10}$$

---

[18]Technically, Equation (6A.9) is only an approximation due to *Jensen's inequality*. That is, expected values of

$$\frac{\$1,210}{1 + \text{Spot rate}} > \frac{\$1,210}{1 + \text{Spot rate expected over year 2}}$$

However, we ignore this very minor issue in the rest of the analysis.

2. Buy a two-year bond but sell at date 1. His *expected* proceeds would be

$$\frac{\$1,000 \times (1.10)^2}{1 + \text{Spot rate expected over year 2}} \tag{6A.11}$$

Given our discussion of forward rates, we can rewrite (6A.11) as

$$\frac{\$1,000 \times 1.08 \times 1.1204}{1 + \text{Spot rate expected over year 2}} \tag{6A.12}$$

(Remember that 12.04 percent was the forward rate over year 2, f_2.)

Under what condition will the return from strategy 1 equal the expected return from strategy 2? In other words, under what condition will formula (6A.10) equal formula (6A.12)?

The two strategies will yield the same expected return only when

$$12.04\% = \text{Spot rate expected over year 2} \tag{6A.13}$$

In other words, if the forward rate equals the expected spot rate, one would expect to earn the same return over the first year whether one invested in a one-year bond, or invested in a two-year bond but sold after one year.

The Expectations Hypothesis

Equation (6A.13) seems fairly reasonable. That is, it is reasonable that investors would set interest rates in such a way that the forward rate would equal the spot rate expected by the marketplace a year from now.[19] For example, imagine that individuals in the marketplace do not concern themselves with risk. If the forward rate, f_2, is less than the spot rate expected over year 2, individuals desiring to invest for one year would always buy a one-year bond. That is, our work above shows that an individual investing in a two-year bond but planning to sell at the end of one year would expect to earn less than if he simply bought a one-year bond.

Equation (6A.13) was stated for the specific case where the forward rate was 12.04 percent. We can generalize this to

Expectations Hypothesis:

$$f_2 = \text{Spot rate expected over year 2} \tag{6A.14}$$

Equation (6A.14) says that the forward rate over the second year is set to the spot rate that people expect to prevail over the second year. This is called the *expectations hypothesis*. It states that investors will set interest rates such that the forward rate over the second year is equal to the one-year spot rate expected over the second year.

Liquidity-Preference Hypothesis

At this point, many students think that Equation (6A.14) *must* hold. However, note that we developed (6A.14) by assuming that investors were risk-neutral. Suppose, alternatively, that investors are averse to risk.

---

[19]Of course, all individuals will have different expectations, so Equation (6A.13) cannot hold for all individuals. However, financial economists generally speak of a consensus expectation. This is the expectation of the market as a whole.

Visit us at www.mcgrawhill.ca/olc/ross

Which of the following strategies would appear more risky for an individual who wants to invest for one year?

1. Invest in a one-year bond.
2. Invest in a two-year bond but sell at the end of one year.

Strategy 1 has no risk because the investor knows that the rate of return must be r_1. Conversely, strategy 2 has much risk; the final return is dependent on what happens to interest rates.

Because strategy 2 has more risk than strategy 1, no risk-averse investor will choose strategy 2 if both strategies have the same expected return. Risk-averse investors can have no preference for one strategy over the other only when the expected return on strategy 2 is *above* the return on strategy 1. Because the two strategies have the same expected return when f_2 equals the spot rate expected over year 2, strategy 2 can only have a higher rate of return when

Liquidity-Preference Hypothesis:

$$f_2 > \text{Spot rate expected over year 2} \qquad (6A.15)$$

That is, in order to induce investors to hold the riskier two-year bonds, the market sets the forward rate over the second year to be above the spot rate expected over the second year. Equation (6A.15) is called the *liquidity-preference hypothesis.*

We developed the entire discussion by assuming that individuals are planning to invest over one year. We pointed out that for such individuals, a two-year bond has extra risk because it must be sold prematurely. What about those individuals who want to invest for two years? (We call these people investors with a two-year *time horizon*.)

They could choose one of the following strategies:

3. Buy a two-year zero-coupon bond.
4. Buy a one-year bond. When the bond matures, they immediately buy another one-year bond.

Strategy 3 has no risk for an investor with a two-year time horizon, because the proceeds to be received at date 2 are known as of date 0. However, strategy 4 has risk since the spot rate over year 2 is unknown at date 0. It can be shown that risk-averse investors will prefer neither strategy 3 nor strategy 4 over the other when

$$f_2 < \text{Spot rate expected over year 2} \qquad (6A.16)$$

Note that introducing risk aversion gives contrary predictions. Relationship (6A.15) holds for a market dominated by investors with a one-year time horizon. Relationship (6A.16) holds for a market dominated by investors with a two-year time horizon. Financial economists have generally argued that the time horizon of the typical investor is generally much shorter than the maturity of typical bonds in the marketplace. Thus, economists view (6A.15) as the better depiction of equilibrium in the bond market with *risk-averse* investors.

However, do we have a market of risk-neutral investors or risk-averse investors? In other words, can the expectations hypothesis of Equation (6A.14) or the liquidity-preference hypothesis of Equation (6A.15) be expected to hold? As we will learn later in this book, economists view investors as being risk-averse for the most part. Yet economists are never satisfied with a casual examination of a theory's assumptions. To them, empirical evidence of a theory's predictions must be the final arbiter.

There has been a great deal of empirical evidence on the term structure of interest rates. Unfortunately (perhaps fortunately for some students), we will not be able to present the evidence in any detail. Suffice it to say that, in our opinion, the evidence supports the liquidity-preference hypothesis over the expectations hypothesis. One simple result might give students the flavour of this research. Consider an individual choosing between one of the following two strategies:

1. Invest in a one-year bond.
2. Invest in a 20-year bond but sell at the end of one year.

(Strategy 2′ is identical to strategy 2 except that a 20-year bond is substituted for a two-year bond.)

The expectations hypothesis states that the expected returns on both strategies are identical. The liquidity-preference hypothesis states that the expected return on strategy 2′ should be above the expected return on strategy 1. Though no one knows what returns are actually expected over a particular time period, actual returns from the past may allow us to infer expectations. The results from January 1926 to December 1999 are illuminating. Over this time period the average yearly return on strategy 1 is 3.8 percent; it is 5.5 percent on strategy 2′.[20] This evidence is generally considered to be consistent with the liquidity-preference hypothesis and inconsistent with the expectations hypothesis.

Application of Term Structure Theory

In explaining term structure theory, it was convenient to use examples of zero-coupon bonds and spot and forward rates. To see the application, we go back to coupon bonds and yields to maturity the way that actual bond data is presented in the financial press.

Figure 6A.3 shows a yield curve for Government of Canada bonds, a plot of bond yields to maturity against time to maturity. Yield curves are observed at a particular date and change shape over time. This yield curve is for November 2006.

Notice that the yield curve is flat, with the long rates approximately equal to the short rates. Term structure theory gives us two reasons why the observed yield curve is flat. Investors expect that rates will stay constant or fall slightly in the future and that there is a liquidity premium.

Now suppose you were advising a friend who was renewing a home mortgage. Suppose further that the alternatives were a one-year mortgage at 8.5 percent and a two-year mortgage

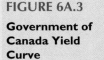

FIGURE 6A.3

Government of Canada Yield Curve

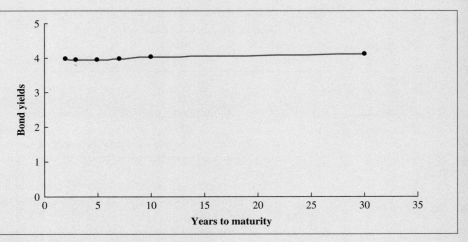

Source: www.bankofcanada.ca. Used with permission.

---

[20]Taken from *Stocks, Bonds, Bills, and Inflation 2000 Yearbook* (Chicago: Ibbotson Associates).

It is important to note that strategy 2′ does not involve buying a 20-year bond and holding it to maturity. Rather, it consists of buying a 20-year bond and selling it one year later, that is, when it has become a 19-year bond. This round-trip transaction occurs 63 times in the 63-year sample from January 1926 to December 1999.

at 9 percent. We know that on average, over the life of a mortgage, rolling over one-year rates will probably be cheaper because the borrower will avoid paying the liquidity premium. Further, the flat yield curve tells us that the market does not expect interest rates will rise.

Appendix Questions and Problems

6.A1   Define the forward rate.

6.A2   What is the relationship between the one-year spot rate, the two-year spot rate, and the forward rate over the second year?

6.A3   What is the expectations hypothesis?

6.A4   What is the liquidity-preference hypothesis?

6.A5   What is the difference between a spot interest rate and the yield to maturity?

6.A6   Assume that the five-year spot rate is 8 percent.
   a. If the forward rate over the sixth year is currently at 6.21 percent, what is the six-year spot rate?
   b. If the forward rate over the fifth year is currently at 7.4 percent, what is the four-year spot rate?

6.A7   The appropriate discount rate for cash flows received one year from today is 11 percent. The appropriate annual discount rate for cash flows received two years from today is 13 percent.
   a. What is the price of a two-year bond that pays an annual coupon of 7 percent?
   b. What is the yield to maturity of this bond?

6.A8   The one-year spot rate equals 9 percent and the two-year spot rate equals 6.5 percent. What should a 4.6 percent coupon two-year bond cost?

6.A9   If the one-year spot rate is 9 percent and the two-year spot rate is 12 percent, what is the forward rate?

6.A10 Assume the following spot rates:

Maturity	Spot Rates (%)
1	5
2	7
3	11

What are the forward rates over each of the 3 years?

6.A11 Consider the following three zero-coupon bonds:

Bond	Face Value	Time to Maturity	Market Price
1	$1,000	one year	$900.00
2	1,000	two years	820.00
3	1,000	three years	699.19

   a. Calculate the one-, two-, and three-year spot rates.
   b. Calculate the forward rate over the second year, and the one corresponding to the third year.
   c. Is the forward rate over the third year the same as the one-year spot rate investors expect to prevail at the end of the second year? Discuss.

6.A12 Consider the bonds from problem 6.A11.
   a. What is the price of the third bond that risk-neutral investors expect to prevail at the end of the second year?
   b. Now assume that investors are risk-averse with a two-year investment horizon. Further assume that for every year at maturity beyond two years, investors demand a 1.5 percent liquidity premium. What is the price of the third bond that the risk-averse investors expect to prevail at the end of the second year?

Chapter 7

Net Present Value and Other Investment Rules

EXECUTIVE SUMMARY

Chapter 5 examined the relationship between $1 today and $1 in the future. For example, a corporate project generating a set of cash flows can be valued by discounting these flows, an approach called the *net present value (NPV)* approach. While we believe that the NPV approach is the best one for evaluating capital budgeting projects, our treatment would be incomplete if we ignored alternative methods. This chapter examines these alternative methods. We first consider the NPV approach as a benchmark. Next we examine four alternatives: payback, accounting rate of return, internal rate of return, and the profitability index.

7.1 Why Use Net Present Value?

This chapter, as well as the next two, focuses on *capital budgeting*, the decision-making process for accepting or rejecting projects. This chapter develops the basic capital budgeting methods, leaving much of the practical application to Chapters 8 and 9. But we don't have to develop these methods from scratch. In Chapter 4, we discussed the basic principles of net present value. Further, in Chapter 5, we pointed out that a dollar received in the future is worth less than a dollar received today. The reason, of course, is that today's dollar can be reinvested, yielding a greater amount in the future. And we showed in Chapter 5 that the exact worth of a dollar to be received in the future is its present value. Furthermore, Section 5.1 suggested calculating the *net present value* of any project. That is, the section suggested calculating the difference between the sum of the present values of the project's future cash flows and the initial cost of the project.

The net present value (NPV) method is the first one to be considered in this chapter. We begin by reviewing the approach with a simple illustration shown in Example 7.1. Next we ask why the method leads to good decisions.

EXAMPLE 7.1

The Alpha Corporation is considering investing in a riskless project costing $100. The project receives $107 in one year and has no other cash flows. The interest rate is 6 percent.

The NPV of the project can easily be calculated as:

$$\$0.94 = -\$100 + \frac{\$107}{1.06} \tag{7.1}$$

From Chapter 5, we know that the project should be accepted since its NPV is positive. Had the NPV of the project been negative, as would have been the case with an interest rate greater than 7 percent, the project should be rejected.

The basic investment rule can be generalized to:

> Accept a project if the NPV is greater than zero.
> Reject a project if NPV is less than zero.

We refer to this as the NPV rule.

Now why does the NPV rule lead to good decisions? Consider the following two strategies available to the managers of Alpha Corporation:

1. Use $100 of corporate cash to invest in the project. The $107 will be paid as a dividend in one year.
2. Forgo the project and pay the $100 of corporate cash as a dividend today.

If strategy 2 is employed, the shareholder might deposit the dividend in his bank for one year. With an interest rate of 6 percent, strategy 2 would produce cash of $106 ($100 × 1.06) at the end of the year. The shareholder would prefer strategy 1, since strategy 2 produces less than $107 at the end of the year.

Thus, our basic point is:

Accepting positive NPV projects benefits the shareholders.

How do we interpret the exact NPV of $0.94? This is the increase in the value of the firm from the project. For example, imagine that the firm today has productive assets worth $V and has $100 of cash. If the firm forgoes the project, the value of the firm today would simply be:

$$\$V + \$100 \tag{7.2}$$

If the firm accepts the project, the firm will receive $107 in one year but will have no cash today. Thus, the firm's value today would be:

$$\$V + \frac{\$107}{1.06} \tag{7.3}$$

The difference between Equation (7.2) and Equation (7.3) is just $0.94, the present value of Equation (7.1). Thus:

The value of the firm rises by the NPV of the project.

Note that the value of the firm is merely the sum of the values of the different projects, divisions, or other entities within the firm. This property, called **value additivity,** is quite important. It implies that the contribution of any project to a firm's value is simply the NPV of the project. As we will see later, alternative methods discussed in this chapter do not generally have this nice property.

One detail remains. We assumed that the project was riskless, a rather implausible assumption. Future cash flows of real-world projects are invariably risky. In other words, cash flows can only be estimated, rather than known. Imagine that the managers of Alpha *expect* the cash flow of the project to be $107 next year. That is, the cash flow could be higher, say $117, or lower, say $97. With this slight change, the project is risky. Suppose the project is about as risky as the stock market as a whole, where the expected return this year is, say 10 percent. Well, 10 percent becomes the discount rate, implying that the NPV of the project would be:

$$-\$2.73 = -\$100 + \frac{\$107}{1.10}$$

Since the NPV is negative, the project should be rejected. This makes sense since a shareholder of Alpha receiving a $100 dividend today could invest it in the stock market, expecting a 10 percent return. Why accept a project with the same risk as the market but with an expected return of only 7 percent?

Conceptually, the discount rate on a risky project is the return that one can expect to earn on a financial asset of comparable risk. This discount rate is often referred to as an *opportunity cost*, since corporate investment in the project takes away the shareholder's opportunity to invest the dividend in a financial asset. If the actual calculation of the discount rate strikes you as extremely difficult in the real world, you are probably right. While you can call a bank to find out the interest rate, whom do you call to find the expected return on the market this year? And, if the risk of the project differs from that of the market, how do you make the adjustment? However, the calculation is by no means impossible. While we forgo the calculation in this chapter, we present it in later chapters of the text.

Having shown that NPV is a sensible approach, how can we tell whether alternative methods are as good as NPV? The key to NPV is its three attributes:

1. *NPV Uses Cash Flows.* Cash flows from a project can be used for other corporate purposes (e.g., dividend payments, other capital-budgeting projects, or payments of corporate interest). By contrast, earnings are an artificial construct. While earnings are useful to accountants, they should not be used in capital budgeting because they do not represent cash.
2. *NPV Uses All the Cash Flows of the Project.* Other approaches ignore cash flows beyond a particular date; beware of these approaches.
3. *NPV Discounts the Cash Flows Properly.* Other approaches may ignore the time value of money when handling cash flows. Beware of these approaches as well.

> **? Concept Questions**
> • **What is the NPV rule?**
> • **Why does this rule lead to good investment decisions?**

7.2 The Payback Period Rule

Defining the Rule

One of the most popular alternatives to NPV is the **payback period rule.** Here is how the payback period rule works.

Consider a project with an initial investment of $50,000 (ie., an initial cash outflow of $50,000). Cash flows are $30,000, $20,000, and $10,000 in the first three years, respectively. These flows are illustrated in Figure 7.1. A useful way of writing down investments like the preceding is with the notation

$$(-\$50,000, \$30,000, \$20,000, \$10,000)$$

The minus sign in front of the $50,000 reminds us that this is a cash outflow for the investor, and the commas between the different numbers indicate that they are received—or if they are cash outflows, that they are paid out—at different times. In this example we are assuming that the cash flows occur one year apart, with the first one occurring the moment we decide to take on the investment.

The firm receives cash flows of $30,000 and $20,000 in the first two years, which add up to the $50,000 original investment. This means that the firm has recovered its investment within two years. In this case two years is the *payback period* of the investment.

FIGURE 7.1

Cash Flows of an Investment Project

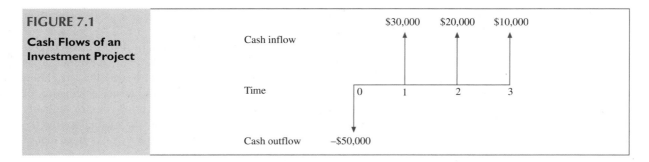

The payback period rule for making investment decisions is simple. A particular cut-off time, say two years, is selected. All investment projects that have payback periods of two years or less are accepted and all of those that pay off in more than two years, if at all, are rejected.

Problems With the Payback Method

There are at least three problems with the payback method. To illustrate the first two problems, we consider the three projects in Table 7.1. All three projects have the same three-year payback period, so they should all be equally attractive—right?

Actually, they are not equally attractive, as can be seen by a comparison of different *pairs* of projects.

Problem 1: Timing of Cash Flows Within the Payback Period   Let us compare project *A* with project *B*. In years 1 through 3, the cash flows of project *A* rise from $20 to $50 while the cash flows of project *B* fall from $50 to $20. Because the large cash flow of $50 comes earlier with project *B,* its net present value must be higher. Nevertheless, we saw above that the payback periods of the two projects are identical. Thus, a problem with the payback period is that it does not consider the timing of the cash flows within the payback period. This shows that the payback method is inferior to NPV because, as we pointed out earlier, the NPV approach *discounts the cash flows properly.*

Problem 2: Payments After the Payback Period   Now consider projects *B* and *C,* which have identical cash flows within the payback period. However, project *C* is clearly preferred because it has the cash flow of $60,000 in the fourth year. Thus, another problem with the payback method is that it ignores all cash flows occurring after the payback period. This flaw is not present with the NPV approach because, as we pointed out earlier, the NPV approach *uses all the cash flows of the project.* The payback method forces managers to have an artificially short-term orientation, which may lead to decisions not in the shareholders' best interests.

Problem 3: Arbitrary Standard for Payback Period   We do not need to refer to Table 7.1 when considering a third problem with the payback approach. Capital markets help us estimate the discount rate used in the NPV method. The riskless rate, perhaps proxied by the yield on a Treasury instrument, would be the appropriate rate for a riskless investment.

Later chapters of this textbook show how to use historical returns in the capital markets in order to estimate the discount rate for a risky project. However, there is no comparable guide for choosing the payback cutoff date, so the choice is somewhat arbitrary.

TABLE 7.1
Expected Cash Flows for Projects A through C

Year	A	B	C
0	−$100	−$100	−$100
1	20	50	50
2	30	30	30
3	50	20	20
4	60	60	60,000
Payback period (years)	3	3	3

Managerial Perspective

Despite its shortcomings, the payback method can be acceptable when making relatively small decisions. The decision to build a small warehouse, for example, or to pay for a tune-up for a truck is the sort of decision that is often made by lower-level management. Typically a manager might reason that a tune-up would cost, say, $200, and if it saved $120 each year in reduced fuel costs, it would pay for itself in less than two years. On such a basis the decision would be made.

Although the treasurer of the company might not have made the decision in the same way, the company endorses such decision making. Why would upper management condone or even encourage such retrograde activity in its employees? One answer would be that it is easy to make decisions using payback. Multiply the tune-up decision into 50 such decisions a month, and the appeal of this simple method becomes clearer.

The payback method also has some desirable features for managerial control. Just as important as the investment decision itself is the company's ability to evaluate the manager's decision-making ability. Under the NPV method, a long time may pass before one decides whether or not a decision was correct. With the payback method we know in two years whether the manager's assessment of the cash flows was correct.

It has also been suggested that firms with good investment opportunities but no available cash may justifiably use payback. For example, the payback method could be used by small, privately held firms with good growth prospects but limited access to the capital markets. Quick cash recovery enhances the reinvestment possibilities for such firms.

Finally, practitioners often argue that standard academic criticisms of payback overstate any real-world problems with the method. For example, textbooks typically make fun of payback by positing a project with low cash inflows in the early years but a huge cash inflow right after the payback cutoff date. This project is likely to be rejected under the payback method, though its acceptance would, in truth, benefit the firm. Project *C* in our Table 7.1 is an example of such a project. Practitioners point out that the pattern of cash flows in these textbook examples is much too stylized to mirror the real world. In fact, a number of executives have told us that, for the overwhelming majority of real-world projects, both payback and NPV lead to the same decision. In addition, these executives indicate that, if an investment like project *C* were encountered in the real world, decision makers would almost certainly make *ad hoc* adjustments to the payback rule so that the project would be accepted.

Notwithstanding all of the preceding rationale, it is not surprising to discover that as the decision grows in importance, which is to say when firms look at bigger projects, NPV becomes the order of the day. When questions of controlling and evaluating the manager become less important than making the right investment decision, payback is used less frequently. For big-ticket decisions, such as whether or not to buy a machine, build a factory, or acquire a company, the payback method is seldom used.

Summary of Payback

The payback method differs from NPV and is therefore conceptually wrong. With its arbitrary cutoff date and its blindness to cash flows after that date, it can lead to some flagrantly foolish decisions if it is used too literally. Nevertheless, because of its simplicity, as well as its other advantages mentioned above, companies often use it as a screen for making the myriad of minor investment decisions they continually face.

Although this means that you should be wary of trying to change approaches such as the payback method when you encounter them in companies, you should probably be careful not to accept the sloppy financial thinking they represent. After this course, you would do your company a disservice if you used payback instead of NPV when you had a choice.

? Concept Questions
- **List the problems of the payback method.**
- **What are some advantages?**

7.3 The Discounted Payback Period Rule

Aware of the pitfalls of the payback approach, some decision makers use a variant called the **discounted payback period rule.** Under this approach, we first discount the cash flows. Then we ask how long it takes for the discounted cash flows to equal the initial investment.

For example, suppose that the discount rate is 10 percent and the cash flows on a project are given by

$$(-\$100, \$50, \$50, \$20)$$

This investment has a payback period of two years, because the investment is paid back in that time.

To compute the project's discounted payback period, we first discount each of the cash flows at the 10 percent rate. In discounted terms, then, the cash flows look like

$$[-\$100, \$50/1.1, \$50/(1.1)^2, \$20/(1.1)^3] = (-\$100, \$45.45, \$41.32, \$15.03)$$

The discounted payback period of the original investment is simply the payback period for these discounted cash flows. The payback period for the discounted cash flows is slightly less than three years since the discounted cash flows over the three years are $101.80 (or $45.45 + $41.32 + $15.03). As long as the cash flows are positive, the discounted payback period will never be smaller than the payback period, because discounting will lower the cash flows.

At first glance the discounted payback may seem like an attractive alternative, but on closer inspection we see that it has some of the same major flaws as the payback. Like payback, discounted payback first requires us to make a somewhat magical choice of an arbitrary cut-off period, and then it ignores all of the cash flows after that date.

If we have already gone to the trouble of discounting the cash flows, any small appeal to simplicity or to managerial control that payback may have has been lost. We might just as well add up the discounted cash flows and use the NPV to make the decision. Although discounted payback looks a bit like the NPV, it is just a poor compromise between the payback method and the NPV.

7.4 The Average Accounting Return (AAR)

Defining the Rule

Another attractive and fatally flawed approach to making financial decisions is the **average accounting return (AAR)**. The average accounting return is the average project earnings after taxes and depreciation, divided by the average book value of the investment during its life. In spite of its flaws, the average accounting return method is worth examining because it is still used in business.

EXAMPLE 7.2

> Consider a company that is evaluating whether or not to buy a store in a newly built mall. The purchase price is $500,000. We will assume that the store has an estimated life of five years and will need to be completely scrapped or rebuilt at the end of that time. The projected yearly sales and expense figures are shown in Table 7.2.

It is worth looking carefully at this table. In fact, the first step in any project assessment is a careful look at the projected cash flows. When the store starts up, it is estimated that first-year sales will be $433,333 and that, after expenses, the before-tax cash flow will be $233,333. After the first year, sales are expected to rise and expenses are expected to fall, resulting in a before-tax cash flow of $300,000. After that, competition from other stores and the loss in novelty will drop before-tax cash flow to $166,667, $100,000, and $33,333, respectively, in the next three years.

To compute the average accounting return on the project, we divide the average net income by the average amount invested. This can be done in three steps.

TABLE 7.2
Projected Yearly Revenue and Costs for Average Accounting Return

	Year 1	Year 2	Year 3	Year 4	Year 5
Revenue	$433,333	$450,000	$266,667	$200,000	$133,333
Expenses	200,000	150,000	100,000	100,000	100,000
Before-tax cash flow	233,333	300,000	166,667	100,000	33,333
Depreciation	100,000	100,000	100,000	100,000	100,000
Earnings before taxes	133,333	200,000	66,667	0	−66,667
Taxes $(T_c = 0.25)$*	33,333	50,000	16,667	0	−16,667
Net income	100,000	150,000	50,000	0	−50,000

$$\text{Average net income} = \frac{(\$100,000 + 150,000 + 50,000 + 0 - 50,000)}{5} = \$50,000$$

$$\text{Average investment} = \frac{\$500,000 + 0}{2} = \$250,000$$

$$\text{AAR} = \frac{\$50,000}{\$250,000} = 20\%$$

*Corporate tax rate $= T_c$. The tax rebate in year 5 of −$16,667 occurs if the rest of the firm is profitable. Here, the loss in the project reduces the taxes of the entire firm.

Step 1: Determining Average Net Income   The net income in any year is the net cash flow minus depreciation and taxes. Depreciation is not a cash outflow.[1] Rather, it is a charge reflecting the fact that the investment in the store becomes less valuable every year.

We assume the project has a useful life of five years, at which time it will be worthless. Because the initial investment is $500,000 and because it will be worthless in five years, we will assume that it loses value at the rate of $100,000 each year. This steady loss in value of $100,000 is called *straight-line depreciation.* We subtract both depreciation and taxes from before-tax cash flow to derive the net income, as shown in Table 7.2. The net income over the five years is $100,000 in the first year, $150,000 in year 2, $50,000 in year 3, zero in year 4, and −$50,000 in the last year. The average net income over the life of the project is therefore

Average Net Income:
[$100,000 + $150,000 + $50,000 + $0 + (−$50,000)]/5 = $50,000

Step 2: Determining Average Investment   We stated earlier that, due to depreciation, the investment in the store becomes less valuable every year. Because depreciation is $100,000 per year, the value at the end of year zero is $500,000, the value at the end of year 1 is $400,000, and so on. What is the average value of the investment over the life of the investment?

The mechanical calculation is

Average Investment:
($500,000 + $400,000 + $300,000 + $200,000 + $100,000 + $0)/6 = $250,000   **(7.4)**

We divide by 6 and not 5, because $500,000 is what the investment is worth at the beginning of the five years and $0 is what it is worth at the beginning of the sixth year. In other words, there are six terms in the parentheses of Equation (7.4). Note that Table 7.2 arrives at the same answer for average investment by averaging the initial investment and ending value. This works here because we assume straight-line depreciation and zero salvage.

Step 3: Determining AAR   The average return is simply

$$AAR = \frac{\$50,000}{\$250,000} = 20\%$$

If the firm had a targeted accounting rate of return greater than 20 percent, the project would be rejected, and if its targeted return were less than 20 percent, it would be accepted.

Analyzing the Average Accounting Return Method

By now you should be able to see what is wrong with the AAR method.

The first and most important flaw with AAR is that it does not work with the right raw materials. It uses net income and book value of the investment, both of which come from the accounting books. Accounting numbers are somewhat arbitrary. For example, certain cash outflows, such as the cost of a building, are depreciated under current accounting rules. Other flows, such as maintenance, are expensed. In real-world situations, the decision to depreciate or expense an item involves judgment. Thus, the basic inputs of the AAR method, income and average investment, are affected by the accountant's judgment. Conversely, the NPV method *uses cash flows.* Accounting judgments do not affect cash flow.

---

[1]The rates of depreciation and tax used in this example are chosen for simplicity. Leasehold improvements are one of the few asset classes for which tax depreciation in Canada is straight-line. We discuss these topics in detail in Appendix 1A and in Chapter 8. Recall from Chapter 2 that depreciation is the special case of amortization applicable to capital assets.

Second, AAR takes no account of timing. In the previous example, the AAR would have been the same if the $100,000 net income in the first year had occurred in the last year. However, delaying an inflow for five years would have lowered the NPV of the investment. As mentioned earlier in this chapter, the NPV approach *discounts properly.*

Third, just as payback requires an arbitrary choice of the cut-off date, the AAR method offers no guidance on what the right targeted rate of return should be. It could be the discount rate in the market. But then again, because the AAR method is not the same as the present value method, it is not obvious that this would be the right choice.

Given these problems, is the AAR method employed in practice? Like the payback method, the AAR (and variations of it) is frequently used as a "backup" to discounted cash flow methods. Perhaps this is so because it is easy to calculate and uses accounting numbers readily available from the firm's accounting system. In addition, both shareholders and the media pay a lot of attention to the overall profitability of a firm. Thus, some managers may feel pressured to select projects that are profitable in the near term, even if the projects come up short in terms of NPV. These managers may focus on the AAR of individual projects more than they should.

? Concept Questions

- **What are the three steps in calculating AAR?**
- **What are some flaws with the AAR method?**

7.5 The Internal Rate of Return (IRR)

Now we come to the most important alternative to the NPV approach: the internal rate of return, universally known as the IRR. The IRR is about as close as you can get to the NPV without actually being the NPV. The basic rationale behind the IRR is that it tries to find a single number that summarizes the merits of a project. That number does not depend on the interest rate that prevails in the capital market. That is why it is called the internal rate of return; the number is internal or intrinsic to the project and does not depend on anything except the cash flows of the project.

For example, consider the simple project (−$100, $110) in Figure 7.2. For a given rate, the net present value of this project can be described as

$$\text{NPV} = -\$100 + \frac{\$110}{1 + r} \tag{7.5}$$

where r is the discount rate.

What must the discount rate be to make the NPV of the project equal to zero?

We begin by using an arbitrary discount rate of 0.08, which yields

$$\$1.85 = \$100 + \frac{\$110}{1.08} \tag{7.6}$$

FIGURE 7.2

Cash Flows for a Simple Project

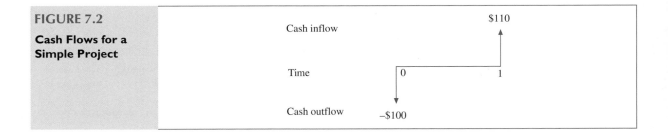

Since the NPV in Equation (7.6) is positive, we now try a higher discount rate, say, 0.12. This yields

$$-\$1.79 = \$100 + \frac{\$110}{1.12} \qquad (7.7)$$

Since the NPV in Equation (7.7) is negative, we lower the discount rate to, say, 0.10. This yields

$$0 = -\$100 + \frac{\$110}{1.10} \qquad (7.8)$$

This trial-and-error procedure tells us that the NPV of the project is zero when r equals 10 percent.[2] Thus, we say that 10 percent is the project's **internal rate of return (IRR).** In general, the IRR is the rate that causes the NPV of the project to be zero. The implication of this exercise is very simple. The firm should be equally willing to accept or reject the project if the discount rate is 10 percent. The firm should accept the project if the discount rate is below 10 percent. The firm should reject the project if the discount rate is above 10 percent.

The general investment rule is clear:

> Accept the project if IRR is greater than the discount rate.
>
> Reject the project if IRR is less than the discount rate.

We refer to this as the **basic IRR rule.** Having mastered the basics of the IRR rule, you should recognize that we used the IRR (without defining it) when we calculated the yield to maturity of a bond in Chapter 6. In fact, the yield to maturity is the bond's IRR.[3]

Now we can try the more complicated example in Figure 7.3. As we did in Equations (7.6) to (7.8), we use trial and error to calculate the internal rate of return.

We try 20 percent and 30 percent, yielding

Discount Rate	NPV
20%	$10.65
30%	−18.39

After much more trial and error, we find that the NPV of the project is zero when the discount rate is 23.37 percent. Thus, the IRR is 23.37 percent. With a 20 percent discount rate the NPV is positive and we accept it. However, if the discount rate is 30 percent, we reject it.

FIGURE 7.3

Cash Flows for a More Complex Project

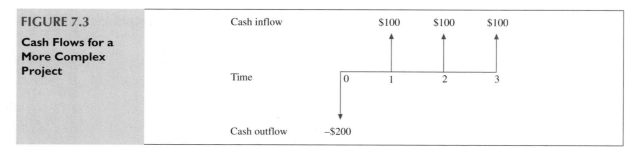

---

[2]Of course, we could have directly solved for r in Equation (7.5) after setting NPV equal to zero. However, with a long series of cash flows, one cannot generally directly solve for r. Instead, one is forced to use a trial-and-error method similar to that in Equations (7.6), (7.7), and (7.8).

[3]Strictly speaking, this is true for bonds with annual coupons. Typically, bonds carry semiannual coupons so yield to maturity is the six-month IRR expressed as a stated rate per year.

Algebraically, IRR is the unknown in the following equation:[4]

$$0 = -\$200 + \frac{\$100}{1 + IRR} + \frac{\$100}{(1 + IRR)^2} + \frac{\$100}{(1 + IRR)^3}$$

Figure 7.4 illustrates what it means to find the IRR for a project. The figure plots the NPV as a function of the discount rate. The curve crosses the horizontal axis at the IRR of 23.37 percent because this is where the NPV equals zero.

It should also be clear that the NPV is positive for discount rates below the IRR and negative for discount rates above the IRR. This means that if we accept projects like this one when the discount rate is less than the IRR, we will be accepting positive NPV projects. Thus, the IRR rule will coincide exactly with the NPV rule.

If this were all there was to it, the IRR rule would always coincide with the NPV rule. This would be a wonderful discovery because it would mean that just by computing the IRR for a project we would be able to tell where it ranks among all of the projects we are considering. For example, if the IRR rule really works, a project with an IRR of 20 percent will always be at least as good as one with an IRR of 15 percent.

But the world of finance is not so kind. Unfortunately, the IRR rule and the NPV rule are the same only for simple examples like the ones above. Several problems with the IRR occur in more complicated situations.

? Concept Questions

• **How does one calculate the IRR of a project?**

FIGURE 7.4

Net Present Value (NPV) and Discount Rates for a Relatively Complex Project

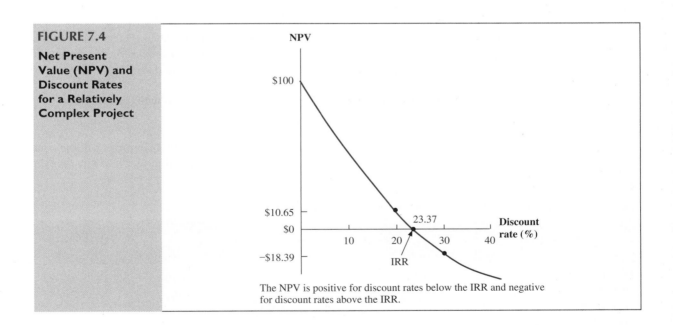

The NPV is positive for discount rates below the IRR and negative for discount rates above the IRR.

---

[4]One can derive the IRR directly for a problem with an initial outflow and either one or two subsequent inflows. In the case of two subsequent inflows, the quadratic formula is needed. In general, however, only trial and error will work for an outflow and three or more subsequent inflows. Hand calculators calculate IRR by trial and error, though at lightning speed.

7.6 Problems with the IRR Approach

Definition of Independent and Mutually Exclusive Projects

An **independent project** is one whose acceptance or rejection is independent of the acceptance or rejection of other projects. For example, imagine that McDonald's is considering putting another hamburger outlet in Beijing to get ready for the 2008 Olympics. Acceptance or rejection of this unit is likely to be unrelated to the acceptance or rejection of any other restaurant in its system. The remoteness of the outlet in question ensures that it will not pull sales away from other outlets.

Now consider the other extreme, **mutually exclusive investments.** What does it mean for two projects, A and B, to be mutually exclusive? You can accept A or you can accept B or you can reject both of them, but you cannot accept both of them. For example, A might be a decision to build an apartment building on a corner lot that you own, and B might be a decision to build a movie theatre on the same lot.

We now present two general problems with the IRR approach that affect both independent and mutually exclusive projects. Next, we deal with two problems affecting mutually exclusive projects only.

Two General Problems Affecting Both Independent and Mutually Exclusive Projects

We begin our discussion with project A, which has the following cash flows:

$$(-\$100, \$130)$$

The IRR for project A is 30 percent. Table 7.3 provides other relevant information on the project. The relationship between NPV and the discount rate is shown for this project in Figure 7.5. As you can see, the NPV declines as the discount rate rises.

Problem 1: Investing or Financing?   Now consider project B, with cash flows of

$$(\$100, -\$130)$$

These cash flows are exactly the reverse of the flows for project A. In project B, the firm receives funds first and then pays out funds later. While unusual, projects of this type do

TABLE 7.3   The Internal Rate of Return and Net Present Value

	Project A			Project B			Project C		
Dates:	0	1	2	0	1	2	0	1	2
Cash flows	−$100	$130		$100	−$130		−$100	$230	−$132
IRR		30%			30%		10%		20%
NPV @ 10%		$18.2			−$18.2				
Accept if market rate		<30%			>30%		>10%		<20%
Financing or investing		Investing			Financing			Mixture	

FIGURE 7.5   **Net Present Value and Discount Rates for Projects A, B, and C**

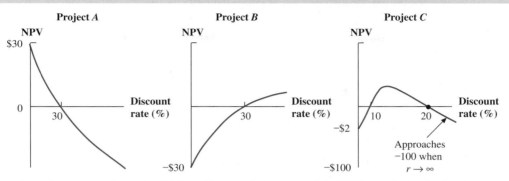

Project *A* has a cash outflow at date 0 followed by a cash inflow at date 1. Its NPV is negatively related to the discount rate.

Project *B* has a cash inflow at date 0 followed by a cash outflow at date 1. Its NPV is positively related to the discount rate.

Project *C* has two changes of sign in its cash flows. It has an outflow at date 0, an inflow at date 1, and an outflow at date 2. Projects with more than one change of sign can have multiple rates of return.

exist. For example, consider a corporation conducting a seminar where the participants pay in advance. Because large expenses are frequently incurred at the seminar date, cash inflows precede cash outflows.

Consider our trial-and-error method to calculate IRR:

$$-\$4 = +\$100 - \frac{\$130}{1.25}$$

$$\$0 = +\$100 - \frac{\$130}{1.30}$$

$$\$3.70 = +\$100 - \frac{\$130}{1.35}$$

As with project *A*, the internal rate of return is 30 percent. However, notice that the net present value is *negative* when the discount rate is *below* 30 percent. Conversely, the net present value is positive when the discount rate is above 30 percent. The decision rule is exactly the opposite of our previous result. For this type of a project, the rule is:

> Accept the project when IRR is less than the discount rate.
>
> Reject the project when IRR is greater than the discount rate.

This unusual decision rule follows from the graph of project *B* in Figure 7.5. The curve is upward sloping, implying that NPV is *positively* related to the discount rate.

The graph makes intuitive sense. Suppose that the firm wants to obtain $100 immediately. It can either (1) conduct project *B* or (2) borrow $100 from a bank. Thus, the project is actually a substitute for borrowing. In fact, because the IRR is 30 percent, taking on project *B* is tantamount to borrowing at 30 percent. If the firm can borrow from a bank at, say, only 25 percent, it should reject the project. However, if a firm can only borrow from a bank at, say, 35 percent, it should accept the project. Thus, project *B* will be accepted if and only if the discount rate is *above* the IRR.[5]

This should be contrasted with project *A*. If the firm has $100 of cash to invest, it can either (1) conduct project *A* or (2) lend $100 to the bank. The project is actually a substitute for lending. In fact, because the IRR is 30 percent, taking on project *A* is tantamount to lending at 30 percent. The firm should accept project *A* if the lending rate is below 30 percent. Conversely, the firm should reject project *A* if the lending rate is above 30 percent.

Because the firm initially pays out money with project *A* but initially receives money with project *B,* we refer to project *A* as an investing-type project and project *B* as a financing-type project. Investing-type projects are the norm. Because the IRR rule is reversed for a financing-type project, we view this type of project as a problem—unless it is understood properly.

Problem 2: Multiple Rates of Return   Suppose the cash flows from a project are

$$(-\$100, \$230, -\$132)$$

Because this project has a negative cash flow, a positive cash flow, and another negative cash flow, we say that the project's cash flows exhibit two changes of sign, or "flip-flops." While this pattern of cash flows might look a bit strange at first, many projects require outflows of cash after receiving some inflows. An example would be a strip-mining project. The first stage in such a project is the initial investment in excavating the mine. Profits from operating the mine are received in the second stage. The third stage involves a further investment to reclaim the land and satisfy the requirements of environmental protection legislation. Cash flows are negative at this stage.

Projects financed by lease arrangements also produce negative cash flows followed by positive ones. We study leasing carefully in a later chapter, but for now we will give you a hint. Using leases for financing can sometimes bring substantial tax advantages. These advantages are often sufficient to make an otherwise bad investment have positive cash flows following an initial outlay. But after a while the tax advantages decline or run out. The cash flows turn negative when this occurs.

It is easy to verify that this project has not one but two IRRs: 10 percent and 20 percent.[6] In a case like this, the IRR does not make any sense. What IRR are we to use: 10 percent or 20 percent? Because there is no good reason to use one over the other, IRR simply cannot be used here.

Why does this project have multiple rates of return? Project *C* generates multiple internal rates of return because both an inflow and an outflow occur after the initial investment. In general, these flip-flops or changes in sign produce multiple IRRs. In theory, a

---

[5]This paragraph implicitly assumes that the cash flows of the project are risk-free. In this way, we can treat the borrowing rate as the discount rate for a firm needing $100. With risky cash flows, another discount rate would be chosen. However, the intuition behind the decision to accept when IRR is less than the discount rate would still apply.

[6]The calculations are

$$0 = -\$100 + \frac{\$230}{1.1} - \frac{\$132}{(1.1)^2}$$

$$= -\$100 + \$209.09 - \$109.09$$

and

$$0 = -\$100 + \frac{\$230}{1.2} - \frac{\$132}{(1.2)^2}$$

$$= -\$100 + \$191.67 - \$91.67$$

Thus, we have multiple rates of return.

cash flow stream with K changes in sign can have up to K sensible internal rates of return (IRRs above -100%).[7] Therefore, since project C has two changes in sign, it can have as many as two IRRs. As we pointed out, projects whose cash flows change sign repeatedly can occur in the real world.

NPV Rule   Of course, we should not be too worried about multiple rates of return. After all, we can always fall back on the NPV rule. Figure 7.5 plots the NPV of project C ($-\$100$, $\$230$, $-\$132$) as a function of the discount rate. As the figure shows, the NPV is zero at both 10 percent and 20 percent and negative outside the range. Thus, the NPV rule tells us to accept the project if the appropriate discount rate is between 10 percent and 20 percent. The project should be rejected if the discount rate lies outside of this range.

Modified IRR   As an alternative to NPV, we now introduce the **modified IRR (MIRR)** method, which handles the multiple-IRR problem by combining cash flows until only one change in sign remains. To see how it works, consider project C again. With a discount rate of, say, 14 percent, the value of the last cash flow, $-\$132$, is:

$$-\$132/1.14 = -\$115.79$$

as of date 1. Since $\$230$ is already received at that time, the "adjusted" cash flow at date 1 is $\$114.21$ ($230 - 115.79$). Thus, the MIRR approach produces the following two cash flows for the project:

$$(-\$100, \$114.21)$$

Note that, by discounting and then combining cash flows, we are left with only one change in sign. The IRR rule can now be applied. The IRR of these two cash flows is 14.21 percent, implying that the project should be accepted given our assumed discount rate of 14 percent.

---

[7]Those of you who are steeped in algebra might have recognized that finding the IRR is like finding the root of a polynomial equation. For a project with cash flows of $(C_0, \ldots, C_T)$, the formula for computing the IRR requires us to find the interest rate, r, that makes

$$\text{NPV} = C_0 + C_1/(1 + r) + \ldots + C_T/(1 + r)^T = 0$$

If we let the symbol x stand for the discount factor,

$$x = 1/(1 + r)$$

then the formula for the IRR becomes

$$\text{NPV} = C_0 + C_1 x + C_2 x^2 + \ldots + C_T x^T = 0$$

Finding the IRR, then, is the same as finding the roots of this polynomial equation. If a particular value x^* is a root of the equation, then, because

$$x = 1/(1 + r)$$

it follows that there is an associated IRR:

$$r^* = (1/x^*) - 1$$

From the theory of polynomials, it is well known that an nth-order polynomial has n roots. Generally, an IRR above -100 percent is considered sensible. Since each root that is positive generates an IRR above -100 percent, any positive root can have a sensible IRR associated with it. Applying Descartes' rule of signs gives the result that a stream of n cash flows can have up to K IRRs above -100 percent, where K is the number of changes in sign for the cash flows.

Of course, project C is relatively simple to begin with, since it has only three cash flows and two changes in sign. However, the same procedure can easily be applied to more complex projects; that is, just keep discounting and combining the later cash flows until only one change of sign remains.

While this adjustment does correct for multiple IRRs, it appears, at least to us, to violate the "spirit" of the IRR approach. As stated earlier, the basic rationale behind the IRR method is that it provides a single number summarizing the merits of a project. That number does not depend on the discount rate. In fact, that is why it is called the internal rate of return; the number is *internal,* or intrinsic, to the project and does not depend on anything except the cash flows of the project. By contrast, MIRR is clearly a function of the discount rate. However, this point is not meant to be a criticism of MIRR. A firm using this adjustment will avoid the multiple-IRR problem, just as a firm using the NPV rule will avoid it.

Are We Ever Safe from the Multiple-IRR Problem?   If the first cash flow for a project is negative—because it is the initial investment—and if all of the remaining flows are positive, there can be only a single, unique IRR, no matter how many periods the project lasts. This is easy to understand by using the concept of the time value of money. For example, it is easy to verify that project A in Table 7.3 has an IRR of 30 percent, because using a 30 percent discount rate gives

$$NPV = -\$100 + \$130/(1.3)$$
$$= 0$$

How do we know that this is the only IRR? Suppose that we were to try a discount rate greater than 30 percent. In computing the NPV, changing the discount rate does not change the value of the initial cash flow of $-\$100$ because that cash flow is not discounted. But raising the discount rate can only lower the present value of the future cash flows. In other words, because the NPV is zero at 30 percent, any increase in the rate will push the NPV into the negative range. Similarly, if we try a discount rate of less than 30 percent, the overall NPV of the project will be positive. Though this example has only one positive flow, the above reasoning still implies a single, unique IRR if there are many inflows (but no outflows) after the initial investment.

If the initial cash flow is positive—and if all of the remaining flows are negative—there can only be a single, unique IRR. This result follows from reasoning similar to that above. Both these cases have only one change of sign or flip-flop in the cash flows. Thus, we are safe from multiple IRRs whenever there is only one sign change in the cash flows.

General Rules   The following chart summarizes our rules:

Flows	Number of IRRs	IRR Criterion	NPV Criterion
First cash flow is negative and all remaining cash flows are positive.	1	Accept if IRR $> r$ Reject if IRR $< r$	Accept if NPV > 0 Reject if NPV < 0
First cash flow is positive and all remaining cash flows are negative.	1	Accept if IRR $< r$ Reject if IRR $> r$	Accept if NVP > 0 Reject if NVP < 0
Some cash flows after first are positive and some cash flows after first are negative.	May be more than 1	No valid IRR	Accept if NPV > 0 Reject if NPV < 0

Note: IRR = Internal rate of return; r = Discount rate; and NPV = Net present value.

Note that the NPV criterion is the same for each of the three cases. In other words, NPV analysis is always appropriate. Conversely, the IRR can be used only in certain cases.

Problems Specific to Mutually Exclusive Projects

As mentioned earlier, two or more projects are mutually exclusive if the firm can, at most, accept only one of them. We now present two problems dealing with the application of the IRR approach to mutually exclusive projects. These two problems are quite similar, though logically distinct.[8]

The Scale Problem   A professor we know motivates class discussions on this topic with the statement: "Students, I am prepared to let one of you choose between two mutually exclusive 'business' propositions. Opportunity 1—You give me $1 now and I'll give you $1.50 back at the end of the class period. Opportunity 2—You give me $10 and I'll give you $11 back at the end of the class period. You can only choose one of the two opportunities. And you cannot choose either opportunity more than once. I'll pick the first volunteer."

Which would you choose? The correct answer is opportunity 2.[9] To see this, look at the following chart:

	Cash Flow at Beginning of Class	Cash Flow at End of Class (90 minutes later)	NPV*	IRR
Opportunity 1	−$1	+$1.50	$0.50	50%
Opportunity 2	−10	+11.00	1.00	10

*We assume a zero rate of interest because the class lasted only 90 minutes. It just seemed like a lot longer.

As we have stressed earlier in the text, one should choose the opportunity with the higher NPV. This is opportunity 2 in the example. Or, as one of the professor's students explained it: "I trust the professor, so I know I'll get my money back. And I have $10 in my pocket right now so I can choose either opportunity. At the end of the class, I'll be able to play two rounds of my favourite electronic game with opportunity 2 and still have my original investment, safe and sound. The profit on opportunity 1 buys only one round.

This business proposition illustrates a defect with the internal rate of return criterion. The basic IRR rule says take opportunity 1, because the IRR is 50 percent. The IRR is only 10 percent for opportunity 2.

Where does IRR go wrong? The problem with IRR is that it ignores issues of scale. While opportunity 1 has a greater IRR, the investment is much smaller. In other words, the high percentage return on opportunity 1 is more than offset by the ability to earn at least a decent return on a much bigger investment under opportunity 2.[10]

Since IRR seems to be misguided here, can we adjust or correct it? We illustrate how in Example 7.3.

---

[8]Another problem with IRR occurs either when long-term interest rates differ from short-term rates (that is, when the term structure of interest rates, presented in Appendix 6A, is not flat) or when the riskiness of the cash flows changes over time. In these circumstances, using IRR is inappropriate because no one discount rate is applicable to all the cash flows

[9]The professor uses real money here. Though many students have done poorly on the professor's exams over the years, no student ever chose opportunity 1. The professor claims that his students are "money players."

[10]A 10 percent return is more than decent over a 90-minute interval!

EXAMPLE 7.3

Jack and Ramona have just purchased the rights to *Corporate Finance: The Motion Picture.* They will produce this major motion picture on either a small budget or a big budget. The estimated cash flows are

	Cash Flow at Date 0	Cash Flow at Date 1	NPV @ 25%	IRR
Small budget	−$10 million	$40 million	$22 million	300%
Large budget	−25 million	65 million	27 million	160%

Because of high risk, a 25 percent discount rate is considered appropriate. Ramona wants to adopt the large budget because the NPV is higher. Jack wants to adopt the small budget because the IRR is higher. Who is right?

For the reasons espoused in the classroom example above, NPV is correct. Hence, Ramona is right. However, Jack is very stubborn where IRR is concerned. How can Ramona justify the large budget to Jack using the IRR approach?

This is where incremental IRR comes in. She calculates the incremental cash flows from choosing the large budget instead of the small budget as

	Cash Flow at Date 0 (in $ millions)	Cash Flow at Date 1 (in $ millions)
Incremental cash flows from choosing large budget instead of small budget	$-25 - (-10) = -15$	$65 - 40 = 25$

This chart shows that the incremental cash flows are −$15 million at date 0 and $25 million at date 1. Ramona calculates incremental IRR as

Formula for Calculating the Incremental IRR:

$$0 = -\$15 \text{ million} + \frac{\$25 \text{ million}}{1 + \text{IRR}}$$

IRR equals 66.67 percent in this equation. Ramona says that the **incremental IRR** is 66.67 percent. Incremental IRR is the IRR on the incremental investment from choosing the large project instead of the small project.

In addition, we can calculate the NPV of the incremental cash flows:

NPV of Incremental Cash Flows:

$$-\$15 \text{ million} + \frac{\$25 \text{ million}}{1.25} = \$5 \text{ million}$$

We know the small-budget picture would be acceptable as an independent project since its NPV is positive. We want to know whether it is beneficial to invest an additional $15 million in order to make the large-budget picture instead. In other words, is it beneficial to invest an additional $15 million in order to receive an additional $25 million next year? First, the calculations above show the NPV of the incremental investment to be positive. Second, the incremental IRR of 66.67 percent is higher than the discount rate of 25 percent. For both reasons, the incremental investment can be justified. The second reason is what Jack needed to hear to be convinced. Hence, the large-budget movie should be made.

In review, we can handle this example (or any mutually exclusive example) in one of three ways:

1. *Compare the NPVs of the two choices.* The NPV of the large-budget picture is greater than the NPV of the small-budget picture; that is, $27 million is greater than $22 million.

2. *Compare the incremental NPV* from making the large-budget picture instead of the small-budget picture. Because incremental NPV equals $5 million, we choose the large-budget picture.

3. *Compare the incremental IRR to the discount rate.* Because the incremental IRR is 66.67 percent and the discount rate is 25 percent, we take the large-budget picture.

All three approaches always give the same decision. However, we must not compare the IRRs of the two pictures. If we did we would make the wrong choice; that is, we would accept the small-budget picture.

While students frequently think that problems of scale are relatively unimportant, the truth is just the opposite. No real-world project comes in one clear-cut size. Rather, the firm has to *determine* the best size for the project. The movie budget of $25 million is not fixed in stone. Perhaps an extra $1 million to hire a bigger star or to film at a better location will increase the movie's gross. Similarly, an industrial firm must decide whether it wants a warehouse of, say, 500,000 square feet or 600,000 square feet. And, earlier in the chapter we imagined McDonald's opening an outlet in Beijing. If it does this, it must decide how big the outlet should be. For almost any project, someone in the firm has to decide on its size, implying that problems of scale abound in the real world.

One final note here. Students ask which project should be subtracted from the other in calculating incremental flows. Notice that we are subtracting the smaller project's cash flows from the bigger project's cash flows. This leaves an *outflow* at date 0. We then use the basic IRR rule on the incremental flows.[11]

The Timing Problem   In Example 7.4 we illustrate another very similar problem with using the IRR approach to evaluate mutually exclusive projects.

EXAMPLE 7.4

Suppose that the Kaufold Corporation has two alternative uses for a warehouse. It can store toxic waste containers (investment A) or electronic equipment (investment B). The cash flows are as follows:

	Year				NPV			
	0	1	2	3	@ 0%	@ 10%	@ 15%	IRR
Investment A	−$10,000	$10,000	$1,000	$ 1,000	$2,000	$669	$109	16.04%
Investment B	− 10,000	1,000	1,000	12,000	4,000	751	−484	12.94

We find that the NPV of investment B is higher with low discount rates, and the NPV of investment A is higher with high discount rates. This is not surprising if you look closely at the cash flow patterns. The cash flows of A occur early, whereas the cash flows of B occur later.

---

[11]Alternatively, we could have subtracted the larger project's cash flows from the smaller project's cash flows. This would have left an *inflow* at date 0, making it necessary to use the IRR rule for financing situations. This would work but we find it more confusing.

If we assume a high discount rate, we favour investment A because we are implicitly assuming that the early cash flow (for example, $10,000 in year 1) can be reinvested at that rate. Because most of investment B's cash flows occur in year 3, B's value is relatively high with low discount rates.[12]

The NPVs and IRRs for both projects appear in Figure 7.6. Project *A* has an NPV of $2,000 at a discount rate of zero. This is calculated by simply adding up the cash flows without discounting them. Project *B* has an NPV of $4,000 at the zero rate. However, the NPV of project *B* declines more rapidly as the discount rate increases than does the NPV of project *A*. As stated above, this is because *B*'s cash flows occur later. Both projects have the same NPV at a discount rate of 10.55 percent. The IRR for a project is the rate at which the NPV equals zero. Because the NPV of *B* declines more rapidly, *B* actually has a lower IRR.

As with the movie example presented above, we can select the better project with one of three different methods:

1. *Compare NPVs of the two projects.* Figure 7.6 aids our decision. If the discount rate is below 10.55 percent, one should choose project *B* because *B* has a higher NPV. If the rate is above 10.55 percent, one should choose project *A* because *A* has a higher NPV.

2. *Compare incremental IRR to discount rate.* Another way of determining that *B* is a better project is to subtract the cash flows of *A* from the cash flows of *B* and then to calculate the IRR. This is the incremental IRR approach we spoke of earlier.

The incremental cash flows are as follows:

| | | | | | NPV of Incremental Cash Flows | | | |
| | | | | | | | | |
Year:	0	1	2	3	@ 0%	@ 10%	@ 15%	IRR
B − *A*	0	−$9,000	0	$11,000	$2,000	$83	−$593	10.55%

This chart shows that the incremental IRR is 10.55 percent. In other words, the NPV on the incremental investment is zero when the discount rate is 10.55 percent. Thus, if the

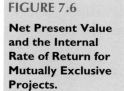

FIGURE 7.6

Net Present Value and the Internal Rate of Return for Mutually Exclusive Projects.

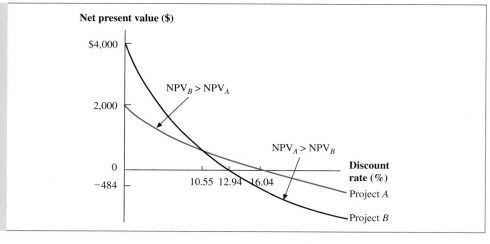

---

[12]It is possible to modify the IRR to specify the reinvestment rate. We do not recommend this modified IRR approach because it does not resolve the timing problem.

relevant discount rate is below 10.55 percent, project *B* is preferred to project *A*. If the relevant discount rate is above 10.55 percent, project *A* is preferred to project *B*.[13]

3. *Calculate NPV on incremental cash flows.* Finally, one could calculate the NPV on the incremental cash flows. The chart that appears with the previous method displays these NPVs. We find that the incremental NPV is positive when the discount rate is either 0 percent or 10 percent. The incremental NPV is negative if the discount rate is 15 percent. If the NPV is positive on the incremental flows, one should choose *B*. If the NPV is negative, one should choose *A*.

In summary, the same decision is reached whether one compares the NPVs of the two projects, compares the incremental IRR to the relevant discount rate, or examines the NPV of the incremental cash flows. However, as shown earlier, one should not compare the IRR of project *A* with the IRR of project *B*.

We suggested earlier that one should subtract the cash flows of the smaller project from the cash flows of the bigger project. What do we do here since the two projects have the same initial investment? Our suggestion in this case is to perform the subtraction so that the first nonzero cash flow is negative. In the Kaufold Corporation example, we achieved this by subtracting *A* from *B*. In this way, we can still use the basic IRR rule for evaluating cash flows.

These examples illustrate problems with the IRR approach in evaluating mutually exclusive projects. Both the professor–student example and the motion picture example illustrate the problem that arises when mutually exclusive projects have different initial investments. The Kaufold Corp. example illustrates the problem that arises when mutually exclusive projects have different cash flow timings. When working with mutually exclusive projects, it is not necessary to determine whether it is the scale problem or the timing problem that exists. Very likely both occur in any real world situation. Instead, the practitioner should simply use either an incremental IRR or an NPV approach.

Redeeming Qualities of the IRR

The IRR probably survives because it fills a need that the NPV does not. People seem to want a rule that summarizes the information about a project in a single rate of return. This single rate provides people with a simple way of discussing projects. For example, one manager in a firm might say to another, "Remodelling the north wing has a 20 percent IRR."

To their credit, however, companies that employ the IRR approach seem to understand its deficiencies. For example, companies frequently restrict managerial projections of cash flows to be negative at the beginning and strictly positive later. Perhaps, then, the ability of the IRR approach to capture a complex investment project in a single number and the ease of communicating that number explain the survival of the IRR.

A Test

To test your knowledge, consider the following two statements:

1. You must know the discount rate to compute the NPV of a project but you compute the IRR without referring to the discount rate.

2. Hence, the IRR rule is easier to apply than the NPV rule because you don't use the discount rate when applying IRR.

---

[13]In this example, we first showed that the NPVs of the two projects are equal when the discount rate is 10.55 percent. We next showed that the incremental IRR is also 10.55 percent. This is not a coincidence; this equality must always hold. The incremental IRR is the rate that causes the incremental cash flows to have zero NPV. The incremental cash flows have zero NPV when the two projects have the same NPV.

The first statement is true. The discount rate is needed to *compute* NPV. The IRR is *computed* by solving for the rate where the NPV is zero. No mention is made of the discount rate in the mere computation. However, the second statement is false. In order to *apply* IRR, you must compare the internal rate of return with the discount rate. Thus, the discount rate is needed for making a decision under either the NPV or IRR approach.

? Concept Questions

- **What is the difference between independent projects and mutually exclusive projects?**
- **What are two problems with the IRR approach that apply to both independent and mutually exclusive projects?**
- **What is the MIRR?**
- **What are two additional problems applying only to mutually exclusive projects?**

7.7 The Profitability Index (PI)

Another method that is used to evaluate projects is called the **profitability index (PI).** It is the ratio of the present value of the future expected cash flows *after* initial investment divided by the amount of the initial investment. The profitability index can be represented as

$$\text{Profitability index(PI)} = \frac{\text{PV of cash flows subsequent to initial investment}}{\text{Initial investment}}$$

EXAMPLE 7.5

Hiram Finnegan Inc. applies a 12 percent cost of capital to two investment opportunities.

Project	Cash Flows ($000,000)			PV @ 12% of Cash Flows Subsequent to Initial Investment ($000,000)	Profitability Index	NPV @ 12% ($000,000)
	C_0	C_1	C_2			
1	−20	70	10	70.5	3.53	50.5
2	−10	15	40	45.3	4.53	35.3

For example, the profitability index is calculated for project 1 as follows. The present value of the cash flows *after* the initial investment are

$$\$70.5 = \frac{\$70}{1.12} + \frac{\$10}{(1.12)^2} \tag{7.9}$$

The profitability index is calculated by dividing the result of Equation (7.9) by the initial investment of $20.[14] This yields

$$3.53 = \frac{\$70.5}{\$20}$$

We consider three possibilities:

1. *Independent projects.* We first assume that we have two independent projects. According to the NPV criterion, both projects should be accepted since NPV is positive in each case. The NPV is positive whenever the profitability index is greater than 1. Thus, the *PI decision rule* is

---

[14]For a "borrowing" type of investment the initial cash flow is an inflow rather than an outlay. In this case, we restate the PI as the present value of the inflows divided by the present value of the outflows.

Accept an independent project if PI > 1.

Reject if PI < 1.

2. *Mutually exclusive projects.* Let us assume that you can now only accept one project. NPV analysis says accept project 1 because this project has the bigger NPV. Because project 2 has the higher PI, the profitability index leads to the wrong selection.

   The problem with the profitability index for mutually exclusive projects is the same as the scale problem with the IRR that we mentioned earlier. Project 2 is smaller than project 1. Because the PI is a ratio, this index misses the fact that project 1 has a larger investment than project 2 has. Thus, like IRR, PI ignores differences of scale for mutually exclusive projects.

   However, as with IRR, the flaw with the PI approach can be corrected using incremental analysis. We write the incremental cash flows after subtracting project 2 from project 1 as follows:

Project	Cash Flows ($000,000)			PV @ 12% of Cash Flows Subsequent to Initial Investment ($000,000)	Profitability Index	NPV @ 12% ($000,000)
	C_0	C_1	C_2			
1 − 2	−10	55	−30	25.2	2.52	15.2

Because the profitability index on the incremental cash flows is greater than 1.0, we should choose the bigger project, that is, project 1. This is the same decision we get with the NPV approach.

3. *Capital rationing.* The two cases above implicitly assumed that the firm could always attract enough capital to make any profitable investments. Now we consider the case when a firm does not have enough capital to fund all positive NPV projects. This is the case of **capital rationing.**

   Imagine that the firm has a third project, as well as the first two. Project 3 has the following cash flows:

Project	Cash Flows ($000,000)			PV @ 12% of Cash Flows Subsequent to Initial Investment ($000,000)	Profitability Index	NPV @ 12% ($000,000)
	C_0	C_1	C_2			
3	−10	5	60	43.4	4.34	33.4

Further, imagine that the projects of Hiram Finnegan Inc. are independent, but the firm has only $20 million to invest. Because project 1 has an initial investment of $20 million, the firm cannot select both this project and another one. Conversely, because projects 2 and 3 have initial investments of $10 million each, both these projects can be chosen. In other words, the cash constraint forces the firm to choose either project 1 or projects 2 and 3.

What should the firm do? Individually, projects 2 and 3 have lower NPVs than project 1 has. However, when the NPVs of projects 2 and 3 are added together, they are higher than the NPV of project 1. Thus, common sense dictates that projects 2 and 3 shall be accepted.

What does our conclusion have to say about the NPV rule or the PI rule? In the case of limited funds, we cannot rank projects according to their NPVs. Instead, we should rank them according to the ratio of present value to initial investment. This is the PI rule.

Both project 2 and project 3 have higher PI ratios than does project 1. Thus, they should be ranked ahead of project 1 when capital is rationed.[15]

The usefulness of the profitability index under capital rationing can be explained in terms of the expression "bang for the buck." In capital budgeting, the profitability index measures the bang (the dollar return) for the buck invested. Hence, it is useful for capital rationing.

It should be noted that the profitability index does not work if funds are also limited beyond the initial time period. For example, if heavy cash outflows elsewhere in the firm were to occur at date 1, project 3 might need to be rejected. In other words, the profitability index cannot handle capital rationing over multiple time periods.

? Concept Questions

- **How does one calculate a project's profitability index?**
- **How is the profitability index applied to independent projects, mutually exclusive projects, and situations of capital rationing?**

7.8 The Practice of Capital Budgeting

So far, this chapter has asked the question: Which capital budgeting methods should companies be using? An equally important question is: Which methods *are* companies using? Table 7.4 goes a long way toward answering this question. As can be seen from the table, approximately three-quarters of large U.S. and Canadian companies use the IRR and NPV methods. An exclusively Canadian study by Jog and Srivastava reached a similar conclusion.[16] This is not surprising, given the theoretical advantages of these approaches. Over

TABLE 7.4
Percent of CFOs Who Always or Almost Always Use a Given Technique

	% Always or Almost Always
Internal rate of return (IRR)	75.6%
Net present value (NPV)	74.9
Payback method	56.7
Discounted payback	29.5
Accounting rate of return	30.3
Profitability index	11.9

Source: Figure 2 from J. R. Graham and C. R. Harvey, "The Theory and Practice of Corporate Finance: Evidence from the Field," *Journal of Financial Economics* 60 (May 2001). Based on a survey of 392 CFOs.

[15]Our approach to PI ranking under capital rationing worked because the initial outlays on the two higher-ranked projects exactly used up the budget of $20 million. If some funds were left over, the PI ranking method could break down. In this case, the solution would be to consider all feasible combinations of projects within the budget and to choose the combination with the highest total NPV.

[16]V. M. Jog and A. K. Srivastava, "Capital Budgeting Practices in Corporate Canada," *Financial Practice and Education* 5 (Fall/Winter 1995), pp. 37–43.

TABLE 7.5
Frequency of Use of Various Capital Budgeting Methods

	Large Firms	Small Firms
Internal rate of return (IRR)	3.41	2.87
Net present value (NPV)	3.42	2.83
Payback method	2.25	2.72
Discounted payback	1.55	1.58
Accounting rate of return	1.25	1.41
Profitability index	0.75	0.78

Firms indicate frequency of use on a scale from 0 (never) to 4 (always). Numbers in table are averages across respondents.
Source: Table 2 from J. R. Graham and C. R. Harvey, "The Theory and Practice of Corporate Finance: Evidence from the Field," *Journal of Financial Economics* 60 (May 2001).

one-half of these companies use the payback method, a rather surprising result given the conceptual problems with this approach. And while discounted payback represents a theoretical improvement over regular payback, the usage here is far less. Perhaps companies are attracted to the user-friendly nature of payback. In addition, the flaws of this approach, as mentioned in the current chapter, may be relatively easy to correct. For example, while the payback method ignores all cash flows after the payback period, an alert manager can make ad hoc adjustments for a project with back-loaded cash flows.

One might expect the capital budgeting methods of large firms to be more sophisticated than the methods of small firms. After all, large firms have the financial resources to hire more sophisticated employees. Table 7.5 provides some support for this idea. Here, firms indicate frequency of use of the various capital budgeting methods on a scale of 0 (never) to 4 (always). Both the IRR and NPV methods are used more frequently, and payback less frequently, in large firms than in small firms. Conversely, large and small firms employ the last three approaches about equally.

The use of quantitative techniques in capital budgeting varies with the industry. As one would imagine, firms that are better able to estimate cash flows precisely are more likely to use NPV. For example, estimation of cash flow in certain aspects of the oil business is quite feasible. Because of this, energy-related firms were among the first to use NPV analysis. Conversely, the flows in the motion picture business are very hard to project. The grosses of great hits like *Shrek, Spiderman, Pirates of the Caribbean* and *Lord of the Rings* were far, far greater than anyone imagined. The big failures like *Waterworld* were unexpected as well. Consequently, NPV analysis is frowned upon in the movie business.

Non-cash-flow factors may occasionally play a role in capital budgeting decisions. Ego is one example of such a factor. Building extremely tall skyscrapers is usually not about economics and practicality and more to do with prestige, making a bold statement, and acquiring bragging rights.[17] Another example of a non-cash-flow factor is over-optimism when entering the restaurant industry. This initial enthusiasm can be an important factor in taking the plunge into a venture that may not look all that great on paper.

---

[17]*National Post,* Monday, July 23, 2001, pp. A1–2.

7.9 SUMMARY AND CONCLUSIONS

1. In this chapter we cover different investment decision rules. We evaluate the most popular alternatives to the NPV: the payback period, the accounting rate of return, the internal rate of return, and the profitability index. In doing so, we learn more about the NPV.

2. While we find that the alternatives have some redeeming qualities, when all is said and done, they are not the NPV rule; for those of us in finance, that makes them decidedly second-rate.

3. Of the competitors to NPV, IRR must be ranked above either payback or accounting rate of return. In fact, IRR always reaches the same decision as NPV in the normal case where the initial outflows of an independent investment project are only followed by a series of inflows.

4. We classified the flaws of IRR into two types. First, we considered the general case applying to both independent and mutually exclusive projects. There appeared to be two problems here:

    a. Some projects have cash inflows followed by one or more outflows. The IRR rule is inverted here: One should accept when the IRR is *below* the discount rate.

    b. Some projects have a number of changes of sign in their cash flows. Here, there are likely to be multiple internal rates of return. The practitioner must use either NPV or modified IRR here.

5. Next, we considered the specific problems with the IRR for mutually exclusive projects. We showed that, due to differences in either size or timing, the project with the highest IRR need not have the highest NPV. Hence, the IRR rule should not be applied. (Of course, NPV can still be applied.)

    However, we then calculated incremental cash flows. For ease of calculation, we suggested subtracting the cash flows of the smaller project from the cash flows of the larger project. In that way, the incremental initial cash flow is negative.

    One can correctly pick the better of two mutually exclusive projects in three other ways:

    a. Choose the project with the higher NPV.

    b. If the incremental IRR is greater than the discount rate, choose the bigger project.

    c. If the incremental NPV is positive, choose the bigger project.

6. We describe the capital rationing as a case where funds are limited to a fixed dollar amount. With capital rationing the profitability index can be a useful method. Of course, a manager can never go wrong by maximizing the total NPV of all company projects.

KEY TERMS

Average accounting return (AAR) 177
Basic IRR rule 180
Capital rationing 193
Discounted payback period rule 176

Incremental IRR 188
Independent project 182
Internal rate of return (IRR) 180
Modified IRR (MIRR) 185

Mutually exclusive investments 182
Payback period rule 173
Profitability index (PI) 192
Value additivity 172

SUGGESTED READING

For a discussion of what capital budgeting techniques are used by large firms, see:
Vijay M. Jog and Ashwani K. Srivastava. "Capital Budgeting Practice in Corporate Canada." *Financial Practice and Education 5* (Fall/Winter 1995), pp. 37–43.
J. R. Graham and C. R. Harvey. "The Theory and Practice of Corporate Finance: Evidence from the Field." *Journal of Financial Economics* 60 (May 2001).

QUESTIONS & PROBLEMS

The Payback Period Rule

7.1 Fuji Software Inc. has the following mutually exclusive projects.

Year	Project A	Project B
0	−$7,500	−$5,000
1	4,000	2,500
2	3,500	1,200
3	1,500	3,000

    a. Suppose Fuji's payback period cutoff is two years. Which of these two projects should be chosen?

    b. Suppose Fuji uses the NPV rule to rank these two projects. Which project should be chosen if the appropriate discount rate is 15 percent?

7.2 An investment project provides cash inflows of $840 per year for eight years. What is the project payback period if the initial cost is $3,000? What if the initial cost is $5,000? What if it is $7,000?

7.3 An investment project has annual cash inflows of $7,000, $7,500, $8,000, and $8,500, and a discount rate of 14 percent. What is the discounted payback period for these cash flows if the initial cost is $8,000? What if the initial cost is $13,000? What if it is $18,000?

7.4 An investment project costs $10,000 and has annual cash flows of $2,100 for six years. What is the discounted payback period if the discount rate is 0 percent? What if the discount rate is 5 percent? If it is 15 percent?

7.5 An investment under consideration has a payback of seven years and a cost of $483,000. If the required return is 12 percent, what is the worst-case NPV? The best case NPV? Explain. Assume the cash flows are conventional.

Average Accounting Return

7.6 Your firm is considering purchasing a machine with the following annual, end-of-year, book investment accounts:

	Purchase Date	Year 1	Year 2	Year 3	Year 4
Gross Investment	$20,000	$20,000	$20,000	$20,000	$20,000
Less: Accumulated Depreciation	0	8,000	9,000	10,000	20,000
Net Investment	$20,000	$12,000	$11,000	$10,000	$ 0

    The machine generates, on average, $4,500 per year in additional net income.

    a. What is the average accounting return for this machine?

    b. What three flaws are inherent in this decision rule?

7.7 The Bluerock Group has invested $8,000 in a high-tech project lasting three years. Depreciation is $4,000, $2,500, and $1,500 in years 1, 2, and 3, respectively. The project generates pre-tax income of $2,000 each year. The pre-tax income already includes the depreciation expense. If the tax rate is 25 percent, what is the project's average accounting return (AAR)?

7.8 Western Printing Co. has an opportunity to purchase a $6 million printing machine. The machine has an economic life of five years and will be worthless after that time. It will generate net income of $275,000 one year from today and the income stream will grow at 8 percent per year thereafter. The company uses straight-line depreciation (i.e., equal depreciation each year). What is the average accounting return of the investment? Should the machine be purchased if Western Printing's average accounting return cutoff is 23 percent?

The Internal Rate of Return

7.9 Fluffy Creatures World Inc. has a project with the following cash flows:

Year	Cash Flows ($)
0	−$8,000
1	4,000
2	3,000
3	2,000

    The company evaluates all projects by applying the IRR rule. If the appropriate interest rate is 8 percent, should the company accept the project?

Visit us at www.mcgrawhill.ca/olc/ross

7.10 Compute the internal rate of return for the cash flows of the following two projects:

	Cash Flows ($)	
Year	Project A	Project B
0	−$2,000	−$1,500
1	1,000	500
2	1,500	1,000
3	2,000	1,500

EXCEL

7.11

Year	Deepwater Fishing	New Submarine Ride
0	−$600,000	−$1,800,000
1	270,000	1,000,000
2	350,000	700,000
3	300,000	900,000

As a financial analyst for BRC, you are asked the following questions:

a. If your decision rule is to accept the project with the greater IRR, which project should you choose?

b. Because you are fully aware of the IRR rule's scale problem, you calculate the incremental IRR for the cash flows. Based on your computation, which project should you choose?

c. To be prudent, you compute the NPV for both projects at a discount rate of 15 percent. Which project should you choose? Is it consistent with the incremental IRR rule?

7.12 Westbrook Petroleum Inc. is trying to evaluate a generation project with the following cash flows:

Year	Cash Flow
0	−$28,000,000
1	53,000,000
2	− 8,000,000

a. If the company requires a 10 percent return on its investments, should it accept this project? Why?

b. Compute the IRR for this project. How many IRRs are there? If you apply the IRR decision rule, should you accept the project or not? What's going on here?

7.13 This problem is useful for testing the ability of financial calculators and computer software. Consider the following cash flows. How many different IRRs are there? (*Hint:* Search between 20 percent and 70 percent.) When should we take this project?

Year	Cash Flow
0	−$ 504
1	2,862
2	−6,070
3	5,700
4	−2,000

7.14 The Enviro Mining Corporation is set to open a gold mine near Banff, Alberta. According to the treasurer, Monty Goldstein, "This is a golden opportunity." The mine will cost $600,000 to open and will have an economic life of 11 years. It will generate a cash inflow of $100,000 at the end of the first year, and the cash inflows are projected to grow at 8 percent per year for the next 10 years. After 11 years, the mine will be abandoned. Abandonment costs will be $50,000 at the end of year 11.

a. What is the IRR for the gold mine?

b. The Enviro Mining Corporation requires a 10 percent return on such undertakings. Should the mine be opened?

7.15 Consider two streams of cash flows, *A* and *B*. Stream *A*'s first cash flow is $5,000 and is received three years from today. Future cash flows in stream *A* grow by 4 percent in perpetuity. Stream *B*'s first cash flow is −$6,000, is received two years from today, and will continue in perpetuity. Assume that the appropriate discount rate is 12 percent.

    a. What is the present value of each stream?

    b. Suppose that the two streams are combined into one project, called *C*. What is the IRR of project *C*?

    c. What is the correct IRR rule for project *C*?

7.16 McLennan's Corp. has a project with the following cash flows:

Year	Cash Flow
0	$20,000
1	−26,000
2	13,000

What is the IRR of the project? What is happening here?

7.17 It is sometimes stated that "the internal rate of return approach assumes reinvestment of the intermediate cash flows at the internal rate of return." Is this claim correct? To answer, suppose you calculate the IRR of a project in the usual way. Next, suppose you do the following:

    a. Calculate the future value (as of the end of the project) of all the cash flows other than the initial outlay assuming they are reinvested at the IRR, producing a single future value figure for the project.

    b. Calculate the IRR of the project using the single future value calculated in the previous step and the initial outlay. It is easy to verify that you will get the same IRR as in your original calculation only if you use the IRR as the reinvestment rate in the previous step.

The Profitability Index

7.18 James plans to open a self-serve grooming centre in a storefront. The grooming equipment will cost $160,000, to be paid immediately. James expects after-tax cash inflows of $40,000 annually for seven years, after which he plans to scrap the equipment and retire to the beaches of Nevis. The first cash inflow occurs at the end of the first year. Assume the required return is 15 percent. What is the project's PI? Should it be accepted?

EXCEL

7.19 Suppose the following two independent investment opportunities are available to Greek Letters Inc. The appropriate discount rate is 10 percent.

Year	Project Alpha	Project Beta
0	−$500	−$2,000
1	300	300
2	700	1,800
3	600	1,700

    a. Compute the profitability index for each of the two projects.

    b. Which project(s) should Greek Letters accept based on the profitability index rule?

7.20 The Robb Computer Corporation is trying to choose between the following two mutually exclusive design projects:

Year	Cash Flow (I)	Cash Flow (II)
0	−$30,000	−$5,000
1	15,000	2,800
2	15,000	2,800
3	15,000	2,800

    a. If the required return is 10 percent and Robb Computer applies the profitability index decision rule, which project should the firm accept?

    b. If the company applies the NPV decision rule, which project should it take?

    c. Explain why your answers in (a) and (b) are different.

7.21 Hanmi Group, a consumer electronics conglomerate, is reviewing its annual budget in wireless technology. It is considering investments in three different technologies to develop wireless communication devices. Consider the following cash flows of the three independent projects for Hanmi. Assume the discount rate for Hanmi is 10 percent. Further, Hanmi Group has only $30 million to invest in new projects this year.

	Cash Flow in Millions ($)		
Year	CDMA	G4	Wi-Fi
0	−$10	−$20	−$30
1	25	20	20
2	15	50	40
3	5	40	100

a. Based on the profitability index decision rule, rank these investments.
b. Based on the NPV, rank these investments.
c. Based on your findings in (a) and (b), what would you recommend to the CEO of Hanmi Group and why.

Comparison of Investment Rules

EXCEL

7.22 Mario Brothers, a game manufacturer, has a new idea for an adventure game. It can market the game either as a traditional board game or as an interactive DVD, but not both. Consider the following cash flows of the two mutually exclusive projects for Mario Brothers. Assume the discount rate for Mario Brothers is 10 percent.

Year	Board Game	DVD
0	−$300	−$1,500
1	400	1,100
2	100	800
3	100	400

a. Based on the payback period rule, which project should be chosen?
b. Based on the NPV, which project should be chosen?
c. Based on the IRR, which project should be chosen?
d. Based on the incremental IRR, which project should be chosen?

7.23 Consider the following cash flows of two mutually exclusive projects for AZ-Motorcars. Assume the discount rate for AZ-Motorcars is 10 percent.

Year	AZM Mini-SUV	AZF Full-SUV
0	−$200,000	−$500,000
1	200,000	200,000
2	150,000	300,000
3	150,000	300,000

a. Based on the payback period, which project should be taken?
b. Based on the NPV, which project should be taken?
c. Based on the IRR, which project should be taken?
d. Based on this analysis, is incremental IRR analysis necessary? If yes, please conduct the analysis.

7.24 The treasurer of Fresh Canned Fruits Inc. has projected the cash flows of projects *A, B,* and *C* as follows.

Year	Project A	Project B	Project C
0	−$100,000	−$200,000	−$100,000
1	70,000	130,000	75,000
2	70,000	130,000	60,000

Suppose the relevant discount rate is 12 percent a year.

a. Compute the profitability index for each of the three projects.

b. Compute the NPV for each of the three projects.

c. Suppose these three projects are independent. Which project(s) should Fresh accept based on the profitability index rule?

d. Suppose these three projects are mutually exclusive. Which project(s) should Fresh accept based on the profitability index rule?

e. Suppose Fresh's budget for these projects is $300,000. The projects are not divisible. Which project(s) should Fresh accept?

7.25 Consider the following cash flows of two mutually exclusive projects for Tokyo Rubber Company. Assume the discount rate for Tokyo Rubber Company is 10 percent.

Year	Dry Prepreg	Solvent Prepreg
0	−$1,000,000	−$500,000
1	600,000	300,000
2	400,000	500,000
3	1,000,000	100,000

a. Based on the payback period, which project should be taken?

b. Based on the NPV, which project should be taken?

c. Based on the IRR, which project should be taken?

d. Based on this analysis, is incremental IRR analysis necessary? If yes, please conduct the analysis.

7.26 Consider two mutually exclusive new product launch projects that Nagano Golf is considering. Assume the discount rate for Nagano Golf is 15 percent.

Project *A*: Nagano NP-30

• Professional clubs that will take an initial investment of $100,000 at time 0.

• Next five years (years 1–5) of sales will generate a consistent cash flow of $40,000 per year.

• Introduction of new product at year 6 will terminate further cash flows from this project.

Project *B*: Nagano NX-20

• High-end amateur clubs that will take an initial investment of $30,000 at time 0.

• Cash flow at year 1 is $20,000. In each subsequent year cash flow will grow at 15 percent per year.

• Introduction of new product at year 6 will terminate further cash flows from this project.

Year	NP-30	NX-20
0	−$100,000	−$30,000
1	40,000	20,000
2	40,000	23,000
3	40,000	26,450
4	40,000	30,418
5	40,000	34,980

Please fill in the following table:

	NP-30	NX-20	Implications
NPV			
IRR			
Incremental IRR			
PI			

7.27 Consider two mutually exclusive R&D projects that ADM is considering. Assume the discount rate for ADM is 15 percent.

Project *A*: Server CPU .13 micron processing project.
- By shrinking the die size to .13 micron, ADM will be able to offer server CPU chips with lower power consumption and heat generation, meaning faster CPUs.

Project *B*: New telecom chip project.
- Entry into this industry will require introduction of a new chip for cell phones.
- The know-how will require a lot of upfront capital, but success of the project will lead to large cash flows later on.

Year	A	B
0	−$100,000	−$200,000
1	50,000	60,000
2	50,000	60,000
3	40,000	60,000
4	30,000	100,000
5	20,000	200,000

Please fill in the following table:

	A	B	Implications
NPV			
IRR			
Incremental IRR			
PI			

7.28 You are a senior manager at Poeing Aircraft and have been authorized to spend up to $200,000 for projects. The three projects you are considering have the following characteristics:

Project *A*: Initial investment of $150,000. Cash flow of $50,000 at year 1 and $100,000 at year 2. This is a plant expansion project, where the required rate of return is 10 percent.

Project *B*: Initial investment of $200,000. Cash flow of $200,000 at year 1 and $111,000 at year 2. This is a new product development project, where the required rate of return is 20 percent.

Project *C*: Initial investment of $100,000. Cash flow of $100,000 at year 1 and $100,000 at year 2. This is a market expansion project, where the required rate of return is 20 percent.
Assume the corporate discount rate is 10 percent.
Please offer your recommendations, backed by your analysis:

	A	B	C	Implications
Payback				
IRR				
Incremental IRR				
PI				
NPV				

MINICASE: Gold Mining Corp.

Randy Goldberg, the owner of Gold Mining Corp., is evaluating a new gold mine in northern Manitoba. Dan Stone, the company's geologist, has just finished his analysis of the mine site. He has estimated that the mine would be productive for eight years, after which the gold would be completely mined. Dan has taken an estimate of the gold deposits to Alma Garrett, the company's financial officer. Alma has been asked by Randy to perform an analysis and present her recommendation on whether the company should open the new mine. Alma has used the estimates provided by Dan to determine the revenues that could be expected from the mine. She has also projected the expense of opening the mine and the annual operating expenses. If the company opens the mine, it will cost $500 million today, and it will have a cash outflow of $80 million nine years from today in costs associated with closing the mine and reclaiming the area surrounding it. All figures are after-tax and the tax rate for Gold Mining is 31 percent. The expected cash flows each year from the mine are shown in the following table. Gold Mining has a 12 percent required return on all of its gold mines.

Year	Cash Flow
0	−$500,000,000
1	60,000,000
2	90,000,000
3	170,000,000
4	230,000,000
5	205,000,000
6	140,000,000
7	110,000,000
8	70,000,000
9	− 80,000,000

1. Construct a spreadsheet to calculate the payback period, internal rate of return, modified internal rate of return, and net present value of the proposed mine.

2. Based on your analysis, should the company open the mine?

3. Most spreadsheets do not have a built-in formula to calculate the payback period. Write a VBA script that calculates the payback period for a project.

Chapter 8

Net Present Value and Capital Budgeting

EXECUTIVE SUMMARY

In January 2006, Sharp Corporation, the world's leading producer of flat panel LCD TVs, announced that it would spend an additional ¥200 billion ($2.03 billion) to build a new production plant. With a total investment of ¥350 billion ($3.55 billion), the production capacity of the new plant would increase from 30,000 to 90,000 glass substrates per month, resulting in the production equivalent of 22 million 32-inch TV sets by 2008. Just days earlier, Matsushita Electric Industrial Co., the world's leading plasma TV manufacturer, announced that it would invest ¥180 billion ($1.82 billion) to build a new plant to produce plasma panels. The new plasma plant would more than double the company's production capacity to 11.1 million units per year. Sharp would not have made such an enormous investment into these facilities if the company felt that the return from these investments was going to be less than the initial costs. The decision of whether or not go through with the expansion is an example of a capital budgeting decision.

Previous chapters discussed the basics of capital budgeting and the net present value approach. We now want to move beyond these basics into the real-world application of these techniques. We want to show you how to use discounted cash flow (DCF) analysis and net present value (NPV) in capital budgeting decisions.

In this chapter, we show how to identify the relevant cash flows of a project, including initial investment outlays, requirements for working capital, and operating cash flows. We look at the effects of depreciation and taxes. We examine the impact of inflation on interest rates and on a project's discount rate, and we show why inflation must be handled consistently in NPV analysis.

8.1 Incremental Cash Flows

Cash Flows—Not Accounting Income

You may not have thought about it, but there is a big difference between corporate finance courses and financial accounting courses. Techniques in corporate finance generally use cash flows, whereas financial accounting generally stresses income or earnings numbers. Certainly, our text has followed this tradition since our net present value techniques discounted cash flows, not earnings. When considering a single project, we discounted the cash flows that the firm receives from the project. When valuing the firm as a whole, we discounted dividends—not earnings—because dividends are the cash flows that an investor receives.

There are many differences between earnings and cash flows. For example, consider a firm buying a building for $100,000 today. The entire $100,000 is an immediate cash outflow. However, assuming straight-line depreciation over 20 years, only $5,000 (or $100,000/20) is considered an accounting expense in the current year.[1] Current earnings are thereby reduced by only $5,000. The remaining $95,000 is expensed over the following 19 years.

Because the seller of the property demands immediate payment, the cost of the project to the firm at date 0 is $100,000. Thus, the full $100,000 figure should be viewed as an immediate outflow for capital budgeting purposes.

In addition, it is not enough to use cash flows. In calculating the NPV of a project, only cash flows that are *incremental* to the project should be used. **Incremental cash flows** are the changes in the firm's cash flows that occur as a direct consequence of accepting the project. That is, we are interested in the difference between the cash flows of the firm with and without the project.

The use of incremental cash flows sounds easy enough, but pitfalls abound in the real world. In this section we describe how to avoid some of the pitfalls of determining incremental cash flows.

Sunk Costs

A **sunk cost** is a cost that has already occurred. Because sunk costs are in the past, they cannot be changed by the decision to accept or reject the project. Just as we "let bygones be bygones," we should ignore such costs. Sunk costs are not incremental cash outflows.

EXAMPLE 8.1

The General Milk Company is currently evaluating the NPV of establishing a line of chocolate milk. As part of the evaluation, the company had paid a consulting firm $100,000 to perform a test marketing analysis. The expenditure was made last year. Is this cost relevant for the capital budgeting decision now confronting the management of General Milk Company?

The answer is no. The $100,000 is not recoverable, so the $100,000 expenditure is a sunk cost, or "spilled milk." Of course, the decision to spend $100,000 for a marketing analysis was a capital budgeting decision itself and was perfectly relevant *before* it was sunk. Our point is that once the company incurred the expense, the cost became irrelevant for any future decision.

Opportunity Costs

Your firm may have an asset that it is considering selling, leasing, or employing elsewhere in the business. If the asset is used in a new project, potential revenues from alternative uses are lost. These lost revenues can meaningfully be viewed as costs. They are called **opportunity costs** because, by taking the project, the firm forgoes other opportunities for using the assets.

---

[1] Recall from Chapter 2 that accountants use the term *amortization* to refer to depreciation and depletion.

EXAMPLE 8.2

Suppose the Pacific Trading Company has an empty warehouse in Vancouver that can be used to store a new line of electronic pinball machines. The company hopes to market the machines to affluent West Coast consumers. Should the cost of the warehouse and land be included in the costs associated with introducing a new line of electronic pinball machines?

The answer is yes. The use of a warehouse is not free; it has an opportunity cost. The cost is the cash that could be raised by the company if the decision to market the electronic pinball machines were rejected and the warehouse and land were put to some other use (or sold). If so, the NPV of the alternative uses becomes an opportunity cost of the decision to sell electronic pinball machines.

Side Effects

Another difficulty in determining incremental cash flows comes from the side effects of the proposed project on other parts of the firm. A side effect is classified as either **erosion** or **synergy.** Erosion occurs when a new product reduces the sales and, hence, the cash flows, of existing products. Synergy occurs when a new project increases the cash flows of existing projects.

EXAMPLE 8.3

Suppose the Innovative Motors Corporation (IMC) is determining the NPV of a new convertible sports car. Some of the customers who would purchase the car are owners of IMC's compact sedan. Are all sales and profits from the new convertible sports car incremental?

The answer is no because some of the cash flow represents transfers from other elements of IMC's product line. This is erosion, which must be included in the NPV calculation. Without taking erosion into account, IMC might erroneously calculate the NPV of the sports car to be, say, $100 million. If half the customers are transfers from the sedan and lost sedan sales have an NPV of −$150 million, the true NPV is −$50 million ($100 million − $150 million).

IMC is also contemplating the formation of a racing team. The team is forecasted to lose money for the foreseeable future, with perhaps the best projection showing an NPV of −$35 million for the operation. However, IMC's managers are aware that the team will likely generate great publicity for all of IMC's products. A consultant estimates that the increase in cash flows elsewhere in the firm has a present value of $65 million. Assuming that the consultant's estimates of synergy are trustworthy, the net present value of the team is $30 million ($65 million − $35 million). The managers should form the team.

Allocated Costs

Frequently a particular expenditure benefits a number of projects. Accountants allocate this cost across the different projects when determining income. However, for capital budgeting purposes, this **allocated cost** should be viewed as a cash outflow of a project only if it is an incremental cost of the project.

EXAMPLE 8.4

> The Voetmann Consulting Corp. devotes one wing of its suite of offices to a library requiring a cash outflow of $100,000 a year in upkeep. A proposed capital budgeting project is expected to generate revenue equal to 5 percent of the firm's overall sales. An executive at the firm, H. Sears, argues that $5,000 (5% × 100,000) should be viewed as the proposed project's share of the library's costs. Is this appropriate for capital budgeting?
>
> The answer is no. One must ask the question: What is the difference between the cash flows of the entire firm with the project and the cash flows of the entire firm without the project? The firm will spend $100,000 on library upkeep whether or not the proposed project is accepted. Since acceptance of the proposed project does not affect this cash flow, the cash flow should be ignored when calculating the NPV of the project.

? Concept Questions
- **What are the four difficulties in determining incremental cash flows?**
- **Define sunk costs, opportunity costs, side effects, and allocated costs.**

8.2 The Majestic Mulch and Compost Company: An Example

We next consider the example of a proposed investment in machinery and related items. Our example involves the Majestic Mulch and Compost Company (MMCC) and power mulching tools.

The MMCC, originally established in 1988 to make composting equipment, is now a leading producer of composters. In 1990 the company introduced "Friends of Grass," its first line of high-performance composters. The MMCC management has sought opportunities in whatever businesses seem to have some potential for cash flow. In 1993, World B. Clean, vice-president of MMCC, identified another segment of the compost market that looked promising and that he felt was not adequately served by larger manufacturers. That market was for power mulching tools, and he believed a large number of composters valued a high-performance mulcher to aid in composting. He also believed that it would be difficult for competitors to take advantage of the opportunity because of MMCC's cost advantages and because of its highly developed marketing skills.

As a result, in late 2000 MMCC decided to evaluate the marketing potential of power mulching tools. MMCC sent a questionnaire to consumers in three markets: Vancouver, Toronto, and Montreal. The results of the three questionnaires were much better than expected and supported the conclusion that the power mulching tools could achieve a 10 to 15 percent share of the market. Of course, some people at MMCC complained about the cost of the test marketing, which was $250,000. However, Clean argued that it was a sunk cost and should not be included in project evaluation.

In any case, the MMCC is now considering investing in a machine to produce power mulching tools. The power mulchers would be produced in a building owned by the firm and located outside Prince George, B.C. It is currently vacant, and has no resale value due to its location. Working with his staff, Clean is preparing an analysis of the proposed new product. He summarizes his assumptions as follows: The cost of the tool-making machine is $800,000. The machine has an estimated market value at the end of eight years of $150,000. Production by year during the eight-year life of the machine is expected to be as follows: 6,000 units, 9,000 units, 12,000 units, 13,000 units, 12,000 units, 10,000 units, 8,000 units, and 6,000 units. The price of power mulchers in the first year will be $100. The power mulching tool market is highly competitive, so Clean believes that the price of power mulchers will increase only 2 percent per year, as compared to the anticipated general inflation rate of 5 percent. Conversely, the materials used to produce power mulchers are becoming more expensive. Because of this, variable production cash outflows are expected to grow 5 percent per year. First-year variable production costs will be $64 per unit, and fixed production costs will be $50,000 each year. The tax rate is 40 percent.

Net working capital is defined as the difference between current assets and current liabilities. Clean finds that the firm must maintain an investment in working capital. Like any manufacturing firm, it will purchase raw materials before production and sale, giving rise to an investment in inventory. It will maintain cash as a buffer against unforeseen expenditures. Its credit sales will generate accounts receivable. Management believes that the investment in the different items of working capital totals $40,000 in year 0, stays at 15 percent of sales at the end of each year, and falls to $0 by the project's end. In other words, the investment in working capital is completely recovered by the end of the project's life.

Projections based on these assumptions and Clean's analysis appear in Tables 8.1 through 8.4. In these tables all cash flows are assumed to occur at the *end* of the year. Because of the large amount of data in these tables, it is important to see how the tables are related. Table 8.1 shows the basic data for both investment and income. Supplementary schedules, as presented in Tables 8.2 and 8.3, help explain where the numbers in Table 8.1 come from. Our goal is to obtain projections of cash flow. The data in Table 8.1 are all that is needed to calculate the relevant cash flows, as shown in Table 8.4.

TABLE 8.1   The Worksheet for Cash Flows of the MMCC*

	Year 0	Year 1	Year 2	Year 3	Year 4	Year 5	Year 6	Year 7	Year 8
I. Income									
(1) Sales revenues		$600,000	$918,000	$1,248,480	$1,379,570	$1,298,919	$1,104,081	$900,930	$689,211
(2) Operating costs		434,000	654,800	896,720	1,013,144	983,509	866,820	736,129	590,327
(3) CCA		80,000	144,000	115,200	92,160	73,728	58,982	47,186	37,749
(4) EBIT		86,000	119,200	236,560	274,266	241,682	178,278	117,615	61,136
(5) Taxes		34,400	47,680	94,624	109,707	96,673	71,311	47,046	24,454
(6) Net income		51,600	71,520	141,936	164,560	145,009	106,967	70,569	36,682
II. Investments									
(7) NWC (end of year)	$40,000	$90,000	$137,700	$187,272	$206,936	$194,838	$165,612	$135,139	$0
(8) Change in NWC*	($40,000)	($50,000)	($47,700)	($49,572)	($19,664)	$12,098	$29,226	$30,473	$135,139
(9) Equipment†	($800,000)								
(10) Aftertax salvage									$150,000
(11) Investment cash flow	($840,000)	($50,000)	($47,700)	($49,572)	($19,664)	$12,098	$29,226	$30,473	$285,139

*All cash flows occur at the end of the year.
†A negative change in net working capital or equipment represents a cash outflow for the company.

TABLE 8.2   Operating Revenues and Costs of the MMCC

(1) Year	(2) Production	(3) Price*	(4) Sales Revenues	(5) Cost Per Unit†	(6) Variable Costs	(7) Fixed Costs	(8) Operating Costs
1	6,000	$100.00	$ 600,000	$64.00	$384,000	$50,000	$ 434,000
2	9,000	102.00	918,000	67.20	604,800	50,000	654,800
3	12,000	104.04	1,248,480	70.56	846,720	50,000	896,720
4	13,000	106.12	1,379,570	74.09	963,144	50,000	1,013,144
5	12,000	108.24	1,298,919	77.79	933,509	50,000	983,509
6	10,000	110.41	1,104,081	81.68	816,820	50,000	866,820
7	8,000	112.62	900,930	85.77	686,129	50,000	736,129
8	6,000	114.87	689,211	90.05	540,327	50,000	590,327

*Prices rise 2 percent a year.
†Unit costs rise 5 percent a year.

TABLE 8.3
Annual Capital Cost Allowance, Power Mulcher Project (Class 8, 20 percent rate)

Year	Beginning UCC	CCA	Ending UCC
1	$400,000	$ 80,000	$320,000
2	720,000	144,000	576,000
3	576,000	115,200	460,800
4	460,800	92,160	368,640
5	368,640	73,728	294,912
6	294,912	58,982	235,930
7	235,930	47,186	188,744
8	188,744	37,749	150,995

TABLE 8.4   Incremental Cash Flows for the MMCC

	Year 0	Year 1	Year 2	Year 3	Year 4	Year 5	Year 6	Year 7	Year 8
(1) Sales revenues [line 1, Table 8.1]		$600,000	$918,000	$1,248,480	$1,379,570	$1,298,919	$1,104,081	$900,930	$689,211
(2) Operating costs [line 2, Table 8.1]		434,000	654,800	896,720	1,013,144	983,509	866,820	736,129	590,327
(3) Taxes [line 5, Table 8.1]		34,400	47,680	94,624	109,707	96,673	71,311	47,046	24,454
(4) Operating cash flow [(1) − (2) − (3)]		131,600	215,520	257,136	256,720	218,737	165,949	117,755	74,430
(5) Investment cash flow	($840,000)	(50,000)	(47,700)	(49,572)	(19,664)	12,098	29,226	30,473	285,139
(6) Total project cash flow	($840,000)	$81,600	$167,820	$207,564	$237,056	$230,835	$195,175	$148,228	$359,570

NPV @ 4% $500,135
NPV @ 10% $188,042
NPV @ 15% $ 2,280
NPV @ 20%   ($137,896)

An Analysis of the Project

Investments   The investment outlays required for the project are summarized in the bottom segment of Table 8.1. They consist of two parts:[2]

1. *The power mulching tool machine.* The purchase requires a cash outflow of $800,000 at year 0. The firm realizes a cash inflow when the machine is sold in year 8. These cash flows are shown in lines 9 and 10 of Table 8.1.
2. *The investment in working capital.* Required working capital appears in line 7. Working capital rises over the early years of the project as expansion occurs. However, all working capital is assumed to be recovered at the end, a common assumption in capital budgeting. In other words, all inventory is sold by the end, the cash balance maintained as a buffer is liquidated, and all accounts receivable are collected. Increases in working capital in the early years must be funded by cash generated elsewhere in the firm. Hence, these increases are viewed as cash *outflows*. Conversely, decreases in working capital in the later years are viewed as cash inflows. All of these cash flows are presented in line 8. A more complete discussion of working capital is provided later in this section. The total cash flow from the above two investments is shown in line 11.

Income, Taxes, and Operating Cash Flow   Next, the determination of income and operating cash flow is presented in the top segment of Table 8.1. While we are ultimately interested in cash flow—not income—we need the income calculation in order to determine taxes. Lines 1 and 2 of Table 8.1 show sales revenues and operating costs, respectively. The projections in these lines are based on the sales revenues and operating costs computed in columns 4 and 8 of Table 8.2. The estimates of revenues and costs follow from assumptions made by the corporate planning staff at MMCC. In other words, the estimates critically depend on the fact that product prices are projected to increase at 2 percent per year and variable costs are projected to increase at 5 percent per year.

Capital cost allowance (depreciation for tax purposes and abbreviated as CCA) of the $800,000 capital investment is based on the amount allowed by the Canada Revenue Agency.[3] CCA calculations are shown in Table 8.3 and are based on a class 8, 20 percent rate. The column labelled CCA is reproduced in line 3 of Table 8.1. Earnings before interest and taxes (EBIT) are calculated in line 4 of Table 8.1. Taxes are provided in line 5 of this table, and net income is calculated in line 6.

Project Cash Flow   Project cash flow is finally determined in Table 8.4. It consists of operating cash flow and investment cash flow. Operating cash flow is determined by subtracting operating costs and taxes from sales revenues as shown in lines 1 through 4 in Table 8.4. Adding investment cash flow from line 11 in Table 8.1 gives total project cash flow on line 6 in Table 8.4.

Net Present Value   It is possible to calculate the NPV of the MMCC power mulcher tool project from these cash flows. As can be seen at the bottom of Table 8.4, the NPV is $188,042 if 10 percent is the appropriate discount rate and −$137,896 if 20 percent is the appropriate discount rate. If the discount rate is 15.07 percent, the project will have a zero

---

[2]If the vacant building had a resale value, this would be included as a third part to this section. Recall from Section 8.1 the discussion of opportunity costs. A positive resale value would be a cash outflow in year 0.

[3]CCA rules are discussed in detail in Appendix 8A.

NPV. In other words, the project's internal rate of return is 15.07 percent. If the discount rate of the MMCC power mulcher tool project is above 15.07 percent, it should not be accepted because its NPV would be negative.

Which Set of Books?

It should be noted that the firm's management generally keeps two sets of books, one for the Canada Revenue Agency (CRA) (called the *tax books*) and another for its annual report (called the *shareholders' books*). The tax books follow the rules of the *Income Tax Act*. The shareholders' books follow the rules of the Canadian Institute of Chartered Accountants (CICA), the governing body in accounting. The two sets of rules differ widely in certain areas. For example, deductible expenses as calculated according to CICA rules are often different from the calculations required by the Act.

Such differences result from the different purposes of the two sets of rules. CICA rules seek to represent the accounting income of the firm according to Generally Accepted Accounting Principles. Tax rules govern the calculation of corporate income tax. Appendix 8A gives a synopsis of the tax rules on CCA.

Which of the two sets of rules on depreciation do we want in order to create the previous tables for MMCC? Clearly, we're interested in the tax rules. Our purpose is to determine net cash flow, and tax payments are a cash outflow. The CICA regulations determine the calculation of accounting income, not cash flow.

A Note on Net Working Capital

The investment in net working capital is an important part of any capital budgeting analysis. While we explicitly considered net working capital in line 7 (Table 8.1) as 15 percent of sales, students may be wondering where such numbers come from. An investment in net working capital arises whenever (1) raw materials and other inventory are purchased prior to the sale of finished goods, (2) cash is kept in the project as a buffer against unexpected expenditures, and (3) credit sales are made, generating accounts receivable rather than cash. (The investment in net working capital is offset to the extent that purchases are made on credit, that is, when accounts payable are created.) This investment in net working capital represents a cash outflow, because cash generated elsewhere in the firm is tied up in the project.

To see how the investment in net working capital is built from its component parts, we focus on year 1. We see in Table 8.1 that MMCC's managers predict sales in year 1 to be $600,000 and operating costs to be $434,000. If both the sales and costs were cash transactions, the firm would receive $166,000 (or $600,000 − $434,000).

However, the managers:

1. Forecast that $100,000 of the sales will be on credit, implying that cash receipts in year 1 will be only $500,000 (or $600,000 − $100,000). The accounts receivable of $100,000 will be collected in year 2.

2. Believe that they can defer payment on $40,000 of the $434,000 of costs, implying that cash disbursements will be only $394,000 (or $434,000 − $40,000). Of course, MMCC will pay off the $40,000 of accounts payable in year 2.

3. Decide that inventory of $25,000 should be left on hand at year 1 to avoid *stockouts* (that is, running out of inventory) and other contingencies.

4. Decide that cash of $5,000 should be earmarked for the project at year 1 to avoid running out of cash.

Thus, net working capital in year 1 is

$100,000	−	$40,000	+	$25,000	+	$5,000	=	$90,000
Accounts receivable		Accounts payable		Inventory		Cash		Net working capital

Because $90,000 of cash generated elsewhere in the firm must be used to offset this requirement for net working capital, MMCC's managers correctly view the investment in net working capital as a cash outflow of the project. As the project grows over time, needs for net working capital increase. Changes in net working capital from year to year represent further cash flows, as indicated by the negative numbers for the first few years of line 8 of Table 8.1. However, in the declining years of the project, net working capital is reduced—ultimately to zero. That is, accounts receivable are finally collected, the project's cash buffer is returned to the rest of the corporation, and all remaining inventory is sold off. This frees up cash in the later years, as indicated by positive numbers in years 5, 6, 7, and 8 on line 8.

Typically, corporate worksheets (such as Table 8.1) treat net working capital as a whole. The individual components of net working capital (receivables, inventory, and so on) do not generally appear in the worksheets. However, the reader should remember that the net working capital numbers in the worksheets are not pulled out of thin air. Rather, they result from a meticulous forecast of the components, just as we illustrated for year 1.

Interest Expense

It may have bothered you that interest expense was ignored in the MMCC example. After all, many projects are at least partially financed with debt, particularly a power mulcher tool machine that is likely to increase the debt capacity of the firm. As it turns out, our approach of assuming no debt financing is rather standard in the real world. Firms typically calculate a project's cash flows under the assumption that the project is only financed with equity. Any adjustments for debt financing are reflected in the discount rate, not the cash flows. The treatment of debt in capital budgeting will be covered in depth later in the text. Suffice it to say at this time that the full ramifications of debt financing are well beyond our current discussion.

? Concept Questions
- **What are the items leading to cash flow in any year?**
- **Why did we determine taxable income when NPV analysis discounts cash flows, not income?**
- **Why is the increase in net working capital viewed as a cash outflow?**

8.3 Inflation and Capital Budgeting

Inflation is an important fact of economic life, and it must be considered in capital budgeting. We begin by considering the relationship between interest rates and inflation.

Interest Rates and Inflation

Suppose that the one-year interest rate that a financial institution pays is 10 percent. This means that an individual who deposits $1,000 at date 0 will get $1,100 (or $1,000 × 1.10) in one year. While 10 percent may seem like a handsome return, one can only put it in perspective after examining the rate of inflation.

Suppose that the rate of inflation is 6 percent over the year and it affects all goods equally. For example, a restaurant that charges $1.00 for a hamburger at date 0 charges $1.06 for the same hamburger at the end of the year. You can use your $1,000 to buy 1,000 hamburgers at date 0. Alternatively, if you put all of your money in the bank, you can buy 1,038 (or $1,100 / $1.06) hamburgers at date 1. Thus, you are only able to increase your hamburger consumption by 3.8 percent by lending to the bank. Since the prices of all goods rise at this 6 percent rate, lending lets you increase your consumption of any single good or any combination of goods by only 3.8 percent. Thus, 3.8 percent is what you are *really* earning through your savings account, after adjusting for inflation. Economists refer to the 3.8 percent number as the **real interest rate.** Economists refer to the 10 percent rate as the **nominal interest rate** or simply the *interest rate.* The above discussion is illustrated in Figure 8.1.

We have used an example with a specific nominal interest rate and a specific inflation rate. In general, the equation relating real and nominal cash flows can be written as

$$1 + \text{Nominal interest rate} = (1 + \text{Real interest rate}) \times (1 + \text{Inflation rate})$$

Rearranging terms, we have

$$\text{Real interest rate} = \frac{1 + \text{Nominal interest rate}}{1 + \text{Inflation rate}} - 1 \qquad \textbf{(8.1)}$$

The equation indicates that the real interest rate in our example is 3.8 percent $(1.10/1.06 - 1)$.

This equation determines the real interest rate precisely. The following equation is an approximation:

$$\text{Real interest rate} \approx \text{Nominal interest rate} - \text{Inflation rate} \qquad \textbf{(8.2)}$$

The symbol $\approx$ indicates that the equation is approximately true. This latter equation calculates the real rate in our example as

$$4\% = 10\% - 6\%$$

The student should be aware that, while Equation (8.2) may seem more intuitive than Equation (8.1), (8.2) is only an approximation.

This approximation is reasonably accurate for low rates of interest and inflation. In our example, the difference between the approximate calculation and the exact one is only 0.2 percent (4 percent − 3.8 percent). Unfortunately, the approximation becomes poor when rates are higher.

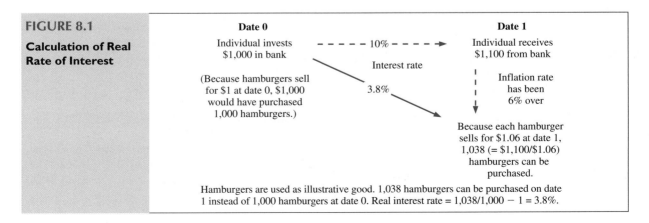

FIGURE 8.1

Calculation of Real Rate of Interest

EXAMPLE 8.5

The little-known monarchy of Gerberovia recently had a nominal interest rate of 300 percent and an inflation rate of 280 percent. According to Equation (8.2), the real interest rate is:

$$300\% - 280\% = 20\% \qquad \text{(Approximate formula)}$$

However, according to Equation (8.1), this rate is:

$$\frac{1 + 300\%}{1 + 280\%} - 1 = 5.26\% \qquad \text{(Exact formula)}$$

How do we know that the second formula is indeed the exact one? Let's think in terms of hamburgers again. Had you deposited $1,000 in a Gerberovian bank a year ago, the account would be worth $4,000 [$1,000 × (1 + 300%)] today. However, while a hamburger cost $1 a year ago, it costs $3.80 (1 + 280%) today. Therefore, you would now be able to buy 1052.6 (4,000/3.80) hamburgers, implying a real interest rate of 5.26 percent.

Cash Flow and Inflation

The above analysis defines two types of interest rates (nominal rates and real rates) and relates them through Equation (8.1). Capital budgeting requires data on cash flows as well as on interest rates. Like interest rates, cash flows can be expressed in either nominal or real terms.

A cash flow is expressed in nominal terms if the actual dollars to be received (or paid out) are given. A cash flow is expressed in real terms if the current or date 0 purchasing power of the cash flow is given.

EXAMPLE 8.6

Ottawa Publishing has just purchased the rights to the next book by famed romantic novelist Barbara Musk. Still unwritten, the book should be available to the public in four years. Currently, romantic novels sell for $10.00 in paperback. The publishers believe that inflation will be 6 percent a year over the next four years. Since romantic novels are so popular, the publishers anticipate that their prices will rise about 2 percent per year more than the inflation rate over the next four years. Not wanting to overprice, Ottawa Publishing anticipates pricing the novel at $13.60 [or $(1.08)^4 \times \$10.00$] four years from now. In other words, the nominal value after four years is the future value calculated using the inflation rate of 8 percent. The firm anticipates selling 100,000 copies.

The expected cash flow in the fourth year of $1.36 million (or $13.60 × 100,000) is a **nominal cash flow** because the firm expects to receive $1.36 million at that time. In other words, a nominal cash flow reflects the actual dollars to be received in the future.

We determine the purchasing power of $1.36 million in four years as

$$\$1.08 \text{ million} = \frac{\$1.36 \text{ million}}{(1.06)^4}$$

The figure $1.08 million is a **real cash flow** since it is expressed in terms of date 0 purchasing power. Extending our hamburger example, the $1.36 million to be received in four years will only buy 1.08 million hamburgers because the price of a hamburger will rise from $1 to $1.26 [or $1 \times (1.06)^4$] over the period.

EXAMPLE 8.7

Gatineau Booksellers, a customer of Ottawa Publishing, recently made leasehold improvements to its store for $2,000,000 to be depreciated by the straight-line method over five years. This implies yearly depreciation of $400,000 (or $2,000,000/5). Is this $400,000 figure a real or nominal quantity?

Depreciation is a *nominal quantity* because $400,000 is the actual tax deduction over each of the next four years. Depreciation becomes a real quantity if it is adjusted for purchasing power.[4] Hence, $316,837 [or $400,000/(1.06)^5] is depreciation in the fourth year, expressed as a real quantity.

Discounting: Nominal or Real?

Our previous discussion showed that interest rates can be expressed in either nominal or real terms. Similarly, cash flows can be expressed in either nominal or real terms. Given these choices, how should one express interest rates and cash flows when performing capital budgeting?

Financial practitioners correctly stress the need to maintain *consistency* between cash flows and discount rates. That is,

> *Nominal* cash flows must be discounted at the *nominal* rate.
>
> *Real* cash flows must be discounted at the *real* rate.

As long as one is consistent, either approach is correct. In order to minimize computational error, it is generally advisable in practice to choose the approach that is easier. This idea is illustrated in Examples 8.8 and 8.9.

EXAMPLE 8.8

Shields Electric forecasts the following nominal cash flows on a particular project:

Date:	0	1	2
Cash flow	−$1,000	$600	$650

The nominal interest rate is 14 percent, and the inflation rate is forecast to be 5 percent. What is the value of the project?

Using Nominal Quantities   The NPV can be calculated as

$$\$26.47 = -\$1,000 + \frac{\$600}{1.14} + \frac{\$650}{(1.14)^2}$$

The project should be accepted.

Using Real Quantities   The real cash flows are

Date:	0	1	2
Cash flow	−$1,000	$571.43	$589.57
		$\left(\dfrac{\$600}{1.05}\right)$	$\left(\dfrac{\$650}{1.05^2}\right)$

---

[4]We use the word *quantity* not *cash flow,* because it is the CCA tax shield, not the depreciation itself, that is a cash flow. Tax shields are defined later in this chapter.

The real interest rate is 8.57143 percent (1.14/1.05 − 1).
The NPV can be calculated as

$$\$26.47 = -\$1,000 + \frac{\$571.43}{1.0857143} + \frac{\$589.57}{(1.0857143)^2}$$

The NPV is the same when cash flows are expressed in real quantities. It must always be the case that the NPV is the same under the two different approaches.

Because both approaches always yield the same result, which one should be used? Students will be happy to learn the following rule: Use the approach that is simpler. In the Shields Electric case, nominal quantities produce a simpler calculation because the problem gave us nominal cash flows to begin with.

EXAMPLE 8.9

Altshuler Inc. used the following data for a capital budgeting project:

Year	0	1	2
Capital expenditure	$1,210		
Revenues (in real terms)		$1,900	$2,000
Cash expenses (in real terms)		950	1,000
Depreciation (straight line)		605	605

The president, David Altshuler, estimates inflation to be 10 percent per year over the next two years. In addition, he believes that the cash flows of the project should be discounted at the nominal rate of 15.5 percent. His firm's tax rate is 40 percent.

Mr. Altshuler forecasts all cash flows in *nominal* terms. Thus, he generates the following spreadsheet:

Year	0	1	2
Capital expenditure	−$1,210		
Revenues		$2,090 (= 1,900 × 1.10)	$2,420 (= 2,000 × (1.10)²)
−Expenses		−1,045 (= 950 × 1.10)	−1,210 (= 1,000 × (1.10)²)
−Depreciation		−605 (= 1,210/2)	−605
Taxable income		440	605
−Taxes (40%)		−176	−242
Income after taxes		264	363
+Depreciation		+605	+605
Cash flow		$ 869	$ 968

$$NPV = -\$1,210 + \frac{\$869}{1.155} + \frac{\$968}{(1.155)^2} = \$268$$

Mr. Altshuler's sidekick, Stuart Weiss, prefers working in real terms. He first calculates the real rate to be 5 percent (= $1.155/1.10 - 1$). Next, he generates the following spreadsheet in *real* quantities:

Year	0	1	2
Capital expenditure	−$1,210		
Revenues		$1,900	$ 2,000
−Expenses		−950	−1,000
−Depreciation		−550 (= 605/1.1)	−500 (= 605/1.1)^2)
Taxable income		400	500
−Taxes (40%)		−160	−200
Income after taxes		240	300
+Depreciation		+550	+500
Cash flow		$ 790	$ 800

$$\text{NPV} = -\$1{,}210 + \frac{\$790}{1.05} + \frac{\$800}{(1.05)^2} = \$268$$

In explaining his calculations to Mr. Altshuler, Mr. Weiss points out:

1. Since the capital expenditure occurs at date 0 (today), its nominal value and its real value are equal.
2. Since yearly depreciation of $605 is a nominal quantity, one converts it to a real quantity by discounting at the inflation rate of 10 percent.
3. It is no coincidence that both Mr. Altshuler and Mr. Weiss arrive at the same NPV number. Both methods must always give the same NPV.

? Concept Questions
- **What is the difference between the nominal and the real interest rate?**
- **What is the difference between nominal and real cash flows?**

8.4 Alternative Definitions of Operating Cash Flow

The analysis in the previous section is quite general and can be adapted to just about any capital investment problem. This section discusses the fact that different definitions of project operating cash flow are commonly used, both in practice and in finance texts.

The different approaches to operating cash flow all measure the same thing. If used correctly, every approach will produce the same answer, although one is not necessarily any better or more useful than another. Unfortunately, the fact that alternative definitions are used sometimes leads to confusion. For this reason, we examine several of these variations next to see how they are related.

In the discussion that follows, keep in mind that cash flow literally means dollars in less dollars out. This is all we are concerned with. Different definitions of operating cash flow simply amount to different ways of manipulating basic information about sales, costs, depreciation, and taxes to get at cash flow.

For a particular project and year under consideration, suppose we have the following estimates:

$$
\begin{aligned}
\text{Sales} &= \$1{,}500 \\
\text{Costs} &= \$700 \\
\text{Depreciation} &= \$600
\end{aligned}
$$

With these estimates, notice that EBIT is:

$$\begin{aligned} \text{EBIT} &= \text{Sales} - \text{Costs} - \text{Depreciation} \\ &= \$1{,}500 - 700 - 600 \\ &= \$200 \end{aligned}$$

Once again, we assume that no interest is paid, so the tax bill is:

$$\begin{aligned} \text{Taxes} &= \text{EBIT} \times T_c \\ &= \$200 \times .34 = \$68 \end{aligned}$$

where T_c, the corporate tax rate, is 34 percent.

When we put all of this together, we see that project operating cash flow, OCF, is:

$$\begin{aligned} \text{OCF} &= \text{EBIT} + \text{Depreciation} - \text{Taxes} \\ &= \$200 + 600 - 68 = \$732 \end{aligned}$$

It turns out there are some other ways to determine OCF that could be (and are) used. We consider these next.

The Bottom-Up Approach

Because we are ignoring any financing expenses, such as interest, in our calculations of project OCF, we can write project net income as:

$$\begin{aligned} \text{Project net income} &= \text{EBIT} - \text{Taxes} \\ &= \$200 - 68 \\ &= \$132 \end{aligned}$$

If we simply add the depreciation to both sides, we arrive at a slightly different and very common expression for OCF:

$$\begin{aligned} \text{OCF} &= \text{Net income} + \text{Depreciation} \\ &= \$132 + 600 \\ &= \$732 \end{aligned} \tag{8.3}$$

This is the *bottom-up* approach. Begin with the accountant's bottom line (net income) and add back any non-cash deductions such as depreciation. It is crucial to remember that this definition of operating cash flow as net income plus depreciation is correct only if there is no interest expense subtracted in the calculation of net income.

The Top-Down Approach

Perhaps the most obvious way to calculate OCF is this:

$$\begin{aligned} \text{OCF} &= \text{Sales} - \text{Costs} - \text{Taxes} \\ &= \$1{,}500 - 700 - 68 = \$732 \end{aligned} \tag{8.4}$$

This is the *top-down* approach, the second variation on the basic OCF definition. Begin with the top of the income statement with sales and work down to net cash flow by subtracting costs, taxes, and other expenses. Along the way, simply leave out any strictly non-cash items such as depreciation.

The Tax Shield Approach

The third variation on our basic definition of OCF is the *tax shield* approach. This approach will be very useful for some problems we consider in the next chapter. The tax shield definition of OCF is:

$$\text{OCF} = (\text{Sales} - \text{Costs}) \times (1 - T_c) + \text{Depreciation} \times T_c \tag{8.5}$$

where T_c is again the corporate tax rate. Assuming that $T_c = 34$ percent, the OCF works out to be:

$$\begin{aligned} \text{OCF} &= (\$1{,}500 - 700) \times .66 + 600 \times .34 \\ &= \$528 + 204 \\ &= \$732 \end{aligned}$$

This approach views OCF as having two components. The first part is what the project's cash flow would be if there were no depreciation expense. In this case, this would-have-been cash flow is $528. The second part of OCF in this approach is the depreciation deduction multiplied by the tax rate. This is called the **depreciation tax shield.** Knowing that depreciation is a non-cash expense, the only cash flow effect of deducting depreciation is to reduce our taxes. At the current 34 percent corporate tax rate, every dollar in depreciation expense saves 34 cents in taxes. So, in the example, the $600 depreciation deduction saves us $600 \times .34 = \$204$ in taxes.

Conclusion

Now that each approach has been used and its been shown that all of these approaches are the same, you may be wondering why everyone does not just agree on one of them. One reason is that different approaches are useful in different circumstances. The best one to use is whichever happens to be the most convenient for the problem at hand.

8.5 Applying the Tax Shield Approach to the Majestic Mulch and Compost Company Project

If you look back over our analysis of MMCC you will see that most of the number crunching involved finding CCA, EBIT, and net income figures. The tax shield approach has the potential to save us considerable time. To realize that potential, we do the calculations in a different order from Table 8.4. Instead of adding the cash flow components down the columns for each year and finding the present value of the total cash flows, we find the present values of each source of cash flows and add the present values. To find the present values we use a discount rate of 15 percent.

To begin, it will be helpful to define the following:

$$\begin{aligned} \text{OCF} &= \text{Operating cash flow} \\ R &= \text{Revenues} \\ E &= \text{Expenses (operating costs)} \\ D &= \text{Depreciation for tax purposes, i.e., CCA}^5 \\ T_c &= \text{Corporate tax rate} \end{aligned}$$

The first source of cash flow is $(R - E)(1 - T_c)$, as shown for each year on the first line of Table 8.5. The figure for the first year is $99,600. (The numbers come from Table 8.1.)

$$\begin{aligned} (R - E)(1 - T_c) &= (\$600{,}000 - \$434{,}000)(1 - 0.40) \\ &= \$99{,}600 \end{aligned}$$

Calculating the present value of the $99,600 for the first year, and adding the present values of the other $(R - E)(1 - T_c)$ figures in Table 8.5 gives a total present value for this source of $682,696, as seen in the lower part of Table 8.5.

---

[5] In this discussion we use the terms *depreciation* and *CCA* interchangeably.

TABLE 8.5   Tax Shield Solution, Power Mulcher Project

	Year 0	Year 1	Year 2	Year 3	Year 4	Year 5	Year 6	Year 7	Year 8
(1) $(R - E)(1 - T_c)$		$99,600	$157,920	$211,056	$219,856	$189,246	$142,356	$98,881	$59,331
(2) Changes in NWC	($40,000)	(50,000)	(47,700)	(49,572)	(19,664)	12,098	29,226	30,473	135,139
(3) Equipment expenditure:	(800,000)								150,000
Totals									
PV of $(R - E)(1 - T_c)$	$682,696								
PV of changes in NWC	(89,100)								
PV of equipment expenditure	(750,965)								
PV of CCA tax shield	159,649								
NPV	$2,280								

The second term is the tax shield on CCA for the first year. Table 8.6 reproduces the first year's tax shield of $32,000 along with the corresponding tax shields for each year. The total present value of the CCA tax shield is shown as $159,649.

The changes in net working capital and equipment expenditure are the same as in Table 8.4. Their present values are shown in the lower part of Table 8.5. The NPV is the sum of the present values of the four sources of cash flow. The answer, $2,280, is identical to what we found in Table 8.4 for a discount rate of 15 percent.

Present Value of the Tax Shield on CCA

Further time savings are made possible by using a formula that replaces the detailed calculation of yearly CCA. The formula is based on the idea that tax shields from CCA continue in perpetuity as long as there are assets remaining in the CCA class.[6] To calculate the present value of the tax shield on CCA, we first find the present value of an infinite stream of tax shields abstracting from two practical implications: the 50 percent rule for CCA and disposal of the asset. We then adjust the formula. The detailed derivation is in Appendix 8B.

TABLE 8.6
Present Value of
Tax Shield on CCA

Year	CCA	0.40 × CCA	PV @ 15 percent
1	$ 80,000	$ 32,000	$ 27,826
2	144,000	57,600	43,554
3	115,200	46,080	30,298
4	92,160	36,864	21,077
5	73,728	29,491	14,662
6	58,982	23,593	10,200
7	47,186	18,874	7,096
8	37,749	15,099	4,936
		PV of tax shield on CCA	$159,649

---

[6]Strictly speaking, the UCC for a class remains positive as long as there are physical assets in the class and the proceeds from disposal of assets are less than total UCC for the class.

C = Total capital cost of the asset that is added to the pool
d = CCA rate for the asset class
T_c = Company's marginal tax rate
k = Discount rate
S = Salvage or disposal value of the asset
n = Asset life in years.

$$\text{PV tax shield on CCA} = \frac{[CdT_c]}{k+d} \times \frac{[1+0.5k]}{1+k} - \frac{SdT_c}{k+d} \times \frac{1}{(1+k)^n} \qquad (8.6)$$

Using the first part of (8.6), the present value of the tax shield on MMCC's project is $170,932 assuming that the tax shield goes on in perpetuity.

$$= \frac{800,000\,(0.40)\,(0.20)}{0.15+0.20} \times \frac{1+0.5+(0.15)}{1+0.15}$$
$$= 182,857 \times 1.075 \times 1.15 = \$170,932$$

The adjustment for the salvage value (second part of 8.6) is

$$- \frac{150,000\,(0.40)\,(0.20)}{0.15+0.20} \times \frac{1}{(1+0.15)^8}$$
$$= -34,286 \times 1/(1.15)^8 = -\$11,208$$

The present value of the tax shield on CCA is the sum of the two present values.[7]

$$\text{Present value of tax shield from CCA} = \$170,932 - \$11,208$$
$$= \$159,724.$$

Total Project Cash Flow Versus Tax Shield Approach

The tax shield approach has three advantages over the total project cash flow approach:

1. Simplifying formulas such as annuities and growing annuities can be applied, where appropriate, to a cash flow source. This is not feasible for the approach we used in the first example, because cash flows from all sources were combined to determine net cash flow for a year. Because the net cash flow for each year (as in line 4 of Table 8.4) is derived from so many sources, no simplifying formula can normally be used to calculate the net present value of all the yearly cash flows.
2. The approach used in the tax shield example can discount cash flows at different rates. This is often necessary due to varying risks associated with different cash flows.
3. The approach used in the first example cannot separate real and nominal flows because cash flows from all sources are combined each year. Thus, one must either make all flows nominal or make all flows real at the start.

---

[7]There is a slight difference between this calculation for the present value of the tax shield on CCA and what we got in Table 8.6 by adding the tax shields over the project life. The difference arises whenever the salvage value of the asset differs from its UCC. The formula solution is more accurate as it takes into account the future CCA on this difference. In this case, the asset was sold for $150,000 and had UCC of $150,995. The $995 left in the pool after eight years creates an infinite stream of CCA. At time 8, this stream has a present value of [$995(0.20)(0.40)]/[0.15 + 0.20] = $227.43. At time 0, the present value of this stream at 15 percent is about $75. To get the precise estimate of the present value of the CCA tax shield, we need to add this to the approximation in Table 8.6: $159,649 + $75 = $159,724. This adjustment could be made initially by adding another line to Table 8.1.

It is our opinion that the tax shield approach is an improvement over the total project cash flow approach. In many cases, the improvement can be substantial, because both time savings and increases in accuracy are involved. The current example appears to allow both benefits. In some situations, however, there is only a slight improvement. For example, suppose that the cash flows from each source are irregular. The tax shield method would not save time, because the cash flows from the individual sources would not fit any simplifying formula. Also, suppose one were very unsure of the appropriate discount rates. Selecting a different discount rate for each cash flow might be unnecessary.[8]

We find that real-world companies use both approaches. Thus, the student should be aware of both procedures, always looking for practical situations where the latter method allows substantial benefits.

? Concept Questions

- **What is the basic difference between the discounting approach in the total project cash flow example and the discounting approach in the tax shield example?**
- **What are the benefits of using each approach?**

8.6 Investments of Unequal Lives: The Equivalent Annual Cost Method

Suppose a firm must choose between two machines of unequal lives. Both machines can do the same job, but they have different operating costs and will last for different time periods. A simple application of the NPV rule suggests taking the machine whose costs have the lower present value. This choice, as illustrated in Example 8.10, might be a mistake, however, because the lower-cost machine may need to be replaced before the other one.

EXAMPLE 8.10

The Downtown Athletic Club must choose between two mechanical tennis ball throwers. Machine *A* costs less than machine *B* but will not last as long. The cash outflows from the two machines are:

Date:	0	1	2	3	4
Machine *A*	$500	$120	$120	$120	
Machine *B*	600	100	100	100	$100

Machine *A* costs $500 and lasts three years. There will be maintenance expenses of $120 to be paid at the end of each of the three years. Machine *B* costs $600 and lasts four years. There will be maintenance expenses of $100 to be paid at the end of each of the four years. We place all costs in *real* terms, an assumption greatly simplifying the analysis. Revenues per year are assumed to be the same, regardless of machine, so they are ignored in the analysis. Note that all numbers in the above chart are *outflows*.

---

[8]One of our colleagues in accounting is particularly critical of those who employ precise methodologies in situations with vague data. He tells the story of an accountant flying over the Grand Canyon who tells his seatmate, "I'll bet you didn't know that the Grand Canyon is two billion and two years old." The seatmate says, "Well, I can understand that it's around two billion years old, but how did you come up with two billion and two?" The accountant replied, "The pilot announced that the Grand Canyon was two billion years old when I took this same flight two years ago."

To get a handle on the decision, let's take the present value of the costs of each of the two machines. Assuming a discount rate of 10 percent, we have:

$$\text{Machine } A: \$798.42 = \$500 + \frac{\$120}{1.1} + \frac{\$120}{(1.1)^2} + \frac{\$120}{(1.1)^3}$$

$$\text{Machine } B: \$916.99 = \$600 + \frac{\$100}{1.1} + \frac{\$100}{(1.1)^2} + \frac{\$100}{(1.1)^3} + \frac{\$100}{(1.1)^4} \qquad \text{(8.7)}$$

Machine *B* has a higher present value of outflows. A naive approach would be to select machine *A* because of its lower present value. However, machine *B* has a longer life so perhaps its cost per year is actually lower.

How might one properly adjust for the difference in useful life when comparing the two machines? Perhaps the easiest approach involves calculating something called the *equivalent annual cost* of each machine. This approach puts costs on a per-year basis.

Equation (8.7) showed that payments of ($500, $120, $120, $120) are equivalent to a single payment of $798.42 at date 0. We now wish to equate the single payment of $798.42 at date 0 with a three-year annuity. Using techniques of previous chapters, we have

$$\$798.42 = C \times A^3_{0.10}$$

$A^3_{0.10}$ is an annuity of $1 a year for three years, discounted at 10 percent. *C* is the unknown—the annuity payment per year such that the present value of all payments equals $798.42. Because $A^3_{0.10}$ equals 2.4869, *C* equals $321.05 ($798.42/2.4869). Thus, a payment stream of ($500, $120, $120, $120) is equivalent to annuity payments of $321.05 made at the *end* of each year for three years. We refer to $321.05 as the *equivalent annual cost* of machine *A*.

This idea is summarized in the chart below:

Date	0	1	2	3
Cash outflows of Machine *A*	$500	$120	$120	$120
Equivalent annual cost of Machine *A*		$321.05	$321.05	$321.05

The Downtown Athletic Club should be indifferent between cash outflows of ($500, $120, $120, $120) and cash outflows of ($0, $321.05, $321.05, $321.05). Alternatively, one can say that the purchase of the machine is financially equivalent to a rental agreement calling for annual lease payments of $321.05. Because the club plans to replace the machine, these payments will go on indefinitely.

Now let's turn to machine *B*. We calculate its equivalent annual cost from

$$\$916.99 = C \times A^4_{0.10}$$

Because $A^4_{0.10}$ equals 3.1699, *C* equals $916.99/3.1699, or $289.28.

As we did above for machine *A*, the following chart can be created for machine *B:*

Date	0	1	2	3	4
Cash outflows of Machine *B*	$600	$100	$100	$100	$100
Equivalent annual cost of Machine *B*		$289.28	$289.28	$289.28	$289.28

The decision is easy once the charts of the two machines are compared. Would you rather make annual lease payments of $321.05 or $289.28? Put this way, the problem becomes a no-brainer. Clearly, a rational person would rather pay the lower amount. Thus, machine *B* is the preferred choice.

Two final remarks are in order. First, it is no accident that we specified the costs of the tennis ball machines in real terms. While *B* would still have been the preferred machine had the costs been stated in nominal terms, the actual solution would have been much more difficult. As a general rule, always convert cash flows to real terms when working through problems of this type.

Second, the above analysis applies only if one anticipates that both machines can be replaced. The analysis would differ if no replacement were possible. For example, imagine that the only company that manufactured tennis ball throwers just went out of business and no new producers are expected to enter the field. In this case, machine *B* would generate revenues in the fourth year whereas machine *A* would not. Here, simple net present value analysis for mutually exclusive projects including both revenues and costs would be appropriate.

The General Decision to Replace (Advanced)

The previous analysis concerned the choice between machine *A* and machine *B*, both of which were new acquisitions. More typically, firms must decide when to replace an existing machine with a new one. This decision is actually quite straightforward. One should replace if the annual cost of the new machine is less than the annual cost of the old machine. As with much else in finance, an example, such as Example 8.11, clarifies this approach better than further explanation.

EXAMPLE 8.11

Consider the situation of BIKE, which must decide whether to replace an existing machine. BIKE currently pays no taxes. The replacement machine costs $9,000 now and requires maintenance of $1,000 at the end of every year for eight years. At the end of eight years the machine would be sold for $2,000. All numbers are in real terms.

The existing machine requires increasing amounts of maintenance each year, and its salvage value falls each year, as shown:

Year	Maintenance	Salvage
Present	$ 0	$4,000
1	1,000	2,500
2	2,000	1,500
3	3,000	1,000
4	4,000	0

This chart tells us that the existing machine can be sold for $4,000 now. If it is sold one year from now, the resale price will be $2,500, and $1,000 must be spent on maintenance during the year to keep it running. For ease of calculation,we assume that this maintenance fee is paid at the end of the year. The machine will last for four more years before it falls apart. In other words, salvage value will be zero at the end of year 4. If BIKE faces an opportunity cost of capital of 15 percent, when should it replace the machine?

As we said above, our approach is to compare the annual cost of the replacement machine with the annual cost of the old machine. The annual cost of the replacement machine is simply its *equivalent annual cost* (EAC). Let's calculate that first.

Equivalent Annual Cost of New Machine   The present value of the cost of the new replacement machine is as follows:

$$PV_{costs} = \$9,000 + \$1,000 \times A^8_{0.15} - \frac{\$2,000}{(1.15)^8}$$

$$= \$9,000 + \$1,000 \times (4.4837) - \$2,000 \times (0.3269)$$

$$= \$12,833$$

Notice that the $2,000 salvage value is an inflow. It is treated as a *negative* number in the above equation because it *offsets* the cost of the machine.

The EAC of a new replacement machine equals

$$PV/8\text{-year annuity factor at }15\% = \frac{PV}{A^8_{0.15}} = \frac{\$12,833}{4.4873} = \$2,860$$

This calculation implies that buying a replacement machine is financially equivalent to renting this machine for $2,860 per year.

Cost of Old Machine   This calculation is a little trickier. If BIKE keeps the old machine for one year, the firm must pay maintenance costs of $1,000 a year from now. But this is not BIKE's only cost from keeping the machine for one year. BIKE will receive $2,500 at date 1 if the old machine is kept for one year but would receive $4,000 today if the old machine were sold immediately. This reduction in sales proceeds is clearly a cost as well.

Thus, the PV of the costs of keeping the machine one more year before selling it equals

$$\$40,000 + \frac{\$1,000}{1.15} - \frac{\$2,500}{1.15} = \$2,696$$

That is, if BIKE holds the old machine for one year, BIKE does *not* receive the $4,000 today. This $4,000 can be thought of as an opportunity cost. In addition, the firm must pay $1,000 a year from now. Finally, BIKE does receive $2,500 a year from now. This last item is treated as a negative number because it offsets the other two costs.

While we normally express cash flows in terms of present value, the analysis to come is made easier if we express the cash flow in terms of its future value one year from now. This future value is

$$\$2,696 \times 1.15 = \$3,100$$

In other words, the cost of keeping the machine for one year is equivalent to paying $3,100 at the end of the year.

Making the Comparison   Now let's review the cash flows. If we replace the machine immediately, we can view our annual expense as $2,860, beginning at the end of the year. This annual expense occurs forever, if we replace the new machine every eight years. This cash flow stream can be written as

	Year 1	Year 2	Year 3	Year 4	
Expenses from replacing machine immediately	$2,860	$2,860	$2,860	$2,860	...

If we replace the old machine in one year, our expense from using the old machine for that final year can be viewed as $3,100, payable at the end of the year. After replacement, our annual expense is $2,860, beginning at the end of two years. This annual expense occurs forever, if we replace the new machine every eight years. This cash flow stream can be written as

	Year 1	Year 2	Year 3	Year 4	. . .
Expenses from using old machine for one year and then replacing it	$3,100	$2,860	$2,860	$2,860	. . .

Put this way, the choice is a no-brainer. Anyone would rather pay $2,860 at the end of the year than $3,100 at the end of the year. Thus, BIKE should replace[9] the old machine immediately in order to minimize the expense at year 1.

Two final points should be made on the decision to replace. First, we have examined a situation where both the old machine and the replacement machine generate the same revenues. Because revenues are unaffected by the choice of machine, revenues do not enter our analysis. This situation is common in business. For example, the decision to replace either the heating system or the air conditioning system in one's home office will likely not affect firm revenues. However, sometimes revenues will be greater with a new machine. The above approach can easily be amended to handle differential revenues.

Second, we want to stress the importance of the above approach. Applications of the above approach are pervasive in business, since *every* machine must be replaced at some point.

Concept Questions

• **What is the equivalent annual cost method of capital budgeting?**

8.7 SUMMARY AND CONCLUSIONS

This chapter discusses a number of practical applications of capital budgeting.

1. Capital budgeting must be conducted on an incremental basis. This means that sunk costs must be ignored, while opportunity costs, side effects, and allocated costs need to be considered.

2. Inflation should be handled consistently. One approach is to express both cash flows and the discount rate in nominal terms. The other approach is to express both cash flows and the discount rate in real terms. Because either approach yields the same NPV calculation, the simpler method should be used. Which method is simpler will generally depend on the nature of the capital budgeting problem.

3. In the total project cash flow example, we computed NPV using the following two steps:
   a. Calculate the net cash flow from all sources for each period.
   b. Calculate the NPV using the cash flows calculated above.

---

[9]One caveat is in order. Perhaps the old machine's maintenance is high in the first year but drops after that. A decision to replace immediately might be premature in that case. Therefore, we need to check the cost of the old machine in future years.

The cost of keeping the existing machine a second year is

$$\text{PV of costs at time 1} = \$2,500 + \frac{\$2,000}{1.15} - \frac{\$1,500}{1.15} = \$2,935$$

which has future value of $3,375 ($2,935 × 1.15).

The costs of keeping the existing machine for years 3 and 4 are also greater than the EAC of buying a new machine. Thus, BIKE's decision to replace the old machine immediately is still valid.

In the tax shield example, we used two different steps:

a. Calculate the present value of each source (for example, revenues and CCA tax shield).

b. Add the present values across the different sources (including initial investment) in order to get NPV.

The second approach has three benefits. Simplifying formulas can often be used. Nominal cash flows and real cash flows can be handled in the same example. Cash flows of varying risk can be used in the same example.

4. A firm should use the equivalent annual cost approach when choosing between two machines of unequal lives.

KEY TERMS

Allocated cost 206	Nominal cash flow 214	Real interest rate 213
Depreciation tax shield 219	Nominal interest rate 213	Sunk cost 205
Erosion 206	Opportunity cost 205	Synergy 206
Incremental cash flow 205	Real cash flow 214	

SUGGESTED READING

An excellent in-depth examination of the capital budgeting decision is contained in:
T. Koller, M. Goodhart, D. Wessels. *Valuation: Measuring and Managing the Value of Companies.* 4th ed. The McKinsey Company, 2005.

QUESTIONS & PROBLEMS

Incremental Cash Flows

8.1   Which of the following should be treated as incremental cash flows when computing the NPV of an investment?

a. The reduction in the sales of the company's other products.

b. The expenditure on plant and equipment.

c. The cost of research and development undertaken in connection with the product during the past three years.

d. The annual CCA expense.

e. Dividend payments.

f. The resale value of plant and equipment at the end of the project's life.

g. Salary and medical costs for production employees on leave.

Practical Application of NPV to Capital Budgeting (no inflation)

8.2   Suppose Mario Lemieux decided to make another comeback with the Pittsburgh Penguins in 2008. The Penguins offer him a two-year contract in January 2008 with the following provisions:

a. $5 million signing bonus

b. $7 million per year for two years

c. Seven years of deferred payments of $3 million per year, starting at the end of year 2

d. A games played bonus provision that totals $1 million per year for the two years of the contract

Assume that Lemieux achieved his bonus requirements both years and he signed the contract right away on January 1, 2008. Assume that cash flows are discounted at 13.75 percent. Ignore any taxes. Lemieux's signing bonus was paid on the day the contract was signed. His salary and bonuses, other than the signing bonus, are paid at the end of the year. What was the present value of this contract in January when Mario Lemieux signed it?

Comparing Mutually Exclusive Projects

EXCEL

8.3   Victoria Enterprises Inc. is evaluating alternative uses for a three-storey manufacturing and warehousing building that it has purchased for $850,000. The company could continue to rent the building to the present occupants for $55,000 per year. These tenants have indicated an interest in staying in the building for at least another 15 years. Alternatively, the company could make improvements to modify the existing structure to use for its own manufacturing and warehousing needs. Victoria's production engineer feels the building could be adapted to handle one of two new product lines. The cost and revenue data for the two product alternatives follow.

	Product A	Product B
Initial cash outlay for building modifications	$100,000	$180,000
Initial cash outlay for equipment	401,000	437,000
Annual pre-tax cash revenues (generated for 15 years)	299,000	365,000
Annual pre-tax cash expenditures (generated for 15 years)	177,000	235,000

The building will be used for only 15 years for either product A or product B. After 15 years, the building will be too small for efficient production of either product line. At that time, Victoria plans to rent the building to firms similar to the current occupants. To rent the building again, Victoria will need to restore the building to its present layout. The estimated cash cost of restoring the building if product A has been undertaken is $18,995; if product B has been produced, the cash cost will be $107,000. These cash costs can be deducted for tax purposes in the year the expenditures occur.

Victoria will depreciate the original building shell (purchased for $850,000) at a CCA rate of 5 percent, regardless of which alternative it chooses. The building modifications fall into CCA class 13 and are depreciated using the straight-line method over a 15-year life. Equipment purchases for either product are in class 8 and have a CCA rate of 20 percent. The firm's tax rate is 36 percent, and its required rate of return on such investments is 15 percent.

For simplicity, assume all cash flows for a given year occur at the end of the year. The initial outlays for modifications and equipment will occur at $t = 0$, and the restoration outlays will occur at the end of year 15. Also, Victoria has other profitable ongoing operations that are sufficient to cover any losses.

Which use of the building would you recommend to management?

Valuation of the Firm

8.4   The Regina Wheat Company (RWC) has wheat fields that currently produce annual profits of $600,500. These fields are expected to produce average annual profits of $600,500 in real terms forever. RWC has no depreciable assets, so the annual cash flow is also $600,500. RWC is an all-equity firm with 275,000 shares outstanding. The appropriate discount rate for its stock is 18 percent. RWC has an investment opportunity with a gross present value of $1.8 million. The investment requires a $1.1 million outlay now. RWC has no other investment opportunities. Assume all cash flows are received at the end of each year. What is the price per share of RWC?

Capital Budgeting with Inflation

8.5   Consider the following cash flows on two mutually exclusive projects.

Year	Project A	Project B
0	−$40,000	−$50,000
1	20,000	8,000
2	16,000	20,000
3	16,000	42,000

Cash flows of project A are expressed in real terms while those of project B are expressed in nominal terms. The appropriate nominal discount rate is 14 percent, and inflation is 4 percent. Which project should you choose?

8.6 Phillips Industries runs a small manufacturing operation. For this year, it expects to have real net cash flows of $150,000. Phillips is an ongoing operation, but it expects competitive pressures to erode its (inflation-adjusted) net cash flows at 7 percent per year. The appropriate real discount rate for Phillips is 11 percent. All net cash flows are received at year-end. What is the present value of the net cash flows from Phillips' operations?

EXCEL

8.7 Larry, a small restaurant owner/manager, is contemplating the purchase of a larger restaurant from its owner, who is retiring. Larry would finance the purchase by selling his existing small restaurant, taking a second mortgage on his house, selling the stocks and bonds that he owns, and, if necessary, taking out a bank loan. Because Larry would have almost all of his wealth in the restaurant, he wants a careful analysis of how much he should be willing to pay for the business. The present owner of the larger restaurant has supplied the following information from the past five years.

Year	Gross Revenue	Profit
−5	$875,000	$ 70,000
−4	891,000	32,000
−3	828,000	6,000
−2	928,000	98,000
Last	998,000	101,000

As with many small businesses, the larger restaurant is structured as a sole proprietorship so no corporate taxes are deducted. The preceding figures have not been adjusted for changes in the price level. There is general agreement that the average profits for the past five years are representative of what can be expected in the future, after adjusting for inflation.

Larry is of the opinion that he could earn at least $3,000 in current dollars per month as a hired manager. Larry feels he should subtract this amount from profits when analyzing the venture. Furthermore, he is aware of statistics showing that for restaurants of this size, approximately 6.5 percent go out of business each year.

Larry has done some preliminary work to value the business. His analysis is as follows:

Year	Profits	Price-Level Factor	Profits (current dollars)	Imputed Managerial Wage	Net Profits
−5	$ 70,000	1.28	$ 89,600	$36,000	$ 53,600
−4	32,000	1.18	37,760	36,000	1,760
−3	6,000	1.09	6,540	36,000	−29,460
−2	98,000	1.04	101,920	36,000	65,920
Last	101,000	1.00	101,000	36,000	65,000

The average net profits for the past five years, expressed in current dollars, are $31,000. Using this average net profit figure, Larry predicted that expected real net profits next year will be $31,000 and that this figure will decline each year after next by 6 percent adjusting the probability of bankruptcy. He decided to discount these expected real net profits at the current risk-free rate of 2 percent.

Visit us at www.mcgrawhill.ca/olc/ross

Based on these calculations, Larry has calculated that the value of the restaurant is $510,000.

a. Do you agree with Larry's assessment of the restaurant? In your answer, consider his treatment of inflation and his deduction of the managerial wage of $3,000 per month.

b. What present value would you place on the revenue stream; in other words, how much would you advise Larry to be willing to pay for the restaurant?

8.8 The Biological Insect Control Corporation (BICC) has hired you as a consultant to evaluate the NPV of its proposed toad ranch. BICC plans to breed toads and sell them as ecologically desirable insect-control mechanisms. It anticipates that the business will continue in perpetuity. Following the negligible start-up costs, BICC expects the following nominal cash flows at the end of the year.

Revenues	$170,000
Labour costs	95,000
Other costs	37,000

The company will rent machinery for $21,500 per year. The rental payments start at the end of year 1 and are expressed in nominal terms. Revenues will increase by 6 percent per year in real terms. Labour costs will increase by 3.5 percent per year in real terms. Other costs will decrease by 1 percent per year in real terms. The rate of inflation is expected to be 4 percent per year. BICC's required rate of return is 9 percent in real terms. There are no taxes. All cash flows occur at year-end. What is the NPV of BICC's proposed toad ranch today?

8.9 You are asked to evaluate the following project for a corporation with profitable ongoing operations. The required investment on January 1 of this year is $44,000. The firm will depreciate the investment at a CCA rate of 20 percent. The firm is in the 34 percent tax bracket.

The price of the product on January 1 will be $300 per unit. That price will stay constant in real terms. Labour costs will be $12 per hour on January 1. They will increase at 1 percent per year in real terms. Energy costs will be $6.15 per physical unit on January 1; they will increase at 3 percent per year in real terms. The inflation rate is 6.5 percent. Revenue is received and costs are paid at year-end.

	Year 1	Year 2	Year 3	Year 4
Physical production, in units	100	200	200	150
Labour input, in hours	2,000	2,000	2,000	2,000
Energy input, physical units	200	200	200	200

The riskless nominal discount rate is 8 percent. The real discount rate for costs and revenues is 4 percent. Calculate the NPV of this project.

8.10 Sparkling Water Inc. sells 4 million bottles of drinking water each year. Each bottle sells at $1.75 and costs per bottle are $0.35. Sales income and costs occur at year-end. Sales income is expected to rise at 7 percent annually, while costs are expected to rise at 5 percent annually. The relevant discount rate is 11 percent. The corporate tax rate is 32 percent. What is Sparkling worth today?

8.11 International Buckeyes is building a factory that can make 1 million buckeyes a year for five years. The factory costs $8 million. In year 1, each buckeye will sell for $3.15. The price will rise 5 percent each year. During the first year, variable costs will be $0.2625 per buckeye and will rise by 3 percent each year. International Buckeyes will depreciate the factory at a CCA rate of 25 percent.

International Buckeyes expects to be able to sell the factory for $751,342.16 at the end of year 5. The proceeds will be invested in a new factory. The discount rate for risky cash flows is 25 percent. The discount rate for riskless cash flows is 20 percent. Cash flows, except the initial investment, occur at the end of the year. The corporate tax rate is 38 percent. What is the net present value of this project?

8.12 Majestic Mining Company is negotiating for the purchase of a new piece of equipment for its current operations. MMC wants to know the maximum price that it should be willing to pay for the equipment. That is, how high must the price be for the equipment to have an NPV of zero? You are given the following facts:

1. The new equipment would replace existing equipment that has a current market value of $27,000.
2. The new equipment would not affect revenues, but before-tax operating costs would be reduced by $14,000 per year for eight years. These savings in cost would occur at year-end.
3. The old equipment is now five years old. It is expected to last for another eight years, and to have no resale value at the end of those eight years. It was purchased for $38,000 and is being depreciated at a CCA rate of 25 percent.
4. The new equipment will also be depreciated at a CCA rate of 25 percent. MMC expects to be able to sell the equipment for $5,000 at the end of eight years. At that time, the firm plans to reinvest in new equipment in the same CCA pool.
5. MMC has profitable ongoing operations.
6. The appropriate discount rate is 11.5 percent.
7. The tax rate is 38 percent.

EXCEL

8.13 After extensive medical and marketing research, Pill Ltd. believes it can penetrate the pain reliever market. It can follow one of two strategies. The first is to manufacture a medication aimed at relieving headache pain. The second strategy is to make a pill designed to relieve headache and arthritis pain. Both products would be introduced at a price of $4.75 per package in real terms. The broader remedy would probably sell 10 million packages a year. This is twice the sales rate for the headache-only medication. Cash costs of production in the first year are expected to be $1.13 per package in real terms for the headache-only brand. Production costs are expected to be $1.70 in real terms for the more general pill. All prices and costs are expected to rise at the general inflation rate of 3.75 percent.

Either strategy would require further investment in plant. The headache-only pill could be produced using equipment that would cost $10.2 million, last three years, and have no resale value. The machinery required to produce the broader remedy would cost $14.5 million and last three years. At this time the firm would be able to sell it for $1 million (in real terms). The production machinery would need to be replaced every three years at constant real costs.

Suppose that, for both projects, the firm will use a CCA rate of 20 percent. The firm faces a corporate tax rate of 36 percent. Management believes the appropriate real discount rate is 13 percent. Which pain reliever should Pill Ltd. produce?

8.14 A machine that lasts four years has the following net cash outflows: $15,000 to purchase the machine and $6,250 for the annual year-end operating cost. At the end of four years, the machine is sold for $2,900; thus, the cash flow at year 4, C_4 is only $3,350.

C_0	C_1	C_2	C_3	C_4
$15,000	$6,250	$6,250	$6,250	$3,350

The cost of capital is 7 percent. What is the present value of the costs of operating a series of such machines in perpetuity?

Replacement with Unequal Lives

EXCEL

8.15 Office Automation Inc. is obliged to choose between two copiers, XX40 or RH45. XX40 costs less than RH45, but its economic life is shorter. The costs and maintenance expenses of these two copiers are given as follows. These cash flows are expressed in real terms.

Copier	Year 0	Year 1	Year 2	Year 3	Year 4	Year 5
XX40	$1500	$250	$250	$250		
RH45	915	105	105	105	$105	$105

Visit us at www.mcgrawhill.ca/olc/ross

The inflation rate is 5 percent and the nominal discount rate is 14 percent. Assume that revenues are the same regardless of the copier, and that whichever copier the company chooses, it will buy the model forever. Which copier should the company choose? Ignore taxes and depreciation.

8.16 Station CJXT is considering the replacement of its old, fully depreciated sound mixer. Two new models are available. Mixer X has a cost of $410,000, a five-year expected life, and after-tax cash flow savings of $120,000 per year. Mixer Y has a cost of $625,000, an eight-year life, and after-tax cash flow savings of $131,000 per year. No new technological developments are expected. The cost of capital is 11.7 percent. Should CJXT replace the old mixer with X or Y?

8.17 Which is better: (1) investing $10,000 in a guaranteed investment certificate (GIC) for one year at 9 percent when expected inflation is 4 percent or (2) investing $10,000 in a GIC at 5 percent when expected inflation is 1 percent? In assessing these alternatives, assume that interest received is taxed at a rate of 38 percent.

8.18 A new electronic process monitor costs $145,000. This cost will be depreciated at 25 percent per year (class 9). The monitor will actually be worthless in five years. The new monitor would save us $57,000 per year before taxes in operating costs. If we require a 14.5 percent return, what is the NPV of the purchase? Assume a tax rate of 40 percent.

8.19 We believe we can sell 12,000 home security devices per year at $31 apiece. They cost $20 each to manufacture (variable cost). Fixed production costs will run $28,000 per year. The necessary equipment costs $150,000 to buy and will be depreciated at a 20 percent CCA rate. The equipment will have zero salvage value after the five-year life of the project. When this project is over, there will still be other assets in the CCA class. We will need to invest $41,500 in net working capital up front, but no additional net working capital investment will be necessary. The discount rate is 15 percent, and the tax rate is 41 percent. What do you think of the proposal?

8.20 This problem is much easier if you are working with a spreadsheet. We are contemplating the purchase of a $1 million computer-based customer order management system. CCA on the system will be calculated at a rate of 30 percent. In five years it will be worth $405,000. When this project is over, there will still be other assets in the CCA class. We would save $500,000 before taxes per year in order processing costs, and we would reduce working capital by $250,000 (a one-time reduction). What is the DCF return on this investment? The relevant tax rate is 38 percent.

8.21 A proposed cost-saving device has an installed cost of $56,300. It is in class 9 for CCA purposes. (CCA rates are given in Table 8A.1.) It will actually function for five years, at which time it will have no value. When this project is over, there will still be other assets in the CCA class. There are no working capital consequences from the investment; the tax rate is 42 percent.
    a. What must the annual pre-tax cost savings be for us to favour the investment? We require a 11 percent return. Hint: This is a variation on the problem of setting a bid price.
    b. Suppose the device will be worth $17,000 in salvage (before taxes). How does this change your answer?

8.22 Klaatu Co. has recently completed a $300,000, two-year marketing study. Based on the results, Klaatu has estimated that 10,000 of its new RUR-class robots could be sold annually over the next eight years at a price of $10,115 each. Variable costs per robot are $7,900; fixed costs total $11.7 million per year.

       Start-up costs include $41 million to build production facilities, $2.2 million in land, and $9 million in net working capital. The $41 million facility is made up of a building valued at $6 million that will belong to CCA class 3 and $35 million of manufacturing equipment (belonging to CCA class 8). (CCA rates are in Appendix 8A.) At the end of the project's life, the facilities (including the land) will be sold for an estimated $10.1 million, assuming the building's value will be $4 million. When this project is over, there will still be other assets in the CCA class. The value of the land is not expected to change.

Finally, start-up would also entail fully deductible expenses of $1.2 million at year 0. An ongoing, profitable business, Klaatu pays taxes at a 37 percent rate. Klaatu uses a 15.5 percent discount rate on projects such as this one. Should Klaatu produce the RUR-class robots?

MINICASE: I.Q. Inc.

In order to maintain its leadership position in the computer peripherals industry, particularly inkjet printers and accessories, I.Q. has begun to develop a new ink for its 8xx line of inkjet printers. As a marketing manager of the 8xx line of inkjet printers and accessories, you are in the position to make a decision whether or not to continue the development. The project is codenamed IQ8Ink.

Research efforts for the IQ8Ink have cost I.Q. Inc. $2 million so far, in addition to a positive test marketing effort costing $0.75 million. However, these are sunk costs and will not impact your decision making. What should be considered are the new investment and future cash inflows. From your observation, you know that you can invest immediately and start production now. You also know that the economic life of this effort is only four years, meaning potentially four years of production.

I.Q.'s CEO, K. Fione, is very pleased with the progress of the 8xx line so far and wishes to congratulate you on a job well done. So, the decision on the development of IQ8Ink is critical. From engineering, you know that you will need to invest another $1 million in production equipment to make this new ink. The equipment will have a useful life of five years and qualifies for a CCA rate of 20 percent. At year 4, you expect to sell the equipment for $0.5 million. For planning purposes, you believe that assets will remain in the equipment's CCA class. Furthermore, the net working capital requirement will increase by $1.2 million immediately and will be recaptured at year 4.

As for the potential customers, there are two distinct segments:

1. New 8xx printers—For every new 8xx printer, one unit of this new ink will be used. (Assume complete retirement of old ink models with no costs associated.) Internal transfer price is at $1.75 now. The variable cost to produce per unit is $0.50.
2. Existing 8xx printers—While competitors exist, offering generic ink, IQ8Ink is superior and will take a large percentage of market share. Wholesale price is at $11 now. The variable cost to produce per unit is the same as above.

Note that on average, ink price and cost rise at 1.5 percent above the inflation rate. In addition, marketing and administration efforts will cost $0.25 million the first year and increase at inflation each subsequent year.

From economic data, inflation is expected to remain constant at 2 percent. I.Q.'s corporate tax rate is 36 percent and the division has a discount rate of 16.5 percent.

Last, you know that production of new 8xx printers will be 300,000 units in the first year and will increase by 10 percent per year. Additionally, the demand for ink from existing 8xx printers is 1 million units in the first year and increases by 12 percent per year. Out of the demand for ink from existing 8xx printers, I.Q. expects to capture 76 percent.

MINICASE: Jimmy's Hot Dog Stands

Jimmy Levitin owns a popular hot dog stand on a trendy section of Melrose Boulevard. Following the success of his first hot dog stand, "Jimmy's," which has been in operation for five years, Jimmy is now considering opening a second hot dog stand in another trendy location, on Sunset Boulevard in the Silver Lake area. Jimmy's market research shows that the clientele in both areas is similar: young professionals, typically without children, who like the traditional aspect of eating hot dogs, but also relish his gourmet, specially manufactured low-fat dogs and the healthy side dishes his stand also sells.

Jimmy's overall plan is to get the second stand up and running for five years, and then sell both stands off to a new owner and retire.

Jimmy estimates that the cost of starting up a second stand will be as follows:

Purchase of real estate (retail food outlet)	$650,000
Installation of specialized kitchen equipment	75,000
Furniture and fittings	37,500

The cost of the real estate was allocated $400,000 to the land and $250,000 to the building. The Building CCA rate is 4%.

On the sale of the building, the proceeds were allocated in the same ratio to land and building as they were in the purchase.

Jimmy estimates that net working capital will increase by $35,000 for the first year for the new outlet. He also estimates that yearly operating costs of the new location would be almost identical to those of his current stand:

Labour costs, inclusive of all overhead costs:	
Kitchen and service staff (4 persons)	$119,000
Raw materials:	
Hot dogs: 200 per day × 7 days	
× 52 weeks	$ 54,600
Drinks	$ 21,000
Other food supplies	76,000
Nonfood supplies	25,000
Total raw materials	$176,600
The revenues at his current location are as follows:	
Sales of hot dogs and other food items	$495,000
Drinks	$104,000
Total revenues	$599,000

In addition to contributing profits, Jimmy expects that opening a second stand will decrease the cost of purchasing gourmet hot dogs from 75 cents to 63 cents in both locations. This is due to economies of scale, since the new outlet would double output over the current level of demand. Jimmy also expects that he will be able to manage both locations himself, avoiding hiring a second manager for the new location.

Assume that:

- The marginal tax rate is 38 percent.
- The required rate of return is 11 percent.
- The CCA rate is 30 percent.
- At the time the business is sold, the real estate will have increased in value at an annual rate of 9.5 percent and the kitchen equipment and furniture will have no value.
- The sale price of the business is the market value of the real estate plus one year's revenue.

What is the NPV of this investment?

Appendix 8A   Capital Cost Allowance

Under the *Income Tax Act,* accounting amortization cannot be used in the calculation of income for income tax purposes. Instead, the Act mandates the use of the Capital Cost Allowance (CCA) system.[10] Capital cost allowance is deducted in determining taxable income. CCA is not the same as depreciation under GAAP so there is no reason why calculation of a firm's income under tax rules has to be the same as under GAAP. For example, taxable corporate income may often be lower than accounting income because the company uses accelerated capital cost allowance rules in computing depreciation for tax purposes while using straight-line depreciation for GAAP reporting.[11]

CCA calculation begins by assigning every asset to a particular class. An asset's class establishes its maximum CCA rate for tax purposes. Leasehold improvements follow straight-line depreciation for CCA. For all other assets, CCA follows the declining balance method. The CCA for each year is computed by multiplying the asset's book value for tax purposes, called *undepreciated capital cost (UCC),* by the appropriate rate.

Intangible assets, such as goodwill and patents, are particularly important to knowledge-based firms like software developers and pharmaceutical companies. Such assets are not subject to CCA. Instead, intangible assets are amortized at an effective rate of 5.25 percent on the declining balance.

---

[10]Recall from Chapter 2 that accountants use the term *amortization* to refer to depreciation and depletion.

[11]Where taxable income is less than accounting income, total taxes (calculated from accounting income) are greater than current taxes (calculated from taxable income). The difference, deferred taxes (or future tax liability) for the year, is added to the deferred tax liability account on the balance sheet.

TABLE 8A.1
Common CCA Classess

Class	Rate	Asset
1	4%	Brick buildings (acquired after 1987)
3	5	Brick buildings (acquired prior to 1988)
6	10	Fences and frame buildings
7	15	Canoes and boats, ships
8	20	Manufacturing and processing equipment
9	25	Electrical equipment and aircraft
10	30	Vans, trucks, and tractors
13	straight-line	Leasehold improvements
16	40	Taxicabs and rental cars
22	50	Excavating equipment
45	45	Computer equipment

Source: *Income Tax Act 2001* (72nd edition).

The CCA system is unique to Canada and differs in many respects from the depreciation method used in the United States. One key difference is that, in the Canadian system, the expected salvage value (what we think the asset will be worth when we dispose of it) and the actual expected economic life (how long we expect the asset to be in service) are not considered in the calculation of capital cost allowance. (Some typical CCA classes and their respective CCA rates are described in Table 8A.1.) Another unique feature of the CCA system is the concept of pooling of assets described in detail below. Calculating CCA on pools of assets rather than for each item simplifies the system.

To illustrate how capital cost allowance is calculated, suppose your firm is considering buying a van costing $24,000, including any set-up costs that must (by law) be capitalized. (No rational, profitable business would capitalize, for tax purposes, anything that could legally be expensed.) Table 8A.1 shows that vans fall in class 10 with a 30 percent CCA rate. To calculate the CCA we need to follow the 50 percent rule, which requires us to figure CCA on only one-half of the asset's installed cost in the first year it is put in use. Notice that we add the other half in the second year. The UCC at the beginning of year 2 is:

$$\text{Beginning UCC} - \text{CCA} + \text{Remaining half of purchase price}$$
$$\$12,000 - 0.30 \times \$12,000 + \$12,000 = \$20,400$$

Table 8A.2 shows the CCA for our van for the first five years.

As we pointed out, in calculating CCA under current tax law, the economic life and future market value of the asset are not issues. As a result, an asset's UCC can differ substantially from its actual market value. With our $24,000 van, UCC after the first year is $8,400 (or $12,000 less the first year's CCA of $3,600). The remaining UCC values are summarized in Table 8A.2. After five years, the van's undepreciated capital cost is $4,898.

TABLE 8A.2
CCA for a Van

Year	Beginning UCC	CCA	Ending UCC
1	$12,000*	$3,600	$ 8,400
2	20,400†	6,120	14,280
3	14,280	4,284	9,996
4	9,996	2,999	6,997
5	6,997	2,099	4,898

*One-half of $24,000.
†Year 1 ending balance plus the remaining half of $24,000.

Capital Cost Allowance in Practice

Since capital cost allowance is deducted in computing taxable income, larger CCA rates reduce taxes and increase cash flows. To illustrate, in a federal budget a few years ago, the minister announced an increase in CCA rates from 30 to 45 percent for computer equipment. The combined federal/provincial corporate tax rate for this sector is 34.5 percent.

EXAMPLE 8A.1

Mississauga Manufacturing was planning to acquire new processing equipment to enhance efficiency and its ability to compete with U.S. firms. The equipment had an installed cost of $1 million. How much additional tax did the new measure save Mississauga in the first year the equipment was put into use?

Under the 50 percent rule, UCC for the first year is $1/2 \times \$1$ million = $500,000. The CCA deductions under the old and new rates are

$$\text{Old rate: CCA} = 0.30 \times \$500,000 = \$150,000$$
$$\text{New rate: CCA} = 0.45 \times \$500,000 = \$225,000$$

Because the firm deducts CCA in figuring taxable income, taxable income will be reduced by the incremental CCA of $75,000. With $75,000 less in taxable income, Mississauga Manufacturing's combined tax bill will drop by $75,000 \times 0.345 = \$25,875$.

Asset Purchases and Sales

When an asset is sold, the UCC in its asset class (or pool) is reduced by what is realized on the asset or by its original cost, whichever is less. This amount is called the *adjusted cost of disposal.* Suppose that we want to sell the van in our earlier example after five years and find that it is worth $6,000. Since the $6,000 price is less than the original cost, the adjusted cost of disposal is $6,000 and the UCC in class 10 is reduced by this amount.

In this case, the $6,000 removed from the pool is $1,102 (or $6,000 − $4,898) more than the undepreciated capital cost of the van we are selling, and future CCA deductions will be reduced as the pool continues. On the other hand, if we sold the van for, say, $4,000, the UCC in class 10 would be reduced by $4,000 and the $898 excess ($4,898 − $4,000) of UCC over the sale price would remain in the pool. In this case, future CCA increases as the declining balance calculations depreciate the $898 excess UCC to infinity.

So far, we have focused on CCA calculations for one asset. In practice, firms often buy and sell assets from a given class in the course of a year. In this case, we apply the net acquisitions rule. From the total installed cost of all acquisitions we subtract the adjusted cost of disposal of all assets in the pool. The result is net acquisitions for the asset class. If net acquisitions is positive, we apply the 50 percent rule and calculate CCA as above. If net acquisitions is negative, the 50 percent rule does not apply.

When an Asset Pool Is Terminated

Suppose your firm decides to contract out all transport and to sell all company vehicles. If the company owns no other class 10 assets, the asset pool in this class is terminated. As before, the adjusted cost of disposal is the net sales proceeds or the total installed cost of all the pool assets, whichever is less. This adjusted cost of disposal is subtracted from the total UCC in the pool. So far, the steps are exactly the same as in our van example where the pool continued. What happens next is different. Unless the adjusted cost of disposal just happens to equal the UCC exactly, a positive or negative UCC balance remains and this has tax implications.

A positive UCC balance remains when the adjusted cost of disposal is less than UCC before the sale. In this case, the firm has a terminal loss equal to the remaining UCC. Because this loss is deductible from income for the year, it results in a tax saving. For example, if we sell the van after two years for $10,000, then the UCC exceeds the market value by $4,280 (or $14,280 − $10,000). In this case, the terminal loss of $4,280—assuming the tax rate is 40 percent—gives rise to a tax saving of 0.40 × $4,280 = $1,712.

A negative UCC balance occurs when the adjusted cost of disposal exceeds UCC in the pool. To illustrate, return to our van example and suppose that this van is the only class 10 asset our company owns when it sells off the pool. In this case, we see that there is a $1,102 excess of adjusted cost of disposal ($6,000 − $4,898) over UCC so the final UCC balance is −$1,102.

The company must pay tax at its ordinary tax rate on this negative balance. Taxes must be paid in this case since the difference in adjusted cost of disposal and UCC is "excess" CCA recaptured when the asset is sold. We overdepreciated the asset by $6,000 − $4,898 = $1,102. Since we deducted $1,102 too much in CCA, we paid $440.80 ($1,102 × 0.4) too little in taxes, and we simply have to make up the difference.[12]

Notice that this is not a tax on a capital gain. As a general rule, a capital gain only occurs if the market price exceeds the original cost. To illustrate a capital gain, suppose that instead of buying the van, our firm purchased a classic car for $50,000. After five years, the classic car will be sold for $75,000. In this case, the sale price exceeds the purchase price so the adjusted cost of disposal is $50,000 and the UCC pool is reduced by this amount. The total negative balance left in the UCC pool is $6,123 − $50,000 = −$43,877 and this is recaptured CCA. In addition, the firm has a capital gain of $75,000 − $50,000 = $25,000, the difference between the sale price and the original cost.

EXAMPLE 8A.2

Staple Supply Ltd. has just purchased a new computerized information system with an installed cost of $160,000. The computer is in class 10 for CCA purposes. What are the yearly capital cost allowances? Based on historical experience, we think that the system will be worth only $10,000 when we get rid of it in four years. What are the tax consequences of the sale if the company has several other computers that will still be in use in four years? Now suppose that Staple Supply will sell all its assets and wind up the company in four years. What is the total after-tax cash flow from the sale?

In Table 8A.3, at the end of year 4 the remaining balance for the specific computer system will be $20,630.[12] The pool is reduced by $10,000, but it will continue to be "depreciated." There are no tax consequences in year 4. This is only the case when the pool is active. If this is the only computer system, we close the pool and claim a terminal loss of $20,630 − $10,000 = $10,630.

TABLE 8A.3
CCA for a Computer System

Year	Beginning UCC	CCA	Ending UCC
1	$ 80,000*	$36,000	$44,000
2	124,000†	53,800	68,200
3	68,200	30,690	37,510
4	37,510	16,880	20,630

[12]In actuality, the capital cost allowance for the entire pool will be calculated at once, without specific identification of each computer system.

The company must pay tax on this capital gain of $25,000. As explained in Appendix 1A, at the time of writing, a corporation is taxed on 50 percent of any capital gains. Using a marginal corporate tax rate of 40 percent, the tax payable is $5,000 (or $25,000 \times 0.50 \times 0.40$).

Appendix Questions

8.A1   What is the difference between capital cost allowance and GAAP depreciation?

8.A2   A company has just invested $210,500 in new manufacturing equipment (class 8). Develop a CCA and UCC schedule (like Table 8A.2) for the first 10 years.

8.A3   Suppose the company decides to sell the equipment after three years for $65,000 and terminates the asset pool. Calculate the tax results.

Appendix 8B   Derivation of the Present Value of CCA Tax Shield Formula

We can use the growing perpetuity formula from Chapter 5 (Equation 5.10) to derive the present value of the CCA tax shield. Recall that when cash flows grow at a constant rate g, the present value of the perpetuity at discount rate k is

$$PV = \frac{\text{1st payment}}{k - g}$$

Since we are temporarily ignoring the half-year rule, the growth rate in CCA payments is equal to $(-d)$, the CCA rate. Since CCA declines over time as the depreciable base (CC) reduces, the growth rate is negative. For example, in Table 8.6

$$
\begin{aligned}
CCA_3 &= CCA_2\,[1 + (-d)] \\
&= 144,000\,[1 + (-0.20)] \\
&= 144,000\,(0.8) = 115,200
\end{aligned}
$$

Given the growth rate as $(-d)$, we need the first payment to complete the formula. This is the first year's tax shield calculating the CCA at rate d on the total cost of the asset added to the depreciation pool, C, and then multiplying by the tax rate, T_c.

$$\text{1st payment} = CdT_c$$

We can now complete the formula.

$$
\begin{aligned}
PV\ (\text{CCA tax shield}) &= \frac{\text{1st payment}}{k - g} \\
&= \frac{CdT_c}{k - (-d)} \\
&= \frac{CdT_c}{k + d}
\end{aligned}
$$

The next step is to extend the formula to adjust for Canada Revenue Agency's 50 percent rule. This rule states that a firm must add one-half of the incremental capital cost of a new project in year 1 and the other half in year 2. The result is that we now calculate present value of the tax shield in two parts. The present value of the stream starting the first year is simply one-half of the original value:

$$PV\ \text{of 1st half} = 0.5\,\frac{CdT_c}{k + d}$$

The PV of the second half (deferred one year) is the same quantity (bracketed term below) discounted back to time zero. The total present value of the tax shield on CCA under the 50 percent rule is the sum of the two present values.

$$\text{PV tax shield on CCA} = \frac{0.5\ CdT_c}{k + d} + \frac{[0.5\ CdT_c]}{[k + d]}\ \frac{1}{(1 + k)}$$

With a little algebra we can simplify the formula to

$$PV = \frac{0.5\ CdT_c}{k + d}[1 + 1/(1 + k)] = \frac{0.5\ CdT_c}{k + d}\left[\frac{1 + k + 1}{1 + k}\right]$$

$$= \frac{CdT_c}{k + d}\ \frac{[1 + 0.5k]}{[1 + k]}$$

The final adjustment for salvage value begins with the present value in the salvage year, *n,* of future tax shields beginning in year, $n + 1$.

$$\frac{SdT_c}{k + d}$$

We discount this figure back to today and subtract it to get the complete formula.[13]

$$\text{PV tax shield on CCA} = \frac{[CdT_c]}{k + d} \times \frac{[1 + 0.5k]}{1 + k} - \frac{SdT_c}{k + d} \times \frac{1}{(1 + k)^n} \qquad (8\text{B}.1)$$

---

[13]By not adjusting the salvage value for the 50 percent rule, we assume there will be no new investment in year *n.*

Chapter 9

Risk Analysis, Real Options, and Capital Budgeting

Chapters 7 and 8 covered the basic principles of capital budgeting, with particular emphasis on the net present value (NPV) approach. However, this is not the end of the story. Real-world practitioners often wonder how much confidence they should place in NPV calculations. This chapter examines sensitivity analysis, scenario analysis, break-even analysis, and Monte Carlo simulations, all of which recognize that, because it is based on estimates, NPV is really a distribution, not a single number. These techniques help the practitioner determine the degree of confidence to be placed in a capital budgeting calculation.

Information is uncovered as a project unfolds, allowing a manager to make sequential decisions over the life of the project. This chapter covers decision trees and real options, capital budgeting techniques that specifically take the sequential nature of decision making into account.

9.1 Decision Trees

There is usually a sequence of decisions in NPV project analysis. This section introduces the device of **decision trees** for identifying these sequential decisions.

Imagine you are the treasurer of the Solar Electronics Corporation (SEC), and the engineering group has recently developed the technology for solar-powered jet engines. The jet engine is to be used with 150-passenger commercial airplanes. The marketing staff has proposed that SEC develop some prototypes and conduct test marketing of the engine. A corporate planning group, including representatives from production, marketing, and engineering, estimates that this preliminary phase will take a year and will cost $100 million. Furthermore, the group believes there is a 75 percent chance that the marketing tests will prove successful.

If the initial marketing tests are *successful,* SEC can go ahead with full-scale production. This investment phase will cost $1,500 million. Production and sales will occur over the next five years. The preliminary cash flow projection appears in Table 9.1. Should SEC go ahead with investment and production on the jet engine, the NPV at a discount rate of 15 percent (in millions) is

$$
\begin{aligned}
\text{NPV} &= -\$1,500 + \sum_{t=1}^{5} \frac{\$900}{(1.15)^t} \\
&= -\$1,500 + \$900 \times A_{0.15}^{5} \\
&= \$1,517
\end{aligned}
$$

TABLE 9.1
Cash Flow Forecasts for Solar Electronics Corporation's Jet Engine Base Case (millions)*

Investment	Year 1	Years 2–6
Revenues		$ 6,000
Variable costs		(3,000)
Fixed costs		(1,791)
Depreciation		(300)
Pre-tax profit		909
Tax ($T_c = 0.34$)		(309)
Net profit		$ 600
Cash flow		$ 900
Initial investment costs	−$1,500	

* Assumptions: (1) Investment is depreciated in years 2 through 6 using the straight-line method for simplicity; (2) tax rate is 34 percent; (3) the company receives no tax benefits on initial development costs.

Note that the NPV is calculated as of date 1, the date at which the investment of $1,500 million is made. Later we bring this number back to date 0.

If the initial marketing tests are *unsuccessful,* SEC's $1,500 million investment has an NPV of −$3,611 million. This figure is also calculated as of date 1. (To save space, we will not provide the raw numbers leading to this calculation.)

Figure 9.1 displays the problem concerning the jet engine as a decision tree. If SEC decides to conduct test marketing, there is a 75 percent probability that the test marketing will be successful. If the tests are successful, the firm faces a second decision: whether to invest $1,500 million in a project that yields $1,517 million NPV or to stop. If the tests

FIGURE 9.1
Decision Tree ($ millions) for SEC

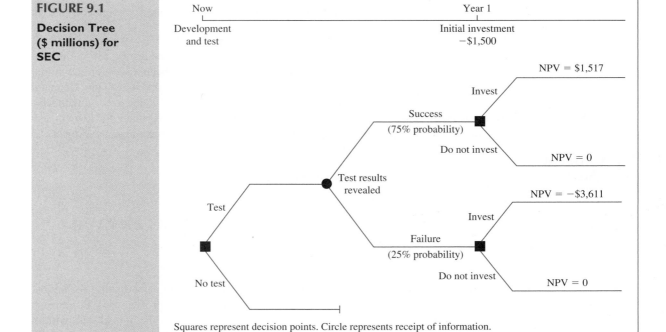

Squares represent decision points. Circle represents receipt of information.
SEC must make two decisions:
  1. Whether to develop and test engine
  2. Whether to invest in full-scale production

are unsuccessful, the firm faces a different decision: whether to invest $1,500 million in a project that yields −$3,611 million NPV or to stop.

To review, SEC has the following two decisions to make:

1. Whether to develop and test the solar-powered jet engine.
2. Whether to invest in full-scale production following the results of the test.

One makes decisions in reverse order with decision trees. Thus we analyze the second-stage investment of $1,500 million first. If the tests are successful, should SEC make the second-stage investment? The answer is obviously yes, since $1,517 million is greater than zero. If the tests are unsuccessful, should the second-stage investment be made? Just as obviously, the answer is no, since −$3,611 million is below zero.

Now we move back to the first stage, where the decision boils down to the question: Should SEC invest $100 million now to obtain a 75 percent chance of $1,517 million one year later? The expected payoff evaluated at date 1 (in millions) is

$$
\begin{pmatrix} \text{Expected} \\ \text{payoff} \end{pmatrix} = \begin{pmatrix} \text{Probability} \\ \text{of} \\ \text{success} \end{pmatrix} \times \begin{pmatrix} \text{Payoff} \\ \text{if} \\ \text{successful} \end{pmatrix} + \begin{pmatrix} \text{Probability} \\ \text{of} \\ \text{failure} \end{pmatrix} \times \begin{pmatrix} \text{Payoff} \\ \text{if} \\ \text{failure} \end{pmatrix}
$$

$$
= (0.75 \times \$1{,}517) + (0.25 \times \$0)
$$

$$
= \$1{,}138
$$

The NPV of testing computed at date 0 (in millions) is

$$
\text{NPV} = -\$100 + \frac{\$1{,}138}{1.15}
$$

$$
= \$890
$$

Since the NPV is a positive number, the firm should test the market for solar-powered jet engines.

Warning   We have used a discount rate of 15 percent for both the testing and the investment decisions. Perhaps a higher discount rate should have been used for the initial test-marketing decision, which is likely to be riskier than the investment decision. Discount rates can also vary when different periods have different levels of risk due to varying macroeconomic conditions. This is especially important for decision trees, where the level of risk from one branch of the tree to another can differ greatly due to the nature of the project.

? Concept Questions
- **What is a decision tree?**
- **How do decision trees handle sequential decisions?**

9.2 Sensitivity Analysis, Scenario Analysis, and Break-Even Analysis

One thrust of this book is that NPV analysis is a superior capital budgeting technique. In fact, because the NPV approach uses cash flows rather than profits, uses all the cash flows, and discounts the cash flows properly, it is hard to find any theoretical fault with it. However, in our conversations with practical businesspeople, we hear the phrase "a false sense of security" frequently. These people point out that the documentation for capital budgeting proposals is often quite impressive. Cash flows are projected down to the last thousand dollars (or even the last dollar) for each year (or even each month). Opportunity costs and side effects are handled quite properly. Sunk costs are ignored—also quite properly. When a high net present value appears at the bottom, one's temptation is to say yes immediately. Nevertheless, the projected cash flow often goes unmet in practice, and the firm ends up with a money loser.

Sensitivity Analysis and Scenario Analysis

How can the firm get the net present value technique to live up to its potential? One approach is **sensitivity analysis** (a.k.a. *what-if analysis* and *BOP analysis*[1]), which examines how sensitive a particular NPV calculation is to changes in underlying assumptions. We illustrate the technique with Solar Electronics' solar-powered jet engine from the previous section. As pointed out earlier, the cash flow forecasts for this project appear in Table 9.1. We begin by considering the assumptions underlying revenues, costs, and after-tax cash flows shown in the table.

Revenues   Sales projections for the proposed jet engine have been estimated by the marketing department as

$$\begin{array}{ccccc} \text{Number of jet} \\ \text{engines sold} \end{array} = \text{Market share} \times \begin{array}{c} \text{Size of jet} \\ \text{engine market} \end{array}$$

$$3000 = 0.30 \times 10{,}000$$

$$\text{Sales revenues} = \begin{array}{c} \text{Number of jet} \\ \text{engines sold} \end{array} \times \begin{array}{c} \text{Price per} \\ \text{engine} \end{array}$$

$$\$6{,}000 \text{ million} = 3000 \times \$2 \text{ million}$$

Thus, it turns out that the revenue estimates depend on three assumptions:

1. Market share
2. Size of jet engine market
3. Price per engine

Costs   Financial analysts frequently divide costs into two types: variable costs and fixed costs. **Variable costs** change as the output changes, and they are zero when production is zero. Costs of direct labour and raw materials are usually variable. It is common to assume that a variable cost is constant per unit of output, implying that total variable costs are proportional to the level of production. For example, if direct labour is variable and one unit of final output requires $10 of direct labour, then 100 units of final output should require $1,000 of direct labour.

Fixed costs are not dependent on the amount of goods or services produced during the period. Fixed costs are usually measured as costs per unit of time, such as rent per month or salaries per year. Naturally, fixed costs are not fixed forever. They are only fixed over a predetermined time period.

The engineering department has estimated variable costs to be $1 million per engine. Fixed costs are $1,791 million per year. The cost breakdowns are

$$\begin{array}{c} \text{Variable} \\ \text{cost} \end{array} = \begin{array}{c} \text{Variable cost} \\ \text{per unit} \end{array} \times \begin{array}{c} \text{Number of jet} \\ \text{engines sold} \end{array}$$

$$\$3{,}000 \text{ million} = \$1 \text{ million} \times 3000$$

---

[1]BOP stands for Best, Optimistic, Pessimistic.

TABLE 9.2
Different Estimates for Solar Electronics' Solar Jet Engine

Variable	Pessimistic	Expected or Best	Optimistic
Market size (per year)	5000	10,000	20,000
Market share	20%	30%	50%
Price	$1.9 million	$2 million	$2.2 million
Variable cost (per plane)	$1.2 million	$1 million	$0.8 million
Fixed cost (per year)	$1,891 million	$1,791 million	$1,741 million
Investment	$1,900 million	$1,500 million	$1,000 million

$$\text{Total cost before taxes} = \text{Variable cost} + \text{Fixed cost}$$
$$\$4,791 \text{ million} = \$3,000 \text{ million} + \$1,791 \text{ million}$$

The above estimates for market size, market share, price, variable cost, and fixed cost, as well as the estimate of initial investment, are presented in the middle column of Table 9.2. These figures represent the firm's expectations or best estimates of the different parameters. For purposes of comparison, the firm's analysts prepared both optimistic and pessimistic forecasts for the different variables. These are also provided in the table.

Standard sensitivity analysis calls for an NPV calculation for all three possibilities of a single variable, along with the expected forecast for all other variables. This procedure is illustrated in Table 9.3. For example, consider the NPV calculation of $8,154 million provided in the upper right-hand corner of this table. This occurs when the optimistic forecast of 20,000 units per year is used for market size. However, the expected forecasts from Table 9.2 are employed for all other variables when the $8,154 million figure is generated. Note that the same number of $1,517 million appears in each row of the middle column of Table 9.3. This occurs because the expected forecast is used for the variable that was singled out, as well as for all other variables.

Table 9.3 can be used for a number of purposes. First, taken as a whole, the table can indicate whether NPV analysis should be trusted. In other words, it reduces the false sense of security we spoke of earlier. Suppose that NPV is positive when the expected forecast for each variable is used. However, further suppose that every number in the pessimistic column is highly negative and every number in the optimistic column is highly positive.

TABLE 9.3
NPV Calculations as of Date 1 (in $ millions) for the Solar Jet Engine Using Sensitivity Analysis

	Pessimistic	Expected or Best	Optimistic
Market size	−$1,802*	$1,517	$8,154
Market share	−696*	1,517	5,942
Price	853	1,517	2,844
Variable cost	189	1,517	2,844
Fixed cost	1,295	1,517	1,628
Investment	1,208	1,517	1,903

Under sensitivity analysis, one input is varied while all other inputs are assumed to meet their expectation. For example, an NPV of −$1,802 occurs when the pessimistic forecast of 5000 is used for market size. However, the expected forecasts from Table 9.2 are used for all other variables when −$1,802 is generated.

* We assume that the other divisions of the firm are profitable, implying that a loss on this project can offset income elsewhere in the firm, thereby reducing the overall taxes of the firm.

Even a single error in this forecast greatly alters the estimate, making one leery of the net present value approach. A conservative manager might well scrap the entire NPV analysis in this situation. Fortunately, this does not seem to be the case in Table 9.3, because all but two of the numbers are positive. Managers viewing the table will likely consider NPV analysis to be useful for the solar-powered jet engine.

Second, sensitivity analysis shows where more information is needed. For example, error in the estimate of investment appears to be relatively unimportant because, even under the pessimistic scenario, the NPV of $1,208 million is still highly positive. By contrast, the pessimistic forecast for market share leads to a negative NPV of $-$696 million, and a pessimistic forecast for market size leads to a substantially negative NPV of $-$1,802 million. Since the effect of incorrect estimates on revenues is so much greater than the effect of incorrect estimates on costs, more information on the factors determining revenues might be needed.

Because of these advantages, sensitivity analysis is widely used in practice. Graham and Harvey[2] report that slightly over 50 percent of the 392 firms in their sample subject their capital budgeting calculations to sensitivity analysis. This number is particularly large when one considers that only about 75 percent of the firms in their sample use NPV analysis.

Unfortunately, sensitivity analysis also suffers from some drawbacks. For example, sensitivity analysis may unwittingly *increase* the false sense of security among managers. Suppose all pessimistic forecasts yield positive NPVs. A manager might feel that there is no way the project can lose money. Of course, the forecasters may simply have an optimistic view of a pessimistic forecast. To combat this, some companies do not treat optimistic and pessimistic forecasts subjectively. Rather, their pessimistic forecasts are always, say, 20 percent less than expected. Unfortunately, the cure in this case may be worse than the disease, because a deviation of a fixed percentage ignores the fact that some variables are easier to forecast than others.

In addition, sensitivity analysis treats each variable in isolation when, in reality, the different variables are likely to be related. For example, if ineffective management allows costs to get out of control, it is likely that variable costs, fixed costs, and investment will all rise above expectation at the same time. If the market is not receptive to a solar-powered jet engine, both market share and price should decline together.

Managers frequently perform **scenario analysis,** a variant of sensitivity analysis, to minimize this problem. Simply put, this approach examines a number of different likely scenarios, where each scenario involves a confluence of factors. As a simple example, consider the effect of a few airline crashes. These crashes are likely to reduce flying in total, thereby limiting the demand for any new engines. Furthermore, even if the crashes did not involve solar-powered aircraft, the public could become more averse to any innovative and controversial technologies. Hence, SEC's market share might fall as well. Perhaps the cash flow calculations would look like those in Table 9.4 under the scenario of a plane crash. Given the calculations in the table, the NPV (in millions) would be

$$-\$2,023 = -\$1,500 - \$156 \times A_{0.15}^5$$

A series of scenarios like this might illuminate issues concerning the project better than the standard application of sensitivity analysis would.

Break-Even Analysis

Our discussion of sensitivity analysis and scenario analysis suggests that there are many ways to examine variability in forecasts. We now present another approach, **break-even**

[2]See Figure 2 of John Graham and Campbell Harvey, "The Theory and Practice of Corporate Finance: Evidence from the Field," *Journal of Financial Economics* (May/June 2001).

TABLE 9.4
Cash Flow Forecast (in $ millions) Under the Scenario of a Plane Crash*

	Year 1	Years 2–6
Revenues		$2,800
Variable costs		−1,400
Fixed costs		−1,791
Depreciation		−300
Pre-tax profit		−691
Tax ($T_c = 0.34$)[†]		235
Net profit		−456
Cash flow		−156
Initial investment cost	−$1,500	

*Assumptions are

    Market size   7000 (70 percent of expectation)
    Market share   20% (2/3 of expectation)
Forecasts for all other variables are the expected forecasts as given in Table 9.2.
[†]Tax loss offsets income elsewhere in firm.

analysis. As its name implies, this approach determines the sales needed to break even. The approach is a useful complement to sensitivity analysis, because it also sheds light on the severity of incorrect forecasts. We calculate the break-even point in terms of both accounting profit and present value.

Accounting Profit   Net profit under four different sales forecasts is

Unit Sales	Net Profit (in $ millions)
0	−$1,380
1000	−720
3000	600
10,000	5,220

A more complete presentation of costs and revenues appears in Table 9.5.

    We plot the revenues, costs, and profits under the different assumptions about sales in Figure 9.2. The revenue and cost curves cross at 2091 jet engines. This is the break-even point, i.e., the point where the project generates no profits or losses. As long as sales are above 2091 jet engines, the project will make a profit.

    This break-even point can be calculated very easily. Because the sale price is $2 million per engine and the variable cost is $1 million per engine,[3] the after-tax difference per engine is

$$(\text{Sale price} - \text{Variable cost}) \times (1 - T_c) = (\$2\text{ million} - \$1\text{ million}) \times (1 - 0.34)$$

$$= \$0.66\text{ million}$$

where T_c is the corporate tax rate of 34 percent. This after-tax difference is called the **contribution margin** because each additional engine contributes this amount to after-tax profit.

    Fixed costs are $1,791 million and depreciation is $300 million, implying that the after-tax sum of these costs is

---

[3]Though the previous section considered both optimistic and pessimistic forecasts for sale price and variable cost, break-even analysis uses just the expected or best estimates of these variables.

TABLE 9.5   Revenues and Costs of Project Under Different Sales Assumptions
(in $ millions, except unit sales)

Year 1			Years 2–6						
Initial Investment	Annual Unit Sales	Revenues	Variable Costs	Fixed Costs	Depreciation	Taxes* ($T_c = 0.34$)	Net Profit	Operating Cash Flows	NPV (evaluated date 1)
$1,500	0	$ 0	$ 0	−$1,791	−$300	$ 711	−$1,380	−$1,080	−$5,120
1,500	1,000	2,000	−1,000	−1,791	−300	371	−720	−420	−2,908
1,500	3,000	6,000	−3,000	−1,791	−300	−309	600	900	1,517
1,500	10,000	20,000	−10,000	−1,791	−300	−2,689	5,220	5,520	17,004

*Loss is incurred in the first two rows. For tax purposes, this loss offsets income elsewhere in the firm.

$$\text{(Fixed costs + Depreciation)} \times (1 - T_c) = (\$1{,}791 \text{ million} + \$300 \text{ million})$$
$$\times (1 - 0.34) = \$1{,}380 \text{ million}$$

That is, the firm incurs costs of $1,380 million, regardless of the number of sales. Because each engine contributes $0.66 million, sales must reach the following level to offset the above costs:

Accounting Profit Break-Even Point:

$$\frac{\text{(Fixed costs + Depreciation)} \times (1 - T_c)}{\text{(Sale price − Variable costs)} \times (1 - T_c)} = \frac{\$1{,}380 \text{ million}}{\$0.66 \text{ million}} = 2091 \qquad (9.1)$$

Thus, 2,091 engines is the break-even point required for an accounting profit.

Present Value   As we stated many times in the text, we are more interested in present value than we are in net profits. Therefore, we must calculate the present value of the cash flows. Given a discount rate of 15 percent, we have

Unit Sales	NPV ($ millions)
0	−5,120
1000	−2,908
3000	1,517
10,000	17,004

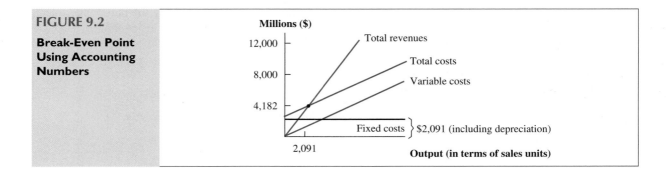

FIGURE 9.2

Break-Even Point Using Accounting Numbers

These NPV calculations are reproduced in the last column of Table 9.5. We can see that the NPV is negative if SEC produces 1000 jet engines and positive if it produces 3000 jet engines. Obviously, the zero NPV point occurs between 1000 and 3000 jet engines.

The present value break-even point can be calculated very easily. The firm originally invested $1,500 million. This initial investment can be expressed as a five-year equivalent annual cost (EAC), determined by dividing the initial investment by the appropriate five-year annuity factor:

$$\text{EAC} = \frac{\text{Initial investment}}{\text{5-year annuity factor at 15\%}} = \frac{\text{Initial investment}}{A_{0.15}^{5}}$$

$$= \frac{\$1,500 \text{ million}}{3.3522} = \$447.5 \text{ million}$$

Note that the EAC of $447.5 million is greater than the yearly depreciation of $300 million. This must occur since the calculation of EAC implicitly assumes that the $1,500 million investment could have been invested at 15 percent.

After-tax costs, regardless of output, can be viewed as

$$\begin{array}{ccccccc} \$1,528 & = & \$447.5 & + & \$1,791 & \times & 0.66 & - & \$300 & \times 0.34 \\ \text{million} & & \text{million} & & \text{million} & & & & \text{million} & \end{array}$$

$$= \quad \text{EAC} \quad + \quad \begin{array}{c}\text{Fixed}\\\text{costs}\end{array} \times (1 - T_c) - \begin{array}{c}\text{Depreci-}\\\text{ation}\end{array} \times T_c$$

That is, in addition to the initial investment's equivalent annual cost of $447.5 million, the firm pays fixed costs each year and receives a depreciation tax shield each year. The depreciation tax shield is written as a negative number since it offsets the costs in the equation. Because each engine contributes $0.66 million to after-tax profit, it will take the following sales to offset the above costs:

Present Value Break-Even Point:

$$\frac{\text{EAC} + \text{Fixed costs} \times (1 - T_c) - \text{Depreciation} \times T_c}{(\text{Sales price} - \text{Variable costs}) \times (1 - T_c)} = \frac{\$1,528 \text{ million}}{\$0.66 \text{ million}} = 2,315 \quad \textbf{(9.2)}$$

Thus, 2315 engines is the break-even point from the perspective of present value.

Why is the accounting break-even point (Equation 9.1) different from the financial break-even point in Equation (9.2)? When we use accounting profit as the basis for the break-even calculation, we subtract depreciation. Depreciation for the solar jet engines project is $300 million. If 2091 solar jet engines are sold, SEC will generate sufficient revenues to cover the $300 million depreciation expense plus other costs. Unfortunately, at this level of sales SEC will not cover the economic opportunity costs of the $1,500 million laid out for the investment. If we take into account that the $1,500 million could have been invested at 15 percent, the true annual cost of the investment is $447.5 million and not $300 million. Depreciation understates the true costs of recovering the initial investment. Thus, companies that break even on an accounting basis are really losing money. They are losing the opportunity cost of the initial investment.

? Concept Questions

- **What is a sensitivity analysis?**
- **Why is it important to perform a sensitivity analysis?**
- **What is a break-even analysis?**
- **Describe how sensitivity analysis interacts with break-even analysis.**

Break-Even Analysis, EAC, and Capital Cost Allowance

So far, in this chapter and the previous one, all our examples with EAC and break-even analysis have featured straight-line depreciation. While this had the advantage of simplifying the examples, it lacks realism for Canada. Here, Example 9.1 shows how to incorporate capital cost allowance into break-even analysis using the EAC approach.

EXAMPLE 9.1

Nack Trucks Inc. is expanding into the business of buying stripped-down truck platforms, which it plans to customize to client specifications and resell. The company will rent its manufacturing facility for $6,000 per month. Truck platforms cost $20,000 each and the typical finished product sells for $42,000.

This new business line would require $60,000 in new equipment. This equipment falls into class 8 with a CCA rate of 20 percent and would be worth about $5,000 after four years. Nack's tax rate is 43.5 percent and the cost of capital is 20 percent.

There is only one major competitor and Nack's sales staff estimate that they could achieve annual sales of 12 units. In order to determine if this sales level will be profitable, we must find the NPV break-even point.

This problem is very similar to the one we solved for SEC in Equation (9.2) above. The key difference is that the depreciation here is based on CCA so we have to replace the term, Depreciation $\times T_c$, in (9.2) with the EAC of the present value of the CCA tax shield: $EAC_{PVCCATS}$. This requires first calculating PVCCATS and then converting to an EAC.

$$\text{PVCCATS} = \frac{\$60,000\,(0.20)\,(0.435)}{0.20 + 0.20} \times \frac{1 \; + \; 0.5\,(0.20)}{1 \; + \; 0.20} - \frac{\$5,000\,(0.20)\,(0.435)}{0.20 + 0.20}$$

$$\times \frac{1}{(1.20)^4} = \$11,438$$

$$EAC_{PVCCATS} = \$11,438/A_{0.20}^4 = \$11,438/2.5887 = \$4,418.38$$

Next we find the EAC of the investment as:

$$[\$60,000 - \$5,000/(1.20)^4]/2.5887 = \$22,246.30$$

Fixed costs after tax are the rent of $6,000 \times 12 = $72,000 per year times $(1 - 0.435)$ = $40,680, and the after-tax contribution margin is ($42,000 - $20,000)(1 - 0.435) = $12,430.

We can now rewrite Equation (9.2) and fill in the numbers:

Present Value Break-Even Point with CCA

$$\frac{\text{EAC} + \text{Fixed costs} \times (1 - T_c) - EAC_{PVCCATS}}{(\text{Sale price} - \text{Variable costs}) \times (1 - T_c)} = \frac{\$22,246.30 + \$40,680 - \$4,418.38}{\$12,430}$$

$$= 4.71 \text{ or } 5 \text{ trucks}$$

Our calculations show that the break-even point is 5 trucks. This is well below targeted sales of 12 trucks, so the expansion looks promising.

9.3 Monte Carlo Simulation

Both sensitivity analysis and scenario analysis attempt to answer the question, "What if?" However, while both analyses are frequently used in the real world, each has its own limitations. Sensitivity analysis allows only one variable to change at a time. By contrast, many variables are likely to move at the same time in the real world. Scenario analysis follows specific scenarios, such as changes in inflation, government regulation, or the number of competitors. While this methodology is often quite helpful, it cannot cover all sources of variability. In fact, projects are likely to exhibit a lot of variability under just one economic scenario.

Monte Carlo simulation is a further attempt to model real-world uncertainty. This approach takes its name from the famous European casino, because it analyzes projects the way one might analyze gambling strategies. Imagine a serious blackjack player who wonders if he should take a third card whenever his first two cards total 16. Most likely, a formal mathematical model would be too complex to be practical here. However, he could play thousands of hands in a casino, sometimes drawing a third card when his first two cards add to 16 and sometimes not drawing that third card. He could compare his winnings (or losses) under the two strategies in order to determine which was better. Of course, since he would probably lose a lot of money performing this test in a real casino, simulating the results from the two strategies on a computer might be cheaper. Monte Carlo simulation of capital budgeting projects is in this spirit.

Imagine that Backyard Barbecues Inc. (BBI), a manufacturer of both charcoal and gas grills, has the blueprint for a new grill that cooks with compressed hydrogen. The CFO, Edward H. Comiskey, being dissatisfied with simpler capital budgeting techniques, wants a Monte Carlo simulation for this new grill. A consultant specializing in the Monte Carlo approach, Lester Mauney, takes him through the five basic steps of the method.

Step 1: Specify the Basic Model

Les Mauney breaks up cash flow into three components: annual revenue, annual costs, and initial investment. The revenue in any year is viewed as:

$$\text{Number of grills sold by entire industry} \times \text{Market share of BBI's hydrogen grill (in percent)} \times \text{Price per hydrogen grill} \qquad (9.3)$$

The cost in any year is viewed as:

$$\text{Fixed manufacturing costs} + \text{Variable manufacturing costs} + \text{Marketing costs} + \text{Selling costs}$$

Initial investment is viewed as:

$$\text{Cost of patent} + \text{Test-marketing costs} + \text{Cost of production facility}$$

Step 2: Specify a Distribution for Each Variable in the Model

Here comes the hard part. Let's start with revenue, which has three components in (9.3). The consultant first models overall market size, that is, the number of grills sold by the entire industry. The trade publication, *Outdoor Food (OF),* reported that 10 million grills

FIGURE 9.3

Probability Distributions for Industrywide Unit Sales, Market Share of BBI's Hydrogen Grill, and Price of Hydrogen Grill

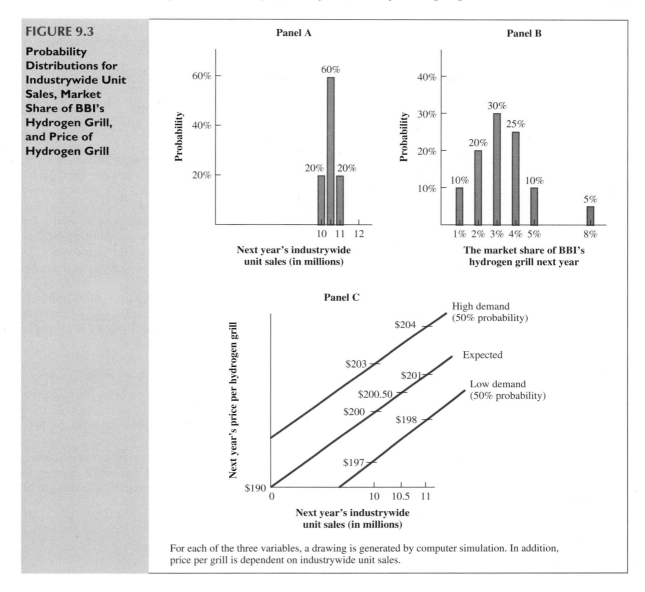

For each of the three variables, a drawing is generated by computer simulation. In addition, price per grill is dependent on industrywide unit sales.

of all types were sold in North America last year and it forecasts sales of 10.5 million next year. Mr. Mauney, using *OF*'s forecast and his own intuition, creates the following distribution for next year's sales of grills by the entire industry:

Probability	20%	60%	20%
Next year's industrywide unit sales	10 million	10.5 million	11 million

The tight distribution here reflects the slow but steady historical growth in the grill market. This probability distribution is graphed in Panel A of Figure 9.3.

Lester Mauney realizes that estimating the market share of BBI's hydrogen grill is more difficult. Nevertheless, after a great deal of analysis, he determines the distribution of next year's market share to be:

Probability	10%	20%	30%	25%	10%	5%
Market share of BBI's hydrogen grill next year	1%	2%	3%	4%	5%	8%

While the consultant assumed a symmetrical distribution for industrywide unit sales, he believes a skewed distribution makes more sense for the project's market share. In his mind, there is always the small possibility that sales of the hydrogen grill will really take off. This probability distribution is graphed in Panel B of Figure 9.3.

The above forecasts assume that unit sales for the overall industry are unrelated to the project's market share. In other words, the two variables are *independent* of each other. Mr. Mauney reasons that, while an economic boom might increase industrywide grill sales and a recession might decrease them, the project's market share is unlikely to be related to economic conditions.

Now Mr. Mauney must determine the distribution of price per grill. Mr. Comiskey, the CFO, informs him that the price will be in the area of $200 per grill, given what other competitors are charging. However, the consultant believes that the price per hydrogen grill will almost certainly depend on the size of the overall market for grills. As in any business, you can usually charge more if demand is high.

After rejecting a number of complex models for price, Mr. Mauney settles on the following specification:

$$\frac{\text{Next year's price}}{\text{per hydrogen grill}} = \$190 + \$1 \times \text{Industrywide unit sales (in millions)} +/-\$3 \quad \textbf{(9.4)}$$

The grill price in (9.4) is dependent on the unit sales of the industry. In addition, random variation is modelled via the term "$+/-\$3$," where a drawing of $+\$3$ and a drawing of $-\$3$ each occur 50 percent of the time. For example, if industrywide unit sales are 11 million, the price per grill would be either:

$$\$190 + \$11 + \$3 = \$204 \qquad (50\% \text{ probability})$$

$$\$190 + \$11 - \$3 = \$198 \qquad (50\% \text{ probability})$$

The relationship between the price of a hydrogen grill and industrywide unit sales is graphed in Panel C of Figure 9.3.

The consultant now has distributions for each of the three components of next year's revenue. However, he needs distributions for future years as well. Using forecasts from *Outdoor Food* and other publications, Mr. Mauney forecasts the distribution of growth rates for the entire industry over the second year to be:

Probability	20%	60%	20%
Growth rate of industrywide unit sales in second year	1%	3%	5%

Given both the distribution of next year's industrywide unit sales and the distribution of growth rates for this variable over the second year, we can generate the distribution of industrywide unit sales for the second year. A similar extension should give Mr. Mauney a distribution for later years as well, though we won't go into the details here. And, just as the consultant extended the first component of revenue (industrywide unit sales) to later years, he would want to do the same thing for market share and unit price.

The above discussion shows how the three components of revenue can be modelled. Step 2 would be complete once the components of cost and of investment are modelled in a similar way. Special attention must be paid to the interactions between variables here, since ineffective management will likely allow the different cost components to rise together. However, since you are probably getting the idea now, we will skip the rest of this step.

Step 3: The Computer Draws One Outcome

As we said above, next year's revenue in our model is the product of three components. Imagine that the computer randomly picks industrywide unit sales of 10 million, a market share for BBI's hydrogen grill of 2 percent and a +$3 random price variation. Given these drawings, next year's price per hydrogen grill will be:

$$\$190 + \$10 + \$3 = \$203$$

and next year's revenue for BBI's hydrogen grill will be:

$$10 \text{ million} \times 0.02 \times \$203 = \$40.6 \text{ million}$$

Of course, we are not done with the entire outcome yet. We would have to perform drawings for revenue in each future year. In addition, we would perform drawings for costs in each future year. Finally, a drawing for initial investment would have to be made as well. In this way, a single outcome would generate a cash flow from the project in each future year.

How likely is it that the specific outcome above would be drawn? We can answer this because we know the probability of each component. Since industry sales of $10 million has a 20 percent probability, a market share of 2 percent also has a 20 percent probability, and a random price variation of +$3 has a 50 percent probability, the probability of these three drawings together in the same outcome is:

$$0.02 = 0.20 \times 0.20 \times 0.50 \tag{9.5}$$

Of course, the probability would get even smaller once drawings for future revenues, future costs, and the initial investment are included in the outcome.

This step generates the cash flow for each year from a single outcome. What we are ultimately interested in is the *distribution* of cash flow each year across many outcomes. We ask the computer to randomly draw over and over again to give us this distribution, which is just what is done in the next step.

Step 4: Repeat the Procedure

While the above three steps generate one outcome, the essence of Monte Carlo simulation is repeated outcomes. Depending on the situation, the computer may be called on to generate thousands or even millions of outcomes. The result of all these drawings is a distribution of cash flow for each future year. This distribution is the basic output of Monte Carlo simulation.

Consider Figure 9.4. Here, repeated drawings have produced the simulated distribution of the third year's cash flow. There would be, of course, a distribution like the one in this figure for each future year. This leaves us with just one more step.

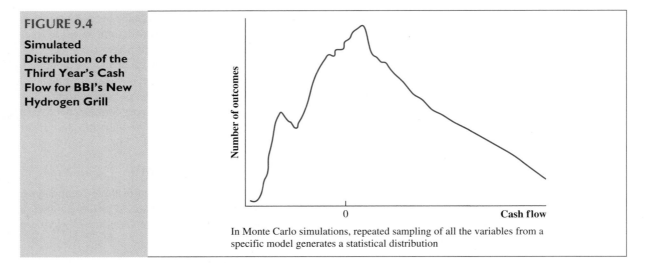

FIGURE 9.4

Simulated Distribution of the Third Year's Cash Flow for BBI's New Hydrogen Grill

In Monte Carlo simulations, repeated sampling of all the variables from a specific model generates a statistical distribution

Step 5: Calculate NPV

Given the distribution of cash flow for the third year in Figure 9.4, one can determine the expected cash flow for this year. In a similar manner, one can also determine the expected cash flow for each future year and can then calculate the net present value of the project by discounting these expected cash flows at an appropriate rate.

Monte Carlo simulation is often viewed as a step beyond either sensitivity analysis or scenario analysis. Interactions between the variables are explicitly specified in Monte Carlo so, at least in theory, this methodology provides a more complete analysis. And, as a byproduct, having to build a precise model deepens the forecaster's understanding of the project.

Since Monte Carlo simulations have been around for at least 35 years, you might think that most firms would be performing them by now. Surprisingly, this does not seem to be the case. In our experience, executives are frequently skeptical of all the complexity. It is difficult to model either the distributions of all variables or the interactions between variables. In addition, the computer output is often devoid of economic intuition. Thus, while Monte Carlo simulations are used in certain real-world situations,[4] the approach is not likely to be "the wave of the future." In fact, Graham and Harvey[5] report that only about 15 percent of the firms in their sample use capital budgeting simulations.

9.4 Real Options

In Chapter 7, we stressed the superiority of net present value (NPV) analysis over other approaches when valuing capital budgeting projects. However, both scholars and practitioners have pointed out problems with NPV. The basic idea here is that NPV analysis, as well as all the other approaches in Chapter 7, ignores the adjustments that a firm can make

---

[4]More than perhaps any other, the pharmaceutical industry has pioneered applications of this methodology. For example, see, Nancy A. Nichols, "Scientific Management at Merck: An Interview with CFO Judy Lewent," *Harvard Business Review* (January/February 1994).

[5]See Figure 2 of Graham and Harvey, *op. cit.*

after a project is accepted. These adjustments are called **real options.**[6] In this respect, NPV underestimates the true value of a project. NPV's conservatism here is best explained through a series of examples.

The Option to Expand

Conrad Willig, an entrepreneur, recently learned of a chemical treatment that causes water to freeze at 30°C, rather than 0°C. Of all the many practical applications for this treatment, Mr. Willig liked more than anything else the idea of hotels made of ice. Conrad estimated the annual cash flows from a single ice hotel to be $2 million, based on an initial investment of $12 million. He felt that 20 percent was an appropriate discount rate, given the risk of this new venture. Assuming that the cash flows were perpetual, Mr. Willig determined the NPV of the project to be:

$$-\$12,000,000 + \$2,000,000/0.20 = -\$2 \text{ million}$$

Most entrepreneurs would have rejected this venture, given its negative NPV. But Conrad was not your typical entrepreneur. He reasoned that NPV analysis missed a hidden source of value. While he was pretty sure that the initial investment would cost $12 million, there was some uncertainty concerning annual cash flows. His cash flow estimate of $2 million per year actually reflected his belief that there was a 50 percent probability that annual cash flows would be $3 million and a 50 percent probability that annual cash flows would be $1 million.

The NPV calculations for the two forecasts are:

Optimistic forecast: $-\$12$ million $+ \$3$ million$/0.20 = \$3$ million

Pessimistic forecast: $-\$12$ million $+ \$1$ million$/0.20 = -\$7$ million

On the surface, this new calculation doesn't seem to help Mr. Willig very much since an average of the two forecasts yields an NPV for the project of:

$$50\% \times \$3 \text{ million} + 50\% \times (-\$7 \text{ million}) = -\$2 \text{ million}$$

(which is just the value he calculated in the first place).

However, if the optimistic forecast turns out to be correct, Mr. Willig would want to *expand.* If he believes that there are, say, 10 locations in the country that can support an ice hotel, the true NPV of the venture would be:

$$50\% \times 10 \times \$3 \text{ million} + 50\% \times (-\$7 \text{ million}) = \$11.5 \text{ million}$$

The idea here, which is represented in Figure 9.5, is both basic and universal. The entrepreneur has the option to expand if the pilot location is successful. For example, think of all the people that start restaurants, most of them ultimately failing. These individuals are not necessarily overly optimistic. They may realize the likelihood of failure but go ahead anyway because of the small chance of starting the next McDonald's or Burger King.

The Option to Abandon

Managers also have the option to abandon existing projects. While abandonment may seem cowardly, it can often save companies a great deal of money. Because of this, the option to abandon increases the value of any potential project.

The above example on ice hotels, which illustrated the option to expand, can also illustrate the option to abandon. To see this, imagine that Mr. Willig now believes that

---

[6]To obtain precise estimates of real option value, it is necessary to use the binomial option pricing model. This is covered in depth in Chapter 24.

FIGURE 9.5

Decision Tree for Ice Hotel

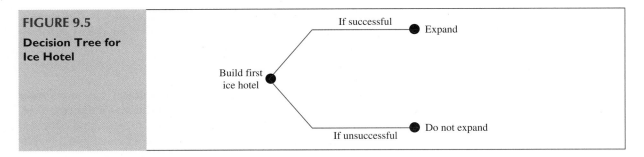

there is a 50 percent probability that annual cash flows will be $6 million and a 50 percent probability that annual cash flows will be −$2 million. The NPV calculations under the two forecasts become:

Optimistic forecast: −$12 million + $6 million/0.2 = $18 million

Pessimistic forecast: −$12 million − $2 million/0.2 = −$22 million

yielding an NPV for the project of:

$$50\% \times \$18 \text{ million} + 50\% \times (-\$22 \text{ million}) = -\$2 \text{ million} \qquad \textbf{(9.6)}$$

Furthermore, now imagine that Mr. Willig wants to own, at most, just one ice hotel, implying that there is no option to expand. Since the NPV in (9.6) is negative, it looks as if he will not build the hotel.

But things change when we consider the abandonment option. As of date 1, the entrepreneur will know which forecast has come true. If cash flows equal those under the optimistic forecast, Conrad will keep the project alive. If, however, cash flows equal those under the pessimistic forecast, he will abandon the hotel. Knowing these possibilities ahead of time, the NPV of the project becomes:

$$50\% \times \$18 \text{ million} + 50\% \times (-\$12 \text{ million} - \$2 \text{ million}/1.20) = \$2.17 \text{ million}$$

Since Mr. Willig abandons after experiencing the cash flow of −$2 million at date 1, he does not have to endure this outflow in any of the later years. Because the NPV is now positive, Conrad will accept the project.

The example here is clearly a stylized one. While many years may pass before a project is abandoned in the real world, our ice hotel was abandoned after just one year. And, while salvage values generally accompany abandonment, we assumed no salvage value for the ice hotel. Nevertheless, abandonment options are pervasive in the real world.

For example, consider the moviemaking industry. As shown in Figure 9.6, movies begin with either the purchase or development of a script. A completed script might cost a movie studio a few million dollars and potentially lead to actual production. However, the great majority of scripts (perhaps well in excess of 80 percent) are abandoned. Why would studios abandon scripts that they had commissioned in the first place? While the studios know ahead of time that only a few scripts will be promising, they don't know which ones. Thus, they cast a wide net, commissioning many scripts to get a few good ones. And, the studios must be ruthless with the bad scripts, since the expenditure here pales in comparison to the huge losses from producing a bad movie.

The few lucky scripts will then move into production, where costs might be budgeted in the tens of millions of dollars, if not much more. At this stage, the dreaded phrase is that on-location production gets "bogged down," creating cost overruns. But the studios are equally ruthless here. Should these overruns become excessive, production is likely to

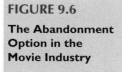

FIGURE 9.6

The Abandonment Option in the Movie Industry

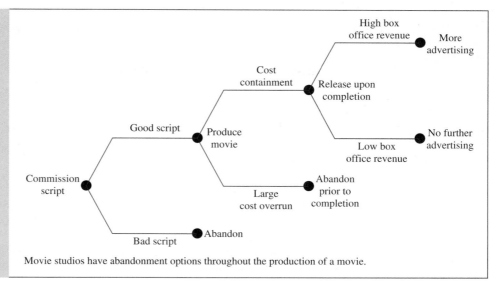

Movie studios have abandonment options throughout the production of a movie.

be abandoned in midstream. Interestingly, abandonment almost always occurs due to high costs, not due to the fear that the movie won't be able to find an audience. Little information on that score will be obtained until the movie is actually released.

Release of the movie is accompanied by significant advertising expenditures, perhaps in the range of $10 to $20 million. Box office success in the first few weeks is likely to lead to further advertising expenditures. Again, the studio has the option, but not the obligation, to increase advertising here. It also has an option to produce a sequel.

Moviemaking is one of the riskiest businesses around, with studios receiving hundreds of millions of dollars in a matter of weeks from a blockbuster while receiving practically nothing during this period from a flop. The above abandonment options contain costs that might otherwise bankrupt the industry.

Timing Options

One often finds urban land that has been vacant for many years. Yet this land is bought and sold from time to time. Why would anyone pay a positive price for land that has no source of revenue? Certainly one could not arrive at this positive value through NPV analysis. However, the paradox can easily be explained in terms of real options.

Suppose that the land's highest and best use is as an office building. Total construction costs for the building are estimated to be $1 million. Currently, net rents (after all costs) are estimated to be $90,000 per year in perpetuity and the discount rate is 10 percent. The NPV of this proposed building would be:

$$-\$1 \text{ million} + \$90,000/0.10 = -\$100,000$$

Since this NPV is negative, one would not currently want to build. In addition, it appears as if the land is worthless. However, suppose that the government is planning a bid for the Summer Olympics. Office rents will likely increase if the bid succeeds. In this case, the property's owner might want to erect the office building after all. Conversely, office rents will remain the same, or even fall, if the bid fails. The owner will not build in this case.

We say that the property owner has a *timing option*. While he does not currently want to build, he will want to build in the future should rents in the area rise substantially. This

FIGURE 9.7

Decision Tree for Vacant Land

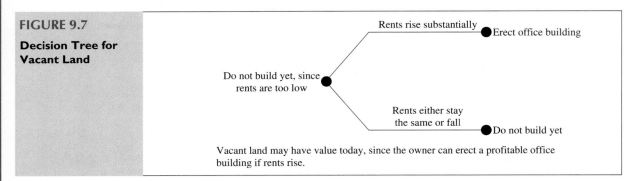

Rents rise substantially → Erect office building

Do not build yet, since rents are too low

Rents either stay the same or fall → Do not build yet

Vacant land may have value today, since the owner can erect a profitable office building if rents rise.

timing option explains why vacant land often has value. While there are costs, such as taxes, from holding raw land, the value of an office building after a substantial rise in rents may more than offset these holding costs. Of course, the exact value of the vacant land depends on both the probability of success in the Olympic bid and the extent of the rent increase. Figure 9.7 illustrates this timing option.

Mining operations almost always provide timing options as well. Suppose you own a copper mine where the cost of mining each tonne of copper exceeds the sales revenue. It's a no-brainer to say that you would not want to mine the copper currently. And since there are costs of ownership such as property taxes, insurance, and security, you might actually want to pay someone to take the mine off your hands. However, we would caution you not to do so hastily. Copper prices in the future might very well increase enough so that production is profitable. Given that possibility, you could likely find someone to pay a positive price for the property today.

? **Concept** Questions

- **What are the different types of real options?**
- **Why does traditional NPV analysis tend to underestimate the true value of a capital project?**

9.5 SUMMARY AND CONCLUSIONS

This chapter discusses a number of practical applications of capital budgeting.

1. Though NPV is the best capital budgeting approach conceptually, it has been criticized in practice for providing managers with a false sense of security. Sensitivity analysis shows NPV under varying assumptions, giving managers a better feel for the project's risks. Unfortunately, sensitivity analysis modifies only one variable at a time, while many variables are likely to vary together in the real world. Scenario analysis examines a project's performance under different scenarios (e.g., war breaking out or oil prices skyrocketing). Finally, managers want to know how bad forecasts must be before a project loses money. Break-even analysis calculates the sales figure at which the project breaks even. Though break-even analysis is frequently performed on an accounting profit basis, we suggest that a net present value basis is more appropriate.

2. Monte Carlo simulation begins with a model of the firm's cash flows, based on both the interactions between different variables and the movement of each individual variable over time. Random sampling generates a distribution of these cash flows for each period, leading to a net present value calculation.

3. We analyze the hidden options in capital budgeting, such as the option to expand, the option to abandon, and timing options. We return to this topic in Chapter 23.

KEY TERMS

Break-even analysis 245
Contribution margin 246
Decision trees 240

Fixed costs 243
Monte Carlo simulation 250
Real options 255

Scenario analysis 245
Sensitivity analysis 243
Variable costs 243

SUGGESTED READING

Two excellent sources on scenario analysis in corporate risk management are:
Rene Stulz. "Rethinking Risk Management." *Journal of Applied Corporate Finance,* 1996
    (Fall), 8–24. Reprinted in *Corporate Hedging in Theory and Practice: Lessons from Metall-
    gesellschaft,* Christopher L. Culp and Merton H. Miller, eds, Risk Publications, London,
    1999.
Gregory W. Brown and Donald H. Chew, eds. *Corporate Risk: Strategies and Management.*
    Risk Publications. London, 1999.

An excellent book on real options is:
Martha Amram and Nalin Kulatilaka. *Real Options: Managing Strategic Investment in an
    Uncertain World.* Boston: Harvard Business School Press (1999).

A fascinating discussion of real options in the movie business can be found in:
Laura Martin. "Film Studio Reel Options." Unpublished manuscript, Credit Suisse First Boston
    (CSFB) (May 11, 2001). Obtainable at www.valuesweep.com.

Two popular software packages for simulation analysis are:
Crystal Ball—www.decionneering.com/crystal_ball/index.html
@Risk—www.palisade.com/risk/default.asp

QUESTIONS & PROBLEMS

Decision Trees

9.1   PR Electronics Inc. has developed a new Pink-Ray DVD. If the Pink-Ray DVD is success-
      ful, the present value of the payoff (when the product is brought to market) is $20 million.
      If the Pink-Ray DVD fails, the present value of the payoff is $5 million. If the product
      goes directly to market, there is a 50 percent chance of success. Alternatively, PR can
      delay the launch by one year and spend $2 million to test market the Pink-Ray DVD. Test
      marketing would allow the firm to improve the product and increase the probability of
      success to 75 percent. The appropriate discount rate is 15 percent. Should the firm conduct
      test marketing?

9.2   The manager for a growing firm is considering the launch of a new product. If the product
      goes directly to market, there is a 50 percent chance of success. For $120,000 the manager
      can conduct a focus group that will increase the product's chance of success to 70 percent.
      Alternatively, the manager has the option to pay a consulting firm $400,000 to research
      the market and refine the product. The consulting firm successfully launches new products
      90 percent of the time. If the firm successfully launches the product, the payoff will be
      $1.2 million. If the product is a failure, the NPV is zero. Which action will result in the
      highest expected payoff to the firm?

9.3   B&B has a new baby powder ready to market. If the firm goes directly to the market with
      the product, there is only a 55 percent chance of success. However, the firm can conduct
      customer segment research, which will take a year and cost $1 million. By going through
      research, B&B will be able to better target potential customers and will increase the prob-
      ability of success to 70 percent. If successful, the baby powder will bring a present value
      profit (at time of initial selling) of $30 million. If unsuccessful, the present value payoff is
      only $3 million. Should the firm conduct customer segment research or go directly to mar-
      ket? The appropriate discount rate is 15 percent.

9.4   Young Canadian screenwriter Christopher Draper has just finished his first script. It has
      action, drama, and humour, and he thinks it will be a blockbuster. He takes the script to
      every motion picture studio in town and tries to sell it but to no avail. Finally, ACME

Studios offers to buy the script for either (a) $7,000 or (b) 1 percent of the movie's profits. There are two decisions the studio will have to make. First is to decide if the script is good or bad, and second if the movie is good or bad. First, there is an 87 percent chance that the script is bad. If it is bad, the studio does nothing more and throws the script out. If the script is good, they will shoot the movie. After the movie is shot, the studio will review it, and there is a 68 percent chance that the movie is bad. If the movie is bad, the movie will not be promoted and will not turn a profit. If the movie is good, the studio will promote heavily; the average profit for this type of movie is $9.5 million. Chris rejects the $7,000 and says he wants the 1 percent of profits. Was this a good decision by Chris?

9.5   The sales of Superspeed Tricycles Inc. are decreasing because of foreign competition. The firm's chief financial officer (CFO) is considering the following mutually exclusive options to maintain market share this year:

- Price the products more aggressively. With this option, there is a 60 percent change that Superspeed will lose only $1.7 million in cash flow due to the decreased revenue. However, there is a 40 percent probability that Superspeed's pricing strategy will fail, and the firm will lose a total of $2 million in cash flow.
- Pay $950,000 for an Ottawa lobbyist to convince the regulators to impose tariffs on the overseas tricycle manufacturers. With the lobbyist, there is a 77 percent chance that Superspeed will lose no cash flow to the foreign competition. If the lobbyist does not succeed, Superspeed will lose $2.5 million in cash flow.

Assume all cash flows occur today, and that Superspeed Tricycles will cease operations after this year. As the assistant to the CFO, which strategy would you recommend to maximize expected cash flow?

Accounting Break-Even Analysis

9.6   Your buddy comes to you with a surefire way to make some quick money and help pay off your student loans. His idea is to sell T-shirts with the words "I get" on them. "You get it?" He says, "You see all those bumper stickers and T-shirts that say 'got milk' or 'got surf.' So this says, 'I get.' It's funny! All we have to do is buy a used silk screen press for $2,000 and we are in business!" Assume there are no fixed costs, and you depreciate the $2,000 in the first period. Taxes are 30 percent.

a. What is the accounting break-even point if each shirt costs $8 to make and you can sell them for $10 apiece?

b. Now assume one year has passed and you have sold 5,000 shirts! You find out that the Dairy Farmers of America have copyrighted the "got milk" slogan and are requiring you to pay $10,000 to continue operations. You expect this craze will last for another three years and that your discount rate is 12 percent.

c. What is the financial break-even point for your enterprise now?

9.7   In each of the following cases, find the unknown variable. Ignore taxes.

Accounting Break-even	Unit Price	Unit Variable Cost	Fixed Costs	Depreciation
130,200	$ 41	$30	$ 820,000	?
135,000	?	56	3,200,000	$1,150,000
5,478	105	?	160,000	105,000

9.8   Fredrikson Inc. has just purchased a $500,000 machine to produce calculators. The machine qualifies for CCA at the rate of 30 percent and will be worth $65,000 after five years. It will produce 24,000 calculators each year. The variable production cost per calculator is $16 and total fixed costs are $1.1 million. The corporate tax rate is 37 percent and the cost of capital is 14 percent. (This is the required PVCCATS calculation. For the firm to break even (in terms of accounting profit), how much should the firm charge per calculator?

9.9   You are considering investing in a company that cultivates abalone for sale to local restaurants. Use the following information:

$$
\begin{aligned}
\text{Sales price per abalone} &= \$3.00 \\
\text{Variable costs per abalone} &= \$0.67 \\
\text{Fixed costs per year} &= \$410,000 \\
\text{EAC}_{\text{PVCCATS}} &= \$21,000 \\
\text{Tax Rate} &= 36\%
\end{aligned}
$$

a. How much abalone must be harvested and sold per year for you to receive any profit (accounting break-even point)?

b. How much profit will you receive if 395,000 abalones are sold per year?

Present Value Break-Even Analysis

9.10 L.J.'s Toys Inc. just purchased a $250,000 machine to produce toy cars. The machine has a CCA rate of 20 percent and will be worth $5,000 after five years. Each toy sells for $30. The variable cost per toy is $6, and the firm incurs fixed costs of $375,000 each year. The corporate tax rate for the company is 29 percent. The appropriate discount rate is 14 percent. Assets will remain in the CCA class after the end of the project. What is the present value break-even point for the project?

EXCEL

9.11 The Cornchopper Company is considering the purchase of a new harvester. Cornchopper has hired you to determine the break-even purchase price (in terms of present value) of the harvester. This break-even purchase price is the price at which the project's NPV is zero. Base your analysis on the following facts:

- The new harvester is not expected to affect revenues, but pre-tax operating expenses will be reduced by $9,500 per year for 10 years.
- The old harvester is now five years old and has a UCC of $33,000.
- The old harvester can be sold for $21,500 today.
- The new harvester has a CCA rate of 20 percent and will be worthless after 12 years.
- The corporate tax rate is 36 percent.
- The firm's required rate of return is 14 percent.
- Assets will remain in the CCA class after the end of the project.

9.12 Niko has purchased a brand new machine to produce its High Flight line of shoes. The machine has an economic life of five years and a CCA rate of 30 percent. The machine costs $350,000 and will be worth $12,500 in five years.

The sale price per pair of shoes is $70, while the variable cost is $7.50. $100,000 of fixed cost per year is attributed to the machine.

Assume that the corporate tax rate is 41 percent and the appropriate discount rate is 8 percent. Assets will remain in the CCA class after the project ends. What is the present value break-even point?

Scenario Analysis

9.13 The CFO of Mercer Inc. is considering an investment of $450,000 in a machine with a CCA rate of 20 percent and a seven-year economic life. The appropriate discount rate is 12 percent, and the corporate tax rate for the company is 37 percent. Assume all revenues and expenses, which are presented below, are received and paid in cash. Assets will remain in the CCA class after the project ends.

	Pessimistic	Expected	Optimistic
Unit sales	22,000	25,000	28,500
Price	$38	$40	$42
Variable costs per unit	$22	$20	$18
Fixed costs per year	$320,000	$300,000	$280,000

a. Calculate the NPV of the project in each of the above scenarios.

b. If each scenario is equally likely, is the machine a worthwhile investment?

EXCEL

9.14 You are the financial analyst for a tennis racquet manufacturer. The company is considering a project using a graphite-like material in its racquets. Given the following information about the market for a racquet with the new material, will you recommend the project?

	Estimate		
	Pessimistic	Expected	Optimistic
Market size	105,000	122,000	135,000
Market share	18%	25%	27%
Selling price	$115	$120	$125
Variable costs per year	$74	$69	$66
Fixed costs per year	$850,000	$800,000	$750,000
Initial investment	$ 1,500,000	$1,500,000	$1,500,000

Assume the appropriate discount rate is 14 percent. The corporate tax rate is 37 percent. The CCA rate is 20 percent and salvage value after five years is $58,000. Assets will remain in the CCA class after the project ends. Each of the three scenarios is equally likely. Assume all revenues and expenses are received and paid in cash.

EXCEL

9.15 Xrco Petroleum has identified a new type of fuel additive and is considering launching this new product. As a marketing manager, you have come up with the following scenarios for the launch. From finance, you know that the tax rate for the company is 40 percent and the effective discount rate is 9 percent. You also know that the CCA rate is 20 percent and that production will occur over the next five years only. After five years, the salvage value will be $110,000. Assets will remain in the CCA class after the project ends. Will you undertake the project?

	Pessimistic	Expected	Optimistic	
Probability of scenario occurring	25%	45%	30%	
Market size	100,000	150,000	200,000	*Per year
Market share	20%	25%	30%	
Price	$100	$120	$140	
Variable cost	$80	$75	$70	
Fixed cost	$10,000	$245,000	$180,000	*Per year
Investment	$1,000,000	$1,000,000	$1,000,000	

9.16 The Big Burrito is planning to purchase a touch screen order system for its drive-thru window that would allow customers to select their order as soon as they arrive. This would reduce customer wait time and increase order accuracy. The touch screen and software would cost the Big Burrito $150,000 and would last five years. There would also be an annual maintenance cost of $5,000. In addition to improved customer service, the Big Burrito would gain two benefits. First, it could totally eliminate the full-time worker who used to accept and enter these orders. His annual salary plus benefits total $30,000 per year. Second, it expects drive-thru sales to increase but it doesn't know by how much. The estimates are:

	Pessimistic	Expected	Optimistic
Revenue increase (decrease)	$(5,000)	$15,000	$20,000
COGS, 25% of revenue increase	(1,250)	3,750	5,000

Net working capital (NWC) is expected to increase by $5,000 in the first year and be recovered at the end of year 5. If the appropriate discount rate is 15 percent and you ignore taxes, should the Big Burrito go ahead with this investment? (See the chart below summarizing this information.)

				Pessimistic			
	Year 0	Year 1	Year 2	Year 3	Year 4	Year 5	NPV
Investments:							
Touch screen system	$(150,000)						
Annual maintenance		$(5,000)	$(5,000)	$(5,000)	$(5,000)	$(5,000)	
Change in NWC		(5,000)				5,000	
Wages saved		30,000	30,000	30,000	30,000	30,000	
Total cash flow from investments	$(150,000)	$20,000	$25,000	$25,000	$25,000	$30,000	
Income:							
Revenue		$(5,000)	$(5,000)	$ (5,000)	$ (5,000)	$ (5,000)	
COGS		1,250	1,250	1,250	1,250	1,250	
Cash flow from operations		$(3,750)	$(3,750)	$ (3,750)	$ (3,750)	$ (3,750)	
Total cash flow from project	$(150,000)	$16,250	$21,250	$21,250	$21,250	$26,250	
PV 15% (CF)	(150,000)	14,130	16,068	13,972	12,150	13,051	($80,629)

The Option to Abandon

9.17 All-Star Games Inc. has hired you to perform a feasibility study of a new video game that requires a $3.5 million initial investment. All-Star expects a total annual operating cash flow of $778,000 for the next 8 years. The relevant discount rate is 11.5 percent. Cash flows occur at year-end.

a. What is the NPV of the new video game?

b. After one year, the estimate of remaining annual cash flows will be revised either upward to $1.5 million or downward to $120,000. Each revision has an equal

Visit us at www.mcgrawhill.ca/olc/ross

probability of occurring. At that time, the video game project can be sold for $800,000. What is the revised NPV given that the firm can abandon the project after one year?

9.18   Allied Products Inc. is considering a new product launch. The firm expects to have annual operating cash flow of $190 million for the next 10 years. Allied Products uses a discount rate of 18 percent for new product launches. The initial investment is $106 million. Assume that the project has no salvage value at the end of its economic life.

   a.   What is the NPV of the new product?

   b.   After the first year, the project can be dismantled and sold for $60 million. If the estimates of remaining cash flows are revised based on the first year's experience, at what level of expected cash flows does it make sense to abandon the project?

9.19   Applied Nanotech is thinking about introducing a new surface-cleaning machine. The marketing department has come up with the estimate that Applied Nanotech can sell 10 units per year at $0.3 million net cash flow per unit for the next five years. The engineering department has come up with the estimate that developing the machine will take a $10 million initial investment. The finance department has estimated that a 25 percent discount rate should be used.

   a.   What is the base-case NPV?

   b.   If unsuccessful, after the first year the project can be dismantled and will have an after-tax salvage value of $8 million. Also, after the first year, expected cash flows will be revised up to 24 units per year or to 0 units, with equal probability. What is the revised NPV?

9.20   Consider the following project for Hand Clapper Inc. The company is considering a four-year project to manufacture clap-command garage door openers. This project requires an initial investment of $8 million that will be depreciated straight-line to zero over the project's life. An initial investment in net working capital of $2 million is required to support spare parts inventory; this cost is fully recoverable whenever the project ends. The company believes it can generate $7 million in pre-tax revenues with $3 million in total pre-tax operating costs. The tax rate is 38 percent, and the discount rate is 16 percent. The market value of the equipment over the life of the project is as follows:

Year	Market Value (millions)
1	$6.50
2	6.00
3	3.00
4	0.00

   a.   Assuming Hand Clapper operates this project for four years, what is the NPV?

   b.   Now compute the project NPVs assuming the project is abandoned after only one year, after two years, and after three years. What economic life for this project maximizes its value to the firm? What does this problem tell you about not considering abandonment possibilities when evaluating project

9.21   Snapplers are planning to enter the bottled water market. They expect to sell 4.5 million bottles per year at a net cash flow of $0.50 apiece for the next five years but they are unsure about the market. At the end of the first year, they will learn if the product is a success or failure. If it is a success, they can revise their forecast to 8 million bottles per year. If it is a failure, unit sales will be 1 million. Success and failure are equally likely. The relevant discount rate is 15 percent and the initial investment required is $3 million. If they abandon the project after year 1, they can recover $1.5 million of the initial investment.

   a.   What is the base case NPV?

   b.   What is the value of the option to abandon?

MINICASE: Bunyan Lumber LLC

B.C. Bunyan Lumber LLC harvests timber and delivers logs to timber mills for sale. The company was founded 95 years ago by Pete Bunyan. The current CEO is Pauline Bunyan, the granddaughter of the founder. The company is currently evaluating a 5000 acre forest it owns in central British Columbia. Paula has asked Shawn Montador, the company's finance officer, to evaluate the project. Pauline's concern is when the company should harvest the timber.

Lumber is sold by the company for its "pond value." Pond value is the amount a mill will pay for a log delivered to the mill location. The price paid for logs delivered to a mill is quoted in dollars per thousands of board feet (MBF), and the price depends on the grade of the logs. The forest B.C. Bunyan Lumber is evaluating was planted by the company 20 years ago and is made up entirely of Douglas fir trees. The table here shows the current price per MBF for the three grades of timber the company feels will come from the stand:

Years from Today to Begin Harvest	Harvest (MBF) Per Acre	Timber Grade		
		1P	2P	3P
20	6	10%	40%	50%
25	7.6	12	42	46
30	9	15	42	43
35	10	16	43	41

The company expects to lose 5 percent of the timber it cuts due to defects and breakage. The forest will be clear-cut when the company harvests the timber. This method of harvesting allows for faster growth of replanted trees. All of the harvesting, processing, replanting, and transportation are to be handled by subcontractors hired by

B.C. Bunyan Lumber. The cost of the logging is expected to be $140 per MBF. A road system has to be constructed and is expected to cost $50 per MBF on average. Sales preparation and administrative costs, excluding office overhead costs, are expected to be $18 per MBF.

As soon as the harvesting is complete, the company will reforest the land. Reforesting costs include the following:

	Per Acre Cost
Excavator piling	$150
Broadcast burning	300
Site preparation	145
Planting costs	225

All costs are expected to increase at the inflation rate.

Assume all cash flows occur at the year of harvest. For example, if the company begins harvesting the timber 20 years from today, the cash flow from the harvest will be received 20 years from today. When the company logs the land, it will immediately replant the land with new saplings. The harvest period chosen will be repeated for the foreseeable future. The company's nominal required return is 10 percent, and the inflation rate is expected to be 3.7 percent per year. B.C. Bunyan Lumber has a 35 percent tax rate.

Clear-cutting is a controversial method of forest management. To obtain the necessary permits, B.C. Bunyan Lumber has agreed to contribute to a conservation fund every time it harvests the lumber. If the company harvested the forest today, the required contribution would be $100,000. The company has agreed that the required contribution will grow by 3.2 percent per year. When should the company harvest the forest?

Visit us at www.mcgrawhill.ca/olc/ross

PART 3

Chapter 10

Risk and Return: Lessons from Market History

EXECUTIVE SUMMARY

We learned in Chapter 5 that riskless cash flows should be discounted at the riskless rate of interest. Because most capital-budgeting projects involve risky flows, a different discount rate must be used. The next four chapters are devoted to determining the discount rate for risky projects.

Past experience indicates that students find the upcoming material among the most difficult in the entire textbook. Because of this, we always teach the material by presenting the results and conclusions first. By seeing where we are going ahead of time, it is easier to absorb the material when we get there. A synopsis of the four chapters follows:

1. Because our ultimate goal is to discount risky cash flows, we must first find a way to measure risk. In the current chapter we measure the variability of an asset by the variance or standard deviation of its returns. If an individual holds only *one* asset, its variance or standard deviation would be the appropriate measure of risk.
2. While Chapter 10 considers one type of asset in isolation, Chapter 11 examines a portfolio of many assets. In this case, we are interested in the *contribution* of the security to the risk of the entire portfolio. Because much of an individual security's variance is dispersed in a large, diversified portfolio, neither the security's variance nor its standard deviation can be viewed as the security's contribution to the risk of a large portfolio. Rather, this contribution is best measured by the security's beta (β). As an example, consider a stock whose returns are high when the returns on a large, diversified portfolio are low—and vice versa. This stock has a negative beta. In other words, it acts as a hedge, implying that the stock actually tends to reduce the risk of the portfolio. However, the stock could have a high variance, implying high risk for an investor holding only this security.
3. Investors will only hold a risky security if its expected return is high enough to compensate for its risk. Given the above, the expected return on a security should be positively related to the security's beta. In fact, the relationship between risk and expected return can be expressed more precisely by the following equation:

$$\begin{matrix} \text{Expected return} \\ \text{on a security} \end{matrix} = \begin{matrix} \text{Risk-free} \\ \text{rate} \end{matrix} + \text{Beta} \times \left(\begin{matrix} \text{Expected return on} \\ \text{market portfolio} \end{matrix} - \begin{matrix} \text{Risk-free} \\ \text{rate} \end{matrix} \right)$$

Because the term in parentheses on the right-hand side is positive, this equation says that the expected return on a security is a positive function of its beta. This equation is frequently referred to as the *capital asset pricing model* (CAPM).
4. We derive the relationship between risk and return in a different manner in Chapter 12. However, many of the conclusions are quite similar. This chapter is based on the *arbitrage pricing theory* (APT).
5. The theoretical ideas in Chapters 10, 11, and 12 are intellectually challenging. Fortunately, Chapter 13, which applies the above theory to the selection of discount rates, is much

simpler. In a world where (*a*) a project has the same risk as the firm, and (*b*) the firm has no debt, the expected return on the stock should serve as the project's discount rate. This expected return is taken from the capital asset pricing model, as presented above.

Because we have a long road ahead of us, the maxim that any journey begins with a single step applies here. We start with the perhaps mundane calculation of a security's return.

10.1 Returns

Dollar Earnings

Suppose Canadian Atlantic Enterprises has several thousand shares of stock outstanding. You purchased some of these shares at the beginning of the year. It's now year-end, and you want to determine how well you've done on your investment.

Over the year, a company may pay cash *dividends* to its shareholders. As a shareholder in Canadian Atlantic Enterprises, you are a part owner of the company. If the company is profitable, it may choose to distribute some of its profits to shareholders. (Dividend policy is detailed in Chapter 19.)

In addition to the dividend, the other part of your return is the *capital gain* or *capital loss* on the stock arising from changes in the value of your investment. For example, consider the cash flows illustrated in Figure 10.1. The stock is selling for $37 per share. If you bought 100 shares, you had a total outlay of $3,700. Suppose that, over the year, the stock paid a dividend of $1.85 per share. By the end of the year, then, you would have received income of

$$\text{Dividend} = \$1.85 \times 100 = \$185$$

Also the value of the stock rose to $40.33 per share by the end of the year. Your 100 shares are now worth $4,033, so you have a capital gain of

$$\text{Capital gain} = (\$40.33 - \$37) \times 100 = \$333$$

On the other hand, if the price had dropped to, say, $34.78, you would have had a capital loss of

$$\text{Capital loss} = (\$34.78 - \$37) \times 100 = -\$222$$

Notice that a capital loss is the same thing as a negative capital gain.

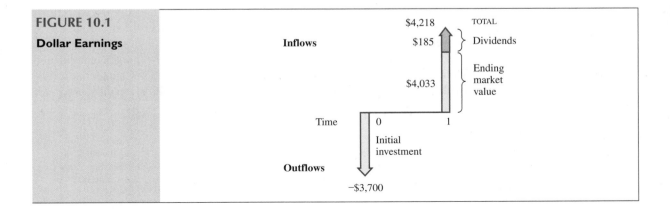

FIGURE 10.1

Dollar Earnings

The total dollar earnings on your investment is the sum of the dividend and the capital gain:

$$\text{Total earnings} = \text{Dividend income} + \text{Capital gain (or loss)}$$

In our first example, the total dollar earnings is thus given by

$$\text{Total dollar earnings} = \$185 + 333 = \$518$$

Notice that, if you sold the stock at the end of the year, the total amount of cash you would have would be your initial investment plus the total return. In the preceding example, then, you would have:

$$\begin{aligned}\text{Total cash if stock is sold} &= \text{Initial investment} + \text{Total dollar earnings} \\ &= \$3,700 + \$518 \\ &= \$4,218\end{aligned}$$

As a check, notice that this is the same as the proceeds from the sale of the stock plus the dividends:

$$\begin{aligned}\text{Proceeds from stock sale} + \text{Dividends} &= \$40.33 \times 100 + \$185 \\ &= \$4,033 + \$185 \\ &= \$4,218\end{aligned}$$

Suppose you hold on to your Canadian Atlantic stock and don't sell it at the end of the year. Should you still consider the capital gain as part of your earnings? Isn't this only a paper gain and not really a cash flow if you don't sell it?

The answer to the first question is a strong yes; the answer to the second is an equally strong no. The capital gain is every bit as much a part of your return as the dividend, and you should certainly count it as part of your return. That you actually decided to keep the stock and not sell it or *realize* the gain in no way changes the fact that, if you want to, you could get the cash value of the stock.[1]

Percentage Returns or Rate of Return

It is usually more convenient to summarize information about returns in percentage terms, rather than dollar terms, because that way your return does not depend on the amount invested. The question we want to answer is, How much do we get for each dollar we invest?

To answer this question, let P_t be the price of the stock at the beginning of the year and let D_{t+1} be the dividend paid on the stock during the year. Consider the cash flows in Figure 10.2. These are the same as those in Figure 10.1, except that we have now expressed everything on a per share basis.

In our example, the price at the beginning of the year was $37 per share and the dividend paid during the year on each share was $1.85. As we discussed in Chapter 5, expressing the dividend as a percentage of the beginning stock price results in the *dividend yield:*

$$\text{Dividend yield} = D_{t+1}/P_t = \$1.85/\$37 = 0.05 = 5\%$$

---

[1] After all, you could always sell the stock at year-end and immediately reinvest by buying the stock back. There is no difference between doing this and just not selling (assuming, of course, that there are no tax consequences from selling the stock). Again, the point is that whether you actually cash out or reinvest by not selling does not affect the return you earn.

FIGURE 10.2

Percentage Returns: Dollar Earnings and Per-Share Return

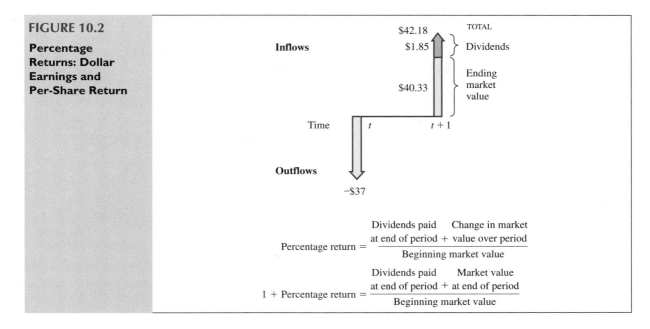

The second component of our percentage return is the capital gains yield. Recall (from Chapter 6) that this is calculated as the change in the price during the year (the capital gain) divided by the beginning price:

$$\text{Capital gains yield} = (P_{t+1} - P_t)/P_t$$
$$= (\$40.33 - \$37)/\$37 = \$3.33/\$37 = 0.09 = 9\%$$

Combining these two results, we find that the *total returns* on the investment in Canadian Atlantic stock during the year, which we will label R_{t+1}, was

$$R_{t+1} = \frac{\text{Div}_{t+1}}{P_t} + \frac{(P_{t+1} - P_t)}{P_t} = 5\% + 9\% = 14\%$$

From now on we will refer to returns in percentage terms.

EXAMPLE 10.1

Suppose a stock begins the year with a price of $25 per share and ends with a price of $35 per share. During the year it paid a $2 dividend per share. What are its dividend yield, its capital gain, and its total return for the year? We can imagine the cash flows in Figure 10.3.

$$R_1 = \frac{\text{Div}_1}{P_0} + \frac{P_1 - P_0}{P_0}$$

$$= \frac{\$2}{\$25} + \frac{\$35 - \$25}{\$25} = \frac{\$12}{\$25}$$

$$= 8\% + 40\% = 48\%$$

Thus, the stock's dividend yield, its capital gain, and its total return are 8 percent, 40 percent, and 48 percent, respectively.

FIGURE 10.3

Cash Flow—An Investment Example

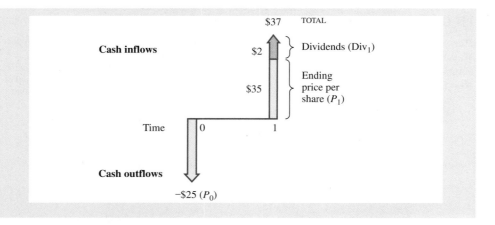

Suppose you had invested $5,000. The total dollar proceeds you would have received on an investment in the stock are $5,000 \times 1.48 = $7,400$. If you know the total return on the stock, you do not need to know how many shares you would have had to purchase to figure out how much money you would have made on the $5,000 investment. You just use the total return.[2]

? Concept Questions

- **What are the two parts of total return?**
- **Why are unrealized capital gains or losses included in the calculation of returns?**
- **What is the difference between a dollar return and a percentage return? Why are percentage returns more convenient?**

10.2 Holding-Period Returns

Investors look to capital market history as a guide to the risks and returns of alternative portfolio strategies. The data set in Table 10.1 could be used in advising large institutional investors. It draws on two major studies: Roger Ibbotson and Rex Sinquefield's examination of rates of return in U.S. financial markets and James Hatch and Robert White's

---

[2]Consider the stock in the previous example. We have ignored the question of when during the year you receive the dividend. Does it make a difference? To explore this question, suppose first that the dividend is paid at the very beginning of the year, and you receive it the moment after you have purchased the stock. Suppose, too, that interest rates are 10 percent, and that immediately after receiving the dividend you lend it out. What will be your total return, including the loan proceeds, at the end of the year?

Alternatively, instead of lending the dividend you could have reinvested it and purchased more of the stock. If that is what you do with the dividend, what will your total return be? (Warning: This does not go on forever, and when you buy more stock with the cash from the dividend on your first purchase, you are too late to get yet another dividend on the new stock.)

Finally, suppose the dividend is paid at year-end. What answer would you get for the total return? As you can see, by ignoring the question of when the dividend is paid when we calculate the return, we are implicitly assuming that it is received at the end of the year and cannot be reinvested during the year. The right way to figure out the return on a stock is to determine exactly when the dividend is received and to include the return that comes from reinvesting the dividend in the stock. This gives a pure stock return without confounding the issue by requiring knowledge of the interest rate during the year.

TABLE 10.1   Annual Market Index Returns, 1948–2006

Year	Statistics Canada Inflation	Canadian Stocks S&P/TSX Composite	Scotia Capital Markets 91-day-T-bill	Scotia Capital Markets long Bonds	U.S. Stocks S&P 500 (C$)	BMO Nesbitt Burns Small Stocks
1948	8.88	12.25	0.40	−0.08	5.50	
1949	1.09	23.85	0.45	5.18	22.15	
1950	5.91	51.69	0.51	1.74	39.18	
1951	10.66	25.44	0.71	−7.89	15.00	
1952	−1.38	0.01	0.95	5.01	13.68	
1953	0.00	2.56	1.54	5.00	−0.99	
1954	0.00	39.37	1.62	12.23	52.62	
1955	0.47	27.68	1.22	0.13	35.51	
1956	3.24	12.68	2.63	−8.87	2.35	
1957	1.79	−20.58	3.76	7.94	−8.51	
1958	2.64	31.25	2.27	1.92	40.49	
1959	1.29	4.59	4.39	−5.07	10.54	
1960	1.27	1.78	3.66	12.19	5.15	
1961	0.42	32.75	2.86	9.16	32.85	
1962	1.67	−7.09	3.81	5.03	−5.77	
1963	1.64	15.60	3.58	4.58	23.19	
1964	2.02	25.43	3.73	6.16	15.75	
1965	3.16	6.67	3.79	0.05	12.58	
1966	3.45	−7.07	4.89	−1.05	−9.33	
1967	4.07	18.09	4.38	−0.48	23.61	
1968	3.91	22.45	6.22	2.14	10.26	
1969	4.79	−0.81	6.83	−2.86	−8.50	
1970	1.31	−3.57	6.89	16.39	−1.96	−11.69
1971	5.16	8.01	3.86	14.84	13.28	15.83
1972	4.91	27.37	3.43	8.11	18.12	44.72
1973	9.36	0.27	4.78	1.97	−14.58	−7.82
1974	12.30	−25.93	7.68	−4.53	−26.87	−26.89
1975	9.52	18.48	7.05	8.02	40.72	41.00
1976	5.87	11.02	9.10	23.64	22.97	22.77
1977	9.45	10.71	7.64	9.04	0.65	39.93
1978	8.44	29.72	7.90	4.10	15.50	44.41
1979	9.69	44.77	11.01	−2.83	16.52	46.04
1980	11.20	30.13	12.23	2.18	35.51	42.86
1981	12.20	−10.25	19.11	−2.09	−5.57	−15.10
1982	9.23	5.54	15.27	45.82	25.84	4.55
1983	4.51	35.49	9.39	9.61	24.07	44.30
1984	3.77	−2.39	11.21	16.90	12.87	−2.33
1985	4.38	25.07	9.70	26.68	39.82	38.98
1986	4.19	8.95	9.34	17.21	16.96	12.33
1987	4.12	5.88	8.20	1.77	−0.96	−5.47
1988	3.96	11.08	8.94	11.30	7.21	5.46
1989	5.17	21.37	11.95	15.17	27.74	10.66
1990	5.00	−14.80	13.28	4.32	−3.06	−27.32
1991	3.78	12.02	9.90	25.30	30.05	18.51
1992	2.14	−1.43	6.65	11.57	18.42	13.01
1993	1.70	32.55	5.63	22.09	14.40	52.26
1994	0.23	−0.18	4.76	−7.39	7.48	−9.21
1995	1.75	14.53	7.39	26.34	33.68	13.88
1996	2.17	28.35	5.02	14.18	23.62	28.66
1997	0.73	14.98	3.20	18.46	39.18	6.97
1998	1.02	−1.58	4.74	12.85	37.71	−17.90
1999	2.58	31.59	4.66	−5.98	14.14	20.29
2000	3.23	7.41	5.49	12.97	−5.67	−4.29
2001	0.60	−12.60	4.70	8.10	−6.50	0.70
2002	4.30	−12.40	2.50	8.70	−22.70	−0.90
2003	1.60	26.70	2.90	6.70	5.30	42.70
2004	2.40	14.50	2.30	7.20	3.30	14.10
2005	2.00	23.29	2.58	5.86	3.80	19.70
2006	1.60	17.30	4.00	4.10	15.70	20.83

Sources: William M. Mercer Ltd., Bloomberg Financial Services, Fortress Small Cap Equity Fund, BMO, and Scotia Capital.

study of Canadian returns.[3] Our data present year-to-year historical rates of return on five important types of financial investments or asset classes:

1. *Canadian common stocks.* The common stock portfolio is based on a sample of the largest companies (in terms of total market value of outstanding stock) in Canada.[4]
2. *U.S. common stocks.* This portfolio consists of 500 of the largest U.S. companies. The full historical series is given in U.S. dollars and in Canadian dollars adjusting for shifts in exchange rates.
3. *Small stocks.* This portfolio, compiled by BMO Nesbitt Burns, includes the bottom fifth of stocks listed on the Toronto Stock Exchange (TSX). The ranking is by market value of equity capitalization—the price of the stock multiplied by the number of shares outstanding.
4. *Long bonds.* This portfolio includes high-quality, long-term corporate, provincial, and Government of Canada bonds.
5. *Canada Treasury bills.* This portfolio consists of Treasury bills (*T-bills* for short) with a three-month maturity.

These returns are not adjusted for transactions costs, inflation, or taxes; thus, they are nominal, pretax returns. In addition to the year-to-year returns on these financial instruments, the year-to-year percentage change in the Statistics Canada Consumer Price Index (CPI) is also computed. This is a commonly used measure of inflation, so we can calculate real returns using this as the inflation rate.

The five asset classes included cover a broad range of investments popular with Canadian individuals and financial institutions. We include U.S. stocks since Canadian investors often invest abroad—particularly in the United States.[5]

Before looking closely at the different portfolio returns, we take a look at the "big picture." Figure 10.4 shows what happened to $1 invested in three of these different portfolios at the beginning of 1957. We work with a sample period of 1957–2006 for two reasons: the years immediately after World War II do not reflect trends today and the TSE 300 (predecessor of the TSX) was introduced in 1956, making 1957 the first really comparable year. This decision is somewhat controversial and we return to it later as we draw lessons from our data. The growth in value for each of the different portfolios over the 50-year period ending in 2006 is given separately. Notice that, to get everything on a single graph, some modification in scaling is used. As is commonly done with financial series, the vertical axis is on a logarithmic scale such that equal distances measure equal percentage changes (as opposed to equal dollar changes) in values.

Looking at Figure 10.4, we see that the common stock investments did the best overall. Every dollar invested in Canadian stocks grew to $107.66 over the 50 years.

At the other end, the T-bill portfolio grew to only $23.43. Long bonds did better with an ending value of $54.72. These values are less impressive when we consider inflation over this period. As illustrated, the price level climbed such that $7.48 is needed just to replace the original $1.

---

[3]The two classic studies are R. G. Ibbotson and R. A. Sinquefield, *Stocks, Bonds, Bills, and Inflation* (Charlottesville, Va.: Financial Analysts Research Foundation, 1982); and J. Hatch and R. White, *Canadian Stocks, Bonds, Bills, and Inflation: 1950–1983* (Charlottesville, Va.: Financial Analysts Research Foundation, 1985). Additional sources are BMO Nesbitt Burns for small capitalization for small stocks, Scotia Capital Markets for Canada Treasury bills and long bonds, and Statistics Canada CANSIM for rates of exchange and inflation.

[4]From 1956 on, the S&P/TSX 60 is used. For earlier years, the data used are a sample provided by the TSE.

[5]Chapter 32 discusses exchange-rate risk and other risks of foreign investments.

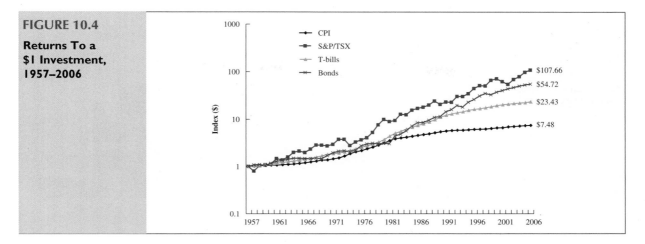

FIGURE 10.4

Returns To a $1 Investment, 1957–2006

Figure 10.4 gives the total value of a $1 investment in the Canadian stock market from 1957 through 2006. In other words, it shows what the total return would have been if the dollar had been left in the stock market and if each year the dividends from the previous year had been reinvested in more stock. If R_t is the return in year t (expressed in decimals), the total you would have from year 1 to year T is the product of the returns in each of the years:

$$(1 + R_1) \times (1 + R_2) \cdots \times (1 + R_t) \times \cdots \times (1 + R_T)$$

For example, if the returns were 11 percent, −5 percent, and 9 percent in a three-year period, a $1 investment at the beginning of the period would, at the end of the three years, be worth

$$
\begin{aligned}
(1 + R_1) \times (1 + R_2) \times (1 + R_3) &= (\$1 + 0.11) \times (\$1 - 0.05) \times (\$1 + 0.09) \\
&= \$1.11 \times \$0.95 \times \$1.09 \\
&= \$1.15
\end{aligned}
$$

Notice that 0.15 (or 15 percent) is the total return and that it includes the return from reinvesting the first-year dividends in the stock market for two more years and reinvesting the second-year dividends for the final year. The 15 percent is called a three-year holding-period return. Table 10.1 gives annual holding-period returns from 1948 to 2006. From this table you can determine holding-period returns for any combination of years.

? Concept Questions

- What was the smallest return observed over the 56 years for each of these investments? When did it occur?
- How many times did large Canadian stocks (common stocks) return more than 30 percent? How many times did they return less than 20 percent?
- What was the longest winning streak (years without a negative return) for large Canadian stocks? For long-term bonds?
- How often did the T-bill portfolio have a negative return?

10.3 Return Statistics

The history of capital market returns is too complicated to be useful in its undigested form. To use the history we must first find some manageable ways of describing it, dramatically condensing the detailed data into a few simple statements.

FIGURE 10.5

Frequency Distribution of Returns on Canadian Common Stocks, 1957–2006

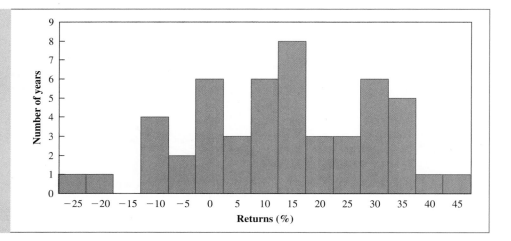

This is where two important numbers summarizing the history come in. The first and most natural number we want to find is some single measure that best describes the past

EXAMPLE 10.2

The returns on Canadian common stocks from 1989 to 1992 were (in decimals) 0.2137, −0.1480, 0.1202, and −0.0143, respectively. The average or mean return over these four years is

$$\overline{R} = \frac{0.2137 - 0.1480 + 0.1202 - 0.0143}{4} = 0.0429$$

annual returns on the stock market. In other words, what is our best estimate of the return that an investor could have realized in a particular year over the 1948–2006 period? This is the *average return*.

Figure 10.5 plots the histogram of the yearly stock market returns from 1957 to 2006. This plot is the **frequency distribution** of the numbers. The height of the graph gives the number of sample observations in the range on the horizontal axis.

Given a frequency distribution like that in Figure 10.5, we can calculate the **average** or **mean** of the distribution. To compute the arithmetic average of the distribution, we add up all of the values and divide the total number (50 in our case, because we have 50 years of data) by T. The bar over the R is used to represent the mean, and the formula is the ordinary formula for the average:

$$\text{Mean} = \overline{R} = \frac{(R_1 + \ldots + R_T)}{T}$$

The arithmetic mean of the 50 annual returns from 1957 to 2006 is 11.10 percent. The arithmetic mean return has the advantage of being easy to calculate and interpret so we use it here in Example 10.2 to measure expected return.[6]

? Concept Questions

• **Why are return statistics useful?**

---

[6]We do have to admit that there is an alternative measure that is more accurate for present purposes: the geometric mean. To compute the geometric mean we link the returns in each of our 50 years geometrically: $[(1 + R_1)(1 + R_2) \ldots (1 + R_{50})]^{1/50} - 1$. This is a superior formula because it reflects mathematically the fact that returns are compounded. The difference between the arithmetic and geometric averages is proportionate to variance. This means that high-variance investments like risky shares will result in the greatest error when using the simplified arithmetic method.

10.4 Average Stock Returns and Risk-Free Returns

Now that we have computed the average return on the stock market, it seems sensible to compare it with the returns on other securities. The most obvious comparison is with the low variability returns in the government bond market. These are free of most of the volatility we see in the stock market.

The Government of Canada borrows money by issuing bonds, which the investing public holds. As we discussed in an earlier chapter, these bonds come in many forms. The ones we'll look at here are called *Treasury bills,* or *T-bills.* Once a week the government sells some bills at an auction. A typical bill is a pure discount bond that will mature in a year or less. Because the government can raise taxes to pay for the debt it incurs—a trick that many of us would like to be able to perform—this debt is virtually free of risk of default. Thus, we call the yield on T-bills the *risk-free return* over a short time (one year or less).[7]

An interesting comparison, then, is between the virtually risk-free return on T-bills and the very risky return on common stocks. This difference between risky returns and risk-free returns is often called the *excess return on the risky asset.* It is called *excess* because it is the additional return resulting from the riskiness of common stocks, and it is interpreted as a **risk premium.**

Table 10.2 shows the average stock return, bond return, T-bill return, and inflation rate from 1957 through 2006. From this we can derive risk premiums. We can see that the average risk premium for common stocks for the entire period was 4.53 percent (11.10 percent − 6.57 percent).

One of the most significant observations of stock market data is this long-run excess of the stock return over the risk-free return. An investor for this period was rewarded for investment in the stock market with an extra or excess return over what would have been achieved by simply investing in T-bills.

Why was there such a reward? Does it mean that it never pays to invest in T-bills and that someone who invested in them instead of in the stock market needs a course in finance? A complete answer to these questions lies at the heart of modern finance, and Chapter 11 is devoted entirely to them. However, part of the answer can be found in the variability of the various types of investments. We see in Table 10.1 many years when an investment in T-bills achieved higher returns than an investment in common stocks. Also, we note that the returns from an investment in common stocks are frequently negative, whereas an investment in T-bills never produces a negative return.[8] So, we now turn our attention to measuring the variability of returns and an introductory discussion of risk.

By looking more closely at Table 10.2, we see that the standard deviation of T-bills is substantially less than that of common stocks. This suggests that the risk of T-bills is below that of common stocks. Because the answer turns on the riskiness of investments in common stock, we now shift our attention to measuring this risk.

? Concept Questions

- **What is the major observation about capital markets that we will seek to explain?**
- **What does the observation tell us about investors for the period from 1957 through 2006?**

---

[7] A Treasury bill with a 90-day maturity is risk-free only during that particular time period.

[8] All our returns are nominal and before-tax. The real, after-tax return on T-bills can be negative.

TABLE 10.2   Average Annual Returns, 1957–2006

Investment	Arithmetic Average Return (%)	Risk Premium (%)	Standard Deviation (%)	Distribution
Canadian common stocks	11.10	4.53	16.03	
U.S. common stocks ($)	12.38	5.81	16.82	
Long bonds	8.78	2.21	10.07	
Small stocks	14.34	7.77	22.29	
Inflation	4.15		3.21	
Treasury bills	6.57	0.00	3.64	

10.5 Risk Statistics

The second number that we use to characterize the distribution of returns is a measure of risk. There is no universally agreed upon definition of risk. One way to think about the risk of returns on common stock is in terms of how spread out the frequency distribution in Figure 10.5 is.[9] The spread or dispersion of a distribution is a measure of how much a particular return can deviate from the mean return. If the distribution is very spread out, the returns that will occur are very uncertain. By contrast, a distribution whose returns are all within a few percentage points of each other is tight, and the returns are less uncertain. The measures of risk we will discuss are variance and standard deviation.

EXAMPLE 10.3

The returns on Canadian common stocks from 1989 to 1992 were (in decimals) 0.2137, −0.1480, 0.1202, and −0.0143, respectively. The variance of this sample is computed as

$$\text{Var} = \frac{1}{T-1}[(R_1 - \overline{R})^2 + (R_2 - \overline{R})^2 + (R_3 - \overline{R})^2 + (R_4 - \overline{R})^2]$$

$$0.0250 = \frac{1}{3}[(0.2137 - 0.0429)^2 + (-0.1480 - 0.0429)^2 + (0.1202 - 0.0429)^2 + (-0.0143 - 0.0429)^2]$$

$$\text{SD} = \sqrt{0.0250} = 0.1508 = 15.08\%$$

Variance and Standard Deviation

The **variance** and its square root, the **standard deviation,** are the most common measures of variability or dispersion. In Example 10.3, we used Var to denote the variance and SD to represent the standard deviation. This formula tells us just what to do: Take each of the T individual returns $(R_1, R_2, \ldots)$ and subtract the average return, $\overline{R}$; square the result, and add them all up. Finally, divide this total by the number of returns less 1 $(T - 1)$. The standard deviation is always just the square root of the variance.[10]

Using the actual stock returns in Table 10.1 for the 50-year period 1957–2006 in the above formula, the resulting standard deviation of stock returns is 16.03 percent. The standard deviation is the standard statistical measure of the spread of a sample, and it will be the measure we use most of the time. Its interpretation is facilitated by a discussion of the normal distribution.

---

[9]Several condensed frequency distributions are also in the extreme right column of Table 10.2.

[10]For small samples, as in this example, you can use a financial calculator to compute the variance and standard deviation. For example, using the Sharp Business/Financial calculator, the steps are:

1. Clear the calculator.
2. Set the calculator to statistics mode by pressing *2nd F MODE* until STAT appears on the display.
3. Set the calculator for statistical calculations by pressing *2nd F TAB decimal point.* The calculator responds by displaying 0.
4. Enter the first observation, 0.2137, and press *M+*. The calculator displays 1, showing that it has recorded the first observation.
5. Enter the second observation, −0.1480, using the +/− key to enter the sign. The calculator displays 2, showing that it has recorded the second observation.
6. Enter the remaining observations.
7. Ask the calculator for the expected return (*R* in the formula) by pressing *x*.
8. Ask the calculator for the standard deviation by pressing σ.

For larger samples, you should use the STDEV command in Excel.

Normal Distribution and Its Implications for Standard Deviation

A large enough sample drawn from a **normal distribution** looks like the bell-shaped curve drawn in Figure 10.6. As you can see, this distribution is *symmetric* about its mean, not *skewed,* and it has a much cleaner shape than the actual distribution of yearly returns drawn in Figure 10.5.[11] Of course, if we had been able to observe stock market returns for 1,000 years, we might have filled in a lot of the jumps and jerks in Figure 10.5 and had a smoother curve.

In classical statistics, the normal distribution plays a central role, and the standard deviation is the usual way of representing the spread of a normal distribution. For the normal distribution, the probability of having a return that is above or below the mean by a certain amount depends only on the standard deviation. For example, the probability of having a return that is within one standard deviation of the mean of the distribution is approximately 0.68 or 2/3, and the probability of having a return that is within two standard deviations of the mean is approximately 0.95.

The 16.03 percent standard deviation we found for stock returns from 1957 through 2006 can now be interpreted in the following way: If stock returns are roughly normally distributed, the probability that a yearly return will fall in the range −4.93 percent to 27.13 percent (11.10 percent plus or minus one standard deviation, 16.03 percent) is about 67 percent. This range is illustrated in Figure 10.6. In other words, there is about one chance in three that the return will be *outside* this range. Based on historical experience and assuming that the past is a good guide to the future, investors who buy shares in large Canadian companies should expect to be outside this range in one year out of every three. This reinforces our earlier observations about stock market volatility. However, there is only a 5 percent chance (approximately) that we would end up outside the range −20.90 percent to 43.16 percent (11.10 percent plus or minus 2 × 16.03%). These points are also illustrated in Figure 10.6.

The distribution in Figure 10.6 is a theoretical distribution, sometimes called the *population.* There is no assurance that the actual distribution of observations in a given sample will produce a histogram that looks exactly like the theoretical distribution. We can see how messy the actual frequency function of historical observations is by observing Figure 10.5. If we were to keep on generating observations for a long enough period of time, however, the aberrations in the sample would disappear, and the actual historical distribution would start to look like the underlying theoretical distribution.

Our comparison illustrates how sampling error exists in any individual sample. In other words, the distribution of the sample only approximates the true distribution; we always measure the truth with some error. For example, we do not know what the true expected return was for common stocks in the 50-year history. However, we are sure that 11.10 percent is a good estimate.

Value at Risk

Figure 10.6 provides the basis for calculating **value at risk (VaR),** a popular risk measurement tool used by banks, insurance companies, and other financial institutions. VaR represents the maximum possible loss in dollars for a given confidence level. To explain where VaR comes from, we start with Figure 10.6, which shows that there is a 95.44 percent probability that the annual return on common stock will lie between a loss of −20.90 percent and a gain of 43.16 percent. This means that there is a 4.56 percent probability

---

[11]Some people define risk as the possibility of obtaining a return below the average. Some measures of risk, such as semivariance, use only the negative deviations from the average return. However, for symmetric distributions, such as the normal distribution, this method of measuring downside risk is equivalent to measuring risk with deviations from the mean on both sides.

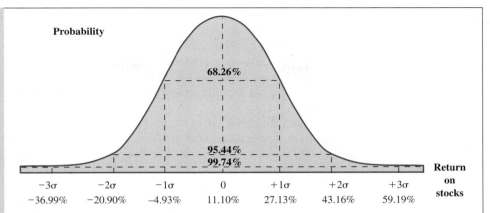

FIGURE 10.6

The Normal Distribution

In the case of a normal distribution, there is a 68.26 percent probability that a return will be within one standard deviation of the mean. In this example, there is a 68.26 percent probability that a yearly return will be between −4.93 percent and 27.13 percent.

There is a 95.44 percent probability that a return will be within two standard deviations of the mean. In this example, there is a 95.44 percent probability that a yearly return will be between −20.90 percent and 43.16 percent.

Finally, there is a 99.74 percent probability that a return will be within three standard deviations of the mean. In this example, there is a 99.74 percent probability that a yearly return will be between −36.99 percent and 59.19 percent.

that the return will lie outside this range. Given that the normal distribution is symmetric, it follows that half that probability (or 2.28 percent) is attached to returns below −20.90 percent. (There is a similar probability of returns higher than 43.16 percent but because we are measuring risk, it is not of concern here.) In brief, if we pick 2.28 percent as our confidence level, Figure 10.6 tells us that returns lower than −20.90 percent will occur only 2.28 percent of the time.

VaR is expressed in dollars so the final piece of information needed is our total exposure to Canadian equities. Suppose that this is $200 million. Multiplying $200 million by a loss of 20.90 percent gives $41.8 million for VaR. In other words, $41.8 million is the most we can lose in one year on our Canadian equity exposure provided we are willing to accept a 2.28 percent chance that our loss could be higher. Canadian banks are required to report VaR in their annual reports.

Further Perspective on Returns and Risk

Table 10.2 presents returns and risks for major asset classes over a reasonably long period of Canadian history. Our discussion of these data suggested that the greater the potential reward, the greater is the risk. In particular, the equity risk premium was 4.53 percent over this period for Canadian stocks.

This may strike you as low as during the 1990s, as well as in the years immediately after World War II, double-digit returns on Canadian and U.S. stocks were common, as Table 10.1 shows. Currently most financial executives and professional investment managers expect lower returns and smaller risk premiums in the future.[12] We agree with their

---

[12]A survey of academic views on the market risk premium is in I. Welch, "Views of Financial Economists on the Equity Risk Premium and Other Issues," *Journal of Business* 73 (October 2000), pp. 501–537. William Mercer surveys professional investment managers in Canada in its annual *Fearless Forecast* available in the Knowledge Center at http://www.mercerhr.com/pressrelease/details.jhtml/dynamic/idContent/1254370;jsessionid=Y1B3XKLO50LFECTGOUGCIIQKMZ0QUJLW.

expectation and this relates to our earlier discussion of which data to use to calculate the market risk premium. In Table 10.1 we display returns data back to 1948 but only go back to 1957 when we calculate risk premiums in Table 10.2. This drops off the high returns experienced in many of the post-war years. If we recalculate the returns and risk premiums in Table 10.2 going all the way back to 1948, we arrive at a market risk premium of 6.98 percent. We discuss the relationship between risk and required return in more detail in the next chapter.

Using U.S. data including the years immediately following World War II and going back to 1926, Appendix 10A (available on the Online Learning Centre at www.mcgrawhill. ca/olc/ross) shows a similar result. The risk premium for this period is higher than for other historical periods.

All this suggests that our estimate of around 4 percent is quite a reasonable prediction for the equity risk premium in Canada looking to the future. However, we do have to acknowledge that this remains a controversial issue about which experts disagree.

? Concept Questions

- Define sample estimates of variance and standard deviation.
- How does the normal distribution help us interpret standard deviation?
- Assuming that long-term bonds have an approximately normal distribution, what is the approximate probability of earning 17 percent or more in a given year? With T-bills, what is this probability?
- Real estate returns appear to be an anomaly, with higher returns and lower standard deviation than common stocks. What factors could explain this?

10.6 More on Average Returns

Thus far in this chapter we have looked closely at simple average returns. But there is another way of computing an average return. The fact that average returns are calculated two different ways leads to some confusion, so our goal in this section is to explain the two approaches and also the circumstances under which each is appropriate.

Arithmetic Versus Geometric Averages

Let's start with a simple example. A particular stock is bought for $100. The first year it falls to $50. The second year it rises back to $100, leaving the buyer right back where he started (no dividends were paid).

What was the average return on this investment? Common sense seems to say that the average return must be exactly zero because you started with $100 and ended with $100. But if we calculate the returns year-by-year, we see that the stock lost 50 percent the first year. The second year, the stock made 100 percent (the stock doubled). The average return over the two years was thus $(-50 \text{ percent} + 100 \text{ percent})/2 = 25$ percent! So which is correct, 0 percent or 25 percent? The answer is that both are correct; they just answer different questions. The 0 percent is called the geometric average return. The 25 percent is called the arithmetic average return. The geometric average return answers the question, *"What was your average compound return per year over a particular period?"* The arithmetic average return answers the question, *"What was your return in an average year over a particular period?"*

Notice that in previous sections, the average returns calculated were all arithmetic averages, so we already know how to calculate them. The following paragraphs will discuss how to how to calculate geometric averages and under which circumstances one average is more meaningful than the other.

Calculating Geometric Average Returns

To illustrate how we calculate a geometric average return, suppose a particular investment had annual returns of 10 percent, 12 percent, 3 percent, and −9 percent over the last four years. The geometric average return over this four-year period is calculated as $(1.10 \times 1.12 \times 1.03 \times .91)^{1/4} - 1 = 3.66$ percent. In contrast, the average arithmetic return we have been calculating is $(.10 + .12 + .03 + .09)/4 = 4.0$ percent.

In general, if we have T years of returns, the geometric average return over these T years is calculated using this formula:

$$\text{Geometric average return} = [(1 + R_1) \times (1 + R_2) \times \cdots \times (1 + R_T)]^{1/T} - 1 \quad (9.1)$$

This formula tells us that four steps are required:

1. Take each of the T annual returns $R_1, R_2, \ldots, R_T$ and add 1 to each (after converting them to decimals).
2. Multiply all the numbers from step 1 together.
3. Take the result from step 2 and raise it to the power of $1/T$.
4. Finally, subtract 1 from the result of step 3. The result is the geometric average return.

EXAMPLE 10.4

Calculating the Geometric Average Return
Calculate the geometric average return for S&P 500 large-cap stocks for 1972–1976 using the numbers given here. First convert percentages to decimal returns, add 1, and then calculate their product.

S&P 500 Returns	Product
18.12%	1.1812
−14.58	×0.8542
−26.87	×0.7313
40.72	×1.4072
22.97	×1.2297
	1.2768

Notice that the number 1.2768 is what our investment is worth after five years if we started with a $1 investment. The geometric average return is then calculated as:

$$\text{Geometric average return} = 1.2768^{1/5} - 1 = .0501, \text{ or } 5.01\%$$

Thus the geometric average return is about 5.01 percent in this example. Here is a tip: If you are using a financial calculator, you can put $1 in as the present value, $1.2768 as the future value, and 5 as the number of periods. Then solve for the unknown rate. You should get the same answer.

TABLE 10.3
Geometric versus Arithmetic Average Returns. 1957–2006

| | Average Return | | |
Investment	Arithmetic (%)	Geometric (%)	Standard deviation (%)
Canadian common stocks	11.10	9.92	16.03
U.S. common stocks (C$)	12.38	11.10	16.82
Long bonds	8.78	8.33	10.07
Small stocks	14.34	12.16	22.29
Inflation	4.15	4.11	3.21
Treasury bills	6.57	6.51	3.64

Average return on small stocks is based on data from 1970 to 2005.

In the examples thus far, the geometric average returns seem to be smaller. It turns out that this will always be true (as long as the returns are not all identical, in which case the two "averages" would be the same). To illustrate, Table 10.3 shows the arithmetic averages and standard deviations from Table 10.1, along with the geometric average returns.

As shown in Table 10.3, the geometric averages are all smaller, but the magnitude of the difference varies quite a bit. The reason is that the difference is greater for more volatile investments. In fact, there is a useful approximation. Assuming all the numbers are expressed in decimals (as opposed to percentages), the geometric average return is approximately equal to the arithmetic average return minus half the variance. For example, looking at Canadian common stocks, the arithmetic average is 11.10 and the standard deviation is 16.03, implying that the variance is 0.4004. The approximate geometric average is thus .1110% − 0.02569/2 = 9.82%, which is quite close to the actual value.

Arithmetic Average Return or Geometric Average Return?

When looking at historical returns, the difference between the geometric and arithmetic average returns is not too hard to understand. The geometric average tells you what you actually earned per year on average, compounded annually. The arithmetic average tells you what you earned in a typical year. You should use whichever one answers the question you want answered.

A somewhat trickier question concerns forecasting the future, and there's a lot of confusion about this point among analysts and financial planners. The problem is this: If we have *estimates* of both the arithmetic and geometric average returns, then the arithmetic average is probably too high for longer periods and the geometric average is probably too low for shorter periods.

The good news is that there is a simple way of combining the two averages, which we call *Blume's formula.*[13] Suppose we calculated geometric and arithmetic return averages from N years of data and we wish to use these averages to form a T-year average return forecast, $R(T)$, where T is less than N. Here's how we do it:

$$R(T) = \frac{T-1}{N-1} \times \text{Geometric Average} + \frac{N-T}{N-1} \times \text{Arithmetic Average}$$

[13]This elegant result is due to Marshal Blume ("Unbiased Estimates of Long-Run Expected Rates of Return," *Journal of the American Statistical Association,* September 1974, pp. 634–638).

For example, suppose that from 25 years of annual returns data, we calculate an arithmetic average return of 12 percent and a geometric average return of 9 percent. From these averages, we wish to make 1-year, 5-year, and 10-year average return forecasts. These three average return forecasts are calculated as follows:

$$R(1) = \frac{1-1}{24} \times 9\% + \frac{25-1}{24} \times 12\% = 12\%$$

$$R(5) = \frac{5-1}{24} \times 9\% + \frac{25-5}{24} \times 12\% = 11.5\%$$

$$R(10) = \frac{10-1}{24} \times 9\% + \frac{25-10}{24} \times 12\% = 10.875\%$$

Thus, we see that 1-year, 5-year, and 10-year forecasts are 12 percent, 11.5 percent, and 10.875 percent, respectively. This concludes our discussion of geometric versus arithmetic averages. One last note: In the future, "average return" means arithmetic average unless explicitly stated otherwise.

10.7   SUMMARY AND CONCLUSIONS

1. This chapter explores capital market history. Such history is useful because it tells us what to expect in the way of returns from risky assets. We summed up our study of market history with two key lessons:

    a. Risky assets, on average, earn a risk premium. There is a reward for bearing risk.

    b. The greater the risk from a risky investment, the greater is the required reward.

    These lessons' implications for the financial manager are discussed in the chapters ahead.

2. The statistical measures in this chapter are necessary building blocks for the next three chapters. Standard deviation and variance measure the variability of the return on an individual security. We will argue that standard deviation and variance are appropriate measures of the risk of an individual security only if an investor's portfolio is composed exclusively of that security.

KEY TERMS

Average (mean) 275	Risk premium 275	Value at risk (VaR) 279
Frequency distribution 274	Standard deviation 277	Variance 277
Normal distribution 278		

SUGGESTED READING

An important record of the performance of financial investments in Canadian capital markets can be found in:

J. E. Hatch and R. W. White. *Canadian Stocks, Bonds, Bills and Inflation: 1950–1983.* Charlottesville, Va.: Financial Analysts Research Foundation, 1985.

The corresponding study for the United States is:

R. G. Ibbotson and R. A. Sinquefield. *Stocks, Bonds, Bills and Inflation* (SBBI). Charlottesville, Va.: Financial Analysts Research Foundation, 1982. (Updated in *SBBI 2003 Yearbook™*. Chicago: Ibbotson Associates.)

What is the equity risk premium? This is the question addressed by:

Bradford Cornell. *The Equity Risk Premium: The Long Term Future of the Stock Market.* New York: John Wiley, 1999; and Robert S. Shiller. *Irrational Exuberance.* Princeton, N.J.: Princeton University Press, 2000.

QUESTIONS & PROBLEMS

Returns

10.1 One year ago, you bought 500 shares of Bobby Inc. stock at $52 per share. You just received a dividend of $1,000 and Bobby stock now sells for $56.
  a. How much did you earn in capital gains?
  b. What was your total dollar return?
  c. What was your percentage return?
  d. Must you sell the stock to include the capital gain in your return?

10.2 One year ago, Mr. Seth Cohen invested $12,500 in 200 shares of First Industries Inc. stock and just received a dividend of $750. Today, he sold the 200 shares at $69.75 per share.
  a. What was his capital gain?
  b. What was his total dollar return?
  c. What was his percentage return?
  d. What was the stock's dividend yield?

10.3 You purchased a stock one year ago at $40 per share. The stock just paid a dividend of $1.75 per share. Today, you sold the stock at $33 per share. What is the percentage return on this stock?

10.4 Refer to Table 10.1 in the text and look at the period from 1973 through 1980.
  a. Calculate the average return for Treasury bills and the average annual inflation rate (consumer price index) for this period.
  b. Calculate the standard deviation of Treasury bill returns and inflation over this period.
  c. Calculate the real return for each year. What is the average real return for Treasury bills?
  d. Many people consider Treasury bills to be risk-free. What do these calculations tell you about the potential risks of Treasury bills?

10.5 Use the information provided in Table 10.1 to compute the nominal and real annual returns from 1979 to 2003 for
  a. Canadian common stock.
  b. Long-term bonds.
  c. Canada Treasury bills.

10.6 Suppose the current interest rate on Canada Treasury bills is 3.9 percent. Table 10.2 shows the average return on Treasury bills from 1957 through 2005 to be 6.80 percent. The average return on common stock during the same period was 10.97 percent. Given this information, what is the current expected return on common stocks?

10.7 Two years ago, General Materials and Standard Fixtures' stock prices were the same. Over the first year, General Materials' stock price increased by 9 percent while Standard Fixtures' stock price decreased by 9 percent. Over the second year, General Materials' stock price decreased by 9 percent and Standard Fixtures' stock price increased by 9 percent. Do these two stocks have the same prices today? Explain.

Average Returns, Expected Returns, and Variance

10.8 During the past seven years, the returns on a portfolio of long-term bonds were the following:

Year	Long-Term Bonds
−7	−4.6%
−6	−1.5
−5	61.9
−4	7.8
−3	24.4
−2	89.9
Last	20.1

a. Calculate the average return for long-term bonds over this period.

b. Calculate the variance and the standard deviation of the returns for long-term bonds during this period.

10.9 The following are the returns during the past seven years on a market portfolio of common stocks and on Treasury bills.

Year	Common Stocks	Treasury Bills
−7	39.1%	11.6%
−6	−6.1	7.1
−5	22.4	8.9
−4	56.8	12.3
−3	7.5	9.1
−2	41.3	7.9
Last	−15.9	6.9

The realized risk premium is the return on the common stocks less the return on the Treasury bills.

a. Calculate the realized risk premium of common stocks over T-bills in each year.

b. Calculate the average risk premium of common stocks over T-bills during the period.

c. Is it possible that this observed risk premium can be negative? Explain.

Average Returns, Expected Returns, and Variance

10.10 The returns on both a portfolio of common stocks and a portfolio of Treasury bills are contingent on the state of the economy, as shown below.

Economic Condition	Probability	Market Return	Treasury Bills
Recession	0.20	−11.2%	3.6%
Normal	0.50	11.4	3.6
Boom	0.30	21.6	3.6

a. Calculate the expected returns on the Treasury bills and on the market.

b. Calculate the expected risk premium.

10.11 Tabulated below are fictional returns on small-company stocks and on large-company common stocks.

Small-Company Stocks (%)	Large-Company Common Stocks (%)
49.1	47.0
30.5	29.1
−5.0	−29.6
−12.0	−0.5
14.0	9.6

a. Calculate the average return for the small-company stocks and for the large-company common stocks.

b. Calculate the variance and standard deviation of the small-company returns and the large company returns.

10.12 The following data are the returns from 1988 through 1993 on four types of capital market instruments: Canadian common stocks, small-cap stocks, long-term bonds, and Canada Treasury bills.

Year	Canadian Common Stocks	Small-Cap Stocks	Long-Term Bonds	Canada T-Bills
1988	11.08	5.46	11.30	8.94
1989	21.37	10.66	15.17	11.95
1990	−14.80	−27.32	4.32	13.28
1991	12.02	18.51	25.30	9.90
1992	−1.43	13.01	11.57	6.65
1993	32.55	52.26	22.09	5.63

Calculate the average return and variance for each type of security.

10.13 Suppose International Trading Company's stock returns follow a normal distribution with a mean of 18.4 percent and a standard deviation of 14.6 percent. What is the range in which roughly 95 percent of the returns fall?

10.14 Go to the "Excel Analytics" link for BCE Inc. (BCE) and download the monthly adjusted stock prices. Assuming you invested $1,000 in BCE at the close 12 months ago, what is your ending investment value? What was the average monthly geometric return over this period? What was the average monthly arithmetic return?

www.mcgrawhill.ca/
edumarketinsight

10.15 Go to the "Excel Analytics" link for Encana (ECA) and download the monthly adjusted stock prices. What was the average monthly return for Encana over the past year? What was the monthly variance of returns? The monthly standard deviation?

MINICASE: A Job at Deck Out My Yacht Corporation

You have recently graduated from business school, and your job search led you to Deck Out My Yacht Corporation. Because you felt the company's business was seaworthy, you accepted a job offer. The first day on the job, while you are finishing your employment paperwork, Alvin Jones, who works in Finance, stops by to inform you about the company's retirement plan.

Retirement plans are offered by many companies and such plans are tax-deferred savings vehicles, meaning that any deposits you make into the plan are deducted from your current pretax income, so no current taxes are paid on the money. For example, assume your salary will be $50,000 per year. If you contribute $3,000, you will pay taxes on only $47,000 in income. There are also no taxes paid on any capital gains or income while you are invested in the plan, but you do pay taxes when you withdraw money at retirement. As is fairly common, the company also has a 5 percent match. This means that the company will match your contribution up to 5 percent of your salary, but you must contribute to get the match.

This plan has several options for investments, most of which are mutual funds. A mutual fund is a portfolio of assets. When you purchase shares in a mutual fund, you are actually purchasing partial ownership of the fund's assets. The return of the fund is the weighted average of the return of the assets owned by the fund, minus any expenses. The largest expense is typically the management fee, paid to the fund manager. The management fee is compensation for the manager, who makes all of the investment decisions for the fund.

Deck Out My Yacht uses Marshall McLaren Financial Services as its plan administrator. Here are the investment options offered for employees:

Company Stock
One option is stock in Deck Out My Yacht. The company is currently privately held. However, when you interviewed with the owner, Larissa Warren, she informed you the company stock was expected to go public in the next three to four years. Until then, a company stock price is simply set each year by the board of directors.

M&M TSX Composite Index Fund
This mutual fund tracks the TSX Composite. Stocks in the fund are weighted exactly the same as the TSX Composite. This means the fund return is approximately the return on the TSX, minus expenses. Because an index fund purchases assets based on the composition of the index it is following, the fund manager is not required to research stocks and make investment decisions. The result is that the fund expenses are usually low. The M&M TSX Composite

Index Fund charges expenses of .15 percent of assets per year.

M&M Small-Cap Fund

This fund primarily invests in small-capitalization stocks. As such, the returns of the fund are more volatile. The fund can also invest 10 percent of its assets in companies based outside the Canada. This fund charges 1.70 percent in expenses.

M&M Large-Company Stock Fund

This fund invests primarily in large-capitalization stocks of companies based in North America. The fund is managed by Robbie McLaren and has outperformed the market in six of the last eight years. The fund charges 1.50 percent in expenses.

M&M Bond Fund

This fund invests in long-term corporate bonds issued by Canadian-domiciled companies. The fund is restricted to investments in bonds with an investment grade credit rating. This fund charges 1.40 percent in expenses.

M&M Money Market Fund

This fund invests in short-term, high-credit quality debt instruments, which include Treasury bills. As such, the return on the money market fund is only slightly higher than the return on Treasury bills. Because of the credit quality and short-term nature of the investments, there is only a very slight risk of negative return. The fund charges .60 percent in expenses.

1. What advantages do the mutual funds offer compared to the company stock?
2. Assume that you invest 5 percent of your salary and receive the full 5 percent match from Deck Out My Yacht. What EAR do you earn from the match? What conclusions do you draw about matching plans?

3. Assume you decide you should invest at least part of your money in large-capitalization stocks of companies based in North America. What are the advantages and disadvantages of choosing the M&M Large-Company Stock Fund compared to the M&M TSX Composite Index Fund?
4. The returns on the M&M Small-Cap Fund are the most volatile of all the mutual funds. Why would you ever want to invest in this fund? When you examine the expenses of the mutual funds, you will notice that this fund also has the highest expenses. Does this affect your decision to invest in this fund?
5. A measure of risk-adjusted performance that is often used is the Sharpe ratio. The Sharpe ratio is calculated as the risk premium of an asset divided by its standard deviation. The standard deviation and return of the funds over the past 10 years are listed here. Calculate the Sharpe ratio for each of these funds. Assume that the expected return and standard deviation of the company stock will be 18 percent and 70 percent, respectively. Calculate the Sharpe ratio for the company stock. How appropriate is the Sharpe ratio for these assets? When would you use the Sharpe ratio?

	10-Year Annual Return	Standard Deviation
M&M TSX Composite Index Fund	11.48%	15.82%
M&M Small-Cap Fund	16.68	19.64
M&M Large-Company Stock Fund	11.85	15.41
M&M Bond Fund	9.67	10.83

6. What portfolio allocation would you choose? Why? Explain your thinking carefully.

Appendix 10A: The Historical Market Risk Premium: The Very Long Run
To access Appendix 10A, please go to the Online Learning Centre at **www.mcgrawhill.ca/olc/ross**.

Chapter 11

Risk and Return: The Capital Asset Pricing Model (CAPM)

EXECUTIVE SUMMARY

The previous chapter achieved two purposes. First, we acquainted you with the history of Canadian capital markets. Second, we presented statistics such as expected return, variance, and standard deviation. Our ultimate goal in the next three chapters is to determine the appropriate discount rate for capital budgeting projects. Because the discount rate on a project is a function of its risk, the discussion in the previous chapter on standard deviation is a necessary first step. However, we shall see that standard deviation is not the final word on risk.

Our next step is to investigate the relationship between the risk and the return of individual securities when these securities are part of a large portfolio. This task is taken up in Chapter 11. The actual treatment of the appropriate discount rate for capital budgeting is reserved for Chapter 13.

The crux of the current chapter can be summarized as follows: An individual who holds one security should use expected return as the measure of the security's return. Standard deviation or variance is the proper measure of the security's risk. An individual who holds a diversified portfolio cares about the *contribution* of each security to the expected return and the risk of the portfolio. It turns out that a security's expected return is the appropriate measure of the security's contribution to the expected return on the portfolio. However, neither the security's variance nor the security's standard deviation is an appropriate measure of a security's contribution to the risk of a portfolio. The contribution of a security to the risk of a portfolio is best measured by beta.

11.1 Individual Securities

In the first part of Chapter 11 we will examine the characteristics of individual securities. In particular, we will discuss:

1. *Expected return.* This is the return that an individual expects a stock to earn over the next period. Of course, because this is only an expectation, the actual return may be either higher or lower. An individual's expectation may simply be the average return per period a security has earned in the past. Alternatively, it may be based on a detailed analysis of a firm's prospects, on some computer-based model, or on special (or inside) information.

2. *Variance and standard deviation.* There are many ways to assess the volatility of a security's return. One of the most common is variance, which is a measure of the

squared deviations of a security's return from its expected return. Standard deviation, which is the square root of the variance, may be thought of as a standardized version of the variance.

3. *Covariance and correlation.* Returns on individual securities are related to one another. Covariance is a statistic measuring the interrelationship between two securities. Alternatively, this relationship can be restated in terms of the correlation between the two securities. Covariance and correlation are building blocks to an understanding of the beta coefficient.

11.2 Expected Return, Variance, and Covariance

Expected Return and Variance

Suppose financial analysts believe that there are four equally likely states of the economy: depression, recession, normal, and boom times. The returns on the Supertech Company are expected to follow the economy closely, while the returns on the Slowpoke Company are not. The return predictions are given below:

	Supertech Returns R_{At}	Slowpoke Returns R_{Bt}
Depression	−20%	5%
Recession	10	20
Normal	30	−12
Boom	50	9

Variance can be calculated in four steps. Calculating expected return is the first step.[1] An additional step is needed to calculate standard deviation. (The calculations are presented in Table 11.1.)

1. Calculate the expected return:

Supertech:

$$\frac{-0.20 + 0.10 + 0.30 + 0.50}{4} = 0.175 = 17.5\%$$

Slowpoke:

$$\frac{0.05 + 0.20 - 0.12 + 0.09}{4} = 0.055 = 5.5\%$$

2. For each company, calculate the deviation of each possible return from the company's expected return given above. This is presented in the third column of Table 11.1.

3. The deviations we have calculated are indications of the dispersion of returns. However, because some are positive and some are negative, it is difficult to work with them in this form. For example, if we were to add up all the deviations for a single company, we would get zero as the sum.

To make the deviations more meaningful, we multiply each one by itself. Now all the numbers are positive, implying that their sum must be positive as well. The squared deviations are presented in the last column of Table 11.1.

---

[1] If the probabilities of all the states are not the same, find the expected return (standard deviation) by multiplying each return (deviation) by its probability.

TABLE 11.1
Calculating Variance and Standard Deviation

(1) State of Economy	(2) Rate of Return	(3) Deviation from Expected Return	(4) Squared Value of Deviation
	Supertech*	**(Expected return = 0.175)**	
	R_{At}	$(R_{At} - \overline{R}_A)$	$(R_{At} - \overline{R}_A)^2$
Depression	−0.20	−0.375	0.140625
		(= −0.20 − 0.175)	[= (−0.375)^2]
Recession	0.10	−0.075	0.005625
Normal	0.30	0.125	0.015625
Boom	0.50	0.325	0.105625
			0.267500
	Slowpoke†	**(Expected return = 0.055)**	
	R_{Bt}	$(R_{Bt} - \overline{R}_B)$	$(R_{Bt} - \overline{R}_B)^2$
Depression	0.05	−0.005	0.000025
		(= 0.05 − 0.055)	[= (−0.005)^2]
Recession	0.20	0.145	0.021025
Normal	−0.12	−0.175	0.030625
Boom	0.09	0.035	0.001225
			0.052900

$$*\overline{R}_A = \frac{-0.20 + 0.10 + 0.30 + 0.50}{4} = 0.175 = 17.5\%$$

$$\text{Var}(R_A) = \sigma_A^2 = \frac{0.2675}{4} = 0.066875$$

$$\text{SD}(R_A) = \sigma_A = \sqrt{0.066875} = 0.2586 = 25.86\%$$

$$^\dagger \overline{R}_B = \frac{0.05 + 0.20 - 0.12 + 0.09}{4} = 0.055 = 5.5\%$$

$$\text{Var}(R_B) = \sigma_B^2 = \frac{0.0529}{4} = 0.013225$$

$$\text{SD}(R_B) = \sigma_B = \sqrt{0.013225} = 0.1150 = 11.50\%$$

4. For each company, calculate the average squared deviation, which is the variance:[2]

Supertech:

$$\frac{0.140625 + 0.005625 + 0.015625 + 0.105625}{4} = 0.066875$$

Slowpoke:

$$\frac{0.000025 + 0.021025 + 0.030625 + 0.001225}{4} = 0.013225$$

Thus, the variance of Supertech is 0.066875, and the variance of Slowpoke is 0.013225.

5. Calculate standard deviation by taking the square root of the variance:

Supertech:

$$\sqrt{0.066875} = 0.2586 = 25.86\%$$

---

[2]In this example, the four states give rise to four possible outcomes for each stock. Had we used past data, the outcomes would have actually occurred. In that case, statisticians argue that the correct divisor is $N - 1$, where N is the number of observations. Thus, the denominator would be 3 (or $4 - 1$) in the case of past data, not 4. Note that the example in Section 10.5 involved past data and we used a divisor of $N - 1$. While this difference causes grief to both students and textbook writers, it is a minor point in practice. In the real world, samples are generally so large that using N or $N - 1$ in the denominator has virtually no effect on the calculation of variance.

Slowpoke:
$$\sqrt{0.013225} = 0.1150 = 11.50\%$$

Algebraically, the formula for variance can be expressed as

$$\text{Var}(R) = \text{Expected value of } (R - \overline{R})^2$$

where $\overline{R}$ is the security's expected return and R is the actual return.

A look at the four-step calculation for variance makes it clear why it is a measure of the spread of the sample of returns. For each observation, we square the difference between the actual return and the expected return. We then take an average of these squared differences.

However, because the variance is still expressed in squared terms, it is difficult to interpret. Standard deviation has a much simpler interpretation, which we will provide shortly. Standard deviation is simply the square root of the variance. The general formula for the standard deviation is

$$\text{SD}(R) = \sqrt{\text{Var}(R)}$$

Covariance and Correlation

The statistical estimates variance and standard deviation measure the variability of individual stocks. We now wish to measure the relationship between the return on one stock and the return on another. To make our discussion more precise, we need a statistical measure of the relationship between two variables. Enter **covariance** and **correlation.**

Covariance and correlation are ways of measuring whether or not two random variables are related and how. We explain these terms by extending an example presented earlier in this chapter in Example 11.1.

EXAMPLE 11.1

We have already determined the expected returns and standard deviations for both Supertech and Slowpoke. (The expected returns are 0.175 and 0.055 for Supertech and Slowpoke, respectively. The standard deviations are 0.2586 and 0.1150, respectively.) In addition, we calculated for each firm the deviation of each possible return from the expected return. Using these data, covariance can be calculated in two steps. An extra step is needed to calculate correlation.

1. For each state of the economy, multiply Supertech's deviation from its expected return and Slowpoke's deviation from its expected return together. For example, Supertech's rate of return in a depression is −0.20, which is −0.375 (or −0.20 − 0.175) from its expected return. Slowpoke's rate of return in a depression is 0.05, which is −0.005 (or 0.05 − 0.055) from its expected return. Multiplying the two deviations together yields 0.001875 [or (−0.375) × (−0.005)]. The actual calculations are given in the last column of Table 11.2. This procedure can be written algebraically as

$$(R_{At} - \overline{R}_A) \times (R_{Bt} - \overline{R}_B) \tag{11.1}$$

where R_{At} and R_{Bt} are the returns on Supertech and Slowpoke in state t. $\overline{R}_A$ and $\overline{R}_B$ are the expected returns on the two securities.

2. Calculate the average value of the four states in the last column. This average is the covariance. That is,[3]

$$\sigma_{AB} = \text{Cov}(R_A, R_B) = \frac{-0.195}{4} = -0.004875$$

[3]As with variance, we divide by N (4 in this example) because the four states give rise to four possible outcomes. However, had we used past data, the correct divisor would be $N - 1$ (3 in this example).

Note that we represent the covariance between Supertech and Slowpoke as either Cov(R_A, R_B) or σ_{AB}. Equation (11.1) illustrates the intuition of covariance. Suppose Supertech's return is generally above its average when Slowpoke's return is above its average, and Supertech's return is generally below its average when Slowpoke's return is below its average. This is indicative of a positive dependency or a positive relationship between the two returns. Note that the term in Equation (11.1) will be *positive* in any state where both returns are *above* their averages. In addition, (11.1) will still be *positive* in any state where both terms are *below* their averages. Thus, a positive relationship between the two returns will give rise to a positive calculation for covariance.

Conversely, suppose Supertech's return is generally above its average when Slowpoke's return is below its average, and Supertech's return is generally below its average when Slowpoke's return is above its average. This is indicative of a negative dependency or a negative relationship between the two returns. Note that the term in Equation (11.1) will be *negative* in any state where one return is above its average and the other return is below its average. Thus, a negative relationship between the two returns will give rise to a negative calculation for covariance.

Finally, suppose there is no relation between the two returns. In this case, knowing whether the return on Supertech is above or below its expected return tells us nothing about the return on Slowpoke. In the covariance formula, then, there will be no tendency for the terms to be positive or negative, and on average they will tend to offset each other and cancel out. This will make the covariance zero.

Of course, even if the two returns are unrelated to each other, the covariance formula will not equal zero exactly in any actual history. This is due to sampling error; randomness alone will make the calculation positive or negative. But for a historical sample that is long enough, if the two returns are not related to each other, we should expect the formula to come close to zero.

TABLE 11.2   Calculating Covariance and Correlation

State of Economy	Rate of Return of Supertech R_{At}	Deviation from Expected Return $(R_{At} - \overline{R}_A)$	Rate of Return of Slowpoke R_{Bt}	Deviation from Expected Return $(R_{Bt} - \overline{R}_B)$	Product of Deviations $(R_{At} - \overline{R}_A)$ $\times (R_{Bt} - \overline{R}_B)$
		(Expected return = 0.175)		(Expected return = 0.055)	
Depression	−0.20	−0.375 (= −0.20 − 0.175)	0.05	−0.005 (= 0.05 − 0.055)	0.001875 (= −0.375 × −0.005)
Recession	0.10	−0.075	0.20	0.145	−0.010875 (= −0.075 × 0.145)
Normal	0.30	0.125	−0.12	−0.175	−0.021875 (= 0.125 × −0.175)
Boom	0.50	0.325	0.09	0.035	0.011375 (= 0.325 × 0.035)
	0.70		0.22		−0.0195

$$\sigma_{AB} = \text{Cov}(R_A, R_B) = \frac{-0.0195}{4} = -0.004875$$

$$\rho_{AB} = \text{Corr}(R_A, R_B) = \frac{\text{Cov}(R_A, R_B)}{\text{SD}(R_A) \times \text{SD}(R_B)} = \frac{-0.004875}{0.2586 \times 0.1150} = -0.1639$$

The covariance formula seems to capture what we are looking for. If the two returns are positively related to each other, they will have a positive covariance, and if they are negatively related to each other, the covariance will be negative. Last, and very important, if they are unrelated, the covariance should be zero.

The formula for covariance can be written algebraically as[4]

$$\sigma_{AB} = \text{Cov}(R_A, R_B) = \text{Expected value of } [(R_A - \overline{R}_A) \times (R_B - \overline{R}_B)]$$

where $\overline{R}_A$ and $\overline{R}_B$ are the expected returns for the two securities, and R_A and R_B are the actual returns. The ordering of the two variables is unimportant. That is, the covariance of A with B is equal to the covariance of B with A. This can be stated more formally as $\text{Cov}(R_A, R_B) = \text{Cov}(R_B, R_A)$ or $\sigma_{AB} = \sigma_{BA}$.

The covariance we calculated is -0.004875. A negative number like this implies that the return on one stock is likely to be above its average when the return on the other stock is below its average, and vice versa. However, the size of the number is difficult to interpret. Like the variance figure, the covariance is in squared deviation units. Until we can put it in perspective, we don't know what to make of it.

We solve the problem by computing the correlation.

3. To calculate the correlation, divide the covariance by the standard deviations of both of the two securities. For our example, we have

$$\rho_{AB} = \text{Corr}(R_A, R_B) = \frac{\text{Cov}(R_A, R_B)}{\sigma_A \times \sigma_B} = \frac{-0.004875}{0.2586 \times 0.1150} = -0.1639 \quad \textbf{(11.2)}$$

where σ_A and σ_B are the standard deviations of Supertech and Slowpoke, respectively. Note that we represent the correlation between Supertech and Slowpoke either as $\text{Corr}(R_A, R_B)$ or ρ_{AB}. As with covariance, the ordering of the two variables is unimportant. That is, the correlation of A with B is equal to the correlation of B with A. More formally, $\text{Corr}(R_A, R_B) = \text{Corr}(R_B, R_A)$ or $\rho_{AB} = \rho_{BA}$.

Because the standard deviation is always positive, the sign of the correlation between two variables must be the same as that of the covariance between the two variables. If the correlation is positive, we say that the variables are *positively correlated;* if it is negative, we say that they are *negatively correlated;* and if it is zero, we say that they are *uncorrelated.* Furthermore, it can be proven that the correlation is always between $+1$ and -1. This is due to the standardizing procedure of dividing by the two standard deviations.

We can compare the correlation between different pairs of securities. For example, it turns out that the correlation between Bank of Montreal and Royal Bank of Canada is much higher than the correlation between Bank of Montreal and Nortel. Hence, we can state that the first pair of securities is more interrelated than the second pair.

Figure 11.1 shows the three benchmark cases for two assets, A and B. The figure shows two assets with return correlations of $+1$, -1, and 0. This implies perfect positive correlation, perfect negative correlation, and no correlation, respectively. The graphs in the figure plot the separate returns on the two securities through time.

---

[4]The covariance formula can also be written using summation notation:

$$\sigma_{AB} = \text{Cov}(R_A, R_B) \sum_{t=1}^{4} P_t(R_{At} - \overline{R}_A)(\overline{R}_{Bt} - \overline{R}_B)$$

where P_t represents the probability of state t occurring.

FIGURE 11.1

Examples of Different Correlation Coefficients

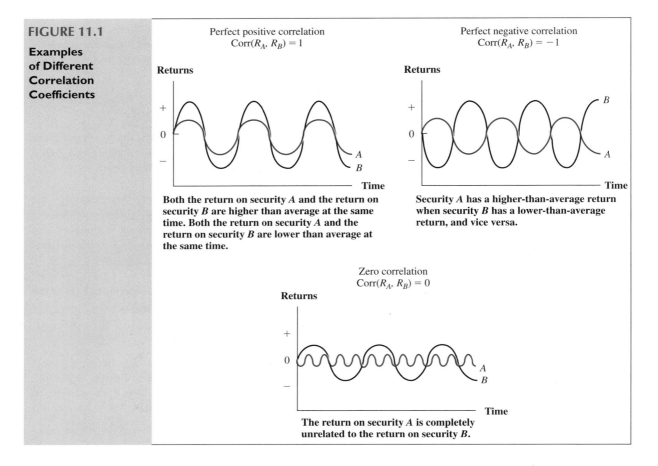

Perfect positive correlation
$\text{Corr}(R_A, R_B) = 1$

Both the return on security *A* and the return on security *B* are higher than average at the same time. Both the return on security *A* and the return on security *B* are lower than average at the same time.

Perfect negative correlation
$\text{Corr}(R_A, R_B) = -1$

Security *A* has a higher-than-average return when security *B* has a lower-than-average return, and vice versa.

Zero correlation
$\text{Corr}(R_A, R_B) = 0$

The return on security *A* is completely unrelated to the return on security *B*.

11.3 The Risk and Return for Portfolios

Suppose that an investor has estimates of the expected returns and standard deviations on individual securities and the correlations between securities. How then does the investor choose the best combination or **portfolio** of securities to hold? Obviously, the investor would like a portfolio with a high expected return and a low standard deviation of return. It is therefore worthwhile to consider

1. The relationship between the expected return on individual securities and the expected return on a portfolio made up of these securities.
2. The relationship between the standard deviations of individual securities, the correlations between these securities, and the standard deviation of a portfolio made up of these securities.

The Example of Supertech and Slowpoke

In order to analyze the above two relationships, we will use the Supertech and Slowpoke example presented previously. The relevant data are in the box below.[5]

---

[5]See Tables 11.1 and 11.2 for actual calculations.

The Expected Return on a Portfolio

The formula for expected return on a portfolio is very simple:

> The expected return on a portfolio is simply a weighted average of the expected returns on the individual securities.

Relevant Data from Example of Supertech and Slowpoke

Item	Symbol	Value
Expected return on Supertech	$\overline{R}_{\text{Super}}$	0.175 = 17.5%
Expected return on Slowpoke	$\overline{R}_{\text{Slow}}$	0.055 = 5.5%
Variance of Supertech	σ^2_{Super}	0.066875
Variance of Slowpoke	σ^2_{Slow}	0.013225
Standard deviation of Supertech	σ_{Super}	0.2586 = 25.86%
Standard deviation of Slowpoke	σ_{Slow}	0.1150 = 11.50%
Covariance between Supertech and Slowpoke	$\sigma_{\text{Super, Slow}}$	−0.004875
Correlation between Supertech and Slowpoke	$\rho_{\text{Super, Slow}}$	−0.1639

EXAMPLE 11.2

Consider Supertech and Slowpoke. From the box above, we find that the expected returns on these two securities are 17.5 percent and 5.5 percent, respectively.

The expected return on a portfolio of these two securities alone can be written as

$$\text{Expected return on portfolio} = X_{\text{Super}}\,(17.5\%) + X_{\text{Slow}}\,(5.5\%)$$

where X_{Super} is the percentage of the portfolio in Supertech and X_{Slow} is the percentage of the portfolio in Slowpoke. If the investor with $100 invests $60 in Supertech and $40 in Slowpoke, the expected return on the portfolio can be written as

$$\text{Expected return on portfolio} = 0.6 \times 17.5\% + 0.4 \times 5.5\% = 12.7\%$$

Algebraically, we can write

$$\text{Expected return on portfolio} = X_A\overline{R}_A + X_B\overline{R}_B \qquad (11.3)$$

where X_A and X_B are the proportions of the total portfolio in the assets A and B, respectively. (Because our investor can only invest in two securities, $X_A + X_B$ must equal 1 or 100 percent.) $\overline{R}_A$ and $\overline{R}_B$ are the expected returns on the two securities.

Now consider two stocks, each with an expected return of 10 percent. The expected return on a portfolio composed of these two stocks must be 10 percent, regardless of the proportions of the two stocks held. This result may seem obvious at this point, but it will become important later. The result implies that you do not reduce or *dissipate* your expected return by investing in a number of securities. Rather, the expected return on your portfolio is simply a weighted average of the expected returns on the individual assets in the portfolio.

Variance and Standard Deviation of a Portfolio

The Variance   The formula for the variance of a portfolio composed of two securities, *A* and *B,* is

The Variance of the Portfolio:
$$\text{Var(portfolio)} = X_A^2\sigma_A^2 + 2X_AX_B\sigma_{A,B} + X_B^2\sigma_B^2$$

Note that there are three terms on the right-hand side of the equation. The first term involves the variance of $A(\sigma_A^2)$, the second term involves the covariance between the two securities $(\sigma_{A,B})$, and the third term involves the variance of $B(\sigma_B^2)$. (It should be noted that $\sigma_{A,B} = \sigma_{B,A}$. That is, the ordering of the variables is not relevant when expressing the covariance between two securities.)

The formula indicates an important point. The variance of a portfolio depends on both the variances of the individual securities and the covariance between the two securities. The variance of a security measures the variability of an individual security's return. Covariance measures the relationship between the two securities. For given variances of the individual securities, a positive relationship or covariance between the two securities increases the variance of the entire portfolio. A negative relationship or covariance between the two securities decreases the variance of the entire portfolio. This important result seems to square with common sense. If one of your securities tends to go up when the other goes down, or vice versa, your two securities are offsetting each other. You are achieving what we call a *hedge* in finance, and the risk of your entire portfolio will be low. However, if both your securities rise and fall together, you are not hedging at all. Hence, the risk of your entire portfolio will be higher.

The variance formula for our two securities, Super and Slow, is

$$\text{Var(portfolio)} = X_{\text{Super}}^2\sigma_{\text{Super}}^2 + 2X_{\text{Super}}X_{\text{Slow}}\sigma_{\text{Super,Slow}} + X_{\text{Slow}}^2\sigma_{\text{Slow}}^2 \quad (11.4)$$

Given our earlier assumption that an individual with $100 invests $60 in Supertech and $40 in Slowpoke, $X_{\text{Super}} = 0.6$ and $X_{\text{Slow}} = 0.4$. Using this assumption and the relevant data from the box on page 294, the variance of the portfolio is

$$0.023851 = 0.36 \times 0.066875 + 2 \times [0.6 \times 0.4 \times (-0.004875)]$$
$$+0.16 \times 0.013225 \quad (11.4')$$

The Matrix Approach   Alternatively, Equation (11.4) can be expressed in the following matrix format:

	Supertech	Slowpoke
Supertech	$X_{\text{Super}}^2\sigma_{\text{Super}}^2$ $0.024075 = 0.36 \times 0.066875$	$X_{\text{Super}}X_{\text{Slow}}\sigma_{\text{Super, Slow}}$ $-0.00117 = 0.6 \times 0.4 \times (-0.004875)$
Slowpoke	$X_{\text{Super}}X_{\text{Slow}}\sigma_{\text{Super, Slow}}$ $-0.00117 = 0.6 \times 0.4 \times (-0.004875)$	$X_{\text{Slow}}^2\sigma_{\text{Slow}}^2$ $0.002116 = 0.16 \times 0.013225$

There are four boxes in the matrix. We can add the terms in the boxes to obtain Equation (11.4), the variance of a portfolio composed of the two securities. The term in the upper left-hand corner contains the variance of Supertech. The term in the lower right-hand corner contains the variance of Slowpoke. The other two boxes contain the covariance terms. These two boxes are identical, indicating why the covariance term is multiplied by 2 in Equation (11.4).

At this point, students often find the box approach to be more confusing than Equation (11.4). However, the box approach is easily generalized to more than two securities, a task we perform later in this chapter.

Standard Deviation of a Portfolio   Given (11.4′), we can now determine the standard deviation of the portfolio's return. This is

$$\sigma_P = \text{SD(portfolio)} = \sqrt{\text{Var(portfolio)}} = \sqrt{0.023851} = 0.1544 = 15.44\% \quad \textbf{(11.5)}$$

The interpretation of the standard deviation of the portfolio is the same as the interpretation of the standard deviation of an individual security. The expected return on our portfolio is 12.7 percent. A return of −2.74 percent (12.7% − 15.44%) is one standard deviation below the mean and a return of 28.14 percent (12.7% + 15.44%) is one standard deviation above the mean. If the return on the portfolio is normally distributed, a return between −2.74 percent and +28.14 percent occurs about 68 percent of the time.[6]

The Diversification Effect   It is instructive to compare the standard deviation of the portfolio with the standard deviation of the individual securities. The weighted average of the standard deviations of the individual securities is

$$\text{Weighted average of standard deviations} = X_{\text{Super}}\sigma_{\text{Super}} + X_{\text{Slow}}\sigma_{\text{Slow}} \quad \textbf{(11.6)}$$
$$0.2012 = 0.6 \times 0.2586 + 0.4 \times 0.115$$

One of the most important results in this chapter relates to the difference between Equations (11.5) and (11.6). In our example, the standard deviation of the portfolio is *less* than a weighted average of the standard deviations of the individual securities.

We pointed out earlier that the expected return on the portfolio is a weighted average of the expected returns on the individual securities. Thus, we get a different type of result for the standard deviation of a portfolio than we do for the expected return on a portfolio.

It is generally argued that our result for the standard deviation of a portfolio is due to diversification. For example, Supertech and Slowpoke are slightly negatively correlated ($\rho = -0.1639$). Supertech's return is likely to be a little below average if Slowpoke's return is above average. Similarly, Supertech's return is likely to be a little above average if Slowpoke's return is below average. Thus, the standard deviation of a portfolio composed of the two securities is less than a weighted average of the standard deviations of the two securities.

The above example has negative correlation. Clearly, there will be less benefit from diversification if the two securities exhibit positive correlation. How high must the positive correlation be before all diversification benefits vanish?

To answer this question, let us rewrite (11.4) in terms of correlation rather than covariance. The covariance can be rewritten as[7]

$$\sigma_{\text{Super, Slow}} = \rho_{\text{Super, Slow}}\sigma_{\text{Super}}\sigma_{\text{Slow}} \quad \textbf{(11.7)}$$

The formula states that the covariance between any two securities is simply the correlation between the two securities multiplied by the standard deviations of each. In other

---

[6]There are only four equally probable returns for Supertech and Slowpoke, so neither security possesses a normal distribution. Thus, probabilities would be slightly different in our example.

[7]As with covariance, the ordering of the two securities is not relevant when expressing the correlation between the two securities. That is, $\rho_{\text{Super, Slow}} = \rho_{\text{Slow, Super}}$.

words, covariance incorporates both (1) the correlation between the two assets and (2) the variability of each of the two securities as measured by standard deviation.

From our calculations earlier in this chapter we know that the correlation between the two securities is -0.1639. Given the variances used in Equation (11.4′), the standard deviations are 0.2586 and 0.115 for Supertech and Slowpoke, respectively. Thus, the variance of a portfolio can be expressed as

Variance of the portfolio's return:

$$= X^2_{Super}\sigma^2_{Super} + 2X_{Super}X_{Slow}\rho_{Super, Slow}\sigma_{Super}\sigma_{Slow} + X^2_{Slow}\sigma^2_{Slow}$$

$$0.023851 = 0.36 \times 0.066875 + 2 \times 0.6 \times 0.4 \times (-0.1639) \quad \textbf{(11.8)}$$
$$\times 0.2586 \times 0.115 + 0.16 \times 0.013225$$

The middle term on the right-hand side is now written in terms of correlation, ρ, not covariance.

Suppose $\rho_{Super, Slow} = 1$, the highest possible value for correlation. Assume all the other parameters in the example are the same. The variance of the portfolio is

$$\text{Variance of the portfolio's return} = 0.040466 = 0.36 \times 0.066875 + 2$$
$$\times (0.6 \times 0.4 \times 1 \times 0.2586 \times 0.115)$$
$$+ 0.16 \times 0.013225$$

The standard deviation is

$$\text{Standard deviation of portfolio's return} = \sqrt{0.040466} = 0.2012 = 20.12\% \quad \textbf{(11.9)}$$

Note that (11.9) and (11.6) are equal. That is, the standard deviation of a portfolio's return is equal to the weighted average of the standard deviations of the individual returns when $\rho = 1$. Inspection of (11.8) indicates that the variance and hence the standard deviation of the portfolio must drop as the correlation drops below 1. This leads to:

As long as $\rho < 1$, the standard deviation of a portfolio of two securities is less than the weighted average of the standard deviations of the individual securities.

In other words, the diversification effect applies as long as there is less than perfect correlation (as long as $\rho < 1$). Thus, our Supertech–Slowpoke example is a case of over-kill. We illustrated diversification with an example with negative correlation. We could have illustrated diversification with an example with positive correlation—as long as it was not perfect positive correlation.

An Extension to Many Assets   The preceding insight can be extended to the case of many assets. That is, as long as correlations between pairs of securities are less than 1, the standard deviation of a portfolio of many assets is less than the weighted average of the standard deviations of the individual securities.

Now consider Table 11.3, which shows the standard deviation of the S&P/TSX 60 and the standard deviations of some of the individual securities listed in the index over a recent 25-year period. Note that all of the individual securities in the table have higher standard deviations than that of the index. In general, the standard deviations of most of the individual securities in an index will be above the standard deviation of the index itself, though a few of the securities could have lower standard deviations than that of the index.

? Concept Questions

• What are the formulas for the expected return, variance, and standard deviation of a portfolio of two assets?
• What is the diversification effect?
• What are the highest and lowest possible values for the correlation coefficient?

TABLE 11.3 Standard Deviations of Annual Returns of Selected TSX Companies over a 25-Year Period	
Abitibi Price Inc.	30.88%
Bank of Montreal	24.23
Bell Canada Enterprises Inc.	21.47
Canadian Pacific Ltd.	26.16
Imperial Oil Ltd.	24.84
Molson Companies Ltd.	24.79
MacMillan Bloedel Ltd.	27.04
Placer Dome Inc.	42.33
S&P/TSX 60	17.04

Source: Calculated from Canadian Financial Markets Research Centre data.

11.4 The Efficient Set for Two Assets

Our results on expected returns and standard deviations are graphed in Figure 11.2. In the figure, there is a dot labelled Slowpoke and a dot labelled Supertech. Each dot represents both the expected return and the standard deviation for an individual security. As can be seen, Supertech has both a higher expected return and a higher standard deviation.

The box or "□" in Figure 11.2 represents a portfolio with 60 percent invested in Supertech and 40 percent invested in Slowpoke. You will recall that we have previously calculated both the expected return and the standard deviation for this portfolio.

The choice of 60 percent in Supertech and 40 percent in Slowpoke is just one of an infinite number of portfolios that can be created. The set of portfolios is sketched by the curved line in Figure 11.3.

Consider portfolio 1. This is a portfolio composed of 90 percent Slowpoke and 10 percent Supertech. Because it is weighted so heavily toward Slowpoke, it appears close to the Slowpoke point on the graph. Portfolio 2 is higher on the curve because it is composed of 50 percent Slowpoke and 50 percent Supertech. Portfolio 3 is close to the Supertech point on the graph because it is composed of 90 percent Supertech and 10 percent Slowpoke.

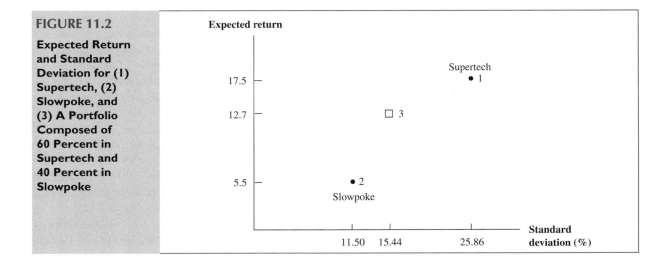

FIGURE 11.2

Expected Return and Standard Deviation for (1) Supertech, (2) Slowpoke, and (3) A Portfolio Composed of 60 Percent in Supertech and 40 Percent in Slowpoke

FIGURE 11.3

Set of Portfolios Composed of Holdings in Supertech and Slowpoke (correlation between the two securities is −0.16)

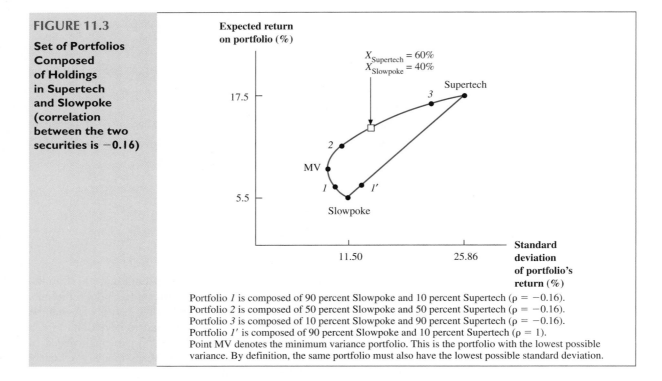

Portfolio *1* is composed of 90 percent Slowpoke and 10 percent Supertech ($\rho = -0.16$).
Portfolio *2* is composed of 50 percent Slowpoke and 50 percent Supertech ($\rho = -0.16$).
Portfolio *3* is composed of 10 percent Slowpoke and 90 percent Supertech ($\rho = -0.16$).
Portfolio *1'* is composed of 90 percent Slowpoke and 10 percent Supertech ($\rho = 1$).
Point MV denotes the minimum variance portfolio. This is the portfolio with the lowest possible variance. By definition, the same portfolio must also have the lowest possible standard deviation.

There are a few important points concerning this graph.

1. We argued that the diversification effect occurs whenever the correlation between the two securities is below 1. The correlation between Supertech and Slowpoke is −0.1639. The diversification effect can be illustrated by comparison with the straight line between the Supertech point and the Slowpoke point. The straight line represents points that would have been generated had the correlation coefficient between the two securities been 1. The diversification effect is illustrated in the figure since the curved line is always to the left of the straight line. Consider point 1'. This represents a portfolio composed of 90 percent in Slowpoke and 10 percent in Supertech if the correlation between the two were exactly 1. We argue that there is no diversification effect if $\rho = 1$. However, the diversification effect applies to the curved line, because point 1 has the same expected return as point 1' but has a lower standard deviation. (Points 2' and 3' are omitted to reduce the clutter in Figure 11.3.)

Though the straight line and the curved line are both represented in Figure 11.3, they do not exist simultaneously. Either $\rho = -0.1639$ and the curve exists or $\rho = 1$ and the straight line exists. In other words, though an investor can choose between different points on the curve if $\rho = -0.1639$, he or she cannot choose between points on the curve and points on the straight line.

2. The point MV represents the minimum variance portfolio. This is the portfolio with the lowest possible variance. By definition, this portfolio must also have the lowest possible standard deviation. (The term *minimum variance portfolio* is standard in the literature, and we will use that term. Perhaps *minimum standard deviation* would actually be better, because standard deviation, not variance, is measured on the horizontal axis of Figure 11.3.)

3. An investor considering a portfolio of Slowpoke and Supertech faces an **opportunity set** or **feasible set** represented by the curved line in Figure 11.3. That is, the investor can

achieve any point on the curve by selecting the appropriate mix between the two securities. He or she cannot achieve any points above the curve because the investor cannot increase the return on the individual securities, decrease the standard deviations of the securities, or decrease the correlation between the two securities. Neither can the investor achieve points below the curve because he or she cannot lower the returns on the individual securities, increase the standard deviations of the securities, or increase the correlation. (Of course, the investor would not want to achieve points below the curve, even if it were possible to do so.)

Were the investor relatively tolerant of risk, he or she might choose portfolio 3. (In fact, the investor could even choose the end point by investing all his or her money in Supertech.) An investor with less tolerance for risk might choose point 2. An investor wanting as little risk as possible would choose MV, the portfolio with minimum variance or minimum standard deviation.

4. Note that the curve is backward bending between the Slowpoke point and MV. This indicates that, for a portion of the feasible set, standard deviation actually decreases as one increases expected return. Students frequently ask, "How can an increase in the proportion of the risky security, Supertech, lead to a reduction in the risk of the portfolio?"

This surprising finding is due to the diversification effect. The returns on the two securities are negatively correlated. One security tends to go up when the other goes down. Thus, an addition of a small amount of Supertech acts as a hedge to a portfolio composed only of Slowpoke. The risk of the portfolio is reduced, implying a backward bending curve. Actually, backward bending always occurs if $\rho \leq 0$. It may or may not occur when $\rho > 0$. Of course, the curve bends backward only for a portion of its length. As one continues to increase the percentage of Supertech in the portfolio, the high standard deviation of this security eventually causes the standard deviation of the entire portfolio to rise.

5. No investor would want to hold a portfolio with an expected return below that of the minimum variance portfolio. For example, no investor would choose portfolio 1. This portfolio has less expected return but more standard deviation than the minimum variance portfolio has. We say that portfolios such as portfolio 1 are *dominated* by the minimum variance portfolio.

Though the entire curve from Slowpoke to Supertech is called the *feasible set,* investors only consider the curve from MV to Supertech. Hence, the curve from MV to Supertech is called the **efficient set.**

Figure 11.3 represents the opportunity set when $\rho = -0.1639$. It is worthwhile to examine Figure 11.4, which shows different curves for different correlations. As can be seen, the lower the correlation, the more bend there is in the curve. This indicates that the diversification effect rises as ρ declines. The greatest bend occurs in the limiting case where $\rho = -1$. This is perfect negative correlation. While this extreme case where $\rho = -1$ seems to fascinate students, it has little practical importance. Most pairs of securities exhibit positive correlation. Strong negative correlation, let alone perfect negative correlation, is an unlikely occurrence indeed.[8]

Note that there is only one correlation between a pair of securities. We stated earlier that the correlation between Slowpoke and Supertech is -0.1639. Thus, the curve in Figure 11.4 representing this correlation is the correct one and the other curves should be viewed as merely hypothetical.

---

[8]A major exception occurs with derivative securities. For example, the correlation between a stock and a put option on the stock is generally strongly negative. Puts will be treated later in the text.

FIGURE 11.4

Opportunity Sets Composed of Holdings in Supertech and Slowpoke

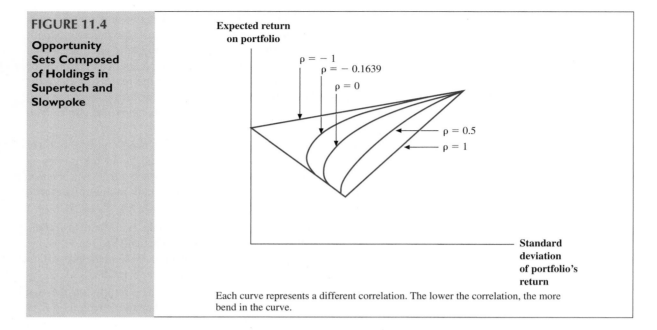

Each curve represents a different correlation. The lower the correlation, the more bend in the curve.

The graphs we examined are not mere intellectual curiosities. Rather, efficient sets can easily be calculated in the real world. As mentioned earlier, data on returns, standard deviations, and correlations are generally taken from past data, though subjective notions can be used to calculate the values of these statistics as well. Once the statistics have been determined, any one of a whole host of software packages can be purchased to generate an efficient set. However, the choice of the preferred portfolio within the efficient set is up to you. As with other important decisions like what job to choose, what house or car to buy, and how much time to allocate to this course, there is no computer program to choose the preferred portfolio.

Application to International Diversification

Research on diversification extends our discussion of historical average risks and returns in Chapter 11 to include foreign investment portfolios. It turns out that the feasible set looks like Figure 11.5, where points like *U* and *L* represent portfolios instead of individual stocks. Portfolio *U* represents 100 percent investment in Canadian equities and portfolio *L* represents 100 percent in foreign equities. The domestic stock portfolio is less risky than the foreign portfolio. Does this mean that Canadian portfolio managers should invest entirely in Canada?

The answer is no because the minimum variance portfolio with approximately 20 percent foreign content dominates portfolio *U,* the 100 percent domestic portfolio. Going from 0 percent to around 20 percent foreign content actually reduces portfolio standard deviation due to the diversification effect. However, portfolio MV is not necessarily optimal. Recognizing these points led pension managers to lobby successfully in 2005 for an end to foreign content restriction.[9]

---

[9]These data come from H. S. Marmer, "International Investing: A New Canadian Perspective," *Canadian Investment Review* (Spring 1991), pp. 47–53; and *Canadian Investment Review* (Winter 1998), pp. 49–51. B. Bruce, "Why Diversify?" *Canadian Investment Review* (Summer 2000), pp. 40–44, takes this case further, arguing for foreign content of 70 percent.

FIGURE 11.5

Efficient Frontier

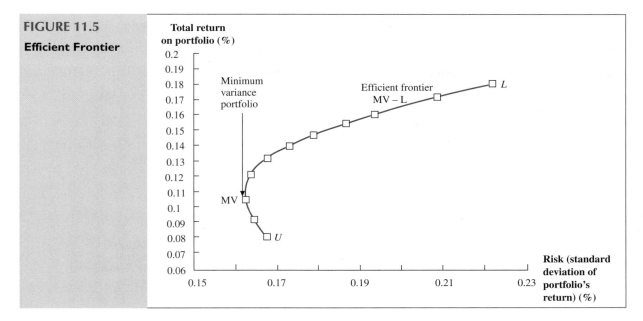

Another point worth pondering concerns the potential pitfalls of using only past data to estimate future returns and correlations. The stock markets of many foreign countries— such as Korea, Thailand, and Indonesia—had phenomenal growth in the early 1990s. Thus, a graph like Figure 11.5 makes a large investment in these foreign markets seem attractive. However, abnormally high returns and low correlations cannot be sustained forever, and the Asian stock markets suffered major declines in the late 1990s. To avoid the forecaster's trap inherent in blind reliance on historical returns, some subjectivity must be used when forecasting future expected returns and correlations. Scenario analysis is a useful tool here.

? Concept Question

• **What is the relationship between the shape of the efficient set for two assets and the correlation between the two assets?**

11.5 The Efficient Set for Many Securities

The previous discussion concerned two securities. We found that a simple curve sketched out all the possible portfolios. Because investors generally hold more than two securities, we should examine the same feasible set when more than two securities are held. The shaded area in Figure 11.6 represents the opportunity set or feasible set when many securities are considered. The shaded area represents all the possible combinations of expected return and standard deviation for a portfolio. For example, in a universe of 100 securities, point 1 might represent a portfolio of, say, 40 securities. Point 2 might represent a portfolio of 80 securities. Point 3 might represent a different set of 80 securities or the same 80 securities held in different proportions. Obviously, the combinations are virtually endless. However, note that all possible combinations fit into a confined region. No security or combination of securities can fall outside of the shaded region. That is, no one can choose a portfolio with an expected return above that given by the shaded region because

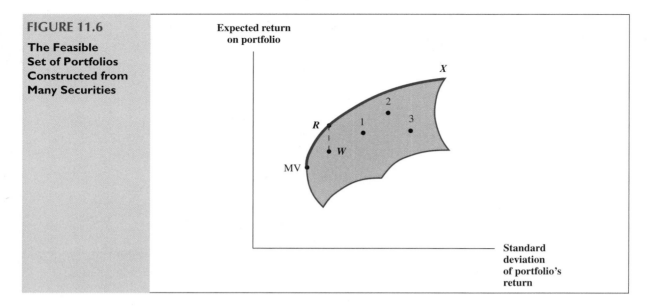

FIGURE 11.6

The Feasible Set of Portfolios Constructed from Many Securities

the expected returns on individual securities cannot be altered. Furthermore, no one can choose a portfolio with a standard deviation below that given in the shaded area. Perhaps more surprisingly, no one can choose an expected return below that given in the curve. In other words, the capital markets actually prevent a self-destructive person from taking on a guaranteed loss.[10]

So far, Figure 11.6 is different from the earlier graphs. When only two securities are involved, all the combinations lie on a single curve. Conversely, with many securities the combinations cover an entire area. However, notice that an individual will want to be somewhere on the upper edge between MV and X. The upper edge, which we indicate in Figure 11.6 by a thick line, is called the *efficient set*. Any point below the efficient set would receive less expected return and the same standard deviation as a point on the efficient set. For example, consider R on the efficient set and W directly below it. If W contains the risk you desire, you should choose R instead in order to receive a higher expected return.

In the final analysis, Figure 11.6 is quite similar to Figure 11.3. The efficient set in Figure 11.3 runs from MV to Supertech. It contains various combinations of the securities Supertech and Slowpoke. The efficient set in Figure 11.6 runs from MV to X. It contains various combinations of many securities. The fact that a whole shaded area appears in Figure 11.6 but not in Figure 11.3 is not an important difference; no investor would choose any point below the efficient set in Figure 11.6 anyway.

We mentioned earlier that an efficient set for two securities can be traced out easily in the real world. The task becomes more difficult when additional securities are included because the number of observations grows. For example, using subjective analysis to estimate expected returns and standard deviations for, say, 100 or 500 securities may very well become overwhelming, and the difficulties with correlations may be greater still. There are almost 5,000 correlations between pairs of securities from a universe of 100 securities.

---

[10]Of course, someone dead set on parting with his money can do so. For example, he can trade frequently without purpose, so that commissions more than offset the positive expected returns on the portfolio.

TABLE 11.4   Matrix Used to Calculate the Variance of a Portfolio

Stock	1	2	3	...	N
1	$X^2_1\sigma_1^2$	$X_1X_2\text{Cov}(R_1,R_2)$	$X_1X_3\text{Cov}(R_1,R_3)$		$X_1X_N\text{Cov}(R_1,R_N)$
2	$X_2X_1\text{Cov}(R_2,R_1)$	$X_2^2\sigma_2^2$	$X_2X_3\text{Cov}(R_2,R_3)$		$X_2X_N\text{Cov}(R_2,R_N)$
3	$X_3X_1\text{Cov}(R_3,R_1)$	$X_3X_2\text{Cov}(R_3,R_2)$	$X_3^2\sigma_3^2$		$X_3X_N\text{Cov}(R_3,R_N)$
⋮					
N	$X_NX_1\text{Cov}(R_N,R_1)$	$X_NX_2\text{Cov}(R_N,R_2)$	$X_NX_3\text{Cov}(R_N,R_3)$		$X_N^2\sigma_N^2$

- The variance of the portfolio is the sum of the terms in all the boxes.
- σi is the standard deviation of stock i.
- $\text{Cov}(R_i, R_j)$ is the covariance between stock i and stock j.
- Terms involving the standard deviation of a single security appear on the diagonal. Terms involving covariance between two securities appear off the diagonal.

Though much of the mathematics of efficient set computation had been derived in the 1950s,[11] the high cost of computer time restricted application of the principles. In recent years, the cost has been drastically reduced and a number of software packages allow the calculation of an efficient set for portfolios of moderate size. By all accounts, these packages sell quite briskly, so that our discussion above would appear to be important in practice.

Variance and Standard Deviation in a Portfolio of Many Assets

Earlier, we calculated the formulas for variance and standard deviation in the two-asset case. Because we considered a portfolio of many assets in Figure 11.6, it is worthwhile to calculate the formulas for variance and standard deviation in the many-asset case. The formula for the variance of a portfolio of many assets can be viewed as an extension of the formula for the variance of two assets.

To develop the formula, we employ the same type of matrix that we used in the two-asset case. This matrix is displayed in Table 11.4. Assuming that there are N assets, we write the numbers 1 through N on the horizontal axis and 1 through N on the vertical axis. This creates a matrix of $N \times N = N^2$ boxes.

Consider, for example, the box with a horizontal dimension of 2 and a vertical dimension of 3. The term in the box is $X_3X_2\text{Cov}(R_3, R_2)$. X_3 and X_2 are the percentages of the entire portfolio that are invested in the third asset and the second asset, respectively. For example, if an individual with a portfolio of $1,000 invests $100 in the second asset, $X_2 = 10\%$ (or $100/$1,000). $\text{Cov}(R_3, R_2)$ is the covariance between the returns on the third asset and the returns on the second asset. Next, note the box with a horizontal dimension of 3 and a vertical dimension of 2. The term in the box is $X_2X_3\text{Cov}(R_2, R_3)$. Because $\text{Cov}(R_3, R_2) = \text{Cov}(R_2, R_3)$, the two boxes have the same value. The second security and the third

---

[11]The classic is Harry Markowitz, *Portfolio Selection* (New York: John Wiley & Sons, 1959). Markowitz shared the Nobel Prize in Economics in 1990 (with William Sharpe) for his work on modern portfolio theory.

TABLE 11.5
Number of Variance and Covariance Terms as a Function of the Number of Stocks in the Portfolio

Number of Stocks in Portfolio	Total Number of Terms	Number of Variance Terms (number of terms on diagonal)	Number of Covariance Terms (number of terms off diagonal)
1	1	1	0
2	4	2	2
3	9	3	6
10	100	10	90
100	10,000	100	9,900
$\vdots$	$\vdots$		
N	N^2	N	$N^2 - N$

In a large portfolio, the number of terms involving covariance between two securities is much greater than the number of terms involving variance of a single security.

security make up one pair of stocks. In fact, every pair of stocks appears twice in the table: once in the lower left-hand side and once in the upper right-hand side.

Suppose that the vertical dimension equals the horizontal dimension. For example, the term in the box is $X_1^2\sigma_1^2$ when both dimensions are 1. Here, σ_1^2 is the variance of the return on the first security.

Thus, the diagonal terms in the matrix contain the variances of the different stocks. The off-diagonal terms contain the covariances. Table 11.5 relates the numbers of diagonal and off-diagonal elements to the size of the matrix. The number of diagonal terms (number of variance terms) is always the same as the number of stocks in the portfolio. The number of off-diagonal terms (number of covariance terms) rises much faster than the number of diagonal terms. For example, a portfolio of 100 stocks has 9900 covariance terms. Since the variance of a portfolio's returns is the sum of all the boxes, it follows that:

> The variance of the return on a portfolio with many securities is more dependent on the covariances between the individual securities than on the variances of the individual securities.

In a large portfolio, the number of terms involving covariance between two securities is much greater than the number of terms involving variance of a single security.

? Concept Questions
- What is the formula for the variance of a portfolio for many assets?
- How can the formula be expressed in terms of a box or matrix?

11.6 Diversification: An Example

The above point can be illustrated by altering the matrix in Table 11.4 slightly. Suppose that we make the following three assumptions:

1. All securities possess the same variance, which we write as $\overline{var}$ In other words, $\sigma_i^2 = \overline{var}$ for every security.

TABLE 11.6   Matrix Used to Calculate the Variance of a Portfolio*

Stock	1	2	3	...	N
1	$(1/N^2)\,\overline{\text{var}}$	$(1/N^2)\,\overline{\text{cov}}$	$(1/N^2)\,\overline{\text{cov}}$		$(1/N^2)\,\overline{\text{cov}}$
2	$(1/N^2)\,\overline{\text{cov}}$	$(1/N^2)\,\overline{\text{var}}$	$(1/N^2)\,\overline{\text{cov}}$		$(1/N^2)\,\overline{\text{cov}}$
3	$(1/N^2)\,\overline{\text{cov}}$	$(1/N^2)\,\overline{\text{cov}}$	$(1/N^2)\,\overline{\text{var}}$		$(1/N^2)\,\overline{\text{cov}}$
⋮					
N	$(1/N^2)\,\overline{\text{cov}}$	$(1/N^2)\,\overline{\text{cov}}$	$(1/N^2)\,\overline{\text{cov}}$		$(1/N^2)\,\overline{\text{var}}$

*When
  a. All securities possess the same variance, which we represent as $\overline{\text{var}}$.
  b. All pairs of securities possess the same covariance, which we represent as $\overline{\text{cov}}$.
  c. All securities are held in the same proportion, which is $1/N$.

2. All covariances in Table 11.4 are the same. We represent this uniform covariance as $\overline{\text{cov}}$. In other words, $\text{Cov}(R_i, R_j) = \overline{\text{cov}}$ for every pair of securities. It can easily be shown that $\overline{\text{var}} > \overline{\text{cov}}$.

3. All securities are equally weighted in the portfolio. Because there are N assets, the weight of each asset in the portfolio is $1/N$. In other words, $X_i = 1/N$ for each security i.

Table 11.6 is the matrix of variances and covariances under these three simplifying assumptions. Note that all of the diagonal terms are identical. Similarly, all of the off-diagonal terms are identical. As with Table 11.4, the variance of the portfolio is the sum of the terms of the boxes in Table 11.6. We know that there are N diagonal terms involving variance. Similarly, there are $N \times (N - 1)$ off-diagonal terms involving covariance. Summing across all the boxes in Table 11.6, we can express the variances of the portfolio as

$$\text{Variance of portfolio} = \underset{\substack{\text{Number of}\\ \text{diagonal}\\ \text{terms}}}{N} \times \underset{\substack{\text{Each}\\ \text{diagonal}\\ \text{term}}}{\left(\frac{1}{N^2}\right)\overline{\text{var}}} + \underset{\substack{\text{Number of}\\ \text{off-diagonal}\\ \text{terms}}}{N(N-1)} \times \underset{\substack{\text{Each}\\ \text{off-diagonal}\\ \text{term}}}{\left(\frac{1}{N^2}\right)\overline{\text{cov}}} \tag{11.10}$$

$$= \left(\frac{1}{N}\right)\overline{\text{var}} + \left(\frac{N^2 - N}{N^2}\right)\overline{\text{cov}}$$

$$= \left(\frac{1}{N}\right)\overline{\text{var}} + \left(1 - \frac{1}{N}\right)\overline{\text{cov}}$$

Equation (11.10) expresses the variance of our special portfolio as a weighted sum of the average security variance and the average covariance.[12] The intuition is confirmed when we increase the number of securities in the portfolio without limit. The variance of the portfolio becomes

$$\text{Variance of portfolio (when } N \to \infty) = \overline{\text{cov}} \tag{11.11}$$

---

[12]Equation (11.10) is actually a weighted average of the variance and covariance terms because the weights, $1/N$ and $1 - 1/N$, sum to 1.

This occurs because (1) the weight on the variance term, $1/N$, goes to 0 as N goes to infinity and (2) the weight on the covariance term, $1 - 1/N$, goes to 1 as N goes to infinity.

Equation (11.11) provides an interesting and important result. In our special portfolio, the variances of the individual securities completely vanish as the number of securities becomes large. However, the covariance terms remain. In fact, the variance of the portfolio becomes the average covariance, $\overline{cov}$. One often hears that one should diversify. You should not put all your eggs in one basket. The effect of diversification on the risk of a portfolio can be illustrated in this example. The variances of the individual securities are diversified away, but the covariance terms cannot be diversified away.

The fact that part, but not all, of one's risk can be diversified away should be explored. Consider Mr. Smith, who brings $1,000 to the roulette table at a casino. It would be very risky if he put all his money on one spin of the wheel. For example, imagine that he put the full $1,000 on red at the table. If the wheel showed red, he would get $2,000, but if the wheel showed black, he would lose everything. Suppose, instead, that he divided his money over 1000 different spins by betting $1 at a time on red. Probability theory tells us that he could count on winning about 50 percent of the time. In other words, he could count on pretty nearly getting all his original $1,000 back.[13]

Now, let's contrast this with our stock market example, which we illustrate in Figure 11.7. The variance of the portfolio with only one security is, of course, var, because the variance of a portfolio with one security is the variance of the security. The variance of the portfolio drops as more securities are added, which is evidence of the diversification effect. However, unlike Mr. Smith's roulette example, the portfolio's variance can never drop to zero. Rather it reaches a floor of $\overline{cov}$, which is the covariance of each pair of securities.[14]

Because the variance of the portfolio asymptotically approaches $\overline{cov}$, each additional security continues to reduce risk. Thus, if there were neither commissions nor other transactions costs, it could be argued that one can never achieve too much diversification. However, there is a cost to diversification in the real world. Commissions per dollar invested fall as one makes larger purchases in a single stock. Unfortunately, one must buy fewer shares of each security when buying more and more different securities. Comparing the costs and benefits of diversification, Meir Statman argues that a portfolio of about 30 stocks is needed to achieve optimal diversification. Sean Cleary and David Copp find that, for Canadian investors, the number of stocks needed is 30 to 50. This higher number is likely because Canadian stocks are more concentrated in a few industries.[15]

We mentioned earlier that $\overline{var}$ must be greater than $\overline{cov}$. Thus, the variance of a security's return can be broken down in the following way:

$$\begin{array}{ccccc} \text{Total risk of} & & \text{Portfolio} & & \text{Unsystematic or} \\ \text{individual security} & = & \text{risk} & + & \text{diversible risk} \\ (\overline{var}) & & (\overline{cov}) & & (\overline{var} - \overline{cov}) \end{array}$$

Total risk, which is $\overline{var}$ in our example, is the risk that one bears by holding one security only. *Portfolio risk* is the risk that one still bears after achieving full diversification, which is $\overline{cov}$ in our example. Portfolio risk is often called **systematic** or **market risk** as well.

---

[13]This example ignores the casino's cut.

[14]Though it is harder to show, this risk reduction effect also applies to the general case where variances and covariances are *not* equal.

[15]Meir Statman, "How Many Stocks Make a Diversified Portfolio?" *Journal of Financial and Quantitative Analysis* (September 1987); Sean Cleary and David Copp, "Diversification with Canadian Stocks: How Much Is Enough?" *Canadian Investment Review* (Fall 1999).

FIGURE 11.7

Relationship Between the Variance of a Portfolio's Return and the Number of Securities in the Portfolio

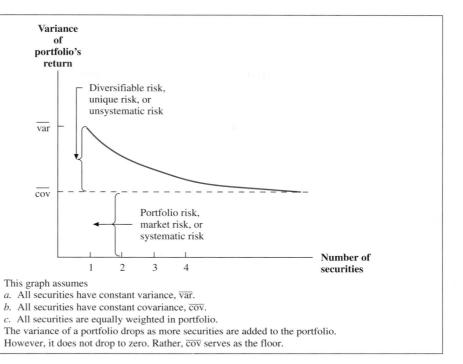

This graph assumes
a. All securities have constant variance, $\overline{var}$.
b. All securities have constant covariance, $\overline{cov}$.
c. All securities are equally weighted in portfolio.
The variance of a portfolio drops as more securities are added to the portfolio.
However, it does not drop to zero. Rather, $\overline{cov}$ serves as the floor.

Diversifiable, unique, or **unsystematic risk** is that risk that can be diversified away in a large portfolio, which must be ($\overline{var} - \overline{cov}$) by definition.

To an individual who selects a diversified portfolio, the total risk of an individual security is not important. When considering adding a security to a diversified portfolio, the individual cares about that portion of the risk of a security that cannot be diversified away. This risk can alternatively be viewed as the *contribution* of a security to the risk of an entire portfolio. We will talk later about the case where securities make different contributions to the risk of the entire portfolio.

Risk and the Sensible Investor

Having gone to all this trouble to show that unsystematic risk disappears in a well-diversified portfolio, how do we know that investors even want such portfolios? Suppose they like risk and don't want it to disappear?

We must admit that, theoretically at least, this is possible, but we will argue that it does not describe what we think of as the typical investor. Our typical investor is **risk averse.** Risk-averse behaviour can be defined in many ways, but we prefer the following example: A fair gamble is one with zero expected return; a risk-averse investor would prefer to avoid fair gambles.

Why do investors choose well-diversified portfolios? Our answer is that they are risk averse, and risk-averse people avoid unnecessary risk, such as the unsystematic risk on a stock. If you do not think this is much of an answer to why investors choose well-diversified portfolios and avoid unsystematic risk, consider whether you would take on such a risk. For example, suppose you had worked all summer and had saved $5,000, which you intended to use for university expenses. Now, suppose someone came up to you and offered to flip a coin for the money: heads, you would double your money, and tails, you would lose it all.

Would you take such a bet? Perhaps you would, but the average investor would not. To induce the typical risk-averse investor to take a fair gamble, you must sweeten the pot. For example, you might need to raise the odds of winning from 50–50 to 70–30 or higher. The risk-averse investor can be induced to take fair gambles only if they are sweetened so that they become unfair to the investor's advantage.

Beyond risk aversion, the tremendous growth of mutual funds and exchange-traded funds in recent years strongly suggests that investors want diversified portfolios. *Mutual funds* pool funds from individual investors, allowing them to own units in large, diversified portfolios. Exchange-traded funds (ETFs) are trusts that track a market index such as the Standard & Poor's 500, the S&P/TSX 60, or the Nikkei. They trade on the New York Stock Exchange and the TSX. By holding such funds, individuals can achieve wide diversification across securities and markets around the world.

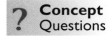

Concept Questions
- **What are the two components of the total risk of a security?**
- **Why doesn't diversification eliminate all risk?**
- **How is risk aversion defined?**

11.7 Riskless Borrowing and Lending

In constructing Figure 11.6, we assume that all the securities on the efficient set are risky. Alternatively, an investor could easily combine a risky investment with an investment in a riskless or risk-free security, such as an investment in Canada Treasury bills. This is illustrated in Example 11.3.

EXAMPLE 11.3

Zorana Sadiq is considering investing in the common stock of Princess Enterprises. In addition, Ms. Sadiq will either borrow or lend at the risk-free rate. The relevant parameters are

	Expected Return on Common Stock of Princess	Guaranteed Return on Risk-Free Asset
Return	14%	3%
Standard deviation	0.20	0

Suppose Ms. Sadiq chooses to invest a total of $1,000; $350 is invested in Princess Enterprises and $650 in the risk-free asset. The expected return on her total investment is simply a weighted average of the two returns:

Expected return on portfolio
composed of one riskless $= 0.069 = (0.35 \times 0.14) + (0.65 \times 0.03)$ **(11.12)**
and one risky asset

Because the expected return on the portfolio is a weighted average of the expected return on the risky asset (Princess Enterprises) and the risk-free return, the calculation is analogous to the way we treated two risky assets. In other words, Equation (11.3) applies here.

Using Equation (11.4), the formula for the variance of the portfolio can be written as

$$X^2_{\text{Princess}}\sigma^2_{\text{Princess}} + 2X_{\text{Princess}}X_{\text{Risk-free}}\sigma_{\text{Princess,Risk-free}} + X^2_{\text{Risk-free}}\sigma^2_{\text{Risk-free}}$$

However, by definition, the risk-free asset has no variability. Thus, both $\sigma_{Princess,Risk\text{-}free}$ and $\sigma^2_{Risk\text{-}free}$ are equal to zero, reducing the above expression to

$$\begin{matrix} \text{Variance of portfolio} \\ \text{composed of one} \\ \text{riskless and one} \\ \text{risky asset} \end{matrix} = X^2_{Princess}\sigma^2_{Princess} = (0.35)^2 \times (0.20)^2 = 0.0049 \qquad (11.13)$$

The standard deviation of the portfolio is

$$\begin{matrix} \text{Standard deviation of} \\ \text{portfolio composed} \\ \text{of one riskless and} \\ \text{one risky asset} \end{matrix} = X_{Princess}\sigma_{Princess} = 0.35 \times 0.20 = 0.07 \qquad (11.14)$$

The relationship between risk and return for one risky and one riskless asset can be seen in Figure 11.8. Ms. Sadiq's split of 35–65 percent between the two assets is represented on a *straight* line between the risk-free rate and a pure investment in Princess Enterprises. Note that, unlike the case of two risky assets, the opportunity set is straight, not curved.

Suppose that, alternatively, Ms. Sadiq borrows $200 at the risk-free rate. Combining this with her original sum of $1,000, she invests a total of $1,200 in Princess Enterprises. Her expected return would be

$$\begin{matrix} \text{Expected return on portfolio} \\ \text{formed by borrowing} \\ \text{to invest in risky asset} \end{matrix} = 16.2\% = 1.20 \times 0.14 + (-0.2) \times 0.03$$

Here, she invests 120 percent of her original investment of $1,000 by borrowing 20 percent of her original investment. Note that the return of 16.2 percent is greater than the 14 percent expected return on Princess Enterprises. This occurs because she is borrowing at 3 percent to invest in a security with an expected return greater than 3 percent.

The standard deviation is

$$\begin{matrix} \text{Standard deviation of portfolio formed} \\ \text{by borrowing to invest in risky asset} \end{matrix} = 1.20 \times 0.2 = 0.24$$

The standard deviation of 0.24 is greater than 0.20, the standard deviation of Princess Enterprises, because borrowing increases the variability of the investment. This investment also appears in Figure 11.8.

So far, we have assumed that Ms. Sadiq is able to borrow at the same rate at which she can lend.[16] Now let us consider the case where the borrowing rate is above the lending rate. The dotted line in Figure 11.8 illustrates the opportunity set for borrowing opportunities in this case. The dotted line is below the solid line because a higher borrowing rate lowers the expected return on the investment.

---

[16]Surprisingly, this appears to be a decent approximation because a large number of investors are able to borrow on margin when purchasing stocks. The borrowing rate on the margin is very near the riskless rate of interest, particularly for large investors. More will be said about this in a later chapter. Also note that portfolio weights can be negative when investors sell a stock short. Short selling involves borrowing the stock and selling it today with the plan to cover the short in the future by buying back the stock at a lower price. With short selling, the line in Figure 11.8 extends to the left of the vertical axis.

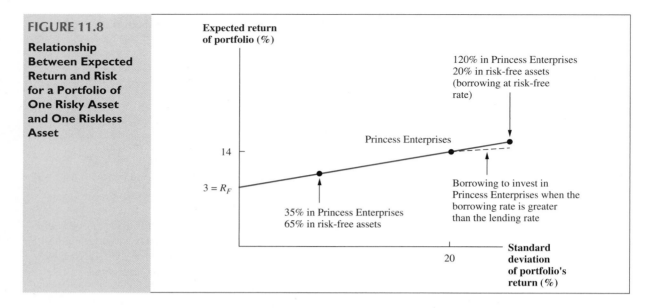

FIGURE 11.8

Relationship Between Expected Return and Risk for a Portfolio of One Risky Asset and One Riskless Asset

The Optimal Portfolio

The previous section analyzed a portfolio of one riskless asset and one risky asset. In reality, an investor is likely to combine an investment in the riskless asset with a portfolio of risky assets. This is illustrated in Figure 11.9.

Consider point Q, representing a portfolio of securities. Point Q is in the interior of the feasible set of risky securities. Let us assume the point represents a portfolio of 30 percent in BCE Inc. (BCE), 45 percent in Canadian Imperial Bank of Commerce (CIBC), and 25 percent in Inco. Individuals combining investments in Q with investments in the

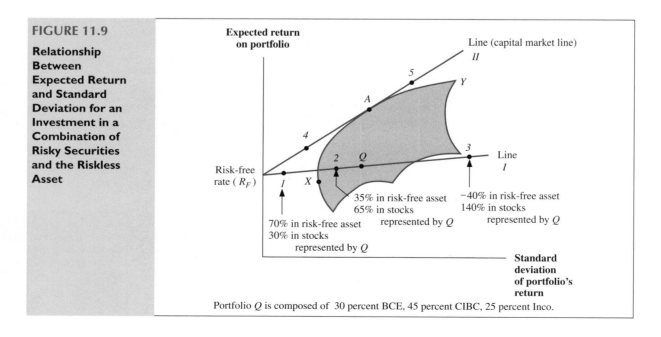

FIGURE 11.9

Relationship Between Expected Return and Standard Deviation for an Investment in a Combination of Risky Securities and the Riskless Asset

Portfolio Q is composed of 30 percent BCE, 45 percent CIBC, 25 percent Inco.

riskless asset would achieve points along the straight line from R_F to Q. We refer to this as line *I*. For example, point 1 represents a portfolio of 70 percent in the riskless asset and 30 percent in stocks represented by Q. An investor with $100 choosing point 1 as his portfolio would put $70 in the risk-free asset and $30 in Q. This can be restated as $70 in the riskless asset, $9 (or 0.3 × $30) in BCE, $13.50 (or 0.45 × $30) in CIBC, and $7.50 (or 0.25 × $30) in Inco. Point 2 also represents a portfolio of the risk-free asset and Q, with more (65 percent) being invested in Q.

Point 3 is obtained by borrowing to invest in Q. For example, an investor with $100 of his or her own would borrow $40 from the bank or broker in order to invest $140 in Q. This can be stated as borrowing $40 and contributing $100 of one's own money in order to invest $42 (or 0.3 × $140) in BCE, $63 (or 0.45 × $140) in CIBC, and $35 (or 0.25 × $140) in Inco.

Though any investor can obtain any point on line *I*, no point on the line is optimal. To see this, consider line *II*, a line running from R_F through *A*. Point *A* represents another portfolio of risky securities. Line *II* represents portfolios formed by combinations of the risk-free asset and the securities in *A*. Points between R_F and *A* are portfolios in which some money is invested in the riskless asset and the rest is placed in *A*. Points past *A* are achieved by borrowing at the riskless rate to buy more of *A* than one could with one's original funds alone.

As drawn, line *II* is tangent to the efficient set of risky securities. Whatever point an individual can obtain on line *I*, he or she can obtain a point with the same standard deviation and a higher expected return on line *II*. In fact, because line *II* is tangent to the efficient set, it provides the investor with the best possible opportunities. In other words, line *II*, which is frequently called the **capital market line,** can be viewed as the efficient set of all assets, both risky and riskless. An investor with a fair degree of risk aversion might choose a point between R_F and *A*, perhaps point 4. An individual with a lower degree of risk aversion might choose a point closer to *A* or even beyond *A*. For example, point 5 is achieved when an individual borrows money to increase an investment in *A*.

The graph illustrates an important point. With riskless borrowing and lending, the portfolio of risky assets held by any investor would always be point *A*. Regardless of the investor's tolerance for risk, he or she would never choose any other point on the efficient set of risky assets (represented by curve *XAY*) or any point in the interior of the feasible region. Rather, the investor would combine the securities of *A* with the riskless assets if he or she had high aversion to risk and would borrow the riskless asset to invest more funds in *A* if he or she had low aversion to risk.

This result establishes what financial economists call the **separation principle.** That is, the investor makes two separate decisions:

1. After estimating (a) the expected return and variances of individual securities and (b) the covariances between pairs of securities, the investor calculates the efficient set of risky assets, represented by curve *XAY* in Figure 11.9, and determines point *A*, the tangency between the risk-free rate and the efficient set of risky assets (curve *XAY*). Point *A* represents the portfolio of risky assets that the investor will hold. This point is determined solely from estimates of returns, variances, and covariances. No personal characteristics, such as degree of risk aversion, are needed in this step.

2. The investor must now determine how to combine point *A*, the portfolio of risky assets, with the riskless asset. He or she could invest some of the funds in the riskless asset and some in portfolio *A*. The investor would end up at a point on the line between R_F and *A* in this case. Alternatively, the investor could borrow at the risk-free rate and contribute some personal funds as well, investing the sum in portfolio *A*. He or she would end up at a

point on line *II* beyond *A*. The investor's position in the riskless asset (that is, the choice of where on the line he or she wants to be) is determined by internal characteristics, such as the investor's ability to tolerate risk.

? Concept Questions

- **What is the formula for the standard deviation of a portfolio composed of one risk-less and one risky asset?**
- **How does one determine the optimal portfolio among the efficient set of risky assets?**

11.8 Market Equilibrium

Definition of the Market Equilibrium Portfolio

The above analysis concerns one investor. Estimates of the expected returns and variances for individual securities and the covariances between pairs of securities are unique to this individual. Other investors would obviously have different estimates of these variables. However, the estimates might not vary much because all investors would be forming expectations from the same data on past price movement and other publicly available information.

Financial economists often imagine a world where all investors possess the same estimates of expected returns, variances, and covariances. Though this can never be literally true, it can be thought of as a useful simplifying assumption in a world where investors have access to similar sources of information. This assumption is called **homogeneous expectations.**[17]

If investors have homogenous expectations, Figure 11.9 would be the same for all individuals. That is, all investors would sketch out the same efficient set of risky assets because they would be working with the same inputs. This efficient set of risky assets is represented by the curve *XAY*. Because the same risk-free rate would apply to everyone, all investors would view point *A* as the portfolio of risky assets to be held.

This point *A* takes on great importance because all investors would purchase the risky securities that it represents. Those investors with a high degree of risk aversion might combine *A* with an investment in the riskless asset, achieving point 4, for example. Others with low aversion to risk might borrow to achieve, say, point 5. Because this is a very important conclusion, we restate it:

In a world with homogenous expectations, all investors would hold the portfolio of risky assets represented by point *A*.

If all investors choose the same portfolio of risky assets, it is possible to determine what that portfolio is. Common sense tells us that it is a market-value weighted portfolio of all existing securities. It is the **market portfolio.**[18]

In practice, financial economists use a broad-based index such as the S&P/TSX 60 as a proxy for the market portfolio. Of course, all investors do not hold the same portfolio in practice. However, we know that a large number of investors hold diversified portfolios,

---

[17]The assumption of homogeneous expectations states that all investors have the same beliefs concerning returns, variances, and covariances. It does not say that all investors have the same aversion to risk.

[18]By "market-value weighted," we mean that the percentage weight of each stock is the market value of the company's equity divided by the total market capitalization.

particularly when mutual funds or pension funds are included. A broad-based index is a good proxy for the highly diversified portfolios of many investors.

Definition of Risk When Investors Hold the Market Portfolio

The previous section states that many investors hold diversified portfolios similar to broad-based indexes. This result allows us to measure the risk of a security in the context of a diversified portfolio as the *beta* of the security. We illustrate beta in Example 11.4.

EXAMPLE 11.4

Consider the following possible returns on both the stock of Jelco Inc. and on the market:

State	Type of Economy	Return on Market (percent)	Return on Jelco, Inc. (percent)
I	Bull	15	25
II	Bull	15	15
III	Bear	−5	−5
IV	Bear	−5	−15

Though the return on the market has only two possible outcomes (15 percent and −5 percent), the return on Jelco has four possible outcomes. It is helpful to consider the expected return on a security for a given return on the market. Assuming each state is equally likely, we have

Type of Economy	Return on Market (percent)	Expected Return on Jelco, Inc. (percent)
Bull	15%	20% = 25% × ½ + 15% × ½
Bear	−5%	−10% = −5% × ½ + (−15%) × ½

Jelco Inc. responds to market movements because its expected return is greater in bullish states than in bearish states. We now calculate exactly how responsive the security is to market movements. The market's return in a bullish economy is 20 percent [15% − (−5%)] greater than the market's return in a bearish economy. However, the expected return on Jelco in a bullish economy is 30 percent [20% − (−10%)] greater than its expected return in a bearish state. Thus, Jelco Inc. has a responsiveness coefficient of 1.5 (30%/20%).

This relationship appears in Figure 11.10. The returns for both Jelco and the market in each state are plotted as four points. In addition, we plot the expected return on the security for each of the two possible returns on the market. These two points, each of which we designate by an X, are joined by a line called the **characteristic line** of the security. The slope of the line is 1.5, the number calculated in the previous paragraph. This responsiveness coefficient of 1.5 is the **beta** of Jelco.

The interpretation of beta from Figure 11.10 is intuitive. The graph tells us that the returns of Jelco are magnified 1.5 times over those of the market. When the market does well, Jelco's stock is expected to do even better. When the market does poorly, Jelco's stock is expected to do even worse. Now imagine an individual with a portfolio near that of the market who is considering the addition of Jelco to his portfolio. Because of Jelco's *magnification factor* of 1.5, he will view this stock as contributing much to the risk of the portfolio. (We will show shortly that the beta of the average security in the market is 1.) Jelco contributes more to the risk of a large, diversified portfolio than does an average security because Jelco is more responsive to movements in the market.

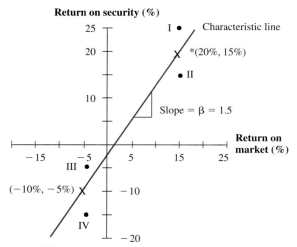

FIGURE 11.10

Performance of Jelco Inc. and the Market Portfolio

The two points marked X represent the expected return on Jelco for each possible outcome of the market portfolio. The expected return on Jelco is positively related to the return on the market. Because the slope is 1.5, we say that Jelco's beta is 1.5. Beta measures the responsiveness of the security's return to movement in the market. *(20%, 15%) refers to the point where the return on the security is 20 perecent and the return on the market is 15 percent.

Further insight can be gleaned by examining securities with negative betas. One should view these securities as either hedges or insurance policies. The security is expected to do well when the market does poorly and vice versa. Because of this, adding a negative-beta security to a large, diversified portfolio actually reduces the risk of the portfolio.[19]

Table 11.7 presents empirical estimates of betas for individual securities. As can be seen, some securities are more responsive to the market than others. For example, Nortel Networks (NT) has a beta of 3.05. This means that, for every 1 percent movement in the market,[20] Nortel is expected to move 3.05 percent in the same direction. Conversely, EPCOR Power has a beta of only 0.11. This means that, for every 1 percent movement in the market, EPCOR Power is expected to move 0.11 percent in the same direction.

We can summarize our discussion of beta by saying:

Beta measures the responsiveness of a security to movements in the market portfolio.

The Formula for Beta

Our discussion so far has stressed the intuition behind beta. The actual definition of beta is

$$\beta_i = \frac{\text{Cov}(R_i, R_M)}{\sigma^2(R_M)} \qquad (11.15)$$

where $\text{Cov}(R_i, R_M)$ is the covariance between the return on asset i and the return on the market portfolio and $\sigma^2(R_M)$ is the variance of the market.

One useful property is that the average beta across all securities, when weighted by the proportion of each security's market value to that of the market portfolio, is 1. That is,

$$\sum_{i=1}^{N} X_i\beta_i = 1 \qquad (11.16)$$

---

[19]Unfortunately, empirical evidence shows that virtually no stocks have negative betas.

[20]Table 11.7 uses the S&P/TSX 60 as the proxy for the market portfolio and obtains betas from the *Financial Post* Investor Suite. Other sources include Bloomberg and Yahoo Finance.

TABLE 11.7
Estimates of Beta for Selected Individual Stocks

Stock	Beta
High-Beta Stocks	
Research in Motion	2.21
Nortel Networks	3.05
Average-beta Stocks	
Bank of Nova Scotia	0.56
Investors Group	0.88
Petro-Canada	0.82
Rogers Communication	1.41
Low-beta stocks	
Canadian Utilities	0.29
Enbridge	0.21
EPCOR Power	0.11

Source: *Financial Post Advisor,* January 2007. Used wish permission.

where X_i is the proportion of security i's market value to that of the entire market and N is the number of securities in the market.

Equation (11.16) is intuitive, once you think about it. If you weight all securities by their market values, the resulting portfolio is the market. By definition, the beta of the market portfolio is 1. That is, for every 1 percent movement in the market, the market must move 1 percent—*by definition.*

A Test

We have put these questions on past corporate finance examinations:

1. What sort of investor rationally views the variance (or standard deviation) of an individual security's return as the security's proper measure of risk?

2. What sort of investor rationally views the beta of a security as the security's proper measure of risk?

A good answer might be something like the following:

> A rational, risk-averse investor views the variance (or standard deviation) of her portfolio's return as the proper measure of the risk of her portfolio. If for some reason or another the investor can hold only one security, the variance of that security's return becomes the variance of the portfolio's return. Hence, the variance of the security's return is the security's proper measure of risk.
>
> If an individual holds a diversified portfolio, she still views the variance (or standard deviation) of her portfolio's return as the proper measure of the risk of her portfolio. However, she is no longer interested in the variance of each individual security's return. Rather, she is interested in the contribution of an individual security to the variance of the portfolio.

Under the assumption of homogeneous expectations, all individuals hold the market portfolio. Thus, we measure risk as the contribution of an individual security to the variance of the market portfolio. This contribution, when standardized properly, is the beta of the security. While very few investors hold the market portfolio exactly, many hold reasonably diversified portfolios. These portfolios are close enough to the market portfolio so that the beta of a security is likely to be a reasonable measure of its risk.

? Concept Questions

- If all investors have homogeneous expectations, what portfolio of risky assets do they hold?
- What is the formula for beta?
- Why is beta the appropriate measure of risk for a single security in a large portfolio?

11.9 Relationship Between Risk and Expected Return (CAPM)

It is commonplace to argue that the expected return on an asset should be positively related to its risk. That is, individuals will hold a risky asset only if its expected return compensates for its risk. In this section, we first estimate the expected return on the stock market as a whole. Next, we estimate expected returns on individual securities.

Expected Return on Market

Financial economists frequently argue that the expected return on the market can be represented as:

$$\overline{R}_M = R_F + \text{Risk premium}$$

In words, the expected return on the market is the sum of the risk-free rate plus some compensation for the risk inherent in the market portfolio. Note that the equation refers to the *expected* return on the market, not the actual return in a particular month or year. Because stocks have risk, the actual return on the market over a particular period can, of course, be below R_F, or can even be negative.

Since investors want compensation for risk, the risk premium is presumably positive. But exactly how positive is it? It is generally argued that the best estimate for the risk premium in the future is the average risk premium in the past. As reported in Chapter 10, the expected return on common stocks was 11.10 percent over 1957–2006. The average risk-free rate over the same time interval was 6.57 percent. Thus, the average difference between the two was 4.53 percent (11.10% − 6.57%). Financial economists find this to be a useful estimate of the difference to occur in the future. We will use it frequently in this text.[21]

For example, if the risk-free rate, generally estimated by the yield on a one-year Treasury bill, is 5 percent, the expected return on the market is

$$5\% + 4.53\% = 9.53\%$$

Expected Return on Individual Security

Now that we have estimated the expected return on the market as a whole, what is the expected return on an individual security? We have argued that the beta of a security is the appropriate measure of risk in a large, diversified portfolio. Since most investors are diversified, the expected return on a security should be positively related to its beta. This is illustrated in Figure 11.11.

Actually, financial economists can be more precise about the relationship between expected return and beta. They posit that, under plausible conditions, the relationship between expected return and beta can be represented by the following equation.[22]

Capital Asset Pricing Model:

$\overline{R}$	=	R_F	+	β	$\times$	$(\overline{R}_M - R_F)$	(11.17)
Expected return on a security	=	Risk-free rate	+	Beta of the security	$\times$	Difference between expected return on market and risk-free rate	

---

[21]This is not the only way to estimate the market-risk premium. In fact, there are several useful ways to estimate the market-risk premium. One could argue that the long-term government bond return is the best measure of the long-term historical risk-free rate. With this empirical version of the CAPM, one would use the current long-term government bond return to estimate the current risk-free rate.

[22]This relationship was first proposed independently by John Lintner and William F. Sharpe.

FIGURE 11.11

Relationship Between Expected Return on an Individual Security and Beta of the Security

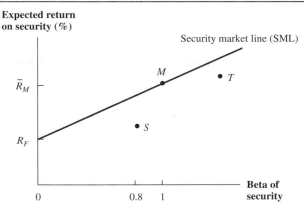

The Security Market Line (SML) is the graphical depiction of the capital asset pricing model (CAPM).
The expected return on a stock with a beta of 0 is equal to the risk-free rate.
The expected return on a stock with a beta of 1 is equal to the expected return on the market.

This formula, which is called the **capital asset pricing model** (or CAPM for short), implies that the expected return on a security is linearly related to its beta. Since the average return on the market has been higher than the average risk-free rate over long periods of time, $\overline{R}_M - R_F$ is presumably positive. Thus, the formula implies that the expected return on a security is *positively* related to its beta. The formula can be illustrated by assuming a few special cases:

- *Assume that* $\beta = 0$. Here $\overline{R} = R_F$, that is, the expected return on the security is equal to the risk-free rate. Because a security with zero beta has no relevant risk, its expected return should equal the risk-free rate.
- *Assume that* $\beta = 1$. Equation (11.17) reduces to $\overline{R} = R_M$. That is, the expected return on the security is equal to the expected return on the market. This makes sense since the beta of the market portfolio is also 1.

Formula (11.17) can be represented graphically by the upward sloping line in Figure 11.11. Note that the line begins at R_F and rises to $\overline{R}_M$ when beta is 1. This line graphically representing the CAPM is frequently called the **security market line** (SML).

As with any line, the SML has both a slope and an intercept. R_F, the risk-free rate, is the intercept. Because the beta of a security is the horizontal axis, $R_M - R_F$ is the slope. The line will be upward sloping as long as the expected return on the market is greater than the risk-free rate. Because the market portfolio is a risky asset, theory suggests that its expected return is above the risk-free rate. In addition, the empirical evidence of the previous chapter showed that the average return per year on the market portfolio over the past 50 years was 4.53 percent above the risk-free rate.

EXAMPLE 11.5

The stock of Aardvark Enterprises has a beta of 1.5 and that of Zebra Enterprises has a beta of 0.7. The risk-free rate is 5 percent, and the difference between the expected return on the market and the risk-free rate is 4.53 percent. The expected returns on the two securities are:

Expected Return for Aardvark:
$$10.44\% = 5\% + 1.2 \times 4.53\%$$ **(11.18)**

Expected Return for Zebra:
$$8.62\% = 5\% + 0.8 \times 4.53\%$$

Three additional points concerning the CAPM should be mentioned:

1. *Linearity.* The intuition behind an upwardly sloping curve is clear. Because beta is the appropriate measure of risk, high-beta securities should have an expected return above that of low-beta securities. However, both Figure 11.11 and Equation (11.17) show something more than an upwardly sloping curve; the relationship between expected return and beta corresponds to a *straight* line.

   It is easy to show that the line of Figure 11.11 is straight. To see this, consider security *S* with, say, a beta of 0.8. This security is represented by a point below the security market line in the figure. Any investor could duplicate the beta of security *S* by buying a portfolio with 20 percent in the risk-free asset and 80 percent in a security with a beta of 1. However, the homemade portfolio would itself lie on the SML. In other words, the portfolio dominates security *S* because the portfolio has a higher expected return and the same beta.

   Now consider security *T* with, say, a beta greater than 1. This security is also below the SML in Figure 11.11. Any investor could duplicate the beta of security *T* by borrowing to invest in a security with a beta of 1. This portfolio must also lie on the SML, thereby dominating security *T*.

   Because no one would hold either *S* or *T,* their stock prices would drop. This price adjustment would raise the expected returns on the two securities. The price adjustment would continue until the two securities lay on the security market line. The preceding example considered two overpriced stocks and a straight SML. Securities lying above the SML are *underpriced.* Their prices must rise until their expected returns lie on the line. If the SML is itself curved, many stocks would be mispriced. In equilibrium, all securities would be held only when prices changed so that the SML became straight. In other words, linearity would be achieved.

2. *Portfolios as well as securities.* Our discussion of the CAPM considered individual securities. Does the relationship in Figure 11.11 and Equation (11.17) hold for portfolios as well?

   Yes. To see this, consider a portfolio formed by investing equally in our two securities, Aardvark and Zebra. The expected return on the portfolio is

   Expected Return on Portfolio:
   $$9.53\% = 0.5 \times 10.44\% + 0.5 \times 8.62\% \qquad \textbf{(11.19)}$$

   The beta of the portfolio is simply a weighted average of the betas of the two securities. Thus we have

   Beta of Portfolio:
   $$1.0 = 0.5 \times 1.2 + 0.5 \times 0.8$$

   Under the CAPM, the expected return on the portfolio is

   $$9.53\% = 5\% + 1.0 \times 4.53\% \qquad \textbf{(11.20)}$$

   Because the expected return in (11.19) is the same as the expected return in (11.20), the example shows that the CAPM holds for portfolios as well as for individual securities.

3. *A potential confusion.* Students often confuse the SML in Figure 11.11 with line *II* in Figure 11.9. Actually, the lines are quite different. Line *II* traces the efficient set of portfolios formed from both risky assets and the riskless asset. Each point on the line represents an entire portfolio. Point *A* is a portfolio composed entirely of risky assets. Every other point on the line represents a portfolio of the securities in *A* combined with

the riskless asset. The axes on Figure 11.9 are the expected return on a *portfolio* and the standard deviation of a *portfolio*. Individual securities do not lie along line *II*.

The SML in Figure 11.11 relates expected return to beta. Figure 11.11 differs from Figure 11.9 in at least two ways. First, beta appears in the horizontal axis of Figure 11.11, but standard deviation appears in the horizontal axis of Figure 11.9. Second, the SML in Figure 11.11 holds both for all individual securities and for all possible portfolios, whereas line *II* in Figure 11.9 holds only for efficient portfolios.

We stated earlier that, under homogeneous expectations, point *A* in Figure 11.9 becomes the market portfolio. In this situation, line *II* is referred to as the capital market line (CML).

? Concept Questions

- **Why is the SML a straight line?**
- **What is the capital asset pricing model?**
- **What are the differences between the capital market line and the security market line?**

11.10   SUMMARY AND CONCLUSIONS

This chapter sets forth the fundamentals of modern portfolio theory and the pricing of capital assets. Our basic points are these:

1. This chapter shows us how to calculate the expected return and variance for individual securities, and the covariance and correlation for pairs of securities. Given these statistics, the expected return and variance for a portfolio of two securities *A* and *B* can be written as

$$\text{Expected return on portfolio} = X_A \overline{R}_A + X_B \overline{R}_B$$
$$\text{Var(portfolio)} = X_A^2 \sigma_A^2 + 2 X_A X_B \sigma_{AB} + X_B^2 \sigma_B^2$$

2. In our notation, *X* stands for the proportion of a security in one's portfolio. By varying *X*, one can trace out the efficient set of portfolios. We graphed the efficient set for the two-asset case as a curve, pointing out that the degree of curvature or bend in the graph reflects the diversification effect: The lower the correlation between the two securities, the greater the bend. The same general shape of the efficient set holds in a world of many assets.

3. Just as the formula for variance in the two-asset case is computed from a 2×2 matrix, the variance formula is computed from an $N \times N$ matrix in the *N*-asset case. We show that, with a large number of assets, there are many more covariance terms than variance terms in the matrix. In fact, the variance terms are effectively diversified away in a large portfolio but the covariance terms are not. Thus, a diversified portfolio can only eliminate some, but not all, of the risk of the individual securities.

4. The efficient set of risky assets can be combined with riskless borrowing and lending. In this case, a rational investor will always choose to hold the portfolio of risky securities represented by point *A* in Figure 11.9. Then he or she can either borrow or lend at the riskless rate to achieve any desired point on line *II* in the figure.

5. The contribution of a security to the risk of a large, well-diversified portfolio is proportional to the covariance of the security's return with the market's return. This contribution, when standardized, is called the beta. The beta of a security can also be interpreted as the responsiveness of a security's return to that of the market.

6. The CAPM states that

$$\overline{R} = R_F + \beta(\overline{R}_M - R_F)$$

In other words, the expected return on a security is positively (and linearly) related to the security's beta.

KEY TERMS

Beta 315
Capital asset pricing model
  (CAPM) 319
Capital market line 313
Characteristic line 315
Correlation 291
Covariance 291

Diversifiable (unique)
  (unsystematic) risk 309
Efficient set 301
Homogeneous
  expectations 314
Market portfolio 314
Opportunity (feasible) set 300

Portfolio 294
Risk averse 309
Security market line
  (SML) 319
Separation principle 313
Systematic (market) risk 308

SUGGESTED READING

The capital asset pricing model was originally published in two classic articles:

W. F. Sharpe. "Capital Asset Prices: A Theory of Market Equilibrium Under Conditions of Risk." *Journal of Finance* (September 1964). (William F. Sharpe shared the Nobel Prize in economics in 1990 with Harry Markowitz for his development of CAPM.)

J. Lintner. "Security Prices, Risk and Maximal Gains from Diversification." *Journal of Finance* (December 1965).

The seminal influence of Harry Markowitz is described in:
"Travels along the Efficient Frontier," *Dow Jones Asset Management* (May/June 1997).

Canadian tests of the capital asset pricing model are reviewed in current investment texts:

Z. Bodie, A. Kane, A. Marcus, S. Perrakis, and P. Ryan. *Investments.* 5th Canadian ed. Whitby, Ontario: McGraw-Hill Ryerson, 2005.

W. F. Sharpe, G. F. Alexander, J. V. Bailey, and D. J. Fowler. *Investments.* 3rd Canadian ed. Scarborough, Ontario: Prentice Hall Canada, 2000.

The Canadian Investment Review *is a source for less technical articles on asset pricing.*

QUESTIONS & PROBLEMS

Expected Return, Variance, and Covariance

11.1   You own a portfolio that has $1,200 invested in stock *A* and $1,900 invested in stock *B*. If the expected returns on these stocks are 11 percent and 16 percent, respectively, what is the expected return on the portfolio?

11.2   You own a portfolio that is 50 percent invested in stock *X,* 30 percent in stock *Y,* and 20 percent in stock *Z.* The expected returns on these three stocks are 11 percent, 17 percent, and 14 percent, respectively. What is the expected return on the portfolio?

11.3   You have $10,000 to invest in a stock portfolio. Your choices are stock *X* with an expected return of 14 percent and stock *Y* with an expected return of 9 percent. If your goal is to create a portfolio with an expected return of 12.2 percent, how much money will you invest in stock *X?* In stock *Y?*

11.4   Based on the following information, calculate the expected return and standard deviation for the two stocks:

State of Economy	Probability of State of Economy	Rate of Return If State Occurs Stock A	Stock B
Recession	.10	.06	−.20
Normal	.60	.07	.13
Boom	.30	.11	.33

11.5   A portfolio is invested 20 percent in stock *G,* 70 percent in stock *J,* and 10 percent in stock *K.* The expected returns on these stocks are 8 percent, 15 percent, and 24 percent, respectively. What is the portfolio's expected return? How do you interpret your answer?

EXCEL

11.6   Based on the following information, calculate the expected return and standard deviation:

State of Economy	Probability of State of Economy	Rate of Return If State Occurs
Depression	.10	−.045
Recession	.20	.044
Normal	.50	.120
Boom	.20	.207

11.7   Consider the following information:

State of Economy	Probability of State of Economy	Rate of Return If State Occurs		
		Stock A	Stock B	Stock C
Boom	.70	.07	.15	.33
Bust	.30	.13	.03	−.06

a. What is the expected return on an equally weighted portfolio of these three stocks?

b. What is the variance of a portfolio invested 20 percent each in A and B, and 60 percent in C?

Portfolios

11.8   You own a portfolio equally invested in a risk-free asset and two stocks. If one of the stocks has a beta of 1.9 and the total portfolio is equally as risky as the market, what must the beta be for the other stock in your portfolio?

11.9   Using information from the previous chapter about capital market history, determine the return on a portfolio that is equally invested in large-company stocks and long-term government bonds. What is the return on a portfolio that is equally invested in small company stocks and Treasury bills?

EXCEL

11.10   Consider the following information about three stocks:

State of Economy	Probability of State of Economy	Rate of Return If State Occurs		
		Stock A	Stock B	Stock C
Boom	.40	.20	.35	.60
Normal	.40	.15	.12	.05
Bust	.20	.01	−.25	−.50

a. If your portfolio is invested 40 percent each in A and B and 20 percent in C, what is the portfolio expected return? The variance? The standard deviation?

b. If the expected T-bill rate is 3.80 percent, what is the expected risk premium on the portfolio?

c. If the expected inflation rate is 3.50 percent, what are the approximate and exact expected real returns on the portfolio? What are the approximate and exact expected real risk premiums on the portfolio?

EXCEL

11.11   You have $100,000 to invest in a portfolio containing stock X, stock Y, and a risk-free asset. You must invest all of your money. Your goal is to create a portfolio that has an expected return of 13.5 percent and that has only 70 percent of the risk of the overall market. If X has an expected return of 31 percent and a beta of 1.8, Y has an expected return of 20 percent and a beta of 1.3, and the risk-free rate is 7 percent, how much money will you invest in stock X? How do you interpret your answer?

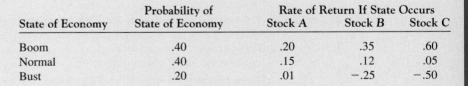

Visit us at www.mcgrawhill.ca/olc/ross

11.12 You want to create a portfolio equally as risky as the market, and you have $1,000,000 to invest. Given this information, fill in the rest of the following table:

Asset	Investment	Beta
Stock A	$200,000	.80
Stock B	$250,000	1.30
Stock C		1.50
Risk-free asset		

11.13 Security F has an expected return of 12 percent and a standard deviation of 34 percent per year. Security G has an expected return of 18 percent and a standard deviation of 50 percent per year.

   a. What is the expected return on a portfolio composed of 30 percent of security F and 70 percent of security G?

   b. If the correlation between the returns of security F and security G is 0.2, what is the standard deviation of the portfolio described in part (a)?

11.14 Based on the following information, calculate the expected return and standard deviation of each of the following stocks. Assume each state of the economy is equally likely to happen. What are the covariance and correlation between the returns of the two stocks?

State of Economy	Investment	Beta
Bear	.063	−.037
Normal	.105	.064
Bull	.156	.253

11.15 Suppose the expected returns and standard deviations of stocks A and B are $E(RA) = .15$, $E(RB) = .25$, $\sigma A = .40$, and $\sigma B = .65$, respectively.

   a. Calculate the expected return and standard deviation of a portfolio that is composed of 40 percent A and 60 percent B when the correlation between the returns on A and B is 0.5.

   b. Calculate the standard deviation of a portfolio that is composed of 40 percent A and 60 percent B when the correlation coefficient between the returns on A and B is −0.5.

   c. How does the correlation between the returns on A and B affect the standard deviation of the portfolio?

11.16 You have been provided the following data about the securities of three firms, the market portfolio, and the risk-free asset:

Security	Expected Return	Standard Deviation	Correlation*	Beta
Firm A	.13	.38	(i)	0.9
Firm B	.16	(ii)	.40	1.1
Firm C	.25	.65	.35	(iii)
The market portfolio	.15	.20	(iv)	(v)
The risk-free asset	.05	(vi)	(vii)	(viii)

*With the market portfolio

   a. Fill in the missing values in the table.

   b. Is the stock of firm A correctly priced according to the capital asset pricing model (CAPM)? What about the stock of firm B? Firm C? If these securities are not correctly priced, what is your investment recommendation for someone with a well-diversified portfolio?

11.17 There are three securities in the market. The following chart shows their possible payoffs:

State	Probability of Outcome	Return on Security 1	Return on Security 2	Return on Security 3
1	.10	.25	.25	.10
2	.40	.20	.15	.15
3	.40	.15	.20	.20
4	.10	.10	.10	.25

   a. What are the expected return and standard deviation of each security?

   b. What are the covariances and correlations between the pairs of securities?

   c. What are the expected return and standard deviation of a portfolio with half of its funds invested in security 1 and half in security 2?

   d. What are the expected return and standard deviation of a portfolio with half of its funds invested in security 1 and half in security 3?

   e. What are the expected return and standard deviation of a portfolio with half of its funds invested in security 2 and half in security 3?

   f. What do your answers in parts (a), (c), (d), and (e) imply about diversification?

CAPM

11.18 Is it possible that a risky asset could have a beta of zero? Explain. Based on the CAPM, what is the expected return on such an asset? Is it possible that a risky asset could have a negative beta? What does the CAPM predict about the expected return on such an asset? Can you give an explanation for your answer?

11.19 A stock has an expected return of 17 percent, a beta of 1.9, and the expected return on the market is 11 percent. What must the risk-free rate be?

11.20 A stock has a beta of 1.2 and an expected return of 16 percent. A risk-free asset currently earns 5 percent.

   a. What is the expected return on a portfolio that is equally invested in the two assets?

   b. If a portfolio of the two assets has a beta of .75, what are the portfolio weights?

   c. If a portfolio of the two assets has an expected return of 8 percent, what is its beta?

   d. If a portfolio of the two assets has a beta of 2.40, what are the portfolio weights? How do you interpret the weights for the two assets in this case? Explain.

11.21 Stock *Y* has a beta of 1.50 and an expected return of 17 percent. Stock *Z* has a beta of .80 and an expected return of 10.5 percent. If the risk-free rate is 5.5 percent and the market risk premium is 7.5 percent, are these stocks correctly priced? What would the risk-free rate be for the two stock to be correctly priced?

11.22 Using the CAPM, show that the ratio of the risk premiums on two assets is equal to the ratio of their betas.

11.23 The market portfolio has an expected return of 12 percent and a standard deviation of 10 percent. The risk-free rate is 5 percent.

   a. What is the expected return on a well-diversified portfolio with a standard deviation of 7 percent?

   b. What is the standard deviation of a well-diversified portfolio with an expected return of 20 percent?

11.24 A portfolio that combines the risk-free asset and the market portfolio has an expected return of 12 percent and a standard deviation of 18 percent. The risk-free rate is 5 percent, and the expected return on the market portfolio is 14 percent. Assume the capital asset pricing model holds. What expected rate of return would a security earn if it had a .45 correlation with the market portfolio and a standard deviation of 40 percent?

11.25 Suppose the risk-free rate is 6.3 percent and the market portfolio has an expected return of 14.8 percent. The market portfolio has a variance of .0498. Portfolio *Z* has a correlation coefficient with the market of .45 and a variance of .1783. According to the capital asset pricing model, what is the expected return on portfolio *Z?*

11.26 Consider the following two stocks:

	Beta	Expected Return
Murck Pharmaceutical	2.1	30%
Pizer Drug Corp	0.9	19%

Assume the capital asset pricing model holds. Based on the CAPM, what is the risk-free rate? What is the expected return on the market portfolio?

11.27 Assume the capital asset pricing model holds.
  a. Draw the security market line for the case where the expected market risk premium is 5 percent and the risk-free rate is 8 percent.
  b. Suppose that an asset has a beta of 1.1 and an expected return of 12 percent. Does the expected return of this asset lie above or below the security market line that you drew in part (a)? Is the security properly priced? If not, explain what will happen in this market.
  c. Suppose that an asset has a beta of 3 and an expected return of 31 percent. Does the expected return of this asset lie above or below the security market line that you drew in part (a)? Is the security properly priced? If not, explain what will happen in this market.

11.28 Suppose the expected return on the market portfolio is 15.1 percent and the risk-free rate is 4.3 percent. Solomon Inc. stock has a beta of 1.8. Assume the capital asset pricing model holds.
  a. What is the expected return on Solomon's stock?
  b. If the risk-free rate decreases to 3.5 percent, what is the expected return on Solomon's stock?

11.29 You have access to the following data concerning the Durham Company and the market portfolio:

  Variance of returns on the market portfolio = 0.05321

  Covariance between the returns on Durham and the market portfolio = 0.0516

  The expected market risk premium is 11.3 percent and the expected return on Treasury bills is 4.9 percent.
  a. Write the equation of the security market line.
  b. What is the required return on Durham Company's stock?

11.30 Johnson Paint stock has an expected return of 19 percent and a beta of 3.5, while Williamson Tire stock has an expected return of 15 percent and a beta of 2.6. Assume the capital asset pricing model holds. What is the expected return on the market? What is the risk-free rate?

11.31 Is the following statement true or false? Explain.

  A risky security cannot have an expected return that is less than the risk-free rate because no risk-averse investor would be willing to hold this asset in equilibrium.

11.32 There are two stocks in the market: stock *A* and stock *B*. The price of stock *A* today is $55. The price of stock *A* next year will be $40 if the economy is in a recession, $60 if the economy is normal, and $70 if the economy is expanding. The probabilities of recession, normal times, and expansion are 0.1, 0.8, and 0.1, respectively. Stock *A* pays no dividends and has a correlation of 1.1 with the market portfolio. Stock *B* has an expected return of 11 percent, a standard deviation of 14 percent, a correlation with the market portfolio of 0.4, and a correlation with stock A of 0.55. The market portfolio has a standard deviation of 10 percent. Assume the CAPM holds.

a. If you are a typical, risk-averse investor with a well-diversified portfolio, which stock would you prefer? Why?

b. What are the expected return and standard deviation of a portfolio consisting of 70 percent of stock A and 30 percent of stock $B?$

c. What is the beta of the portfolio in part (b)?

Advanced (requires calculus)

11.33 Assume stocks A and B have the following characteristics:

Stock	Expected Return (%)	Standard Deviation %
A	6	11
B	12	22

The covariance between the returns on the two stocks is 0.001.

a. Suppose an investor holds a portfolio consisting of only stock A and stock B. Find the portfolio weights, X_A and X_B, such that the variance of his portfolio is minimized. (Hint: Remember that the sum of the two weights must equal 1.)

b. What is the expected return on the minimum variance portfolio?

c. If the covariance between the returns on the two stocks is -0.02, what are the minimum variance weights?

d. What is the variance of the portfolio in part (c)?

NOTE: While these problems can be calculated manually, it is recommended that a spreadsheet program such as Excel® be used for calculations.

STANDARD
&POOR'S

www.mcgrawhill.ca/
edumarketinsight

11.34 Go to the "Excel Analytics" link for Nexen Inc. (NXY) and Thomson Corp. (TOC) and download the monthly adjusted stock prices. Copy the monthly returns for each stock into a new spreadsheet. Calculate the covariance and correlation between the two stock returns. Would you expect a higher or lower correlation if you had chosen Petro-Canada (PCA) instead of Thomson Corp.? What is the standard deviation of a portfolio 75 percent invested in NXY and 25 percent in TOC? What about a portfolio equally invested in the two stocks? What about a portfolio 25 percent in NXY and 75 percent in TOC?

11.35 Go to the "Excel Analytics" link for Encana Corp (ECA) and download the monthly adjusted stock prices. Copy the monthly returns for ECA and the monthly S&P 500 returns in a new spreadsheet. Calculate the beta of ECA for the entire period of data available. Now download the monthly stock prices for Research In Motion Limited (RIM) and calculate the beta for this company. Are the betas similar? Would you have expected the beta for ECA to be higher or lower than the beta for RIM? Why?

Appendix 11A: Is Beta Dead?
To access Appendix 11A, please go to the Online Learning Centre at
www.mcgrawhill.ca/olc/ross.

Visit us at www.mcgrawhill.ca/olc/ross

MINICASE: A Job at Deck Out My Yacht, Part 2

You are discussing your retirement plan with Alvin Jones when he mentions that Maureen Buffett, a representative from Marshall McLaren Financial Services, is visiting Deck Out My Yacht today. You decide that you should meet with Maureen, so Alvin sets up an appointment for you later in the day. When you sit down with Maureen, she discusses the various investment options available in the company's retirement plan. You mention to Maureen that you researched Deck Out My Yacht before you accepted your new job. You are confident in management's ability to lead the company.

Analysis of the company has led to your belief that the company is growing and will achieve a greater market share in the future. You also feel you should support your employer. Given these considerations, along with the fact that you are a conservative investor, you are leaning toward investing 100 percent of your retirement amount in Deck Out My Yacht.

Assume the risk-free rate is the historical average risk-free rate (Chapter 10). The correlation between the bond fund and large-cap stock fund is .27. Note that the spreadsheet graphing and "solver" functions may assist you in answering the following questions.

1. Considering the effects of diversification, how should Maureen respond to the suggestion that you invest 100 percent of your retirement savings in Deck Out My Yacht stock?
2. Maureen's response to investing your retirement savings entirely in Deck Out My Yacht stock has convinced you that this may not be the best alternative. Because you are a conservative investor, you tell Maureen that a 100 percent investment in the bond fund may be the best alternative. Is it?
3. Using the returns for the M&M Large-Cap Stock Fund and the M&M Bond Fund, graph the opportunity set of feasible portfolios.
4. After examining the opportunity set, you notice that you can invest in a portfolio consisting of the bond fund and the large-cap stock fund that will have exactly the same standard deviation as the bond fund. This portfolio will also have a greater expected return. What are the portfolio weights and expected return of this portfolio?
5. Examining the opportunity set, notice there is a portfolio that has the lowest standard deviation. This is the minimum variance portfolio. What are the portfolio weights, expected return, and standard deviation of this portfolio? Why is the minimum variance portfolio important?
6. A measure of risk-adjusted performance that is often used is the Sharpe ratio. The Sharpe ratio is calculated as the risk premium of an asset divided by its standard deviation. The portfolio with the highest possible Sharpe ratio on the opportunity set is called the Sharpe optimal portfolio. What are the portfolio weights, expected return, and standard deviation of the Sharpe optimal portfolio? How does the Sharpe ratio of this portfolio compare to the Sharpe ratios of the bond fund and the large-cap stock fund? Do you see a connection between the Sharpe optimal portfolio and the CAPM? What is the connection?

Chapter 12

An Alternative View of Risk and Return: The Arbitrage Pricing Theory

EXECUTIVE SUMMARY

The previous two chapters showed how variable returns on securities are. This variability is measured by variance and by standard deviation. Next, we discussed how the returns on securities are interdependent. We measured the degree of interdependence between a pair of securities by covariance and by correlation. This interdependence led to a number of interesting results. First, we showed that diversification in stocks can eliminate some, but not all, risk. By contrast, we showed that diversification in a casino can eliminate all risk. Second, the interdependence of returns led to the capital asset pricing model (CAPM). This model posits a positive (and linear) relationship between the beta of a security and its expected return.

The CAPM was developed in the early 1960s.[1] An alternative to the CAPM, is the *arbitrage pricing theory (APT)*.[2] For our purposes, the differences between the two models stem from the APT's treatment of the interrelationship among the returns on securities.[3] The APT assumes that returns on securities are generated by a number of industrywide and marketwide factors. Correlation between a pair of securities occurs when these two securities are affected by the same factor or factors. By contrast, though the CAPM allows correlation among securities, it does not specify the underlying factors causing the correlation.

Both the APT and the CAPM imply a positive relationship between expected return and risk. In our (perhaps biased) opinion, the APT allows this relationship to be developed in a particularly intuitive manner. In addition, the APT views risk more generally than just as the standardized covariance or beta of a security with the market portfolio. Therefore, we offer this approach as an alternative to the CAPM.

[1] In particular, see Jack Treynor, "Toward a Theory of the Market Value of Risky Assets," unpublished manuscript (1961); William F. Sharpe, "Capital Asset Prices: A Theory of Market Equilibrium Under Conditions of Risk," *Journal of Finance* (September 1964); and John Lintner, "The Valuation of Risky Assets and the Selection of Risky Investments in Stock Portfolios and Capital Budgets," *Review of Economics and Statistics* (February 1965).

[2] See Stephen A. Ross, "The Arbitrage Theory of Capital Asset Pricing," *Journal of Economic Theory* (December 1976).

[3] This is by no means the only difference in the assumptions of the two models. For example, the CAPM usually assumes either that the returns on assets are normally distributed or that investors have quadratic utility functions. The APT does not require either assumption. Instead it is based on the more general principle that when assets are priced correctly, it is not possible to make arbitrage profits without taking on risk. While this and other differences are quite important in research, they are not relevant to the material presented in our text.

12.1 Factor Models: Announcements, Surprises, and Expected Returns

We learned in the previous chapter how to construct portfolios and how to evaluate their returns. We now step back and examine the returns on individual securities more closely. By doing this we will find that the portfolios inherit and alter the properties of the securities they comprise.

To be concrete, let us consider the return on the stock of a company called Quebec Supply. What will determine this stock's return in, say, the coming month?

The return on any stock traded in a financial market consists of two parts. First, the *normal* or *expected return* from the stock is the part of the return that shareholders in the market predict or expect. It depends on all of the information shareholders have that bears on the stock, and it uses all of our understanding of what will influence the stock in the next month.

The second part is the *uncertain* and *risky return* on the stock. This is the portion that comes from information that will be revealed within the month. The list of such information is endless, but here are some examples:

- News about Quebec Supply's research.
- Statistics Canada figures released on the gross national product (GNP).
- Announcement of the latest federal deficit-reduction plans.
- Discovery that a rival's product has been tampered with.
- News that Quebec Supply's sales figures are higher than expected.
- A sudden drop in interest rates.
- The unexpected retirement of Quebec Supply's founder and president.

A way to write the return on Quebec Supply's stock in the coming month, then, is

$$R = \overline{R} + U$$

where R is the actual total return in the month, $\overline{R}$ is the expected part of the return, and U stands for the unexpected part of the return.

Some care must be exercised in studying the effects of these and other news items on the return. For example, Statistics Canada might give us GNP or unemployment figures for this month, but how much of that is new information for shareholders? Surely, at the beginning of the month, shareholders will have some idea or forecast of what the monthly GNP will be. To the extent to which the shareholders had forecast the government's announcement, that forecast should be factored into the expected part of the return as of the beginning of the month, $\overline{R}$. On the other hand, insofar as the announcement by the government is a surprise and to the extent to which it influences the return on the stock, it will be part of U, the unanticipated part of the return.

As an example, suppose shareholders in the market had forecast that the GNP increase this month would be 0.5 percent. If GNP influences our company's stock, this forecast will be part of the information shareholders use to form the expectation, $\overline{R}$, of monthly return. If the actual announcement this month is exactly 0.5 percent, the same as the forecast, then the shareholders learned nothing new, and the announcement is not news. It is like hearing a rumour about a friend when you knew it all along. Another way of saying this is that shareholders had already discounted the announcement. This use of the word *discount* is different from that in computing present value, but the spirit is similar. When we discount a dollar in the future, we say that it is worth less to us because of the time value of money.

When we discount an announcement or a news item in the future, we mean that it has less impact on the market because the market already knew much of it.

On the other hand, suppose Statistics Canada announced that the actual GNP increase during the month was 1.5 percent. Now shareholders have learned something—that the increase is one percentage point higher than they had forecast. This difference between the actual result and the forecast, one percentage point in this example, is sometimes called the *innovation* or *surprise*.

Any announcement can be broken into two parts: the anticipated or expected part, and the surprise or innovation:

$$\text{Announcement} = \text{Expected part} + \text{Surprise}$$

The expected part of any announcement is part of the information the market uses to form the expectation, $\overline{R}$, of the return on the stock. The surprise is the news that influences the unanticipated return on the stock, U.

To take another example, if shareholders know in January that the president of a firm is going to resign, the official announcement in February will be fully expected and will be discounted by the market. Because the announcement was expected before February, its influence on the stock will have taken place before February. The announcement itself in February will contain no surprise, and the stock's price should not change at all at the announcement in February.

When we speak of news, then, we refer to the surprise part of any announcement and not to the portion that the market has expected and therefore has already discounted.

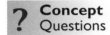 **Concept Questions**

- **What are the two basic parts of a return?**
- **Under what conditions will some news have no effect on common stock prices?**

12.2 Risk: Systematic and Unsystematic

The unanticipated part of the return, that portion resulting from surprises, is the true risk of any investment. After all, if we had already got what we had expected, there would be no risk and no uncertainty.

There are important differences, though, among various sources of risk. Look at our previous list of news stories. Some of these stories are directed specifically at Quebec Supply, and some are more general. Which of the news items are of specific importance to Quebec Supply?

Announcements about interest rates or GNP are clearly important for nearly all companies, whereas the news about Quebec Supply's president, its research, its sales, or the affairs of a rival company are of specific interest to Quebec Supply. We will divide these two types of announcements and the resulting risk, then, into two components: a systematic portion, called *systematic risk,* and the remainder, which we call *specific* or *unsystematic risk.* The following definitions describe the difference:

- A *systematic risk* is any risk that affects a large number of assets, each to a greater or lesser degree.
- An *unsystematic risk* is a risk that specifically affects a single asset or a small group of assets.[4]

---

[4]In the previous chapter, we briefly mentioned that unsystematic risk is risk that can be diversified away in a large portfolio. This result will also follow from the present analysis.

Uncertainty about general economic conditions, such as GNP, interest rates, or inflation, is an example of systematic risk. These conditions affect nearly all stocks to some degree. An unanticipated or surprise increase in inflation affects wages and the costs of the supplies that companies buy, the value of the assets that companies own, and the prices at which companies sell their products. These forces to which all companies are susceptible are the essence of systematic risk.

In contrast, the announcement of a small oil strike by a company may very well affect that company alone or a few other companies. Certainly, it is unlikely to have an effect on the world oil market. To stress that such information is unsystematic and affects only some specific companies, we sometimes call it an *idiosyncratic risk.*

The distinction between a systematic risk and an unsystematic risk is never as exact as we make it out to be. Even the most narrow and peculiar bit of news about a company ripples through the economy. It reminds us of the tale of the war that was lost because one horse lost a shoe; even a minor event may have an impact on the world. But this degree of hair-splitting should not trouble us much. To paraphrase a judge's comment on pornography, we are not able to define systematic and unsystematic risk exactly, but we know them when we see them.

This permits us to break down the risk of Quebec Supply's stock into its two components: the systematic and the unsystematic. As is traditional, we will use the Greek epsilon, ε, to represent the unsystematic risk and write

$$R = \bar{R} + U$$
$$= \bar{R} + m + \varepsilon$$

where we have used the letter m to stand for the systematic risk. Sometimes systematic risk is referred to as *market risk.* This emphasizes the fact that m influences all assets in the market to some extent.

The important point about the way we have broken the total risk, U, into its two components, m and ε, is that ε, because it is specific to the company, is unrelated to the specific risk of most other companies. For example, the unsystematic risk on Quebec Supply's stock, ε_Q, is unrelated to the unsystematic risk of Bank of Montreal's stock, ε_{BMO}. The risk that Quebec Supply's stock will go up or down because of a discovery by its research team—or its failure to discover something—probably is unrelated to any of the specific uncertainties that affect Bank of Montreal's stock.

Using the terms of the previous chapter, this means that the unsystematic risks of Quebec Supply's stock and Bank of Montreal's stock are unrelated to each other, or uncorrelated. In the symbols of statistics,

$$\text{Corr}(\varepsilon_Q, \varepsilon_{BMO}) = 0$$

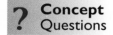

Concept Questions
- **Describe the difference between systematic risk and unsystematic risk.**
- **Why is unsystematic risk sometimes referred to as** *idiosyncratic risk?*

12.3 Systematic Risk and Betas

The fact that the unsystematic parts of the returns on two companies are unrelated to each other does not mean that the systematic portions are unrelated. On the contrary, because both companies are influenced by the same systematic risks, individual companies' systematic risks and, therefore, their total returns will be related.

For example, a surprise about inflation will influence almost all companies to some extent. How sensitive is Quebec Supply's stock return to unanticipated changes in inflation? If Quebec Supply's stock tends to go up on news that inflation is exceeding expectations, we would say that it is positively related to inflation. If the stock goes down when inflation exceeds expectations and up when inflation falls short of expectations, it is negatively related. In the unusual case where a stock's return is uncorrelated with inflation surprises, inflation has no effect on it.

We capture the influence of a systematic risk like inflation on a stock by using the **beta coefficient.** The beta coefficient, β, tells us the response of the stock's return to a systematic risk. In the previous chapter, beta measured the responsiveness of a security's return to a specific risk factor, the return on the market portfolio. We used this type of responsiveness to develop the capital asset pricing model. Because we now consider many types of systematic risks, our current work can be viewed as a generalization of what we did in the previous chapter.

If a company's stock is positively related to the risk of inflation, that stock has a positive inflation beta. If it is negatively related to inflation, its inflation beta is negative, and if it is uncorrelated with inflation, its inflation beta is zero.

It is not hard to imagine stocks with positive and negative inflation betas. The stock of a company owning gold mines will probably have a positive inflation beta because an unanticipated rise in inflation is usually associated with an increase in gold prices. On the other hand, an automobile company facing stiff foreign competition might find that an increase in inflation means that the wages it pays are higher, but that it cannot raise its prices to cover the increase. This profit squeeze, as the company's expenses rise faster than its revenues, would give its stock a negative inflation beta.

Some companies that have few assets and that act as brokers—buying items in competitive markets and reselling them in other markets—might be relatively unaffected by inflation, because their costs and their revenues would rise and fall together. Their stocks would have an inflation beta of zero.

Some structure is useful at this point. Suppose we have identified three systematic risks on which we want to focus. We may believe that these three are sufficient to describe the systematic risks that influence stock returns. Three likely candidates are inflation, GNP, and interest rates. Thus, every stock will have a beta associated with each of these systematic risks: an inflation beta, a GNP beta, and an interest-rate beta. We can write the return on the stock, then, in the following form:

$$
\begin{aligned}
R &= \overline{R} + U \\
&= \overline{R} + m + \varepsilon \\
&= \overline{R} + \beta_I F_I + \beta_{GNP} F_{GNP} + \beta_r F_r + \varepsilon
\end{aligned}
$$

where we have used β_I to denote the stock's inflation beta, β_{GNP} for its GNP beta, and β_r to stand for its interest-rate beta. In the equation, F stands for a surprise, whether it be in inflation, GNP, or interest rates.

Let us go through an example to see how the surprises and the expected return add up to produce the total return, R, on a given stock. To make it more familiar, suppose that the return is over a horizon of a year and not just a month. Suppose that at the beginning of the year, inflation is forecast to be 5 percent for the year. GNP is forecast to increase by 2 percent, and interest rates are expected not to change. Suppose the stock we are looking at has the following betas:

$$
\begin{aligned}
\beta_I &= 2.0 \\
\beta_{GNP} &= 1.0 \\
\beta_r &= -1.8
\end{aligned}
$$

The magnitude of the beta describes how great an impact a systematic risk has on a stock's returns. A beta of $+1$ indicates that the stock's return rises and falls one for one with the systematic factor. This means, in our example, that because the stock has a GNP beta of 1, it experiences a 1 percent increase in return for every 1 percent surprise increase in GNP. If its GNP beta were -2, it would fall by 2 percent when there was an unanticipated increase of 1 percent in GNP, and it would rise by 2 percent if GNP experienced a surprise 1 percent decline.

Next let's suppose that during the year the following occurs: Inflation rises by 7 percent, GNP rises by only 1 percent, and interest rates fall by 2 percent. Lastly, suppose that we learn some good news about the company (perhaps that it's succeeding rapidly with some new business strategy) and that this unanticipated development contributes 5 percent to its return. In other words,

$$\varepsilon = 5\%$$

Let us assemble all of this information to find what return the stock had during the year.

First, we must determine what news or surprises took place in the systematic factors. From our information we know that

$$\text{Expected inflation} = 5\%$$
$$\text{Expected GNP change} = 2\%$$
$$\text{Expected change in interest rates} = 0\%$$

This means that the market had discounted these changes, and the surprises will be the difference between what actually takes place and these expectations:

$$
\begin{aligned}
F_I &= \text{Surprise in inflation} \\
&= \text{Actual inflation} - \text{Expected inflation} \\
&= 7\% - 5\% \\
&= 2\%
\end{aligned}
$$

Similarly,

$$
\begin{aligned}
F_{\text{GNP}} &= \text{Surprise in GNP} \\
&= \text{Actual GNP} - \text{Expected GNP} \\
&= 1\% - 2\% \\
&= -1\%
\end{aligned}
$$

and

$$
\begin{aligned}
F_r &= \text{Surprise in change in interest rates} \\
&= \text{Actual change} - \text{Expected change} \\
&= -2\% - 0\% \\
&= -2\%
\end{aligned}
$$

The total effect of the systematic risks on the stock return, then, is

$$
\begin{aligned}
m &= \text{Systematic risk portion of return} \\
&= \beta_I F_I + \beta_{\text{GNP}} F_{\text{GNP}} + \beta_r F_r \\
&= [2 \times 2\%] + [1 \times (-1\%)] + [(-1.8) \times (-2\%)] \\
&= 6.6\%
\end{aligned}
$$

Combining this with the unsystematic risk portion, the total risky portion of the return on the stock is

$$m + \varepsilon = 6.6\% + 5\% = 11.6\%$$

Last, if the expected return on the stock for the year is, say, 4 percent, the total return from all three components is

$$R = \bar{R} + m + \varepsilon$$
$$= 4\% + 6.6\% + 5\%$$
$$= 15.6\%$$

The model we have been looking at is called a **factor model,** and the systematic sources of risk, designated *F,* are called the *factors.* To be perfectly formal, a *k-factor model* is a model where each stock's return is generated by

$$R = \bar{R} + \beta_1 F_1 + \beta_2 F_2 + \ldots + \beta_k F_k + \varepsilon$$

where ε is specific to a particular stock and uncorrelated with the ε-term for other stocks. In our preceding example, we had a three-factor model. We used inflation, GNP, and the change in interest rates as examples of systematic sources of risk (or factors). Researchers have not settled on what is the correct set of factors. Like so many other questions, this might be one of those matters that never are laid to rest.

In practice, researchers frequently use a one-factor model for returns. They do not use all of the sorts of economic factors we used previously as examples; instead, they use an index of stock market returns—like the S&P/TSX 60 or even a more broadly based index with more stocks in it—as the single factor. Using the single-factor model we can write returns as

$$R = \bar{R} + \beta(R_{\text{S\&P/TSX 60}} - \bar{R}_{\text{S\&P/TSX 60}}) + \varepsilon$$

Where there is only one factor (the returns on the S&P/TSX 60 Index), we do not need to put a subscript on the beta. In this form (with minor modifications) the factor model is called a **market model.** This term is employed because the index that is used for the factor is an index of returns on the whole (stock) market. The market model is written as

$$R = \bar{R} + \beta(R_M - \bar{R}_M) + \varepsilon$$

where R_M is the return on the market portfolio.[5] The single β is called the *beta coefficient.*

? **Concept Questions**

- **What is an inflation beta? A GNP beta? An interest-rate beta?**
- **What is the difference between a *k*-factor model and the market model?**
- **Define the beta coefficient.**

12.4 Portfolios and Factor Models

Now let us see what happens to portfolios of stocks when each of the stocks follows a one-factor model. For purposes of discussion, we will take the coming one-month period and examine returns. We could have used a day, a year, or any other time period. If the period represents the time between decisions, however, we would rather it be short than long—a month is a reasonable time frame to use.

---

[5]Alternatively, the market model could be written as

$$R = \alpha + \beta R_M + \varepsilon$$

Here alpha (α) is an intercept term equal to $\bar{R} - \beta\bar{R}_M$.

We will create portfolios from a list of N stocks, and we will use a one-factor model to capture the systematic risk. The ith stock in the list will therefore have returns

$$R_i = \bar{R}_i + \beta_i F + \varepsilon_i \qquad (12.1)$$

where we have subscripted the variables to indicate that they relate to the ith stock. Notice that the factor F is not subscripted. The factor that represents systematic risk could be a surprise in GNP, or we could use the market model and let the factor be the difference between the S&P/TSX 60 return and what we expect that return to be, $R_{\text{S\&P/TSX 60}} - \bar{R}_{\text{S\&P/TSX 60}}$. In either case, the factor applies to all stocks.

The β_i is subscripted because it represents the unique way the factor influences the ith stock. To recapitulate our discussion of factor models, if β_i is zero, the returns on the ith stock are

$$R_i = \bar{R} + \varepsilon_i$$

In words, the ith stock's returns are unaffected by the factor, F, if β_i is zero. If β_i is positive, positive changes in the factor raise the ith stock's returns, and declines lower them. Conversely, if β_i is negative, its returns and the factor move in opposite directions.

Figure 12.1 illustrates the relationship between a stock's excess returns, $R_i - \bar{R}_i$, and the factor F for different betas, where $\beta_i > 0$. The lines in Figure 12.1 plot Equation (12.1) on the assumption that there has been no unsystematic risk. That is, $\varepsilon_i = 0$. Because we are assuming positive betas, the lines slope upward, indicating that the return on the stock rises with F. Notice that, if the factor is zero ($F = 0$), the line passes through zero on the y-axis.

Now let us see what happens when we create stock portfolios where each stock follows a one-factor model. Let x_i be the proportion of security i in the portfolio. That is, if

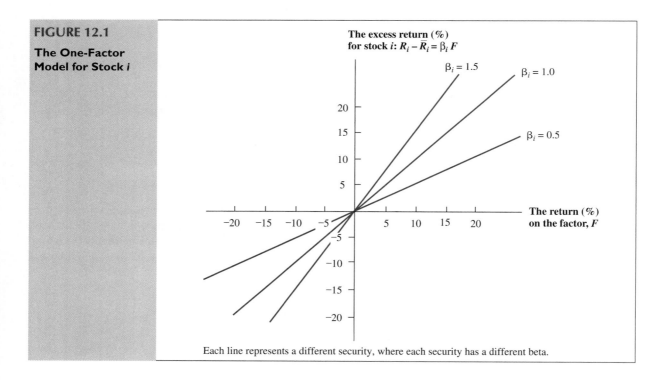

FIGURE 12.1

The One-Factor Model for Stock *i*

Each line represents a different security, where each security has a different beta.

an individual with a portfolio of \$100 wants \$20 in TransCanada Pipelines Ltd., we say $X_{TCPL} = 20\%$. Because the Xs represent the proportions of wealth we are investing in each of the stocks, we know that they must add up to 100 percent or 1. That is,

$$X_1 + X_2 + X_3 + \ldots + X_N = 1$$

We know that the portfolio return is the weighted average of the returns on the individual assets in the portfolio:

$$R_P = X_1 R_1 + X_2 R_2 + X_3 R_3 + \ldots + X_N R_N \tag{12.2}$$

Equation (12.2) expresses the return on the portfolio as a weighted average of the returns on the individual assets. We saw from Equation (12.1) that each asset's return is determined by both the factor F and the unsystematic risk of ε_i. Thus, by substituting Equation (12.1) for each R_i in Equation (12.2), we have

$$R_P = X_1(\overline{R}_1 + \beta_1 F + \varepsilon_1) + X_2(\overline{R}_2 + \beta_2 F + \varepsilon_2) + \tag{12.3}$$
$$\text{(Return on stock 1)} \quad \text{(Return on stock 2)}$$

$$X_3(\overline{R}_3 + \beta_3 F + \varepsilon_3) + \ldots + X_N(\overline{R}_N + \beta_N F + \varepsilon_N)$$
$$\text{(Return on stock 3)} \qquad \text{(Return on stock } N)$$

Equation (12.3) shows us that the return on a portfolio is determined by three sets of parameters:

1. The expected return on each individual security, $\overline{R}_i$.
2. The beta of each security multiplied by the factor F.
3. The unsystematic risk of each individual security, ε_i.

We express Equation (12.3) in terms of these three sets of parameters as

Weighted Average of Expected Returns:

$$R_P = X_1 \overline{R}_1 + X_2 \overline{R}_2 + X_3 \overline{R}_3 + \ldots + X_N \overline{R}_N \tag{12.4}$$

(Weighted Average of Betas)*F:*

$$+ (X_1 \beta_1 + X_2 \beta_2 + X_3 \beta_3 + \ldots + X_N \beta_N)F$$

Weighted Average of Unsystematic Risks:

$$+ X_1 \varepsilon_1 + X_2 \varepsilon_2 + X_3 \varepsilon_3 + \ldots + X_N \varepsilon_N$$

This rather imposing equation is actually straightforward. The first row is the weighted average of each security's expected return. The items in the parentheses of the second row represent the weighted average of each security's beta. This weighted average is, in turn, multiplied by the factor F. The third row represents a weighted average of the unsystematic risks of the individual securities.

Where does uncertainty appear in Equation (12.4)? There is no uncertainty in the first row because only the expected value of each security's return appears there. Uncertainty in the second row is reflected by only one item, F. That is, while we know that the expected value of F is zero, we do not know what its value will be over a particular time period. Uncertainty in the third row is reflected by each unsystematic risk, ε_i.

Portfolios and Diversification

In the previous sections of this chapter, we expressed the return on a single security in terms of our factor model. Portfolios were treated next. Because investors generally hold diversified portfolios, we now want to know what Equation (12.4) looks like in a large or diversified portfolio.[6]

As it turns out, something unusual happens to Equation (12.4)—the third row actually *disappears* in a large portfolio. To see this, consider the gambler of the previous chapter who divides $1,000 by betting on red over many spins of the roulette wheel. For example, he may participate in 1000 spins, betting $1 at a time. Though we do not know ahead of time whether a particular spin will yield red or black, we can be confident that red will win about 50 percent of the time. Ignoring the house take, the investor can be expected to end up with just about his original $1,000.

Though we are concerned with stocks, not roulette wheels, the same principle applies. Each security has its own unsystematic risk, where the surprise for one stock is unrelated to the surprise of another stock. By investing a small amount in each security, the weighted average of the unsystematic risks will be very close to zero in a large portfolio.[7]

Although the third row completely vanishes in a large portfolio, nothing unusual occurs in either row 1 or row 2. Row 1 remains a weighted average of the expected returns on the individual securities as securities are added to the portfolio. Because there is no uncertainty at all in the first row, there is no way for diversification to cause this row to vanish. The terms inside the parentheses of the second row remain a weighted average of the betas. They do not vanish, either, when securities are added. Because the factor F is unaffected when securities are added to the portfolios, the second row does not vanish.

Why does the third row vanish while the second row does not, though both rows reflect uncertainty? The key is that there are many unsystematic risks in row 3. Because these risks are independent of each other, the effect of diversification becomes stronger as we add more assets to the portfolio. The resulting portfolio becomes less and less risky, and the return becomes more certain. However, the systematic risk, F, affects all securities because it is outside the parentheses in row 2. Because one cannot avoid this factor by investing in many securities, diversification does not occur in this row.

EXAMPLE 12.1

The above material can be further explained by an example similar in spirit to the diversification example of the previous chapter. We keep our one-factor model but make three specific assumptions:

1. All securities have the same expected return of 10 percent. This assumption implies that the first row of Equation (12.4) must also equal 10 percent because this row is a weighted average of the expected returns of the individual securities.

2. All securities have a beta of 1. The sum of the terms inside parentheses in the second row of (12.4) must equal 1 because these terms are a weighted average of the individual betas. Since the terms inside the parentheses are multiplied by F, the value of the second row is $1 \times F = F$.

3. In this example, we focus on the behaviour of one individual, Walter Bagehot. Being a new observer of the economic scene, Mr. Bagehot decides to hold an equally weighted portfolio. That is, the proportion of each security in his portfolio is $1/N$.

---

[6]Technically, we can think of a large portfolio as one where an investor keeps increasing the number of securities without limit. In practice, effective diversification would occur if at least a few dozen securities were held.

[7]More precisely, we say that the weighted average of the unsystematic risk approaches zero as the number of equally weighted securities in a portfolio approaches infinity.

FIGURE 12.2

Diversification and the Portfolio Risk for an Equally Weighted Portfolio

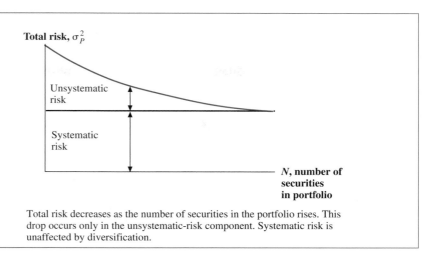

Total risk decreases as the number of securities in the portfolio rises. This drop occurs only in the unsystematic-risk component. Systematic risk is unaffected by diversification.

We can express the return on Mr. Bagehot's portfolio as

Return on Walter Bagehot's Portfolio:

$$R_P = 10\% + F + \left(\frac{1}{N}\varepsilon_1 + \frac{1}{N}\varepsilon_2 + \frac{1}{N}\varepsilon_3 + \ldots + \frac{1}{N}\varepsilon_N\right) \qquad (12.4')$$

From   From   From row 3 of (12.4)
row 1   row 2
of (12.4) of (12.4)

We mentioned above that, as N increases without limit, row 3 of (12.4) becomes equal to zero. Thus, the return to Walter Bagehot's portfolio when the number of securities is very large is

$$R_P = 10\% + F \qquad (12.4'')$$

The key to diversification is exhibited in (12.4"). The unsystematic risk of row 3 vanishes,[8] while the systematic risk of row 2 remains.

This is illustrated in Figure 12.2. Systematic risk, captured by variation in the factor, F, is not reduced through diversification. Conversely, unsystematic risk diminishes as securities are added, vanishing as the number of securities becomes infinite. Our result is analogous to the diversification example of the previous chapter. In that chapter, we said that undiversifiable or systematic risk arises from positive covariances between securities. In this chapter, we say that systematic risk arises from a common factor F. Because a common factor causes positive covariances, the arguments of the two chapters are parallel.

? Concept Questions

- **How can the return on a portfolio be expressed in terms of a factor model?**
- **What risk is diversified away in a large portfolio?**

---

[8]The variance of row 3 is

$$\frac{1}{N^2}\sigma_\varepsilon^2 + \frac{1}{N^2}\sigma_\varepsilon^2 + \frac{1}{N^2}\sigma_\varepsilon^2 + \ldots + \frac{1}{N^2}\sigma_\varepsilon^2 = \frac{1}{N^2}N\sigma_\varepsilon^2$$

where σ_ε^2 is the variance of each ε. This can be rewritten as σ_ε^2/N, which tends to 0 as N goes to infinity.

12.5 Betas and Expected Returns

The Linear Relationship

We have argued many times that the expected return on a security compensates for its risk. In the previous chapter we showed that market beta (the standardized covariance of the security's returns with those of the market) was the appropriate measure of risk under the assumptions of homogeneous expectations and riskless borrowing and lending. The capital asset pricing model, which posited these assumptions, implied that the expected return on a security was positively (and linearly) related to its beta. We will find a similar relationship between risk and return in the one-factor model of this chapter.

We begin by noting that the relevant risk in large and well-diversified portfolios is all systematic because unsystematic risk is diversified away. An implication is that, when a well-diversified shareholder considers changing holdings of a particular stock, the security's unsystematic risk can be ignored.

Notice that we are not claiming that stocks, like portfolios, have no unsystematic risk. Neither are we saying that the unsystematic risk of a stock will not affect its returns. Stocks do have unsystematic risk, and their actual returns do depend on the unsystematic risk. Because this risk washes out in a well-diversified portfolio, however, shareholders can ignore this unsystematic risk when they consider whether or not to add a stock to their portfolio. Therefore, if shareholders are ignoring the unsystematic risk, only the systematic risk of a stock can be related to its *expected* return.

This relationship is illustrated in the security market line of Figure 12.3. Points *P, C, A,* and *L* all lie on the line emanating from the risk-free rate of 10 percent. The points representing each of these four assets can be created by combinations of the risk-free rate and any of the other three assets. For example, since *A* has a beta of 2.0 and *P* has a beta of 1.0, a portfolio of 50 percent in asset *A* and 50 percent in the riskless rate has the same beta as asset *P*. The risk-free rate is 10 percent and the expected return on security *A* is 35 percent, implying that the combination's return of 22.5 percent [or (10% + 35%)/2] is identical to security *P*'s expected return. Because security *P* has both the same beta and the same expected return as a combination of the riskless asset and security *A*, an individual is equally inclined to add a small amount of security *P* and to add a small amount of this

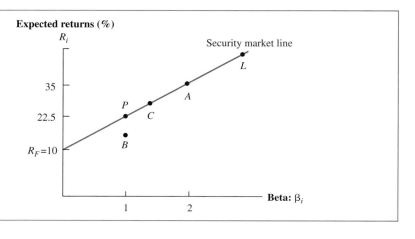

FIGURE 12.3

A Graph of Beta and Expected Return for Individual Stocks Under the One-Factor Model

combination to a portfolio. However, the unsystematic risk of security *P* need not be equal to the unsystematic risk of the combination of security *A* and the risk-free rate because unsystematic risk is diversified away in a large portfolio.

Of course, the potential combinations of points on the security market line are endless. One can duplicate *P* by combinations of the risk-free rate and either *C* or *L* (or both of them). One can duplicate *C* (or *A* or *L*) by borrowing at the risk-free rate to invest in *P*. The infinite number of points on the security market line that are not labelled can be used as well.

Now consider security *B*. Because its expected return is below the line, no investor would hold it. Instead, the investor would prefer security *P*, a combination of security *A* and the riskless asset or some other combination. Thus, security *B*'s price is too high. Its price will fall in a competitive market, forcing its expected return back up to the line in equilibrium.

Because we know that the return on any zero-beta asset is R_F and the expected return on asset *P* is $\overline{R}_p$, it can easily be shown that

$$\overline{R} = R_F + \beta(\overline{R}_P - R_F) \tag{12.5}$$

In Equation (12.5), $\overline{R}$ can be thought of as the expected return on any security or portfolio lying on the security market line. β is the beta of that security or portfolio.

The Market Portfolio and the Single Factor

In the CAPM, the beta of a security measures the security's responsiveness to movements in the market portfolio. In the one-factor model of the APT, the beta of a security measures its responsiveness to the factor. We now relate the market portfolio to the single factor.

A large, diversified portfolio has no unsystematic risk because the unsystematic risks of the individual securities are diversified away. Assuming that no security has a disproportionate market share, the market portfolio is fully diversified and contains no unsystematic risk.[9] In other words, the market portfolio is perfectly correlated with the single factor, implying that the market portfolio is really a scaled-up or scaled-down version of the factor. After scaling properly, we can treat the market portfolio as the factor itself.

The market portfolio, like every security or portfolio, lies on the security market line. When the market portfolio is the factor, the beta of the market portfolio is 1 by definition. This is shown in Figure 12.4. (We deleted the securities and the specific expected returns from Figure 12.3 for clarity; the two graphs are otherwise identical.) With the market portfolio as the factor, Equation (12.5) becomes

$$\overline{R} = R_F + \beta(\overline{R}_M - R_F)$$

where $\overline{R}_M$ is the expected return on the market. This equation shows that the expected return on any asset, $\overline{R}$, is linearly related to the security's beta. The equation is identical to that of the CAPM, which we developed in the previous chapter.

? Concept Questions

• **What is the relationship between the one-factor model and the CAPM?**

---

[9]This assumption is generally plausible in the real world. For example, even the market value of a large company like Royal Bank of Canada is only a small fraction of the market value of the S&P/TSX 60 index.

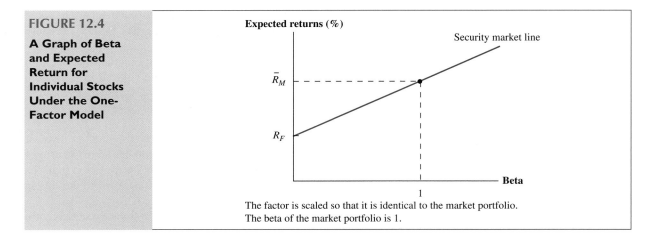

FIGURE 12.4

A Graph of Beta and Expected Return for Individual Stocks Under the One-Factor Model

Expected returns (%)

Security market line

$\bar{R}_M$

R_F

Beta

1

The factor is scaled so that it is identical to the market portfolio.
The beta of the market portfolio is 1.

12.6 The Capital Asset Pricing Model and the Arbitrage Pricing Theory

The CAPM and the APT are alternative models of risk and return. It is worthwhile to consider the differences between the two models, both in terms of pedagogy and in terms of application.

Differences in Pedagogy

We feel that the CAPM has at least one strong advantage from the student's point of view. The derivation of the CAPM necessarily brings the reader through a discussion of efficient sets. The treatment—beginning with the case of two risky assets, moving to the case of many risky assets, and finishing when a riskless asset is added to the many risky ones—is of great intuitive value. This sort of presentation is not as easily accomplished with the APT.

However, the APT has an offsetting advantage. The model adds factors until the unsystematic risk of any security is uncorrelated with the unsystematic risk of every other security. Under this formulation, it is easily shown that (1) unsystematic risk steadily falls (and ultimately vanishes) as the number of securities in the portfolio increases but (2) the systematic risks do not decrease. This result was also shown in the CAPM, though the intuition was cloudier because the unsystematic risks could be correlated across securities.

Differences in Application

One advantage of the APT is that it can handle multiple factors while the CAPM ignores them. Although the bulk of our presentation in this chapter focused on the one-factor model, a multifactor model is probably more reflective of reality. That is, one must abstract from many marketwide and industrywide factors before the unsystematic risk of one security becomes uncorrelated with the unsystematic risks of other securities. Under this multifactor version of the APT, the relationship between risk and return can be expressed as

$$\bar{R} = R_F + (\bar{R}_1 - R_F)\beta_1 + (\bar{R}_2 - R_F)\beta_2 + (\bar{R}_3 - R_F)\beta_3 + \ldots + (\bar{R}_K - R_F)\beta_K \qquad (12.6)$$

In this equation, β_1 stands for the security's beta with respect to the first factor, β_2 stands for the security's beta with respect to the second factor, and so on. For example, if the first factor is GNP, β_1 is the security's GNP beta. The term $\bar{R}_1$ is the expected return on a security (or portfolio) whose beta with respect to the first factor is 1 and whose beta with respect to all other factors is zero. Because the market compensates for risk, $(\bar{R}_1 - \bar{R}_F)$ will be positive in the normal case.[10] (An analogous interpretation can be given to $\bar{R}_2$, $\bar{R}_3$, and so on.)

The equation states that the security's expected return is related to the security's factor betas. The intuition in Equation (12.6) is straightforward. Each factor represents risk that cannot be diversified away. The higher a security's beta with regard to a particular factor is, the higher is the risk that the security bears. In a rational world, the expected return on the security should compensate for this risk. The above equation states that the expected return is a summation of the risk-free rate plus the compensation for each type of risk that the security bears.

As an example, consider a classic U.S. study where the factors were monthly growth in industrial production (IP), change in expected inflation ($\Delta\,EI$), unanticipated inflation (UI), unanticipated change in the risk premium between risky bonds and default-free bonds (URP), and unanticipated change in the difference between the return on long-term government bonds and the return on short-term government bonds (UBR).[11] Using the period 1958–84, the empirical results of the study indicated that the expected monthly return on any stock, $\bar{R}_s$, can be described as

$$\bar{R}_s = 0.0041 + 0.0136\beta_{IP} - 0.0001\beta_{\Delta EI} - 0.0006\beta_{UI} + 0.0072\beta_{URP} - 0.0052\beta_{UBR}$$

Suppose a particular stock had the following betas: $\beta_{IP} = 1.1$, $\beta_{\Delta EI} = 2$, $\beta_{UI} = 3$, $\beta_{URP} = 0.1$, $\beta_{UBR} = 1.6$. The expected monthly return on that security would be

$$\begin{aligned}\bar{R}_s &= 0.0041 + 0.0136 \times 1.1 - 0.0001 \times 2 - 0.0006 \times 3\\ &\quad + 0.0072 \times 0.1 - 0.0052 \times 1.6 = 0.0095\end{aligned}$$

Assuming that one of the firm's projects has risk equivalent to that of the firm, this value of 0.0095 (i.e., 0.95 percent) can be used as the monthly discount rate for the project. (Because annual data are often supplied for capital budgeting purposes, the annual rate of 0.120 [or $(1.0095)^{12} - 1$] might be used instead.)[12]

A classic Canadian study identified five similar factors:

1. The rate of growth in industrial production.
2. The changes in the slope of the term structure of interest rates (the difference between the returns on long-term and short-term Canada bonds).
3. The default risk premium for bonds (measured as the difference between the yield on long-term Canada bonds and the yield on the ScotiaMcLeod corporate bond index.
4. Inflation (measured as the growth of the consumer price index).
5. The value-weighted return on the market portfolio (S&P/TSX 60).[13]

Using the period 1970–84, the empirical results of the study indicated that expected monthly returns on a sample of 100 TSX stocks could be described as a function of the risk premiums associated with these five factors.

---

[10]Actually,$(\bar{R}_i - R_F)$ could be negative in the case where factor i is perceived as a hedge of some sort.

[11]N. Chen, R. Roll, and S. Ross, "Economic Forces and the Stock Market," *Journal of Business* (July 1986).

[12]Strictly speaking, we must assume that the firm has no debt. We discuss the impact of debt on betas in Chapters 13 and 18.

[13]E. Otuteye, "How Economic Forces Explain Canadian Stock Returns," *Canadian Investment Review* (Spring 1991), pp. 93–99. An earlier Canadian study supportive of the APT is L. Kryzanowski and M. C. To, "General Factor Models and the Structure of Security Returns," *Journal of Financial and Quantitative Analysis* (March 1983), pp. 31–52.

Because many factors appear on the right side of the APT equation, the APT formulation explained expected returns in this Canadian sample more accurately than did the CAPM. However, as we mentioned earlier, one can't easily determine which are the appropriate factors. The factors in the above study were included for reasons of both common sense and convenience. They were not derived from theory, and the choice of factors varies from study to study. A more recent Canadian study, for example, includes changes in a U.S. stock index and in exchange rates as factors.[14]

By contrast, use of the market index in the CAPM formulation is implied by the theory of the previous chapter. We suggested in earlier chapters that the S&P/TSX 60 Index mirrors stock market movements quite well. Using an update of the Hatch and White results first reported in Chapter 10, Chapter 11 easily calculated expected returns on different securities from the CAPM.[15]

? Concept Questions

- **What are the advantages and disadvantages of the CAPM and the APT?**
- **What conclusions can be drawn from empirical tests of APT?**

12.7 Parametric Approaches to Asset Pricing

Empirical Models

The CAPM and the APT by no means exhaust the models and techniques used in practice to measure the expected return on risky assets. Both the CAPM and the APT are *risk-based models.* They each measure the risk of a security by its beta(s) on some systematic factor(s), and they each argue that the expected excess return must be proportional to the beta(s). As we have seen, this is intuitively appealing and has a strong basis in theory, but there are alternative approaches.

Most of these alternatives can be lumped under the broad heading of parametric or empirical methods. The word *empirical* refers to the fact that these approaches are based less on some theory of how financial markets work and more on simply looking for regularities and relations in the past history of market data. In these approaches the researcher specifies some parameters or attributes associated with the securities in question and then examines the data directly for a relation between these attributes and expected returns. For example, an extensive amount of research has been done on whether the expected return on a firm is related to its size. Is it true that small firms have higher average returns than large firms? Researchers have also examined a variety of accounting measures such as the ratio of the price of a stock to the accounting earnings, the P/E ratio, and the closely related ratio of the market value of the stock to the book value of the company, the M/B ratio.[16] Here it might be argued that companies with low P/Es or low M/Bs are "undervalued" and can be expected to have higher returns in the future.

---

[14]L. Kryzanowski, S. Lalancette, and M.C. To, "Performance Attribution Using an APT with Prespecified Macrofactors and Time-Varying Risk Premia and Betas," *Journal of Financial and Quantitative Analysis* 32 (June 1997), pp. 205–224.

[15]Though many researchers assume that surrogates for the market portfolio are easily found, Richard Roll, "A Critique of the Asset Pricing Theory's Tests," *Journal of Financial Economics* (March 1977), argues that the absence of a universally acceptable proxy for the market portfolio seriously impairs application of the CAPM. After all, the market must include real estate, racehorses, and other assets that are not in the stock market.

[16]E. F. Fama and K. R. French, "Common Risk Factors in the Returns on Stocks and Bonds," *Journal of Financial Economics* 33:1, pp. 3–56 and "Multifactor Explanations of Asset Pricing Anomalies," *Journal of Finance* 51:1, pp. 55–84.

To use the empirical approach to determine the expected return, we would estimate the following equation:

$$\overline{R}_i = R_F + k_{P/E}(P/E)_i + k_{M/B}(M/B)_i + k_{size}(size)_p$$

where $\overline{R}_i$ is the expected return of firm i, and where the ks are coefficients that we estimate from stock market data. Notice that this is the same form as Equation (12.6) with the firm's attributes in place of betas and with the ks in place of the excess factor portfolio returns.

When tested with data, these parametric approaches seem to do quite well, and when comparisons are made between using parameters and using betas to predict stock returns, the parameters, such as P/E and M/B, seem to work better. There are a variety of possible explanations for these results, and the issues have certainly not been settled. Critics of the empirical approach are skeptical of what they call *data mining*. The particular parameters that researchers work with are often chosen because they have been shown to be related to returns. For instance, suppose that you were asked to explain the change in GMAT test scores over the past 40 years in some particular province. Suppose that to do this you searched through all of the data series you could find. After much searching, you might discover, for example, that the change in the scores was directly related to the jackrabbit population in Alberta. We know that any such relation is purely accidental, but if you search long enough and have enough choices, you will find something even if it's not really there. It's a bit like staring at clouds. After a while you will see clouds that look like anything you want, clowns, bears, or whatever, but all you are really doing is data mining.

Needless to say, the researchers on these matters defend their work by arguing that they have not mined the data and have been very careful to avoid such traps by not snooping at the data to see what will work.

Of course, as a matter of pure theory, since anyone in the market can easily look up the P/E ratio of a firm, one would certainly not expect to find that firms with low P/Es did better than firms with high P/Es simply because they were undervalued. In an efficient market in which prices reflect all public information, such public measures of undervaluation would be quickly exploited and would not be expected to last.

Perhaps a better explanation for the success of empirical approaches lies in a synthesis of the risk-based approaches and the empirical methods. In an efficient market, risk and return are related, hence perhaps the parameters or attributes that appear to be related to returns are also better measures of risk. For example, if we were to find that low P/E firms outperformed high P/E firms and that this was true even for firms that had the same beta(s), then we have at least two possible explanations. First, we could simply discard the risk-based theories as incorrect. Furthermore, we could argue that markets are inefficient and that buying low P/E stocks provides us with an opportunity to make higher than predicted returns. Second, we could argue that *both* views of the world are correct and that the P/E is really just a better way to measure systematic risk, i.e., beta(s), than directly estimating beta from the data.

Style Portfolios

In addition to their use as a platform for estimating expected returns, stock attributes are also widely used as a way of characterizing money management styles. For example, a portfolio that has a P/E ratio much in excess of the market average might be characterized as a high P/E or a growth stock portfolio. Similarly, a portfolio made up of stocks with an average P/E less than that for a market index might be characterized as a low P/E or a value portfolio.

To evaluate how well a portfolio manager is doing, often his or her performance is compared with the performance of some basic indexes. For example, the portfolio returns of a manager who purchases large Canadian stocks might be compared against the performance of the S&P/TSX 60 Index. In such a case the S&P/TSX 60 is said to be the *benchmark* against which his or her performance is measured. Similarly, an international manager might be compared against some common index of international stocks. In choosing an appropriate benchmark, care should be taken to identify a benchmark that contains only those types of stocks that the manager targets as representative of his or her style and that are also available to be purchased. A manager who was told not to purchase any stocks in the S&P/TSX 60 Index would not consider a comparison against the S&P/TSX 60 to be legitimate.

Increasingly, too, managers are compared not only against an index, but also against a peer group of similar managers. The performance of a fund that advertises itself as a growth fund might be measured against the performance of a large sample of similar funds. For instance, the performance over some period is commonly assigned to quartiles. The top 25 percent of the funds are said to be in the first quartile, the next 25 percent in the second quartile, the next 25 percent in the third quartile, and the worst-performing 25 percent of the funds in the last quartile. If the fund we are examining happens to have performance that falls in the second quartile, then we speak of it as a second-quartile manager.

Similarly, we call a fund that purchases low M/B stocks a value fund and would measure its performance against a sample of similar value funds. These approaches to measuring performance are relatively new, and they are part of an active and exciting effort to refine our ability to identify and use investment skills.

? **Concept Questions**
- Empirical models are sometimes called factor models. What is the difference between a factor as we have used it previously in this chapter and an attribute as we use it in this section?
- What is data mining and why might it overstate the relation between some stock attribute and returns?
- What is wrong with measuring the performance of a Canadian growth stock manager against a benchmark composed of U.S. stocks?

12.8 SUMMARY AND CONCLUSIONS

The previous chapter developed the capital asset pricing model (CAPM). As an alternative, this chapter develops the arbitrage pricing theory (APT).

1. The APT assumes that stock returns are generated according to factor models. For example, we might describe a stock's return as

$$R = \bar{R} + \beta_I F_I + \beta_{GNP} F_{GNP} + \beta_r F_r + \varepsilon$$

where I, GNP, and r stand for inflation, gross national product, and the interest rate, respectively. The three factors F_I, F_{GNP}, and F_r represent systematic risk because these factors affect many securities. The term ε is considered unsystematic risk because it is unique to each individual security.

2. For convenience, we frequently describe a security's return according to a one-factor model:

$$R = \bar{R} + \beta F + \varepsilon$$

3. As securities are added to a portfolio, the unsystematic risks of the individual securities offset each other. A fully diversified portfolio has no unsystematic risk but still has systematic risk. This result indicates that diversification can only eliminate some, but not all, of the risk of individual securities.

4. For this reason, the expected return on a stock is positively related to its systematic risk. In a one-factor model, the systematic risk of a security is simply the beta of the CAPM. Thus, the implications of the CAPM and the one-factor APT are identical. However, each security has many risks in a multifactor model. The expected return on a security is positively related to the beta of the security with each factor.

5. Empirical or parametric models that capture the relations between returns and stock attributes such as P/E or M/B ratios can be estimated directly from the data without any appeal to theory. These ratios are also used to measure the style of a portfolio manager and to construct benchmarks and samples against which his or her performance is measured.

KEY TERMS

Beta coefficient 333
Factor model 335
Market model 335

SUGGESTED READING

Complete treatments of the APT can be found in the following articles:
S. A. Ross. "Return, Risk and Arbitrage." In Friend and Bicksler, eds. *Risk and Return in Finance.* New York: Heath Lexington, 1974.
S. A. Ross. "The Arbitrage Theory of Asset Pricing." *Journal of Economic Theory* (December 1976).

Two less technical discussions of APT are:
D. H. Bower, R. S. Bower, and D. Logue. "A Primer on Arbitrage Pricing Theory." *Midland Corporate Finance Journal* (Fall 1984).
R. Roll and S. Ross. "The Arbitrage Pricing Theory Approach to Strategic Portfolio Planning." *Financial Analysts Journal* (May/June 1984).

Discussions of Canadian tests of APT are found in:
Z. Bodie, A. Kane, A. J. Marcus, S. Perrakis, and P. J. Ryan. *Investments.* 5th Canadian ed. Whitby, Ontario: McGraw-Hill Ryerson, 2005.
L. Kryzanowski, S. Lalancette, and M. C. To, "Performance Attribution Using an APT With Prespecified Macrofactors and Time-Varying Risk Premia and Betas." *Journal of Financial and Quantitative Analysis* 32, (June 1997).
E. Otuteye. "How Economic Forces Explain Canadian Stock Returns." *Canadian Investment Review* (Spring 1991).
B. F. Smith. "A Study of the Arbitrage Stocks." In M. J. Robinson and B. F. Smith, eds., *Canadian Capital Markets,* London, Ontario: Ivey Business School, 1993.

A Canadian take on investment styles is:
H. Marmer. "Talk Isn't Cheap." *Canadian Investment Review* 8 (Spring 1995), pp.17–22

QUESTIONS & PROBLEMS

Factor Models and Risk

12.1 A researcher has determined that a two-factor model is appropriate to determine the return of a stock. The factors are the percentage change in GNP and an interest rate. GNP is expected to grow by 3 percent, and the interest rate is expected to be 4.5 percent. A stock has a beta of 1.2 on the percentage change in GNP and a beta of -0.8 on the interest rate. If the expected rate of return for the stock is 11 percent, what is the revised expected return of the stock if GNP actually grows by 4.2 percent and interest rates are 4.6 percent?

12.2 Suppose a three-factor model is appropriate to describe the returns of a stock. Information about those three factors is presented in the following chart:

Factor	Beta of Factor	Expected Value	Actual Value
GNP	0.000586	$5,396	$5,436
Inflation	−1.40	3.1%	3.8%
Interest Rates	−0.67	9.5%	10.3%

  a. What is the systematic risk of the stock return?
  b. Suppose unexpected bad news about the firm was announced that causes the stock price to drop by 2.6 percent. If the expected return of the stock is 9.5 percent, what is the total return on this stock?

12.3 Suppose a factor model is appropriate to describe the returns on a stock. The current expected return on the stock is 10.5 percent. Information about those factors is presented in the following chart:

Factor	Beta of Factor	Expected Value	Actual Value
Growth in GNP	2.04	3.5%	4.8%
Inflation	−1.90	7.1%	7.8%

  a. What is the systematic risk of the stock return?
  b. The firm announced that its market share had unexpectedly increased from 23 percent to 27 percent. Investors know from past experience that the stock return will increase by 0.36 percent for every 1 percent increase in its market share. What is the unsystematic risk of the stock?
  c. What is the total return on this stock?

12.4 Suppose stock returns can be explained by the following three-factor model:

$$R_i = R_F + \beta_1 F_1 + \beta_2 F_2 + \beta_3 F_3$$

Assume there is no firm-specific risk. The information for each stock is presented here:

	β_1	β_2	β_3
Stock A	1.20	0.90	0.20
Stock B	0.80	1.40	−0.30
Stock C	0.95	−0.05	1.50

The risk premiums for the factors are 5.5 percent, 4.2 percent, and 4.9 percent, respectively. If you create a portfolio with 20 percent invested in stock A, 20 percent invested in stock B, and the remainder in stock C, what is the expression for the return of your portfolio? If the risk-free rate is 5 percent, what is the expected return of your portfolio?

12.5 Suppose stock returns can be explained by a two-factor model. The firm specific risks for all stocks are independent. The following table shows the information for two diversified portfolios:

	β_1	β_2	E(R)
Portfolio A	0.75	1.20	18%
Portfolio B	1.60	−0.20	14%

If the risk-free rate is 6 percent, what are the risk premiums for each factor in this model?

12.6 The following three stocks are available in the market:

	E(R)	β
Stock A	10.5%	1.20
Stock B	13.0%	0.98
Stock C	15.7%	1.37
Market	14.2%	1.00

Assume the market model is valid.
a. Write the market model equation for each stock.
b. What is the return on a portfolio with weights of 30 percent stock A, 45 percent stock B, and 25 percent stock C?
c. Suppose the return on the market is 15 percent and there are no unsystematic surprise in the returns. What is the return on each stock? What is the return on the portfolio?

12.7 You are forming an equally weighted portfolio of stocks. Many stocks have the same beta of 0.84 for factor 1 and the same beta of 1.69 for factor 2. All stocks also have the same expected return of 11 percent. Assume a two-factor model describes the return on each of these stocks.
a. Write the equation of the returns on your portfolio if you place only five stocks in it.
b. Write the equation of the returns on your portfolio if you place in it a very large number of stocks that all have the same expected returns and the same betas.

The APT

12.8 There are two stock markets, each driven by the same common force F with an expected value of zero and standard deviation of 10 percent. There are many securities in each market; thus you can invest in as many stocks as you wish. Due to restrictions, however, you can invest in only one of the two markets. The expected return on every security in both markets is 10 percent.

The returns for each security i in the first market are generated by the relationship

$$R_{1i} = 0.10 + 1.5F + \varepsilon_{1i}$$

where $\varepsilon_1 i$ is the term that measures the surprises in the returns of stock i in market 1. These surprises are normally distributed; their mean is zero. The returns for security j in the second market are generated by relationship

$$R_{2j} = 0.10 + 0.5F + \varepsilon_{2j}$$

where $\varepsilon_2 j$ is the term that measures the surprises in the returns of stock j in market 2. These surprises are normally distributed; their mean is zero. The standard deviation of $\varepsilon_1 i$ and $\varepsilon_2 j$ for any two stocks, i and j, is 20 percent.
a. If the correlation between the surprises in the returns of any two stocks in the first market is zero, and if the correlation between the surprises in the returns of any two stocks in the second market is zero, in which market would a risk-averse person prefer to invest? (Note: The correlation between ε_{1i} and ε_{1j} for any i and j is zero, and the correlation between ε_{2i} and ε_{2j} for any i and j is zero.)
b. If the correlation between $\varepsilon_1 i$ and $\varepsilon_1 j$ in the first market is 0.9 and the correlation between ε_{2i} and ε_{2j} in the second market is zero, in which market would a risk-averse person prefer to invest?
c. If the correlation between ε_{1i} and ε_{1j} in the first market is zero and the correlation between ε_{2i} and ε_{2j} in the second market is 0.5, in which market would a risk-averse person prefer to invest?
d. In general, what is the relationship between the correlations of the disturbances in the two markets that would make a risk-averse person equally willing to invest in either of the two markets?

12.9   Assume that the following market model adequately describes the return-generating behaviour of risky assets:

$$R_{it} = \alpha_i + \beta_i R_{Mt} + \varepsilon_{it}$$

Here:

R_{it} = The return for the ith asset at time t.

R_{Mt} = The return on a portfolio containing all risky assets in some proportion at time t.

R_{Mt} and ε_{it} are statistically independent.

Short selling (i.e., negative positions) is allowed in the market. You are given the following information:

Asset	β_i	$E(R_i)$	$Var(\varepsilon_i)$
A	0.7	8.41%	0.0100
B	1.2	12.06	0.0144
C	1.5	13.95	0.0225

The variance of the market is 0.0121 and there are no transaction costs.

a. Calculate the standard deviation of returns for each asset.
b. Calculate the variance of return of three portfolios containing an infinite number of asset types A, B, or C, respectively.
c. Assume the risk-free rate is 3.3 percent and the expected return on the market is 10.6 percent. Which asset will not be held by rational investors?
d. What equilibrium state will emerge such that no arbitrage opportunities exist? Why?

12.10. Assume that the returns of individual securities are generated by the following two-factor model:

$$R_{it} = E(R_{it}) + \beta_{i1}F_{1t} + \beta_{i2}F_{2t}$$

Here:

R_{it} is the return for security i at time t.

F_{1t} and F_{2t} are market factors with zero expectation and zero covariance.

In addition, assume that there is a capital market for four securities, and the capital market for these four assets is perfect in the sense that there are no transaction costs and short sales (i.e., negative positions) are permitted. The characteristics of the four securities follow:

Security	β_1	β_2	$E(R)$
1	1.0	1.5	20%
2	0.5	2.0	20
3	1.0	0.5	10
4	1.5	0.75	10

a. Construct a portfolio containing (long or short) securities 1 and 2, with a return that does not depend on the market factor, F_{1t}, in any way. (*Hint:* Such a portfolio will have $\beta_1 = 0$.) Compute the expected return and β_2 coefficient for this portfolio.
b. Following the procedure in (a), construct a portfolio containing securities 3 and 4 with a return that does not depend on the market factor F_{1t}. Compute the expected return and β_2 coefficient for this portfolio.
c. There is a risk-free asset with expected return equal to 5 percent, $\beta_1 = 0$, and $\beta_2 = 0$. Describe a possible arbitrage opportunity in such detail that an investor could implement it.
d. What effect would the existence of these kinds of arbitrage opportunities have on the capital markets for these securities in the short and long run? Graph your analysis.

MINICASE: The Fama–French Multifactor Model and Mutual Fund Returns

Dawn Browne, an investment broker, has been approached by client Jack Wong about the risk of his U.S. investments. Dawn has recently read several articles concerning the risk factors that can potentially affect asset returns, and she has decided to examine Jack's mutual fund holdings. Jack is currently invested in the Fidelity Magellan Fund (FMAGX), the Fidelity Low-Priced Stock Fund (FLPSX), and the Baron Small Cap Fund (BSCFX).

Dawn would like to estimate the well-known multifactor model proposed by Eugene Fama and Ken French to determine the risk of each mutual fund. Here is the regression equation for the multifactor model she proposes to use:

$$R_{it} - R_{Ft} = \alpha_i + \beta_1(R_{Mt} - R_{Ft}) + \beta_2(SMB_t) + \beta_3(HML_t) + \varepsilon_t$$

In the regression equation, R_{it} is the return of asset i at time t, R_{Ft} is the risk-free rate at time t, and RM_t is the return on the market at time t. Thus, the first risk factor in the Fama–French regression is the market factor often used with the CAPM.

The second risk factor, SMB or "small minus big," is calculated by taking the difference in the returns on a portfolio of small-cap stocks and a portfolio of big-cap stocks. This factor is intended to pick up the so-called small firm effect. Similarly, the third factor, HML or "high minus low," is calculated by taking the difference in the returns between a portfolio of "value" stocks and a portfolio of "growth" stocks. Stocks with low market-to-book ratios are classified as value stocks and vice versa for growth stocks. This factor is included because of the historical tendency for value stocks to earn a higher return.

In models such as the one Dawn is considering, the alpha (α) term is of particular interest. It is the regression intercept; but more important, it is also the excess return the asset earned. In other words, if the alpha is positive, the asset earned a return greater than it should have given its level of risk; if the alpha is negative, the asset earned a return lower than it should have given its level of risk. This measure is called "Jensen's alpha," and it is a very widely used tool for mutual fund evaluation.

1. For a large-company stock mutual fund, would you expect the betas to be positive or negative for each of the factors in a Fama–French multifactor model?

2. The Fama–French factors and risk-free rates are available at Ken French's Web site: mba.tuck. dartmouth.edu/pages/faculty/ken.french/. Download the monthly factors and save the most recent 60 months for each factor. The historical prices for each of the mutual funds can be found on various Web sites, including finance.yahoo.com. Find the prices of each mutual fund for the same time as the Fama–French factors and calculate the returns for each month. Be sure to include dividends. For each mutual fund, estimate the multifactor regression equation using the Fama–French factors. How well do the regression estimates explain the variation in the return of each mutual fund?

3. What do you observe about the beta coefficients for the different mutual funds? Comment on any similarities or differences.

4. If the market is efficient, what value would you expect for alpha? Do your estimates support market efficiency?

5. Which fund has performed best considering its risk? Why?

Risk, Return, and Capital Budgeting

EXECUTIVE SUMMARY

Our text has devoted a number of chapters to net present value (NPV) analysis. We argued that a dollar to be received in the future is worth less than a dollar received today for two reasons. First, there is the simple time value of money argument in a riskless world. If you have a dollar today, you can invest it in the bank and receive more than a dollar by some future date. Second, a risky dollar is worth less than a riskless dollar. Consider a firm expecting a $1 cash flow. If actuality exceeds expectations (revenues are especially high or expenses are especially low), perhaps $1.10 or $1.20 will be received. If actuality falls short of expectations, perhaps only $0.80 or $0.90 will be received. This risk is unattractive to the typical firm.

Our work on NPV allowed us to value riskless cash flows precisely, discounting by the riskless interest rate. However, because most real-world cash flows in the future are risky, business demands a procedure for discounting risky cash flows. This chapter applies the concept of net present value to risky cash flows.

We begin by reviewing previous chapters' words on NPV. We've learned that the basic NPV formula for an investment that generates incremental cash flows (C_t) in future periods is

$$NPV = C_0 + \sum_{t=1}^{T} \frac{C_t}{(1 + r)^t}$$

For risky projects, expected incremental cash flows $\overline{C}_t$ are placed in the numerator, and the NPV formula becomes

$$NPV = C_0 + \sum_{t=1}^{T} \frac{\overline{C}_t}{(1 + r)^t}$$

The discount rate depends on three sources of capital—equity, debt, and preferred shares. Since equity is the only source that can provide 100 percent of the financing and because it is the most complex of the three, we start with the cost of equity. The costs of debt and preferred shares are considered subsequently.

In this chapter, we will show that the discount rate used to determine the NPV of a risky project can be computed from the CAPM (or APT). For example, if an all-equity firm is seeking to value a risky project, such as renovating a warehouse, the firm will determine the required return, r_S, on the project by using the SML. We call r_S the firm's **cost of equity** capital.

When firms finance with both debt and equity, the discount rate to use is the project's overall cost of capital. The overall cost of capital is a weighted average of the cost of debt, the cost of equity, and the cost of preferred shares.

FIGURE 13.1

Choices of a Firm With Extra Cash

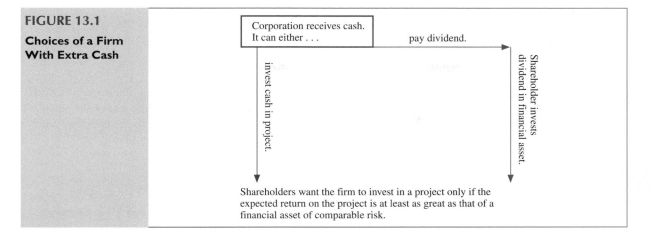

Corporation receives cash. It can either . . .

pay dividend.

invest cash in project.

Shareholder invests dividend in financial asset.

Shareholders want the firm to invest in a project only if the expected return on the project is at least as great as that of a financial asset of comparable risk.

13.1 The Cost of Equity Capital

Whenever a firm has extra cash, it can take one of two actions. It can pay out the cash immediately as a dividend or the firm can invest extra cash in a project, paying out the future cash flows of the project as dividends. Which procedure would the shareholders prefer? If they can reinvest the dividend in a financial asset (a stock or bond) with the same risk as that of the project, the shareholders would desire the alternative with the higher expected return. In other words, the project should be undertaken only if its expected return is greater than that of a financial asset of comparable risk. This is illustrated in Figure 13.1. A very simple capital budgeting rule follows: The discount rate of a project should be the expected return on a financial asset of comparable risk.

From the firm's perspective, the expected return is the cost of equity capital. If we use the CAPM for returns, the expected return on the stock will be

$$\overline{R} = R_F + \beta \times (\overline{R}_M - R_F) \tag{13.1}$$

where $\overline{R}_M - R_F$ is the excess market return and R_F is the risk-free rate.[1]

We now have the tools to estimate a firm's cost of equity capital. To do this, we need to know three things:

- The risk-free rate, R_F.
- The market risk premium, $\overline{R}_M - R_F$.
- The company beta, β_i.

EXAMPLE 13.1

Suppose the stock of the Quatram Company, a publisher of university textbooks, has a beta of 1.3. The firm is 100 percent equity financed; that is, it has no debt. Quatram is considering a number of capital budgeting projects that will double its size. Because these new projects are similar to the firm's existing ones, the average beta on the new projects is assumed to be equal to Quatram's existing beta. The market risk premium is 8.5 percent and the risk-free rate is 7 percent. What is the appropriate discount rate for these new projects?

---

[1]Of course, we can use the k-factor APT model (Chapter 12) and estimate several beta coefficients. However, for our purposes it is sufficient to estimate a single beta.

Now we can estimate the cost of equity r_S for Quatram as

$$r_s = 7\% + (8.5\% \times 1.3)$$
$$= 7\% + 11.05\%$$
$$= 18.05\%$$

Two key assumptions were made in this example: (1) The beta risk of the new projects is the same as the risk of the firm, and (2) the firm is all-equity financed. Given these assumptions, it follows that the cash flows of the new projects should be discounted at the 18.05 percent rate.

EXAMPLE 13.2

Suppose Alpha Air Freight is an all-equity firm with a beta of 1.21. Further suppose the market risk premium is 4 percent, and the risk-free rate is 6 percent. We can determine the expected return on the common stock of Alpha Air Freight by using the SML of Equation (13.1). We find that the expected return is

$$6\% + (1.21 \times 4.0\%) = 10.8\%$$

Because this is the return that shareholders can expect in the financial markets on a stock with a β of 1.21, it is the return they expect on Alpha Air Freight's stock.

Further suppose Alpha is evaluating the following independent projects:

Project	Project's Beta (β)	Project's Expected Cash Flows Next Year	Project's Internal Rate of Return	Project's NPV When Cash Flows Are Discounted at 10.8%	Accept or Reject
A	1.21	$140	40%	$26.4	Accept
B	1.21	120	20	8.3	Accept
C	1.21	109	9	−1.6	Reject

Each project initially costs $100 and has a life of one year. All projects are assumed to have the same risk as the firm as a whole. Because the cost of equity capital is 10.8 percent, projects in an all-equity firm are discounted at this rate. Projects A and B have positive NPVs, and C will have a negative NPV. Thus, only A and B will be accepted.[2] This is illustrated in Figure 13.2.

---

[2]In addition to the SML, the dividend valuation model presented earlier in the text can be used to represent the firm's cost of equity capital. Using this model, the present value (P) of the firm's expected dividend payments can be expressed as

$$P = \frac{\text{Div}_1}{(1 + r_s)} + \frac{\text{Div}_2}{(1 + r_s)^2} + \ldots + \frac{\text{Div}_N}{(1 + r_s)^N} + \ldots \qquad (a)$$

where r_s is the required return of shareholders and the firm's cost of equity capital. If the dividends are expected to grow at a constant rate, g, equation (a) reduces to

$$P = \frac{\text{Div}_1}{r_s - g} \qquad (b)$$

Equation (b) can be reformulated as

$$r_S = \frac{\text{Div}_1}{P} + g \qquad (c)$$

We can use equation (c) to estimate r_S. Div_1/P is the dividend yield expected over the next year. An estimate of the cost of equity capital is determined from an estimate of Div_1/P and g.

Although there is considerable debate, many consider the dividend valuation model to be both less theoretically sound and more difficult to apply than the SML. Hence, examples in this chapter calculate cost of equity capital using the SML approach.

FIGURE 13.2

Using the Security Market Line to Estimate the Risk-Adjusted Discount Rate for Risky Projects

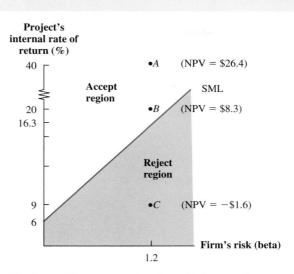

The diagonal line represents the relationship between the cost of equity capital and the firm's beta. An all-equity firm should accept an investment-type project whose internal rate of return is-greater than the cost of equity capital, and should reject an investment-type project whose internal rate of return is less than the cost of equity capital. (The above graph assumes that all projects are as risky as the firm.)

? Concept Questions

- What choices are available to a firm when extra cash is received?
- When estimating the cost of equity for Quatram, what key assumptions were made?

13.2 Estimation of Beta

In the previous example we assumed that the company beta was known. Of course, beta must be estimated in the real world. We pointed out earlier that the beta of a security is the standardized covariance of a security's return with the return on the market portfolio. The formula for security i, first given in Chapter 11, is

$$\text{Beta of security } i = \frac{\text{Cov}(R_i, R_M)}{\text{Var}(R_M)} = \frac{\sigma_{i,M}}{\sigma_M^2}$$

In words, the beta is the covariance of a security with the market, divided by the variance of the market. Because we calculated both covariance and variance in earlier chapters, calculating beta involves no new material.

EXAMPLE 13.3 (ADVANCED)

Suppose we sample the returns of the General Tool Company and the S&P/TSX 60 Index for four years. They are tabulated as follows:

Year	General Tool Company R_G	S&P/TSX Index R_M
1	−10%	−40%
2	3	−30
3	20	10
4	15	20

We can calculate beta in six steps:[3]

1. Calculate average return on each asset:

Average Return on General Tool:

$$\frac{-0.10 + 0.03 + 0.20 + 0.15}{4} = 0.07 \text{ (or 7\%)}$$

Average Return on Market Portfolio:

$$\frac{-0.40 - 0.30 + 0.10 + 0.20}{4} = -0.10 \text{ (or } -10\%)$$

2. For each asset, calculate the deviation of each return from the asset's average return determined above. This is presented in columns 3 and 5 of Table 13.1.
3. Multiply the deviation of General Tool's return by the deviation of the market's return. This is presented in column 6. This procedure is analogous to our calculation of covariance in an earlier chapter. The procedure will be used in the numerator of the beta calculation.
4. Calculate the squared deviation of the market's return. This is presented in column 7. This procedure is analogous to our calculation of variance in Chapter 10. The procedure will be used in the denominator of the beta calculation.

TABLE 13.1   Calculating Beta

(1) Year	(2) Rate of Return on General Tool (R_G)	(3) General Tool's Deviation from Average Return* $(R_G - \overline{R}_G)$	(4) Rate of Return on Market Portfolio	(5) Market Portfolio's Deviation from Average Return† $(R_M - \overline{R}_M)$	(6) Deviation of General Tool Multiplied by Deviation of Market Portfolio	(7) Squared Deviation of Market Portfolio
1	−0.10	−0.17 (−0.10 − 0.07)	−0.40	−0.30	0.051 [(−0.17) × (−0.30)]	0.090 [(−0.30) × (−0.30)]
2	0.03	−0.04	−0.30	−0.20	0.008	0.040
3	0.20	0.13	0.10	0.20	0.026	0.040
4	0.15	0.08	0.20	0.30	0.024	0.090
	Avg = 0.07		Avg = −0.10		Sum: 0.109	Sum: 0.260

Beta of General Tool: $0.419 = \dfrac{0.109}{0.260}$.

*Average return for General Tool is 0.07.

†Average return for market is −0.10.

---

[3]We present these calculations as an illustration. Chapter 11 discusses beta calculation with statistical software.

5. Take the sum of column 6 and the sum of column 7. They are

Sum of Deviation of General Tool Multiplied by Deviation of Market Portfolio:
$$0.051 + 0.008 + 0.026 + 0.024 = 0.109$$
Sum of Squared Deviation of Market Portfolio:
$$0.090 + 0.040 + 0.040 + 0.090 = 0.260$$

6. The beta is the sum of column 6 divided by the sum of column 7. This is

Beta of General Tool:
$$0.419 = \frac{0.109}{0.260}$$

Measuring Company Betas

The basic method of measuring company betas is to estimate:

$$\frac{\mathrm{Cov}(R_{it}, R_{Mt})}{\mathrm{Var}(R_{Mt})}$$

using $t = 1, 2, \ldots, T$ observations

Problems
1. Betas may vary over time.
2. The sample size may be inadequate.
3. Betas are influenced by changing financial leverage and business risk.

Solutions
1. Problems 1 and 2 (above) can be moderated by more sophisticated statistical techniques.
2. Problem 3 can be lessened by adjusting for changes in business and financial risk.
3. Look at average beta estimates of several comparable firms in the industry.

? Concept Questions
- How does one calculate the discount rate from the beta?
- What are the two key assumptions we used when calculating the discount rate?
- What are the six steps needed to calculate beta?

Beta Estimation in Practice

The General Tool Company discussed in the previous example is fictional. It is instructive to see how betas are determined for actual real-world companies. Figure 13.3 plots monthly returns for four large firms against monthly returns on the S&P/TSX Composite. As mentioned in Chapter 11, each firm has its own characteristic line. The slope of the characteristic line is beta, as estimated using the technique of Table 13.1. This technique is called *regression*. Though we have not shown it in the table, one can also determine the intercept (commonly called alpha) of the characteristic line by regression. Since a line can be created from its intercept and slope, the regression allows one to estimate the characteristic line of a firm.

We use five years of monthly data for each plot. While this choice is arbitrary, it is in line with calculations performed in the real world. Practitioners know that the accuracy of the beta coefficient is suspect when too few observations are used. Conversely, since firms may change their industry over time, observations from the distant past are out-of-date.

FIGURE 13.3 Plots of Five Years of Monthly Returns on Four Individual Securities Against Five Years of Monthly Returns of the Broad S&P/TSX Composite Index

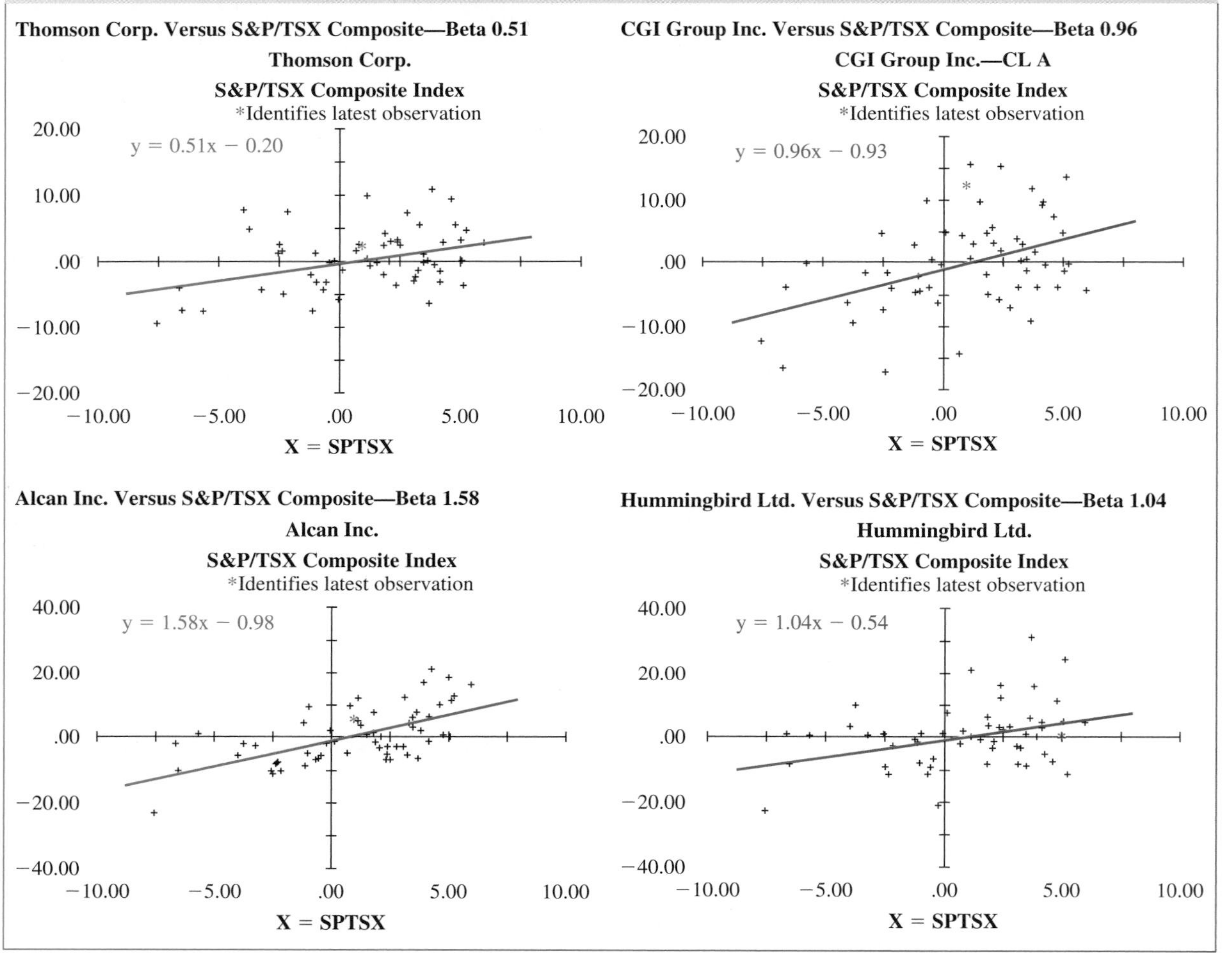

Source: Bloomberg LP.

The mechanics for calculating betas are quite simple. People in business frequently estimate beta by using commercially available computer programs. Certain hand-held calculators are also able to perform the calculation. In addition, a large number of services sell or even give away estimates of beta for different firms.

We stated in Chapter 11 that the average beta across all stocks in an index is 1. Of course, this need not be true for a subset of the index. For example, of the four securities in our figure, two have betas above 1 and two have betas below 1. Since beta is a measure of the risk of a single security for someone holding a large, diversified portfolio, our results indicate that The Thomson Corp. has relatively low risk and CGI Group Inc. has relatively high risk. A more detailed discussion of the determinants of beta is presented in Section 13.3.

Stability of Beta

We stated above that the beta of a firm is likely to change if the firm changes its industry. It is also interesting to ask the reverse question: Does the beta of a firm stay the same if its industry stays the same?

Take the case of Alcan Inc., a large firm that for the most part has stayed in the same industries for many decades. While Alcan is just one company, most analysts argue that betas are generally stable for firms remaining in the same industry. However, this is not to say that, as long as a firm stays in the same industry, its beta will *never* change. Changes in product line, changes in technology, or changes in the market may affect a firm's beta. For example, the deregulation of the airline industry has increased the betas of airline firms. Furthermore, as we will show in a later section, an increase in the leverage of a firm (i.e., the amount of debt in its capital structure) will increase the firm's beta.

Using an Industry Beta

Our approach of estimating the beta of a company from its own past data may seem commonsensical to you. However, it is frequently argued that one can better estimate a firm's beta by involving the whole industry. Consider Table 13.2, which shows the betas of some of the more prominent firms in the Canadian financial services industry. The average beta across all of the firms in the table is 0.56. Imagine a financial executive at National Bank of Canada trying to estimate the firm's beta. Because beta-estimation is subject to random variation, the executive may be uncomfortable with the estimate of 0.45. However, the error in beta-estimation on a single stock is much higher than the error for a portfolio of securities. This is because the error arises from unsystematic risk, which is greatly reduced in a portfolio, as we showed in Chapter 11. Thus, the executive of National Bank may use the industry beta of 0.56 as the estimate of her own firm's beta. (As it turns out, the choice is unimportant here, since the industry beta is quite close to that of the firm.)

By contrast, consider Bank of Montreal (BMO). Assuming a risk-free rate of 5 percent and a risk premium of 3.84 percent, BMO might estimate its cost of equity capital as:

$$5\% + 0.09 \times 3.84\% = 5.35\%$$

However, if BMO believed that the industry beta contained less estimation error, it could estimate its cost of equity capital as:

$$5\% + 0.56 \times 3.84\% = 7.15\%$$

The difference is substantial here, perhaps presenting a difficult choice for a financial executive at BMO.

While there is no formula for selecting the right beta, there is a very simple guideline. If one believes that the operations of the firm are similar to the operations of the rest of the industry, one should use the industry beta simply to reduce estimation error.[4] However, if an executive believes that the operations of the firm are fundamentally different from those in the rest of the industry, the firm's beta should be used.

In Canada, we often find large firms, such as Bombardier, Nortel, and Air Canada, which dominate their respective industries. For such firms, industry betas would not work well.

? Concept Questions

- What is the disadvantage of using too few observations when estimating beta?
- What is the disadvantage of using too many observations when estimating beta?
- What is the disadvantage of using the industry beta as the estimate of the beta of an individual firm?

[4] As we will see later, an adjustment must be made when the debt level in the industry is different from that of the firm.

Company	Beta
Bank of Montreal	0.54
Canadian Imperial Bank of Commerce	0.71
National Bank of Canada	0.48
Toronto-Dominion Bank	1.00
AGF Management Ltd.	1.21
Power Financial	0.64
Fairfax Financial	1.92
Bank of Nova Scotia	0.56
Investors Group	0.89
RBC Financial Group	0.59
Equally Weighted Portfolio	0.85

TABLE 13.2
Betas for Firms in the Financial Services Industry

Source: www.fpinformat.ca.

13.3 Determinants of Beta

The regression analysis approach in the previous section does not tell us where beta comes from. The beta of a stock does not come out of thin air. Rather, it is determined by the characteristics of the firm. If the firm is not traded on an exchange because it is a subsidiary of a larger firm or too small to be listed, examining these characteristics may be the best way to estimate beta.[5] We consider three factors: the cyclical nature of revenues, operating leverage, and financial leverage.

Cyclicality of Revenues

The revenues of some firms are quite cyclical. That is, these firms do well in the expansion phase of the business cycle and do poorly in the contraction phase. Empirical evidence suggests high-tech firms, retailers, and mining firms fluctuate with the business cycle. Firms in industries such as utilities and food are less dependent upon the cycle. Because beta is the standardized covariability of a stock's return with the market's return, it is not surprising that highly cyclical stocks have high betas.

It is worthwhile to point out that cyclicality is not the same as variability. For example, a movie studio has highly variable revenues because hits and flops are not easily predictable. However, because the revenues of a studio are more dependent on the quality of its releases than on the phase of the business cycle, motion picture companies are not particularly cyclical. In other words, stocks with high standard deviations need not have high betas, a point we have stressed before.

Operating Leverage

We distinguished fixed costs from variable costs earlier in the text. At that time, we mentioned that fixed costs do not change as quantity changes. Conversely, variable costs increase as the quantity of output rises. This difference between variable costs and fixed costs allows us to define operating leverage.

---

[5]An interesting example occurred in the debate over the cost of equity for Teleglobe in 1991 hearings before the Canadian Radio-Television and Telecommunications Commission. The debate was continued in C. S. Patterson, "The Cost of Equity Capital of a Non-Traded Unique Entity"; in L. Booth, "Estimating the Cost of Equity Capital of a Non-Traded Unique Entity"; and in C. S. Patterson, "Reply"; all in *Canadian Journal of Administrative Sciences* 10 (June 1993).

EXAMPLE 13.4

Consider a firm that can choose either technology A or technology B when making a particular product. The relevant differences between the two technologies are displayed below:

Technology A	Technology B
Fixed cost: $1,000/year	Fixed cost: $2,000/year
Variable cost: $8/unit	Variable cost: $6/unit
Price: $10/unit	Price: $10/unit
Contribution margin: $2 (or $10 − $8)	Contribution margin: $4 (or $10 − $6)

Technology A has lower fixed costs and higher variable costs than does technology B. Perhaps technology A involves less mechanization than does B. Or, the equipment in A may be leased whereas the equipment in B must be purchased. Alternatively, perhaps technology A involves few employees but many subcontractors, whereas B involves only highly skilled employees who must be retained in bad times. Because technology B has both lower variable costs and higher fixed costs, we say that it has higher **operating leverage**.[6]

Figure 13.4 graphs costs under both technologies. The slope of each total-cost line represents variable costs under a single technology. The slope of A's line is steeper, indicating greater variable costs.

Because the two technologies are used to produce the same products, a unit price of $10 applies for both cases. We mentioned in an earlier chapter that contribution margin is the difference between price and variable cost. It measures the incremental profit from one additional unit. The contribution margin in B is greater because its technology is riskier. An unexpected sale increases profit by $2 under A but increases profit by $4 under B. Similarly, an unexpected sale cancellation reduces profit by $2 under A but reduces profit by $4 under B. This is illustrated in Figure 13.5. This figure shows the change in earnings before interest and taxes for a given change in volume. The slope of the right-hand graph is greater, indicating that technology B is riskier.

FIGURE 13.4

Costs With Two Different Technologies

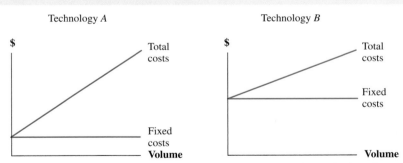

Technology A has higher variable costs and lower fixed costs than does technology B. Technology B has higher operating leverage.

---

[6]The actual definition of operating leverage is

$$\frac{\text{Change in EBIT}}{\text{EBIT}} \times \frac{\text{Sales}}{\text{Change in sales}}$$

where EBIT is earnings before interest and taxes. That is, operating leverage measures the percentage change in EBIT for a given percentage change in sales or revenues. It can be shown that operating leverage increases as fixed costs rise and as variable costs fall.

FIGURE 13.5

Illustration of the Effect of a Change in Volume on the Change in Earnings Before Interest and Taxes (EBIT)

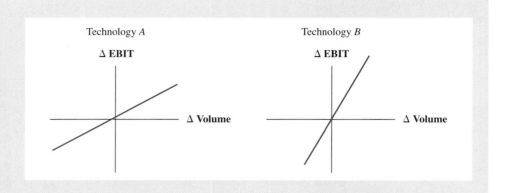

The cyclicality of a firm's revenues is a determinant of the firm's beta. Operating leverage magnifies the effect of cyclicality on beta. As mentioned earlier, business risk is generally defined as the risk of the firm without financial leverage. Business risk depends both on the responsiveness of the firm's revenues to the business cycle and on the firm's operating leverage.

While the above discussion concerns firms, it applies to projects as well. If one cannot estimate a project's beta in another way, one can examine the project's revenues and operating leverage. Those projects whose revenues appear strongly cyclical and whose operating leverage appears high are likely to have high betas. Conversely, weak cyclicality and low operating leverage imply low betas. As mentioned earlier, this approach is unfortunately qualitative in nature. Because start-up projects have little data, quantitative estimates of their betas generally are not feasible.

Financial Leverage and Beta

As suggested by their names, operating leverage and financial leverage are analogous concepts. Operating leverage refers to the firm's fixed costs of *production*. Financial leverage is the extent to which a firm relies on debt. Because a levered firm must make interest payments regardless of the firm's sales, financial leverage refers to the firm's fixed costs of *finance*.

In our discussion of beta, we have been implicitly using the firm's **equity beta.** This is the beta of the common stock of the firm. Actually, a firm has an asset beta as well as an equity beta. As the name suggests, the **asset beta** is the beta of the assets of the firm. The asset beta may also be thought of as the beta of the common stock if the firm had been financed with equity only.

Imagine an individual who owns all of the firm's debt and all of its equity. In other words, this individual owns the entire firm. What is the beta of this investor's portfolio of the firm's debt and equity?

As with any portfolio, the beta of this portfolio is a weighted average of the betas of the individual items in the portfolio. Hence, we have

$$\beta_{\text{Portfolio}} = \beta_{\text{Asset}} = \frac{\text{Debt}}{\text{Debt} + \text{Equity}} \times \beta_{\text{Debt}} + \frac{\text{Equity}}{\text{Debt} + \text{Equity}} \times \beta_{\text{Equity}} \quad (13.2)$$

where β_{Equity} is the beta of the equity of the *levered* firm. Notice that the beta of debt is multiplied by Debt/(Debt + Equity), the percentage of debt in the capital structure. Similarly, the beta of equity is multiplied by the percentage of equity in the capital structure.

Because the portfolio is the levered firm, the beta of the portfolio is equal to the beta of the levered firm. This is what we refer to as the firm's *asset beta*.

The beta of debt is very low in practice. If we make the commonplace assumption that the beta of debt is zero, we have

$$\beta_{\text{Asset}} = \frac{\text{Equity}}{\text{Debt} + \text{Equity}} \times \beta_{\text{Equity}} \qquad (13.3)$$

Because Equity/(Debt + Equity) must be below 1 for a levered firm, it follows that $\beta_{\text{Asset}} < \beta_{\text{Equity}}$. In words, the beta of the unlevered firm must be less than the beta of the equity in an otherwise identical levered firm. Rearranging the above equation, we have

$$\beta_{\text{Equity}} = \beta_{\text{Asset}}\left(1 + \frac{\text{Debt}}{\text{Equity}}\right)$$

The equity beta will always be greater than the asset beta with financial leverage.[7]

EXAMPLE 13.5

Consider a tree-growing company, Rapid Cedars Inc., which is currently all equity and has a beta of 0.8. The firm has decided to move to a capital structure of one part debt to two parts equity. Because the firm is staying in the same industry, its asset beta should remain at 0.8. However, assuming a zero beta for its debt, its equity beta would become

$$\beta_{\text{Equity}} = \beta_{\text{Asset}}\left(1 + \frac{\text{Debt}}{\text{Equity}}\right)$$
$$1.2 = 0.8\left(1 + \frac{1}{2}\right)$$

If the firm had one part debt to one part equity in its capital structure, its equity beta would be

$$1.6 = 0.8\,(1 + 1)$$

However, as long as it stayed in the same industry, its asset beta would remain at 0.8. The effect of leverage, then, is to increase the equity beta.

? Concept Questions
- **What are determinants of equity betas?**
- **What is the difference between an asset beta and an equity beta?**

13.4 Extensions of the Basic Model

The Firm Versus the Project: *Vive la Différence*

We now assume that the risk of a project differs from that of the firm, while keeping the all-equity assumption. We began the chapter by pointing out that each project should be paired with a financial asset of comparable risk. If a project's beta differs from that of the

---

[7]It can be shown that the relationship between a firm's asset beta and its equity beta with corporate taxes is

$$\beta_{\text{Equity}} = \beta_{\text{Asset}}\left[1 + (1 - T_c)\frac{\text{Debt}}{\text{Equity}}\right]$$

See Chapter 18 for more details.

firm, the project should be discounted at the rate commensurate with its own beta. This is a very important point because firms frequently speak of a *corporate discount rate. (Hurdle rate, cutoff rate, benchmark,* and *cost of capital* are frequently used synonymously.) Unless all projects in the corporation are of the same risk, choosing the same discount rate for all projects is incorrect.

EXAMPLE 13.6

D. D. Ronnelley Co., a publishing firm, may accept a project in computer software. Noting that computer software companies have high betas, the publishing firm views the software venture as more risky than the rest of its business. It should discount the project at a rate commensurate with the risk of software companies. For example, it might use the average beta of a portfolio of publicly traded software firms. On the other hand, if all projects in D. D. Ronnelley Co. were discounted at the same rate, a bias would result. The firm would accept too many high-risk projects (software ventures) and reject too many low-risk projects (books and magazines). This point is illustrated in Figure 13.6.

FIGURE 13.6

Relationship Between the Firm's Cost of Capital and the Security Market Line

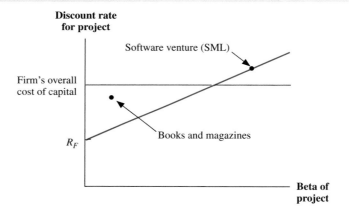

Use of a firm's cost of capital may lead to incorrect capital budgeting decisions. Projects with high risk, such as the software venture for D. D. Ronnelley Co., should be discounted at a high rate. By using the firm's cost of equity, the firm is likely to accept too many high-risk projects.

Projects with low risk should be discounted at a low rate. By using the firm's cost of capital, the firm is likely to reject too many low-risk projects.

The D. D. Ronnelley example assumes that the proposed project fits nicely into a particular industry, allowing the industry beta to be used. Unfortunately, many projects cannot be categorized so neatly. The beta of a new project may be greater than the beta of existing firms in the same industry because the very newness of the project likely increases its responsiveness to economywide movements. For example, a start-up computer venture may fail in a recession while Computerland, Corel, or IBM Canada will still be around. Conversely, in an economywide expansion, the venture may grow much faster than the established computer firms.

In addition, a new project may constitute its own industry. For example, do recent ventures that allow shopping by TV belong in the television industry, in the retail industry, or in an entirely new industry? We do not think the answer can easily be determined before the home shopping networks have had years of experience.

What beta should be used when an industrywide beta is not appropriate? One approach, which considers the determinants of the project's beta, was treated earlier in this chapter. Unfortunately, that approach is only qualitative in nature.

The Cost of Debt

The cost of debt is the return that the firm's long-term creditors demand on new borrowing. In principle, the beta for the firm's debt can be determined and then the SML could be used to estimate the required return on debt just as the required return on equity is estimated. In practice, this is not necessary.

Unlike a firm's cost of equity, its cost of debt can normally be observed either directly or indirectly, because the cost of debt is simply the interest rate the firm must pay on new borrowing, and we can observe the interest rates in the financial markets. For example, if the firm already has bonds outstanding, then the yield to maturity on those bonds is the market-required rate on the firm's debt.

Alternatively, if the firm's bonds were rated, say, *A,* the interest rate can be figured out by finding out what the rate is for newly issued *A*-rated bonds. Either way, there is no need to actually estimate a beta for the debt since the rate can be directly observed.

There is one thing to be careful about. The coupon rate on the firm's outstanding debt is irrelevant. This just tells us roughly what the firm's cost of debt was back when the bonds were issued, not what the cost of debt is today. This is why it is important to look at the yield on the debt in today's marketplace.

The Cost of Preferred Stock

Determining the cost of fixed rate preferred stock is quite straightforward. Preferred stock has a fixed dividend paid every period forever, so a share of preferred stock is essentially a perpetuity. The cost of preferred stock, r_P, is thus:

$$r_P = B / P_0$$

where B is the fixed dividend and P_0 is the current price per share of the preferred stock. Notice that the cost of preferred stock is simply equal to the dividend yield on the preferred stock. Alternatively, preferred stocks are rated in much the same way as bonds, so the cost of preferred stock can be estimated by observing the required returns on other, similarly rated shares of preferred stock.

The Weighted Average Cost of Capital

Now that we have the costs associated with the main sources of capital that the firm employs, we need to worry about the specific mix.

Because the average cost of capital for a firm is a weighting of its cost of equity and its cost of debt, it is usually referred to as the **weighted average cost of capital** (r_{WACC}). From now on we will use this term.

One of the implications of using WACC for a project is the assumption that money is raised in the optimal proportions. For instance, if the optimal weight for debt is 25 percent, raising $100 million means that $25 million will come from new debt and $75 million from common and preferred shares. Practically speaking, the firm would not raise these sums simultaneously by issuing both debt and equity. Instead, the firm may issue just debt, or just equity, which, at that point, has the effect of upsetting the optimal debt ratio. Issuing just one type of security and temporarily upsetting the optimal weights presents no problem as long as a subsequent issue takes the firm back to the optimal ratio for which it is striving. The point is that the firm's capital structure weights may fluctuate within some range in the short term, but the target weights should always be used in computing WACC.

Financial analysts frequently focus on a firm's total capitalization, which is the sum of its long-term debt and equity. This is particularly true in determining the cost of capital; short-term liabilities are often ignored in the process. Some short-term liabilities such as accounts payable and accrued wages rise automatically with sales increases and have already been incorporated into cash flow estimates. The reason for ignoring them in calculating the cost of capital is to avoid the error of double counting. Other current liabilities, short-term bank borrowing, for example, are excluded because they support seasonal needs and are not part of the permanent capital structure. It should be noted that if a firm used short-term bank loans as a part of its permanent financing, the cost would be included as part of the cost of debt.

The Capital Structure Weights

We use the symbol S (for stock) to stand for the market value of the firm's equity. We calculate this by taking the number of shares and multiplying it by the price per share. The procedure is the same for preferred shares, denoted by the symbol P. Similarly, we use the symbol B (for bonds) to stand for the market value of the firm's debt. For long-term debt, we calculate this by multiplying the market price of a single bond by the number of bonds outstanding.

For multiple bond issues (as there normally would be), we repeat this calculation for each and then add the results. If there is debt that is not publicly traded (because it was privately placed with a life insurance company, for example), we must observe the yields on similar, publicly traded debt and estimate the market value of the privately held debt using this yield as the discount rate.

Finally, the symbol V (for value) stands for the combined market value of the debt, equity and preferred:

$$V = S + B + P$$

If we divide both sides by V, we can calculate the percentages of the total capital represented by the debt, equity and preferred:

$$100\% = S/V + B/V + P/V$$

These percentages can be interpreted just like portfolio weights, and they are often called the capital structure weights.

The correct way to proceed is to use the market values of the debt and equity. The reason for this is that the market values measure the management's success in achieving its goal: maximizing shareholder wealth. Under certain circumstances, such as a privately owned company, it may not be possible to get reliable estimates of these quantities. Even for publicly traded firms, market value weights present some difficulties. If there is a major shift in stock or bond prices, market value weights may fluctuate significantly so that the weighted average cost of capital is quite another number by the time a weekend is over. In fact, some practitioners encounter some of these difficulties in computing WACC using market value weights, book values are usually the best alternative when market values are not readily available.

Taxes and the Weighted Average Cost of Capital

The previous result is called the unadjusted WACC because it does not consider the impact of debt on taxes. When determining the discount rate on after-tax cash flows, the discount rate also needs to be expressed on an after-tax basis.

As discussed previously in Chapter 2, the interest paid by a corporation is deductible for tax purposes. Payments to shareholders, such as dividends paid, are not. Thus, in determining an after-tax discount rate, we need to distinguish between the pre-tax and after-tax cost of debt.

To illustrate, suppose a firm borrows $1 million at 9 percent interest. The corporate tax rate is 40 percent. What is the after-tax interest rate on this loan? The total interest bill would be $90,000 per year. This amount is tax deductible, however, so the $90,000 interest reduces our tax bill by $0.40 \times \$90,000 = \$36,000$. The after-tax interest bill is thus $\$90,000 - \$36,000 = \$54,000$. The after-tax interest rate is $54,000 / $1 million = 5.4\%$.

Notice that the after-tax rate is simply equal to the pre-tax rate multiplied by one minus the tax rate. For example, using the preceding numbers, the after-tax interest rate is $9\% \times (1 - 0.40) = 5.4\%$.

The symbol T_C is used to denote the corporate tax rate. Thus, once the effect of taxes is factored into the WACC, the equation is:

$$\text{WACC} = (S/V) \times r_S + (B/V) \times r_B \times (1 - T_C) + (P/V) \times r_P$$

This WACC has a very straightforward interpretation. It is the overall return that the firm must earn on its existing assets to maintain the value of its stock. It is also the required return on any investments by the firm that have essentially the same risks as existing operations. So, if the cash flows were being evaluated from a proposed expansion of existing operations, this would be the discount rate used in the evaluation.

EXAMPLE 13.7

Consider a firm whose debt has a market value of $40 million and whose stock has a market value of $60 million (3 million outstanding shares of stock, each selling for $20 per share). The firm pays a 15 percent rate of interest on its new debt and has a beta of 1.41. The corporate tax rate is 34 percent. (Assume that the SML holds, that the risk premium on the market is 9.5 percent, and that the current Treasury bill rate is 11 percent.) What is this firm's r_{WACC}?

To compute the r_{WACC} using Equation (13.4), we must know: (1) the after-tax cost of debt, $r_B \times (1 - T_C)$; (2) the cost of equity, r_S; and (3) the proportions of debt and equity used by the firm. These three values are computed below.

1. The pre-tax cost of debt is 15 percent, implying an after-tax cost of 9.9 percent $[15\% \times (1 - 0.34)]$.
2. The cost of equity capital is computed by using the SML:

$$r_S = R_F + \beta \times [\bar{R}_M - R_F]$$
$$= 11\% + 1.41 \times 9.5\%$$
$$= 24.40\%$$

3. The proportions of debt and equity are computed from the market values of debt and equity. Because the market value of the firm is $100 million ($40 million + $60 million), the proportions of debt and equity are 40 and 60 percent, respectively.

The cost of equity, r_S, is 24.40 percent, and the after-tax cost of debt, $r_B \times (1 - T_C)$, is 9.9 percent. B is $40 million and S is $60 million. Therefore,

$$r_{WACC} = \frac{B}{V} \times r_B \times (1 - T_C) + \frac{S}{V} \times r_S$$

$$= \left(\frac{40}{100} \times 9.9\%\right) + \left(\frac{60}{100} \times 24.40\%\right) = 18.60\%$$

This procedure is presented in chart form next:

(1) Financing Components	(2) Market Values	(3) Weight	(4) Cost of Capital (after corporate tax)	(5) WACC
Debt	$ 40,000,000	0.40	15% × (1 − 0.34) = 9.9%	3.96%
Equity	60,000,000	0.60	11% + 1.41 × 9.5% = 24.40%	14.64
	$100,000,000	1.00		18.60%

The weights we used in the previous example were market-value weights. Market-value weights are more appropriate than book-value weights because the market values of the securities are closer to the actual dollars that would be received from their sale. Actually it is useful to think in terms of "target" market weights. These are the market weights expected to prevail over the life of the firm or project.

EXAMPLE 13.8

Suppose that a firm has both a current and a target debt–equity ratio of 0.6, a cost of debt of 15.15 percent, and a cost of equity of 20 percent. The corporate tax rate is 34 percent.

Our first step calls for transforming the debt-to-equity (B/S) ratio to a debt-to-value ratio. A B/S ratio of 0.6 implies 6 parts debt for 10 parts equity. Since value is equal to the sum of the debt plus the equity, the debt-to-value ratio is $\frac{6}{6 + 10} = 0.375$.

Similarly, the equity-to-value ratio is $\frac{10}{6 + 10} = 0.625$. The r_{WACC} will then be

$$r_{WACC} = \left(\frac{S}{V}\right) \times r_S + \left(\frac{B}{V}\right) \times r_B \times (1 - T_C)$$

$$= 0.625 \times 20\% + 0.375 \times 15.15\% \times (0.66) = 16.25\%$$

Suppose the firm is considering taking on a warehouse renovation costing $50 million that is expected to yield cost savings of $12 million a year for six years. Using the NPV equation and discounting the six years of expected cash flows from the renovation at the r_{WACC}, we have[8]

$$NPV = -\$50 + \frac{\$12}{(1 + r_{WACC})} + \ldots + \frac{\$12}{(1 + r_{WACC})^6}$$

$$= -\$50 + \$12 \times A^6_{0.1625}$$

$$= -\$50 + (12 \times 3.66)$$

$$= -\$6.07$$

Should the firm take on the warehouse renovation? The project has a negative NPV using the firm's r_{WACC}. This means that the financial markets offer superior projects in the same risk class (namely, the firm's risk class). The answer is clear: The firm should reject the project.

---

[8]This discussion of WACC has been implicitly based on perpetual cash flows. However, an important paper by J. Miles and R. Ezzel, "The Weighted Average Cost of Capital, Perfect Capital Markets and Project Life: A Clarification," *Journal of Financial and Quantitative Analysis* (September 1980), shows that the WACC is appropriate even when cash flows are not perpetual.

? Concept Questions

- **What is the relationship between the firm's cost of capital and the security market line (SML)?**
- **When calculating a firm's WACC, why are market-value weights more appropriate than book-value weights?**

13.5 Estimating the Cost of Capital for Rogers Communications

We will illustrate the practical application of the weighted average cost of capital by calculating it for Rogers Communications. The firm provides various services through its subsidiaries including wireless communications, cable television, home phone, and broadband Internet. The company also owns the Toronto Blue Jays and Sportsnet, a sports dedicated channel. These subsidiaries helped Rogers to attain $8,763 billion in revenue for 12 months ended September 30, 2006. In this application, market values for Rogers were observed as of September 30, 2006 and we calculate the WACC for that day.[9]

Complications and compromises arise in applying formulas in practice. As a cross-listed telecommunications company, Rogers does business in a number of currencies and across many borders; its financing reflects its multinational nature. Ideally, we should calculate the market value of all sources of financing and determine the relative weights of each source. If any difficulties arise in finding the market value of some non-traded bonds for Rogers, it would require us to use book values for debt.[10]

A related issue is the degree of precision we can attach to our measures of the cost of capital. Although we will make the computation carrying two decimal points, in reality our estimates are not that precise. When we use the final answer in capital budgeting, sensitivity analysis is highly recommended.

To find the market value weight of equity, we start by finding the total market value of all common stock. The market values are calculated as the number of shares times the share price. The figures for Rogers as of September 30, 2006, were 56,233,894 class A voting common shares and 261,130,061 class B non-voting common shares. Multiplying each by its price gives:

Security	Shares Outstanding	Market Price	Market Value (millions)
Class A shares	56,233,894	$65.81	$ 3,700
Class B shares	261,130,061	$61.20	15,981
			$19,681

---

[9]Information comes from www.globeinvestor.com, www.finance.yahoo.com and Rogers' Third Quarter 2006 Results at www.rogers.com. When calculating the cost of capital, it is common to ignore short-term financing, such as payables and accruals. We also ignore short-term debt unless it is a permanent source of financing. For simplicity, leases are not included in long-term debt for the purposes of this analysis.

[10]It is more important to use the market value for the calculation of equity weights than the calculation of debt weights, as the market value of common equity may differ markedly from its book value. For Rogers, we were fortunate to have access to the market values of the bonds through Bloomberg. Table 13.3 displays a complete list of all 22 bonds that Rogers has outstanding in addition to the amount outstanding, the weights and the weighted average cost of debt. Some of the YTM were estimated (as indicated) because the information was not present on the Bloomberg Financial Services program. This information enables us to use the market values instead of the book values, which helps to calculate a more applicable cost of debt.

To find the market value weight of debt, we must find the total market value of all the outstanding long-term debt. The before-tax cost of debt is what it would cost Rogers to issue long-term debt today. We estimate the cost of debt based on the weighted average current yield to maturities of the outstanding debt. Multiplying the bond yields by the weight of the outstanding debt is shown in Table 13.3.

The purpose of calculating the weighted average cost of debt is to estimate the cost of debt going forward. Using the amount of debt outstanding calculated in Table 13.3, the relative weighting of the debt and the equity is:

Security	Market Value (millions)	Weight (%)
Debt	$ 6,245.07	24.09%
Equity	19,681.00	75.91
	$25,926.07	100.00%

As you can see from the weights, Rogers uses common equity for 75.91 percent of its financing needs. Note that the calculation is simplified as both classes of common stock are combined.

TABLE 13.3   Weighted Average Cost of Debt for Rogers Communications

Issuer	Coupon	Price	Maturity	YTM	Amount Outstanding (millions)	Weight of Each Individual Debt	Weighted Average Cost of Debt
Rogers Cable Inc.	8.750	119.00	5/1/2032	7.124	$ 200.00	3.20%	0.228%
	6.750	101.13	3/15/2015	6.574	280.00	4.48	0.295
	5.500	94.50	3/15/2014	6.440	350.00	5.60	0.361
^	6.250	98.00	6/15/2016	6.613	350.00	5.60	0.371
	6.250	99.50	6/15/2013	6.341	350.00	5.60	0.355
	6.250	94.02	6/15/2013	7.396	350.00	5.60	0.415
	7.875	106.63	5/1/2012	6.443	350.00	5.60	0.361
	7.250	107.48	12/15/2011	5.569	175.00	2.80	0.156
Rogers Cantel	9.750	125.16	6/1/2016	6.157	154.90	2.48	0.153
	7.500	106.75	3/15/2015	6.450	550.00	8.81	0.568
Rogers Wireless	6.375	94.11	3/1/2014	7.422	0.67	0.01	0.001
	6.375	94.11	3/1/2014	7.422	0.67	0.01	0.001
	6.375	99.01	3/1/2014	6.544	749.33	12.00	0.785
	7.250	105.13	12/15/2012	6.238	470.00	7.53	0.469
	8.000	106.63	12/15/2012	6.674	400.00	6.41	0.427
	7.625	109.69	12/15/2011	5.456	459.50	7.36	0.401
	7.625	109.69	12/15/2011	5.456	0.50	0.01	0.000
	7.625	109.69	12/15/2011	5.456	0.50	0.01	0.000
	9.625	113.25	5/1/2011	6.250	496.00	7.94	0.496
	9.625	113.25	5/1/2011	6.250	4.00	0.06	0.004
	9.625	113.25	5/1/2011	6.250	4.00	0.06	0.004
*	FLOAT	102.42	12/15/2010	7.880	550.00	8.81	0.694
					$6,245.07	100.00%	6.547%

^Denotes that the price of the bond was estimated. The YTM was then calculated using this assumed price.
*The yield to maturity is approximated.

The before-tax cost of debt is an estimate of what it would cost Rogers to issue long-term debt today. To convert to an after-tax cost, we use the average tax rate for Rogers during 2005–06 of 36.1 percent:

$$r_B \times (1 - T_C) = 6.547\% \, (1 - 0.361) = 4.18\%$$

To determine the cost of common stock for Rogers we use the CAPM and the firm beta as Rogers is quite unique in Canada:

$$
\begin{aligned}
\beta &= 1.39^{11} \\
\text{Market risk premium} &= 4.32\%^{12} \\
\text{Risk-free rate} &= 4.16\%^{13} \\
r_S &= r_f + \beta(\text{market risk premium}) \\
&= 4.16\% + 1.39 \times (4.32\%) \\
&= 10.16\%
\end{aligned}
$$

To find the weighted average cost of capital, we weight the cost of each source:

$$
\begin{aligned}
r_{\text{WACC}} &= \frac{S}{V} \times r_S + \frac{B}{V} \times r_B \times (1 - T_C) \\
r_{\text{WACC}} &= 0.7591 \times 10.16\% + 0.2409 \times 4.18\% \\
r_{\text{WACC}} &= 8.72\%
\end{aligned}
$$

? Concept Questions

- **What compromises are necessary in computing WACC for Rogers?**

13.6 Reducing the Cost of Capital

Chapters 10–13 develop the idea that both the expected return on a stock and the cost of capital of the firm are positively related to risk. Recently, a number of academics have argued that expected return and cost of capital are negatively related to liquidity as well.[14] In addition, these scholars make the interesting point that, although it is quite difficult to lower the risk of a firm, it is much easier to increase the liquidity of the firm's stock. Therefore, they suggest that a firm can actually lower its cost of capital through liquidity enhancement. We develop this idea next.

What Is Liquidity?

Anyone who owns his or her own home probably thinks of liquidity in terms of the time it takes to buy or sell the home. For example, condominiums in large metropolitan areas are generally quite liquid. Particularly in good times, a condominium may sell within days of

---

[11] From www.fpinfomart.ca.

[12] This is the weighted average of the geometric and arithmetic risk premiums from Chapter 10 for the period 1957–2006. Blume's formula, found in Chapter 10, is used to calculate the average for a ten year forecast horizon using 50 years of past data.

[13] This is the Government of Canada 10-year benchmark bond yield from www.bankofcanada.ca. The 10-year benchmark bond yield is used because we are assuming that the new project will be long-term, having approximately a ten year lifespan. In a situation like this, we want to match the project length to that of the appropriate risk-free rate.

[14] For example, see Y. Amihud and H. Mendelson, "The Liquidity Route to a Lower Cost of Capital," *Journal of Applied Corporate Finance* (Winter 2000); M. J. Brennan and C. Tamarowski, "Investor Relations, Liquidity, and Stock Prices," *Journal of Applied Corporate Finance* (Winter 2000); and G. Jacoby, D. J. Fowler, and A. A. Gottesman, "The Capital Asset Pricing Model and the Liquidity Effect: A Theoretical Approach," *Journal of Financial Markets* 3 (2000).

being placed on the market. By contrast, single-family homes in suburban areas may take weeks or months to sell. Special properties such as multimillion dollar "executive homes" may take longer still.

The concept of liquidity is similar, but not identical, in stocks. Here, we speak of the *cost* of buying and selling instead. That is, those stocks that are expensive to trade are considered less liquid than those that trade cheaply. What do we mean by the cost to trade? We generally think of three costs here: brokerage fees, the bid–ask spread, and market-impact costs.

Brokerage fees are the easiest to understand, because you must pay a broker to execute a trade. More difficult is the bid–ask spread. Consider the New York Stock Exchange (NYSE), where all trades on a particular stock must go through the stock's specialist, who is physically on the floor of the exchange.[15] If you want to trade 100 shares of XYZ Co., your broker must get the *quote* from XYZ's specialist. Suppose the specialist provides a quote of 100–100.07. This means that you can buy from the specialist at $100.07 per share and sell to the specialist at $100 per share. Note that the specialist makes money here, since she buys from you at $100 and sells to you (or to someone else) at $100.07. The gain to the specialist is a cost to you, because you are losing $0.07 dollar per share over a round-trip transaction (over a purchase and a subsequent sale).

Finally, we have *market-impact costs*. Suppose that a trader wants to sell 10,000 shares instead of just 100 shares. Here, the specialist has to take on extra risk when buying. First, she has to pay out $100,000 (10,000 × $100), cash which may not be easily available to her. Second, the trader may be selling this large amount because she has special information that the stock will fall imminently. The specialist bears the risk of losing a lot of money on that trade. Consequently, to compensate for these risks, the specialist may not buy at $100/share but at a lower price. Similarly, the specialist may be willing to sell a large block of stock only at a price above $100.07. The price drop associated with a large sale and the price rise associated with a large purchase are the market-impact costs.

Liquidity, Expected Returns, and the Cost of Capital

The cost of trading a nonliquid stock reduces the total return that an investor receives. That is, if one buys a stock for $100 and sells it later for $105, the gain before trading costs is $5. If one must pay a dollar of commission when buying and another dollar when selling, the gain after trading costs is only $3. Both the bid–ask spread and market-impact costs would reduce this gain still further.

As we will see later, trading costs vary across securities. In the last four chapters, we have stressed that investors demand a high expected return as compensation when investing in high-risk, e.g., high-beta, stocks. Because the expected return to the investor is the cost of capital to the firm, the cost of capital is positively related to beta. Now, we are saying the same thing for trading costs. Investors demand a high expected return when investing in stocks with high trading costs, i.e., low liquidity. And, this high expected return implies a high cost of capital to the firm. This idea is illustrated in Figure 13.7.

Liquidity and Adverse Selection

Liquidity varies across stocks, because the factors determining liquidity vary across stocks. Although there are a number of factors, we focus on just one, *adverse selection*. As mentioned before, the specialist will lose money on a trade if the trader has information that

---

[15]On the Toronto Stock Exchange, trading is fully automated and there are no specialists. The issue of order execution remains an important one, as shown in L. Kryzanowski, "Trade Costs and Investment Performance," *Canadian Investment Review* (Summer 2001).

FIGURE 13.7

Liquidity and the Cost of Capital

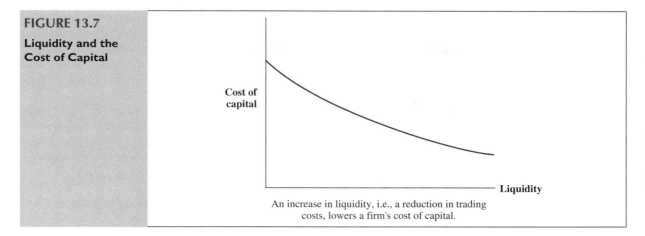

An increase in liquidity, i.e., a reduction in trading costs, lowers a firm's cost of capital.

the specialist does not have. If you have special information that the stock is worth $110 in the preceding example, you will want to buy shares at $100.07. The specialist is obligated to sell to you at this price, which is considerably below the true price of $110. Conversely, if you know that the stock is worth only $90 and you currently own 100 shares, you will be happy to sell these shares to the specialist at $100. Again, the specialist loses, since she pays $100/share for a stock worth only $90. In either of these cases, we say that the specialist has been *picked off,* or has been subject to adverse selection.

The specialist must protect herself in some way here. Of course, she cannot forbid informed individuals from trading, because she does not know ahead of time who these investors are. Her next best alternative is to widen the bid–ask spread, thereby increasing the costs of trading to *all* traders—both informed and uninformed. That is, if the spread is widened to, say 99.98–100.11, each trader pays a round-trip cost of $0.13 per share.

The key here is that the spread should be positively related to the ratio of informed to uninformed traders. That is, informed traders will pick off the specialist and uninformed traders will not. Thus, informed traders in a stock raise the required return on equity, thereby increasing the cost of capital.

What the Corporation Can Do

The corporation has an incentive to lower trading costs because—given the preceding discussion—a lower cost of capital should result. Amihud and Mendelson identify two general strategies for corporations. First, they argue that firms should try to bring in more uninformed investors. Stock splits may be a useful tool here. Imagine that a company has 1 million shares outstanding with a price per share of $100. Because investors generally buy in round lots of 100 shares, these investors would need $10,000 ($100 × 100 shares) for a purchase. A number of small investors might be "priced out" of the stock, although large investors would not be. Thus, the ratio of large investors to small investors would be high. Because large investors are generally more likely than small investors to be informed, the ratio of informed investors to uninformed investors will likely be high.

A 2:1 stock split would give two shares of stock for every one that the investor previously held. Because every investor would still hold the same proportional interest in the firm, each investor would be no better off than before. Thus, it is likely that the price per share will fall to $50 from $100. Here, an individual with 100 shares worth $10,000 ($100 × 100 shares) finds herself still worth $10,000 (= $50 × 200 shares) after the split.

However, a round lot becomes more affordable, thereby bringing more small and uninformed investors into the firm. Consequently, the adverse selection costs are reduced, allowing the specialist to lower the bid–ask spread. In turn, it is hoped that the expected return on the stock, and the cost of equity capital, will fall as well. If this happens, the stock might actually trade at a price slightly above $50.

Companies can also attract small investors by facilitating stock purchases through the Internet. Direct stock purchase plans and dividend reinvestment programs handled online allow small investors the opportunity to buy securities cheaply.

Secondly, companies can disclose more information. This narrows the gap between uninformed and informed investors, thereby lowering the cost of capital. Suggestions include providing greater financial data on corporate segments and more management forecasts. An interesting study by Coller and Yohn[16] concludes that the bid–ask spread is reduced after the release of these forecasts.

This section would not be complete without a discussion of security analysts. These analysts are employed by brokerage houses to follow the companies in individual industries. For example, an analyst for a particular brokerage house might follow all the firms in, say, the transportation industry. This analyst distributes reports and other information to the clients of the brokerage house. Virtually all brokerage houses have analysts following the major industries. Again, through dissemination of the information, these analysts narrow the gap between the informed and the uninformed investors, thereby tending to reduce the bid–ask spread.

Although all major industries are covered, the smaller firms in these industries are often ignored, implying a higher bid–ask spread and a higher cost of capital for these firms. Analysts frequently state that they avoid following companies that release little information, pointing out that these companies are more trouble than they are worth. Thus, it behooves companies that are not followed to release as much information as possible to security analysts in the hopes of attracting their interest. Friendliness toward security analysts would be very helpful as well. The argument here is not to get the analysts to make buy recommendations. Rather, it is simply to interest the analysts in following the company, thereby reducing the information asymmetry between informed and uninformed investors.

? Concept Questions

- **What is liquidity?**
- **What is the relation between liquidity and expected returns?**
- **What is adverse selection?**
- **What can a corporation do to lower its cost of capital?**

13.7 SUMMARY AND CONCLUSIONS

Earlier chapters on capital budgeting assumed that projects generate riskless cash flows. The appropriate discount rate in those cases is the riskless interest rate. Of course, most cash flows from real-world capital budgeting projects are risky. This chapter discusses the discount rate when cash flows are risky.

1. A firm with excess cash can either pay a dividend or make a capital expenditure. Because shareholders can reinvest the dividend in risky financial assets, the expected return on a capital budgeting project should be at least as great as the expected return on a financial asset of comparable risk.

---

[16]M. Coller and T. Yohn, "Management Forecasts and Information Asymmetry: An Examination of Bid–Ask Spreads," *Journal of Accounting Research* (Fall 1997).

2. The expected return on any asset is dependent upon its beta. Thus, we showed how to estimate the beta of a stock. The appropriate procedure employs regression analysis on historical returns.

3. We considered the case of a project whose beta risk was equal to that of the firm. If the firm is unlevered, the discount rate on the project is equal to

$$R_F + \beta \times (\overline{R}_M - R_F)$$

where $\overline{R}_M$ is the expected return on the market portfolio and R_F is the risk-free rate. In words, the discount rate on the project is equal to the CAPM's estimate of the expected return on the security.

4. If the project's beta differs from that of the firm, the discount rate should be based on the project's beta. The project's beta can sometimes be estimated by determining the average beta of the project's industry.

5. The beta of a company is a function of a number of factors. Perhaps the three most important are
   • Cyclicality of revenues
   • Operating leverage
   • Financial leverage.

6. Sometimes one should not use the average beta of the project's industry as an estimate of the beta of the project. In this case, one can estimate the project's beta by considering the project's cyclicality of revenues and its operating leverage. This approach is qualitative in nature.

7. If a firm uses debt, the discount rate to use is the r_{WACC}. In order to calculate r_{WACC}, the cost of equity and the cost of debt applicable to a project must be estimated. Assuming a scale-enhancing project, the cost of equity can be estimated using the SML for the firm's equity. Conceptually, a dividend growth model could be used as well, though it is likely to be far less accurate in practice. In Chapter 18, three well-known approaches for incorporating debt are presented.

8. A number of academics have argued that expected returns are negatively related to liquidity, where high liquidity is equivalent to low costs of trading. These scholars have further suggested that firms can reduce their cost of capital by lowering these trading costs. Practical suggestions include stock splits, more complete dissemination of information, and more effective assistance to security analysts.

Visit us at www.mcgrawhill.ca/olc/ross

KEY TERMS

Asset beta 362
Cost of equity 352
Equity beta 362

Operating leverage 361
Weighted average cost of capital (r_{WACC}) 365

SUGGESTED READING

The following article contains a superb discussion of some of the subtleties of using WACC for project evaluation:
J. Miles and R. Ezzel. "The Weighted Average Cost of Capital, Perfect Capital Markets and Project Life: A Clarification." *Journal of Financial and Quantitative Analysis* 15 (September 1980).

The following article provides a comprehensive survey of capital budgeting in practice, including the determination of the cost of capital:
J. R. Graham and C. R. Harvey. "The Theory and Practice of Corporate Finance: Evidence from the Field." *Journal of Financial Economics* (May 2001).

Estimates of the cost of capital under both the capital asset pricing model and the arbitrage pricing theory are contained in:
E. F. Fama and K. R. French. "Industry Cost of Capital." *Journal of Financial Economics* (February 1997).

One of the best "how-to" guides is:

T. Copeland, T. Koller, and J. Murrin. *Valuation: Measuring and Managing the Value of Companies.* 2nd ed. New York: John Wiley & Sons, 1995.

A good discussion of liquidity issues for stocks listed on the Toronto Stock Exchange is:

L. Kryzanowski. "Trade Costs and Investment Performance." *Canadian Investment Review* (Summer 2001).

QUESTIONS & PROBLEMS

Beta and the Cost of Equity

13.1   Furniture Depot Inc. is an all-equity firm with a beta of 1.6. The market risk premium is 9 percent and the risk-free rate is 5 percent. The company is considering a project that will generate annual after-tax cash flows of $510,000 at year-end for five years. The project requires an immediate investment of $1.45 million. If the project has the same risk as the firm as a whole, should Furniture Depot undertake the project?

13.2   The Dybvig Corporation's common stock has a beta of 1.3. If the risk-free rate is 4.5 percent and the expected return on the market is 12 percent, what is Dybvig's cost of equity capital?

13.3   The correlation between the returns on Ceramics Craftsman Inc. and the returns on the S&P/TSX 60 is 0.910. The variance of the returns on Ceramics Craftsman Inc. is 0.005112, and the variance of the returns on the S&P/TSX 60 is 0.001668. What is the beta of Ceramics Craftsman stock?

EXCEL

13.4   The returns from the past 13 quarters on Mercantile Bank Corporation and the market are listed below.

Mercantile	Market
−0.009	0.023
0.051	0.058
−0.001	−0.020
−0.045	−0.050
0.085	0.071
0.000	0.012
−0.080	−0.075
0.020	0.050
0.125	0.120
0.110	0.049
−0.100	−0.030
0.040	0.028

The covariance of Mercantile Bank Corporation's return with the market's return is 0.038711. The market variance is 0.038588. The expected returns on Mercantile and the market are 0.016333 and 0.019667, respectively.

a. What is the beta of Mercantile Bank Corporation stock?

b. Is Mercantile's beta higher or lower than the beta of the average stock?

13.5   If you use the stock beta and the security market line to compute the discount rate for a project, what assumptions are you implicitly making?

13.6   Lang Cosmetics is evaluating a project to produce a perfume line. Lang currently produces no body-scent products and is an all-equity firm.

a. Should Lang Cosmetics use its stock beta to evaluate the project?

b. How should Lang Cosmetics compute the appropriate beta to evaluate the project?

13.7   The following table lists possible rates of return on Compton Technology's stock and debt and on the market portfolio. The probability of each state is also listed.

State	Probability	Return on Stock (%)	Return on Debt (%)	Return on the Market (%)
1	0.15	4%	7%	6%
2	0.25	9	7	9
3	0.30	19	9	15
4	0.30	16	11	19

a. What is the beta of Compton Technology debt?

b. What is the beta of Compton Technology stock?

c. If the debt-to-equity ratio of Compton Technology is 0.5, what is the asset beta of Compton Technology? Assume no taxes.

The Cost of Debt

13.8 Bobby Inc. is trying to determine its cost of debt. The firm has a debt issue outstanding with 12 years to maturity that is quoted at 105 percent of face value. The issue makes semiannual payments and has a coupon rate of 8 percent annually. What is Bobby's pre-tax cost of debt? If the tax rate is 35 percent, what is the after-tax cost of debt?

13.9 Basketball Backboards Corp. issued a 30-year, 10 percent semiannual bond 7 years ago. The bond currently sells for 108 percent of its face value. The company's tax rate is 35 percent.

a. What is the pre-tax cost of debt?

b. What is the after-tax cost of debt?

c. Which is more relevant, the pre-tax or the after-tax cost of debt? Why?

13.10 For the firm in the previous problem, suppose the book value of the debt issue is $20 million. In addition, the company has a second debt issue on the market, a zero coupon bond with seven years left to maturity; the book value of this issue is $80 million and the bonds sell for 58 percent of par. What is the company's total book value of debt? The total market value? What is your best estimate of the after-tax cost of debt now?

Weighted Average Cost of Capital

13.11 Mullineaux Corporation has a target capital structure of 55 percent common stock and 45 percent debt. Its cost of equity is 16 percent, and the cost of debt is 9 percent. The relevant tax rate is 35 percent. What is Mullineaux's WACC?

13.12 Filler Manufacturing has a target debt–equity ratio of .60. Its cost of equity is 18 percent, and its cost of debt is 10 percent. If the tax rate is 35 percent, what is Filler's WACC?

13.13 Winnipeg Brew has 9.5 million shares of common stock outstanding. The current share price is $53, and the book value per share is $5. Winnipeg Brew also has two bond issues outstanding. The first bond issue has a face value of $75 million and an 8 percent coupon and sells for 93 percent of par. The second issue has a face value of $60 million and a 7.5 percent coupon and sells for 96.5 percent of par. The first issue matures in 10 years, the second in 6 years.

a. What are Winnipeg Brew's capital structure weights on a book value basis?

b. What are Winnipeg Brew's capital structure weights on a market value basis?

c. Which are more relevant, the book or market value weights? Why?

13.14 In the previous problem, suppose the company's stock has a beta of 1.2. The risk-free rate is 5.2 percent, and the market risk premium is 9 percent. Assume that the overall cost of debt is the weighted average implied by the two outstanding debt issues. Both bonds make semiannual payments. The tax rate is 35 percent. What is the company's WACC?

13.15 Kose Inc. has a target debt–equity ratio of .80. Its WACC is 10.5 percent, and the tax rate is 35 percent.

Visit us at www.mcgrawhill.ca/olc/ross

   a. If Kose's cost of equity is 15 percent, what is its pre-tax cost of debt?

   b. If instead you know that the after-tax cost of debt is 6.4 percent, what is the cost of equity?

13.16 Given the following information for Huntington Power Co., find the WACC. Assume the company's tax rate is 35 percent.

Debt:	4,000 7 percent coupon bonds outstanding, $1,000 par value, 20 years to maturity, selling for 103 percent of par; the bonds make semiannual payments.
Common stock:	90,000 shares outstanding, selling for $57 per share; the beta is 1.10.
Preferred Shares:	10,000 shares of 6.5 percent preferred with a current price of $100, and a par value $100.
Market:	8 percent market risk premium and 6 percent risk-free rate.

13.17 Titan Mining Corporation has 9 million shares of common stock outstanding and 120,000 8.5 percent semiannual bonds outstanding, par value $1,000 each. The common stock currently sells for $34 per share and has a beta of 1.20, and the bonds have 15 years to maturity and sell for 93 percent of par. The market risk premium is 10 percent, T-bills are yielding 5 percent, and Titan Mining's tax rate is 35 percent.

   a. What is the firm's market value capital structure?

   b. If Titan Mining is evaluating a new investment project that has the same risk as the firm's typical project, what rate should the firm use to discount the project's cash flows?

13.18 Och Inc. is considering a project that will result in initial after-tax cash savings of $3.5 million at the end of the first year, and these savings will grow at a rate of 5 percent per year indefinitely. The firm has a target debt–equity ratio of .65, a cost of equity of 15 percent, and an after-tax cost of debt of 5.5 percent. The cost-saving proposal is somewhat riskier than the usual project the firm undertakes; management uses the subjective approach and applies an adjustment factor of −2 percent to the cost of capital for such risky projects. Under what circumstances should Och take on the project?

13.19 The Primetime Sanders Investment Bank has the following financing outstanding. What is the WACC for the company?

Debt:	50,000 bonds with an 8 percent coupon rate and a current price of $119.80; the bonds have 25 years to maturity. 150,000 zero coupon bonds with a price of 13.85 and 30 years until maturity.
Preferred stock:	120,000 shares of 6.5 percent preferred with a current price of $112, and a $100 par value.
Common stock:	2,000,000 shares of common stock; the current price is $65, and the beta of the stock is 1.1.
Market:	The corporate tax rate is 40 percent, the market risk premium is 9 percent, and the risk-free rate is 4 percent.

13.20 This is a comprehensive project evaluation problem bringing together much of what you have learned in this and previous chapters. Suppose you have been hired as a financial consultant to Defense Electronics Inc. (DEI), a large, publicly traded firm that is the market share leader in radar detection systems (RDSs). The company is looking at setting up a manufacturing plant overseas to produce a new line of RDSs. This will be a five-year project. The company bought some land three years ago for $7 million in anticipation of using it as a toxic dump site for waste chemicals, but it built a piping system to safely discard the chemicals instead. If the company sold the land today, it would receive $6.5 million after taxes. In five years the land can be sold for $4.5 million after taxes and reclamation costs.

Visit us at www.mcgrawhill.ca/olc/ross

The company wants to build its new manufacturing plant on this land; the plant will cost $15 million to build. The following market data on DEI's securities are current:

Debt:	15,000 bonds 7 percent coupon rate outstanding, 15 years to maturity, selling for 92 percent of par; the bonds have a $1,000 par value each and make semiannual payments.
Common stock:	300,000 shares outstanding, selling for $75 per share; the beta is 1.3.
Preferred stock:	20,000 shares of 5 percent preferred stock outstanding, selling for $72 per share.
Market:	8 percent expected market risk premium; 5 percent risk-free rate.

DEI's tax rate is 35 percent. The project requires $900,000 in initial net working capital investment to become operational.

a. Calculate the project's initial time 0 cash flow, taking into account all side effects.
b. The new RDS project is somewhat riskier than a typical project for DEI, primarily because the plant is being located overseas. Management has told you to use an adjustment factor of +2 percent to account for this increased riskiness. Calculate the appropriate discount rate to use when evaluating DEI's project.
c. The manufacturing plant has an eight-year tax life, and DEI uses straight-line depreciation. At the end of the project (i.e., the end of year 5), the plant can be scrapped for $5 million. What is the after-tax salvage value of this manufacturing plant?
d. The company will incur $400,000 in annual fixed costs. The plan is to manufacture 12,000 RDSs per year and sell them at $10,000 per machine; the variable production costs are $9,000 per RDS. What is the annual operating cash flow (OCF) from this project?
e. DEI's comptroller is primarily interested in the impact of DEI's investments on the bottom line of reported accounting statements. What will you tell her is the accounting break-even quantity of RDSs sold for this project?
f. Finally, DEI's president wants you to throw all your calculations, assumptions, and everything else into the report for the chief financial officer; all he wants to know is the RDS project's internal rate of return, IRR, and net present value, NPV. What will you report?

MINICASE: AlliedProducts

AlliedProducts Inc. has recently won approval from Transport Canada for its Enhanced Ground Proximity Warning System (GPWS). This system is designed to give airplane pilots additional warning of approaching ground danger and, thus, help prevent crashes. AlliedProducts has spent $15 million in research and development over the past four years developing GPWS. The GPWS will be put on the market beginning this year and AlliedProducts expects it to stay on the market for five years.

As a financial analyst specializing in the aerospace industry for United Pension & Investment Inc., you are asked by your managing partner, Adam Smith, to evaluate the potential of this new GPWS project.

Initially, AlliedProducts will need to acquire $47 million in production equipment to make the GPWS.

The equipment is expected to have a seven-year useful life. This equipment can be sold for $9 million at the end of five years. AlliedProducts intends to sell two different versions of the GPWS:

1. NEW GPWS intended for installation in new aircraft. The selling price is $76,000 per system and the variable cost to produce it is $52,000 per system. (Assume cash flows occur at year-end.)
2. UPGRADE GPWS intended for installation on existing aircraft with an older version ground proximity radar in place. The selling price of the Upgrade system is $35,000 per system and the variable cost to produce it is $23,500 per system.

AlliedProducts intends to raise prices at the same rate as inflation. Variable costs will also increase with inflation. In addition, the GPWS project will also incur $3 million in marketing and general administration costs the first year (expected to increase at the same rate as inflation).

AlliedProducts' corporate tax rate is 38 percent. Assume the equity beta of 1.27 listed in Value Line Investment Survey (the latest edition) is considered the best estimate of AlliedProducts' beta. A five-year Canada bond has a rate of 4.90 percent and the S&P/TSX recent years' historical average excess return (i.e., the market return less the Canada bond rate) is 4.7 percent. Annual inflation is expected to remain constant at 2.1 percent. Further suppose that AlliedProducts' cost of debt (before tax) is 6.2 percent and (this is somewhat unrealistic) its debt-to-equity ratio is 50 percent and will remain 50 for at least five years.

Commercial Aircraft Market

The state of the economy has a major impact on the airplane manufacturing industry. Airline industry analysts have the following production expectations, depending on the annual state of the economy for the next five years:

State of economy	Probability of State	New Aircraft (year 1)	Annual Growth
Strong growth	0.12	350	0.17
Moderate growth	0.48	250	0.12
Mild recession	0.32	150	0.05
Severe recession	0.08	50	0.01

While probabilities of each state of the economy do not change during the next five years, airplane production for each state will increase, as shown in the table, each year after year 1. Transport Canada requires that each of these planes have a new ground proximity warning system, of which there are a number of manufacturers besides AlliedProducts.

AlliedProducts estimates that there are approximately 12,500 existing aircraft that comprise the market for its GPWS Upgrade package. Due to federal regulations, all existing aircraft will require an upgraded ground proximity warning system within the next five years, again, not necessarily from AlliedProducts. AlliedProducts believes the upgrades of the existing aircraft fleet will be spread evenly over the five years (the time value of money would suggest manufacturers defer purchasing upgrades until the fifth year; however, consumer demand for the additional safety will induce earlier upgrades).

For CCA purposes, production equipment is in class 8. The immediate initial working capital requirement is $2 million, and thereafter the net working capital requirements will be 5 percent of sales.

AlliedProducts has a number of competitors in both the New GPWS and Upgrade GPWS markets but expects to dominate with a 47 percent market share.

Assignment

a. First, use the CAPM to determine the appropriate discount rate for this project. Then, use computer spreadsheets, such as Excel or Lotus 1-2-3, to analyze.

b. Will the GPWS project improve the wealth of Allied-Products' shareholders, such as your firm—United Pension & Investment Inc.?

Appendix 13A   Economic Value Added and the Measurement of Financial Performance

Chapter 13 shows how to calculate the appropriate discount rate for capital budgeting and other valuation problems. We now consider the measurement of financial performance. We introduce the concept of economic value added, which uses the same discount rate developed for capital budgeting. We begin with a simple example.

Calculating Economic Value Added

Many years ago, Henry Bodenheimer started Bodie's Blimps, one of the largest high-speed blimp manufacturers. Because growth was so rapid, Henry put most of his effort into capital budgeting. His approach to capital budgeting parallelled that of Chapter 13. He forecasted cash flows for various projects and discounted them at the cost of capital appropriate to the beta of the blimp business. However, these projects have grown rapidly, in some cases becoming whole divisions. He now needs to evaluate the performance of these divisions in order to reward his division managers. How does he perform the appropriate analysis?

Henry is aware that capital budgeting and performance measurement are essentially mirror images of each other. Capital budgeting is forward-looking by nature because one must estimate future cash flows to value a project. By contrast, performance measurement is backward-looking. As Henry stated to a group of his executives, "Capital budgeting is like looking through the windshield while driving a car. You need to know what lies farther down the road to calculate a net present value. Performance measurement is like looking into the rearview mirror. You find out where you have been."

Henry first measured the performance of his various divisions by return on assets (ROA), an approach that we treated in Appendix 2A. For example, if a division had earnings after tax of $1,000 and had assets of $10,000, the ROA would be[17]

$$\frac{\$1,000}{\$10,000} = 10\%.$$

He calculated the ROA ratio for each of his divisions, paying a bonus to each of his division managers based on the size of that division's ROA. However, while ROA was generally effective in motivating his managers, there were a number of situations where it appeared that ROA was counterproductive.

For example, Henry always believed that Sharon Smith, head of the supersonic division, was his best manager. The ROA of Smith's division was generally in the high double digits, but the best estimate of the weighted average cost of capital for the division was only 20%. Furthermore, the division had been growing rapidly. However, as soon as Henry paid bonuses based on ROA, the division stopped growing. At that time, Smith's division had after-tax earnings of $2,000,000 on an asset base of $2,000,000, for an ROA of 100% ($2 million/$2 million).

Henry found out why the growth stopped when he suggested a project to Smith that would earn $1,000,000 per year on an investment of $2,000,000. This was clearly an attractive project with an ROA of 50% ($1 million/$2 million). He thought that Smith would jump at the chance to place his project into her division, because the ROA of the project was much higher than the cost of capital of 20%. However, Smith did everything she could to kill the project. And, as Henry later figured out, Smith was rational to do so. Smith must have realized that if the project were accepted, the division's ROA would become

$$\frac{\$2,000,000 + \$1,000,000}{\$2,000,000 + \$2,000,000} = 75\%$$

Thus, the ROA of Smith's division would fall from 100% to 75% if the project were accepted, with Smith's bonus falling in tandem.

Henry was later exposed to the economic value-added (EVA) approach,[18] which seems to obviate this particular problem. The formula for EVA is

$$[\text{ROA} - \text{Weighted average cost of capital}] \times \text{Total capital}$$

Without the new project, the EVA of Smith's division would be:

$$[100\% - 20\%] \times \$2,000,000 = \$1,600,000$$

---

[17]Earnings after tax is EBIT $(1 - T_c)$ where EBIT is earnings before interest and taxes and T_c is the tax rate. Stern Stewart and other EVA users refer to EBIT $(1 - T_c)$ as net operating profit after tax.

[18]Stern Stewart & Company have a copyright on the terms *economic value added* and *EVA*. Details on the Stern Stewart & Company EVA can be found in J. M. Stern, G. B. Stewart, and D. A. Chew, "The EVA Financial Management System," *Journal of Applied Corporate Finance* (Summer 1999).

Visit us at www.mcgrawhill.ca/olc/ross

This is an annual number. That is, the division would bring in $1.6 million above and beyond the cost of capital to the firm each year.

With the new project included, the EVA jumps to

$$[75\% - 20\%] \times \$4,000,000 = \$2,200,000$$

If Sharon Smith knew that her bonus was based on EVA, she would now have an incentive to accept, not reject, the project. Although ROA appears in the EVA formula, EVA differs substantially from ROA. The big difference is that ROA is a percentage number and EVA is a dollar value. In the preceding example, EVA increased when the new project was added even though the ROA actually decreased. In this situation, EVA correctly incorporates the fact that a high return on a large division may be better than a very high return on a smaller division. The situation here is quite similar to the scale problem in capital budgeting that we discussed in Section 6.6.

Further understanding of EVA can be achieved by rewriting the EVA formula. Because ROA multiplied by total capital is equal to earnings after tax, we can write the EVA formula as:

$$\text{Earnings after tax} - \text{Weighted average cost of capital} \times \text{Total capital}$$

Thus, EVA can simply be viewed as earnings after capital costs. Although accountants subtract many costs (including depreciation) to get the earnings number shown in financial reports, they do not subtract out capital costs. One can see the logic of accountants, because the cost of capital is very subjective. By contrast, costs such as COGS (cost of goods sold), SGA (sales, general, and administration), and even depreciation can be measured more objectively.[19] However, even if the cost of capital is difficult to estimate, it is hard to justify ignoring it completely. After all, this textbook argues that the cost of capital is a necessary input to capital budgeting. Shouldn't it also be a necessary input to performance measurement?

This example argues that EVA can increase investment for those firms that are currently underinvesting. However, there are many firms in the reverse situation; the managers are so focused on increasing earnings that they take on projects for which the profits do not justify the capital outlays. These managers either are unaware of capital costs or, knowing these costs, choose to ignore them. Because the cost of capital is right in the middle of the EVA formula, managers will not easily ignore these costs when evaluated on an EVA system.

One other advantage of EVA is that it is so stark; the number is either positive or it is negative. Plenty of divisions have negative EVAs for a number of years. Because these divisions are destroying more value than they are creating, a strong point can be made for liquidating these divisions. Although managers are generally emotionally opposed to this type of action, EVA analysis makes liquidation harder to ignore.

In Example 13A.1, International Trade Corporation has a negative EVA—it is destroying shareholder value. The following paragraph discusses real corporate examples of value creators and value destroyers.

In 2003, the Corporate Renaissance Group identified Leon's Furniture Limited, Cognos Inc., and Sceptre Investment Counsel Ltd. as the top consistent value creators based on EVA. In comparison, Canlan Ice Sports Corp., Napier Environmental Technologies, and Asia Pacific Resources were identified as the most consistent value destroyers based on EVA performance. The top seven consistent value creators and consistent value destroyers are in Table 13A.1.

---

[19]Some EVA users add back depreciation and other non-cash items. A Canadian example is: B. A. Schofield, "Evaluating Stocks," *Canadian Investment Review* (Spring 2000).

EXAMPLE 13A.1

Assume the following figures for the International Trade Corporation

$$EBIT = \$2.5 \text{ billion}$$
$$T_c = 0.4$$
$$r_{WACC} = 11\%$$
$$\text{Total capital contributed} = \text{Total debt} + \text{Equity}$$
$$= \$10 \text{ billion} + \$10 \text{ billion}$$
$$= \$20 \text{ billion}$$

Now we can calculate International Trade's EVA:

$$EVA = EBIT (1 - T_c) - r_{WACC} \times \text{Total capital}$$
$$= (\$2.5 \text{ billion} \times 0.6) - (0.11 \times \$20 \text{ billion})$$
$$= \$1.5 \text{ billion} - \$2.2 \text{ billion}$$
$$= -\$700 \text{ million}$$

Despite being listed as a consistent value creator, Biovail's stock price has dropped from a high of approximately $90 per share in October of 2002 to $30 per share in May of 2006. The exact opposite of Biovail would be F N X Mining Co. Inc. The company's stock price rose to a high of $16 per share in February 2006 from a low of almost $6 per share in June 2003. These are two examples that show that it is not always possible to predict a share price turnaround by using EVA. It is important to note that Table 13A.1 sets out to compare past EVA with future stock performance.

Some Caveats on EVA

The preceding discussion puts EVA in a very positive light. However, one can certainly find much to criticize with EVA as well. We now focus on two well-known problems with EVA. First, the preceding example uses EVA for performance measurement, where we believe it properly belongs. To us, EVA seems a clear improvement over ROA and other financial ratios. However, EVA has little to offer for capital budgeting because EVA focuses only on current earnings. By contrast, net present value analysis uses projections of all future cash flows, where the cash flows will generally differ from year to year. Thus, as far as capital budgeting is concerned, NPV analysis has a richness that EVA does not have. Although supporters may argue that EVA correctly incorporates the weighted average cost of capital, one must remember that the discount rate in NPV analysis is the same weighted

TABLE 13A.1

Consistent Value Creators and Value Destroyers Based on EVA

Consistent Value Creators 1995–2002 Company	Consistent Value Destroyers 1995–2002 Company
Leon's Furniture	Canlan Ice Sports Corp.
Cognos Inc.	Napier Environmental Technologies
Sceptre Investment Counsel Ltd.	Asia Pacific Resources Ltd.
Pason Systems Inc.	Ballard Power Systems Inc.
Dupont Canada Inc.	F N X Mining Co. Inc.
Metro Inc.	Sterlite Gold Ltd.
Biovail Corporation	Aldeavision Inc.

Source: V. Jog, "Value and Wealth Creation in Canada," *Canadian Investment Review,* Winter 2003, pp. 45–50.

TABLE 13A.2

Selected Economic Value Added Users

United States	Canada
Bausch & Lomb	Alcan Aluminum
Briggs and Stratton Corp.	Cogeco Inc.
Coca-Cola Company	Domtar Inc.
Eli Lilly & Co.	Grand & Toy
Dun & Bradstreet Corp.	Long Manufacturing
JC Penny	Robin Hood Multifoods
Monsanto	
Rubbermaid Inc.	
Sprint	
Toys R Us	
U.S. Postal Service	
Whirlpool	

Source: Adapted from sternstewart.com.

average cost of capital. That is, both approaches take the cost of equity capital based on beta and combine it with the cost of debt to get an estimate of this weighted average.

A second problem with EVA is that it may increase the shortsightedness of managers. Under EVA, a manager will be well rewarded today if earnings are high today. Future losses may not harm the manager, because there is a good chance that she will be promoted or have left the firm by then. Thus, the manager has an incentive to run a division with more regard for short-term than long-term value. By raising prices or cutting quality, the manager may increase current profits (and, therefore, current EVA). However, to the extent that customer satisfaction is reduced, future profits (and therefore future EVA) are likely to fall. However, one should not be too harsh with EVA here, because the same problem occurs with ROA. A manager who raises prices or cuts quality will increase current ROA at the expense of future ROA. The problem, then, is not EVA per se but with the use of accounting numbers in general. Because shareholders want the discounted present value of all cash flows to be maximized, managers with bonuses based on some function of current profits or current cash flows are likely to behave in a shortsighted way.

Despite these shortcomings EVA or something similar is used widely by corporations in the U.S. and Canada. Table 13A.2 lists some examples.

? Concept Questions

- Why is capital budgeting important to a firm?
- What is the major difference between EVA and ROA
- What are the advantages of using EVA?
- What are the well-known problems of EVA?

SUGGESTED READING

More on economic value added can be found in:

J. M. Stern, G. B. Stewart, and D. A. Chew. "The EVA Financial Management System." *Journal of Applied Corporate Finance* (Summer 1999), and at www.sternstewart.com.

Useful Canadian articles on EVA are:

H. M. Armitage and V. Jog. "Economic Value Creation—What Every Management Accountant Should Know." *CMA Magazine* (October 1996).

V. Jog. "Value Creation and the Credibility of Financial Reporting in Canada." *Canadian Investment Review,* Fall 2002.

D. Keys, M. Azamhuzjaev, and J. Mackey. "EVA, To Boldly Go." *CMA Magazine* (September 1999).

B. A. Schofield. "Evaluating Stocks." *Canadian Investment Review* (Spring 2000).

PART 4

Chapter 14

Corporate Financing Decisions and Efficient Capital Markets

EXECUTIVE SUMMARY

The section on value concentrated on the firm's capital budgeting decisions—the left-hand side of the balance sheet of the firm. This chapter begins our analysis of corporate-financing decisions—the right-hand side of the balance sheet. We take the firm's capital budgeting decision as fixed in this section of the text.

The point of this chapter is to introduce the concept of *efficient capital markets* and its implications for corporate finance. Efficient capital markets are those in which market prices reflect available information. This means that market prices reflect the underlying present value of securities, and there is no way to make unusual or excess profits by using the available information.

This concept has profound implications for financial managers, because market efficiency eliminates many value-enhancing strategies of firms. In particular, we show that in an efficient market:

1. Stock price should not be affected by a firm's choice of accounting method.
2. Financial managers cannot time issues of bonds and stocks.
3. Firms cannot expect to gain through speculation in currency and bond markets.
4. Financial managers should pay attention to the information in market prices.

However, the evidence on market efficiency is not one-sided. A very influential school of thought, known as *behavioural finance,* argues that markets are simply not efficient. Ultimately, whether or not capital markets are efficient is an empirical question. We will describe several studies examining efficient markets.

14.1 Can Financing Decisions Create Value?

Earlier parts of the book show how to evaluate projects according to the net present value criterion. The real world is a competitive place where projects with positive net present value are not always easy to come by. However, through hard work or through good fortune, a firm can identify winning projects. For example, to create value from capital budgeting decisions, the firm is likely to:

1. Locate an unsatisfied demand for a particular product or service.
2. Create a barrier to make it more difficult for other firms to compete.
3. Produce products or services at lower cost than competition.
4. Be the first to develop a new product.

The next five chapters concern *financing* decisions. Typical financing decisions include how much debt and equity to sell, what types of debt and equity to sell, and when to sell debt and equity. Just as the net present value criterion was used to evaluate capital budgeting projects, we now want to use the same criterion to evaluate financing decisions.

Though the procedure for evaluating financing decisions is identical to the procedure for evaluating projects, the results are different. It turns out that the typical firm has many more capital expenditure opportunities with positive net present values than financing opportunities with positive net present values. In fact, we later show that some plausible financial models imply that no valuable financial opportunities exist at all.

Though this dearth of profitable financing opportunities will be examined in detail later, a few remarks are in order now. We maintain that there are basically three ways to create valuable financing opportunities:

1. *Fool investors.* Assume that a firm can raise capital either by issuing stock or by issuing a more complex security, say, a combination of stock and warrants. Suppose that, in truth, 100 shares of stock are worth the same as 50 units of our complex security. If investors have a misguided, overly optimistic view of the complex security, perhaps the 50 units can be sold for more than the 100 shares of stock can. Clearly, this complex security provides a valuable financing opportunity because the firm is getting more than fair value for it.

   Financial managers try to package securities to receive the greatest value. A cynic might view this as attempting to fool investors. However, empirical evidence suggests that investors cannot easily be fooled. Thus, one must be skeptical that value can easily be created.

   The theory of efficient capital markets expresses this idea. In its extreme form, it says that all securities are appropriately priced at all times, implying that the market as a whole is very shrewd indeed. Thus, corporate managers should not attempt to create value by fooling investors. Instead, managers must create value in other ways.

2. *Reduce costs or increase subsidies.* We show later in the book that certain forms of financing have greater tax advantages than other forms. Clearly, a firm packaging securities to minimize taxes can increase firm value. In addition, any financing technique involves other costs. For example, investment bankers, lawyers, and accountants must be paid. A firm packaging securities to minimize these costs can also increase firm value.

   Finally, any financing vehicle that provides subsidies is valuable. This last possibility is illustrated in Example 14.1 below.

EXAMPLE 14.1

Suppose Mississauga Electronics Company is thinking about relocating its plant to Mexico where labour costs are lower. In the hope that it can stay in Ontario, the company has submitted an application to the province to guarantee a five-year bank term loan for $2 million. With a provincial guarantee, a chartered bank has offered to make the loan at an interest rate of 5 percent. This is an attractive rate because the normal cost of debt capital for Mississauga Electronics Company is 10 percent. What is the NPV of this potential financing transaction?

If the provincial loan guarantee is provided and the term loan is made to Mississauga Electronics Company,

$$NPV = \$2,000,000 - \left[\frac{\$100,000}{1.1} + \frac{\$100,000}{(1.1)^2} + \frac{\$100,000}{(1.1)^3} + \frac{\$100,000}{(1.1)^4} + \frac{\$2,100,000}{(1.1)^5}\right]$$

$$= \$2,000,000 - \$1,620,921$$
$$= \$379,079$$

This transaction has a positive NPV. The Mississauga Electronics Company obtains subsidized financing where the amount of the subsidy is $379,079.

3. *Create a new security.* There has been a surge in financial innovation in the past two decades. For example, in a speech on financial innovation, the late Nobel laureate Merton Miller asked the rhetorical question, "Can any twenty-year period in recorded history have witnessed even a tenth as much new development? Where corporations once issued only straight debt and straight common stock, they now issue zero-coupon, inflation-linked bonds, adjustable rate notes, floating rate notes, putable bonds, credit-enhanced debt securities, receivable-backed securities, convertible adjustable preferred stock, and adjustable rate convertible debt—to name just a few!"[1] And, financial innovation has occurred even more rapidly in the years following Miller's speech.

Though the advantage of each instrument is different, one general theme is that these new securities cannot easily be duplicated by combinations of existing securities. Thus, a previously unsatisfied clientele may pay extra for a specialized security catering to its needs. For example, putable bonds let the purchaser sell the bond at a fixed price back to the firm. This innovation creates a price floor, allowing the investor to reduce his or her downside risk. Perhaps risk-averse investors or investors with little knowledge of the bond market would find this feature particularly attractive.

Corporations gain from developing unique securities by issuing these securities at high prices. However, we believe that the value captured by the innovator is small in the long run because the innovator usually cannot patent or copyright the idea. Soon, many firms will be issuing securities of the same kind, forcing prices down as a result.

This brief introduction sets the stage for the next five chapters of the book. The rest of this chapter examines the efficient capital markets hypothesis. We show that if capital markets are efficient, corporate managers cannot create value by fooling investors. This is quite important, because managers must create value in other, perhaps more difficult ways. The following four chapters concern the costs and subsidies of various forms of financing. A discussion of new financing instruments is postponed until later chapters of the text.

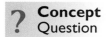 **Concept** Question

• **List the three ways financing decisions can create value.**

14.2 A Description of Efficient Capital Markets

An efficient capital market is one in which stock prices fully reflect available information. To illustrate how an efficient market works, suppose the F-stop Camera Corporation (FCC) is attempting to develop a camera that will double the speed of the autofocusing system now available. FCC believes this research has a positive NPV.

Now consider a share of stock in FCC. What determines the willingness of investors to hold shares of FCC at a particular price? One important factor is the probability that FCC will be the company to develop the new autofocusing system first. In an efficient market we would expect the price of the shares of FCC to rise if this probability increases.

Suppose a well-known engineer is hired by FCC to help develop the new autofocusing system. In an efficient market, what will happen to FCC's share price when this is announced? If the well-known scientist is paid a salary that fully reflects her contribution to the firm, the price of the stock will not necessarily change. Suppose, instead, that hiring the

---

[1]M. Miller, "Financial Innovation: The Last Twenty Years and the Next," *Journal of Financial and Quantitative Analysis* (December 1986). However, Peter Tufano, "Securities Innovations: A Historical and Functional Perspective," *Journal of Applied Corporate Finance* (Winter 1995), shows that many securities commonly believed to have been invented in the 1970s and 1980s can be traced as far back as the 1830s.

scientist is a positive-NPV transaction. In this case, the price of shares in FCC will increase because the firm can pay the scientist a salary below her true value to the company.

When will the increase in the price of FCC's shares take place? Assume that the hiring announcement is made in a press release on Wednesday morning. In an efficient market, the price of shares in FCC will *immediately and correctly* adjust to this new information. Investors should not be able to buy the stock on Wednesday afternoon and make a profit on Thursday. This would imply that it took the stock market a day to realize the implication of the FCC press release. The efficient market hypothesis predicts that the price of shares of FCC stock on Wednesday afternoon will already reflect the information contained in the Wednesday morning press release.

The **efficient market hypothesis (EMH)** has implications for investors and for firms.

- Because information is reflected in prices immediately, investors should only expect to obtain a normal rate of return. Awareness of information when it is released does an investor no good. The price adjusts before the investor has time to trade on it.
- Firms should expect to receive the fair value for securities that they sell. *Fair* means that the price they receive for the securities they issue is the present value. Thus, valuable financing opportunities that arise from fooling investors are unavailable in efficient capital markets.

EXAMPLE 14.2

Suppose Nortel announces it has invented a digital switch that is 30 times faster than existing switches. The price of a share of Nortel should increase immediately to a new equilibrium level.

Figure 14.1 presents three possible adjustments in stock prices in reaction to good news. The solid line represents the path taken by the stock in an efficient market. In this case the price adjusts immediately to the new information so that no further changes take place in the price of the stock. The dotted line depicts a delayed reaction. Here it takes the market 30 days to absorb the information fully. Finally, the broken line illustrates an overreaction and subsequent correction back to the true price. The broken line and the dotted line show the paths that the stock price might take in an inefficient market. If the price of the stock takes several days to adjust, trading profits would be available to investors who bought at the date of the announcement and sold once the price settled back to the equilibrium.[2]

Foundations of Market Efficiency

Figure 14.1 shows the consequences of market efficiency. But what are the conditions that *cause* market efficiency? Andrei Shleifer argues that there are three conditions, any one of which will lead to efficiency:[3] (1) rationality, (2) independent deviations from rationality, and (3) arbitrage. A discussion of these conditions follows.

---

[2]Now you should understand the following short story. A student was walking down the hall with his finance professor when they both saw a $20 bill on the floor. As the student bent down to pick it up, the professor shook his head slowly and, with a look of disappointment on his face, said patiently to the student, "Don't bother. If it were really there, someone else would have already picked it up."

The moral of the story reflects the logic of the efficient market hypothesis: If you think you have found a pattern in stock prices or a simple device for picking winners, you probably have not. If there were such a simple way to make money, someone else would have found it before. Furthermore, if people tried to exploit the information, their efforts would become self-defeating and the pattern would disappear.

[3]Andrei Shleifer, *Inefficient Markets: An Introduction to Behavioral Finance,* Oxford University Press, Oxford, United Kingdom (2000).

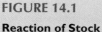

Reaction of Stock Price to New Information in Efficient and Inefficient Markets

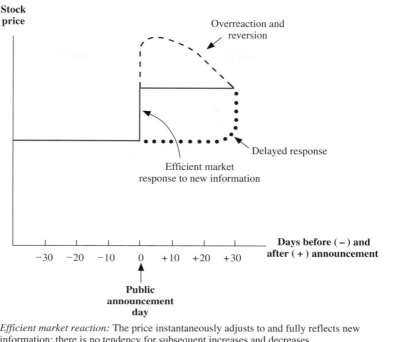

Efficient market reaction: The price instantaneously adjusts to and fully reflects new information; there is no tendency for subsequent increases and decreases.
Delayed reaction: The price partially adjusts to the new information; thirty days elapse before the price completely reflects the new information.
Overreaction: The price overadjusts to the new information; there is a bubble in the price sequence.

Rationality   Imagine that all investors are rational. When new information is released in the marketplace, all investors will adjust their estimates of stock prices in a rational way. In our example, investors will use the information in FCC's press release, in conjunction with existing information on the firm, to determine the NPV of FCC's new venture. If the information in the press release implies that the NPV of the venture is $10 million and there are 2 million shares, investors will calculate that the NPV is $5 per share. While FCC's old price might be, say, $40, no one would now transact at that price. Anyone interested in selling would only sell at a price of at least $45 ($40 + $5). And anyone interested in buying would now be willing to pay up to $45. In other words, the price would rise by $5. And the price would rise immediately, since rational investors would see no reason to wait before trading at the new price.

Of course, we all know times when family members, friends, and yes, even ourselves seem to behave less than perfectly rationally. Thus, perhaps it is too much to ask that *all* investors behave rationally. But the market will still be efficient if the following scenario holds.

Independent Deviations from Rationality   Suppose that FCC's press release is not all that clear. How many new cameras are likely to be sold? At what price? What is the likely cost per camera? Will other camera companies be able to develop competing products? How long will this likely take? If these, and other, questions cannot be answered easily, it will be difficult to estimate NPV.

Now imagine that, with so many questions going unanswered, many investors do not think clearly. Some investors might get caught up in the romance of a new product, hoping, and ultimately believing, in sales projections well above what is rational. They would overpay for new shares. And if they needed to sell shares (perhaps to finance current consumption), they would do so only at a high price. If these individuals dominate the market, the stock price would likely rise beyond what market efficiency would predict.

However, due to emotional resistance, investors could just as easily react to new information in a pessimistic manner. After all, business historians tell us that investors were initially quite skeptical about the benefits of the telephone, the copier, the automobile, and the motion picture. Certainly, they could be overly skeptical about this new camera. If investors were primarily of this type, the stock price would likely rise less than market efficiency would predict.

But suppose that about as many individuals were irrationally optimistic as were irrationally pessimistic. Prices would likely rise in a manner consistent with market efficiency, even though most investors would be classified as less than fully rational. Thus, market efficiency does not require rational individuals, only countervailing irrationalities.

However, this assumption of offsetting irrationalities at *all* times may be unrealistic. Perhaps, at certain times most investors are swept away by excessive optimism and, at other times, are caught in the throes of extreme pessimism. But even here, there is an assumption that will produce efficiency.

Arbitrage   Imagine a world with two types of individuals: the irrational amateurs and the rational professionals. The amateurs get caught up in their emotions, at times believing irrationally that a stock is undervalued and at other times believing the opposite. If the passions of the different amateurs do not cancel each other out, these amateurs, by themselves, would tend to carry stocks either above or below their efficient prices.

Now let's bring in the professionals. Suppose professionals go about their business methodically and rationally. They study companies thoroughly, they evaluate the evidence objectively, they estimate stock prices coldly and clearly, and they act accordingly. If a stock is underpriced, they would buy it. If overpriced, they would sell it (or even sell it short).[4] And their confidence would likely be greater than that of the amateurs. While an amateur might risk only a small sum, these professionals might risk large ones, *knowing* as they do that the stock is mispriced. Furthermore, they would be willing to rearrange their entire portfolio in search of a profit. If they find that General Motors is underpriced, they might sell the Ford stock they own (or even sell Ford short) in order to buy GM. *Arbitrage* is the word that comes to mind here, since arbitrage generates profit from the simultaneous purchase and sale of different, but substitute, securities. If the arbitrage of professionals dominates the speculation of amateurs, markets would still be efficient.[5]

? **Concept Questions**

- **Can you define an efficient market?**
- **Name the three foundations of market efficiency.**

---

[4]When an investor short-sells a stock, his position is such that he gains from a fall in the stock and loses from a rise in the stock. Thus, short-selling a stock can be viewed as the opposite of buying a stock.

[5]Because Ford and GM are different companies, the arbitrage here is not riskless. For this reason, it is sometimes termed "quasi-arbitrage."

14.3 The Different Types of Efficiency

In our previous discussion, we assumed that the market responds immediately to all available information. In actuality, certain information may affect stock prices more quickly than other information. To handle differential response rates, researchers separate information into different types. The most common classification system uses three types: information on past prices, publicly available information, and all information. The effect of these three information sets on prices is examined below.

The Weak Form

Imagine a trading strategy that recommends buying a stock when it has gone up three days in a row and recommends selling a stock when it has gone down three days in a row. This strategy uses only information on past prices. It does not use any other information, such as earnings forecasts, merger announcements, or money supply figures. A capital market is said to be *weakly efficient* or to satisfy **weak-form efficiency** if it fully incorporates the information in past stock prices. Thus, the above strategy would not be able to generate profits if weak-form efficiency holds.

Often weak-form efficiency is represented mathematically as

$$P_t = P_{t-1} + \text{Expected return} + \text{Random error}_t \qquad (14.1)$$

Equation (14.1) states that the price today is equal to the sum of the last observed price plus the expected return on the stock plus a random component occurring over the interval. The last observed price could have occurred yesterday, last week, or last month, depending on one's sampling interval. The expected return is a function of a security's risk and is based on the models of risk and return in previous chapters. The random component is due to new information on the stock. It could be either positive or negative and has an expectation of zero. The random component in any one period is unrelated to the random component in any past period. Hence, this component is not predictable from past prices. If stock prices follow (14.1), they are said to follow a **random walk.**[6]

Weak-form efficiency is about the weakest type of efficiency that we would expect a financial market to display because historical price information is the easiest kind of information about a stock to acquire. If it were possible to make extraordinary profits simply by finding the patterns in the stock price movements, everyone would do it, and any profits would disappear in the scramble. An exception to this statement occurred in the hot high-tech market of the late 1990s. Some investors were able to achieve superior returns following momentum strategies based on the idea that stocks that went up yesterday are likely also to go up today. Day trading became very popular in this "momentum market."[7]

The effect of competition can be seen in Figure 14.2. Suppose the price of a stock displayed a cyclical pattern, as indicated by the wavy curve. Shrewd investors would buy at the low points, forcing those prices up. Conversely, they would sell at the high points, forcing prices down. Via competition, the cyclical regularities would be eliminated, leaving only random fluctuations.

---

[6]For purposes of this text, the random walk can be considered synonymous with weak-form efficiency. Technically, the random walk is a slightly more restrictive hypothesis because it assumes that stock returns are identically distributed through time.

[7]A Canadian study on momentum is M. Inglis and S. Cleary, "Momentum in Canadian Stock Returns," *Canadian Journal of Administrative Sciences,* September 1998, pp. 279–291.

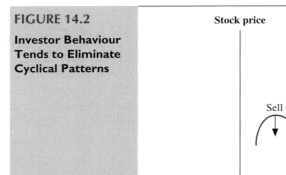

FIGURE 14.2

Investor Behaviour Tends to Eliminate Cyclical Patterns

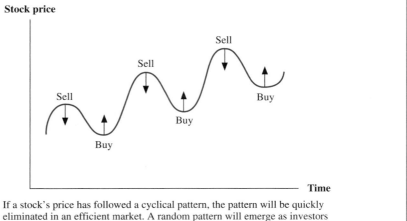

If a stock's price has followed a cyclical pattern, the pattern will be quickly eliminated in an efficient market. A random pattern will emerge as investors buy at the trough and sell at the peak of a cycle.

The Semistrong and Strong Forms

If weak-form efficiency is controversial, even more contentious are the two stronger types of efficiency: **semistrong-form efficiency** and **strong-form efficiency.** A market is semistrong-form efficient if prices reflect (incorporate) all publicly available information, including published accounting statements for the firm as well as historical price information. A market is strong-form efficient if prices reflect all information, public or private.

The information set of past prices is a subset of the information set of publicly available information, which in turn is a subset of all information. This is shown in Figure 14.3. Thus, strong-form efficiency implies semistrong-form efficiency, and semistrong-form efficiency implies weak-form efficiency. The distinction between semistrong-form efficiency and weak-form efficiency is that semistrong-form efficiency requires not only that the market be efficient with respect to historical price information, but also that *all* of the information available to the public be reflected in price.

To illustrate the different forms of efficiency, imagine an investor who always sold a particular stock after its price had risen. A market that was only weak-form efficient and not semistrong-form efficient would still prevent such a scheme from generating positive NPV. According to weak-form efficiency, a recent price rise does not imply that the stock is overvalued.

Now consider a firm reporting increased earnings. An individual might consider investing in the stock after hearing of the news release. However, if the market is semistrong efficient, the price should rise immediately upon the news release. Thus, the investor would end up paying the higher price, eliminating all chance for a profit.

At the furthest end of the spectrum is strong-form efficiency, which incorporates the other two types of efficiency. This form says that anything that is pertinent to the value of the stock and that is known to at least one investor is, in fact, fully incorporated into the stock value. A strict believer in strong-form efficiency would deny that an insider who knew whether a company mining operation had struck gold could profit from that information. Such a devotee of the strong-form efficient market hypothesis might argue that as soon as the insider tried to trade on his or her information, the market would recognize what was happening, and the price would shoot up before he or she could buy any of the stock. Alternatively, sometimes believers in strong-form efficiency take the view that there are no such things as secrets and that as soon as the gold is discovered, the secret gets out.

FIGURE 14.3

Relationship Among Three Different Information Sets

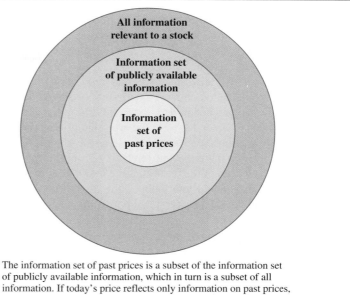

The information set of past prices is a subset of the information set of publicly available information, which in turn is a subset of all information. If today's price reflects only information on past prices, the market is weak-form efficient. If today's price reflects all publicly available information, the market is semistrong-form efficient. If today's price reflects all information, both public and private, the market is strong-form efficient.

Semistrong-form efficiency implies weak-form efficiency and strong-form efficiency implies semistrong-form efficiency.

One reason to expect that markets are weak-form efficient is because it is so cheap and easy to find patterns in stock prices. Anyone who can program a computer and knows a little bit of statistics can search for such patterns. It stands to reason that if there were such patterns, people would find and exploit them, in the process causing them to disappear.

Semistrong-form efficiency, though, uses much more sophisticated information and reasoning than weak-form efficiency. An investor must be skilled at economics and statistics, and steeped in the idiosyncrasies of individual industries and companies and their products. Furthermore, to acquire and use such skills requires talent, ability, and time. In the jargon of the economist, such an effort is costly and the ability to be successful at it is probably in scarce supply.

As for strong-form efficiency, this is just farther down the road than semistrong-form efficiency. It is difficult to believe that the market is so efficient that someone with truly valuable inside information cannot prosper by using it. It is also difficult to find direct evidence concerning strong-form efficiency. What we have tends to be unfavourable to this hypothesis of market efficiency.

Some Common Misconceptions About the Efficient Market Hypothesis

No idea in finance has attracted as much attention as that of efficient markets, and not all of the attention has been flattering. To a certain extent this is because much of the criticism has been based on a misunderstanding of what the hypothesis does and does not say. We illustrate three misconceptions below.

The Efficacy of Dart Throwing   When the notion of market efficiency was first publicized and debated in the popular financial press, it was often characterized by the following quote: "Throwing darts at the financial page will produce a portfolio that can be expected to do as well as any managed by professional security analysts."[8] This is almost, but not quite, true.

All the efficient market hypothesis really says is that, on average, the manager will not be able to achieve an abnormal or excess return. The excess return is defined with respect to some benchmark expected return that could come from the security market line (SML) of Chapter 11, from the arbitrage pricing theory (APT) of Chapter 12, or from some other asset pricing model. The investor must still decide how risky a portfolio he or she wants and what expected return it will normally have. A random dart thrower might wind up with all of the darts sticking into one or two high-risk stocks that deal in genetic engineering. Would you really want all of your stock investments in two such stocks? (Beware, though—a professional portfolio manager could do the same.)

The failure to understand this has often led to a confusion about market efficiency. For example, sometimes it is wrongly argued that market efficiency means that it does not matter what you do because the efficiency of the market will protect the unwary. However, as someone once remarked, "The efficient market protects the sheep from the wolves, but nothing can protect the sheep from themselves."

What efficiency does say is that the price a firm will obtain when it sells a share of its stock is a fair price in the sense that it reflects the value of that stock given the information that is available about it. Shareholders need not worry that they are paying too much for a stock with a low dividend or some other characteristic, because the market has already incorporated it into the price. However, investors still have to worry about such things as their level of risk exposure and their degree of diversification.

Price Fluctuations   Much of the public is skeptical of efficiency because stock prices fluctuate from day to day. However, this price movement is in no way inconsistent with efficiency, because a stock in an efficient market adjusts to new information by changing price. In fact, the absence of price movements in a changing world might suggest an inefficiency.

Shareholder Disinterest   Many laypersons are skeptical that the market price can be efficient if only a fraction of the outstanding shares change hands on any given day. However, the number of traders in a stock on a given day is generally far fewer than the number of people following the stock. This is true because an individual will trade only when his or her appraisal of the value of the stock differs enough from the market price to justify incurring brokerage commissions and other transactions costs. Furthermore, even if the number of traders following a stock is small relative to the number of outstanding shareholders, the stock can be expected to be efficiently priced as long as a number of interested traders use the publicly available information. That is, the stock price can reflect the available information even if many shareholders never follow the stock and are not considering trading in the near future.

? Concept Questions

- How would you describe the three forms of the efficient market hypothesis?
- What could make markets inefficient?
- Does market efficiency mean you can throw darts at a *National Post* listing of Toronto Stock Exchange stocks to pick a portfolio?
- What does it mean to say that the price you pay for a stock is fair?

---

[8]B. G. Malkiel, *A Random Walk Down Wall Street,* 8th ed. (New York: Norton, 2003).

14.4 The Evidence

The record on the efficient market hypothesis is extensive, and in large measure it is reassuring to advocates of the efficiency of markets. The studies done by academics fall into broad categories. First, there is evidence as to whether changes of stock prices are predictable or random. Second are *event studies.* Third is the record of professionally managed investment firms. Fourth, there are *anomalies* (evidence contrary to the efficient market hypothesis). The final category is tests of whether insiders beat the market.

The Weak Form

The random walk hypothesis, as expressed in Equation (14.1), implies that a stock's price movement in the past is unrelated to its price movement in the future. The work of Chapter 10 allows us to test this implication. In that chapter, we discussed the concept of correlation between the returns on two different stocks. For example, the correlation between the return on Stelco and the return on Dofasco is likely to be high because both stocks are in the steel industry. Conversely, the correlation between the return on Stelco and the return on the stock of, say, a European fast-food chain is likely to be low.

Financial economists frequently speak of **serial correlation,** which involves only one security. This is the correlation between the current return on a security and the return on the same security over a later period. A positive coefficient of serial correlation for a particular stock indicates a tendency toward *continuation.* That is, a higher-than-average return today is likely to be followed by higher-than-average returns in the future. Similarly, a lower-than-average return today is likely to be followed by lower-than-average returns in the future.

A negative coefficient of serial correlation for a particular stock indicates a tendency toward *reversal.* A higher-than-average return today is likely to be followed by lower-than-average returns in the future, and so forth. Both significantly positive and significantly negative serial correlation coefficients are indications of market inefficiencies; in either case, returns today can be used to predict future returns.

Serial correlation coefficients for stock returns near zero would be consistent with the random walk hypothesis. Thus, a current stock return that is higher than average is as likely to be followed by lower-than-average returns as by higher-than-average returns. Similarly, a current stock return that is lower than average is as likely to be followed by higher-than-average returns as by lower-than-average returns.

Correlation coefficients can, in principle, vary between -1 and 1, and the reported coefficients are quite small. A Canadian study, for example, found an average correlation coefficient of -0.01 for daily stock returns for TSX stocks.[9] Correlation coefficients like this one are so small relative to both estimation errors and transactions costs that the results are generally considered to be consistent with weak-form efficiency.

The weak form of the efficient market hypothesis has been tested in many other ways as well. Our view of the literature is that the evidence, taken as a whole, is consistent with weak-form efficiency.

This finding raises an interesting thought: If price changes are truly random, why do so many technical analysts believe that prices follow patterns? The work of both psychologists and statisticians suggests that most people simply do not know what randomness looks like. For example, consider Figure 14.4. The top graph was generated by a computer using random numbers and Equation 14.1. Yet we have found that people examining the chart generally see patterns. Different people see different patterns and forecast different future price movements.

---

[9]Stephen R. Foerster, "The Daily and Monthly Return Behaviour of Canadian Stocks," in *Canadian Capital Markets,* Michael J. Robinson and Brian F. Smith, eds. (London, Ontario: Western Business School, 1993), pp. 1–28.

FIGURE 14.4

Simulated and Actual Stock Price Movements

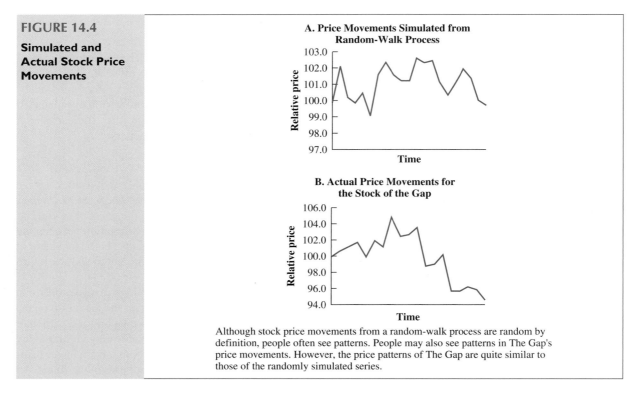

A. Price Movements Simulated from Random-Walk Process

B. Actual Price Movements for the Stock of the Gap

Although stock price movements from a random-walk process are random by definition, people often see patterns. People may also see patterns in The Gap's price movements. However, the price patterns of The Gap are quite similar to those of the randomly simulated series.

However, in our experience, viewers are all quite confident of the patterns they see. Next consider the bottom graph, which tracks actual movements in The Gap's stock price. This graph may look quite non-random to some, suggesting weak-form inefficiency. However, it also bears a close visual resemblance to the simulated series, and statistical tests indicate that it indeed behaves like a purely random series. Thus, in our opinion, people claiming to see patterns in stock price data are probably seeing optical illusions.

The Semistrong Form

The semistrong form of the efficient market hypothesis implies that prices should reflect all publicly available information. We present two types of tests of this form.

Event Studies   The *abnormal return (AR)* of a given stock on a particular day can be measured by subtracting the market's return on the same day (R_m)—as measured by the market index—from the actual return (R) of the stock on that day:[10] We write this algebraically as:

$$AR = R - R_m$$

A way to think of the tests of the semistrong form is to examine the following system of relationships:

Information released at time $t - 1 \rightarrow AR_{t-1}$
Information released at time $t \rightarrow AR_t$
Information released at time $t + 1 \rightarrow AR_{t+1}$

---

[10]The abnormal return can also be measured by using the market model. In this case the abnormal return is

$$AR = R - (\alpha + \beta R_m)$$

where AR stands for a stock's abnormal return and where the arrows indicate that the return in any time period is related only to the information released during that period.

According to the efficient market hypothesis, a stock's abnormal return at time t, AR_t, should reflect the release of information at the same time, t. Any information released before then, though, should have no effect on abnormal returns in this period, because all of its influence should have been felt before. In other words, an efficient market would already have incorporated previous information into prices. Because a stock's return today cannot depend on what the market does not yet know, the information that will be known only in the future cannot influence the stock's return either. Hence the arrows point in the direction that is shown, with information in any one time period affecting only that period's abnormal return. *Event studies* are statistical studies that examine whether the arrows are as shown or whether the release of information influences returns on other days.

As an example, consider the study by Szewczyk, Tsetsekos, and Zantout[11] on dividend omissions. Figure 14.5 shows the plot of *cumulative abnormal returns (CAR)* for a sample of companies announcing dividend omissions. Since dividend omissions are generally considered to be bad events, we would expect that abnormal returns would be negative around the time of the announcement. They are, as evidenced by a drop in the CAR on both the day before the announcement (day -1) and the day of the announcement (day 0).[12] However, note that there is virtually no movement in the CARs in the days following the announcement. This implies that the bad news is fully incorporated into the stock price by the announcement day, a result consistent with market efficiency.

Over the years, this type of methodology has been applied to a large number of events. Announcements of dividends, earnings, mergers, capital expenditures, and new issues of stock are a few examples of the vast literature in the area.[13] The early event studies generally supported the view that the market is semistrong form (and therefore also weak form) efficient. However, a number of more recent studies present evidence that the market does not react to all relevant information immediately. Some conclude from this that the market is not efficient. Others argue that this conclusion is unwarranted, given statistical and methodological problems in the studies. This issue will be addressed in more detail later in the chapter.

---

[11]Samuel A. Szewczyk, George P. Tsetsekos, and Zaher Z. Zantout, "Do Dividend Omissions Signal Future Earnings or Past Earnings?" Journal of Investing (Spring 1997).

[12]An astute reader may wonder why the abnormal return is negative on day –1, as well as on day 0. To see why, first note that the announcement date is generally taken in academic studies to be the publication date of the story in the *Wall Street Journal* (*WSJ*). Then consider a company announcing a dividend omission via press release at noon on Tuesday. The stock should fall on Tuesday. The announcement will be reported in the *WSJ* on Wednesday, because the Tuesday edition of the *WSJ* has already been printed. For this firm, the stock price falls on the day *before* the announcement in the *WSJ*.

Alternatively, imagine another firm announcing a dividend omission via press release on Tuesday at 8 p.m. Since the stock market is closed at that late hour, the stock will fall on Wednesday. Because the *WSJ* will report the announcement on Wednesday, the stock price falls on the day of the announcement in the *WSJ*.

Since firms may make announcements either during trading hours or after trading hours, stocks should fall on both day -1 and day 0 relative to publication in the *WSJ*.

[13]Some event studies suggest that stock market prices respond to information too slowly for the market to be efficient. For example, Eli Bartov, Suresh Radhakrishnan, and Itzhak Krinsky, "Investor Sophistication and Patterns in Stock Returns After Earnings Announcements," *The Accounting Review* 75 (January 2000); and V. Mehrotra, W. W. Yu, and C. Zhang, "Market Reactions to the *Financial Post's* 'Hot Stock' Column," *Canadian Journal of Administrative Sciences* 16 (June 1999), pp. 118–131.

FIGURE 14.5   Cumulative Abnormal Returns for Companies Announcing Dividend Omissions

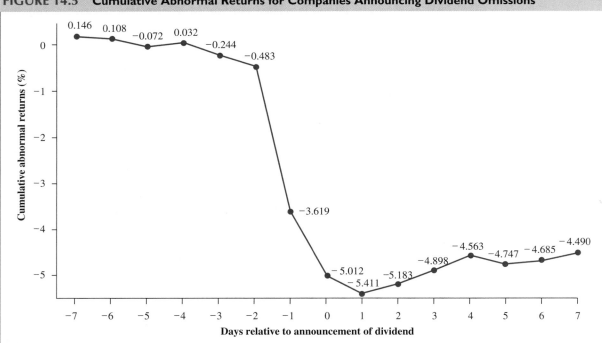

Cumulative abnormal returns (CARs) fall on both the day before the announcement and the day of the announcement of dividend omissions. CARs have very little movement after the announcement date. This pattern is consistent with market efficiency.

Source: Exhibit 2 in S. H. Szewczyk, George P. Tsetsekos, and Zaher Zantout, "Do Dividend Omissions Signal Future Earnings or Past Earnings?" *Journal of Investing* (Spring 1997).

The Record of Mutual Funds   If the market is efficient in the semistrong form, then no matter what publicly available information mutual fund managers use to pick stocks, their average returns should be the same as those of the average investor in the market as a whole. We can test efficiency, then, by comparing the performance of these professionals with that of a market index.

Consider Figure 14.6, which presents the performance of various types of U.S. mutual funds relative to the stock market as a whole. The far left of the figure shows that the universe of all funds covered in the study underperforms the market by 2.13 percent per year, after an appropriate adjustment for risk. Thus, rather than outperforming the market, the evidence shows underperformance. This underperformance holds for a number of types of funds as well. Returns in this study are net of fees, expenses, and commissions, so fund returns would be higher if these costs were added back. However, the study shows no evidence that funds, as a whole, are *beating* the market. Canadian studies of mutual fund performance reach the same conclusion.[14] Canadian pension fund managers also generally fail to outperform the market index.[15]

Perhaps nothing rankles successful stock market investors more than to have some professor tell them that they are not necessarily smart, just lucky. However, while Figure 14.6

---

[14]A Canadian study is G. Athanassakos, P. Carayannopoulos, and M. Racine, "Mutual Fund Performance: The Canadian Experience Between 1985 and 1996," *Canadian Journal of Financial Planning of the CAFP* 1 (June 2000), pp. 5–9.

[15]Vijay M. Jog, "Investment Performance of Pension Funds—A Canadian Study," *Canadian Journal of Administrative Sciences* 3 (June 1986).

FIGURE 14.6   Annual Return Performance* of Different Types of U.S. Mutual Funds Relative to a Broad-Based Market Index (1963–1998)

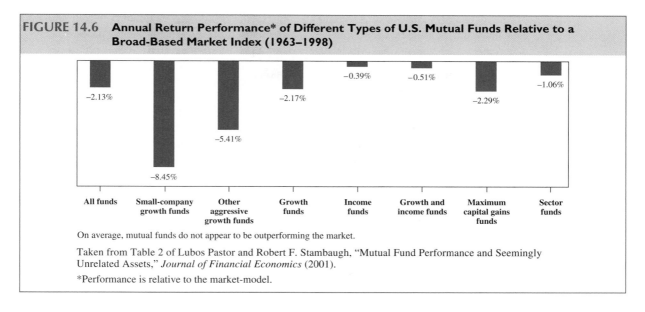

On average, mutual funds do not appear to be outperforming the market.

Taken from Table 2 of Lubos Pastor and Robert F. Stambaugh, "Mutual Fund Performance and Seemingly Unrelated Assets," *Journal of Financial Economics* (2001).

*Performance is relative to the market-model.

represents only one study, there have been a host of papers on mutual funds. The overwhelming evidence here is that mutual funds do not beat broad-based indexes on average.

By and large, mutual fund managers rely on publicly available information. Thus, the finding that they do not outperform the market indexes is consistent with semistrong-form and weak-form efficiency. This research has two important practical implications. First, it does not imply that mutual funds are bad investments for individuals. Though these funds fail to achieve better returns than some indexes of the market, they do permit the investor to buy a portfolio that has a large number of stocks in it (the phrase "a well-diversified portfolio" is often used). They might also be very good at providing a variety of services such as keeping custody and records of all of the stocks.

Second, the research underpins the growth of a particular kind of mutual fund, an index fund, which follows a passive investment strategy of investing in the market index. For example, TD Canadian Index Fund invests in the S&P/TSX Composite Total Return Index, and its performance tracks that of the index. The fund has lower expenses than an actively managed fund because it does not employ analysts to pick stocks. Investors who believe in semistrong-form efficiency prefer index investing because it implies that analysts will not beat the market consistently.

The Strong Form

Even the most enthusiastic adherents to the efficient market hypothesis would not be surprised to find that markets are inefficient in the strong form. After all, if an individual has information that no one else has, it is likely that he or she can profit from it. For example, in late 2001, the U.S. FDA announced that a key anti-cancer drug produced by ImClone Systems had not passed a regulatory test and the stock dropped sharply. In the days before the announcement, ImClone's ex-CEO, Sam Waksal, and his friend, lifestyle guru Martha Stewart, sold the company's stock. By selling her 3928 shares before the announcement, Ms. Stewart saved around US$50,000. Mr. Waksal was convicted of insider trading and Ms. Stewart was found guilty of obstructing a criminal investigation. Ironically, ImClone later received FDA approval for the new drug and its stock recovered.

Officers, directors, and major shareholders of a firm are considered insiders who may have information that is not public. In order to promote informational and allocational efficiency, the Ontario Securities Commission (and its counterparts in other provinces) and the U.S. Securities and Exchange Commission have regulations on insider trading. Insiders are allowed to buy and sell shares in their companies based on their general outlook but are prohibited from trading on specific pieces of information that have not yet become news. To enforce these regulations, the OSC, the SEC, and other securities commissions all require insiders to reveal any trading they might do in their own company's shares.

Researchers have used these records to test the hypothesis of strong-form market efficiency. If the strong form of the efficient market hypothesis holds, insiders should not be able to profit by trading on their information. By examining the record of insider trades, we can see whether they made abnormal returns. A number of studies support the view that these trades were abnormally profitable. Thus, strong-form efficiency does not seem to be substantiated by the evidence.[16]

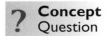

Concept Question

• **What conclusions about market efficiency can be drawn from available evidence?**

14.5 The Behavioural Challenge to Market Efficiency

In Section 14.2 and 14.3 we presented three conditions, any one of which will lead to market efficiency. In that section a case was made that at least one of the conditions is likely to hold in the real world. However, there is definitely disagreement. Many members of the academic community argue that none of the three conditions is likely to hold in reality. This point of view is based on what is called *behavioural finance*. Let us examine the behavioural view of each of these three conditions.

Rationality   Are people really rational? Not always. Just travel to Atlantic City or Las Vegas to see people gambling, sometimes with large sums of money. The casino's take implies a negative expected return for the gambler. Because gambling is risky and has a negative expected return, it can never be on the efficient frontier. In addition, gamblers will often bet on black at a roulette table after black has occurred a number of consecutive times, thinking that the run will continue. This strategy is faulty because roulette tables have no memory.

But, of course, gambling is only a sideshow as far as finance is concerned. Is there irrationality in financial markets as well? The answer may well be yes. Many investors do not achieve the degree of diversification that they should. Others trade frequently, generating both commissions and taxes. In fact, taxes can be handled optimally by selling losers and holding onto winners. Although some individuals invest with tax minimization in mind, plenty of them do just the opposite. Many are more likely to sell their winners than their losers, a strategy leading to high tax payments.[17] The behavioural view is not that *all* investors are irrational. Rather, it is that some, perhaps many, investors are.[18]

---

[16]H. N. Seyhun, Investor Intelligence from Insider Trading, MIT Press: Cambridge, Mass, 1998, studies strong-form efficiency on the NYSE. Arturo Bris, "Do Insider Trading Laws Work?" Yale ICF Working Paper No. 00-19, shows that insider trading in Canada offers higher profits than in the U.S.

[17]For example, see Brad Barber and Terrance Odean, "The Courage of Misguided Convictions," *Financial Analysts Journal* (November/December 1999).

[18]Irrationality may explain current research which shows that stock returns vary directly with the amount of sunlight during different seasons; see Mark J. Kamstra, Lisa A. Kramer, and Maurice D. Levi, "Winter Blues: A SAD Stock Market Cycle," *American Economic Review* (March 2003).

Independent Deviations from Rationality   Are deviations from rationality generally random, thereby likely to cancel out in a whole population of investors? To the contrary, psychologists have long argued that people deviate from rationality in accordance with a number of basic principles. Not all of these principles have an application to finance and market efficiency, but at least two seem to do so.

The first principle, called *representativeness,* can be explained with the gambling example just used. The gambler believing a run of black will continue is in error because the probability of a black spin is still only about 50 percent. Gamblers behaving in this way exhibit the psychological trait of representativeness—drawing conclusions from insufficient data. In other words, the gambler believes the small sample he observed is more representative of the population than it really is.

How is this related to finance? Perhaps a market dominated by representativeness leads to bubbles. People see a sector of the market—for example, Internet stocks—having a short history of high revenue growth and extrapolate that it will continue forever. When the growth inevitably stalls, prices have nowhere to go but down.

The second principle is *conservatism,* which means that people are too slow in adjusting their beliefs to new information. Suppose that your goal since childhood was to become a dentist. Perhaps you came from a family of dentists, perhaps you liked the security and relatively high income that comes with that profession or perhaps teeth always fascinated you. As things stand now, you could probably look forward to a long and productive career in that occupation. However, suppose a new drug was developed that would prevent tooth decay. That drug would clearly reduce the demand for dentists. How quickly would you realize the implications as stated here? If you were emotionally attached to dentistry, you might adjust your beliefs slowly. Family and friends could tell you to switch out of predental courses in college, but you just might not be psychologically ready to do that. Instead, you might cling to your rosy view of dentistry's future.

Perhaps there is a relationship to finance here. For example, many studies report that prices seem to adjust slowly to the information contained in earnings announcements.[19] Could it be that because of conservatism, investors are slow in adjusting their beliefs to new information? More will be said about this in the next section.

Arbitrage   In Section 14.2 we suggested that professional investors, knowing that securities are mispriced, could buy the underpriced ones while selling correctly priced (or even overpriced) substitutes. This might undo any mispricing caused by emotional amateurs.

Trading of this sort is likely to be more risky than it appears at first glance. Suppose professionals generally believed that McDonald's stock was underpriced. They would buy it while selling their holdings in, say, Burger King and Wendy's. However, if amateurs were taking opposite positions, prices would adjust to correct levels only if the positions of amateurs were small relative to those of the professionals. In a world of many amateurs, a few professionals would have to take big positions to bring prices into line, perhaps even engaging heavily in short selling. Buying large amounts of one stock and short selling large amounts of other stocks is quite risky, even if the two stocks are in the same industry. Here, unanticipated bad news about McDonald's and unanticipated good news about the other two stocks would cause the professionals to register large losses.

In addition, if amateurs mispriced McDonald's today, what is to prevent McDonald's from being even *more* mispriced tomorrow? This risk of further mispricing, even in the presence of no new information, may also cause professionals to cut back their arbitrage

---

[19]For example, see Vijay Singal, *Beyond the Random Walk* (New York: Oxford University Press, 2004), Chapter 4.

positions. As an example, imagine a shrewd professional who believed Internet stocks were overpriced in 1998. Had he bet on a decline at that time, he would have lost in the near term: Prices rose through March of 2000. Yet, he would have eventually made money because prices later fell. However, near-term risk may reduce the size of arbitrage strategies.

In conclusion, the arguments presented here suggest that the theoretical underpinnings of the efficient capital markets hypothesis, presented in Section 14.2, might not hold in reality. That is, investors may be irrational, irrationality may be related across investors rather than cancelling out across investors, and arbitrage strategies may involve too much risk to eliminate market efficiencies.

14.6 Empirical Challenges to Market Efficiency

Section 14.4 presented empirical evidence supportive of market efficiency. We now present evidence challenging this hypothesis. (Adherents of market efficiency generally refer to results of this type as *anomalies*.)

1. *Limits to arbitrage:* Royal Dutch Petroleum and Shell Transport merged their interests in 1907, with all subsequent cash flows being split on a 60 percent–40 percent basis between the two companies. However, both companies continued to be publicly traded. You might imagine that the market value of Royal Dutch would always be 1.5 (=60/40) times that of Shell. That is, if Royal Dutch ever became overpriced, rational investors would buy Shell instead of Royal Dutch. If Royal Dutch were underpriced, investors would buy Royal Dutch. In addition, arbitrageurs would go further by buying the underpriced security and selling the overpriced security short.

   However, Figure 14.7 shows that Royal Dutch and Shell have rarely traded at parity (i.e., 60/40) over the 1962 to 2004 period. Why would these deviations occur? As stated in the previous section, behavioural finance suggests that there are limits to arbitrage. That is, an investor buying the overpriced asset and selling the underpriced asset does not have a sure thing. Deviations from parity could actually *increase* in the short run, implying losses for the arbitrageur. The well-known statement, "Markets can stay irrational longer than you can stay solvent," attributed to John Maynard Keynes, applies here. Thus, risk considerations may force arbitrageurs to take positions that are too small to move prices back to parity.

   Academics have documented a number of these deviations from parity. Froot and Dabora show similar results for both the twin companies of Unilever N.V. and Unilever PLC and for two classes of SmithKline Beecham stock.[20] Lamont and Thaler present similar findings for 3Com and its subsidiary Palm Inc.[21] Other researchers find price behaviour in closed-end mutual funds suggestive of parity deviations.

2. *Earnings surprises:* Common sense suggests that prices should rise when earnings are reported to be higher than expected and prices should fall when the reverse occurs. However, market efficiency implies that prices will adjust immediately to the announcement, while behavioural finance would predict another pattern. Kolasinski and Li rank companies by the extent of their *earnings surprise*—that is, the difference between current

---

[20]Kenneth A. Froot and Emil M. Dabora, "How Are Stock Prices Affected by the Location of Trade?" *Journal of Financial Economics* 53 (August 1999).

[21]Owen Lamont and Richard Thaler, "Can the Market Add and Subtract? Mispricing in Tech Stock Carve-Outs," *Journal of Political Economy* (April 2003).

FIGURE 14.7

Deviations of the Ratio of the Market Value of Royal Dutch to the Market Value of Shell from Parity

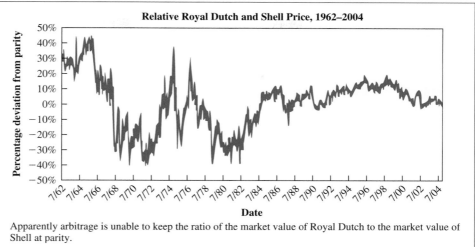

Apparently arbitrage is unable to keep the ratio of the market value of Royal Dutch to the market value of Shell at parity.

Source: Author calculations.

quarterly earnings and quarterly earnings four quarters ago, divided by the current stock price.[22] They form a portfolio of companies with the most extreme positive surprises and another portfolio of companies with the most extreme negative surprises. Figure 14.8 shows returns from buying the two portfolios, net of the return on the overall market. As can be seen, prices adjust slowly to the earnings announcements, with the portfolio with the positive surprises outperforming the portfolio with the negative surprises over both the next month and the next six months. Many other researchers obtain similar results.

Why do prices adjust slowly? Behavioural finance suggests that investors exhibit conservatism because they are slow to adjust to the information contained in the announcements.

3. *Size:* In 1981, two important papers presented evidence that in the United States, the returns on stocks with small market capitalizations were greater than the returns on stocks with large market capitalizations over most of the 20th century.[23] Table 10.3 shows that Canadian stocks with small market capitalizations outperformed stocks with large market capitalizations[24] over the period from 1970 to 2003. The difference in returns is perhaps 5–10 percent per year. While much of the differential performance is merely compensation for the extra risk of small stocks, a number of researchers have argued that not all of it can be explained by risk differences.[25] In addition, Kleim presented evidence that most of the difference in performance occurs in the month of

---

[22]Adam Kolasinski and Xu Li, "Do Managers Detect Mispricing? Evidence from Insider Trading and Post-Earnings-Announcement Drift" (Massachusetts Institute of Technology: unpublished paper, 2005).

[23]See R. W. Banz, "The Relationship between Return and Market Value of Common Stocks," *Journal of Financial Economics* (March 1981), and M. R. Reinganum, "Misspecification of Capital Asset Pricing: Empirical Anomalies Based on Earnings Yields and Market Values," *Journal of Financial Economics* (March 1981).

[24]Market capitalization is the price per share of stock multiplied by the number of shares outstanding.

[25]D. B Keim, "Size-Related Anomalies and Stock Return Seasonality: Further Empirical Evidence," *Journal of Financial Economics* (June 1983). See also J. Jaffe, D. Keim, and R. Westerfield, "Earnings Yields, Market Values and Stock Returns," *Journal of Finance* (March 1989). They find that firms with high earnings yields and small market capitalizations have abnormally high returns.

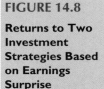

FIGURE 14.8

Returns to Two Investment Strategies Based on Earnings Surprise

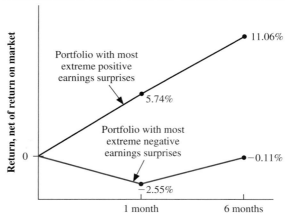

This figure shows returns net of the market return to a strategy of buying stocks with extremely high positive earnings surprise (the difference between current quarterly earnings and quarterly earnings four quarters ago, divided by the current stock price) and to a strategy of buying stocks with extremely high negative earnings surprise. The graph shows a slow adjustment to the information in the earnings announcement.

Source: Adapted from Table 1 of Adam Kolasinski and Xu Li, "Do Manager's Detect Mispricing? Evidence from Insider Trading and Post-Earnings-Announcement Drift" (Massachusetts Institute of Technology: unpublished paper, 2005).

January. Jog shows that this *size effect* (also called the *small capitalization effect* or *January effect*) is international. It has been documented for Canada and in most stock exchanges around the world occurring immediately after the close of the tax year.[26] While the effect is small relative to commissions on stock purchases and sales, investors who have decided to buy small-capitalization stocks can exploit the anomaly by buying in December rather than in January.

4. *Value versus growth:* A number of papers have argued that stocks with high book value-to-stock-price ratios and/or high earnings-to-price ratios (generally called *value stocks*) outperform stocks with low ratios (*growth stocks*). For example, Fama and French find that for 12 of 13 major international stock markets, the average return on stocks with high book-value-to-stock-price ratios is above the average return on stocks with low book-value-to-stock-price ratios.[27] Figure 14.9 shows these returns for the world's five largest stock markets. Value stocks have outperformed growth stocks in each of these five markets.

Because the return difference is so large and because these ratios can be obtained so easily for individual stocks, the results may constitute strong evidence against

---

[26]Vijay Jog, "Stock Pricing Anomalies Revisited," *Canadian Investment Review* (Winter 1998). Stephen R. Foerster and David C. Porter, "Calendar and Size-Based Anomalies in Canadian Stock Returns," in *Canadian Capital Markets,* Michael J. Robinson and Brian F. Smith, eds. (London, Ontario: Western Business School, 1993), pp.133–40, supports these findings with the TSX-Western database. George Athanassakos, "Seasons for Stocks," *Canadian Investment Review* 10 (Fall 1997), pp. 29–33, relates the effect of institutional trading. S. Elfakhani, L.J. Lockwood, and R.S. Zaher, "Small Firm and Value Effects in the Canadian Stock Market," *Journal of Financial Research* 21 (Fall 1998), pp. 277–291.

[27]Taken from Table III of Eugene F. Fama and Kenneth R. French, "Value versus Growth: The International Evidence," *Journal of Finance* 53 (December 1998).

FIGURE 14.9

Annual Dollar Returns* (in percent) on Low Book-to-Price Firms and High Book-to-Price Firms in Selected Countries

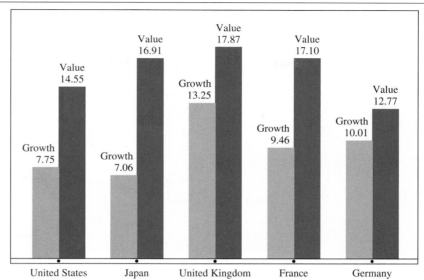

High book-to-price stocks (frequently called value stocks) outperform low book-to-price (growth) stocks in different countries.

Source: Eugene F. Fama and Kenneth R. French, "Value Versus Growth: The International Evidence," *Journal of Finance* (December 1998).

*Dollar returns are expressed as the excess over the return on U.S. Treasury bills.

market efficiency. However, a number of current papers suggest that the unusual returns are due to biases in the commercial databases, not to a true inefficiency.[28] Since the debate revolves around the details of data collection, we will not pursue the issue further. However, it is safe to say that no conclusion is warranted at this time. As with so many other topics in finance and economics, further research is needed.

5. *Crashes and bubbles:* The stock market crash of October 19, 1987, is extremely puzzling. The market dropped between 20 percent and 25 percent on a Monday following a weekend during which little surprising news was released. A drop of this magnitude for no apparent reason is not consistent with market efficiency. Because the crash of 1929 is still an enigma, it is doubtful that the more recent 1987 debacle will be explained anytime soon. The recent comments of an eminent historian are apt here: When asked what, in his opinion, the effect of the French Revolution of 1789 was, he replied that it was too early to tell.

   Perhaps the two stock market crashes are evidence consistent with the **bubble theory** of speculative markets. That is, security prices sometimes move wildly above their true values. Eventually, prices fall back to their original level, causing great losses for investors. Consider, for example, the behaviour of Internet stocks of the late 1990s. Figure 14.10 shows values of an index of Internet stocks from 1996 through 2002. The index rose over 10-fold from January 1996 to its high in March 2000 before retreating to approximately its original level in 2002. For comparison, the figure also

---

[28]For example, S. P. Kothari, J. Shanken, and R. G. Sloan, "Another Look at the Cross-Section of Expected Stock Returns," *Journal of Finance* 50 (March 1995), pp. 185–224; document survivorship bias arises because databases do not include the lower returns on companies that went out of business during the sample period.

FIGURE 14.10

Value of Index of Internet Stocks

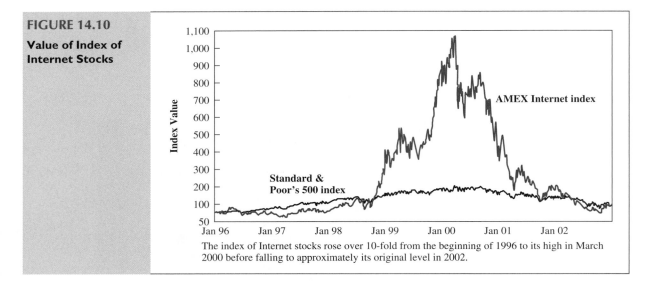

The index of Internet stocks rose over 10-fold from the beginning of 1996 to its high in March 2000 before falling to approximately its original level in 2002.

shows price movement for the Standard & Poor 500 index. While this index rose and fell over the same period, the price movement was quite muted relative to that of Internet stocks.

Many commentators describe the rise and fall of Internet stocks as a *bubble*. Is it correct to do so? Unfortunately, there is no precise definition of the term. Some academics argue that the price movement in the figure is consistent with rationality. Prices rose initially, they say, because it appeared that the Internet would soon capture a large chunk of international commerce. Prices fell when later evidence suggested this would not occur quite so quickly. However, others argue that the initial rosy scenario was never supported by the facts. Rather, prices rose due to nothing more than "irrational exuberance."

Bubbles can occur in other markets as well. For example, at the time of writing in the winter of 2007, a number of analysts were concerned about a bubble in real estate prices in Vancouver, Calgary and Edmonton. The idea that real estate has departed from market efficiency received support from a recent study identifying positive correlation in real estate returns in the Greater Toronto Area over the period 1982 to 2001.[29] Even in normal markets we would not expect to observe the same level of efficiency as in stock markets because real estate is illiquid and not standardized.

14.7 Reviewing the Differences

It is fair to say that the controversy over efficient capital markets has not yet been resolved. Rather, academic financial economists have sorted themselves into three camps, with some adhering to market efficiency, some believing in behavioural finance, and others (perhaps the majority) not yet convinced that either side has won the argument. This state of affairs

---

[29]J. Brox, E. Carvalho, and M. Duckett, "Testing Weak-Form Efficiency in Greater Toronto Area Residential Real Estate," University of Waterloo, Department of Economics, Working Paper, 2003.

is certainly different from, say, 20 years ago, when market efficiency went unchallenged. In addition, the controversy here is perhaps the most contentious of any area of financial economics.

Because of the controversy, it does not appear that our textbook, or any textbook, can easily resolve the differing points of view. However, we can illustrate the differences between the camps by relating the two psychological principles mentioned earlier, representativeness and conservatism, to stock returns.

Representativeness

This principle implies overweighting the results of small samples, as with the gambler who thinks a few consecutive spins of black on the roulette wheel make black a more likely outcome than red on the next spin. Financial economists have argued that representativeness leads to *overreaction* in stock returns. We mentioned earlier that financial bubbles are likely overreactions to news. Internet companies showed great revenue growth for a short time in the late 1990s, causing many to believe that this growth would continue indefinitely. Stock prices rose (too much) at this point. When at last investors realized that this growth could not be sustained, prices plummeted.

Conservatism

This principle states that individuals adjust their beliefs too slowly to new information. A market composed of this type of investor would likely lead to stock prices that *underreact* in the presence of new information. The example concerning earnings surprises may illustrate this underreaction. Prices rose slowly following announcements of positive earnings surprises. Announcements of negative surprises had a similar, but opposite, reaction.

The Academic Viewpoints

The academic camps have different views of these results. The efficient market believers stress that representativeness and conservatism have opposite implications for stock prices. Which principle, they ask, should dominate in any particular situation? In other words, why should investors overreact to news about Internet stocks but underreact to earnings news? Proponents of market efficiency say that unless behaviourists can answer these two questions satisfactorily, we should not reject market efficiency in favour of behavioural finance. In addition, Eugene Fama[30] reviewed the academic studies on anomalies, finding that about half of them show overreaction and half show underreaction. He concluded that this evidence is consistent with the market efficiency hypothesis that anomalies are chance events.

Adherents of behavioural finance see things a little differently. First, they point out that the three theoretical foundations of market efficiency appear to be violated in the real world. Second, there are simply too many anomalies, with a number of them being replicated in out-of-sample tests. This argues against anomalies being mere chance events. Finally, though the field has not yet determined why either overreaction or underreaction should dominate in a particular situation, much progress has already been made in a short time.[31]

---

[30]Eugene F. Fama, "Market Efficiency, Long-Term Returns, and Behavioral Finance," *Journal of Financial Economics* 49 (September 1998).

[31]Excellent reviews of this progress can be found in Andrei Shleifer, *Inefficient Markets: An Introduction to Behavioral Finance,* op. cit. and in Nicholas Barberis and Richard Thaler, "A Survey of Behavioral Finance," in the *Handbook of the Economics of Finance,* eds. George Constantinides, Milton Harris, and Rene Stultz (Amsterdam: North Holland, 2003).

A Random Talk With Burton Malkiel

How will the technology bubble be remembered?

Historians will record the Internet bubble of the late 1990s as one of the greatest bubbles of all time. Valuations became truly unbelievable. During the Nifty Fifty craze, the well-known growth stocks may have sold at 60-, 70- or even 80-times earnings. During the Internet bubble, stocks would sell at 60-, 70- or 80-times sales. Priceline.com, one of the Internet companies that sold discounted airline tickets, was valued at one time with a market capitalization that was larger than the combined market capitalizations of Delta Airlines, American Airlines and United Airlines. At its low, Priceline sold for about a dollar a share. You even had enormous multi-billion dollar capitalizations from companies that had essentially no sales at all. They were just selling on a promise.

People confused the correct idea that the Internet was real, that it was going to mean some profound changes in the way we live and shop and get information, to saying that the ordinary rules of valuation didn't apply. Whatever business you are in, an asset can only be worth the present value of the cash flows that are going to be generated in the future.

Look at reports that were issued by Wall Street firms. You find statements such as "the old metrics are different this time." That has certainly proved to be wrong. Most of these Internet stocks today are selling at a tiny fraction of their high market valuations. It is not clear that any of them have a business model that is going to allow them to make money. In one sense, Amazon.com is a very successful company. But they have yet to show that they are able to make any money.

To be sure, the same thing happened in our past history. There were many people who laid railroad tracks during the railroad-ization of North America. There was overbuilding and most of them collapsed. We had hundreds of automobile manufacturers at one time.

But what didn't happen in the past were the market valuations assigned to these companies. Why did firms like Morgan Stanley and Merrill Lynch put out buy recommendations on all of these stocks when they were at or near their peaks? The real problem is that their well-known analysts were paid a lot of money, not necessarily to make correct judgments about whether stocks were good buys or not, but rather based on their success in bringing investment banking clients into the firm. Who knows whether they knew better or not? But there was a clear conflict of interest.

Here's another thing—the CNBC effect. You had people talking about these extraordinary gains, and [producers] didn't want a fuddy duddy value manager being interviewed on CNBC. [They] wanted the person who said Amazon.com has a price target of $500 a share. Those were the people who got on those shows. That fed the public enthusiasm. There were some people who got it right. They were generally the value managers who actually underperformed the market as a whole very badly during that period.

How did institutional investors compare to retail investors?

The retail investors probably did a bit worse. Some of the institutional investors were sucked up in the enthusiasm and probably did overweight some of these stocks. But I think the real damage occurred with individual investors. It really worries me how sensitive the public money flows are to recent performance.

Having said that, everyone is ranked each quarter in the institutional business versus everyone else. The institutions—not quite to the extent that the public is—are not immune at all. Presumably the savvy institutions should be precisely the ones who lean against the wind. But if you look at the cash balances of mutual fund managers and institutional money managers, you find almost invariably their lowest cash balances are just at the peak of the market. They're almost perfect contrarian indicators.

I can remember arguments that I had with institutional investors in 1999, when I'd talk about the Pricelines of the world. People would say "You don't understand the value of the first mover. What a brilliant idea Priceline has. Don't worry that they're losing money now." Very clearly, there is soul searching to be done by the institutions.

Burton Malkiel is the Chemical Bank Chairman's Professor of Economics at Princeton University and author of *A Random Walk Down Wall Street*. His comments are excerpted (with permission) from *Canadian Investment Review,* Summer 2001.

14.8 Implications for Corporate Finance

Accounting and Efficient Markets

The accounting profession provides firms with a significant amount of leeway in their reporting practices. For example, companies may choose either the percentage-of-completion or the completed-contract method for construction projects. They may depreciate physical assets by either accelerated or straight-line depreciation. Financial institutions may exercise considerable judgment in setting aside loan loss provisions.

Accountants have frequently been accused of misusing this leeway in the hopes of boosting earnings and stock prices. For example, U.S. Steel (now USX Corporation) switched from straight-line to accelerated depreciation after World War II, because its high reported profits at that time attracted much government scrutiny. It switched back to straight-line depreciation in the 1960s after years of low reported earnings.

In the 1930s, Canada's largest life insurance company, Sun Life, experienced a major drop in the market value of its common stock portfolio that effectively erased the company's capital. To allow the company to remain in business, federal regulators changed the accounting rules for insurance companies to allow Sun Life to backdate the prices of its investments until the market improved.[32]

Despite such examples, accounting choice should not affect stock price provided two conditions hold. First, enough information must be provided in the annual report and other public sources so that financial analysts can construct earnings under the alternative accounting methods. This appears to be the case for many, though not necessarily all, accounting choices. Second, the market must be efficient in the semistrong form. In other words, the market must appropriately use all of this accounting information in determining the market price.

Of course, the issue of whether accounting choice affects stock price is ultimately an empirical matter. A number of academic papers have addressed this issue. Kaplan and Roll found that the switch from accelerated to straight-line depreciation generally did not affect stock prices significantly.[33] Several other accounting procedures have been studied. Hong, Kaplan, and Mandelker found no evidence that the stock market was affected by the artificially higher earnings reported using the pooling method, compared to the purchase method, for reporting mergers and acquisitions.[34] Cheung found no association between security returns and inflation accounting disclosures in Canada.[35] In summary, the above empirical evidence suggests that accounting changes do not fool the market.[36]

Stock price is also likely to be affected if a company either withholds useful information or provides incorrect information that cannot be corrected based on public sources.

---

[32]Lawrence Kryzanowski and Gordon S. Roberts, "Capital Forbearance: A Depression-Era Case Study of Sun Life," *Canadian Journal of Administrative Sciences* (April 1998).

[33]R. S. Kaplan and R. Roll, "Investor Evaluation of Accounting Information: Some Empirical Evidence," *Journal of Business* 45 (April 1972).

[34]H. Hong, R. S. Kaplan, and G. Mandelker, "Pooling vs. Purchase: The Effects of Accounting for Mergers on Stock Prices," *Accounting Review* 53 (1978).

[35]J. K. Cheung, "Inflation Accounting Disclosures and Stock Price Adjustments: Some Canadian Results," *Accounting and Finance* 26 (November 1986).

[36]These excellent studies are slightly off the mark for our purposes. They test the hypothesis that, in aggregate, stock prices are invariant to accounting changes. The efficient market hypothesis actually makes a stronger statement. As long as earnings can be reconstructed under alternative accounting methods, each stock should be unaffected by a change in accounting.

In many such cases of deliberate misrepresentation, the market obtains more accurate information of its own. One example in which this did occur involved the Northland Bank. Prior to its failure in 1985, the bank used questionable accounting to cover up its exposure to bad energy loans in Western Canada. According to the Estey Commission, which investigated the bank failure, "The financial statements became gold fillings covering cavities in the assets and in the earnings of the bank." Yet research on stock prices prior to the collapse has shown that stock market investors were aware that the bank was highly risky.[37]

More recently, companies like Enron, WorldCom, Global Crossing, and Xerox have reported fraudulent numbers. There was no way for financial analysts to construct alternative earnings numbers because these analysts were unaware how the reported numbers were determined.

The Timing Decision

Imagine a firm whose managers are contemplating the date to issue equity. This decision is frequently called the *timing* decision. If managers believe that their stock is overpriced, they are likely to issue equity immediately. Here, they are creating value for their current stockholders because they are selling stock for more than it is worth. Conversely, if the managers believe that their stock is underpriced, they are more likely to wait, hoping that the stock price will eventually rise to its true value.

However, if markets are efficient, securities are always correctly priced. Since efficiency implies that stock is always sold for its true worth, the timing decision becomes unimportant. Figure 14.11 shows three possible stock price adjustments to the issuance of new stock. Market efficiency implies that the stock price of the issuing firm, on average, neither rises nor falls after issuance of the stock. Of course, market efficiency is ultimately an empirical issue.

Surprisingly, a recent paper has called market efficiency into question. Ritter[38] presents evidence that annual returns over the five years following an IPO are, on average, approximately 2 percent less for the issuing company than the return on a non-issuing company of similar market capitalization. In addition, Ritter examines seasoned equity offerings (SEO), i.e., publicly traded companies that issue additional stock. They find that, over the five years following an SEO, the annualized return on the issuing firm's stock is between 3 and 4 percent less than the return on a comparable non-issuing company. The evidence of the Loughran and Ritter paper suggests that corporate managers issue stock when it is overpriced. In other words, they are successfully able to time the market. The evidence that managers time their IPOs is less compelling: Returns following IPOs are closer to those of their control group.

Does the ability of a corporate official to issue an SEO when the security is overpriced indicate that the market is inefficient in the semistrong form or the strong form? The answer is actually somewhat more complex than it may first appear. On one hand, officials are likely to have special information that the rest of us do not have, suggesting that the market need only be inefficient in the strong form. On the other hand, if the market were truly semistrong efficient, the price would drop immediately and completely upon the announcement of an upcoming SEO. That is, rational investors would realize that stock is being issued because corporate officials have special information that the stock is

---

[37]R. Giammarino, E. Schwartz, and J. Zechner, "Market Valuation of Bank Assets and Deposit Insurance in Canada," *Canadian Journal of Economics* 22 (February 1989), pp. 109–26.

[38]J. R. Ritter, "Investment Banking and Security Issuance," Chapter 9 of *Handbook of the Economics of Finance*, eds. G. Constantinides, M. Harris, and R. Stulz (Amsterdam: North Holland, 2003).

FIGURE 14.11

Three Stock Price Adjustments

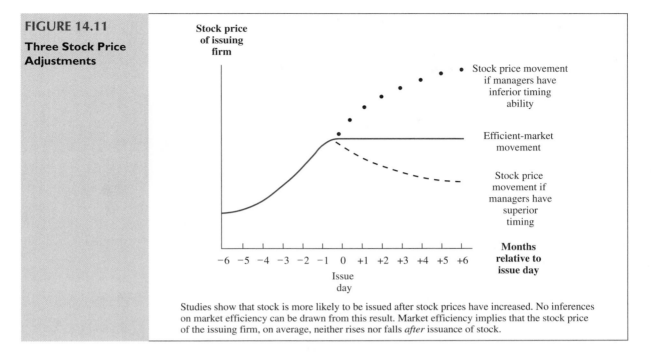

Studies show that stock is more likely to be issued after stock prices have increased. No inferences on market efficiency can be drawn from this result. Market efficiency implies that the stock price of the issuing firm, on average, neither rises nor falls *after* issuance of stock.

overpriced. Indeed, many empirical studies report a price drop on the announcement date. However, Figure 14.12 shows a further price drop in the subsequent years, suggesting that the market is inefficient in the semistrong form.

Speculation and Efficient Markets

We normally think of individuals and financial institutions as the primary speculators in financial markets. However, industrial corporations speculate as well. For example, many companies make interest rate bets. If the managers of a firm believe that interest rates are likely to rise, they have an incentive to borrow because the present value of the liability will fall with the rate increase. In addition, these managers will have an incentive to borrow long term rather than short term in order to lock in the low rates for a longer period. The thinking can get more sophisticated. Suppose that the long-term rate is already higher than the short-term rate. The manager might argue that this differential reflects the market's view that rates will rise. However, perhaps he anticipates a rate increase even greater than what the market anticipates, as implied by the upward-sloping term structure. Again, the manager will want to borrow long term rather than short term.

Firms also speculate in foreign currencies. Suppose that the CFO of a multinational corporation based in the United States believes that the euro will decline relative to the dollar. She would probably issue euro-denominated debt rather than dollar-denominated debt because she expects the value of the foreign liability to fall. Conversely, she would issue debt domestically if she believes foreign currencies will appreciate relative to the dollar.

We are perhaps getting a little ahead of our story: The subtleties of the term structure and exchange rates are treated in other chapters, not this one. However, the big picture question is this: What does market efficiency have to say about such activity? The answer is clear. If financial markets are efficient, managers should not waste their time trying

FIGURE 14.12

Returns on Initial Public Offerings (IPOs) and Seasoned Equity Offerings (SEOs) in Years Following Issue

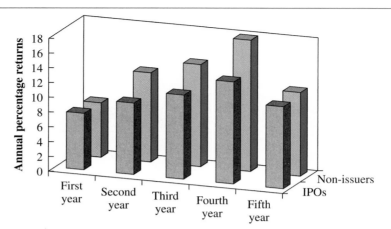

The average raw returns for 7042 IPOs from 1970 to 2000 and their matching non-issuing firms during the five years after the issue. The first-year return does not include the return on the day of issue.

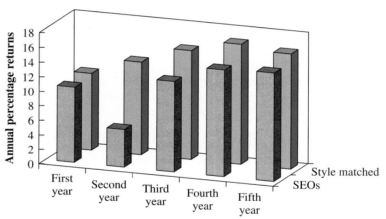

The average raw returns for 7502 SEOs from 1970 to 2000 and their matching non-issuing firms during the five years after the issue. The first-year return does not include the return on the day of issue. On average, IPOs underperform their control groups by about 2 percent per year in the five years following issuance. SEOs underperform by about 3 percent to 4 percent per year.

Source: Jay Ritter, "Investment Banking and Security Issuance," Chapter 9 of *Handbook of the Economics of Finance,* eds. George Constantinides, Milton Harris, and Rene Stulz (Amsterdam: North Holland, 2003).

to forecast the movements of interest rates and foreign currencies. Their forecasts will likely be no better than chance. And they will be using up valuable executive time. This is not to say, however, that firms should flippantly pick the maturity or the denomination of their debt in a random fashion. A firm must *choose* these parameters carefully. However, the choice should be based on other rationales, not on an attempt to beat the market. For example, a firm with a project lasting five years might decide to issue five-year debt. A firm might issue yen-denominated debt because it anticipates expanding into Japan in a big way.

The same thinking applies to acquisitions. Many corporations buy up other firms because they think these targets are underpriced. Unfortunately, the empirical evidence suggests that the market is too efficient for this type of speculation to be profitable. And the acquirer never pays just the current market price. The bidding firm must pay a premium above market to induce a majority of shareholders of the target firm to sell their shares. However, this is not to say that firms should never be acquired. Rather, managers should consider an acquisition if there are benefits (synergies) from the union. Improved marketing, economies in production, replacement of bad management, and even tax reduction are typical synergies. These synergies are distinct from the perception that the acquired firm is underpriced.

One final point should be mentioned. We talked earlier about empirical evidence suggesting that SEOs are timed to take advantage of overpriced stock. This makes sense—managers are likely to know more about their own firms than the market does. However, while managers may have special information about their own firms, it is unlikely that they have special information about interest rates, foreign currencies, and other firms. There are simply too many participants in these markets, many of whom are devoting all of their time to forecasting. Managers typically spend most of their effort running their own firms, with only a small amount of time devoted to studying financial markets.

Information in Market Prices

The previous section argued that it is quite difficult to forecast future market prices. However, the current and past prices of any asset are known—and of great use. Consider, for example, Becher's study of bank mergers.[39] The author finds that stock prices of acquired banks rise about 23 percent on average upon the first announcement of a merger. This is not surprising because companies are generally bought out at a premium above current stock price. However, the same study shows that prices of acquiring banks fall almost 5 percent on average upon the same announcement. This is pretty strong evidence that bank mergers do not benefit, and may even hurt, acquiring companies. The reason for this result is unclear, though perhaps acquirers simply overpay for acquisitions. Regardless of the reason, the *implication* is clear. A bank should think deeply before acquiring another bank.

Furthermore, suppose you are the CFO of a company whose stock price drops much more than 5 percent upon announcement of an acquisition. The market is telling you that the merger is bad for your firm. Serious consideration should be given to cancelling the merger, even if, prior to the announcement, you thought the merger was a good idea.

Of course, mergers are only one type of corporate event. Managers should pay attention to the stock price reaction to any of their announcements, whether it concerns a new venture, a divestiture, a restructuring, or something else.

This is not the only way in which corporations can use the information in market prices. Suppose you are on the board of directors of a company whose stock price has declined precipitously since the current chief executive officer (CEO) was hired. In addition, the prices of competitors have risen over the same time. Though there may be extenuating circumstances, this can be viewed as evidence that the CEO is doing a poor job. Perhaps he should be fired. If this seems harsh, consider that Warner, Watts, and Wruck find a strong negative correlation between managerial turnover and prior stock

---

[39]David A. Becher, "The Valuation Effects of Bank Mergers," *Journal of Corporate Finance* 6 (2000).

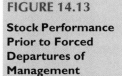

FIGURE 14.13

Stock Performance Prior to Forced Departures of Management

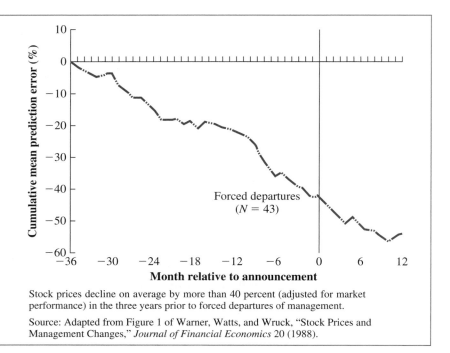

Stock prices decline on average by more than 40 percent (adjusted for market performance) in the three years prior to forced departures of management.

Source: Adapted from Figure 1 of Warner, Watts, and Wruck, "Stock Prices and Management Changes," *Journal of Financial Economics* 20 (1988).

performance.[40] Figure 14.13 shows that stocks fall on average about 40 percent in price (relative to market movements) in the three years prior to the forced departure of a top manager.

If managers are fired for bad stock price performance, perhaps they are rewarded for stock price appreciation. Hall and Liebman state,

> Our main empirical finding is that CEO wealth often changes by millions of dollars for typical changes in firm value. For example, the median total compensation for CEOs is about $1 million if their firm's stock has a 30th percentile annual return (-7.0 percent) and is $5 million if the firm's stock has a 70th percentile annual return (20.5 percent). Thus, there is a difference of about $4 million in compensation for achieving a moderately above average performance relative to a moderately below average performance.[41]

Market efficiency implies that stock prices reflect all available information. We recommend using this information as much as possible in corporate decisions. And at least with respect to executive firings and executive compensation, it looks as if real-world corporations do pay attention to market prices. The following box summarizes some key issues in the efficient markets debate:

? Concept Question

- **What are three implications of the efficient market hypothesis for corporate finance?**

---

[40]Jerold B. Warner, Ross L. Watts, and Karen H. Wruck, "Stock Prices and Top Management Changes," *Journal of Financial Economics* 20 (1988).

[41]Brian J. Hall and Jeffrey B. Liebman, "Are CEOs Really Paid Like Bureaucrats?" *Quarterly Journal of Economics* (August 1998), p. 654.

Efficient Market Hypothesis: A Summary

Does Not Say

- Prices are uncaused.
- Investors are foolish and too stupid to be in the market.
- All shares of stock have the same expected returns.
- Investors should throw darts to select stocks.
- There is no upward trend in stock prices.

Does Say

- Prices reflect underlying value.
- Financial managers cannot time stock and bond sales.
- Managers cannot profitably speculate in foreign currencies.
- Managers cannot boost stock prices through creative accounting.

Why Doesn't Everybody Believe It?

- There are optical illusions, mirages, and apparent patterns in charts of stock market returns.
- The truth is less interesting.
- There is evidence against efficiency.
  - Two different, but financially identical, classes of stock of the same firm selling at different prices.
  - Earnings surprises.
  - Small versus large stocks.
  - Value versus growth stocks.
  - Crashes and bubbles.

Three Forms

Weak form: Current prices reflect past prices; chartism (technical analysis) is useless.
Semistrong form: Prices reflect all public information; most fundamental analysis is useless.
Strong form: Prices reflect all that is knowable; nobody consistently makes superior profits.

14.9 SUMMARY AND CONCLUSIONS

1. An efficient financial market processes the information available to investors and incorporates it into the prices of securities. Market efficiency has two general implications. First, in any given time period, a stock's abnormal return depends on information or news received by the market in that period. Second, an investor who uses the same information as the market cannot expect to earn abnormal returns. In other words, systems for playing the market are doomed to fail.

2. What information does the market use to determine prices? The weak form of the efficient market hypothesis says that the market uses the past history of prices and is therefore efficient with respect to these past prices. This implies that stock selection based on patterns of past stock-price movements is not better than random stock selection.

3. The semistrong form states that the market uses all publicly available information in setting prices.

4. Strong-form efficiency states that the market uses all of the information that anybody knows about stocks, even inside information.

5. Much evidence from different financial markets supports weak-form and semistrong-form efficiency but not strong-form efficiency.

6. Behavioural finance states that the market is not efficient. Adherents argue that:

    a. Investors are not rational.

    b. Deviations from rationality are similar across investors.

    c. Arbitrage, being costly, will not eliminate inefficiencies.

7. Behaviourists point to many studies, including those showing that small stocks outperform large stocks, value stocks outperform growth stocks, and stock prices adjust slowly to earnings surprises, as empirical confirmation of their beliefs.

8. Four implications of market efficiency for corporate finance are:

    a. Managers cannot fool the market through creative accounting.

    b. Firms cannot successfully time issues of debt and equity.

    c. Managers cannot profitably speculate in foreign currencies and other instruments.

    d. Managers can reap many benefits by paying attention to market prices.

    e. A firm can sell as many bonds or shares of stock as it desires without depressing prices significantly.

KEY TERMS

Bubble theory 405	Random walk 391	Serial correlation 395
Efficient market hypothesis (EMH) 388	Semistrong-form efficiency 392	Strong-form efficiency 392
		Weak-form efficiency 391

SUGGESTED READING

The concept of market efficiency is important. Classic review articles include:

E. F. Fama. "Efficient Capital Markets: A Review of Theory and Empirical Work." *Journal of Finance* (May 1970).

E. F. Fama. "Efficient Capital Markets: II." *Journal of Finance* (December 1991).

An entertaining yet informative book on efficient markets is:

B. G. Malkiel. *A Random Walk Down Wall Street.* 8th ed. New York: Norton, 2003.

An excellent review of research on market efficiency in Canada is:

Z. Bodie, A. Kane, A. J. Marcus, S. Perrakis, and P. J. Ryan. *Investments.* 5th Canadian ed. Whitby, ON: McGraw-Hill Ryerson, 2005.

QUESTIONS & PROBLEMS

Efficient Capital Markets

14.1   *a.* What rule should a firm follow when making financing decisions?

      b. How can firms create valuable financing opportunities?

14.2   Prospectors Inc. is a publicly traded gold prospecting company in the Northwest Territories. Although the firm's searches for gold usually fail, the prospectors occasionally find a rich vein of ore. What pattern would you expect to observe for Prospectors' cumulative abnormal returns if the market is efficient?

14.3   Your broker commented that well-managed firms are better investments than poorly managed firms. As evidence your broker cited a recent study examining 100 small manufacturing firms that eight years earlier had been listed in an industry magazine as the best-managed small manufacturers in the country. In the ensuing eight years, the 100 firms listed have not earned more than the normal market return. Your broker continued to say that if the firms were well managed, they should have produced better-than-average returns. If the market is efficient, do you agree with your broker?

14.4   Ansari Aerotechnologies, an aerospace-technology firm, announced this morning that it has hired the world's most knowledgeable and prolific space researchers. Before today, Ansari's stock has been selling for $70. Assume no other information is received over the next week and the stock market as a whole does not move.

      a. What do you expect will happen to Ansari's stock?

      b. Consider the following scenarios:

         1. The stock price jumps to $108 on the day of the announcement. In subsequent days it floats up to $123, then falls down to $95

         2. The stock price jumps to $95 and remains at that level.

         3. The stock price gradually climbs to $95 over the week.

Which scenario(s) indicate market efficiency? Which do not? Why?

14.5 TransTrust Corp. has changed how it accounts for inventory. Taxes are unaffected, although the resulting earnings report released this quarter is 20 percent higher than what it would have been under the old accounting system. There is no other surprise in the earnings report, and the change in the accounting treatment was publicly announced. If the market is efficient, will the stock price be higher when the market learns that the reported earnings are higher?

14.6 When the 56-year-old founder of Gulf & Western Inc. died of a heart attack, the stock price immediately jumped from $18 per share to $20.25, a 12.5 percent increase. This is evidence of market inefficiency because an efficient stock market would have anticipated his death and adjusted the price beforehand. Assume that no other information is received and the stock market as a whole does not move. Is this statement about market efficiency true or false? Explain.

14.7 For each of the following scenarios, discuss whether profit opportunities exist from trading in the stock of the firm under the conditions that (1) the market is not weak-form efficient, (2) the market is weak form but not semistrong-form efficient, (3) the market is semistrong form but not strong-form efficient, and (4) the market is strong-form efficient.

   a. The stock price has risen steadily each day for the past 30 days.
   b. The financial statements for a company were released three days ago, and you believe you've uncovered some anomalies in the company's inventory and cost control reporting techniques that are causing the firm's true liquidity strength to be understated.
   c. You observe that the senior management of a company has been buying a lot of the company's stock on the open market over the past week.

14.8 In the middle to late 1990s the performance of the pros was unusually poor—on the order of 90 percent of all equity mutual funds underperformed a passively managed index fund. How does this bear on the issue of market efficiency?

14.9 On January 27, 1985, the following announcement was made: "Early today the Justice Department reached a decision in the Universal Product Care (UPC) case. UPC has been found guilty of discriminatory practices in hiring. For the next five years, UPC must pay $2 million each year to a fund representing victims of UPC's policies." Assuming the market is efficient, should investors not buy UPC stock after the announcement because the litigation will cause an abnormally low rate of return? Explain.

14.10 SDM Ltd. is going to adopt a bone density scanner device that can greatly improve hospital efficiency. Do you think the lead engineer can profit from purchasing the firm's stock before the news release on the device? After reading the announcement in *The National Post,* should you be able to earn an abnormal return from purchasing the stock if the market is efficient?

14.11 The Durkin Investing Agency has been the best stock picker in the country for the past two years. Before this rise to fame occurred, the Durkin newsletter had 300 subscribers. Those subscribers beat the market consistently, earning substantially higher returns after adjustment for risk and transaction costs. Subscriptions have skyrocketed to 30,000. Now, when the Durkin Investing Agency recommends a stock, the price instantly rises several points. The subscribers currently earn only a normal return when they buy recommended stock because the price rises before anybody can act on the information. Briefly explain this phenomenon. Is Durkin's ability to pick stocks consistent with market efficiency?

14.12 Suppose the market is semistrong-form efficient. Can you expect to earn excess returns if you make trades based on

   a. Your broker's information about record earnings for a stock?
   b. Rumours about a merger of a firm?
   c. Yesterday's announcement of a successful new product test?

14.13 Imagine that a particular macroeconomic variable that influences your firm's net earnings is positively serially correlated. Assume market efficiency. Would you expect price changes in your stock to be serially correlated? Why or why not?

14.14 The efficient market hypothesis implies that all mutual funds should obtain the same expected risk-adjusted returns. Therefore, we can simply pick mutual funds at random. Is this statement true or false? Explain.

14.15 Assume that markets are efficient. During a trading day Green Jacket Golf Inc. announces that it has lost a contract for a large golfing project that, prior to the news, it was widely believed to have secured. If the market is efficient, how should the stock price react to this information if no additional information is released?

14.16 Some people argue that the efficient market hypothesis cannot explain the 1987 market crash or the high price-to-earnings ratio of Internet stocks during the late 1990s. What alternative hypothesis is currently used for these two phenomena?

The Evidence

14.17 Air Canada, WestJet, and Transat A. T. Inc. announced purchases of planes on July 18 (7/18), February 12 (2/12), and October 7 (10/7), respectively. Given the information below, calculate the cumulative abnormal return (CAR) for these stocks as a group. Graph the result and provide an explanation. All of the stocks have a beta of 1 and no other announcements are made.

	Transat			Air Canada			WestJet	
Date	Market Return	Company Return	Date	Market Return	Company Return	Date	Market Return	Company Return
7/12	−0.3	−0.5	2/8	−0.9	−1.1	10/1	0.5	0.3
7/13	0.1	0.2	2/9	−1.0	−1.1	10/2	0.4	0.6
7/16	0.5	0.7	2/10	0.4	0.2	10/3	1.1	1.1
7/17	−0.5	−0.3	2/11	0.6	0.8	10/6	0.1	−0.3
7/18	−2.2	1.1	2/12	−0.3	−0.1	10/7	−2.2	−0.3
7/19	−0.9	−0.7	2/15	1.1	1.2	10/8	0.5	0.5
7/20	−1.0	−1.1	2/16	0.5	0.5	10/9	−0.3	−0.2
7/23	0.7	0.5	2/17	−0.3	−0.2	10/10	0.3	0.1
7/24	0.2	0.1	2/18	0.3	0.2	10/13	0.1	−0.1

14.18 The following diagram shows the cumulative abnormal returns (CAR) for 386 oil exploration companies announcing oil discoveries over the period from 1950 to 1980. Month 0 in the diagram is the announcement month. Assume that no other information is received and the stock market as a whole does not move. Is the diagram consistent with market efficiency? Why or why not?

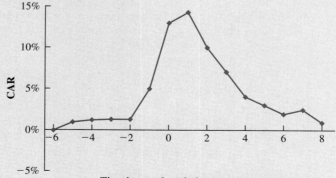

Time in months relative to event month

14.19 The following figures present the results of four cumulative abnormal returns (CAR) studies. Indicate whether the results of each study support, reject, or are inconclusive about the semistrong form of the efficient market hypothesis. In each figure, time 0 is the date of an event.

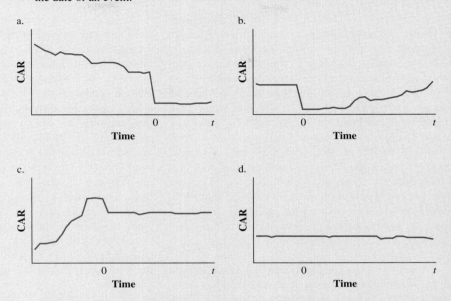

14.20 A study analyzed the behaviour of the stock prices of firms that had lost antitrust cases. Included in the diagram are all firms that lost the initial court decision, even if the decision was later overturned on appeal. The event at time 0 is the initial, preappeal court decision. Assume no other information was released, aside from that disclosed in the initial trial. The stock prices all have a beta of 1. Is the diagram consistent with market efficiency? Why or why not?

14.21 On January 23, 1998, Royal Bank of Canada and Bank of Montreal announced their plans for a merger. On April 17 of the same year, CIBC and TD Bank announced plans for a second merger. Both proposed mergers were later rejected by the finance minister and did not occur.

   Using the S&P database or an alternative source, download daily data for returns on each of these four banks and for the TSX 60 Index for January and April of 1998. Assuming that the banks' betas were approximately equal to 1, find the cumulative excess returns associated with each announcement. What conclusions can you draw?

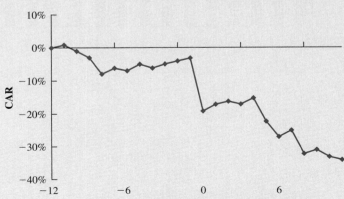

Time in months relative to event month

Visit us at www.mcgrawhill.ca/olc/ross

MINICASE: Your Retirement Plan at Deck Out My Yacht

You have been at your job for Deck Out My Yacht for a week now and have decided you need to sign up for the company's retirement plan. Even after your discussion with the Marshall McLaren Financial Services representative, you are still unsure which investment option you should choose. Recall that the options available to you are stock in Deck Out My Yacht, the M&M TSX Composite Index Fund, the M&M Small-Cap Fund, the M&M Large-Company Stock Fund, the M&M Bond Fund, and the M&M Money Market Fund. You have decided that you should invest in a diversified portfolio, with 70 percent of your investment in equity, 25 percent in bonds, and 5 percent in the money market fund. You have also decided to focus your equity investment on large-cap stocks, but you are debating whether to select the TSX/S&P Composite Index Fund or the Large-Company Stock Fund.

In thinking it over, you understand the basic difference in the two funds. One is a purely passive fund that replicates a widely followed large-cap index, the TSX Composite, and has low fees. The other is actively managed with the intention that the skill of the portfolio manager will result in improved performance relative to an index. Fees are higher in the latter fund. You are just not certain which way to go, so you ask Blake Price, who works in the company's finance area, for advice.

After discussing your concerns, Blake gives you some information comparing the performance of equity mutual funds and the F&F Passive TSX Composite Fund. The F&F Passive TSX Composite Fund is the largest fictitious equity index mutual fund based on the TSX. It replicates the TSX Composite, and its return is only negligibly different from the TSX Composite. Fees are very low. As a result, the fund is essentially identical to the M&M TSX Composite Index Fund offered in the retirement plan, but it has been in existence for much longer, so you can study its track record for over two decades. The graph below summarizes Blake's comments by showing the percentage of equity mutual funds that outperformed the fund over the previous 10 years. So for example, from January 1979 to December 1988, about 70 percent of equity mutual funds outperformed the fund. Blake suggests that you study the graph and answer the following questions:

1. What implications do you draw from the graph for mutual fund investors?
2. Is the graph consistent or inconsistent with market efficiency? Explain carefully.
3. What investment decision would you make for the equity portion of your retirement plan? Why?

Ratio of Managed Equity Funds Beating the F&F
Passive TSX Composite Fund: 10-Year Returns

Chapter 15

Long-Term Financing:
An Introduction

EXECUTIVE SUMMARY

This chapter introduces the basic sources of long-term financing: common stock, preferred stock, and long-term debt. Later chapters discuss these topics in more detail. Perhaps no other area is more perplexing to new students of finance than corporate securities such as shares of stock, bonds, and debentures. Although the concepts are simple and logical, the language is strange and unfamiliar.

The purpose of this chapter is to describe the basic features of long-term financing. We begin with a look at common stock, preferred stock, and long-term debt and then briefly consider patterns of the different kinds of long-term financing. We also describe the income trust form of organization, which grew rapidly in Canada between 2001 and 2006. Discussion of more complex forms of long-term finance, such as convertibles and leases, is reserved for later chapters.

15.1 Common Stock

The term **common stock** (or **common shares**) means different things to different people, but is usually applied to stock that has no special preference either in dividends or in bankruptcy. A description of the common stock of Enbridge Inc. is presented in the table below.

Enbridge Inc. Shareholders' Equity at Book Value, 2006
(in $ thousands)

Share Capital	
Preferred shares	$ 125,000
Common shares	2,416,100
Contributed surplus	18,300
Retained earnings	2,322,700
Foreign currency translation adjustment	(135,800)
Reciprocal shareholding	(135,700)
Total shareholders' equity	$ 4,610,600

Source: Enbridge Annual Report 2006.

Owners of common stock in a corporation are referred to as *shareholders* or *stockholders*. They receive stock certificates for the *shares* they own. There can be a stated value on each stock certificate called the *par value,* but more typically in Canada, there is no particular par value assigned to stock.

As we discussed in Chapter 1, common shareholders are protected by *limited liability.* If the company goes bankrupt, the creditors cannot seek payment of the firm's debt from its common shareholders. On the other hand, the common shareholders are the residual claimants and almost always lose 100 percent of their investment if the firm goes bankrupt.

Authorized Versus Issued Common Stock

Shares of common stock are the fundamental ownership units of the corporation. The articles of incorporation of a new corporation must state the number of shares of common stock the corporation is authorized to issue.

The board of directors of the corporation, after a vote of the shareholders, can amend the articles of incorporation to increase the number of shares authorized; there is no legal limit to the number of shares that can be authorized this way. In a recent year, for example, Enbridge Inc. had authorized an unlimited amount of common shares, but had issued 351,800,000 shares. There is no requirement that all of the authorized shares ever be issued.

Retained Earnings

In 2006, Enbridge Inc. paid out around 67 percent of its net income as dividends; the rest is retained in the business and is called **retained earnings.** The cumulative amount of retained earnings (since original incorporation) was $2,322.7 million in 2006.

The sum of accumulated retained earnings, contributed surplus (if any), share capital, and adjustments to equity is the total shareholders' equity of the firm, which is usually referred to as the firm's **book value of equity** (or *net worth*). The book value of equity represents an accountant's measure of the amount contributed directly and indirectly to the corporation by equity investors.

To illustrate some of these definitions, suppose Western Redwood Corporation was formed in 1976 with 10,000 shares of stock issued and sold for $1 per share. By 2007 the company had been profitable and had retained profits of $100,000. Shareholders' equity of Western Redwood Corporation in 2007 is as follows:

Western Redwood Corporation Equity Accounts, 2007	
Common stock (10,000 shares outstanding)	$ 10,000
Retained earnings	100,000
Total shareholders' equity	$110,000

$$\text{Book value per share} = \frac{\$110,000}{10,000} = \$11$$

Now suppose the company has profitable investment opportunities and decides to sell 10,000 shares of new stock to raise the necessary funding. The current market price is $20 per share. The table below shows the effects of the sale of stock on the balance sheet.

Western Redwood Corporation, 2007, After Sale of Stock	
Common stock (20,000 shares outstanding)	$210,000
Retained earnings	100,000
Total shareholders' equity	$310,000

$$\text{Book value per share} = \frac{\$310,000}{20,000} = \$15.50$$

What happened?

1. Since 10,000 shares of new stock were issued at a book value of $20, a total of $200,000 was added to common stock.

2. The book value per share was higher than the previous book value of $11 because the market price of the new stock was higher than the book value.

Market Value, Book Value, and Replacement Value

The total book value of common equity for Enbridge Inc. in 2006 was $4,610,600,000. The company had outstanding 351,800,000 common shares.

The book value per share was thus

$$\frac{\text{Total common shareholders' equity}}{\text{Shares outstanding}} = \frac{\$4,610,600,000}{351,800,000} = \$13.10$$

Enbridge Inc. is a publicly owned company. Its common stock and equity preferred stock trade on the Toronto Stock Exchange (TSX); its common stock also trades on the New York Stock Exchange (NYSE). Thousands of shares change hands every day. Market prices of Enbridge's common shares were between $30.96 and $40.57 per share during 2006. Thus, the market prices were above the book value.

In addition to market and book values, you may hear the term *replacement value.* This refers to the current cost of replacing the assets of the firm. Market, book, and replacement value are equal at the time when a firm purchases an asset. After that time, these values will diverge. The market–to–book-value ratio of common stock and Tobin's Q (market value of assets/replacement value of assets), introduced in Appendix 2A, are indicators of the success of the firm. A market-to-book or Tobin's Q ratio greater than 1 indicates the firm has done well with its investment decisions.

Shareholders' Rights

Shareholders elect directors who, in turn, hire management to carry out their directives. Shareholders, therefore, control the corporation through the right to elect the directors; generally only shareholders have this right.

Directors are elected at an annual shareholders' meeting by a vote of those people who hold a majority of shares present and are entitled to vote. The exact mechanism for electing directors differs across companies. The two most important methods are *cumulative voting* and *straight voting.*[1]

The value of a share of common stock in a corporation is directly related to the general rights of shareholders. In addition to the right to vote for directors, shareholders usually have the following rights:

1. The right to share proportionally in dividends paid.
2. The right to share proportionally in assets remaining after liabilities have been paid in a liquidation.
3. The right to vote on matters of great importance to shareholders, such as a merger, usually decided at the annual meeting or a special meeting.
4. The right to share proportionally in any new stock sold when approved by the board of directors. Called the *preemptive right,* this right is detailed in Chapter 20.

---

[1]Outside Canada and the United States, other factors besides proportionate ownership can be important in electing directors. For example, in 1989, T. Boone Pickens, a well-known U.S. takeover specialist, acquired over 20 percent of the shares of Koito, an important auto parts manufacturer in Japan. When Pickens requested that three executives from his firm go on the Koito board, Tamotsu Aoyama, a Koito director replied, "It is necessary to build a trusting relationship first. In Japan, it is not possible to just say, 'I'm a major shareholder' and get a seat on the board right away." *The Globe and Mail* (April 27, 1989).

EXAMPLE 15.1

Imagine that a corporation has two shareholders: MacDonald with 25 shares and Laurier with 75 shares. Both want to be on the board of directors. Laurier does not want MacDonald to be a director. Let us assume that there are four directors to be elected and each shareholder nominates four candidates.

Cumulative Voting   The effect of **cumulative voting** is to permit minority participation. If cumulative voting is permitted, the total number of votes that each shareholder may cast is determined first. That number is usually calculated as the number of shares (owned or controlled) multiplied by the number of directors to be elected. Each shareholder can distribute these votes as he or she wishes over one or more candidates. MacDonald will get $25 \times 4 = 100$ votes, and Laurier is entitled to $75 \times 4 = 300$ votes. If MacDonald gives all his votes to himself, he is assured of a directorship. It is not possible for Laurier to divide 300 votes among the four candidates in such a way as to preclude MacDonald's election to the board.

In general, if there are N directors up for election, then $1/(N + 1)$ percent of the stock (plus one share) will guarantee you a seat. In our current example, this is $1/(4 + 1) = 20\%$. With cumulative voting, the more seats that are up for election at one time, the easier it is to win one.

Straight Voting   If **straight voting** is permitted, MacDonald may cast 25 votes for each candidate and Laurier may cast 75 votes for each. As a consequence, Laurier will elect all of the candidates.

Straight voting can freeze out minority shareholders; that is the rationale for cumulative voting. But devices have been worked out to minimize its impact. One such device is to *stagger* the voting for the board of directors. Staggering permits a fraction of the directorships to come to a vote at a particular time. It has two basic effects:

1. Staggering makes it more difficult for a minority to elect a director when there is cumulative voting.

2. Staggering makes successful takeover attempts less likely by making the election of new directors more difficult.

Proxy Voting   A **proxy** is the legal grant of authority by a shareholder to someone else to vote his or her shares. For convenience, the actual voting in large public corporations usually is done by proxy.

Many companies, such as BCE Inc., have hundreds of thousands of shareholders. Shareholders can come to the annual meeting and vote in person, or they can transfer their right to vote to another party by proxy.

Obviously, management always tries to get as many proxies transferred to it as possible. However, if shareholders are not satisfied with management's position on a particular issue or with the corporate governance of the firm, an outside group of shareholders can try to obtain as many votes as possible via proxy. They can vote to direct management actions or more drastically to replace management or change the company's governance. Under the umbrella of the Canadian Coalition for Good Governance large pension funds like the Ontario Teachers' Pension Board or British Columbia Investment Management Corporation have developed detailed proxy voting guidelines.

Dividends

A distinctive feature of corporations is that they issue shares of stock and are authorized by law to pay dividends to the holders of those shares. **Dividends** paid to shareholders represent a return on the capital directly or indirectly contributed to the corporation by the shareholders. The payment of dividends is at the discretion of the board of directors.

Here are some important characteristics of dividends:

1. Unless a dividend is declared by the board of directors of a corporation, it is not a liability of the corporation. A corporation cannot *default* on an undeclared dividend. As a consequence, corporations cannot become *bankrupt* because of nonpayment of dividends. The amount of the dividend and even whether it is paid are decisions based on the business judgment of the board of directors.

2. The payment of dividends by the corporation is not a business expense. Dividends are not deductible for corporate tax purposes. In short, dividends are paid out of after-tax profits of the corporation.

3. Dividends received by individual shareholders are partially sheltered by a dividend tax credit discussed in detail in Appendix 1A. Canadian corporations that own shares in other companies are permitted to exclude from taxable income 100 percent of the dividend amounts they receive from taxable Canadian corporations. The purpose of this provision is to avoid the double taxation of dividends.

Classes of Shares

Some firms have more than one class of common shares. Often, the classes are created with unequal voting rights. For example, Canadian Tire Corporation has two classes of common shares, both publicly traded. The majority of the voting common shares were distributed among offspring of the company founder and the rest are held by Canadian Tire dealers, pension funds, and the general public. The nonvoting, Canadian Tire A shares are more widely held.[2]

There are a number of other Canadian corporations with restricted (nonvoting or limited-voting) stock. Nonvoting shares must receive dividends no lower than dividends on voting shares. Some companies pay a higher dividend on the nonvoting shares. In 2007, Canadian Tire's dividend rate was $0.74 per share on both classes of stock.

A primary reason for creating dual classes of stock has to do with control of the firm. If such stock exists, management of a firm can raise equity capital by issuing nonvoting or limited-voting stock while maintaining control. Amoako-Adu and Smith show that firms going public with dual classes of shares in Canada are often family controlled.[3] Examples of such Canadian companies include Bombardier, Magna International, Rogers Communications, Shaw Communications, and Celestica.

Lease, McConnell, and Mikkelson found the market prices of U.S. stocks with superior voting rights to be about 5 percent higher than the prices of otherwise identical stocks with inferior voting rights.[4] However, DeAngelo and DeAngelo found some

---

[2]For example, on one day in mid-2001, 997,200 shares of the nonvoting stock traded, but not a single share of the voting stock changed hands.

[3]B. Amoako-Adu and B. Smith, "Dual Class Firms: Capitalization, Ownership Structure and Recapitalization Back Into Single Class," *Journal of Banking and Finance* 25 (June 2001), pp. 1083–1111.

[4]R. C. Lease, J. J. McConnell, and W. H. Mikkelson, "The Market Value of Control in Publicly Traded Corporations," *Journal of Financial Economics* (April 1983).

Bombardier Didn't Heed Teachers on Share Structure

As one of Canada's first families of business now knows, the country's biggest money managers are starting to play hardball on corporate governance.

Bombardier Inc. executives made the rounds at the big pension funds this winter, as newly named CEO Paul Tellier explored the idea of selling stock to rebuild a debt-heavy balance sheet. The **Ontario Teachers Pension Plan Board** was among the first stops.

Brian Gibson, senior vice-president of the $68-billion fund, revealed this week at the Association of Investment Management and Research annual conference in Arizona that Teachers made Bombardier a simple offer.

Teachers was willing to invest more than $1-billion in Bombardier, long-term backing that would solve the transportation conglomerate's financial woes. However, the money was conditional on the Bombardier clan, led by company chairman Laurent Beaudoin, bidding adieu to a dual share structure.

To win Teachers' support, Mr. Beaudoin would have to set aside a corporate hierarchy that gives the founder's heirs almost two-thirds of the votes, when they hold just 22 per cent of Bombardier's equity.

"When multiple-voting-share companies get into trouble, investors have an opportunity to offer up a financial lifeline, but in return, demand that governance change for the better," Mr. Gibson explained. "Unfortunately, the Canadian experience has been that these companies can come to market and manage to raise money with no strings attached."

That's exactly what played out at Bombardier. Its executives found several pension funds willing to buy stock on terms more generous than what was available in the public market. But all the money managers wanted to see the dual share structure eliminated. The founding family refused to give up what it regards as a birthright, but most investors regard as an affront to the basic tenet of one share, one vote.

Bombardier eventually sold $1.2-billion worth of subordinate voting shares to the public, at $3.25 a share, just above the 52-week low. In a capital-intensive industry, where your cost of funding is a key criterion for success, Bombardier opted for family interests over the best equity deal.

As a result of the stock sale, existing shareholders suffered massive dilution. But with the dual share structure, members of a Bombardier clan who were at the controls when the company went off the rails were able to maintain the status quo on ownership.

While he's a bit frustrated with shortsighted shareholders who don't make full use of their clout, content instead to remain second-class owners, Mr. Gibson is philosophical about the setback at Bombardier.

"It will take time to change governance," he said. The Teachers fund manager also observed that "multiple share structures and good governance aren't mutually exclusive. We're seeing many of these companies take steps to increase the independence of directors and put higher standards in place in the boardroom."

There have even been a few wins on dual share structures, which are found at many Canadian family-owned companies, including index heavyweights, such as Magna International Inc. and the cable plays. Sceptre Investments said last week it would move to a single class of shares as its founders retired.

Funds such as Teachers aren't taking this activist stance on simple principle. Mr. Gibson said: "We're taking these steps because where we've been active on governance, we've made a lot of money."

Teachers has $3-billion tied up in a stock portfolio that sees the fund take a hands-on role in the boardroom. Holdings include Nexen Inc., where the fund helped unravel the oil company's knotted ownership, mining play Inmet Mining Corp. and tech company Macdonald Dettwiler & Associates Ltd. Over 12 years, this portfolio has put up stellar results, better than any other unit of the fund.

The concept of good governance translating into good money may be enough to bring Canada's business families onside the next time multiple voting shares are up for debate.

awillis@globeandmail.ca.

Andrew Willis writes for *The Globe and Mail*. His comments are reproduced with permission from the May 15, 2003, edition.

evidence that the market value of differences in voting rights may be much higher when control of the firm is involved.[5] Smith and Amoako-Adu found similar results for TSX

---

[5]H. DeAngelo and L. DeAngelo, "Managerial Ownership of Voting Rights: A Study of Public Corporations with Dual Classes of Common Stock," *Journal of Financial Economics* 14 (1985).

stocks.[6] Maynes, Robinson, and White conducted a study of voting rights in Canada that reinforced the importance of control.[7]

Since it is only necessary to own 51 percent of the voting stock to control a company, nonvoting shareholders could be left out in the cold in the event of a takeover bid for the company. To protect the nonvoting shareholders, most companies have a **coattail** provision giving nonvoting shareholders the right either to vote or to convert their shares into voting shares that can be tendered to the takeover bid. In the Canadian Tire case, all Class A shareholders become entitled to vote and the coattail provision is triggered if a bid is made for "all or substantially all" of the voting shares.

The effectiveness of coattails was tested in 1986 when the Canadian Tire Dealers Association offered to buy 49 percent of the voting shares from the founding Billes family. In the absence of protection, the nonvoting shareholders stood to lose substantially. The dealers bid at a large premium for the voting shares, which were trading at $40 before the bid. Nonvoting shares were priced at $14. Further, since the dealers were the principal buyers of Canadian Tire products, control of the company would have allowed them to adjust prices to benefit themselves over the nonvoting shareholders.

The key question was whether the bid triggered the coattail. The dealers and the Billes family argued that the offer was for 49 percent of the stock, not for "all or substantially all" of the voting shares. In the end the Ontario Securities Commission ruled that the offer was unfair to holders of the A shares (a view upheld in two court appeals). As a result, investors believe that coattails have protective value but remain skeptical that they afford complete protection.[8]

Canadian Tire is not an isolated example. Amoako-Adu and Smith document other cases of shareholder disputes involving dual classes of shares and identify a trend of dual-class firms reclassifying their shares into a single class. Their study suggests that reclassifying the shares makes them more attractive to potential investors.

? **Concept**
    Questions

- **What is a company's book value?**
- **What rights do shareholders have?**
- **What is a proxy?**
- **Why do firms issue nonvoting shares? How are they valued?**

15.2 Corporate Long-Term Debt: The Basics

Securities issued by corporations may be classified roughly as *equity* or *debt*. This distinction is basic to much of the modern theory and practice of corporate finance.

At its crudest level, debt represents something that must be repaid; it is the result of borrowing money. When corporations borrow, they contract to make regularly scheduled interest payments and to repay the original amount borrowed (that is, the *principal*). The person or firm making the loan is called a *creditor* or *lender*.

---

[6]Brian F. Smith and Ben Amoako-Adu, "Relative Prices of Dual Class Shares," *Journal of Financial and Quantitative Analysis* 30 (June 1995), pp. 223–239.

[7]Elizabeth Maynes, Chris Robinson, and Alan White, "How Much Is a Share Vote Worth?" *Canadian Investment Review* (Spring 1990), pp. 49–56.

[8]A Canadian study consistent with this conclusion is: Chris Robinson, John Rumsey, and Alan White, "Market Efficiency in the Valuation of Corporate Control: Evidence from Dual Class Equity," *Canadian Journal of Administrative Sciences* 13, pp. 251–263.

Interest Versus Dividends

The corporation borrowing the money is called a *debtor* or *borrower.* The amount owed the creditor is a liability of the corporation; however, it is a liability of limited value. The corporation can legally default at any time on its liability (for example, by not paying interest) and hand over the assets to the creditors.[9] This can be a valuable option. The creditors benefit if the assets have a value greater than the value of the liability, but only foolish management would default in this circumstance. On the other hand, the corporation and the equity investors benefit if the value of the assets is less than the value of the liabilities, because equity investors are able to walk away from the liabilities and default on their payment.

From a financial point of view, the main differences between debt and equity are the following:

1. Debt is not an ownership interest in the firm. Creditors do not usually have voting power. The device used by creditors to protect themselves is the loan contract (the *indenture*).

2. The corporation's payment of interest on debt is considered a cost of doing business and is fully tax deductible. Thus, interest expense is paid out to creditors before the corporate tax liability is computed. Dividends on common and preferred stock are paid to shareholders after the tax liability has been determined. Dividends are considered a return to shareholders on their contributed capital. Because interest expense can be used to reduce taxes, the government (that is, the Canada Revenue Agency) is providing a direct tax subsidy on the use of debt when compared to equity. This point is discussed in detail in the next two chapters.

3. Unpaid debt is a liability of the firm. If it is not paid, the creditors can legally claim the assets of the firm. This action may result in *liquidation* and *bankruptcy.* Thus, one of the costs of issuing debt is the possibility of *financial failure,* which does not arise when equity is issued.

Is It Debt or Equity?

Sometimes it is not clear whether a particular security is debt or equity. For example, suppose a 50-year bond is issued with interest payable solely from corporate income if and only if earned, and repayment is subordinate to all other debts of the business. Corporations are very adept at creating hybrid securities that look like equity but are called *debt.* Obviously, the distinction between debt and equity is important for tax purposes. When corporations try to create a debt security that is really equity, they are trying to obtain the tax benefits of debt while eliminating its bankruptcy costs.

Basic Features of Long-Term Debt

Long-term corporate debt usually is denominated in $1,000-units called the *principal* or *face value.* Long-term debt is a promise by the borrowing firm to repay the principal amount by a certain date, called the *maturity date.* Long-term debt almost always has a par value equal to the face value, and debt price is often expressed as a percentage of the par value. For example, it might be said that Telus debt is selling at 106.75, which means that a bond with a par value of $1,000 can be purchased for $1,067.50. In this case, the debt is

---

[9]In practice, creditors can make a claim against the assets of the firm and a court will administer the legal remedy.

Equity Versus Debt

Feature	Equity	Debt
Income	Dividends	Interest
Tax status	Dividends are taxed as personal income. Dividends are not a business expense.	Interest is taxed as personal income. Interest is a business expense, and corporations can deduct interest when computing corporate tax liability.
Control	Common stock and preferred stock usually have voting rights.	Control is exercised with loan agreement.
Default	Firms cannot be forced into bankruptcy for nonpayment of dividends.	Unpaid debt is a liability of the firm. Nonpayment may result in creditors forcing the firm into bankruptcy.
Bottom line:	Tax status favours debt, but default favours equity. Control features of debt and equity are different, but one is not better than the other.	

selling at a premium because market price is greater than the par value. Debt can also sell at a discount with respect to par value.

The borrower using long-term debt generally pays interest at a rate expressed as a fraction of par value. Thus, at $1,000 par value, Telus' 7.5 percent debt means that $75 of interest is paid to holders of debt, usually in semiannual installments (for example, $37.50 on June 30 and December 31). The payment schedules are in the form of coupons that are detached from the debt certificates and sent to the company for payment.[10]

Different Types of Debt

Typical debt securities are called *notes, debentures,* or *bonds.* In legal language, a debenture is an unsecured corporate debt, whereas a bond is secured by a mortgage on the corporate property. However, in common usage, the word *bond* is used indiscriminately and often refers to both secured and unsecured debt. A note usually refers to a short-term obligation, perhaps under seven years.

Debentures and bonds are long-term debt. *Long-term debt* is any obligation that is payable more than one year from the date it was originally issued and is sometimes called *funded debt.* Debt that is due in less than one year is unfunded and is accounted for as a current liability. Some debt is perpetual and has no specific maturity. This type of debt is referred to as a *consol.*

Repayment

Bonds can be repaid at maturity or earlier through the use of a sinking fund. A *sinking fund* is an account managed on behalf of the issuer by a bond trustee (generally a trust company) for the purpose of retiring all or part of the bonds prior to their stated maturity. The trustee retires the debt either by buying bonds in the market or by calling some of the

---

[10]Chapter 6 presents valuation formulas for debt.

debt. From an investor's viewpoint, a sinking fund reduces the risk that the company will be unable to repay the principal at maturity. Since it involves regular purchases, a sinking fund also improves the marketability of the bonds.

Debt may be extinguished before maturity through a *call provision* giving the firm the right to pay a specific amount (the *call price*) to *retire* (*extinguish*) the debt before the stated maturity date. The call price is generally higher than the par value of the debt. Debt that is callable at 105 is debt that the firm can buy back from the holder at a price of $1,050 per debenture or bond, regardless of what the market value of the debt might be. Call prices are always specified when the debt is originally issued. However, lenders are given a five-year to ten-year call protection period during which the debt cannot be called away.

Many long-term corporate bonds outstanding in Canada have call provisions as we just described. New corporate debt features a different call provision referred to as a **Canada plus call.** This new approach is designed to replace the traditional call feature by making it unattractive for the issuer ever to call the bonds. Unlike the standard call, with the Canada call the exact amount of the call premium is not set at the time of issuance. Instead, the Canada plus call stipulates that, in the event of a call, the issuer must provide a call premium that will compensate investors for the difference in interest between the original bond and new debt issued to replace it. This compensation cancels the borrower's benefit from calling the debt and the result is that call will not occur.

Seniority

In general terms, **seniority** indicates preference in position over other lenders. Some debt is **subordinated.** In the event of default, holders of subordinated debt must give preference to other specified creditors. Usually, this means that the subordinated lenders will be paid off only after the specified creditors have been compensated. However, debt cannot be subordinated to equity.

Security

Security is a form of attachment to property; it provides that the property can be sold in the event of default to satisfy the debt for which security is given. A mortgage is used for security in tangible property; for example, debt can be secured by mortgages on plant and equipment. Holders of such debt have prior claim on the mortgaged assets in case of default. Debentures are not secured by a mortgage. Thus, if mortgaged property is sold in the event of default, debenture holders will obtain something only if the mortgage bondholders have been fully satisfied.

Indenture

The written agreement between the corporate debt issuer and the lender, setting forth maturity date, interest rate, and all other terms, is called an *indenture.* We treat this in detail in later chapters. For now, we note that

1. The indenture completely describes the nature of the indebtedness.

2. It lists all restrictions placed on the firm by the lenders. These restrictions are placed in *restrictive covenants.* Examples are

    a.   Restrictions on further indebtedness.

    b.   A maximum on the amount of dividends that can be paid.

    c.   A minimum level of working capital.

EXAMPLE 15.2

The following table shows some of the many long-term debt securities of Rogers Communications Inc., a Canadian leader in wireless communications and broadband services, in February 2007 (in millions).

9.625% secured senior note due 2011	$496
7.875% secured senior note due 2012	350
7.25% secured senior note due 2012	470
6.75% secured senior debt due 2015	280
8.75% secured senior debentures due 2032	200

As can be seen, Rogers has a number of different notes and debentures which vary in time to maturity, amount, and coupon rate.

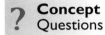

Concept Questions

- **What is corporate debt? Describe its general features.**
- **Why is it sometimes difficult to tell whether a particular security is debt or equity?**

15.3 Preferred Shares

Preferred shares have preference over common shares in the payment of dividends and in the distribution of corporate assets in the event of liquidation. *Preference* means that holders of the preferred shares must receive a dividend (in the case of an ongoing firm) before holders of common shares are entitled to anything. If the firm is liquidated, preferred shareholders rank behind all creditors but ahead of common shareholders.

Preferred shares are a form of equity from legal, tax, and regulatory standpoints. However, holders of preferred shares often have no voting privileges.

Stated Value

Preferred shares have a stated liquidating value, for example, $25 per share. The cash dividend is described in terms of dollars per share. For example, CIBC "$2.25 preferred" translates easily into a dividend yield of 9 percent of the stated $25 value.

Cumulative and Noncumulative Dividends

A preferred dividend is not like interest on a bond. The board of directors may decide not to pay the dividends on preferred shares, and the decision may have nothing to do with the current net income of the corporation.

Dividends payable on preferred shares are either *cumulative* or *noncumulative;* most are cumulative. If preferred dividends are cumulative and are not paid in a particular year, they will be carried forward as an arrearage. Usually both the cumulated (past) preferred dividends plus the current preferred dividends must be paid before the common shareholders can receive anything.

Unpaid preferred dividends are not debts of the firm. Directors elected by the common shareholders can defer preferred dividends indefinitely. However, in such cases

1. Common shareholders must also forgo dividends.
2. Holders of preferred shares are often granted voting and other rights if preferred dividends have not been paid for some time.

Because preferred shareholders receive no interest on the cumulated dividends, some have argued that firms have an incentive to delay paying preferred dividends.

Are Preferred Shares Really Debt?

A good case can be made that preferred shares are really debt in disguise, a kind of equity bond. Preferred shareholders receive a stated dividend only; and, if the corporation is liquidated, they get a stated value. Often, preferreds carry credit ratings much like bonds. Furthermore, preferred shares are sometimes convertible into common shares. Preferreds are often callable by the issuer, and the holder often has the right to sell the preferred shares back to the issuer at a set price.

In addition, in recent years, many new issues of preferred shares have had obligatory sinking funds. Such a sinking fund effectively creates a final maturity since the entire issue will ultimately be retired.

On top of all of this, preferred shares with adjustable dividends have been offered in recent years. One example is the *CARP* (*c*umulative, *a*djustable *r*ate, *p*referred). There are various types of floating rate preferred, some of which are quite innovative in the way that the dividend is determined. For example, dividends on Royal Bank of Canada First Preferred Shares Series C (old) were set at two-thirds of the bank's average Canadian prime rate with a floor dividend of 6.67 percent per year.

For all these reasons, preferred shares seem to be a lot like debt. In comparison to debt, the yields on preferred shares are generally lower. For example, the Royal Bank has another series of preferred shares with a $1.52 stated dividend. In February 2007, the market price of the $1.175 Royal Bank preferred was about $25.58. This gave a yield of about 4.6 percent, considerably below the yield on Royal Bank long-term debt (about 5.3 percent at that time).

Despite the apparently low yields, corporate investors have an incentive to hold preferred shares issued by other corporations as opposed to holding their debt since 100 percent of the dividends they receive are exempt from income taxes.[11] Because individual investors do not receive this tax break, most preferred shares in Canada are purchased by corporate investors.[12] Corporate investors pay a premium for preferred shares because of the tax exclusion on dividends; as a consequence, yields are low.

Preferred Shares and Taxes

Turning to the issuer's point of view, a tax loophole encourages corporations that are lightly taxed or not taxable due to losses or tax shelters to issue preferred shares. Such low-tax companies can make little use of the tax deduction on interest. However, they can issue preferred shares and enjoy lower financing costs since preferred dividends are significantly lower than interest payments.

In 1987 the federal government attempted to close the tax loophole by introducing a tax of 40 percent of the preferred dividends to be paid by the issuer of preferred stock. The tax is refunded (through a deduction) to taxable issuers only. The effect of this and associated tax changes was to narrow but not close the loophole.

Table 15.1 shows how Zero Tax Ltd., a corporation not paying any income taxes, can issue preferred shares attractive to Full Tax Ltd., a second corporation taxable at a combined federal and provincial rate of 45 percent. The example assumes that Zero Tax is seeking

---

[11]In the United States, the corporate dividend exclusion is only for 80 percent. I. Fooladi and G. Roberts, "On Preferred Stock," *Journal of Financial Research* 9 (Winter 1986), pp. 319–24, argue that this difference in tax law explains why Canadian firms finance much more heavily with preferred shares.

[12]Preferred dividends paid to individual investors qualify for the dividend tax credit.

TABLE 15.1
Tax Loophole on
Preferred Stock

	Preferred	Debt
Issuer: Zero Tax Ltd.		
Preferred dividend/interest paid	$ 67.00	$ 100.00
Dividend tax at 40%	26.80	0.00
Tax deduction on interest	0.00	0.00
Total financing cost	$ 93.80	$ 100.00
After-tax cost	9.38%	10.00%
Purchaser: Full Tax Ltd.		
Before-tax income	$ 67.00	$ 100.00
Tax	0.00	45.00
After-tax income	$ 67.00	$ 55.00
After-tax yield	6.70%	5.50%

$1,000 in financing through either debt or preferred stock and that Zero Tax can issue either debt with a 10 percent coupon or preferred stock with a 6.7 percent dividend.[13]

Table 15.1 shows that with preferred shares financing, Zero Tax pays out 6.7% × $1,000 = $67.00 in dividends and 40% × $67.00 = $26.80 in tax on the dividends for a total after-tax outlay of $93.80. This represents an after-tax cost of $93.80/$1,000 = 9.38%. Debt financing is more expensive with an outlay of $100 and an after-tax yield of 10 percent. So Zero Tax is better off issuing preferred stock.

From the point of view of the purchaser, Full Tax Ltd., the preferred dividend is received tax-free for an after-tax yield of 6.7 percent. If it bought debt issued by Zero Tax instead, Full Tax would pay income tax of $45 for a net after-tax receipt of $55 or 5.5 percent. So again, preferred shares are better than debt.

Of course, if we change the example to make the issuer fully taxable, the after-tax cost of debt will drop to 5.5 percent, making debt financing more attractive. This reinforces our point that the tax motivation for issuing preferred shares is limited to lightly taxed companies.

Beyond Taxes

For fully taxed firms, the fact that dividends are not an allowable deduction from taxable corporate income is the most serious obstacle to issuing preferred shares, but there are several reasons beyond taxes why preferreds are issued.

We can start by discussing some supply factors. First, regulated public utilities can pass the tax disadvantage of issuing preferred shares on to their customers because of the way pricing formulas are set up in regulatory environments. Consequently, a substantial amount of straight preferred shares are issued by utilities, particularly in the United States.

Second, firms issuing preferred shares can avoid the threat of bankruptcy that might otherwise exist if debt were relied on. Unpaid preferred dividends are not debts of a corporation, and preferred shareholders cannot force a corporation into bankruptcy because of unpaid dividends.

---

[13]We set the preferred dividend at around two-thirds of the debt yield to reflect market prices as exemplified by the Royal Bank issue discussed earlier. Further discussion of preferred shares and taxes in Canada appears in I. Fooladi, P. A. McGraw, and G. S. Roberts, "Preferred Share Rules Freeze Out the Individual Investor," *CA Magazine* (April 11, 1988), pp. 38–41.

A third reason for issuing preferred shares concerns control of the firm. Since preferred shareholders often cannot vote, preferreds may be a means of raising equity without surrendering control.

On the demand side, for tax reasons discussed earlier, most preferred shares are owned by corporations. Some of the new types of adjustable-rate preferreds are ideally suited for corporations needing short-term investments for temporarily idle cash.

? Concept Questions

- **What are preferred shares?**
- **Why are preferred shares arguably more like debt than equity?**
- **Why is it attractive for firms that are not paying taxes to issue preferred shares?**
- **What are three reasons unrelated to taxes why preferred shares are issued?**

15.4 Income Trusts

Starting in 2001, the income trust, a non-corporate form of business organization, has been growing in importance in Canada. At the end of 2004, there were over 200 income trusts listed on the Toronto Stock Exchange, with a sector market capitalization of $118 billion.[14] Within this sector, the fastest growing component is business income trusts that took this form of business organization, traditionally popular in real estate and oil and gas, and applied it to businesses like telephone listing, container ports, restaurant chains, and other businesses usually organized as corporations. In response to the growing importance of this sector, recent provincial legislation extended limited liability protection, previously limited to corporate shareholders, to trust unitholders. Along the same lines, at the end of 2005, the TSX began to include income trusts in its benchmark S&P / TSX composite index.

Income Trust Income and Taxation

Business income trusts are structured so that income is taxed only once in the hands of unitholders. To achieve this, the operating entity (taxed as a corporation) pays the income trust interest, royalties, or lease payments, which are usually tax deductible. Since the operating entity usually pays the income trust enough to reduce operating income to zero, the operating company pays virtually no tax. The interest, royalties, or lease payments received by the trust are not taxable because it is not a corporation but a partnership. Rather, this cash flow is passed through to the unitholders, resulting in the desired level of taxation.

Table 15.2 compares income trust taxation against the tax treatment of dividends to show how the net amount received by investors is the same under current tax rates. However, at the end of October 2006, the federal government announced plans to tax income trusts as corporations. Applicable in 2011 to trusts in existence in October 2006 and immediately to new trusts, these plans are expected (at the time of writing) either to put an end to new trust conversions, or reduce the number of corporations converting to income trusts.[15] As a result, companies such as BCE that were in the process of converting to

---

[14]For more on income trusts see J. Fenwick and B. Kalymon, "A Note on Income Trusts," Ivey Publishing, 2004; and Department of Finance, "Tax and Other Issues Related to Publicly Listed Flow-Through Entities (Income Trusts and Limited Partnerships)," September 8, 2005.

[15]ScotiaMcLeod, "Federal Government to Implement New Tax Fairness Plan," November 1, 2006.

TABLE 15.2
Taxation of Income Trust Distributions vs. Dividends

	Dividends paid by large corporations	Interest and taxable distribution of income trusts
A. Income	$100	$100
B. Corporate income tax[1]	32	0
C. Amount distributed to investor	68	100
D. Amount included in income	99	100
E. Personal income tax (46%[2] of D)	46	46
F. Dividend tax credit	(32)[3]	0
G. Net personal income tax	14	46
H. Total tax paid (B + G)	46	46
I. Investor's net receipt	54	54

[1]The combined average federal–provincial corporate income tax rate in 2010.
[2]The average top federal–provincial personal income tax rate.
[3]Assumes that the provinces and territories increase their dividend tax credits for eligible dividends to equal their general corporate income tax rates.

Source: http://www.fin.gc.ca/budget06/bp/bpc3be.htm#dividends.

income trusts reversed their decisions. For Telus Corp., the plan to convert to an income trust was already reflected in the stock price. When the federal announcement was made, the stock price dropped from $64.93 to $56.15 on November 1, 2006. This shows that before the tax changes, investors were willing to pay an additional $8.78 for the tax advantage offered by an income trust. It also demonstrates the effect that the government can have on dividend policy and capital structure decisions.

Income trust structure has worked well for trusts in stable businesses with stock cash flow generating abilities; examples are Yellow Pages Income Fund or Boston Pizza Royalty Fund. As cash flows fluctuate in riskier industries, trusts have had to reduce or suspend distributions. When this happened to Halterm—a trust based on the container port business in Halifax—in 2003, the unit price dropped by 59 percent.[16]

15.5 Patterns of Long-Term Financing

Firms use cash flow for capital spending and net working capital. According to Zyblock's study of financing patterns in the U.S. and Canada,[17] Canadian firms spent $102.7 billion on capital and working capital in a recent year. Of this amount, around two-thirds or $70.1 billion came from **internal financing** (or cash flow), defined as net income plus depreciation minus dividends. Because total spending exceeded internal financing, there was a financial gap. In the year studied, the financial gap was $32.6 billion (i.e., $102.7 billion – $70.1 billion). To fill the financial gap, firms borrowed $12.1 billion in short- and long-term debt and issued new equity (net of share buybacks) of $20.5 billion.

---

[16]R. Carrick, "Halterm Income Fund provides a cautionary tale for investors," *The Globe and Mail,* Report on Business, March 27, 2003.

[17]M. Zyblock, "Corporate Financial Leverage: A Canada–U.S. Comparison, 1961–1996," Statistics Canada, Analytical Studies Branch, Research Paper Series (December 1997).

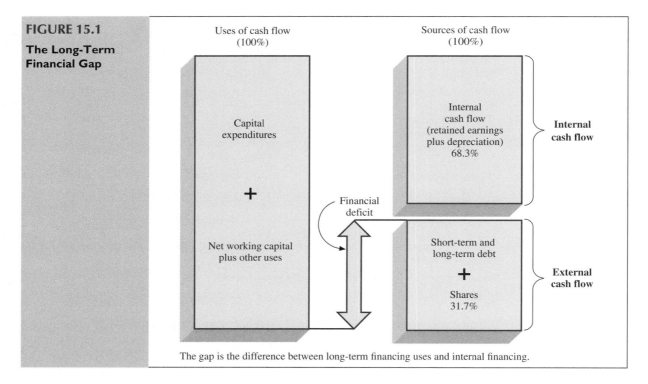

FIGURE 15.1

The Long-Term Financial Gap

The gap is the difference between long-term financing uses and internal financing.

Figure 15.1 depicts the financial gap. It shows that Canadian firms generate the majority of their funds internally.

These data are consistent with the results of a survey by Gordon Donaldson on how firms establish long-term financing strategies.[18] He found that:

1. The first form of financing used by firms for positive-NPV projects is internally generated cash flow (net income plus depreciation minus dividends).

2. When a firm has insufficient cash flow from internal sources, it sells off part of its investment in marketable securities.

3. As a last resort, a firm will use externally generated cash flow. First, debt is used. Common stock is used last.

These observations, when taken together, suggest a pecking order to long-term financing strategy. At the top of the **pecking order** is using internally generated cash flow; at the bottom is issuing new equity.

? Concept Questions

- **What is the financial gap?**
- **What are the major sources of corporate financing? What trends have emerged in recent years?**

---

[18]G. G. Donaldson, *Corporate Debt Capacity: A Study of Corporate Debt Policy and Determination of Corporate Debt Capacity* (Boston: Harvard Graduate School of Business Administration, 1961). See also S. C. Myers, "The Capital Structure Puzzle," *Journal of Finance* (July 1984).

15.6 SUMMARY AND CONCLUSIONS

The basic sources of long-term financing are long-term debt, preferred stock, and common stock. This chapter describes the essential features of each.

1. We emphasize that common shareholders have:
   - Residual risk and return in a corporation
   - Voting rights
   - Limited liability if the corporation elects to default on its debt and must transfer some or all of the assets to the creditors

2. Long-term debt involves contractual obligations set out in indentures. There are many kinds of debt, but the essential feature is that debt involves a stated amount that must be repaid. Interest payments on debt are considered a business expense and are tax deductible.

3. Preferred stock has some of the features of debt and some of the features of common equity. Holders of preferred stock have preference in liquidation and in dividend payments compared to holders of common equity.

4. Firms need financing for fixed assets, current assets, and investment in affiliates along with other uses. Most of the financing is provided from internally generated cash flow. The percentage mix of financing has remained relatively stable in Canada.

KEY TERMS

Book value of equity 422	Cumulative voting 424	Proxy 424
Canada plus call 430	Dividends 425	Retained earnings 422
Coattail 427	Internal financing 435	Seniority 430
Common stock (common shares) 421	Pecking order 436	Straight voting 424
	Preferred shares 431	Subordinated (debt) 430

SUGGESTED READING

Evidence on the financial structure of industrial corporations is found in:
M. Zyblock. "Corporate Financial Leverage: A Canada–U.S. Comparison, 1961–1996." Statistics Canada, Analytical Studies Branch, Research Paper Series (December 1997).

For a highly readable discussion of voting and nonvoting shares in Canada, see:
Elizabeth Maynes, Chris Robinson, and Alan White. "How Much Is a Share Vote Worth?" *Canadian Investment Review* (Spring 1990).

QUESTIONS & PROBLEMS

15.1   The Brice Co. equity accounts in 2007 are:

Common shares (2,500,000 shares outstanding)	$ 4,000,000
Retained earnings	195,000,000
Total	$199,000,000

Suppose the company decides to issue 3000 new common shares. The current price is $46 per share. Show the effect on the different accounts. What is the market-to-book ratio after the share issue?

15.2   In the previous question, suppose the company buys 100 of its own shares. What would happen to the accounts shown?

15.3   Which usually has a higher yield: preferred stock or corporate bonds? Why is there a difference? Who are the main investors in preferred stock? Why?

15.4   What are the main differences between corporate debt and equity? Why do some clever firms try to issue equity in the guise of debt? Why might preferred stock be called an equity bond?

15.5   The Babel Tower Company has $14 million of positive-NPV projects. Based on the historical pattern of long-term financing for Canadian industrial firms, what financing strategy will Babel probably use?

EXCEL

15.6   Ulrich Ltd.'s articles of incorporation authorize the firm to issue 750,000 shares of common stock, of which 325,000 shares have been issued at $5.90. In the quarter that ended last week, Ulrich earned net income of $360,000; 21 percent of that income was paid as a dividend. Prior to the close of the books, Ulrich had $3,545,000 in retained earnings.
   a. Create the equity statement for Ulrich.
   b. Create a new equity statement that reflects the sale of 35,000 authorized but unissued shares at the price of $4 per share.

15.7   The shareholders of the Unicorn Company need to elect nine new directors. There are 2.5 million shares outstanding. How many shares do you need to be certain that you can elect at least one director if:
   a. Unicorn has straight voting?
   b. Unicorn has cumulative voting?

15.8   Power Inc. is going to elect six board members next month. Betty Brown owns 32 percent of the total shares outstanding. How confident can she be that one of her candidate friends will be elected under the cumulative voting rule? And will her friend be elected for certain if the voting procedure is changed to the staggering rule, under which shareholders vote on three board members at a time?

15.9   As an apprentice financial engineer, what new types of securities do you think might appeal to investors? What problems would have to be overcome to issue such securities?

15.10   Manhattan Pizza Pies Income Trust generated $34,456,750 in net income before last year. If corporate tax is 36 percent, personal dividend tax is 23 percent, and taxes on personal income and interest are 44 percent, what would be the amount distributed to income trust unitholders? What amount would investors received after taxes have been paid? What would be the total tax paid to the government if Manhattan was not an income trust but a corporation?

15.11   The Distribution Company is currently structured as a corporation. It is considering restructuring the company to become an income trust, but is unsure if this would benefit shareholders. Company executives have hired Johnny Mack as a consultant. They tell him that the corporate tax rate is currently 35 percent, last year's net income before tax is $576,879 and there are 7000 outstanding shares. If the company decides to restructure into an income trust, one share will become one income trust unit. Dividends are taxed at 22 percent and income and interest income is taxed at 41 percent.
   a. Is it worth it for the Distribution Company to restructure into an income trust?
   b. If the answer to (a) is yes, how much more would an investor gain if that investor owned 1000 units?
   c. At what corporate tax rate would the company be indifferent to restructuring into an income trust?

15.12   An investor pays tax at a marginal combined federal–provincial rate of 41 percent. Long-term corporate bonds currently yield 6.6 percent. Because preferred shares issued by the same corporations are riskier, the investor seeks an increase in after-tax yield (for preferreds over bonds) of 1.5 percent. If a preferred share issue is as attractive as a bond issued by the same company, what dividend yield (before tax) must the preferred shares have? (Refer to Appendix 1A for relevant tax rates.)

15.13   Refer to Enbridge Inc.'s (ENB) statement of shareholders' equity in Section 15.1.
   a. Suppose that the company issues 8 million new common shares at today's market price. Prepare a new version of the table to reflect this financing. (Obtain the current price from a financial newspaper or from S&P.)
   b. Now suppose that instead Enbridge Inc. buys 2.6 million shares. These shares are cancelled. Revise the table to reflect this change.

Chapter 16

Capital Structure: Basic Concepts

EXECUTIVE SUMMARY

Previous chapters of this book examined the capital budgeting decision. We pointed out that this decision concerns the left-hand side of the balance sheet. The previous two chapters began our discussion of the capital structure decision,[1] which deals with the right-hand side of the balance sheet.

In general, a firm can choose among many alternative capital structures. It can issue a large amount of debt or it can issue very little debt. It can issue floating-rate preferred stock, warrants, convertible bonds, caps, and collars. It can arrange lease financing, bond swaps, and forward contracts. Because the number of instruments is so large, the variations in capital structures are endless. We simplify the analysis by considering only common stock and straight debt in this chapter. The "bells and whistles," as they are called on Bay Street, must await later chapters of the text. The capital structure decision we consider is the decision to rely on debt. We examine the factors that are important in the choice of a firm's debt-to-equity ratio.

Our results in this chapter are basic. First, we discuss the capital structure decision in a world with neither taxes nor other capital market imperfections. Surprisingly, we find that the capital structure decision is a matter of *indifference* in this world. We next argue that there is a feature in Canadian tax law that subsidizes debt financing. Finally, we show that an increase in the firm's value from debt financing leads to an increase in the value of the equity.

16.1 The Capital Structure Question and the Pie Theory

How should a firm choose its debt–equity ratio? More generally, what is the best capital structure for the firm? We call our approach to the capital structure question the **pie model.** If you are wondering why we chose this name, just take a look at Figure 16.1. The pie in question is the sum of the financial claims of the firm (debt and equity in this case). We define the value of the firm to be this sum. Hence, the value of the firm, *V,* is

$$V = B + S \qquad (16.1)$$

where B is the market value of the debt and S is the market value of the equity. Figure 16.1 presents two possible ways of slicing this pie between stock and debt. If company management's goal is to make the firm as valuable as possible, then the firm should pick the debt–equity ratio that makes the pie—the total value, V—as big as possible.

---

[1] It is conventional to refer to choices regarding debt and equity as *capital structure decisions.* However, the term *financial structure decisions* would be more accurate, and we use the terms interchangeably.

FIGURE 16.1

Two Pie Models of Capital Structure

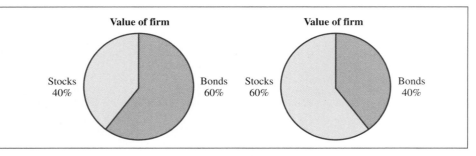

This discussion begs two important questions:

1. Why should the shareholders in the firm care about maximizing the value of the entire firm? After all, the value of the firm is, by definition, the sum of both the debt and the equity. Instead, why should the shareholders not prefer the strategy that maximizes their interests only?

2. What is the ratio of debt to equity that maximizes the shareholders' interests?

Let us examine each of the two questions in turn.

? Concept Question

• **What is the pie model of capital structure?**

16.2 Maximizing Firm Value Versus Maximizing Shareholder Interests

The following example illustrates that the capital structure that maximizes the value of the firm is the one that financial managers should choose for the shareholders.

EXAMPLE 16.1

Suppose the market value of the J.J. Sprint Company is $1,000. The company currently has no debt, and each of J. J. Sprint's 100 shares of stock sells for $10. A company such as J. J. Sprint with no debt is called an *unlevered* company. Further suppose that J. J. Sprint plans to borrow $500 and pay the $500 proceeds to shareholders as an extra cash dividend of $5 per share. After the issuance of debt, the firm becomes *levered*. The investments of the firm will not change as a result of this transaction. What will the value of the firm be after the proposed restructuring?

Management recognizes that, by definition, only one of three outcomes can occur from restructuring. Firm value after restructuring can be either (1) greater than the original firm value of $1,000, (2) equal to $1,000, or (3) less than $1,000. After consulting with investment bankers, management believes that restructuring will not change firm value more than $250 in either direction. Thus, it views firm values of $1,250, $1,000, and $750 as the relevant range. The original capital structure and these three possibilities under the new capital structure are presented below.

	No Debt (original capital structure)	Debt Plus Dividend (three possibilities after restructuring)		
		I	II	III
Debt	$ 0	$ 500	$ 500	$500
Equity	1,000	750	500	250
Firm value	$1,000	$1,250	$1,000	$750

Note that the value of equity is below $1,000 under any of the three possibilities. This can be explained in one of two ways. First, the chart shows the value of the equity *after* the extra cash dividend is paid. Since cash is paid out, a dividend represents a partial liquidation of the firm. Consequently, there is less value in the firm for the equityholders after the dividend payment. Second, in the event of a future liquidation, stockholders will be paid only after bondholders have been paid in full. Thus, the debt is an encumbrance of the firm, reducing the value of the equity.

Of course, management recognizes that there are infinite possible outcomes. These three are to be viewed as *representative* outcomes only. We can now determine the payoff to shareholders under the three possibilities:

	Payoff to Shareholders After Restructuring		
	I	II	III
Capital gains	−$250	−$500	−$750
Dividends	500	500	500
Net gain or loss to shareholders	$250	$ 0	−$250

No one can be sure ahead of time which of the three outcomes will occur. However, imagine that managers believe that outcome I is most likely. They should definitely restructure the firm because the shareholders gain $250. That is, although the value of the stock declines by $250 to $750, they receive $500 in dividends. Their net gain is $250 = −$250 + $500. Also, notice that the value of the firm rises by $250.

Alternatively, imagine that managers believe that outcome III is most likely. In this case they should not restructure the firm because the shareholders expect a $250 loss. That is, the stock falls by $750 to $250 and they receive $500 in dividends. Their net loss is −$250 = −$750 + $500. Also, notice that the value of the firm falls by $250.

Finally, imagine that the managers believe that outcome II is most likely. Restructuring would not affect the shareholders' interest because the net gain to shareholders in this case is zero. Also, notice that the value of the firm is unchanged if outcome II occurs.

This example explains why managers should attempt to maximize the value of the firm. In other words, it answers Question (1) in Section 16.1. In this example, changes in capital structure benefit the shareholders if and only if the value of the firm increases. Conversely, these changes hurt the shareholders if and only if the value of the firm decreases. This result holds generally for capital structure changes of many different types.[2] Thus, managers should choose the capital structure that they believe will have the highest firm value because this capital structure is most beneficial to the firm's shareholders.

Note however that the example does not tell us which of the three outcomes is likely to occur. Thus, it does not tell us whether debt should be added to J. J. Sprint's capital

---

[2]This result may not hold exactly in the more complex case where debt has a significant possibility of default, leading to possible agency conflicts between shareholders and bondholders. Issues of default are treated in the next chapter.

structure. In other words, it does not answer Question (2) in Section 16.1. This second question is treated in the next section.

? Concept Question

- **Why should financial managers choose the capital structure that maximizes the value of the firm?**

16.3 Financial Leverage and Firm Value: An Example

Leverage and Returns to Shareholders

The previous section shows that the capital structure producing the highest firm value is the one that maximizes shareholder wealth. In this section, we wish to determine that optimal capital structure. We begin by illustrating the effect of capital structure on returns to shareholders. We will use a detailed example, which we encourage students to study carefully. Once we have mastered this example, we will be ready to determine the optimal capital structure.

Trans Can Corporation currently has no debt in its capital structure. The firm is considering issuing debt to buy back some of its equity. Both its current and proposed capital structures are presented in Table 16.1. The firm's assets are $8,000. There are 400 shares of the all-equity firm, implying a market value per share of $20. The proposed debt issue is for $4,000, leaving $4,000 in equity. The interest rate is 10 percent.

The effect of economic conditions on earnings per share is shown in Table 16.2 for the current capital structure (all-equity). Consider first the middle column where earnings are *expected* to be $1,200. Since assets are $8,000, the return on assets (ROA) is 15 percent (= $1,200/$8,000). Because assets equal equity for this all-equity firm, return on equity (ROE) is also 15 percent. Earnings per share (EPS) are $3.00 (= $1,200/400). Similar calculations yield EPS of $1.00 and $5.00 in the cases of recession and expansion, respectively.

The case of leverage is presented in Table 16.3. ROA in the three economic states is identical in Tables 16.2 and 16.3, because this ratio is calculated before interest is considered. Since debt is $4,000 here, interest is $400 (= 0.10 × $4,000). Thus, earnings after interest are $800 (= $1,200 − $400) in the middle (expected) case. Since equity is $4,000, ROE is 20 percent ($800/$4,000). Earnings per share are $4.00 (= $800/200). Similar calculations yield earnings of $0 and $8.00 for recession and expansion, respectively.

Tables 16.2 and 16.3 show that the effect of financial leverage depends on the company's earnings before interest. If earnings before interest are equal to $1,200, the return on

TABLE 16.1
Financial Structure of Trans Can Corporation

	Current	Proposed
Assets	$8,000	$8,000
Debt	$ 0	$4,000
Equity (market and book)	$8,000	$4,000
Interest rate	10%	10%
Market value/share	$ 20	$ 20
Shares outstanding	400	200

The proposed capital structure has leverage, whereas the current structure is all equity.

TABLE 16.2
Trans Can's Current Capital Structure: No Debt

	Recession	Expected	Expansion
Return on assets (ROA)	5%	15%	25%
Earnings	$ 400	$1,200	$2,000
Return on equity (ROE) = Earnings/Equity	5%	15%	25%
Earnings per share (EPS)	$1.00	$ 3.00	$ 5.00
Point in Figure 16.2	A	B	C

equity (ROE) is higher under the proposed structure. If earnings before interest are equal to $400, the ROE is higher under the current structure.

This idea is represented in Figure 16.2. The solid line represents the case of no leverage. The line begins at the origin, indicating that earnings per share (EPS) would be zero if earnings before interest and taxes (EBIT) were zero. The EPS rises in tandem with a rise in EBIT. The no-debt line in Figure 16.2 plots points A, B, and C representing the three cases presented in Table 16.2.

The dotted line represents the case of $4,000 of debt. Here, EPS is negative if EBIT is zero. This follows because $400 of interest must be paid regardless of the firm's profits. The debt line in Figure 16.2 plots points D, E, and F representing the three cases presented in Table 16.3.

Now consider the slopes of the two lines. The slope of the dotted line (the line with debt) is higher than the slope of the solid line. This occurs because the levered firm has *fewer* shares of stock outstanding than does the unlevered firm. Therefore, any increase in EBIT leads to a greater rise in EPS for the levered firm because the earnings increase is distributed over fewer shares of stock.

Because the dotted line has a lower intercept but a higher slope, the two lines must intersect. The *break-even* point occurs at $800 of EBIT. Were earnings before interest to be $800, both firms would produce $2 of earnings per share (EPS). Because $800 is break-even, earnings above $800 lead to greater EPS for the levered firm. Earnings below $800 lead to greater EPS for the unlevered firm.

The Choice Between Debt and Equity

Tables 16.2 and 16.3 and Figure 16.2 are important because they show the effect of leverage on earnings per share. Students should study the tables and figure until they feel comfortable with the calculation of each number in them. However, we have not yet presented the punch line. That is, we have not yet stated which capital structure is better for Trans Can.

TABLE 16.3
Trans Can's Proposed Capital Structure: Debt = $4,000

	Recession	Expected	Expansion
Return on assets (ROA)	5%	15%	25%
Earnings before interest and taxes (EBIT)	$400	$1,200	$2,000
Interest	−400	−400	−400
Earnings after interest	$ 0	$ 800	$1,600
Return on equity (ROE)			
= Earnings after interest/Equity	0	20%	40%
Earnings per share (EPS)	0	$ 4.00	$ 8.00
Point in Figure 16.2	D	E	F

FIGURE 16.2

Financial Leverage: EPS and EBIT for the Trans Can Corporation

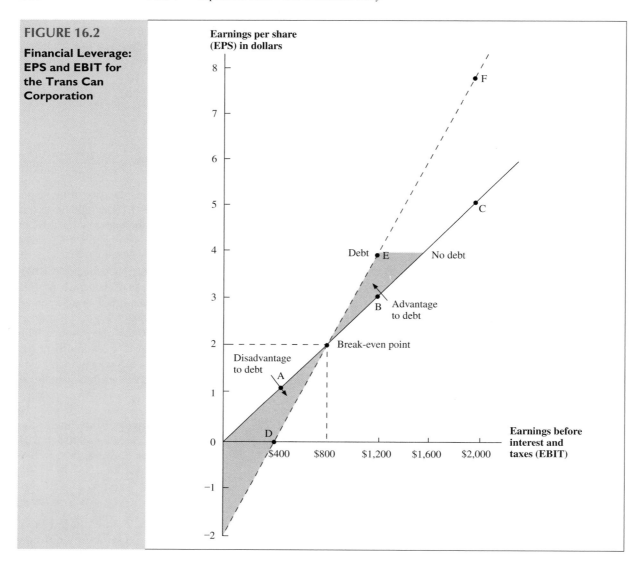

At this point, many students believe that leverage is beneficial, because EPS is expected to be $4.00 with leverage and only $3.00 without leverage. However, leverage also creates *risk.* Note that in a recession, EPS is higher ($1.00 versus 0) for the unlevered firm. Thus, a risk-averse investor might prefer the all-equity firm, while a risk-neutral (or less risk-averse) investor might prefer leverage. Given this ambiguity, which capital structure *is* better?

Modigliani and Miller (MM) have a convincing argument that a firm cannot change the total value of its outstanding securities by changing the proportions of its capital structure. In other words, the value of the firm is always the same under different capital structures. In *still* other words, no capital structure is any better or worse than any other capital structure for the firm's shareholders. This rather pessimistic result is the famous **MM Proposition I.**[3]

---

[3]The original paper is F. Modigliani and M. Miller, "The Cost of Capital, Corporation Finance and the Theory of Investment," *American Economic Review* (June 1958).

Their argument compares a simple strategy, which we call Strategy *A,* with a two-part strategy, which we call Strategy *B.* Both of these strategies for shareholders of Trans Can are illuminated in Table 16.4. Let us now examine the first strategy.

Strategy A—Buy 100 shares of the levered equity. This entitles the shareholder to the cash flows from Trans Can supposing that the company goes ahead with adding debt.

The first line in the top panel of Table 16.4 shows EPS for the proposed levered equity in the three economic states. The second line shows the earnings in the three states for an individual buying 100 shares. The next line shows that the cost of these 100 shares is $2,000.

Let us now consider the second strategy, which has two parts to it.

Strategy B—This strategy gives the investor shares in Trans Can assuming no debt is added to the corporate capital structure. The debt goes on the investor's personal balance sheet in proportions chosen to replicate the cash flows from Strategy *A.*

1. Borrow $2,000 from either a bank or, more likely, a brokerage house. (If the brokerage house is the lender, we say that this is *going on margin.*)

2. Use the borrowed proceeds plus your own investment of $2,000 (a total of $4,000) to buy 200 shares of the current unlevered equity at $20 per share.

The bottom panel of Table 16.4 shows payoffs under Strategy *B,* which we call the *homemade leverage* strategy. First, observe the middle column, which indicates that 200 shares of the unlevered equity are *expected* to generate $600 of earnings. Assuming that the $2,000 is borrowed at a 10 percent interest rate, the interest expense is $200 (= 0.10 × $2,000). Thus, the net earnings are expected to be $400. A similar calculation generates net earnings of either $0 or $800 in recession or expansion, respectively.

Now, let us compare these two strategies, both in terms of earnings per year and in terms of initial cost. The top panel of the table shows that Strategy *A* generates earnings of $0, $400, and $800 in the three states. The bottom panel of the table shows that Strategy *B* generates the *same* net earnings in the three states.

The top panel of the table shows that Strategy *A* involves an initial cost of $2,000. Similarly, the bottom panel shows an *identical* net cost of $2,000 for Strategy *B.*

TABLE 16.4   Payoff and Cost to Shareholders of Trans Can Corporation Under the Proposed Structure and Under the Current Structure with Homemade Leverage

Strategy A: Buy 100 Shares of Levered Equity	Recession	Expected	Expansion
EPS of *levered* equity (taken from last line of Table 16.3)	$0	$ 4	$ 8
Earnings per 100 shares	$0	$400	$800
Initial cost = 100 shares @ $20/share = $2,000			

Strategy B: Homemade Leverage	Recession	Expected	Expansion
Earnings per 200 shares in current *unlevered* Trans Can	$1 × 200 = $ 200	$3 × 200 = $ 600	$5 × 200 = $ 1,000
Interest at 10% on $2,000	−200	−200	−200
Net earnings	$ 0	$ 400	$ 800
Initial cost = 200 shares @ $20/share − $2,000 = $2,000			
Cost of stock Amount borrowed			

Investor receives the same payoff whether she (1) buys shares in a levered corporation or (2) buys shares in an unlevered firm and borrows on personal account. Her initial investment is the same in either case. Thus, the firm neither helps nor hurts her by adding debt to capital structure.

This shows a very important result. Both the cost and the payoff from the two strategies are the same. Thus, one must conclude that Trans Can is neither helping nor hurting its shareholders by restructuring. In other words, an investor is not receiving anything from corporate leverage that he or she could not receive on his or her own.

Note that, as shown in Table 16.1, the equity of the unlevered firm is valued at $8,000. Since the equity of the levered firm is $4,000 and its debt is $4,000, the value of the levered firm is also $8,000. Now suppose that, for whatever reason, the value of the levered firm were actually greater than the value of the unlevered firm. Here, Strategy *A* would cost more than Strategy *B*. In this case, an investor would prefer to borrow on his own account and invest in the stock of the unlevered firm. He would get the same net earnings each year as if he had invested in the stock of the levered firm. However, his cost would be less. The strategy would not be unique to our investor. Given the higher value of the levered firm, no rational investor would invest in the stock of the levered firm. Anyone desiring shares in the levered firm would get the same dollar return more cheaply by borrowing to finance a purchase of the unlevered firm's shares. The equilibrium result would be, of course, that the value of the levered firm would fall, and the value of the unlevered firm would rise until they became equal. At this point, individuals would be indifferent between Strategy *A* and Strategy *B*.

This example illustrates the basic result of Modigliani–Miller (MM) and is commonly called their Proposition I. We state this proposition as:

> **MM Proposition I (no taxes): The value of the levered firm is the same as the value of the unlevered firm.**

This is perhaps the most important result in all of corporate finance. In fact, it is generally considered the beginning point of modern managerial finance. Before MM, the effect of leverage on the value of the firm was considered complex and convoluted. Modigliani and Miller show a blindingly simple result: If levered firms are priced too high, rational investors will arbitrage by borrowing on their personal accounts to buy shares in unlevered firms. This substitution is oftentimes called *homemade leverage*. As long as individuals borrow (and lend) on the same terms as the firms, they can duplicate the effects of corporate leverage on their own.

The example of Trans Can Corporation shows that leverage does not affect the value of the firm. Since we showed earlier that shareholders' welfare is directly related to the firm's value, the example indicates that changes in capital structure cannot affect the shareholders' welfare.

A Key Assumption

The MM result hinges on the assumption that individuals can borrow as cheaply as corporations. If, alternatively, individuals can only borrow at a higher rate, one can easily show that corporations can increase firm value by borrowing.

Is this assumption of equal borrowing costs a good one? Individuals who want to buy stock and borrow can do so by establishing a margin account with the broker. Under this arrangement, the broker lends the individual a portion of the purchase price. For example, the individual might buy $10,000 of stock by investing $6,000 of her own funds and borrowing $4,000 from the broker. Should the stock be worth $9,000 on the next day, the individual's net worth or equity in the account would be $5,000 = $9,000 − $4,000.[4]

---

[4]We are ignoring the one-day interest charge on the loan.

The broker fears that a sudden price drop will cause the equity in the individual's account to be negative, implying that the broker may not get her loan repaid in full. To guard against this possibility, stock exchange rules require that the individual make additional cash contributions (replenish her margin account) as the stock price falls. Because (1) the procedures for replenishing the account have developed over many years, and (2) the broker holds the stock as collateral, there is little default risk to the broker.[5] In particular, if margin contributions are not made on time, the broker can sell the stock in order to satisfy her loan. Therefore, brokers generally charge low interest, with many rates being only slightly above the risk-free rate.

By contrast, corporations frequently borrow using illiquid assets (e.g., plant and equipment) as collateral. The costs to the lender of initial negotiation and ongoing supervision, as well as of working out arrangements in the event of financial distress, can be quite substantial. Thus, it is difficult to argue that individuals must borrow at higher rates than can corporations.[6]

? Concept Questions

- Describe financial leverage.
- What is levered equity?
- How can a shareholder of Trans Can undo the company's financial leverage?

16.4 Modigliani and Miller: Proposition II (No Taxes)

Risk to Equityholders Rises with Leverage

At a Trans Can corporate meeting, a corporate officer said, "Well, maybe it does not matter whether the corporation or the individual levers—as long as some leverage takes place. Leverage benefits investors. After all, an investor's expected return rises with the amount of the leverage present." He then pointed out that, as shown in Tables 16.2 and 16.3, the expected return on unlevered equity is 15 percent while the expected return on levered equity is 20 percent.

However, another officer replied, "Not necessarily. Though the expected return rises with leverage, the *risk* rises as well." This point can be seen from an examination of Tables 16.2 and 16.3. With earnings before interest and taxes (EBIT) varying between $400 and $2,000, earnings per share (EPS) for the shareholders of the unlevered firm vary between $1.00 and $5.00. EPS for the shareholders of the levered firm vary between $0 and $8.00. This greater range for the EPS of the levered firm implies greater risk for the levered firm's shareholders. In other words, levered shareholders have better returns in good times than do unlevered shareholders but have worse returns in bad times. The two tables also show greater range for the ROE of the levered firm's shareholders. The above interpretation concerning risk applies here as well.

The same insight can be taken from Figure 16.2. The slope of the line for the levered firm is greater than the slope of the line for the unlevered firm. This means that the levered shareholders have better returns in good times than do unlevered shareholders but have worse returns in bad times, implying greater risk with leverage. In other words, the slope

---

[5]Had this text been published before October 19, 1987, when stock prices declined by more than 20 percent, we might have used the phrase "virtually no" risk instead of "little."

[6]One caveat is in order. Initial margin or borrowing is currently limited by law to 50 percent of value. Certain companies, like financial institutions, borrow over 90 percent of their firm's market value. Individuals borrowing against the stock of all-equity corporations cannot duplicate the debt of these highly levered corporations.

of the line measures the risk to shareholders, since the slope indicates the responsiveness of ROE to changes in firm performance (earnings before interest and taxes).

Proposition II: Required Return to Equityholders Rises with Leverage

Since levered equity has greater risk, it should have a greater expected return as compensation. In our example, the market *requires* only a 15 percent expected return for the unlevered equity, but it requires a 20 percent expected return for the levered equity.

This type of reasoning allows us to develop **MM Proposition II.** Here, MM argue that the expected return on equity is positively related to leverage, because the risk to equityholders increases with leverage.

To develop this position recall from Chapter 13 that the firm's weighted average cost of capital, r_{WACC}, can be written as:[7]

$$\frac{B}{B+S} \times r_B + \frac{S}{B+S} \times r_S \qquad (16.2)$$

where

r_B is the interest rate, also called the cost of debt

r_S is the expected return on equity or stock, also called the *cost of equity* or the *required return on equity*

B is the value of the firm's debt or bonds

S is the value of the firm's stock or equity

Equation (16.2) is quite intuitive. It simply says that a firm's weighted average cost of capital is a weighted average of its cost of debt and its cost of equity. The weight applied to debt is the proportion of debt in the capital structure, and the weight applied to equity is the proportion of equity in the capital structure. Calculations of r_{WACC} from Equation (16.2) for both the unlevered and the levered firm are presented in Table 16.5.

TABLE 16.5
Cost of Capital Calculations for Trans Can

$$r_{WACC} = \frac{B}{B+S} \times r_B + \frac{S}{B+S} \times r_S$$

Unlevered firm: $15\% = \frac{0}{\$8,000} \times 10\%^* + \frac{\$8,000}{\$8,000} \times 15\%†$

Levered firm: $15\% = \frac{\$4,000}{\$8,000} \times 10\%^* + \frac{\$4,000}{\$8,000} \times 20\%‡$

*10% is the interest rate.

†From the "Expected" column in Table 16.2, we learn that expected earnings after interest for the unlevered firm are $1,200. From Table 16.1, we learn that equity for the unlevered firm is $8,000. Thus, r_S for the unlevered firm is:

$$\frac{\text{Expected earnings after interest}}{\text{Equity}} = \frac{\$1,200}{\$8,000} = 15\%$$

‡From the "Expected" column in Table 16.3, we learn that expected earnings after interest for the levered firm are $800. From Table 16.1, we learn that equity for the levered firm is $4,000. Thus r_S for the levered firm is:

$$\frac{\text{Expected earnings after interest}}{\text{Equity}} = \frac{\$800}{\$4,000} = 20\%$$

[7] Since we do not have taxes here, the cost of debt is r_B, not $r_B(1 - T_C)$ as it was in Chapter 13.

An implication of MM Proposition I is that r_{WACC} is a constant for a given firm, regardless of the capital structure.[8] For example, Table 16.5 shows that r_{WACC} for Trans Can is 15 percent, with or without leverage.

Let us now define r_0 to be the *cost of capital for an all-equity firm.* For the Trans Can Corp., r_0 is calculated as:

$$r_0 = \frac{\text{Expected earnings to unlevered firm}}{\text{Unlevered equity}} = \frac{\$1,200}{\$8,000} = 15\%$$

As can be seen from Table 16.5, r_{WACC} is equal to r_0 for Trans Can. In fact, r_{WACC} must *always* equal r_0 in a world without corporate taxes.

Proposition II states the expected return of equity, r_S, in terms of leverage. The exact relationship, derived by setting $r_{WACC} = r_0$ and then rearranging Equation (16.2), is[9]

MM Proposition II (no taxes):

$$r_S = r_0 + \frac{B}{S}(r_0 - r_B) \tag{16.3}$$

Equation (16.3) implies that the required return on equity is a linear function of the firm's debt-to-equity ratio. Examining Equation (16.3), we see that if r_0 exceeds the debt rate, r_B, then the cost of equity rises with increases in the debt–equity ratio, *B/S*. Normally, r_0 should exceed r_B. That is, because even unlevered equity is risky, it should have an expected return greater than that of riskless debt. Note that Equation (16.3) holds for Trans Can in its levered state:

$$0.20 = 0.15 + \frac{\$4,000}{\$4,000}(0.15 - 0.10)$$

Figure 16.3 graphs Equation (16.3). As you can see, we have plotted the relation between the cost of equity, r_S, and the debt–equity ratio, *B/S,* as a straight line. What we witness in Equation (16.3) and illustrate in Figure 16.3 is the effect of leverage on the cost of equity. As the firm raises the debt–equity ratio, each dollar of equity is levered with additional debt. This raises the risk of equity and therefore the required return, r_S, on the equity.

Figure 16.3 also shows that r_{WACC} is unaffected by leverage, a point we made above. (It is important for students to realize that r_0, the cost of capital for an all-equity firm, is represented by a single dot on the graph. By contrast, r_{WACC} is an entire line.)

---

[8]This statement holds in a world of no taxes. It does not hold in a world with taxes, a point to be brought out later in this chapter (see Figure 16.5).

[9]This can be derived from Equation (16.2) by setting $r_{WACC} = r_0$, yielding:

$$\frac{B}{B+S}r_B + \frac{S}{B+S}r_S = r_0. \tag{16.2}$$

Multiplying both sides by $(B + S)/S$ yields:

$$\frac{B}{S}r_B + r_S = \frac{B+S}{S}r_0.$$

We can rewrite the right-hand side as

$$\frac{B}{S}r_B + r_S = \frac{B}{S}r_0 + r_0.$$

Moving $(B/S)r_B$ to the right-hand side and rearranging yields:

$$r_S = r_0 + \frac{B}{S}(r_0 - r_B). \tag{16.3}$$

FIGURE 16.3

The Cost of Equity, the Cost of Debt, and the Weighted Average Cost of Capital: MM Proposition II with No Corporate Taxes

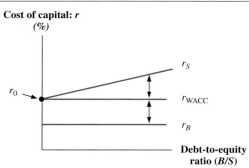

Cost of capital: r
$(\%)$

r_S

r_0

r_{WACC}

r_B

Debt-to-equity
ratio (B/S)

$$r_S = r_0 + \frac{B}{S}(r_0 - r_B)$$

r_S is the cost of equity.
r_B is the cost of debt.
r_0 is the cost of capital for an all-equity firm.
r_{WACC} is a firm's weighted average cost of capital. In a world with no taxes,
r_{WACC} for a levered firm is equal to r_0.
r_0 is a single point while r_S, r_B, and r_{WACC} are all entire lines.
The cost of equity capital, r_S, is positively related to the firm's debt–equity ratio. The firm's weighted average cost of capital, r_{WACC}, is invariant to the firm's debt–equity ratio.

Example Illustrating Proposition I and Proposition II

EXAMPLE 16.2

Luteran Motors, an all-equity firm, has an expected cash flow of $10 million per year in perpetuity. There are 10 million shares outstanding, implying expected annual cash flow of $1 per share. The cost of capital for this unlevered firm is 10 percent. The firm will soon build a new plant for $4 million. The plant is expected to generate additional cash flow of $1 million per year. These figures can be described as

Current Company	New Plant
Cash flow: $10 million	Initial outlay: $4 million
Number of outstanding shares: 10 million	Additional annual cash flow: $1 million

The project's net present value is

$$-\$4 \text{ million} + \frac{\$1 \text{ million}}{0.1} = \$6 \text{ million}$$

assuming that the project is discounted at the same rate as the firm as a whole. Before the market knows of the project, the *market value balance sheet* of the firm is

LUTERAN MOTORS
Balance Sheet (all equity)

Old assets: $\dfrac{\$10 \text{ million}}{0.1} = \$100 \text{ million}$	Equity: $100 million (10 million shares of stock)

The value of the firm is $100 million, because the cash flows of $10 million per year are capitalized at 10 percent. A share of stock sells for $10 (or $100 million/10 million) because there are 10 million shares outstanding.

The market value balance sheet is a useful tool of financial analysis. Because students are often thrown off guard by it initially, we recommend extra study here. The key is that the market value balance sheet has the same form as the balance sheet that accountants use. That is, assets are placed on the left-hand side, whereas liabilities and owners' equity are placed on the right-hand side. In addition, the left-hand side and the right-hand side must be equal. The difference is in the numbers. Accountants value items in terms of historical cost (original purchase price less depreciation), whereas financial people value items in terms of market value.

The firm will issue $4 million of either equity or debt. Let us consider the effect of equity and debt financing in turn.

Share Financing   Imagine that the firm announces that, in the near future, it will raise $4 million in equity in order to build a new plant. The stock price will rise to reflect the positive net present value of the plant. According to efficient markets, the increase occurs immediately. That is, the rise occurs on the day of the announcement, not on the date of either the onset of construction of the power plant or the forthcoming stock offering. The market value balance sheet becomes

LUTERAN MOTORS

Balance Sheet (upon announcement of equity issue to construct plant)

Old assets	$100 million	Equity	$106 million
			(10 million shares of stock)
NPV of plant:			
$-\$4 \text{ million} + \dfrac{\$1 \text{ million}}{0.1} =$ 6 million			
Total assets	$106 million		

Note that the NPV of the plant is included in the market value balance sheet. Because the new shares have not yet been issued, the number of outstanding shares remains 10 million. The price per share has now risen to $10.60 (or $106/10 million) to reflect news concerning the plant.

Shortly thereafter, $4 million of stock is floated. Because the stock is selling at $10.60 per share, 377,358 (or $4 million/$10.60) shares of stock are issued. Imagine that funds are put in the bank *temporarily* before being used to build the plant. The market value balance sheet becomes

LUTERAN MOTORS

Balance Sheet (upon issuance of stock but before construction begins on plant)

Old assets	$100 million	Equity	$110 million
			(10,377,358 shares of stock)
NPV of plant	6 million		
Proceeds from new issue of stock	4 million		
(currently invested in bank)			
Total assets	$110 million		

The number of shares outstanding is now 10,377,358 because 377,358 new shares were issued. The price per share is $10.60 ($110,000,000/10,377,358). Note that the price has not changed. This is consistent with efficient capital markets, because stock price should only move due to new information.

Of course, the funds are placed in the bank only temporarily. Shortly after the new issue, the $4 million is given to a contractor who builds the plant. To avoid problems in discounting, we assume that the plant is built immediately. The balance sheet then becomes

LUTERAN MOTORS

Balance Sheet (upon completion of the plant)

Old assets	$100 million	Equity	$110 million
PV of plant: $\frac{\$1\ \text{million}}{0.1} =$ 10 million			(10,377,358 shares of stock)
Total assets	$110 million		

Though total assets do not change, the composition of the assets does change. The bank account has been emptied to pay the contractor. The present value of cash flows of $1 million a year from the plant is reflected as an asset worth $10 million. Because the building expenditures of $4 million have already been paid, they no longer represent a future cost. Hence, they no longer reduce the value of the plant. According to efficient capital markets, the price per share of stock remains $10.60.

Expected yearly cash flow from the firm is $11 million, $10 million of which comes from the old assets and $1 million from the new. The expected return to equityholders is

$$r_S = \frac{\$11\ \text{million}}{\$110\ \text{million}} = 0.10$$

Because the firm is all equity, $r_S = r_0 = 0.10$.

Debt Financing   Alternatively, imagine that the firm announces that, in the near future, it will borrow $4 million at 6 percent to build a new plant. This implies yearly interest payments of $240,000 (or $4,000,000 \times 6\%$). Again the stock price rises immediately to reflect the positive net present value of the plant. Thus, we have

LUTERAN MOTORS

Balance Sheet (upon announcement of debt issue to construct plant)

Old assets	$100 million	Equity	$106 million
NPV of plant: $-\$4\ \text{million} + \frac{\$1\ \text{million}}{0.1} =$ 6 million			(10 million shares of stock)
Total assets	$106 million		

The value of the firm is the same as in the equity financing case because (1) the same plant is to be built and (2) MM prove that debt financing is neither better nor worse than equity financing.

At some point, $4 million of debt is issued. As before, the funds are placed in the bank temporarily. The market value balance sheet becomes

LUTERAN MOTORS

Balance Sheet (upon debt issuance but before construction begins on plant)

Old assets	$100 million	Debt	$4 million
NPV of plant	6 million	Equity	106 million
			(10 million shares of stock)
Proceeds from debt issue			
(currently invested in bank)	4 million		
Total assets	$110 million	Debt plus equity	$110 million

Note that debt appears on the right-hand side of the balance sheet. The stock price is still $10.60, in accordance with our discussion of efficient capital markets.

Finally, the contractor receives $4 million and builds the plant. The market value balance sheet becomes

LUTERAN MOTORS

Balance Sheet (upon completion of the plant)

Old assets	$100 million	Debt	$4 million
PV of plant	10 million	Equity	106 million
			(10 million shares of stock)
Total assets	$110 million	Debt plus equity	$110 million

The only change here is that the bank account has been depleted to pay the contractor. The equityholders expect yearly cash flow after interest of

$$\underset{\substack{\text{Cash flow on}\\\text{old assets}}}{\$10,000,000} + \underset{\substack{\text{Cash flow on}\\\text{new assets}}}{\$1,000,000} - \underset{\substack{\text{Interest:}\\\$4\text{ million} \times 6\%}}{\$240,000} = \$10,760,000$$

The equityholders expect to earn a return of

$$\frac{\$10,760,000}{\$106,000,000} = 10.15\%$$

This return of 10.15 percent for levered equityholders is higher than the 10 percent return for the unlevered equityholders. This result is sensible because, as we argued earlier, levered equity is riskier. In fact, the return of 10.15 percent should be exactly what MM Proposition II predicts. This prediction can be verified by plugging values into

$$r_S = r_0 + \frac{B}{S}(r_0 - r_B) \tag{16.3}$$

We obtain

$$10.15\% = 10\% + \frac{\$4,000,000}{\$106,000,000} \times (10\% - 6\%)$$

This example was useful for two reasons. First, we wanted to introduce the concept of market value balance sheets, a tool that will prove useful elsewhere in the text. Among other things, this technique allows one to calculate the price per share of a new issue of stock. Second, the example illustrates three aspects of Modigliani and Miller:

1. The example is consistent with MM Proposition I because the value of the firm is $110 million after either equity or debt financing.

2. Students are often more interested in stock price than in firm value. We show that the stock price is always $10.60, regardless of whether debt or equity financing is used.

3. The example is consistent with MM Proposition II. The expected return to equityholders rises from 10 to 10.15 percent, just as Equation (16.3) states.

MM: An Interpretation

The Modigliani–Miller results indicate that managers of a firm cannot change its value by repackaging the firm's securities. Though this idea was considered revolutionary when it was originally proposed in the late 1950s, the MM model and arbitrage proof have since met with wide acclaim.[10]

MM argue that the firm's overall cost of capital cannot be reduced as debt is substituted for equity, even though debt appears to be cheaper than equity. The reason for this is that, as the firm adds debt, the remaining equity becomes more risky. As this risk rises, the cost of equity capital rises as a result. The increase in the cost of the remaining equity capital offsets the higher proportion of the firm financed by low-cost debt. In fact, MM prove that the two effects exactly offset each other, so that both the value of the firm and the firm's overall cost of capital are invariant to leverage.

MM use an interesting analogy to food. They consider a dairy farmer with two choices. Either he can sell whole milk or, by skimming, he can sell a combination of cream and low-fat milk. Though the farmer can get a high price for the cream, he gets a low price for the low-fat milk, implying no net gain. In fact, imagine that the proceeds from the whole-milk strategy were less than those from the cream–low-fat milk strategy. Arbitrageurs would buy the whole milk, perform the skimming operation themselves, and resell the cream and low-fat milk separately. Competition between arbitrageurs would tend to boost the price of whole milk until proceeds from the two strategies became equal. Thus, the value of the farmer's milk is invariant with the way in which the milk is packaged.

Food found its way into this chapter earlier, when we viewed the firm as a pie.[11] MM argue that the size of the pie does not change, no matter how shareholders and bondholders divide it. MM say that a firm's capital structure is irrelevant; it is what it is by some historical accident. The theory implies that firms' debt–equity ratios could be anything. They are what they are because of whimsical and random managerial decisions about how much to borrow and how much stock to issue.

Although scholars are always fascinated with far-reaching theories, students are perhaps more concerned with real-world applications. Do real-world managers follow MM by treating capital structure decisions with indifference? Unfortunately for the theory, virtually all companies in certain industries, such as banking, choose high debt-to-equity ratios. Conversely, companies in other industries, such as pharmaceuticals, choose low debt-to-equity ratios. In fact, almost any industry has a debt-to-equity ratio to which companies in that industry adhere. Thus, companies do not appear to be selecting their degree of leverage in a frivolous or random manner. Because of this, financial economists (including MM themselves) have argued that real-world factors may have been left out of the theory.

---

[10]Franco Modigliani and Merton Miller have each won the Nobel Prize in Economics, in part for their work on capital structure.

[11]Other authors have also brought food into discussions on capital structure. For example, Stewart Myers in "The Search for Optimal Capital Structure," *Midland Corporate Finance Journal* (Spring 1983), used chicken. Abstracting from the extra costs in cutting up poultry, he argues that all of the chicken parts should, in sum, sell for no more than a whole chicken.

In Professor Miller's Words . . .

The Modigliani–Miller results are not easy to understand fully. This point is related in a story told by Merton Miller.

"How difficult it is to summarize briefly the contribution of the [Modigliani–Miller] papers was brought home to me very clearly last October after Franco Modigliani was awarded the Nobel Prize in Economics in part—but, of course, only in part—for the work in finance. The television camera crews from our local stations in Chicago immediately descended upon me. 'We understand,' they said, 'that you worked with Modigliani some years back in developing these M and M theorems and we wonder if you could explain them briefly to our television viewers.'

" 'How briefly?' I asked.

" 'Oh, take ten seconds,' was the reply.

"Ten seconds to explain the work of a lifetime! Ten seconds to describe two carefully reasoned articles, each running to more than thirty printed pages and each with sixty or so long footnotes! When they saw the look of dismay on my face, they said, 'You don't have to go into details. Just give us the main points in simple, common-sense terms.'

"The main point of the first or cost-of-capital article was, in principle at least, simple enough to make. It said that in an economist's ideal world of complete and perfect capital markets and with full and symmetric information among all market participants, the total market value of all the securities issued by a firm was governed by the earning power and risk of its underlying real assets and was independent of how the mix of securities issued to finance it was divided between debt instruments and equity capital. . . .

"Such a summary, however, uses too many short-handed terms and concepts, like perfect capital markets, that are rich in connotations to economists but hardly so to the general public. So I thought, instead, of an analogy that we ourselves had invoked in the original paper. . . .

" 'Think of the firm,' I said, 'as a gigantic tub of whole milk. The farmer can sell the whole milk as is.

Or he can separate out the cream and sell it at a considerably higher price than the whole milk would bring. (That's the analog of a firm selling low-yield and hence high-priced debt securities.) But, of course, what the farmer would have left would be skim milk with low butterfat content and that would sell for much less than whole milk. That corresponds to the levered equity. The M and M proposition says that if there were no costs of separation (and, of course, no government dairy support programs), the cream plus the skim milk would bring the same price as the whole milk.'

"The television people conferred among themselves and came back to inform me that it was too long, too complicated, and too academic.

" 'Don't you have anything simpler?' they asked. I thought of another way that the M and M proposition is presented these days, which emphasizes the notion of market completeness and stresses the role of securities as devices for 'partitioning' a firm's payoffs in each possible state of the world among the group of its capital suppliers.

" 'Think of the firm,' I said, 'as a gigantic pizza, divided into quarters. If now you cut each quarter in half into eighths, the M and M proposition says that you will have more pieces but not more pizza.'

"Again there was a whispered conference among the camera crew, and the director came back and said:

" 'Professor, we understand from the press release that there were two M and M propositions. Can we try the other one?' "

[Professor Miller tried valiantly to explain the second proposition, though this was apparently even more difficult to get across. After his attempt:]

"Once again there was a whispered conversation. They shut the lights off. They folded up their equipment. They thanked me for giving them the time. They said that they'd get back to me. But I knew that I had somehow lost my chance to start a new career as a packager of economic wisdom for TV viewers in convenient ten-second bites. Some have the talent for it . . . and some just don't."

Source: GSB Chicago, University of Chicago (Autumn 1986).

Summary of Modigliani–Miller Propositions Without Taxes

Assumptions:

- No taxes
- No transaction costs
- Individuals and corporations borrow at same rate
- Complete information
- Perpetual cash flow
- No default risk

Results:

Proposition I: $V_L = V_U$ (Value of levered firm equals value of unlevered firm)

Proposition II: $r_S = r_0 + \frac{B}{S}(r_0 - r_B)$

Intuition:

Proposition I: Through homemade leverage, individuals can either duplicate or undo the effects of corporate leverage.

Proposition II: The cost of equity rises with leverage, because the risk to equity rises with leverage.

Though many of our students have argued that individuals can only borrow at rates above the corporate borrowing rate, we disagreed with this argument earlier in the chapter. But when we look elsewhere for unrealistic assumptions in the theory, we find two:[12]

1. Taxes were ignored.
2. Bankruptcy costs and other agency costs were not considered.

We will turn to taxes shortly. Bankruptcy costs and other agency costs will be treated in the next chapter. The boxed section above presents a summary of the main Modigliani–Miller results without taxes.

? Concept Questions
- **Why does the expected return on equity rise with firm leverage?**
- **What is the exact relationship between the expected return on equity and firm leverage?**
- **How are market value balance sheets set up?**

16.5   Taxes

The Basic Insight

The previous part of this chapter showed that firm value is unrelated to debt in a world without taxes. We now show that, in the presence of corporate taxes, the firm's value is positively related to its debt. The basic intuition can be seen from a pie chart, such as the one in Figure 16.4. Consider the all-equity firm on the left. Here, both equityholders and

---

[12]MM were aware of both of these issues, as can be seen in their original paper.

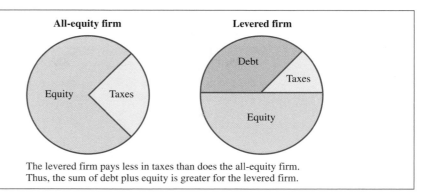

FIGURE 16.4

Two Pie Models of Capital Structure Under Corporate Taxes

The levered firm pays less in taxes than does the all-equity firm. Thus, the sum of debt plus equity is greater for the levered firm.

Canada Revenue Agency (CRA) have claims on the value of the firm. The value of the all-equity firm is, of course, that owned by the equityholders. The proportion going to taxes is simply a cost.

The pie on the right for the levered firm shows three claims: equityholders, debtholders, and taxes. The value of the levered firm is the sum of the value of the debt and the value of the equity. In selecting between the two capital structures in the picture, a financial manager should select the one with the higher value. Assuming that the total area is the same for both pies, value is maximized for that capital structure paying the least in taxes. In other words, the manager should choose the capital structure that minimizes taxes.

We will show that, due to Canadian tax law allowing interest to be deducted from taxable income, the proportion of the pie allocated to taxes is less for the levered firm than it is for the unlevered firm. Thus, managers should select high leverage.

Taxation of Corporate Income

EXAMPLE 16.3

The Water Products Company has a corporate tax rate, T_C, of 40 percent and expected earnings before interest and taxes (EBIT) of $1 million. Its entire earnings after taxes are paid out as dividends.

The firm is considering two alternative capital structures. Under Plan I, Water Products has no debt in its capital structure. Under Plan II, the company would have $4,000,000 of debt, B. The cost of debt, r_B, is 10 percent for both plans.

The chief financial officer for Water Products makes the following calculations:

	Plan I	Plan II
Earnings before interest and taxes (EBIT)	$1,000,000	$1,000,000
Interest ($r_B B$)	0	(400,000)
Earnings before taxes (EBT) = (EBIT − $r_B B$)	1,000,000	600,000
Taxes ($T_C = 0.40$)	(400,000)	(240,000)
Earnings after corporate taxes (EAT) = [(EBIT − $r_B B$) × (1 − T_C)]	600,000	360,000
Total cash flow to both shareholders and bondholders [EBIT × (1 − T_C) + $T_C r_B B$]	$ 600,000	$ 760,000

The most relevant numbers for our purposes are the two on the bottom line. Here, we see that more cash flow reaches the owners of the firm (both shareholders and bondholders) under Plan II.

The difference is $160,000 = $760,000 − $600,000. It does not take us long to realize the source of this difference. Water Products pays less taxes under Plan II ($240,000) than it does under Plan I ($400,000). The difference here is $160,000 = $400,000 − $240,000.

This difference occurs because interest totally escapes corporate taxation, whereas earnings after interest but before corporate taxes (EBT) are taxed at the 40 percent rate.[13] We express this relationship algebraically below.

Present Value of the Tax Shield

The discussion above shows a tax advantage to debt or, equivalently, a tax disadvantage to equity. We now want to value this advantage. The dollar interest is:

$$\text{Interest} = \underbrace{r_B}_{\text{Interest rate}} \times \underbrace{B}_{\text{Amount borrowed}}$$

This interest is $400,000 (10% × $4,000,000) for Water Products. All this interest is tax-deductible. That is, whatever the taxable income of Water Products would have been without the debt, the taxable income is now $400,000 *less* with the debt.

Because the corporate tax rate is 0.40 in our example, the reduction in corporate taxes is $160,000 (0.40 × $400,000). This number is identical to the reduction in corporate taxes calculated previously.

Algebraically, the reduction in corporate taxes is:

$$\underbrace{T_C}_{\text{Corporate tax rate}} \times \underbrace{r_B \times B}_{\text{Dollar amount of interest}} \qquad \textbf{(16.4)}$$

That is, whatever the taxes that a firm would pay each year without debt, the firm will pay $T_C r_B B$ less with the debt of B. Expression (16.4) is often called the *tax shield from debt*. Note that it is an *annual* amount.

As long as the firm expects to be in a positive tax bracket, we can assume that the cash flow in Expression (16.4) has the same risk as the interest on the debt. Thus, its value can be determined by discounting at the interest rate, r_B. Assuming that the cash flows are perpetual, the present value of the tax shield is:

$$\frac{T_C r_B B}{r_B} = T_C B \qquad \textbf{(16.5)}$$

Value of the Levered Firm

We have just calculated the present value of the tax shield from debt. Our next step is to calculate the value of the levered firm. From Equations (16.5 and 16.7) the after-tax cash flow to the shareholders and bondholders in the levered firm is

$$\text{EBIT} \times (1 - T_C) + T_C r_B B \qquad \textbf{(16.6)}$$

---

[13]Note that shareholders actually receive more under Plan I ($600,000) than under Plan II ($360,000). Students are often bothered by this since it seems to imply that shareholders are better off without leverage. However, remember that there are more shares outstanding in Plan I than in Plan II. A full-blown model would show that earnings per share are higher with leverage.

The first term in Expression (16.6) is the after-tax cash flow in the unlevered firm. The value of an unlevered firm (that is, a firm with no debt) is the present value of EBIT $\times (1 - T_C)$,

$$V_U = \frac{\text{EBIT} \times (1 - T_C)}{r_0} \qquad (16.7)$$

where

$$V_U = \text{Present value of an unlevered firm}$$
$$\text{EBIT} \times (1 - T_C) = \text{Firm cash flows after corporate taxes}$$
$$T_C = \text{Corporate tax rate}$$
$$r_0 = \text{The cost of capital to an all-equity firm (as can be seen from the formula, } r_0 \text{ now discounts } \textit{after-tax} \text{ cash flows)}$$

The second part of the cash flows, $T_C r_B B$, is the tax shield. To determine its present value, the tax shield should be discounted at r_B.

As a consequence, we have[14]

MM Proposition I (Corporate Taxes):

$$V_L = \frac{\text{EBIT} \times (1 - T_C)}{r_0} + \frac{T_C r_B B}{r_B} \qquad (16.8)$$
$$= V_U + T_C B$$

Equation (16.8) is **MM Proposition I under corporate taxes.** The first term in Equation (16.8) is the value of the cash flows of the firm with no debt tax shield. In other words, this term is equal to V_U, the value of the all-equity firm. The value of the firm is the value of an all-equity firm plus $T_C B$, the tax rate times the value of the debt. $T_C B$ is the present value of the tax shield in the case of perpetual cash flows.[15]

The Water Products example reveals that, because the tax shield increases with the amount of debt, the firm can raise its total cash flow and its value by substituting debt for equity. We now have a clear example of why the capital structure does matter: By raising

---

[14]This relationship holds when the debt level is assumed to be constant through time. A different formula would apply if the debt–equity ratio were assumed to be a constant over time. For a deeper treatment of this point, see J. A. Miles and J. R. Ezzell, "The Weighted Average Cost of Capital, Perfect Capital Markets and Project Life," *Journal of Financial and Quantitative Analysis* (September 1980).

[15]The following example calculates the present value if we assume the debt has a finite life. Suppose the Maxwell Company has $1 million in debt with an 8 percent coupon rate. If the debt matures in two years and the cost of debt capital, r_B, is 10 percent, what is the present value of the tax shields if the corporate tax rate is 40 percent? The debt is amortized in equal installments over two years.

Year	Loan Balance	Interest	Tax Shield	Present Value of Tax Shield
0	$1,000,000			
1	500,000	$80,000	0.4 $\times$ $80,000	$29,090.91
2	0	40,000	0.4 $\times$ $40,000	13,223.14
				$42,314.05

The present value of the tax savings is

$$\text{PV} = \frac{0.40 \times \$80,000}{1.10} + \frac{0.40 \times \$40,000}{(1.10)^2} = \$42,314.05$$

The Maxwell Company's value is higher than that of a comparable unlevered firm by $42,314.05.

the debt–equity ratio, the firm can lower its taxes and thereby increase its total value. The strong forces that operate to maximize the value of the firm would seem to push it toward an all-debt capital structure.

EXAMPLE 16.4

Divided Airlines is currently an unlevered firm. It is considering a capital restructuring to allow $200 of debt. The company expects to generate $166.67 in cash flows before interest and taxes, in perpetuity. The corporate tax rate is 40 percent, implying after-tax cash flows of $100. Its cost of debt capital is 10 percent. Unlevered firms in the same industry have a cost of equity capital of 20 percent. What will the new value of Divided Airlines be?

The value of Divided Airlines will equal[16]

$$V_L = \frac{\text{EBIT} \times (1 - T_C)}{r_0} + T_C B$$

$$= \frac{\$100}{0.20} + (0.40 \times \$200)$$

$$= \$500 + \$80$$

$$= \$580$$

Because $V_L = B + S$, the value of levered equity, S, is equal to $580 - \$200 = \$380$. The value of Divided Airlines as a function of leverage is shown in Figure 16.5.

FIGURE 16.5

The Effect of Financial Leverage on Firm Value: MM with Corporate Taxes in the Case of Divided Airlines

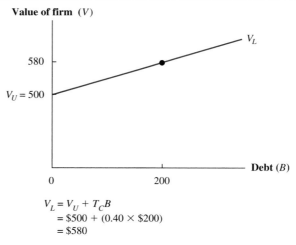

$$V_L = V_U + T_C B$$
$$= \$500 + (0.40 \times \$200)$$
$$= \$580$$

Debt reduces Divided's tax burden. As a result, the value of the firm is positively related to debt.

Expected Return and Leverage Under Corporate Taxes

MM Proposition II under no taxes posits a positive relationship between the expected return on equity and leverage. This result occurs because the risk of equity increases with

---

[16]Note that, in a world with taxes, r_0 is used to discount after-tax cash flows.

leverage. The same intuition also holds in a world of corporate taxes. The exact formula is[17]

MM Proposition II (Corporate Taxes):

$$r_S = r_0 + \frac{B}{S} \times (1 - T_C) \times (r_0 - r_B) \tag{16.9}$$

Applying the **MM Proposition II under corporate taxes** formula to Divided Airlines, we get

$$r_S = 0.2316 = 0.20 + \frac{200}{380} \times (1 - 0.40) \times (0.20 - 0.10)$$

This calculation is illustrated in Figure 16.6.

Whenever $r_0 > r_B$, r_S increases with leverage, a result that we also found in the no-tax case. As stated earlier in this chapter, r_0 should exceed r_B. That is, since equity (even unlevered equity) is risky, it should have an expected return greater than that on the less risky debt.

We can check this calculation by discounting at r_S to determine the value of the levered equity. The algebraic formula for levered equity is

$$S = \frac{(\text{EBIT} - r_B B) \times (1 - T_C)}{r_S} \tag{16.10}$$

The numerator is the expected cash flow to levered equity after interest and taxes. The denominator is the rate at which the cash flow to equity is discounted.

---

[17]This relationship can be shown as follows: Given MM Proposition I under taxes, a levered firm's market value balance sheet can be written as

V_U = Value of unlevered firm	B = Debt
$T_C B$ = Tax shield	S = Equity

The value of the unlevered firm is simply the value of the assets without benefit of leverage. The balance sheet indicates that the firm's value increases by $T_C B$ when debt of B is added. The expected cash flow from the left-hand side of the balance sheet can be written as

$$V_U r_0 + T_C B r_B \tag{a}$$

Because assets are risky, their expected rate of return is r_0. The tax shield has the same risk as the debt, so its expected rate of return is r_B.
The expected cash to bondholders and shareholders together is

$$S r_S + B r_B \tag{b}$$

Expression (b) reflects the fact that stock earns an expected return of r_s and debt earns the interest rate r_B.

Because all cash flows are paid out as dividends in our no-growth perpetuity model, the cash flows going into the firm equal those going to stakeholders. Hence (a) and (b) are equal:

$$S r_S + B r_B = V_U r_0 + T_C B r_B \tag{c}$$

Dividing both sides of (c) by S, subtracting $B r_B$ from both sides, and rearranging yields

$$r_S = \frac{V_U}{S} \times r_0 - (1 - T_C) \times \frac{B}{S} r_B \tag{d}$$

Because the value of the levered firm, V_L, equals $V_U + T_C B = B + S$, it follows that $V_U = S + (1 - T_C) \times B$. Thus, (d) can be rewritten as

$$r_S = \frac{S + (1 - T_C) \times B}{S} \times r_0 - (1 - T_C) \times \frac{B}{S} r_B \tag{e}$$

Bringing the terms involving $(1 - T_C) \times \frac{B}{S}$ together produces Equation (16.8).

For Divided Airlines we get[18]

$$\frac{(\$166.67 - 0.10 \times \$200)(1 - 0.40)}{0.2316} = \$380$$

the same result we obtained earlier.

The Weighted Average Cost of Capital, r_{WACC}, and Corporate Taxes

In Chapter 13, we defined the weighted average cost of capital (with corporate taxes) as

$$r_{\text{WACC}} = \frac{B}{V_L}r_B(1 - T_C) + \frac{S}{V_L}r_S$$

Note that the cost of debt capital, r_B, is multiplied by $(1 - T_C)$ because interest is tax-deductible at the corporate level. However, the cost of equity, r_S, is not multiplied by this factor because dividends are not deductible. In the no-tax case, r_{WACC} is not affected by leverage. However, since debt is tax-advantaged relative to equity, it can be shown that r_{WACC} declines with leverage in a world with corporate taxes. This result can be seen in Figure 16.6.

For Divided Airlines,

$$r_{\text{WACC}} = \left(\frac{200}{580} \times 0.10 \times 0.60\right) + \left(\frac{380}{580} \times 0.2316\right)$$
$$= 0.1724$$

Divided Airlines has reduced its r_{WACC} from 0.20 (with no debt) to 0.1724 with reliance on debt. This result is intuitively pleasing because it suggests that, when a firm lowers its r_{WACC}, the firm's value will increase. Using the r_{WACC} approach, we can confirm that the value of Divided Airlines is $580:

$$V_L = \frac{\text{EBIT} \times (1 - T_C)}{r_{\text{WACC}}} = \frac{166.67 (1 - 0.4)}{0.1724}$$
$$= \$580$$

FIGURE 16.6

The Effect of Financial Leverage on the Cost of Debt and Equity Capital

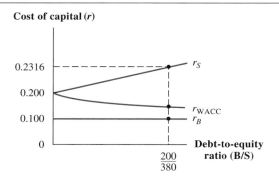

Financial leverage adds risk to the firm's equity. As compensation, the cost of equity rises with the firm's risk.

$$r_S = r_0 + \frac{B}{S}(1 - T_C)(r_0 - r_B)$$

$$= 0.20 + \left(\frac{200}{380} \times 0.60 \times 0.10\right)$$

$$= 0.2316$$

---

[18]The calculation suffers slightly from rounding error because we only carried the discount rate, 0.2316, out to four decimal places.

Stock Price and Leverage Under Corporate Taxes

At this point, students often believe the numbers—or at least are too intimidated to dispute them. However, they think we have asked the wrong question. "Why are we choosing to maximize the value of the firm?" they will say. "If managers are looking out for the shareholders' interest, why aren't they trying to maximize stock price?" If this question occurred to you, you have come to the right section.

Our response is twofold. First, we showed in the first section of this chapter that the capital structure that maximizes firm value is also the one that most benefits the interests of the shareholders.[19]

However, that general explanation is not always convincing to students. As a second procedure, we calculate the stock price of Divided Airlines both before and after the exchange of debt for stock. We do this by presenting a set of market value balance sheets. The market value balance sheet for the company in its all-equity form can be represented as

DIVIDED AIRLINES
Balance Sheet (all-equity firm)

Physical assets	Equity $500
$\frac{166.67}{0.20} \times (1 - 0.40) = \$500$	(100 shares)

Assuming that there are 100 shares outstanding, each share is worth $5 = \$500/100$.

Next imagine that the company announces that, in the near future, it will issue $200 of debt to buy back $200 of stock. We know from our previous discussion that the value of the firm will rise to reflect the tax shield of debt. In efficient capital markets, the increase occurs immediately. That is, the rise occurs on the day of the announcement, not on the date of the debt-for-equity exchange. The market value balance sheet now becomes

DIVIDED AIRLINES
Balance Sheet
(upon announcement of debt issue)

Physical assets	$500	Equity	$580
Present value of tax shield	80		(100 shares)
Total assets	$580		

Note that the debt has not yet been issued. Therefore, only equity appears on the right-hand side of the balance sheet. Each share is now worth $580/100 = \$5.80$, implying that the shareholders have benefited by $80. The equityholders gain because they are the owners of a firm that has improved its financial policy.

The introduction of the tax shield to the balance sheet is frequently perplexing to students. Although physical assets are tangible, the ethereal nature of the tax shield bothers many students. However, remember that an asset is any item with value. The tax shield has value because it reduces the stream of future taxes. The fact that one cannot touch the

---

[19]At that time, we pointed out that this result may not exactly hold in the more complex case where debt has a significant possibility of default. Issues of default are treated in the next chapter.

shield in the way that one can touch a physical asset is a philosophical, not a financial, consideration.

At some point, the exchange of debt for equity occurs. Debt of $200 is issued, and the proceeds are used to buy back shares. How many shares of stock are repurchased? Because shares are now selling at $5.80 each, the number of shares that the firm acquires is $200/$5.80 = 34.48. This leaves 65.52 (or 100 − 34.48) shares of stock outstanding. The market value balance sheet is now

DIVIDED AIRLINES
Balance Sheet
(after exchange has taken place)

Physical assets	$500	Equity	$ 380
Present value of tax shield	80	(100 − 34.48 = 65.52 shares)	
		Debt	200
Total assets	$580	Debt plus equity	$580

Each share of stock is worth $380/65.52 = $5.80 after the exchange. Notice that the stock price does not change on the exchange date. As we mentioned above, the stock price moves on the date of the announcement only. Because the shareholders participating in the exchange receive a price equal to the market price per share after the exchange, they do not care whether they exchange their stock or not.

A summary of the main results of Modigliani–Miller with corporate taxes is presented in the following boxed section.

Summary of Modigliani–Miller Propositions with Corporate Taxes

Assumptions:

• Corporations are taxed at the rate T_C, on earnings after interest.

• No transaction costs.

• Individuals and corporations borrow at same rate.

• Complete information.

• Perpetual cash flows.

• No default risk.

Results:

Proposition I: $V_L = V_U + T_C B$

　(for a firm with perpetual debt)

Proposition II: $r_S = r_0 + \dfrac{B}{S}(1 - T_C)(r_0 - r_B)$

Intuition:

Proposition I:　Since corporations can deduct interest payments but not dividend payments, corporate leverage lowers tax payments.

Proposition II: The cost of equity rises with leverage, because the risk to equity rises with leverage.

The Divided Airlines example was provided for two reasons. First, it shows that an increase in the value of the firm from debt financing leads to an increase in the price of the stock. In fact, the shareholders capture the entire $80 tax shield. Second, we wanted to provide more work with market value balance sheets.

? Concept Questions

- **What makes a levered firm more valuable than an otherwise identical unlevered firm?**
- **What is MM Proposition I under corporate taxes?**
- **What is MM Proposition II under corporate taxes?**

16.6 SUMMARY AND CONCLUSIONS

1. We began our discussion of the capital structure decision by arguing that the particular capital structure that maximizes the value of the firm can also be the one that provides the most benefit to the shareholders.

2. In a world of no taxes, the famous Proposition I of Modigliani and Miller proves that the value of the firm is unaffected by the debt-to-equity ratio. In other words, a firm's capital structure is a matter of indifference in that world. The authors obtain their results by showing that either a high or a low corporate ratio of debt to equity can be offset by homemade leverage. The result hinges on the assumption that individuals can borrow at the same rate as corporations, an assumption we believe to be quite plausible.

3. MM's Proposition II in a world without taxes states

$$r_S = r_0 + \frac{B}{S}(r_0 - r_B)$$

This implies that the expected rate of return on equity (also called the *cost of equity* or the *required return on equity*) is positively related to the firm's leverage. This makes intuitive sense, because the risk of equity rises with leverage, a point illustrated by the differently sloped lines of Figure 16.2.

4. While the above work of MM is quite elegant, it does not explain the empirical findings on capital structure very well. MM imply that the capital structure decision is a matter of indifference, while the decision appears to be a weighty one in the real world. Still, learning the MM theory has been far from a waste of time. MM's arguments are a starting point; they show what does not matter and allow us to relax the assumptions so we can see exactly what does matter in the real world. To achieve real-world relevance, we next considered corporate taxes.

5. In a world with corporate taxes but no bankruptcy costs, firm value is an increasing function of leverage. The formula for the value of the firm is

$$V_L = V_U + T_C B$$

Expected return on levered equity can be expressed as

$$r_S = r_0 + \frac{B}{S} \times (1 - T_C) \times (r_0 - r_B)$$

Here, value is positively related to leverage. This result implies that firms should have a capital structure almost entirely composed of debt. Because real-world firms select more moderate levels of debt, the next chapter considers modifications to the results of this chapter.

KEY TERMS

MM Proposition I 444
MM Proposition II 448
MM Proposition I
  (corporate taxes) 459

MM Proposition II
  (corporate taxes) 461

Pie model 439

SUGGESTED READING

The classic papers by Modigliani and Miller are:
F. Modigliani and M. H. Miller. "The Cost of Capital, Corporation Finance, and the Theory of Investment." *American Economic Review* (June 1958).
———. "Corporate Income Taxes and the Cost of Capital: A Correction." *American Economic Review* (June 1963).

A more recent perspective on the above papers is provided by
M. Miller. "Modigliani–Miller Propositions After 30 Years." in D. Chew, ed., *The New Corporate Finance: Where Theory Meets Practice.* 3rd ed. (New York: McGraw-Hill, 2001).

QUESTIONS & PROBLEMS

Capital Structure Without Taxes

16.1   Alpha Corporation and Beta Corporation are identical in every way except their capital structures. Alpha Corporation, an all-equity firm, has 5000 shares of stock outstanding, currently worth $20 per share. Beta Corporation uses leverage in its capital structure. The market value of Beta's debt is $25,000, and its cost of debt is 13 percent. Each firm is expected to have earnings before interest of $35,000 in perpetuity. Neither firm pays taxes. Assume that every investor can borrow at 13 percent per year.
    a. What is the value of Alpha Corporation?
    b. What is the value of Beta Corporation?
    c. What is the market value of Beta Corporation's equity?
    d. How much will it cost to purchase 20 percent of each firm's equity?
    e. Assuming each firm meets its earnings estimates, what will be the dollar return to each position in part (d) over the next year?
    f. Construct an investment strategy in which an investor purchases 20 percent of Alpha's equity and replicates both the cost and dollar return of purchasing 20 percent of Beta's equity.
    g. Is Alpha's equity more or less risky than Beta's equity? Explain.

16.2   Acetate Inc. has equity with a market value of $30 million and debt with a market value of $9 million. Treasury bills that mature in one year yield 7 percent per year, and the expected return on the market portfolio over the next year is 21 percent. The beta of Acetate's equity is 0.85. The firm pays no taxes.
    a. What is Acetate's debt–equity ratio?
    b. What is the firm's weighted average cost of capital?
    c. What is the cost of capital for an otherwise identical all-equity firm?

16.3   Levered Inc. and Unlevered Inc. are identical in every way except their capital structures. Each company expects to earn $96 million before interest per year in perpetuity, with each company distributing all its earnings as dividends. Levered's perpetual debt has a market value of $275 million and costs 8 percent per year. Levered has 4.8 million shares outstanding, currently worth $98 per share. Unlevered has no debt and 10.4 million shares outstanding, currently worth $76 per share. Neither firm pays taxes. Is Levered's stock a better buy than Unlevered's stock?

Break-Even EBIT and Leverage

16.4   Taylor Corp. is comparing two different capital structures. Plan 1 would result in 900 shares of stock and $12,000 of debt. Plan 2 would result in 650 shares of stock and $15,000 of debt. The interest rate on debt is 10 percent. Ignoring taxes, compare both of these plans to an all-equity plan assuming that EBIT will be $9,500. The all-equity plan would result in 1100 shares of stock outstanding.

a. Which of the three plans has the highest EPS? The lowest?

b. Assume that Taylor Corp. will be subject to a 25 percent tax rate. Which of the three plans has the highest EPS? The lowest?

16.5   The Veblen Company and the Knight Company are identical in every respect except that Veblen is not levered. The market value of Knight Company's 6 percent bonds is $1 million. Financial information for the two firms appears here. All earnings streams are perpetuities. Neither firm pays taxes. Both firms distribute all earnings available to common shareholders immediately.

	Veblen	**Knight**
Projected operating income	$ 300,000	$ 300,000
Year-end interest on debt	—	60,000
Market value of stock	2,400,000	1,714,000
Market value of debt	—	1,000,000

a. An investor who can borrow at 6 percent per year wishes to purchase 5 percent of Knight's equity. Can he increase his dollar return by purchasing 5 percent of Veblen's equity if he borrows so that the initial net costs of the two strategies are the same?

b. Given the two investment strategies in (a), which will investors choose? When will this process cease?

EXCEL

16.6   Grimsley Inc. is an all-equity firm with 150,000 shares of common stock outstanding, worth $45 per share. Neither the firm nor its shareholders pays any taxes. Consider three shareholders of Grimsley—Ms. Cannon, Ms. Finley, and Ms. Lease. All three individuals can borrow and lend at 17 percent per annum, the same rate at which the firm lens and borrows. The values of their holdings in Grimsley and of their personal borrowing and lending positions are listed below:

	Value of Grimsley Shares	**Total Borrowing**	**Total Lending**
Ms. Cannon	$13,500	$2,500	$ 0
Ms. Finley	58,500	0	6,000
Ms. Lease	23,580	0	0

Grimsley's management recently decided to alter the firm's capital structure so that the debt-to equity ratio of the firm is 0.25. In order to do this, Grimsley issued $900,000 in debt yielding 17 percent per annum and used the funds to repurchase 20,000 shares.

The three shareholders wish to alter their positions so that their payoffs after the restructuring equal their payoffs prior to the restructuring. Assume that Grimsley immediately distributes all earnings available to shareholders at the end of the year and that the restructuring will have no effect on the firm's earnings before taxes. Show the values of each of the investors' shares in Grimsley, as well as their borrowing and lending positions, after they have adjusted their portfolios.

16.7   Rayburn Manufacturing Inc. is currently an all-equity firm that pays no taxes. The market value of the firm's equity is $5 million. The cost of this unlevered equity is 17 percent per annum. Rayburn plans to issue $1,000,000 in debt and use the proceeds to repurchase stock. The cost of debt is 11 percent per annum.

a. After Rayburn repurchases, what will the firm's weighted average cost of capital be?

b. After the repurchase, what will the cost of equity be? Explain.

c. Use your answer to (b) to compute Rayburn's weighted average cost of capital after the repurchase. Is this answer consistent with (a)?

16.8   Strom Inc. is an all-equity firm with 300,000 shares of common stock outstanding. Each share is worth $20. The firm pays no taxes. The approprirate discount rate for the firm's unlevered equity is 13 percent. Strom's earnings last year were $810,000, and management expects earnings will remain the same per annum in perpetuity. Strom is planning to buy a competitor's business for $342,500. Once acquired, the competitor's facilities are expected to increase Strom's earnings by $126,000 per year. The competitor is also an all-equity firm with the same risks as Strom and a required return on its equity of 13 percent.

a. Construct the market value balance sheet in order to fund the buyout.

b. Suppose Strom decides to issue equity in order to fund the buyout.
   1. According to the efficient markets hypothesis, what will Strom's stock price be immediately after the announcement?
   2. Construct Strom's market value balance sheet immediately after the announcement.
   3. How many shares will Strom need to issue in order to fund the buyout?
   4. Construct Strom's market value balance sheet after the equity issue but before the purchase is finalized.
   5. Construct Strom's market value balance sheet after the purchase is finalized.
   6. What is the expected return to Strom's equityholders after the buyout?
   7. What is Strom's weighted average cost of capital after the buyout?

c. Suppose Strom decides to issue 11 percent debt in order to fund the buyout.
   1. Construct Strom's market value balance sheet immediately after the announcement.
   2. Construct Strom's market value balance sheet after the debt issue but before the purchase is finalized.
   3. Construct Strom's market value balance sheet after the purchase is finalized.
   4. What is the expected return to Strom's equityholders after the buyout?
   5. What is Strom's weighted average cost of capital after the buyout?

EXCEL

16.9   The Yukon Power Company, an all-equity firm, is planning to build a new power plant. Financial data pertaining to the company and the new power plant are listed below. Assume all earnings are paid out as dividends.

Company Date	
Annual expected earnings (in perpetuity)	$34 million
Number of shares outstanding	13 million
New Power Plant	
Initial outlay	$25 million
Added annual expected earnings (in perpetuity)	5 million

The new power plant has the same risk as existing assets. The current required rate of return on the firm's equity is 11 percent. Assume there are no taxes and no costs of bankruptcy.

a. Construct Yukon's market value balance sheet before the firm announces that it will build the new power plant. What is the price per share of Yukon Power's equity?

b. Suppose Yukon Power decides to issue equity to fund the initial outlay for the power plant.
   1. Construct Yukon Power's market value balance sheet immediately after the announcement. What is the new price per share of the firm's equity?
   2. How many shares will Yukon Power need to issue in order to fund the outlay?
   3. Construct Yukon Power's market value balance sheet after the equity issue but before the outlay is made.

  4. Construct Yukon Power's market value balance sheet after the outlay has been made.
  5. What will the value of Yukon Power be if the common stock is issued to finance the construction of the new power plant?
  c. Suppose Yukon Power decides to issue $25 million of 7 percent bonds in order to fund the initial outlay for the power plant.
  1. Construct Yukon Power's market value balance sheet immediately after the announcement.
  2. Construct Yukon Power's market value balance sheet after the debt issue but before the outlay is made.
  3. Construct Yukon Power's market value balance sheet after the outlay has been made.
  4. What will the value of Yukon Power be if debt is issued to finance the construction of the new power plant?
  5. Calculate the rate of return required by equityholders after both the debt issue and the completion of the new plant.
  6. Calculate the firm's weighted average cost of capital after both the debt issue and the completion of the new plant.

16.10 In a world with no taxes, no transaction costs, and no costs of financial distress, is the following statement true, false, or uncertain? If a firm issues equity to repurchase some of its debt, the price per share of the firm's stock will rise because the shares are less risky. Explain.

16.11 Locomotive Corporation is planning to repurchase part of its common stock by issuing corporate debt. As a result, the firm's debt–equity ratio is expected to rise from 40 percent to 55 percent. The firm currently has $8.5 million worth of debt outstanding. The cost of this debt is 8.5 percent per year. Locomotive expects to have an EBIT of $4 million per year in perpetuity. Locomotive pays no taxes.
  a. What is the market value of Locomotive Corporation before and after the repurchase announcement?
  b. What is the expected return on the firm's equity before the announcement of the stock repurchase plan?
  c. What is the expected return on the equity of an otherwise identical all-equity firm?
  d. What is the expected return on the firm's equity after the announcement of the stock repurchase plan?

Capital Structure With Corporate Taxes

16.12 Green Manufacturing Inc. plans to announce that it will issue $3 million of perpetual debt and use the proceeds to repurchase common stock. The bonds will sell at par with a 4.65 percent annual coupon rate. Green is currently an all-equity firm worth $14 million with 750,000 shares of common stock outstanding. After the sale of the bonds, Green will maintain the new capital structure indefinitely. Green currently generates annual pre-tax earnings of $1.5 million. This level of earnings is expected to remain constant in perpetuity. Green is subject to a corporate tax rate of 36 percent.
  a. What is the expected return on Green's equity before the announcement of the debt issue?
  b. Construct Green's market value balance sheet before the announcement of the debt issue. What is the price per share of the firm's equity?
  c. Construct Green's market value balance sheet immediately after the announcement of the debt issue.
  d. What is Green's stock price per share immediately after the repurchase announcement?
  e. How many shares will Green repurchase as a result of the debt issue? How many shares of common stock will remain after the repurchase?

Visit us at www.mcgrawhill.ca/olc/ross

    f. Construct the market value balance sheet after the restructuring.

    g. What is the required return on Green's equity after the restructuring?

16.13 The market value of a firm with $600,000 of debt is $1.9 million. The pre-tax interest rate on debt is 12 percent per annum, and the company is in the 34 percent tax bracket. The company expects $386,000 of earnings before interest and taxes every year in perpetuity.

    a. What would the value of the firm be if it were financed entirely with equity?

    b. What amount of the firm's annual earnings is available to shareholders?

16.14 An all-equity firm has 200,000 shares of common stock outstanding, currently worth $20 per share. Its equityholders require an 18 percent return. The firm decides to issue $1.2 million of 11 percent debt and use the proceeds to repurchase common stock. According to Modigliani–Miller, what is the market value of the firm's equity after the repurchase? Assume a 31 percent corporate tax rate.

16.15 Strider Publishing Company, an all-equity firm, expects perpetual earnings before interest and taxes (EBIT) of $1.8 million per year. Strider's after-tax, all-equity discount rate is 18 percent. The firm is subject to a 36 percent corporate tax rate.

    a. What is the value of Strider Publishing?

    b. If Strider issues $750,000 of debt and uses the proceeds to repurchase stock, what will the value of the firm be?

    c. Explain any difference in your answers to (a) and (b).

    d. What assumptions are you making when valuing Strider?

16.16 Robson Inc. expects perpetual earnings before interest and taxes of $1.6 million per year. The firm's pre-tax cost of debt is 7 percent per annum, and its annual interest expense is $250,000. Company analysts estimate that the unlevered cost of Robson's equity 14 percent. Robson is subject to a 34 percent corporate tax rate.

    a. What is the value of this firm?

    b. If there are no costs of financial distress or bankruptcy, what percentage of the firm's capital structure would be financed by debt?

    c. Is the conclusion in (b) applicable to the real world?

16.17 The Appalachian Company expects perpetual earnings before interest and taxes (EBIT) of $6 million per year. The firm's after-tax, all-equity discount rate (r_0) is 14 percent. Appalachian is subject to a corporate tax rate of 35 percent. The pre-tax cost of the firm's debt capital is 11 percent per annum, and the firm has $9 million of debt in its capital structure.

    a. What is Appalachian's value?

    b. What is Appalachian's cost of equity (r_S)?

    c. What is Appalachian's weighted average cost of capital (r_{WACC})?

16.18 Williamson, Inc., has a debt-to-equity ratio of 3.5. The firm's weighted average cost of capital (r_{WACC}) is 14.6 percent, and its pre-tax cost of debt is 9.8 percent. Williamson is subject to a corporate tax rate of 35 percent.

    a. What is Williamson's cost of equity capital (r_S)?

    b. What is Williamson's unlevered cost of equity capital (r_0)?

    c. What would Williamson's weighted average cost of capital (r_{WACC}) be if the firm's debt-to-equity ratio were 0.75? What if it were 1.5?

16.19 GeneralTools (GT) expects earnings before interest and taxes (EBIT) of $210,000 every year in perpetuity. The firm currently has no debt, but it can borrow at 10 percent per annum. GT's cost of equity (r_0) is 23 percent, and the firm is subject to a corporate tax rate of 36 percent.

    a. What is the value of the firm?

    b. What will the value of GT be if it borrows $210,000 and uses the proceeds to repurchase equity?

MINICASE: Danielson Real Estate Recapitalization

Danielson Real Estate Company was founded 25 years ago by the current CEO, Gregory Danielson. The company purchases real estate, including land and buildings, and rents the property to tenants. The company has shown a profit every year for the past 18 years, and the shareholders are satisfied with the company's management. Prior to founding Danielson Real Estate, Gregory was the founder and CEO of a failed llama farming operation. The resulting bankruptcy made him extremely averse to debt financing. As a result, the company is entirely equity financed, with 15 million shares of common stock outstanding. The stock currently trades at $32.50 per share.

Danielson is evaluating a plan to purchase a huge tract of land in southeastern Saskatchewan for $100 million. The land will subsequently be leased to tenant farmers. This purchase is expected to increase Danielson's annual pre-tax earnings by $25 million in perpetuity. Kim Weyand, the company's new CFO, has been put in charge of the project. Kim has determined that the company's current cost of capital is 12.5 percent. She feels that the company would be more valuable if it included debt in its capital structure, therefore she is evaluating whether the company should issue debt to entirely finance the project. Based on some conversations with investment banks, she thinks that the company can issue bonds at par value with an 8 percent coupon rate. Based on her analysis, she also believes that a capital structure in the range of 70 percent equity/30 percent debt would be optimal. If the company goes beyond 30 percent debt, its bonds would carry a lower rating and a much higher coupon because the possibility of financial distress and the associated costs would rise sharply. Danielson has a 38 percent corporate tax rate.

1. If Danielson wishes to maximize its total market value, would you recommend that it issue debt or equity to finance the land purchase? Explain.
2. Construct Danielson's market value balance sheet before it announces the purchase.
3. Suppose Danielson decides to issue equity to finance the purchase.
   a. What is the net present value of the project?
   b. Construct Danielson's market value balance sheet after it announces that the firm will finance the purchase using equity. What would be the new price per share of the firm's stock? How many shares will Danielson need to issue to finance the purchase?
   c. Construct Danielson's market value balance sheet after the equity issue but before the purchase has been made. How many shares of common stock does Danielson have outstanding? What is the price per share of the firm's stock?
   d. Construct Danielson's market value balance sheet after the purchase has been made.
4. Suppose Danielson decides to issue debt to finance the purchase.
   a. What will the market value of the company be if the purchase is financed with debt?
   b. Construct Danielson's market value balance sheet after both the debt issue and the land purchase. What is the price per share of the firm's stock?
5. Which method of financing maximizes the per share stock price of Danielson's equity?

16.20 Locate the annual balance sheets for BCE Inc. (BCE), Magna International Inc. (MGA), and Telus Corp. (TU). For each company calculate the long-term debt-to-equity ratio for the prior two years. Why would these companies use such different capital structures?

STANDARD &POOR'S

www.mcgrawhill.ca/ edumarketinsight

16.21 Look up Thomson Corp. (TOC) and download the annual income statements. For the most recent year, calculate the marginal tax rate, EBIT, and find the total interest expense. From the annual balance sheets calculate the total long-term debt (including the portion due within one year). Using the interest expense and total long-term debt, calculate the average cost of debt. The current beta of Thomson is 0.63. Use this beta and the historical average risk-free rate and market risk premium found in Chapter 10 to calculate the levered cost of equity. Now calculate the unlevered cost of equity. What is the unlevered value of Thomson? What is the interest tax shield and the value of the levered Thomson?

Chapter 17

Capital Structure: Limits to the Use of Debt

EXECUTIVE SUMMARY

A student might ask whether the MM theory with taxes predicts the capital structures of typical firms. The answer is, unfortunately, no. The theory states that $V_L = V_U + T_C B$. One can always increase firm value by increasing leverage, implying that firms should issue maximum debt. This is inconsistent with the real world, where firms generally employ only moderate amounts of debt.

However, the MM theory tells us *where to look* when searching for the determinants of capital structure. For example, the theory ignores bankruptcy and its attendant costs. These costs can get out of hand for a highly levered firm like Eaton's or Canada 3000. The moderate leverage of most firms can now easily be explained.

In addition, the MM theory ignores personal taxes. In the real world, the *personal* tax rate on interest is higher than the *effective* personal tax rate on equity distributions. Thus, the personal tax penalties to bondholders tend to offset the tax benefits to debt at the corporate level. Even when bankruptcy costs are ignored, this idea can be shown to imply that there is an optimal amount of debt for the economy as a whole. The implications of bankruptcy costs and personal taxes are examined in this chapter.

17.1 Costs of Financial Distress

Bankruptcy Risk or Bankruptcy Cost?

As mentioned throughout the previous chapter, debt provides tax benefits to the firm. However, debt puts pressure on the firm, because interest and principal payments are obligations. If these obligations are not met, the firm may risk some sort of financial distress. The ultimate distress is *bankruptcy,* in which ownership of the firm's assets is legally transferred from the shareholders to the bondholders. These debt obligations are fundamentally different from stock obligations. While shareholders like and expect dividends, they are not legally entitled to dividends in the way bondholders are legally entitled to interest and principal payments.

We show in Example 17.1 that bankruptcy costs, or, more generally, financial distress costs, tend to offset the advantages to debt. We begin by positing a simple illustration of bankruptcy. All taxes are ignored to focus only on the costs of debt.

EXAMPLE 17.1

The Knight Corporation plans to be in business for one more year. It forecasts a cash flow of either $100 or $50 in the coming year, each occurring with 50 percent probability. Previously issued debt requires payments of $49 of interest and principal. The Day Corporation has identical cash flow prospects but has $60 of interest and principal obligations. The cash flows of these two firms can be represented as

	Knight Corp.		Day Corp.	
	Boom Times (prob. 50%)	Recession (prob. 50%)	Boom Times (prob. 50%)	Recession (prob. 50%)
Cash flow	$100	$50	$100	$50
Payment of interest and principal on debt	49	49	60	50
Distribution to shareholders	$ 51	$ 1	$ 40	$ 0

The Day Corporation will be bankrupt in a recession. Note that, under the law, corporations have limited liability. Thus, Day's bondholders will receive only $50 in a recession; they cannot get the additional $10 from the shareholders.[1]

We assume that (1) both bondholders and shareholders are risk neutral and (2) the interest rate is 10 percent. Due to this risk neutrality, cash flows to both shareholders and bondholders are to be discounted at the 10 percent rate.[2] We can evaluate the debt, the equity, and the entire firm for both Knight and Day as follows:

$$S_{\text{KNIGHT}} = \$23.64 = \frac{\$51 \times \frac{1}{2} + \$1 \times \frac{1}{2}}{1.10} \qquad S_{\text{DAY}} = \$18.18 = \frac{\$40 \times \frac{1}{2} + 0 \times \frac{1}{2}}{1.10}$$

$$B_{\text{KNIGHT}} = \$44.54 = \frac{\$49 \times \frac{1}{2} + \$49 \times \frac{1}{2}}{1.10} \qquad B_{\text{DAY}} = \$50 = \frac{\$60 \times \frac{1}{2}}{1.10} + \frac{\$60 \times \frac{1}{2} + \$50 \times \frac{1}{2}}{1.10}$$

$$V_{\text{KNIGHT}} = \$68.18 \qquad V_{\text{DAY}} = \$68.18$$

Note that the two firms have the same value, even though Day runs the risk of bankruptcy. Furthermore, notice that Day's bondholders are valuing the bonds with their eyes open. Though the promised payment of principal and interest is $60, the bondholders are willing to pay only $50. Hence, their *promised* return or yield is

$$\frac{\$60}{\$50} - 1 = 20\%$$

Day's debt can be viewed as a *junk bond,* because the probability of default is so high. As with all junk bonds, bondholders demand a high promised yield.

---

[1]There are situations in which the limited liability of a corporation can be "pierced." Typically, fraud or misrepresentation must be present.

[2]Normally, one assumes that investors are averse to risk. In that case, the cost of debt capital, r_B, is less than the cost of equity capital, r_S, which rises with leverage as shown in the previous chapter. In addition, r_B may rise when the increase in leverage allows the possibility of default.

For simplicity, we assume *risk neutrality* in this example. This means that investors are indifferent to whether risk is high, low, or even absent. Here, $r_S = r_B$, because risk-neutral investors do not demand compensation for bearing risk. In addition, neither r_S nor r_B rises with leverage. Because the interest rate is 10 percent, our assumption of risk neutrality implies that $r_S = 10\%$ as well.

Though financial economists believe that investors are risk averse, they frequently develop examples based on risk neutrality to isolate a point unrelated to risk. This is our approach, because we want to focus on bankruptcy costs—not bankruptcy risk. The same qualitative conclusions from this example can be drawn in a world of risk aversion, albeit with much more difficulty for the reader.

The Day example is not realistic because it ignores an important cash flow, to be discussed below. A more realistic set of numbers might be

DAY CORP.

	Boom Times (prob. 50%)	Recession (prob. 50%)	
Cash flow	$100	$50	$S_{DAY} = \$18.18 = \dfrac{\$40 \times \frac{1}{2} + 0 \times \frac{1}{2}}{1.10}$
Debt repayment	60	35	$B_{DAY} = \$43.18 = \dfrac{\$60 \times \frac{1}{2} + \$35 \times \frac{1}{2}}{1.10}$
Distribution to shareholders	$ 40	$ 0	$V_{DAY} = \$61.36$

Why do the bondholders receive only $35 in a recession? If cash flow is only $50, bondholders will be informed that they are not paid in full. These bondholders are likely to hire lawyers to negotiate or even to sue the company. Similarly, the firm is likely to hire lawyers to defend itself. Further costs will be incurred if the case gets to a bankruptcy court. These fees are always paid before the bondholders get paid. In this example, we are assuming that bankruptcy costs total $15 (or $50 − $35).

The value of the firm is now $61.36, an amount below the $68.18 figure calculated earlier. By comparing Day's value in a world with no bankruptcy costs against Day's value in a world with these costs, we conclude

The possibility of bankruptcy has a negative effect on the value of the firm. However, it is not the risk of bankruptcy itself that lowers value. Rather, it is the costs associated with bankruptcy that lower value.

The explanation follows from our pie example. In a world of no bankruptcy costs, the bondholders and the shareholders share the entire pie. However, bankruptcy costs eat up some of the pie in the real world, leaving less for the shareholders and bondholders.

Because the bondholders are aware that they receive little in a recession, they pay a lower price. In this case, their promised return is

$$\frac{\$60}{\$43.18} - 1 = 39.0\%$$

The bondholders are paying a fair price if they are realistic about both the probability and the cost of bankruptcy. It is the *shareholders* who bear these future bankruptcy costs. To see this, imagine that Day Corp. was originally all equity. The shareholders want the firm to issue debt with a promised payment of $60 and use the proceeds to pay a dividend. If there had been no bankruptcy costs, our results show that bondholders would pay $50 to purchase debt with a promised payment of $60. Hence, a dividend of $50 could be paid to the shareholders. However, if bankruptcy costs exist, bondholders would only pay $43.18 for the debt. In that case, only a dividend of $43.18 could be paid to the shareholders. Because the dividend is less when bankruptcy costs exist, the shareholders are hurt by bankruptcy costs

? Concept Questions

- **What does risk neutrality mean?**
- **Can one have bankruptcy risk without bankruptcy costs?**
- **Why do we say that shareholders bear bankruptcy costs?**

17.2 Description of Costs

The example above showed that bankruptcy costs can lower the value of the firm. In fact, the same general result holds even if a legal bankruptcy is prevented. Thus, *financial distress costs* may be a better phrase than *bankruptcy costs.* It is worthwhile to describe these costs in more detail.

Direct Costs of Financial Distress: Legal and Administrative Costs of Liquidation or Reorganization

As mentioned earlier, lawyers are involved throughout all the stages before and during bankruptcy. With fees often in the hundreds of dollars an hour, these costs can add up quickly. In addition, administrative and accounting fees can substantially add to the total bill. And if a trial takes place, we must not forget expert witnesses. Each side may hire a number of these witnesses to testify about the fairness of a proposed settlement. Their fees can easily rival those of lawyers or accountants. (However, we personally look upon these witnesses more kindly, because they are frequently drawn from the ranks of finance professors.)

Perhaps one of the most well-publicized bankruptcies in recent years concerned a municipality—Orange County, California—not a corporation. This bankruptcy followed large bond-trading losses in the county's financial portfolio. The *Los Angeles Times* stated:

> Orange County taxpayers lost [U.S.] $1.69 billion, and their government, one year ago today, sank into bankruptcy. Now they are spending millions more to get out of it.
>
> Accountants pore over fiscal ledgers at $325 an hour. Lawyers toil into the night—at $385 an hour. Financial advisors from one of the nation's most prominent investment houses labor for the taxpayers at $150,000 a month. Clerks stand by the photocopy machines, running up bills that sometimes exceed $3,000.
>
> Total so far: $29 million. And it's nowhere near over.
>
> The multi-pronged effort to lift Orange County out of the nation's worst municipal bankruptcy has become a money-eating machine, gobbling up taxpayer funds at a rate of $2.4 million a month. That's $115,000 a day.
>
> County administrators are not alarmed.
>
> They say Orange County's bankruptcy was an epic disaster that will require equally dramatic expenditures of taxpayer cash to help it survive. While they have refused to pay several thousand dollars' worth of claimed expenses—lavish dinners, big hotel bills—they have rarely questioned the sky-high hourly fees. They predict the costs could climb much higher.
>
> Indeed, participants in the county's investment pool have agreed to create a separate $50 million fund to pay the costs of doing legal battle with Wall Street.[3]

Bankruptcy costs in the private sector are often far larger than those in Orange County. For example, as of 2005, the direct costs of Enron's and Worldcom's bankruptcies were commonly estimated to exceed $1 billion and $600 million, respectively.

A number of academic studies have measured the direct costs of financial distress. While large in absolute amount, these costs are actually small as a percentage of firm value. White, Altman, and Weiss estimate the direct costs of financial distress to be about 3 percent of market value for U.S. firms. Fisher and Martel find that the costs are closer to

---

[3]"The High Cost of Going Bankrupt," *Los Angeles Times Orange County Edition,* December 6, 1995. Taken from Lexis/Nexis. All amounts are in U.S. dollars.

6 percent of firm value for a sample of Canadian bankruptcies.[4] In a study of direct financial distress costs of 20 railroad bankruptcies, Warner finds that net financial distress costs were, on average, 1 percent of the market value of the firm seven years before bankruptcy and were somewhat larger percentages as bankruptcy approached (for example, 2.5 percent of the market value of the firm three years before bankruptcy).[5] Of course, few firms end up in bankruptcy. Thus, the preceding cost estimates must be multiplied by the probability of bankruptcy to yield the *expected* cost of bankruptcy. Warner states:

> Suppose, for example, that a given railroad picks a level of debt such that bankruptcy would occur on average once every 20 years (i.e., the probability of going bankrupt is 5 percent in any given year). Assume that when bankruptcy occurs, the firm would pay a lump sum penalty equal to 3 percent of its now current market value. . . .
>
> [Then], the firm's expected cost of bankruptcy is equal to fifteen one-hundredths of one percent of its now current market value.

Indirect Costs of Financial Distress

Impaired Ability to Conduct Business   Bankruptcy hampers conduct with customers and suppliers. Sales are frequently lost because of both fear of impaired service and loss of trust. For example, many loyal Chrysler customers switched to other manufacturers when Chrysler skirted insolvency in the 1970s. These buyers questioned whether parts and servicing would be available were Chrysler to fail. Sometimes the taint of impending bankruptcy is enough to drive customers away. For example, gamblers avoided Atlantis casino in Atlantic City after it became technically insolvent. Gamblers are a superstitious bunch. Many reasoned, "If the casino itself cannot make money, how can I expect to make money there?" A particularly outrageous story concerned two unrelated stores, both named Mitchells. When one Mitchells declared bankruptcy, customers stayed away from both stores. In time, the second store was forced to declare bankruptcy as well.

Though these costs clearly exist, it is quite difficult to measure them. Altman has estimated that both direct and indirect costs are frequently greater than 20 percent of firm value.[6]

Andrade and Kaplan estimate total distress costs to be between 10 percent and 20 percent of firm value.[7] Bar-Or estimates expected future distress costs for firms that are

---

[4]M. J. White, "Bankruptcy Costs and the New Bankruptcy Code," *Journal of Finance* (May 1983); and E. I. Altman, " A Further Empirical Investigation of the Bankruptcy Cost Question," *Journal of Finance* (September 1984). More recently, Lawrence A. Weiss, "Bankruptcy Resolution: Direct Costs and Violation of Priority of Claims," *Journal of Financial Economics* 27 (1990), estimates that direct costs of bankruptcy are 3.1 percent of the value of the firm. Canadian bankruptcies are examined in: T. C. G. Fisher and J. Martel, "The Bankruptcy Decision: Empirical Evidence from Canada," Working Paper, Wilfrid Laurier University (November 2000).

[5]J. B. Warner, "Bankruptcy Costs: Some Evidence," *Journal of Finance* (May 1977).

[6]David M. Cutler and Lawrence H. Summers, "The Costs of Conflict Resolution and Financial Distress: Evidence from the Texaco–Pennzoil Litigation," *Rand Journal of Economics* 19 (1988), estimate the indirect costs of Texaco's 1987 bankruptcy to be about 9 percent of the firm's value. Steven N. Kaplan, "Campeau's Acquisition of Federated: Value Added or Destroyed," *Journal of Financial Economics* 24 (1989), finds the indirect costs of financial distress for Campeau to be very small.

The work of L. Lang and R. Stulz, "Contagious and Competitive Intra-Industry Effects of Bankruptcy Announcements: An Empirical Analysis," *Journal of Financial Economics* (August 1992) and T. Opler and S. Titman, "Financial Distress and Corporate Performance," *Journal of Finance* (July 1994) suggest indirect financial distress costs are substantial. T. Opler, "Controlling Financial Distress Costs in LBOs," *Financial Management* (Autumn 1993) shows that LBO financing techniques can be expected to reduce the costs of financial distress.

[7]Gregor Andrade and Steven N. Kaplan, "How Costly is Financial (Not Economic) Distress? Evidence from Highly Leveraged Transactions That Became Distressed," *Journal of Finance* (October 1998).

currently healthy to be 8 to 10 percent of operating value, a number below the estimates of either Altman or Andrade and Kaplan.[8] However, unlike Bar-Or, these authors consider distress costs for firms already in distress, not expected distress costs for currently healthy firms.

Agency Costs

When a firm has debt, conflicts of interest arise between shareholders and bondholders, and shareholders are tempted to pursue selfish strategies. These conflicts of interest, which are magnified when financial distress occurs, impose **agency costs** on the firm. We describe three kinds of selfish strategies that shareholders use to hurt the bondholders and help themselves. These strategies are costly because they will lower the market value of the whole firm.

Selfish Investment Strategy 1: Incentive to Take Large Risks   Firms near bankruptcy often take great chances, because they feel that they are playing with someone else's money. A good example of this occurred in the failure of two banks in Western Canada in 1985. Because they were allowed to stay in business although they were economically insolvent, the banks had nothing to lose by taking great risks. Because of these and other failures, the Canada Deposit Insurance Corporation declared a multibillion-dollar deficit in late 1993.[9]

To see how the incentive to take risk works, imagine a levered firm considering two mutually exclusive projects: a low-risk one and a high-risk one. There are two equally likely outcomes: recession and boom. The firm is in such dire straits that, should a recession hit, it will come near to bankruptcy with one project and actually fall into bankruptcy with the other. The cash flows for the firm if the low-risk project is taken can be described as

Value of Entire Firm if Low-Risk Project Is Chosen

	Probability	Value of Firm	=	Stock	+	Bonds
Recession	0.5	$100	=	$ 0	+	$100
Boom	0.5	$200	=	$100	+	$100

If recession occurs, the value of the firm will be $100, and if boom occurs, the value of the firm will be $200. The expected value of the firm is $150 (or $0.5 \times \$100 + 0.5 \times \$200$).

The firm has promised to pay bondholders $100. Shareholders will obtain the difference between the total payoff and the amount paid to the bondholders. The bondholders have the prior claim on the payoffs, and the shareholders have the residual claim.

Now suppose that a riskier project can be substituted for the low-risk project. The payoffs and probabilities are as follows:

Value of Entire Firm if High-Risk Project Is Chosen

	Probability	Value of Firm	=	Stock	+	Bonds
Recession	0.5	$ 50	=	$ 0	+	$ 50
Boom	0.5	$240	=	$140	+	$100

The expected value of the firm is $145 (or $0.5 \times \$50 + 0.5 \times \$240$), which is lower than the expected value with the low-risk project. Thus, the low-risk project would

---

[8]Yuval Bar-Or, "An Investigation of Expected Financial Distress Costs," unpublished paper, Wharton School, University of Pennsylvania (March 2000).

[9]The same thing happened on a grander scale in the U.S. savings and loan debacle. Edward J. Kane, *The Savings and Loan Mess* (Washington, D.C.: Urban Institute Press, 1989), estimates that closing S&Ls when they first became insolvent, thus preventing them from gambling with deposits insured with taxpayers' money, would have saved half of the over U.S. $100 billion bill for cleaning up the industry.

**TABLE 17.1
Example
Illustrating
Incentive to
Underinvest**

	Firm Without Project		Firm With Project	
	Boom	Recession	Boom	Recession
Firm cash flows	$5,000	$2,400	$6,700	$4,100
Bondholders' claim	4,000	2,400	4,000	4,000
Shareholders' claim	$1,000	$ 0	$2,700	$ 100

The project has positive NPV. However, much of its value is captured by bondholders. Rational managers, acting in the shareholders' interest, will reject the project.

be accepted if the firm were all equity. However, note that the expected value of the stock is $70 (or $0.5 \times \$0 + 0.5 \times \$140$) with the high-risk project, but only $50 (or $0.5 \times \$0 + 0.5 \times \$100$) with the low-risk project. Given the firm's present levered state, shareholders will select the high-risk project.

The key is that, relative to the low-risk project, the high-risk project increases firm value in a boom and decreases firm value in a recession. The increase in value in a boom is captured by the shareholders, because the bondholders are paid in full (they receive $100) regardless of which project is accepted. Conversely, the drop in value in a recession is lost by the bondholders, because they are paid in full with the low-risk project but receive only $50 with the high-risk one. The shareholders will receive nothing in a recession anyway, whether the high-risk or low-risk project is selected. Thus, financial economists argue that shareholders expropriate value from the bondholders by selecting high-risk projects.

Selfish Investment Strategy 2: Incentive Toward Underinvestment   Shareholders of a firm with a significant probability of bankruptcy often find that new investment helps the bondholders at the shareholders' expense. The simplest case might be a real estate owner facing imminent bankruptcy. If he took $100,000 out of his own pocket to refurbish the building, he could increase the building's value by, say, $150,000. Though this investment has a positive net present value, he will turn it down if the increase in value cannot prevent bankruptcy. "Why," he asks, "should I use my own funds to improve the value of a building that the bank will soon repossess?"

This idea is formalized by the following simple example. Consider a firm with $4,000 of principal and interest payments due at the end of the year. It will be pulled into bankruptcy by a recession because its cash flows will be only $2,400 in that state. The firm's cash flows are presented in the left-hand side of Table 17.1. The firm could avoid bankruptcy in a recession by raising new equity to invest in a new project. The project costs $1,000 and brings in $1,700 in either state, implying a positive net present value. Clearly it would be accepted in an all-equity firm.

However, the project hurts the shareholders of the levered firm. To see this, imagine that the old shareholders contribute the $1,000 *themselves*.[10] The expected value of the shareholders' interest without the project is $500 (or $0.5 \times \$1,000 + 0.5 \times \$0$). The expected value with the project is $1,400 (or $0.5 \times \$2,700 + 0.5 \times \$100$). The shareholders' interest rises by only $900 (or $\$1,400 - \$500$) while costing $1,000.

The key is that the shareholders contribute the full $1,000 investment, but the shareholders and bondholders *share* the benefits. The shareholders take the entire gain if boom times occur. Conversely, the bondholders reap most of the cash flow from the project in a recession.

---

[10]The same qualitative results will be obtained if the $1,000 is raised from new shareholders. However, the arithmetic becomes much more difficult since we must determine how many new shares are issued.

The discussion of Selfish Strategy 1 is quite similar to the discussion of Selfish Strategy 2. In both cases, an investment strategy for the levered firm is different from the one for the unlevered firm. Thus, leverage results in distorted investment policy. Whereas the unlevered corporation always chooses projects with positive net present value, the levered firm may deviate from this policy.

Selfish Investment Strategy 3: Milking the Property   Another strategy is to pay out extra dividends or other distributions in times of financial distress, leaving less in the firm for the bondholders. This is known as *milking the property,* a phrase taken from real estate. Strategies 2 and 3 are very similar. In Strategy 2, the firm chooses not to raise new equity. Strategy 3 goes one step further, because equity is actually withdrawn through the dividend.

Summary of Selfish Strategies   The above distortions occur only when there is a probability of bankruptcy or financial distress. Thus, these distortions *should not* affect, say, Bell Canada Enterprises (BCE) because bankruptcy is not a realistic possibility for a diversified blue-chip firm such as this. In other words, BCE's debt will be virtually risk-free, regardless of the projects it accepts. The same argument could be made for regulated utilities like TransCanada Corporation that are protected by federal and provincial energy boards. However, biotechnology firms like Viventia Biotech and other high-tech companies might be very affected by these distortions. Viventia has significant future investment opportunities as compared to assets in place and faces intense competition and uncertain future revenues. Because the distortions are related to financial distress, we included them in the earlier section, "Indirect Costs of Financial Distress."

Who pays the cost of selfish investment strategies? We argue that it is ultimately the shareholders. Rational bondholders know that when financial distress is imminent, they cannot expect help from shareholders. Rather, shareholders are likely to choose investment strategies that reduce the value of the bonds. Bondholders protect themselves accordingly by raising the interest rate that they require on the bonds. Because the shareholders must pay these higher rates, they ultimately bear the costs of selfish strategies.

For firms that face these distortions, debt financing will be difficult and costly to obtain. These firms will have low leverage ratios.

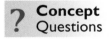

Concept Questions
- **What is the main direct cost of financial distress?**
- **What are the indirect costs of financial distress?**
- **Who pays the costs of selfish strategies?**

17.3 Can Costs of Debt Be Reduced?

Each of the costs of financial distress we mentioned above is substantial in its own right. The sum of them may well affect debt financing severely. Thus, managers have an incentive to reduce these costs. We now turn to some of their methods. However, it should be mentioned at the outset that these methods can, at most, reduce the costs of debt. They cannot eliminate them entirely.

Protective Covenants

Because the shareholders must pay higher interest rates as insurance against their own selfish strategies, they frequently make arrangements with bondholders in hopes of lowering rates. These agreements, called **protective covenants,** are incorporated as part of the loan document (or *indenture*) between shareholders and bondholders. The covenants must be taken seriously since a broken covenant can lead to default. Protective covenants can be classified into two types: negative covenants and positive covenants.

A **negative covenant** limits or prohibits actions that the company may take. Here are some typical negative covenants:

1. Limitations are placed on the amount of dividends a company may pay.
2. The firm may not pledge any of its assets to other lenders.
3. The firm may not merge with another firm.
4. The firm may not sell or lease its major assets without approval by the lender.
5. The firm may not issue additional long-term debt of equal or higher seniority.

A **positive covenant** specifies an action that the company agrees to take or a condition the company must abide by. Here are some examples:

1. The company agrees to maintain its working capital at a minimum level.
2. The company must furnish periodic financial statements to the lender.
3. The company must segregate and maintain specified assets as security for the debt.

These lists of covenants are not exhaustive. We have seen loan agreements with more than 30 covenants. Smith and Warner examined public issues of debt and found that 91 percent of the bond indentures included covenants that restricted the issuance of additional debt, 23 percent restricted dividends, 39 percent restricted mergers, and 36 percent limited the sale of assets.[11] A list of typical bond covenants and their uses appears in Table 17.2.

Protective covenants should reduce the costs of bankruptcy, ultimately increasing the value of the firm. Thus, shareholders are likely to favour all reasonable covenants. To see this, consider three choices by shareholders to reduce bankruptcy costs.

1. *Issue no debt.* Because of the tax advantages to debt, this is a very costly way of avoiding conflicts.
2. *Issue debt with no restrictive and protective covenants.* In this case, the market price of debt will be much lower (and the cost of debt much higher) than would otherwise be true.
3. *Write protective and restrictive covenants into the loan contracts.* If the covenants are clearly written, the creditors may receive protection without large costs being imposed on the shareholders. They will happily accept a lower interest rate. Roberts and Viscione found that secured debt (bonds with positive covenant 3 above) carried lower yields than unsecured bonds.[12]

Thus, bond covenants, even if they reduce flexibility, can increase the value of the firm. They can be the lowest-cost solution to the shareholder–bondholder conflict.

Consolidation of Debt

One reason why bankruptcy costs are so high is that different creditors (and their lawyers) fight with each other. This problem can be alleviated if one lender or at most a few lenders can shoulder the entire debt. Should financial distress occur, negotiating costs are minimized under this arrangement. In addition, bondholders can purchase stock as well. In

---

[11]C. W. Smith and J. B. Warner, "On Financial Contracting: An Analysis of Bond Covenants," *Journal of Financial Economics* 7 (1979).

[12]G. S. Roberts and J. A. Viscione, "The Impact of Seniority and Security Covenants on Bond Yields," *Journal of Finance* (December 1984).

TABLE 17.2   Loan Covenants

Covenant Type	Shareholder Action or Firm Circumstances	Reason for Covenant

Financial-statement signals
  1. Working capital requirement
  2. Interest coverage
  3. Minimum net worth
	As the firm approaches financial distress, shareholders may want the firm to make high-risk investments.	Shareholders lose value before bankruptcy; bondholders are hurt much more in bankruptcy than shareholders (limited liability); bondholders are hurt by *distortion of investment that leads to increases in risk.*

Restrictions on asset disposition
  1. Limit dividends
  2. Limit sale of assets
  3. Collateral and mortgages
	Shareholders attempt to transfer corporate assets to themselves.	This limits the ability of shareholders to transfer assets to themselves and to *underinvest.*

Restrictions on switching assets	Shareholders attempt to increase risk of the firm.	Increased firm risk helps shareholders; bondholders hurt by *distortion of investment that leads to increases in risk.*

Dilution
  1. Limit on leasing
  2. Limit on further borrowing
	Shareholders may attempt to issue new debt of equal or greater priority.	This restricts *dilution of the claim of existing bondholders.*

this way, shareholders and debtholders are not pitted against each other, because they are not separate entities. This appears to be the approach in Japan where large banks generally take significant stock positions in the firms to which they lend money.[13] Debt–equity ratios in Japan are far higher than those in Canada and the United States.

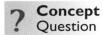 **Concept Question**

• **How can covenants and debt consolidation reduce debt agency costs?**

17.4 Integration of Tax Effects and Financial Distress Costs

Modigliani and Miller argue that the firm's value rises with leverage in the presence of corporate taxes. Because this implies that all firms should choose maximum debt, the theory does not predict the behaviour of firms in the real world. Other authors have suggested that bankruptcy and related costs reduce the value of the levered firm.

The integration of tax effects and distress costs appears in Figure 17.1. At the top of the figure, the diagonal straight line in the figure represents the value of the firm in a world without bankruptcy costs. The ∩-shaped curve represents the value of the firm with these costs. This curve rises as the firm moves from all-equity to a small amount of debt. Here, the present value of the distress costs is minimal because the probability of distress is so small. However, as more and more debt is added, the present value of these costs rises at an *increasing* rate. At some point, the increase in the present value of these costs from an additional dollar of debt equals the increase in the present value of the tax shield. This is the debt level maximizing the value of the firm and is represented by B^* in Figure 17.1. In other words, B^* is the optimal amount of debt. Bankruptcy costs increase faster than the

---

[13]Canadian and U.S. banks are becoming increasingly interested in taking equity options when lending to higher-risk firms. Convertible bonds (discussed in Chapter 25) include an equity option partly as a way of controlling agency costs.

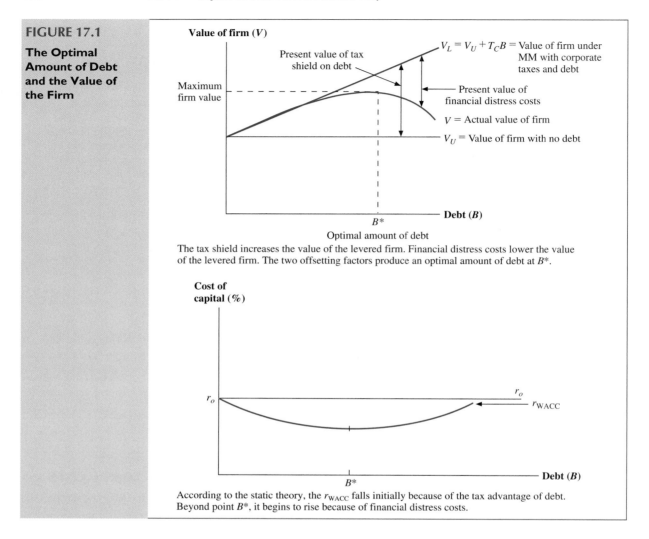

FIGURE 17.1

The Optimal Amount of Debt and the Value of the Firm

Value of firm (V)

Present value of tax shield on debt

$V_L = V_U + T_C B$ = Value of firm under MM with corporate taxes and debt

Maximum firm value

Present value of financial distress costs

V = Actual value of firm

V_U = Value of firm with no debt

Debt (B)

B^*

Optimal amount of debt

The tax shield increases the value of the levered firm. Financial distress costs lower the value of the levered firm. The two offsetting factors produce an optimal amount of debt at B^*.

Cost of capital (%)

r_o

r_o

r_{WACC}

B^*

Debt (B)

According to the static theory, the r_{WACC} falls initially because of the tax advantage of debt. Beyond point B^*, it begins to rise because of financial distress costs.

tax shield beyond this point, implying a reduction in firm value from further leverage. At the bottom of Figure 17.1, the weighted average cost of capital (r_{WACC}) goes down as debt is added to the capital structure. After reaching B^* the weighted average cost of capital goes up. The optimal amount of debt also produces the lowest weighted average cost of capital.

Our discussion implies that a firm's capital structure decisions involve a trade-off between the tax benefits of debt and the costs of financial distress. In fact, this approach is frequently called the *trade-off* or the *static trade-off theory* of capital structure. The implication is that there is an optimum amount of debt for any individual firm. This amount of debt becomes the firm's target debt level. (In the real world of finance, this optimum is frequently referred to as the firm's *debt capacity*.) Because financial distress costs cannot be expressed in a precise way, no formula has yet been developed to determine a firm's optimal debt level exactly. However, the last section of this chapter offers some rules of thumb for selecting a debt–equity ratio in the real world. Our situation is reminiscent of a quote of John Maynard Keynes. He reputedly said that, although most historians would agree that Queen Elizabeth I was both a better monarch and an unhappier woman than Queen Victoria, no one has yet been able to express the statement in a precise and rigorous formula.

Pie Again

Critics of the MM theory often say that MM fails when we add such real-world issues as taxes and bankruptcy costs. Taking that view, however, blinds critics to the real value of the MM theory. The pie approach offers a more constructive way of thinking about these matters and the role of capital structure.

Taxes are just another claim on the cash flows of the firm. Let G (for government and taxes) stand for the market value of the government's claim to the firm's taxes. Bankruptcy costs are another claim on the cash flows. Let us label their value with an L (for lawyers). The cash flows to the claim L rise with the debt–equity ratio.

The pie theory says that all of these claims are paid from only one source, the cash flows (CF) of the firm. Algebraically, we must have

$$\text{CF} = \text{Payments to shareholders}$$
$$+$$
$$\text{Payments to bondholders}$$
$$+$$
$$\text{Payments to the government}$$
$$+$$
$$\text{Payments to lawyers}$$
$$+$$
$$\text{Payments to any and all other claimants}$$
$$\text{to the cash flows of the firms}$$

Figure 17.2 shows the new pie. No matter how many slices we take and no matter who gets them, they must still add up to the total cash flow. The value of the firm, V_T, is unaltered by the capital structure. Now, however, we must be broader in our definition of the firm's value:

$$V_T = S + B + G + L$$

We previously wrote the firm's value as

$$S + B$$

when we ignored taxes and bankruptcy costs.

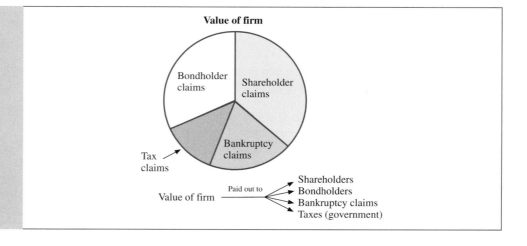

FIGURE 17.2

The Pie Model with Real-World Factors

Value of firm

Bondholder claims

Shareholder claims

Tax claims

Bankruptcy claims

Value of firm —— Paid out to → Shareholders
→ Bondholders
→ Bankruptcy claims
→ Taxes (government)

Nor have we even begun to exhaust the list of financial claims to the firm's cash flows. To give an unusual example, everyone reading this book has an economic claim to the cash flows of Ford Motor Company of Canada. After all, if you are injured in an accident, you might sue Ford. Win or lose, Ford will expend resources dealing with the matter. If you think this is farfetched and unimportant, ask yourself what Ford might be willing to pay every man, woman, and child in the country to have them promise that they would never sue the company, no matter what happened. The law does not permit such payments, but that does not mean that a value to all of those potential claims does not exist. We guess that it would run into billions of dollars, and, for Ford or any other company, there should be a slice of the pie labelled *LS* for "potential lawsuits."

This is the essence of the MM intuition and theory: V is $V(CF)$ and depends on the total cash flow of the firm. The capital structure cuts it into slices.

There is, however, an important difference between claims such as those of shareholders and bondholders on the one hand and those of government and potential litigants in lawsuits on the other. The first set of claims are **marketed claims,** and the second set are **nonmarketed claims.** One difference is that the marketed claims can be bought and sold in financial markets, and the nonmarketed claims cannot.

When we speak of the value of the firm, generally we are referring just to the value of the marketed claims, V_M, and not the value of nonmarketed claims, V_N. What we have shown is that the total value,

$$V_T = S + B + G + L$$
$$= V_M + V_N$$

is unaltered. But, as we saw, the value of the marketed claims, V_M, can change with changes in the capital structure in general and the debt–equity ratio in particular.

By the pie theory, any increase in V_M must imply an identical decrease in V_N. In an efficient market, we showed that the capital structure will be chosen to maximize the value of the marketed claims, V_M. We can equivalently think of the efficient market as working to minimize the value of the nonmarketed claims, V_N. These are taxes and bankruptcy costs in the previous example, but they also include all the other nonmarketed claims such as the *LS* claim.

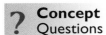

Concept Questions
- **List all the claims to the firm's assets.**
- **Describe marketed claims and nonmarketed claims.**
- **How can a firm maximize the value of its marketed claims?**

17.5 Signalling

The previous section pointed out that the corporate leverage decision involves a trade-off between a tax subsidy and financial distress costs. This idea was graphed in Figure 17.1, where the marginal tax subsidy of debt exceeds the distress costs of debt for low levels of debt. The reverse holds for high levels of debt. The firm's capital structure is optimized where the marginal subsidy to debt equals the marginal cost.

Let's explore this idea a little more. What is the relationship between a company's profitability and its debt level? A firm with low anticipated profits will likely take on a low level of debt. A small interest deduction is all that is needed to offset all of this firm's pre-tax profits. And, too much debt would raise the firm's expected distress costs. A more successful firm would probably take on more debt. This firm could use the extra interest to reduce the taxes from its greater earnings. And, being more financially secure, this firm would find its extra debt increasing the risk of bankruptcy only slightly. In other words, rational firms raise debt levels (and the concomitant interest payments) when profits are expected to increase.

How do investors react to an increase in debt? Rational investors are likely to infer a higher firm value from a higher debt level. Thus, these investors are likely to bid up a firm's stock price after the firm has, say, issued debt in order to buy back equity. We say that investors view debt as a *signal* of firm value.

Now we get to the incentives of managers to fool the public. Consider a firm whose level of debt is optimal. That is, the marginal tax benefit of debt exactly equals the marginal distress costs of debt. However, imagine that the firm's manager desires to increase the firm's current stock price, perhaps because he knows that many of his shareholders want to sell their stock soon. This manager might want to increase the level of debt just to make investors *think* that the firm is more valuable than it really is. If the strategy works, investors will push up the price of the stock.

The above implies that firms can fool investors by taking on *some* additional leverage. Now let's ask the big question. Are there benefits to extra debt but no costs, implying that all firms will take on as much debt as possible? The answer, fortunately, is that there are costs as well. Imagine that a firm has issued extra debt just to fool the public. At some point the market will learn that the company is not that valuable after all. At this time, the stock price should actually fall *below* what it would have been had the debt never been increased. Why? Because the firm's debt level is now above the optimal level. That is, the marginal tax benefit of debt is below the marginal cost of debt. Thus, if the current shareholders plan to sell, say, half of their shares now and retain the other half, an increase in debt will help them on immediate sales but likely hurt them on later ones.

Now here is the important point: We said earlier that, in a world where managers do not attempt to fool investors, valuable firms issue more debt than less valuable ones. It turns out that, even when managers attempt to fool investors, the more valuable firms will still want to issue more debt than the less valuable firms. That is, while all firms will increase debt levels somewhat to fool investors, the costs of extra debt prevent the less valuable firms from issuing more debt than the more valuable firms issue. Thus, investors can still treat debt level as a signal of firm value. In other words, investors can still view an announcement of debt as a positive sign for the firm.

The above is a simplified example of debt signalling and one can argue that it is too simplified. For example, perhaps the shareholders of some firms want to sell most of their stock immediately while the shareholders of other firms want to sell only a little of theirs now. It is impossible to tell here whether the firms with the most debt are the most valuable or merely the ones with the most impatient shareholders. Since other objections can be brought up as well, signalling theory is best validated by empirical evidence. And, fortunately, the empirical evidence tends to support the theory.

For example, consider the evidence concerning **exchange offers.** Firms often change their debt levels through exchange offers, of which there are two types. The first type of offer allows shareholders to exchange some of their stock for debt, thereby increasing leverage. The second type allows bondholders to exchange some of their debt for stock, decreasing leverage. Figure 17.3 shows the stock price behaviour of firms that change their proportions of debt and equity via exchange offers. The solid line in the figure indicates that stock prices rise substantially on the date when an exchange offering increasing leverage is announced. (This date is referred to as date 0 in the figure.) Conversely, the dotted line in the figure indicates that stock price falls substantially when an offer decreasing leverage is announced.

FIGURE 17.3

Stock Returns at the Time of Announcements of Exchange Offers

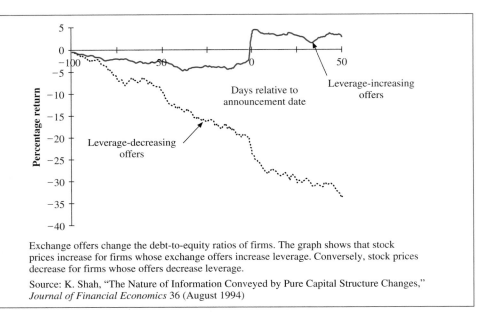

Exchange offers change the debt-to-equity ratios of firms. The graph shows that stock prices increase for firms whose exchange offers increase leverage. Conversely, stock prices decrease for firms whose offers decrease leverage.

Source: K. Shah, "The Nature of Information Conveyed by Pure Capital Structure Changes," *Journal of Financial Economics* 36 (August 1994)

The market infers from an increase in debt that the firm is better off, leading to a stock price rise. Conversely, the market infers the reverse from a decrease in debt, implying a stock price fall. Thus, we say that managers signal information when they change leverage.

? Concept Questions

- **Do managers have an incentive to fool investors by issuing additional debt?**
- **Is there a cost to issuing additional debt?**
- **What empirical evidence suggests that managers signal information through debt levels?**

17.6 Shirking, Perquisites, and Bad Investments: A Note on Agency Cost of Equity

The previous section introduced the static trade-off model, in which a rise in debt increases both the tax shield and the costs of distress. We now extend the trade-off model by considering an important agency cost of equity. A discussion of this cost of equity is contained in a well-known quote from Adam Smith.[14]

> The directors of such [joint-stock] companies, however, being the managers of other people's money than of their own, it cannot well be expected that they should watch over it with the same anxious vigilance with which the partners in a private copartnery frequently watch over their own. Like the stewards of a rich man, they are apt to consider attention to small matters as not for their master's honor, and very easily give themselves a dispensation from having it. Negligence and profusion, therefore, must always prevail, more or less, in the management of the affairs of such a company.

---

[14]Adam Smith, *The Wealth of Nations* [1776], Cannon edition (New York: Modern Library, 1937), p. 700, as quoted in M. C. Jensen and W. Meckling, "Theory of the Firm: Managerial Behavior, Agency Costs, and Ownership Structure," *Journal of Financial Economics* 3 (1978).

This elegant prose can be restated in modern vocabulary. An individual will work harder for a firm if he or she is one of its owners rather than just an employee. In addition, the individual will work harder as the owner of a larger percentage of the company. This idea has an important implication for capital structure, which we illustrate with Example 17.2.

EXAMPLE 17.2

Ms. Pagell is an owner–entrepreneur running a computer-services firm worth $1 million. She currently owns 100 percent of the firm. Because of the need to expand, she must raise another $2 million. She can either issue $2 million of debt at 12 percent interest or issue $2 million in stock. The cash flows under the two alternatives are presented below:

	Debt Issue				Stock Issue			
	Cash Flow	Interest	Cash Flow to Equity	Cash Flow to Ms. Pagell (100% of equity)	Cash Flow	Interest	Cash Flow to Equity	Cash Flow to Ms. Pagell (33⅓% of equity)
6-hour days	$300,000	$240,000	$ 60,000	$ 60,000	$300,000	0	$300,000	$100,000
10-hour days	400,000	240,000	160,000	160,000	400,000	0	400,000	133,333

Like any entrepreneur, Ms. Pagell can choose the degree of intensity with which she works. In our example, she can work either 6 or 10 hours per day. With the debt issue, the extra work brings her $100,000 (or $160,000 − $60,000) more income. However, with a stock issue she retains only a one-third interest in the equity. Thus, the extra work brings her only $33,333 (or $133,333 − $100,000). Being only human, she is likely to work harder if she issues debt. In other words, she has more incentive to *shirk* if she issues equity.

In addition, she is likely to obtain more *perquisites* (a big office, a company car, more expense account meals) if she issues stock. If she is a one-third shareholder, two-thirds of these costs are paid by the other shareholders. If she is the sole owner, any additional perquisites reduce her equity stake.

Finally, she is more likely to take on capital budgeting projects with negative net present values. It might seem surprising that a manager with any equity interest at all would take on negative NPV projects, since stock price would clearly fall. However, managerial salaries generally rise with firm size, indicating that managers have an incentive to accept some unprofitable projects after all the profitable ones have been taken on. That is, when an unprofitable project is accepted, the loss in stock value to a manager with only a small equity interest may be less than the increase in salary. In fact, it is our opinion that losses from accepting bad projects are far greater than losses from either shirking or excessive perquisites. Hugely unprofitable projects have bankrupted whole firms, something that even the largest of expense accounts is unlikely to do.

Thus, as the firm issues more equity, our entrepreneur will likely increase leisure time, work-related perquisites, and unprofitable investments. These three items are called agency costs, because managers of the firm are agents of the shareholders.[15]

---

[15]As previously discussed, agency costs are generally defined as the costs from the conflicts of interest among shareholders, bondholders, and managers.

This example is quite applicable to a small company considering a large stock offering. Because an owner–manager will greatly dilute his or her share in the total equity in this case, a significant drop in work intensity or a significant increase in fringe benefits is possible. Conversely, consider a large company like Royal Bank issuing shares for the umpteenth time. The typical manager has such a small percentage stake in the firm that any temptation for negligence is unlikely to change with the share issue.

Who bears the burden of these agency costs? If the new shareholders enter with their eyes open, they do not. Knowing that Ms. Pagell may work short hours, they will pay only a low price for the stock. Thus, it is the owner who is hurt by agency costs.

We saw earlier that shareholders reduce bankruptcy costs, agency cost of debt, through protective covenants. Analogously, owners try to control the agency cost of equity. Firms going public for the first time may allow monitoring by new shareholders. Owners may retain a large portion of the stock to convince new shareholders that no shirking is planned. For large firms, the monitoring role is played by the board of directors although there is considerable controversy over boards' effectiveness in this role.[16] Another common approach is to use stock options and bonuses linked to stock price performance to bring the interests of management in line with those of the shareholders. However, though these techniques may reduce the agency costs of equity, they are unlikely to eliminate them.

It is commonly suggested that leveraged buyouts (LBOs) significantly reduce the agency cost of equity. In an LBO, a purchaser (sometimes a team of existing management) buys out the shareholders at a price above the current market. In other words, the company goes private since the stock is placed in the hands of only a few people. Because the managers now own a substantial chunk of the business, they are likely to work harder than when they were simply hired hands.

Effect of Agency Costs of Equity on Debt–Equity Financing

Before our discussion of agency costs of equity in the current section, we stated that the change in the value of the firm when debt is substituted for equity is (1) the tax shield on debt minus (2) the increase in the costs of financial distress (including the agency costs of debt). Now, the change in the value of the firm is (1) the tax shield on debt plus (2) the reduction in the agency costs of equity minus (3) the increase in the costs of financial distress (including the agency costs of debt). The optimal debt–equity ratio would be higher in a world with agency costs of equity than in a world without these costs. However, because the agency costs of debt are so significant, the costs of equity do not imply 100 percent debt financing.

Free Cash Flow

Any reader of murder mysteries knows that a criminal must have both motive and opportunity. The above discussion was about motive. Managers with only a small ownership interest have an incentive for wasteful behaviour. For example, they bear only a small portion of the costs of, say, excessive expense accounts, and reap all of the benefits.

Now let's talk about opportunity. A manager can only pad his expense account if the firm has the cash flow to cover it. Thus, we might expect to see more wasteful activity in a firm with a capacity to generate large cash flows than in one with a capacity to generate only small flows. This very simple idea, which is formally called the *free cash flow hypothesis,* has attracted the attention of the academic community.[17]

---

[16]We discuss shareholder activism in Chapter 30.

[17]The seminal article is Michael C. Jensen, "Agency Costs of Free Cash Flow, Corporate Finance and Takeovers," *American Economic Review* 76 (1986), pp. 323–39.

A fair amount of academic work supports the hypothesis. For example, a frequently cited paper found that firms with high free cash flow are more likely to make bad acquisitions than are firms with low free cash flow.[18] A related Canadian study reports that firms with high free cash flow are more likely to undertake investments with low returns.[19]

The hypothesis has important implications for capital structure. Since dividends leave the firm, they reduce free cash flow. Thus, according to the free cash flow hypothesis, an increase in dividends should benefit the shareholders by reducing the ability of managers to pursue wasteful activities. Furthermore, since interest and principal also leave the firm, debt reduces free cash flow as well. In fact, interest and principal should have a greater effect than dividends have on the free-spending ways of managers, because bankruptcy will occur if the firm is unable to make future debt payments. By contrast, a future dividend reduction will cause fewer problems to the managers, since the firm has no legal obligation to pay dividends. Because of this, the free cash flow hypothesis argues that a shift from equity to debt will boost firm value.[20]

In summary, the free cash flow hypothesis provides still another reason for firms to issue debt. We previously discussed the costs of equity; new equity dilutes the holdings of managers, increasing their *motive* to waste corporate resources. We now state that debt reduces free cash flow, because the firm must make interest and principal payments. The free cash flow hypothesis implies that debt reduces the *opportunity* for managers to waste resources.

? Concept Questions
- **What are agency costs?**
- **Why are shirking and perquisites considered an agency cost of equity?**
- **How do agency costs of equity affect the firm's debt–equity ratio?**
- **What is the free cash flow hypothesis?**

17.7 The Pecking-Order Theory

Although the trade-off theory has dominated corporate finance circles for a long time, attention is also being paid to the *pecking-order theory*.[21] To understand this view of the world, let's put ourselves in the position of a corporate financial manager whose firm needs new capital. The manager faces a choice between issuing debt and issuing equity. Previously, we evaluated the choice in terms of tax benefits, distress costs, and agency costs. However, there is one consideration that we have so far neglected: timing.

Imagine the manager saying:

> I want to issue stock in one situation only—when it is overvalued. If the stock of my firm is selling at $50 per share, but I think that it is actually worth $60, I will not issue stock. I would

---

[18]L. Lang, R. Stulz, and R. Walkling, "Managerial Performance, Tobin's Q and the Gains in Tender Offers," *Journal of Financial Economics* (1989).

[19]R. S. Chirinko and H. Schaller, "A Revealed Preference Approach to Understanding Corporate Governance Problems: Evidence from Canada," Center for Economic Studies and Ifo Institute for Economic Research Working Paper 826, Massachusetts Institute of Technology, 2002.

[20]A number of papers provide empirical support for these implications of the free cash flow hypothesis. In particular, see K. Lehn and Poulsen, "Free Cash Flow and Shareholder Value in Going-Private Transactions," *Journal of Finance* (July 1989); L. Lang and R. Litzenberger, "Dividend Announcements: Cash Flow Signalling vs. Free Cash Flow Hypothesis," *Journal of Financial Economics* (September 1989); and T. Nohel and V. Tarhan, "Share Repurchases and Firm Performance: New Evidence on the Agency Costs of Free Cash Flow," *Journal of Financial Economics* 49 (August 1998).

[21]The pecking-order theory is generally attributed to S. C. Myers, "The Capital Structure Puzzle," *Journal of Finance* 39 (July 1984).

actually be giving new shareholders a gift, because they would receive stock worth $60, but would only have to pay $50 for it. More importantly, my current shareholders would be upset, because the firm would be receiving $50 in cash, but giving away something worth $60. So if I believe that my stock is undervalued, I would issue bonds. Bonds, particularly those with little or no risk of default, are likely to be priced correctly. Their value is primarily determined by the marketwide interest rate, a variable that is publicly known.

But, suppose that our stock is selling at $70. Now I'd like to issue stock. If I can get some fool to buy our stock for $70 while the stock is really only worth $60, I will be making $10 for our current shareholders.

Now, although this may strike you as a cynical view, it seems to square well with reality. Before insider trading and disclosure laws were adopted, many managers were alleged to have unfairly trumpeted their firm's prospects prior to equity issuance. And, even today, managers seem more willing to issue equity after the price of their stock has risen than after their stock has fallen in price. For example, in 2001, high-tech stock prices were down from their highs and such well-known firms as PMC-Sierra, Lucent Technologies, and Nortel Networks all issued debt. Thus, timing might be an important motive in equity issuance, perhaps even more important than those motives in the trade-off model. After all, the firm in the preceding example *immediately* makes $10 by properly timing the issuance of equity. Ten dollars' worth of agency costs and bankruptcy cost reduction might take many years to realize.

The key that makes the example work is asymmetric information; in an exception to the efficient market hypothesis from Chapter 14, the manager must know more about his firm's prospects than does the typical investor. If the manager's estimate of the true worth of the company is no better than the estimate of a typical investor, any attempts by the manager to time will fail. This assumption of asymmetry is quite plausible. Managers should know more about their company than do outsiders, because managers work at the company every day. (One caveat is that some managers are perpetually optimistic about their firm, blurring good judgment.)

But we are not finished with this example yet; we must consider the investor. Imagine an investor saying:

I make investments carefully, because it involves my hard-earned money. However, even with all the time I put into studying stocks, I can't possibly know what the managers themselves know. After all, I've got a day job to be concerned with. So, I watch what the managers do. If a firm issues stock, the firm was likely overvalued beforehand. If a firm issues debt, it was likely undervalued.

When we look at both issuers and investors, we see a kind of poker game, with each side trying to outwit the other. There are two prescriptions to the issuer in this poker game. The first one, which is fairly straightforward, is to issue debt instead of equity when the stock is undervalued. The second, which is more subtle, is to issue debt also when the firm is *overvalued.* After all, if a firm issues equity, investors will infer that the stock is overvalued. They will not buy it until the stock has fallen enough to eliminate any advantage from equity issuance. In fact, only the most overvalued firms have any incentive to issue equity. Should even a moderately overpriced firm issue equity, investors will infer that this firm is among the *most* overpriced, causing the stock to fall more than is deserved. Thus, the end result is that virtually no one will issue equity.[22]

This result that essentially all firms should issue debt is clearly an extreme one. It is as extreme as (1) the Modigliani–Miller (MM) result that, in a world without taxes, firms

[22]In the interest of simplicity, we have not presented our results in the form of a rigorous model. For a deeper explanation, refer to S. C. Myers. "The Capital Structure Puzzle," *Journal of Finance* (July 1984).

are indifferent to capital structure and (2) the MM result that, in a world of corporate taxes but no financial distress costs, all firms should be 100 percent debt-financed. Perhaps we in finance have a penchant for extreme models!

But, just as one can temper MM's conclusions by combining financial distress costs with corporate taxes, we can temper those of the pure pecking-order theory. This pure version assumes that timing is the financial manager's only consideration. In reality, a manager must consider taxes, financial distress costs, and agency costs as well. Thus, a firm may issue debt only up to a point. If financial distress becomes a real possibility beyond that point, the firm may issue equity instead.

Rules of the Pecking Order

For expository purposes, we have oversimplified by comparing equity to *riskless* debt. Managers cannot use special knowledge of their firm to determine if this type of debt is mispriced, because the price of riskless debt is determined solely by the marketwide interest rate. However, in reality, corporate debt has the possibility of default. Thus, just as managers have a tendency to issue equity when they think it is overvalued, managers also have a tendency to issue debt when they think it is overvalued.

When would managers view their debt as overvalued? Probably in the same situations when they think their equity is overvalued. For example, if the public thinks that the firm's prospects are rosy but the managers see trouble ahead, these managers would view their debt—as well as their equity—as being overvalued. That is, the public might see the debt as nearly risk-free, whereas the managers see a strong possibility of default.

Thus, investors are likely to price a debt issue with the same skepticism that they have when pricing an equity issue. The way managers get out of this box is to finance projects out of retained earnings. You don't have to worry about investor skepticism if you can avoid going to investors in the first place. Thus, the first rule of the pecking order is:

Rule 1

Use internal financing.

However, although investors fear mispricing of both debt and equity, the fear is much greater for equity. Corporate debt still has relatively little risk compared to equity because, if financial distress is avoided, investors receive a fixed return. Thus, the pecking-order theory implies that, if outside financing is required, debt should be issued before equity.[23] Only when the firm's debt capacity is reached should the firm consider equity.

Of course, there are many types of debt. For example, because convertible debt is more risky than straight debt, the pecking-order theory implies that one should issue straight debt before issuing convertibles. Thus, the second rule of pecking-order theory is:

Rule 2

Issue the safest securities first.

Implications

There are a number of implications associated with the pecking-order theory that are at odds with the trade-off theory.

1. *There is no target amount of leverage.* According to the trade-off model, each firm balances the benefits of debt, such as the tax shield, with the costs of debt, such as distress costs. The optimal amount of leverage occurs where the marginal benefit of debt equals the marginal cost of debt.

---

[23]We discuss convertible debt in Chapter 25.

By contrast, the pecking-order theory does not imply a target amount of leverage. Rather, each firm chooses its leverage ratio based on financing needs. Firms first fund projects out of retained earnings. This should lower the percentage of debt in the capital structure, because profitable, internally funded projects raise both the book value and the market value of equity. Additional cash needs are met with debt, clearly raising the debt level. However, at some point the debt capacity of the firm may be exhausted, giving way to equity issuance. Thus, the amount of leverage is determined by the happenstance of available projects. Firms do not pursue a target ratio of debt to equity.

2. *Profitable firms use less debt.* Profitable firms generate cash internally, implying less need for outside financing. Because firms desiring outside capital turn to debt first, profitable firms end up relying on less debt. The trade-off model does not have this implication. The greater cash flow of more profitable firms creates greater debt capacity. These firms will use that debt capacity to capture the tax shield and the other benefits of leverage. Two empirical papers find that in the real world, more profitable firms are less levered,[24] a result consistent with the pecking-order theory.

3. *Companies like financial slack.* The pecking-order theory is based on the difficulties of obtaining financing at a reasonable cost. A skeptical investing public thinks a stock is overvalued if the managers try to issue more of it, thereby leading to a stock price decline. Because this happens with bonds but to a lesser extent, managers rely first on bond financing. However, firms can issue only so much debt before encountering the potential costs of financial distress.

Wouldn't it be easier to have the cash ahead of time? This is the idea behind *financial slack.* Because firms know that they will have to fund profitable projects at various times in the future, they accumulate cash today. They are then not forced to go to the capital markets when a project comes up. However, there is a limit to the amount of cash a firm will want to accumulate. As mentioned earlier in this chapter, too much free cash may tempt managers to pursue wasteful activities.

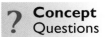

Concept Questions

• **What is the pecking-order theory?**
• **What are the problems of issuing equity according to this theory?**
• **What is financial slack?**

17.8 Growth and the Debt–Equity Ratio

While the trade-off between the tax shield and bankruptcy costs (as illustrated in Figure 17.1) is the "standard model" of capital structure, it has its critics. For example, some point out that bankruptcy costs in the real world appear to be much smaller than the tax subsidy. Thus, the model implies that the optimal debt/value ratio should still be near 100 percent, an implication at odds with reality.[25]

---

[24]See L. S. Sunder and S. C. Myers, "Testing Static Trade-off Against Pecking Order Models of Capital Structure," *Journal of Financial Economics* (February 1999); and E. F. Fama and K. R. French, "Testing Trade-off and Pecking Order Predictions about Dividends and Debt," unpublished paper, University of Chicago (November 1999). Most recently, Armen Hovakimian, Tim Opler, and Sheridan Titman, "The Debt–Equity Choice," *Journal of Financial and Quantitative Analysis* (March 2001) find that while pecking order considerations affect firm debt levels in the short run, firms tend to move to target debt ratios in a manner consistent with the trade-off model.

[25]See Merton Miller's Presidential Address to the American Finance Association, reprinted as "Debt and Taxes," *Journal of Finance* (May 1977).

Perhaps the pecking-order theory is more consistent with the real world here. That is, firms are likely to have more equity in their capital structure than implied by the static trade-off theory, because internal financing is preferred to external financing.

In addition, growth can imply significant equity financing, even in a world with low bankruptcy costs.[26] The basic idea is that growth accrues to the shareholders, increasing the value of equity. Because the value of debt does not change, the debt–equity ratio falls. To explain the idea, we first consider an example of a no-growth firm. Next, we examine the effect of growth on firm leverage.

No-Growth

Imagine a world of perfect certainty[27] where a firm has earnings before interest and taxes (EBIT) of $100. In addition, the firm has issued $1,000 of debt at an interest rate of 10 percent, implying interest payments of $100 per year. The cash flows to the firm are:

Date	1	2	3	4 . . .
Earnings before interest and taxes (EBIT)	$100	$100	$100	$100 . . .
Interest	−100	−100	−100	−100 . . .
Taxable income	$ 0	$ 0	$ 0	$ 0 . . .

The firm has issued just enough debt so that all EBIT is paid out as interest. Since interest is tax-deductible, the firm pays no taxes. In this example, the equity is worthless because shareholders receive no cash flows. Since debt is worth $1,000, the firm is also valued at $1,000. Therefore, the debt-to-value ratio is 100 percent (= $1,000/$1,000).

Had the firm issued less than $1,000 of debt, the corporation would have positive taxable income and, consequently, would have ended up paying some taxes. Had the firm issued more than $1,000 of debt, interest would have exceeded EBIT, causing default. Consequently, the optimal debt-to-value ratio is 100 percent.

Growth

Now imagine another firm that also has EBIT of $100 at date 1 but is growing at 5 percent per year.[28] To eliminate taxes, this firm also wants to issue enough debt so that interest equals EBIT. Since EBIT is growing at 5 percent per year, interest must also grow at this rate. This is achieved by increasing debt by 5 percent per year.[29] The debt and income levels are:

Date	0	1	2	3	4 . . .
Debt	$1,000	$1,050	$1,102.50	$1,157.63 . . .	
New debt issued		50	52.50	55.13 . . .	
EBIT		$ 100	$ 105	$ 110.25	$115.76 . . .
Interest		−100	−105	−110.25	−115.76 . . .
Taxable income		$ 0	$ 0	$ 0	$ 0

Note that interest on a particular date is always 10 percent of the debt on the previous date. Debt is set so that interest is exactly equal to EBIT. As in the no-growth case, the

---

[26]This new idea is introduced and analyzed in J. L. Berens and C. L. Cuny, "Inflation, Growth, and Capital Structure," *Review of Financial Sudies* 8 (Winter 1995).

[27]The same qualitative results occur under uncertainty, though the mathematics is more troublesome.

[28]For simplicity, assume that growth is achieved without earnings retention. The same conclusions would be reached with retained earnings, though the arithmetic would become more involved. Of course, growth without earnings retention is less realistic than growth with retention.

[29]Since the firm makes no real investment, the new debt is used to buy back shares of stock.

levered firm has the maximum amount of debt at each date. Default would occur if interest payments were increased.

Because growth is 5 percent per year, the value of the firm is:[30]

$$V_{Firm} = \frac{\$100}{0.10 - 0.05} = \$2,000$$

The equity at date 0 is the difference between the value of the firm at that time, $2,000, and the debt of $1,000. Hence, equity must be equal to $1,000[31] implying a debt-to-value ratio of 50 percent (= $1,000/$2,000). Note the important difference between the no-growth and the growth example. The no-growth example has no equity; the value of the firm is simply the value of the debt. With growth, there is equity as well as debt.

As we mentioned earlier, any further increase in debt would lower the value of the firm in a world with bankruptcy costs. Thus, with growth, the optimal amount of debt is less than 100 percent. Note, however, that bankruptcy costs need not be as large as the tax subsidy. In fact, even with infinitesimally small bankruptcy costs, firm value would decline if promised interest rose above $100 in the first year. The key to this example is that *today's* interest is set equal to *today's* income. While the introduction of future growth opportunities increases firm value, it does not increase the current level of debt needed to shield today's income from today's taxes. Since equity is the difference between firm value and debt, growth increases the value of equity.

The above example captures an essential feature of the real world: growth. The same conclusion is reached in a world of inflation but no growth opportunities.[32] The result of this section, that 100 percent debt financing is suboptimal, holds whether growth opportunities and/or inflation are present. Since most firms have growth opportunities and since inflation has been with us for most of the last 100 years, this section's example is based on realistic assumptions. The basic point is this: High-growth firms will have lower debt ratios than low-growth firms.

? Concept Question

- How do growth opportunities decrease the advantage of debt financing?

---

[30]The firm can also be valued by a variant of Equation (16.7):

$$V_L = V_U \qquad\qquad + PV \ of \ Tax \ Shield$$
$$= \frac{\$100(1 - T_C)}{0.10 - 0.05} + \frac{T_C \times \$100}{0.10 - 0.05} = \$2,000$$

Because of firm growth, both V_U and PV of the tax shield are growing perpetuities.

[31]Students are often surprised that equity has value when taxable income is zero. Actually, the equityholders are receiving cash flow each period, since new debt is used to buy back stock.

[32]Notice that we restricted the debt to bonds with level coupon payments. Suppose, instead, that the firm had begun at date 0 by issuing debt-carrying coupons of $105 in year 1, $110.25 in year 2, $115.76 in year 3, and so on. Since there is no uncertainty in our example, these coupons are just the annual EBIT of the firm. At an interest rate of 10 percent such a bond would carry a price of $2,000, which is the entire value of the firm. Thus, the proceeds from the bond issue would equal the value of the firm and the firm would be capitalized as an all-debt firm.

Keep in mind that the important feature of debt is that it is a contractual commitment by the firm to make scheduled payments to the holder. While these payments are usually in the form of level coupons, they also may vary over time. Technically, the same conclusion is reached under inflation in a world with financial institutions similar to those in Canada. But the conclusion will not hold if indexed bonds are issued and/or only real payments are tax-deductible.

17.9 Personal Taxes

So far in the chapter, we have considered corporate taxes only. Unfortunately, tax law does not let us off that easily. Income to individuals is taxed at federal marginal rates up to 29 percent. Combining the provincial tax rate with the federal tax rate, the marginal rates can be as high as 48 percent.[33] Furthermore, tax law offers a dividend tax credit to individuals. To see the effect of personal taxes on capital structure, we have reproduced our Water Products example (from Section 16.5) below.

	Plan I	Plan II
Earnings before interest and taxes (EBIT)	$1,000,000	$1,000,000
Interest (r_BB)	0	(400,000)
Earnings before taxes (EBT = EBIT − r_BB)	1,000,000	600,000
Taxes ($T_C = 0.40$)	(400,000)	(240,000)
Earnings after corporate taxes	600,000	360,000
EAT = (EBIT − r_BB) × (1 − T_C)		
Total cash flow to both shareholders and bondholders		
[EBIT × (1 − T_C) + $T_C r_B B$]	$ 600,000	$ 760,000

As presented above, this example considers corporate taxes but not personal taxes. To treat these personal taxes, we first assume that all earnings after taxes are paid out as dividends, and that both dividends and interest are taxed at the same personal rate. (We assume 36 percent.)

	Plan I	Plan II
Dividends	$ 600,000	$ 360,000
Personal taxes on dividends		
(Personal rate = 36%)	(216,000)	(129,600)
Dividends after personal taxes	$ 384,000	$ 230,400
Interest	0	$ 400,000
Taxes on interest	0	(144,000)
Interest after personal taxes	0	256,000
Total cash flow to both bondholders and shareholders		
after personal taxes	$ 384,000	$ 486,400

Total taxes paid at both corporate and personal levels are

Plan I:	$400,000	+	$216,000			=	$616,000
	Corporate taxes		Personal taxes on dividends				

Plan II:	$240,000		$129,600		$144,000	=	$513,600
	Corporate taxes	+	Personal taxes on dividends	+	Personal taxes on interest		

Total cash flow to all investors after personal taxes is greater under Plan II. This must be the case because (1) total cash flow was higher when personal taxes were ignored and

---

[33]Appendix 1A gives more detail on taxes.

(2) all cash flows (both interest and dividends) are taxed at the same personal tax rate. Thus, the conclusion that debt increases the value of the firm still holds.

However, the analysis to this point assumed that all earnings are paid out in dividends, and the personal tax rate on dividends was the same as the personal tax rate on interest. In reality, dividends may be deferred through retention of earnings, and a dividend tax credit exists. Thus, the effective personal tax rate on distributions to shareholders is below the personal tax rate on interest.[34]

To illustrate this tax rate differential, let us assume that the effective personal tax rate on distributions to shareholders, T_S, is 10 percent and the personal tax rate on interest, T_B, is 50 percent. The cash flows for the two plans are

	Plan I	Plan II
Distributions to shareholders	$ 600,000	$ 360,000
Personal taxes on shareholder distributions (at 10% tax rate)	(60,000)	(36,000)
Distribution to shareholders after personal taxes	540,000	324,000
Interest	0	400,000
Taxes on interest (at 50% tax rate)	0	(200,000)
Interest after personal taxes	0	200,000
Add back shareholder distributions after personal taxes	540,000	324,000
Total cash flow to all investors after personal taxes	$ 540,000	$ 524,000

Total taxes paid at both personal and corporate levels are

Plan I:	$400,000	+	$60,000			= $460,000
	Corporate taxes		Personal taxes on dividends			

Plan II:	$240,000		$36,000		$200,000	= $476,000
	Corporate taxes	+	Personal taxes on dividends	+	Personal taxes on interest	

In this scenario, the total cash flows are higher under Plan I than under Plan II. Though the example is expressed in terms of cash flows, we would expect the value of the firm to be higher under Plan I than under Plan II because lower total taxes are paid. The increase in corporate taxes under the all-equity plan is more than offset by the decrease in personal taxes.

Interest receives a tax deduction at the corporate level. Equity distributions are taxed at a lower rate than interest at the personal level. The above examples illustrate that total tax at all levels may either increase or decrease with debt, depending on the tax rates and tax credits in effect.

The Miller Model

Valuation Under Personal and Corporate Taxes   The previous example calculated *cash flows* for the two plans under personal and corporate taxes. However, we have made

---

[34]Positive NPV investments financed by deferring dividends will lead to capital gains also taxed at a lower rate. We discuss this in more detail in Chapter 19.

no attempt to determine firm value so far. It can be shown that the value of the levered firm can be expressed in terms of an unlevered firm as[35]

$$V_L = V_U + \left[1 - \frac{(1 - T_C) \times (1 - T_S)}{(1 - T_B)} \right] \times B \qquad (17.1)$$

T_B is the personal tax rate on ordinary income, such as interest, and T_S is the personal tax rate on equity distributions.

If we set $T_B = T_S$, Equation (17.1) simplifies to

$$V_L = V_U + T_C B \qquad (17.2)$$

which is the result we calculated for a world of no personal taxes. Hence, the introduction of personal taxes does not affect our valuation formula as long as equity distributions are taxed identically to interest at the personal level.

However, the gain from leverage is reduced when $T_S < T_B$. Here, more taxes are paid at the personal level for a levered firm than for an unlevered firm. In fact, imagine that $(1 - T_C) \times (1 - T_S) = 1 - T_B$. Equation (17.1) tells us there is no gain from leverage at all! In other words, the value of the levered firm is equal to the value of the unlevered firm. The gain from leverage disappears because the lower corporate taxes for a levered firm are *exactly* offset by higher personal taxes. These results are presented in Figure 17.4. More details of the Miller model are in Appendix 17B, which can be accessed at www. mcgrawhill.ca/olc/ross.

EXAMPLE 17.3

Acme Industries anticipates a perpetual pre-tax earning stream of $100,000 and faces a 45 percent corporate tax rate. Investors discount the earnings stream after corporate taxes at 15 percent. The personal tax rate on equity distributions is 30 percent and the personal tax rate on interest is 47 percent. Acme currently has an all-equity capital structure but is considering borrowing $120,000 at 10 percent.

---

[35]Shareholders receive

$$(\text{EBIT} - r_B B) \times (1 - T_C) \times (1 - T_S)$$

Bondholders receive

$$r_B B \times (1 - T_B)$$

Thus, the total cash flow to all stakeholders is

$$(\text{EBIT} - r_B B) \times (1 - T_C) \times (1 - T_S) + r_B B \times (1 - T_B)$$

which can be rewritten as

$$\text{EBIT} \times (1 - T_C) \times (1 - T_S) + r_B B \times (1 - T_B) \times \left[1 - \frac{(1 - T_C) \times (1 - T_S)}{1 - T_B} \right] \qquad (a)$$

The first term in Equation (*a*) is the cash flow from an unlevered firm after all taxes. The value of this stream must be V_U, the value of an unlevered firm. An individual buying a bond for B receives $r_B B \times (1 - T_B)$ after all taxes. Thus, the value of the second term in (*a*) must be

$$B \times \left[1 - \frac{(1 - T_C) \times (1 - T_S)}{1 - T_B} \right]$$

Therefore, the value of the stream in Equation (*a*), which is the value of the levered firm, must be

$$V_U + \left[1 - \frac{(1 - T_C) \times (1 - T_S)}{1 - T_B} \right] \times B$$

FIGURE 17.4

Gains From Financial Leverage With Both Corporate and Personal Taxes

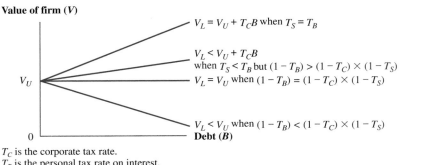

Value of firm (V)

$V_L = V_U + T_C B$ when $T_S = T_B$

$V_L < V_U + T_C B$ when $T_S < T_B$ but $(1 - T_B) > (1 - T_C) \times (1 - T_S)$

$V_L = V_U$ when $(1 - T_B) = (1 - T_C) \times (1 - T_S)$

$V_L < V_U$ when $(1 - T_B) < (1 - T_C) \times (1 - T_S)$

Debt (B)

T_C is the corporate tax rate.
T_B is the personal tax rate on interest.
T_S is the personal tax rate on dividends and other equity distributions.
Both personal taxes and corporate taxes are included. Bankruptcy costs and agency costs are ignored. The effect of debt on firm value depends on T_S, T_C, and T_B.

The value of the all-equity firm is[36]

$$V_U = \frac{\$100,000 \times (1 - 0.45)}{0.15} = \$366,667$$

The value of the levered firm is

$$V_1 = \$366,667 + \left[1 - \frac{(1 - 0.45) \times (1 - 0.30)}{(1 - 0.47)} \right] \times \$120,000 = \$399,497$$

The advantage to leverage here is $\$399,497 - \$366,667 = \$32,830$. This is much smaller than the $\$54,000 = 0.45 \times \$120,000 = T_C \times B$, which would have been the gain in a world with no personal taxes.

Acme had previously considered the choice years earlier when $T_B = 60$ percent and $T_S = 18$ percent. Here

$$V_1 = \$366,667 + \left[1 - \frac{(1 - 0.45) \times (1 - 0.18)}{(1 - 0.60)} \right] \times \$120,000 = \$351,367$$

In this case the value of the levered firm V_1 is $\$351,367$, which is *less than* the value of the unlevered firm, $V_U = \$366,667$. Hence, Acme was wise not to increase leverage years ago. Leverage causes a loss of value in this case because the personal tax rate on interest is much higher than the personal tax rate on equity distributions. In other words, the reduction in corporate taxes from leverage is more than offset by the increase in taxes from leverage at the personal level.

Which one is the most applicable to Canada? While the numbers are different for different firms in different provinces, Chapter 1 showed that interest income is taxed at the full marginal rate, around 43 percent before surtaxes for the top bracket. Equity distributions take the form of either dividends or capital gains, and both are taxed more lightly than interest. As we showed in Appendix 1A, dividend income is sheltered by the dividend tax credit. Capital gains are taxed at 50 percent of the marginal tax rate.

---

[36]Alternatively, we could have said that investors discount the earnings stream after both corporate and personal taxes at $10.5\% = [15\% \times (1 - 0.30)]$:

$$V_U = \frac{\$100,000 \times (1 - 0.45) \times (1 - 0.30)}{0.105} = \$366,667$$

FIGURE 17.5

Value of the Firm Under the Miller Model When Interest Deductibility Is Limited to Earnings

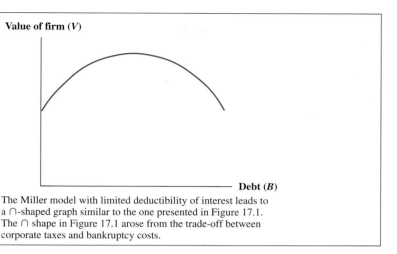

Value of firm (*V*)

Debt (*B*)

The Miller model with limited deductibility of interest leads to a ∩-shaped graph similar to the one presented in Figure 17.1. The ∩ shape in Figure 17.1 arose from the trade-off between corporate taxes and bankruptcy costs.

While the exact numbers depend on the type of portfolio chosen, our first scenario for Acme is a reasonable tax scenario for Canadian investors and companies.[37] In Canada, personal taxes reduce, but do not eliminate, the advantage to corporate leverage. This result is still unrealistic. It suggests that firms should add debt, moving out on the second line from the top in Figure 17.3, until 100 percent leverage is reached. Firms do not do this. One reason is that interest on debt is not the firm's only tax shield. Investment tax credits, capital cost allowance, and depletion allowances give rise to tax shields regardless of the firm's decision on leverage. Because these other tax shields exist, increased leverage brings with it a risk that income will not be high enough to utilize the debt tax shield fully. The result is that firms will use a limited amount of debt.[38]

The results of limited tax deductibility are provided in Figure 17.5. Firm value should rise when debt is first added to the capital structure. However, as more and more debt is issued, the full deductibility of the interest becomes less likely. Firm value still increases, but at a lower and lower rate. At some point, the probability of tax deductibility is low enough that an incremental dollar of debt is as costly to the firm as an incremental dollar of equity. Firm value then decreases with further leverage.

This graph looks surprisingly like the curve in Figure 17.1 where the trade-off between the tax shield and bankruptcy costs is illustrated. Thus, a key change in assumptions may explain why firms are not 100 percent debt financed under the current tax law.

? Concept Question

- **How do personal taxes change the conclusions of the Modigliani–Miller model about capital structure?**

---

[37]Support for this scenario comes from M. H. Wilson, "Draft Legislation, Regulations, and Explanatory Notes Respecting Preferred Share Financing," (Ottawa: Department of Finance, April 1988).

[38]This argument was first advanced by H. DeAngelo and R. Masulis, "Optimal Capital Structure Under Corporate and Personal Taxation," *Journal of Financial Economics* (March 1980), pp. 3–30. Empirical testing in Canada has so far failed to find strong support for the argument: A. H. R. Davis, "The Corporate Use of Debt Substitutes in Canada: A Test of Competing Versions of the Substitution Hypothesis," *Canadian Journal of Administrative Sciences* 11 (March 1994), pp. 105–15.

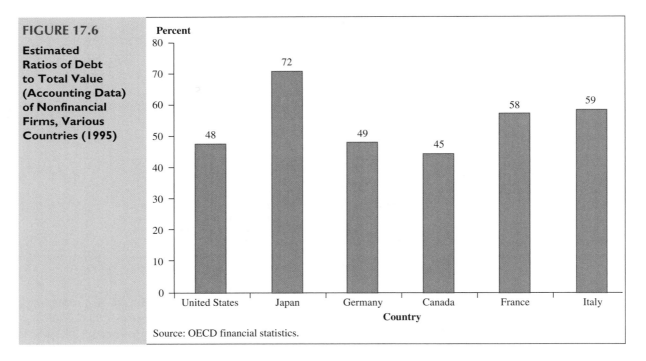

FIGURE 17.6

Estimated Ratios of Debt to Total Value (Accounting Data) of Nonfinancial Firms, Various Countries (1995)

Source: OECD financial statistics.

17.10   How Firms Establish Capital Structure

The theories of capital structure are among the most elegant and sophisticated in the field of finance. Financial economists should (and do!) pat themselves on the back for contributions in this area. However, the practical applications of the theories are less than fully satisfying. Consider that our work on net present value produced an exact formula for evaluating projects. Conversely, the most we can say on capital structure is provided in either Figure 17.1 or Figure 17.5; the optimal capital structure involves a trade-off between taxes and costs of debt. No exact formula is available for evaluating the optimal debt–equity ratio. For this reason, we turn to empirical evidence.

The following empirical regularities are worthwhile to consider when formulating capital structure policy:

1. *Most Canadian firms have low debt–equity ratios.* Figure 17.6 shows debt to total value ratios (measured at book values) for large industrial corporations in the United States, Japan, Germany, Canada, France, and Italy. In all countries, firms have debt ratios well below 100 percent. Although most corporations have debt in their capital structures, they still pay substantial taxes. Thus, it is clear that corporations have not issued debt up to the point that tax shelters have been completely used up, and we conclude that there must be limits to the amount of debt corporations can issue.[39]

2. *A number of firms use no debt.* Agrawal and Nagarajan[40] examined approximately 100 firms on the New York Stock Exchange without long-term debt. They found that these

[39]For further insight, see John Graham, "How Big Are the Tax Benefits of Debt?" *Journal of Finance* (2000).

[40]Anup Agrawal and Nandu Nagarajan, "Corporate Capital Structure, Agency Costs, and Ownership Control: The Case of All-Equity Firms," *Journal of Finance* 45 (September 1990).

TABLE 17.3
Book Value Debt/Equity Ratios for Selected Industries in Canada, Fourth Quarter 2005

Industry	Ratio
All industries	0.916
Non-financial	0.989
Agriculture, forestry, fishing, and hunting	1.296
Oil and gas extraction and support activities	0.967
Mining (except oil and gas)	0.454
Utilities	0.905
Construction	2.006
Manufacturing	0.618
Wholesale trade	0.855
Retail trade	1.072
Transportation and warehousing	1.454
Information and cultural industries	1.238
Real estate and rental and leasing	2.061
Professional, scientific, and technical services	0.846
Administrative and support, waste management and remediation services	1.427
Educational, healthcare, and social assistance services	0.930
Arts, entertainment, and recreation	2.393
Accommodation and food services	3.592
Repair, maintenance, and personal services	0.838
Insurance carriers and related activities	0.177

Source: "Book value debt/equity ratios for selected industries in Canada 2005," adapted from the Statistics Canada publication "Quarterly Financial Statistics for Enterprises," Catalogue 61-008, Fourth Quarter 2005, Vol. 16, No. 4, April 2006.

firms are averse to leverage of any kind, with little short-term debt as well. In addition, they have levels of cash and marketable securities well above their levered counterparts. Typically, the managers of these firms have high equity ownership. Furthermore, there is significantly greater family involvement in all-equity firms than in levered firms.

Thus, a story emerges. Managers of all-equity firms are less diversified than the managers of similar, but levered, firms. Because of this, significant leverage represents an added risk that the managers of all-equity firms are loath to accept.

3. *There are differences in the capital structures of different industries.* There are very significant interindustry differences in debt ratios that persist over time. As can be seen in Table 17.3, debt ratios tend to be very low in high-growth industries with ample future investment opportunities such as mining—this is true even when the need for external finance is great. Industries with relatively few investment opportunities and slow growth, such as accommodation and food services, tend to use higher levels of debt.

4. *Most corporations employ target debt–equity ratios.* Graham and Harvey asked 392 chief financial officers (CFOs) of U.S. and Canadian corporations whether their firms use target debt–equity ratios, with the results being presented in Figure 17.7.[41] As can be seen, the great majority of the firms use targets, though the strictness of the targets varies across companies. Only 19 percent of the firms avoid target ratios. Results elsewhere in the paper indicate that large firms are more likely than small firms to employ these targets. The CFOs did not specify what they meant by either *flexible* or *strict*

[41]John Graham and Campbell Harvey, "The Theory and Practice of Corporate Finance," *Journal of Financial Economics* (May/June 2001).

FIGURE 17.7

Survey Results on the Use of Target Debt–Equity Ratios

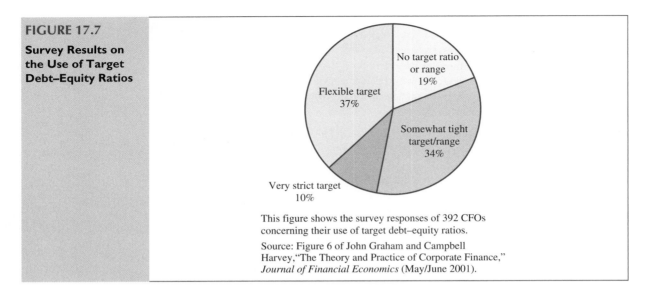

No target ratio
or range
19%

Flexible target
37%

Somewhat tight
target/range
34%

Very strict target
10%

This figure shows the survey responses of 392 CFOs concerning their use of target debt–equity ratios.

Source: Figure 6 of John Graham and Campbell Harvey, "The Theory and Practice of Corporate Finance," *Journal of Financial Economics* (May/June 2001).

targets. However, elsewhere in the study, the respondents indicated that, by and large, they did not rebalance in response to changes in their firm's stock price, suggesting some flexibility in target ratios.

How should companies establish target debt–equity ratios? While there is no mathematical formula for establishing a target ratio, we present three important factors affecting the ratio:

- *Taxes.* As pointed out earlier, firms can only deduct interest for tax purposes to the extent of their profits before interest. Thus, highly profitable firms are more likely to have larger target ratios than less profitable firms.[42]

- *Types of Assets.* Financial distress is costly, with or without formal bankruptcy proceedings. The costs of financial distress depend on the types of assets that the firm has. For example, if a firm has a large investment in land, buildings, and other tangible assets, it will have smaller costs of financial distress than a firm with a large investment in research and development. Research and development typically has less resale value than land; thus, most of its value disappears in financial distress. Therefore, firms with large investments in tangible assets are likely to have higher target debt–equity ratios than firms with large investments in research and development.

- *Uncertainty of Operating Income.* Firms with uncertain operating income have a high probability of experiencing financial distress, even without debt. Thus, these firms must finance mostly with equity. For example, pharmaceutical firms have uncertain operating income because no one can predict whether today's research will generate new drugs. Consequently, these firms issue little debt. By contrast, the operating income of firms in regulated industries, such as utilities, generally has little uncertainty. Relative to other industries, utilities use a great deal of debt.

---

[42]By contrast, the pecking-order theory argues that profitable firms will employ less debt because they can invest out of retained earnings. However, the pecking-order theory argues against the use of *target* ratios in the first place.

The Decision to Use More Debt:
The Case of Campeau Corporation's Acquisition of Federated

To illustrate the application of capital structure theory, we examine what actually happens when a particular firm decides to use more debt.[43] Let's look at Campeau Corp.'s experiences. Campeau's increased reliance on debt in the acquisition of Federated Department Stores illustrates many important points of this chapter.

On May 3, 1988, after a series of acquisition events, Campeau Corp. purchased Federated Department Stores (a U.S. chain) for $8.17 billion; $7.96 billion (97 percent of the purchase) was financed with debt. In his analysis of this acquisition, Kaplan estimates that after the acquisition, Federated assets increased in value by $1.8 billion. Possible sources of increased value include tax benefits and profits from selling off assets that were undervalued on Federated's balance sheet.

However, even with this large increase in value, Federated had to file for protection under Chapter 11 of U.S. bankruptcy laws in 1990. The biggest reason why Federated filed for bankruptcy was that cash flow was not sufficient to meet the required debt service. Furthermore, Campeau did not have other assets to make up the shortfall. Kaplan argues that if Campeau had financed the acquisition with a mix of debt and equity (as opposed to 97 percent debt), Federated would not have had to file for bankruptcy: "The Federated purchase illustrates that a highly leveraged transaction can increase value, but still not be able to make its debt payments."

Benefits

First we examine benefits of Campeau's acquisition of Federated:

1. *Asset sales to more efficient managers.* After purchasing Federated, Campeau proceeded to sell many of the operating divisions. These sales of assets to other department stores and related businesses appear to have increased value. One reason is that Campeau's purchase of Federated came after the stock market crash of 1987; the stock and bond markets may have undervalued Federated. A less convincing argument why value was created

is that the purchasers overpaid for the assets sold. In fact, the companies that bought assets showed good post-purchase performance. However, this potential source of value cannot be overlooked.

2. *Lower agency costs.* It is often argued that leverage reduces the agency cost of equity. The new debt from the acquisition forced managers to maximize resources and cash flow.

3. *Tax benefits.* It is well known that new debt can increase a firm's value by reducing taxes. Although Campeau retired some Federated debt with asset sales, most of the asset sales were also financed with debt, and interest tax shields were created and maintained.

Costs

Next we examine costs of the acquisition:

1. *Financial distress.* When firms such as Campeau increase their reliance on debt, they also increase the likelihood of financial distress. Financial distress can be formal bankruptcy, which happened to Federated on January 15, 1990. Bankruptcy costs include court costs (direct costs) and loss of market share (indirect costs). According to Kaplan's estimate, bankruptcy costs were relatively modest, reducing Campeau's gain from the acquisition from the original $1.8 billion to $1.6 billion when Federated emerged from bankruptcy in 1992.

2. *Financial slack.* The debt Campeau used to finance the Federated acquisition was well beyond industry norms. In fact, after the purchase, Campeau used up all of Federated's financial slack, which caused the bankruptcy filing. One key area of concern after using up the financial slack is capital expenditures. Cuts in capital expenditures by Federated during the Campeau period may have hurt its assets' market value.

Part of Campeau's purchase of Federated can be analyzed in terms of asset sales, tax benefits, and the costs of financial distress. However, the Campeau experience shows that agency costs and financial slack are also factors in the firm's decision to use more debt.

---

[43]This section draws on Steven N. Kaplan, "Campeau's Acquisition of Federated: Value Destroyed or Value Added," *Journal of Financial Economics* 25 (1989), pp. 191–212; and a follow-up article (by the same author): "Campeau's Acquisition of Federated: Post-Bankruptcy Results," *Journal of Financial Economics* 35 (1994), pp. 123–136.

One final note is in order. Because no formula supports them, the preceding points may seem too nebulous to assist financial decision making. Instead, many real-world firms simply base their capital structure decisions on industry averages. While this may strike some as a cowardly approach, it at least keeps firms from deviating far from accepted practice. After all, the existing firms in any industry are the survivors. Therefore, one should pay at least some attention to their decisions.

? Concept
Questions

- List the empirical regularities we observe for corporate capital structure.
- What are the factors to consider in establishing a debt–equity ratio?

17.11 SUMMARY AND CONCLUSIONS

1. We mentioned in the last chapter that, according to theory, firms should create all-debt capital structures under corporate taxation. Because firms generally assume moderate amounts of debt in the real world, the theory must have been missing something at that point. We state in this chapter that costs of financial distress cause firms to restrain their issuance of debt. These costs are of two types: direct and indirect. Lawyers' and accountants' fees during the bankruptcy process are examples of direct costs. We mention four examples of indirect costs:

   - Impaired ability to conduct business.
   - Incentive to take on risky projects.
   - Incentive toward underinvestment.
   - Distribution of funds to shareholders prior to bankruptcy.

2. Because the above costs are substantial and the shareholders ultimately bear them, firms have an incentive for cost reduction. We suggest three cost-reduction techniques:

   - Protective covenants.
   - Repurchase of debt prior to bankruptcy.
   - Consolidation of debt.

3. Because costs of financial distress can be reduced but not eliminated, firms will not finance entirely with debt. Figure 17.1 illustrates the relationship between firm value and debt. In the figure, firms select the debt-to-equity ratio at which firm value is maximized.

4. Signalling theory argues that profitable firms are likely to increase their leverage, since the extra interest payments will offset some of the pre-tax profits. Rational shareholders will infer higher firm value from a higher debt level. Thus, investors view debt as a signal of firm value.

5. Managers owning a small proportion of a firm's equity can be expected to work less, maintain more lavish expense accounts, and accept more pet projects with negative NPVs than managers owning a large proportion of equity. Since new issues of equity dilute a manager's percentage interest in the firm, the above agency costs are likely to increase when a firm's growth is financed through new equity, rather than through new debt.

6. The pecking-order theory implies that managers prefer internal to external financing. If external financing is required, managers tend to choose the safest securities, such as debt. Firms may accumulate slack to avoid external equity.

7. Berens and Cuny argue that significant equity financing can be explained by real growth and inflation, even in a world of low bankruptcy costs.

8. The results so far have ignored personal taxes. If distributions to equityholders are taxed at a lower effective personal tax rate than are interest payments, the tax advantage to debt at the corporate level is partially offset. In fact, the corporate tax advantage to debt is eliminated if

$$(1 - T_C) \times (1 - T_S) = (1 - T_B)$$

9. Debt-to-equity ratios vary across industries. We present three factors determining the target debt-to-equity ratio:

   a. *Taxes.* Firms with high taxable income should rely more on debt than firms with low taxable income.

b. *Types of Assets.* Firms with a high percentage of intangible assets such as research and development should have low debt. Firms with primarily tangible assets should have higher debt.

c. *Uncertainty of Operating Income.* Firms with high uncertainty of operating income should rely mostly on equity.

KEY TERMS

Agency costs 477

Exchange offers 485

Marketed claims 484

Negative covenant 480

Nonmarketed claims 484

Positive covenant 480

Protective covenants 479

SUGGESTED READING

A review of the literature on taxes and capital structure, among other topics, can be found in:
John R. Graham. "Taxes and Corporate Finance: A Review." *Review of Financial Studies* (2003).

Merton Miller's Nobel lecture is reprinted as:
M. Miller. "Leverage." *Journal of Finance* (June 1991).

The pecking-order theory is presented in:
S. Myers. "The Capital Structure Puzzle." *Journal of Finance* (July 1984).

Signalling theory is presented in:
S. Ross. "The Determination of Financial Structure: The Incentive Signal Approach." *Bell Journal of Economics* (1977).

Free cash flow theory is presented in:
Michael C. Jensen. "The Agency Costs of Free Cash Flow: Corporate Finance and Takeovers." *American Economic Review* (May 1986).

Different theories of capital structure are empirically tested in:
Eugene Fama, and Kenneth R. French. "Testing Tradeoff and Pecking Order Predictions about Dividends and Debt." *Review of Financial Studies* (2002).

QUESTIONS & PROBLEMS

Costs of Financial Distress

17.1   What are the direct and indirect costs of bankruptcy? Briefly explain each.

17.2   Edwards Construction currently has debt outstanding with a market value of $80,000 and a cost of 12 percent. The company has an EBIT rate of $9,600 that is expected to continue in perpetuity. Assume there are no taxes.
   a. What is the value of the company's equity? What is the debt-to-value ratio?
   b. What are the equity value and debt-to-value ratio if the company's growth rate is 5 percent?
   c. What are the equity value and debt-to-value ratio if the company's growth rate is 10 percent?

17.3   Do you agree or disagree with the following statement: A firm's shareholders will never want the firm to invest in projects with negative net present values. Why?

17.4   Suppose the president of Troy Corporation states that the company should increase the amount of debt in its capital structure because of the tax-advantaged status of its interest payments. His argument is that this action would increase the value of the company. How would you respond?

17.5   Due to large losses incurred in the past several years, Ebbers Corporation has $2.5 billion in tax loss carryforwards. This means that the next $2.5 billion of the firm's income will be free from corporate income taxes. Security analysts estimate that it will take many years for the firm to generate $2.5 billion in earnings. The firm has a moderate amount of debt in its capital structure. The firm's CEO is wants to issue debt to raise the funds needed to finance an upcoming project.
   a. What are the advantages and disadvantages of the CEO's decision?
   b. What measures can the shareholders of Ebbers Corporation undertake to minimize the costs of debt?
   c. How would the advantages and disadvantages be different if the CEO chose to issue equity?

17.6   Good Time Company is a regional chain department store. It will remain in business for one more year. The probability of a boom year is 55 percent and the probability of a recession is 45 percent. It is projected that the company will generate a total cash flow of $290 million in a boom year and $110 million in a recession. The company's required debt payment at the end of the year is $162 million. The market value of the company's outstanding debt is $118.93 million. The company pays no taxes. Assume a discount rate of 13 percent.

a. What payoff do bondholders expect to receive in the event of a recession?
b. What is the promised return on the company's debt?
c. What is the expected return on the company's debt?

17.7   Nass Corporation and Warsaw Corporation are identical firms except that Warsaw is more levered. Both companies will remain in business for one more year. The companies' economists agree that the probability of the continuation of the current expansion is 70 percent for the next year, and the probability of a recession is 30 percent. If the expansion continues, each firm will generate earnings before interest and taxes (EBIT) of $3.6 million. If a recession occurs, each firm will generate earnings before interest and taxes (EBIT) of $900,000. Nass's debt obligation requires the firm to pay $1,250,000 at the end of the year. Warsaw's debt obligation requires the firm to pay $1.6 million at the end of the year. Neither firm pays taxes. Assume a discount rate of 16.7 percent.

a. What are the potential payoffs in one year to Nass's shareholders and bondholders? What about those for Warsaw's?
b. Nass's CEO recently stated that Nass's value should be higher than Warsaw's because the firm has less debt and therefore less bankruptcy risk. Do you agree or disagree with this statement?
c. Assuming that both firms pay taxes, how do the existence of financial distress costs and agency costs affect Modigliani and Miller's theory?

17.8   Space Rock Corporation's economists estimate that a good business environment and a bad business environment are almost equally likely for the coming year. The managers of Space Rock must choose between two mutually exclusive projects. Assume that the project Fountain chooses will be the firm's only activity and that the firm will close one year from today. Space Rock is obligated to make a $450 payment to bondholders at the end of the year. The projects have the same systematic risk but different volatilities. Consider the following information pertaining to the two projects:

Low-Risk Project

Economy	Probability	Project Payoff	Value of Firm		Value of Equity	Value of Debt
Bad	0.47	$450	$450	=	$ 0	$450
Good	0.53	$725	$725	=	$275	$450

High-Risk Project

Economy	Probability	Project Payoff	Value of Firm		Value of Equity	Value of Debt
Bad	0.47	$150	$150	=	$ 0	$150
Good	0.53	$800	$800	=	$350	$450

a. What is the expected value of the firm if the low-volatility project is undertaken? What if the high-volatility project is undertaken? Which of the two strategies maximizes the expected value of the firm?
b. What is the expected value of the firm's equity if the low-volatility project is undertaken? What is it if the high-volatility project is undertaken?
c. Which project would Space Rock's shareholders prefer? Explain.

d. Suppose bondholders are fully aware that shareholders might choose to maximize equity value rather than total firm value and opt for the high-volatility project. To minimize this agency cost, the firm's bondholders decide to use a bond covenant to stipulate that the bondholders can demand a higher payment if Space Rock chooses to take on the high-volatility project. What payment to bondholders would make shareholders indifferent between the two projects?

Personal Taxes

EXCEL

17.9 Wealth Factor Enterprises is an all-equity firm that is considering issuing $15 million of perpetual 9 percent debt. The firm will use the proceeds of the bond sale to repurchase equity. Wealth Factor distributes all earnings available to shareholders immediately as dividends. The firm will generate $2.8 million of earnings before interest and taxes (EBIT) every year in perpetuity. Wealth Factor is subject to a corporate tax of 37 percent. Financial information for the firm under each of its two possible financial structures is shown below:

	Unlevered	Levered
EBIT	$2,800,000	$2,800,000
Interest	–	1,350,000
EBT	$2,800,000	$1,450,000
Taxes	1,036,000	536,500
Net Income	$1,764,000	$ 913,500

a. Suppose the personal tax rate on interest income (T_B) and equity distributions (T_S) is 30 percent.
   1. Which plan to equityholders prefer?
   2. Which plan generates the greater tax revenue?
   3. Suppose equityholders demand a 20 percent return after personal taxes on the firm's unlevered equity. What is the value of the firm under each plan?
b. Suppose $T_B = 0.55$ and $T_S = 0.20$.
   1. What is the annual after-tax cash flow to equityholders under each plan?
   2. What is the annual after-tax cash flow to debtholders under each plan?
c. Suppose there are no corporate taxes and $T_B = 0.55$ and $T_S = 0.20$.
   1. What is the annual after-tax cash flow to equityholders under each plan?
   2. How does this scenario compare to Part (B) where there is a 37 percent corporate tax on profits?

17.10 When bankruptcy costs are considered, the general expression for the value of a levered firm in a world in which the tax rate on equity distributions (T_S) equals zero is:

$$V_L = V_U + [1 - \{(1 - T_C)/(1 - T_B)\}] \times B - C(B)$$

where

V_L	=	The value of a levered firm
V_U	=	The value of an unlevered firm
B	=	The market vlaue of the firm's debt
T_C	=	The tax rate on corporate income
T_B	=	The personal tax rate on interest income
$C(B)$	=	The present value of the costs of financial distress

Assume all investors are risk-neutral.

a. In their no-tax model, what do Modigliani and Miller assume about T_C, T_B, and $C(B)$? What do these assumptions imply about a firm's optimal debt–equity ratio?
b. In their model with corporate taxes, what do Modigliani and Miller assume about T_C, T_B, and $C(B)$? What do these assumptions imply about a firm's optimal debt–equity ratio?
c. Consider an all-equity firm that is certain to be able to use interest deductions to reduce its corporate tax bill. If the corporate tax rate is 40 percent, the personal tax

rate on interest income is 22 percent, and there are no costs of financial distress, by how much will the value of the firm change if it issues $1 million in debt and uses the proceeds to repurchase equity?

d. Consider another all-equity firm that does not pay taxes due to large tax-loss carryforwards from previous years. The personal tax rate on interest income is 22 percent, and there are no costs of financial distress. What would be the change in value of this firm from adding $1 of perpetual debt rather than $1 of equity?

17.11 Overnight Publishing Company (OPC) has $3 million in excess cash. The firm plans to use this cash either to retire all of its outstanding debt or to repurchase equity. The firm's debt is held by one institution that is willing to sell it back to OPC for $3 million. The institution will not charge OPC any transaction costs. Once OPC becomes an all-equity firm, it will remain unlevered forever. If OPC does not retire the debt, the company will use the $3 million in cash to buy back some of its stock on the open market. Repurchasing stock also has no transaction costs. The company will generate $1,800,000 of annual earnings before interest and taxes in perpetuity regardless of its capital structure. The firm immediately pays out all earnings as dividends at the end of each year. OPC is subject to a corporate tax rate of 39 percent, and the required rate of return on the firm's unlevered equity is 16 percent. The personal tax rate on interest income is 24 percent, and there are no taxes on equity distribution. Assume there are no bankruptcy costs.

a. What is the value of OPC if it chooses to retire all of its debt and become an unlevered firm?

b. What is the value of OPC it is decides to repurchase stock instead of retiring its debt? (*Hint:* Use the equation for the value of a levered firm with personal tax on interest income from the previous problem.)

c. Assume that expected bankruptcy costs have a present value of $450,000. How does this influence OPC's decision?

17.12 Bilbo Inc. is an all-equity firm with 1000 shares of common stock outstanding. Investors require a 19 percent return on Bilbo's unlevered equity. The company distributes all of its earnings to equityholders as dividends at the end of each year. Frodo estimates that its annuals earnings before interest and taxes (EBIT) will be $1,100, $2,050, or $4,000 with probabilities of 0.15, 0.45, and 0.40, respectively. The firm's expectations about earnings will be unchanged in perpetuity. There are no corporate or personal taxes.

a. What is the value of the firm?

b. Suppose Bilbo issues $8,000 of debt at an interest rate of 10 percent and uses the proceeds to repurchase 550 shares of common stock.

1. What is the new value of the firm?
2. What is the new value of the firm's equity?
3. What is the required return on the firm's levered equity?
4. What is the firm's weighted average cost of capital?

c. Suppose that Bilbo's earnings are subject to a corporate tax rate of 37 percent.

1. Will the presence of corporate taxes increase or decrease the value of the firm? Why?
2. What is the value of the firm?

d. Suppose that, in addition to a tax on corporate income of 37 percent, interest income is taxes at 31 percent and the effective tax rate on equity is 17 percent. Assume the introduction of the personal tax rate does not affect the required return on the firm's equity. What is the value of Bilbo in a world with personal and corporate taxes?

17.13 Cores Brewing Company is an all-equity firm that has been ordered by environmental regulators to stop polluting a local river. It must now spend $125 million on pollution-control equipment. The company has three alternatives for obtaining the needed $125 million:

• Sell $125 million of perpetual, corporate bonds with a 20 percent coupon payable at the end of every year. Interest income on these bonds is subject to personal tax rate of 16.5 percent.

- Sell $125 million of perpetual pollution-control bonds with a 16 percent coupon payable at the end of every year. The interest on these bonds is not taxable to investors.
- Sell $125 million of common stock with a 10.25 percent current dividend yield.

Cores Brewing Company is subject to a corporate tax rate of 38 percent. Equity distributions are not taxable to investors. The president of Cores wants to sell common stock because it carries the lowest rate. Mr. Gregories, the company's treasurer, suggests bond financing because of the tax shield offered by the debt. His analysis shows that the value of the firm would increase by $47.5 million (0.38 × $125 million) if Cores issued debt instead of equity. A newly hired financial analyst, Ms. Jackson, agrees with Mr. Gregories and adds that it does not matter which type of debt is issued since the yields will be bid up to reflect taxes.

a. Comment on the analysis of the president, Mr. Gregories, and Ms. Jackson.

b. Should Cores be indifferent about which financing plan it chooses? If not, rank the three alternatives and give the benefits and cost of each.

17.14 Jack Blackburn, CEO of the Weinberg Company, is evaluating his firm's capital structure. He expects that Weinberg will have perpetual earnings before interest and taxes of $850,000. The after-tax required return on Weinberg's equity if it were an all-equity firm is 9.7 percent. Currently, the firm has $1.7 million in debt outstanding and is subject to a corporate tax rate of 39 percent. The personal tax rate on interest income is 17.5 percent, and the personal tax rate on equity distributions is zero. The present value of the combined financial distress and agency costs associated with the debt are approximately 6 percent of the total value of the debt.

a. What is the value of the firm?

b. What is the added value of Weinberg's debt?

17.15 Stratford Textile Corporate (STC) has decided to relocate to Nunavut in four years. Because of transportation costs and a nonexistent secondary market for used textile machines, all of STC's machines will be worthless after four years. Mr. O'Toole, a plan engineer, recommends that one of the following two machines should be purchased for use in the existing plan over the next four years:

	Heavy-Duty Model	Light-Weight Model
Expected annual cost savings	$740	$716
Economic life	4 years	2.5 years
Price of machine	$1,050	$525

The machines carry a CCA rate of 20 percent. STC is subject to a corporate tax rate of 39 percent. STC obtained the following information for its analysis of various investments and financial proposals:

Asset	Expected Return	Variance	Covariance with Market Return
Risk-free asset	0.1		
Market Portfolio	0.2	0.05	
STC common stock			0.044

STC, an all-equity firm, has a market value of $10.7 million.

a. What is STC's cost of capital?

b. Which of the two machines should STC purchase?

c. The CFO of STC is considering the sale of $2 million of 9.4 percent perpetual bonds and using the proceeds to repurchase STC stock. If this plan is adopted:

1. What is the new value of he firm?

2. What is the value of the firm's equity?

MINICASE: Two-Line Pass Inc.'s Capital Budgeting

Robert McKenzie is the founder and CEO of Two-Line Pass Inc., a regional sports restaurant company. Robert is considering opening several new restaurants. David Dregger, the company's CFO, has been put in charge of the capital budgeting analysis. He has examined the potential for the company's expansion and determined that the success of the new restaurants will depend critically on the state of the economy over the next few years.

McKenzie currently has a bond issue outstanding with a face value of $23 million that is due in one year. Covenants associated with this bond issue prohibit the issuance of any additional debt. This restriction means that the expansion will be entirely financed with equity at a cost of $11 million. David has summarized his analysis in the following table, which shows the value of the company in each state of the economy next year, both with and without expansion:

Economic Growth	Probability	Without Expansion	With Expansion
Low	0.25	$20,000,000	$24,500,000
Normal	0.50	$33,400,000	$45,000,000
High	0.25	$42,500,000	$55,000,000

1. What is the expected value of the company in one year, with and without expansion? Would the company's shareholders be better off with or without expansion? Why?
2. What is the expected value of the company's debt in one year, with and without the expansion?
3. One year from now, how much value creation is expected from the expansion? How much value is expected for stockholders? Bondholders?
4. If the company announces that it is not expanding, what do you think will happen to the price of its bonds? What will happen to the price of the bonds if the company does expand?
5. If the company opts not to expand, what are the implications for the company's future borrowing needs? What are the implications if the company does expand?
6. Because of the bond covenant, the expansion would have to be financed with equity. How would it affect your answer if the expansion were financed with cash on hand instead of new equity?

d. Suppose that, because of the new debt, the firm will face costs associated with possible financial distress. These costs can be expressed as 3 percent of the levered firm value calculated in (c). Do these costs imply that STC should remain unlevered?

Appendix 17A: Some Useful Formulas of Financial Structure
Appendix 17B: The Miller Model and the Graduated Income Tax
To access Appendix 17A and 17B, please go to the Online Learning Centre at **www.mcgrawhill.ca/olc/ross.**

Chapter 18

Valuation and Capital Budgeting for the Levered Firm

EXECUTIVE SUMMARY

Instructors often structure the basic course in corporate finance around the two sides of the balance sheet. The left-hand side of the balance sheet contains assets. Chapters 5–9 treat capital budgeting, which is a decision concerning the long-term assets of the firm. Chapters 10–13 cover the discount rate for a project, so those chapters also concern the left-hand side of the balance sheet. The right-hand side of the balance sheet contains liabilities and owner's equity. Chapters 14–17 examine the debt-versus-equity decision, which is a decision about the right-hand side of the balance sheet.

While the preceding chapters of this textbook have, for the most part, treated the capital budgeting decision separately from the capital structure decision, the two decisions are actually related. As we will see, a project of an all-equity firm might be rejected, while the same project might be accepted for a levered but otherwise identical firm. This could occur because the cost of capital frequently decreases with leverage, as we saw in Chapter 16, thereby turning some negative NPV projects into positive NPV projects.

Chapters 5–9 implicitly assumed that the firm is financed with only equity. The goal of this chapter is to value a project, or the firm itself, when leverage is employed. We point out that there are three standard approaches to valuation under leverage: the adjusted present value (APV) method, the flow to equity (FTE) method, and the weighted average cost of capital (WACC) method. These three approaches may seem, at first glance, to be quite different. However, we show that, if applied correctly, all three approaches provide the same value estimate.

The three methods discussed below can be used to value either the firm as a whole or a project. The example below discusses project value, though everything we say applies to an entire firm as well.

18.1 Adjusted Present Value (APV) Approach

The **adjusted present value (APV)** method is best described by the following formula:

$$APV = NPV + NPVF$$

In words, the value of a project to a levered firm (APV) is equal to the value of the project to an unlevered firm (NPV) plus the net present value of the financing side effects (NPVF). There are four major side effects and we covered the first two in Chapters 16 and 17:

1. *The tax subsidy to debt.* This was discussed in Chapter 16, where we pointed out that, for perpetual debt, the value of the tax subsidy is $T_C B$. (T_C is the corporate tax rate, and B is

the value of the debt.) The material on valuation under corporate taxes in Chapter 16 is actually an application of the APV approach.

2. *The costs of financial distress.* The possibility of financial distress, and bankruptcy in particular, arises with debt financing. As stated in the previous chapter, financial distress imposes costs, thereby lowering value.

3. *The costs of issuing new securities.* As we will discuss in detail in Chapter 20, investment bankers participate in the public issuance of corporate debt. These bankers must be compensated for their time and effort, a cost that lowers the value of the project.

4. *Subsidies to debt financing.* The interest rate on debt issued by the provinces and the federal government is substantially below the yield on debt issued by risky private corporations. Frequently, corporations are able to obtain loan guarantees from government, lowering their borrowing costs to a government rate. This subsidy adds value.

While each of these four side effects is important, the tax deduction to debt almost certainly has the highest dollar value in practice. For this reason, the following example considers the tax subsidy, but not the other three side effects.[1]

Consider a project of the Victoria Corporation with the following characteristics:

Sales = \$500,000 per year for the indefinite future
Cash costs = 72% of sales
Initial investment = \$440,000
$T_C = 40\%$
$r_0 = 20\%$, where r_0 is the cost of capital for a project of an all-equity firm

If both the project and the firm are financed with only equity, the project's cash flow is

Sales	\$500,000
Cash costs	−360,000
Operating income	140,000
Corporate tax (40% tax rate)	−56,000
Unlevered cash flow (UCF)	\$ 84,000

The distinction in Chapter 5 between present value and net present value is quite important for this example. As pointed out in Chapter 5, the *present value* of a project is determined before the initial investment at date 0 is subtracted. The initial investment is subtracted for the calculation of *net* present value.

Given a discount rate of 20 percent, the present value of the project is the present value of unlevered cash flow (UCF)[2]

$$\frac{\$84,000}{0.20} = \$420,000$$

The project's NPV (that is, its value to an all-equity firm) is

$$\$420,000 - \$440,000 = -\$20,000$$

Since the NPV is negative, the project would be rejected by an all-equity firm.

Now imagine that the firm finances the project with exactly \$116,666.67 in debt, so that the remaining investment of \$323,333.33 (or \$440,000 − \$116,666.67) is financed with equity. The *net* present value of the project under leverage, which we call *APV*, is

$$
\begin{aligned}
\text{APV} &= \text{NPV} + T_C \times B \\
\$26,666.67 &= -\$20,000 + 0.40 \times \$116,666.67
\end{aligned}
$$

---

[1]The BDE example of Section 18.6 handles both flotation costs and interest subsidies.

[2]UCF is often referred to as free cash flow.

That is, the value of the project when financed with some leverage is equal to the value of the project when financed with all equity plus the tax shield from the debt. Since this number is positive, the project should be accepted.

You may be wondering why we chose such a precise amount of debt. Actually, we chose it so that the ratio of debt to the present value of the project under leverage is 0.25.[3]

In this example, debt is a fixed proportion of the present value of the project, not a fixed proportion of the initial investment of $440,000. This is consistent with the goal of a target debt-to-*market*-value ratio, which we find in the real world. For example, chartered banks typically lend to real estate developers a fixed percentage of the market value of a project, not a fixed percentage of the initial investment.

? Concept Questions
- **How is the APV method applied?**
- **What additional information beyond NPV does one need to calculate APV?**

18.2 Flow to Equity (FTE) Approach

The **flow to equity (FTE)** approach is an alternative capital budgeting approach. The formula simply calls for discounting the cash flow from the project to the equityholders of the levered firm at the cost of equity capital, r_S. For a perpetuity, this becomes

$$\frac{\text{Cash flow from project to equityholders of the levered firm}}{r_S}$$

There are three steps to the FTE approach.

Step 1: Calculating Levered Cash Flow (LCF)[4]

Assuming an interest rate of 10 percent, the perpetual cash flow to equityholders in our example is

Sales	$500,000.00
Cash costs	−360,000.00
Interest (10% × $116,666.67)	−11,666.67
Income after interest	128,333.33
Corporate tax (0.40 tax rate)	−51,333.33
Levered cash flow	$ 77,000.00

---

[3]We choose 0.25 as an example, here. The present value of the project after the initial investment has been made is $466,666.67 (or $26,666.67 + $440,000). Thus, the debt-to-value ratio of the project is 0.25 (or $116,666.67/$466,666.67).

This level of debt can be calculated directly. Note that

Present value of levered project	=	Present value of unlevered project	+	T_C	×	B
$V_{\text{With debt}}$	=	$420,000	+	0.40 × 0.25	×	$V_{\text{With debt}}$

Rearranging the last line, we have

$$V_{\text{With debt}} (1 - 0.40 \times 0.25) = \$420,000$$
$$V_{\text{With debt}} = \$466,666.67$$

Since debt is 0.25 of value, debt is $116,666.67 (or 0.25 × $466,666.67).

[4]We use the term *levered cash flow (LCF)* for simplicity. A more complete term would be *cash flow from the project to the equityholders of a levered firm*. Similarly, a more complete term for *unlevered cash flow (UCF)* would be *cash flow from the project to the equityholders of an unlevered firm*.

Alternatively, one can calculate levered cash flow directly from unlevered cash flow (UCF). The key here is that the difference between the cash flow that equityholders receive in an unlevered firm and the cash flow that equityholders receive in a levered firm is the after-tax interest payment. (Repayment of principal does not appear in this example, since the debt is perpetual.) One writes this algebraically as

$$UCF - LCF = (1 - T_C)r_B B$$

The term on the right-hand side of this expression is the after-tax interest payment. Thus, since cash flow to the unlevered equityholders (UCF) is $84,000 and the after-tax interest payment is $7000 [(0.60) 0.10 × $116,666.67], cash flow to the levered equityholders (LCF) is

$$\$84,000 - \$7,000 = \$77,000$$

which is exactly the number we calculated earlier.

Step 2: Calculating r_S

The next step is to calculate the discount rate, r_S. Note that we assumed that the discount rate on unlevered equity, r_0, is 0.20. As we saw in Chapter 16, the formula for r_S is

$$r_S = r_0 + \frac{B}{S}(1 - T_C)(r_0 - r_B)$$

Note that our target debt-to-value ratio of $\frac{1}{4}$ implies a target debt-to-equity ratio of $\frac{1}{3}$. Applying the above formula to this example, we have

$$r_S = 0.20 + \tfrac{1}{3}(0.60)(0.20 - 0.10) = 0.22$$

Step 3: Valuation

The present value of the project's LCF is

$$\frac{LCF}{r_S} = \frac{\$77,000}{0.22} = \$350,000$$

Since the initial investment is $440,000 and $116,666.67 is borrowed, the firm must advance the project $323,333.33 (or $440,000 − $116,666.67) out of its own cash reserves. The *net* present value of the project is simply the difference between the present value of the project's LCF and the investment not borrowed. Thus, the NPV is

$$\$350,000.00 - \$323,333.33 = \$26,666.67$$

which is identical to the result found with the APV approach.

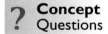

Concept Questions

- **How is the FTE method applied?**
- **What information is needed to calculate FTE?**

18.3 Weighted Average Cost of Capital (WACC) Method

Finally, one can value a project using the **weighted average cost of capital (WACC)** method. While this method was discussed in Chapters 13 and 16, it is worthwhile to review it here. The WACC approach begins with the insight that projects of levered firms are simultaneously financed with both debt and equity. The cost of capital is a weighted average of the cost of debt and the cost of equity. As seen in Chapters 13 and 16, the cost of equity is r_S. Ignoring taxes, the cost of debt is simply the borrowing rate, r_B. However, with corporate taxes, the appropriate cost of debt is $(1 - T_C)r_B$, the after-tax cost of debt.

The formula for determining the weighted average cost of capital, r_{WACC}, is

$$r_{\text{WACC}} = \frac{S}{S + B}r_S + \frac{B}{S + B}r_B(1 - T_C)$$

The weight for equity, $S/(S + B)$, and the weight for debt, $B/(S + B)$, are target ratios. Target ratios are generally expressed in terms of market values, not book values.

The formula calls for discounting the *unlevered* cash flow of the project (UCF) at the weighted average cost of capital, r_{WACC}. The net present value of the project can be written algebraically as

$$\sum_{t=1}^{\infty} \frac{\text{UCF}_t}{(1 + r_{\text{WACC}})^t} - \text{Initial investment}$$

If the project is a perpetuity, the net present value is

$$\frac{\text{UCF}}{r_{\text{WACC}}} - \text{Initial investment}$$

We previously stated that the target debt-to-value ratio of our project is and $\frac{1}{4}$ the corporate tax rate is 0.40, implying that the weighted average cost of capital is

$$r_{\text{WACC}} = \frac{3}{4} \times 0.22 + \frac{1}{4} \times 0.10(0.60) = 0.18$$

Note that r_{WACC}, 0.18, is lower than the cost of equity capital for an all-equity firm, 0.20. This must always be the case, since debt financing provides a tax subsidy that lowers the average cost of capital.[5]

We previously determined the UCF of the project to be $84,000, implying that the present value of the project is

$$\frac{\$84,000}{0.18} = \$466,666.67$$

Since this initial investment is $440,000, the NPV of the project is

$$\$466,666.67 - \$440,000 = \$26,666.67$$

In this example, all three approaches yield the same value.

? Concept Question
- **How is the WACC method applied?**

18.4 A Comparison of the APV, FTE, and WACC Approaches

Capital budgeting techniques in the early chapters of this text applied to all-equity firms. Capital budgeting for the levered firm could not be handled early in the book because the effects of debt on firm value were deferred until the previous two chapters. We learned

---

[5]This is based on MM Proposition I abstracting from the impact of personal taxes.

there that debt increases firm value through tax benefits but decreases value through bankruptcy and related costs.

In the present chapter, we provide three approaches to capital budgeting for the levered firm. The adjusted present value (APV) approach first values the project on an all-equity basis. That is, the project's after-tax cash flows under all-equity financing (UCF) are placed in the numerator of the capital budgeting equation. The discount rate, assuming all-equity financing, appears in the denominator. At this point, the calculation is identical to that performed in the early chapters of this book. We then add the net present value of the debt. We point out that the net present value of the debt is likely to be the sum of four parameters: tax effects, flotation costs, bankruptcy costs, and interest subsidies.

The flow to equity (FTE) approach discounts the after-tax cash flow from a project going to the equityholders of a levered firm (LCF). LCF is the residual to equityholders after interest has been deducted. The discount rate is r_S, the cost of capital to the equityholders of a levered firm. For a firm with leverage, r_S must be greater than r_0, the cost of capital for an unlevered firm. This follows from our material in Chapter 16 showing that leverage raises the risk to the equityholders.

The last approach is the weighted average cost of capital (WACC) method. This technique calculates the project's after-tax cash flows assuming all-equity financing (UCF). The UCF is placed in the numerator of the capital budgeting equation. The denominator, r_{WACC}, is a weighted average of the cost of equity capital and the cost of debt capital. The tax advantage of debt is reflected in the denominator because the cost of debt capital is determined net of corporate tax. The numerator does not reflect debt at all.

All three approaches perform the same task: valuation in the presence of debt financing. And, as illustrated by the previous example, all three provide the same valuation estimate. However, as we saw before, the approaches are markedly different in technique. Because of this, students often ask questions of the following sort: "How can this be? How can the three approaches look so different and yet give the same answer?" We believe that the best way to handle questions like these is through the following two points.

1. *APV versus WACC.* Of the three approaches, APV and WACC display the greatest similarity. After all, both approaches put the unlevered cash flow (UCF) in the numerator. However, the APV approach discounts these flows at r_0, yielding the value of the unlevered project. Adding the present value of the tax shield gives the value of the project under leverage. The WACC approach discounts UCF at r_{WACC}, which is lower than r_0.

   Thus, both approaches adjust the basic NPV formula for unlevered firms in order to reflect the tax benefit of leverage. The APV approach makes this adjustment directly. It simply adds in the present value of the tax shield as a separate term. The WACC approach makes the adjustment in a more subtle way. Here, the discount rate is lowered below r_0. Although we do not provide a proof in the textbook, it can be shown that these two adjustments always have the same quantitative effect.

2. *Entity being valued.* The FTE approach appears at first glance to be far different from the other two. For both the APV and the WACC approaches, the initial investment is subtracted out in the final step ($440,000 in our example). However, for the FTE approach, only the firm's contribution to the initial investment ($323,333.33 = $440,000 − $116,666.67) is subtracted out. This occurs because under the FTE approach, only the future cash flows to the levered equityholders (LCF) are valued. By contrast, future cash flows to the unlevered equityholders (UCF) are valued in both the APV and WACC approaches. Thus, since LCFs are net of interest payments, whereas UCFs are not, the initial investment under the FTE approach is correspondingly reduced by debt financing. In this way, the FTE approach produces the same answer that the other two approaches do.

A Suggested Guideline

The net present value of our project is exactly the same under each of the three methods. In theory, this should always be the case.[6] However, one method usually provides an easier computation than another, and, in many cases, one or more of the methods is virtually impossible computationally.

To illustrate, consider when it is best to use the WACC and FTE approaches. If the risk of a project stays constant throughout its life, it is plausible to assume that r_0 remains constant throughout the project's life. This assumption of constant risk appears to be reasonable for many real-world projects.[7] In addition, if the debt-to-value ratio remains constant over the life of the project, both r_S and r_{WACC} will remain constant as well. Under this latter assumption, either the FTE or the WACC approach is easy to apply. However, if the debt-to-value ratio varies from year to year, both r_S and r_{WACC} vary from year to year as well. Using the FTE or the WACC approach when the denominator changes every year is computationally quite complex, and when computations become complex, the error rate rises. Thus, both the FTE and WACC approaches present difficulties when the debt-to-value *ratio* changes over time.

The APV approach is based on the *level* of debt in each future period. Consequently, when the debt level can be specified precisely for future periods, the APV approach is quite easy to use. However, when the debt level is uncertain, the APV approach becomes more problematic.[8] For example, when the debt-to-value ratio is a constant, the debt level varies with the value of the project. Since the value of the project in a future year cannot be easily forecast, the level of debt cannot be easily forecast either.

Thus, we suggest the following guideline:

> Use WACC or FTE if the firm's target debt-to-value *ratio* applies to the project over its life. Use APV if the project's *level* of debt is known over the life of the project.

There are a number of situations where the APV approach is preferred. For example, in a leveraged buyout (LBO) the firm begins with a large amount of debt but rapidly pays down the debt over a number of years. Since the schedule of debt reduction in the future is known when the LBO is arranged, tax shields in every future year can be easily forecast. Thus, the APV approach is easy to use here. By contrast, the WACC and FTE approaches are virtually impossible to apply to LBOs, since the debt-to-equity ratio cannot be expected to be constant over time. In addition, situations involving interest subsidies and flotation costs are much easier to handle with the APV approach. (The BDE example in Section 18.6 applies the APV approach to subsidies and flotation costs.) Finally, the APV approach handles the lease-versus-buy decision much more easily than does either the FTE or the WACC approach. (A full treatment of the lease-versus-buy decision appears in Chapter 22.)

The preceding examples are special cases. Typical capital budgeting situations are more amenable to either the WACC or the FTE approach than to the APV approach. Financial managers generally think in terms of target debt–value *ratios*. If a project does

---

[6]See R. A. Taggart, "Capital Budgeting and the Financing Decision," *Financial Management* (Summer 1977).

[7]Exceptions include projects involving decision trees and real options discussed in Chapter 9.

[8]For example, when we introduced APV in Section 18.1, we set the optimal debt level at 25 percent of the present value of the project with leverage. In a sense, we "cheated" as this present value was not known at that point. For more on this point, see L. D. Booth, "Capital Budgeting Frameworks for the Multinational Corporation," *Journal of International Business Studies* (Fall 1982).

The Three Methods of Capital Budgeting with Leverage

1. **Adjusted Present Value (APV) Method**

$$\sum_{t=1}^{\infty} \frac{\text{UCF}_t}{(1 + r_0)^t} + \text{Additional effects of debt} - \text{Initial investment}$$

UCF_t = The project's cash flow at date t to the equityholders of an unlevered firm
r_0 = Cost of capital for project in an unlevered firm

2. **Flow to Equity (FTE) Method**

$$\sum_{t=1}^{\infty} \frac{\text{LCF}_t}{(1 + r_S)^t} - (\text{Initial investment} - \text{Amount borrowed})$$

LCF_t = The project's cash flow at date t to the equityholders of a levered firm
r_S = Cost of equity capital with leverage

3. **Weighted Average Cost of Capital (WACC) Method**

$$\sum_{t=1}^{\infty} \frac{\text{UCF}_t}{(1 + r_{\text{WACC}})^t} - \text{Initial investment}$$

r_{WACC} = Weighted average cost of capital

Notes:
1. The middle term in the APV formula implies that the value of a project with leverage is greater than the value of the project without leverage. Since $r_{\text{WACC}} < r_0$, the WACC formula implies that the value of a project with leverage is greater than the value of the project without leverage.
2. In the FTE method, cash flow *after interest* (LCF) is used. Initial investment is reduced by *amount borrowed* as well.

Guidelines:
1. Use WACC or FTE if the firm's target debt-to-value *ratio* applies to the project over its life.
2. Use APV if the project's *level* of debt is known over the life of the project.

better than expected, both its value and its debt capacity will likely rise. The manager will increase debt correspondingly here. Conversely, the manager would be likely to reduce debt if the value of the project were to decline unexpectedly. Of course, because financing is a time-consuming task, the ratio cannot be adjusted on a day-to-day or a month-to-month basis. Rather, the adjustment can be expected to occur over the long run. As mentioned before, the WACC and FTE approaches are more appropriate than is the APV approach when a firm focuses on a target debt–value ratio.

Summing up, we recommend that the WACC and the FTE approaches, rather than the APV approach, be used in most real-world situations. In addition, frequent discussions with business executives have convinced us that the WACC is by far the most widely used method in the real world. Thus, practitioners seem to agree with us that, outside of the special situations mentioned above, the APV approach is a less important method of capital budgeting.

- **What is the main difference between APV and WACC?**
- **What is the main difference between the FTE approach and the other two approaches?**
- **When should the APV method be used?**
- **When should the FTE and WACC approaches be used?**

18.5 Capital Budgeting When the Discount Rate Must Be Estimated

The previous sections of this chapter introduced APV, FTE, and WACC—the three basic approaches to valuing a levered firm. However, one important detail remains. The example in Sections 18.1 through 18.3 *assumed* a discount rate. We now want to show how this rate is determined for real-world firms with leverage, with an application to the three preceding approaches. Example 18.1 brings together the work in Chapters 10–13 on the discount rate for unlevered firms with that in Chapter 16 on the effect of leverage on the cost of capital.

EXAMPLE 18.1

World-Wide Enterprises (WWE) is a large conglomerate thinking of entering the widget business, where it plans to finance projects with a debt-to-value ratio of 25 percent (or, alternatively, a debt-to-equity ratio of $\frac{1}{3}$). As a diversified conglomerate, WWE has a beta approximately equal to 1.0. However, the widget business is more risky than WWE's current operations and requires its own measure of risk. There is currently one firm in the widget industry, Alberta Widgets (AW). This firm is financed with 40 percent debt and 60 percent equity. The beta of AW's equity is 1.5.[9] AW has a borrowing rate of 12 percent, and WWE expects to borrow for its widget venture at 10 percent. The corporate tax rate for both firms is 0.40, the market risk premium is 8.5 percent, and the riskless interest rate is 8 percent. What is the appropriate discount rate for WWE to use for its widget venture?

As explained in Sections 18.1 through 18.3, a corporation may use one of three capital budgeting approaches: APV, FTE, or WACC. The appropriate discount rates for these three approaches are r_0, r_S, and r_{WACC}, respectively. Since AW is WWE's only competitor in widgets, we look at AW's cost of capital to calculate r_0, r_S, and r_{WACC} for WWE's widget venture. The four-step procedure below will allow us to calculate all three discount rates.

1. *Determining AW's cost of equity capital.* First, we determine AW's cost of equity capital, using the security market line (SML) of Chapter 11:

AW's Cost of Equity Capital:

$$r_S = R_F + \beta \times (\overline{R}_M - R_F)$$
$$20.75\% = 8\% + 1.5 \times 8.5\%$$

where $\overline{R}_M$ is the expected return on the market portfolio and R_F is the risk-free rate.

2. *Determining AW's hypothetical all-equity cost of capital.* However, we must standardize the above number in some way, since AW and WWE's widget ventures have different target

[9]An alternative approach is to estimate beta for the project using projected operating and financial leverage. Cleveland Patterson, "The Cost of Equity Capital of a Non-Traded Entity: A Canadian Study," *Canadian Journal of Administrative Sciences* 10 (June 1993), pp. 116–21, applies this approach to estimate the cost of equity for Teleglobe Canada Inc. We discussed this in Chapter 13.

debt-to-value ratios. The easiest approach is to calculate the hypothetical cost of equity capital for AW, assuming all-equity financing. This can be determined from MM's Proposition II under taxes (from Chapter 16):

AW's Cost of Capital if All-Equity:

$$r_S = r_0 + \frac{B}{S}(1 - T_C)\,(r_0 - r_B)$$

$$20.75\% = r_0 + \frac{0.4}{0.6}(0.60)\,(r_0 - 12\%)$$

In the examples of Chapter 16, the unknown in this equation was r_S.[10] However, for this example, the unknown is r_0. By solving the equation, one finds that $r_0 = 0.1825$. Of course, r_0 is less than r_S because the cost of equity capital would be less when the firm employs no leverage.

At this point, firms in the real world generally make the assumption that the business risk of their venture is about equal to the business risk of the firms already in the business. Applying this assumption to our problem, we assert that the hypothetical discount rate of WWE's widget venture if the venture is all-equity financed is also 0.1825.[11] This discount rate will be employed if WWE uses the APV approach, since the APV approach calls for r_0, the project's cost of capital in a firm with no leverage.

3. *Determining r_S for WWE's widget venture.* Alternatively, WWE might use the FTE approach, where the discount rate for levered equity is determined from

Cost of Equity Capital for WWE's Widget Venture:

$$r_S = r_0 + \frac{B}{S}(1 - T_C)\,(r_0 - r_B)$$

$$19.9\% = 18.25\% + \frac{1}{3}\,(0.60)\,(18.25\% - 10\%)$$

Note that the cost of equity capital for WWE's widget venture, 0.199, is less than the cost of equity capital for AW, 0.2075. This occurs because AW has a higher debt-to-equity ratio. (As mentioned above, both firms are assumed to have the same business risk.)

4. *Determining r_{WACC} for WWE's widget venture.* Finally, WWE might use the WACC approach. The appropriate calculation here is

r_{WACC} for WWE's Widget Venture:

$$r_{\mathrm{WACC}} = \frac{B}{S + B}r_B\,(1 - T_C) + \frac{S}{S + B}r_S$$

$$16.425\% = \frac{1}{4}10\%\,(0.60) + \frac{3}{4} \times 19.9\%$$

The preceding example shows how the three discount rates, r_0, r_S, and r_{WACC}, are determined in the real world. These are the appropriate rates for the APV, FTE, and WACC approaches, respectively. Note that r_S for Alberta Widgets is determined first, because the

---

[10]In this example we are assuming that the debt betas for AW and WWE are zero. This assumption is not strictly correct because the cost of debt for AW and WWE is assumed to be higher than the risk-free rate. As a practical matter, most academic research suggests debt betas are very close to zero.

[11]Alternatively, a firm might assume that its venture would be somewhat riskier since it is a new entrant. Thus, the firm might select a discount rate slightly higher than 0.1825. Of course, no exact formula exists for adjusting the discount rate upwards.

cost of equity capital can be determined from the beta of the firm's stock. As discussed in Chapter 13, beta can easily be estimated for any publicly traded firm, such as AW.

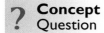

Concept Question

- **What adjustments are required in capital budgeting for a project with beta different from the firm's?**

18.6 APV Example

As mentioned above, the APV approach is effective in situations where flotation costs and subsidized financing arise. The FTE and the WACC approaches are less effective in these situations. Example 18.2 illustrates where the APV approach works well.

EXAMPLE 18.2

Suppose BDE is considering a $30 million project that will last five years. This investment will be depreciated at a CCA rate of 20 percent. Projected net operating revenue is $5.5 million annually. The tax rate is 40 percent. There is no salvage value at the end of the project. The risk-free rate is 5 percent and the cost of equity is 10 percent. This is often called the *cost of unlevered equity* since we assume initially that the firm has no debt.

All-Equity Value

Assuming that the project is financed with 100 percent equity, its value is

$$-\$30,000,000 + \frac{\$5,500,000}{0.1}\left[1 - \frac{1}{(1.1)^5}\right] + \text{CCATS}$$

$$= -\$30,000,000 + \$20,849,327 + \frac{\$30,000,000 \times 0.2 \times 0.4}{0.1 + 0.2} \times \frac{1 + 0.5 \times 0.1}{1 + 0.1}$$

$$= -\$30,000,000 + \$20,849,327 + \$7,636,364$$

$$= -\$1,514,309$$

An all-equity firm would clearly *reject* this project because the NPV is negative. And equity flotation costs (not considered yet) would only make the NPV more negative. However, debt financing may add enough value to the project to justify acceptance. We consider the effects of debt below.

Additional Effects of Debt

BDE can obtain a five-year, balloon payment loan for $22,500,000 after flotation costs. The interest rate is the risk-free cost of debt of 5 percent. The flotation costs are 1 percent of the amount raised. We look at three ways in which debt financing alters the NPV of the project.

Flotation Costs   The following formula gives us the flotation costs:

$$\$22,500,000 = (1 - 0.01) \times \text{Amount raised}$$

$$\text{Amount raised} = \frac{\$22,500,000}{0.99} = \$22,727,273$$

So flotation costs are $227,273 and in the text we added these to the initial outlay, reducing NPV.

The APV method refines the estimate of flotation costs by recognizing that they generate a tax shield. Flotation costs are paid immediately but are deducted from taxes by amortizing over the life of the loan. In this example, the annual tax deduction for flotation costs is $227,273/5 years = $45,455. At a tax rate of 40 percent, the annual tax shield is $45,455 × 0.40 = $18,182.

To find the net flotation costs of the loan, add the present value of the tax shield to the flotation costs:

$$\text{Net flotation costs} = -\$227{,}273 + \frac{\$18{,}182}{0.05} \times \left[1 - \frac{1}{(1.05)^5}\right]$$

$$= -\$227{,}273 + \$78{,}719 = -\$148{,}554$$

The net present value of the project after debt flotation costs but before the benefits of debt is

$$-\$1{,}514{,}309 - \$148{,}554 = -\$1{,}662{,}863$$

Tax Subsidy   The loan of $22,500,000 is received at date 0. Annual interest at 5 percent is $1,125,000. The interest cost after tax is $675,000 [or $1,125,000 × (1 − 0.40)]. The loan has a balloon payment of the full principal at the end of five years. The loan gives rise to three sets of cash flows: the loan received, the annual interest cost after taxes, and the repayment of principal. The net present value of the loan is simply the sum of three present values:

$$\text{NPV(loan)} = \begin{matrix}+\text{Amount} \\ \text{borrowed}\end{matrix} - \begin{matrix}\text{Present value} \\ \text{of after-tax} \\ \text{interest payments}\end{matrix} - \begin{matrix}\text{Present value} \\ \text{of loan} \\ \text{repayments}\end{matrix} \qquad \text{(18.1)}$$

$$= +\$22{,}500{,}000 - \frac{\$675{,}000}{0.05} \times \left[1 - \frac{1}{(1.05)^5}\right] - \frac{\$22{,}500{,}000}{(1.05)^5}$$

$$= +\$22{,}500{,}000 - \$2{,}922{,}397 - \$17{,}629{,}339 = \$1{,}948{,}264$$

The NPV of the loan is positive, reflecting the interest tax shield.[12]

The adjusted present value of the project with this financing is

$$\text{APV} = \text{All-equity value} - \text{Flotation costs of debt} + \text{NPV (loan)}$$
$$\$285{,}401 = -\$1{,}514{,}309 - \$148{,}554 + \$1{,}948{,}264$$

Though we previously saw that an all-equity firm would reject the project, a firm would *accept* the project if a $22,500,000 loan could be obtained.

Because the loan discussed above was at the market rate of 5 percent, we have considered only two of the three additional effects of debt (flotation costs and tax subsidy) so far. We now examine another loan for which the third effect arises.

Non–Market Rate Financing   In Canada, a number of companies can obtain subsidized financing from federal or provincial governments. For example, in 2001, loan subsidies from the federal government enabled Bombardier to beat its Brazilian rival, Embraer, in winning billion-dollar contracts for its regional jets from Air Wisconsin and Northwest

---

[12]The NPV (loan) must be zero in a no-tax world, because interest provides no tax shield there. To check this intuition we calculate

$$0 = \$22{,}500{,}000 - \frac{\$1{,}125{,}000}{0.05}\left[1 - \frac{1}{(1.05)^5}\right] - \frac{\$22{,}500{,}000}{(1.05)^5}$$

Airlines.[13] Suppose that the BDE project is deemed socially beneficial and a federal minister grants the firm a $22,500,000 loan at 4 percent interest. In addition, the government absorbs all flotation costs. Clearly, the company will choose this loan over the one we previously calculated. At 4 percent interest, annual interest payments are $22,500,000 × 0.04 = $900,000. After-tax payments are $540,000 = $900,000 × (1 − 0.40). Using Equation (18.1),

$$\text{NPV(loan)} = \begin{array}{c} +\text{Amount} \\ \text{borrowed} \end{array} - \begin{array}{c} \text{Present value} \\ \text{of after-tax} \\ \text{interest payments} \end{array} - \begin{array}{c} \text{Present value} \\ \text{of loan} \\ \text{repayments} \end{array}$$

$$= +\$22,500,000 - \frac{\$540,000}{0.05} \times \left[1 - \frac{1}{(1.05)^5}\right] - \frac{\$22,500,000}{(1.05)^5}$$

$$= +\$22,500,000 - \$2,337,917 - \$17,629,339 = \$2,532,744$$

Notice that we still discount the cash flows at 5 percent when the firm is borrowing at 4 percent. This is done because 5 percent is the fair market rate (the rate at which the firm could borrow *without* benefit of subsidization). The adjusted present value of the subsidized loan is larger than the net present value of the earlier loan because the firm is now borrowing at the below-market rate of 4 percent. Note that the NPV (loan) calculation captures both the tax effect *and* the non–market rate effect.

The adjusted present value of the project with subsidized debt financing is

$$\begin{array}{ccccccc} \text{APV} & = & \text{All-equity value} & - & \text{Flotation costs of debt} & + & \text{NPV (loan)} \\ \$1,018,435 & = & -\$1,514,309 & - & 0 & + & \$2,532,744 \end{array}$$

Subsidized financing has enhanced the NPV substantially. The result is that the government debt subsidy program will likely achieve its result—encouraging the firm to invest in the kind of project the government wishes to encourage.

The above example illustrates the adjusted present value approach. The approach begins with the present value of a project for the all-equity firm. Next, the effects of debt are added in. The approach is intuitively appealing because individual components are calculated separately and added together in a simple way. And, if the debt from the project can be specified precisely, the present value of the debt can be calculated precisely.

? Concept Question

• **How do flotation costs and subsidized financing affect APV?**

18.7 Beta and Leverage

Chapter 13 provides the formula for the relationship between the beta of the common stock and the leverage of the firm in a world without taxes:

The No-Tax Case:

$$\beta_{\text{Equity}} = \beta_{\text{Asset}}\left(1 + \frac{\text{Debt}}{\text{Equity}}\right) \tag{18.2}$$

---

[13]K. Leger, "Canada, Brazil both claim win in subsidy war," *National Post,* July 27, 2001.

As pointed out in Chapter 13, this relationship holds under the assumption that the beta of debt is zero.

Since firms must pay corporate taxes in practice, it is worthwhile to provide the relationship with corporate taxes. It can be shown that the relationship between the beta of the unlevered firm and the beta of the levered equity is[14]

The Corporate-Tax Case:

$$\beta_{\text{Equity}} = \left[1 + \frac{(1 - T_C)\text{Debt}}{\text{Equity}} \right] \beta_{\text{Unlevered firm}} \qquad (18.3)$$

when (1) the corporation is taxed at the rate of T_C and (2) the debt has a zero beta.

Because $[1 + (1 - T_C)\text{Debt/Equity}]$ must be more than 1 for a levered firm, it follows that $\beta_{\text{Unlevered firm}} < \beta_{\text{Equity}}$. The corporate-tax case of Equation (18.3) is quite similar to the no-tax case of Equation (18.2), because the beta of levered equity must be greater than the beta of the unlevered firm in either case. The intuition that leverage increases the risk of equity applies in both cases.

However, notice that the two equations are not equal. It can be shown that leverage increases the equity beta less rapidly under corporate taxes. This occurs because, under taxes, leverage creates a *riskless* tax shield, thereby lowering the risk of the entire firm.

EXAMPLE 18.3

Alberta Petroleum Ltd. is considering a scale-enhancing project. The market value of the firm's debt is $100 million, and the market value of the firm's equity is $200 million. The debt is considered riskless. The corporate tax rate is 40 percent. Regression analysis indicates that the beta of the firm's equity is 2. The risk-free rate is 10 percent, and the expected market premium is 8.5 percent. What would be the project's discount rate in the hypothetical case that Alberta Petroleum is all-equity?

---

[14]This result holds only if the beta of debt equals zero. To see this, note that

$$V_U + T_C B = V_L = B + S \qquad (a)$$

where
$\quad V_U = $ Value of unlevered firm
$\quad V_L = $ Value of levered firm
$\quad B = $ Value of debt in a levered firm
$\quad S = $ Value of equity in a levered firm

As we stated in the text, the beta of the levered firm is a weighted average of the debt beta and the equity beta:

$$\frac{B}{B + S} \times \beta_B + \frac{S}{B + S} \times \beta_S$$

where β_B and β_S are the betas of the debt and the equity of the levered firm, respectively. Because $V_L = B + S$, we have

$$\frac{B}{V_L} \times \beta_B + \frac{S}{V_L} \times \beta_S \qquad (b)$$

The beta of the levered firm can also be expressed as a weighted average of the beta of the unlevered firm and the beta of the tax shield:

$$\frac{V_U}{V_U + T_C B} \times \beta_U + \frac{T_C B}{V_U + T_C B} \times \beta_B$$

where β_U is the beta of the unlevered firm. This follows from equation (a). Because $V_L = V_U + T_C B$, we have

$$\frac{V_U}{V_L} \times \beta_U + \frac{T_C B}{V_L} \times \beta_B \qquad (c)$$

We can equate Equations (b) and (c) because both represent the beta of a levered firm. Equation (a) tells us that $V_U = S + (1 - T_C) \times B$. Under the assumption that $\beta_B = 0$, equating (b) and (c) and using Equation (a) yields Equation (18.3).

We can answer this question in two steps:

1. *Determining beta of a hypothetical all-equity firm.* Rearranging Equation (18.3), we have

Unlevered Beta:

$$\frac{\text{Equity}}{\text{Equity} + (1 - T_C) \times \text{Debt}} \times \beta_{\text{Equity}} = \beta_{\text{Unlevered firm}} \qquad (18.4)$$

$$\frac{\$200\text{ million}}{\$200\text{ million} + (1 - 0.40) \times \$100\text{ million}} \times 2 = 1.54$$

2. *Determining the discount rate.* We calculate the discount rate from the security market line (SML) as

Discount Rate:

$$r_S = R_F + \beta \times [\overline{R}_M - R_F]$$
$$23.09\% = 10\% + 1.54 \times 8.5\%$$

The Project Is Not Scale-Enhancing

Because Example 18.3 assumed that the project is scale-enhancing, we began with the beta of the firm's equity. If the project is not scale-enhancing, we could begin with the equity betas of firms in the industry of the project. For each firm, the hypothetical beta of the unlevered equity could be calculated by Equation (18.4). The SML could then be used to determine the project's discount rate from the average of these betas.

EXAMPLE 18.4

The J. Lowes Corporation, which currently manufactures staples, is considering a $1 million investment in a project in the aircraft adhesives industry. The corporation estimates unlevered after-tax cash flows (UCF) of $300,000 per year in perpetuity from the project. The firm will finance the project with a debt-to-value ratio of 0.5 (or, equivalently, a debt-to-equity ratio of 1:1).

The three competitors in this new industry are currently unlevered, with betas of 1.2, 1.3, and 1.4. Assuming a risk-free rate of 5 percent, a market-risk premium of 9 percent, and a corporate tax rate of 40 percent, what is the net present value of the project?

We can answer this question in five steps.

1. *Calculating the average unlevered beta in the industry.* The average unlevered beta across all three existing competitors in the aircraft adhesives industry is

$$\frac{1.2 + 1.3 + 1.4}{3} = 1.3$$

2. *Calculating the levered beta for J. Lowes' new project.* Assuming the same unlevered beta for this new project as for the existing competitors, we have, from Equation (18.3),

Levered Beta:

$$\beta_{\text{Equity}} = [1 + \frac{(1 - T_C)\text{Debt}}{\text{Equity}}]\beta_{\text{Unlevered firm}}$$

$$2.08 = (1 + \frac{0.6 \times 1}{1}) \times 1.3$$

3. *Calculating the cost of levered equity for the new project.* We calculate the discount rate from the security market line (SML) as

Discount Rate:

$$r_S = R_F + \beta \times [\bar{R}_M - R_F]$$
$$0.237 = 0.05 + 2.08 \times 0.09$$

4. *Calculating the WACC for the new project.* The formula for determining the weighted average cost of capital, r_{WACC}, is

$$r_{WACC} = \frac{B}{V}r_B(1 - T_C) + \frac{S}{V}r_S$$
$$0.134 = \frac{1}{2} \times 0.05 \times 0.6 + \frac{1}{2} \times 0.237$$

5. *Determining the project's value.* Because the cash flows are perpetual, the NPV of the project is

$$\frac{\text{Unlevered cash flows (UCF)}}{r_{WACC}} - \text{Initial investment}$$

$$\frac{\$300,000}{0.134} - \$1 \text{ million} = \$1.24 \text{ million}$$

? Concept Question

• **How is beta adjusted for leverage and corporate taxes?**

18.8 SUMMARY AND CONCLUSIONS

Earlier chapters showed how to calculate net present value for projects of all-equity firms. We pointed out in the last two chapters that the introduction of taxes and bankruptcy costs changes a firm's financing decisions and means that rational corporations should employ some debt. Because of the benefits and costs associated with debt, the capital budgeting decision is different for levered firms than for unlevered firms. The present chapter has discussed three methods for capital budgeting by levered firms: the adjusted present value (APV), flows to equity (FTE), and weighted average cost of capital (WACC) approaches.

1. The APV formula can be written as

$$\sum_{t=1}^{\infty}\frac{UCF_t}{(1 + r_0)^t} + \text{Additional effects of debt} - \text{Initial investment}$$

There are four additional effects of debt:
• Tax shield from debt financing.
• Flotation costs.
• Bankruptcy costs.
• Benefit of non–market-rate financing.

2. The FTE formula can be written as

$$\sum_{t=1}^{\infty}\frac{LCF_t}{(1 + r_S)^t} - (\text{Initial investment} - \text{Amount borrowed})$$

3. The WACC formula can be written as

$$\sum_{t=1}^{\infty}\frac{UCF_t}{(1 + r_{WACC})^t} - \text{Initial investment}$$

4. Corporations frequently follow these guidelines:
   • Use WACC or FTE if the firm's target debt-to-value *ratio* applies to the project over its life.
   • Use APV if the project's *level* of debt is known over the life of the project.
5. The APV method is used frequently for special situations like interest subsidies, LBOs, and leases. The WACC and FTE methods are commonly used for more typical capital budgeting situations. The APV approach is a rather unimportant method for typical capital budgeting situations.
6. The beta of the equity of the firm is positively related to the leverage of the firm.
7. The beta of a project is the same as the firm's beta only in the case of scale-enhancing projects. Otherwise, one must begin with unlevered betas for firms in the same industry as the project.

KEY TERMS

Adjusted present value (APV) 511   Flow to equity (FTE) 513   Weighted average cost of capital (WACC) 514

SUGGESTED READING

The following article contains a superb discussion of some of the subtleties of using WACC for project valuation:
J. Miles and R. Ezzell. "The Weighted Average Cost of Capital, Perfect Capital Markets and Project Life: A Clarification." *Journal of Financial and Quantitative Analysis* 15 (September 1980).

The following article presents the practical aspects of the APV approach:
T.A. Luehrman. "Using APV: A Better Tool for Valuing Operations." *Harvard Business Review* (May/June 1997).

A fascinating article on the merits of the APV and WACC approaches is:
I. Inselbag and H. Kaufold. "Two DCF Approaches in Valuing Companies Under Alternative Financing Strategies (and How to Choose Between Them)." *Journal of Applied Corporate Finance* (Spring 1997).

This article points out some important limitations of APV:
L. D. Booth. "Capital Budgeting Frameworks for the Multinational Corporation." *Journal of International Business Studies* (Fall 1982).

QUESTIONS & PROBLEMS

Adjusted Present Value (APV)

18.1   GM and Ford are competing to sell a fleet of next-generation crossover vehicles to Budget. The vehicles will be in an asset class with a CCA rate of 25 percent and will be sold after five years. Budget expects that the crossover vehicles will have no salvage value. The car rental company expects a fleet of 30 vehicles to generate $430,000 per year in pre-tax income. Budget is in the 38 percent tax bracket and the firm's overall required return is 9.875 percent. The addition of the new fleet will not add to the risk of the firm. Treasury bills are priced to yield 4.25 percent.
   a. What is the maximum price that Budget should be willing to pay for the fleet?
   b. Suppose the price of the fleet is $1.1 million; both suppliers are charging this price. Budget is able to issue $850,000 in debt to finance the project. The bonds can be issued at par and will carry a seven percent interest rate. Budget will incur no costs to issue the debt and no costs of financial distress. What is the APV of this project if Budget uses debt to finance the auto purchase?
   c. To entice Budget to buy crossovers from Ford, Ford is willing to finance their purchase up to $700,000 at 6 percent. Now what is the maximum price that Budget is willing to pay Ford Canada for the fleet of crossover vehicles?

EXCEL

18.2   Sammoth Corporation has established a joint venture with Rocky Avenue Construction Inc. to build a toll bridge in New Brunswick. The initial investment in equipment is $42 million. The equipment will be fully depreciated using the straight-line method over its economic life of five years. Earnings before interest, taxes, and depreciation collected from the toll bridge are projected to be $4.34 million per annum for 30 years

Visit us at www.mcgrawhill.ca/olc/ross

starting from the end of the first year. The corporate tax rate is 38 percent. The required rate of return for the project under all-equity financing is 14.5 percent. The pre-tax cost of debt for the joint partnership is 9.5 percent. To encourage investment in the country's infrastructure, the Canadian government will subsidize the project with an $18 million, 18-year loan at an interest rate of 6 percent per year. All principal will be repaid in one balloon payment at the end of year 18. What is the adjusted present value of this project?

18.3   For the company in the previous problem, what is the value of being able to issue subsidized debt instead of having to issue debt at the terms it would normally receive? Assume the face amount and maturity of the debt issue are the same.

18.4   Raging Bull Inc. has produced rodeo supplies for over 20 years. The company currently has a debt–equity ratio of 45 percent and is in the 40 percent tax bracket. The required return on the firm's levered equity is 15.75 percent. Raging Bull is planning to expand its production capacity. The equipment to be purchased is expected to generate the following unlevered cash flows:

Year	Cash Flow
0	−$27,000,000
1	9,000,000
2	15,000,000
3	12,000,000

The company has arranged a $14 million debt issue to partially finance the expansion. Under the loan, the company would pay interest of 8.8 percent at the end of each year on the outstanding balance at the beginning of the year. The company would also make year-end principal payments of $5.51 million per year, completely retiring the issue by the end of the third year. Using the adjusted present value method, should the company proceed with the expansion?

EXCEL

18.5   Peatco is considering a $3.1 million project that will be depreciated at a CCA rate of 35 percent over the three-year life of the project. The project will generate pre-tax earnings of $980,000 per year, and it will not change the risk level of the firm. Peatco can obtain a three-year, 8 percent loan to finance the project; the bank will charge Peatco fees of 0.75 percent of the gross proceeds of the loan. The fee must be paid upfront, not from the loan proceeds. If Peatco financed the project with all equity, its cost of capital would be 15 percent. The tax rate is 38 percent and the risk-free rate is 4.6 percent.
   a. Using the APV method, determine whether or not Peatco should undertake the project.
   b. After hearing that Peatco would not be initiating the project in their town, the city council voted to subsidize Peatco's loan. Under the city's proposal, Peatco will pay the same fees, but the rate of the loan will be 5.5 percent. Should Peatco accept the city's offer and begin the project?

18.6   Jiminy Inc., an all-equity firm, is considering a $2.4 million investment that will be depreciated at a CCA rate of 30 percent over four-year life. The project is expected to generate earnings before taxes and depreciation of $850,000 per year for four years. The investment will not change the risk level of the firm. The company can obtain a four-year, 9.5 percent loan to finance the project (all principal will be repaid in one balloon payment at the end of the fourth year) or Jiminy can obtain a two-year, 8.75 percent loan (one-tenth of the principal repaid at the end of the first year) followed another two-year loan at 9.6 percent (one-tenth the principal is repaid at the end of the first year). In either case, the bank will charge the firm a total of $24,000 in flotation fees, which will be amortized over the four-year life of the loan. If the company financed the project entirely with equity, the firm's cost of capital would be 12 percent. The corporate tax rate is 30 percent.
   a. Using the adjusted present value method, determine whether the company should undertake the project obtaining a four-year loan.
   b. Using the adjusted present value method, determine whether the company should undertake the project obtaining two consecutive two-year loans.
   c. Which borrowing option is better for Jiminy?

Flow to Equity

18.7   The Torino Pizza Club owns three identical restaurants popular for their specialty pizzas. Each restaurant has a debt–equity ratio of 40 percent and makes interest payments of $29,500 at the end of each year. The cost of the firm's levered equity is 19 percent. Each store estimates that annual sales will be $1 million; annual cost of goods sold will be $450,000; and annual general and administrative costs will be $325,000. These cash flows are expected to remain the same forever. The corporate tax rate is 36 percent.
    a. Use the flow to equity approach to determine the value of the company's equity.
    b. What is the total value of the company?
    c. What is the main difference between the FTE approach and the other two approaches?

Weighted Average Cost of Capital

18.8   If Wild West Widgets Inc. were an all-equity company, it would have a beta of 1.1. The company has a target debt–equity ratio of 0.36. The expected return on the market portfolio is 13 percent, and Treasury bills currently yield 7 percent. The company has two bond issues outstanding: one that matures in 20 years and has a 9 percent coupon rate and one that matures in 25 years and has a 10.5 percent coupon rate. The first bond currently sells for $975 and the second bond sells at $984. Both bonds have the same amount outstanding. The corporate tax rate is 36 percent.
    a. What is the company's cost of debt?
    b. What is the company's cost of equity?
    c. What is the company's weighted average cost of capital?

18.9   Environmental Power Corporation (EPC) is considering a $50 million project in its power systems division. James Watt, the company's chief financial officer, has evaluated the project and determined that the project's unlevered cash flows will be $3.5 million per year in perpetuity. Mr. Watt has devised two possibilities for raising the initial investment: issuing 10-year bonds or issuing common stock. NEC's pre-tax cost of debt is 7.2 percent, and its cost of equity is 10.9 percent. The company's target debt-to-value ratio is 80 percent. The project has the same risk as NEC's existing businesses, and it will support the same amount of debt. NEC is in the 34 percent tax bracket. Should NEC accept the project?

18.10   Klingon Corporation's stock returns have a covariance with the market portfolio of 0.048. The standard deviation of the returns on the market portfolio is 20 percent, and the expected market risk premium is 7.5 percent. The company has bonds outstanding with a total market value of $30 million and a yield to maturity of 8 percent. The company also has 5 million shares of common stock outstanding, each selling for $20. The company's CEO considers the firm's current debt–equity ratio optimal. The corporate tax rate is 35 percent, and Treasury bills currently yield 6 percent. The company is considering the purchase of additional equipment that would cost $40 million. The expected unlevered cash flows from the equipment are $13 million per year for five years. Purchasing the equipment will not change the risk level of the firm.
    a. Use the weighted average cost of capital approach to determine whether Klingon should purchase the equipment.
    b. Suppose the company decides to fund the purchase of the equipment entirely with debt. What is the cost of capital for the project now? Explain.

18.11   Sammy the Mechanic Inc. has compiled the following information on its financing costs:

Type of Financing	Book Value	Market Value	Before-Tax Cost
Long-term debt	$ 2,000,000	$ 2,000,000	9%
Short-term debt	9,000,000	8,000,000	7
Common stock	6,000,000	22,000,000	14
Total	$17,000,000	$32,000,000	

The company is in the 35 percent tax bracket and has a target debt–equity ratio of 60 percent. The target short-term debt/long-term debt ratio is 20 percent.
    a. What is the company's weighted average cost of capital using book value weights?

Visit us at www.mcgrawhill.ca/olc/ross

    b. What is the company's weighted average cost of capital using market value weights?

    c. What is the company's weighted average cost of capital using target capital structure weights?

    d. What is the difference between WACCs? Which is the correct WACC to use for project evaluation?

A Comparison of the APV, FTE, and WACC Approaches

18.12 Pop Industries just issued $160,000 of perpetual 10 percent debt and used the proceeds to repurchase stock. The company expects to generate $75,000 of earnings before interest and taxes in perpetuity. The company distributes all its earnings as dividends at the end of each year. The firm's unlevered cost of capital is 18 percent, and the corporate tax rate is 40 percent.

    a. What is the value of the company as an unlevered firm?

    b. Use the adjusted present value method to calculate the value of the company with leverage.

    c. What is the required return on the firm's levered equity?

    d. Use the flow to equity method to calculate the value of the company's equity.

18.13 Dillon Inc.'s current required return is 20 percent, and the firm distributes all of its earnings as dividends at the end of each year. The company is an unlevered firm with expected annual earnings before taxes of $35 million in perpetuity. There are 1.5 million shares of common stock outstanding and is subject to a corporate tax rate of 35 percent. The firm is planning a recapitalization under which it will issue $40 million of perpetual 9 percent debt and use the proceeds to buy back shares.

    a. Calculate the value of the company before the recapitalization plan is announced. What is the value of equity before the announcement? What is the price per share?

    b. Use the APV method to calculate the company value after the recapitalization plan is announced. What is the value of equity after the announcement? What is the price per share?

    c. How many shares will be repurchased? What is the value of equity after the repurchase has been completed? What is the price per share?

    d. Use the flow to equity method to calculate the value of the company's equity after the recapitalization.

18.14 Mojave Mocha Company has a debt–equity ratio of 0.45. The required return on the company's unlevered equity is 17 percent, and the pre-tax cost of the firm's debt is 9 percent. Sales revenue for the company is expected to remain stable indefinitely at last year's level of $23,500,000. Variable costs amount to 60 percent of sales. The tax rate is 40 percent, and the company distributes all its earnings as dividends at the end of each year.

    a. If the company were financed entirely by equity, how much would it be worth?

    b. What is the required return on the firm's levered equity?

    c. Use the weighted average cost of capital method to calculate the value of the company. What is the value of the company's equity? What is the value of the company's debt?

    d. Use the flow to equity method to calculate the value of the company's equity.

    e. What is the main difference between the WACC and APV methods?

Capital Budgeting for Projects That Are Not Scale-Enhancing

18.15 Blue Angel Inc., a private firm in the holiday gift industry, is considering a new project. The company currently has a target debt–equity ratio of .40, but the industry target debt–equity ratio is .35. The industry average beta is 1.2. The market risk premium is 8 percent, and the risk-free rate is 7 percent. Assume all companies in this industry can issue debt at the risk-free rate. The corporate tax rate is 40 percent. The project requires an initial outlay of $450,000 and is expected to result in a $75,000 cash inflow at the end of the first year. The project will be financed at Blue Angel's target debt–equity ratio. Annual cash flows from the project will grow at a constant rate of 5 percent until the end of the fifth year and remain constant forever thereafter. Should Blue Angel invest in the project?

The NPV of Loans

18.16 Jack Lantern, CFO of Halloween Enterprises, is evaluating a 12-year, 8.4 percent loan with gross proceeds of $5,312,500. The interest payments on the loan will be made annually. Flotation costs are estimated to be 0.75 percent of gross proceeds and will be amortized using a straight-line schedule over the 12-year life of the loan. The company has a tax rate of 31 percent, and the loan will not increase the risk of financial distress for the company.

    a. Calculate the net present value of the loan excluding flotation costs.

    b. Calculate the net present value of the loan including flotation costs.

Beta and Leverage

18.17 North Pole Fishing Equipment Corporation and South Pole Fishing Equipment Corporation would have identical equity betas of 1.25 if both were all equity financed. The market value information for each company is shown here:

	North Pole	South Pole
Debt	$1,400,000	$2,600,000
Equity	$2,600,000	$1,400,000

The expected return on the market portfolio is 12.40 percent, and the risk-free rate is 5.30 percent. Both companies are subject to a corporate tax rate of 35 percent. Assume the beta of debt is zero.

    a. What are the two types of risk that are measured by a levered beta?

    b. What is the equity beta of each of the two companies?

    c. What is the required rate of return on each of the two companies' equity?

18.18 D.B. Incorporated and A.P. Co. both have the same beta of 1.47. The equity beta of D.B. is 2.02 and the equity beta of A.P. is 1.87. The corporate tax rate is 37 percent for both companies, the expected return on the market portfolio is 9 percent and the risk-free rate is 4.25 percent. Assuming that the beta of debt is zero, what the debt-to-equity ratio for both companies?

STANDARD & POOR'S

www.mcgrawhill.ca/ edumarketinsight

18.19 Use the Financial Post Advisor to locate the annual income statements for MDS Inc. (MDS) and calculate the marginal tax rate for the company for the last year. Assume that the marginal text rate for next year will be the same as last year's effective tax rate. Next, find the beta for MDS. Using the current debt and equity from the most recent annual balance sheet, calculate the unlevered beta for MDS.

18.20 Use the Financial Post Advisor to locate balance sheets and stock market information for Rogers Communications. Calculate book-value weights for the firm's capital structure. Assume that the marginal tax rate for next year will be the same as last year's effective tax rate. Find the market value of Rogers' stock and its market capitalization. Assuming that the debt is trading at its book value, calculate the market-value weights. How do they compare with the book-value weights? Using the beta and information provided in Table 10.2, what is the cost of equity for the company. Using the company's long term debt note disclosure, what is the current cost of debt for the company? Find the weighted average cost of capital for Rogers using each set of weights in turn. Explain the difference between the two WACCs. Which is the correct WACC to use for capital budgeting analysis?

18.21 Repeat your calculations using market-value weights in Problem 18.17 for two of BCE's competitors in the integrated telecommunications industry. How does WACC differ among these three firms? What explains the differences?

Appendix 18A: The Adjusted-Present-Value Approch to Valuing Leveraged Buyouts

To access Appendix 18A, please go to the Online Learning Centre at **www.mcgrawhill.ca/olc/ross.**

Visit us at www.mcgrawhill.ca/olc/ross

MINICASE: The Leveraged Buyout of Miku Products Group Inc.

Miku Products Group Inc. (MPG) was founded 17 years ago by Joe Miku and originally sold snack foods such as potato chips and pretzels. Through acquisitions, the company has grown into a conglomerate with major divisions in the snack food industry, car audio systems, health products, and building supplies. Additionally, the company has several smaller divisions. In recent years the company has been underperforming, but the company's management does not seem to be aggressively pursuing opportunities to improve operations (and the stock price).

Mack Fleury is a financial analyst specializing in identifying potential buyout targets. He believes that two major changes are needed at Miku. First, he thinks that the company would be better off if it sold several divisions and concentrated on its core competencies in snack foods and car audio systems. Second, the company is financed entirely with equity. Because the cash flows of the company are relatively steady, Mack thinks the company's debt–equity ratio should be at least .25. He believes these changes would significantly enhance shareholder wealth, but he also believes that the existing board and company management are unlikely to take the necessary actions. As a result, Mack thinks the company is a good candidate for a leveraged buyout.

A leveraged buyout (LBO) is the acquisition by a small group of equity investors of a public or private company. Generally, an LBO is financed primarily with debt. The new shareholders service the heavy interest and principal payments with cash from operations and/or asset sales. Shareholders generally hope to reverse the LBO within three to seven years by way of a public offering or sale of the company to another firm. A buyout is, therefore, likely to be successful only if the firm generates sufficient cash to service the debt in the early years and if the company is attractive to other buyers a few years down the road.

Mack has suggested the potential LBO to his partners, Fran Mae and Horatio Caruso. Fran and Horatio have asked Mack to provide projections of the cash flows for the company. Mack has provided the following estimates (in millions):

	2007	2008	2009	2010	2011	2012
Sales	$1,751	$1,861	$1,973	$2,088	$2,204	$2,324
Costs	490	540	591	624	657	692
Depreciation	301	316	332	348	366	384
EBT	$ 960	$1,005	$1,050	$1,116	$1,181	$1,247
Capital expenditures	$ 187	$ 174	$ 151	$ 149	$ 132	$ 165
Change in NWC	−$ 88	−$ 7	$ 94	$ 51	$ 13	$ 97
Asset sales	$ 900	$ 713				

At the end of six years, Mack estimates that the growth rate in cash flows will be 3.2 percent per year. The capital expenditures are for new projects and the replacement of equipment that wears out. Additionally, the company would realize cash flow from the sale of several divisions. Even though the company will sell these divisions, overall sales should increase because of a more concentrated effort on the remaining divisions.

After plowing through the company's financials and various pro forma scenarios, Fran and Horatio feel that in six years they will be able to sell the company to another party or take it public again. They are also aware that they will have to borrow a considerable amount of the purchase price. The interest payments on the debt for each of the next six years if the LBO is undertaken will be these (in millions):

	2007	2008	2009	2010	2011	2012
Interest Payments	$1,260	$1,501	$1,100	$1,050	$1,310	$1,127

The company currently has a required return on assets of 16 percent. Because of the high debt level, the debt will carry a yield to maturity of 12.925 percent for the next three years. When the debt is refinanced in three years, it will carry a yield to maturity of 10.5 percent for the next three years. Finally, when the debt is refinanced again in 2012, it is believed that the new yield to maturity will be 8 percent. MPG currently has 257 million shares of stock outstanding that sell for $26 per share. The corporate tax rate is 34 percent. If Mack, Fran, and Horatio decide to undertake the LBO, what is the most they should offer per share?

Chapter 19

Dividends and Other Payouts

EXECUTIVE SUMMARY

In recent years, Canadian corporations have paid out about 33 percent of their net income as cash dividends. However, a significant number of firms pay no cash dividends while many pay dividends in excess of their net income. Corporations view the dividend decision as quite important, because it determines what funds flow to investors and what funds are retained by the firm for reinvestment. Dividend policy can also provide information to the shareholder concerning firm performance.

However, dividends cannot be viewed in isolation. Companies currently devote about 40 percent of net income to share repurchases as well, a percentage much higher than that of only a few decades ago. Thus, dividends and repurchases must be seen as alternative payouts competing for corporate cash flows.

This chapter examines corporate policy concerning dividends and other payouts. The first four sections of the chapter deal with two issues. We discuss the practical aspects of both dividends and share repurchases. We also establish the irrelevance of any payout policy in a world of perfect capital markets. We move on to a world of personal taxes in Section 19.5, where the advantage of repurchases over dividends is presented. This advantage is perhaps the reason for the rapid growth in repurchases in recent years. However, dividends have hardly vanished, leading us to a search for the benefits of a high-dividend policy in the next two sections.

19.1 Different Types of Dividends

The term *dividend* usually refers to cash distributions of earnings. If a distribution is made from sources other than current or accumulated retained earnings, the term *distribution* rather than *dividend* is used. However, it is acceptable to refer to a distribution from earnings as a *dividend* and refer to a distribution from capital as a *liquidating dividend.* More generally, any direct payment by the corporation to the shareholders may be considered part of dividend policy.

The most common type of dividend is in the form of cash. Public companies usually pay **regular cash dividends** four times a year. Sometimes firms pay a regular cash dividend and an *extra cash dividend.* Paying a cash dividend reduces corporate cash and retained earnings shown on the balance sheet—except in the case of a liquidating dividend (where the common shares account may be reduced).[1]

Another type of dividend, paid out in shares of stock, is referred to as a **stock dividend.** It is not a true dividend, because no cash leaves the firm. Rather, a stock dividend increases

---

[1]Bond covenants restrict payment of liquidating dividends, as we discuss in Chapter 21.

the number of shares outstanding, thereby reducing the value of each share. A stock dividend is commonly expressed as a ratio; for example, with a 2 percent stock dividend, a shareholder receives one new share for every 50 currently owned.

When a firm declares a **stock split,** it increases the number of shares outstanding. For example, in a two-for-one split, each shareholder receives one additional share of stock for each share held originally, so a two-for-one stock split is equivalent to a 100 percent stock dividend.

After a stock split, each share is entitled to a smaller percentage of the firm's cash flow, so the stock price should fall. For example, if the managers of a firm whose stock is selling at $50 declare a 2:1 stock split, the price of a share of stock should fall to about $25. A stock split strongly resembles a stock dividend except it is usually much larger.

19.2 Standard Method of Cash Dividend Payment

The decision of whether to pay a dividend rests in the hands of the board of directors of the corporation. A dividend is distributable to shareholders of record on a specific date. When a dividend has been declared, it becomes a liability of the firm and cannot be easily rescinded by the corporation. The amount of the dividend is expressed as dollars per share (*dividend per share*), as a percentage of the market price (*dividend yield*), or as a percentage of earnings per share (*dividend payout*).

The mechanics of a dividend payment can be illustrated by the example in Figure 19.1 and the following chronology:

1. **Declaration date.** On January 15 (the declaration date), the board of directors passes a resolution to pay a dividend of $1 per share on February 16 to all holders of record on January 30.

2. **Date of record.** The corporation prepares a list on January 30 of all individuals believed to be shareholders as of this date. The word *believed* is important here, because the dividend will not be paid to those individuals whose notification of purchase is received by the company after January 30.

3. **Ex-dividend date.** The procedure on the date of record would be unfair if efficient investment dealers could notify the corporation by January 30 of a trade occurring on January 29, whereas the same trade might not reach the corporation until February 2 if executed by a less efficient dealer. To eliminate this problem, all investment dealers entitle

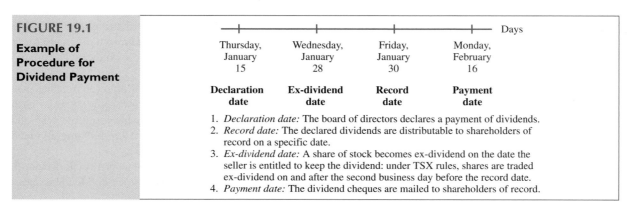

FIGURE 19.1

Example of Procedure for Dividend Payment

	Thursday, January 15	Wednesday, January 28	Friday, January 30	Monday, February 16	Days
	Declaration date	Ex-dividend date	Record date	Payment date	

1. *Declaration date:* The board of directors declares a payment of dividends.
2. *Record date:* The declared dividends are distributable to shareholders of record on a specific date.
3. *Ex-dividend date:* A share of stock becomes ex-dividend on the date the seller is entitled to keep the dividend: under TSX rules, shares are traded ex-dividend on and after the second business day before the record date.
4. *Payment date:* The dividend cheques are mailed to shareholders of record.

shareholders to receive the dividend if they purchased the stock three business days before the date of record. The second day before the date of record (Wednesday, January 28, in our example) is called the *ex-dividend date.* Before this date the stock is said to trade *cum dividend* (Latin for "with dividend").[2]

4. **Date of payment.** The dividend cheques are mailed to the shareholders on February 16.

Obviously, the ex-dividend date is important, because an individual purchasing the security before the ex-dividend date will receive the current dividend, whereas another individual purchasing the security on or after this date will not receive the dividend. The stock price should fall on the ex-dividend date.[3] It is worthwhile to note that this drop is an indication of efficiency, not inefficiency, because the market rationally attaches value to a cash dividend. In a world with neither taxes nor transaction costs, the stock price is expected to fall by the amount of the dividend:

Before ex-dividend date: Price = $(P + 1)$
On or after ex-dividend date: Price = P

This is illustrated in Figure 19.2.

The amount of the price drop is a matter for empirical investigation. Elton and Gruber have argued that, due to personal taxes, the stock price should drop by less than the dividend.[4] For example, consider the case with no capital gains taxes. On the day before a stock goes ex-dividend, shareholders must decide either to buy immediately and pay tax on the forthcoming dividend, or to buy tomorrow, thereby missing the dividend. If all investors are in a 30 percent bracket for dividends and the quarterly dividend is $1, the stock price should

FIGURE 19.2

Price Behaviour Around the Ex-Dividend Date for a $1 Cash Dividend

Perfect-world case

Ex-date

Price = $(P+1)$

$1 is the ex-dividend price drop

Price = P

The stock price will fall by the amount of the dividend on the ex-date (time 0). If the dividend is $1 per share, the price will be equal to *P* on the ex-date.

Before ex-date (-1)   Price = $(P + 1)$
Ex-date (0)   Price = P

---

[2]The three-day period between the last *cum dividend* date and the record date is consistent with three-day settlement of stock purchases and sales (T + 3) in effect at the time of writing in 2001. With new computers, U.S. and Canadian exchanges are planning to speed settlement to one day (T + 1) by mid-2004, according to R. Carrick in "There's no need to be wary of T + 1," *The Globe and Mail,* March 1, 2001, B16. When this occurs, the lag for dividends will also drop to one day.

[3]The stock price typically falls within the first few minutes of the ex-dividend day.

[4]N. Elton and M. Gruber, "Marginal Stockholder Tax Rates and the Clientele Effect," *Review of Economics and Statistics* 52 (February 1970).

fall by $0.70 on the ex-dividend date. If the stock price falls by this amount on the ex-dividend date, then purchasers will receive the same return from either strategy.[5]

As an example of the price drop on the ex-dividend date, consider the example of Microsoft. The stock went ex dividend on November 15, 2004, with a total dividend of US$3.08 per share, consisting of a US$3 special dividend and a US$.08 regular dividend. The following stock price chart shows the price of Microsoft stock on each of the four days prior to the ex-dividend date and on the ex-dividend date:

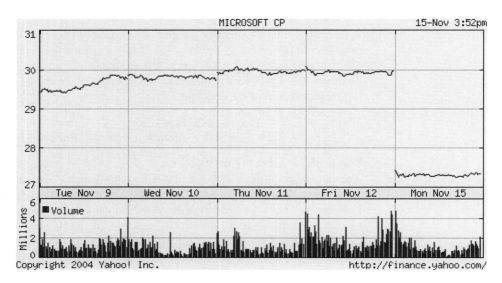

The stock closed at US$29.97 on November 12 (a Friday) and opened at US$27.34 on November 15, a drop of US$2.63. With a 15 percent tax rate on dividends, we would have expected a drop of US$2.62, and the actual price drop was almost exactly that amount.

? Concept Questions
- **Describe the procedure of a dividend payment.**
- **Why should the price of a stock change when it goes ex-dividend?**

19.3 The Benchmark Case: An Illustration of the Irrelevance of Dividend Policy

A powerful argument can be made that dividend policy does not matter. This will be illustrated with the York Corporation, an all-equity firm in existence for 10 years. The financial managers know at the present time (date 0) that the firm will dissolve in one year (date 1). At date 0, the managers are able to forecast cash flows with perfect certainty. The managers

---

[5]The situation is more complex when capital gains are considered. The individual pays capital gains taxes upon a subsequent sale. Because the price drops on the ex-dividend date, the original purchase price is higher if the purchase is made before the ex-dividend date, and the individual will reap, and pay taxes on, lower capital gains. Elton and Gruber show that the price drop is increased slightly when capital gains taxes are considered. L. D. Booth and D. J. Johnston, "The Ex-Dividend Day Behavior of Canadian Stock Prices: Tax Changes and Clientele Effects," *Journal of Finance* 39 (June 1984), find that personal taxes on dividends are the main factor in determining the price drop with a small adjustment for capital gains tax. We return to personal taxes later in the chapter.

know that the firm will receive a cash flow of $10,000 immediately and another $10,000 next year. They believe that York has no additional positive NPV projects it can use to its advantage.[6]

Current Policy: Dividends Set Equal to Cash Flow

At the present time, dividends (Div) at each date are set equal to the cash flow of $10,000. The NPV of the firm can be calculated by discounting these dividends. The firm's value can be expressed as

$$V_0 = \text{Div}_0 + \frac{\text{Div}_1}{1 + r_S}$$

where Div_0 and Div_1 are the cash flows paid out in dividends, and r_S is the discount rate. The first dividend is not discounted because it will be paid immediately.

Assuming $r_S = 10\%$, the value of the firm can be calculated by

$$\$19,090.91 = \$10,000 + \frac{\$10,000}{1.1}$$

If 1000 shares are outstanding, the value of each share is

$$\$19.09 = \$10 + \frac{\$10}{1.1} \tag{19.1}$$

To simplify the example, we assume that the ex-dividend date is the same as the date of payment. After the imminent dividend is paid, the stock price will immediately fall to $9.09 (or $19.09 − $10). Several of York's board members have expressed dissatisfaction with the current dividend policy and have asked you to analyze an alternative policy.

Alternative Policy: Initial Dividend Is Greater Than Cash Flow

Another policy is for the firm to pay a dividend of $11 per share immediately, which is, of course, a total dividend of $11,000. Because the cash runoff is only $10,000, the extra $1,000 must be raised in one of a few ways. Perhaps the simplest would be to issue $1,000 of bonds or stock now (at date 0). Assume that stock is issued and the new shareholders will desire enough cash flow at date 1 to let them earn the required 10 percent return on their date 0 investment.[7] The new shareholders will demand $1,100 of the date 1 cash flow, leaving only $8,900 to the old shareholders.[8] The dividends to the old shareholders will be

	Date 0	Date 1
Aggregate dividends to old shareholders	$11,000	$8,900
Dividends per share	11.00	8.90

The present value of the dividends per share is therefore

$$\$19.09 = \$11 + \frac{\$8.90}{1.1} \tag{19.2}$$

Students often find it instructive to determine the price at which the new stock is issued. Because the new shareholders are not entitled to the immediate dividend, they would pay $8.09 (or $8.90/1.1) per share. Thus, 123.61 (or $1,000/$8.09) new shares are issued.

---

[6]York's investment in physical assets is fixed.

[7]The same results would occur after an issue of bonds, though the argument would be less easily resolved.

[8]Because the new shareholders buy at date 0, their first (and only) dividend is at date 1.

The Indifference Proposition

Note that the NPVs of Equations (19.1) and (19.2) are equal. This leads to the initially surprising conclusion that the change in dividend policy did not affect the value of a share of stock. However, upon reflection, the result seems quite sensible. The new shareholders are parting with their money at date 0 and receiving it back with the appropriate return at date 1. In other words, they are taking on a zero-NPV investment. As illustrated in Figure 19.3, old shareholders are receiving additional funds at date 0 but must pay the new shareholders their money with the appropriate return at date 1. Because the old shareholders must pay back principal plus the appropriate return, the act of issuing new stock at date 0 will neither increase nor decrease the value of the old shareholders' holdings. That is, they are giving up a zero-NPV investment to the new shareholders. An increase in dividends at date 0 leads to the necessary reduction of dividends at date 1, so the value of the old shareholders' holdings remains unchanged.

This illustration is based on the pioneering work of Modigliani and Miller (MM).[9] Although our presentation is in the form of a numerical example, the MM paper proves

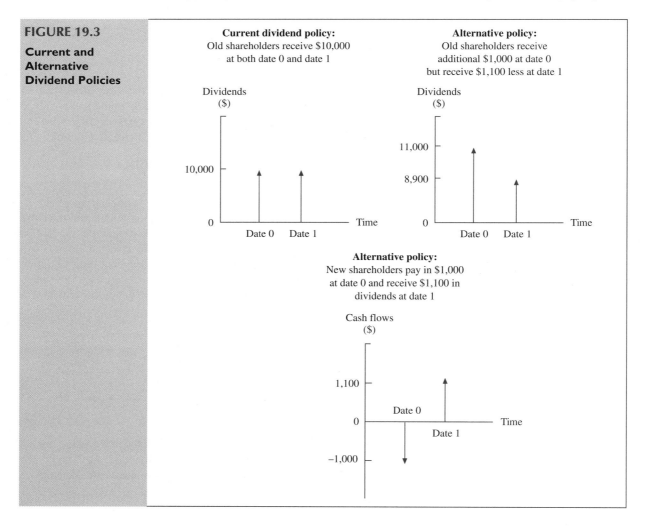

FIGURE 19.3

Current and Alternative Dividend Policies

---

[9]M. H. Miller and F. Modigliani, "Dividend Policy, Growth and the Valuation of Shares," *Journal of Business* (October 1961). Yes, this is the same MM who gave us a capital structure theory.

that investors are indifferent to dividend policy in the general algebraic case. MM make the following assumptions:

1. There are neither taxes nor brokerage fees, and no single participant can affect the market price of the security through his or her trades. Economists say that perfect markets exist when these conditions are met.

2. All individuals have the same beliefs concerning future investments, profits, and dividends. As mentioned in Chapter 11, these individuals are said to have *homogenous expectations.*

3. The investment policy of the firm is set ahead of time, and is not altered by changes in dividend policy.

Homemade Dividends

To illustrate the indifference investors have toward dividend policy in our example, we used net present value equations. An alternative, and perhaps more intuitively appealing, explanation avoids the mathematics of discounted cash flows.

Suppose individual investor *X* prefers dividends per share of $10 at both dates 0 and 1. Would she be disappointed when informed that the firm's management is adopting the alternative dividend policy (dividends of $11 and $8.90 on the two dates, respectively)? Not necessarily, because she could easily reinvest the $1 of unneeded funds received on date 0, yielding an incremental return of $1.10 at date 1. Thus, she would receive her desired net cash flow of $11 − $1 = $10 at date 0 and $8.90 + $1.10 = $10 at date 1.

Conversely, imagine investor *Z,* who prefers $11 of cash flow at date 0 and $8.90 of cash flow at date 1, and who finds that management will pay dividends of $10 at both dates 0 and 1. He can sell off shares of stock at date 0 to receive the desired amount of cash flow. That is, if at date 0 he sells off shares (or fractions of shares) totalling $1, his cash flow at date 0 becomes $10 + $1 = $11. Because a sale of $1 of stock at date 0 will reduce his dividends by $1.10 at date 1, his net cash flow at date 1 will be $10 − $1.10 = $8.90.

The example illustrates how investors can make **homemade dividends.** In this instance, corporate dividend policy is being undone by a potentially dissatisfied shareholder. This homemade dividend is illustrated in Figure 19.4. Here the firm's cash flows of $10 at both date 0 and date 1 are represented by point *A*. This point also represents the initial dividend payout. Alternatively, as we just saw, the firm could pay out $11 at date 0 and $8.90 at date 1, a strategy represented by point *B*. Similarly, by either issuing new stock or buying back old stock, the managers of the firm could achieve a dividend payout represented by any point on the diagonal line.

The same diagonal line also represents the choices available to the shareholder. For example, if the shareholder receives a dividend distribution of ($11, $8.90), he or she can either reinvest some of the dividends to move down and to the right on the graph or sell off shares of stock and move up and to the left.

Many corporations actually assist their shareholders in creating homemade dividend policies by offering *automatic dividend reinvestment plans* (ADPs or DRIPs). As the name suggests, with such a plan, shareholders have the option of automatically reinvesting some or all of their cash dividend in shares of stock.

Under a new-issue dividend reinvestment plan, investors buy new stock issued by the firm and receive a small discount—usually under 5 percent. This makes dividend reinvestment very attractive to investors who do not need cash flow from dividends. Since the 5 percent discount compares favourably with issue costs for new stock (which will be discussed in Chapter 20), dividend reinvestment plans are popular with large companies that periodically seek new common stock.[10]

---

[10]Reinvested dividends are still taxable.

FIGURE 19.4

Homemade Dividends: A Trade-Off Between Dividends at Date 0 and Dividends at Date 1

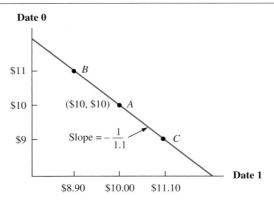

This graph illustrates both (1) how managers can vary dividend policy and (2) how individuals can undo the firm's dividend policy.

Managers varying dividend policy. A firm paying out all cash flows immediately is at point *A* on the graph. The firm could achieve point *B* by issuing stock to pay extra dividends or achieve point *C* by buying back old stock with some of its cash.

Individuals undoing the firm's dividend policy. Suppose the firm adopts the dividend policy represented by point *B:* dividends of $11 at date 0 and $8.90 at date 1. An investor can reinvest $1 of the dividends at 10 percent, which will place her at point *A*. Suppose, alternatively, the firm adopts the dividend policy represented by point *A*. An individual can sell off $1 of stock at date 0, placing him at point *B*. No matter what dividend policy the firm establishes, a shareholder can undo it.

Investment dealers also use financial engineering to create homemade dividends (or homemade capital gains). **Stripped common shares** entitle holders to receive either all the dividends from one or a group of well-known companies or an installment receipt that packages any capital gain in the form of a call option. The call option gives the investor the right to buy the underlying shares at a fixed price and so is valuable if the shares appreciate beyond that price.

The implications of Figure 19.4 can be summarized in two sentences:

1. By varying dividend policy, the managers can achieve any payout along the diagonal line in Figure 19.4.

2. Either by reinvesting excess dividends at date 0 or by selling off shares of stock at this date, any individual investor can achieve any net cash payout along the diagonal line.

Thus, because both the corporation and the individual investor can move only along the diagonal line, dividend policy in this model is irrelevant. The changes the managers make in dividend policy can be undone by an individual who, by either reinvesting dividends or selling off stock, can move to any desired point on the diagonal line.

A Test

You can test your understanding by examining these true statements:

- Dividends are relevant.
- Dividend policy is irrelevant.

The first statement follows from common sense. Clearly, investors prefer higher dividends to lower dividends at any single date if the dividend level is held constant at every other date. In other words, if the dividend per share at a given date is raised while the dividend per share for each other date is held constant, the stock price will rise. This act can be accomplished by management decisions that improve productivity, increase tax savings, or strengthen product marketing.

The second statement makes sense once we realize that dividend policy cannot raise the dividend per share at one date while holding the dividend level per share constant at all other dates. Rather, dividend policy merely establishes the trade-off between dividends at one date and dividends at another date. As we saw in Figure 19.4, an increase in date 0 dividends can be accomplished only by a decrease in date 1 dividends. The extent of the decrease is such that the present value of all dividends is not affected.

Thus, in this simple world, dividend policy does not matter. That is, managers choosing to raise or to lower the current dividend do not affect the current values of their firms. This theory is a powerful one, and the work of MM is considered a classic in modern finance. With relatively few assumptions, a rather surprising result is shown to be perfectly true.[11] Because we want to examine many real-world factors ignored by MM, their work is only a starting point in this chapter's discussion of dividends. The next part of the chapter investigates these real-world considerations.

Dividends and Investment Policy

The argument above shows that an increase in dividends through issuing new shares neither helps nor hurts the shareholders. Similarly, a reduction in dividends through share repurchase neither helps nor hurts shareholders.

What about reducing capital expenditures to increase dividends? Earlier chapters show that a firm should accept all positive NPV projects. To do otherwise would reduce the value of the firm. Thus, we have an important point:

> Firms should never give up a positive NPV project to increase a dividend (or to pay a dividend for the first time).

This idea was implicitly considered by Miller and Modigliani. As we pointed out, one of the assumptions underlying their dividend-irrelevance proposition was, "The investment policy of the firm is set ahead of time and is not altered by changes in dividend policy."

? Concept Questions
- **How can an investor make homemade dividends?**
- **Are dividends irrelevant?**
- **What assumptions are needed to show that dividend policy is irrelevant?**

19.4 Repurchase of Stock

Instead of paying dividends, a firm may use cash to repurchase shares of its own stock. Share repurchases have taken on increased importance in recent years. Consider Figure 19.5, which shows the average ratios of both dividends to earnings and repurchases to earnings for U.S. industrial firms for the years 1984 to 2004. As can be seen, the ratio of repurchases to earnings was far less than the ratio of dividends to earnings in the early years. However, by 1998, the ratio of repurchases to earnings exceeded the ratio of dividends to earnings.

---

[11]One of the real contributions of MM has been to shift the burden of proof. Before MM, firm value was believed to be influenced by its dividend policy. After MM, it became clear that establishing a correct dividend policy was not obvious at all.

FIGURE 19.5

Ratios of Various Payouts to Earnings

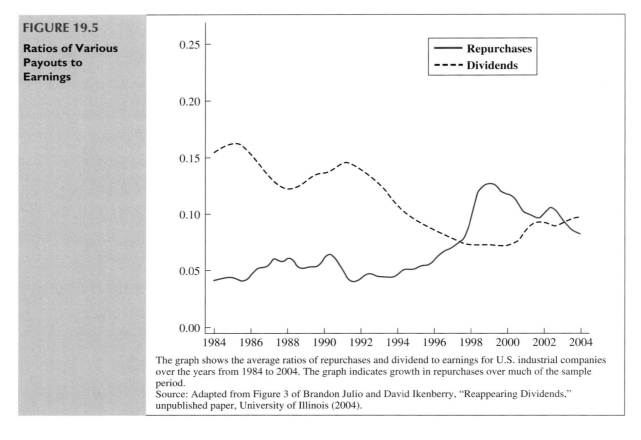

The graph shows the average ratios of repurchases and dividend to earnings for U.S. industrial companies over the years from 1984 to 2004. The graph indicates growth in repurchases over much of the sample period.
Source: Adapted from Figure 3 of Brandon Julio and David Ikenberry, "Reappearing Dividends," unpublished paper, University of Illinois (2004).

This trend reversed after 1999, with the ratio of repurchases to earnings falling slightly below the ratio of dividends to earnings by 2004.

Share repurchases are typically accomplished in one of two ways. First, companies may simply purchase their own stock, just as anyone would buy shares of a particular stock. In these *open-market purchases,* the firm does not reveal itself as the buyer. Thus, the seller does not know whether the shares were sold back to the firm or to just another investor.

Second, the firm could institute a *tender offer.* Here, the firm announces to all of its shareholders that it is willing to buy a fixed number of shares at a specific price. For example, suppose Arts and Crafts (A&C) Inc. has 1 million shares of stock outstanding, with a stock price of $50 per share. The firm makes a tender offer to buy back 300,000 shares at $60 per share. A&C chooses a price above $50 to induce shareholders to sell, that is, tender, their shares. In fact, if the tender price is set high enough, shareholders may very well want to sell more than the 300,000 shares. In the extreme case where all outstanding shares are tendered, A&C will buy back 3 out of every 10 shares that a shareholder has.

We now consider an example of a repurchase presented in the theoretical world of a perfect capital market. We next discuss the real-world factors involved in the repurchase decision.

Dividend Versus Repurchase: Conceptual Example

Imagine that Telephonic Industries has excess cash of $300,000 (or $3 per share) and is considering an immediate payment of this amount as an extra dividend. The firm forecasts that, after the dividend, earnings will be $450,000 per year, or $4.50 for each of the

TABLE 19.1
Dividend Versus Repurchase Example for Telephonic Industries

	For Entire Firm	Per Share
Extra Dividend		**(100,000 shares outstanding)**
Proposed dividend	$ 300,000	$ 3.00
Forecasted annual earnings after dividend	450,000	4.50
Market value of stock after dividend	2,700,000	27.00
Repurchase		**(90,000 shares outstanding)**
Forecasted annual earnings after repurchase	$ 450,000	$ 5.00
Market value of stock after repurchase	2,700,000	30.00

100,000 shares outstanding. Because the price–earnings ratio is 6 for comparable companies, the shares of the firm should sell for $27 after the dividend is paid. These figures are presented in the top half of Table 19.1. Since the dividend is $3 per share, the stock would have sold for $30 a share *before* payment of the dividend.

Alternatively, the firm could use the excess cash to repurchase some of its own stock. Imagine that a tender offer of $30 a share is made. Here, 10,000 shares are repurchased so that the total number of shares remaining is 90,000. With fewer shares outstanding, the earnings per share will rise to $5. The price–earnings ratio remains at 6, since both the business and financial risks of the firm are the same in the repurchase case as they were for the dividend case.[12] Thus the price of a share after the repurchase is $30. These results are presented in the bottom half of Table 19.1.

If commissions, taxes, and other imperfections are ignored in our example, the shareholders are indifferent between a dividend and a repurchase. With dividends, each shareholder owns a share worth $27 and receives $3 in dividends, so that the total value is $30. This figure is the same as both the amount received by the selling shareholders and the value of the stock for the remaining shareholders in the repurchase case.

This example illustrates the important point that, in a perfect market, the firm is indifferent between a dividend payment and a share repurchase. This result is quite similar to the indifference propositions established by MM for debt versus equity financing and for dividends versus capital gains.

You may often read in the popular financial press that a repurchase agreement is beneficial because earnings per share increase. Earnings per share do rise for Telephonic Industries if a repurchase is substituted for a cash dividend: The EPS is $4.50 after a dividend and $5 after the repurchase. This result holds because the drop in shares after a repurchase implies a reduction in the denominator of the EPS ratio.

However, the financial press frequently places undue emphasis on EPS figures in a repurchase agreement. Given the irrelevance propositions we have discussed, an increase in EPS need not be beneficial. When a repurchase is financed by excess cash, we showed that, in a perfect capital market, the total value to the shareholder is the same under the dividend payment strategy as under the repurchase strategy.

Dividends Versus Repurchases: Real-World Considerations

We recently referred to Figure 19.5, which showed the recent growth in share repurchases. Why do some firms choose repurchases over dividends? Here are perhaps five of the most common reasons.

---

[12]Chapter 6 discusses use of the P/E ratio to value stocks.

1. Flexibility It is well known that firms view dividends as a commitment to their shareholders and are quite hesitant to reduce an existing dividend. Repurchases do not represent a similar commitment. Thus, a firm with a permanent increase in cash flow is likely to increase its dividend. Conversely, a firm whose cash flow increase is only temporary is likely to repurchase shares of stock.[13]

2. Executive Compensation Executives are frequently given stock options as part of their overall compensation. Let's revisit the Telephonic Industries example of Table 19.1, where the firm's stock was selling at $30 when the firm was considering either a dividend or a repurchase. Further imagine that Telephonic had granted 1000 stock options to its CEO, Ralph Taylor, two years before the decision was made. At that time the stock price was, say, only $20. This means that Mr. Taylor can buy 1000 shares for $20 a share at any time between the grant of the options and their expiration, a procedure called *exercising* the options.[14] His gain from exercising is directly proportional to the rise in the stock price above $20. As we saw in the example, the price of the stock would fall to $27 following a dividend but would remain at $30 following a repurchase. The CEO would clearly prefer a repurchase to a dividend because the difference between the stock price and the exercise price of $20 would be $10 ($30 − $20) following the repurchase but only $7 ($27 − $20) following the dividend. Existing stock options will always have greater value when the firm repurchases shares instead of paying a dividend,[15] since the stock price will be greater after a repurchase than after a dividend. De Jong, Van Dijk, and Veld surveyed the 500 largest nonfinancial corporations in Canada on their share repurchase and dividend policies. They found that firms offering significant executive stock options tend to prefer repurchasing shares over paying dividends.[16]

3. Offset to Dilution In addition, the exercise of stock options increases the number of shares outstanding. In other words, exercise causes dilution of the stock. Firms frequently buy back shares of stock to offset this dilution. However, it is hard to argue that this is a valid reason for repurchase. As we showed in Table 19.1, repurchase is neither better nor worse for the shareholders than a dividend. Our argument holds whether or not stock options have been exercised previously.[17]

4. Repurchase as Investment Many companies buy back stock because they believe that a repurchase is their best investment. This occurs more frequently when managers believe that the stock price is temporarily depressed. Here, it is likely thought that (1) investment opportunities in nonfinancial assets are few, and (2) the firm's own stock price should rise with the passage of time.

The fact that some companies repurchase their stock when they believe it is undervalued does not imply that the management of the company must be correct; only empirical studies

[13]See Murali Jagannathan, Clifford P. Stephens, and Michael Weisbach, "Financial Flexibility and the Choice Between Dividends and Stock Repurchases," *Journal of Financial Economics* 57 (2000) and Wayne Guay and Jarrod Harford, "The Cash-Flow Permanence of Dividend Increases Versus Repurchases," *Journal of Financial Economics* 57 (2000) for both an explanation of and empirical support for flexibility.

[14]The exercise price of an executive stock option is generally set equal to the market price at the time of the grant.

[15]See George W. Fenn and Nellie Liang, "Corporate Payout Policy and Managerial Stock Incentives," *Journal of Financial Economics* 60 (2001).

[16]Abe De Jong, Ronald Van Dijk, and Chris Veld, "The Dividend and Share Repurchase Policies of Canadian Firms: Empirical Evidence Based on a New Research Design," Erasmus Research Institute of Management, ERS-2001-88-F&A.

[17]See Kathleen Kahle, "When a Buyback Isn't a Buyback: Open Market Repurchases and Employee Options," *Journal of Financial Economics* 63 (2002).

can make this determination. The immediate stock market reaction to the announcement of a stock repurchase is usually quite favourable. In addition, some empirical work has shown that the long-term stock price performance of securities after a buyback is better than the stock price performance of comparable companies that do not repurchase.[18]

5. Taxes Since taxes for both dividends and share repurchases are treated in depth in the next section, suffice it to say at this point that repurchases provide a tax advantage over dividends.

? Concept Questions

- **In a perfect capital market, are repurchases preferred to dividends?**
- **What are five reasons for preferring repurchases to dividends in the real world?**

19.5 Personal Taxes, Issuance Costs, and Dividends

The model we used to determine the level of dividends assumed that there were no taxes, no transactions costs, and no uncertainty. It concluded that dividend policy is irrelevant. Although this model helps us to grasp some fundamentals of dividend policy, it ignores many factors that exist in reality. We begin our investigation of these real-world considerations with the effect of taxes on the level of a firm's dividends.

In Canada, both dividends and capital gains are taxed at effective rates *less than* the marginal tax rate. For dividends, we showed in Chapter 1 that individual investors face a lower tax rate due to the dividend tax credit. Capital gains in the hands of individuals are taxed at 50 percent of the marginal tax rate. Since taxation takes place only when capital gains are realized, capital gains are very lightly taxed in Canada. Thus, for individual shareholders, the *effective* tax rate on dividend income is higher than the tax rate on capital gains.[19]

To facilitate our discussion of dividend policy in the presence of personal taxes, we classify firms into two groups based on whether they have sufficient cash to pay a dividend.

Firms Without Sufficient Cash to Pay a Dividend

It is simplest to begin with a firm without cash owned by a single entrepreneur. If this firm should decide to pay a dividend of $100, it must raise capital. The firm might choose among a number of different stock and bond issues in order to pay the dividend. However, for simplicity, we assume that the entrepreneur contributes cash to the firm by issuing stock to himself. This transaction, diagrammed in the left-hand side of Figure 19.6, would clearly be a *wash* in a world of no taxes. Here $100 cash goes into the firm when stock is issued and is immediately paid out as a dividend. Thus, the entrepreneur neither benefits nor loses when the dividend is paid, a result consistent with Miller–Modigliani.

Now assume that dividends are taxed at 30 percent. The firm still receives $100 on issuance of stock. However, the $100 dividend is not fully credited to the entrepreneur.

---

[18]For Canada, see David Ikenberry, Josef Lakonishok, and Theo Vermaelen, "Stock Repurchases in Canada: Performance and Strategic Trading," *Journal of Finance,* October 2000; and William McNally, Brian F. Smith, and Thomas Barnes, "The Short-Run Impact of Open Market Purchase Trades," Working Paper, Wilfrid Laurier University, 2004.

[19]L. D. Booth and D. J. Johnston, "Ex-Dividend Day Behavior," (1984) found that dividends are taxed more heavily than capital gains for the marginal investor. Subsequent tax reforms have narrowed, but not eliminated, this difference.

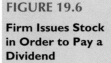

FIGURE 19.6

Firm Issues Stock in Order to Pay a Dividend

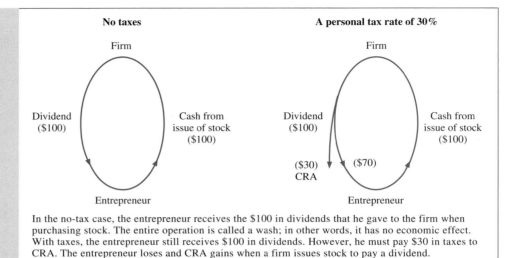

In the no-tax case, the entrepreneur receives the $100 in dividends that he gave to the firm when purchasing stock. The entire operation is called a wash; in other words, it has no economic effect. With taxes, the entrepreneur still receives $100 in dividends. However, he must pay $30 in taxes to CRA. The entrepreneur loses and CRA gains when a firm issues stock to pay a dividend.

Instead, the dividend payment is taxed, implying that the owner receives only $70 net after tax. Thus, the entrepreneur loses $30.

Although our example is a bit simplistic, financial economists generally agree that, in a world of personal taxes, one should not issue shares to pay a dividend.

The flotation costs of issuing shares add to this effect. Investment bankers must be paid when new capital is raised. Thus, the net receipts due to the firm from a new issue are less than 100 percent of total capital raised. These costs are examined in a later chapter. Because the size of new issues can be lowered by a reduction in dividends, we have another argument in favour of a low-dividend policy.

Of course, our advice not to finance dividends through new share issues might need to be modified somewhat in the real world. A company with a large and steady cash flow for many years in the past might be paying a regular dividend. If the cash flow unexpectedly dried up for a single year, should new stock be issued so that dividends could be continued? While our previous discussion would imply that new shares should not be issued, many managers might issue the stock anyway for practical reasons. In particular, shareholders might prefer stable dividends. Thus, managers might be forced to issue stock to achieve this stability, knowing full well the adverse tax consequences.

Firms With Sufficient Cash to Pay a Dividend

The previous discussion argues that, in a world with personal taxes, one should not issue stock to pay a dividend. Does the tax disadvantage of dividends imply the stronger policy, "Never pay dividends in a world with personal taxes"?

We argue that this prescription does not necessarily apply to firms with excess cash. To see this, imagine a firm with $1 million in extra cash after selecting all positive NPV projects and determining the level of prudent cash balances. The firm might consider the following alternatives to a dividend:

1. *Select additional capital budgeting projects.* Because the firm has already taken all the available positive NPV projects, it must invest its excess cash in negative NPV projects. This is clearly a policy at variance with the principles of corporate finance and represents an example of the agency costs of equity introduced in Chapter 17. Jensen

has suggested that many managers choose to take on negative NPV projects in lieu of dividends, doing their shareholders a disservice in the process.[20] It is frequently argued that managers who adopt negative NPV projects are ripe for takeover, leveraged buy-outs, and proxy fights.

2. *Acquire other companies.* To avoid the payment of dividends, a firm might use excess cash to acquire another company. This strategy has the advantage of acquiring profitable assets. However, a firm often incurs heavy costs when it embarks on an acquisition program. In addition, acquisitions are invariably made above the market price. Premiums of 20 to 80 percent are not uncommon. Because of this, a number of researchers have argued that mergers are not generally profitable to the acquiring company, even when firms are merged for a valid business purpose.[21] Therefore, a company making an acquisition merely to avoid a dividend is unlikely to benefit its shareholders.

3. *Purchase financial assets.* The strategy of purchasing financial assets in lieu of a dividend payment can be illustrated in Example 19.1.

EXAMPLE 19.1

The Regional Electric Company has $1,000 of extra cash. It can retain the cash and invest it in Treasury bills yielding 8 percent, or it can pay the cash to shareholders as a dividend. Shareholders can also invest in Treasury bills with the same yield. Suppose, realistically, that the tax rate is 44 percent on ordinary income like interest on Treasury bills for both the company and individual investors and the individual tax rate *on dividends* is 30 percent. How much cash will investors have after five years under each policy?

If dividends are paid now, shareholders will receive $1,000 before taxes, or $1,000 × (1 − 0.30) = $700 after taxes. This is the amount they will invest. If the rate on T-bills is 8 percent before taxes, then the after-tax return is 8% × (1 − 0.44) = 4.48% per year. Thus, in five years, the shareholders will have

$$\$700 \times (1 + 0.0448)^5 = \$871.49$$

If Regional Electric Company retains the cash, invests in Treasury bills, and pays out the proceeds five years from now, then $1,000 will be invested today. However, since the corporate tax rate is 44 percent, the after-tax return from the T-bills will be 8% × (1 − 0.44) = 4.48% per year. In five years, the investment will be worth

$$\$1,000 \times (1 + 0.0448)^5 = \$1,244.99$$

If this amount is then paid out as a dividend, the shareholders will receive (after tax)

$$\$1244.99 \times (1 - 0.30) = \$871.49$$

In this case, dividends will be the same after tax whether the firm pays them now or later after investing in Treasury bills. The reason is that the firm invests exactly as profitably as the shareholders on their own (on an after-tax basis).[22]

---

[20]M. C. Jensen, "Agency Costs of Free Cash Flows, Corporate Finance and Takeovers," *American Economic Review* (May 1986), pp. 323–29.

[21]Richard Roll, "The Hubris Hypothesis of Corporate Turnovers," *Journal of Business* (1986), pp. 197–216, explores this idea in depth.

[22]Personal taxes have no impact on dividend policy in our example because the dividend tax credit reduces the personal tax rate on dividends. For a detailed discussion of this *tax integration* effect, see René Huot, *Understanding Income Tax,* 1992–93 ed. (Scarborough: Carswell Thomson Professional Publishing, 1992), pp. N48–N50.

This example shows that for a firm with extra cash, the dividend payout decision will depend on personal and corporate tax rates. Assuming all other things are the same, when personal tax rates are higher than corporate tax rates, a firm has an incentive to reduce dividend payouts. This would have occurred if we changed our example to have the firm invest in preferred stock instead of T-bills. (Recall from Chapter 1 that corporations enjoy a 100 percent exclusion of dividends from taxable income.) However, if personal tax rates on dividends are lower than corporate tax rates (for investors in lower tax brackets or tax-exempt investors), a firm has incentive to pay out any excess cash in dividends.

4. *Repurchase shares.* The example we described in the previous section showed that investors are indifferent between share repurchase and dividends in a world without taxes and transaction costs. However, under current tax law, shareholders generally prefer a repurchase to a dividend. A repurchase has a significant tax advantage over a cash dividend. A dividend is taxed, and a shareholder has no choice about whether or not to receive the dividend. In a repurchase, a shareholder pays taxes only if (1) the shareholder actually chooses to sell, and (2) the shareholder has a taxable capital gain on the sale.

Summary on Personal Taxes

This section suggests that, because of personal taxes, firms have an incentive to reduce dividends. For example, they might increase capital expenditures, acquire other companies, or purchase financial assets. However, due to financial considerations and legal constraints, rational firms with large cash flows will likely exhaust these activities with plenty of cash left over for dividends.

It is harder to explain why firms pay dividends instead of repurchasing shares. The tax savings from buybacks are significant. On the other hand, there may be other, more subtle benefits from dividends and we consider these below.

? Concept Questions
- **List four alternatives to paying a dividend with excess cash.**
- **Indicate a problem with each of these alternatives.**

19.6 Expected Return, Dividends, and Personal Taxes

The material presented so far in this chapter can properly be called a discussion of *dividend policy*. That is, it is concerned with the level of dividends chosen by the firm. A related, but distinctly different, question is, What is the relationship between the expected return on a security and its dividend yield? To answer this question, we consider a situation in which dividends are taxed at 30 percent and capital gains are not taxed at all—a scenario that is not unrealistic for many Canadian individual investors.[23] We ignore corporate taxes for the time being.

---

[23]L. D. Booth and D. J. Johnston, "Ex-Dividend Day Behavior," find a "very low effective tax rate on capital gains" in the 1970s. A. Protopapadakis, "Some Indirect Evidence of Effective Capital Gains Tax Rates," *Journal of Business* (April 1983), finds that, for the United States, "the effective marginal tax rates on capital gains fluctuated between 3.4 percent and 6.6 percent between 1960 and 1978 and that capital gains are held, on average, between 24 and 31 years before they are reported" (p. 127).

Suppose a shareholder is considering the stocks of firm G, which pays no dividend, and firm D, which pays a dividend. Firm G stock currently sells for $100; next year's price is expected to be $120. The shareholder in firm G thus expects a $20 capital gain. With no dividend, the return is $20/$100 = 20%. If capital gains are not taxed, the pre-tax and after-tax returns must be the same.[24]

Suppose firm D stock is expected to pay a $20 dividend next year. The stock's price is expected to be $100 after the dividend payment. If the stocks of firm G and firm D are equally risky, the market prices must be set so that their *after-tax* expected returns are equal. The after-tax return on firm D must thus be 20 percent.

What will be the price of stock in firm D? The after-tax dividend is $20 \times (1 - 0.30)$ = $14, so our investor will have a total of $114 after taxes. At a 20 percent required rate of return (after taxes), the present value of this after-tax amount is

$$\text{Present value} = \$114/1.20 = \$95$$

The market price of firm D's stock thus must be $95.

Because the investor receives $120 from firm D at date 1 ($100 in value of stock plus $20 in dividends) before personal taxes, the expected pre-tax return on the security equals

$$\frac{\$120}{\$95} - 1 = 26.32\%$$

Table 19.2 shows the calculations.

This example shows that the expected *pre-tax* return on a security with a high dividend yield is greater than the expected *pre-tax* return on an otherwise identical security

TABLE 19.2
Effect of Dividend Yield on Pre-Tax Expected Returns

	Firm G (no dividend)	Firm D (all dividend)
Assumptions:		
Expected price at date 1	$120	$100
Dividend at date 1 (before tax)	0	$20
Dividend at date 1 (after tax)	0	$14
Price at date 0	$100	(to be solved)
Analysis:		
We solve that the price of firm D at date 0 is $95,* allowing us to calculate		
Capital gain	$20	$100 − $95 = $5
Total gain before tax	$20	$20 + $5 = $25
(both dividend		
and capital gain)		
Total percentage return (before tax)	$\frac{\$20}{\$100} = 0.20$	$\frac{\$25}{\$95} = 0.2632$
Total gain after tax	$20	$14 + $5 = $19
Total percentage return (after tax)	$\frac{\$20}{\$100} = 0.20$	$\frac{\$19}{\$95} = 0.20$

Stocks with high dividend yields will have higher pre-tax expected returns than stocks with low dividend yields. This is referred to as the *grossing up effect.*

*We solve for the price of firm D at date 0 as

$$P_0 = \frac{\$100 + \$20 \times (1 - 0.30)}{1.20} = \$95$$

---

[24]Under current tax law, if the shareholder in firm G does not sell the shares for a gain, it will be an unrealized capital gain, which is not taxed.

with a low dividend yield.[25] Our conclusion is consistent with efficient capital markets because much of the pre-tax return for a security with a high dividend yield is taxed away. One implication is that an individual in a zero tax bracket should invest in securities with high dividend yields. There is at least casual evidence that pension funds, which are not subject to taxes, select securities with high dividend yields.

Does the above example suggest that corporate managers should avoid paying dividends? One might think so at first glance, because firm *G* sells at a higher price at date 0 than does firm *D*. However, by deferring a potential $20 dividend, firm *D* might increase its stock price at date 0 by far less than $20. For example, this is likely to be the case if firm *D*'s best use for its cash is to pay $20 for a company whose market price is far below $20. (In a previous section we explain why managers might do this.) Moreover, our prior discussion showed that deferring dividends to purchase bonds or shares of stock is justified only when personal taxes go down by more than corporate taxes rise. Thus, our example does *not* imply that dividends should be avoided.

Some Evidence on Dividends and Taxes in Canada

Is our example showing higher pre-tax returns for stocks that pay dividends realistic for Canadian capital markets? Since tax laws change from budget to budget, we must be cautious in interpreting research results. Prior to 1972, capital gains were untaxed in Canada (as in our simplified example). Morgan found that stocks that paid dividends had higher pre-tax returns prior to 1972. From 1972 to 1977, Morgan detected no difference in pre-tax returns.[26]

In 1985, a lifetime exemption on capital gains was introduced. Amoako-Adu, Rashid, and Stebbins found that anticipation of this tax break for capital gains caused investors to bid up the prices of low-dividend yield stocks. Firms responded by lowering their dividend payouts, according to Adjaoud and Zeghal.[27]

Appendix 1A shows how the dividend tax credit works to reduce taxes on dividends received from Canadian firms. Table 1A.3 shows how the dividend tax credit lowers the effective tax rate on dividends for investors in different tax brackets. For top-bracket investors there is a moderate reduction as compared to ordinary income. These investors face a far lower effective tax rate on capital gains because gains are taxed only when shares are sold. For these reasons, we believe that, from the viewpoint of individual investors, higher dividends require higher pre-tax returns.

Another way of measuring the effective tax rates on dividends and capital gains in Canada is to look at ex-dividend day price drops. We showed earlier that, ignoring taxes, a stock price should drop by the amount of the dividend when it goes ex-dividend. This is because the price drop offsets what investors lose by waiting to buy the stock until it goes ex-dividend. If dividends are taxed and capital gains are tax-free, the price drop should be lower, equal to the after-tax value of the dividend. However, if gains are taxed too, the

---

[25]Dividend yield is defined as

$$\frac{\text{Annual dividends per share}}{\text{Current price per share}}$$

Note that this differs slightly from Chapter 6, where Div in the numerator represented next year's dividend.

[26]I. G. Morgan, "Dividends and Stock Price Behaviour in Canada," *Journal of Business Administration* 12 (Fall 1989).

[27]B. Amoako-Adu, M. Rashid, and M. Stebbins, "Capital Gains Tax and Equity Values: Empirical Test of Stock Price Reaction to the Introduction and Reduction of Capital Gains Tax Exemption," *Journal of Banking and Finance* 16 (1992), pp. 275–87; F. Adjaoud and D. Zeghal, "Taxation and Dividend Policy in Canada: New Evidence," *Finance Economie Comptabilité,* (2nd Semester, 1999), 141–54.

price drop needs to be adjusted for the gains tax. An investor who waits for the stock to go ex-dividend buys at a lower price and hence has a larger capital gain when the stock is sold later.

In research designed to infer tax rates from ex-dividend day behaviour, Booth and Johnston concluded that marginal investors who set prices are taxed more heavily on dividends than on capital gains.[28] This supports our argument: Individual investors likely look for higher pre-tax returns on dividend-paying than on non-dividend–paying stocks.[29]

? Concept Questions

- **What are the tax benefits of low dividends?**
- **Explain the relationship between a stock's dividend yield and its pre-tax return.**

19.7 Real-World Factors Favouring a High-Dividend Policy

In the previous section, we pointed out that taxes must be paid by the recipient of a dividend. Since the tax rate on dividends is above the *effective* tax rate on capital gains, financial managers will seek out ways to reduce dividends. While we discussed the problems with taking on more capital budgeting projects, acquiring other firms, and hoarding cash, we stated that share repurchase has many of the benefits of a dividend with less of a tax disadvantage. In this section, we consider reasons why a firm might pay its shareholders high dividends, even in the presence of personal taxes on these dividends.

Desire for Current Income

It has been argued that many individuals desire current income. The classic example is the group of retired people and others living on a fixed income, proverbially known as "widows and orphans." The argument further states that these individuals would bid up the stock price should dividends rise and bid down the stock price should dividends fall.

Miller and Modigliani point out that this argument does not hold in their theoretical model. An individual preferring high current cash flow but holding low-dividend securities could easily sell off shares to provide the necessary funds. Thus, in a world of no transactions costs, a high–current-dividend policy would be of no value to the shareholder.

However, the current income argument does have relevance in the real world. The sale of stock involves brokerage fees and other transactions costs—direct cash expenses that could be avoided by an investment in high-dividend securities. In addition, the

---

[28]Booth and Johnston, "Ex-Dividend Day Behavior." Their research also showed that interlisted stocks, traded on exchanges in both the United States and Canada, tended to be priced by U.S. investors and not be affected by Canadian tax changes. J. Lakonishok and T. Vermaelen, "Tax Reforms and Ex-Dividend Day Behavior," *Journal of Finance* (September 1983), pp. 1157–58, gives a competing explanation in terms of tax arbitrage by short-term traders.

[29]For the U.S., M. Brennan, "Taxes, Market Valuation and Corporate Financial Policy," *National Tax Journal* (December 1970); and R. Litzenberger and K. Ramaswamy, "The Effect of Personal Taxes and Dividends on Capital Asset Prices: Theory and Empirical Evidence," *Journal of Financial Economics* (June 1979), found a positive association between expected pretax returns and dividend yields. A number of more recent studies also assign an important role to transactions costs in determining ex-dividend day returns. See also R. Bali and G. L. Hite, "Ex-Dividend Day Stock Price Behavior: Discreteness or Tax-Induced Clienteles?" *Journal of Financial Economics* (February 1998); and M. Frank and R. Jagannathan, "Why Do Stock Prices Drop By Less Than the Value of the Dividend? Evidence From a Country Without Taxes," *Journal of Financial Economics* (February 1998). D. W. French and N. V. Delcoure, "Decimalization and the Ex-Dividend-Day Behavior of Stock Prices," New Mexico State University Working Paper (2002).

expenditure of one's time when selling securities might further lead many investors to buy high-dividend securities.

However, to put this argument in perspective, it should be remembered that financial intermediaries such as mutual funds can perform repackaging transactions at low cost. Such intermediaries could buy low-dividend stocks and, by a controlled policy of realizing gains, pay their investors at a higher rate.

Behavioural Finance

Suppose it turned out that the transaction costs in selling no-dividend securities could not account for the preference of investors for dividends. Would there still be a reason for high dividends? We introduced the topic of behavioural finance in Chapter 14, pointing out that the ideas of behaviourists represent a strong challenge to the theory of efficient capital markets. It turns out that behavioural finance also has an argument for high dividends.

The basic idea here concerns *self-control,* a concept that, though quite important in psychology, has received virtually no emphasis in finance. While we cannot review all that psychology has to say about self-control, let's focus on one example—losing weight. Suppose Alfred Martin, a university student, just got back from the Christmas break more than a few pounds heavier than he would like. Everyone would probably agree that diet and exercise are the two ways to lose weight. But how should Alfred put this approach into practice? (We'll focus on exercise though the same principle would apply to diet as well.) One way, let's call it the economists' way, would involve trying to make rational decisions. Each day, Al would balance the costs and the benefits of exercising. Perhaps he would choose to exercise on most days, since losing the weight is important to him. However, when he is too busy with exams, he might rationally choose not to exercise because he cannot afford the time. And, he wants to be socially active as well. So he may rationally choose to avoid exercise on days when parties and other social commitments become too time-consuming.

This seems sensible—at first glance. The problem is that he must make a choice every day and there may simply be too many days when his lack of self-control gets the better of him. He may tell himself that he doesn't have the time to exercise on a particular day, simply because he is starting to find exercise boring, not because he really doesn't have the time. Before long, he is avoiding exercise on most days—and overeating in reaction to the guilt from not exercising!

Is there an alternative? One way would be to set rigid rules. Perhaps Alfred decides to exercise five days a week—*no matter what.* While this is not necessarily the best approach for everyone, there is no question that many of us, perhaps most of us, live by a set of rules. For example, Shefrin and Statman[30] suggest some typical rules:

—Jog at least two miles a day
—Do not consume more than 1200 calories per day
—Bank the wife's salary and only spend from the husband's paycheque
—Save at least 2 percent of every paycheque for children's university education and never withdraw from this fund
—Never touch a drop.

What does this have to do with dividends? Investors must also deal with self-control. Suppose a retiree wants to consume $20,000 a year from savings, in addition to the Canada Pension Plan and her pension. On one hand, she could buy stocks with a dividend yield high

---

[30]Hersh M. Shefrin and Meir Statman, "Explaining Investor Preference for Cash Dividends," *Journal of Financial Economics* 13 (1984).

enough to generate $20,000 in dividends. On the other hand, she could place her savings in no-dividend stocks, selling off $20,000 each year for consumption. Though these two approaches seem equivalent financially, the second one may allow for too much leeway. If lack of self-control gets the better of her, she might sell off too much, leaving little for her later years. Better, perhaps, to short-circuit this possibility by investing in dividend-paying stocks, with a firm personal rule of *never* "dipping into principal." While behaviourists do not claim that this approach is for everyone, they argue that enough people think this way to explain why firms pay dividends, even though, as we said earlier, dividends are tax-disadvantaged.

Does behavioural finance argue for increased stock repurchases as well as increased dividends? The answer is no, since investors will sell the stock that firms repurchase. As we said above, selling stock involves too much leeway. Investors might sell too many shares of stock, leaving little for the later years. Thus, the behaviourist argument may explain why companies pay dividends in a world with personal taxes.

Agency Costs

Although shareholders, bondholders, and management form firms for mutually beneficial reasons, one party may later gain at the other's expense. For example, take the potential conflict between bondholders and shareholders. Bondholders would like shareholders to leave as much cash as possible in the firm so that this cash would be available to pay the bondholders during times of financial distress. Conversely, shareholders would like to keep this extra cash for themselves. That's where dividends come in. Managers, acting on behalf of the shareholders, may pay dividends simply to keep the cash away from the bondholders. In other words, a dividend can be viewed as a wealth transfer from bondholders to shareholders. There is empirical evidence for this view of things. For example, DeAngelo and DeAngelo find that firms in financial distress are reluctant to cut dividends.[31] Of course, bondholders know of the propensity of shareholders to transfer money out of the firm. To protect themselves, bondholders frequently create protective covenants in loan agreements stating that dividends can be paid only if the firm has earnings, cash flow, and working capital above prespecified levels.

Although the managers may be looking out for the shareholders in any conflict with bondholders, the managers may pursue selfish goals at the expense of shareholders in other situations. For example, as discussed in Chapter 17, managers might pad expense accounts, take on pet projects with negative NPVs, or, more simply, not work very hard. Managers find it easier to pursue these selfish goals when the firm has plenty of free cash flow. After all, one cannot squander funds if the funds are not available in the first place. And, that is where dividends come in. Several scholars have suggested that dividends can serve as a way for the board of directors to reduce agency costs.[32] By paying dividends equal to the amount of "surplus" cash flow, a firm can reduce management's ability to squander the firm's resources.[33]

---

[31]H. DeAngelo and L. DeAngelo, "Dividend Policy and Financial Distress: An Empirical Investigation of Troubled NYSE Firms," *Journal of Finance* 45 (1990).

[32]Michael Rozeff, "How Companies Set Their Dividend Payout Ratios," in *The Revolution in Corporate Finance,* edited by Joel M. Stern and Donald H. Chew (New York: Basil Blackwell, 1986). See also Robert S. Hansen, Raman Kumar, and Dilip K. Shome, "Dividend Policy and Corporate Monitoring: Evidence from the Regulated Electric Utility Industry," *Financial Management* (Spring 1994).

[33]Current research shows that in many other countries where shareholders have weaker legal rights, the focal agency conflict is not between shareholders and managers but rather between controlling shareholders and other shareholders. In such countries, dividends are seen as a way of prying wealth loose from the hands of controlling shareholders: R. LaPorta, F. Lopez-de-Silanes, A. Schleifer, and R.W. Vishny, "Agency Problems and Dividend Policies Around the World," *Journal of Finance* (2000).

While the above discussion suggests a reason for increased dividends, the same argument applies to share repurchases as well. Managers, acting on behalf of shareholders, can just as easily keep cash from bondholders through repurchases as through dividends. And the board of directors, also acting on behalf of shareholders, can reduce the cash available to spendthrift managers just as easily through repurchases as through dividends. Thus, the presence of agency costs is not an argument for dividends over repurchases. Rather, agency costs imply firms may well increase either dividends or share repurchases rather than hoard large amounts of cash.

Information Content of Dividends and Dividend Signalling

Information Content   While there are many things researchers do not know about dividends, there is one thing that we know for sure: The stock price of a firm will generally rise when the firm announces an increase in the dividend and will generally fall when a dividend reduction is announced. For example, Asquith and Mullins estimate that stock prices rise following announcements of dividend initiations.[34] Stock prices rose when their sample of U.S. firms started or resumed dividends. Deshpande and Jog obtained the same result for a Canadian sample.[35] Healy and Palepu and Michael, Thaler, and Womack find that stock prices fall about 7 percent following announcements of dividend omissions.[36]

The question is: How should one *interpret* this empirical evidence? Consider the following three positions on dividends:

1. From the homemade dividend argument of MM, dividend policy is irrelevant, given that future earnings (and cash flows) are held constant.

2. Because of tax effects, a firm's stock price is negatively related to the current dividend when future earnings (or cash flows) are held constant.

3. Because of shareholders' desire for current income, a firm's stock price is positively related to its current dividend, even when future earnings (or cash flows) are held constant.

At first glance, the empirical evidence that stock prices rise when dividend increases are announced may seem consistent with position 3 and inconsistent with positions 1 and 2. In fact, many writers have argued this. However, other authors have countered that the observation itself is consistent with all three positions. They point out that companies do not like

---

[34]P. Asquith and D. Mullins, Jr., "The Impact of Initiating Dividend Payments on Shareholder Wealth," *Journal of Business* (January 1983).

[35]S. D. Deshpande and V. M. Jog, "The Information Content of Dividend Resumptions: The Canadian Evidence," *Proceedings of the Finance Division of the Administrative Sciences Association of Canada* 7 (1986), pp. 151–62. This topic has spawned a large volume of research. Selected examples are G. Charest, "Dividend Information, Stock Returns and Market Efficiency," *Journal of Financial Economics* 6 (1978); G. Charest, "Returns to Dividend Changing Stocks on the Toronto Stock Exchange," *Journal of Business Administration* 12 (Fall 1980), pp. 1–18; R. Pettit, "Dividend Announcements, Security Performance, and Capital Market Efficiency," *Journal of Finance* (1972); J. Ahroney and I. Swary, "Quarterly Dividend and Earnings Announcements and Stockholders' Returns: An Empirical Analysis," *Journal of Finance* (March 1980); C. Kwan, "Efficient Market Tests of the Informational Content of Dividends: Critique and Extensions," *Journal of Financial and Quantitative Analysis* 16 (1981); and F. Adjaoud, "The Information Content of Dividends: A Canadian Test," *Canadian Journal of Administrative Sciences* 16 (1984), pp. 338–51

[36]P. M. Healy and K. G. Palepu, "Earnings Information Conveyed by Dividend Initiations and Omissions," *Journal of Financial Economics* 21 (1988) and R. Michaely, R. H. Thaler, and K. Womack, "Price Reactions to Dividend Initiations and Omissions: Overreactions or Drift," *Journal of Finance* 50 (1995).

to cut a dividend. Thus, firms will raise the dividend only when future earnings, cash flow, and so on are expected to rise enough so that the dividend is not likely to be reduced later to its original level. A dividend increase is management's *signal* to the market that the firm is expected to do well.

It is the expectation of good times, and not only the shareholders' affinity for current income, that raises stock price. The rise in the stock price following the dividend signal is called the **information content effect** of the dividend. To recapitulate, imagine that the stock price is unaffected or even negatively affected by the level of dividends, given that future earnings (or cash flows) are held constant. Nevertheless, the information content effect implies that stock price may rise when dividends are raised—if dividends simultaneously cause shareholders to *increase* their expectations of future earnings and cash flows.

Canadian managers behave consistently with the theory of dividend signalling. In 1989, for example, the Bank of Montreal's earnings per share dropped from $4.89 the previous year to $0.04 due to increased loan loss provisions for lesser developed country debt. Yet the annual dividend was increased slightly from $2.00 to $2.12 per share. The payout ratio skyrocketed to 5300 percent ($2.12/$0.04). Management signalled the market that earnings would recover in 1990, which they did.

Dividend Signalling   We just argued that the market infers a rise in earnings and cash flows from a dividend increase, leading to a higher stock price. Conversely, the market infers a decrease in cash flows from a dividend reduction, leading to a fall in stock price. This raises an interesting corporate strategy: Could management increase dividends just to make the market *think* that cash flows will be higher, even when management knows that cash flows will not rise?

While this strategy may seem dishonest, academics take the position that managers frequently attempt the strategy. Academics begin with the following accounting identity for an all-equity firm:[37]

$$\text{Cash flow}^{37} = \text{Capital expenditures} + \text{Dividends} \qquad \textbf{(19.3)}$$

Equation (19.3) must hold if a firm is neither issuing nor repurchasing stock. That is, the cash flow from the firm must go somewhere. If it is not paid out in dividends, it must be used in some expenditure. Whether the expenditure involves a capital budgeting project or a purchase of Treasury bills, it is still an expenditure.

Imagine that we are in the middle of the year and investors are trying to make some forecast of cash flow over the entire year. These investors may very well use (19.3) to estimate cash flow. For example, suppose that the firm announces current dividends will be $50 million and the market believes that capital expenditures are $80 million. The market would then determine cash flow to be $130 million (50 + 80).

Now, suppose that the firm had, alternatively, announced a dividend of $70 million. The market might assume that cash flow remains at $130 million, implying capital expenditures of $60 million (130 − 70). Here, the increase in dividends would hurt stock price, since the market anticipates valuable capital expenditures will be crowded out. Alternatively, the market might assume that capital expenditures remain at $80 million, implying the estimate of cash flow to be $150 million (70 + 80). Stock price would likely rise here, since stock prices usually increase with cash flow. In general, academics believe that models where investors assume capital expenditures remain the same are more realistic. Thus, an increase in dividends improves stock price.

---

[37]The correct representation of (19.3) involves cash flow, not earnings. However, with little loss of understanding, we could discuss dividend signalling in terms of earnings, not cash flow.

Now we come to the incentives of managers to fool the public. Suppose you are a manager who wants to boost stock price, perhaps because you are planning to sell some of your personal holdings of the company's stock immediately. You might increase dividends so that the market would raise its estimate of cash flow, thereby also boosting the current stock price.

If this strategy is appealing, would anything prevent you from raising dividends without limit? The answer is yes, because there is also a *cost* to raising dividends. That is, the firm will have to forgo some of its profitable projects. Remember that cash flow in (19.3) is a constant, so that an increase in dividends is obtained only by a reduction in capital expenditures. At some point the market will learn that cash flow has not increased but, instead, profitable capital expenditures have been cut. Once the market absorbs this information, stock price should fall below what it would have been had dividends never been raised. Thus, if you plan to sell, say, half of your shares and retain the other half, an increase in dividends should help you on the immediate sale but hurt you when you sell your remaining shares years later. Thus, your decision on the level of dividends will be based, among other things, on the timing of your personal stock sales.

The above is a simplified example of dividend signalling, where the manager sets dividend policy based on maximum benefit for himself.[38] Alternatively, a given manager may have no desire to sell his shares immediately, but knows that, at any one time, plenty of ordinary shareholders will want to do so. Thus, for the benefit of shareholders in general, a manager will always be aware of the trade-off between current and future stock price. And this, then, is the essence of signalling with dividends. It is not enough for a manager to set dividend policy in order to maximize the true (or intrinsic) value of the firm. He must also consider the effect of dividend policy on the current stock price, even if the current stock price does not reflect true value.

Does a motive to signal imply that managers will increase dividends rather than share repurchases? The answer is likely no, since most academic models imply that dividends and share repurchases are perfect substitutes.[39] Rather, these models indicate that managers will consider reducing capital spending (even projects with positive NPVs) in order to increase either dividends or share repurchases.

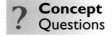

Concept Questions

- What are the real-world factors favouring a high-dividend policy?

19.8   The Clientele Effect: A Resolution of Real-World Factors?

In the previous two sections, we pointed out that the existence of personal taxes favours a low-dividend policy, whereas other factors favour high dividends. The financial profession had hoped that it would be easy to determine which of these sets of factors dominates.

[38]Papers examining fully developed models of signalling include S. Bhattacharya, "Imperfect Information, Dividend Policy, and 'The Bird in the Hand' Fallacy," *Bell Journal of Economics* 10 (1979); S. Bhattacharya, "Nondissipative Signaling Structure and Dividend Policy," *Quarterly Journal of Economics* 95 (1980), p. 1; S. Ross, "The Determination of Financial Structure: The Incentive Signalling Approach," *Bell Journal of Economics* 8 (1977), p. 1; M. Miller and K. Rock, "Dividend Policy Under Asymmetric Information," *Journal of Finance* (1985).

[39]Signalling models where dividends and repurchases are not perfect substitutes are contained in Franklin Allen, Antonio Bernardo, and Ivo Welch, "A Theory of Dividends Based on Tax Clienteles," *Journal of Finance* (2002) and John Kose and Joseph Williams, "Dividends, Dilution and Taxes: A Signaling Equilibrium," *Journal of Finance* (1985).

Unfortunately, after years of research, no one has been able to conclude which of the two is more important. This is surprising, since one might be skeptical that the two sets of factors would cancel each other out so perfectly.

However, one particular idea, known as the *clientele effect,* implies that the two sets of factors are likely to cancel each other out after all. To understand this idea, let's separate those investors in high-tax brackets from those in low-tax brackets. Individuals in high-tax brackets likely prefer either no or low dividends. Low–tax-bracket investors generally fall into three categories. First, there are individual investors in low brackets. They are likely to prefer some dividends if they desire current income. Second, pension funds pay no taxes on either dividends or capital gains. Because they face no tax consequences, pension funds will also prefer dividends if they have a preference for current income. Finally, Canadian corporations can exclude 100 percent of their dividend income received from other Canadian corporations but cannot exclude any of their capital gains. Thus, corporations would prefer to invest in high-dividend stocks, even without a preference for current income.

Suppose that 40 percent of all investors prefer high dividends and 60 percent prefer low dividends, yet only 20 percent of firms pay high dividends while 80 percent pay low dividends. Here, the high-dividend firms will be in short supply; thus their stock should be bid up while the stock of low-dividend firms should be bid down.

However, the dividend policies of all firms need not be fixed in the long run. In this example, we would expect enough low-dividend firms to increase their payout so that 40 percent of the firms pay high dividends and 60 percent of the firms pay low dividends. After this has occurred, no type of firm will be better off from changing its dividend policy. Once payouts of corporations conform to the desires of shareholders, no single firm can affect its market value by switching from one dividend strategy to another.

Clienteles are likely to form in the following way:

Group	Stocks
Individuals in high-tax brackets	Zero-to-low-payout stocks
Individuals in low-tax brackets	Low-to-medium-payout stocks
Tax-free institutions	Medium-payout stocks
Corporations	High-payout stocks

To see if you understand the clientele effect, consider the following question: "In spite of the theoretical argument that dividend policy is irrelevant or that firms should not pay dividends, many investors like high dividends. Because of this fact, a firm can boost its share price by having a higher dividend payout ratio." True or false?

The statement is likely to be false. As long as there are already enough high-dividend firms to satisfy dividend-loving investors, a firm will not be able to boost its share price by paying high dividends. A firm can boost its stock price only if an unsatisfied clientele exists. There is no evidence that this is the case.

Our discussion of clienteles followed from the fact that tax brackets vary across investors. If shareholders care about taxes, stocks should attract clienteles based on dividend yield. Is there any evidence that this is the case?

Consider Figure 19.7. Here, John Graham and Alok Kumar[40] rank common stocks by their dividend yields (the ratio of dividend to stock price) and place them into five portfolios, called quintiles. The bottom quintile contains the 20 percent of stocks with the lowest dividend yields; the next quintile contains the 20 percent of stocks with the next

[40]John Graham and Alok Kumar, "Do Dividend Clienteles Exist? Evidence on Dividend Preferences of Retail Investors," *Journal of Finance* 61 (June 2006) pp. 1305–1336.

FIGURE 19.7

Preferences of Investors for Dividend Yield

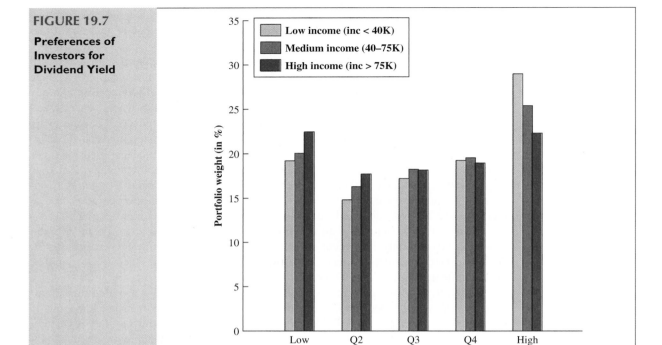

All stocks are ranked on their dividend yields and placed into five quintile portfolios. The figure shows the weight of each quintile in the portfolios of low-, medium-, and high-income investors. Relative to those with lower income, high-income investors place a greater percentage of their assets in low-dividend stocks and a smaller percentage in high-dividend stocks.

Source: Adapted from Figure 2 of John Graham and Alok Kumar, "Do Dividend Clienteles Exist? Evidence on Dividend Preferences of Retail Investors," forthcoming *Journal of Finance* 61 (June 2006), pp. 1305–1336

lowest dividend yields; and so on. The figure shows the weight of each quintile in the portfolios of low-, medium-, and high-income investors. As can be seen, relative to low-income investors, high-income investors put a greater percentage of their assets into low-dividend securities. Conversely, again relative to low-income investors, high-income investors put a smaller percentage of their assets into high-dividend securities.

? Concept Questions

- **How does the market react to unexpected dividend changes? What does this tell us about dividends? About dividend policy?**
- **What is a dividend clientele?**
- **All things considered, would you expect a risky firm with significant, but highly uncertain growth prospects to have a low or high dividend payout?**

19.9 What We Know and Do Not Know About Dividend Policy

Corporate Dividends Are Substantial

We pointed out earlier in the chapter that shareholder income taxes and new issue flotation costs are two important practical considerations favouring low dividends. Nevertheless, dividends in the U.S. and Canada are substantial. A current study by Fama and French

IN THEIR OWN WORDS

Why Cognos Incorporated Pays No Dividend

Cognos Inc. is a $922.1 million software provider founded in 1969. The company's common shares are listed as COGN on the NASDAQ. Cognos has never paid any cash dividends on its stock. Between 2003 and 2004, the company grew 24 percent and in the future will continue to retain earnings in order to help finance its business. The practice of not issuing dividends is common for high-tech companies.

Why Rogers Communications Pays Dividends

Rogers Communications Inc. is Canada's premier cable television provider and generates more than $5,099.3 million in revenue. The company's common stock is listed as RCI.A on the TSX. In 2003, Rogers Communications announced that it would begin paying a semiannual dividend to shareholders for the first time in company history. On June 10, 2004, Rogers Communications paid shareholders a cash dividend of $0.10 a share. The company changed its dividend policy in response to its strong financial performance over an extended period of time. At the same time, it wanted to provide its shareholders with an additional opportunity for a return on their investment. Since 2004, Rogers has increased its cash dividend to $ 0.16 per share.

Sources: www.cognos.com and www.rogers.com/

documents that the average firm listed on the New York Stock Exchange, American Stock Exchange, or Nasdaq paid out approximately 43 percent of its earnings over a 25-year period ending in 1998.[41]

Fewer Companies Pay Dividends

Although dividends are substantial, Fama and French (FF) point out that the percentage of companies paying dividends has fallen over the last few decades.[42] FF argue that the decline was caused primarily by an explosion of small, currently unprofitable companies that have recently listed on various stock exchanges. For the most part, firms of this type do not pay dividends. Figure 19.8 shows that the proportion of dividend payers among U.S. industrial firms dropped substantially from 1984 to 2002.

This figure, presented in a paper by Julio and Ikenberry (JI),[43] also shows an *increase* in the proportion of dividend payers from 2002 to 2004. One obvious explanation is the cut in the U.S. maximum tax rate on dividends to 15 percent, signed into law in May 2003. However, JI downplay the effect of the tax cut, suggesting a number of other reasons. Furthermore, the resurgence in dividend payers has been observed only over the two-year period from 2002 to 2004. Perhaps this trend is just a statistical aberration.

Figure 19.8 does not imply that dividends across *all* firms declined from 1984 to 2002. DeAngelo, DeAngelo, and Skinner[44] point out that while small firms have shied away from dividends, the largest firms have substantially increased their dividends over

[41]E. F. Fama and K. R. French , "Disappearing Dividends: Changing Firm Characteristics or Lower Propensity to Pay," *Journal of Financial Economics* (April 2001).

[42]E. F. Fama and K. R. French, "Disappearing Dividends: Changing Firm Characteristics or Lower Propensity to Pay?" *Journal of Financial Economics* (April 2001).

[43]Brandon Julio and David Ikenberry, "Reappearing Dividends," unpublished paper, University of Illinois (July 2004).

[44]Harry DeAngelo, Linda DeAngelo, and Douglas Skinner, "Are Dividends Disappearing? Dividend Concentration and the Consolidation of Earnings," *Journal of Financial Economics* (2004).

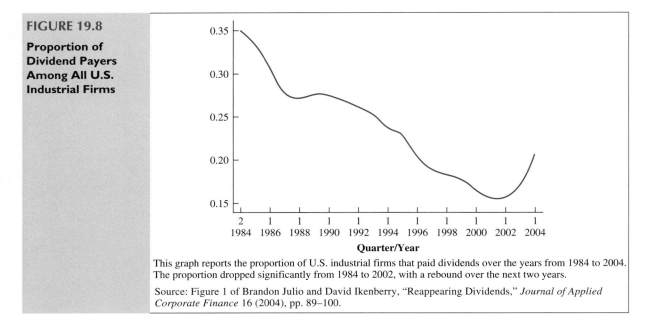

FIGURE 19.8

Proportion of Dividend Payers Among All U.S. Industrial Firms

This graph reports the proportion of U.S. industrial firms that paid dividends over the years from 1984 to 2004. The proportion dropped significantly from 1984 to 2002, with a rebound over the next two years.

Source: Figure 1 of Brandon Julio and David Ikenberry, "Reappearing Dividends," *Journal of Applied Corporate Finance* 16 (2004), pp. 89–100.

recent decades. This increase has created such concentration in dividends that the top 25 dividend-paying firms accounted for more than 50 percent of aggregate dividends in the United States in 2000. DeAngelo and colleagues conclude (p. 425), "Industrial firms exhibit a two-tier structure in which a small number of firms with very high earnings collectively generates the majority of earnings and dominates the dividend supply, while the vast majority of firms has at best a modest collective impact on aggregate earnings and dividends."

In the last part of the twentieth century, Canadian firms also reduced dividend payout ratios from historic highs as documented by Foerster and Sapp.[45] This trend appears to be reversing however, as companies like Bank of Montreal announce increases in their target payout ratios.

Corporations Smooth Dividends

In 1956, John Lintner[46] made two important observations concerning dividend policy. First, real-world companies typically set long-run target ratios of dividends to earnings. A firm is likely to set a low target ratio if it has many positive NPV projects relative to available cash flow and a high ratio if it has few positive NPV projects. Second, managers know that only part of any change in earnings is likely to be permanent. Because managers need time to assess the permanence of any earnings rise, dividend changes appear to lag earnings changes by a number of periods.

---

[45]Stephen R. Foerster and Stephen G. Sapp, "The changing role of dividends: A firm-level study from the nineteenth to the twenty-first century," *Canadian Journal of Economics,* Volume 39, November 2006, pp. 1316–1344.

[46]J. Lintner, "Distribution and Incomes of Corporations Among Dividends, Retained Earnings, and Taxes," *American Economic Review* (May 1956).

EXAMPLE 19.2

Calculator Graphics Inc. (CGI) has a target payout ratio of 0.30. Last year's earnings per share were $10, and in accordance with the target, CGI paid dividends of $3 per share last year. However, earnings have jumped to $20 this year. Since the managers do not believe that this increase is permanent, they do *not* plan to raise dividends all the way to $6 (0.30 × $20). Rather, their speed of adjustment coefficient, *s*, is 0.5, implying that the *increase* in dividends from last year to this year will be:

$$0.5 \times (\$6 - \$3) = \$1.50$$

That is, the increase in dividends is the product of the speed of adjustment coefficient, 0.50, times the difference between what dividends would be with full adjustment [$6 (0.30 × $20)] and last year's dividends. Since dividends will increase by $1.50, dividends this year will be $4.50 ($3 + $1.50).

Now, suppose that earnings stay at $20 next year. The increase in dividends next year will be:

$$0.5 \times (\$6 - \$4.50) = \$0.75$$

In words, the increase in dividends from this year to next year will be the speed of adjustment coefficient (0.50) times the difference between what dividends would have been next year with full adjustment ($6) and this year's dividends ($4.50). Since dividends will increase by $0.75, dividends next year will be $5.25 ($4.50 + $0.75). In this way, dividends will slowly rise every year, if earnings in all future years remain at $20. However, dividends will reach $6 only at infinity.

Taken together, Lintner's observations suggest that two parameters describe dividend policy: the target payout ratio (*t*) and the speed of adjustment of current dividends to the target (*s*). Dividend changes will tend to conform to the following model:

$$\text{Div}_1 - \text{Div}_0 = s \cdot (t\text{EPS}_1 - \text{Div}_0) \qquad (19.4)$$

where Div_1 and Div_0 are dividends in the next year and dividends in the current year, respectively. EPS_1 is earnings per share in the next year.

The limiting cases occur when $s = 1$ and $s = 0$. If $s = 1$, the actual change in dividends will be equal to the target change in dividends. Here, the full adjustment occurs immediately. If $s = 0$, $\text{Div}_1 = \text{Div}_0$. In other words, there is no change in dividends at all. Real-world companies can be expected to set s between 0 and 1.

An implication of Lintner's model is that the dividends-to-earnings ratio rises when a company begins a period of bad times, and the ratio falls when a company reaches a period of good times. Thus, dividends display less variability than do earnings. In other words, firms smooth dividends.

Payouts Provide Information to the Market

We previously observed that the price of a firm's stock frequently rises when its current dividend is increased or a share repurchase is announced. Conversely, the price of a firm's stock can fall significantly when its dividend is cut. In other words, there is information content in dividend changes. One reason may be that investors are looking at current dividends for clues concerning the level of future earnings and dividends.

A Sensible Dividend Policy

The knowledge of the finance profession varies across topic areas. For example, capital budgeting techniques are both powerful and precise. A single net present value equation can accurately determine whether a multimillion-dollar project should be accepted or rejected. The capital asset pricing model and the arbitrage pricing model provide empirically validated relationships between expected return and risk.

Conversely, the field has less knowledge of capital structure policy. Though a number of elegant theories relate firm value to the level of debt, no formula can be used to calculate the firm's optimum debt–equity ratio. Our profession is forced too frequently to employ rules of thumb, such as treating the industry's average ratio as the optimal one for the firm. The field's knowledge of dividend policy is, perhaps, similar to its knowledge of capital structure policy. We do know that:

1. Firms should avoid having to cut back on positive NPV projects to pay a dividend, with or without personal taxes.

2. Firms should avoid issuing stock to pay a dividend in a world with personal taxes.

3. Repurchases should be considered when there are few positive new investment opportunities and there is a surplus of unneeded cash.

The preceding recommendations suggest that firms with many positive NPV projects relative to available cash flow should have low payout ratios. Firms with fewer positive NPV projects relative to available cash flow might want to consider higher payouts. In addition, there is some benefit to dividend stability, and unnecessary changes in dividend payout are avoided by most firms.

However, there is no formula for calculating the optimal dividend-to-earnings ratio. In addition, there is no formula for determining the optimal mix between repurchases and dividends. It can be argued that, for tax reasons, firms should always substitute stock repurchases for dividends. However, while the volume of repurchases has greatly increased over time, dividends do not appear to be on the way out. At the present time, the dollar volume of dividends is only slightly less than that of repurchases.

The Pros and Cons of Paying Dividends

Pros	Cons
1. Cash dividends can underscore good results and provide support to stock price.	1 Dividends are taxed move heavily than capital gains.
2. Dividends may attract institutional investors who prefer some return in the form of dividends. A mix of institutional and individual investors may allow a firm to raise capital at lower cost because of the ability of the firm to reach a wider market.	**2.** Dividends can reduce internal sources of financing. Dividends may force the firm to forgo positive NPV projects or to rely on costly external equity financing.
3. Stock price usually increases with the announcement of a new or increased dividend.	**3.** Once established, dividend cuts are hard to make without adversely affecting a firm's stock price.
4. Dividends absorb excess cash flow and may reduce agency costs that arise from conflicts between management and shareholders.	

19.10   SUMMARY AND CONCLUSIONS

1. The dividend policy of the firm is irrelevant in a perfect capital market because the shareholder can effectively undo the firm's dividend strategy. If a shareholder receives a greater dividend than desired, he or she can reinvest the excess. Conversely, if the shareholder receives a smaller dividend than desired, he or she can sell off extra shares of stock. This argument is due to MM and is similar to their homemade leverage concept, discussed in Chapter 16.

2. Shareholders will be indifferent between dividends and share repurchases in a perfect capital market.

3. Since dividends in Canada are taxed when paid to individuals, companies should not issue stock in order to pay out a dividend.

4. Also because of taxes, firms have an incentive to reduce dividends. For example, they might consider increasing capital expenditures, acquiring other companies, or purchasing financial assets. However, due to financial considerations and legal constraints, rational firms with large cash flows will likely exhaust these activities with plenty of cash left over for dividends.

5. In a world with personal taxes, a strong case can be made for repurchasing shares instead of paying dividends.

6. Nevertheless, there are a number of justifications for dividends even in a world with personal taxes:

   a. Investors in no-dividend stocks incur transaction costs when selling off shares for current consumption.

   b. Behavioural finance argues that investors with limited self-control can meet current consumption needs via high-dividend stocks while adhering to a policy of "never dipping into principal."

   c. Managers, acting on behalf of shareholders, can pay dividends to keep cash from bondholders. The board of directors, also acting on behalf of shareholders, can use dividends to reduce the cash available to spendthrift managers.

   d. Managers may increase dividends to boost current stock price, even at the expense of projects with positive NPVs. This strategy is called signalling.

7. The stock market reacts positively to increases in dividends (or an initial payment) and negatively to decreases in dividends. This suggests that there is information content in dividend payments.

8. High (low) dividend firms should arise to meet the demands of dividend-preferring (capital gains-preferring) investors. Because of these clienteles, it is not clear that a firm can create value by changing its dividend policy.

KEY TERMS

Clienteles 557	Ex-dividend date 534	Stock dividend 533
Date of payment 535	Homemade dividends 539	Stock split 534
Date of record 534	Information content effect 555	Stripped common shares 540
Declaration date 534	Regular cash dividends 533	

SUGGESTED READING

The breakthrough in the theory of dividend policy is contained in:
M. Miller and F. Modigliani. "Dividend Policy, Growth, and the Valuation of Shares." *Journal of Business* (October 1961).

A survey of dividend policy can be found in:
Franklin Allen and Roni Michaely. "Dividend Policy." In R. A. Jarrow, V. Maksimovic, and W. T. Ziemba (eds.). *Handbooks in Operations Research and Management Science: Finance.* Amsterdam: Elsevier Science (1995), 793–838.

Current trends in dividend policy are examined in:
Eugene F. Fama and Kenneth R. French. "Disappearing Dividends: Changing Firm Characteristics or Lower Propensity to Pay?" *Journal of Financial Economics* (April 2001).

Visit us at www.mcgrawhill.ca/olc/ross

B. Amoako-Adu, M. Rashid, and M. Stebbins, "Capital Gains Tax and Equity Values: Empirical Test of Stock Price Reaction to the Introduction and Reduction of Capital Gains Tax Exemption." *Journal of Banking and Finance* 16 (1992), 275–87.

A current study of share repurchases in Canada is:

D. Ikenberry, J. Lakonishok, and T. Vermaelen, "Stock Repurchases in Canada: Performance and Strategic Trading." *Journal of Finance* (October 2000).

QUESTIONS & PROBLEMS

The Mechanics of Dividend Payouts

19.1   Identify and describe each of the following dates that are associated with a dividend payment on common stock:

February 16
February 24
February 26
March 14

19.2   On April 5, the board of directors of National Park Golf Club declared a dividend of $0.50 per share payable on Tuesday, May 4, to shareholders of record as of Tuesday, April 20. Supposed Mr. Peterson bought 350 shares of National Park on April 6 for $9.87 a share. Assume there are no taxes, no transaction costs, and no news between your purchase and the sale of the stock. If he were to sell his stocks on April 16, for how much would Mr. Peterson be able to sell his stock?

19.3   If increases in dividends tend to be followed by (immediate) increases in share prices, how can it be said that dividend policy is irrelevant?

19.4   The O'Toole Company belongs to a risk class for which the appropriate discount rate is 10 percent. O'Toole currently has 200,000 outstanding shares selling at $750 each. The firm is contemplating the declaration of a $3.75 dividend at the end of the fiscal year that just began. Assume there are no taxes on dividends. Answer the following questions based on the Miller and Modigliani model, which is discussed in the text.
   a. What will be the price of the stock on the ex-dividend date if the dividend is declared?
   b. What will be the price of the stock at the end of the year if the dividend is not declared?
   c. If O'Toole makes $2 million of new investments at the beginning of the period, earns net income of $1 million, and pays the dividend at the end of the year, how many shares of new stock must the firm issue to meet its funding needs?
   d. Is it realistic to use the MM model in the real world to value stock? Why or why not?

19.5   On February 17, the board of directors of Unidentified Fliers Corp. declared a dividend a dividend of $1.76 per share payable on March 18 to all holders of record on March 1. All investors are in the 34 percent tax bracket.
   a. What is the ex-dividend date?
   b. Ignoring personal taxes, how much should the stock price drop on the ex-dividend date?

The Benchmark Case: An Illumination of the Irrelevance of Dividend Policy

19.6   The growing perpetuity model expresses the value of a share of stock as the present value of the expected dividends from that stock. How can you conclude that dividend policy is irrelevant when this model is valid?

19.7   Cavendish Corporation stock, of which Roger Rabbit owns 460 shares, will pay $2-per-share dividend one year from today. Two years from now Cavendish will close its doors; shareholders will receive liquidating dividends of $18.5673 per share. The required rate of return on Cavendish stock is 13 percent.
   a. What is the current price of Cavendish stock?
   b. You prefer to receive equal amounts of money in each of the next two years. How will you accomplish this?

EXCEL

19.8   The net income of Novis Corporation is $36,000. The company has 9000 outstanding shares and a 100 percent payout policy. The expected value of the firm one year from now is $1,640,300. The appropriate discount rate for Novis is 12 percent, and the dividend tax rate is zero.

a.   What is the current value of the firm assuming the current dividend has not yet been paid?

b.   What is the ex-dividend price of Novis's stock if the board follows its current policy?

c.   At the dividend declaration meeting, several board members claimed that the dividend is too meager and is probably depressing Novis's price. They proposed that Novis sell enough new shares to finance a $4.25 dividend.

   1.   Comment on the claim that the low dividend is depressing the stock price. Support your argument with calculations.

   2.   If the proposal is adopted, at what price will the new shares sell? How many will be sold?

19.9   Gibbons Enterprises has a current period cash flow of $11 million and pays no dividends. The present value of the company's future cash flows is $115 million. The company is entirely financed with equity and has 13 million shares outstanding. Assume the dividend tax rate is zero.

a.   What is the share price of the Gibson stock?

b.   Suppose the board of directors announces its plan to pay out 50 percent of its current cash flow as cash dividends to its shareholders. How can Jeff Miller, who owns 100,000 shares of Gibbons stock, achieve a zero payout policy on his own?

Taxes, Issuance Costs and Dividends

19.10   National Business Machine Co. (NBM) has $2.5 million of extra cash after taxes have been paid. NBM has two choices to make use of this cash. One alternative is to invest the cash in financial assets. One alternative is to invest the cash in financial assets. The resulting investment income will be paid out as a special dividend at the end of three years. In this case, the firm can invest in Treasury bills yielding 5 percent, or a 10 percent preferred stock. Only 36 percent of the dividends from investing in preferred stock would be subject to corporate taxes. Another alternative is to pay out the cash as dividends and let the shareholders invest on their own in Treasury bills with the same yield. The corporate tax rate is 34 percent, and the individual tax rate is 26 percent. Should the cash be paid today or in three years? Which of the two options generates the highest after-tax income for the shareholders?

19.11   In their 1970 paper on dividends and taxes, Elton and Gruber reported that the ex-dividend date drop in a stock's price as a percentage of the dividend should equal the ratio of 1 minus the ordinary income tax rate to 1 minus the capital gains rate; that is,

$$\frac{P_b - P_e}{D} = \frac{1 - T_0}{1 - T_c}$$

where

P_e = The ex-dividend stock price

P_b = The stock price before it trades ex-dividend

D = The amount of the dividend

T_o = The tax rate on ordinary income

T_c = The effective tax rate on capital gains

Note: As we pointed out in the text, effective tax rate of capital gains is less than the actual tax rate, because their realization may be postponed. Indeed, because investors could postpone their realizations indefinitely, the effective rate could be zero.

a.   If $T_o = T_c = 0$, how much will the stock's price fall?

b.   If $T_o \neq 0$ and $T_c = 0$, how much will it fall?

  c. Explain the results you found in (a) and (b).

  d. Do the results of Elton and Gruber's study imply that firms will maximize shareholder wealth by not paying dividends?

19.12 After completing its capital spending for the year, Carlson Manufacturing has $1,000 extra cash. Carlson's managers must choose between investing the cash in Treasury bonds that yield 9 percent or paying the cash out to investors who would invest in the bonds themselves.

  a. If the corporate tax rate is 33 percent, what personal tax rate would make the investors equally willing to receive the dividend or to let Carlson invest the money?

  b. Is the answer to (a) reasonable? Why or why not?

  c. Suppose the only investment choice is a preferred stock that yields 13 percent. The corporate dividend exclusion of 72 percent applies. What personal tax rate will make the stockholders indifferent to the outcome of Carlson's dividend decision?

  d. Is this a compelling argument for a low dividend payout ratio? Why or why not?

Real-World Factors Favouring a High Dividend Policy

19.13 The bird-in-the-hand argument, which states that a dividend today is safer than the uncertain prospect of a capital gain tomorrow, is often used to justify high dividend payout ratios. Explain the fallacy behind this argument.

19.14 The desire for current income is not a valid explanation of preference for high current dividend policy because investors can always create homemade dividends by selling a portion of their stocks. Is this statement true or false? Why?

19.15 Your aunt is in a high tax bracket and would like to minimize the tax burden of her investment portfolio. She is willing to buy and sell to maximize her after-tax returns, and she has asked for your advice. What would you suggest she do?

A Resolution of Real-World Factors

19.16 In the May 4, 1981, issue of *Fortune,* an article entitled "Fresh Evidence That Dividends Don't Matter" stated, "All told, 115 companies of the 500 [largest industrial corporations] raised their payout every year during the period [1970–1989]. Investors in this . . . group would have fared somewhat better than investors in the 500 as a whole: the median total [annual compound] return of the 115 was 10.7% during the decade versus 9.4% for the 500." Is this evidence that investors prefer dividends to capital gains? Why or why not?

19.17 Last month, PEI Power Corp., which had been having trouble with cost overruns on a nuclear power plant that it had been building, announced that it was "temporarily suspending payments due to the cash flow crunch associated with its investment program." The company's stock price dropped from $29.50 to $24 when this announcement was made. How would you interpret this change in the stock price?

19.18 Southern Established Inc. have been paying out regular quarterly dividends ever since 1983. It just doubled the dividend in the current fiscal quarter and a much larger increase is to be on the way. Southern's stock price rose from $31.75 to $38.00 when the dividend increase was announced. Explain the possible reasons for this price increase.

19.19 Spike Higginson owns Envirotechno stock because its price has been steadily rising over the past few years and he expects this performance to continue. Spike is trying to convince Sandy Doons to purchase some Envirotechno stock, but she is reluctant because Envirotechno has never paid a dividend. She depends on steady dividends to provide her with income.

  a. What preferences are these two investors demonstrating?

  b. What argument should Spike use to convince Sandy that Envirotechno stock is the stock for her?

  c. Why might Spike's argument not convince Sandy?

19.20 If the market places the same value on $1 of dividends as on $1 of capital gains, then firms with different payout ratios will appeal to different clienteles of investors. One clientele is as good as another; therefore, a firm cannot increase its value by changing its dividend policy. Yet empirical investigations reveal a strong correlation between dividend payout ratios and other firm characteristics. For example, small, rapidly growing firms that have recently gone public almost always have payout ratios that are zero; all earnings are reinvested in the business. Explain this phenomenon if dividend policy is irrelevant.

19.21 In spite of the theoretical argument that dividend policy should be irrelevant, the fact remains that many investors like high dividends. If this preference exists, a firm can boost its share price by increasing its dividend payout ratio. Explain the fallacy in this argument.

19.22 The Sharpe Co. just paid a dividend of $2.25 per share of stock. Its target payout ratio is 35 percent. The company expects to have an earnings per share of $6.50 one year from now.
    a. If the adjustment rate is .275 as defined in the Lintner model, what is the dividend one year from now?
    b. If the adjustment rate is .6 instead, what is the dividend one year from now?
    c. Which adjustment rate is more conservative? Why?

19.23 Worthington Corporation has declared an annual dividend of $0.80 per share. For the year just ended, earnings were $7 per share.
    a. What is Worthington's payout ratio?
    b. Suppose Worthington has 7 million shares outstanding. Borrowing for the coming year is planned at $18 million. What are planned investment outlays assuming a residual dividend policy? What target capital structure is implicit in these calculations?

19.24 Falling Zeppelins Corporation follows a strict residual dividend policy. Its debt–equity ratio is 3.
    a. If earnings for the year are $180,000, what is the maximum amount of capital spending possible with no new equity?
    b. If planned investment outlays for the coming year are $760,000, will Falling Zeppelins pay a dividend? If so, how much?
    c. Does Falling Zeppelins maintain a constant dividend payout? Why or why not?

19.25 Find the annual income statement for Newmont Mining Corp (NEM), CAE Inc. (CAE) and Nortel Networks Limited (NT). What are the EPS for each company for the last 5 years? What are the dividends for each company over the past five years? Why would these companies have such different dividend policies? Is there anything unusual about the dividends for Nortel? How could the company pay dividends with negative earnings?

Visit us at www.mcgrawhill.ca/olc/ross

MINICASE: Electronic Timing Inc.

Electronic Timing Inc. (ETI) is a small company founded 15 years ago by electronics engineers Tom Miller and Jessica Kerr. ETI manufactures integrated circuits to capitalize on the complex mixed-signal design technology and has recently entered the market for frequency timing generators, or silicon timing devices, which provide the timing signals or "clocks" necessary to synchronize electronic systems. Its clock products originally were used in PC video graphics applications, but the market subsequently expanded to include motherboards, PC peripheral devices, and other digital consumer electronics, such as digital television boxes and game consoles. ETI also designs and markets custom application-specific integrated circuits (ASICs) for industrial customers. The ASIC's design combines analog and digital, or mixed-signal, technology. In addition to Tom and Jessica, Nolan Pittman, who provided capital for the company, is one of the three principal owners. Each owns 25 percent of the 1 million shares outstanding. Several other individuals, including current employees, own the remaining company shares.

Recently, the company designed a new computer motherboard. The company's design is both more efficient and less expensive to manufacture, and the ETI design is expected to become standard in many personal computers. After investigating the possibility of manufacturing the new motherboard, ETI determined that the costs involved in building a new plant would be prohibitive. The owners also decided that they were unwilling to bring in another large outside owner. Instead, ETI sold the design to an outside firm. The sale of the motherboard design was completed for an after-tax payment of $30 million.

1. Tom believes the company should use the extra cash to pay a special one-time dividend. How will this proposal affect the stock price? How will it affect the value of the company?

2. Jessica believes that the company should use the extra cash to pay off debt and upgrade and expand its existing manufacturing capability. How would Jessica's proposals affect the company?

3. Nolan is in favour of a share repurchase. He argues that a repurchase will increase the company's P/E ratio, return on assets, and return on equity. Are his arguments correct? How will a share repurchase affect the value of the company?

4. Another option discussed by Tom, Jessica, and Nolan would be to begin a regular dividend payment to shareholders. How would you evaluate this proposal?

5. One way to value a share of stock is the dividend growth, or growing perpetuity, model. Consider the following: The dividend payout ratio is 1 minus b, where b is the "retention" or "plowback" ratio. So, the dividend next year will be the earnings next year, E_1, times 1 minus the retention ratio. The most commonly used equation to calculate the sustainable growth rate is the return on equity times the retention ratio. Substituting these relationships into the dividend growth model, we get the following equation to calculate the price of a share of stock today:

$$P_0 = \frac{E_1(1 - b)}{r_S - \text{ROE} \times b}$$

What are the implications of this result in terms of whether the company should pay a dividend or upgrade and expand its manufacturing capability? Explain.

6. Does the question of whether the company should pay a dividend depend on whether the company is organized as a corporation or an LLC?

Appendix 19A: Stock Dividends and Stock Splits
To access Appendix 19A, please go to the Online Learning Centre at **www.mcgrawhill.ca/olc/ross**.

PART 5

Chapter 20

Issuing Equity Securities to the Public

EXECUTIVE SUMMARY

This chapter looks at how corporations issue securities to the investing public. The general procedures for debt and equity are quite similar. This chapter focuses on equity, but the procedures for debt and equity are basically the same.

Since issuing securities is a specialized activity not undertaken on a daily basis, issuing corporations generally seek assistance from an investment dealer. Depending on the type of security and the alternatives chosen, the assistance from the investment dealer may include a variety of services, including advice on (1) which securities to issue, (2) how to structure and price the deal, and (3) complying with disclosure requirements set by regulators. In addition, investment dealers offer the issuer various forms of protection against receiving substantially less than the issue price or failing to sell the entire issue.

The new securities could be a primary market, public issue sold directly to the public with the help of an investment dealer. Once registered with provincial regulatory authorities, the newly issued securities may be traded on secondary markets (stock exchanges or over the counter). In contrast, in a private placement, debt or equity (common or preferred shares) is sold directly to a small number of buyers.

A company's first issue of public equity is called an *initial public offering (IPO)*. IPOs come in cycles: in the late 1990s dot-com companies dominated the scene. Starting in 2001, income trusts took over and in 2003, the largest IPO was Yellow Pages Income Fund, which raised $935 million. In a public offering of debt or equity, the investment dealer will generally act as an underwriter taking on some, or all, of the pricing risk in the new issue. The underwriter does this by buying the issue and reselling it. The underwriter takes all the pricing risk in a special type of public offering called a *bought deal*.

Instead of marketing to the general public, a corporation can sell common stock to its existing shareholders by what is called a *rights offer*. Rights offerings are usually cheaper and faster than underwritten public offerings in part because they are marketed to a narrower audience that already has shown interest in the stock. Through the 1970s, rights offerings were easily the most popular method of raising new equity in Canada.

In the 1980s, the Ontario Securities Commission (OSC) introduced a streamlined reporting and registration system for large companies that issue securities regularly, called Prompt Offering Prospectus (POP). With deregulation and the advantages of POP, growing competition among underwriters promoted dramatic growth in the popularity of bought deals over rights offers. Today, the majority of equity dollars raised in Canada use POP and are bought deals.

20.1 The Public Issue

A firm issuing securities must satisfy a number of requirements set out by provincial regulations and statutes and enforced by provincial securities commissions. Regulation of the securities market in Canada is carried out by provincial commissions and through provincial securities acts. However, only eight of the provinces have commissions, due in large part to an absence of exchanges in some provinces. This is in contrast to the United States, where regulation is handled by a federal body, the Securities and Exchange Commission (SEC). The regulators' goal is to promote the efficient flow of information about securities and the smooth functioning of securities markets.

All companies listed on the Toronto Stock Exchange come under the jurisdiction of the Ontario Securities Commission. The *Securities Act* sets forth the provincial regulations for all new securities issues involving the province of Ontario and the Toronto Stock Exchange (TSX). The OSC administers the act. Other provinces have similar legislation and regulating bodies, but the OSC is the most noteworthy because of the TSX's scope.[1] In general terms, the OSC rules seek to ensure that investors receive all material information on new issues in the form of a registration statement and prospectus. The Canadian Securities Administrators (CSA) coordinates regulation and, at the time of writing in June 2004, the CSA has completed a draft for Uniform Securities Legislation, which would streamline practices across jurisdictions. Of particular note is the proposed "passport system," which would allow a prospectus that is approved in one province to be immediately approved in all other provinces, making it valid across Canada.

The OSC's responsibility for efficient information flow goes beyond new issues. It continues to regulate the trading of securities after they have been issued to ensure adequate disclosure of information. For example, in June 2004, the OSC announced that it would extend a cease-trade order that stops management and insiders from the Hollinger group of companies from trading shares.

Another informational role of the OSC is gathering and publishing insider reports filed by major shareholders, officers, and directors of TSX-listed firms. To ensure efficient functioning of markets, the OSC oversees the training and supervision that investment dealers provide for their personnel. It also monitors investment dealers' capital positions. Increasing market volatility and the popularity of bought deals in which the dealer assumes all the price risk make capital adequacy important. The Investment Dealers Association of Canada is a national self-regulatory agency for the securities industry. Its mandate is to protect investors and ensure integrity of the marketplace, as well as promote fair and competitive capital markets.[2]

20.2 The Basic Procedure for a New Issue

There is a series of steps involved in issuing securities to the public, which is depicted in Table 20.1. In general terms, the basic procedure is as follows:

1. Management's first step in issuing any securities to the public is to obtain approval from the board of directors. The firm must also engage an underwriter.

2. The firm must prepare and distribute copies of a preliminary **prospectus** to the OSC and to potential investors. The preliminary prospectus contains some of the financial information that will be contained in the final prospectus; it does not contain the price at which the

---

[1]The TSX is Canada's largest stock exchange. The TSX Group, the company that owns and operates the TSX, also operates the TSX Venture Exchange where smaller companies list their stock because they are not able to meet the TSX requirements. In addition to equity exchanges, the Montreal Exchange specializes in the trading of derivatives, and the Winnipeg Commodities Exchange is focused on trading commodities such as wheat and rice.

[2]Source: http:www.ida.ca.

TABLE 20.1   The Process of Raising Capital

Steps in Public Offering	Time	Activities
1. Preunderwriting conferences	Several months	The amount of money to be raised and the type of security to be issued are discussed. The underwriting syndicate and selling group are put together. The underwriting contract is negotiated. Board approval is obtained.
2. Registration statements filed and approved	A 20-day waiting period	The registration statement contains all relevant financial and business information.
3. Pricing the issue	Usually not before the last day of the registration period	For seasoned offerings the price is set close to the prevailing market price. For initial public offerings intensive research and analysis are required.
4. Public offering and sale	Shortly after the last day of the registration period	In a typical firm commitment contract, the underwriter buys a stipulated amount of stock from the firm and sells it at a higher price. The selling group assists in the sale.
5. Market stabilization	Usually 30 days after the offering	The underwriter stands ready to place orders to buy at a specified price on the market.

security will be offered. The preliminary prospectus is sometimes called a **red herring,** in part because bold red letters are printed on the cover warning that the OSC has neither approved nor disapproved of the securities. The OSC studies the preliminary prospectus and notifies the company of any changes required. This process is usually completed within about two weeks.

3. Once the revised, final prospectus meets with the OSC's approval, a price is determined and a full-fledged selling effort gets underway. A final prospectus must accompany the delivery of securities or confirmation of sale, whichever comes first.

Tombstone advertisements are used by underwriters during and after the waiting period. The **tombstone** contains the name of the company whose securities are involved. Figure 20.1 shows a tombstone featuring a deal by Ernst & Young Orenda Corporate Finance.

The POP System

In 1982, the SEC approved its shelf registration system designed to reduce repetitive filing requirements for large companies. In 1983, the OSC introduced the POP (Prompt Offering Prospectus) system with a similar goal. The eight provinces with securities commissions all have compatible legislation allowing certain securities issuers prompt access to capital markets without the necessity of preparing a full preliminary and final prospectus prior to a distribution.

The POP system, accessible only by large companies, lets issuers file annual and interim financial statements regardless of whether they issue securities in a given year. To use the POP system, issuers must have been reporting for 36 months and have complied with the continuous disclosure requirements. Because the OSC has an extensive file of information on these companies, only a short prospectus is required when securities are issued. As we stated earlier, POP offerings in the form of bought deals became quite popular in the late 1980s.

In the early 1990s, securities regulators in Canada and the SEC in the United States introduced a Multi-Jurisdictional Disclosure System (MJDS). Under MJDS, large issuers in the two countries are allowed to issue securities in both countries under disclosure documents satisfactory to regulators in the home country. In its day, this was an important

FIGURE 20.1

An Excerpt of a Tombstone Advertisement

This announcement is neither an offer to sell nor a solicitation of an offer to buy any of these securities. The offering is made only by the Prospectus.

New Issue

11,500,000 Shares

World Wrestling Federation Entertainment, Inc.

Class A Common Stock

Price $17.00 Per Share

Copies of the Prospectus may be obtained in any State in which this announcement is circulated from only such of the Underwriters, including the undersigned, as may lawfully offer these securities in such State.

U.S. Offering

9,200,000 Shares

This portion of the underwriting is being offered in the United States and Canada.

Bear, Stearns & Co. Inc.

Credit Suisse First Boston

Merrill Lynch & Co.

Wit Capital Corporation

Allen & Company Incorporated	Banc of America Securities LLC	Deutsche Banc Alex. Brown
Donaldson, Lufkin & Jenrette	A.G. Edwards & Sons, Inc.	Hambrecht & Quist ING Barings
Prudential Securities	SG Cowen Wasserstein Perella Securities, Inc.	Advest, Inc.
Axiom Capital Management, Inc.	Blackford Securities Corp.	J.C. Bradford & Co.
Joseph Charles & Assoc., Inc.	Chatsworth Securities LLC	Gabelli & Company, Inc.
Gaines, Berland Inc. Jefferies & Company, Inc.	Josephthal & Co. Inc.	Neuberger Berman, LLC
Raymond James & Associates, Inc.		Sanders Morris Mundy
Tucker Anthony Cleary Gull		Wachovia Securities, Inc.

International Offering

2,300,000 Shares

This portion of the underwriting is being offered outside of the United States and Canada.

Bear, Stearns International Limited

Credit Suisse First Boston

Merrill Lynch International

simplification of filing requirements for certain large Canadian companies. While MJDS is based on a model of companies issuing securities simultaneously at home and in foreign markets, in 2004, many Canadian companies were cross-listed on the NYSE or Nasdaq. Cross-listing refers to the practice of listing a firm's shares for trading on other exchanges usually in foreign countries. For Canadian firms, cross-listing opens up the alternative of issuing in larger U.S. stock markets. Possible advantages for U.S. listing include greater liquidity, lower trading costs, greater visibility, and greater investor protection under more stringent U.S. securities laws such as Sarbanes-Oxley on corporate governance. U.S. listing also brings possible disadvantages in the form of higher accounting and compliance costs. On balance, it remains undecided whether U.S. listing adds shareholder value.[3]

? Concept Questions

- • **What are the basic procedures in selling a new issue?**
- • **What is a preliminary prospectus?**
- • **What are the POP system and MJDS and what advantages do they offer?**

20.3 The Cash Offer

If the public issue of securities is a cash offer, underwriters are usually involved. Underwriters perform the following services for corporate issuers:

1. Formulating the method used to issue the securities.
2. Pricing the new securities.
3. Selling the new securities.

Typically, the underwriter buys the securities for less than the offering price and accepts the risk of not being able to sell them. Because underwriting involves risk, underwriters combine to form an underwriting group called a **syndicate** or a **banking group** to share the risk and help to sell the issue.

In a syndicate, one or more managers arrange or co-manage the offering. The lead manager typically has the responsibility for packaging and executing the deal. The other underwriters in the syndicate serve primarily to distribute the issue.

The difference between the underwriter's buying price and the offering price is called the **spread** or **discount.** It is the basic compensation received by the underwriter.

In Canada, firms often establish long-term relationships with their underwriters. With the growth in popularity of bought deals, competition among underwriters has increased. At the same time, mergers among investment dealers have reduced the number of underwriters. For example, RBC Dominion Securities grew through merger with six other investment dealers and a major capital injection by the Royal Bank.

Types of Underwriting

Two basic types of underwriting are involved in a cash offer: regular underwriting and a bought deal.

Regular Underwriting   With **regular underwriting** the banking group of underwriters buys the securities from the issuing firm and resells them to the public for the purchase price plus an underwriting spread. Regular underwriting includes an "out clause," which

---

[3]A positive view is in: Michael R. King and Dan Segal, "Corporate Governance, International Cross Listing and Home Bias," *Canadian Investment Review,* Winter 2003. Usha R. Mittoo challenges the positive view in: "The Value of U.S. Listing: Does a U.S. Listing Improve Stock Performance in the Long Run?" *Canadian Investment Review,* Fall 2003. Supporting the challenge, a recent paper finds that companies tend to cross-list in markets similar to their home country's where diversification benefits are small: Sergei Sarkissian and Michael J. Schill, "The Overseas Listing Decision: New Evidence of Proximity Preference," *Review of Financial Studies* 17, Fall 2004.

gives the banking group the option to decline the issue if the price drops dramatically. In this case, the deal is usually withdrawn. The issue might be repriced and/or reoffered at a later date. **Firm-commitment underwriting** is like regular underwriting without the out clause.

A close counterpart to regular underwriting is called **best-efforts underwriting.** The underwriter is legally bound to use "best efforts" to sell the securities at the agreed-upon offering price. Beyond this, the underwriter does not guarantee any particular amount of money to the issuer. This form of underwriting is more common with initial public offerings (IPOs).

Bought Deal   In a **bought deal,** the issuer sells the entire issue to one investment dealer or to a group that then attempts to resell it. As in firm-commitment underwriting, the investment dealer assumes all the price risk. The dealer has usually "premarketed" the prospective issue to a few large institutional investors. Issuers in bought deals are large, well-known firms that qualify for the use of POP to speed up OSC filings. For these reasons, bought deals are usually executed swiftly. Bought deals are the most popular form of underwriting in Canada today.

The Selling Period

While the issue is being sold to the public, the underwriting group agrees not to sell securities for less than the offering price until the syndicate dissolves. The principal underwriter is permitted to buy shares if the market price falls below the offering price. The purpose would be to support the market and stabilize the price from temporary downward pressure. If the issue remains unsold after a time (for example, 30 days), members can leave the group and sell their shares at whatever price the market will allow.

The Overallotment Option

Many underwriting contracts contain an *overallotment option* or *Green Shoe provision* that gives members of the underwriting group the option to purchase additional shares at the offering price less fees and commissions.[4] The stated reason for the overallotment option is to cover excess demand and oversubscriptions. The option has a short maturity (around 30 days) and is limited to about 10 percent of the original number of shares issued.

The overallotment option is a benefit to the underwriting syndicate and a cost to the issuer. If the market price of the new issue rises immediately, the overallotment option allows the underwriters to buy additional shares from the issuer and immediately resell them to the public.

Investment Dealers

Investment banks are at the heart of new security issues. They provide advice, market the securities (after investigating the market's receptiveness to the issue), and underwrite the proceeds. They accept the risk that the market price may fall between the date the offering price is set and the time the issue is sold.

In addition, investment banks have the responsibility of pricing fairly. When a firm goes public, particularly for the first time, the buyers know relatively little about the firm's operations. After all, it is not rational for a buyer of, say, only 1000 shares of stock to study the company at length. Instead, the buyer must rely on the judgment of the investment

---

[4]The term *Green Shoe provision* sounds exotic, but the origin is relatively mundane. It comes from the Green Shoe Company, which once granted such an option.

TABLE 20.2
Top IPO
Underwriters for
2005 and 2006
Based on All IPO
Deals on TSX and
TSX Venture*

2006	2005
1. CIBC World Markets	CIBC World Markets
2. RBC Dominion Securities	BMO Nesbitt Burns
3. TD Securities	RBC Dominion Securities
4. Canaccord Capital	TD Securities
5. BMO Nesbitt Burns	Scotia Capital
6. Scotia Capital	National Bank Financial
7. National Bank Financial	Canaccord Capital
8. Raymond James	Blackmont Capital
9. Blackmont Capital	Raymond James
10. Desjardins Securities	HSBC Securities
11. Wellington West	Desjardins Securities
12. HSBC Securities	Wellington West
13. GMP Securities	Dundee Securities
14. Dundee Securities	Richardson Partners
15. Sprott Securities	GMP Securities
16. Goldman Sachs	Genuity Capital
17. Berkshire Securities	Sprott Securities
18. Research Capital	Research Capital
19. Haywood Securities	Haywood Securities
20. Peters & Co.	Berkshire Securities

*Rankings based on estimated commission dollars.
Source: *Investment Executive,* April 2007. Used with permission.

bank, which has presumably examined the firm in detail. Given this asymmetry of information, what prevents the investment banker from pricing the issued securities too high? While the underwriter has a short-run incentive to price high, it has a long-run incentive to make sure that its customers do not pay too much; they might desert the underwriter in future deals if they lose money on this one. Thus, as long as investment banks plan to stay in business over time, it is in their self-interest to price fairly.

In other words, financial economists argue that each investment bank has a reservoir of "reputation capital."[5] Mispricing of new issues, as well as unethical dealings, is likely to reduce this reputation capital.

One measure of this reputation capital is the pecking order among the investment banks. MBA students are aware of this order because they know that accepting a job with a top-tier firm is universally regarded as more prestigious than accepting a job with a lower-tier firm.

Table 20.2 lists the largest underwriters in Canada based on revenue in 2005 and 2006. The table shows that CIBC World Markets was the leading underwriter.

The Offering Price and Underpricing

Determining the correct offering price is an underwriter's hardest task. The issuing firm faces a potential cost if the offering price is set too high or too low. If the issue is priced below the true market price, the issuer's existing shareholders will experience an

[5]For example, see R. Carter, F. H. Dark, and A. K. Singh, "Underwriter Reputation, Initial Returns and the Long-Run Performance of IPO Stocks," *Journal of Finance* 53 (1998); and R. Beatty and J. Ritter, "Investment Banking, Reputation, and the Underpricing of Initial Public Offerings," *Journal of Financial Economics* (1986).

opportunity loss when they sell their shares for less than they are worth. If the issue is priced too high, it may be unsuccessful and have to be withdrawn. Of course, this is the underwriter's problem under a bought deal.

Underpricing is a fairly common occurrence and it clearly helps new shareholders earn a higher return on the shares they buy. However, to the existing shareholders of the issuing firm, underpricing is an indirect cost of issuing new securities. In the case of an IPO, underpricing reduces the proceeds received by the original owners.

The Decision to Go Public

When a private company grows to a certain size, it may consider the advantages of going public by issuing common stock through an **initial public offering (IPO).** One important advantage is that public firms have greater access to new capital once their shares are valued on secondary markets. Further, publicly traded firms must meet OSC and other disclosure requirements that reduce information risk for potential investors. In addition, going public makes it possible for the firm's principal owners to sell some of their shares and diversify their personal portfolios while retaining control of the company.

Going public also has disadvantages. Public firms are subject to stricter disclosure and other potentially costly regulatory requirements.

On balance, most large companies in Canada are public. When a firm decides to go public, it does so through an IPO.

Pricing IPOs

Determining the correct offering price is the most difficult thing the lead investment bank must do for an initial public offering. The issuing firm faces a potential cost if the offering price is set too high or too low. If the issue is priced too high, it may be unsuccessful and be withdrawn. If the issue is priced below the true market price, the issuer's existing shareholders will experience an opportunity loss.

Table 20.3 draws on studies by Jay R. Ritter at the University of Florida. In general, the studies found that IPOs are underpriced compared to their prices in the aftermarket immediately after the offering period.

Another dramatic example of underpricing came with the IPO of Tim Hortons in March 2006. The Canadian corporate icon announced the pricing of its initial public offering of 29 million shares of common stock at a price of $27 per share. The stock closed at

TABLE 20.3
Number of Offerings, Average First-Day Return, and Gross Proceeds of Initial Public Offerings: 1975–2005

Year	Number of Offerings*	Average First-Day Return, %[†]	Gross Proceeds ($ in millions)[‡]
1975–1979	112	5.7	1,124
1980–1989	2380	6.8	61,880
1990–1999[1]	4146	21.1	291,531
2000–2005[1]	959	29.0	193,310
1975–2005	**7597**	**17.3**	**547,845**

*The number of offerings excludes IPOs with an offer price of less than $5.00, ADRs, best-efforts offers, unit offers, Regulation A offerings (small issues raising less than $1.5 million during the 1980s), real estate investment trusts (REITs), partnerships, and closed-end funds.

[†]First-day returns are computed as the percentage return from the offering price to the first closing market price.

[‡]Gross proceeds data are from Securities Data Co. and exclude overallotment options but include the international tranche, if any. No adjustments for inflation have been made.

[1]The years 1990–1999 and 2000–2005 are affected by the Internet bubble. Refer to Table 20.4 for more details.

Source: Professor Jay R. Ritter, University of Florida.

Jay R. Ritter on IPO Underpricing Around the World

The United States is not the only country in which initial public offerings of common stock (IPOs) are underpriced. The phenomenon exists in every country with a stock market, although the extent of underpricing varies from country to country.

In general, countries with developed capital markets have more moderate underpricing than those with emerging markets. During the Internet bubble of 1999–2000, however, underpricing in the developed capital markets increased dramatically. In the U.S., for example, the average first-day return during 1999–2000 was 65 percent. At the same time that underpricing in the developed capital markets increased, the underpricing of IPOs sold to residents of China moderated. The Chinese average has come down to a mere 257 percent, which is lower than it had been in the early and mid-1990s. After the bursting of the Internet bubble in mid-2000, the level of underpricing in the U.S., Germany, and other developed capital markets has returned to more traditional levels, and the volume of IPOs slowed to a trickle in 2001–2003.

The table below gives a summary of the average first day returns on IPOs for 38 countries around the world, with the figures collected from a number of studies by various authors. In countries where the first-day price change is limited by regulations, the return is measured until price limits are no longer binding.

Country	Sample size	Time Period	Average First-Day Return	Country	Sample Size	Time Period	Average First-Day Return
Australia	381	1976–1995	12.1%	Malaysia	401	1980–1998	104.1%
Austria	76	1984–1999	6.5	Mexico	37	1987–1990	33.0
Belgium	86	1984–1999	14.6	Netherlands	143	1982–1999	10.2
Brazil	62	1979–1990	78.5	New Zealand	201	1979–1999	23.0
Canada	500	1971–1999	6.3	Nigeria	63	1989–1993	19.1
Chile	55	1982–1997	8.8	Norway	68	1984–1996	12.5
China	432	1990–2000	256.9	Philippines	104	1987–1997	22.7
Denmark	117	1984–1998	5.4	Poland	149	1991–1998	35.6
Finland	99	1984–1997	10.1	Portugal	21	1992–1998	10.6
France	571	1983–2000	11.6	Singapore	128	1973–1992	31.4
Germany	407	1978–1999	27.7	South Africa	118	1980–1991	32.7
Greece	129	1987–1994	51.7	Spain	99	1986–1998	10.7
Hong Kong	334	1980–1996	15.9	Sweden	251	1980–1994	34.1
India	98	1992–1993	35.3	Switzerland	120	1983–2000	34.9
Indonesia	106	1989–1994	15.1	Taiwan	293	1986–1998	31.1
Israel	285	1990–1994	12.1	Thailand	292	1987–1997	46.7
Italy	164	1985–2000	23.9	Turkey	138	1990–1996	13.6
Japan	1,689	1970–2001	28.4	United Kingdom	3,122	1959–2001	17.4
Korea	477	1980–1996	74.3	United States	14,840	1960–2001	18.4

Jay R. Ritter is Cordell Professor of Finance at the University of Florida. An outstanding scholar, he is well-respected for his insightful analyses of new issues and companies going public.

$33.10 after one day of trading—a 22.6 percent increase from the IPO price. However, there is much more to the IPO process. It is not just about what the market will bear at the time but also about trying to get the company launched for the long term and building a good investor base.[6]

---

[6]Pricing information was obtained through Bloomberg LP. Historical prices and price changes can also be found at finance.yahoo.com.

Underpricing: A Possible Explanation

There are several possible explanations for underpricing, but so far there is no agreement among scholars as to which explanation is correct. There are two important facts associated with the underpricing puzzle that are key elements to a unifying theory. First, much of the apparent underpricing is concentrated in smaller issues. This point is documented in Table 20.4, which shows that underpricing tends to be attributable to firms with few or no sales in the prior year. These firms tend to be young firms with uncertain future prospects. The increased uncertainty in some way probably attracts risk-averse investors only if underpricing exists. Second, when the price of a new issue is too low, the issue is often *oversubscribed*. This means investors will not be able to buy all of the shares they want, and the underwriters will allocate the shares among investors. The average investor will find it difficult to get shares in an oversubscribed offering because there will not be enough shares to go around. Although initial public offerings have positive initial returns on average, a significant fraction of them have price drops. An investor submitting an order for all new issues may find that he or she will be allocated more shares in issues that go down in price.

Consider this tale of two investors. Ms. Smarts knows precisely what companies are worth when their shares are offered. Mr. Average knows only that prices usually rise one month after the IPO. Armed with this information, Mr. Average decides to buy 1000 shares of every IPO. Does Mr. Average actually earn an abnormally high average return across all initial offerings?

The answer is no, and at least one reason is Ms. Smarts. For example, because Ms. Smarts knows that company *XYZ* is underpriced, she invests all her money in its IPO. When the issue is oversubscribed, the underwriters must allocate the shares between Ms. Smarts and Mr. Average. If they do this on a pro rata basis and if Ms. Smarts has bid for twice as many shares as Mr. Average, she will get two shares for each one Mr. Average receives. The net result is that when an issue is underpriced, Mr. Average cannot buy as much of it as he wants.

TABLE 20.4   Average First-Day Returns, Categorized by Sales, for IPOs: 1980–2005*

Annual Sales of Issuing Firms	Number of Firms	1980–1989 First-Day Average Return	Number of Firms	1990–1998 First-Day Average Return	Number of Firms	1999–2000 First-Day Average Return	Number of Firms	2001–2005 First-Day Average Return
0 ≤ Sales < $10 m	393	10.1%	671	17.2%	328	69.8%	77	6.1%
$10 m ≤ Sales < $20 m	253	8.7	377	18.7	139	79.9	27	10.5
$20 m ≤ Sales < $50 m	492	7.6	777	18.7	152	74.5	70	9.7
$50 m ≤ Sales < $100 m	345	6.5	574	13.0	89	60.4	72	16.1
$100 m ≤ Sales < $200 m	241	4.6	444	11.9	54	35.5	79	14.7
$200 m ≤ Sales	278	3.5	628	8.7	87	26.0	209	10.9
All	2002	7.1%	3471	14.8%	849	64.6%	534	11.3%

*Data are from Securities Data Co., with corrections by the authors. Sales, measured in millions, are for the last twelve months prior to going public. All sales have been converted into dollars of 2003 purchasing power, using the Consumer Price Index. There are 6854 IPOs, after excluding IPOs with an offer price of less than $5.00 per share, units, REITs, ADRs, closed-end funds, banks and S&Ls, firms not listed on CRSP within six months of the offer date, and 140 firms with missing sales. The average first-day return is 18.5 percent.

Source: Professor Jay R. Ritter, University of Florida.

Ms. Smarts also knows that company *ABC* is overpriced. In this case, she avoids its IPO altogether, and Mr. Average ends up with a full 1000 shares. To summarize, Mr. Average receives fewer shares when more knowledgeable investors swarm to buy an underpriced issue, but he gets all he wants when the smart money avoids the issue. This is called the *winner's curse,* and it explains much of the reason why IPOs have such a large average return. When the average investor wins and gets his allocation, it is because those who knew better avoided the issue. To counteract the winner's curse and attract the average investor, underwriters underprice issues.[7]

? Concept Questions

- **Suppose a stockbroker calls you up out of the blue and offers to sell "all the shares you want" of a new issue. Do you think the issue will be more or less underpriced than average?**
- **What factors determine the degree of underpricing?**

20.4 The Announcement of New Equity and the Value of the Firm

It seems reasonable to believe that new long-term financing is arranged by firms after positive net present value projects are put together. As a consequence, when the announcement of external financing is made, the firm's market value should go up. As discussed in an earlier chapter, this is precisely the opposite of what actually happens in the case of new equity financing. Asquith and Mullins, Masulis and Korwar, and Mikkelson and Partch have all found that the market value of existing U.S. equity drops on the announcement of a new issue of common stock.[8] Studies by Mittoo and by Derosiers, L'Her, and Sauriol obtain a similar result for TSX stocks.[9] Plausible reasons for this strange result include:

1. *Managerial information.* If managers have superior information about the market value of the firm, they may know when the firm is overvalued. If they do, they might attempt to issue new shares of stock when the market value exceeds the correct value. This will benefit existing shareholders. However, the potential new shareholders are not stupid. They will infer overvaluation from the new issue, thereby bidding down the stock price on the announcement date of the issue.

2. *Debt capacity.* The stereotypical firm chooses a debt-to-equity ratio that balances the tax shield from the debt with the cost of financial distress. When the managers of a firm have special information that the probability of financial distress has risen, the firm is more likely to raise capital through stock than through debt. If the market infers this chain of events, the stock price should fall on the announcement date of an equity issue.

---

[7]This explanation was first suggested in K. Rock, "Why New Issues Are Underpriced," *Journal of Financial Economics* 15 (1986).

[8]P. Asquith and D. Mullins, "Equity Issues and Offering Dilution," *Journal of Financial Economics* 15 (1986); R. Masulis and A. N. Korwar, "Seasoned Equity Offerings: An Empirical Investigation," *Journal of Financial Economics* 15 (1986); and W. H. Mikkelson and M. M. Partch, "The Valuation Effects of Security Offerings and the Issuance Process," *Journal of Financial Economics* 15 (1986).

[9]Usha R. Mittoo, "Seasoned Equity Offerings and the Cost of Equity in the Canadian Market," in Paul Halpern, ed., *Financing Growth in Canada,* University of Calgary Press, 1997; and Stéphanie Desrosiers, Jean-Francois L'Her, and Lorraine Sauriol, "SEOs: Bearers of Long-Term Bad News," *Canadian Investment Review,* Spring 2004.

3. *Falling earnings.*[10] When managers raise capital in amounts that are unexpectedly large (as most unanticipated financings will be) and if investors have a reasonable fix on the firm's upcoming investments and dividend payouts (as they do because capital expenditure announcements are often well known, as are future dividends), the unanticipated financings are roughly equal to unanticipated shortfalls in earnings (this follows directly from the firm's sources and uses of funds identity). Therefore, an announcement of a new stock issue will also reveal a future earnings shortfall.

20.5 The Cost of Issuing Securities

Issuing securities to the public isn't free, and the costs of different methods are important determinants of which method is used. These costs associated with *floating* a new issue are generically called *flotation* costs. In this section, we take a closer look at the flotation costs associated with equity sales to the public.

The costs of selling stock fall into six categories: (1) the spread, (2) other direct expenses, (3) indirect expenses, (4) abnormal returns, (5) underpricing, and (6) the overallotment option. We look at these costs first for American and then for Canadian equity sales.

The Costs of Issuing Securities

Spread	The spread consists of direct fees paid by the issuer to the underwriting syndicate—the difference between the price the issuer receives and the offer price.
Other direct expenses	These are direct costs, incurred by the issuer, that are not part of the compensation to underwriters. These costs include filing fees, legal fees, and taxes—all reported on the prospectus.
Indirect expenses	These costs are not reported on the prospectus and include the costs of management time spent working on the new issue.
Abnormal returns	In a seasoned issue of stock, the price drops on average by 3 percent on the announcement of the issue.
Underpricing	For initial public offerings, losses arise from selling the stock below the correct value.
Overallotment (Green Shoe) option	The Green Shoe option gives the underwriters the right to buy additional shares at the offer price to cover overallotments.

Table 20.5 reports the direct costs of new equity issues in 1990–2003 for publicly traded U.S. firms. The percentages in Table 20.5 are as reported in the prospectuses of the issuing companies. These costs only include the spread (underwriter discount) and other direct costs, including legal fees, accounting fees, printing costs, SEC registration costs, and taxes. Not included are indirect expenses, abnormal returns, underpricing, and the overallotment option.

As indicated in Table 20.5, the direct costs alone can be very large, particularly for smaller (less than $10 million) issues. For this group, the direct costs, as reported by the companies, average a little more than 13 percent. This means the company, net of costs, receives 87 percent of the proceeds of the sale on average. On a $10 million issue, this is over $1 million in direct expenses—a substantial cost.

---

[10]Robert S. Haugen and Claire Crutchley, "Corporate Earnings and Financings, An Empirical Analysis," *Journal of Business* 20 (1990).

TABLE 20.5
Direct Costs as a Percentage of Gross Proceeds for Seasonal Equity Offered by U.S. Companies: 1990–2003

Proceeds (in $ millions)	Number of issues	Gross Spread	Other Direct Expense	Total Direct Cost
2 – 9.99	267	7.56%	5.32%	12.88%
10 – 19.99	519	6.32	2.49	8.81
20 – 39.99	904	5.73	1.51	7.24
40 – 59.99	677	5.28	0.92	6.20
60 – 79.99	489	5.07	0.74	5.81
80 – 99.99	292	4.95	0.61	5.56
100 – 199.99	657	4.57	0.43	5.00
200 – 499.99	275	3.99	0.27	4.26
500 and up	83	3.48	0.16	3.64
Total	4163	5.37%	1.35%	6.72%

Source: Inmoo Lee, Scott Lockhead, Jay Ritter, and Quanshui Zhao, "The Costs of Raising Capital," *Journal of Financial Research I* (Spring 1996), calculations and updates by the authors.

TABLE 20.6
Costs of Going Public in Canada: 1984–97

Fees	6.00%
Underpricing (first day trading return)	7.88
Total	13.88%

Sources: Fees are from L. Kryzanowski and I. Rakita, "Is the U.S. 7% Solution Equivalent to the Canadian 6% Solution?" *Canadian Investment Review,* Fall 1999, pp. 27–34. Underpricing is from V. Jog and A. Srivastava, "The Mixed Results of Canadian IPOs," *Canadian Investment Review,* Winter 1997–98, pp. 22–26 and the website of J. Ritter: www.bear.cba.ufl.edu/ritter/index.html.

Table 20.5 tells only part of the story. For IPOs, the effective costs can be much greater because of the indirect costs. Table 20.6 reports both the direct costs of going public and the degree of underpricing based on IPOs that occurred on the TSX between 1984 and 1997. These figures understate the total cost because the study did not consider indirect expenses or the overallotment option.

The total costs of going public over these years averaged just under 14 percent. This is roughly comparable to the U.S. figures for smaller IPOs. Once again we see that the costs of issuing securities can be considerable.

Overall, three conclusions emerge from our discussion of underwriting:

1. Substantial economies of size are evident. Larger firms can raise equity more easily.

2. The cost associated with underpricing can be substantial and can exceed the direct costs.

3. The issue costs are higher for an initial public offering than for a seasoned offering.

? Concept Questions

- **What are the different costs associated with security offerings?**
- **What lessons do we learn from studying issue costs?**

20.6 Rights

When new shares of common stock are sold to the general public, the proportional ownership of existing shareholders will likely be reduced. However, if a **pre-emptive right** is contained in the firm's articles of incorporation, then the firm must first offer any new issue of common stock to existing shareholders. If the articles of incorporation do not include a pre-emptive right, the firm has a choice of offering the issue of common stock directly to existing shareholders or to the public. In some industries, regulatory authorities set rules concerning rights. For example, prior to the 1980 *Bank Act,* chartered banks were required to raise equity exclusively through rights offerings.

An issue of common stock offered to existing shareholders is called a *rights offering.* In a rights offering, each shareholder is issued one right for every share owned. The rights give the shareholder an *option* to buy a specified number of new shares from the firm at a specified price within a specified time, after which time the rights are said to expire.

The terms of the rights offering are evidenced by certificates known as *rights.* Such rights are often traded on securities exchanges or over the counter.

The Mechanics of a Rights Offering

To illustrate the various considerations a financial manager has in a rights offering, we will examine the situation faced by the National Power Company, whose abbreviated initial financial statements are given in Table 20.7.

As the table shows, National Power earns $2 million after taxes and has 1 million shares outstanding. Earnings per share are thus $2. The stock sells for $20 (10 times earnings). To fund a planned expansion, the company intends to raise $5 million of new equity funds by a rights offering.

To execute a rights offering, the financial manager of National Power must answer the following questions:

1. What price should the existing shareholders be allowed to pay for a share of new stock?
2. How many rights will be required to purchase one share of stock?
3. What effect will the rights offering have on the existing price of the stock?

Subscription Price

In a rights offering, the **subscription price** is the price that existing shareholders are allowed to pay for a share of stock. A rational shareholder will only subscribe to the rights

TABLE 20.7
National Power Company Financial Statement Before Rights Offering

NATIONAL POWER COMPANY
Balance Sheet

Assets		Shareholders' Equity	
		Common stock	$ 5,000,000
		Retained earnings	10,000,000
Total	$15,000,000	Total	$15,000,000

Income Statement

Earnings before taxes	$ 3,333,333
Taxes (40%)	$ 1,333,333
Net income	$ 2,000,000
Earnings per share	$ 2
Shares outstanding	1,000,000
Market price per share	$ 20
Total market value	$20,000,000

offering if the subscription price is below the market price of the stock on the offer's expiration date. For example, if the stock price at expiration is $13 and the subscription price is $15, no rational shareholder will subscribe. Why pay $15 for something worth $13? National Power chooses a price of $10, which is well below the current market price of $20. As long as the market price does not fall by half before expiration, the rights offering will succeed.

Number of Rights Needed to Purchase a Share

National Power wants to raise $5 million in new equity. Suppose that the subscription price is set at $10 per share. How National Power arrived at that price is something we will discuss below, but notice that the subscription price is substantially less than the current $20 per share market price.

At $10 per share, National Power will have to issue 500,000 new shares. This can be determined by dividing the total amount of funds to be raised by the subscription price:

$$\text{Number of new shares} = \frac{\text{Funds to be raised}}{\text{Subscription price}} = \frac{\$5,000,000}{\$10} = 500,000 \text{ shares} \qquad (20.1)$$

Because shareholders always get one right for each share of stock they own, 1 million rights will be issued by National Power. To determine how many rights will be needed to buy one new share of stock, we can divide the number of existing outstanding shares of stock by the number of new shares:

$$\text{Number of rights needed to buy a share of stock} = \frac{\text{Old shares}}{\text{New shares}} = \frac{1,000,000}{500,000} = 2 \text{ rights} \qquad (20.2)$$

Thus, a shareholder will need to give up two rights plus $10 to receive a share of new stock. If all shareholders do this, National Power will raise the required $5 million.

It should be clear that the subscription price, the number of new shares, and the number of rights needed to buy a new share of stock are interrelated. For example, National Power can lower the subscription price. If so, more new shares must be issued to raise $5 million in new equity. Several alternatives are worked out here:

Subscription Price	New Shares	Rights Needed to Buy a Share of Stock
$20	250,000	4
10	500,000	2
5	1,000,000	1

The Value of a Right

Rights clearly have value. In the case of National Power, the right to be able to buy a share of stock worth $20 for $10 is definitely worth something.

Suppose a shareholder of National Power owns two shares of stock just before the rights offering. This situation is depicted in Table 20.8. Initially, National Power costs $20 per share, so the shareholder's total holding is worth 2 × $20 = $40. The National Power rights offer gives shareholders with two rights the opportunity to purchase one additional share for $10. The additional share does not carry a right.

The shareholder who has two shares will receive two rights. The holding of the shareholder who exercises these rights and buys the new share would increase to three shares. The total investment would be $40 + $10 = $50 (the $40 initial value plus the $10 paid to the company).

TABLE 20.8
**The Value
of Rights for
the Individual
Shareholder**

Initial Position	
Number of shares	2
Share price	$20
Value of holding	$40
Terms of offer	
Subscription price	$10
Number of rights issued	2
Number of rights for a new share	2
After offer	
Number of shares	3
Value of holdings	$50
Share price	$16.67
Value of a right	
Old price—New price	$20 − $16.67 = $3.33

The shareholder now holds three shares, all of which are identical because the new share does not have a right and the rights attached to the old shares have been exercised. Since the total cost of buying these three shares is $40 + $10 = $50, the price per share must end up at $50/3 = $16.67 (rounded to two decimal places).

Table 20.9 summarizes what happens to National Power's stock price. If all shareholders exercise their rights, the number of shares will increase to 1 million + 0.5 million = 1.5 million. The value of the firm will increase to $20 million + $5 million = $25 million. The value of each share will thus drop to $25 million/1.5 million = $16.67 after the rights offering.

The difference between the old share price of $20 and the new share price of $16.67 reflects the fact that the old shares carried rights to subscribe to the new issue. The difference must equal the value of one right, that is, $20 − $16.67 = $3.33.

Although holding no shares of outstanding National Power stock, an investor who wants to subscribe to the new issue can do so by buying some rights. Suppose an outside investor buys two rights. This will cost $3.33 × 2 = $6.67 (accounting for previous rounding). If the investor exercises the rights at a subscription price of $10, the total cost would be $10 + $6.67 = $16.67. In return for this expenditure, the investor will receive a share of the new stock, which, as we have seen, is worth $16.67.

TABLE 20.9
**National Power
Company Rights
Offering**

Initial Position	
Number of shares	1 million
Share price	$20
Value of firm	$20 million
Terms of offer	
Subscription price	$10
Number of rights issued	1 million
Number of rights for a share	2
After offer	
Number of shares	1.5 million
Share price	$16.67
Value of firm	$25 million
Value of one right	$20 − $16.67 = $3.33

EXAMPLE 20.1

In the National Power example, suppose the subscription price was set at $8. How many shares will have to be sold? How many rights would you need to buy a new share? What is the value of a right? What will the price per share be after the rights offer?

To raise $5 million, $5 million/$8 = 625,000 shares will need to be sold. There are 1 million shares outstanding, so it will take 1 million/625,000 = 8/5 = 1.6 rights to buy a new share of stock. (You can buy five new shares for every eight you own.) After the rights offer, there will be 1.625 million shares worth $25 million all together, so the per share value is $25/1.625 = $15.38 each. The value of a right in this case is the $20 original price less the $15.38 ending price ($4.62).

Theoretical Value of a Right   We can summarize the discussion in Example 20.1 with an equation for the theoretical value of a right during the rights-on period:

$$R_0 = (M_0 - S)/(N + 1) \qquad (20.3)$$

where

M_0 = Common share price during the rights-on period
S = Subscription price
N = Number of rights required to buy one new share

We illustrate the use of Equation (20.3) by checking our answer for the value of one right in the National Power example:

$$R_0 = (\$20 - 8)/(1.6 + 1) = \$4.62$$

This is the same answer we got earlier.

Ex-Rights

National Power's rights have a substantial value. In addition, the rights offering will have a large impact on the market price of National Power's stock. It will drop by $3.33 on the day when the shares trade **ex-rights.**

The standard procedure for issuing rights is similar to that for paying a dividend. It begins with the firm's setting a **holder-of-record date.** Following stock exchange rules, the stock typically goes ex-rights four trading days before the holder-of-record date. If the stock is sold before the ex-rights date—rights-on, with rights, or cum rights—the new owner will receive the rights. After the ex-rights date, an investor who purchases the shares will not receive the rights.

EXAMPLE 20.2

The Lagrange Point Co. has proposed a rights offering. The stock currently sells for $40 per share. Under the terms of the offer, shareholders will be allowed to buy one new share for every five that they own at a price of $25 per share. What is the value of a right? What is the ex-rights price?

You can buy five rights-on shares for 5 × $40 = $200 and then exercise the rights for another $25. Your total investment is $225, and you end up with six ex-rights shares. The ex-rights price per share is $225/6 = $37.50 per share. The rights are thus worth $40 − $37.50 = $2.50 apiece.

Using Equation (20.3) we have

$$R_0 = (\$40 - \$25)/(5 + 1) = \$2.50$$

Value of Rights After Ex-Rights Date

When the stock goes ex-rights, its price drops by the value of one right. Until the rights expire, holders can buy one share at the subscription price by exercising N rights. In equation form[11]

$$M_e = M_0 - R_0 \tag{20.4}$$
$$R_e = (M_e - S)/N \tag{20.5}$$

where M_e is the common share price during the ex-rights period.

Checking the formula using this example gives

$$M_e = \$40 - \$2.50 = \$37.50$$
$$R_e = (\$37.50 - \$25)/5 = \$2.50$$

EXAMPLE 20.3

In the previous example, suppose you could buy the rights for only $0.25 instead of the $2.50 we calculated. What could you do?

You can get rich quick, because you have found a money machine. Here is the recipe: Buy five rights for $1.25. Exercise them and pay $25 to get a new share. Your total investment to get one ex-rights share is 5 × $0.25 + $25 = $26.25. Sell the share for $37.50 and pocket the $11.25 difference. Repeat as desired.

A variation on this theme actually occurred in the course of a rights offering by a major Canadian chartered bank in the mid-1980s. The bank's employee stock ownership plan had promoted share ownership by tellers and clerical staff who were unfamiliar with the workings of rights offerings. When they received notification of the rights offering, many employees did not bother to respond until they were personally solicited by other, more sophisticated employees who bought the rights for a fraction of their value. We do not endorse the ethics behind such transactions. But the incident does show why it pays for everyone who owns stock to understand the workings of rights offers.

The Underwriting Arrangements

Rights offerings are typically arranged using **standby underwriting.** In standby underwriting, the issuer makes a rights offering, and the underwriter makes a firm commitment to "take up" (that is, purchase) the unsubscribed portion of the issue. The underwriter usually gets a **standby fee** and additional amounts based on the securities taken up.

Standby underwriting protects the firm against undersubscription. This can occur if investors throw away rights or if bad news causes the stock's market price to fall below the subscription price.

In practice, a small percentage (less than 10 percent) of shareholders fail to exercise valuable rights. This can probably be attributed to ignorance or vacations. Furthermore, shareholders are usually given an **oversubscription privilege,** which enables them to purchase unsubscribed shares at the subscription price. The oversubscription privilege makes it unlikely that the corporate issuer would have to turn to its underwriter for help.

---

[11]During the ex-rights period, a right represents a short-lived option to buy the stock. Equation (20.5) gives the minimum value of this option. The market value of rights is generally higher, as explained in our discussion of options in Chapter 23.

Effects on Shareholders

Shareholders can exercise their rights or sell them. In either case, the shareholder will not win or lose by the rights offering. The hypothetical holder of two shares of National Power has a portfolio worth $40. If the shareholder exercises the rights, he or she ends up with three shares worth a total of $50. In other words, by spending $10, the investor's holding increases in value by $10, which means that the shareholder is neither better nor worse off.

On the other hand, if the shareholder sells the two rights for $3.33 each, he or she obtains $3.33 × 2 = $6.67 and ends up with two shares worth $16.67 and the cash from selling the right:

$$
\begin{aligned}
\text{Shares held} &= 2 \times \$16.67 = \$33.33 \\
\text{Rights sold} &= 2 \times \$\ 3.33 = \underline{\quad 6.67} \\
\text{Total} \qquad &= \qquad\qquad \$40.00
\end{aligned}
$$

The new $33.33 market value plus $6.67 in cash is exactly the same as the original holding of $40. Thus, shareholders cannot lose or gain from exercising or selling rights.

It is obvious that after the rights offering, the new market price of the firm's stock will be lower than it was before the rights offering. As we have seen, however, shareholders have suffered no loss because of the rights offering. The lower the subscription price, the greater is the price decline of a rights offering. It is important to emphasize that because shareholders receive rights equal in value to the price drop, the rights offering does not hurt shareholders.

There is one last issue. How do we set the subscription price in a rights offering? If you think about it, in theory, the subscription price really does not matter. It has to be below the market price of the stock for the rights to have value, but, beyond this, the price is arbitrary. In principle, it can be as low as we care to make it as long as it is not zero.

In practice, however, the subscription price is typically 20 to 25 percent below the prevailing stock price. Once we recognize market inefficiencies and frictions, a subscription price too close to the share price may result in undersubscription due simply to market imperfections.

Cost of Rights Offerings

Until the early 1980s, rights offerings were the most popular method of raising new equity in Canada for seasoned issuers. (Obviously, rights offerings cannot be used for IPOs.) The reason was lower flotation costs from the simpler underwriting arrangements. In the late 1980s and early 1990s, with the rise of POP, bought deals replaced rights offers as the prevalent form of equity issue.

In the United States, firms use general cash offers much more often than rights offerings. This reliance on general cash offers has caused considerable debate among researchers because, as in Canada, rights offerings are usually much cheaper in terms of flotation costs. One study has found that firms making underwritten rights offers suffered substantially larger price drops than did firms making underwritten cash offers.[12] This is a hidden cost, and it may be part of the reason that underwritten rights offers are uncommon in the United States. Alternatively, as in Canada, the introduction of streamlined offer procedures through POP is likely a factor.[13]

---

[12]Robert S. Hansen, "The Demise of the Rights Issue," *Review of Financial Studies* 1 (Fall 1988), pp. 289–309.

[13]This argument is from: N. D. Ursel and D. J. Trepanier, "Securities Regulation Reform and the Decline of Rights Offerings," *Canadian Journal of Administrative Science* 18 (June 2001).

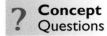

Concept Questions

- How does a rights offering work?
- What questions must financial management answer in a rights offering?
- How is the value of a right determined?
- When does a rights offering affect the value of a company's shares?
- Does a rights offer cause a share price decrease? How are existing shareholders affected by a rights offer?

20.7 The Private Equity Market

The previous sections of this chapter assumed that a company is big enough, successful enough, and old enough to raise capital in the public equity market. Of course, there are many firms that have not reached this stage and cannot use the public equity market. For start-up firms or firms in financial trouble, the public equity market is often not available.[14] This has created a trend towards more private equity buyouts, and has increased the profile of private equity firms and the private equity process. For example, at the time of writing, Sobeys Inc. announced that it will go private. Bell Canada Enterprises is entertaining offers from the Ontario Teachers' Pension Plan, while Hudson's Bay, Four Seasons Hotels, and Intrawest have already made the switch. In the United States, about US$602 billion of shares vanished in 2006 courtesy of stock buybacks, and Barclays Capital reports that 6 percent of the U.S. stock market could disappear this year if recent trends continue.[15]

Private Placement

Private placements avoid the costly procedures associated with the registration requirements that are part of public issues. The Ontario Securities Commission (OSC) and the U.S. Securities and Exchange Commission (SEC) restrict private placement issues to no more than a couple of dozen knowledgeable investors, including institutions such as insurance companies and pension funds. The biggest drawback of privately placed securities is that the securities cannot be easily resold. Most private placements involve debt securities, but equity securities can also be privately placed.

The Private Equity Firm

A large amount of private equity investment is undertaken by professional private equity managers representing large institutional investors such as mutual funds and pension funds. The limited partnership is the dominant form of intermediation in this market. Typically, the institutional investors act as the limited partners and the professional managers act as general partners. The general partners are firms that specialize in funding and managing equity investments in closely held private firms. The private equity market has been important for both traditional start-up companies and established public firms. Thus, the private equity market can be divided into venture equity and nonventure equity markets. A large part of the nonventure market is made up of firms in financial distress. Firms in financial distress are not likely to be able to issue public equity and typically cannot use traditional forms of debt such as bank loans or public debt. For these firms, the best alternative is to find a private equity market firm.

---

[14]S. E. Pratt, "Overview and Introduction to the Venture Capital Industry," *Guide to Venture Capital Sources,* 10th ed., 1987 (Venture Economics, Laurel Avenue, Box 348, Wellesley Hills, MA 02181).

[15]Ian McGugan, "Cheap money is good for you," *Canadian Business.* Toronto: Summer 2007.

Suppliers of Venture Capital

Venture capital is an important part of the private equity market. Venture capital activity varies by industry, with high-tech making up the largest component. There are at least five types of suppliers of venture capital. First, a few old-line, wealthy families have traditionally provided start-up capital to promising businesses. These families have been involved in venture capital for the better part of the last century, if not longer.

Second, a number of private partnerships and corporations have been formed to provide investment funds. The organizer behind the partnership might raise capital from institutional investors, such as insurance companies and pension funds. Alternatively, a group of individuals might provide the funds to be ultimately invested with budding entrepreneurs.

Stories used to abound about how easily an individual could obtain venture capital. Though that may have been the case in an earlier era, it is certainly not the case today. Venture capital firms employ various screening procedures to prevent inappropriate funding. For example, because of the large demand for funds, many venture capitalists have at least one employee whose full-time job consists of reading business plans. Only the very best plans can expect to attract funds. Maier and Walker and Riding indicate that only about 2 to 3 percent of requests actually receive financing.[16]

Third, large industrial or financial corporations have established venture capital subsidiaries. Chartered banks, for example, participate in the venture capital market through affiliates. Other firms, such as Bell Canada Enterprises (BCE), invest in firms developing related technological innovations. Merchant banks such as Onex and Ontario Teachers' Merchant Bank provide venture capital financing.

Fourth, around one-third of venture capital activity has some government involvement. *Crown-related firms* are government-owned. Although capital growth is important to these firms, their mandates include investing in depressed areas and targeting particular industries. *Hybrids* have a mix of government and private-sector support. These firms include labour sponsored venture capital firms. Sponsored by labour unions and established to fund small and medium-sized businesses and promote job creation, these funds offer a 30 percent tax credit to individual investors. Anderson and Tian argue that labour sponsored funds are unattractive to investors due to poor performance and high fees.[17]

Fifth, participants in an informal venture capital market have recently been identified.[18] Rather than belonging to any venture capital firm, these investors (often referred to as *angels*) act as individuals when providing financing. However, they should not, by any means, be viewed as isolated. Wetzel and others indicate that there is a rich network of angels, continually relying on each other for advice. A number of researchers have stressed that, in any informal network, there is likely one knowledgeable and trustworthy individual who, when backing a venture, brings a few less experienced investors in with him. Riding argues that the prototypical angel has income over $175,000, net worth over

---

[16]J. B. Maier and D. Walker, "The Role of Venture Capital in Financing Small Business," *Journal of Business Venturing* (Summer 1987); A. Riding in "Roundtable on Angel Investment in Canada," *Canadian Investment Review* (Fall 2000).

[17]Scott Anderson and Yisong Tian, "Incentive Fees, Valuation and Performance of Labour Sponsored Investment Funds," *Canadian Investment Review,* Fall 2003. For more on this issue including a contrary view see: Scot Blythe, "Labour-sponsored performance fees stir controversy," http://www.advisor.ca/product/current/article.jsp?content=20030801_132552_2684#, August 2003.

[18]See W. E. Wetzel, "The Informal Venture Capital Market: Aspects of Scale and Market Efficiency," *Journal of Business Venturing* (Fall 1987).

$1,000,000, and substantial business experience and knowledge. As one might expect, the informal venture capitalist is able to tolerate high risks.

Though this informal market may seem small and unimportant, it is perhaps the largest of all sources of venture capital. The size of each contribution is smaller here, typically ranging from $10,000 to $150,000.

Stages of Financing

Lo identifies five stages in venture capital financing:[19]

1. *Seed-money stage.* A small amount of financing needed to prove a concept or develop a product. Marketing is not included in this stage.

2. *Start-up and first-round financing.* Financing for firms that started within the past year. Funds are likely to pay for marketing and product development expenditures. Additional money to begin sales and manufacturing after a firm has spent its start-up funds.

3. *Second-round financing.* Funds earmarked for working capital for a firm that is currently selling its product but still losing money.

4. *Third-round financing.* Financing for a company that is at least breaking even and is contemplating an expansion. This stage is also known as mezzanine financing.

5. *Fourth-round financing.* Money provided for firms that are likely to go public within half a year. This round is also known as bridge financing.

Although these categories may seem vague to the reader, we have found that the terms are well accepted within the industry. For example, the venture capital firms listed in Pratt's *Guide to Venture Capital* indicate which of the above stages they are interested in financing.

The penultimate stage in venture capital finance is the initial public offering.[20] Venture capitalists are very important participants in initial public offerings. Venture capitalists rarely sell all of the shares they own at the time of the initial public offering. Instead, they usually sell out in subsequent public offerings. However, there is considerable evidence that venture capitalists can successfully time IPOs by taking firms public when the market values are highest (see Figure 20.2).[21] Venture capital investment in Canada went from $2.65 billion in 1999 to $5.78 billion in 2000 at the height of the tech boom. By 2005, it was back down to $1.83 billion.[22]

? Concept Questions

- **What are the different sources of venture capital financing?**
- **What are the different stages for companies seeking venture capital financing?**
- **What is the private equity market?**

---

[19]Joseph Lo, "Note on Venture Capital," Richard Ivey School of Business, 9B04N005, 2004.

[20]A very influential paper by Christopher Barry, Chris J. Muscarella, John W. Peavey III, and Michael R. Vetsuypens, "The Role of Venture Capital in the Creation of Public Companies: Evidence From the Going Public Process," *Journal of Financial Economics* 27 (1990), shows that venture capitalists do not usually sell shares at the time of the initial public offering, but they usually have board seats and act as advisors to managers.

[21]This successful timing ability adds another anomaly to the efficient markets hypothesis.

[22]Joseph Lo, "Note on Venture Capital," Richard Ivey School of Business, 9B04N005, 2004. Additional information available at the Canadian Venture Capital & Private Equity Association website. 2005 data were obtained from http://www.cvca.ca/files/News/RNathan_Presentation_press_conference_Feb_14_2006.pdf.

FIGURE 20.2

Initial Public Offerings by Venture Capital-Backed Biotechnology Firms, January 1978 to January 1992

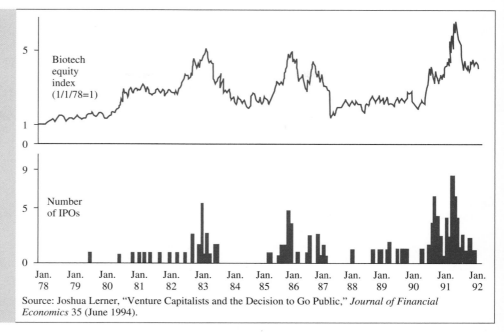

Source: Joshua Lerner, "Venture Capitalists and the Decision to Go Public," *Journal of Financial Economics* 35 (June 1994).

20.8 SUMMARY AND CONCLUSIONS

This chapter looks at how corporate securities are issued.

1. The costs of issuing securities can be quite large. They are much lower (as a percentage) for larger issues.

2. For large issues, the bought deal type of underwriting is far more prevalent than regular underwriting. This is probably connected to the savings available through prompt offering prospectuses and concentrated selling efforts.

3. Direct and indirect costs of going public can be substantial. However, once a firm is public, it can raise additional capital more easily than private firms.

4. Rights offerings are cheaper than general cash offers. Even so, most new equity issues in the United States are underwritten general cash offers. In Canada, the bought deal is cheaper and dominates the new issue market.

5. Venture capitalists are an increasingly important influence in start-up firms and subsequent financing.

KEY TERMS

Best-efforts underwriting 574
Bought deal 574
Ex-rights 585
Firm-commitment
  underwriting 574
Holder-of-record date 585
Initial public offering
  (IPO) 576

Oversubscription privilege 586
Pre-emptive right 581
Prospectus 570
Red herring 571
Regular underwriting 573
Spread (discount) 573
Standby fee 586
Standby underwriting 586

Subscription price 582
Syndicate (banking group) 573
Tombstone 571
Venture capital 589

SUGGESTED READING

For further reading on underwriting in Canada and the role of the OSC, see:
Ontario Securities Commission Annual Reports.

Summaries of relevant research on going public are found in:
L. Kryzanowski and I. Rakita. "Is the U.S. 7% Solution Equivalent to the Canadian 6% Solution?" *Canadian Investment Review* (Fall 1999), pp. 27–34.

Jay Ritter and Ivo Welch. "A Review of IPO Activity, Pricing, and Allocation." *Journal of Finance* (August 2002).

T. J. Jenkinson and A. Ljungqvist. *Going Public: The Theory and Evidence on How Companies Raise Equity Finance* (Second Revised Edition). Oxford University Press, 2001.

Interesting discussions of venture capital investment are in:
J. Lo. "Note on Venture Capital." Richard Ivey School of Business, 9B04N005, 2004.

P. Gompers and J. Lerner. *The Venture Capital Cycle.* MIT Press, 1999.

QUESTIONS & PROBLEMS

Rights Offerings

20.1 Junk Inc. is proposing a rights offering. Presently there are 350,000 shares outstanding at $85 each. There will be 70,000 new shares offered at $70 each.
 a. What is the new market value of the company?
 b. How many rights are associated with one of the new shares?
 c. What is the ex-rights price?
 d. What is the value of a right?
 e. Why might a company have a rights offering rather than a general cash offer?

20.2 The Black-Radler Joint Venture Corporation has announced a rights offer to raise $30 million for a tabloid, the *Corporate Embezzler*. This "newspaper" will review potential articles from freelance authors after the author pays a nonrefundable reviewing fee of $60 per page. The stock currently sells for $20 per share, and there are 5.2 million shares outstanding.
 a. What is the maximum possible subscription price? What is the minimum?
 b. If the subscription price is set at $15 per share, how many shares must be sold? How many rights will it take to buy one share?
 c. What is the ex-rights price? What is the value of a right?
 d. Show how a shareholder with 1000 shares before the offering and no desire (or money) to buy additional shares is not harmed by the rights offer.

20.3 Iron Curtains Co. has concluded that additional equity financing will be needed to expand operations and that the needed funds will be best obtained through a rights offering. It has correctly determined that as a result of the rights offering, the share price will fall from $80 to $74.50 ($80 is the rights-on price; $74.50 is the ex-rights price, also known as the *when-issued* price). The company is seeking $15 million in additional funds with a per-share subscription price equal to $40. How many shares are there currently, before the offering? (Assume that the increment to the market value of the equity equals the gross proceeds from the offering.)

20.4 A company's stock currently sells for $65 per share. Last week the firm issued rights to raise new equity. To purchase a new share, a shareholder must remit $20 and three rights.
 a. What is the ex-rights stock price?
 b. What is the price of one right?
 c. When will the price drop occur? Why will it occur then?

20.5 Summit Corp.'s stock is currently selling at $13 per share. There are 1 million shares outstanding. The firm is planning to raise $2 million to finance a new project. What are the ex-rights stock price, the value of a right, and the appropriate subscription prices under the following scenarios?
 a. Two shares of outstanding stock are entitled to purchase one additional share of the new issue.
 b. Four shares of outstanding stock are entitled to purchase one additional share of the new issue.
 c. How does the shareholders' wealth change from part (a) to part (b)?

20.6 Scoobatank and Stuff Manufacturing is considering a rights offer. The company has determined that the ex-rights price would be $52. The current price is $55 per share, and there are 5 million shares outstanding. The rights offer would raise a total of $60 million. What is the subscription price?

20.7 Space and Time Machines (STM) wants to raise $3.65 million via a rights offering. The company currently has 490,000 shares of common stock outstanding that sell for $30 per share. Its underwriter, George Orwell, has set a subscription price of $22 per share and will charge STM a 6 percent spread. If you currently own 6000 shares of stock in the company and decide not to participate in the rights offering, how much money can you get by selling your rights?

20.8 Mitsi Inventory Systems Inc. has announced a rights offer. The company has announced that it will take four rights to buy a new share in the offering at a subscription price of $40. At the close of business the day before the ex-rights day, the company's stock sells for $80 per share. The next morning you notice that the stock sells for $72 per share and the rights sell for $6 each. Are the stock and/or the rights correctly priced on the ex-rights day? Describe a transaction in which you could use these prices to create an immediate profit.

20.9 Show that the value of a right can be written as:

$$\text{Value of a right} = P_{RO} - P_X = (P_{RO} - P_S)/(N + 1)$$

where P_{RO}, P_S, and P_X stand for the rights-on price, the subscription price, and the ex-rights price, respectively, and N is the number of rights needed to buy one new share at the subscription price.

New Issues

20.10 Suppose the Copernicus Company has 24,000 shares of stock. Each share is worth $42 and the company's market value of equity is $1,008,000. Suppose the firm issues 6000 shares of new stock at the following prices: $42, $38, $45. What will be the effect of each of the alternative offering prices on the existing price per share?

Initial Public Offerings

20.11 In 1980, a certain assistant professor of finance bought 12 initial public offerings of common stock. He held each of these for approximately one month and then sold. The investment rule he followed was to submit a purchase order for every firm commitment initial public offering of oil and gas exploration companies. There were 22 of these offerings, and he submitted a purchase order for approximately $1,000 in stock for each of the companies. With 10 of these, no shares were allocated to this assistant professor. With 5 of the 12 offerings that were purchased, fewer than the requested number of shares were allocated.

The year 1980 was very good for oil and gas exploration company owners: On average, for the 22 companies that went public, the stocks were selling for 80 percent above the offering price a month after the initial offering date. The assistant professor looked at his performance record and found that the $8,400 invested in the 12 companies had grown to $10,000, representing a return of only about 20 percent (commissions were negligible). Did he have bad luck, or should he have expected to do worse than the average initial public offering investor? Explain.

20.12 Suppose that super rock group Life Sentence decided to issue an IPO. The underwriter was Merrill Lynch. This IPO ended up being underpriced by about 54 percent.
a. Should Life Sentence be upset at Merrill Lynch over the underpricing?
b. Would it affect your thinking to know that the group was incorporated less than four years earlier, had only $30 million in revenues for the first nine months of 2007, and had never earned a profit? Additionally, the band only had one album, *Death Row*, which had won three People's Choice awards and two Grammy awards, but there had been no stated intentions of releasing another album. Instead the band wanted to concentrate on merchandise and promoting their tours.

MINICASE: Deck Out My Yacht Goes Public

Deck Out My Yacht has been discussing the future. The company has been experiencing fast growth, and the future looks like clear sailing. However, the fast growth means that the company's growth can no longer be funded by internal sources, thus management has decided the time is right to take the company public. To this end, they have entered into discussions with the investment bank of Boom, Regatta & Grounding. The company has a working relationship with Laurin Boom, the underwriter who assisted with the company's previous bond offering. Boom, Regatta & Grounding have helped numerous small companies in the IPO process allowing management to feel confident with this choice.

Boom tells management about the process. Although Boom, Regatta & Grounding charged an underwriter fee of 4 percent on the bond offering, the underwriter fee is 7 percent on all initial stock offerings of the size of Deck Out My Yacht's initial offering. Boom estimates that the company can expect to pay about $1,450,000 in legal fees and expenses, $16,000 in OSC registration fees, and $12,000 in other filing fees. Additionally, to be listed on the TSX, the company must pay $160,000. There are also transfer agent fees of $8,500 and engraving expenses of $490,000. The company should also expect to pay $65,000 for other expenses associated with the IPO.

Finally, Boom tells management that to file with the OSC the company must provide three years' worth of audited financial statements. The costs of the audit are unknown. Boom is then told that the company provides audited financial statements as part of its bond indenture, and the company pays $210,000 per year for the outside auditor.

1. During the discussion of the potential IPO and Deck Out My Yacht's future, management decides that the optimal amount that should be raised is $50 million. However, if the company needs more cash soon, a secondary offering close to the IPO could be potentially problematic. Instead, it was suggested that the company should raise $80 million in the IPO. How can we calculate the optimal size of the IPO? What are the advantages and disadvantage of increasing the size of the IPO to $80 million?

2. After deliberation, management has decided that the company should use a firm commitment offering with Boom, Regatta & Grounding as the lead underwriter. The IPO will be for $60 million. Ignoring underpricing, how much will the IPO cost the company as a percentage of the funds received?

3. Many of the employees of Deck Out My Yacht have shares of stock in the company because of an existing employee stock purchase plan. To sell the stock, the employees can tender their shares to be sold in the IPO at the offering price, or the employees can retain their stock and sell it in the secondary market after East Deck Out My Yacht goes public (once the 180-day lockup expires). You have been asked to advise the employees about which option is best. What would you suggest to the employees?

c. How would it affect your thinking to know that in addition to the 2 million shares offered in the IPO, Life Sentence had an additional 12 million shares outstanding? Of the 12 million shares, 4 million shares were owned by Universal Studios, and the remaining 8 million shares were owned by the four band members.

20.13 Hot Dog Stands Inc. and Lemonade Stands Inc. have announced IPOs at $12 per share. One of these is undervalued by $1.20, while the other is overvalued by $0.60. But street vendors are not your specialty, so you have no way of knowing which is which. You plan on buying 1000 shares of each. If an issue is underpriced, it will be rationed, and you will only get half your order. If you get 1000 shares in both, what will be your profit? What profit do you actually expect? What principle have you illustrated?

20.14 The boxed material contains the cover page and summary of the prospectus for the initial public offering of the Pest Investigation Control Corporation (PICC), which is going public tomorrow with an initial public offering managed by investment dealer Erlanger and Ritter.

Prospectus PICC
200,000 shares
Pest Investigation Control Corporation

Of the shares being offered hereby, all 200,000 are being sold by the Pest Investigation Control Corporation Inc. ("the Company"). Before the offering there has been no public market for the shares of PICC, and no guarantee can be given that any market will develop.

These securities have not been approved or disapproved by the OSC nor has the commission passed upon the accuracy or adequacy of this prospectus.

This is an initial public offering. The common shares are being offered, subject to prior sale, when, as, and if delivered to and accepted by the Underwriters and subject to approval of certain legal matters by their Counsel and by Counsel for the Company. The Underwriters reserve the right to withdraw, cancel, or modify such offer and to reject offers in whole or in part.

	Price to Public	Underwriting Discount	Proceeds to Company*
Per share	$11.00	$1.10	$9.90
Total	$2,200,000	$220, 000	$1,980,000

*Before deducting expenses estimated at $27,000 payable by the company.

ERLANGER AND RITTER, INVESTMENT DEALERS
April 12, 2007
Prospectus Summary

The Company   The Pest Investigation Control Corporation (PICC) breeds and markets toads and tree frogs as ecologically safe insect-control mechanisms.

The Offering   200,000 shares of common stock, no par value.

Listing   The company will trade over the counter.

Shares Outstanding   As of March 31, 2007, 400,000 shares of common stock were outstanding. After the offering, 600,000 shares of common stock will be outstanding.

Use of Proceeds   To finance expansion of inventory and receivables and general working capital, and to pay for country club memberships for certain finance professors.

a. Assume that you know nothing about PICC other than the information contained in the prospectus. Based on your knowledge of finance, what is your prediction for the price of PICC tomorrow? Briefly explain your answer.

b. Assume that you have several thousand dollars to invest. When you get home from class tonight, you find that your stockbroker, whom you have not talked to for weeks, has left a message that PICC is going public tomorrow and that she can get you several hundred shares at the offering price if you call her back first thing in the morning. Discuss the merits of this opportunity.

Chapter 21

Long-Term Debt

EXECUTIVE SUMMARY

The previous chapter introduced the mechanics of new long-term financing, with an emphasis on equity. This chapter takes a closer look at long-term debt instruments.

The chapter begins with a review of the basic features of long-term debt and a description of some important aspects of publicly issued long-term bonds. We also discuss forms of long-term financing that are not publicly issued: term loans and private placement bonds. These are directly placed with lending institutions, such as chartered banks and life insurance companies.

All bond agreements have protective covenants. These are restrictions on the firm that protect the bondholder. We present several types of protective covenants in this chapter.

Most publicly issued corporate bonds have call provisions, which enable a company to buy back its bonds at a predetermined call price. This chapter attempts to answer two questions about call provisions:

1. Should firms issue callable bonds?
2. When should such bonds be called?

Financial engineering has produced many different kinds of long-term bonds. We discuss zero-coupon bonds, floating-rate bonds, and other special types of bonds and then analyze what types of bonds are best in different circumstances.

21.1 Long-Term Debt: A Review

Long-term debt securities are promises by the issuing firm to repay principal and to pay interest on the unpaid balance. The *maturity* of a long-term debt instrument refers to the length of time the debt remains outstanding with some unpaid balance. Debt securities can be *short-term* (maturities of one year or less) or *long-term* (maturities of more than one year).[1] Short-term debt is sometimes referred to as *unfunded debt;* long-term debt is sometimes called *funded debt.*[2]

The two major forms of long-term debt are public issue and privately placed debt. We discuss public issue bonds first, and most of what we say about them holds true for privately placed long-term debt as well. The main difference between publicly issued and privately placed debt is that private debt is directly placed with a lending institution.

There are many other attributes of long-term debt, including security, seniority, call features, sinking funds, ratings, and protective covenants. The boxed material on the next page illustrates many of these attributes.

---

[1]In addition, people often refer to *intermediate-term debt,* which has a maturity of more than one year and less than three to five years.

[2]The word *funding* generally implies long-term. Thus, a firm planning to *fund* its debt requirements may be replacing short-term debt with long-term debt.

Features of Loblaw Companies—Medium-Term Notes (Unsecured) Issue

Terms		Explanation
Amount of Issue	$300 million	The company will issue $300 million of bonds.
Issue Date	1/18/05	The bonds will be sold on January 18, 2005.
Maturity Date	1/18/36	The bonds will be paid in 31 years.
Annual Coupon	5.90	Each bondholder will receive $59.00 per bond per year.
Face Value	$1,000	The denomination of the bonds is $1,000.
Issue Price	99.859	The issue price will be 99.859% of the $1,000 face value per bond.
Yield to Maturity	5.91%	If the bond is held to maturity, bondholders will receive a stated annual rate of return equal to 5.91%.
Coupon Payment	1/18 and 7/18	Coupons of $59.00/2 = $29.50 will be paid semi-annually on these dates.
Security	Unsecured	The bonds are debentures.
Call Provision	Canada Yield Price at Canada plus 0.27%	Redeemable at the Company's option at the price calculated to provide a yield to maturity equal to Canada yield or equivalent maturity plus 0.27%
Rating	DBRS A	The bond is of satisfactory credit quality, but is not as high as AA.

Source: www.sedar.com.

21.2 The Public Issue of Bonds

The general procedures followed in a **public issue** of bonds are the same as those for stocks. The issue must be registered with the OSC and any other relevant provincial securities commissions, there must be a prospectus, and so on. The registration statement for a public issue of bonds, however, is different from the one for common stock. For bonds, the registration statement must indicate an indenture.

An **indenture** is a written agreement between the corporation (the borrower) and a trust company. It is sometimes referred to as the *deed of trust*.[3] The trust company is appointed by the corporation to represent the bondholders. The trust company must (1) be sure the terms of the indenture are obeyed, (2) manage the sinking fund, and (3) represent bondholders if the company defaults on its payments.

The typical bond indenture can be a document of several hundred pages. It generally includes:

1. The basic terms of the bonds.
2. A description of property used as security.
3. The seniority of the bonds.

___
[3]The terms *loan agreement* and *loan contract* are usually used for privately placed debt and term loans.

4. Details of the protective covenants.

5. The sinking fund arrangements.

6. The call provision.

Each of these is discussed below.

The Basic Terms

Bonds usually have a *face value* of $1,000. This is also called the *principal value* and it is stated on the bond certificate. In addition, the *par value* (i.e., initial accounting value) of a bond is the same as the face value.

Transactions between bond buyers and bond sellers determine the market value of the bond. Actual bond market values depend on the general level of interest rates, among other factors, and need not equal the face value. Because the Canadian corporate bond market is quite illiquid, there is a good chance that it is not fully efficient. For this reason, there is likely a good payoff for investment dealers and issuers who pioneer financial engineering innovations. The bond price is quoted as a percentage of the face value. Though interest is paid only twice a year, interest *accrues* continually over the year. This is illustrated in Example 21.1 below.

EXAMPLE 21.1

Suppose the Black Corporation has issued 100 bonds. The amount stated on each bond certificate is $1,000. The total face value or principal value of the bonds is $100,000. Further suppose the bonds are currently *priced* at 100, which means 100 percent of $1,000. This means that buyers and sellers are holding bonds at a price per bond of $1,000. If interest rates rise, the price of the bond might fall to, say, 97, which means 97 percent of $1,000 (or $970).

Suppose the bonds have a stated interest rate of 7 percent due on January 1, 2050. The bond indenture might read:

> The bond will mature on January 1, 2050, and will be limited in aggregate principal amount to $100,000. Each bond will bear interest at the rate of 7.0 percent per annum from January 1, 1990, or from the most recent Interest Payment Date to which interest has been paid or provided for. Interest is payable semiannually on July 1 and January 1 of each year.

Suppose an investor bought the bonds on April 1, 2004. Since the last coupon payment on January 1, three months of interest had accrued. These three months represented half of a semiannual coupon period. The stated semiannual rate was 7 percent or 3.5 percent per semiannual period so accrued interest over the three months is $\frac{1}{2} \times 3.5\% = 1.75\%$. Therefore, the buyer of the bond had to pay a price of 100 percent plus the 1.75 percent of accrued interest ($17.50).[4] On July 1, the buyer received an interest payment of $35. This can be viewed as the sum of the $17.50 he or she paid the seller plus the three months of interest, $17.50 for holding the bond from April 1 to July 1.

As is typical of corporate bonds, the Black bonds are **registered.** The indenture might read:

> Interest is payable semiannually on July 1 and January 1 of each year to the person in whose name the bond is registered at the close of business on June 15 or December 15, respectively.

---

[4]To be precise, accrued interest in Canada is computed based on a day count. Since 2004 was a leap year, there were 91 days between the last coupon payment on January 1 and the settlement date on April 1. The coupon period was 182 days. Accrued interest was: $91/182 \times 3.5\% \times \$1000 = \$17.50$.

This means that the company has a registrar who will record the ownership of each bond. The company will pay the interest and principal by cheque mailed directly to the address of the owner of record.

When a bond is registered with attached coupons, the bondholder must separate a coupon from the bond certificate and send it to the company registrar (paying agent). Some bonds are in **bearer** form. This means that ownership is not recorded in the company books. As with a registered bond with attached coupons, the holder of the bond certificate separates the coupon and sends it in to the company to receive payment.

There are two drawbacks to bearer bonds. First, they can easily be lost or stolen. Second, because the company does not know who owns its bonds, it cannot notify bondholders of important events. Consider, for example, Mr. and Mrs. Smith, who go to their safety deposit box and clip the coupon on their 12 percent, $1,000 bond issued by the Black Company. They send the coupon to the paying agent and feel richer. A few days later, a notice comes from the paying agent that the bond was retired and its principal paid off one year earlier. In other words, the bond no longer exists. Mr. and Mrs. Smith must forfeit one year of interest. (Of course, they can turn their bond in for $1,000.)

However, bearer bonds have the advantage of secrecy because even the issuing company does not know who the bond's owners are. This secrecy is particularly vexing to taxing authorities because tax collection on interest is difficult if the holder is unknown.

Security

Debt securities are also classified according to the *collateral* protecting the bondholder. Collateral is a general term for the assets that are pledged as security for payment of debt. For example, *collateral trust bonds* involve a pledge of common stock held by the corporation.

EXAMPLE 21.2

Suppose Railroad Holding Company owns all of the common stock of Track Inc.; that is, Track Inc. is a wholly owned subsidiary of the Railroad Holding Company. Railroad issues debt securities that pledge the common stock of Track Inc. as collateral. The debts are collateral trust bonds; a trust company will hold them. If Railroad Holding Company defaults on the debt, the trust company will be able to sell the stock of Track Inc. to satisfy Railroad's obligation.

Mortgage securities are secured by a mortgage on real estate or other long-term assets of the borrower.[5] The legal document that describes such a mortgage is called a *mortgage-trust indenture* or *trust deed.* The mortgage can be *closed-end,* so that there is a limit as to the amount of bonds that can be issued. More frequently it is *open-end,* without limit to the amount of bonds that may be issued.

EXAMPLE 21.3

Suppose the Yukon Land Company has buildings and land worth $10 million and a $4 million mortgage on these properties. If the mortgage is closed-end, the Yukon Land Company cannot issue more bonds on this property.

If the bond indenture contains no clause limiting the amount of additional bonds that can be issued, it is an open-end mortgage. In this case, the Yukon Land Company can issue additional

---

[5]A set of railroad cars is an example of "other long-term assets" used as security.

bonds on its property, making the existing bonds riskier. For example, if additional mortgage bonds of $2 million are issued, the property has been pledged for a total of $6 million of bonds. If Yukon Land Company must liquidate its property for $4 million, the original bondholders will receive 4/6, or 67 percent, of their investment. If the mortgage had been closed-end, they would have received 100 percent of the stated value.

The value of a mortgage depends on the market value of the underlying property. For this reason, mortgage bonds sometimes require that the property be properly maintained and insured. Of course, a building and equipment bought in 1914 for manufacturing slide rules might not have much value, no matter how well the company maintains it. The value of any property ultimately depends on its next best economic use. Bond indentures cannot easily insure against losses in economic value.

Sometimes mortgages are on specific property, for example, a single building. More often, blanket mortgages are used. A blanket mortgage pledges many assets owned by the company.

Some bonds represent unsecured obligations of the company. A **debenture** is an unsecured bond, for which no specific pledge of property is made. Debenture holders have a claim on property not otherwise pledged: the property that remains after mortgages and collateral trusts are taken into account. Almost all public bonds issued by industrial and finance companies are debentures. However, most utility bonds are secured by a pledge of assets.

Seniority

In general terms, *seniority* indicates preference in position over other lenders, and debts are sometimes labelled "senior" or "junior" to indicate seniority. Some debt is *subordinated,* as in, for example, a subordinated debenture.

In the event of default, holders of subordinated debt must give preference to other special creditors. Usually, this means that the subordinated lenders are paid off from cash flow and asset sales only after the specified creditors have been compensated. However, debt cannot be subordinated to equity.

Protective Covenants

A **protective covenant** is that part of the indenture or loan agreement that limits certain actions of the borrowing company. Protective covenants can be classified into two types: negative covenants and positive covenants. A **negative covenant** limits or prohibits actions that the company may take. Here are some typical examples:

1. Limitations are placed on the amount of dividends a company may pay.
2. The firm cannot pledge any of its assets to other lenders.
3. The firm cannot merge with another firm.
4. The firm may not sell or lease its major assets without approval by the lender.
5. The firm cannot issue additional long-term debt.

A **positive covenant** specifies an action that the company agrees to take or a condition the company must abide by. Here are some examples:

1. The company agrees to maintain its working capital at a minimum level.
2. The company must furnish periodic financial statements to the lender.

The financial implications of protective covenants were treated in detail in the chapters on capital structure. In that discussion, we argued that protective covenants can benefit shareholders because, if bondholders are assured that they will be protected in times of financial stress, they will accept a lower interest rate.

The Sinking Fund

Bonds can be entirely repaid at maturity, at which time the bondholder will receive the stated value of the bond, or they can be repaid before maturity. Early repayment is more typical.

In a direct placement of debt the repayment schedule is specified in the loan contract. For public issues, the repayment takes place through the use of a sinking fund and a call provision.

A **sinking fund** is an account managed by the bond trustee for the purpose of repaying the bonds. Typically, the company makes yearly payments to the trustee. The trustee can purchase bonds in the market or can select bonds randomly using a lottery and purchase them, generally at face value. There are many different kinds of sinking fund arrangements:

- Most sinking funds start between 5 and 10 years after the initial issuance.
- Some sinking funds establish equal payments over the life of the bond.
- Most high-quality bond issues establish payments to the sinking fund that are not sufficient to redeem the entire issue. As a consequence, there is the possibility of a large *balloon* payment at maturity.

Sinking funds have two opposing effects on bondholders:

1. *Sinking funds provide extra protection to bondholders.* A firm experiencing financial difficulties would have trouble making sinking fund payments. Thus, sinking fund payments provide an early warning system to bondholders.

2. *Sinking funds give the firm an attractive option.* If bond prices fall below the face value, the firm will satisfy the sinking fund by buying bonds at the lower market prices. If bond prices rise above the face value, the firm will buy the bonds back at the lower face value.

The Call Provision

A *call provision* lets the company repurchase or *call* the entire bond issue at a predetermined price over a specified period.

Historically, the call price was set above the bond's face value of $1,000. The difference between the call price and the face value is the **call premium.** For example, if the call price is 105 (that is, 105 percent of $1,000), the call premium is 50. The amount of the call premium usually becomes smaller over time. One typical arrangement is to set the call premium initially equal to the annual coupon payment and then make it decline to zero over the life of the bond.

Call provisions are not usually operative during the first few years of a bond's life. For example, a company may be prohibited from calling its bonds for the first 10 years. This is referred to as a **deferred call.** During this period, the bond is said to be **call protected.**

Many long-term corporate bonds outstanding in Canada have call provisions as we just described. New corporate debt features a different call provision referred to as a **Canada plus call.** This new approach is designed to replace the traditional call feature by making it unattractive for the issuer ever to call the bonds. Unlike the standard call, with the Canada call the exact amount of the call premium is not set at the time of issuance. Instead, the Canada plus call stipulates that, in the event of a call, the issuer must provide a call premium that will compensate investors for the difference in interest between the original bond and new debt issued to replace it. This compensation cancels the borrower's benefit from calling the debt, and the result is that call will not occur.

The Canada plus call takes its name from the formula used to calculate the difference in the interest; to determine the new, lower interest rate, the formula adds a premium to the yield on Canadas. We give a numerical example of a Canada plus call in Section 21.3.

? Concept Questions

- **Do bearer bonds have any advantage? Why might Mr. "I Like to Keep My Affairs Private" prefer to hold bearer bonds?**
- **What advantages and disadvantages do bondholders derive from provisions of sinking funds?**
- **What is a call provision? What is the difference between the call price and the stated price?**

21.3 Bond Refunding

Replacing all or part of an issue of outstanding bonds is called bond **refunding.** Usually, the first step in a typical bond refunding is to call the entire issue of bonds at the call price. Bond refunding raises two questions:

1. Should firms issue callable bonds?
2. Given that callable bonds have been issued, when should the bonds be called?

We attempt to answer these questions in this section.

Should Firms Issue Callable Bonds?

Common sense tells us that call provisions have value. First, many publicly issued bonds have call provisions. Second, it is obvious that a call works to the advantage of the issuer. If interest rates fall and bond prices go up, the option to buy back the bonds at the call price is valuable. In bond refunding, firms will typically replace the called bonds with a new bond issue. The new bonds will have a lower coupon rate than the called bonds.

However, bondholders will take the call provision into account when they buy the bond. For this reason, we can expect that bondholders will demand higher interest rates on callable bonds than on noncallable bonds. In fact, financial economists view call provisions as being zero-sum in efficient capital markets.[6] Any expected gains to the issuer from being allowed to refund the bond at lower rates will be offset by higher initial interest rates. We illustrate the zero-sum aspect of callable bonds in Example 21.4.

EXAMPLE 21.4

Suppose Janine Intercable Company intends to issue perpetual bonds of $1,000 face value at a 10 percent interest rate.[7] Annual coupons have been set at $100. There is an equal chance that, by the end of the year, interest rates will either

1. Fall to 6.67 percent. If so, the bond price will increase to $1,500.
2. Increase to 20 percent. If so, the bond price will fall to $500.

---

[6]See A. Kraus, "An Analysis of Call Provisions and the Corporate Refunding Decision," *Midland Corporate Finance Journal* 1 (Spring 1983), p. 1.

[7]Recall that perpetual bonds have no maturity date; their market price equals coupon/yield.

Noncallable Bond   Suppose the market price of the noncallable bond is the expected price it will have next year plus the coupon, all discounted at the current 10 percent interest rate.[8] The value of the noncallable bond is

Value of Noncallable Bond:

$$\frac{\text{First-year coupon} + \text{Expected price at end of year}}{1 + r}$$

$$= \frac{\$100 + (0.5 \times \$1,500) + (0.5 \times \$500)}{1.10}$$

$$= \$1,000$$

Callable Bond   Now suppose the Janine Intercable Company decides to issue callable bonds. The call premium is set at $100 over par value and the bonds can be called *only* at the end of the first year.[9] In this case, the call provision will allow the company to buy back its bonds at $1,100 ($1,000 par value plus the $100 call premium). Should interest rates fall, the company will buy for $1,100 a bond that would be worth $1,500 in the absence of a call provision. Of course, if interest rates rise, Janine would not want to call the bonds for $1,100, because they are worth only $500 on the market.

Suppose rates fall and Janine calls the bonds by paying $1,100. If the firm simultaneously issues new bonds with a coupon of $100, it will bring in $1,500 (or $100/0.0667) at the 6.67 percent interest rate. This will allow Janine to pay an extra dividend to shareholders of $400 (or $1,500 − $1,100). In other words, if rates fall from 10 percent to 6.67 percent, exercise of the call will transfer $400 of potential bondholder gains to the shareholders.

When investors purchase callable bonds, they realize that they will forfeit their anticipated gains to shareholders if the bonds are called. As a consequence, they will not pay $1,000 for a callable bond with a coupon of $100.

How high must the coupon on the callable bond be so that it can be issued at the par value of $1,000? We can answer this in three steps.

Step 1: Determining End-of-Year Value If Interest Rates Drop   If the interest rate drops to 6.67 percent by the end of the year, the bond will be called for $1,100. The bondholder will receive both this amount and the annual coupon payment. If we let C represent the coupon on the callable bond, the bondholder gets the following at the end of the year:

$$\$1,100 + C$$

Step 2: Determining End-of-Year Value If Interest Rates Rise   If interest rates rise to 20 percent, the value of the bondholder's position at the end of the year is

$$\frac{C}{0.20} + C$$

That is, the perpetuity formula tells us that the bond will sell at $C/0.20$. In addition, the bondholder receives the coupon payment at the end of the year.

Step 3: Solving for C   Because interest rates are equally likely to rise or to fall, the expected value of the bondholder's end-of-year position is

$$(\$1,100 + C) \times 0.5 + \left(\frac{C}{0.20} + C\right) \times 0.5$$

---

[8]We are assuming that the current price of the noncallable bonds is the expected value discounted at the risk-free rate of 10 percent. This is equivalent to assuming that the risk is unsystematic and carries no risk premium.

[9]Normally, bonds can be called over a period of many years. Our assumption that the bond can only be called at the end of the first year is introduced for simplicity.

Using the current interest rate of 10 percent, we set the present value of these payments equal to par:

$$\$1,000 = \frac{(\$1,100 + C) \times 0.5 + \left(\dfrac{C}{0.20} + C\right) \times 0.5}{1.10}$$

C is the unknown in the equation. The equation holds if $C = \$157.14$. In other words, callable bonds can sell at par only if their coupon rate is 15.714 percent.

The Paradox Restated   If Janine issues a noncallable bond, it will only need to pay a 10 percent interest rate. By contrast, Janine must pay an interest rate of 15.7 percent on a callable bond. The interest rate differential makes an investor indifferent between the two bonds in our example. Because the return to the investor is the same with either bond, the cost of debt capital is the same to Janine with either bond. Thus, our example suggests that there is neither an advantage nor a disadvantage from issuing callable bonds.

If this analysis is correct, why are callable bonds issued in the real world? This question has vexed financial economists for a long time. We now consider four specific reasons why a company might use a call provision:

1. Superior interest rate predictions.
2. Taxes.
3. Financial flexibility for future investment opportunities.
4. Less interest-rate risk.

Superior Interest Rate Forecasting   Company insiders may know more about interest rate changes on its bonds than does the investing public. For example, managers may be better informed about potential changes in the firm's credit rating. Thus, a company may prefer the call provision at a particular time because it believes that the expected fall in interest rates (the probability of a fall multiplied by the amount of the fall) is greater than the bondholders believe.

Although this is possible, there is reason to doubt that inside information is the rationale for call provisions. Suppose firms really had superior ability to predict changes that would affect them. Bondholders would infer that a company expected an improvement in its credit rating whenever it issued callable bonds. Bondholders would require an increase in the coupon rate to protect them against a call if this occurred. As a result, we would expect that there would be no financial advantage to the firm from callable bonds over noncallable bonds.

Of course, there are many non–company-specific reasons why interest rates can fall. For example, the interest-rate level is connected to the anticipated inflation rate. But it is difficult to see how companies could have more information about the general level of interest rates than other participants in the bond markets.

Taxes   Call provisions may have tax advantages if the bondholder is taxed at a lower rate than the company. We have seen that callable bonds have higher coupon rates than noncallable bonds. Because the coupons provide a deductible interest expense to the corporation and are taxable income to the bondholder, the corporation will gain more than a bondholder in a low tax bracket will lose. Presumably, some of the tax saving can be passed on to the bondholders in the form of a high coupon.

Future Investment Opportunities   As we have explained, bond indentures contain protective covenants that restrict a company's investment opportunities. For example, protective covenants may limit the company's ability to acquire another firm or to sell certain assets (for example, a division of the company). If the covenants are sufficiently restrictive, the cost to the shareholders in lost net present value can be large. However, if bonds are callable, the company can buy back the bonds at the call price and take advantage of a superior investment opportunity.[10]

Less Interest-Rate Risk   The call provision will reduce the sensitivity of a bond's value to changes in the level of interest rates. As interest rates increase, the value of a noncallable bond will fall. Because the callable bond has a higher coupon rate, the value of a callable bond will fall less than the value of a noncallable bond. Kraus has argued that, by reducing the sensitivity of a bond's value to changes in interest rates, the call provision may reduce the risk to shareholders as well as bondholders.[11] He argues that, because the bond is a liability of the corporation, the equityholders bear risk as the bond changes value over time. Thus, it can be shown that, under certain conditions, reducing the risk of bonds through a call provision will also reduce the risk of equity.

Calling Bonds: When Does It Make Sense?

The value of the company is the value of the stock plus the value of the bonds. From the Modigliani–Miller theory and the pie model in earlier chapters, we know that firm value is unchanged by how it is divided between these two instruments. Therefore, maximizing shareholder wealth means minimizing the value of the callable bonds. In a world with no transactions costs, it can be shown that the company should call its bonds whenever the callable bond value exceeds the call price. This policy minimizes the value of the callable bonds.

The preceding analysis is modified slightly by including the costs from issuing new bonds. These extra costs change the refunding rule to allow bonds to trade at prices above the call price. The objective of the company is to minimize the sum of the value of the callable bonds plus new issue costs. It has been observed that many real-world firms do not call their bonds when the market value of the bonds reaches the call price. Perhaps these issue costs are an explanation. Also, when a bond is called, the holder has about 30 days to surrender the bond and receive the call price in cash. In 30 days the market value of the bonds could fall below the call price. If so, the firm is giving away money. To forestall this possibility, it can be argued that firms should wait until the market value of the bond exceeds the call price before calling bonds.

EXAMPLE 21.5

The Nipigon Lake Mining Co. has a $20 million outstanding bond issue bearing a 16 percent coupon that it issued in 1987. The bonds mature in 2017 but are callable in 2008 for a 6 percent call premium. Nipigon Lake's investment banker has given assurance that up to $30 million of new nine-year bonds maturing in 2014 can be sold carrying a 7 percent coupon. To eliminate timing problems with the two issues, the new bonds will be sold a month before the old bonds

[10]This argument is from Z. Bodie and R. A. Taggart, "Future Investment Opportunities and the Value of the Call Provision on a Bond," *Journal of Finance* 33 (1978), p. 4.

[11]A. Kraus, "An Analysis of Call Provisions and the Corporate Refunding Decision," *Midland Corporate Finance Journal* 1 (Spring 1983). Kraus points out that the call provision will not always reduce the equity's interest-rate risk. If the firm as a whole bears interest-rate risk, more of this risk may be shifted from equityholders to bondholders with noncallable debt. In this case, equityholders may actually bear more risk with callable debt.

are to be called. Nipigon Lake will have to pay the coupons on both issues during this month but can defray some of the cost by investing the issue at 3 percent, the short-term interest rate. Flotation costs for the $20 million new issue would total $1,125,000, and Nipigon Lake's marginal tax rate is 40 percent. Construct a framework to determine whether it is in Nipigon Lake's best interest to call the previous issue.

In constructing a framework to analyze a refunding operation, there are three steps: cost of refunding, interest savings, and the NPV of the refunding operation. Following the logic of our capital budgeting analysis in Chapter 8, we calculate the after-tax cash flows from each step and discount them at the after-tax cost of debt. All work described here is illustrated in Table 21.1.

Cost of Refunding   The first step in this framework consists of the call premium, the flotation costs, the related tax savings, and any extra interest that must be paid or can be earned.

Call Premium   The call premium = $0.06 \times (\$20,000,000) = \$1,200,000$
Note that a call premium is not a tax-deductible expense.

Flotation Costs   Although flotation costs are a one-time expense, for tax purposes they are amortized over the life of the issue or five years, whichever is less. For Nipigon Lake, flotation costs amount to $1,125,000. This results in an annual expense for the first five years after the issue:

$$\$1,125,000/5 = \$225,000$$

Flotation costs produce an annual tax shield of $90,000:

$$\$225,000 \times (0.4) = \$90,000$$

TABLE 21.1   Bond Refunding Worksheet

	Amount Before Tax	Amount After Tax	Time Period	4.2 Percent PV Factor	PV
PV Cost of Refunding					
Call premium		$1,200,000	0	1.0000	$1,200,000
Flotation costs on new issue		1,125,000	0	1.0000	1,125,000
Tax savings on new issue flotation costs		−90,000	1−5	4.4269	−398,423
Extra interest on old issue	$266,667	160,000	0	1.0000	160,000
Interest on short-term investment	−50,000	−30,000	0	1.0000	230,000
Total after-tax investment					$2,056,577
Interest savings for the refunding issue: $t = 1 - 9$					
Interest on old bond	3,200,000	1,920,000			
Interest on new bond	1,400,000	840,000			
Net interest savings	$1,800,000	$1,080,000	1−9	7.3680	$7,957,474
NPV for refunding operation					
NPV = PV of interest savings − PV of cost refunding					$5,900,897

Tax Savings   The tax savings on the flotation costs are a five-year annuity and will be discounted at the after-tax cost of debt (7% (1 − 0.40) = 4.2%). [12] This amounts to a savings of $398,423. Therefore, the total flotation costs of issuing debt are

Flotation costs	$1,125,000
PV of tax savings	(398,423)
Total after-tax cost	$726,577

Additional interest   Extra interest paid on old issue totals:[13]

$$\$20,000,000 \times \left(8\% \times \tfrac{1}{6}\right) = \$266,667$$

After-tax interest: $266,667 × (1 − 0.40) = $160,000

By investing the proceeds of the new issue at short-term interest rates, some of this expense can be avoided:

$$\$20,000,000 \times \left(3\% \times \tfrac{1}{12}\right) = \$50,000$$

After-tax investment proceeds: $50,000 × (1 − 0.40) = $30,000

The total additional interest is

Extra interest paid	$160,000
Extra interest earned	(30,000)
Total additional interest	$130,000

These three items amount to a total after-tax investment of

Call premium	$1,200,000
Flotation costs	726,577
Additional interest	130,000
Total investment	$2,056,577

Interest Savings on New Issue

Interest on old bond = $20,000,000 × 16% = $3,200,000
Interest on new bond = $20,000,000 × 7% = $1,400,000
Annual savings = $1,800,000
After-tax savings = $1,800,000 × (1 − 0.40) = $1,080,000
PV of annual savings over 9 years = $1,080,000 × 7.3680 = $7,957,474

NPV for the Refunding Operation

Interest savings	$7,957,474
Investment	(2,056,577)
NPV	$5,900,897

Nipigon Lake can save almost $6 million by proceeding with a call on its old bonds. The 16 percent original interest rate used in this example closely follows the actual interest

---

[12]Since we assume that the refunding costs as well as the principal are financed by the new debt issue, we use the after-tax cost of debt as the discount rate. This is consistent with the Adjusted Present Value approach as shown in A. R. Ofer and R. A. Taggart, "Bond Refunding: A Clarifying Analysis," *Journal of Finance* 32 (March 1977).

[13]Since we do not know in which month the bond will be called, it is reasonable to assume that it represents 1/6 of a semiannual coupon period.

rates during the 1980s. The example illustrates why firms would want to include a call provision when interest rates are very high.

Canada Plus Call

In our example, the Nipigon Lake Mining bond had a traditional call feature. Here we illustrate how a Canada plus call would make calling the debt unattractive. Suppose, that when the bonds were issued in 1987, Nipigon debt carried a yield 75 basis points above comparable Canadas. To set up a Canada plus call, Nipigon agreed in 1987 to compensate investors based on a yield of Canada plus 75 basis points if the bonds were ever called.

In our example, by 2008, rates on 10-year Canadas have fallen to 6.25 percent and Nipigon could issue new nine-year debt at 7 percent. Given this information, we can now calculate the annual interest penalty Nipigon would have to pay to call the debt:

$$16\% - [\text{Canada} + 0.75] = 16\% - [6.25 + 0.75] = 9.00\%$$

In dollars this is 9 percent of $20,000,000 or $1.8 million. This $1.8 million is precisely the annual savings from calling the debt with the traditional call calculated earlier. Our example shows that, with the Canada plus call, calling the bond will not save Nipigon interest costs. This raises the question of why firms simply do not issue noncallable bonds rather than going to the trouble of setting up a Canada call. One answer could be that they wish to retain the flexibility to call debt for other reasons such as reorganizing their capital structures.

? Concept Questions
- **What are the advantages to a firm of having a call provision?**
- **What are the disadvantages to bondholders of having a call provision?**
- **Why does a Canada plus call effectively make calling debt unattractive?**

21.4 Bond Ratings

Firms frequently pay to have their debt rated. The two leading bond-rating firms in Canada are Standard & Poor's (S&P) and Dominion Bond Rating Service (DBRS). Moody's, a large U.S. bond rater, often rates Canadian companies that raise funds in U.S. bond markets.[14] The debt ratings depend upon (1) the likelihood that the firm will default and (2) the protection afforded by the loan contract in the event of default. The ratings are constructed from information supplied by the corporation, primarily the financial statements of the firm. The rating classes are shown in Table 21.2.

The highest rating debt can have is AAA. Debt rated AAA is judged to be the best quality and to have the lowest degree of risk. The lowest rating, C or D, indicates that the firm is in default. Since the 1980s, a growing part of corporate borrowing has taken the form of *low-grade bonds*. These bonds are also known as either *high-yield bonds* or *junk bonds*. Low-grade bonds are corporate bonds that are rated below *investment grade* by the major rating agencies (that is, below BBB for Standard & Poor's or Baa for Moody's).

Bond ratings are important, because bonds with lower ratings tend to have higher interest costs. However, the most recent evidence is that bond ratings merely reflect bond risk. There is no conclusive evidence that bond ratings affect risk.[15] It is not surprising that

---

[14]They also rate bonds issued by the individual provinces and the federal government.

[15]M. Weinstein, "The Systematic Risk of Corporate Bonds," *Journal of Financial and Quantitative Analysis* (September 1981); J. P. Ogden, "Determinants of Relative Interest Rate Sensitivity of Corporate Bonds," *Financial Management* (Spring 1987); and F. Reilly and M. Joehnk, "The Association Between Market-Based Risk Measures for Bonds and Bond Ratings," *Journal of Finance* (December 1976).

**TABLE 21.2
Descriptions of
Ratings Used by
Dominion Bond
Rating Service**

The DBRS® long-term debt rating scale is meant to give an indication of the risk that a borrower will not fulfill its full obligations in a timely manner, with respect to both interest and principal commitments. Every DBRS rating is based on quantitative and qualitative considerations relevant to the borrowing entity. Each rating category is denoted by the subcategories "high" and "low." The absence of either a "high" or "low" designation indicates the rating is in the "middle" of the category. The AAA and D categories do not utilize "high," "middle," and "low" as differential grades.

AAA	Long-term debt rated AAA is of the highest credit quality, with exceptionally strong protection for the timely repayment of principal and interest. Earnings are considered stable, the structure of the industry in which the entity operates is strong, and the outlook for future profitability is favourable. There are few qualifying factors present that would detract from the performance of the entity. The strength of liquidity and coverage ratios is unquestioned and the entity has established a credible track record of superior performance. Given the extremely high standard that DBRS has set for this category, few entities are able to achieve a AAA rating.
AA	Long-term debt rated AA is of superior credit quality, and protection of interest and principal is considered high. In many cases they differ from long-term debt rated AAA only to a small degree. Given the extremely restrictive definition DBRS has for the AAA category, entities rated AA are also considered to be strong credits, typically exemplifying above-average strength in key areas of consideration and unlikely to be significantly affected by reasonably foreseeable events.
A	Long-term debt rated "A" is of satisfactory credit quality. Protection of interest and principal is still substantial, but the degree of strength is less than that of AA rated entities. While "A" is a respectable rating, entities in this category are considered to be more susceptible to adverse economic conditions and have greater cyclical tendencies than higher-rated securities.
BBB	Long-term debt rated BBB is of adequate credit quality. Protection of interest and principal is considered acceptable, but the entity is fairly susceptible to adverse changes in financial and economic conditions, or there may be other adverse conditions present which reduce the strength of the entity and its rated securities.
BB	Long-term debt rated BB is defined to be speculative and non-investment grade, where the degree of protection afforded interest and principal is uncertain, particularly during periods of economic recession. Entities in the BB range typically have limited access to capital markets and additional liquidity support. In many cases, deficiencies in critical mass, diversification, and competitive strength are additional negative considerations.
B	Long-term debt rated B is considered highly speculative and there is a reasonably high level of uncertainty as to the ability of the entity to pay interest and principal on a continuing basis in the future, especially in periods of economic recession or industry adversity.
CCC CC C	Long-term debt rated in any of these categories is very highly speculative and is in danger of default of interest and principal. The degree of adverse elements present is more severe than long-term debt rated B. Long-term debt rated below B often have features which, if not remedied, may lead to default. In practice, there is little difference between these three categories, with CC and C normally used for lower ranking debt of companies for which the senior debt is rated in the CCC to B range.
D	A security rated D implies the issuer has either not met a scheduled payment of interest or principal or that the issuer has made it clear that it will miss such a payment in the near future. In some cases, DBRS may not assign a D rating under a bankruptcy announcement scenario, as allowances for grace periods may exist in the underlying legal documentation. Once assigned, the D rating will continue as long as the missed payment continues to be in arrears, and until such time as the rating is suspended, discontinued, or reinstated by DBRS.

Source: Used with permission of Dominion Bond Rating Service, www.dbrs.com.

the stock prices and bond prices of firms do not show any unusual behaviour on the days around a rating change. Because the ratings are based on publicly available information, they probably do not, in themselves, supply new information to the market.[16]

Junk Bonds

The investment community in the United States has labelled bonds with a Standard & Poor's rating of BB and below or a Moody's rating of Ba and below as **junk bonds.** These bonds are also called *high-yield* or *low-grade*—we shall use all three terms interchangeably. Junk bonds come into existence when investment grade bonds are downgraded (fallen angels) or through new bond issues rated BB or lower. Issuance of junk bonds has grown greatly in recent years, leading to increased public interest in this form of financing. This interest is not limited to the United States. Although the junk bond market in Canada is not nearly as developed, there has been a rising trend through the 1990s and into the first half of the twenty-first century of more and more companies issuing high-yield debt.[17]

In our opinion, the growth in junk-bond financing can better be explained by the activities of one man than by a number of economic factors. While a graduate student at the University of Pennsylvania's Wharton School in the 1970s, Michael Milken observed a large difference between the return on high-yield bonds and the return on safer bonds. Believing that this difference was greater than what the extra default risk would justify, he concluded that institutional investors would benefit from purchases of junk bonds.

His later employment at Drexel Burnham Lambert allowed him to develop the junk-bond market. Milken's salesmanship simultaneously increased the demand for junk bonds among institutional investors and the supply of junk bonds among corporations. However, with the collapse of the junk-bond market and with Michael Milken's conviction for securities fraud, Drexel found it necessary to declare bankruptcy.

The U.S. junk-bond market revived in 1993 with smaller issues by foreign companies and smaller U.S. issuers. This market took on increased importance when junk bonds were used to finance mergers, going-private transactions, and other corporate restructurings. While a firm can only issue a small amount of high-grade debt, the same firm can issue much more debt if low-grade financing is allowed as well. Therefore, the use of junk bonds lets acquirers effect takeovers that they could not do with only traditional bond-financing techniques. Drexel was particularly successful with this technique, primarily because its huge base of institutional clients allowed it to raise large sums of money quickly.

At this time, it is not clear how the great growth in junk-bond financing has altered the returns on these instruments. On the one hand, financial theory indicates that the expected return on an asset should be negatively related to its marketability.[18] Because trading volume in junk bonds has greatly increased in recent years, their marketability has risen as well. This should lower the expected return on junk bonds, thereby benefiting corporate issuers. On the other hand, the increased interest in junk-bond financing by corporations

---

[16]M. Weinstein, "The Effect of a Ratings Change Announcement on Bond Price," *Journal of Financial Economics* 5 (1977). However, Robert W. Holthausen and Richard W. Leftwich, "The Effect of Bond Rating Changes on Common Stock Prices," *Journal of Financial Economics* 17 (September 1986), find that bond rating downgrades are associated with abnormal negative returns of the stock of the issuing firm.

[17]D. Hamilton and Sharon Ou, "Default Rates of Canadian Corporate Bond Issuers," *Canadian Investment Review* (Summer 2004).

[18]For example, see Y. Amihud and H. Mendelson, "Asset Pricing and the Bid-Ask Spread," *Journal of Financial Economics* (December 1986).

TABLE 21.3   Annual Default Rates By Whole-Letter Rating, 1989–2003 (%)

Canada	1989	1990	1991	1992	1993	1994	1995	1996	1997	1998	1999	2000	2001	2002	2003
Aaa	0.0	0.0	0.0	0.0	0.0	0.0	0.0	0.0	0.0	0.0	0.0	0.0	0.0	0.0	0.0
Aa	0.0	0.0	0.0	0.0	0.0	0.0	0.0	0.0	0.0	0.0	0.0	0.0	0.0	0.0	0.0
A	0.0	0.0	0.0	0.0	0.0	0.0	0.0	0.0	0.0	0.0	0.0	0.0	0.0	0.0	0.0
Baa	0.0	0.0	0.0	0.0	0.0	0.0	0.0	0.0	0.0	0.0	0.0	2.4	0.0	4.0	0.0
Ba	0.0	0.0	0.0	0.0	0.0	0.0	12.5	0.0	0.0	0.0	4.7	0.0	0.0	0.0	0.0
B	40.0	100.0	0.0	0.0	0.0	0.0	0.0	0.0	0.0	5.9	0.0	0.0	7.1	0.0	4.4
Caa-C	0.0	0.0	0.0	0.0	0.0	0.0	0.0	0.0	0.0	0.0	17.4	53.3	44.4	50.0	0.0
Investment-Grade	0.0	0.0	0.0	0.0	0.0	0.0	0.0	0.0	0.0	0.0	0.0	0.9	0.0	1.6	0.0
Speculative-Grade	33.3	50.0	0.0	0.0	0.0	0.0	3.7	0.0	0.0	3.4	4.6	11.6	10.0	7.7	1.8
All Corporate	2.1	1.9	0.0	0.0	0.0	0.0	1.1	0.0	0.0	1.3	1.8	5.0	3.5	3.4	0.6

United States	1989	1990	1991	1992	1993	1994	1995	1996	1997	1998	1999	2000	2001	2002	2003
Aaa	0.0	0.0	0.0	0.0	0.0	0.0	0.0	0.0	0.0	0.0	0.0	0.0	0.0	0.0	0.0
Aa	0.0	0.0	0.0	0.0	0.0	0.0	0.0	0.0	0.0	0.0	0.0	0.0	0.0	0.0	0.0
A	0.0	0.0	0.0	0.0	0.0	0.0	0.0	0.0	0.0	0.0	0.0	0.0	0.3	0.3	0.0
Baa	0.6	0.0	0.3	0.0	0.0	0.0	0.0	0.0	0.0	0.0	0.2	0.4	0.3	1.1	0.0
Ba	2.8	3.2	5.4	0.3	0.6	0.3	0.6	0.0	0.2	0.5	1.0	1.1	1.6	1.2	1.2
B	8.5	16.0	14.5	9.3	5.9	4.1	5.2	1.5	2.4	4.5	6.0	6.7	9.2	4.8	2.4
Caa-C	25.0	58.8	36.8	26.7	28.6	2.7	12.0	14.6	11.9	16.5	20.5	19.5	34.0	23.9	20.8
Investment-Grade	0.2	0.0	0.1	0.0	0.0	0.0	0.0	0.0	0.0	0.0	0.1	0.2	0.2	0.6	0.0
Speculative-Grade	5.5	10.0	10.4	5.1	3.8	2.1	3.6	1.9	2.2	3.9	5.8	7.1	11.1	7.3	5.4
All Corporate	2.4	4.2	4.0	1.7	1.3	0.7	1.4	0.7	0.8	1.6	2.6	3.2	4.8	3.2	2.2

(the increase in the supply of junk bonds) is likely to raise the expected returns on these assets. The net effect of these two forces is unclear.[19]

Table 21.3 presents data on annual default rates on investment grade (fallen angels) and junk bonds in Canada and the U.S. from 1989 through 2003. The table shows that junk bond defaults came in cycles peaking in 1990 and 2000–2001 for both countries. In Table 21.4, we see cumulative default rates by bond age for both countries. Comparing default rates in the two countries shows that, in Canada, investment grade bonds were less likely to default and the reverse was true for speculative grade bonds. Most of the Canadian defaults by dollar amount were in the telecommunications industry.

We discussed the costs of issuing securities in Chapter 20 and established that the costs of issuing debt are substantially less than the costs of issuing equity. Table 21.5 clarifies several questions regarding the costs of issuing debt securities. It contains a breakdown of direct costs for bond issues in the U.S. after the investment and noninvestment grades have been separated.

---

[19]The actual risk of junk bonds is not known with certainty because it is not easy to measure the default rate. Paul Asquith, David W. Mullins, Jr., and Eric D. Wolff, "Original Issue High Yield Bonds: Aging Analysis of Defaults, Exchanges, and Calls," *Journal of Finance* (September 1989), show that the default rate on junk bonds can be greater than 30 percent over the life of the bond. They look at cumulative default rates and find that of all junk bonds issued in 1977 and 1978, 34 percent had defaulted by December 31, 1988. Edward I. Altman, "Setting the Record Straight on Junk Bonds: A Review of the Research on Default Rates and Returns," *Journal of Applied Corporate Finance* (Summer 1990), shows that yearly default rates of 5 percent are consistent with cumulative default rates of over 30 percent.

TABLE 21.4   Average Cumulative Default Rates By Whole-letter Rating, 1989–2003 (%)

Canada	Year 1	Year 2	Year 3	Year 4	Year 5	United States	Year 1	Year 2	Year 3	Year 4	Year 5
Aaa	0.0	0.0	0.0	0.0	0.0	Aaa	0.0	0.0	0.0	0.0	0.0
Aa	0.0	0.0	0.0	0.0	0.0	Aa	0.0	0.0	0.0	0.0	0.1
A	0.0	0.0	0.0	0.0	0.0	A	0.0	0.1	0.3	0.4	0.5
Baa	0.8	1.8	3.0	3.5	4.2	Baa	0.2	0.7	1.1	1.7	2.2
Ba	1.0	2.2	5.3	8.2	10.7	Ba	1.4	4.0	6.8	8.9	10.9
B	2.8	9.1	13.9	19.3	24.6	B	6.4	14.3	22.5	27.4	32.8
Caa-C	29.5	49.6	64.0	79.7	85.5	Caa-C	22.0	34.8	44.9	53.4	59.8
Investment-Grade	0.3	0.5	0.9	1.0	1.2	Investment-Grade	0.1	0.3	0.5	0.7	1.0
Speculative-Grade	5.3	11.3	16.6	22.2	26.3	Speculative-Grade	5.9	12.0	17.4	21.7	25.4
All Corporates	1.8	3.7	5.5	7.1	8.2	All Corporates	2.4	4.9	7.0	8.6	9.9

Source: D. Hamilton and Sharon Ou, "Default Rates of Canadian Corporate Bond Issuers," *Canadian Investment Review* (Summer 2004).

First, there are substantial economies of scale here as well. Second, investment-grade issues have much lower direct costs, particularly for straight bonds. Finally, there are relatively few noninvestment-grade issues in the smaller size categories.

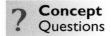

Concept Questions

- **List and describe the different bond-rating classes.**
- **Why don't bond prices change when bond ratings change?**
- **Are the costs of bond issues related to their ratings?**

21.5 Some Different Types of Bonds

Thus far, we have mostly considered "plain vanilla" bonds. In this section, we look at two more unusual types, the products of financial engineering: zero-coupon bonds and floating-rate bonds.[20] We discuss convertible bonds with embedded call options in Chapter 25.

Zero-Coupon Bonds

A bond that pays no coupons at all must be offered at a price that is much lower than its stated value. Such bonds are called **zero-coupon bonds** or just **zeros**.[21]

Suppose the DDB Company issues a $1,000 face value five-year zero-coupon bond. The initial price is set at $713. It is straightforward to check that, at this price, the bonds yield 7 percent to maturity. The total interest paid over the life of the bond is $1,000 − $713 = $287.

For tax purposes, the issuer of a zero-coupon bond deducts interest every year even though no interest is actually paid. Similarly, the owner must pay taxes on interest accrued every year as well, even though no interest is actually received.[22] This second tax feature makes taxable zero-coupon bonds less attractive to taxable investors. However, they are still

---

[20]For more on financial engineering, see John D. Finnerty, "Financial Engineering in Corporate Finance: An Overview," in *Handbook of Financial Engineering,* eds. C. W. Smith and C. W. Smithson (New York: Harper Business, 1990).

[21]A bond issued with a very low coupon rate (as opposed to a zero coupon rate) is an original-issue, discount (OID) bond.

[22]Calculation of yearly interest on a zero-coupon bond is governed by tax law and is not necessarily the true compound interest.

TABLE 21.5   Average Gross Spreads and Total Direct Costs for U.S. Debt Issues: 1990–2003

Proceeds ($ in millions)	Convertible Bonds						Straight Bonds					
	Investment Grade			Noninvestment Grade			Investment Grade			Noninvestment Grade		
	Number of Issues	Gross Spread	Total Direct Cost	Number of Issues	Gross Spread	Total Direct Cost	Number of Issues	Gross Spread	Total Direct Cost	Number of Issues	Gross Spread	Total Direct Cost
2–9.99	0	—	—	0	—	—	40	0.62%	1.90%	0	—	—
10–19.99	0	—	—	1	4.00%	5.67%	68	0.50	1.35	2	2.74%	4.80%
20–39.99	0	—	—	11	3.47	5.02	119	0.58	1.21	13	3.06	4.36
40–59.99	3	1.92%	2.43%	21	3.33	4.48	132	0.39	0.86	12	3.01	3.93
60–79.99	4	1.65	2.09	47	2.78	3.40	68	0.57	0.97	43	2.99	4.07
80–99.99	3	0.89	1.16	9	2.54	3.19	100	0.66	0.94	56	2.74	3.66
100–199.99	28	2.22	2.55	50	2.57	3.00	341	0.55	0.80	321	2.71	3.39
200–499.99	26	1.99	2.18	17	2.62	2.85	173	0.50	0.81	156	2.49	2.90
500 and up	12	1.96	2.09	1	2.50	2.57	97	0.28	0.38	0	2.45	2.71
Total	76	1.99%	2.26%	157	2.81%	3.47%	1138	0.51%	0.85%	623	2.68%	3.35%

Source: Inmoo Lee, Scott Lockhead, Jay Ritter, and Quanshui Zhao, "The Costs of Raising Capital," *Journal of Financial Research* 19 (Spring 1996); updated by the authors.

a very attractive investment for tax-exempt investors with long-term dollar-denominated liabilities, such as pension funds, because the future dollar value is known with relative certainty. Zero-coupon bonds, often in the form of stripped coupons or Guaranteed Investment Certificates (GICs), are attractive to individual investors for tax-sheltered Registered Retirement Savings Plans (RRSPs).

Because zero-coupon bonds have no intermediate coupon payments, they are quite attractive to certain investors and quite unattractive to others. For example, consider an insurance company forecasting death benefit payments of $1,000,000 five years from today. The company would like to be sure that it will have the funds to pay off the liability in five years. It could buy five-year zero-coupon bonds with a face value of $1,000,000. The company is matching assets with liabilities here, a procedure that eliminates interest rate risk. That is, regardless of the movement of interest rates, the firm's set of zeros will always be able to pay off the $1,000,000 liability.

Conversely, the firm would be at risk if it bought coupon bonds instead. For example, if it bought five-year coupon bonds, it would need to reinvest the coupon payments through to the fifth year. Because interest rates in the future are not known with certainty today, one cannot be sure if the sum of bond principal plus coupon accumulation will be worth more or less than $1,000,000 by the fifth year. This type of risk is called reinvestment risk.

Consider a couple saving for their child's university education in 15 years. They *expect* that, with inflation, four years of university should cost $150,000 in 15 years. Thus, they buy 15-year zero-coupon bonds with a face value of $150,000.[23] If they have forecasted inflation perfectly (and if costs keep pace with inflation), their child's tuition will be fully funded. However, if inflation rises more than expected, the tuition would be more than $150,000. Because the zero-coupon bonds produce a shortfall, the child might end up working his way through school. As an alternative, the parents might have considered rolling over Treasury bills. Because the yields on Treasury bills rise and fall with the inflation rate, this simple strategy is likely to cause less risk than the strategy with zeros.

The key to these examples is the distinction between nominal and real quantities. The insurance company's liability is $1,000,000 in *nominal* dollars. Because the face value of a zero-coupon bond is a nominal quantity, the purchase of zeros eliminates risk. However, it is easier to forecast university costs in real terms than in nominal terms. Thus, a zero-coupon bond is a poor choice to reduce the financial risk of a child's university education.

Floating-Rate Bonds

The conventional bonds discussed in this chapter have *fixed dollar obligations* because the coupon rate is set as a fixed percentage of the par value. Similarly, the principal is set equal to the par value. Under these circumstances, the coupon payment and principal are completely fixed.

With **floating-rate bonds (floaters),** the coupon payments are adjustable. The adjustments are tied to the Treasury bill rate or another short-term interest rate. For example, in 2004 RBC Financial Group had outstanding $250 million in floating-rate notes maturing in 2083. The coupon rate was set at 40 basis points over the 30-day Bankers' Acceptance rate.

The majority of these *floaters* have put provisions and floor-and-ceiling provisions:

1. With a *put provision* the holder has the right to redeem his or her note at par on the coupon payment date. Frequently, the investor is prohibited from redeeming at par during the first few years of the bond's life.

---

[23]A more precise strategy would be to buy zeros maturing in years 15, 16, 17, and 18, respectively. In this way, the bonds might mature just in time to meet tuition payments. Further, taxes are ignored in this example.

2. With floor-and-ceiling provisions the coupon rate is subject to a minimum and maximum. For example, the minimum coupon rate might be 8 percent and the maximum rate might be 14 percent.

The popularity of floating-rate bonds is connected to *inflation risk.* When inflation is higher than expected, issuers of fixed-rate bonds tend to make gains at the expense of lenders, and when inflation is less than expected, lenders make gains at the expense of borrowers. Because the inflation risk of long-term bonds is borne by both issuers and bondholders, it is in their interests to devise loan agreements that minimize inflation risk.[24]

Floaters reduce inflation risk because the coupon rate is tied to the current interest rate, which, in turn, is influenced by the rate of inflation. This can most clearly be seen by considering the formula for the present value of a bond. As inflation increases the interest rate (the denominator of the formula), inflation increases a floater's coupon rate (the numerator of the formula). Hence, bond value is hardly affected by inflation. Conversely, the coupon rate of fixed-rate bonds cannot change, implying that the prices of these bonds are at the mercy of inflation.

As an alternative, an individual who is concerned with inflation risk can invest in short-term notes, such as Treasury bills, and *roll them over.*[25] The investor can accomplish essentially the same objective by buying a floater that is adjusted to the LIBOR or T-bill rate. However, the purchaser of a floater can reduce transactions costs relative to rolling over short-term Treasury bills because floaters are long-term bonds. The same type of reduction in transactions costs makes floaters attractive to some corporations.[26] They benefit from issuing a floater instead of issuing a series of short-term notes.

In an earlier section, we discussed callable bonds. Because the coupon on floaters varies with marketwide interest rates, floaters always sell at or near par. Therefore, it is not surprising that floaters do not generally have call features.

Financial Engineering and Bonds

Since bonds are financial contracts, the possible features are only limited by the imagination of the parties involved. As a result, bonds can be fairly exotic, particularly some more recent issues. We discuss a few of the more common features and types next.

Income bonds are similar to conventional bonds, except that coupon payments are dependent on company income. Specifically, coupons are paid to bondholders only if the firm's income is sufficient. In Canada, income bonds are usually issued by firms in the process of reorganization to try to overcome financial distress. The firm can skip the interest payment on an income bond without being in default. Interest paid on income bonds is not tax deductible by the issuer. Since firms in financial distress generally have little taxable income, this disadvantage is reduced. Purchasers of income bonds must pay tax on interest received.

A *convertible bond* can be swapped for a fixed number of shares of stock anytime before maturity at the holder's option. Convertibles are a debt/equity hybrid that allow the holder to profit if the issuer's stock price rises.

A *retractable bond* or *put bond* allows the holder to force the issuer to buy the bond back at a stated price. As long as the issuer remains solvent, the put feature sets a floor

---

[24]See B. Cornell, "The Future of Floating Rate Bonds," in *The Revolution in Corporate Finance,* ed. by J. M. Stern and D. H. Chew, Jr. (New York: Basil Blackwell, 1986).

[25]That is, the investor could buy a bill, receive the face value at maturity, use these proceeds to buy a second bill, receive the face value from the second bill at maturity, and so on.

[26]Cox, Ingersoll, and Ross developed a framework for pricing floating-rate notes; see J. Cox, J. Ingersoll, and S. A. Ross, "An Analysis of Variable Rate Loan Contracts," *Journal of Finance* 35 (May 1980).

price for the bond. It is therefore just the reverse of the call provision. Canada Savings Bonds (CSBs) are an example of retractable bonds. Holders of CSBs may sell them back to the Bank of Canada at any time (through any financial institution) at their par value plus accrued interest.

A *stripped real-return bond* is a zero-coupon bond with inflation protection. These bonds, issued by the Government of Canada for the first time in 1993, have their principal indexed to inflation. Investors receive a known amount in real terms. This feature is designed to make zeros more attractive to investors such as the couple saving for their child's university education in our earlier example.[27]

A given bond may have many unusual features. For example, Merrill Lynch created a popular bond called a *liquid yield option* note or LYON ("lion"). Figuratively speaking, a LYON has everything but the kitchen sink; this bond is a callable, puttable, convertible, zero-coupon, subordinated note. In 1991, Rogers Communications Inc. issued the first LYON in Canada. Two of the most recent exotic bonds are CoCo bonds, which have a coupon payment, and NoNo bonds, which are zero coupon bonds. CoCo and NoNo bonds are contingent convertible, puttable, callable, subordinated bonds. The contingent convertible clause is similar to the normal conversion feature, except the contingent feature must be met. For example, a contingent feature may require that the company stock trade at 110 percent of the conversion price for 20 out of the most recent 30 days. Valuing a bond of this sort can be quite complex, and the yield to maturity calculation is often meaningless. To illustrate, in 2006, a NoNo issued by Merrill Lynch was selling at a price of $939.99, with a yield to maturity of negative 1.63 percent. At the same time, a NoNo issued by Countrywide Financial was selling for $1,640, which implied a yield to maturity of negative 59 percent!

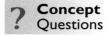 **Concept Questions**

- Why might a zero-coupon bond be attractive to investors?
- How might a put feature affect a bond's coupon? How about a convertibility feature? Why?
- What is the attraction of a floating-rate bond?

21.6 Direct Placement Compared to Public Issues

Earlier in this chapter, we described the mechanics of issuing debt to the public. However, a large portion of debt is privately placed. There are two basic forms of direct private long-term financing: term loans and private placements.

Term loans are direct business loans. These loans have maturities of one to five years. Most term loans are repayable during the life of the loan. The lenders include chartered banks, insurance companies, trust companies, and other lenders that specialize in corporate finance. The interest rate on a term loan may be either a fixed or floating rate.

Private placements are very similar to term loans except that the maturity is longer. Unlike term loans, privately placed debt usually employs an investment dealer. The dealer facilitates the process but does not underwrite the issue. A private placement does not require a full prospectus. Instead, the firm and its investment dealer only need to draw up an offering memorandum briefly describing the issuer and the issue. Most privately placed debt is sold to *exempt purchasers.* These are large insurance companies, pension funds, and other institutions that, as sophisticated market participants, do not require the protection provided by studying a full prospectus.

---

[27]Barry Critchley, "Indexing Gives These Bonds a Real Return," *The Financial Post* (November 27, 1993), p. 17.

Following are the important differences between direct private long-term financing (term loans and private debt placements) and public issues of debt:

1. Registration costs are lower for direct financing. A term loan avoids the cost of OSC registration altogether. Private debt placements require an offering memorandum, but this is cheaper than preparing a full prospectus.

2. Direct placement is likely to have more restrictive covenants.

3. It is easier to renegotiate a term loan or a private placement in the event of a default. It is harder to renegotiate a public issue because hundreds of holders are usually involved.

4. Life insurance companies and pension funds dominate the private placement segment of the bond market. Chartered banks are significant participants in the term loan market.

5. The costs of distributing bonds are lower in the private market because fewer buyers are involved and the issue is not underwritten.

The interest rates on term loans and private placements are usually higher than those on an equivalent public issue. This reflects the trade-off between a higher interest rate and more flexible arrangements in the event of financial distress, as well as the lower costs and lower liquidity associated with private placements.

? Concept Questions
- **What are the differences between private and public bond issues?**
- **A private placement is more likely to have restrictive covenants than is a public issue. Why?**

21.7 Long-Term Syndicated Bank Loans

Most bank loans are for less than a year. They serve as a short-term "bridge" for the acquisition of inventory and are typically self-liquidating—that is, when the firm sells the inventory, the cash is used to repay the bank loan. We talk about the need for short-term bank loans in the next section of the text. Now we focus on long-term bank loans.

First, we introduce the concept of commitment. Most bank loans are made with a commitment to a firm. That commitment establishes a line of credit and allows the firm to borrow up to a predetermined limit. Most commitments are in the form of a revolving credit commitment (i.e., a revolver) with a fixed term of up to three years or more. Revolving credit commitments are drawn or undrawn depending on whether the firm has a current need for the funds.

Now we turn to the concept of syndication. Very large banks such as Citigroup and Royal Bank of Canada typically have a larger demand for loans than they can supply, and small regional banks frequently have more funds on hand than they can profitably lend to existing customers. Basically, they cannot generate enough good loans with the funds they have available. As a result, a very large bank may arrange a loan with a firm or country and then sell portions of it to a syndicate of other banks. With a syndicated loan, each bank has a separate loan agreement with the borrowers.

A syndicated loan is a corporate loan made by a group (or syndicate) of banks and other institutional investors. A syndicated loan may be publicly traded. It may be a line of credit and be "undrawn" or it may be drawn and used by a firm. Syndicated loans are always rated investment grade. However, a *leveraged* syndicated loan is rated speculative grade (i.e., it is "junk"). Every week, the *Wall Street Journal* reports on the number of syndicated loan deals, credit costs, and yields, as seen in Figure 21.1. In addition, syndicated loan prices are reported for a group of publicly traded loans.

FIGURE 21.1

Wall Street Journal Reports

Syndicated-Loan Market/*Trends & Prices*

Syndicated loans are corporate loans that are bought or traded by a group, or "syndicate," of banks and/or institutional investors. Investment-grade loans are investment grade or unrated loans priced at or below the London interbank offered rate (Libor) plus 1.50 percentage points (150 basis points). Leveraged loans are speculative grade or unrated loans priced at or above Libor plus 1.51 percentage points.

Forward Calendar

A leading indicator of activity, showing new investment-grade deals mandated or in the market.

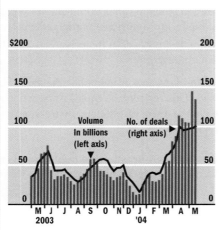

Credit Costs

Market share of high grade loans as a percentage of the investment grade market for loans. Three-year deals are replacing five-year deals, when it comes to multiyear credit facilities.

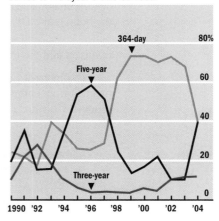

Notes: Final data points on left-hand chart are as of May14; final data points on right-hand chart are year to date.
Sources: Banc of America Securities LLC, Loan Pricing Corp.

The Week's Biggest Movers

Biggest gainers and losers among widely quoted syndicated loans in secondary trading, in the week ended Friday. Listed are the biggest movers among the 114 loans with at least five bids. All loans listed are B-term, or sold to institutional investors.

	LOAN RATING MOODY'S/S&P	COUPON	MATURITY	AVERAGE BID (pct. pts.)	WEEKLY CHANGE (pct.pts.)
Adelphia commun[1]	N.R./N.R.	L+300	June30, '09	97.35	-0.44
Armkel	Ba2/BB-	L+325	March 28, '09	101.25	+0.21
Boyd Gaming	Ba2/BB+	L+200	May 13, '08	100.13	-0.25
Calpine Const Fin	N.R./N.R.	L+600	Aug. 07, '09	104.95	-0.92
Calpine	N.R./B	L+350	July 08, '07	100.02	-0.69
Centennial Cellular[2]	B2/B-	L+275	Jan. 15, '11	99.33	-0.67
Centerpoint Energy	Bal/N.R.	L+350	Oct. 15, '06	101.54	-0.39
Charter Commun[2]	B2/N.R.	L+325	March 31, '11	98.91	-0.71
CHS/Comm Hlth Sys	Ba3/BB-	L+250	July 16, '10	101.40	-0.22
Dex Media East	B1/BB-	L+250	May 08, '09	101.22	-0.27
Dex Media West	B1/BB-	L+275	Sept. 09, '10	101.32	-0.21
DIRECTV Holdings	Ba2/BB-	L+225	March 03, '10	101.35	-0.18
Dobson Commun	N.R./B-	L+325	Oct. 30, '10	99.46	-0.38

	LOAN RATING MOODY'S/S&P	COUPON	MATURITY	AVERAGE BID (pct. pts.)	WEEKLY CHANGE (pct.pts.)
Huntsman 1CI	N.R./B+	L+400	June 30, '07	100.39	-0.76
Iasis Healthcarre	B1/B+	L+425	Jan. 29, '09	100.47	-0.38
Merisant	B1/B+	L+275	Jan. 11,'10	100.40	-0.27
Nalco	B1/BB-	L+250	Oct. 20, '10	100.19	-0.54
Nextel Partners[2]	B1/B	L+300	Nov. 12,'10	100.45	-0.55
Olympus Cable Hldgs	N.R./N.R.	L+300	Sept. 30, '10	97.11	-0.32
Primedia	N.R./B	L+275	June 30, '09	95.80	-3.50
Reliant Resources	N.R./N.R.	L+400	March 15, '07	97.67	-0.23
Solo Cup	B1/N.R.	L+250	Feb. 09, '11	101.40	-0.19
United Rentals NA	Ba3/BB	L+225	Aug. 31,'11	100.93	-0.17
VWR International	N.R./N.R.	L+275	April 07, '11	101.22	-0.18
Warner Music Group	B1/N.R.	L+275	March 01, '11	101.13	-0.17

[1]Century Cable [2]Operating Co.
Source: LSTA/LPC Mark-To-Market Pricing

Unchanged   **1914**

Advncers   132

Decliners   398

Total loans with at least one bid: 2444
Average change in bids: −0.05 percentage point

Note: These are the averages of indicative bid prices provided by bank-loan traders and expressed as a percentage of the par, or face, value. Coupon, or interest rate, is in 1/100s of a percentage point over Libor, or London interbank offered rate. All ratings are for specific loans and not for the company itself except as noted with an (a). These prices do not represent actual trades no are they offers to trade; rather they are estimated values provided by dealers.

Source: LST/LPC Mark-To-Market Pricing

Source: *Wall Street Journal*, May 18, 2004. Used with permission.

Syndicated loans are comparable to bonds in many respects. Altman and Suggitt report slightly higher default rates for syndicated loans. Gottesman and Roberts show that features like maturity and security impact rates on syndicated loans similarly to bonds.[28]

? Concept Questions

- **What are the features of syndicated bank loans?**

21.8 SUMMARY AND CONCLUSIONS

This chapter describes important aspects of long-term debt financing.

1. The written agreement describing the details of the long-term debt contract is called an *indenture*. Some of the main provisions are security, repayment, protective covenants, and call provisions.

2. There are many ways in which shareholders can take advantage of bondholders. Protective covenants are designed to protect bondholders from management decisions that favour shareholders at bondholders' expense.

3. Unsecured bonds are called *debentures* or *notes*. They are general claims on the company's value. Most public corporate bonds are unsecured. In contrast, utility bonds are usually secured. Mortgage bonds are secured by tangible property, and collateral trust bonds are secured by financial securities such as stocks and bonds. If the company defaults on secured bonds, the trustee can repossess the assets. This makes secured bonds more valuable.

4. Long-term bonds usually provide for repayment of principal before maturity. This is accomplished by a sinking fund. With a sinking fund, the company retires a certain number of bonds each year. A sinking fund protects bondholders because it reduces the average maturity of the bond, and its payment signals the financial condition of the company.

5. Most publicly issued bonds are callable. A callable bond is less attractive to bondholders than a noncallable bond. A callable bond can be bought back by the company at a call price that is less than the true value of the bond. As a consequence, callable bonds are priced to obtain higher stated interest rates for bondholders than noncallable bonds.

   Generally, companies should exercise the call provision whenever the bond's value is greater than the call price.

   There is no single reason for call provisions. Sensible reasons include taxes, greater flexibility, management's ability to predict interest rates, and the fact that callable bonds are less sensitive to interest rate changes.

6. There are many different types of bonds, including floating-rate bonds, deep-discount bonds, and income bonds. This chapter also compares private placement with public issuance.

KEY TERMS

Bearer bond 599	Income bonds 615	Refunding 602
Call premium 601	Indenture 597	Registered bond 598
Call protected 601	Junk bonds 610	Sinking fund 601
Canada plus call 601	Negative covenant 600	Term loans 616
Debenture 600	Positive covenant 600	Zero-coupon bonds
Deferred call 601	Private placements 616	(zeros) 612
Floating-rate bonds	Protective covenant 600	
(floaters) 614	Public issue 597	

[28]A. Gottesman and G. S. Roberts, "Loan Rates and Collateral," *Financial Review* 42 (2007); and "Maturity and Corporate Loan Pricing," *Financial Review* 39 (2004).

SUGGESTED READING

The following provide complete coverage of bonds and the bond market:

F. J. Fabozzi, and T. D. Fabozzi, eds. *The Handbook of Fixed Income Securities*. 6th ed. McGraw-Hill, 2000.

A. Bodie, A. Kane, A. J. Marcus, S. Perrakis, and P. J. Ryan. *Investments*. 5th Canadian ed. McGraw-Hill, 2005.

QUESTIONS & PROBLEMS

Public Issue of Bonds

21.1 Raeo Corp. bonds trade at 100 today. The bonds pay semiannual interest on January 1 and July 1. The coupon on the bonds is 6 percent. How much will you pay for a Raeo bond if today is

    a. March 1?

    b. October 1?

    c. July 1?

    d. August 15?

21.2 Sinking funds have both positive and negative characteristics to the bondholders. Why?

21.3 Which of the following are characteristics of public issues, and which are characteristics of direct financing?

    a. Require OSC registration.

    b. Higher interest cost.

    c. Higher fixed cost.

    d. Quicker access to funds.

    e. Active secondary market.

    f. Easily renegotiated.

    g. Lower flotation costs.

    h. Require regular amortization.

    i. Ease of repurchase at favourable prices.

    j. High total cost to small borrowers.

    k. Flexible terms.

    l. Require less intensive investigation.

21.4 What is a call premium? During what period of time is a bond said to be call-protected?

21.5 What is a Canada plus call? How does it remove the issuer's incentive to call debt?

21.6 A company is contemplating a long-term bond issue. It is debating whether to include a call provision. What are the benefits to the company from including a call provision? What are the costs? How do these answers change for a put provision?

21.7 How does a bond issuer decide on the appropriate coupon rate to set on its bonds? Explain the difference between the coupon rate and the required return on a bond.

21.8 Companies pay rating agencies such as Moody's and S&P to rate their bonds, and the costs can be substantial. However, companies are not required to have their bonds rated in the first place; doing so is strictly voluntary. Why do you think they do it?

21.9 Recently several companies have issued bonds with 100-year maturities. Critics charge that the issuers are really selling equity in disguise. What are the issues here? Why would a company want to sell "equity in disguise"?

Bond Refunding

21.10 Bowdeen Manufacturing intends to issue callable, perpetual bonds with annual coupon payments. The bonds are callable at $1,250. One-year interest rates are 11 percent. There is a 60 percent probability that long-term interest rates one year from today will be 13 percent, and a 40 percent probability that long-term interest rates will be 9 percent. Assume that if interest rates fall the bonds will be called. What coupon rate should the bonds have in order to sell at par value?

21.11 Bobcageon Industries has decided to borrow money by issuing perpetual bonds with a coupon rate of 8 percent, payable annually. The one-year interest rate is 8 percent. Next year, there is a 35 percent probability that interest rates will increase to 9 percent, and there is a 65 percent probability that they will fall to 6 percent.

a. What will the market value of these bonds be if they are noncallable?

b. If the company instead decides to make the bonds callable in one year, what coupon will be demanded by the bondholders for the bonds to sell at par? Assume that the bonds will be called if interest rates rise and that the call premium is equal to the annual coupon.

c. What will be the value of the call provision to the company?

21.12 Old Business Ventures Inc. has an outstanding perpetual bond with a 10 percent coupon rate that can be called in one year. The bonds make annual coupon payments. The call premium is set at $150 over par value. There is a 40 percent chance that the interest rate will in one year will be 12 percent, and a 60 percent chance that the interest rate will be 7 percent. If the current interest rate is 10 percent, what is the current market price of the bond?

21.13 In 2001, Whitby Enterprises issued $5 million in bonds. At issue, the bonds carried a yield of 70 basis points above comparable Government of Canada bonds yielding 9.53 percent. When Whitby originally issued the debt, the company agreed to compensate investors on a yield of Canada plus 70 basis points if the bonds were ever called. By 2007, rates on comparable Canadas fell to 6.5 percent and Whitby could issue new debt at 7.2 percent. Given this information, calculate the annual interest penalty Whitby would have to pay to call the debt. Is calling the debt in the best interests of Whitby?

EXCEL

21.14 An outstanding issue of Executive Airlines debentures has a call provision attached. The total principal value of the bonds is $260 million, and the bonds have an annual coupon rate of 9 percent. The total cost of refunding would be 13 percent of the principal amount raised. The appropriate tax rate for the company is 37 percent. How low does the borrowing cost need to drop to justify refunding with a new bond issue?

21.15 KIC Inc. plans to issue $5 million of bonds with a coupon rate of 12 percent and 30 years to maturity. The current market interest rate on these bonds is 11 percent. In one year, the interest rate on the bonds will be either 14 percent or 7 percent with equal probability. Assume investors are risk-neutral.

a. If the bonds are noncallable, what is the price of the bonds today?

b. If the bonds are callable one year from today at $1,450, will their price be greater than or less than the price you computed in (a)? Why?

EXCEL

21.16 Margret Kimberly, CFO of Puget Sound Associates, is considering whether or not to refinance the two currently outstanding corporate bonds of the firm. The first one is an 8 percent perpetual bond with a $1,000 face value with $75 million outstanding. The second one is a 9 percent perpetual bond with the same face value with $87.5 million outstanding. The call premiums for the two bonds are 8.5 percent and 9.5 percent of the face value, respectively. The transaction costs of the refundings are $10 million and $12 million, respectively. The current interest rates for the two bonds are 7 percent and 7.25 percent, respectively. Which bond should Ms. Kimberly recommend be refinanced? What is the NPV of the refunding?

Some Different Types of Bonds

21.17 What is a "junk bond"? What are some of the controversies created by junk-bond financing?

21.18 Describe the following types of bonds:

a. Floating rate

b. Deep discount

c. Income

MINICASE: Financing the Expansion of East Coast Yachts with a Bond Issue

Billie Rickard, the owner of East Coast Yachts and main competitor to Deck Out My Yacht, has decided to expand her operations. She asked her newly hired financial analyst, Darren Dunn, to enlist an underwriter to help sell $30 million in new 20-year bonds to finance new construction. Darren has entered into discussions with Wilson Molina, an underwriter from the firm of Molina, Molina & Rodriguez, about which bond features East Coast Yachts should consider and also what coupon rate the issue will likely have. Although Darren is aware of bond features, he is uncertain of the costs and benefits of some features, so he is not sure how each feature would affect the coupon rate of the bond issue.

1. You are Wilson's assistant, and he has asked you to prepare a memo to Darren describing the effect of each of the following bond features on the coupon rate of the bond. He would also like you to list any advantages or disadvantages of each feature.
   a. The security of the bond—that is, whether the bond has collateral.
   b. The seniority of the bond.
   c. The presence of a sinking fund.
   d. A call provision with specified call dates and call prices.
   e. A deferred call accompanying the call provision in (d).
   f. A make-whole call provision.
   g. Any positive covenants. Also, discuss several possible positive covenants East Coast Yachts might consider.

h. Any negative covenants. Also, discuss several possible negative covenants East Coast Yachts might consider.
   i. A conversion feature (*Note:* East Coast Yachts is not a publicly traded company).
   j. A floating-rate coupon.
   Darren is also considering whether to issue coupon bearing bonds or zero coupon bonds. The YTM on either bond issue will be 8 percent. The coupon bond would have an 8 percent coupon rate. The company's tax rate is 37 percent.

2. How many of the coupon bonds must East Coast Yachts issue to raise the $30 million? How many of the zeroes must it issue?

3. In 20 years, what will be the principal repayment due if East Coast Yachts issues the coupon bonds? What if it issues the zeroes?

4. What are the company's considerations in issuing a coupon bond compared to a zero coupon bond?

5. Suppose East Coast Yachts issues the coupon bonds with a make-whole call provision. The make-whole call rate is the T-bill rate plus 0.40 percent. If East Coast calls the bonds in 7 years when the T-bill rate is 5.6 percent, what is the call price of the bond? What if it is 9.1 percent?

6. Are investors really made whole with a make-whole call provision?

7. After considering all the relevant factors, would you recommend a zero coupon issue or a regular coupon issue? Why? Would you recommend an ordinary call feature or a make-whole call feature? Why?

General Topics

21.19 *a.* In an efficient market callable and noncallable bonds will be priced in such a way that there will be no advantage or disadvantage to the call provision. Comment.
   b. If interest rates fall, will the price of noncallable bonds move up higher than that of callable bonds? Why or why not?

STANDARD &POOR'S

www.mcgrawhill.ca/
edumarketinsight

21.20 Look under the Sedar link for Bell Canada Enterprises (BCE) and find the most recent bond issue for the company. What was the amount of bonds issued? What are the coupon rate, maturity date, payment dates, ranking, and restrictive covenants on the bonds? What are the risk factors of the bonds outlined in the prospectus?

Chapter **22**

Leasing

EXECUTIVE SUMMARY

From aircraft to zithers, almost any asset that can be purchased can be leased. When we take vacations or business trips, renting a car for a few days frequently seems convenient. This is an example of a short-term lease. After all, buying a car and selling it a few days later would be a great nuisance.

Corporations lease both short-term and long-term, but this chapter is primarily concerned with long-term leasing over a period of more than five years. Long-term leasing is a method of financing property, plant, and equipment. Computers and communications equipment make up the largest sector of equipment leasing in Canada. Next comes aircraft leases—big-ticket items ranging to $200 million for a Boeing 787 Dreamliner. Leasing is popular in financing furniture and fixtures as well as manufacturing, transportation, and construction equipment. Over $103 billion in assets were under lease in Canada in 2006, according to the Canadian Finance and Lease Association.

Every lease contract has two parties: the **lessee** and the **lessor.** The lessee is the user of the equipment, and the lessor is the owner. Typically, the lessee first decides on the asset needed and then negotiates a lease contract with a lessor. From the lessee's standpoint, long-term leasing is similar to buying the equipment with a secured loan. The terms of the lease contract are compared to what a banker might arrange with a secured loan. Thus, long-term leasing is a form of financing.

Many questionable advantages are claimed for long-term leasing, such as "leasing provides 100 percent financing," or "leasing conserves capital." However, the principal benefit of long-term leasing is tax reduction. Leasing allows those who need equipment, but cannot take full advantage of the tax benefits associated with ownership, to transfer the tax benefits to a party who can. If the corporate income tax were repealed, long-term leasing would decline dramatically.

22.1 Types of Leases

The Basics

A **lease** is a contractual agreement between a lessee and a lessor. The agreement establishes that the lessee has the right to use an asset and in return must make periodic payments to the lessor, the owner of the asset. The lessor is either the asset's manufacturer or an independent leasing company.[1] If the lessor is an independent leasing company, it must buy the asset from a manufacturer and deliver it to the lessee.

As far as the lessee is concerned, it is the use of the asset that is important, not the ownership. The use of an asset can be obtained by a lease contract. Because the user can

---

[1] Independent of the manufacturer, the leasing company may be owned by a chartered bank. Under the current *Bank Act,* banks are allowed to own leasing subsidiaries but prohibited from leasing vehicles through their branch networks.

also buy the asset, leasing and buying involve alternative financing arrangements for the use of an asset. This is illustrated in Figure 22.1.

The example in Figure 22.1 is common in the computer industry. Firm *U,* the lessee, might be a hospital, a law firm, or any other firm that uses computers. The lessor is an independent leasing company that purchased the equipment from a manufacturer such as IBM or Apple. Leases of this type are called **direct leases.** In the figure, the lessor issued both debt and equity to finance the purchase.

Of course, a manufacturer like IBM could lease its *own* computers, though we do not show this situation in the example. Leases of this type are called **sales-type leases.** In this case, IBM would compete with the independent computer-leasing company.

Operating Leases

Years ago, a lease that provided an operator along with the equipment was called an **operating lease.** Today, an operating lease (or service lease) is difficult to define precisely, but this form of leasing has several important characteristics:

1. Operating leases are usually not fully amortized. This means that the payments required under the terms of the lease are not enough to recover the full cost of the asset for the lessor. This occurs because the term or life of the operating lease is usually less than the economic life of the asset. Thus, the lessor must expect to recover the costs of the asset by renewing the lease or by selling the asset for its residual value.

2. Operating leases usually require the lessor to maintain and insure the leased assets.

3. Perhaps the most interesting feature of an operating lease is the cancellation option. This option gives the lessee the right to cancel the lease contract before the expiration date. If the option to cancel is exercised, the lessee must return the equipment to the lessor. The value of a cancellation clause depends on whether future technological and/or economic conditions are likely to make the value of the asset to the lessee less than the value of the future lease payments under the lease.

FIGURE 22.1   Buying Versus Leasing

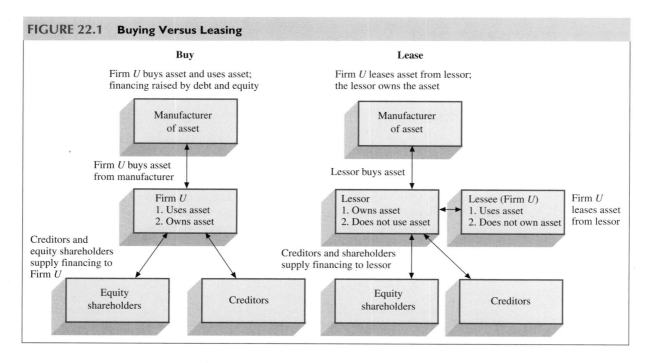

To leasing practitioners, these characteristics constitute an operating lease. However, accountants use the term in a slightly different way, as we will see shortly.

Financial Leases

Financial leases are the exact opposite of operating leases, as is seen from their important characteristics:

1. Financial leases do not provide for maintenance or service by the lessor.

2. Financial leases are fully amortized.

3. The lessee usually has a right to renew the lease on expiration.

4. Generally, financial leases cannot be cancelled. In other words, the lessee must make all payments or face the risk of bankruptcy.

The characteristics of a financial lease (particularly the fact that it is fully amortized) make it very similar to debt financing, so the name is a sensible one. Two special types of financial leases are the sale and lease-back arrangement and the leveraged lease.

Sale and Lease-Back   A **sale and lease-back** occurs when a company sells an asset it owns to another firm and immediately leases it back. In a sale and lease-back, two things happen:

1. The lessee receives cash from the sale of the asset.

2. The lessee makes periodic lease payments, thereby retaining use of the asset.

For example, in January 1989, Air Canada arranged a sale and lease-back of four Boeing 767-200ER aircraft. The purchaser was a Canadian financial institution and the transaction proceeds were $260 million. Further examples include Canadian universities and hospitals that set up sale and lease-back deals for library books and medical equipment.[2] With a sale and lease-back, the lessee may have the option to repurchase the leased assets at the end of the lease.

Leveraged Leases   A **leveraged lease** is a three-sided arrangement among the lessee, the lessor, and the lenders:

1. As in other leases, the lessee uses the assets and makes periodic lease payments.

2. As in other leases, the lessor purchases the assets, delivers them to the lessee, and collects the lease payments. However, the lessor puts up no more than 40 to 50 percent of the purchase price.

3. The lenders supply the remaining financing and receive interest payments from the lessor. Thus, the arrangement on the right-hand side of Figure 22.1 would be a leveraged lease if the bulk of the financing were supplied by creditors.

The lenders in a leveraged lease typically use a nonrecourse loan. This means that the lessor is not obligated to the lender in case of a default. However, the lender is protected in two ways:

1. The lender has a first lien on the asset.

2. In the event of loan default, the lease payments are made directly to the lender.

---

[2]Tax law changes subsequently restricted sale and lease-backs and heavy equipment and aircraft leasing in Canada; we discuss this later. *The Globe and Mail's Report on Business* (January 9, 1989), p. B2; B. Critchley and B. Baxter, "Why the SLB Ban?" *The Financial Post* (April 28, 1989), p. B6; and G. Athanassakos and M. Klatt, "Lease or Buy? How Recent Tax Changes Have Affected the Decision," *Canadian Tax Journal* 41 (1993), pp. 444–53.

The lessor puts up only part of the funds but gets the lease payments and all of the tax benefits of ownership. Lease payments are used to service the nonrecourse loan. The lessee benefits because, in a competitive market, the lease payment is lowered when the lessor saves taxes.

? Concept Questions

- **What are the differences between an operating lease and a financial lease?**
- **What is a sale and lease-back agreement?**
- **How does a leveraged lease work?**

22.2 Accounting and Leasing

Before 1979, leasing was frequently called **off–balance-sheet financing.** As the name implies, a firm could arrange to use an asset through a lease without disclosing the existence of the lease contract on the balance sheet. Lessees only had to report information on leasing activity in the footnotes of their financial statements.

Of course, this meant that firms could acquire the use of a substantial number of assets and incur a substantial long-term financial commitment through financial leases yet not disclose the impact of these arrangements in their financial statements. Operating leases, being cancellable at little or no penalty, do not involve any significant financial commitment. So operating leases did not generate much concern about complete disclosure. As a result, the accounting profession wanted to distinguish clearly between operating and financial leases to ensure that the impact of financial leases was included in the financial statements.

In 1979, the Canadian Institute of Chartered Accountants implemented new rules for lease accounting (CICA 3065). The basic idea is that all financial leases (called *capital leases* in CICA 3065) must be "capitalized." This requirement means that the present value of the lease payments must be calculated and reported along with debt and other liabilities on the right-hand side of the lessee's balance sheet.[3] The same amount must be shown as an asset on the left-hand side of the balance sheet. Operating leases are not disclosed on the balance sheet. Exactly what constitutes a financial or operating lease for accounting purposes is discussed below.

The accounting implications of CICA 3065 are illustrated in Table 22.1. Imagine a firm that has $100,000 in assets and no debt, implying that the equity is also $100,000. The firm needs a truck costing $100,000 that it can lease or buy. The top of the table shows the balance sheet assuming that the firm borrows the money and buys the truck.

If the firm leases the truck, then one of two things will happen. If the lease is an operating lease, then the balance sheet will look like the one in the centre of the table. In this case, neither the asset (the truck) nor the liability (the lease payments) appears. If the lease is a capital (financial) lease, then the balance sheet would look like the one at the bottom of the table, where the truck is shown as an asset and the present value of the lease payments is shown as a liability.

Accountants generally argue that a firm's financial strength is inversely related to the amount of its liabilities. Since the lease liability is hidden with an operating lease, the balance sheet of a firm with an operating lease *looks* stronger than the balance sheet of a firm with an otherwise-identical capital lease. Given the choice, firms would probably classify

---

[3]The income statement is also affected. The asset created is amortized over the lease life and reported income is adjusted downward.

all their leases as operating ones. Because of this tendency, CICA 3065 states that a lease must be classified as a capital one if at least one of the following four criteria is met:

1. The lease transfers ownership of the property to the lessee by the end of the term of the lease.

2. The lessee has an option to purchase the asset at a price below fair market value (bargain purchase price option) when the lease expires.

3. The lease term is 75 percent or more of the estimated economic life of the asset.

4. The present value of the lease payments is at least 90 percent of the asset's fair market value at the start of the lease.[4]

A firm might be tempted to try to cook the books by taking advantage of the somewhat arbitrary distinction between operating leases and capital leases. Suppose a trucking firm wants to lease the $100,000 truck in our example in Table 22.1. The truck is expected to last for 15 years. A (perhaps unethical) financial manager could try to negotiate a lease contract for 10 years with lease payments having a present value of $89,000. These terms would get around criteria 3 and 4. If criteria 1 and 2 are similarly circumvented, the arrangement would be an operating lease and would not show up on the balance sheet.

Does this sort of gimmickry pay? The semistrong form of the efficient capital markets hypothesis implies that stock prices reflect all publicly available information. As we discussed earlier in this text, the empirical evidence generally supports this form of the hypothesis. Though operating leases do not appear in the firm's balance sheet, information on these leases must be disclosed elsewhere in the annual report. All of this suggests that attempts to keep leases off the balance sheet will not affect stock price in an efficient capital market.

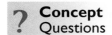 **Concept Questions**

- Define the terms *capital lease* and *operating lease*.
- How are capital leases reported in a firm's financial statements?

TABLE 22.1
Leasing and the Balance Sheet

Balance Sheet				
1. Initial balance sheet (the company buys a $100,000 truck with debt)				
Truck	$100,000	Debt		$100,000
Other assets	100,000	Equity		100,000
Total assets	$200,000	Total debt plus equity		$200,000
2. Operating lease (the company has an operating lease for the truck)				
Truck	$ 0	Debt		$ 0
Other assets	100,000	Equity		100,000
Total assets	$100,000	Total debt plus equity		$100,000
3. Capital (financial) lease (the company has a capital lease for the truck)				
Assets under		Obligations under		
capital lease	$100,000	capital lease		$100,000
Other assets	100,000	Equity		100,000
Total assets	$200,000	Total debt plus equity		$200,000

In the first case, a $100,000 truck is purchased with debt. In the second case, an operating lease is used; no balance sheet entries are created. In the third case, a capital (financial) lease is used; the lease payments are capitalized as a liability, and the leased truck appears as an asset.

---

[4]For more accounting information on leases, see T. H. Beechy and J. E. D. Conrod, Chapter 17: "Accounting for Leases" in *Intermediate Accounting Vol. II,* 3rd ed., McGraw-Hill Ryserson, 2005.

22.3 Taxes and Leases

The lessee can deduct lease payments for income tax purposes if the lease is qualified under tax law. The tax shields associated with lease payments are critical to the economic viability of a lease, so guidelines are an important consideration. Tax rules on leasing have changed considerably in the past few years and further changes may occur. The discussion that follows summarizes the rules in force at the time of writing.

Essentially, the Canada Revenue Agency (CRA) requires that a lease be primarily for business purposes and not merely for tax avoidance. In particular, CRA is on the lookout for leases that are really conditional sales agreements in disguise. The reason is that, in a lease, the lessee gets a tax deduction on the full lease payment. In a conditional sales agreement, only the interest portion of the payment is deductible. If CRA detects one or more of the following, the lease will be disallowed:[5]

1. The lessee automatically acquires title to the property after payment of a specified amount in the form of rentals.

2. The lessee is required to buy the property from the lessor during or at the termination of the lease.

3. The lessee has the right during or at the expiration of the lease to acquire the property at a price less than fair market value.

These rules also apply to sale and lease-back agreements. CRA auditors will rule that a sale and lease-back is really a secured loan if they find one of the above clauses in the agreement.

Once leases are qualified for tax purposes, lessors still must be aware of further tax regulations limiting their use of CCA tax shields on leased assets. Current regulations allow lessors to deduct CCA from leasing income only. Any unused CCA tax shields cannot be passed along to other companies owned by the same parent holding company.

CCA rules limit the tax advantages of sale and lease-backs. The rules place strict limits on a lessor's CCA write-offs on expensive assets, such as aircraft. The result is that big deals are done offshore, such as through U.S. lessors, where the restriction does not apply.

? Concept Questions
- **Why is the Canada Revenue Agency concerned about leasing?**
- **What are some standards the Canada Revenue Agency uses in evaluating a lease?**

22.4 The Cash Flows of Financial Leasing

To begin our analysis of the leasing decision, we need to identify the relevant cash flows. The first part of this section illustrates how this is done. A key point, and one to watch for, is that taxes are a very important consideration in a lease analysis.

---

[5]Note that the Canada Revenue Agency tax rules are different from the CICA's accounting rules. For more details on these conditions, see Interpretation Bulletin IT-233R and updates.

The Incremental Cash Flows

Consider the business decision facing TransCanada Distributors, a distribution firm that runs a fleet of company cars for its sales staff. Business has been expanding and the firm needs 50 more cars to provide basic transportation in support of sales. The type of car required can be purchased wholesale for $20,000. TransCanada has determined that each car can be expected to generate $12,000 per year in added sales for the next five years.

TransCanada has a corporate tax rate (combined federal and provincial) of 40 percent. The cars would qualify for a CCA rate of 40 percent and, due to the hard-driving habits of TransCanada's sales staff, the cars would have no residual value after five years. Financial Lease Co. has offered to lease the cars to TransCanada for lease payments of $5,000 per year for each car over the five-year period. Lease payments are made at the beginning of the year. With the lease, TransCanada would remain responsible for maintenance, insurance, and operating expenses.

Susan Smart, a recently hired MBA, has been asked to compare the direct incremental cash flows from leasing the cars to the cash flows associated with buying them. The first thing she realizes is that, because TransCanada will have the cars either way, the $12,000 saving will be realized whether the cars are leased or purchased. Thus, this sales increase and any other operating costs or revenues can be ignored in the analysis because they are not incremental.

Upon reflection, Ms. Smart concludes that there are only three important cash flow differences between financial leasing and buying.[6]

1. If the cars are leased, TransCanada must make a lease payment of $5,000 each year. However, lease payments are fully tax deductible, so there is a tax shield of $2,000 on each lease payment. The after-tax lease payment is $5,000 − $2,000 = $3,000. This is a cost of leasing instead of buying.[7]

2. If the cars are leased, TransCanada does not own them and cannot depreciate them for tax purposes.

3. If the cars are leased, TransCanada does not have to spend $20,000 apiece today to buy them. This is a benefit to leasing.

Table 22.2 shows the CCA and undepreciated capital cost (UCC) schedule for one car. Notice that under the half-year rule the eligible UCC is only $10,000 when the car is put

TABLE 22.2
Tax Shield on CCA for Car

Year	UCC	CCA	Tax Shield
0	$10,000	$4,000	$1,600
1	16,000	6,400	2,560
2	9,600	3,840	1,536
3	5,760	2,304	922
4	3,456	1,382	553
5	2,074		830

---

[6]There is fourth consequence that we do not discuss here. If the car has a nontrivial salvage value and we lease, we give up that salvage value. This is another cost of leasing instead of buying.

[7]Lease payments are made at the beginning of the year, as shown in Table 22.3. Firms pay taxes later, but our analysis ignores this difference for simplicity.

in use in period 0.[8] Table 22.2 also shows the tax shield on CCA for each year. For example, in period zero, the tax shield is $4,000 \times 0.40 = 1,600$. The tax shields for years 1 through 4 are calculated in the same way. In year 5, the car is scrapped for a zero salvage value. We assume that the asset pool is closed at this time, so there is a tax shield on the terminal loss of $2,074 \times 0.40 = 830$.[9] All these tax shields are lost to TransCanada if it leases so they are a cost of leasing.

The cash flows from leasing instead of buying are summarized in Table 22.3. Notice that the car's cost shows up with a positive sign in year 0, reflecting the fact that TransCanada *saves* $15,400 by leasing instead of buying. We could have expressed the cash flows from the purchase relative to the cash flows from leasing. These cash flows would be

	Year					
	0	1	2	3	4	5
Net cash flows from purchase alternative relative to lease alternative	−$15,400	$5,560	$4,536	$3,922	$3,553	$830

Of course, the cash flows here are the opposite of those in the bottom line of Table 22.3. Depending on our purpose, we may look at either the purchase relative to the lease or vice versa. Students should become comfortable with either viewpoint.

Now that we have the cash flows, we can make our decision by discounting the flows properly. However, because the discount rate is tricky, we take a detour in the next section before moving back to the TransCanada case. There we show that cash flows in the lease-versus-buy decision should be discounted at the after-tax interest rate—the after-tax cost of debt capital.

TABLE 22.3
Incremental Cash Flows for TransCanada from Leasing One Car Instead of Buying

	Year					
	0	1	2	3	4	5
Investment	$20,000					
Lease payment	−5,000	−$5,000	−$5,000	−$5,000	−$5,000	
Payment shield	2,000	2,000	2,000	2,000	2,000	
Forgone tax shield	−1,600	−2,560	−1,536	−922	−553	−$830
Total cash flow	$15,400	−$5,560	−$4,536	−$3,922	−$3,553	−$830

Concept Questions

- What are the cash flow consequences of leasing instead of buying?
- Explain why the $15,400 in Table 22.3 has a positive sign.

---

[8]The purchased car is put in use in period 0 to be consistent with the leasing alternative under which the first payment is made in period 0. Note that the UCC starts in period 0 here. In Chapter 8, the UCC starts at period 1 but does not include period 0. Both labelling methods are accurate and will result in the same CCA calculations.

[9]If the pool were continued, the remaining UCC of $2,074 would be depreciated to infinity as explained in Appendix 8A. To make the example simple and easy to follow, we assume that the asset pool will be closed. In practice, however, it is unrealistic to assume that the asset pool will be closed and would be depreciated to infinity. We illustrate this later.

22.5 A Detour on Discounting and Debt Capacity with Corporate Taxes

The analysis of leases is difficult, so both financial practitioners and academics have made conceptual errors. These errors revolve around taxes. We hope to avoid their mistakes by beginning with the simplest type of example, a loan for one year. Though this example is unrelated to our lease-versus-buy situation, principles developed here will apply directly to lease–buy analysis.

Present Value of Riskless Cash Flows

Consider a corporation that lends $100 for a year. If the interest rate is 11 percent, the firm will receive $111 at the end of the year. Of this amount, $11 is interest and the remaining $100 is the original principal. A corporate tax rate of 40 percent implies taxes on the interest of $4.40 (or 0.40 × $11). Thus, the firm ends up with $106.60 (or $111 − $4.40) after taxes on a $100 investment.

Now, consider a company that borrows $100 for a year. With an 11 percent interest rate, the firm must pay $111 to the bank at the end of the year. However, the borrowing firm can take the $11 of interest as a tax deduction. The corporation pays $4.40 (or 0.40 × $11) less in taxes than it would have paid had it not borrowed the money at all. Thus, considering this reduction in taxes, the firm must pay $106.60 (or $111 − $4.40) on a $100 loan. The cash flows from both lending and borrowing are displayed in Table 22.4.

The above two paragraphs show a very important result: The firm is indifferent between receiving $100 today or $106.60 next year. If it received $100 today, it could lend it out, thereby receiving $106.60 after corporate taxes at the end of the year. Conversely, if it knows today that it will receive $106.60 at the end of the year, it could borrow $100 today. The after-tax interest and principal payments on the loan would be paid with the $106.60 that the firm will receive at the end of the year. Because of the interchangeability illustrated above, we say that a payment of $106.60 next year has a present value of $100. Because $100 = $106.60/1.066, a riskless cash flow should be discounted at the after-tax interest rate of 0.066 [or 0.11 × (1 − 0.40)].

TABLE 22.4
Lending and Borrowing in a World with Corporate Taxes (with 11 percent interest rate and 40 percent corporate tax rate)

Date 0	Date 1
Lending example	
Lend −$100	Receive +$100.00 of principal
	Receive +$ 11.00 of interest
6.6% lending rate	Pay −$ 4.40 (= −0.40 × $11) in taxes
	+$106.60
After-tax lending rate is 6.6%.	
Borrowing example	
Borrow +$100	Pay −$100.00 of principal
	Pay −$ 11.00 of interest
6.6% borrowing rate	Receive +$ 4.40 (= 0.40 × $11) as a tax rebate
	−$106.60
After-tax borrowing rate is 6.6%.	

General principle: In a world with corporate taxes, riskless cash flows should be discounted at the after-tax interest rate.

Our discussion considers a specific example. The general principle is

> In a world with corporate taxes, the firm should discount riskless cash flows at the after-tax riskless rate of interest.

Optimal Debt Level and Riskless Cash Flows (Advanced)

In addition, our simple example can illustrate a related point concerning the optimal debt level. Consider a firm that has just determined that the current level of debt in its capital structure is optimal. Immediately following that determination, the firm is surprised to learn that it will receive a guaranteed payment of $106.60 in one year from, say, a tax-exempt government lottery. This future windfall is an asset that, like any asset, should raise the firm's optimal debt level. How much does this payment raise the firm's optimal level?

Our analysis above implies that the firm's optimal debt level must be $100 more than it previously was. That is, the firm could borrow $100 today, perhaps paying the entire amount out as a dividend. It would owe the bank $111 at the end of the year. However, because it receives a tax rebate of $4.40 (or 0.40 × $11), its net repayment will be $106.60. Thus, its borrowing of $100 today is fully offset by next year's government lottery proceeds of $106.60. In other words, the lottery proceeds act as an irrevocable trust that can service the increased debt. Note that we need not know the optimal debt level before the lottery was announced. We are merely saying that, whatever this prelottery optimal level was, the optimal debt level is $100 more after the lottery announcement.

Of course, this is just one example. The general principle is[10]

> In a world with corporate taxes, one determines the increase in the firm's optimal debt level by discounting a future guaranteed after-tax inflow at the after-tax riskless interest rate.

Conversely, suppose that a second and unrelated firm is surprised to learn that it must pay $106.60 next year to the government for back taxes. Clearly, this additional liability impinges on the second firm's debt capacity. By the same reasoning, it follows that the second firm's optimal debt level must be lowered by exactly $100.

? Concept Questions
• **How should one discount a riskless cash flow?**

22.6 NPV Analysis of the Lease-Versus-Buy Decision

The detour leads to a simple method for evaluating leases: discount all cash flows at the after-tax interest rate. From the bottom line of Table 22.3, TransCanada's incremental cash flows from leasing versus purchasing are

	Year					
	0	1	2	3	4	5
Net cash flows from lease alternative relative to purchase alternative	$15,400	−$5,560	−$4,536	−$3,922	−$3,553	−$830

[10]This principle holds for riskless or guaranteed cash flows only. Unfortunately, there is no easy formula for determining the increase in optimal debt level from a *risky* cash flow.

Let us assume that TransCanada can either borrow or lend at the 11 percent interest rate. If the corporate tax rate is 40 percent, the correct discount rate is the after-tax rate of 6.6 percent we used earlier [$11\% \times (1 - 0.40)$]. When 6.6 percent is used to compute the NPV of the lease, we have

$$NPV = \$15,400 - \frac{\$5,560}{(1.066)} - \frac{\$4,536}{(1.066)^2} - \frac{\$3,922}{(1.066)^3} - \frac{\$3,553}{(1.066)^4} -$$
$$\frac{\$830}{(1.066)^5} = -\$399.61 \tag{22.1}$$

Because the net present value of the incremental cash flows from leasing relative to purchasing is negative, TransCanada prefers to purchase.

Equation (22.1) is the correct approach to lease-versus-buy analysis. However, students are often bothered by three things. First, they question whether the cash flows in Table 22.3 are truly riskless. Second, they wonder how the cash flow and calculations would change when the asset pool stays open and salvage is not zero. We examine these two issues next. Third, they feel that this approach lacks intuition. We address this concern a little later.

The Discount Rate

Because we discounted at the after-tax riskless rate of interest, we have implicitly assumed that the cash flows in the TransCanada example are riskless. Is this appropriate?

A lease payment is like the debt service on a secured bond issued by the lessee, and the discount rate should be approximately the same as the interest rate on such debt. In general, this rate will be slightly higher than the riskless rate considered in the previous section. The various tax shields could be somewhat riskier than the lease payments for two reasons. First, the value of the CCA tax benefits depends on TransCanada's ability to generate enough taxable income to use them. Second, the corporate tax rate may change. For these two reasons, a firm might be justified in discounting the CCA tax benefits at a rate higher than that used for the lease payments. However, our experience is that, in practice, companies discount both the CCA shield and lease payments at the same rate. This implies that financial practitioners view the above two risks as minor. We adopt the pragmatic convention of discounting the two flows at the same rate—the after-tax interest rate on secured debt issued by the lessee.

At this point some students still ask the question, Why not use r_{WACC} as the discount rate in lease-versus-buy analysis? But r_{WACC} should not be used for lease analysis because the cash flows are more like debt-service cash flows than operating cash flows, so the risk is much less. The discount rate should reflect the risk of the incremental cash flows.

Asset Pool and Salvage Value

The TransCanada example where the asset pool is assumed to close and the salvage value of the vehicle is assumed to be zero at the end of four years is simplistic. In reality, this may occur in some circumstances but in most situations the asset pool will remain open and the car will have some resale value. To illustrate, we assume that the vehicle will have approximately a $1,000 resale value.

Assuming that the asset pool will not close after the lease is complete, Table 22.5 shows the incremental cash flows for TransCanada excluding the forgone tax shield.

The present value of these payments, using the 6.6 percent discount rate calculated earlier is

$$PV = \$17,000.00 - \frac{\$3,000.00}{1.066} - \frac{\$3,000.00}{(1.066)^2} - \frac{\$3,000.00}{(1.066)^3} - \frac{\$4,000.00}{(1.066)^4} = \$5,971.42$$

TABLE 22.5
Incremental Cash Flows for TransCanada from Leasing One Car Instead of Buying

	0	1	2	3	4
Investment	$20,000				
Lease payment	−5,000	−$5,000	−$5,000	−$5,000	−$5,000
Payment shield	2,000	2,000	2,000	2,000	2,000
Salvage value					−1,000
	$17,000	−$3,000	−$3,000	−$3,000	−$4,000

Assuming that the salvage value for the vehicle is $1,000 at the end of four years, the present value of the CCA tax shield is

$$
\begin{aligned}
\text{PV} &= \frac{[CdT_c]}{k + d} \times \frac{[1 + 0.5k]}{1 + k} - \frac{SdT_c}{k + d} \times \frac{1}{(1 + k)^n} \\
&= \frac{(\$20,000)(0.40)(0.40)}{0.066 + 0.40} \times \frac{[1 + 0.5(0.066)]}{1 + 0.066} - \frac{(\$1,000)(0.40)(0.40)}{0.066 + 0.40} \times \frac{1}{(1 + 0.066)^4} \\
&= \$6,866.95 \times 0.9690 - \$343.35 \times 0.7744 \\
&= \$6,388.48
\end{aligned}
$$

These revised calculations show that the net present value of leasing one car instead of buying amounts to $5,971.42 − $6388.48 = −$417.06 when the vehicle has a salvage value of $1,000. Given that the NPV is negative, it would be better to buy the vehicle than to lease. The result is quite close to our previous answer where it was also more beneficial to buy than lease.

22.7 Debt Displacement and Lease Valuation

The Basic Concept of Debt Displacement (Advanced)

The previous analysis allows one to calculate the right answer in a simple manner. Although simplicity is an important benefit, the analysis has little intuitive appeal. To remedy this, we hope to make lease–buy analysis more intuitive by considering the issue of debt displacement.

A firm that purchases equipment will generally issue debt to finance the purchase and the debt becomes a liability of the firm. A lessee incurs a liability equal to the present value of all future lease payments. This comparison suggests that leases displace debt. The balance sheets in Table 22.6 illustrate how leasing might affect debt.

Suppose a firm initially has $100,000 of assets and a 150 percent optimal debt–equity ratio. The firm's debt is $60,000, and its equity is $40,000. Suppose the firm must use a new $10,000 machine. The firm has two alternatives:

1. *The firm can purchase the machine.* If it does, it will finance the purchase with a secured loan and with equity. The debt capacity of the machine is assumed to be the same as for the firm as a whole.

2. *The firm can lease the asset and get 100 percent financing.* That is, the present value of the future lease payments will be $10,000.

If the firm finances the machine with both secured debt and new equity, its debt will increase by $6,000 and its equity by $4,000. Its optimal debt–equity ratio of 150 percent will be maintained.

TABLE 22.6
Debt Displacement Elsewhere in the Firm When a Lease Is Instituted

Assets		Liabilities	
Initial situation			
Current	$ 50,000	Debt	$ 60,000
Fixed	50,000	Equity	40,000
Total	$100,000	Total	$100,000
Buy with secured loan			
Current	$ 50,000	Debt	$ 66,000
Fixed	50,000	Equity	44,000
Machine	10,000		
Total	$110,000	Total	$110,000
Lease			
Current	$ 50,000	Lease	$ 10,000
Fixed	50,000	Debt	56,000
Machine	10,000	Equity	44,000
Total	$110,000	Total	$110,000

This example shows that leases reduce the level of debt elsewhere in the firm. Though the example illustrates a point, it is not meant to show a *precise* method for calculating debt displacement.

Conversely, consider the lease alternative. Because the lessee views the lease payment as a liability, the lessee thinks in terms of a *liability-to-equity* ratio, not just a debt-to-equity ratio. As mentioned above, the present value of the lease liability is $10,000. If the leasing firm is to maintain a liability-to-equity ratio of 150 percent, debt elsewhere in the firm must fall by $4,000 when the lease is instituted. Because debt must be repurchased, net liabilities only rise by $6,000 (or $10,000 − $4,000) when $10,000 of assets are placed under lease.[11]

Debt displacement is a hidden cost of leasing. If a firm leases, it will not use as much regular debt as it would otherwise. The benefits of debt capacity will be lost, particularly the lower taxes associated with interest expense.

Optimal Debt Level in the TransCanada Example (Advanced)

The previous section showed that leasing displaces debt. Though the section illustrated a point, it was not meant to show the precise method for calculating debt displacement. Below, we describe the precise method for calculating the difference in optimal debt levels between purchase and lease in the TransCanada example.

From the last line of Table 22.3, we know that the cash flows from the *purchase* alternative relative to the cash flows from the lease alternative are[12]

	Year					
	0	1	2	3	4	5
Net cash flows from purchase alternative relative to lease alternative	−$15,400	$5,560	$4,536	$3,922	$3,553	$830

---

[11]In practice, growing firms generally will not repurchase debt when instituting a lease. Rather, they will issue less debt in the future than they would have without the lease.

[12]The last line of Table 22.3 presents the cash flows from the lease alternative relative to the purchase alternative. As pointed out earlier, our cash flows are now reversed because we are now presenting the cash flows from the purchase alternative relative to the lease alternative.

An increase in the optimal debt level at year 0 occurs because the firm learns at that time of guaranteed cash flows beginning at year 1. Our detour on discounting and debt capacity taught us to calculate this increased debt level by discounting the future riskless cash inflows at the after-tax interest rate. Thus, the additional debt level of the purchase alternative relative to the lease alternative is

$$\text{Increase in optimal debt level from purchase alternative} = \$15{,}799.61 = \frac{\$5{,}560}{(1.066)} + \frac{\$4{,}536}{(1.066)^2} + \frac{\$3{,}922}{(1.066)^3} + \frac{\$3{,}553}{(1.066)^4} + \frac{\$830}{(1.066)^5}$$

That is, whatever the optimal amount of debt under the lease alternative, the optimal amount of debt will be $15,799.61 higher under the purchase alternative.

This result can be stated in another way. Imagine there are two identical firms except that one firm purchases a corporate car and the other leases it. From Table 22.3, we know that the purchasing firm generates more cash flow after taxes in each of the five years than does the leasing firm. Further, imagine that the same bank lends money to both firms. The bank should lend the purchasing firm more money because it has a greater cash flow each period. How much extra money should the bank lend the purchasing firm so that the incremental loan can be paid off by the extra cash flows shown in Table 22.3? The answer is exactly $15,799.61, the increase in the optimal debt level we calculated earlier.

To see this, Table 22.7 works through the example on a year-by-year basis. Because the purchasing firm borrows $15,799.61 more at year 0 than does the leasing firm, the purchasing firm will pay interest of $1737.96 (or $15,799.61 × 0.11) at year 1 on the additional debt. The interest allows the firm to reduce its taxes by $695.18 (or $1,737.96 × 0.40), leaving an after-tax interest expense of $1,042.78 (or $1,737.96 − $695.18) at year 1.

We know from Table 22.3 that the purchasing firm generates $5,560 more cash at year 1 than does the leasing firm. Because the purchasing firm has the extra $5,560 coming in at year 1 but must pay interest on its loan, how much of the loan can the firm repay at year 1 and still have the same cash flow as the leasing firm has? The purchasing firm can repay $4,517.33 of the loan at year 1 and still have the same net cash flow that the leasing firm has. After the repayment, the purchasing firm will have a remaining balance of $11,282.38 (or $15,799.61 − $4,517.33) at year 1. For each of the five years, this sequence of cash flows is displayed in Table 22.7. The outstanding balance goes to zero over the five

TABLE 22.7
Calculation of Increase in Optimal Debt Level if TransCanada Purchases Instead of Leases

	Year					
	0	1	2	3	4	5
Outstanding balance of loan	$15,799.61	$11,282.38**	$7,491.02	$4,063.43	$ 778.62	$ 0.00
Interest		1,737.96	1,241.06	824.01	446.98	85.65
Tax deduction on interest		695.18	496.42	329.60	178.79	34.26
After-tax interest expenses		1,042.77	744.64	494.41	268.19	51.39
Extra cash that purchasing firm generates over leasing firm (from Table 22.3)		5,560.00	4,536.00	3,922.00	3,553.00	830.00
Repayment of loan		$ 4,517.23*	$3,791.36	$3,427.59	$3,284.81	$778.61

* $4,517.23 = $5,560.00 − $1,042.77
** $11,282.38 = $15,799.61 − $4,517.23

years. Thus, the cash flows shown at the bottom of Table 22.3, which represent the extra cash from purchasing instead of leasing, fully amortize the loan of $15,799.61.

Our analysis of debt capacity has two purposes. First, we want to show the additional debt capacity from purchasing, and we just completed this task. Second, we want to determine whether or not the lease is preferred to the purchase. This decision rule follows easily from our discussion. By leasing the equipment and having $15,799.61 less debt than under the purchase alternative, the firm has exactly the same cash flow in years 1 to 5 that it would have through a levered purchase. Thus, we can ignore cash flows beginning in year 1 when comparing the lease alternative with the purchase-with-debt alternative. However, the cash flows differ between the alternatives at year 0. These differences are

1. *The purchase cost at year 0 of $15,400 is avoided by leasing.* This should be viewed as a cash inflow under the leasing alternative.
2. *The firm borrows $15,799.61 less at year 0 under the lease alternative than it can under the purchase alternative.* This should be viewed as a cash outflow under the leasing alternative.

Because the firm borrows $15,799.61 less by leasing but saves only $15,400 on the equipment, the lease alternative requires an extra cash outflow at year 0 relative to the purchase alternative of −$399.61 (or $15,400 − $15,799.61). Because cash flows in later years from leasing are identical to those from purchasing with debt, the firm should purchase.

This conclusion can be expressed another way by looking at the cash flows of the purchase alternative relative to those from the lease. Point 2 means that these incremental cash flows can service a loan of $15,799.61. However, buying instead of leasing requires an outlay of only $15,400 in year 0. Therefore, buying instead of leasing generates a surplus in year 0 (NPV) of $399.61.

This is exactly the same answer we got earlier in this chapter when we discounted all cash flows at the after-tax interest rate. Of course, this is no coincidence because the increase in the optimal debt level is also determined by discounting all flows at the after-tax interest rate. The following box presents both methods. (The numbers in the box are in terms of the NPV of the lease relative to the purchase. Thus, a negative NPV indicates that the purchase alternative should be taken.)

Two Methods for Calculating Net Present Value of Lease Relative to Purchase

Method 1: Discount all cash flows at the after-tax interest rate

$$-\$399.61 = \$15,400 - \text{PV (cash flows) at } 6.6\%$$
$$= \$15,400 - \$15,799.61$$

Method 2: Compare the purchase price with the reduction in optimal debt level under the leasing alternative

$$-\$399.61 = \$15,400 - \$15,799.61$$

$$\underset{\substack{\text{Purchase} \\ \text{price}}}{} - \underset{\substack{\text{Reductin in} \\ \text{optimal debt} \\ \text{level if leasing}}}{}$$

Note: Because we are calculating the NPV of the lease relative to the purchase, a negative value indicates that the purchase alternative is preferred.

22.8 Does Leasing Ever Pay? The Base Case

We previously looked at the lease-versus-buy decision from the perspective of the potential lessee, TransCanada Industries. We now turn things around and look at the lease from the perspective of the lessor, Financial Leasing. The cash flows associated with the lease from the lessor's perspective are shown in Table 22.8. First, the lessor must buy each car for $20,000, so there is a $20,000 outflow today. Next, Financial Leasing depreciates the machine at a CCA rate of 40 percent to obtain the CCA tax shields shown. Finally, the lessor receives a lease payment of $5,000 each year on which it pays taxes at a 40 percent tax rate. The after-tax lease payment received is $3,000.

Now examine the total cash flows to Financial Leasing, as displayed in the bottom line of Table 22.8. Readers with a good memory will notice something very interesting. These cash flows are exactly the opposite of those of TransCanada, as displayed in the bottom line of Table 22.3. Readers with a healthy sense of skepticism may be thinking something very interesting: "If the cash flows of the lessor are exactly the opposite of those of the lessee, the combined cash flow of the two parties must be zero each year. Thus, there does not seem to be any joint benefit to this lease. Because the net present value to the lessee was −$399.61, the NPV to the lessor must be $399.61. The joint NPV is $0 (or −$399.61 + 399.61). There does not appear to be any way for the NPV of both the lessor and the lessee to be positive at the same time. Because one party would inevitably lose money, the leasing deal could never fly."

This is one of the most important results of leasing. Though Table 22.8 concerns one particular leasing deal, the principle can be generalized. As long as (1) both parties are subject to the same interest and tax rates and (2) transaction costs are ignored, there can be no leasing deal that benefits both parties. However, there is a lease payment for which both parties would calculate an NPV of zero. For that lease payment, TransCanada would be indifferent to whether it leased or bought, and Financial Leasing would be indifferent to whether it leased or not. To find the indifference lease payment, we rerun our leasing spreadsheet from Table 22.8, setting the NPV of leasing equal to zero. Table 22.9 shows that the indifference lease payment is $4,849.25.

A student with a healthy sense of skepticism might say, "This textbook appears to be arguing that leasing is not beneficial. Yet, we know that leasing occurs frequently in the real world. Maybe, just maybe, the textbook is wrong." Although we will not admit to being wrong (what textbook would!), we freely admit to being incomplete at this point. The next section considers factors that create benefits to leasing.

TABLE 22.8
Cash Flows to the Lessor

	Year					
	0	1	2	3	4	5
Investment	−$20,000.00					
Lease payment	5,000.00	$5,000	$5,000	$5,000	$5,000	
Payment shield	−2,000.00	−2,000	−2,000	−2,000	−2,000	
Forgone tax shield	1,600.00	2,560	1,536	922	553	$830
Total cash flow	−$15,400.00	$5,560	$4,536	$3,922	$3,553	$830
NPV	$ 399.61					

TABLE 22.9
Indifference Lease Payments

	Year					
	0	1	2	3	4	5
Investment	$20,000.00					
Lease payment	−4,849.25	−$4,849.25	−$4,849.25	−$4,849.25	−$4,849.25	
Payment shield	1,939.70	1,939.70	1,939.70	1,939.70	1,939.70	
Forgone tax shield	−1,600.00	−2,560.00	−1,536.00	−922.00	−553.00	−$830.00
Total cash flow	$15,490.45	−$5,469.55	−$4,445.55	−$3,831.55	−$3,462.55	−$830.00
NPV	$ 0.00					

22.9 Reasons for Leasing

Proponents of leasing make many claims about why firms should lease assets rather than buy them. Some of the reasons given to support leasing are good, and some are not. We discuss here the reasons for leasing we think are good and some that we think are not so good.

Good Reasons for Leasing

If leasing is a good choice, it is because one or more of the following is true:

1. Taxes may be reduced by leasing.
2. The lease contract may reduce certain types of uncertainty.
3. Transactions costs can be higher for buying an asset and financing it with debt or equity than for leasing the asset.

Tax Advantages   By far the most important reason for long-term leasing is tax avoidance. If the corporate income tax were repealed, long-term leasing would become much less important. A lease contract is not a zero sum game between the lessee and lessor when their effective tax rates differ. In this case, the lease can be structured so that both sides benefit. Any tax benefits from leasing can be split between the two firms by setting the lease payments at the appropriate level, and the shareholders of both firms will benefit from this tax transfer arrangement.

This works because a lease contract swaps two sets of tax shields. The lessor obtains the CCA tax shields due to ownership. The lessee receives the tax shield on lease payments made. In a full-payout lease, the total dollar amounts of the two sets of tax shields may be roughly the same, but the critical difference is the timing. CCA tax shields are accelerated deductions reducing the tax burden in early years. Lease payments, on the other hand, reduce taxes by the same amount in every year. As a result, the ownership tax shields often have a greater present value provided the firm is fully taxed.

The basic logic behind structuring a leasing deal makes a firm in a high tax bracket want to act as the lessor. Low-tax (or untaxed) firms will be lessees, because they will not be able to use the tax advantages of ownership, such as CCA and debt financing. These ownership tax shields are worth less to the lessee in this case because the lessee faces a lower tax rate or may not have enough taxable income to absorb the accelerated tax shields in the early years.

Overall, less tax is paid by the lessee and lessor combined, and this tax savings occurs sooner rather than later. The lessor gains on the tax side; the lessee may lose but the amount of any loss is less than the lessor gains. To make the lease attractive, the lessor must pass on some of the tax savings in the form of lower lease payments. In the end, the lessor gains by keeping part of the tax savings, the lessee gains through a lower lease payment, and both gains are paid for through a reduction in tax revenue.

To see how this would work in practice, recall the example of Section 22.8 and the situation of Financial Leasing. The value of the lease it proposed to TransCanada was $399.61. However, the value of the lease to TransCanada was exactly the opposite, −$399.61. Since the lessor's gains came at the expense of the lessee, no deal could be arranged. However, if TransCanada paid no taxes and the lease payments were reduced to $4,874 from $5,000, both Financial Leasing and TransCanada would find there is positive NPV in leasing.

To see this, we can rework Table 22.8 with a zero tax rate. This would occur when TransCanada has enough alternative tax shields to reduce taxable income to zero for the foreseeable future.[13] In this case, notice that the cash flows from leasing are simply the lease payments of $4,874 because no CCA tax shield is lost and the lease payment is not tax deductible. The cash flows from leasing are thus:

	Year					
	0	1	2	3	4	5
Cost of car	$20,000					
Lease payment	−4,874	−$4,874	−$4,874	−$4,874	−$4,874	0
Cash flow	$15,126	−$4,874	−$4,874	−$4,874	−$4,874	0

The value of the lease for TransCanada is

$$NPV = \$15,126 - \$4,874 \times A_{0.11}^{4}$$
$$= \$4.68$$

which is positive. Notice that the discount rate here is 11 percent because TransCanada pays no taxes; in other words, this is both the pre-tax and after-tax rate.

From Table 22.10, the value of the lease to Financial Leasing can be worked out as +$61.54. The discount rate for Financial Leasing is the after-tax rate of 6.6 percent.

TABLE 22.10
Revised Cash Flows to Lessor

	Year					
	0	1	2	3	4	5
Cost of car	−$20,000.00					
Lease payment	4,874.00	$4,874.00	$4,874.00	$4,874.00	$4,874.00	
Payment shield	−1,949.60	−1,949.60	−1,949.60	−1,949.60	−1,949.60	
CCA tax shield	1,600.00	2,560.00	1,536.00	922.00	553.00	$830.00
Total cash flow	−$15,475.60	$5,484.40	$4,460.40	$3,846.40	$3,477.40	$830.00
NPV lessor	$ 61.54					

---

[13]Strictly speaking, the UCC of the cars would be carried on the books until the firm were able to claim CCA. However, the present value of this deferred CCA tax shield would be low, so for the sake of simplicity, we ignore it here.

As a consequence of different tax rates, the lessee (TransCanada) gains $4.68, and the lessor (Financial Leasing) gains $61.54. What this example shows is that the lessor and the lessee can gain if their tax rates are different. The lease contract allows the lessor to take advantage of the CCA and interest tax shields that cannot be used by the lessee. Some of the tax gains to the lessor are passed on to the lessee in the form of lower lease payments.

Because both parties can gain when tax rates differ, the lease payment is agreed upon through negotiation. Before negotiation begins, each party needs to know the *reservation payment* of both parties. This is the payment such that one party will be indifferent to whether it entered the lease deal or not. In other words, this is the payment such that the value of the lease is zero. These payments are calculated below.

Reservation Payment of Lessee   We now solve for L_{MAX}, the payment such that the value of the lease to the lessee is zero. When the lessee is in a zero tax bracket, his cash flows, in terms of L_{MAX}, are:

	Year					
	0	1	2	3	4	5
Cost of machine	$20,000					
Lease payment		$-L_{\text{MAX}}$	$-L_{\text{MAX}}$	$-L_{\text{MAX}}$	$-L_{\text{MAX}}$	$-L_{\text{MAX}}$

This chart implies that:

$$\text{Value of lease} = \$20,000 - L_{\text{MAX}} \times A_{0.11}^{5}$$

The value of the lease equals zero when:

$$L_{\text{MAX}} = \frac{\$20,000}{A_{0.11}^{5}} = \$5,411.41$$

After performing this calculation, the lessor knows that he will never be able to charge a payment above $5,411.41.

Reservation Payment of Lessor   We now solve for L_{MIN}, the payment such that the value of the lease to the lessor is zero. The cash flows to the lessor, in terms of L_{MIN}, are:

	Year					
	0	1	2	3	4	5
Cost of machine	$-$20,000					
CCA tax shield		$ 1,600	$2,560	$1,536	$922	$533	$830
After-tax lease payment ($T_c = 0.40$)		$L_{\text{MIN}} \times (0.60)$	$L_{\text{MIN}} \times (0.60)$	$L_{\text{MIN}} \times (0.60)$	$L_{\text{MIN}} \times (0.60)$	$L_{\text{MIN}} \times (0.60)$

This chart implies that:

$$\text{Value of lease} = -\$20,000 + \text{PV}_{\text{CCA Tax Shield}} + L_{\text{MIN}} \times (0.60) \times A_{0.066}^{5}$$

The value of the lease equals zero when

$$L_{\text{MIN}} = \frac{\$20,000 - \$7130.05}{0.60 \times A_{0.066}^{5}}$$

$$= \frac{\$12,869.95}{2.487}$$

$$= \$5,174.89$$

After performing this calculation, the lessee knows that the lessor will never agree to a lease payment below $5,174.89.

A Reduction of Uncertainty   We have noted that the lessee does not own the property when the lease expires. The value of the property at this time is called the *residual value* and belongs to the lessor. When the lease contract is signed, there may be substantial uncertainty as to what the residual value of the asset will be. Thus, under a lease contract, this residual risk is borne by the lessor. Conversely, the user bears this risk when purchasing.

It is common sense that the party best able to bear a particular risk should do so. If the user firm has little risk aversion, it will not suffer by purchasing. However, if it is highly averse to risk, the user should find a third-party lessor more capable of assuming this burden.

This latter situation frequently arises when the user is a small or newly formed firm. Because the risk of the entire firm is likely to be quite high and because the principal shareholders are likely to be undiversified, the firm desires to minimize risk wherever possible. A potential lessor (such as a large, publicly held financial institution) is far more capable of bearing the risk. Conversely, this situation is unlikely when the user is a blue-chip corporation. That potential lessee is more able to bear risk.

Transactions Costs   The costs of changing an asset's ownership are generally greater than the costs of writing a lease agreement. Consider the choice that confronts a person who lives in Vancouver but must do business in Toronto for two days. Renting a hotel room for two nights is clearly cheaper than buying a condominium for two days and then selling it.

Unfortunately, leases generate agency costs as well. For example, the lessee might misuse or overuse the asset, since the lessee has no interest in the asset's residual value. This cost will be implicitly paid by the lessee through a high lease payment. Although the lessor can reduce these agency costs through monitoring, monitoring itself is costly.

Thus, leasing is most beneficial when the transaction costs of purchase and resale outweigh the agency costs and monitoring costs of a lease. Flath argues that this occurs in short-term leases but not in long-term leases.[14]

Bad Reasons for Leasing

Leasing and Accounting Income   In Section 22.2 ("Accounting and Leasing"), we pointed out that a firm's balance sheet shows fewer liabilities with an operating lease than with either a capitalized lease or a purchase financed with debt. We indicated that a firm desiring to project a strong balance sheet might select an operating lease. In addition, the firm's return on assets (ROA) is generally higher with an operating lease than with either a capitalized lease or a purchase. To see this, we examine, in turn, the numerator and denominator of the ROA formula.

With an operating lease, lease payments are treated as an expense. If the asset is purchased, both capital cost allowance and interest charges are expenses. At least in the early part of the asset's life, the yearly lease payment is generally less than the sum of yearly capital cost allowance and yearly interest. Thus, accounting income, the numerator of the ROA formula, is higher with an operating lease than with a purchase. Because accounting expenses with a capitalized lease are analogous to CCA and interest if the asset is purchased, accounting income does not increase when a lease is capitalized.

In addition, leased assets do not appear on the balance sheet with an operating lease. Thus, the total asset value of a firm, the denominator of the ROA formula, is smaller with an operating lease than it is with either a purchase or a capitalized lease. These two effects cause the firm's ROA to be higher with an operating lease than with either a purchase or a capitalized lease.

Of course, in an efficient capital market, accounting information cannot be used to fool investors. It is unlikely, then, that leasing's impact on accounting numbers should

---

[14]D. Flath, "The Economics of Short Term Leasing," *Economic Inquiry* 18 (April 1980).

create value for the firm. Savvy investors should be able to see through attempts by management to improve the firm's financial statements.

One Hundred Percent Financing   It is often claimed that leasing provides 100 percent financing, while secured equipment loans require an initial down payment. However, we argued earlier that leases tend to displace debt elsewhere in the firm. Our earlier analysis suggests that leases do not permit a greater level of total liabilities than do purchases with borrowing.

Other Reasons   There are, of course, many special reasons for some companies to find advantages in leasing. For example, leasing may be used to circumvent capital expenditure control systems set up by bureaucratic firms.

Leasing Decisions in Practice

The reduction-of-uncertainty motive for leasing is the one that is most often cited by corporations. For example, computers have a way of becoming technologically outdated very quickly, and computers are very commonly leased instead of purchased. In a U.S. survey, 82 percent of the responding firms cited the risk of obsolescence as an important reason for leasing, whereas only 57 percent cited the potential for cheaper financing.[15]

Yet, cheaper financing based on shifting tax shields is an important motive for leasing. One piece of evidence is Canadian lessors' strong reaction to 1989 changes in tax laws restricting sale and lease-backs. Further evidence comes from a study by Dipchand, Gudikunst, and Roberts analyzing decisions taken by Canadian railroads to lease rolling stock. They examined 20 lease contracts and found that, in 17 cases, leasing provided cheaper financing than debt.[16] Shanker confirmed the importance of taxes in leasing decisions.[17] Looking at financial information for Canadian firms between 1985 and 1995, she showed that firms with lower marginal tax rates tend to use more lease financing.

? **Concept** Questions

• **Summarize the good and bad arguments for leasing.**

22.10 Some Unanswered Questions

Our analysis suggests that the primary advantage of long-term leasing results from the differential tax rates of the lessor and the lessee. Other valid reasons for leasing are lower contracting costs and risk reduction. There are several questions our analysis has not specifically answered.

Are the Uses of Leases and of Debt Complementary?

Ang and Peterson find that firms with high debt tend to lease frequently as well.[18] This result should not be puzzling. The corporate attributes that support high debt capacity may also make leasing advantageous. Thus, even though leasing displaces debt (that is, leasing

[15]T. K. Mukherjee, "A Survey of Corporate Leasing Analysis," *Financial Management* 20 (Autumn 1991), pp. 96–107.

[16]C. R. Dipchand, A. C. Gudikunst, and G. S. Roberts, "An Empirical Analysis of Canadian Railroad Leases," *Journal of Financial Research* 3 (Spring 1980), pp. 57–67.

[17]L. Shanker, "Tax Effects and the Leasing Decisions of Canadian Corporations," *Canadian Journal of Administrative Sciences* 14 (June 1997), pp. 195–205.

[18]J. Ang and P. P. Peterson, "The Leasing Puzzle," *Journal of Finance* 39 (September 1984).

and borrowing are substitutes) for an individual firm, high debt and extensive leasing can go hand in hand.

Why Are Leases Offered by Both Manufacturers and Third-Party Lessors?

The offsetting effects of taxes can explain why both manufacturers and third-party lessors offer leases:

1. For manufacturer lessors, the basis for determining capital cost allowance is the manufacturer's cost. For third-party lessors, the basis is the sales price that the lessor paid to the manufacturer. Because the sales price is generally greater than the manufacturer's cost, this is an advantage to third-party lessors.

2. However, the manufacturer must recognize a profit for tax purposes when selling the asset to the third-party lessor. The manufacturer's profit for some equipment can be deferred if the manufacturer becomes the lessor. This provides an incentive for manufacturers to lease.

Why Are Some Assets Leased More Commonly Than Others?

Certain assets appear to be leased more frequently than others. Smith and Wakeman have looked at nontax incentives affecting leasing.[19] Their analysis suggests that asset and firm characteristics are important in the lease-or-buy decision:

1. The more sensitive is the value of an asset to use and maintenance decisions, the more likely it is that the asset will be purchased instead of leased. Ownership provides a better incentive to minimize maintenance costs than does leasing.

2. Price discrimination opportunities may be important. Leasing may be a way for a manufacturer to charge a lower price to one group of customers who lease its product while keeping prices up for other customers who buy.

22.11   SUMMARY AND CONCLUSIONS

A large fraction of equipment is leased rather than purchased. This chapter describes the institutional arrangements surrounding leases and shows how to evaluate leases financially.

1. Leases can be separated into two types: financial and operating. Financial leases are generally longer-term, fully amortized, and not cancellable. In effect, the lessor obtains economic but not legal ownership. Operating leases are usually shorter-term, partially amortized, and cancellable and can be likened to a rental agreement.

2. When a firm purchases an asset with debt, both the asset and the liability appear on the firm's balance sheet. If a lease meets at least one of a number of criteria, it must be capitalized. This means that the present value of the lease appears as both an asset and a liability. A lease escapes capitalization if it does not meet any of these criteria. Leases not meeting the criteria are called *operating leases,* though the accountant's definition differs somewhat from the practitioner's definition. Operating leases do not appear on the balance sheet. For cosmetic reasons, many firms prefer that a lease be called *operating.*

[19]C. W. Smith, Jr., and L. M. Wakeman, "Determinants of Corporate Leasing Policy," *Journal of Finance* (July 1985).

3. Firms generally lease for tax purposes. To protect its interests, the Canada Revenue Agency allows financial arrangements to be classified as leases only if a number of criteria are met.

4. We showed that risk-free cash flows should be discounted at the after-tax, risk-free rate. Because both lease payments and CCA tax shields are nearly riskless, all relevant cash flows in the lease–buy decision should be discounted at a rate near this after-tax rate. We use the practical convention of discounting at the after-tax interest rate on the lessee's secured debt.

5. Though this method is simple, it lacks certain intuitive appeal. In an optional section, we present an alternative, more intuitively appealing method. Relative to a lease, a purchase generates debt capacity. This increase in debt capacity can be calculated by discounting the difference between the cash flows of the purchase and the cash flows of the lease using the after-tax interest rate. The increase in debt capacity from a purchase is compared to the extra outflow at year 0 from a purchase.

6. If the lessor is in the same tax bracket as the lessee, the cash flows to the lessor are exactly the opposite of the cash flows to the lessee. Thus, the value of the lease to the lessee plus the value of the lease to the lessor must be zero. While this suggests that leases can never fly, there are actually at least three good reasons for leasing:

   a. Differences in tax brackets between lessor and lessee.
   b. Shift of risk bearing to the lessor.
   c. Minimization of transactions costs.

We also document a number of bad reasons for leasing.

KEY TERMS

Debt displacement 635	Lessor 623	Operating lease 624
Direct lease 624	Leveraged lease 625	Sale and lease-back 625
Financial lease 625	Off–balance-sheet	Sales-type lease 624
Lease 623	financing 626	
Lessee 623		

SUGGESTED READING

A classic article on lease valuation is:
S. Myers, D. A. Dill, and A. J. Bautista. "Valuation of Financial Lease Contracts." *Journal of Finance* (June 1976).

A good review and discussion of leasing is contained in:
C. W. Smith, Jr., and L. M. Wakeman. "Determinants of Corporate Leasing Policy." *Journal of Finance* (July 1985).

The survey evidence mentioned in this chapter is from:
T. K. Mukherjee. "A Survey of Corporate Leasing Analysis." *Financial Management* (Autumn 1991).

Another useful reading is:
K. V. Sivarama and R. C. Moyer. "Bankruptcy Costs and Financial Leasing Decisions." *Financial Management* (1994).

QUESTIONS & PROBLEMS

22.1   Discuss the validity of each of the following statements:
   a. Leasing reduces risk and can reduce a firm's cost of capital.
   b. Leasing provides 100 percent financing.
   c. Firms that do a large amount of leasing will not do much borrowing.
   d. If the tax advantages of leasing were eliminated, leasing would disappear.
   e. Leasing may encourage lessees to pay more attention to maintenance.
   f. Due to competition, a firm is not likely to get a better deal leasing than purchasing.

Use the following information to work the next six problems:

   You work for a nuclear research laboratory that is contemplating leasing a diagnostic scanner. (Leasing is common with expensive, high-tech equipment.) The scanner costs

$1,264,310 and qualifies for a 30 percent CCA rate. Because of radiation contamination, the scanner will be completely valueless in four years. You can lease it for $376,100 per year for four years.

22.2   Assume that the tax rate is 36 percent. You can borrow at 8 percent pre-tax. Should you lease or buy? Assume there are no other assets in the CCA pool.

22.3   What are the cash flows from the lease from the lessor's viewpoint? Assume a 41 percent tax bracket.

22.4   What would the lease payment have to be for both lessor and lessee to be indifferent to the lease?

EXCEL

22.5   Assume that your company does not contemplate paying taxes for the next several years. What are the cash flows from leasing in this case?

22.6   Combining the information in Questions 22.3 and 22.5, over what range of lease payments will the lease be profitable for both parties?

22.7   Rework Problem 22.2 assuming that the scanner qualifies for a special CCA rate of 50 percent per year.

22.8   An asset costs $91.42. The CCA rate for this asset is 20 percent. The asset's useful life is three years. It will have no salvage value. The corporate tax rate on ordinary income is 41 percent. The interest rate on risk-free cash flows is 5 percent. Assume that there are other assets in the CCA pool and therefore the pool is not terminated.
    a. What set of lease payments will make the lessee and the lessor equally well off?
    b. Show the general condition that will make the value of a lease to the lessor the negative of the value to the lessee.
    c. Assume that the lessee pays no taxes and the lessor is in the 39 percent tax bracket. For what range of lease payments does the lease have a positive NPV for both parties?

EXCEL

22.9   High electricity costs have made Farmer Corporation's chicken-plucking machine economically worthless. There are only two machines available to replace it.

        The International Plucking Machine (IPM) model is available only on a lease basis. The annual, end-of-year payments are $2,000 for five years. This machine will save Farmer $5,900 per year through reductions in electricity costs in each of the five years.

        As an alternative, Farmer can purchase a more energy-efficient machine from Basic Machine Corporation (BMC) for $15,500. This machine will save $9,000 per year in electricity costs. Farmer's bank has offered to finance the machine with a $15,500 loan. The interest rate on the loan will be 8 percent on the remaining balance with five annual principal payments of $3,100.

        Farmer has a target debt-to-asset ratio of 71 percent. As a small business, Farmer is in the 30 percent combined federal–provincial tax bracket. After five years, both machines are worthless. CCA for chicken-plucking machines is at the rate of 30 percent. The savings that Farmer will enjoy are known with certainty because Farmer has a long-term chicken purchase agreement with Kanes Food Products Inc., and a four-year back-log of orders. Assume that there are other assets in the CCA pool and therefore the pool is not terminated.
    a. Should Farmer lease the IPM machine or purchase the more efficient BMC machine?
    b. Does your answer depend on the form of financing for direct purchase?
    c. How much debt is displaced by this lease?

22.10   Tollufson Corporation has decided to purchase a new machine that costs $3 million. The machine will be worthless after three years. CCA for this type of machine is 40 percent. Tollufson is in the 38 percent combined tax bracket. The Royal Canadian Bank has offered Tollufson a three-year loan for $3 million. The repayment schedule is three yearly principal repayments of $1 million and an interest charge of 10 percent on the outstanding balance of the loan at the beginning of each year. The marketwide rate of interest is 10 percent. Both principal repayments and interest are due at the end of each year.

York Leasing Corporation offers to lease the same machine to Tollufson. Lease payments of $1.18 million per year are due at the end of each of the three years of the lease. Assume that there are no other assets in the CCA pool.

a. Should Tollufson lease the machine or buy it with bank financing?

b. What is the annual lease payment that will make Tollufson indifferent to whether it leases the machine or purchases it?

EXCEL

22.11 Timberland Corporation is a furniture manufacturer that is considering installing a milling machine for $460,000. The machine has a CCA rate of 20 percent and will be worthless after seven years. Timberland has been financially distressed and thus the company does not expect to get tax shields over the next seven years. Canadian Leasing Company has offered to lease the machine over seven years. The corporate tax rate for Timberland is 37 percent. The appropriate before-tax interest rate is 7 percent for both firms. Lease payments occur at the end of the year. What is Timberland's reservation price? What is Canadian's reservation price? What is the negotiating range of the lease?

MINICASE: The Decision to Lease or Buy at USB 2.0 Computers

USB 2.0 Computers has decided to proceed with the manufacture and distribution of the virtual keyboard (VK) the company has developed. To undertake this venture, the company needs to obtain equipment for the production of the microphone for the keyboard. Because of the required sensitivity of the microphone and its small size, the company needs specialized equipment for production.

Nick Warf, the company president, has found a vendor for the equipment. Clapton Acoustical Equipment has offered to sell USB 2.0 Computers the necessary equipment at a price of $5 million. Because of the rapid development of new technology, the equipment falls in Class 20. At the end of four years, the market value of the equipment is expected to be $600,000. Alternatively, the company can lease the equipment from Hendrix Leasing. The lease contract calls for four annual payments of $1.3 million due at the beginning of the year. Additionally, USB 2.0 Computers must make a security deposit of $300,000 that will be returned when the lease expires. USB 2.0 Computers can issue bonds with a yield of 10 percent, and the company has a marginal tax rate of 37 percent.

1. Should USB 2.0 buy or lease the equipment?
2. Nick mentions to James Hendrix, the president of Hendrix Leasing, that although the company will need the equipment for four years, he would like a lease contract for two years instead. At the end of the two years, the lease could be renewed. Nick would also like to eliminate the security deposit, but

he would be willing to increase the lease payments to $2.3 million for each of the two years. When the lease is renewed in two years, Hendrix would consider the increased lease payments in the first two years when calculating the terms of the renewal. The equipment is expected to have a market value of $2 million in two years. Why might Nick prefer this lease? What are the potential ethical issues concerning the new lease terms?

3. In the leasing discussion, James informs Nick that the contract could include a purchase option for the equipment at the end of the lease. Hendrix Leasing offers three purchase options:

   a. An option to purchase the equipment at the fair market value.

   b. An option to purchase the equipment at a fixed price. The price will be negotiated before the lease is signed.

   c. An option to purchase the equipment at a price of $250,000. How would the inclusion of a purchase option affect the value of the lease?

4. James also informs Nick that the lease contract can include a cancellation option. The cancellation option would allow USB 2.0 Computers to cancel the lease on any anniversary date of the contract. In order to cancel the lease, USB 2.0 Computers would be required to give 30 days notice prior to the anniversary date. How would the inclusion of a cancellation option affect the value of the lease?

Appendix 22A: APV Approach to Leasing
To access Appendix 22A, please go to the Online Learning Centre at
www.mcgrawhill.ca/olc/ross.

PART 6

Chapter 23

Options and Corporate Finance: Basic Concepts

EXECUTIVE SUMMARY

In the summer of 2000, General Mills (GM) made a share offer to acquire the Pillsbury division of Diageo PLC. Although the offer was generous, the managers of Diageo were worried about the possibility of a decline in GM's stock price. The deal eventually went through, due to a creative financing technique called a contingent value rights (CVR). Although CVRs may seem arcane, they are really straightforward applications of options, a topic to be examined in this chapter.

Options are special contractual arrangements giving the owner the right to buy or sell an asset at a fixed price any time on or before a given date. Stock options, the most familiar type, are options to buy and sell shares of common stock. Ever since 1973, stock options have been traded on organized exchanges.

Corporate securities are very similar to the stock options that are traded on organized exchanges. Almost every issue of corporate bonds and stocks has option features. In addition, capital structure decisions and capital budgeting decisions can be viewed in terms of options.

We start this chapter with a description of different types of publicly traded options. We identify and discuss the factors that determine their values. Next, we show how common stocks and bonds can be thought of as options on the underlying value of the firm. This leads to several new insights concerning corporate finance. For example, we show how certain corporate decisions can be viewed as options. General Mills' issuance of a CVR is one of these corporate decisions.

23.1 Options

An **option** is a contract giving its owner the right to buy or sell an asset at a fixed price on or before a given date. For example, an option on a building might give the buyer the right to buy the building for $1 million on, or any time before, the Saturday prior to the third Wednesday in January 2015. Options are a unique type of financial contract because they give the buyer the right, but not the *obligation,* to do something. The buyer uses the option only if it is advantageous; otherwise the option can be discarded.

There is a special vocabulary associated with options. Here are some important definitions:

1. **Exercising the option.** The act of buying or selling the underlying asset via the option contract is referred to as *exercising the option.*

2. **Strike or exercise price.** The fixed price in the option contract at which the holder can buy or sell the underlying asset is called the *strike price* or *exercise price.*

3. **Expiration date.** The maturity date of the option is referred to as the *expiration date.* After this date, the option is dead.

4. **American and European options.** An *American option* may be exercised at any time up to and including the expiration date. A *European option* differs from an American option in that it can be exercised only on the expiration date.

23.2 Call Options

The most common type of option is a **call option.** A call option gives the owner the right to buy an asset at a fixed price during a particular time period. There is no restriction on the kind of asset, but the most common options traded on exchanges are on stocks and bonds. Usually the assets involved are shares of common stock.

For example, call options on Alcan stock are traded on the Montreal Exchange and cleared through the Canadian Derivatives Clearing Corporation (CDCC). Alcan does not issue (that is, sell) call options on its common stock. Instead, individual investors are the original buyers and sellers of these options. A representative call option on Alcan stock enables an investor to buy 100 shares of Alcan from the option seller (or writer) on or before October 22, 200X, at an exercise price of $60. Like all options traded on the CDCC, the Alcan calls are American options, which can be exercised at any time during their life. This is a valuable option if there is some probability that the price of Alcan common stock will exceed $60 on or before October 22, 200X.

Virtually all stock option contracts specify that the exercise price and number of shares be adjusted for stock splits and stock dividends. To illustrate, suppose that Alcan stock was selling for $57 on the day the option was purchased. Further, suppose that the next day it split three for one. Each share would drop in price to $19, and the probability that the stock would rise over $57 per share in the near future would become very remote. To protect the option holder from such an occurrence, call options are typically adjusted for stock splits and stock dividends. In the case of a three-for-one split, the exercise price would become $20 (or $60/3). Furthermore, the option contract would now include 300 shares, instead of the original 100 shares.[1]

The Value of a Call Option at Expiration

What is the value of a call option contract on common stock at expiration? The answer depends on the value of the underlying stock when the option expires.

We define S_T as the market price of the underlying common stock on the expiration date, T. Of course, this price is not known prior to expiration. Suppose that a particular call option can be exercised at an exercise price of $50. If the value of the common stock at expiration, S_T, is greater than the exercise price of $50, the option will be worth the difference, $S_T - \$50$. When $S_T > \$50$, the call is said to be *in the money*.

For example, suppose that the stock price on expiration day is $60. The option holder has the right to buy the stock from the option seller for $50.[2] Because the stock is selling in the market for $60, the option holder will exercise the option, that is, buy the stock for $50. The holder can then sell the stock for $60 and pocket the difference of $10 (or $60 - \$50$).[3]

---

[1]No adjustment is made for the payment by Alcan of cash dividends to shareholders. This failure to adjust hurts holders of call options, though, of course, they should know the terms of option contracts before buying.

[2]We use the words *buyer, owner,* and *holder* interchangeably.

[3]This example assumes that the call lets the holder purchase one share of stock at $50. In reality, a call lets the holder purchase 100 shares at $50 per share. The profit would then equal $1,000 [or ($60 - \$50) \times 100$].

Of course, it is also possible that the value of the common stock will turn out to be less than the exercise price. If $S_T < \$50$, the call is *out of the money*. The holder will not exercise in this case. For example, if the stock price at the expiration date is $40, no rational investor would exercise. Why pay $50 for stock worth only $40? An option holder has no obligation to exercise the call and can *walk away* from the option. As a consequence, if $S_T < \$50$ on the expiration date, the value of the call option will be 0. In this case, the value of the call option is not $S_T - \$50$, as it would be if the holder of the call option had the *obligation* to exercise the call.

The payoff of a call option at expiration is

	Payoff on the Expiration Date	
	If $S_T \leq \$50$	If $S_T > \$50$
Call option value	0	$S_T - \$50$

Figure 23.1 plots the value of the call at expiration against the value of the stock. It is referred to as the *hockey stick diagram* of call option values. If $S_T < \$50$, the call is out of the money and worthless. If $S_T > \$50$, the call is in the money and rises one-for-one with increases in the stock price. Notice that the call can never have a negative value. It is a *limited liability instrument,* which means that all the holder can lose is the initial amount paid for it.

Suppose Mr. Optimist holds a one-year call option for 100 shares of Alcan common stock. It is a European call option and can be exercised at $60 per share. Assume that the expiration date has arrived. What is the value of the Alcan call option on the expiration date? If Alcan is selling for $65 per share, Mr. Optimist can exercise the option—purchase 100 shares of Alcan at $60 per share—and then immediately sell the shares at $65. Mr. Optimist will have made $500 (or 100 shares × $5).

Alternatively, assume that Alcan is selling for $50 per share on the expiration date. If Mr. Optimist still holds the call option, he will throw it away. The value of the Alcan call on the expiration date will be zero in this case.

FIGURE 23.1

The Value of a Call Option on the Expiration Date

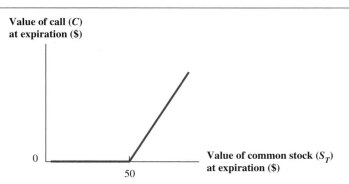

If $S_T > \$50$, then call option value $= S_T - \$50$. If $S_T \leq \$50$, then call option value $= 0$.

A call option gives the owner the right to buy an asset at a fixed price during a particular time period.

? **Concept Questions**
- **What is a call option?**
- **How is a call option's price related to the underlying stock price at the expiration date?**

23.3 Put Options

A **put option** can be viewed as the opposite of a call option. Just as a call gives the holder the right to buy the stock at a fixed price, a put gives the holder the right to *sell* the stock for a fixed exercise price during the life of the option.

The Value of a Put Option at Expiration

The circumstances that determine the value of a put option are the opposite of those for a call option, because a put option gives the holder the right to sell shares. Let us assume that the exercise price of the put is $50. If the price, S_T, of the underlying common stock at expiration is greater than the exercise price, it would be foolish to exercise the option and sell shares at $50. In other words, the put option is worthless if $S_T > \$50$. The put is out of the money in this case. However, if $S_T < \$50$, the put is in the money. In this case, it will pay to buy shares at S_T and use the option to sell them at the exercise price of $50. For example, if the stock price at expiration is $40, the holder should buy the stock in the open market at $40. By immediately exercising, he receives $50 for the sale. His profit is $10 (or $50 − $40).

The payoff of a put option at expiration is

	Payoff on the Expiration Date	
	If $S_T < \$50$	If $S_T \geq \$50$
Put option value	$\$50 - S_T$	0

Figure 23.2 plots the values of a put option for all possible values of the underlying stock. It is instructive to compare Figure 23.2 with Figure 23.1 for the call option. The call option is valuable whenever the stock is above the exercise price, and the put is valuable when the stock price is below the exercise price.

FIGURE 23.2

The Value of a Put Option on the Expiration Date

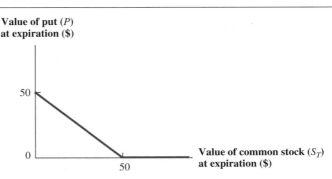

If $S_T \geq \$50$, then the put option value = 0. If $S_T < \$50$, then the put option value = $\$50 - S_T$.

A put option gives the owner the right to *sell* an asset at a fixed price during a particular time period.

In 2001, the shares of Bombardier, the world's largest manufacturer of plane and train equipment, traded at $25.10. By the time of writing in June 2007, huge losses had driven the share price down to about $5. Suppose that Ms. Pessimist foresaw Bombardier's troubles and bought one put contract allowing the sale of 100 Bombardier shares at $12 each through June 2007. At the expiration date, Ms. Pessimist exercised her put contract, which was then in the money. She bought 100 shares of Bombardier for $4 and, on the same day, sold the shares at the exercise price of $12 per share. Her profit was $800 [or 100 shares × ($12 − $4)]. The value of the put contract at expiration was $800. Similarly, if put options were not available to Ms. Pessimist, she could have shortsold the Bombardier stock to achieve a comparable result.

? **Concept Questions**

- **What is a put option?**
- **How is a put option's price related to the underlying stock price at the expiration date?**

23.4 Selling Options

An investor who sells (or *writes*) a call on common stock promises to deliver the shares if required to do so by the call-option holder. Notice that the seller is *obligated* to deliver if the option is exercised. The seller of a call option obtains a cash payment from the holder (or buyer) at the time the option is bought. If, at the expiration date, the price of the common stock is below the exercise price, the call option will not be exercised and the seller's liability is zero.

If, at the expiration date, the price of the common stock is greater than the exercise price, the holder will exercise the call and the seller must give the holder shares of stock in exchange for the exercise price. Here the seller loses the difference between the stock price and the exercise price. For example, assume that the stock price is $60 and the exercise price is $50. Knowing that exercise is imminent, the option seller buys stock in the open market at $60. By being obligated to sell at $50, the option seller loses $10 (or $50 − $60).

Conversely, an investor who sells a put on common stock agrees to purchase shares of common stock if the put holder should so request. The seller loses on this deal if the stock price falls below the exercise price and the holder puts the stock to the seller. For example, assume that the stock price is $40 and the exercise price is $50. The holder of the put will exercise in this case. In other words, the holder will sell the underlying stock at the exercise price of $50. This means that the seller of the put must buy the underlying stock at the exercise price of $50. Because the stock is only worth $40, the loss here is $10 (or $40 − $50).

The values of the "sell-a-call" and "sell-a-put" positions are depicted in Figure 23.3. The graph on the left-hand side of the figure shows that the seller of a call loses nothing when the stock price at expiration date is below $50. However, the seller loses a dollar for every dollar that the stock rises above $50. The graph in the centre of the figure shows that the seller of a put loses nothing when the stock price at expiration date is above $50. However, the seller loses a dollar for every dollar that the stock falls below $50.

It is worthwhile to spend a few minutes comparing the graphs in Figure 23.3 to those in Figures 23.1 and 23.2. The graph of selling a call (the graph in the left-hand side of Figure 23.3) is the mirror image over the horizontal axis of the graph of buying a call (Figure 23.1). This occurs because options are a zero-sum game. The seller of a call loses what the buyer makes. Similarly, the graph of selling a put (the middle graph in

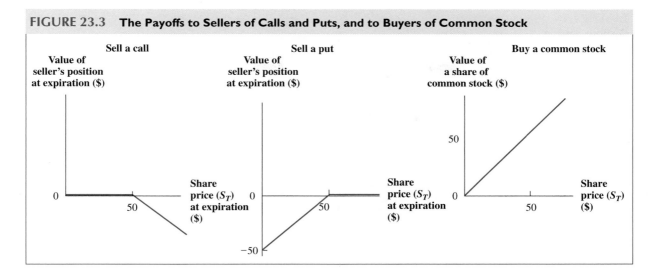

FIGURE 23.3   **The Payoffs to Sellers of Calls and Puts, and to Buyers of Common Stock**

Figure 23.3) is the mirror image of the graph of buying a put (Figure 23.2). Again, the seller of a put loses what the buyer makes.

Figure 23.3 also shows the value at expiration of simply buying common stock. Notice that buying the stock is the same as buying a call option on the stock with an exercise price of zero. This is not surprising. If the exercise price is 0, the call holder can buy the stock for nothing, which is really the same as owning it.

23.5 Stock Option Quotations

Now that we understand the definitions for calls and puts, let's look at the exchanges where they are traded. In the 1970s and 1980s, organized trading in options grew from literally zero into some of the world's largest markets. The tremendous growth in interest in derivative securities resulted from the greatly increased volatility in financial markets we discussed in Chapter 1.[4] Exchange trading in options began in 1973 on the Chicago Board Options Exchange (CBOE). The CBOE is still the largest organized options market, and options are traded in a number of other places today, including London, Paris, Tokyo, and Hong Kong.

Option trading in Canada began in 1975. Today options are traded on the Montreal Exchange and cleared through the Canadian Derivatives Clearing Corp. (CDCC). The CDCC stands between option buyers and sellers. Put and call options involving stock in some of the best-known corporations in Canada are traded daily. Almost all such options are American (as opposed to European).

To illustrate how options are quoted on the CDCC, Table 23.1 presents information on the options of Alcan.

The first thing listed in Table 23.1 is the company identifier, Alcan (AL). This tells us that these options involve the right to buy or sell shares of stock in Alcan (AL), which

---

[4]Our discussion of trends in options trading draws on L. Gagnon, "Exchange-Traded Financial Derivatives in Canada: Finally Off the Launching Pad," *Canadian Investment Review* (Fall 1990), pp. 63–70.

TABLE 23.1
Options Listing Friday, May 04, 2007

Stock Options 10 Most Active Options Company	Volume				Interest
iShares Energy	8,175				30,423
Suncor Energy	3,595				20,054
EnCana	3,508				53,615
Kinross Gold	3,170				33,424
Petro-Canada	2,433				38,086
Barrick	2,185				36,357
Goldcorp	2,018				50,052
TeckComin B SV	2,006				69,633
Cdn Nat Res	1,600				36,536
Natl Bank	1,311				22,925

CDCC Trades					
Total	62,342				1,663,434

Agrico-Eagle (AEM) — 39.67

Strike	Expiry	Put/Call	Volume	Bid	Ask	Open Int.
38	May	P	30	0.4	0.55	50
40	May	P	46	1.15	1.3	329
42	May	C	23	0.3	0.4	113
36	June	P	3	0.5	0.65	70
38	June	C	1	2.95	3.15	120
40	June	C	18	1.85	2.05	219
40	June	P	10	2	2.15	190
42	June	C	10	1.1	1.25	289
44	June	C	50	0.6	0.75	612
40	Sept	C	10	3.75	3.9	55
42	Sept	C	20	2.85	3.05	162
44	Sept	C	15	2.15	2.35	124
40	Dec	P	5	4.25	4.5	29

Total Option Vol. 287   Total Open Int. 6,540

Alcan (AL) — 67.55

Strike	Expiry	Put/Call	Volume	Bid	Ask	Open Int.
62	May	C	100	5.65	5.8	2,611
62	May	P	20	0.1	0.2	337
64	May	C	21	3.85	4	2,535
64	May	P	6	0.4	0.45	475
66	May	C	26	2.35	2.45	540
66	May	P	92	0.85	1	200
68	May	C	23	1.25	1.3	124
68	May	P	50	1.75	1.9	90
70	May	P	10	3.05	3.2	22
64	June	C	1	4.65	4.85	157
66	June	P	66	1.75	1.9	214
68	June	C	37	2.3	2.35	315
68	June	P	55	2.65	2.8	67
70	June	C	22	1.45	1.5	57
62	July	C	8	6.9	7.05	2,073
66	July	C	80	4.15	4.3	743
68	July	C	14	3.05	3.2	386
70	July	C	45	2.15	2.25	52
62	Oct	C	2	8.35	8.5	73
66	Oct	C	20	5.8	5.9	135
66	Oct	P	63	3.5	3.65	85
70	Oct	C	5	3.7	3.8	214

Total Option Vol. 868   Total Open Int. 25,533

Alcan LEAPS 2008 (CLA) — 66.35

Strike	Expiry	Put/Call	Volume	Bid	Ask	Open Int.
62	Jan	C	0	9.4	9.65	421
62	Jan	P	0	2.75	2.9	62
64	Jan	C	0	8.1	8.3	289
64	Jan	P	0	3.35	3.55	70
66	Jan	C	55	6.85	7	108
66	Jan	P	85	4.1	4.3	50
68	Jan	C	45	5.75	5.9	1,176
68	Jan	P	25	4.95	5.2	112
70	Jan	C	37	4.75	4.95	56
70	Jan	P	1	5.95	6.2	0

Total Option Vol. 303   Total Open Int. 13,373

Source: www.nationalpost.ca.

are listed on the Toronto Stock Exchange (TSX). Beside the company identifier is the stock's closing price. As of the close of business (in Toronto), Alcan was selling for $67.55 per share.

On the next line is the strike (or exercise) price. The Alcan options listed here have exercise prices ranging from $62 to $70. To the right of the exercise price is the expiration date. June means the option expires in June. At the bottom is an option marked Oct, meaning it expires in October. All CDCC options expire on the third Friday of the expiration month.

For Agrico-Eagle, the company listed above Alcan, the first option is a put option; the third is a call option. The first option would be described as the "Agrico-Eagle, $38 put." The price for this option is approximately $0.48 (estimated centre value between the "Bid" and the "Ask"). If you pay the $0.48, then you have the right any time between now and the third Friday of June to sell one share of Agrico-Eagle stock for $38. Actually, trading takes place in round lots (multiples of 100 shares), so one option *contract* costs $0.48 × 100 = $48.

The other quotations are similar. For example, the $42 May call option (the third option) costs approximately $0.35. If you pay $0.35 × 100 = $35, then you have the right to buy 100 shares of Agrico-Eagle stock at any time between now and the third Friday in May at a price of $42 per share.

LEAPS

The Montreal Exchange also offers long-lived options called LEAPS (Long-term Equity AnticiPation Securities). LEAPS are exactly the same as the call or put options already discussed except that they have much longer lives.

Table 23.1 shows quotes for Alcan LEAPS expiring in 2008. When these quotations were made in May 2007, the Alcan LEAPS had maturities of just under nine months.

23.6 Combinations of Options

Puts and calls can serve as building blocks for more complex option contracts. For example, Figure 23.4 illustrates the payoff from buying a put option on a stock and simultaneously buying the stock.

If the share price is greater than the exercise price, the put option is worthless, and the value of the combined position is equal to the value of the common stock. If instead the exercise price is greater than the share price, the decline in the value of the shares will be exactly offset by the rise in value of the put.

The strategy of buying a put and buying the underlying stock is called a *protective put.* It is as if one is buying insurance for the stock. The stock can always be sold at the exercise price, regardless of how far the market price of the stock falls.

Note that the combination of buying a put and buying the underlying stock has the same *shape* in Figure 23.4 as the call purchase in Figure 23.1. To pursue this point, let's consider the graph for buying a call, which is shown at the far left of Figure 23.5. This graph is the same as Figure 23.1. Now, let's try the strategy of:

(Leg A) Buying a call.

(Leg B) Buying a zero-coupon bond with a face value of $50 that matures on the same day that the option expires.

FIGURE 23.4   Payoff to the Combination of Buying Puts and Buying Stock

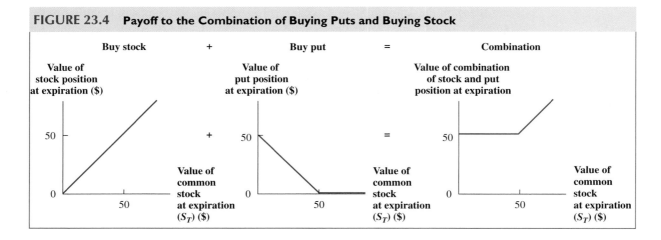

We have drawn the graph of Leg A of this strategy at the far left of Figure 23.5, but what does the graph of Leg B look like? It looks like the middle graph of the figure. That is, anyone buying this zero-coupon bond will be guaranteed to get $50, regardless of the price of the stock at expiration.

What does the graph of *simultaneously* buying both Leg A and Leg B of this strategy look like? It looks like the far-right graph of Figure 23.5. That is, the investor receives a guaranteed $50 from the bond, regardless of what happens to the stock. In addition, the investor receives a payoff from the call of $1 for every $1 that the price of the stock rises above the exercise price of $50.

The far-right graph of Figure 23.5 looks *exactly* like the far-right graph of Figure 23.4. Thus, an investor gets the same payoff from the strategy of Figure 23.4, and the strategy of Figure 23.5, regardless of what happens to the price of the underlying stock. In other words, the investor gets the same payoff from

1. Buying a put and buying the underlying stock.
2. Buying a call and buying a zero-coupon bond.

FIGURE 23.5   Payoff to the Combination of Buying a Call and Buying a Zero-Coupon Bond

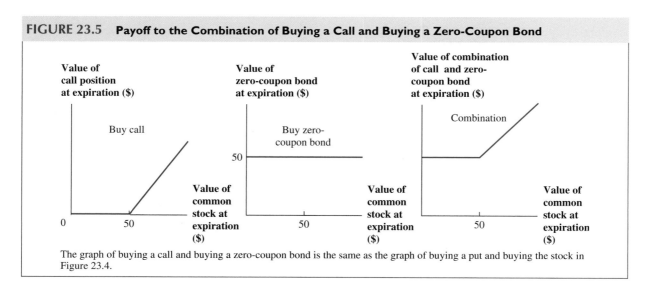

The graph of buying a call and buying a zero-coupon bond is the same as the graph of buying a put and buying the stock in Figure 23.4.

If investors have the same payoffs from the two strategies, the two strategies must have the *same* cost. Otherwise, all investors will choose the strategy with the lower cost and avoid the strategy with the higher cost. This leads to the interesting result that:

$$\underbrace{\text{Price of underlying stock} + \text{Price of put}}_{\text{Cost of first strategy}} = \underbrace{\text{Price of call} + \text{Present value of exercise price}}_{\text{Cost of second strategy}} \qquad (23.1)$$

This relationship is known as **put–call parity** and is one of the most fundamental relationships concerning options. It says that there are two ways of buying a protective put. You can buy a put and buy the underlying stock simultaneously. Here, your total cost is the price of the underlying stock plus the price of the put. Or you can buy the call and buy a zero-coupon bond. Here, your total cost is the price of the call plus the price of the zero-coupon bond. The price of the zero-coupon bond is equal to the present value of the exercise price, i.e., the present value of $50 in our example.

Equation (23.1) is a very precise relationship. It holds only if the put and the call have both the same exercise price and the same expiration date. In addition, the maturity date of the zero-coupon bond must be the same as the expiration date of the options. Also we are assuming that the underlying stock pays no dividends and that the call and the put are European.[5]

To see how fundamental put–call parity is, let's rearrange the formula, yielding:

$$\text{Price of underlying stock} = \text{Price of call} - \text{Price of put} + \text{Present value of exercise price}$$

This relationship now states that you can replicate the purchase of a share of stock by buying a call, selling a put, and buying a zero-coupon bond. (Note that, because a minus sign comes before "Price of put," the put is sold, not bought.) Investors in this three-legged strategy are said to have purchased a *synthetic* stock.

Let's do one more transformation:

Covered-Call Strategy

$$\text{Price of underlying stock} - \text{Price of call} = -\text{Price of put} + \text{Present value of exercise price}$$

Many investors like to buy a stock and write the call on the stock simultaneously. This is a conservative strategy known as *selling a covered call.* The preceding put–call parity relationship tells us that this strategy is equivalent to selling a put and buying a zero-coupon bond. Figure 23.6 develops the graph for the covered call. You can verify that the covered call can be replicated by selling a put and simultaneously buying a zero-coupon bond.

Of course, there are other ways of rearranging the basic put–call relationship. For each rearrangement, the strategy on the left-hand side is equivalent to the strategy on the right-hand side. The beauty of put–call parity is that it shows how any strategy in options can be achieved in two different ways.

? **Concept Question**

• **What is put–call parity?**

---

[5]These assumptions can be relaxed but doing so would take us beyond the scope of this text.

FIGURE 23.6   **Payoff to the Combination of Buying a Stock and Writing a Call**

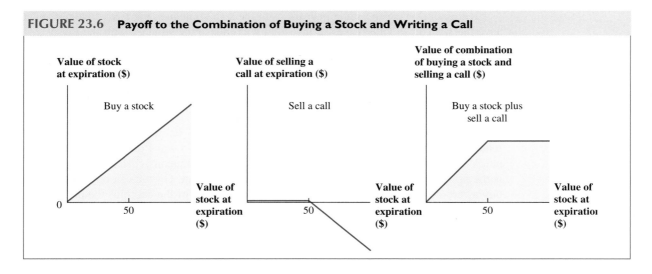

23.7 Valuing Options

In the last section, we determined what options are worth on the expiration date. Now we wish to evaluate the value of options when you buy them well before expiration.[6] We begin by considering the upper and lower bounds on the value of a call.

Bounding the Value of an American Call

Lower Bound   Consider an American call that is in the money prior to expiration. For example, assume that the stock price is $60 and the exercise price is $50. In this case, the option cannot sell below $10. To see this, note the simple strategy if the option sells at, say, $9.

Date	Transaction	
Today	(1) Buy call	−$ 9
Today	(2) Exercise call, that is, buy underlying stock at exercise price	−$50
Today	(3) Sell stock at current market price	+$60
Arbitrage profit		+$ 1

The type of profit that is described in this transaction is an *arbitrage profit*. Arbitrage profits come from transactions that have no risk or cost and cannot occur regularly in normal, well-functioning financial markets.[7] The excess demand for these options would quickly force the option price up to at least $10 (or $60 − $50).[8]

---

[6]Our discussion in this section is of American options, because they are traded in the real world. As necessary, we will indicate differences for European calls.

[7]Paul Halpern and Stuart Turnbull, "Empirical Tests of Boundary Conditions for Toronto Stock Exchange Options," *Journal of Finance* 40 (June 1985), tested these boundary conditions for TCO options in the late 1970s when Canadian options trading was relatively new. While they detected arbitrage opportunities, it is unlikely that these persist today.

[8]Note that this lower bound is strictly true for an American option but not for an European option.

In practice, the price of the option is likely to be above $10. Investors will rationally pay more than $10 because of the possibility that the stock will rise above $60 before expiration.

Upper Bound   Is there an upper boundary for the option price as well? It turns out that the upper boundary is the price of the underlying stock. That is, an option to buy common stock cannot have a greater value than the common stock itself. A call option can be used to buy common stock with a payment of an exercise price. It would be foolish to buy stock this way if the stock could be purchased directly at a lower price. The upper and lower bounds are represented in Figure 23.7. In addition, these bounds are summarized in the bottom half of Table 23.2 on page 661.

The Factors Determining Call Option Values

The previous discussion indicated that the price of a call option must fall somewhere in the shaded region of Figure 23.7. We now determine more precisely where in the shaded region it should be. The factors that determine a call's value can be broken into two sets. The first set contains the features of the option contract. The two basic contractual features are the expiration date and the exercise price. The second set of factors affecting the call price reflects characteristics of the stock and the market.

Exercise Price   An increase in the exercise price reduces the value of the call. For example, imagine that there are two calls on a stock selling at $60. The first call has an exercise price of $50 and the second one has an exercise price of $40. Which call would you rather have? Clearly, you would rather have the call with an exercise price of $40, because that one is $20 ($60 − $40) in the money. In other words, the call with an exercise price of $40 should sell for more than an otherwise identical call with an exercise price of $50.

Expiration Date   The value of an American call option must be at least as great as the value of an otherwise identical option with a shorter term to expiration. Consider two American calls: One has a maturity of nine months and the other expires in six months.

FIGURE 23.7

The Upper and Lower Boundaries of Call Option Values

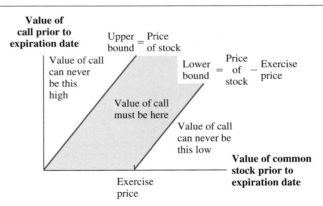

The precise option value will depend on five factors:
1. Exercise price.
2. Expiration date.
3. Stock price.
4. Risk-free interest rate.
5. Variance of the stock.

The nine-month call offers the same rights as the six-month call, and also has an additional three months within which these rights can be exercised. It cannot be worth less and will generally be more valuable.[9]

Stock Price   Other things being equal, the higher the stock price, the more valuable the call option will be. For example, if a stock is worth $80, a call with an exercise price of $100 isn't worth very much. If the stock soars to $120, the call becomes much more valuable.

Now consider Figure 23.8, which shows the relationship between the call price and the stock price prior to expiration. The curve indicates that the call price increases as the stock price increases. Furthermore, it can be shown that the relationship is represented, not by a straight line, but by a *convex* curve. That is, the increase in the call price for a given change in the stock price is greater when the stock price is high than when the stock price is low.

There are two special points on the curve in Figure 23.8:

1. *The stock is worthless.* The call must be worthless if the underlying stock is worthless. That is, if the stock has no chance of attaining any value, it is not worthwhile to pay the exercise price in order to obtain the stock.
2. *The stock price is* very *high relative to the exercise price.* In this situation, the owner of the call knows that he will end up exercising the call. He can view himself as the owner of the stock now, with one difference. He must pay the exercise price at expiration.

Thus, the value of his position, i.e., the value of the call, is:

$$\text{Stock price} - \text{Present value of exercise price}$$

These two points on the curve are summarized in the bottom half of Table 23.2.

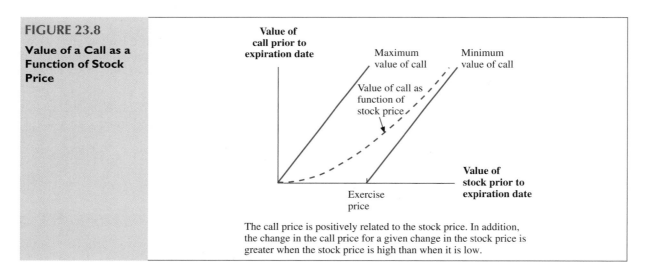

FIGURE 23.8

Value of a Call as a Function of Stock Price

The call price is positively related to the stock price. In addition, the change in the call price for a given change in the stock price is greater when the stock price is high than when it is low.

---

[9]This relationship need not hold for a European call option. Consider a firm with two otherwise identical European call options: one expiring at the end of May and the other expiring a few months later. Further, assume that a *huge* dividend is paid in early June. If the first call is exercised at the end of May, its holder will receive the underlying stock. If he does not sell the stock, he will receive the large dividend shortly thereafter. However, the holder of the second call will receive the stock through exercise after the dividend is paid. Because the market knows that the holder of this option will miss the dividend, the value of the second call option could be less than the value of the first.

TABLE 23.2
Factors Affecting American Option Values

Increase in	Call Option*	Put Option*
Value of underlying asset (stock price)	+	−
Exercise price	−	+
Stock volatility	+	+
Interest rate	+	−
Time to exercise date	+	+

In addition to the preceding, we have presented the following four relationships for American calls:

1. The call price can never be greater than the stock price (*upper bound*).
2. The call price can never be less than either zero or the difference between the stock price and the exercise price (*lower bound*).
3. The call is worth zero if the stock is worth zero.
4. When the stock price is much greater than the exercise price, the call price tends toward the difference between the stock price and the present value of the exercise price.

The Key Factor: The Variability of the Underlying Asset The greater the variability of the underlying asset, the more valuable the call option will be. Consider the following example. Suppose that, just before the call expires, the stock price will be either $100 with probability 0.5 or $80 with probability 0.5. What will be the value of a call with an exercise price of $110? Clearly, it will be worthless because no matter what happens to the stock, its price will always be below the exercise price.

Now let us see what happens if the stock is more variable. Suppose that we add $20 to the best case and take $20 away from the worst case. Now the stock has a one-half chance of being worth $60 and a one-half chance of being worth $120. We have spread the stock returns, but, of course, the expected value of the stock has stayed the same:

$$(^1/_2 \times \$80) + (^1/_2 \times \$100) = \$90 = (^1/_2 \times \$60) + (^1/_2 \times \$120)$$

Notice that the call option has value now because there is a one-half chance that the stock price will be $120, or $10 above the exercise price of $110. This illustrates a very important point. There is a fundamental distinction between holding an option on an underlying asset and holding the underlying asset. If investors in the marketplace are risk-averse, a rise in the variability of the stock will decrease its market value. However, the holder of a call receives payoffs from the positive tail of the probability distribution. As a consequence, a rise in the variability in the underlying stock increases the market value of the call.

This result can also be seen from Figure 23.9. Consider two stocks, *A* and *B,* each of which is normally distributed. For each security, the figure illustrates the probability of different stock prices on the expiration date.[10] As we see, stock *B* has more volatility than does stock *A*. This means that stock *B* has higher probability of both abnormally high returns and abnormally low returns. Let us assume that options on each of the two securities have the same exercise price. To option holders, a return much below average on stock *B* is no worse than a return only moderately below average on stock *A*. In either situation, the option expires out of the money. However, to option holders, a return much above average on stock *B* is better than a return only moderately above average on stock *A*.

---

[10]This graph assumes that, for each security, the exercise price is equal to the expected stock price. This assumption is employed merely to facilitate the discussion. It is not needed to show the relationship between a call's value and the volatility of the underlying stock.

FIGURE 23.9

Distribution of Common-Stock Price at Expiration for Both Security *A* and Security *B*, Whose Options Have the Same Exercise Price

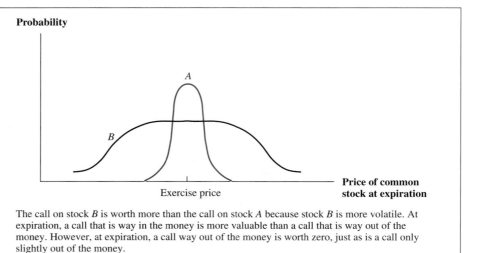

The call on stock *B* is worth more than the call on stock *A* because stock *B* is more volatile. At expiration, a call that is way in the money is more valuable than a call that is way out of the money. However, at expiration, a call way out of the money is worth zero, just as is a call only slightly out of the money.

Because a call's price at the expiration date is the difference between the stock price and the exercise price, the value of the call on *B* at expiration will be higher in this case.

The Interest Rate   Call prices are also a function of the level of interest rates. The higher the risk-free rate is, the more the call is worth. Normally, we think of asset values going down as rates rise. In this case, the exercise price is a cash outflow, a liability. The current value of that liability goes down as the discount rate goes up. This makes the call worth more.

A Quick Discussion of Factors Determining Put Option Values

Given our extended discussion of the factors influencing a call's value, we can easily examine these factors' effect on puts. Table 23.2 summarizes the five factors influencing prices of both American calls and American puts. The effect of three factors on puts are the opposite of the effect of these three factors on calls:

1. The put's market price *decreases* as the stock price increases because puts are in the money when the stock sells below the exercise price.

2. The market value of a put with a high exercise price is *greater* than the value of an otherwise identical put with a low exercise price for the reason given in (1) above.

3. A high interest rate *adversely* affects the value of a put. The ability to sell a stock at a fixed exercise price sometime in the future is worth less if the present value of the exercise price is diminished by a high interest rate.

The effect of the other two factors on puts is the same as the effect of these factors on calls:

4. The value of an American put with a distant expiration date is greater than an otherwise identical put with an earlier expiration.[11] The longer time to maturity gives the put holder more flexibility, just as it did in the case of a call.

---

[11]Though this result must hold in the case of an American put, it need not hold for a European put.

5. Volatility of the underlying stock increases the value of the put. The reasoning is analogous to that for a call. At expiration, a put that is deep in the money is more valuable than a put only slightly in the money. However, at expiration, a put way out of the money is worth zero, just as is a put only slightly out of the money.

? Concept Questions

- **List the factors that determine the value of options.**
- **Why does a stock's variability affect the value of options written on it?**

23.8 An Option Pricing Formula

We have explained *qualitatively* that the value of a call option is a function of five variables:

1. The current price of the underlying asset, which for stock options is the price of the shares of common stock.
2. The exercise price.
3. The time to the expiration date.
4. The variance of the underlying asset.
5. The risk-free interest rate.

It is time to replace the qualitative model with a precise option valuation model. The model we choose is the famous Black–Scholes option pricing model. Myron Scholes and Robert Merton shared the 1997 Nobel Prize in Economics for their pioneering work on option pricing models. You can put numbers into the Black–Scholes model and get values back.

The Black–Scholes model is represented by a rather imposing formula. A derivation of the formula is simply not possible in this textbook, as students will be happy to learn. However, some appreciation for the achievement as well as some intuitive understanding is in order.

In the early chapters of this book, we showed how to discount capital budgeting projects using the net present value formula. We also used this approach to value stocks and bonds.

A Nobel for Peace of Mind

Two of [1997's] Nobel prizes [honoured] efforts to protect millions of people against unforeseen dangers. The first . . . the peace prize, . . . went to the campaign against land mines. But it's the effort celebrated by the prize in economics that has had a far greater influence on daily lives.

Jokes about the real-world relevance of charts and graphs aside, economist Myron Scholes, raised in Canada, and his colleague Robert Merton have been honoured for shaping the options market. It reduces risk in everything from farming to investing in stocks.

Options are rights to choose whether to buy or sell a fixed quantity of something—pigs, savings bonds, whatever—at a fixed price, by a certain date. Since 1973, when Mr. Scholes co-published a formula for determining, rather than guessing the price of an option, the once-small market has ballooned to $200-billion annually.

How are options useful? They have, for example, allowed pig producers to shelter themselves from a drop in the price of pork. They have also allowed the Ontario Teachers' Pension Plan—probably Canada's biggest buyer of options—to shelter retirement savings from a dollar plunge.

How do they work? Take the pig example. A farmer fattening pigs in January plans to sell them in March. He can guess the price per pig will be $100 in March. But even a pig expert can be wrong about his market, and he'd prefer not to take the mistake on the chin. So the farmer buys options to sell his pigs for $100 in March. Come March, if the market price is higher, he won't exercise the option. If it's lower, he has guaranteed himself the "strike price" of $100 per pig.

Now, the price of that guarantee is tough to peg in January. Enter the Black–Scholes model: The option price is the farmer's desired $100 March price minus the March price dictated by what's called the futures market. Say the futures price is $75—the option's worth $25. But not so fast. It's tougher to guess the March price in January than in February because there's more time for interest rates, disease, and other things to influence it. So the option is cheaper in January, more expensive in February. Consequently, a "probability function" is calculated onto the $25, and voila, the option price.

There's genius in simplicity, and the model is so good that it's programmed into traders' calculators. But options or derivatives can become quite complicated. Finance eggheads are constantly inventing new kinds. And buyers and sellers must pay close attention to the assets from which the options are derived—pigs, interest rates, whatever. It was only three years ago that the Ukrainian (Fort William) Credit Union lost $2-million on derivatives trades. California's Orange County fared far worse, losing about $2-billion.

On the whole, though, the Nobel committee was wise to honour such a great achievement, that of protecting people from hugely consequential risks.

Source: The Globe and Mail (October 16, 1997). Used with permission.

Why, students sometimes ask, can't the same NPV formula be used to value puts and calls? It is a good question because the earliest attempts at valuing options used NPV. Unfortunately, the attempts were simply not successful because no one could determine the appropriate discount rate. An option is generally riskier than the underlying stock, but no one knew exactly how much riskier.

Black and Scholes attacked the problem by pointing out that a strategy of borrowing to finance a stock purchase duplicates the risk of a call. Then, knowing the price of a stock already, one can determine the price of a call such that its return is identical to that of the stock-with-borrowing alternative.

We illustrate the intuition behind the Black–Scholes approach by considering a simple example in which a combination of a call and a stock eliminates all risk. This example works because we let the future stock price be one of only two values. Hence, the example is called a *two-state option model*. By eliminating the possibility that the stock price can take on other values, we are able to duplicate the call exactly.

A Two-State Option Model

Consider the following example. Suppose the current market price of a stock is $50 and the stock will be either $60 or $40 at the end of the year. Further, imagine a call option on this stock with a one-year expiration date and a $50 exercise price. Investors can borrow at 10 percent. Our goal is to determine the value of the call.

In order to value the call correctly, we need to examine two strategies. The first is to simply buy the call. The second is to:

a. Buy one-half a share of stock.

b. Borrow $18.18, implying a payment of principal and interest at the end of the year of $20 ($18.18 × 1.10).

As you will see shortly, the cash flows from the second strategy exactly match the cash flows from buying a call. (A little later we will show how we came up with the exact fraction of a share of stock to buy and the exact borrowing amount.) Because the cash flows match, we say that we are *duplicating* the call with the second strategy.

At the end of the year, the future payoffs are set out as follows:

	Future Payoffs	
Initial Transactions	If Stock Price Is $60	If Stock Price Is $40
1. Buy a call	$60 − $50 = $10	0
2. Buy ½ share of stock	$\frac{1}{2}$ × $60 = $30	$\frac{1}{2}$ × $40 = $20
Borrow $18.18 at 10%	−($18.18 × 1.10) = −$20	−$20
Total from stock and borrowing strategy	$10	0

Note that the future payoff structure of the "buy-a-call" strategy is duplicated by the strategy of "buy stock" and "borrow." That is, under either strategy, an investor would end up with $10 if the stock price rose and $0 if the stock price fell. Thus, these two strategies are equivalent as far as traders are concerned.

Now, if two strategies always have the same cash flows at the end of the year, how must their initial costs be related? The two strategies must have the *same* initial cost. Otherwise, there will be an arbitrage possibility. We can easily calculate this cost for our strategy of buying stock and borrowing. This cost is:

$$\text{Buy } \tfrac{1}{2} \text{ share of stock} \quad \tfrac{1}{2} \times \$50 = \quad \$25.00$$
$$\text{Borrow } \$18.18 \qquad\qquad\qquad\qquad\quad -\underline{\$18.18}$$
$$\$\ \ 6.82$$

Because the call option provides the same payoffs at expiration as does the strategy of buying stock and borrowing, the call must be priced at $6.82. This is the value of the call option in a market without arbitrage profits.

We left two issues unexplained in the preceding example.

Determining the Delta   How did we know to buy one-half share of stock in the duplicating strategy? Actually, the answer is easier than it might at first appear. The call price at the end of the year will be either $10 or $0, whereas the stock price will be either $60 or $40. Thus, the call price has a potential swing of $10 ($10 − $0) next period, whereas the stock price has a potential swing of $20 ($60 − $40). We can write this in terms of the following ratio:

Delta

$$\frac{\text{Swing of call}}{\text{Swing of stock}} = \frac{\$10 - \$0}{\$60 - \$40} = \frac{1}{2}$$

This ratio is called the *delta* of the call. In words, a $1 swing in the price of the stock gives rise to a $\$\frac{1}{2}$swing in the price of the call. Because we are trying to duplicate the call with the stock, it seems sensible to buy one-half share of stock instead of buying one call. In other words, the risk of buying one-half share of stock should be the same as the risk of buying one call.

Determining the Amount of Borrowing   How did we know how much to borrow? Buying one-half share of stock brings us either $30 or $20 at expiration, which is exactly $20 more than the payoffs of $10 and $0, respectively, from the call. To duplicate the call through a purchase of stock, we should also borrow enough money so that we have to pay back exactly $20 of interest and principal. This amount of borrowing is merely the present value of $20, which is $18.18 ($20/1.10).

Now that we know how to determine both the delta and the amount borrowed, we can write the value of the call as:

$$
\begin{array}{cccccccc}
\text{Value of call} & = & \text{Stock price} & \times & \text{Delta} & - & \text{Amount borrowed} & \\
\$6.82 & = & \$50 & \times & \frac{1}{2} & - & \$18.18 & \textbf{(23.2)}
\end{array}
$$

We will find this intuition very useful in explaining the Black–Scholes model.

Risk-Neutral Valuation   Before leaving this simple example, we should comment on a remarkable feature. We found the exact value of the option without even knowing the probability that the stock would go up or down! If an optimist thought the probability of an up move was very high and a pessimist thought it was very low, they would still agree on the option value. How could that be? The answer is that the current $50 stock price already balances the views of the optimists and the pessimists. The option reflects that balance because its value depends on the stock price.

This insight provides us with another approach to valuing the call. If we don't need the probabilities of the two states to value the call, perhaps we can select *any* probabilities we want and still come up with the right answer. Suppose we selected probabilities such that the return on the stock is equal to the risk-free rate of 10 percent. We know that the stock return given a rise is 20 percent ($60/$50 − 1) and the stock return given a fall is −20 percent ($40/$50 − 1). Thus, we can solve for the probability of a rise necessary to achieve an expected return of 10 percent as:

$$10\% = \text{Probability of a rise} \times 20\% + (1 - \text{Probability of rise}) \times -20\%$$

Solving this formula, we find that the probability of a rise is 3/4 and the probability of a fall is 1/4. If we apply these probabilities to the call, we can value it as:

$$\text{Value of call} = \frac{\frac{3}{4} \times \$10 + \frac{1}{4} \times \$0}{1.10} = \$6.82$$

the same value that we got from the duplicating approach.

Why did we select probabilities such that the expected return on the stock was 10 percent? We wanted to work with the special case where investors are *risk-neutral*. This case occurs when the expected return on *any* asset (including both the stock and the call) is equal to the risk-free rate. In other words, this case occurs when investors demand no additional compensation beyond the risk-free rate, regardless of the risk of the asset in question.

What would have happened if we had assumed that the expected return on a stock was greater than the risk-free rate? The value of the call would still be $6.82. However, the calculations would be difficult. For example, if we assumed that the expected return on the stock was, say, 11 percent, we would have had to derive the expected return on the call. Although the expected return on the call would be higher than 11 percent, it would take a lot of work to determine it precisely. Why do any more work than you have to? Because we can't think of any good reason, we (and most other financial economists) choose to assume risk-neutrality.

Thus, the preceding material allows us to value a call in the following two ways:

1. Determine the cost of a strategy to duplicate the call. This strategy involves an investment in a fractional share of stock financed by partial borrowing.
2. Calculate the probabilities of a rise and a fall under the assumption of risk-neutrality.

Use those probabilities, in conjunction with the risk-free rate, to discount the payoffs of the call at expiration.

The Black–Scholes Model

The above example illustrates the duplicating strategy. Unfortunately, such a two-state (or binomial) strategy such as this will not work in the real world over, say, a one-year time frame, because there are many more than two possibilities for next year's stock price. However, the number of possibilities is reduced as the time period is shortened. In fact, the assumption that there are only two possibilities for the stock price over the next infinitesimal instant is quite plausible.[12]

In our opinion, the fundamental insight of Black and Scholes is to shorten the time period. They show that a specific combination of stock and borrowing can indeed duplicate a call over an infinitesimal time horizon. Because the price of the stock will change over the first instant, another combination of stock and borrowing is needed to duplicate the call over the second instant and so on. By adjusting the combination from moment to moment, they can continually duplicate the call. It may boggle the mind that a formula can (1) determine the duplicating combination at any moment and (2) value the option based on this duplicating strategy. Suffice it to say that their dynamic strategy allows them to value a call in the real world just as we showed how to value the call in the two-state model.

This is the basic intuition behind the Black–Scholes model. Because the actual derivation of their formula is, alas, far beyond the scope of this text, we simply present the formula itself. The formula is

Black–Scholes Model:

$$C = SN(d_1) - Ee^{-rt}N(d_2)$$

where

$$d_1 = [\ln(S/E) + \left(r + \tfrac{1}{2}\sigma^2\right)t]/\sqrt{\sigma^2 t}$$
$$d_2 = d_1 - \sqrt{\sigma^2 t}$$

This formula for the value of a call, C, is one of the most complex in finance. However, it involves only five parameters:

1. S = Current stock price
2. E = Exercise price of call
3. r = Continuously compounded risk-free rate of return (annualized)
4. σ^2 = Variance (per year) of the continuous return on the stock
5. t = Time (in years) to expiration date

In addition, there is the statistical concept:

$N(d)$ = Probability that a standardized, normally distributed, random variable will be less than or equal to d

Rather than discuss the formula in its algebraic state, we illustrate with Example 23.3.

---

[12] A full treatment of this assumption can be found in John C. Hull, *Options, Futures and Other Derivatives,* 6th ed. Upper Saddle River, N.J.: Prentice Hall (2006).

EXAMPLE 23.3

Consider Private Equipment Company (PEC). On October 4, of year 0, the PEC April $49 call option had a closing value of $4. The stock itself was selling at $50. On October 4 the option had 199 days to expiration (maturity date is April 21, year 1). The annual risk-free interest rate (continuously compounded) is 7 percent.

The above information determines three variables directly:

1. The stock price, *S*, is $50.
2. The exercise price, *E*, is $49.
3. The risk-free rate, *r*, is 0.07.

In addition, the time to maturity, *t*, can be calculated quickly. The formula calls for *t* to be expressed in years.

4. We express the 199-day interval in years as *t* = 199/365.

In the real world, an option trader would know *S* and *E* exactly. Traders generally view Canada Treasury bills as riskless, so a current quote would be obtained for the interest rate. The trader would also know (or could count) the number of days to expiration exactly. Thus, the fraction of a year to expiration, *t*, could be calculated quickly.

The problem comes in determining the variance of the stock's return. The formula calls for the variance measured between the purchase date of October 4 and the expiration date. Unfortunately, this represents the future, so the correct value for variance is simply not available. Instead, traders frequently estimate variance from past data, just as we calculated variance in an earlier chapter. In addition, some traders may use intuition to adjust their estimate. For example, if anticipation of an upcoming event is currently increasing the volatility of the stock, the trader might adjust the estimate of variance upward. (This problem was most severe right after the October 19, 1987, crash. The stock market was quite risky in the aftermath, so estimates using precrash data were too low.)

The above discussion was intended merely to mention the difficulties in variance estimation, not to present a solution.[13] For our purposes, we assume that a trader has come up with an estimate of variance.

5. The variance of Private Equipment Co. has been estimated to be 0.09 per year.

Using the above five parameters, we calculate the Black–Scholes value of the PEC option in three steps:

Step 1: Calculate d_1 *and* d_2. These values can be determined by a straightforward, albeit tedious, insertion of our parameters into the basic formula. We have

$$d_1 = \left[\ln\left(\frac{S}{E}\right) + \left(r + \frac{1}{2}\sigma^2\right)t\right]/\sqrt{\sigma^2 t}$$

$$= \left[\ln\left(\frac{50}{49}\right) + \left(0.07 + \frac{1}{2} \times 0.09\right) \times \frac{199}{365}\right]/\sqrt{0.09 \times \frac{199}{365}}$$

$$= [0.0202 + 0.0627]/0.2215 = 0.3742$$

$$d_2 = d_1 - \sqrt{\sigma^2 t}$$

$$= 0.1527$$

---

[13]A more in-depth attempt to estimate variance can be found in J. Hull, *Options, Futures and Other Derivative Securities*, 6th ed. (Upper Saddle River, N.J.: Prentice-Hall, 2006).

FIGURE 23.10

**Graph of
Cumulative
Probability**

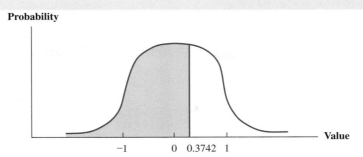

Shaded area represents cumulative probability. Because the probability is
0.6459 that a drawing from the standard normal distribution will be below
0.3742, we say that N(0.3742) = 0.6459. That is, the cumulative probability of
0.3742 is 0.6459.

Step 2: Calculate $N(d_1)$ *and* $N(d_2)$. The values $N(d_1)$ and $N(d_2)$ can best be understood by examining Figure 23.10. The figure shows the normal distribution with an expected value of 0 and a standard deviation of 1. This is frequently called the **standardized normal distribution.** We mentioned in an earlier chapter that the probability that a drawing from this distribution will be between −1 and +1 (within one standard deviation of its mean, in other words) is 68.26 percent.

Now, let us ask a different question: What is the probability that a drawing from the standardized normal distribution will be *below* a particular value? For example, the probability that a drawing will be below 0 is clearly 50 percent because the normal distribution is symmetric. Using statistical terminology, we say that the **cumulative probability** of 0 is 50 percent. Statisticians say N(0) = 50%. It turns out that

$$N(d_1) = N(0.3742) = 0.6459$$
$$N(d_2) = N(0.1527) = 0.5607$$

The first value means that there is a 64.59 percent probability that a drawing from the standardized normal distribution will be below 0.3742. The second value means that there is a 56.07 percent probability that a drawing from the standardized normal distribution will be below 0.1527. More generally, N(d) is the notation that a drawing from the standardized normal distribution will be below d. In other words, N(d) is the cumulative probability of d. Note that d_1 and d_2 in our example are slightly positive, so $N(d_1)$ and $N(d_2)$ are slightly greater than 0.50.

We can determine the cumulative probability from Table 23.3. For example, consider d = 0.37. This can be found in the table as 0.3 on the vertical and 0.07 on the horizontal. The value in the table for d = 0.37 is 0.1443. This value is *not* the cumulative probability of 0.37. One must first make an adjustment to determine cumulative probability. That is,

$$N(0.37) = 0.50 + 0.1443 = 0.6443$$
$$N(-0.37) = 0.50 - 0.1443 = 0.3557$$

Unfortunately, our table only handles two significant digits, whereas our value of 0.3742 has four significant digits. Hence, we must interpolate to find N(0.3742). Because N(0.37) = 0.6443 and N(0.38) = 0.6480, the difference between the two values is 0.0037 (0.6480 − 0.6443). Because 0.3742 is 42 percent of the way between 0.37 and 0.38, we interpolate as[14]

$$N(0.3743) = 0.6443 + 0.42 \times 0.0037 = 0.6459$$

---

[14]This method is called *linear interpolation*. It is only one of a number of possible methods of interpolation.

TABLE 23.3   Cumulative Probabilities of the Standard Normal Distribution Function

d	0.00	0.01	0.02	0.03	0.04	0.05	0.06	0.07	0.08	0.09
0.0	0.0000	0.0040	0.0080	0.0120	0.0160	0.0199	0.0239	0.0279	0.0319	0.0359
0.1	0.0398	0.0438	0.0478	0.0517	0.0557	0.0596	0.0636	0.0675	0.0714	0.0753
0.2	0.0793	0.0832	0.0871	0.0910	0.0948	0.0987	0.1026	0.1064	0.1103	0.1141
0.3	0.1179	0.1217	0.1255	0.1293	0.1331	0.1368	0.1406	0.1443	0.1480	0.1517
0.4	0.1554	0.1591	0.1628	0.1664	0.1700	0.1736	0.1772	0.1808	0.1844	0.1879
0.5	0.1915	0.1950	0.1985	0.2019	0.2054	0.2088	0.2123	0.2157	0.2190	0.2224
0.6	0.2257	0.2291	0.2324	0.2357	0.2389	0.2422	0.2454	0.2486	0.2517	0.2549
0.7	0.2580	0.2611	0.2642	0.2673	0.2704	0.2734	0.2764	0.2794	0.2823	0.2852
0.8	0.2881	0.2910	0.2939	0.2967	0.2995	0.3023	0.3051	0.3078	0.3106	0.3133
0.9	0.3159	0.3186	0.3212	0.3238	0.3264	0.3289	0.3315	0.3340	0.3365	0.3389
1.0	0.3413	0.3438	0.3461	0.3485	0.3508	0.3531	0.3554	0.3577	0.3599	0.3621
1.1	0.3643	0.3665	0.3686	0.3708	0.3729	0.3749	0.3770	0.3790	0.3810	0.3830
1.2	0.3849	0.3869	0.3888	0.3907	0.3925	0.3944	0.3962	0.3980	0.3997	0.4015
1.3	0.4032	0.4049	0.4066	0.4082	0.4099	0.4115	0.4131	0.4147	0.4162	0.4177
1.4	0.4192	0.4207	0.4222	0.4236	0.4251	0.4265	0.4279	0.4292	0.4306	0.4319
1.5	0.4332	0.4345	0.4357	0.4370	0.4382	0.4394	0.4406	0.4418	0.4429	0.4441
1.6	0.4452	0.4463	0.4474	0.4484	0.4495	0.4505	0.4515	0.4525	0.4535	0.4545
1.7	0.4554	0.4564	0.4573	0.4582	0.4591	0.4599	0.4608	0.4616	0.4625	0.4633
1.8	0.4641	0.4649	0.4656	0.4664	0.4671	0.4678	0.4686	0.4693	0.4699	0.4706
1.9	0.4713	0.4719	0.4726	0.4732	0.4738	0.4744	0.4750	0.4756	0.4761	0.4767
2.0	0.4773	0.4778	0.4783	0.4788	0.4793	0.4798	0.4803	0.4808	0.4812	0.4817
2.1	0.4821	0.4826	0.4830	0.4834	0.4838	0.4842	0.4846	0.4850	0.4854	0.4857
2.2	0.4861	0.4866	0.4830	0.4871	0.4875	0.4878	0.4881	0.4884	0.4887	0.4890
2.3	0.4893	0.4896	0.4898	0.4901	0.4904	0.4906	0.4909	0.4911	0.4913	0.4916
2.4	0.4918	0.4920	0.4922	0.4925	0.4927	0.4929	9.4931	0.4932	0.4934	0.4936
2.5	0.4938	0.4940	0.4941	0.4943	0.4945	0.4946	0.4948	0.4949	0.4951	0.4952
2.6	0.4953	0.4955	0.4956	0.4957	0.4959	0.4960	0.4961	0.4962	0.4963	0.4964
2.7	0.4965	0.4966	0.4967	0.4968	0.4969	0.4970	0.4971	0.4972	0.4973	0.4974
2.8	0.4974	0.4975	0.4976	0.4977	0.4977	0.4978	0.4979	0.0479	0.4980	0.4981
2.9	0.4981	0.4982	0.4982	0.4982	0.4984	0.4984	0.4985	0.4985	0.4986	0.4986
3.0	0.4987	0.4987	0.4987	0.4988	0.4988	0.4989	0.4989	0.4989	0.4990	0.4990

$N(d)$ represents areas under the standard normal distribution function. Suppose that $d_1 = 0.24$. This table implies a cumulative probability of $0.5000 + 0.0948 = 0.5948$. If d_1 is equal to 0.2452, we must estimate the probability by interpolating between $N(0.25)$ and $N(0.24)$.

Step 3: Calculate C. We have

$$C = S \times [N(d_1)] - Ee^{-rt} \times [N(d_2)]$$
$$= \$50 \times [N(d_1)] - \$49 \times [e^{-0.07 \times (199/365)}] \times N(d_2)$$
$$= (\$50 \times 0.6459) - (\$49 \times 0.9626 \times 0.5607)$$
$$= \$32.295 - \$26.447$$
$$= \$5.85$$

The estimated price of $5.85 is greater than the $4 actual price, implying that the call option is underpriced. A trader believing in the Black–Scholes model would buy a call. Of course, the Black–Scholes model is fallible. Perhaps the disparity between the model's estimate and the market price reflects error in the model's estimate of variance.

The previous example stressed the calculations involved in using the Black–Scholes formula. Is there any intuition behind the formula? Yes, and that intuition follows from the stock purchase and borrowing strategy in our binomial (two-state) example.[15] The first line of the Black–Scholes equation is:

$$C = S \times \mathrm{N}(d_1) - Ee^{-rt}\,\mathrm{N}(d_2)$$

which is exactly analogous to Equation (23.2):

$$\text{Value of call} = \text{Stock price} \times \text{Delta} - \text{Amount borrowed} \qquad \textbf{(23.2)}$$

that we presented in the two-state example. It turns out that $\mathrm{N}(d_1)$ is the delta in the Black–Scholes model. $\mathrm{N}(d_1)$ is 0.6459 in the previous example. In addition, $Ee^{-rt}\mathrm{N}(d_2)$ is the amount that an investor must borrow to duplicate a call. In the previous example, this value is $26.45 ($49 \times 0.9626 \times 0.5607$). Thus, the model tells us that we can duplicate the call of the preceding example by both:

1. Buying 0.6459 share of stock.
2. Borrowing $26.45.

It is no exaggeration to say that the Black–Scholes formula is among the most important contributions in finance. It allows anyone to calculate the value of an option given a few parameters. The attraction of the formula is that four of the parameters are observable: the current price of the stock, S, the exercise price, E, the interest rate, r, and the time to expiration date, t. Only one of the parameters must be estimated: the variance of return, σ^2.

To see how truly attractive this formula is, note what parameters are not needed. First, the investor's risk aversion does not affect value. The formula can be used by anyone, regardless of willingness to bear risk. Second, it does not depend on the expected return on the stock! Investors with different assessments of the stock's expected return will nevertheless agree on the call price. As in the two-state example, this is because the call depends on the stock price and that price already balances investors' divergent views.

? Concept Questions

- How does the two-state option model work?
- What is the formula for the Black–Scholes option pricing model?

23.9 Stocks and Bonds as Options

The previous material in this chapter described, explained, and valued publicly traded options. This is important material to any finance student because much trading occurs in these listed options. The study of options has another purpose for the student of corporate finance.

You may have heard the one-liner about the elderly gentleman who was surprised to learn that he had been speaking prose all of his life. The same can be said about the corporate finance student and options. Although options were formally defined for the first time

---

[15]Another intuitive approach to the Black–Scholes formula views $\mathrm{N}(d_1)$ and $\mathrm{N}(d_2)$ as probabilities that the option will expire in the money and be exercised. For example, when the stock price is high, these probabilities are close to unity and the call value is the stock price minus the present value of the exercise price. At the other extreme, when the stock price is low, the probabilities are near zero and call is almost worthless. For more on this intuition, see Z. Bodie, A. Kane, A.J. Marcus, S. Perrakis, and P.J. Ryan, *Investments,* 5th Canadian Edition, McGraw Hill Ryerson, Toronto, 2005, p. 691.

in this chapter, many corporate policies discussed earlier in the text were actually options in disguise. Though it is beyond the scope of this chapter to recast all of corporate finance in terms of options, the rest of the chapter considers three topics in which implicit options play an important role:

1. Stocks and bonds as options.
2. Capital structure decisions as options.
3. Capital budgeting decisions as options.

We begin by illustrating the implicit options in stocks and bonds through Example 23.4.

EXAMPLE 23.4

The Popov Company has been awarded the concessions at next year's Olympic Games in Antarctica. Because the firm's principals live in Antarctica and because there is no other concession business on that continent, their enterprise will disband after the games. The firm has issued debt to help finance this venture. Interest and principal due on the debt next year will be $800, at which time the debt will be paid off in full. The firm's cash flows next year are forecasted as

	Popov's Cash Flow Schedule			
	Very Successful Games	Moderately Successful Games	Moderately Unsuccessful Games	Outright Failure
Cash flow before interest and principal	$1,000	$850	$700	$550
Interest and principal	800	800	700	550
Cash flow to shareholders	$ 200	$ 50	$ 0	$ 0

As can be seen, the principals forecasted four equally likely scenarios. If either of the first two scenarios occurs, the bondholders will be paid in full. The extra cash flow goes to the shareholders. However, if either of the last two scenarios occurs, the bondholders will not be paid in full. Instead, they will receive the firm's entire cash flow, leaving the shareholders with nothing.

This example is similar to the bankruptcy examples presented in our chapters on capital structure. Our new insight is that the relationship between the common stock and the firm can be expressed in terms of options. We consider call options first because the intuition is easier. The put option scenario is treated next.

The Firm Expressed in Terms of Call Options

Shareholders   We now show that stock can be viewed as a call option on the firm. To illustrate this, Figure 23.11 graphs the cash flow to the shareholders as a function of the cash flow to the firm. The shareholders receive nothing if the firm's cash flows are less than $800; here, all of the cash flows go to the bondholders. However, the shareholders earn a dollar for every dollar that the firm receives above $800. The graph looks exactly like the call option graph (Figure 23.5) that we considered earlier in this chapter.

But what is the underlying asset upon which the stock is a call option? The underlying asset is the firm itself. That is, we can view the bondholders as owning the firm. However, the shareholders have a call option on the firm with an exercise price of $800.

If the firm's cash flow is above $800, the shareholders will choose to exercise this option. In other words, they will buy the firm from the bondholders for $800. Their net

FIGURE 23.11

Cash Flow to Shareholders of Popov Corporation as a Function of Cash Flow of Firm

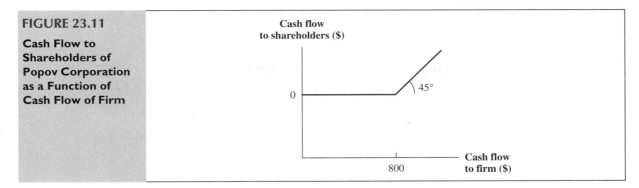

cash flow is the difference between the firm's cash flow and their $800 payment. This will be $200 (or $1,000 − $800) if the games are very successful and $50 (or $850 − $800) if the games are moderately successful.

If the value of the firm's cash flows is less than $800, the shareholders will not choose to exercise their option. Instead, they will walk away from the firm, as would any call option holder. The bondholders then receive the firm's entire cash flow.

This view of the firm is a novel one, and students are frequently bothered by it on first exposure. However, we encourage students to keep looking at the firm in this way until the view becomes second nature to them.

Bondholders   What about the bondholders? Our earlier cash flow schedule showed that they get the entire cash flow of the firm if it is less than $800. Should the firm earn more than $800, the bondholders receive only $800. That is, they are entitled only to interest and principal. This schedule is graphed in Figure 23.12.

In keeping with our view that the shareholders have a call option on the firm, what does the bondholders' position consist of? The bondholders' position can be described by two claims:

1. They own the firm.
2. They have written a call against the firm with an exercise price of $800.

As we mentioned above, the shareholders walk away from the firm if cash flows are less than $800. Thus, the bondholders retain ownership in this case. However, if the cash

FIGURE 23.12

Cash Flow to Bondholders as a Function of Cash Flow of Firm

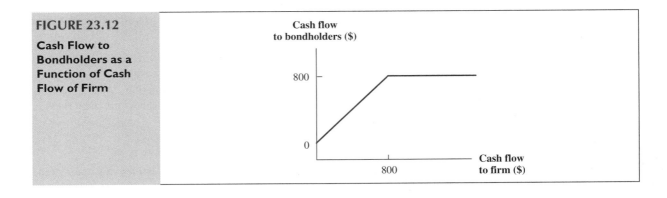

flows are greater than $800, the shareholders exercise their option. They call the stock away from the bondholders for $800.

The Firm Expressed in Terms of Put Options

The above analysis expresses the positions of the shareholders and the bondholders in terms of call options. We can now express the situation in terms of put options.

Shareholders   The shareholders' position can be expressed by three claims:

1. They own the firm.
2. They owe $800 in interest and principal to the bondholders.

If the debt were risk-free, these two claims would fully describe the shareholders' situation. However, because of the possibility of default, we have a third claim as well:

3. The shareholders own a put option on the firm with an exercise price of $800. The group of bondholders is the seller of the put.

Now consider two possibilities.

Cash Flow Is Less Than $800   Because the put has an exercise price of $800, the put is in the money. The shareholders "put" (that is, sell) the firm to the bondholders. Normally, the holder of a put receives the exercise price when the asset is sold. However, the shareholders already owe $800 to the bondholders. Thus, the debt of $800 is simply cancelled—and no money changes hands—when the stock is delivered to the bondholders. Because the shareholders give up the stock in exchange for extinguishing the debt, the shareholders end up with nothing if the cash flow is below $800.

Cash Flow Is Greater Than $800   Because the put is out of the money in this case, the shareholders do not exercise. Thus, the shareholders retain ownership of the firm but pay $800 to the bondholders as interest and principal.

Bondholders   The bondholders' position can be described by two claims:

1. The bondholders are owed $800.
2. They have sold a put option on the firm to the shareholders with an exercise price of $800.

Cash Flow Is Less Than $800   As mentioned above, the shareholders will exercise the put in this case. This means that the bondholders are obligated to pay $800 for the firm. Because they are owed $800, the two obligations offset each other. Thus, the bondholders simply end up with the firm.

Cash Flow Is Greater Than $800   Here, the shareholders do not exercise the put. Thus, the bondholders merely receive the $800 that is due them.

Expressing the bondholders' position in this way is illuminating. With a riskless default-free bond, the bondholders are owed $800. Thus, we can express the risky bond in terms of a riskless bond and a put:

$$\text{Value of risky bond} = \text{Value of default-free bond} - \text{Value of put option}$$

That is, the value of the risky bond is the value of the default-free bond less the value of the shareholders' option to sell the company for $800.

A Resolution of the Two Views

We have argued above that the positions of the shareholders and the bondholders can be viewed either in terms of calls or in terms of puts. These two viewpoints are summarized in Table 23.4.

We have found from past experience that it is generally harder for students to think of the firm in terms of puts than in terms of calls. Thus, it would be helpful if there were a way to show that the two viewpoints are equivalent. Fortunately there is *put–call parity*. In an earlier section we presented the put–call parity relationship as Equation (23.1), which we now repeat:

$$\begin{matrix} \text{Value of} \\ \text{common stock} \end{matrix} + \begin{matrix} \text{Value of put} \\ \text{on common stock} \end{matrix} - \begin{matrix} \text{Value of call} \\ \text{on common stock} \end{matrix} = \begin{matrix} \text{Present value of} \\ \text{exercise price} \end{matrix} \quad \textbf{(23.1)}$$

Using the results of this section, Equation (23.1) can be rewritten as

$$\underbrace{\begin{matrix} \text{Value of call} \\ \text{on firm} \end{matrix}}_{\substack{\text{Shareholders'} \\ \text{position in terms} \\ \text{of call options}}} = \underbrace{\begin{matrix} \text{Value of} \\ \text{firm} \end{matrix} + \begin{matrix} \text{Value of put} \\ \text{on firm} \end{matrix} - \begin{matrix} \text{Value of} \\ \text{default-free bond} \end{matrix}}_{\substack{\text{Shareholders' position} \\ \text{in terms of put options}}} \quad \textbf{(23.2)}$$

Going from Equation (23.1) to Equation (23.2) involves a few steps. First, we treat the firm, not the stock, as the underlying asset in this section. Second, the exercise price is now $800, the principal and interest on the firm's debt. Taking the present value of this amount at the riskless rate yields the value of a default-free bond. Third, the order of the terms in Equation (23.1) is rearranged in Equation (23.2).

Note that the left-hand side of Equation (23.2) is the shareholders' position in terms of call options, as shown in Table 23.4. The right-hand side of Equation (23.2) is the shareholders' position in terms of put options, as shown in the table. Thus, put–call parity shows that viewing the shareholders' position in terms of call options is equivalent to viewing the shareholders' position in terms of put options.

Now, let's rearrange terms in Equation (23.2) to yield

$$\underbrace{\begin{matrix} \text{Value of} \\ \text{firm} \end{matrix} - \begin{matrix} \text{Value of call} \\ \text{on firm} \end{matrix}}_{\substack{\text{Bondholders' position in} \\ \text{terms of call options}}} = \underbrace{\begin{matrix} \text{Value of} \\ \text{default-free bond} \end{matrix} - \begin{matrix} \text{Value of put} \\ \text{on firm} \end{matrix}}_{\substack{\text{Bondholders' position in} \\ \text{terms of put options}}} \quad \textbf{(23.3)}$$

The left-hand side of Equation (23.3) is the bondholders' position in terms of call options, as shown in Table 23.4. The right-hand side of the equation is the bondholders' position in terms of put options, as shown in Table 23.4. Thus, put–call parity shows that viewing the bondholders' position in terms of call options is equivalent to viewing the bondholders' position in terms of put options.

A Note on Loan Guarantees

In the Popov example above, the bondholders bore the risk of default. Of course, bondholders generally ask for an interest rate that is high enough to compensate them for bearing risk. When firms experience financial distress, they can no longer attract new debt at moderate interest rates. Thus, firms experiencing distress have frequently sought loan guarantees from the government. Our framework can be used to understand these guarantees.

TABLE 23.4
Positions of Shareholders and Bondholders in Popov Company in Terms of Calls and Puts

Shareholders	Bondholders
Positions viewed in terms of call options	
1. Shareholders own a call on the firm with exercise price of $800.	1. Bondholders own the firm.
	2. Bondholders have sold a call on the firm to the shareholders.
Positions viewed in terms of put options	
1. Shareholders own the firm.	1. Bondholders are owed $800 in interest and principal.
2. Shareholders owe $800 in interest and principal to bondholders.	2. Bondholders have sold a put on the firm to the shareholders.
3. Shareholders own a put option on the firm with exercise price of $800.	

If the firm defaults on a guaranteed loan, the government must make up the difference. In other words, a government guarantee converts a risky bond into a riskless bond. What is the value of this guarantee?

Recall that, with option pricing,

$$\begin{array}{ccc} \text{Value of} \\ \text{default-free bond} \end{array} = \begin{array}{c} \text{Value of} \\ \text{risky bond} \end{array} + \begin{array}{c} \text{Value of} \\ \text{put option} \end{array}$$

This equation shows that the government is assuming an obligation that has a cost equal to the value of a put option.

Our analysis differs from that of either politicians or company spokespersons. They generally say that the guarantee will cost the taxpayer nothing because the guarantee enables the firm to attract debt, thereby staying solvent. However, it should be pointed out that, though solvency may be a strong possibility, it is never a certainty. Thus, at the time the guarantee is made, the government's obligation has a cost in terms of present value. To say that a guarantee costs the government nothing is like saying that a put on the stock of, say, Royal Bank, has no value because the stock is *likely* to rise in price.

Federal and provincial governments provide guarantees for bank loans to companies whose survival is considered important to the public interest. Who benefits from a typical loan guarantee?

1. If existing risky debt is guaranteed, all gains accrue to the existing bondholders or creditors. The shareholders gain nothing because the limited liability of corporations absolves the shareholders of any obligation in bankruptcy.

2. If new debt is being issued and guaranteed, the new debtholders do not gain. Rather, in a competitive market, they must accept a low interest rate because of the debt's low risk. The shareholders gain here because they are able to issue debt at a low interest rate. In addition, some of the gains accrue to the old bondholders because the firm's value is greater than would otherwise be true. Therefore, if shareholders want all the gains from loan guarantees, they should renegotiate or retire existing bonds before the guarantee is in place.

Deposit Insurance as a Loan Guarantee   When you lend money to a financial institution (by making a deposit), your loan is guaranteed (up to $60,000) by the federal government provided your institution is a member of the Canada Deposit Insurance Corporation (CDIC). As we argued above, loan guarantees are not cost-free. This point was made abundantly clear to the government when two banks in Western Canada collapsed in 1985, the Principal Group collapsed in 1987, and Central Guaranty Trust collapsed in 1992.

We also pointed out that, since the put option allows a risky firm to borrow at subsidized rates, it is an asset to the shareholders. The more volatile the firm, the greater the value of the put option and the more the guarantee is worth to the shareholders. Following this logic, Giammarino, Schwartz, and Zechner modified the Black–Scholes model to value the put option in CDIC deposit insurance for Canadian banks in the mid-1980s. They found that financial markets provided early warning of bank failures as the value of the put option increased significantly before bank failure occurred. Their research also showed that, by charging the same premium for all financial institutions regardless of risk, the CDIC subsidized riskier banks and likely encouraged risk taking.[14]

One result is that accountants in Canada, urged on by the auditor general, are forcing government agencies to report guarantees and other contingent liabilities in their financial statements. This may induce greater caution in extending guarantees in the first place.

? Concept Questions

- How can the firm value be expressed in terms of call options?
- How can the firm value be expressed in terms of put options?
- How does put–call parity relate these two expressions?
- Why are government loan guarantees not free? Why do such guarantees often encourage firms to increase their risk?

23.10   Capital Structure Policy and Options

Recall our chapters on capital structure where we showed how managers, acting on behalf of the shareholders, can take advantage of bondholders. A number of these strategies can be explained in terms of options. As an illustration, this section examines one such strategy, the choice between a high-risk project and a low-risk project.

Selecting High-Risk Projects

Imagine a levered firm considering two mutually exclusive projects: a low-risk one and a high-risk one. There are two equally likely outcomes: recession and boom. The firm is in such dire straits that, should a recession hit, it will come near to bankruptcy if the low-risk project is selected and will actually fall into bankruptcy if the high-risk project is selected. The cash flows for the firm if the low-risk project is taken can be described as

	Probability	Value of Firm	=	Stock	+	Bonds
		Low-Risk Project				
Recession	0.5	$400	=	0	+	$400
Boom	0.5	$800	=	$400	+	$400

If a recession occurs, the value of the firm will be $400, and if a boom occurs, the value of the firm will be $800. The expected value of the firm is $600 (or $0.5 \times \$400 + 0.5 \times \$800$). The firm has promised to pay the bondholders $400. Shareholders will obtain the

---

[16]R. Giammarino, E. Schwartz, and J. Zechner, "Market Valuation of Bank Assets and Deposit Insurance in Canada," *Canadian Journal of Economics* (February 1989), pp. 109–27.

difference between the total payoff and the amount paid to the bondholders. The bondholders have the prior claim on the payoffs, and the shareholders have the residual claim.

Now suppose that a riskier project can be substituted for the low-risk project. The payoffs and probabilities are as follows:

		High-Risk Project				
	Probability	Value of Firm	=	Stock	+	Bonds
Recession	0.5	$ 200	=	0	+	$200
Boom	0.5	$1,000	=	$600	+	$400

The expected value of the firm is $600 (or 0.5 × $200 + 0.5 × $1,000), which is identical to the value of the firm with the low-risk project. However, note that the expected value of the stock is $300 (or 0.5 × 0 + 0.5 × $600) with the high-risk project, but only $200 (or 0.5 × 0 + 0.5 × $400) with the low-risk project. Given the firm's present levered state, shareholders will select the high-risk project.

The shareholders benefit at the expense of the bondholders when the high-risk project is accepted. The explanation is quite clear: The bondholders suffer dollar for dollar when the firm's value falls short of the $400 bond obligation. However, the bondholders' payments are capped at $400 when the firm does well.

This can be explained in terms of call options. We argued earlier in this chapter that the value of a call rises with an increase in the volatility of the underlying asset. Because the stock is a call option on the firm, a rise in the volatility of the firm increases the value of the stock. In our example, the value of the stock is higher if the high-risk project is accepted.

Table 23.4 showed that the value of a risky bond can be viewed as the difference between the value of the stock and the value of a call on the firm. Because a call's value rises with the risk of the underlying asset, the value of the bond should decline if the firm increases its risk. In our example, the bondholders are hurt when the high-risk project is accepted.

? Concept Question

- How can options be used to explain strategies like selecting high-risk projects?

23.11   Mergers and Options

Mergers are structured either as *cash-for-stock* transactions or as *stock-for-stock* transactions. The selling shareholders receive cash from the buyer in the first type of transaction and receive stock in the buying company in the second type of transaction. In the first half of 2000, General Mills (GM) was attempting to acquire the Pillsbury division of Diageo PLC. GM wanted a stock-for-stock transaction and initially offered Diageo 141,000,000 shares of GM's stock. Given that GM was trading at that time at $42.55 per share, the shareholders of Diageo would receive consideration of about $6 billion ($42.55 × 141 million). Although this amount was more than satisfactory to Diageo's management, they were upset with the risk inherent in stock-for-stock transactions. That is, General Mills' shares might be overpriced at $42.55, implying the possibility of a price decline at a later date.

To allay these fears, GM decided to "insure" Diageo's shareholders with a contingent value rights (CVR) plan of up to $642 million or $4.55 ($642 million/141 million) per share.

FIGURE 23.13   **Cash Payment to Each Newly Issued Share of GM Stock in Acquisition of Pillsbury Division of Diageo PLC**

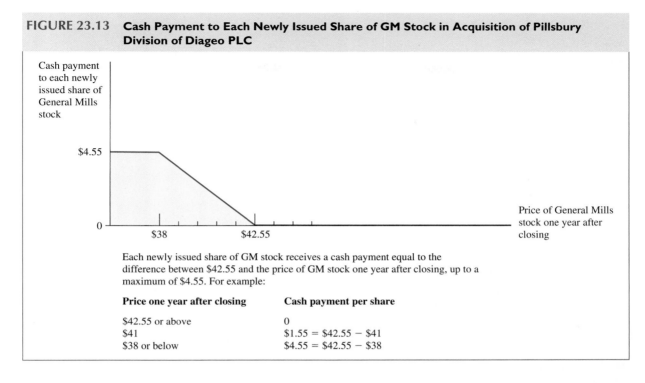

Each newly issued share of GM stock receives a cash payment equal to the difference between $42.55 and the price of GM stock one year after closing, up to a maximum of $4.55. For example:

Price one year after closing	Cash payment per share
$42.55 or above	0
$41	$1.55 = $42.55 − $41
$38 or below	$4.55 = $42.55 − $38

Under this plan, each of the 141 million GM shares issued to Diageo's shareholders would receive in cash the difference between $42.55 and the price of GM's shares one year after the deal's closing date, up to a maximum of $4.55. For example, if GM's shares traded at $40 one year after closing, each newly issued share of GM would receive $2.55 ($42.55 − $40) in cash. Thus, because the cash payment of $2.55 goes with each newly issued share worth $40, the total package is still worth $42.55. However, because the maximum payment is $4.55, no additional insurance is provided for stock price drops below $38 ($42.55 − $4.55). For example, if the stock falls to $36, the total package is worth only $40.55 ($36 + $4.55). In Figure 23.13 the cash payment per share of newly issued GM stock is graphed as a function of GM's stock price one year after the closing date. The total package (price of one share of GM's stock plus the cash payment) is shown in Figure 23.14.

The contingent value rights plan can be viewed in terms of puts. That is, the CVR plan implies that each newly issued share of GM's stock receives a put on GM's stock with an exercise price of $42.55 while selling a put on GM with an exercise price of $38. This idea is illustrated in Figure 23.15. If GM's stock price ends up below $42.55, the cash payoff from each put with an exercise price of $42.55 is equal to the difference between $42.55 and the ending price of GM. However, should the price fall below $38, the put with an exercise price of $38 will also be in the money. Each newly issued share of GM's stock receives a put with an exercise price of $42.55 and writes a put with an exercise price of $38, so each share receives cash of $4.55 ($42.55 − $38) should GM's stock price drop below $38.

Diageo's management liked the contingent value rights plan enough to accept the merger with the CVR agreement attached. This example shows that creative financing techniques, such as the use of puts in this case, can be used to accommodate a seller who would otherwise be reluctant.

FIGURE 23.14

Total Value of a Newly Issued Share of GM Stock, Including the Cash Payment

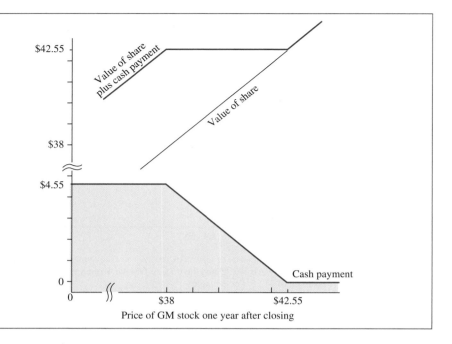

Price of GM stock one year after closing

? Concept Question

• **How can a contingent value rights plan assist in a merger?**

FIGURE 23.15

Payoffs to Implied Puts in General Mills' Acquisition of Pillsbury

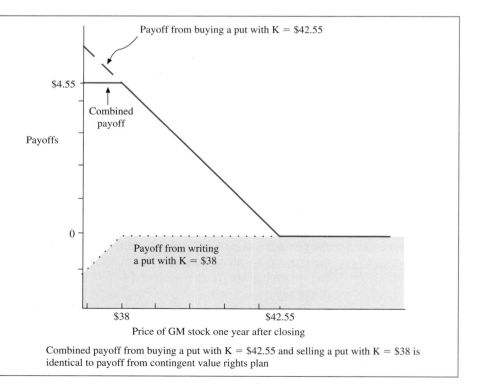

Price of GM stock one year after closing

Combined payoff from buying a put with K = $42.55 and selling a put with K = $38 is identical to payoff from contingent value rights plan

23.12   Investment in Real Projects and Options

Our discussion begins with a quick review of the material on capital budgeting presented earlier in the text. We first considered projects where forecasts for future cash flows were made at date 0. The expected cash flow in each future period was discounted at an appropriate risky rate, yielding an NPV calculation. For independent projects, a positive NPV meant acceptance and a negative NPV meant rejection.

This approach treated risk through the discount rate. We later considered decision-tree analysis, an approach that handles risk in a more sophisticated way. We pointed out that the firm will make investment and operating decisions on a project over its entire life. We value a project today, assuming that future decisions will be optimal. However, we do not yet know what these decisions will be, because much information remains to be discovered. The firm's ability to delay its investment and operating decisions until the release of information is an option. We now illustrate this option through Example 23.5.

EXAMPLE 23.5

Exoff Oil Corporation is considering the purchase of an oil field in a remote northern area. The seller has listed the property for $10,000 and is eager to sell immediately. Initial drilling costs are $500,000. The firm anticipates that 10,000 barrels of oil can be extracted each year for many decades. Because the termination date is so far in the future and so hard to estimate, the firm views the cash flow stream from the oil as a perpetuity. With oil prices at US$40 per barrel (C$53) and extraction costs at C$49 a barrel, the firm anticipates a net margin of $4 per barrel. Because the firm budgets capital in real terms, it assumes that its cash flow per barrel will always be $4. The appropriate real discount rate is 10 percent. The firm has enough tax credits from bad years in the past so that it will not need to pay taxes on any profits from the oil field. Should Exoff buy the property?

The NPV of the oil field to Exoff is

$$-\$110,000 = -\$10,000 - \$500,000 + \frac{\$4 \times 10,000}{0.10} \qquad (23.4)$$

According to this analysis, Exoff should not purchase the land.

Though this approach uses the standard capital budgeting techniques of this and other textbooks, it is actually inappropriate for this situation. To see this, consider the analysis of Kirtley Thornton, a consultant to Exoff. He agrees that the price of oil is *expected* to rise at the rate of inflation. However, he points out that the next year is quite perilous for oil prices. On the one hand, OPEC is considering a long-term agreement that would raise oil prices to C$68 per barrel in real terms for many years in the future. On the other hand, National Motors recently indicated that cars using a mixture of sand and water for fuel are currently being tested. Thornton argues that oil will be priced at $5 in real terms for many years, should this development prove successful. Full information on both these developments will be released in exactly one year.

Should oil prices rise to $68 a barrel, the NPV of the project would be

$$\$1,390,000 = -\$10,000 - \$500,000 + \frac{(\$68 - \$49) \times 10,000}{0.10}$$

However, should oil prices fall to $5 a barrel, the NPV of the oil field will be even more negative than it is today.

Mr. Thornton makes two recommendations to Exoff's board:

1. The land should be purchased.
2. The drilling decision should be delayed until information on both OPEC's new agreement and National Motors' new automobile are developed.

He explains his recommendations to the board by first assuming that the land has already been purchased. He argues that, under this assumption, the drilling decision should be delayed. Second, he investigates his assumption that the land should have been purchased in the first place. This approach, examining the second decision (whether to drill) after assuming that the first decision (to buy the land) has been made, was also used in our earlier presentation on decision trees. Let us now work through Mr. Thornton's analysis.

Assume that the land has already been purchased. If the land has already been purchased, should drilling begin immediately? If drilling begins immediately, the NPV is −$110,000. If the drilling decision is delayed until new information is released in a year, the optimal choice can be made at that time. If oil prices drop to $5 a barrel, Exoff should not drill. Instead, the firm walks away from the project, losing nothing beyond its $10,000 purchase price for the land. If oil prices rise to $68, drilling should begin.

Mr. Thornton points out that, by delaying, the firm will only invest the $500,000 of drilling costs if oil prices rise. Thus, by delaying, the firm saves $500,000 in the case where oil prices drop. He concludes that, once the land is purchased, the drilling decision should be delayed.[17]

Should the land have been purchased in the first place? We now know that, if the land is purchased, it is optimal to defer the drilling decision until the release of information. Given that we know this optimal decision concerning drilling, should the land be purchased in the first place? Without knowing the exact probability that oil prices will rise, Mr. Thornton is nevertheless confident that the land should be purchased. The NPV of the project at $68 oil prices is $1,390,000, whereas the cost of the land is only $10,000. Kirtley believes that an oil price rise is possible, though by no means probable. Even so, he argues that the high potential return is clearly worth the risk.

This example presents an approach that is similar to our decision-tree analysis of the Solar Equipment Company in a previous chapter. Our purpose here is to discuss this type of decision in an option framework. When Exoff purchases the land, it is actually purchasing a call option. That is, once the land has been purchased, the firm has an option to buy an active oil field at an exercise price of $500,000. As it turns out, one should generally not exercise a call option immediately.[18] In this case, the firm delays exercise until relevant information concerning future oil prices is released.

This section points out a serious deficiency in classical capital budgeting: net present value calculations typically ignore the flexibility that real-world firms have. In our example, the standard techniques generated a negative NPV for the land purchase. Yet, by allowing the firm the option to change its investment policy according to new information, the land purchase can easily be justified.

---

[17]Actually, there are three separate effects here. First, the firm avoids drilling costs in the case of low oil prices by delaying the decision. This is the effect discussed by Mr. Thornton. Second, the present value of the $500,000 payment is less when the decision is delayed, even if drilling eventually takes place. Third, the firm loses one year of cash inflows through delay.

The first two arguments support delaying the decision. The third argument supports immediate drilling.

In this example, the first argument greatly outweighs the other two arguments. Thus, Mr. Thornton avoided the second and third arguments in his presentation.

[18]Actually, it can be shown that a call option on a stock that pays no dividend should never be exercised before expiration. However, for a dividend-paying stock, it may be optimal to exercise prior to the ex-dividend date. The analogy applies to our example of an option in real assets.

The firm would receive cash flows from oil earlier if drilling begins immediately. This is equivalent to the benefit from exercising a call on a stock prematurely in order to capture the dividend. However, in our example, this dividend effect is far outweighed by the benefits from waiting.

We urge the reader to look for hidden options in projects. Because options are beneficial, managers are shortchanging their firm's projects if capital budgeting calculations ignore flexibility.

? Concept Question

• **Why are the hidden options in projects valuable?**

23.13 SUMMARY AND CONCLUSIONS

This chapter serves as an introduction to options.

1. The most familiar options are puts and calls. These options give the holder the right to sell or buy shares of common stock at a given exercise price. American options can be exercised at any time up to and including the expiration date. European options can be exercised only on the expiration date.

2. Options can be held either in isolation or in combination. We focused on the strategy of
   • Buying a put
   • Buying the stock
   • Selling a call

   where the put and call have both the same exercise price and the same expiration date. This strategy yields a riskless return because the gain or loss on the call precisely offsets the gain or loss on the stock-and-put combination. In equilibrium, the return on this strategy must be exactly equal to the riskless rate. From this, the put–call parity relationship was established:

$$\text{Value of stock} + \text{Value of put} - \text{Value of call} = \text{Present value of exercise price}$$

3. The value of an option depends on five factors:
   • The price of the underlying asset.
   • The exercise price.
   • The expiration date.
   • The variability of the underlying asset.
   • The interest rate on risk-free bonds.

   The Black–Scholes model can determine the intrinsic price of an option from these five factors.

4. Much of corporate financial theory can be presented in terms of options. In this chapter we pointed out that
   a. Common stock can be represented as a call option on the firm.
   b. Shareholders enhance the value of their call by increasing the risk of their firm.
   c. Real projects have hidden options that enhance value.

KEY TERMS

American options 649	Exercising the option 648	Put option 651
Call option 649	Expiration date 648	Standardized normal
Cumulative probability 669	Option 648	distribution 669
European options 649	Put–call parity 657	Strike or exercise price 648

SUGGESTED READING

The path-breaking article on options is:
Fischer Black and Myron Scholes. "The Pricing of Options and Corporate Liabilities." *Journal of Political Economy* 81 (May–June 1973).

For a detailed discussion of options, read:
J. Hull. *Options, Futures and Other Derivative Securities.* 6th ed. Upper Saddle River, N.J.: Prentice-Hall, 2006.

Visit us at www.mcgrawhill.ca/olc/ross

QUESTIONS & PROBLEMS

Options: General

23.1 Define the following terms associated with options.

  a. Option
  b. Exercise
  c. Strike price
  d. Expiration date
  e. Call option
  f. Put option

23.2 What is the difference between an American option and a European option?

23.3 You notice that shares of stock in the Patel Corporation are going for $50 per share. Call options with an exercise price of $35 per share are selling for $10. What's wrong here? Describe how you can take advantage of this mispricing if the option expires today.

23.4 A call option on Futura Corporation, a non–dividend-paying stock, currently trades for $5. The expiration date of the option is February 14 of next year. The exercise price of the option is $47.

  a. If this is an American option, on what dates can the option be exercised?
  b. If this is a European option, on what dates can the option be exercised?
  c. Suppose the current price of Futura Corporation's stock is $48. Is this option worthless?

23.5 Consider a European call option on stock *A* that expires on December 21 and has a strike price of $60.

  a. If stock *A* is trading at $65 on December 21, what is the payoff to the owner of the option?
  b. If stock *A* is trading at $65 on December 21, what is the payoff to the seller of the option?
  c. If stock *A* is trading at $55 on December 21, what is the payoff to the owner of the option?
  d. If stock *A* is trading at $55 on December 21, what is the payoff to the seller of the option?
  e. Draw the payoff diagram to the owner of this option with respect to the stock price at expiration.
  f. Draw the payoff diagram to the seller of this option with respect to the stock price at expiration.
  g. If the seller of a call option never receives cash at expiration, why would anyone ever sell a call option?

23.6 Consider a European put option on stock *A* that expires on December 21 and has a strike price of $50.

  a. If stock *A* is trading at $55 on December 21, what is the payoff to the owner of the option?
  b. If stock *A* is trading at $55 on December 21, what is the payoff to the seller of the option?
  c. If stock *A* is trading at $45 on December 21, what is the payoff to the owner of the option?
  d. If stock *A* is trading at $45 on December 21, what is the payoff to the seller of the option?
  e. Draw the payoff diagram to the owner of this option with respect to the stock price at expiration.
  f. Draw the payoff diagram to the seller of this option with respect to the stock price at expiration.

23.7 Use the option quote information shown here to answer the questions that follow. The stock is currently selling for $114.

Option	Expiration	Strike Price	Calls Vol.	Calls Last	Put Vol.	Put Last
Letron Inc.						
	February	110	85	7.60	40	.60
	March	110	61	8.80	22	1.55
	May	110	22	10.25	11	2.85
	August	110	3	13.05	3	4.70

  a. Suppose you buy 10 contracts of the February 110 call option. How much will you pay, ignoring commissions?

    b. In part (a), suppose that Letron stock is selling for $140 per share on the expiration date. How much is your options investment worth? What if the terminal stock price is $125? Explain.

    c. Suppose you buy 10 contracts of the August 110 put option. What is your maximum gain? On the expiration date, Letron is selling for $104 per share. How much is your options investment worth? What is your net gain?

    d. In part (c), suppose you *sell* 10 of the August 110 put contracts. What is your net gain or loss if Letron is selling for $103 at expiration? For $132? What is the break-even price—that is, the terminal stock price that results in a zero profit?

23.8 McLemore Industries has a zero coupon bond issue that matures in two years with a face value of $30,000. The current value of the company's assets is $13,000, and the standard deviation of the return on assets is 60 percent per year.

    a. Assume the risk-free rate is 5 percent per year, compounded continuously. What is the value of a risk-free bond with the same face value and maturity as the company's bond?

    b. What price would the bondholders have to pay for a put option on the firm's assets with a strike price equal to the face value of the debt?

    c. Using the answers from (a) and (b), what is the value of the firm's debt? What is the continuously compounded yield on the company's debt?

    d. From an examination of the value of the assets of McLemore Industries, and the fact that the debt must be repaid in two years, it seems likely that the company will default on its debt. Management has approached bondholders and proposed a plan whereby the company would repay the same face value of debt, but the repayment would not occur for five years. What is the value of the debt under the proposed plan? What is the new continuously compounded yield on the debt? Explain why this occurs.

23.9 Brozik Corp. has a zero coupon bond that matures in five years with a face value of $60,000. The current value of the company's assets is $57,000, and the standard deviation of its return on assets is 50 percent per year. The risk-free rate is 6 percent per year, compounded continuously.

    a. What is the value of a risk-free bond with the same face value and maturity as the current bond?

    b. What is the value of a put option on the firm's assets with a strike price equal to the face value of the debt?

    c. Using the answers from (a) and (b), what is the value of the firm's debt? What is the continuously compounded yield on the company's debt?

    d. Assume the company can restructure its assets so that the standard deviation of its return on assets increases to 60 percent per year. What happens to the value of the debt? What is the new continuously compounded yield on the debt? Reconcile your answers in (c) and (d).

    e. What happens to bondholders if the company restructures its assets? What happens to shareholders? How does this create an agency problem?

23.10 You are given the following information concerning options on a particular stock:

Stock price	=	$86
Exercise price	=	$90
Risk-free rate	=	6% per year, compounded continuously
Maturity	=	6 months
Standard deviation	=	53% per year

    a. What is the intrinsic value of the call option? Of the put option?

    b. What is the time value of the call option? Of the put option?

    c. Does the call or the put have the larger time value component? Would you expect this to be true in general?

23.11 Ms. Eisner sold 11 BCE put options and bought 4 BCE call options. Both options have the same exercise price of $51 and the same expiration date. Draw the payoff diagram with respect to the price of BCE stock at expiration.

23.12 Mr. Chang bought two Magna European call contracts and one Magna European put contract, both of which expire in three months. Each contract is for 100 options. The exercise price of each call is $71, and the exercise price of each put is $74.

    a. What is the payoff of Mr. Chang's position at expiration if the market price of Magna stock on the expiration date is $65? What if the market price is $72? What if the market price is $80?

    b. Draw Mr. Chang's payoff diagram with respect to the stock price at expiration.

23.13 Louise holds a six-month European call option contract on Hurricanes Inc., a non–dividend-paying common stock. Each contract is for 100 options. The exercise price of each call option is $10, and the option will expire in moments. Assume there are no transaction costs or taxes associated with the contract.

    a. What is her cash flow at expiration if the stock is selling for $13?

    b. If the stock is selling for $9, what should Louise do?

23.14 The market price of an American call option written on Stock ABC with a strike price of $50 and 6 months until expiration is $9.50. ABC's stock is currently trading for $57.

    a. Is there an arbitrage opportunity? If so, describe what you would do to take advantage of the mispricing.

    b. What do arbitrage opportunities such as this imply about the lower bound on the price of American call options?

    c. What is the upper bound on the price of American call options? Explain.

23.15 List the five factors that determine the value of an American call option. State how a change in each factor affects the option's value.

23.16 List the five factors that determine the value of an American put option. State how a change in each factor affects the option's value.

Put–Call Parity

23.17 General Eclectics Inc. has both European call and put options traded on the Montreal Exchange. Both options have the same exercise price of $43 and both expire in one year. General Eclectic's stock does not pay dividends. The call and the put are currently selling for $8 and $2, respectively. The risk-free interest rate is 5 percent per annum. What should the stock price of General Eclectics Inc. be in order to prevent arbitrage?

23.18 A stock is currently selling for $61 per share. A call option with an exercise price of $65 sells for $4.12 and expires in three months. If the risk-free rate of interest is 2.6 percent per year, compounded continuously, what is the price of a put option with the same exercise price?

23.19 A put option that expires in six months with an exercise price of $50 sells for $4.89. The stock is currently priced at $53, and the risk-free rate is 3.6 percent per year, compounded continuously. What is the price of a call option with the same exercise price?

23.20 A put option and a call option with an exercise price of $70 and three months to expiration sell for $2.87 and $4.68, respectively. If the risk-free rate is 4.8 percent per year, compounded continuously, what is the current stock price?

The Two-State Option Pricing Model

EXCEL

23.21 Maverick Manufacturing Inc. must purchase gold in three months for use in its operations. Maverick's management has estimated that if the price of gold were to rise above $375 per ounce, the firm would go bankrupt. The current price of gold is $350 per ounce. The firm's chief financial officer believes that the price of gold will either rise to $400 per ounce or fall to $325 per ounce over the next three months. Management wishes to eliminate any risk of the firm going bankrupt. Maverick can borrow and lend at the risk-free EAR of 16.99 percent.

    a. Should the company buy a call option or a put option on gold? To avoid bankruptcy, what strike price and time to expiration would the company like this option to have?

    b. How much should such an option sell for in the open market?

    c. If no options currently trade on gold, is there a way for the company to create a synthetic option with identical payoffs to the option just described? If there is, how would the firm do it?

    d. How much does the synthetic option cost? Is this greater than, less than, or equal to what the actual option costs? Does this make sense?

23.22 T-bills currently yield 5.5 percent. Stock in Nina Manufacturing is currently selling for $55 per share. There is no possibility that the stock will be worth less than $50 per share in one year.

    a. What is the value of a call option with a $45 exercise price? What is the intrinsic value?

    b. What is the value of a call option with a $35 exercise price? What is the intrinsic value?

    c. What is the value of a put option with a $45 exercise price? What is the intrinsic value?

23.23 The price of Ervin Corp. stock will be either $75 or $95 at the end of the year. Call options are available with one year to expiration. T-bills currently yield 6 percent.

    a. Suppose the current price of Ervin stock is $80. What is the value of the call option if the exercise price is $70 per share?

    b. Suppose the exercise price is $90 in part (a). What is the value of the call option now?

23.24 Rob wishes to buy a European put option on Organics Inc., a non–dividend-paying common stock, with a strike price of $50 and six months until expiration. Organics' common stock is currently selling for $40 per share, and Rob expects that the stock price will either rise to $70 or fall to $25 in six months. Rob can borrow and lend at the risk-free EAR of 18 percent.

    a. What should the put option sell for today?

    b. If no options currently trade on the stock, is there a way to create a synthetic put option with identical payoffs to the put option just described? If there is, how would you do it?

    c. How much does the synthetic put option cost? Is this greater than, less than, or equal to what the actual put option costs? Does this make sense?

EXCEL

23.25 Ken is interested in buying a European call option written on Southeastern Airlines Inc., a non–dividend-paying common stock, with a strike price of $110 and one year until expiration. Currently, Southeastern's stock sells for $100 per share. In one year Ken knows that Southeastern's stock will be trading at either $125 per share or $80 per share. Ken is able to borrow and lend at the risk-free EAR of 2.5 percent.

    a. What should the call option sell for today?

    b. If no options currently trade on the stock, is there a way to create a synthetic call option with identical payoffs to the call option just described? If there is, how would you do it?

    c. How much does the synthetic call option cost? Is this greater than, less than, or equal to what the actual call option costs? Does this make sense?

The Black–Scholes Option Pricing Model

23.26 What are the prices of a call option and a put option with the following characteristics?

Stock price	=	$86
Exercise price	=	$90
Risk-free rate	=	6% per year, compounded continuously
Maturity	=	6 months
Standard deviation	=	53% per year

23.27 A call option has an exercise price of $80 and matures in six months. The current stock price is $84, and the risk-free rate is 5 percent per year, compounded continuously. What is the price of the call if the standard deviation of the stock is 0 percent per year?

23.28 An investor is said to take a position in a "collar" if she buys the asset, buys an out-of-the-money put option on the asset, and sells an out-of-the-money call option on the asset. The two options should have the same time to expiration. Suppose Marie wishes to purchase a collar on Hollywood Inc., a non–dividend-paying common stock, with six months until expiration. She would like the put to have a strike price of $52 and the call to have a strike price of $90. The current price of Hollywood's stock is $67 per share. Marie can borrow and lend at the continuously compounded risk-free rate of 11 percent per annum, and the annual standard deviation of the stock's return is 53 percent. Use the Black–Scholes model to calculate the total cost of the collar that Marie is interested in buying. What is the effect of the collar?

23.29 A stock is currently priced at $50. The stock will never pay a dividend. The risk-free rate is 12 percent per year, compounded continuously, and the standard deviation of the stock's return is 60 percent. A European call option on the stock has a strike price of $100 and no expiration date, meaning that it has an infinite life. Based on Black–Scholes, what is the value of the call option? Do you see a paradox here? Do you see a way out of the paradox?

23.30 Myron Fisher is interested in purchasing a European call option on Meriwether and Associates Inc., a non–dividend-paying common stock, with a strike price of $50 and one year until expiration. Meriwether's stock is currently trading at $55 per share, and the annual variance of its continuously compounded returns is 0.0099. Treasury bills that mature in one year yield a continuously compounded interest rate of 9 percent per annum. Use the Black–Scholes model to calculate the price of the call option that Myron is interested in buying.

23.31 John Goodfriend is interested in purchasing a European call option on Mozer Inc., a non–dividend-paying common stock, with a strike price of $25 and six months until expiration. Mozer's stock is currently trading at $18 per share, and the annual variance of its continuously compounded returns is 0.30. Treasury bills that mature in six months yield a continuously compounded interest rate of 8 percent per annum. Use the Black–Scholes model to calculate the price of the call option that John is interested in buying.

23.32 David is interested in purchasing a European call option on Divine Vines Inc., a non–dividend-paying common stock, with a strike price of $35 and three months until expiration. Divine's stock is currently trading at $64 per share, and the annual variance of its continuously compounded returns is 0.36. Treasury bills that mature in three months yield a continuously compounded interest rate of 6 percent per annum.
  a. Use the Black–Scholes model to calculate the price of the call option that David is interested in buying.
  b. What does put–call parity imply about the price of a put with a strike price of $35 and three months until expiration?

23.33 Marilyn wishes to buy a European call option on Scuba Solutions Inc., a non–dividend-paying common stock, with a strike price of $35 and one year until expiration. Scuba Solutions is currently selling for $37 per share and Marilyn's estimate of the annual variance of its continuously compounded returns is 0.0416. Marilyn can borrow and lend at the continuously compounded risk-free rate of 8 percent per annum.
  a. Use the Black–Scholes model to calculate the price of the call option that Marilyn is interested in buying.
  b. Suppose Marilyn's estimate of the annual variance of the continuously compounded returns on Scuba's stock changes to 0.11. What is the new Black–Scholes price of the call option?
  c. Does an increase in the volatility (variance) of the underlying asset increase or decrease the Black–Scholes price of a call option?
  d. Scuba's stock price suddenly drops to $20 per share after an announcement that the company will be shutting down its Mediterranean diving operations. Using Marilyn's new estimate of variance (0.11), calculate the Black–Scholes price of the call option.

Application of Options to Corporate Finance
23.34 It is said that the equityholders of a levered firm can be thought of as holding a call option on the firm's assets. Explain what is meant by this statement.

23.35 Weber Real Estate Inc., a construction firm financed by both debt and equity, is undertaking a new project. If the project is successful, the value of the firm in one year will be $550 million but if the project is a failure, the firm will be worth only $370 million. The current value of Weber is $421 million, a figure that includes the prospects for the new project. Weber has outstanding zero coupon bonds due in one year with a face value of $387 million. Treasury bills that mature in one year yield 8 percent EAR. Weber pays no dividends.
  a. Use the two-state option pricing model to find the current value of Weber's debt and equity.
  b. Suppose Weber has 510,000 shares of common stock outstanding. What is the price per share of the firm's equity?

    c. Compare the market value of Weber's debt to the present value of an equal amount of debt that is riskless with one year until maturity. Is the firm's debt worth more than, less than, or the same as the riskless debt? Does this make sense? What factors might cause these two values to be different?

    d. Suppose that in place of the proceeding project, Weber's management decides to undertake a project that is even more risky. The value of the firm will either increase to $750 million or decrease to $300 million by the end of the year. Surprisingly, management concludes that the value of the firm today will remain at exactly $400 million if this risky project is substituted for the less risky one. Use the two-state option pricing model to determine the value of the firm's debt and equity if the firm plans on undertaking this new project. Which project do bondholders prefer?

23.36 Consider a firm that is financed by both debt and equity. The firm is worth $1.1 million today and currently has 700 zero-coupon bonds outstanding that mature in six months. Each bond has a face value of $1,000. The firm pays no dividends. The annual variance of the firm's continuously compounded asset returns is 0.14, and Treasury bills that mature in six months yield a continuously compounded interest rate of 14 percent per annum. Use the Black–Scholes model to calculate the individual values of the firm's debt and equity.

MINICASE: Big Red Dog Manufacturing Options

You are currently working for Big Red Dog Manufacturing. The company, which went public five years ago, engages in the design, production, and distribution of lighting equipment and specialty products worldwide. Because of recent events, Mal Clissold, the company president, is concerned about the company's risk, so he asks for your input.

In your discussion with Mal, you explain that the CAPM proposes that the market risk of the company's stock is the determinant of its expected return. Even though Mal agrees with this, he argues that his portfolio consists entirely of Big Red Dog stock and options, so he is concerned with the total risk, or standard deviation, of the company's stock. Furthermore, even though he has calculated the standard deviation of the company's stock for the past five years, he would like an estimate of the stock's volatility moving forward.

Mal states that you can find the estimated volatility of the stock for future periods by calculating the implied standard deviation of option contracts on the company stock. When you examine the factors that affect the price of an option, all of the factors except the standard deviation of the stock are directly observable in the market. You can also observe the option price as well. Mal states that because you can observe all of the option factors except the standard deviation, you can simply solve the Black–Scholes model and find the implied standard deviation.

To help you find the implied standard deviation of the company's stock, Mal has provided you with the following option prices on four call option that expire in six months. The risk-free rate is 6 percent, and the current stock price is $50.

Strike Price	Option Price
$30	$23.00
40	16.05
50	9.75
55	7.95

1. How many different volatilities would you expect to see for the stock?

2. Unfortunately, solving for the implied standard deviation is not as easy as Mal suggests. In fact, there is no direct solution for the standard deviation of the stock even if we have all other variables for the Black–Scholes model. Mal would still like you to estimate the implied standard deviation of the stock. To do this, set up a spreadsheet using the Solver function in Excel to calculate the implied volatilities for each of the options.

3. Are all of the implied volatilities for the options the same? What are the possible reasons that can cause different volatilities for these options?

4. After you discuss the importance of volatility on option prices, your boss mentions that he has heard of the VIX. What is the VIX and what does it represent? You might need to visit the Chicago Board Options Exchange (CBOE) at www.cboe.com to help with your answer.

5. When you are on the CBOE website, look for the option quotes for the VIX. What does the implied volatility of a VIX option represent?

Chapter **24**

Options and Corporate Finance: Extensions and Applications

EXECUTIVE SUMMARY

This chapter extends the analysis of options contained in Chapter 23. We describe four different types of options found in common corporate finance decisions.

- Executive stock options and compensation.
- The embedded option in a start-up company.
- The options in simple business contracts.
- The option to shut down and reopen a project.

Option features are pervasive in corporate finance decisions. They are involved in decisions of whether to build, expand, or close a factory, to buy productive assets like trucks or machines, to drill for oil or mine for gold, or to construct a building. Sometimes they are involved in decisions about how to pay managers and other employees. In this chapter we do not argue that the NPV approach should be completely jettisoned. In fact, many decisions have few embedded options and, in these cases, optionality can be ignored. However, in many cases, options are an important aspect of the decision and must be separately valued. In practice, there is a decision continuum. At one end of the continuum are decisions with little optionality and at the other are decisions with significant optionality.

In the previous chapter, we presented a few examples of options in corporate finance. We saw that stock is a call option on the firm. We showed that the value of this option could be increased by selecting high-risk rather than low-risk projects. We discussed the embedded option in oil exploration.

However, although the previous chapter presented these options, we made no attempt to *value* them. In this chapter, we will value four embedded options. The first two are handled with the Black–Scholes model. We use the binomial (two-state) model to value the last two options. Although the Black–Scholes model is more well known, the binomial model is probably used more frequently in the real world. The Black–Scholes model works well on only a narrow set of problems. The flexibility of the binomial model allows it to be applied to a wider range of situations. However, binomial approaches often use complex numerical analyses involving large amounts of computer time when applied to portfolios of options in actual companies. In this regard, binomial approaches are less elegant than the Black–Scholes approach.

24.1 Executive Stock Options

Why Options?

Executive compensation is usually made up of base salary plus some or all of the following elements:

- Long-term compensation
- Annual bonuses
- Retirement contributions
- Options

The final component of compensation, options, is by far the biggest part of total compensation for many top executives. Table 24.1 lists Canadian CEOs who held the largest stock option grants at the beginning of 2006. The rank is in terms of the highest-paid CEOs at S&P/TSX Composite index companies.

Knowing the face value of an option does not automatically allow us to determine the market value of the option. We also need to know the exercise price before valuing the option according to either the Black–Scholes model or the binomial model. However, the exercise price is generally set equal to the market price of the stock on the date the executive receives the options. In the next section, we value options under the assumption that the exercise price is equal to the market price of the underlying stock.

Starting in the late 1990s, options in the stock of the company were increasingly granted to executives as an alternative to increases in base pay. Ninety percent of firms listed on the Toronto Stock Exchange had a bonus plan and used stock options.[1] Some of the reasons given for using options are:

1. Options make executives share the same interests as the shareholders. By aligning their interests, it is argued that executives will make better decisions for the benefit of the shareholders.

2. Using options allows the company to lower the executive's base pay. This removes pressures on morale caused by great disparities between the salaries of executives and those of other employees.

3. Options put an executive's pay at risk, rather than guaranteeing it independent of the performance of the firm.

4. In principle, under current U.S. and Canadian tax laws, options are a tax-efficient way to pay employees. Under current tax law, if an executive is given options to purchase the company stock and the options are "at the money," they are not considered part of taxable income. The options are taxed only when they are eventually exercised.

Until recently, options had the advantage of creating no charge against earnings and for this reason were popular with start-up companies short of cash. This changed for Canadian public companies in 2004 when the Canadian Accounting Standards Board began to require the expensing of stock options.

Research studies in the U.S., Canada, and other countries find that, over the 1990s, the use of executive stock options generally served its goal of helping to tie executive

---

[1]X. Zhou, "CEO Pay, Firm Size, and Corporate Performance: Evidence from Canada," University of Sydney, Australia, October 2000.

TABLE 24.1 Canadian CEOs with the Greatest Stock Option Grants

HOW TO READ THE CHART

This is a ranking of the 15 highest-paid CEOs at S&P/TSX composite index companies for fiscal 2006. Some firms do not appear because they have not yet reported their executive compensation data for 2006. Data come from the companies' annual shareholder proxy circulars. For companies without CEOs, data are for the most senior executive. Where there are two names, the company has co-CEOs. When CEOs have changed during the year, data are shown for the CEO (former or current) who was in the job for the greatest portion of 2006. Data include payments, if disclosed, to executives working for management firms hired to operate the company, or to CEOs who are indirectly paid through a consulting or management firm they control.

Currency: For companies that report in U.S. dollars, amounts are converted to Canadian dollars at the average exchange rate for 2006 ($1.1341). For companies with irregular year-ends (not Dec. 31), U.S. dollars are converted at the exchange rate at the company's year-end.
Salary is base salary.
Bonus is annual bonus.
Percentage change is the change from 2005 total salary and bonus. No number is shown if the executive was not in the same position for all of 2005 and 2006. Other includes all other payments and the cash value of other benefits, such as insurance premiums, car and housing allowances and termination or retirement payments.
Share units/long-term incentive plan (LTIP) is the total value of all shares, share units, trust units, long-term incentive plan payouts or other equity-based payments. If companies do not disclose the cash value of shares or units granted, they are assumed to be the value at the fiscal year-end. Option gains are the net profit after the exercise of stock options, stock appreciation rights or equivalent income trust rights. New option grant is the number of stock options or trust unit rights granted in 2006. Value of new options is the estimated future value of option grants. It is based on companies' estimated average fair values or options granted during the year, normally calculated using the Black-Scholes formula. Where no value is shown, the company did not disclose the average fair value per option.

		Salary	Bonus	Subtotal	% change	Other	Share units/ LTIP	Option gains	Total	New Opt. grant #	Value of new options
1	James Balsillie	Research In Motion Ltd.	$561,032	$0	$561,032	+12%	$0	0	$54,148,433	$54,709,465	150,000	$5,463,697
2	Glenn Murphy	Shoppers Drug Mart Corp.	$1,200,000	$1,479,000	$2,679,000	+15%	$68,937	0	$31,694,010	$34,441,947	0	$0
3	Michael Lazaridis	Research In Motion Ltd.	$561,032	$0	$561,032	+12%	$0	0	$32,429,277	$32,990,309	150,000	$5,463,697
4	Paul Desmarais Jr.	Power Corp. of Canada	$933,000	$1,200,000	$2,133,000	+33%	$493,490	0	$21,366,170	$23,992,660	290,125	$2,115,011
5	John Lederer	Loblaw Cos. Ltd.	$966,575	$0	$966,575	—	$12,308088	5,000,000	$3,391,593	$21,666,256	0	$0
6	Dominic D'Alessandro	Manulife Financial Corp.	$1,228,610	$4,539,210	$5,767,820	+23%	$53,034	3,900,000	$10,573,210	$20,294,064	458,532	$3,900,000
7	Bradley Langille	Gammon Lake Resources Inc.	$300,308	$363,510	$663,818	—	$0	0	$19,282,500	$19,946,318	0	$0
8	Ian Telfer	Goldcorp Inc.	$973,171	$1,313,781	$2,286,952	—	$14,895	0	$14,878,250	$17,180,097	300,000	$2,521,734
9	Edward Rogers	Rogers Communications Inc.	$1,488,462	$4,162,500	$5,650,962	+62%	$1,287	0	$10,723,980	$16,376,229	314,500	$2,795,905
10	Andre Desmarais	Power Corp. of Canada	$933,000	$1,200,000	$2,133,000	+33%	$621,490	0	$13,477,274	$16,231,764	290,125	$2,115,011
11	Richard George	Suncor Energy Inc.	$1,177,077	$2,000,000	$3,177,077	+11%	$226,012	4,275,180	$7,826,743	$15,505,012	79,000	$1,964,707
12	Gerald Schwartz	Onex Corp.	$755,950	$12,929,728	$13,685,678	+29%	$0	0	$0	$13,685,678	0	$0
13	Tony Comper	Bank of Montreal	$1,000,000	$1,600,000	$2,600,000	-4%	$675,171	2,700,000	$7,497,201	$13,472,372	149,800	$2,800,000
14	Richard Waugh	Bank of Nova Scotia	$1,000,000	$1,600,000	$2,600,000	+4%	$775,156	3,150,000	$6,846,357	$13,371,513	232,988	$3,150,000
15	Raymond McFeetors	Great-West Lifeco Inc.	$1,481,440	$1,900,000	$3,381,440	+22%	$159,030	0	$9,081,328	$12,621,798	0	$0

Source: Reprinted with permission from The Globe and Mail.

Janet McFarland and Paul Waldie on RIM Options Backdating

Canadian and U.S. regulators will continue to investigate Research in Motion Ltd. despite the BlackBerry maker announcing a change to its board of directors and taking a $250-million (U.S.) accounting charge because of major problems with stock option grants.

James Balsillie, RIM's co-chief executive officer, admitted yesterday his company backdated stock options granted to employees. He said it was an error due to a misunderstanding of accounting rules.

The admission makes RIM the first major Canadian company to get caught up in an options backdating scandal that has swept through the United States, leading to charges against some executives and forcing billions of dollars in earnings to be restated. More than 40 U.S. executives and directors have resigned or been fired after internal reviews of options backdating problems.

Research in Motion's Jim Balsillie is stepping down as chairman, and will retain the title of co-chief executive officer, and continue to sit as a director.

RIM's special committee of the board, which conducted a seven-month internal probe of stock option practices, said yesterday no one at the company will lose his or her job over the options problems.

The review found instances in which "hindsight was used" to select favourable dates to grant stock options, resulting in employees getting options that were already valuable when they were granted.

Options are supposed to be granted with an exercise price equal to the company's share price, so they only become valuable in the future if the share price rises. Backdating occurs when companies look backward to pick a favourable date in the past to grant options.

While RIM's special committee described a number of instances of improper options-granting practices, it said it found no "intentional misconduct" on the part of any director or employee.

The company hopes to put its stock options issues in the past, but regulators say they are continuing to probe RIM's options practices.

Both the U.S. Securities and Exchange Commission and the Ontario Securities Commission are reviewing RIM.

RIM announced a series of board and executive changes yesterday. Mr. Balsillie will remain co-CEO but will give up the title of chairman to an as-yet unnamed independent director, while chief financial officer Dennis Kavelman will leave his position to become chief operating officer. RIM also announced it has appointed two new independent directors and is searching for two others.

As well, the company announced Mr. Balsillie and co-CEO Mike Lazaridis will pay $5-million each to cover the company's costs of investigating the options problems. The special committee report said all option grants, except those to the co-CEOs, were made under Mr. Balsillie's authority, and were not approved by the board as the company had previously reported.

The company said its executives will also repay all the benefit they received from options that were incorrectly priced. While that amount hasn't been revealed, Mr. Balsillie said his own obligation will be "far, far less" than the $5-million he has volunteered to pay to cover the investigation costs.

Mr. Balsillie said the mistake stemmed from his belief that options could be dated on the day they were promised to an executive, and said he was surprised to discover they should have been dated when they were actually approved by the board and granted.

But the special committee report does not attribute all the company's backdating problems to a mistaken belief that options were to be priced at the time they were promised to an executive or future hire.

Indeed, the report says the company was "inconsistent" about when it chose a date to determine the exercise price of its options. In some cases, the report says, options were repriced after an employee joined the company to provide the employee with "better pricing." In limited cases, the company repriced options to existing executives after they were granted if the stock price decreased.

The report says that after 2002, 63 percent of options granted to existing executives contained "incorrect measurement dates" for accounting purposes.

Janet McFarland and Paul Waldie are columnists at *The Globe and Mail*. Their comments are excerpted with permission from the March 5, 2007 *Report on Business*. Reprinted with permission from *The Globe and Mail*.

compensation to company performance.[2] Still, options have come in for considerable criticism. Corporate governance experts worry that options sometimes encourage executives to focus too much on short-term actions to raise share prices. For example, in September 2004, Molson and Coors were proposing a friendly merger supported by top executives at both companies. Critics of the proposed merger discounted the support by Dan O'Neill, Molson CEO, pointing out that the merger would increase the value of his stock options by $2.6 million.[3]

Further, after the end of the tech bubble, the decline in stock prices, especially in the tech sector, had made options granted earlier almost worthless in motivating employees. In response, many companies are currently emphasizing cash compensation. More controversially, others are offering employees an opportunity to exchange their options for new ones with exercise prices at or near the current, lower share price. Compensation plans are supposed to motivate executives and provide an incentive for future performance that will enrich both shareholders and the executive. When companies issue stock options to executives that are already in-the-money, the incentive to increase shareholder value and business performance is not there.

In response to the criticism of stock options, some companies are switching to rewarding their employees with shares. The idea is to retain the alignment of interests while getting away from the short-term focus of options.

Valuing Executive Compensation

In this section, we value executive stock options. Not surprisingly, the complexity of the total compensation package often makes valuation a difficult task. The economic value of the options depends on factors such as the volatility of the underlying stock and the exact terms of the option grant.

We attempt to estimate the economic value of the options held by U.S. executives. To do so, we employ the Black–Scholes option pricing formula from Chapter 23. Of course, we are missing many features of the particular plans, and the best we can hope for is a rough estimate. Simple matters such as requiring the executive to hold the option for a fixed period, the freeze-out period, before exercising, can significantly diminish the value of a standard option. Equally important, the Black–Scholes formula has to be modified if the stock pays dividends and is no longer applicable if the volatility of the stock is changing randomly over time. Intuitively, a call option on a dividend-paying stock is worth less than a call on a stock that pays no dividends: All other things being equal, the dividends will lower the stock price. Nevertheless, let us see what we can do.

EXAMPLE 24.1

Consider James Kilts, the chief executive officer (CEO) of Gillette, who was granted 2 million options. The average stock price at the time of the options grant was $39.71. We will assume that his options are at the money. The risk-free rate is 5 percent and the options expire in five years. The preceding information implies that:

1. The stock price (S) of $39.71 equals the exercise price (E).
2. The risk-free rate $r = 0.05$.
3. The time interval $t = 5$.

---

[2]The most current study for Canada is: X. Zhou, "CEO Pay, Firm Size, and Corporate Performance: Evidence from Canada," University of Sydney, Australia, October 2000. A widely cited U.S. study is: K.J. Murphy, "Executive Compensation," in *Handbook of Labor Economics,* vol. 3, eds. O. Ashenfelter and D. Card (Amsterdam: North Holland).

[3]D. Decloet, "Merger Would Pay Millions to Molson, Coors Chiefs," *Report on Business, Globe and Mail,* September 20, 2004, B1.

In addition, the variance of Gillette is estimated to be $(0.2168)^2 = .0470$

This information allows us to value James Kilts's options using the Black–Scholes model:

$$C = SN(d_1) - Ee^{-rt}N(d_2)$$

$$d_1 = [(r + 1/2\sigma^2)t]/\sqrt{\sigma^2 t} = 0.758$$

$$d_2 = d_1 - \sqrt{\sigma^2 t} = 0.273$$

$$N(d_1) = 0.776$$

$$N(d_2) = 0.608$$

$$e^{-.05 \times 5} = 0.7788$$

$$C = \$39.71 \times .776 - \$39.71 \times (0.7788 \times 0.608) = \$12.03$$

Thus the value of a call option on one share of Gillette stock is \$12.03. Because Mr. Kilts was granted options on 2 million shares, the market value of his options, as estimated by the Black–Scholes formula, is about \$24 million (= 2 million × \$12.03).

We assume that all of the options are "at the money," so that their exercise prices are the current stock values. The total exercise prices are thus equal to the reported face value. We take the risk-free interest rate as 5 percent and assume that the options all have a maturity of five years. Finally, we ignore the dilution from exercising them as warrants and value them as call options. The last required input, the volatility or standard deviation of the stock, σ, is estimated from the historical returns on each of the stocks. Table 24.2 lists the volatilities for each stock and the estimated value of the stock grants. As can be seen, these values, while large by ordinary standards, are significantly less than the corresponding face values. Notice that the ordering by face value is not the same as that by economic value. For example, whereas Sumner Redstone of Viacom ranks fourth in grant value, Table 24.2 shows that he ranks second in Black–Scholes value—the difference being caused by Viacom's high standard deviation.

The values computed in Table 24.2 are the economic values of the options if they were to trade in the market. The real question is this: Whose value are we talking about? Are these the costs of the options to the company? Are they the values of the options to the executives?

Suppose that a company computes the fair market value of the options as we have done and suppose, for purposes of illustration, that we ignore warrant dilution[4] and that the options are in the money and are worth \$25 each. Suppose further that the CEO holds 1 million such options for a total value of \$25 million. This is the amount that the options would trade at in the financial markets and the amount that traders and investors would be willing to pay. If the company were very large, it would not be unreasonable for it to view this as the cost of granting the options to the CEO. Of course, in return, the company expects the CEO to improve the value of the company to its shareholders by more than this amount. As we have seen, perhaps the main purpose of options is to align the interests of management with those of the shareholders of the firm. Under no circumstances, though, is the \$25 million necessarily a fair measure of what they are worth to the CEO.

As an illustration, suppose that the CEO of ABC has options on 1 million shares with an exercise price of \$30 per share and the current price of ABC is \$50 per share. If the options were exercised today, they would be worth \$20 million (an underestimate of their market value). Suppose, in addition, the CEO owns \$5 million in company stock and has

---

[4]See Chapter 25 for a discussion of warrant dilution.

TABLE 24.2   **Value of 2005 Top 10 Option Grants***

Company	CEO	Grant Value of Options Granted (millions)[†]	Annual Stock Standard Deviation (%/year)	Black–Scholes Value (millions)[‡]
Wells Fargo & Co.	Richard Kovacevich	$108.8	20.09	$32
Viacom International Inc.	Sumner Redstone	74.0	30.86	27
Gillette Company	James Kilts	79.4	21.68	24
United HealthGroup Inc.	William McGuire	77.2	21.77	23
Capital One Financial Corporation	Richard Fairbank	46.6	43.78	21
U.W. Bancorp	Jerry Grundhofer	52.3	25.70	17
Dell Computer Corporation	Kevin Rollins	41.7	35.79	17
Countrywide Financial Corporation	Angelo Mozilo	44.6	30.84	16
American Express Company	Kenneth Chenault	41.3	26.32	14
Anheuser-Busch Companies, Inc.	Patrick Stokes	45.3	15.05	12

*Based on the 200 largest U.S. industrial and service corporations.
[†]Grant value of options granted is the number of options times the stock price.
[‡]Stock option award includes reload/restoration options as well as other features that are not being valued here.
Source: Pearl Meyer & Partners.

$5 million in other assets. The CEO clearly has a very undiversified personal portfolio. By the standards of modern portfolio theory having 25/30 or about 83 percent of your personal wealth in one stock and its options is unnecessarily risky.

While the CEO is wealthy by most standards, significant shifts in the stock value will have dramatic impacts on the CEO's economic well-being. If the value drops from $50 per share down to $30 per share, the current exercise value of the options on 1 million shares drops from $20 million down to zero. Ignoring the fact that if the options have more time to mature they will not lose all of this value, we nevertheless have a rather startling decline in the CEO's net worth from about $30 million down to $8 million ($5 million in other assets plus stock that is now worth $3 million). But that is the very purpose of the options and the stock holdings given to the CEO, namely to make the CEO's fortunes rise and fall with those of the company. That is why the company requires executives to hold the options, at least for a freeze-out period, and not simply sell them to realize their value.

The implication is that when options are a large portion of an executive's net worth and the executive is forced by the company to be undiversified, the total value of the position is worth less to the executive than the fair financial market value. As a purely financial matter, an executive might be happier with $5 million in cash rather than $20 million in options. At the least, the executive could then diversify his or her personal portfolio.

? Concept Question

• Why do companies issue options to executives if they cost the company more than they are worth to the executive? Why not just give cash and split the difference? Wouldn't that make both the company and the executive better off?

24.2 Valuing a Start-Up

Michel Normand was not your typical MBA student. Since childhood, he had had one ambition: to open a restaurant that sold wild game and other exotic meats prepared in a French style. He went to business school because he realized that, although he knew 101 ways to cook rabbit, he didn't have the business skills necessary to run a restaurant. He was extremely focused, with each course at graduate school being important to him only to the extent that it could further his dream.

While taking his school's course in entrepreneurship, he began to develop a business plan for his restaurant, which he now called Chez Michel. He thought about marketing, he thought about raising capital, he thought about dealing with future employees. He even devoted a great deal of time to designing the physical layout of the restaurant. Of course, his business plan would not be complete without financial projections. After much thought, he came up with the projections shown in Table 24.3.

The table starts with sales projections, which rise from $300,000 in the first year to a steady state of $1 million a year. Cash Flows From Operations are shown in the next line, although we leave out the intermediate calculations needed to move from line 1 to line 2. After subtracting Working Capital, the table shows Net Cash Flows in line 4. Net Cash Flows are negative initially, as is quite common in start-ups, but they become positive by Year 3. However, the rest of the table presents the unfortunate truth. The cash flows from the restaurant yield a present value of $582,561, assuming a discount rate of 20 percent. Unfortunately, the cost of the building is greater, at $700,000, implying a negative *net* present value of −$117,439.

The projections indicate that Michel's lifelong dream may not come to pass. He cannot expect to raise the capital needed to open his restaurant, and if he did obtain the funding, the restaurant would likely go under anyway. Michel checked and rechecked the numbers, hoping vainly to discover either a numerical error or a cost-saving omission that would move his venture from the red to the black. In fact, Michel saw that, if anything, his forecasts are generous, because a 20 percent discount rate and an infinitely long-lived building are on the optimistic side.

It wasn't until Michel took a course in corporate strategy that he realized the hidden value in his venture. In that course, his instructor repeatedly stated the importance of positioning a firm to take advantage of new opportunities. Although Michel didn't see

TABLE 24.3 Financial Projections for Chez Michel

	Year 1	Year 2	Year 3	Year 4	All Future Years
(1) Sales	$300,000	$600,000	$900,000	$1,000,000	$1,000,000
(2) Cash flows from operations	−$100,000	−$ 50,000	+$ 75,000	+$ 250,000	+$ 250,000
(3) Increase in working capital	$ 50,000	$ 20,000	$ 10,000	$ 10,000	0
(4) Net cash flows (2) − (3)	−$150,000	−$ 70,000	$ 65,000	$ 240,000	$ 250,000
Present value of net cash flows in years 1–4 (discounted at 20%)			−$ 20,255		
Present value of terminal value $\left[\dfrac{\$250,000}{0.20} \times \dfrac{1}{(1.20)^4} \right]$			+$602,816		
Present value of restaurant			$582,561		
−Cost of building			−$700,000		
Net present value of restaurant			−$117,439		

the connection at first, he finally realized the implications for Chez Michel. His financial projections were based on expectations. There was a 50 percent probability that wild game would be more popular than he thought, in which case actual cash flows would exceed projections. And, there was a 50 percent probability that the meat would be less popular, in which case the actual flows would fall short of projections.

If the restaurant did poorly, it would probably fold in a few years, because he would not want to keep losing money forever. However, if the restaurant did well, he would be in a position to expand. If wild game proved popular in one locale, it would likely prove popular in other locales as well. Thus, he noticed two options: the option to abandon under bad conditions and the option to expand under good conditions. Although both options can be valued according to the principles of the previous chapter, we focus on the option to expand because it is probably much more valuable.

Michel reasoned that consumer reaction to wild game and exotic meats would be mixed. Some more adventurous individuals would welcome the chance to try new dishes, while others would likely be won over once they understood that these meats are far lower in cholesterol than traditional meats are. Still, some consumers would undoubtedly resist the idea of eating the meat of wild animals. He forecast that, although he could expand quickly if the first restaurant proved successful, the market would limit him to 30 additional restaurants.

Michel believes that this expansion will occur about four years from now. He believes that he will need three years of operating the first restaurant to (1) get the initial restaurant running smoothly and (2) have enough information to place an accurate value on the restaurant. If the first restaurant is successful enough, he will need another year to obtain outside capital. Thus, he will be ready to build the 30 additional units around the fourth year.

Michel will value his enterprise, including the option to expand, according to the Black–Scholes model. From Table 24.3, we see that each unit cost $700,000, implying a total cost over the 30 additional units of $21,000,000 (30 × $700,000). The present value of the cash inflows from these 30 units is $17,476,830 (30 × $582,561), according to the table. However, because the expansion will occur around the fourth year, this present-value calculation is provided from the point of view of four years in the future. The present value as of today is $8,428,255 [$17,476,830/(1.20)^4], assuming a discount rate of 20 percent per year. Thus, Michel views his potential restaurant business as an option, where the exercise price is $21,000,000 and the value of the underlying asset is $8,428,255. The option is currently out of the money, a result that follows from the negative value of a typical restaurant, as calculated in Table 24.2. Of course, Michel is hoping that the option will move into the money within four years.

Michel needs three additional parameters to use the Black–Scholes model: r, the annual continuously compounded interest rate; t, the time to maturity; and σ, the standard deviation of the underlying asset. Michel uses the yield on a four-year zero-coupon bond, which is 3.5 percent, as the estimate of the interest rate. The time to maturity is four years. The estimate of standard deviation is a little trickier, because there are no historical data on wild game restaurants. Michel finds that the average annual standard deviation of the returns on publicly traded restaurants is 0.35. Because Chez Michel is a new venture, he reasons that the risk here would be somewhat greater. He finds that the average annual standard deviation for restaurants that have gone public in the last few years is 0.45. Because Michel's restaurant is newer still, he uses a standard deviation of 0.50.

There are now enough data to value Michel's venture. The value according to the Black–Scholes model is $1,455,196. The actual calculations are shown in Table 24.4. This value should be used with caution as it is not as precise as it looks. The Black–Scholes

TABLE 24.4   Valuing a Start-Up Firm (Chez Michel) as an Option

Facts

1. The value of a single restaurant is negative, as indicated by the net-present-value calculation in Table 24.3 of −$117,439. Thus, the restaurant would not be funded if there were no possibility of expansion.
2. If the pilot restaurant is successful, Michel Normand plans to create 30 additional restaurants around year 4. This leads to the following observations:
   a. The total cost of 30 units is $21,000,000 (30 × $700,000).
   b. The present value of future cash flows as of year 4 is $17,476,830 (30 × $582,561).
   c. The present value of these cash flows today is $8,428,255 [$17,476,830/(1.20)^4].

Here, we assume that cash flows from the project are discounted at 20% per annum.

   Thus, the business is essentially a call option, where the exercise price is $21,000,000 and the underlying asset is worth $8,428,255.

3. Michel Normand estimates the standard deviation of the return on Chez Michel's stock to be 0.50.

Parameters of the Black–Scholes model:

$$S \text{ (stock price)} = \$8,428,255$$
$$E \text{ (exercise price)} = \$21,000,000$$
$$t \text{ (time to maturity)} = 4 \text{ years}$$
$$\sigma \text{ (standard deviation)} = 0.50$$
$$r \text{ (continuously compounded interest rate)} = 3.5\%$$

Calculation from the Black–Scholes model:

$$C = SN(d_1) - Ee^{-rt}N(d_2)$$
$$d_1 = [\ln(S/E) + (r + 1/2\sigma^2)t]/\sqrt{\sigma^2 t}$$
$$d_2 = d_1 - \sqrt{\sigma^2 t}$$
$$d_1 = \left[\ln\frac{8,428,255}{21,000,000} + (0.035 + {}^1\!/_2 (0.50)^2)4\right]4 / \sqrt{(0.50)^2 \cdot 4} = -0.27293$$
$$d_2 = -0.27293 - \sqrt{(0.50)^2 \cdot 4} = -1.27293$$
$$N(d_1) = N(-0.27293) = 0.3936$$
$$N(d_2) = N(-1.27293) = 0.1020$$
$$C = \$8,428,255 \times 0.3936 - \$21,000,000 \times e^{-0.035 \times 4} \times 0.1020$$
$$= \$1,455,196$$

Value of business including cost of pilot restaurant = $1,455.196 − $117,439
$$= \$1,337,757$$

model is based on a number of assumptions that hold quite well for short-lived options on exchange-listed stocks but are more difficult to justify for real options like opening a restaurant.[5]

Of course, Michel must start his pilot restaurant before he can take advantage of this option. Thus, the net value of the call option less the negative present value of the pilot restaurant is $1,337,757 ($1,455,196 − $117,439). Because this value is large and positive, Michel decides to stay with his dream of Chez Michel. He knows that the probability that the restaurant will fail is greater than 50 percent. Nevertheless, the option to expand is

---

[5]In particular, the underlying asset is not traded; its price does not follow a continuous process; the variance may not be constant over the extended life of the option and the option cannot be exercised without delay. For more on how violations of these assumptions affect valuation of real options see A. Damodaran, *Investment Valuation,* John Wiley & Sons, New York, 1996, pp. 375–76.

important enough that his restaurant business has value. And, if he needs outside capital, he probably can attract the necessary investors.

This finding leads to the appearance of a paradox. If Michel approaches investors to invest in a single restaurant with no possibility of expansion, he will probably not be able to attract capital. After all, Table 24.3 shows a net present value of −$117,439. However, if Michel thinks bigger, he will likely be able to attract all the capital that he needs. But this is really not a paradox at all. By thinking bigger, Michel is offering investors the option, not the obligation, to expand.

The example we have chosen may seem frivolous and, certainly, we added off-beat characteristics for interest. However, if you think that business situations involving options are unusual or unimportant, let us state emphatically that nothing can be further from the truth. The notion of embedded options is at the heart of business. There are two possible outcomes for virtually every business idea. On the one hand, the business may fail, in which case the managers will probably try to shut it down in the most cost-efficient way. On the other hand, the business may prosper, in which case the managers will try to expand. Thus, virtually every business has both the option to abandon and the option to expand. You may have read pundits claiming that the net present value approach to capital budgeting is wrong or incomplete. Although criticism of this type frequently irritates the finance establishment, the pundits definitely have a point. If virtually all projects have embedded options, only an approach such as the one we have outlined can be appropriate. Ignoring the options is likely to lead to serious undervaluation.

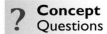

Concept Questions

- **What are the two options that many businesses have?**
- **Why does a strict NPV calculation typically understate the value of a firm or project?**

24.3 More on the Binomial Model

Earlier in this chapter, we examined two applications of options: executive compensation and the start-up decision. In both cases we valued an option using the Black–Scholes model. Although this model is justifiably well known, it is not the only approach to option valuation. As mentioned in the previous chapter, the binomial (two-state) model is an alternative and—in some situations—a superior approach to valuation. The rest of this chapter examines two applications under this binomial model.

Heating Oil

Two-Date Example   Consider Anthony Meyer, a typical heating-oil distributor, whose business consists of buying heating oil at the wholesale level and reselling the oil to homeowners at a slightly higher price. Most of his revenue comes from sales during the winter. Today, September 1, heating oil sells for $1.00 per gallon. In this example, Anthony Meyer hedges his risk using options on heating oil. These options are traded on the New York Mercantile Exchange denominated in U.S. dollars and expressing quantities of heating oil in U.S. gallons. For this reason, we use gallons here and, when we refer to dollars, we mean U.S. dollars.[6] Of course, this price is not fixed. Rather, oil prices will vary from September 1 until December 1, the time when his customers will probably be making their big winter purchases of heating oil. Let's simplify the situation by assuming that Anthony believes

---

[6]Technically speaking, the underlying asset for the options is a futures contract on heating oil. We discuss futures in Chapter 26.

that oil prices will be either at $1.37 or $0.73 on December 1. Figure 24.1 portrays this possible price movement. This potential price range represents a great deal of uncertainty, because Anthony has no idea which of the two possible prices will actually occur. However, this price variability does not translate into that much risk, because he is able to pass price changes on to his customers. That is, he will charge his customers more if he ends up paying $1.37 per gallon than if he ends up paying $0.73 per gallon.

Of course, Anthony is avoiding risk by passing on that risk to his customers. His customers accept this risk, perhaps because they are each too small to negotiate a better deal with Anthony. This is not the case with CECO, a large electric utility in his area. CECO approaches Anthony with the following proposition. The utility would like to be able to buy *up to* 6 million gallons of oil from him at $1.05 per gallon on December 1.

Although this arrangement represents a lot of oil, both Mr. Meyer and CECO know that Anthony can expect to lose money on it. If prices rise to $1.37 per gallon, the utility will happily buy all 6 million gallons from Anthony at only $1.05 per gallon, clearly creating a loss for the distributor. However, if oil prices decline to $0.73 per gallon, the utility will not buy any oil from Anthony. After all, why should CECO pay $1.05 per gallon to Anthony when the utility can buy all the oil it wants at $0.73 per gallon in the open market? In other words, CECO is asking for a *call option* on heating oil. To compensate Anthony for the risk of loss, the two parties agree that CECO will pay him $500,000 up front for the right to buy up to 6 million gallons of oil at $1.05 per gallon.

Is this a fair deal? Although small distributors may evaluate a deal like this by "gut feel," we can evaluate it more quantitatively using the binomial model described in the previous chapter. In that chapter, we pointed out that option problems can be handled most easily by assuming *risk-neutral pricing*. Under this approach, we first note that oil will either rise 37 percent ($1.37/$1.00 − 1) or fall −27 percent ($0.73/$1.00 − 1) from September 1 to December 1. We can think of these two numbers as the possible returns on heating oil. In addition, we introduce two new terms, u and d. We define u as $1 + 0.37 = 1.37$ and d as $1 - 0.27 = 0.73$.[7] Using the methodology of the previous chapter, we value the contract in the following two steps.

Step 1: Determining the Risk-Neutral Probabilities   We determine the probability of a price rise such that the expected return on oil exactly equals the risk-free rate. Assuming an 8 percent annual interest rate, which implies a 2 percent rate over the next three months, we can solve for the probability of a rise as:[8]

$$2\% = \text{Probability of rise} \times 0.37 + (1 - \text{Probability of rise}) \times (-0.27)$$

Solving this equation, we find that the probability of a rise is approximately 45 percent, implying that the probability of a fall is 55 percent. In other words, if the probability of a price rise is 45 percent, the expected return on heating oil is 2 percent. In accordance with what we said in the previous chapter, these are the probabilities that are consistent with a world of risk-neutrality. That is, under risk-neutrality, the expected return on any asset would equal the riskless rate of interest. No one would demand an expected return above this riskless rate, because risk-neutral individuals do not need to be compensated for risk-bearing.

Step 2: Valuing the Contract   If the price of oil rises to $1.37 on December 1, CECO will want to buy oil from Anthony at $1.05 per gallon. Anthony will lose $0.32 per gallon,

---

[7]As we will see later, here u and d are consistent with a standard deviation of the annual return on heating oil of 0.63.

[8]For simplicity, we ignore both storage costs and a convenience yield.

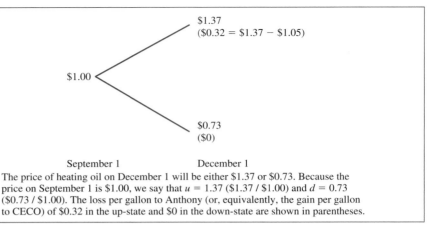

The price of heating oil on December 1 will be either $1.37 or $0.73. Because the price on September 1 is $1.00, we say that u = 1.37 ($1.37 / $1.00) and d = 0.73 ($0.73 / $1.00). The loss per gallon to Anthony (or, equivalently, the gain per gallon to CECO) of $0.32 in the up-state and $0 in the down-state are shown in parentheses.

because he buys oil in the open market at $1.37 per gallon, only to resell it to CECO at $1.05 per gallon. This loss of $0.32 is shown in parentheses in Figure 24.1. Conversely, if the market price of heating oil falls to $0.73 per gallon, CECO will not buy any oil from Anthony at all. That is, CECO would not want to pay $1.05 per gallon to Anthony when the utility could buy heating oil in the open market at $0.73 per gallon. Thus, we can say that Anthony neither gains nor loses if the price drops to $0.73. The gain or loss of zero is placed in parentheses under the price of $0.73 in Figure 24.1. In addition, as mentioned earlier, Anthony receives $500,000 up front.

Given these numbers, the value of the contract to Anthony can be calculated as:

$$[0.45 \times (\$1.05 - \$1.37) \times 6 \text{ million} + 0.55 \times 0]/1.02 + \$500,000 = -\$347,000 \quad \textbf{(24.1)}$$

Value of the call option

As in the previous chapter, we are valuing an option using risk-neutral pricing. The cash flows of −$0.32 ($1.05 − $1.37) and $0 per gallon are multiplied by their risk-neutral probabilities. The entire first term in Equation (24.1) is then discounted at $1.02 because the cash flows in that term occur on December 1. The $500,000 is not discounted, because Anthony receives it today, September 1. Because the present value of the contract is negative, Anthony would be wise to reject the contract.

As stated before, the distributor has sold a call option to CECO. The first term in the preceding equation, which equals −$847,000, can be viewed as the value of this call option. It is a negative number because the equation looks at the option from Anthony's point of view. Therefore, the value of the call option would be +$847,000 to CECO. On a per-gallon basis, the value of the option to CECO is:

$$[0.45 (\$1.37 - \$1.05) + 0.55 \times 0]/1.02 = \$0.141 \quad \textbf{(24.2)}$$

Equation (24.2) shows that CECO will gain $0.32 ($1.37 − $1.05) per gallon in the up-state, because CECO can buy heating oil worth $1.37 for only $1.05 under the contract. By contrast, the contract is worth nothing to CECO in the down-state, because the utility will not pay $1.05 for oil selling for only $0.73 in the open market. Using risk-neutral pricing, the formula tells us that the value of the call option on one gallon of heating oil is $0.141.

Three-Date Example   Although the preceding example captures a number of aspects of the real world, it has one deficiency. It assumes that the price of heating oil can take

FIGURE 24.2

**Movement of
Heating-Oil Prices
in a Three-Date
Model**

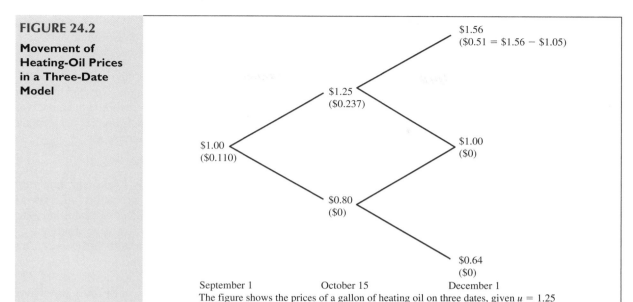

$1.56
($0.51 = $1.56 − $1.05)

$1.25
($0.237)

$1.00
($0.110)

$1.00
($0)

$0.80
($0)

$0.64
($0)

September 1   October 15   December 1

The figure shows the prices of a gallon of heating oil on three dates, given $u = 1.25$ and $d = 0.80$. There are three possible prices for heating oil on December 1. For each one of these three prices, we calculate the price on December 1 of a call option on a gallon of heating oil with an exercise price of $1.05. These numbers are in parentheses. Call prices at earlier dates are determined by the binomial model and are also shown in parentheses.

on only two values on December 1. This is clearly not plausible, because oil can take on essentially any value in reality. Although this deficiency seems glaring at first glance, it actually is quite correctable; all one has to do is to introduce more intervals over the three-month period of our example.

For example, consider Figure 24.2, which shows the price movement of heating oil over two intervals of 1½ months each.[9] As shown in the figure, the price will be either $1.25 or $0.80 on October 15. We refer to $1.25 as the price in the *up-state* and $0.80 as the price in the *down-state*. Thus, heating oil has returns of 25 percent ($1.25/$1) and −20 percent ($0.80/$1) in the two states.

We assume the same variability as we move forward from October 15 to December 1. That is, given a price of $1.25 on October 15, the price on December 1 will be either $1.56 ($1.25 × 1.25) or $1 ($1.25 × 0.80). Similarly, given a price of $0.80 on October 15, the price on December 1 will be either $1 ($0.80 × 1.25) or $0.64 ($0.80 × 0.80). This assumption of constant variability is quite plausible, because the rate of new information affecting heating oil (or most commodities or assets) is likely to be similar from month to month.

Note that there are three possible prices on December 1, but there are two possible prices on October 15. Also note that there are two paths, both generating a price of $1 on December 1. The price could rise to $1.25 on October 15 before falling back down to $1 on December 1 or, alternatively, the price could fall to $0.80 on October 15 before going back up to $1 on December 1. In other words, the model has symmetry, where an up-movement followed by a down-movement yields the same price on December 1 as a down-movement followed by an up-movement.

---

[9]Though it is not apparent at first glance, we will see later that the price movement in Figure 24.2 is consistent with the price movement in Figure 24.1.

How do we value CECO's option in this three-date example? We employ the same procedure that we used in the two-date example, although we will now need an extra step because of the extra date:

Step 1: Determining the Risk-Neutral Probabilities   As we did in the two-date example, we determine what the probability of a price rise would be such that the expected return on heating oil exactly equals the riskless rate. However, in this case, we work with an interval of 1½ months. Assuming an 8 percent annual rate of interest, which implies a 1 percent rate over a 1½ month interval,[10] we can solve for the probability of a rise as:

$$1\% = \text{Probability of rise} \times 0.25 + (1 - \text{Probability of rise}) \times (-0.20)$$

Solving the equation, we find that the probability of a rise here is 47 percent, implying that the probability of a fall is 53 percent. In other words, if the probability of a rise is 47 percent, the expected return on heating oil is 1 percent per each 1½-month interval. Again, these probabilities are determined under the assumption of risk-neutral pricing.

Note that the probabilities of 47 percent and 53 percent hold for both the interval from September 1 to October 15 and the interval from October 15 to December 1. This is the case because the return in the up-state is 25 percent and the return in the down-state is −20 percent for each of the two intervals. Thus, the preceding equation must apply to each of the intervals separately.

Step 2: Valuing the Option as of October 15   As indicated in Figure 24.2, the option to CECO will be worth $0.51 per gallon on December 1 if the price of heating oil has risen to $1.56 on that date. That is, CECO can buy oil from Anthony at $1.05 when it would otherwise have to pay $1.56 in the open market. However the option will be worthless on December 1 if the price of a gallon of heating oil is either $1 or $0.64 on that date. Here, the option is out of the money because the exercise price of $1.05 is above either $1 or $0.64.

Using these implicit option prices on December 1, we can calculate the value of the call option on October 15. If the price of a gallon of heating oil is $1.25 on October 15, Figure 24.2 shows us that the call option will either be worth $0.51 or $0 on December 1. Thus, if the price of heating oil is $1.25 on October 15, the value of the option on one gallon of heating oil at that time is:

$$[0.47 \times 0.51 + 0.53 \times 0]/1.01 = \$0.237$$

Here, we are valuing an option using the same risk-neutral pricing approach that we used in the earlier two-date example. This value of $0.237 is shown in parentheses in Figure 24.2

We also want to value the option on October 15 if the price at that time is $0.80. However, the value here is clearly zero, as indicated by the calculation:

$$[0.47 \times \$0 + 0.53 \times \$0]/1.01 = 0$$

This is obvious, once one looks at Figure 24.2. We see from the figure that the call must end up out of the money on December 1 if the price of heating oil is $0.80 on October 15. Thus, the call must have zero value on October 15 if the price of heating oil is $0.80 on that date.

Step 3: Valuing the Option on September 1   In the previous step, we saw that the price of the call on October 15 would be $0.237 if the price of a gallon of heating oil were $1.25

---

[10]For simplicity, we ignore interest compounding.

on that date. Similarly, the price of the option on October 15 would be $0 if oil were selling at $0.80 on that date. From these values, we can calculate the call option value on September 1 as:

$$[0.47 \times \$0.237 + 0.53 \times \$0]/1.01 = \$0.110$$

Notice that this calculation is completely analogous to the calculation of the option value in the previous step, as well as the calculation of the option value in the two-date example that we presented earlier. In other words, the same approach applies regardless of the number of intervals used. As we will see later, we can move to many intervals, which produces greater realism, yet still maintain the same basic methodology.

The previous calculation has given us the value to CECO of its option on one gallon of heating oil. Now we are ready to calculate the value of the contract to Anthony. Given the calculations from the previous equation, the contract's value can be written as:

$$-\$0.110 \times 6,000,000 + \$500,000 = -\$160,000$$

That is, Anthony is giving away an option worth $0.110 for each of the 6 million gallons of heating oil. In return, he is receiving only $500,000 up front. On balance, he is losing $160,000. Of course, the value of the contract to CECO is the opposite, so the value to this utility is $160,000.

Extension to Many Dates   We have looked at the contract between CECO and Anthony using both a two-date example and a three-date example. The three-date case is more realistic because more possibilities for price movements are allowed here. However, why stop at just three dates? Moving to 4 dates, 5 dates, 50 dates, 500 dates, and so on, should give us ever more realism. Note that, as we move to more dates, we are merely shortening the interval between dates without increasing the overall time period of three months (September 1 to December 1).

For example, imagine a model with 90 dates over the three months. Here, each interval is approximately one day long, because there are about 90 days in a three-month period. The assumption of two possible outcomes in the binomial model is more plausible over a one-day interval than it is over a 1½-month interval, let alone a three-month interval. Of course, we could probably achieve greater realism still by going to an interval of, say, one hour or one minute.

How does one adjust the binomial model in order to accommodate increases in the number of intervals? It turns out that two simple formulas relate u and d to the standard deviation of the return of the underlying asset:[11]

$$u = e^{\sigma/\sqrt{n}} \text{ and } d = 1/u$$

where σ is the standard deviation of the annualized return on the underlying asset (heating oil, in this case) and n is the number of intervals over a year.

When we created the heating oil example, we assumed that the annualized standard deviation of the return on heating oil was 0.63 (or, equivalently, 63 percent). Because there are four quarters in a year, $u = e^{0.63/\sqrt{4}} = 1.37$ and $d = 1/1.37 = 0.73$, as shown in the two-date example of Figure 24.1. In the three-date example of Figure 24.2, where each interval is 1½ months long, $u = e^{0.63/\sqrt{8}} = 1.25$ and $d = 1/1.25 = 0.80$. Thus, the binomial model

---

[11]See John C. Hull, *Options, Futures, and Other Derivatives,* 6th ed. (Upper Saddle River, N.J.: Prentice Hall, 2006) for a derivation of these formulas.

TABLE 24.5
Value of a Call on One Gallon of Heating Oil

Number of Intervals*	Call Value
1	$ 0.141
2	0.110
3	0.122
4	0.116
6	0.114
10	0.114
20	0.114
30	0.114
40	0.114
50	0.113
99	0.113
Black–Scholes Infinity	0.113

In this example, the value of the call according to the binomial model varies as the number of intervals increases. However, the value of the call converges rapidly to the Black–Scholes value. Thus, the binomial model, even with only a few intervals, appears to be a good approximation to Black–Scholes.

*The number of intervals is always one less than the number of dates.

can be applied in practice if the standard deviation of the return of the underlying asset can be estimated.

We stated earlier that the value of the call option on a gallon of heating oil was estimated to be $0.141 in the two-date model and $0.110 in the three-date model. How does the value of the option change as we increase the number of intervals, while keeping the time period constant at three months (from September 1 to December 1)? We have calculated the value of the call for various time intervals[12] in Table 24.5. The realism increases with the number of intervals, because the restriction of only two possible outcomes is more plausible over a short interval than over a long one. Thus, the value of the call when the number of intervals is 99 or infinity is likely more realistic than this value when the number of intervals is, say, 1 or 2. However, a very interesting phenomenon can be observed from the table. Although the value of the call changes as the number of intervals increases, convergence occurs quite rapidly. The call's value when the number of intervals is 6 is almost identical to the value when there are 99 intervals. Thus, a small number of intervals appears serviceable for the binomial model.

What happens when the number of intervals goes to infinity, implying that the length of the interval goes to zero? It can be proved mathematically that one ends up with the value of the Black–Scholes model. This value is also presented in Table 24.5. Thus, one can argue that the Black–Scholes model is the best approach to value the heating-oil option. It is also quite easy to apply. We can use a calculator to value options with Black–Scholes, whereas we must generally use a computer program for the binomial model. However, as shown in Table 24.5, the values from the binomial model, even with relatively few intervals, are quite close to the Black–Scholes value. Thus, although Black–Scholes may save us time, it does not materially affect our estimate of value.

At this point it seems as if the Black–Scholes model is preferable to the binomial model. Who wouldn't want to save time and still get a slightly more accurate value?

---

[12]In this discussion we have used both intervals and *dates*. To keep the terminology straight, remember that the number of intervals is always one less than the number of dates. For example, if a model has two dates, it only has one interval.

However, such is not always the case. There are plenty of situations where the binomial model is preferred to the Black–Scholes model. One such situation is presented in the next section.

24.4 Shutdown and Reopening Decisions

Some of the earliest and most important examples of special options occur in the natural resources and mining industries.

Valuing a Gold Mine

The "Woe Is Me" gold mine was founded in 1888 on one of the richest veins of gold in the West. Twenty years later, by 1908, the mine had been depleted, but occasionally, depending on the price of gold, it is reopened. When this example was created in 2003, gold was not actively mined at Woe Is Me, but its stock was still trading on the exchange under the ticker symbol "WOE." WOE had no debt and, with a stock price of $12 per share and 20 million outstanding shares, it had a market value of $240 million. WOE owns about 160 acres of land surrounding the mine and has a 100-year government lease to mine gold on the land. However, land in that area has a market value of only a few thousand dollars. WOE holds cash and securities and other assets worth about $30 million. What could possibly explain why a company with $30 million in assets and a closed gold mine that was producing no cash flows whatsoever had a market value of $240 million?

The answer lies in the options that WOE implicitly owns in the gold mine. The 2003 price of gold was about $320 per ounce and the cost of extraction and processing at the mine was about $350 per ounce.[13] It is no wonder that the mine is closed. Every ounce of gold extracted cost $350 and could be sold for only $320, for a loss of $30 per ounce. Presumably if the price of gold were to rise, the mine could be opened. It costs $2 million to open the mine and when it is opened, production is 50,000 ounces per year. Geologists believe that the amount of gold in the mine is essentially unlimited, and WOE has the right to mine it for the next hundred years. Under the terms of its lease, WOE cannot stockpile gold and it must sell each year all the gold it mines that year. Closing the mine requires equipment to be mothballed and some environmental precautions to be put in place and costs $1 million. We will refer to the $2 million required to open the mine as the entry fee or investment and the $1 million to close it as the closing or abandonment cost. (There is no way to avoid the abandonment cost by simply keeping the mine open and not operating.)

From a financial perspective, WOE is really just a package of options on the price of gold disguised as a company and a mine. The basic option is a call on the price of gold where the exercise price is the $350 extraction cost. The option is complicated by having an exercise fee of $2 million—the opening cost—whenever it is exercised and a closing fee of $1 million when it is abandoned. It is also complicated by the fact that it is a perpetual option with no final maturity.

The Abandonment and Opening Decisions

Before trying to figure out the exact value of the option implicit in WOE or, for that matter, in any real option problem, it is useful to see what we can glean by just applying common sense. To begin with, the mine should only be opened when the price of gold is sufficiently above the extraction cost of $350 per ounce. Because it costs $2 million to open the mine,

---

[13]Gold is quoted in U.S. dollars so all the prices in this example are in U.S. dollars.

the mine should not be opened whenever the price of gold is only slightly above $350. At a gold price of, say, $350.10, the mine would not be opened because the $0.10 profit per ounce translates into $5,000 per year (50,000 ounces × $0.10/ounce). This would not even cover the $2 million opening costs. More significantly, though, the mine probably would not be opened if the price rose to $360 per ounce even though a $10 profit per ounce—$500,000 million per year—would pay the $2 million opening costs at any reasonable discount rate. The reason is that here, as in all option problems, volatility plays a significant role. Because the gold price is volatile the price has to rise sufficiently above $350 per ounce to make it worth opening the mine. If the price at which the mine is opened is too close to the extraction price of $350 per ounce, say at $360 per ounce, then we would wind up opening the mine every time the price jogged above $360 and find ourselves operating at a loss or facing a closing decision whenever the gold price jogged $10 per ounce (only 3 percent) down.

The estimated volatility of the return on gold is about 15 percent per year. This means that a single annual standard deviation movement in the gold price is 15 percent of $320 or $48 per year. Surely with this amount of random movement in the gold price, a threshold of $352 is much too low to open the mine. A similar logic applies to the closing decision. If the mine is open, then we will clearly keep it open as long as the gold price is above the extraction cost of $350 per ounce since we are profiting on every ounce of gold mined. But, we also will not close the mine down simply because the gold price drops below $350 per ounce. We will tolerate a running loss to keep alive the possibility that the gold price will rise above $350 and to avoid the necessity of having to pay the $1 million abandonment cost only to have to then pay another $2 million to reopen the mine.

To summarize, if the mine is currently closed, then it will be opened—at a cost of $2 million—whenever the price of gold rises sufficiently above the extraction cost of $350 per ounce. If the mine is currently operating, then it will be closed down—at a cost of $1 million—whenever the price of gold falls sufficiently below the extraction cost of $350 per ounce. Our problem is to first find these two threshold prices at which we open a closed mine and close an open mine. We call these prices *popen* and *pclose* respectively, where

$$\text{popen} > \$350/\text{ounce} > \text{pclose}$$

In other words, we open the mine if the gold price option is sufficiently in the money and we close it when the option is sufficiently out of the money.

Valuing the Simple Gold Mine

Here is what has to be done in order both to determine popen and pclose and to value the mine:

Step 1   Find the risk-free interest rate and the volatility. We will use a semiannual interest rate of 3.4 percent and a volatility of 15 percent per year for gold.

Step 2   Construct a binomial tree and fill it out with gold prices. Suppose, for example, that we set the steps of the tree six months apart. If the annual volatility is 15 percent, u is equal to $e^{0.15\sqrt{2}}$, which is approximately equal to 1.11. The other parameter, d, is 0.90 (1/1.11). Figure 24.3 illustrates the tree. Starting at the current price of $320, the first 11 percent increase takes the price to $355 in six months. The first 10 percent decrease takes the price to $288. Subsequent steps are up 11 percent or down 10 percent from the previous price. The tree extends for the 100-year life of the lease or 200 six-month steps.

Using our analysis from the previous section, we now compute the risk-adjusted probabilities for each step. Given a semiannual interest rate of 3.4 percent, we have

$$3.4\% = \text{Probability of a rise} \times 0.11 + (1 - \text{Probability of a rise}) \times -0.10.$$

FIGURE 24.3   A Binomial Tree for Gold Prices

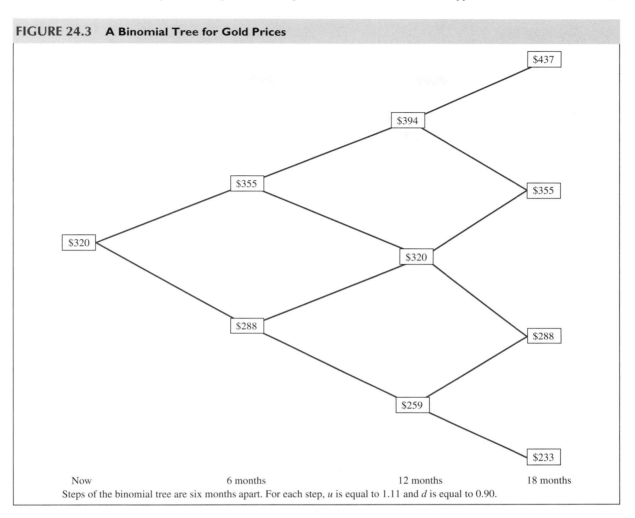

Steps of the binomial tree are six months apart. For each step, *u* is equal to 1.11 and *d* is equal to 0.90.

Solving this equation gives us 0.64 for the probability of a rise, implying that the probability of a fall is 0.36. These probabilities are the same for each six-month interval. In other words, if the probability of a rise is 0.64, the expected return on gold is 3.4 percent per each six-month interval. These probabilities are determined under the assumption of risk-neutral pricing. In other words, if investors are risk-neutral, they will be satisfied with an expected return equal to the risk-free rate, because the extra risk of gold will not concern them.

Step 3   Now we turn on the computer and let it simulate, say, 5000 possible paths through the tree. At each node, the computer has a 0.64 probability of picking an "up" movement in the price and a corresponding 0.36 probability of picking a "down" movement in the price. A typical path might be represented by whether the price rose or fell each six-month period over the next 100 years and it would be a list like

up, up, down, up, down, down, . . . , down

where the first "up" meant the price rose from $320 to $355 in the first six months, the next "up" meant it again went up in the second half of the year from $355 to $394, and so on, ending with a down move in the last half of year 100.

With 5000 such paths we will have a good sample of all the future possibilities for movement in the gold price.

Step 4   Next we consider possible choices for the threshold prices, popen and pclose. For popen, we let the possibilities be

$$\text{popen} = \$360 \text{ or } \$370 \text{ or } \ldots \text{ or } \$500$$

a total of 15 values. For pclose we let the probabilities be

$$\text{pclose} = \$340 \text{ or } \$330 \text{ or } \ldots \text{ or } \$100$$

a total of 25 values.

We picked these choices because they seemed reasonable and because increments of $10 for each seemed sensible. To be precise, though, we should let the threshold prices change as we move through the tree and get closer to the 100-year end. Presumably, for example, if we decided to open the mine with one year left on the lease, the price of gold should be at least high enough to cover the $2 million opening costs in the coming year. Since we mine 50,000 ounces per year, in year 99 we will only open the mine if the gold price is at least $40 above the extraction cost, or $390.

While this will become important at the end of the lease, using a constant threshold shouldn't have too big an impact on the value with 100 years to go and we will stick with our approximation of constant threshold prices.

Step 5   We calculate the value of the mine for each pair of choices of popen and pclose. For example, if popen = $410 and pclose = $290, we use the computer to keep track of the cash flows if we opened the mine whenever it was closed and the gold price rose to $410, and closed the mine whenever it was open and the gold price fell to $290. We do this for each of the 5,000 paths we simulated in Step 4.

For example, consider the path illustrated in Figure 24.4 of

up, up, down, up, up, down, down, down, down

As can be seen from the figure, the price reaches a peak of $437 in 2½ years, only to fall to $288 over the following four six-month intervals. If popen = $410 and pclose = $290, the mine will be opened when the price reaches $437, necessitating a cost of $2 million. However, the firm can sell 25,000 ounces of gold at $437 at that time, producing a cash flow of $2.175 million [25,000 × ($437 − $350)]. When the price falls to $394 six months later, the firm sells another 25,000 ounces, yielding a cash flow of $1.1 million [25,000 × ($394 − $350)]. The price continues to fall, with the price reaching $320 a year later. Here, the firm realizes a cash outflow, because production costs are $350 per ounce. Next, the price falls to $288. Because this is below pclose of $290, the mine is closed at a cost of $1 million. Of course, the price of gold will fluctuate in further years, leading to the possibility of future mine openings and closings.

This path is just a possibility. It may or may not occur in any simulation of 5000 paths. For each of these 5000 paths that the computer simulated, we have a sequence of semiannual cash flows using a popen of $410 and a pclose of $290. We calculate the present value of each of these cash flows, discounting at the interest rate of 3.4 percent. Summing up across all the cash flows, we have the present value of the gold mine for one path.

We then take the average present value of the gold mine across all the 5000 simulated paths. This number is the expected value of the mine from following a policy of opening the mine whenever the gold price hits $410 and closing it at a price of $290.

Step 6   The final step is to compare the different expected discounted cash flows from Step 5 for the range of possible choices for popen and pclose and to pick the highest one.

FIGURE 24.4   A Possible Path for the Price of Gold

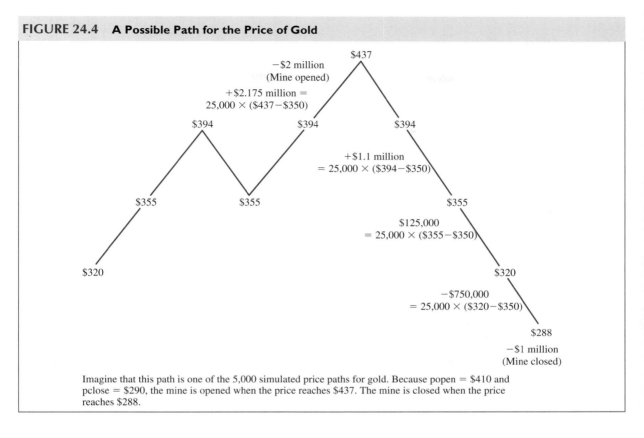

Imagine that this path is one of the 5,000 simulated price paths for gold. Because popen = $410 and pclose = $290, the mine is opened when the price reaches $437. The mine is closed when the price reaches $288.

This is the best estimate of the expected value of the mine. The value for pclose and popen corresponding to this estimate is our best estimate (within $10) of the points at which to open a closed mine and to shut an open one.

As mentioned in Step 3, there are 15 different values for popen and 25 different values for pclose, implying 375 (15 × 25) different pairs. Consider Table 24.6, which shows the present values associated with the 20 best pairs. The table indicates that the best pair is popen = $400 and pclose = $140, with a present value of $1.467 billion. This number represents the average present value across 5,000 simulations, all assuming the preceding values of popen and pclose. The next best pair is popen = $460 and pclose = $300, with a present value of $1.459 billion. The third best pair has a somewhat lower present value still, and so on.

Of course, our estimate of the value of the mine is $1.467 billion, the present value of the best pair of choices. The market capitalization (price × number of shares outstanding) of WOE should reach this value if the market makes the same assumptions that we did. Note that the value of the firm is quite high using an option framework. However, as stated earlier, WOE would appear worthless if a regular discounted cash-flow approach were used. This occurs because the initial price of gold of $320 is below the extraction cost of $350.

This example is not easy, either in terms of concepts or in terms of implementation. However, we believe that the extra work involved in mastering this example is worth it, because it illustrates the type of modelling that actually occurs in corporate finance departments in the real world.

Furthermore, the example illustrates the benefits of the binomial approach. One merely calculates the cash flows associated with each of a number of simulations, discounts the

TABLE 24.6
Valuation of Woe Is Me (WOE) Gold Mine for the 20 Best Choices of popen and pclose

popen	pclose	Estimated Value of Gold Mine
$400	$140	$1,466,720,900
460	300	1,459,406,200
380	290	1,457,838,700
370	100	1,455,131,900
360	190	1,449,708,200
420	150	1,448,711,400
430	340	1,448,450,200
430	110	1,445,396,500
470	200	1,435,687,400
500	320	1,427,512,000
410	290	1,426,483,500
420	290	1,423,865,300
400	160	1,423,061,900
360	320	1,420,748,700
360	180	1,419,112,000
380	280	1,417,405,400
450	310	1,416,238,000
450	280	1,409,709,800
440	220	1,408,269,100
440	240	1,403,398,100

For our simulation, WOE opens the mine whenever the gold price rises above popen and closes the mine whenever the gold price falls below pclose.

cash flows from each simulation, and averages present values across the simulations. Because the Black–Scholes model is not amenable to simulations, it cannot be used for this type of problem. In addition, there are a number of other situations where the binomial model is more appropriate than is the Black–Scholes model. For example, it is well known that the Black–Scholes model cannot properly handle options with dividend payments prior to the expiration date. This model also does not adequately handle the valuation of an American put. By contrast, the binomial model can easily handle both these situations.

Thus, any student of corporate finance should be well versed with both models. The Black–Scholes model should be used whenever appropriate, because it is simpler to use than is the binomial model. However, for the more complex situations where the Black–Scholes model breaks down, the binomial model becomes a necessary tool.

24.5 SUMMARY AND CONCLUSIONS

This chapter extends the intuitions of one of the most significant concepts in finance: option pricing theory. We describe four different types of special options:

- Executive stock options.
- The embedded option in a start-up company.
- The option in simple business contracts.
- The option to shut down and reopen a project.

We try to keep the presentation simple and straightforward from a mathematical point of view. We extend the binomial approach to option pricing in Chapter 23 to many periods. This adjustment brings us closer to the real world, because the assumption of only two prices at the end of an interval is more plausible when the interval is short.

SUGGESTED READING

Excellent practical material on real options can be found in:
Martha Amran and Nalin Kulatilaka. *Real Options.* Cambridge: Harvard Business School Press, 1999.
Real Options in Petroleum, www.puc-rio.br/marco.ind/main.html
S. R. Grenadier and A. M. Weiss. "Investment in Technological Innovations: An Option Pricing Approach." *Journal of Financial Economics* 44 (June 1997), 397–416.

A more academic treatment can be found in:
Michael Brennan and L. Trigeorgis, eds. *Flexibility, Natural Resources, and Strategic Options.* Oxford: Oxford University Press, 1998.
Tom Copeland and Vladimir Antikarov. *Real Options: A Practitioner's Guide.* Texere LLC, 2001.

Two further, useful articles are:
Abolhassen Jalilvand. "Why Firms Use Derivatives: Evidence from Canada." *Canadian Journal of Administrative Sciences* 16 (September 1999), 213–228.
Robert C. Merton. "Applications of Option Pricing Theory: Twenty-Five Years Later." *American Economic Review* 88 (1998), 323–349.

QUESTIONS & PROBLEMS

Executive Stock Options

24.1 Gary Levin is the chief executive officer of Mountainbrook Trading Company. The board of directors has just granted Mr. Levin 25,000 at-the-money European call options on the company's stock, which is currently trading at $55 per share. The stock pays no dividends. The options will expire in four years, and the standard deviation of the returns on the stock is 42 percent. Treasury bills that mature in four years currently yield a continuously compounded interest rate of 5.4 percent.
   a. Use the Black–Scholes model to calculate the value of the stock options.
   b. You are Mr. Levin's financial adviser. He must choose between the previously mentioned stock option package and an immediate $550,000 bonus. If he is risk-neutral, which would you recommend?
   c. How would your answer to (b) change if Mr. Levin were risk-averse and he could not sell the options prior to expiration?

24.2 Jared Lazarus has just been named the new chief executive officer of BluBell Fitness Centres Inc. In addition to an annual salary of $400,000, his three-year contract states that his compensation will include 10,000 at-the-money European call options on the company's stock that expire in three years. The current stock price is $40 per share, and the standard deviation of the returns on the firm's stock is 68 percent. The company does not pay a dividend. Treasury bills that mature in three years yield a continuously compounded interest rate of 5 percent. Assume that Mr. Lazarus's annual salary payments occur at the end of the year and that these cash flows should be discounted at a rate of 9 percent. Using the Black–Scholes model to calculate the value of the stock options, determine the total value of the compensation package on the date the contract is signed.

Binomial Model

24.3 Gaswoks Inc. has been approached to sell up to 50 million litres of gasoline in three months at a price of $1.00 per litre. Gasoline is currently selling on the wholesale market at $0.96 per litre and has a standard deviation of 61 percent. If the risk-free rate is 4.3 percent per year, what is the value of this option?

24.4 There is an American put option on a stock that expires in two months. The stock price is $63, and the standard deviation of the stock returns is 65 percent. The option has a strike price of $70, and the risk-free interest rate is a 5 percent annual percentage rate. What is the price of the put option today using one-month steps? (*Hint:* How will you find the value of the option if it can be exercised early? When would you exercise the option early?)

Real Options

24.5 Jet Black is an international conglomerate with a petroleum division and is currently competing in an auction to win the right to drill for crude oil on a large piece of land in one year. The current market price of crude oil is $55 per barrel, and the land is believed to contain 125,000 barrels of oil. If found, the oil would cost $10 million to extract. Treasury bills that mature in one year yield a continuously compounded interest rate of 6.5 percent, and the standard deviation of the returns on the price of crude oil is 50 percent. Use the Black–Scholes model to calculate the maximum bid that the company should be willing to make at the auction.

24.6 Sardano and Sons is a large, publicly held company that is considering leasing a warehouse. One of the company's divisions specializes in manufacturing steel, and this particular warehouse is the only facility in the area that suits the firm's operations. The current price of steel is $3,600 per tonne. If the price of steel falls over the next six months, the company will purchase 400 tonnes of steel and produce 4800 steel rods. Each steel rod will cost $120 to manufacture, and the company plans to sell the rods for $360 each. It will take only a matter of days to produce and sell the steel rods. If the price of steel rises or remains the same, it will not be profitable to undertake the project, and the company will allow the lease to expire without producing any steel rods. Treasury bills that mature in six months yield a continuously compounded interest rate of 4.5 percent, and the standard deviation of the returns on steel is 45 percent. Use the Black–Scholes model to determine the maximum amount that the company should be willing to pay for the lease.

24.7 The Webber Company is an international conglomerate with a real estate division that owns the right to erect an office building on a parcel of land in downtown Sacramento over the next year. This building would cost $10.5 million to construct. Due to low demand for office space in the downtown area, such a building is worth approximately $10 million today. If demand increases, the building would be worth $12.5 million a year from today. If demand decreases, the same office building would be worth only $8 million in a year. The company can borrow and lend at the risk-free rate of 2.1 percent effective annual rate. A local competitor in the real estate business has recently offered $750,000 for the right to build an office building on the land. Should the company accept this offer? Use a two-state model to value the real option.

24.8 You are in discussions to purchase an option on an office building with a strike price of $47 million. The building is currently valued at $45 million. The option will allow you to purchase the building either six months from today or one year from today. Six months from today, accrued rent payments from the building in the amount of $500,000 will be made to the owners. If you exercise the option in six months, you will receive the accrued rent payments; otherwise the payment will be made to be current owners. A second accrued rent payment of $500,000 will be paid one year from today with the same payment terms. The standard deviation of the value of the building is 25 percent, and the risk-free rate is an 8 percent annual percentage rate. What is the price of the option today using six-month steps? (*Hint:* The value of the building in six months will be reduced by the accrued rent payment if you do not exercise the option at that time.)

MINICASE: Exotic Cuisine Employee Stock Options

John Sparks, a newly minted MBA, has taken a management position with Exotic Cuisines Inc., a restaurant chain that just went public last year. The company's restaurants specialize in exotic main dishes, using ingredients such as kangaroo, buffalo, and ostrich. A concern John had going in was that the restaurant business is very risky. However, after some due diligence, John discovered a common misperception about the restaurant industry. It is widely thought that 90 percent of new restaurants close within three years; however, recent evidence suggests the failure rate is closer to 60 percent over three years. So it is a risky business, although not as risky as John originally thought.

During John's interview process, one of the benefits mentioned was employee stock options. Upon signing the employment contract, John received options with a strike price of $50 for 10,000 shares of company stock. As is fairly common, John's stock options have a three-year vesting period and a 10-year expiration, meaning that John cannot exercise the options for three years, and John loses them if he leaves before they vest. After the three-year vesting period, he can exercise the options at any time. Thus, the employee stock options are European (and subject to forfeit) for the first three years and American afterward. Of course, John cannot sell the options, nor can he enter into any sort of hedging agreement. If John leaves the company after the options vest, he must exercise within 90 days or forfeit.

Exotic Cuisines stock is currently trading at $25.38 per share, a slight increase from the initial offering price last year. There are no market-traded options on the company's stock. Because the company has been traded for only about a year, John is very reluctant to use the historical returns to estimate the standard deviation of the stock's return. However, he has estimated that the average annual standard deviation for restaurant company stocks is about 55 percent. Because Exotic Cuisines is a newer restaurant chain, John decides to use a 60 percent standard deviation in John's calculations. The company is relatively young, and he expects that all earnings will be reinvested back into the company for the near future. Therefore, he expects no

dividends will be paid for at least the next 10 years. A three-year T-Bill currently has a yield of 3.8 percent, and a 10-year Government of Canada bond has a yield of 4.4 percent.

1. John is trying to value his options. What minimum value would John assign? What is the maximum value John would assign?

2. Suppose that in three years the company's stock is trading at $60. At that time should John keep the options or exercise them immediately? What are some of the important determinants in making such a decision?

3. John's options, like most employee stock options, are not transferable or tradable. Does this have a significant effect on the value of the options? Why?

4. Why do you suppose employee stock options usually have a vesting provision? Why must they be exercised shortly after you depart the company even after they vest?

5. A controversial practice with employee stock options is re-pricing. What happens is that a company experiences a stock price decrease, which leaves employee stock options far out of the money or "underwater." In such cases, many companies have "re-priced" or "re-struck" the options, meaning that the company leaves the original terms of the option intact but lowers the strike price. Proponents of re-pricing argue that because the option is very unlikely to end in the money because of the stock price decline, the motivational force is lost. Opponents argue that re-pricing is in essence a reward for failure. How do you evaluate this argument? How does the possibility of re-pricing affect the value of an employee stock option at the time it is granted?

6. As we have seen, much of the volatility in a company's stock price is due to systematic or marketwide risks. Such risks are beyond the control of a company and its employees. What are the implications for employee stock options? Can you recommend an improvement over traditional employee stock options?

Visit us at www.mcgrawhill.ca/olc/ross

Chapter 25

Warrants and Convertibles

EXECUTIVE SUMMARY

In this chapter, we study two financing instruments: warrants and convertibles. A warrant gives the holder the right to buy common stock for cash. In this sense, it is very much like a call. Warrants are generally issued with privately placed bonds, though they are also packaged with new issues of common stock and preferred stock. In the case of new issues of common stock, warrants are sometimes given to investment bankers as compensation for underwriting services.

A convertible bond gives the holder the right to exchange the bond for common stock. It is therefore a mixed security blurring the traditional line between stocks and bonds. There is also convertible preferred stock.

The chapter describes the basic features of warrants and convertibles. It also discusses some of the most important questions concerning these securities:

1. How can warrants and convertibles be valued?
2. What impact do warrants and convertibles have on the value of the firm?
3. What are the differences among warrants, convertibles, and call options?
4. Why do some companies issue bonds with warrants and convertible bonds?
5. Under what circumstances are warrants and convertibles converted into common stock?

25.1 Warrants

Warrants are securities that give holders the right, but not the obligation, to buy shares of common stock directly from a company at a fixed price for a given period of time. Each warrant specifies the number of shares that the holder can buy, the exercise price, and the expiration date.

The preceding description of warrants makes it clear that they are similar to call options. The differences in contractual features between warrants and the call options that trade through the Montreal Exchange and the Canadian Derivative Clearing Corporation (CDCC) are small. For example, warrants have longer maturity periods.[1] Some warrants are actually perpetual, meaning that they never expire at all.

Warrants are referred to as *equity kickers* because they are usually issued in combination with privately placed bonds.[2] In most cases, warrants are attached to the bonds when issued. The loan agreement will state whether the warrants are detachable from the bond, that is, whether they can be sold separately. Usually, the warrant can be detached immediately.

---

[1] Warrants are usually protected against stock splits and stock dividends in the same way that call options are.

[2] Warrants are also issued with publicly distributed bonds and new issues of common and preferred shares.

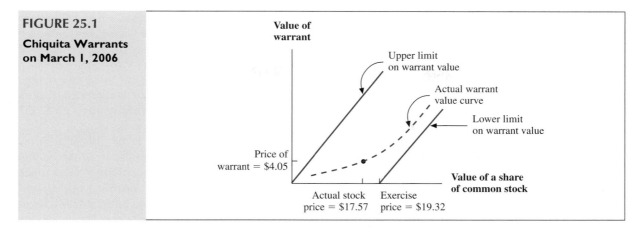

FIGURE 25.1

Chiquita Warrants on March 1, 2006

Including warrants with an issue of securities makes the issue more attractive. With the growth of financial engineering, warrant issuers are creating new varieties. Some warrant issues give investors the right to buy the issuers' bonds instead of their stock. In addition, warrants are issued on their own instead of as sweeteners in a bond issue.

During a corporate reorganization, famed banana company Chiquita Brands International issued warrants. Each warrant gave the holder the right to purchase one share of stock at an exercise price of $19.32. The warrants expire on March 19, 2009. On March 1, 2006, Chiquita Brands stock closed at $17.57, and the price of a warrant was $4.05.

The relationship between the value of Chiquita's warrants and its stock price can be viewed as similar to the relationship between a call option and the stock price, described in a previous chapter. Figure 25.1 depicts the relationship for Chiquita's warrants. The lower limit on the value of the warrants is zero if Chiquita's stock price is below $19.32 per share. If the price of Chiquita's stock rises above $19.32 per share, the lower limit is the stock price minus $19.32. The upper limit is the price of Chiquita's stock. A warrant to buy one share of stock cannot sell at a price above the price of the underlying stock.

The price of Chiquita's warrants on March 1, 2006, was higher than the lower limit. How far the warrant price lies above the lower limit will depend on

1. The variance of Chiquita's stock returns.
2. The time to the warrant's expiration date.
3. The risk-free rate of interest.
4. The stock price of Chiquita.
5. The exercise price.

These are the same factors that determine the value of a call option.

25.2 The Difference Between Warrants and Call Options

From the holder's point of view, warrants are similar to call options on common stock. A warrant, like a call option, gives its holder the right to buy common stock at a specified price. Warrants usually have an expiration date, though in most cases they are issued with longer lives than call options. From the firm's point of view, however, a warrant is very different from a call option on the company's common stock.

The most important difference between call options and warrants is that call options are issued by individuals and warrants are issued by firms. When a warrant is exercised, a firm must issue new shares of stock. Each time a warrant is exercised, then, the number of shares outstanding increases.

To illustrate, suppose the Endrun Company issues a warrant giving holders the right to buy one share of common stock at $25. Further, suppose the warrant is exercised. Endrun must print one new stock certificate. In exchange for the stock certificate, it receives $25 from the holder.

In contrast, when a call option is exercised, there is no change in the number of shares outstanding. Suppose Ms. Eager holds a call option on the common stock of the Endrun Company. The call option gives Ms. Eager the right to buy one share of the common stock for $25. If Ms. Eager chooses to exercise the call option, a seller, say Mr. Swift, is obligated to give her one share of Endrun's common stock in exchange for $25. If Mr. Swift does not already own a share, he must enter the stock market and buy one. The call option is a side bet between buyers and sellers on the value of the Endrun Company's common stock. When a call option is exercised, one investor gains and the other loses. The total number of shares outstanding of the Endrun Company remains constant, and no new funds are made available to the company.

EXAMPLE 25.1

To see how warrants affect the value of the firm, imagine that Mr. Canuck and Ms. America are two investors who have together purchased six ounces of platinum. At the time they bought the platinum, Mr. Canuck and Ms. America each contributed one-half of the cost, which we will assume was $3,000 for six ounces, or $500 an ounce. (They each contributed $1,500.) They incorporated, printed two share certificates, and named the firm the CA Company. Each certificate represents a one-half claim to the platinum. Mr. Canuck and Ms. America each own one certificate. They have formed a company with platinum as its only asset.

A Call Is Issued   Suppose Mr. Canuck later decides to sell to Mrs. North a call option issued on Mr. Canuck's share. The call option gives Mrs. North the right to buy Mr. Canuck's share for $1,800 within the next year. If the price of platinum rises above $600 per ounce, the firm will be worth more than $3,600 and each share will be worth more than $1,800. If Mrs. North decides to exercise her option, Mr. Canuck must turn over his stock certificate and receive $1,800.

How would the firm be affected by the exercise? The number of shares will remain the same. There will still be two shares, now owned by Ms. America and Mrs. North. If the price of platinum rises to $700 an ounce, each share will be worth $2,100 (or $4,200/2). If Mrs. North exercises her option at this price, she will profit by $300.

A Warrant Is Issued Instead   This story changes if a warrant is issued. Suppose that Mr. Canuck does not sell a call option to Mrs. North. Instead, Mr. Canuck and Ms. America have a shareholders' meeting. They vote that CA Company will issue a warrant and sell it to Mrs. North. The warrant will give Mrs. North the right to receive a share of the company at an exercise price of $1,800.[3] If Mrs. North decides to exercise the warrant, the firm will issue another share certificate and give it to Mrs. North in exchange for $1,800.

From Mrs. North's perspective, the call option and the warrant *seem* to be the same. The exercise prices of the warrant and the call are the same: $1,800. It is still advantageous for

---

[3]The sale of the warrant brings cash into the firm. We assume that the sale proceeds immediately leave the firm through a cash dividend to Mr. Canuck and Ms. America. This simplifies the analysis, because the firm with warrants then has the same total value as the firm without warrants.

Mrs. North to exercise the option when the price of platinum exceeds $600 per ounce. However, we will show that Mrs. North actually makes less in the warrant situation due to dilution.

The CA Company must also consider dilution. Suppose the price of platinum increases to $700 an ounce and Mrs. North exercises her warrant. Two things will occur:

1. Mrs. North will pay $1,800 to the firm.
2. The firm will print one share certificate and give it to Mrs. North. The certificate will represent a one-third claim on the platinum of the firm.

Because Mrs. North contributes $1,800 to the firm, the value of the firm increases. It is now worth

$$\text{New value of firm} = \text{Value of platinum} + \text{Contribution by Mrs. North}$$
$$= \quad \$4,200 \quad + \quad \$1,800$$
$$= \quad \$6,000$$

Because Mrs. North has a one-third claim on the firm's value, her share is worth $2,000 (or $6,000/3). By exercising the warrant, Mrs. North gains $2,000 − $1,800 = $200. This is illustrated in Table 25.1.

Dilution   Why does Mrs. North only gain $200 in the warrant case while gaining $300 in the call option case? The key is dilution, that is, the creation of another share. In the call option case, she contributes $1,800 and receives one of the two outstanding shares. That is, she receives a share worth $2,100 (or 1/2 × $4,200). Her gain is $300 (or $2,100 − $1,800). We rewrite this gain as

Gain on Exercise of Call:
$$\frac{\$4,200}{2} - \$1,800 = \$300 \tag{25.1}$$

In the warrant case, she contributes $1,800 and receives a newly created share. She now owns one of the three outstanding shares. Because the $1,800 remains in the firm, her share

TABLE 25.1
Effect of Call Option and Warrant on the CA Company

Value of Firm if:	Price of Platinum per Share	
	$ 700	$ 600
No warrant or option		
Mr. Canuck's share	$2,100	$1,800
Ms. America's share	2,100	1,800
Firm	$4,200	$3,600
Call option		
Mr. Canuck's claim	$ 0	$1,800
Ms. America's claim	2,100	1,800
Mrs. North's claim	2,100	0
Firm	$4,200	$3,600
Warrant		
Mr. Canuck's share	$2,000	$1,800
Ms. America's share	2,000	1,800
Mrs. North's share	2,000	0
Firm	$6,000	$3,600

If the price of platinum is $700, the value of the firm is equal to the value of six ounces of platinum plus the excess dollars paid into the firm by Mrs. North. This amount is $4,200 + $1,800 = $6,000.

is worth $2,000 [($4,200 + $1,800)/3]. Her gain is $200 ($2,000 − $1,800). We rewrite this gain as

Gain on Exercise of Warrant:

$$\frac{\$4,200 + \$1,800}{2 + 1} - \$1,800 = \$200 \qquad (25.2)$$

Warrants also affect accounting numbers. Warrants and (as we shall see) convertible bonds cause the number of shares to increase. This causes the firm's net income to be spread over a larger number of shares, thereby decreasing earnings per share. Firms with significant amounts of warrants and convertible issues must report earnings on a *primary* basis and a *fully diluted* basis.

How the Firm Can Hurt Warrant Holders

The platinum firm owned by Mr. Canuck and Ms. America has issued a warrant to Mrs. North that is *in the money* and about to expire. One way that Mr. Canuck and Ms. America can hurt Mrs. North is to pay themselves a large dividend. This could be funded by selling a substantial amount of platinum. The value of the firm would fall, and the warrant would be worth much less.

? Concept Questions
- **What is the key difference between a warrant and a traded call option?**
- **Why does dilution occur when warrants are exercised?**
- **How can the firm hurt warrant holders?**

25.3 Warrant Pricing and the Black–Scholes Model (Advanced)

We now wish to express the gains from exercising a call and a warrant in more general terms. The gain on a call can be written as

Gain from Exercising a Single Call:

$$\frac{\text{Firm's value net of debt}}{\#} - \text{Exercise price} \qquad (25.3)$$

(Value of a share of stock)

Equation (25.3) generalizes Equation (25.1). We define the *firm's value net of debt* to be the total firm value less the value of the debt. The total firm value is $4,200 in our example and there is no debt. The # stands for the number of shares outstanding, which is 2 in our example. The ratio on the left is the value of a share of stock.

The gain on a warrant can be written as

Gain from Exercising a Single Warrant:

$$\frac{\text{Firm's value net of debt} + \text{Exercise price} \times \#_w}{\# + \#_w} - \text{Exercise price} \qquad (25.4)$$

(Value of a share of stock after warrant is exercised)

Equation (25.4) generalizes (25.2). The numerator of the left-hand term is the firm's value net of debt *after* the warrant is exercised. It is the sum of the firm's value net of debt *prior* to the warrant's exercise plus the proceeds the firm receives from the exercise. The proceeds equal the product of the exercise price multiplied by the number of warrants. The number of warrants appears as $\#_w$. (Our analysis uses the plausible assumption that all warrants in the money will be exercised.) Note that $\#_w = 1$ in our numerical example. The denominator, $\# + \#_w$, is the number of shares outstanding *after* the exercise of the warrants. The ratio on the left is the value of a share of stock after exercise. By rearranging terms, Equation (25.4) can be rewritten as[4]

Gain from Exercising a Single Warrant:

$$\frac{\#}{\# + \#_w} \times \left(\frac{\text{Firm's value net of debt}}{\#} - \text{Exercise price} \right) \qquad \textbf{(25.5)}$$

(Gain from a call on a firm with no warrants)

Equation (25.5) relates the gain on a warrant to the gain on a call. Note that the term within parentheses is Equation (25.3). Thus, the gain from exercising a warrant is a proportion of the gain from exercising a call in a firm without warrants. The proportion $\#/(\# + \#_w)$ is the ratio of the number of shares in the firm without warrants to the number of shares after all the warrants have been exercised. This ratio must always be less than 1. Thus, the gain on a warrant must be less than the gain on an identical call in a firm without warrants. Note that $\#/(\# + \#_w) = 200/300 = \frac{2}{3}$ in our example, which explains why Mrs. North gains $300 on her call yet gains only $200 on her warrant.

Our discussion to this point implies that the Black–Scholes model must be adjusted for warrants. When a call option is issued to Mrs. North, we know that the exercise price is $1,800 and the time to expiration is one year. Though we have posited neither the price of the stock, the variance of the stock, nor the interest rate, we could easily provide these data for a real world situation. Thus, we could use the Black–Scholes model to value Mrs. North's call.

Suppose that the warrant is to be issued tomorrow to Mrs. North. We know the number of warrants to be issued, the warrant's expiration date, and the exercise price. Using our assumption that the warrant proceeds are immediately paid out as a dividend, we could use the Black–Scholes model to value the warrant. We would first calculate the value of an identical call. The warrant price is the call price multiplied by the ratio $\#/(\# + \#_w)$. As stated earlier, this ratio is $\frac{2}{3}$ in our example.

Concept Question

• **How can the Black–Scholes model be used to value warrants?**

25.4 Convertible Bonds

A **convertible bond** is similar to a bond with warrants. The most important difference is that a bond with warrants can be separated into distinct securities, but a convertible bond cannot. A convertible bond gives the holder the right to exchange it for a given number of shares of stock at any time up to and including the maturity date of the bond.

Preferred stock can frequently be converted into common stock. A share of convertible preferred stock is the same as a convertible bond except that it has no maturity date.

---

[4]To derive (25.5), one should separate "Exercise price" in (25.4). This yields

$$\frac{\text{Firm's value net of debt}}{\# + \#_w} - \frac{\#}{\# + \#_w} \times \text{Exercise price}$$

By rearranging terms, one can obtain (25.5).

EXAMPLE 25.2

Oceandoor Technology is one of the most important manufacturers of rigid magnetic disk drives for computers. Its stock is traded over the counter (OTC).

On November 1, 2006, Oceandoor raised $300 million by issuing 6.75 percent convertible subordinated debentures due in 2022. It planned to use the proceeds to invest in new plant and equipment. Like typical debentures, they had a sinking fund and were callable. Oceandoor's bonds differed from other debentures in their convertible feature: Each bond was convertible into 23.53 shares of common stock of Oceandoor anytime before maturity. The number of shares received for each bond (23.53 in this example) is called the **conversion ratio.**

Bond traders also speak of the **conversion price** of the bond. This is calculated as the ratio of the face value of the bond to the conversion ratio. Because the face value of each Oceandoor bond was $1,000, the conversion price was $42.50 (= $1,000/23.53). The bondholders of Oceandoor could give up bonds with a face value of $1,000 and receive 23.53 shares of Oceandoor common stock. This was equivalent to paying $42.50 (= $1,000/23.53) for each share of Oceandoor common stock received.

When Oceandoor issued its convertible bonds, its common stock was trading at $22.625 per share. The conversion price of $42.5 was 88 percent higher than the actual common stock price. This 88 percent is referred to as the **conversion premium.** It reflects the fact that the conversion option in Oceandoor convertible bonds was *out of the money.* This conversion premium is typical.

Convertibles are almost always protected against stock splits and stock dividends. If Oceandoor's common stock had been split two for one, the conversion ratio would have been increased from 23.53 to 47.06.

Conversion ratio, conversion price, and *conversion premium* are well-known terms in the financial community. For that reason alone, the student should master the concepts they represent. However, conversion price and conversion premium implicitly assume that the bond is selling at par. If the bond is selling at another price, the terms have little meaning. By contrast, *conversion ratio* can have a meaningful interpretation regardless of the price of the bond.

? Concept Question

- **What are the conversion ratio, the conversion price, and the conversion premium?**

25.5 The Value of Convertible Bonds

The value of a convertible bond can be described in terms of three components: straight bond value, conversion value, and option value.[5] We examine these three components below.

Straight Bond Value

The straight bond value is what the convertible bonds would sell for if they could not be converted into common stock. It will depend on the general level of interest rates and on the default risk. Suppose that straight debentures issued by Oceandoor had been rated A,

---

[5]For a similar treatment see Richard Brealey and Stewart Myers, *Principles of Corporate Finance,* 7th ed. (Boston: McGraw-Hill, 2003), Chapter 23; and James C. Van Horne, *Financial Market Rates and Flows,* 2nd ed. (Englewood Cliffs, N.J.: Prentice-Hall, 1987), Chapter 11.

FIGURE 25.2

Minimum Value of a Convertible Bond Versus the Value of the Stock for a Given Interest Rate

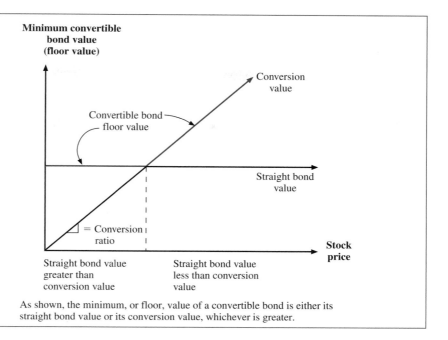

As shown, the minimum, or floor, value of a convertible bond is either its straight bond value or its conversion value, whichever is greater.

and A-rated bonds were priced to yield 4 percent per six months on November 1, 2006. The straight bond value of Oceandoor convertible bonds can be determined by discounting the $33.75 semiannual coupon payment and principal amount at 4 percent:

$$
\begin{aligned}
\text{Straight bond} &= \sum_{t=1}^{32} \frac{\$33.75}{1.04^t} + \frac{\$1{,}000}{(1.04)^{32}} \\
&= \$33.75 \times A_{0.04}^{32} + \frac{\$1{,}000}{(1.04)^{32}} \\
&= \$603.23 + \$285.06 \\
&= \$888.29
\end{aligned}
$$

The straight bond value of a convertible bond is a minimum value. The price of Oceandoor's convertible could not have gone lower than the straight bond value.

Figure 25.2 illustrates the relationship between straight bond value and stock price. In Figure 25.2 we have been somewhat dramatic and implicitly assumed that the convertible bond is default-free. In this case the straight bond value does not depend on the stock price and so it is graphed as a straight line.

Conversion Value

The value of convertible bonds depends on conversion value. **Conversion value** is what the bonds would be worth if they were immediately converted into common stock at current prices. Typically, we compute conversion value by multiplying the number of shares of common stock that will be received when the bond is converted by the current price of the common stock.

On November 1, 2006, each Oceandoor convertible bond could have been converted into 23.53 shares of Oceandoor common stock. Oceandoor common stock was selling for $22.625. Thus, the conversion value was 23.53 × $22.625 = $532.37. A convertible cannot sell for less than its conversion value. Arbitrage prevents this from happening.

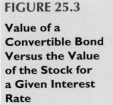

FIGURE 25.3

Value of a Convertible Bond Versus the Value of the Stock for a Given Interest Rate

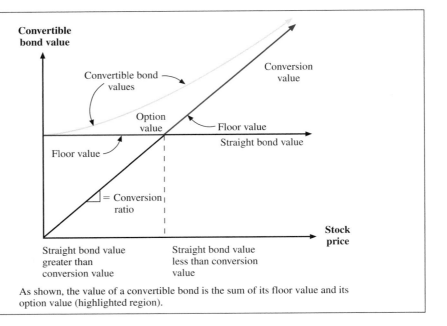

As shown, the value of a convertible bond is the sum of its floor value and its option value (highlighted region).

If Oceandoor's convertible sold for less than $532.37, investors would have bought the bonds and converted them into common stock and sold the stock. The profit would have been the difference between the value of the stock sold and the bond's conversion value.

Thus, convertible bonds have two minimum values: the straight bond value and the conversion value. The conversion value is determined by the value of the firm's underlying common stock. This is illustrated in Figure 25.2. As the value of common stock rises and falls, the conversion price rises and falls with it. When the value of Oceandoor's common stock increased by $1, the conversion value of its convertible bonds increased by $23.53.

Option Value

The value of a convertible bond will generally exceed both the straight bond value and the conversion value.[6] This occurs because holders of convertibles need not convert immediately. Instead, by waiting they can take advantage of whichever is greater in the future: the straight bond value or the conversion value. This option to wait has value, and it raises the value over both the straight bond value and the conversion value.

When the value of the firm is low, the value of convertible bonds is most significantly influenced by their underlying value as straight debt. However, when the value of the firm is very high, the value of convertible bonds is mostly determined by their underlying conversion value. In the language of Bay Street, the convertible is "trading off the stock." This is illustrated in Figure 25.3.

The bottom portion of the figure implies that the value of a convertible bond is the maximum of its straight bond value and its conversion value, plus its option value:

$$\begin{matrix} \text{Value of} \\ \text{convertible bond} \end{matrix} = \begin{matrix} \text{The greater of (straight bond} \\ \text{value or conversion value)} \end{matrix} + \begin{matrix} \text{Option} \\ \text{value} \end{matrix}$$

---

[6]The most plausible exception is when conversion would provide the investor with a dividend much greater than the interest available prior to conversion. The optimal strategy here could very well be to convert immediately, implying that the market value of the bond would exactly equal the conversion value. Other exceptions occur when the firm is in default or the bondholders are forced to convert.

EXAMPLE 25.3

Suppose the Moulton Company has outstanding 1000 shares of common stock and 100 bonds. Each bond has a face value of $1,000 at maturity. They are pure discount bonds and pay no coupons. At maturity each bond can be converted into 10 shares of newly issued common stock.

What circumstances will make it advantageous for holders of Moulton's convertible bonds to convert to common stock at maturity?

If the holders of the convertible bonds convert, they will receive $100 \times 10 = 1000$ shares of common stock. Because there were already 1000 shares, the total number of shares outstanding becomes 2000 upon conversion. Thus, converting bondholders own 50 percent of the value of the firm, V. If they do not convert, they will receive $100,000 or V, whichever is less. The choice for the holders of Moulton's bonds is obvious. They should convert if 50 percent of V is greater than $100,000. This will be true whenever V is greater than $200,000. This is illustrated as follows:

Payoff to Convertible Bondholders and Stockholders of the Moulton Company

	(1)	(2)	(3)
	$V \leq \$100,000$	$\$100,000 < V \leq \$200,000$	$V > \$200,000$
Decision:	Bondholders will not convert	Bondholders will not convert	Bondholders will convert
Convertible bondholders	V	$100,000	$0.5V$
Stockholders	0	$V - \$100,000$	$0.5V$

? Concept Questions
- **What three elements make up the value of a convertible bond?**
- **Describe the payoff structure of convertible bonds.**

25.6 Reasons for Issuing Warrants and Convertibles

The reasons for issuing convertible debt and warrants are a topic with great potential for confusion. To separate fact from fantasy, we present a rather structured argument. In this section and the next one we focus on convertible debt. Given the similarities between convertible debt and warrants, discussed in Section 25.4, the arguments apply to warrants as well. We first compare convertible debt with straight debt. Then we compare convertible debt with equity. For each comparison, we ask: In what situations is the firm better off with convertible debt and in what situations is it worse off?

Convertible Debt Versus Straight Debt

Convertible debt pays a lower interest rate than does otherwise identical straight debt. For example, if the interest rate is 10 percent on straight debt, the interest rate on convertible debt might be 9 percent. Investors will accept a lower interest rate on a convertible because of the potential gain from conversion.

Imagine a firm that seriously considers both convertible debt and straight debt and then finally decides to issue convertibles. When will this decision benefit the firm and when will it hurt the firm? We consider two situations.

The Stock Price Later Rises So That Conversion Is Indicated   The firm clearly likes to see the stock price rise. However, it would have benefited even more had it previously issued straight debt instead of a convertible. While the firm paid out a lower interest rate than it would have with straight debt, it will be obligated to sell the convertible holders a chunk of the equity below its current market price.

The Stock Price Later Falls or Does Not Rise Enough to Justify Conversion   The firm hates to see the stock price fall. However, as long as the stock price does fall, the firm is glad that it had previously issued convertible debt instead of straight debt. This is because the interest rate on convertible debt is lower. Because conversion does not take place, our comparison of interest rates is all that is needed.

Summary   Compared to straight debt, the firm is worse off having issued convertible debt if the underlying stock subsequently does well. The firm is better off having issued convertible debt if the underlying stock subsequently does poorly. In an efficient market, one cannot predict future stock price. Thus, we cannot argue that convertibles either dominate or are dominated by straight debt.

Convertible Debt Versus Common Stock

Next, imagine a firm that seriously considers both convertible debt and common stock and then finally decides to issue convertibles. When will this decision benefit the firm and when will it hurt the firm? We consider our two situations.

The Stock Price Later Rises So That Conversion Is Indicated   The firm is better off having previously issued a convertible instead of equity. To see this, consider the Brascan case. The firm could have issued stock for $16. Instead, by issuing a convertible, the firm effectively received $20 for a share upon conversion.[7]

The Stock Price Later Falls or Does Not Rise Enough to Justify Conversion   No firm wants to see the stock price fall. However, given that the price did fall, the firm would have been better off if it had previously issued stock instead of a convertible. The firm would have benefited by issuing stock above its later market price. That is, the firm would have received more than the subsequent worth of the stock. However, the drop in stock price did not affect the value of the convertible much because the straight bond value serves as a floor.

Summary   Compared with equity, the firm is better off having issued convertible debt if the underlying stock subsequently does well. The firm is worse off having issued convertible debt if the underlying stock subsequently does poorly. One cannot predict future stock price in an efficient market. Thus, we cannot argue that issuing convertibles is better or worse than issuing equity. The above analysis is summarized in Table 25.2.

Modigliani–Miller (MM) pointed out that, abstracting from taxes and bankruptcy costs, the firm is indifferent between issuing stock or issuing debt. The MM relationship is a quite general one. Their pedagogy could be adjusted to show that the firm is indifferent to whether it issues convertibles or issues other instruments. To conserve space (and the patience of students), we have omitted a full-blown proof of MM in a world with convertibles. However, the above results are perfectly consistent with MM. Now we turn to the real-world view of convertibles.

---

[7]This $20 is based on the conversion price in reference to the bond's issue value at par.

TABLE 25.2
The Cases For and Against Convertible Bonds (CBs)

	If Firm Subsequently Does Poorly	If Firm Subsequently Prospers
Convertible bonds (CBs)	No conversion occurs because of low stock price.	Conversion occurs because of high stock price.
Compared to:		
Straight bonds	CBs provide cheap financing because coupon rate is lower.	CBs provide expensive financing because bonds are converted, which dilutes existing equity.
Common stock	CBs provide expensive financing because firm could have issued common stock at high prices.	CBs provide cheap financing because firm issues stock at high prices when bonds are converted.

The "Free Lunch" Story

The previous discussion suggests that issuing a convertible bond is no better and no worse than issuing other instruments. Unfortunately, many corporate executives fall into the trap of arguing that issuing convertible debt is actually better than issuing alternative instruments. This is a free lunch type of explanation, of which we are quite critical.

EXAMPLE 25.4

The stock price of RW Company is $20. Suppose that this company can issue subordinated debentures at 10 percent. It can also issue convertible bonds at 6 percent with a conversion value of $800. The conversion value means that the holders can convert a convertible bond into 40 (or $800/$20) shares of common stock.

A company treasurer who believes in free lunches might argue that convertible bonds should be issued because they represent a cheaper source of financing than either subordinated bonds or common stock. The treasurer will point out that if the company does poorly and the price does not rise above $20, the convertible bondholders will not convert the bonds into common stock. In this case, the company will have obtained debt financing at below-market rates by attaching worthless equity kickers. On the other hand, if the firm does well and the price of its common stock rises to $25 or above, convertible holders will convert. The company will issue 40 shares. The company will receive a bond with face value of $1,000 in exchange for issuing 40 shares of common stock, implying a conversion price of $25. The company will have issued common stock *de facto* at $25 per share, or 20 percent above the $20 common stock price prevailing when the convertible bonds were issued. This enables it to lower its cost of equity capital. Thus, the treasurer happily points out, regardless of whether the company does well or poorly, convertible bonds are the cheapest form of financing.

Although this argument may sound quite plausible at first glance, there is a flaw. The treasurer is comparing convertible financing *with straight debt* when the stock subsequently falls. However, the treasurer compares convertible financing *with common stock* when the stock subsequently rises. This is an unfair mixing of comparisons. By contrast, our analysis of Table 25.2 was fair, because we examined both stock increases and decreases when comparing a convertible with each alternative instrument. We found that no single alternative dominated convertible bonds in *both* up and down markets.

The "Expensive Lunch" Story

Suppose we stand the treasurer's argument on its head by comparing (1) convertible financing with straight debt when the stock rises and (2) convertible financing with equity when the stock falls.

From Table 25.2, we see that convertible debt is more expensive than straight debt when the stock subsequently rises. The firm's obligation to sell convertible holders a chunk of the equity at a below-market price more than offsets the lower interest rate on a convertible.

Also from Table 25.2, we see that convertible debt is more expensive than equity when the stock subsequently falls. Had the firm issued stock, it would have received a price higher than its subsequent worth. Therefore, the expensive lunch story implies that convertible debt is an inferior form of financing. Of course, we dismiss both the free lunch and the expensive lunch arguments.

A Reconciliation

In an efficient financial market there is neither a free lunch nor an expensive lunch. Convertible bonds can be neither cheaper nor more expensive than other instruments. A convertible bond is a package of straight debt and an option to buy common stock. The difference between the market value of a convertible bond and the value of a straight bond is the price investors pay for the call option feature. In an efficient market this is a fair price.

In general, if a company prospers, issuing convertible bonds will turn out to be worse than issuing straight bonds and better than issuing common stock. In contrast, if a company does poorly, convertible bonds will turn out to be better than issuing straight bonds and worse than issuing common stock.

? Concept Questions

- What is wrong with the simple view that it is cheaper to issue a bond with a warrant or a convertible feature because the required coupon is lower than on straight debt?
- What is wrong with the free lunch story?
- What is wrong with the expensive lunch story?

25.7 Why Are Warrants and Convertibles Issued?

Research on firms that issue convertible bonds and warrants shows that they are different from other firms. Here are some of the differences:

1. The bond ratings of firms using convertibles are lower than those of other firms.[8]
2. Convertibles tend to be used by smaller firms with high growth rates and more financial leverage.[9]
3. Convertibles are usually subordinated and unsecured.

---

[8]E. F. Brigham, "An Analysis of Convertible Debentures," *Journal of Finance* 21 (1966).

[9]W. H. Mikkelson, "Convertible Calls and Security Returns," *Journal of Financial Economics* 9 (September 1981), p. 3, established this result for U.S. convertible bonds. R. G. Storey and C. R. Dipchand, "Factors Related to the Conversion Record of Convertible Securities," *Journal of Financial Research* (Winter 1978), studied the conversion record in Canada over the period 1946–75. They found that 70 percent of the convertible issues were converted, suggesting that most issuers experienced growth.

The kind of company that uses convertibles and warrants provides clues to why they are issued. Sensible explanations involve matching cash flows, risk synergy, and agency costs.

Matching Cash Flows

If financing is costly, it makes sense to issue securities whose cash flows match those of the firm. A young, risky, aspiring growth firm might prefer to issue convertibles or bonds with warrants because these will have lower initial interest costs. When the firm is successful, the convertibles (or warrants) will be converted. This causes expensive dilution, but it occurs when the firm can best afford it.

Risk Synergy

Another argument for convertible bonds and bonds with warrants is that they are useful when it is very costly to assess the risk of the issuing company. Suppose you are evaluating a new product offered by a start-up company. The new product is a biogenetic virus that may increase the yields of corn crops in northern climates. It may also cause cancer. This type of product is difficult to value properly. Thus, the risk of the company is very hard to determine—it may be high, or it may be low. If you could be sure the risk of the company was high, you would price the bonds for a high yield, say 15 percent. If it was low, you would price them at a lower yield, say 10 percent.

Convertible bonds and bonds with warrants can protect somewhat against mistakes of risk evaluation. Convertible bonds and bonds with warrants have two components: a straight bond and a call option on the company's underlying stock. If the company turns out to be a low-risk company, the straight bond component will have high value and the call option will have low value. However, if the company turns out to be a high-risk company, the straight bond component will have low value and the call option will have high value. This is illustrated in Table 25.3.

However, although risk has effects on value that cancel each other out in convertibles and bonds with warrants, the market and the buyer nevertheless must make an assessment of the firm's potential in order to value securities. It is not clear that the effort involved is that much less than is required for a straight bond.

Agency Costs

Convertible bonds can resolve agency problems associated with raising money. In a previous chapter, we showed that a straight bond is like a risk-free bond minus a put option on the assets of the firm. This creates an incentive for creditors to force the firm into low-risk activities. In contrast, holders of common stock have incentives to adopt high-risk projects. High-risk projects with negative NPV transfer wealth from bondholders to shareholders.

TABLE 25.3
A Hypothetical Case of the Yields on Convertible Bonds

	Firm Risk	
	Low	High
Straight bond yield	10%	15%
Convertible bond yield	6	7

Note: The yields on straight bonds reflect the risk of default. The yields on convertibles are not sensitive to default risk.

If these conflicts cannot be resolved, the firm may be forced to pass up profitable investment opportunities. However, because convertible bonds have an equity component, less expropriation of wealth can occur when convertible debt is issued instead of straight debt.[10] In other words, convertible bonds mitigate agency costs. One implication of this approach is that convertible bonds should have fewer restrictive debt covenants than do straight bonds. Casual empirical evidence seems to bear this out.

Backdoor Equity

A popular theory of convertibles views them as backdoor equity.[11] The basic story is that young, small, high-growth firms cannot usually issue debt on reasonable terms due to high financial distress costs. However, the owners may be unwilling to issue equity if current stock prices are too low. This is the same as the argument in Table 25.2 that convertibles offer cheap financing relative to common stock if the firm subsequently prospers. It also suggests that issuing convertibles signals that a firm expects high growth.

Lewis, Ragolski, and Seward examine the risk shifting and backdoor equity theories of convertible bond debt. They find evidence for both theories.

In May 2004, Gemini Energy Corp. issued $10 million of convertible debt. The issue had a 10-year maturity and a coupon rate of 10 percent. The bonds were convertible to common shares at $4. At the time of issue, Gemini was trading in Toronto at $3.60 a share. There are many explanations for why convertible debt made sense for Gemini. One of the biggest reasons is that, although it is far from a small firm, it faced high financing costs. Moreover, with its share value lower than years before (in 2000, the shares traded at over $100), convertibles were viewed as backdoor equity.

? Concept Question
- **Why do firms issue convertible bonds and bonds with warrants?**

25.8 Conversion Policy

There is one aspect of convertible bonds that we have omitted so far. Firms are frequently granted a call option on the bond. The typical arrangements for calling a convertible bond are simple. When the bond is called, the holder has about 30 days to choose between the following:

1. Converting the bond to common stock at the conversion ratio.
2. Surrendering the bond and receiving the call price in cash.

What should bondholders do? It should be clear that if the conversion value of the bond is greater than the call price, conversion is better than surrender; and if the conversion value is less than the call price, surrender is better than conversion. If the conversion value is greater than the call price, the call is said to **force conversion.**

---

[10]A. Barnea, R. A. Haugen, and L. Senbet, *Agency Problems and Financial Contracting,* Prentice-Hall Foundations of Science Series (New York: Prentice-Hall, 1985), Chapter VI.

[11]J. Stein, "Convertible Bonds as Backdoor Equity Financing," *Journal of Financial Economics,* 32 (1992). See also Craig M. Lewis, Richard J. Ragolski, and James K. Seward, "Understanding the Design of Convertible Debt," *The Journal of Applied Corporate Finance* (Spring 1998).

What should financial managers do? Calling the bonds does not change the value of the firm as a whole. However, an optimal call policy can benefit the shareholders at the expense of the bondholders. Because we are speaking of dividing a pie of fixed size, the optimal call policy is very simple: Do whatever the bondholders do not want you to do.

Bondholders would love the shareholders to call the bonds when the bonds' market value is below the call price. Shareholders would be giving bondholders extra value. Alternatively, should the value of the bonds rise above the call price, the bondholders would love the shareholders not to call the bonds, because bondholders would be allowed to hold onto a valuable asset.

There is only one policy left. This is the policy that maximizes shareholder value and minimizes bondholder value. This policy is

> Call the bond when its value is equal to the call price.

It is a puzzle that firms do not always call convertible bonds when the conversion value reaches the call price. Ingersoll examined the call policies of 124 firms between 1968 and 1975.[12] In most cases he found that the company waited to call the bonds until the conversion value was much higher than the call price. The median company waited until the conversion value of its bonds was 44 percent higher than the call price. This is not even close to the above strategy. Why?

The reason is that if firms attempt to implement the above optimal strategy, it may not be truly optimal. Recall that bondholders have 30 days to decide whether to convert bonds to common stock or to surrender bonds for the call price in cash. In 30 days the stock price could drop, forcing the conversion value below the call price. If so, the convertible is "out of the money" and the firm is giving away money. The firm would be giving up cash for common stock worth much less. Because of this possibility, firms in the real world usually wait until the conversion value is substantially above the call price before they trigger the call.[13] This is sensible.

? Concept Questions

- **Why will convertible bonds not be voluntarily converted to stock before expiration?**
- **When should firms force conversion of convertibles? Why?**

---

[12]J. Ingersoll, "An Examination of Corporate Call Policies on Convertible Bonds," *Journal of Finance* (May 1977). See also M. Harris and A. Raviv, "A Sequential Signalling Model of Convertible Debt Policy," *Journal of Finance* (December 1985). Harris and Raviv describe a signalling equilibrium that is consistent with Ingersoll's result. They show that managers with favourable information will delay calls to avoid depressing stock prices.

[13]See Paul Asquith, "Convertible Bonds Are Not Called Late," *Journal of Finance* (September 1995). On the other hand, the stock market usually reacts negatively to the announcement of a call. For example, see A. K. Singh, A. R. Cowan, and N. Nayan, "Underwritten Calls of Convertible Bonds," *Journal of Financial Economics* (March 1991); and M. A. Mazzeo and W. T. Moore, "Liquidity Costs and Stock Price Response to Convertible Security Calls," *Journal of Business* (July 1992).

Ederington, Caton, and Campbell test various theories on when it is optimal to call convertibles. They find evidence consistent for the preceding 30-day "safety margin" theory. They also find that calls of in-the-money convertibles are highly unlikely if dividends to be received (after conversion) exceed the company's interest payment. See Louis H. Ederington, Gary L. Caton, and Cynthia J. Campbell, "To Call or Not to Call Convertible Debt," *Financial Management* (Spring 1997).

25.9 SUMMARY AND CONCLUSIONS

1. A warrant gives the holder the right to buy shares of common stock at an exercise price for a given period of time. Typically, warrants are issued in a package with privately placed bonds. Afterward, they become detached and trade separately.

2. A convertible bond is a combination of a straight bond and a call option. The holder can give up the bond in exchange for shares of stock.

3. Convertible bonds and warrants are like call options. However, there are some important differences:

   a. Warrants and convertible securities are issued by corporations. Call options are traded between individual investors.
      1. Warrants are usually issued privately and are combined with a bond. In most cases, the warrants can be detached immediately after the issue. In some cases, warrants are issued with preferred stock, with common stock, in executive compensation programs, or as stand-alone issues.
      2. Convertibles are bonds that can be converted into common stock.
      3. Call options are sold separately by individual investors (called *writers* of call options).

   b. Warrants and call options are exercised for cash. The holder of a warrant gives the company cash and receives new shares of the company's stock. The holder of a call option gives another individual cash in exchange for shares of stock. When someone converts a bond, it is exchanged for common stock. As a consequence, bonds with warrants and convertible bonds have different effects on corporate cash flow and capital structure.

   c. Warrants and convertibles cause dilution to the existing shareholders. When warrants are exercised and convertible bonds converted, the company must issue new shares of common stock. The percentage ownership of the existing shareholders will decline. New shares are not issued when call options are exercised.

4. Many arguments, both plausible and implausible, are given for issuing convertible bonds and bonds with warrants. One plausible rationale for such bonds has to do with risk. Convertibles and bonds with warrants are associated with risky companies. Lenders can do several things to protect themselves from high-risk companies:

   a. They can require high yields.
   b. They can lend less or not at all to firms whose risk is difficult to assess.
   c. They can impose severe restrictions on such debt.

   Another useful way to protect against risk is to issue bonds with equity kickers. This gives the lenders the chance to benefit from risks and reduces the conflicts between bondholders and shareholders concerning risk.

5. A puzzle particularly vexes financial researchers: Convertible bonds usually have call provisions. Companies appear to delay calling convertibles until the conversion value greatly exceeds the call price. From the shareholders' standpoint, the optimal call policy would be to call the convertibles when the conversion value equals the call price.

KEY TERMS

Conversion premium 722	Conversion value 723	Force conversion 730
Conversion price 722	Convertible bond 721	Warrants 716
Conversion ratio 722		

SUGGESTED READING

The following articles analyze when it is optimal to force conversion of convertible bonds:
P. Asquith. "Convertible Bonds Are Not Called Late." *Journal of Finance* (September 1995).
M. Brennan and E. Schwartz. "Convertible Bonds: Valuation and Optimal Strategies for Call Conversion." *Journal of Finance* (December 1977).

Michael Brennan examines the conventional arguments for and against convertible bonds and offers a new "risk synergy" rationale in:

M. Brennan. "The Case for Convertibles." In J. M. Stern and D. H. Chew, eds., *The Revolution in Corporate Finance.* New York: Basil Blackwell, 1986.

For more on convertibles, see:

John D. Finnerty and D. R. Emery. *A Practitioner's Guide to Debt Management.* Boston: Harvard Business School Press, 2001.

QUESTIONS & PROBLEMS

Warrants

25.1   Explain the following limits on the prices of warrants:

    a. If the stock price is below the exercise price of the warrant, the lower bound on the price of a warrant is zero.

    b. If the stock price is above the exercise price of the warrant, the lower bound on the price of a warrant is the difference between the stock price and the exercise price.

    c. An upper bound on the price of any warrant is the current value of the firm's stock.

25.2   What is the primary difference between a warrant and a traded call option? Why is this important? What is dilution?

25.3   A warrant gives its owner the right to purchase three shares of common stock at an exercise price of $32 per share. The current market price of the stock is $39. What is the minimum value of the warrant?

25.4   General Modems has five-year warrants that currently trade in the open market. Each warrant gives its owner the right to purchase one share of common stock for an exercise price of $35.

    a. Suppose the stock is currently trading for $33 per share. What is the lower limit on the price of the warrant? What is the upper limit?

    b. Suppose the stock is currently trading for $39 per share. What is the lower limit on the price of the warrant? What is the upper limit?

25.5   Survivor Inc., an all-equity firm, has three shares of stock outstanding. Yesterday, the firm's assets consisted of five ounces of platinum, currently worth $1,000 per ounce. Today, the company issued Ms. Wu a warrant for its fair value of $1,000. The warrant gives Ms. Wu the right to buy a single share of the firm's stock for $2,100 and can be exercised only on its expiration date one year from today. The firm used the proceeds from the issuance to immediately purchase an additional ounce of platinum.

    a. What was the price of a single share of stock *before* the warrant was issued?

    b. What was the price of a single share of stock immediately *after* the warrant was issued?

    c. Suppose platinum is selling for $1,100 per ounce on the warrant's expiration date in one year. What will be the value of a single share of stock on the warrant's expiration date?

25.6   The capital structure of Ricketti Enterprises consists of 11 million shares of common stock and 1.1 million warrants. Each warrant gives its owner the right to purchase one share of common stock for an exercise price of $15.50. The current stock price is $16.96, and each warrant is worth $3.05. What is the new stock price if all warrant holders decide to exercise today? Assume the market does not expect the warrants to be exercised, since the price per warrant is above the exercise price of each warrant.

EXCEL

25.7   Superior Clamps Inc. has a capital structure consisting of 4.4 million shares of common stock and 550,000 warrants. Each warrant gives its owner the right to purchase one share of newly issued common stock for an exercise price of $22. The warrants are European and will expire one year from today. The market value of the company's assets is $96.8

million, and the annual variance of the returns on the firm's assets is 0.076. Treasury bills that mature in one year yield a continuously compounded interest rate of 6.7 percent. The company does not pay a dividend. Use the Black–Scholes model to determine the value of a single warrant.

25.8   A warrant with six months until expiration entitles its owner to buy 20 shares of the issuing firm's common stock for an exercise price of $42 per share. If the current market price is $29 per share, will the market price of the warrant equal zero?

25.9   Omega Airline's capital structure consists of 1.8 million shares of common stock and zero coupon bonds with a face value of $12 million that mature in six months. The firm just announced that it will issue warrants with an exercise price of $114 and six months until expiration to raise the funds to pay off its maturing debt. Each warrant can be exercised only at expiration and gives its owner the right to buy a single newly issued share of common stock. The firm will place the proceeds from the warrant issue immediately into Treasury bills. The market value balance sheet shows that the firm will have assets worth $192 million after the announcement. The company does not pay dividends. The standard deviation of the returns on the firm's assets is 64 percent, and Treasury bills with a six-month maturity yield 5.4 percent. How many warrants must the company issue today to be able to use the proceeds from the sale to pay off the firm's debt obligation in six months?

Convertible Bonds

25.10   What happens to the price of a convertible bond if interest rates increase?

25.11   If a convertible bond has conversion price of $64.85, what is the conversion ratio of the bond? Suppose that this is a callable, convertible bond. If the stock price volatility increases, how will this affect the price of the bond?

25.12   Hannon Home Products recently issued $430,000 worth of 7.5 percent convertible debentures. Each convertible bond has a face value of $1,000. Each convertible bond can be converted into 24.25 shares or common stock anytime before maturity. The stock price is $31.25, and the market value of each bond is $1,180.
   a. What is the conversion ratio?
   b. What is the conversion price?
   c. What is the conversion premium?
   d. What is the conversion value?
   e. If the stock price increases by $2, what is the new conversion value?

25.13   An analyst has recently informed you that at the issuance of a company's convertible bonds, one of the two following sets of relationships existed:

	Scenario 1	Scenario 2
Face value of each convertible bond	$1,000	$1,000
Straight value of each convertible bond	925	975
Market value of each convertible bond	1,000	890

Assume the bonds are available for immediate conversion. Which of the two scenarios do you believe is more likely? Why?

25.14   Heart & Soul Fitness Centre Inc. issued convertible bonds with a conversion price of $25. The bonds are available for immediate conversion. The current price of the company's common stock is $22 per share. The current market price of the convertible bonds is $990. The convertible bonds' straight value is not known.
  a. What is the minimum price that each of the convertible bonds should sell for?
  b. Explain the difference between the current market price of each convertible bond and the value of the common stock into which it can be immediately converted.

25.15   JG Corp. has just issued a 30-year callable, convertible bond with a coupon rate of 7 percent annual coupon payments. The bond has a conversion price of $125. The company's stock is selling for $32 per share. The owner of the bond will be forced to convert if the bond's conversion value is ever greater than or equal to $1,100. The required return on an otherwise identical nonconvertible bond is 12 percent.
  a. What is the minimum value of the bond?
  b. If the stock price were to grow by 15 percent per year forever, how long would it take for the bond's conversion value to exceed $1,100?

25.16   Tom Allan is the chief executive officer of Home Improvement Construction and owns 690,000 shares of stock. The company currently has 4 million shares of stock and convertible bonds with a face value of $22 million outstanding. The convertible bonds have a conversion price of $22, and the stock is currently selling for $26.
  a. What percentage of the firm's common stock does Mr. Allan own?
  b. If the company decides to call the convertible bonds and force conversion, what percentage of the firm's common stock will Mr. Allan own? He does not own any convertible bonds.

25.17   Ty Cott has been hired to value a new 25-year callable, convertible bond. The bond has a 6.80 percent coupon rate, payable annually. The conversion price is $150, and the stock currently sells for $44.75. The stock price is expected to grow at 12 percent per year. The bond is callable at $1,200; but based on prior experience, it won't be called unless the conversion value is $1,300. The required return on this bond is 10 percent. What value should Ty assign to this bond?

25.18   A $1,000 par convertible debenture has a conversion price for common stock of $170 per share. If the common stock is currently selling for $62 per share, what is the conversion value of the convertible bond?

25.19   MGH Medical Supplies Inc. recently issued a single zero-coupon convertible bond due 10 years from today. The convertible bond, which is currently trading for $400 in the open market, has a face value of $1,000 and can be converted into 25 shares of common stock. Each share of MGH's common stock is currently selling for $12, and otherwise identical nonconvertible bonds yield 11 percent per annum (effective annual yield).
  a. What is the straight value of the convertible bond?
  b. What is its conversion value?
  c. What is its option value?

25.20   Financial institutions sometimes take warrants or call options on the borrower's shares when making a loan. In Canada, this practice is particularly popular with Schedule 2 (foreign-owned) chartered banks. The warrants or call options can be exercised to enhance the lender's return beyond the interest paid. Why do you think that some financial institutions and borrowers prefer this blend of return over simply attaching a higher interest rate to the loan? Explain briefly.

MINICASE: S&S Air's Convertible Bond

Chris Guthrie was recently hired by S&S Air Inc. to assist the company with its short-term financial planning and to evaluate the company's performance. Chris graduated from business school five years ago with a finance degree. He has been employed in the finance department of Ford Motor Company of Canada since then.

S&S Air was founded 10 years ago by two friends, Mark Sexton and Todd Story. The company has manufactured and sold light airplanes over this period, and the company's products have received high reviews for safety and reliability. The company has a niche market in that it sells primarily to individuals who own and fly their own airplanes. The company has two models: the Birdie, which sells for $53,000, and the Eagle, which sells for $78,000.

S&S Air trades on the TSX Venture at $19 per share, but the company needs new funds for investment opportunities. In consultation with Tonisha Jones of underwriter Raines & Warren, Chris decided that a convertible bond issue with a 20-year maturity is the way to go. He met with the owners, Mark and Todd, and presented his analysis of the convertible bond issue. Chris looked at comparable publicly traded companies and determined that the average PE ratio for the industry is 12.5. Earnings per share for the company are $1.60. With this in mind, Chris concluded that the conversion price should be $25 per share.

Several days later, Todd, Mark, and Chris met again to discuss the potential bond issue. Both Todd and Mark have researched convertible bonds and have questions for Chris. Todd begins by asking Chris if the convertible bond issue will have a lower coupon rate than a comparable bond without a conversion feature. Chris replies that to sell the bond at par value, the convertible bond issue would require a 6 percent coupon rate with a conversion value of $800, while a plain vanilla bond would have a 7 percent coupon rate. Todd nods in agreement, and he explains that the convertible bonds are a win–win form of financing. He states that if the value of the company stock does not rise above the conversion price,

the company has issued debt at a cost below the market rate (6 percent instead of 7 percent). If the company's stock does rise to the conversion value, the company has effectively issued stock above the current value.

Mark immediately disagrees, arguing that convertible bonds are a no-win form of financing. He argues that if the value of the company stock rises to $25, the company is forced to sell stock at the conversion price. This means the new shareholders (those who bought the convertible bonds) benefit from a bargain price. Put another way, if the company prospers, it would have been better to have issued straight debt so that the gains would not be shared.

Chris has gone back to Tonisha for help. As Tonisha's assistant, you have been asked to prepare another memo answering the following questions:

1. Why do you think Chris is suggesting a conversion price of $25?
2. What is the floor value of the S&S Air convertible bond?
3. What is the conversion ratio of the bond?
4. What is the conversion premium of the bond?
5. What is the value of the option?
6. Is there anything wrong with Todd's argument that it is cheaper to issue a bond with a convertible feature because the required coupon is lower?
7. Is there anything wrong with Mark's argument that a convertible bond is a bad idea because it allows new shareholders to participate in gains made by the company?
8. How can you reconcile the arguments made by Todd and Mark?
9. During the debate, a question comes up concerning whether the bonds should have an ordinary (not make-whole) call feature. Chris confuses everybody by stating, "The call feature lets S&S Air force conversion, thereby minimizing the problem Mark has identified." What is he talking about? Is he making sense?

Chapter 26

Derivatives and Hedging Risk

EXECUTIVE SUMMARY

Managing risk is one of the most important tasks confronting corporate management, and financial markets are always willing to introduce new products to meet a need, either real or perceived. Consider credit derivatives, also known as credit default swaps. A credit derivative is an option-like instrument that allows the seller of the derivative to put an underlying bond to the purchaser if a credit event, such as bankruptcy, occurs. Credit derivatives were practically unheard of in 2000, but the notional value of these instruments had grown to US$35.1 trillion by April 2007. Of course, the market for currency and interest rate swaps, which allows for the exchange of currencies or interest payments, had grown even larger, with a notional value of over $200 trillion. In this chapter, we explore a variety of derivative contracts that allow a company's management to control risk.

Derivatives, Hedging, and Risk

The name *derivatives* is self-explanatory. A derivative is a financial instrument whose payoffs and values are derived from, or depend on, something else. Often we speak of the thing that the derivative depends on as the *primitive* or the *underlying*. For example, in Chapter 23 we studied how options work. An option is a derivative. The value of a call option depends on the value of the underlying stock on which it is written. Actually, call options are quite complicated examples of derivatives. The vast majority of derivatives are simpler than call options. Most derivatives are forward or futures agreements or what are called swaps, and we will study each of these in some detail.

Why do firms use derivatives? The answer is that derivatives are tools for changing the firm's risk exposure. Derivatives are to finance what scalpels are to surgery. By using derivatives, the firm can cut away unwanted portions of risk exposure and even transform the exposures into quite different forms. A central point in finance is that risk is undesirable. In our chapters on risk and return, we pointed out that individuals would choose risky securities only if the expected return compensated for the risk. Similarly, a firm should accept a project with high risk only if the return on the project compensates for this risk. Not surprisingly, then, firms are usually looking for ways to reduce their risk. When the firm reduces its risk exposure, it is said to be **hedging.** Hedging offsets the firm's risk, such as the risk in a project, by one or more transactions in the financial markets.

The use of derivatives became so prominent in the early 1990s that academics, governments, and regulatory agencies began to look much more closely at the risks associated with these financial instruments. In 1993, the Group of 30 (a non-profit organization of senior executives, regulators, and academics) published *Derivatives: Practices and Principles,* a study that has helped to shape the field of risk management. The report's findings resulted in 20 recommendations that included topics such as the role of boards of directors and senior management, the implementation of independent risk management functions, and the various risks that derivative transactions entail; all to provide a guideline for dealers and end-users in how to use derivatives effectively.[1]

Derivatives can also be used merely to change or even increase the firm's risk exposure. When this occurs, the firm is *speculating* on the movement of some economic variables—those that underlie the derivative. For example, if a derivative is purchased that will rise in value if interest rates rise, and if the firm has no offsetting exposure to interest rate changes, then the firm is speculating that interest rates will rise and result in a profit on its derivatives position. Using derivatives to translate an opinion about whether interest rates or some other economic variable will rise or fall is the opposite of hedging—it is risk enhancing. Speculating on your views on the economy and using derivatives to profit if that view turns out to be correct is not necessarily wrong, but the speculator should always remember that sharp tools cut deep, and if the opinions on which the derivatives position is based turn out to be incorrect, then the consequences can prove costly. Efficient market theory teaches how difficult it is to predict what markets will do. Most of the sad experiences with derivatives occurred not from their use as instruments for hedging and offsetting risk, but, rather, from speculation.

26.1 Forward Contracts

We can begin our discussion of hedging by considering forward contracts. You have probably been dealing in forward contracts your whole life without knowing it. To illustrate, suppose you walk into a bookstore on, say, February 1 to buy the best-seller *Eating Habits of the Rich and Famous.* The cashier tells you that the book is currently sold out, but he takes your phone number, saying that he will reorder it for you. He says the book will cost $10. If you agree on February 1 to pick up and pay $10 for the book when called, you and the cashier have engaged in a **forward contract.** That is, you have agreed both to pay for the book and to pick it up when the bookstore notifies you. Since you are agreeing to buy the book at a later date, you are *buying* a forward contract on February 1. In commodity parlance, you will be **taking delivery** when you pick up the book. The book is called the **deliverable instrument.**

The cashier, acting on behalf of the bookstore, is selling a forward contract. (Alternatively, we say that he is writing a forward contract.) The bookstore has agreed to turn the book over to you at the predetermined price of $10 as soon as it arrives. The act of turning the book over to you is called **making delivery.** Table 26.1 illustrates the book purchase.

TABLE 26.1
Illustration of Book Purchase as a Forward Contract

February 1	Date When Book Arrives
Buyer agrees to 1. Pay the purchase price of $10. 2. Receive book when book arrives.	Buyer 1. Pays purchase price of $10. 2. Receives book.
Seller agrees to 1. Give up book. 2. Accept payment of $10 when book arrives.	Seller 1. Gives up book. 2. Accepts payment of $10.

Note that cash does not change hands on February 1. Cash changes hands when the book arrives.

---

[1]For a detailed list of the G-30's report recommendations, visit http://riskinstitute.ch/00007070.htm.

Note that the agreement takes place on February 1. The price is set and the conditions for sale are set at that time. In this case, the sale will occur when the book arrives. In other cases, an exact date of sale would be given. However, *no* cash changes hands on February 1; cash changes hands only when the book arrives.

Though forward contracts may have seemed exotic to you before you began this chapter, you can see that they are quite commonplace. Forward contracts occur frequently in business. Every time a firm orders an item that cannot be delivered immediately, a forward contract takes place. Sometimes, particularly when the order is small, an oral agreement will suffice. Other times, particularly when the order is larger, a written agreement is necessary.

Note that a forward contract is not an option. Both the buyer and the seller are obligated to perform under the terms of the contract. In contrast, the buyer of an option *chooses* whether or not to exercise the option.

A forward contract should be contrasted with a **cash transaction,** that is, a transaction where exchange is immediate. Had the book been on the bookstore's shelf, your purchase of it would have been a cash transaction.

? Concept Questions
- **What is a forward contract?**
- **Give examples of forward contracts in your life.**

26.2 Futures Contracts

A variant of the forward contract takes place on financial exchanges. Contracts on exchanges are usually called **futures contracts.** For example, consider Table 26.2, which provides data on trading in wheat for Thursday, September 15, 20X1. Let us focus on the September futures contract, which is illustrated in the first row of the table. The first trade of the day in the contract was for $4.11 per bushel. The price reached a high of $4.16¼ during the day and reached a low of $4.07. The last trade was also at $4.07. In other words, the contract *closed* or *settled* at $4.07. The price dropped 6¼ cents per bushel during the day, indicating that the price closed the previous day at $4.13¼ ($4.07 + $0.0625). The contract had been trading for slightly less than a year. During that time, the price reached a high of $4.21 per bushel and a low of $2.72 per bushel. The open interest indicates the number of *contracts outstanding.* The number of contracts outstanding at the close of September 15 was 423.

TABLE 26.2   Data on Wheat Futures Contracts, Thursday, September 15, 20X1

						Lifetime		
	Open	High	Low	Settle	Change	High	Open Low	Interest
Sept	411	416¼	407	407	−6¼	421	272	423
Oct	427	432¼	422	423¼	−5½	432¼	289	47,454
Mar X2	430½	436	426½	427	−4¼	436	323	42,823
May	409	443½	404	405	−5½	420	330	3,422
July	375	376½	369	370¾	−6¾	395	327	4,805

Though we are discussing a futures contract, let us work with a forward contract first. Suppose you wrote a *forward* contract for September wheat at $4.07. From our discussion on forward contracts, this would mean that you would agree to turn over an agreed-upon number of wheat bushels for $4.07 per bushel on some specified date in the remainder of the month of September.

A futures contract differs somewhat from a forward contract. First, the seller can choose to deliver the wheat on any day during the delivery month, that is, the month of September. This gives the seller leeway that he would not have with a forward contract. When the seller decides to deliver, he notifies the exchange clearinghouse that he wants to do so. The clearinghouse then notifies an individual who bought a September wheat contract that she must stand ready to accept delivery within the next few days. Though each exchange selects the buyer in a different way, the buyer is generally chosen in a random fashion. Because there are so many buyers at any one time, the buyer selected by the clearinghouse to take delivery almost certainly did not originally buy the contract from the seller now making delivery.

Second, futures contracts are traded on an exchange whereas forward contracts are generally traded off an exchange. Because of this, there is generally a liquid market in futures contracts. A buyer can net out her futures position with a sale. A seller can net out his futures position with a purchase. This procedure is analogous to the *netting-out* process in the options markets. However, the buyer of an options contract can also walk away from the contract by not exercising it. If a buyer of a futures contract does not subsequently sell her contract, she must take delivery. In practice, over 95 percent of futures contracts are not settled through delivery. Most are offset by other contracts before the delivery date.

Third, and most important, the prices of futures contracts are **marked to the market** on a daily basis. That is, suppose that the price falls to $4.05 on Friday's close. Because all buyers lost two cents per bushel on that day, they each must turn over the two cents per bushel to their brokers within 24 hours, who subsequently remit the proceeds to the clearinghouse. Because all sellers gained two cents per bushel on that day, they each receive two cents per bushel from their brokers. Their brokers are subsequently compensated by the clearinghouse. Because there is a buyer for every seller, the clearinghouse must break even every day.

Now suppose that the price rises to $4.12 on the close of the following Monday. Each buyer receives seven cents ($4.12 − $4.05) per bushel and each seller must pay seven cents per bushel. Finally, suppose that, on Monday, a seller notifies his broker of his intention to deliver.[2] The delivery price will be $4.12, which is Monday's close.

There are clearly many cash flows in futures contracts. However, after all the dust settles, the *net price* to the buyer must be the price at which she bought originally. That is, an individual buying at Thursday's closing price of $4.07 and being called to take delivery on Monday pays two cents per bushel on Friday, receives seven cents per bushel on Monday, and takes delivery at $4.12. Her net outflow per bushel is −$4.07 (−$0.02 + $0.07 − $4.12), which is the price at which she contracted on Thursday. (Our analysis ignores the time value of money.) Conversely, an individual selling at Thursday's closing price of $4.07 and notifying his broker concerning delivery the following Monday receives two cents per bushel on Friday, pays seven cents per bushel on Monday, and makes delivery at $4.12. His net inflow per bushel is $4.07 ($0.02 − $0.07 + $4.12), which is the price at which he contracted on Thursday.

---

[2]He will deliver on Wednesday, two days later.

Illustration of Example Involving Marking to Market in Futures Contracts

Both buyer and seller originally transact at Thursday's closing price. Delivery takes place at Monday's closing price.*

	Thursday, September 19	Friday, September 20	Monday, September 23	Delivery (notification given by seller on Monday)
Closing price:	$4.07	$4.05	$4.12	
Buyer	Buyer purchases futures contract at closing price of $4.07/bushel.	Buyer must pay two cents/bushel to clearinghouse within one business day.	Buyer receives seven cents/bushel from clearinghouse within one business day.	Buyer pays $4.12/bushel and receives grain.

Buyer's net payment of −$4.07 (or −$0.02 + $0.07 − $4.12) is the same as if buyer purchased a forward contract for $4.07/bushel.

Seller	Seller sells futures contract at closing price of $4.07/bushel.	Seller receives two cents/bushel from clearinghouse within one business day.	Seller pays nine cents/bushel to clearinghouse within one business day.	Seller receives $4.12/bushel and delivers grain within one business day.

Seller's net receipts of $4.07 (or $0.02 − $0.07 + $4.12) are the same as if seller sold a forward contract for $4.07/bushel.

*For simplicity, we assume that buyer and seller both (1) initially transact at the same time and (2) meet in delivery process. This is actually very unlikely to occur in the real world because the clearinghouse assigns the buyer to take delivery in a random manner.

These details are presented in the box above. For simplicity, we assumed that the buyer and seller who initially transact on Thursday's close meet in the delivery process.[3] The point in the example is that the buyer's net payment of $4.07 per bushel is the same as if she purchased a forward contract for $4.07. Similarly, the seller's net receipt of $4.07 per bushel is the same as if he sold a forward contract for $4.07 per bushel. The only difference is the timing of the cash flows. The buyer of a forward contract knows that he will make a single payment of $4.07 on the expiration date. He will not need to worry about any other cash flows in the interim. Conversely, though the cash flows to the buyer of a futures contract will net to exactly $4.07 as well, the pattern of cash flows is not known ahead of time.

The mark-to-the-market provision on futures contracts has two related effects. The first concerns differences in net present value. For example, a large price drop immediately following purchase means an immediate outpayment for the buyer of a futures contract. Though the net outflow of $4.07 is still the same as under a forward contract, the

---

[3]As pointed out earlier, this is actually very unlikely to occur in the real world.

present value of the cash outflows is greater to the buyer of a futures contract. Of course, the present value of the cash outflows is less to the buyer of a futures contract if a price rise followed purchase.[4] Though this effect could be substantial in certain theoretical circumstances, it appears to be of quite limited importance in the real world.[5]

Second, the firm must have extra liquidity to handle a sudden outflow prior to expiration. This added risk may make the futures contract less attactive.

Students frequently ask, "Why in the world would managers of the commodity exchanges ruin perfectly good contracts with these bizarre mark-to-the-market provisions?" Actually, the reason is a very good one. Consider the forward contract of Table 26.1 concerning the bookstore. Suppose that the public quickly loses interest in *Eating Habits of the Rich and Famous*. By the time the bookstore calls the buyer, other stores may have dropped the price of the book to $6. Because the forward contract was for $10, the buyer has an incentive not to take delivery on the forward contract. Conversely, should the book become a hot item selling at $15, the bookstore may simply not call the buyer.

As indicated, forward contracts have a very big flaw. Whichever way the price of the deliverable instrument moves, one party has an incentive to default. There are many cases in which defaults have occurred. One famous case concerned Coca-Cola. When the company began in the early twentieth century, Coca-Cola made an agreement to supply its bottlers and distributors with cola syrup at a constant price *forever*. Of course, subsequent inflation would have caused Coca-Cola to lose large sums of money had it honoured the contract. After much legal effort, Coke and its bottlers put an *inflation escalator clause* in the contract. Another famous case concerned Westinghouse. It seems the firm had promised to deliver uranium to certain utilities at a fixed price. The price of uranium skyrocketed in the 1970s, making Westinghouse lose money on every shipment. Westinghouse defaulted on its agreement. The utilities took Westinghouse to court but did not recover anything near what Westinghouse owed them.

The mark-to-the-market provisions minimize the chance of default on a futures contract. If the price rises, the seller has an incentive to default on a forward contract. However, after paying the clearinghouse, the seller of a futures contract has little reason to default. If the price falls, the same argument can be made for the buyer. Because changes in the value of the underlying asset are recognized daily, there is no accumulation of loss, and the incentive to default is reduced.

Because of this default issue, forward contracts generally involve individuals and institutions who know and can trust each other. But as W. C. Fields said, "Trust everybody, but cut the cards." Lawyers earn a handsome living writing supposedly airtight forward contracts, even among friends. The genius of the mark-to-the-market system is that it can prevent default where it is most likely to occur—among investors who do not know each other. Early textbooks on futures contracts usually included a statement such as "No major default has ever occurred on the commodity exchanges." No textbook published after the Hunt Brothers defaulted on silver contracts in 1980 can make that claim. Nevertheless, the extremely low default rate in futures contracts is truly impressive.

Futures contracts are traded in three areas: agricultural commodities, metals and petroleum, and financial assets. The extensive array of futures contracts is listed in Table 26.3.

---

[4]The direction is reversed for the seller of a futures contract. However, the general point that the net present value of cash flows may differ between forward and futures contracts holds for sellers as well.

[5]See John C. Cox, John E. Ingersoll, and Steven A. Ross. "The Relationship Between Forward and Future Prices," *Journal of Financial Economics* (1981).

TABLE 26.3
Futures Contracts Listed in *The Globe and Mail*

Contract	Contract Size	Exchange*
Agricultural (grain and oilseeds):		
Corn	5000 bushels	CBOT
Oats	5000 bushels	CBOT, Minneapolis
Soybeans	5000 bushels	CBOT
Soybean meal	100 tons	CBOT
Soybean oil	60,000 lbs.	CBOT
Wheat	5000 bushels	CBOT
Wheat	5000 bushels	KC
Wheat	5000 bushels	Minneapolis
White wheat	5000 bushels	Minneapolis
Barley	20 metric tonnes	WPG
Flaxseed	20 metric tonnes	WPG
Canola	20 metric tonnes	WPG
Wheat	20 metric tonnes	WPG
Western barley	20 metric tonnes	WPG
Agricultural (livestock and meat):		
Cattle (feeder)	50,000 lbs.	CME
Cattle (live)	40,000 lbs.	CME
Hogs	40,000 lbs.	CME
Pork bellies	40,000 lbs.	CME
Agricultural (food, fibre, and wood):		
Cocoa	10 metric tonnes	CSCE
Coffee	37,500 lbs.	CSCE
Cotton	50,000 lbs.	NYCE
Orange juice	15,000 lbs.	NYCE
Sugar (world)	112,000 lbs.	CSCE
Sugar (domestic)	112,000 lbs.	CSCE
Lumber	80,000 board feet	CME
Metals and petroleum:		
Copper (standard)	25,000 lbs.	COMEX
Gold	100 troy oz.	COMEX
Platinum	50 troy oz.	NYM
Palladium	100 troy oz.	NYM
Silver	5000 troy oz.	COMEX
Liquid propane	42,000 U.S. gal.	NYM
Natural gas	10,000 mmbtu	NYM
Crude oil (light sweet)	1000 barrels	NYM
Heating oil	42,000 gallons	NYM
Gasoline unleaded	42,000 gallons	NYM
Financial:		
British pound	62,500 pounds	CME
Australian dollar	100,000 dollars	IMM
Canadian dollar	100,000 dollars	CME
Japanese yen	12.5 million yen	CME
Swiss franc	125,000 francs	CME
German mark	125,000 marks	CME
3-month banker's acceptances	$1 million	ME
1-month banker's acceptances	$3 million	ME

Continued

TABLE 26.3
Continued

Contract	Contract Size	Exchange*
Government of Canada bond (5- & 10-year)	$100,000	ME
Eurodollar	$1 million	IMM
U.S. Dollar Index	1,000 times index	FINEX
CRB Index	500 times index	NYFE
Treasury bonds	$100,000	CBOT
90-day T-bills	$5 million	CME
5-year Treasury notes	$100,000	CBT
Treasury bonds	$50,000	MCE
Treasury bonds	$1 million	IMM
Financial indexes:		
Municipal bonds	1000 times Bond Buyer Index	CBOT
S&P 500 Index	250 times index	CME
NYSE Composite	50 times index	NYFE
Nikkei Index	$5 times index	CME

*CBOT: Chicago Board of Trade; KC: Kansas City; WPG: Winnipeg; CME: Chicago Merchantile Exchange; CSCE: Coffee, Sugar, and Cocoa Exchange; NYCE: New York Cotton Exchange; COMEX: Commodity Exchange in New York; NYM: New York Merchantile; IPEL: International Petroleum Exchange of London; IMM: International Monetary Market in Chicago; FINEX: Financial Instrument Exchange in New York; NYFE: New York Futures Exchange; ME: Montreal Exchange.

? Concept Questions

- **What is a futures contract?**
- **How is a futures contract related to a forward contract?**
- **Why do exchanges require futures contracts to be marked to market?**

26.3 Hedging

Now that we have determined how futures contracts work, we turn to hedging. There are two types of hedges: long and short. We discuss the short hedge first in Example 26.1.

EXAMPLE 26.1

In June, WildCan, an Alberta junior oil producer, anticipates pumping 1 million barrels of oil for the quarter closing at the end of September. WildCan's CFO, Michael Oleschuk, has two alternatives:

1. *Write futures contracts against anticipated production.* The September crude oil contract (1000 barrels) on the New York Mercantile Exchange is trading at US$37.80 a barrel on June 1. The CFO executes the following transaction:

Date of Transaction	Transaction	Price Per Barrel
June 1	Write 10 September futures contracts	US$37.80

2. *Produce the oil without writing a futures contract.* Alternatively, the CFO could have pumped the oil without benefit of a futures contract. The risk would be quite great here since no one knows what the cash price in September will be. If prices rise, he will profit. Conversely, he will lose if prices fall.

We say that strategy 2 is an unhedged position because there is no attempt to use the futures markets to reduce risk. Conversely, strategy 1 involves a hedge. That is, a position in the futures market offsets the risk of a position in the physical (that is, in the actual) commodity.

Though hedging may seem quite sensible to you, it should be mentioned that not everyone hedges. The CFO of WildCan might reject hedging for at least two reasons.

First, he may simply be uninformed about hedging. Not everyone in business understands the hedging concept. Some executives do not want to use futures markets for hedging their inventories because they feel that the risks are too great.[6] However, we disagree. While there are large price fluctuations in these markets, hedging actually reduces the risk that an individual holding inventories bears.

Second, the CFO may have a special insight or some special information that commodity prices will rise. He would not be wise to lock in a price of US$37.80 if he expects the cash price in September to be well above this price.

Strategy 1 is called a **short hedge,** because WildCan reduces its risk by taking a short position in a futures contract. The short hedge is very common in business. It occurs whenever someone either anticipates receiving inventory or is holding inventory. WildCan was anticipating the production of crude oil. A refiner of gasoline may hold large quantities of crude, which are already paid for. However, the price to be received for gasoline is not known because no one knows what the market price will be when it is produced. The manufacturer may write futures contracts to lock in a sales price.

A mortgage banker may assemble mortgages slowly before selling them in bulk to a financial institution. Movements of interest rates affect the value of the mortgages during the time they are in inventory. The mortgage banker could sell Government of Canada bond futures contracts in order to offset this interest rate risk. (This last example is treated later in this chapter.)

EXAMPLE 26.2

On April 1, Alberta Chemical agreed to sell petrochemicals to a major customer in the future. The delivery dates and the prices have been determined. Because oil is a basic ingredient of the production process, Alberta Chemical will need to have large quantities of oil on hand. The firm can get the oil in one of two ways:

1. *Buy the oil as the firm needs it.* This is an unhedged position because, as of April 1, the firm does not know the prices it will later have to pay for the oil. Oil is quite a volatile commodity, so Alberta Chemical is bearing a good bit of risk. The key to this risk-bearing is that the sales price has already been fixed. Thus, Alberta Chemical cannot pass on increased costs to the consumer.

2. *Buy futures contracts.*[7] The firm can buy futures contracts with expiration months corresponding to the dates on which inventory is needed. A futures contract locks in the purchase price to Alberta Chemical. Because there is a crude oil futures contract for every month,

---

[6]B. Kalymon, *Global Innovation and the Impact on Canada's Financial Markets* (Toronto: Wiley, 1989), Chapter 1, found that many Canadian managers expressed this view when hedging markets were relatively new.

[7]Alternatively, the firm could buy the oil on April 1 and store it. This would eliminate the risk of price movement, because the firm's oil costs would be fixed upon the immediate purchase. However, this strategy is often inferior to strategy 2 because storage costs often exceed the difference between the futures contract quoted on April 1 and the April 1 cash price.

selecting the correct futures contract is not difficult. Many other commodities have only five contracts per year, frequently necessitating buying contracts one month away from the month of production.

As mentioned earlier, Alberta Chemical is interested in hedging the risk of fluctuating oil prices because it cannot pass any cost increases on to the consumer. Suppose, alternatively, that Alberta Chemical was not selling petrochemicals on fixed contract. Instead, imagine that the petrochemicals were to be sold at currently prevailing prices. The price of petrochemicals should move directly with oil prices, because oil is a major component. Because cost increases are likely to be passed on to the consumer, Alberta Chemical would probably not want to hedge in this case. Instead, the firm is likely to choose strategy 1, buying oil as it is needed. If oil prices increase between April 1 and September 1, Alberta Chemical will, of course, find that its inputs have become quite costly. However, in a competitive market, its revenues are likely to rise as well.

Strategy 2 is called a **long hedge** because one takes a long position in a futures contract to reduce risk. In other words, one takes a long position in the futures market. In general, a firm institutes a long hedge when it is committed to a fixed purchase price. One class of situations involves actual written contracts with customers, such as Alberta Chemical had. Alternatively, a firm may find that it cannot easily pass on costs to consumers or does not want to pass on these costs.

For example, a group of students opened a small meat market called What's Your Beef near the University of Pennsylvania in the late 1970s.[8] You may recall that this was a time of volatile consumer prices, especially food prices. Knowing that their fellow students were particularly budget-conscious, the owners vowed to keep food prices constant, regardless of price movements in either direction. They accomplished this by purchasing futures contracts in various agricultural commodities.

Hedging with Futures Versus Hedging with Options

When comparing hedging with futures to hedging with options, there are two key differences between the contracts. The first is that a futures contract creates an obligation between both parties to complete the transaction. One party must deliver the asset and the other party must pay for it. With an option, the transaction occurs only if the owner of the option chooses to exercise it.

The second difference between an option contract and a future contract is that the buyer of an option contract gains a valuable right and must pay the seller for that right. The price of the option is frequently called the option premium. With a future contract, the buyer sets up the account with the investment dealer and the value in the account changes as the price of the asset fluctuates from changes in the market.

? Concept Questions

- Define *short* and *long hedges.*
- Under what circumstances is each of the two hedges used?

---

[8]Ordinarily, an unusual firm name in this textbook is a tipoff that it is fictional. This, however, is a true story.

26.4 Interest Rate Futures Contracts

In this section, we consider interest rate futures contracts. Our examples deal with futures contracts on Government of Canada bonds because of their high popularity. We first price Canada bonds and Canada bond forward contracts. Differences between futures and forward contracts are explored. We then provide hedging examples using Canada government bond (CGB) futures traded on the Montreal Exchange.

Pricing of Government of Canada Bonds

As explained in Chapter 6, a Government of Canada bond pays semiannual interest over its life. In addition, the face value of the bond is paid at maturity. Consider a 20-year, 8 percent coupon bond that was issued on March 1. The first payment is to occur in six months, that is, on September 1. The value of the bond can be determined as

Pricing of a Canada Bond:

$$P_{CGB} = \frac{\$40}{1 + r_1} + \frac{\$40}{(1 + r_2)^2} + \cdots + \frac{\$40}{(1 + r_{39})^{39}} + \frac{\$1,040}{(1 + r_{40})^{40}} \tag{26.1}$$

Because this 8 percent coupon bond pays interest of $80 a year, the semiannual coupon is $40. Principal is paid at maturity along with the last semiannual coupon. The price of the Canada bond, P_{CGB}, is determined by discounting each payment at the appropriate spot rate. Because the payments are semiannual, each spot rate is expressed in semiannual terms. That is, imagine a flat term structure where the effective annual yield is 12 percent for all maturities. Because each spot rate, r, is expressed in semiannual terms, each spot rate is $\sqrt{1.12} - 1 = 5.83\%$. Because coupon payments occur every six months, there are 40 spot rates over the 20-year period.

Pricing of Forward Contracts

Now, imagine a *forward* contract where, on March 1, you agree to buy a new 20-year, 8 percent coupon Canada bond in six months, that is, on September 1. As with typical forward contracts, you will pay for the bond on September 1, not March 1. The cash flows from both the Canada bond issued on March 1 and the forward contract that you purchase on March 1 are presented in Figure 26.1. The cash flows on the Canada bond begin exactly six months earlier than do the cash flows on the forward contract. The bond is purchased with cash on March 1 (date 0). The first coupon payment occurs on September 1 (date 1). The last coupon payment occurs at date 40, along with the face value of $1,000. The forward contract compels you to pay $P_{FORW.CONT.}$, the price of the forward contract, on September 1 (date 1). You receive a new Canada bond at that time. The first coupon payment from the bond you receive occurs on March 1 of the following year (date 2). The last coupon payment occurs at date 41, along with the face value of $1,000.

Given the 40 spot rates, Equation (26.1) showed how to price a Canada bond. How does one price the forward contract on a Canada bond? Just as we saw earlier in the text that net present value analysis is used to price bonds, we will now show that net present value analysis can be used to price forward contracts. Given the cash flows for the forward contract in Figure 26.1, the price of the forward contract must satisfy the following equation:

$$\frac{P_{FORW.CONT.}}{1 + r_1} = \frac{\$40}{(1 + r_2)^2} + \frac{\$40}{(1 + r_3)^3} + \cdots + \frac{\$40}{(1 + r_{40})^{40}} + \frac{\$1,040}{(1 + r_{41})^{41}} \tag{26.2}$$

FIGURE 26.1

Cash Flows for Both a Canada Bond and a Forward Contract on a Canada Bond

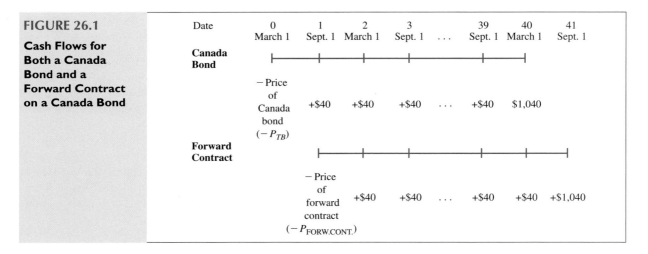

The right-hand side of Equation (26.2) discounts all the cash flows from the delivery instrument (the Canada bond issued on September 1) back to date 0 (March 1). Because the first cash flow occurs at date 2 (March 1 of the subsequent year), it is discounted by $1/(1 + r_2)^2$. The last cash flow of $1,040 occurs at date 41, so it is discounted by $1/(1 + r_{41})^{41}$. The left-hand side represents the cost of the forward contract as of date 0. Because the actual payment occurs at date 1, it is discounted by $1/(1 + r_1)$.

Students often ask, "Why are we discounting everything back to date 0, when we are actually paying for the forward contract on September 1?" The answer is simply that we apply the same techniques to Equation (26.2) that we apply to all capital budgeting problems; we want to put everything in today's (date 0's) dollars. Given that the spot rates are known in the marketplace, traders should have no more trouble pricing a forward contract by Equation (26.2) than they would have pricing a bond by Equation (26.1).

Forward contracts are similar to the underlying bonds themselves. If the entire term structure of interest rates unexpectedly shifts upward on March 2, the Canada bond issued the previous day should fall in value. This can be seen from Equation (26.1). A rise in each of the spot rates lowers the present value of each of the coupon payments. Hence, the value of the bond must fall. Conversely, a fall in the term structure of interest rates increases the value of the bond.

The same relationship holds with forward contracts, as can be seen from rewriting Equation (26.2) as

$$P_{\text{FORW.CONT.}} = \frac{\$40 \times (1 + r_1)}{(1 + r_2)^2} + \frac{\$40 \times (1 + r_1)}{(1 + r_3)^3}$$
$$+ \ldots + \frac{\$40 \times (1 + r_1)}{(1 + r_{40})^{40}} + \frac{\$1,040 \times (1 + r_1)}{(1 + r_{41})^{41}} \qquad (26.3)$$

We went from (26.2) to (26.3) by multiplying both the left- and the right-hand sides by $(1 + r_1)$. If the entire term structure of interest rates unexpectedly shifts upward on March 2, the first term on the right-hand side of Equation (26.3) should fall in value.[9] That is, both r_1 and r_2 will rise an equal amount. However, r_2 enters as a *squared* term, $1/(1 + r_2)^2$,

---

[9] We are assuming that each spot rate shifts by the same amount. For example, suppose that, on March 1, $r_1 = 5\%$, $r_2 = 5.4\%$, and $r_3 = 5.8\%$. Assuming that all rates increase by 0.5 percent on March 2, r_1 becomes 5.5 percent ($5\% + 0.5\%$), r_2 becomes 5.9 percent, and r_3 becomes 6.3 percent.

so an increase in r_2 more than offsets the increase in r_1. As we move further to the right, an increase in any spot rate, r_i, more than offsets an increase in r_1. Here, r_i enters as the *i*th power, $1/(1 + r_i)^i$. Thus, as long as the entire term structure shifts upward by an equal amount on March 2, the value of a forward contract must fall on that date. Conversely, as long as the entire term structure shifts downward by an equal amount on March 2, the value of a forward contract must rise.

Futures Contracts

Our discussion so far has concerned a forward contract in Canada bonds, that is, a forward contract where the deliverable instrument is a Canada bond. What about a futures contract on such a bond?[10] We stated earlier that futures contracts and forward contracts are quite similar, though there are a few differences between the two.

First, futures contracts are generally traded on exchanges, whereas forward contracts are not traded on an exchange. In this case, the Canada bond futures contract is traded on the Montreal Exchange. Table 26.4 shows a listing for CGB 10-year futures. The terminology is similar to what we presented earlier for wheat futures. For the bond futures contract, the delivery month is September 2007. The delivery vehicle is a CGB with maturity between 7.75 and 9.75 years and the face value is $100,000. The listing shows that the settle (closing) price for the futures contract was $106.41 per $100 of par value. Open interest shows that 92,416 contracts were outstanding at this time.

Second, futures contracts generally allow the seller a period of time in which to deliver, whereas forward contracts generally call for delivery on a particular day. The seller of a Canada bond futures contract can choose to deliver on any business day during the delivery month.[11] Third, futures contracts are subject to the mark-to-the-market convention, whereas forward contracts are not. Traders in Canada bond futures contracts must adhere to this convention. Fourth, there is generally a liquid market for futures contracts allowing contracts to be quickly netted out. That is, a buyer can sell a futures contract at any time and a seller can buy back a futures contract at any time. On the other hand, because forward markets are generally quite illiquid, traders cannot easily net out their positions. The popularity of the Canada bond futures contract has produced a reasonably liquid market, and positions of some size can be netted out quite easily.

Our discussion is not intended to be an exhaustive list of differences between forward contracts and futures contracts on Canada bonds. Rather, it is intended to show that the

TABLE 26.4
Listing for Government of Canada Bonds (CGB), 10-Year Futures

Lifetime			Daily					
High	Low	Month	Open	High	Low	Settle	Chg.	Prev. Open Int.
Interest Rate								
Canadian Govt. Bonds 10 Year (ME)								
$100,000, points of 100%; 0.01 = $41.10 per contract								
108.39	**105.67**	**Sept07**	**106.25**	**106.46**	**106.12**	**106.41**	**+0.27**	**92,416**
Vol. 4018			Prev. vol. 7636					

---

[10]Futures contracts on bonds are also called interest rate futures contracts.

[11]Delivery occurs two days after the seller notifies the clearinghouse of the intention to deliver.

two types of contracts share fundamental characteristics. Though there are differences, the two instruments should be viewed as variations of the same species, not different species. Thus, the pricing equation of (26.3), which is exact for the forward contract, should be a decent approximation for the futures contract.

Hedging in Interest Rate Futures

Now that we have covered the basic institutional details of bond futures, we are ready for examples of hedging. Our examples feature bond futures rather than forward contracts because the greater liquidity of futures, discussed above, makes them better suited for hedging.

EXAMPLE 26.3

Peter James is a mortgage officer for a small credit union. On March 1, he made a commitment to lend $1 million on May 1 in a mortgage on a piece of commercial property. The loan is a 10-year mortgage at 6 percent, the going interest rate on mortgages at the time. Thus, the mortgage is made at par. Though the borrower would not use the term, we could say that Mr. James is buying a forward contract on a mortgage. That is, he agrees on March 1 to give $1 million to the borrower on May 1 in exchange for principal and interest every month for the next 10 years.

Like many small mortgage lenders, Peter James has no intention of keeping the $1 million loan on his credit union's balance sheet. Rather, he intends to sell the mortgage to an insurance company. Thus, the insurance company will actually lend the funds and will receive principal and interest over the next 10 years. Mr. James sets April 30 as a deadline for making the sale because the borrowers expect the funds on the following day.

Suppose that Mr. James sells the mortgage to the Great Saskatchewan Life Insurance Company on April 15. What price will the insurance company pay for the mortgage?

You may think that the insurance company will obviously pay $1 million. However, suppose interest rates have risen above 6 percent by April 15. The insurance company will buy the mortgage at a discount. For example, suppose the insurance company agrees to pay only $940,000 for the mortgage. Because the mortgage banker agreed to lend a full $1 million to the borrower, the difference of $60,000 (or $1 million − $940,000) represents a loss to the credit union.

Alternatively, suppose that interest rates fall below 6 percent by April 15. The mortgage can be sold at a premium under this scenario. If the insurance company buys the mortgage at $1.05 million, the mortgage banker will have made an unexpected profit of $50,000 (or $1.05 million − $1 million).

Because Peter James cannot forecast interest rates, this risk is something that he would like to avoid. The risk is summarized in Table 26.5.

Seeing the interest rate risk, students at this point may ask, "What does the mortgage banker get out of this loan to offset his risk-bearing?" Mr. James wants to sell the mortgage to the insurance company so that he can get two fees. The first is an *origination fee,* which is paid to the mortgage banker from the insurance company on April 15, that is, on the date the loan is sold. An industry standard in certain locales is 1 percent of the value of the loan, that is, $10,000 (or 1% × $1 million). In addition, Mr. James will act as a collection agent for the insurance company. For this service, he will receive a small portion of the outstanding balance of the loan each month. For example, if he is paid 0.03 percent of the loan each month, he will receive $300 (0.03% × $1 million) in the first month. As the outstanding balance of the loan declines, he will receive less.

TABLE 26.5 **Effects of Changing Interest Rate on Peter James, Mortgage Banker**	Mortgage interest rate on April 15	Above 6%	Below 6%
	Sale price to Great Saskatchewan Life Insurance Company	Below $1 million (We assume $940,000.)	Above $1 million (We assume $1.05 million.)
	Effect on mortgage banker	He loses because he must lend full $1 million to borrowers.	He gains because he lends only $1 million to borrowers.
	Dollar gain or loss	Loss of $60,000 ($1 million − $940,000)	Gain of $50,000 ($1.05 million − $1 million)

The interest rate on March 1, the date when the loan agreement was made with the borrowers, was 6 percent. April 15 is the date the mortgages were sold to Great Saskatchewan Life Insurance Company.

Though Mr. James will earn profitable fees on the loan, he bears interest rate risk. He loses money if interest rates rise after March 1, and he profits if interest rates fall after March 1. To hedge this risk, he writes June Government of Canada bond futures contracts on March 1. As with mortgages, Government of Canada bond futures contracts fall in value if interest rates rise. Because he *writes* the contract, he makes money on these contracts if they fall in value. Therefore, with an interest rate rise, the loss he endures in the mortgages is offset by his gain in the futures market.

In the opposite case, Government of Canada bond futures contracts rise in value if interest rates fall. Because he writes the contracts, he suffers losses on them when rates fall. With an interest rate fall, the profit he makes on the mortgages is offset by the loss he suffers in the futures markets.

The details of this hedging transaction are presented in Table 26.6. The column on the left is labelled "Cash Markets," because the deal in the mortgage market is transacted off an exchange. The column on the right shows the offsetting transactions in the futures markets. Consider the first row. The mortgage banker enters into a forward contract on March 1. He simultaneously writes Government of Canada bond futures contracts. Ten contracts are written because the deliverable instrument on each contract is $100,000 of Government of Canada bonds. The total is $1 million (or 10 × $100,000), which is equal to the value of the mortgages. Mr. James would prefer to write May Government of Canada bond futures contracts. Here, Government of Canada bonds would be delivered on the futures contract during the same month that the loan is funded. Because there is no May Government of Canada bond futures contract, Mr. James achieves the closest match through a June contract.[12]

If held to maturity, the June contract would obligate the mortgage banker to deliver Government of Canada bonds in June. Interest rate risk ends in the cash market when the loans are sold. Interest rate risk must be terminated in the futures market at that time. Thus, Mr. James nets out his position in the futures contract as soon as the loan is sold to Great Saskatchewan Life Insurance.

---

[12]The Government of Canada bond futures contract is by no means the only instrument available to use for hedging. In Canada, there are also futures on banker's acceptances, which are short-term paper. These futures can be used to hedge interest rate risk in the same way that Government of Canada bond futures are used. As well, the expiration months vary with the instrument.

	Cash Markets	Futures Markets
TABLE 26.6 **Illustration of Hedging Strategy for Peter James, Mortgage Banker**		
March 1	Mortgage banker makes forward contract to lend $1 million at 6 percent for 10 years. The loans are to be funded on May 1. No cash changes hands on March 1.	Mortgage banker writes 10 June Government of Canada bond futures contracts.
April 15	Loans are sold to Great Saskatchewan Life Insurance Company. Mortgage banker will receive sale price from Saskatchewan on the May 1 funding date.	Mortgage banker buys back all the futures contracts.
If interest rates rise:	Loans are sold at a price below $1 million. Mortgage banker *loses* because he receives less than the $1 million he must give to borrowers.	Each futures contract is bought back at a price below the sales price, resulting in *profit*. Mortgage banker's profit in futures market offsets loss in cash market.
If interest rates fall:	Loans are sold at a price above $1 million. Mortgage banker *gains* because he receives more than the $1 million he must give to borrowers.	Each futures contract is bought back at a price above the sales price, resulting in *loss*. Mortgage banker's loss in futures market offsets gain in cash market.

Risk is clearly reduced via an offsetting transaction in the futures market. However, is risk totally eliminated? The answer would be yes if losses in the cash markets were exactly offset in the futures markets and vice versa. This is unlikely to happen because mortgages and Government of Canada bonds are not identical instruments. First, mortgages may have different maturities than Government of Canada bonds. Second, Government of Canada bonds have a different payment stream than do mortgages. Principal is only paid at maturity on Government of Canada bonds, whereas principal is paid every month on mortgages. Because mortgages pay principal continuously, these instruments have a shorter *effective* time to maturity than do Government of Canada bonds of equal maturity.[13] Third, mortgages have default risk whereas Government of Canada bonds do not. The term structure applicable to instruments with default risk may change even when the term structure for risk-free assets remains constant. Fourth, mortgages may be paid off early and hence have a shorter *expected maturity* than Canada bonds of equal maturity.

Because mortgages and Government of Canada bonds are not identical instruments, they are not identically affected by interest rates.[14] If Canada bonds are less volatile than

---

[13]Alternatively, we can say that mortgages have shorter duration than do Government of Canada bonds of equal maturity. A precise definition of duration is provided later in this chapter.

[14]In formal terminology, this type of risk is called *basis risk*. When Mr. James hedges mortgages with Government of Canada bond futures, he is said to be cross-hedging his position, because he is not using identical instruments.

mortgages, a financial consultant may advise Mr. James to write more than 10 Government of Canada bond futures contracts. Conversely, if these bonds are more volatile, the consultant may state that fewer than 10 futures contracts are indicated. An optimal ratio of futures contracts to mortgages will reduce risk as much as possible. However, because the price movements of mortgages and Government of Canada bonds are not perfectly correlated, Mr. James' hedging strategy cannot eliminate all risk.

The strategy we described is called a *short hedge* because Mr. James sells futures contracts in order to reduce risk. Though it involves an interest rate futures contract, this short hedge is analogous to short hedges in agricultural and metallurgical futures contracts. We argued at the beginning of this chapter that individuals and firms institute short hedges to offset inventory price fluctuation. Once Mr. James makes a contract to lend money, the mortgage effectively becomes his inventory. He writes a futures contract to offset the price fluctuation of his inventory.

We now consider a long hedge in Example 26.4.

EXAMPLE 26.4

Canada Wide Ltd. is a large conglomerate with thousands of employees. Nadia Comeau manages the firm's pension fund. In the next three months, Canada Wide's pension fund is expecting to purchase $25 million in long-term Government of Canada bonds because the pension fund managers have been selling securities for the past month, and they feel that they have too much cash on hand. Ms. Comeau's pension fund group faces problems similar to those facing Mr. James' firm. However, in this case, we will be dealing with a long hedge instead of a short hedge.

As with Mr. James, changing interest rates will affect Ms. Comeau. If interest rates fall before she purchases the long-term Canada bonds, the price of the bonds will increase, and she will be paying more than was expected. Conversely, if interest rates rise, the price of long-term Canada bonds will fall, and the bonds can be purchased for less than expected.

The details are provided in the left-hand column of Table 26.7. Like Mr. James, Ms. Comeau finds the risk excessive. Therefore, she offsets her decision to purchase bonds with a transaction

TABLE 26.7
Illustration of Futures Hedge for Nadia Comeau, Pension Fund Manager

		Cash Markets	Future Markets
March 1		Nadia Comeau decides to purchase $25 million in long-term bonds over the next three months.	Pension fund manager buys 250 Government of Canada bond futures contracts.
April 15		Pension fund manager purchases $25 million in long-term Canada bonds.	Pension fund manager sells all futures contracts.
If interest rates rise:		Pension fund manager gains because the price of bonds will have fallen.	Futures contracts are sold at a price below purchase price, resulting in loss. Pension fund manager's loss in futures market offsets gain in cash market.
If interest rates fall:		Pension fund manager loses because the price of bonds will have risen.	Futures contracts are sold at a price above purchase price, resulting in gain. Pension fund manager's gain in futures market offsets loss in cash market.

in the futures markets. Because she loses in the cash market when interest rates fall, she buys futures contracts to reduce the risk. When interest rates fall, the value of her futures contracts increases. The gain in the futures market offsets the loss in the cash market. Conversely, she gains in the cash markets when interest rates rise. The value of her futures contracts decreases when interest rates rise, offsetting her gain.

We call this a *long hedge* because Ms. Comeau offsets risk in the cash markets by buying a futures contract. Though it involves an interest rate futures contract, this long hedge is analogous to long hedges in agricultural and metallurgical futures contracts. We argued at the beginning of this chapter that individuals and firms institute long hedges when their finished goods are to be sold at a fixed price. Once Ms. Comeau makes the decision to purchase Government of Canada bonds, she has the ability to fix her purchase price. She buys a futures contract to offset the price fluctuation of the bonds.

? Concept Questions

- **How are forward contracts on bonds priced?**
- **What are the differences between forward contracts on bonds and futures contracts on bonds?**
- **Give examples of hedging with futures contracts on bonds.**

26.5 Duration Hedging

The prior section concerned the risk of interest rate changes. We now wish to explore this risk in a more precise manner. In particular, we want to show that the concept of duration is a prime determinant of interest rate risk. We begin by considering the effect of interest rate movements on bond prices.

The Case of Zero-Coupon Bonds

Suppose that interest rates are 10 percent across all maturities. A one-year, pure discount bond pays $110 at maturity. A five-year, pure discount bond pays $161.05 at maturity. Both of these bonds are worth $100, as given by[15]

Value of One-Year, Pure Discount Bond:
$$\$100 = \frac{\$110}{1.10}$$

Value of Five-Year, Pure Discount Bond:
$$\$100 = \frac{\$161.05}{(1.10)^5}$$

Which bond value will change more when interest rates move? To find out, we calculate the values of these bonds when interest rates are either 8 or 12 percent. The results are presented in Table 26.8. As can be seen, the five-year bond has greater price swings than does the one-year bond. That is, both bonds are worth $100 when interest rates are 10 percent. The five-year bond is worth more than the one-year bond when interest rates are 8 percent

---

[15]Alternatively, we could have chosen bonds that pay $100 at maturity. Their values would be $90.91 (or $100/1.10) and $62.09 [or $100/(1.10)^5]. However, our comparisons to come are made easier if both have the same initial price.

TABLE 26.8
Value of a Pure Discount Bond as a Function of Interest Rate

Interest Rate	One-Year Pure Discount Bond	Five-Year Pure Discount Bond
8%	$\$101.85 = \dfrac{\$110}{1.08}$	$\$109.61 = \dfrac{\$161.05}{(1.08)^5}$
10%	$\$100.00 = \dfrac{\$1.10}{1.10}$	$\$100.00 = \dfrac{\$161.05}{(1.10)^5}$
12%	$98.21 = \dfrac{\$110}{1.12}$	$\$91.38 = \dfrac{\$161.05}{(1.12)^5}$

For a given interest rate change, a five-year pure discount bond fluctuates more in price than does a one-year pure discount bond.

and worth less than the one-year bond when interest rates are 12 percent. We state that the five-year bond is subject to greater price volatility. This point, which was mentioned in passing in an earlier section of the chapter, is not difficult to understand. The interest rate term in the denominator, $1 + r$, is taken to the fifth power for a five-year bond and only to the first power for the one-year bond. Thus, the effect of a changing interest rate is magnified for the five-year bond. The general rule is:

> The percentage price changes in long-term pure discount bonds are greater than the percentage price changes in short-term pure discount bonds.

The Case of Two Bonds with the Same Maturity but with Different Coupons

The previous example concerned pure discount bonds of different maturities. We now want to see the effect of different coupons on price volatility. To abstract from the effect of differing maturities, we consider two bonds with the same maturity but with different coupons.

Consider a five-year, 10 percent coupon bond and a five-year, 1 percent coupon bond. When interest rates are 10 percent, the bonds are priced at

Value of Five-Year, 10-Percent Coupon Bond:
$$\$100 = \frac{\$10}{1.10} + \frac{\$10}{(1.10)^2} + \frac{\$10}{(1.10)^3} + \frac{\$10}{(1.10)^4} + \frac{\$110}{(1.10)^5}$$

Value of Five-Year, 1-Percent Coupon Bond:
$$\$65.88 = \frac{\$1}{1.10} + \frac{\$1}{(1.10)^2} + \frac{\$1}{(1.10)^3} + \frac{\$1}{(1.10)^4} + \frac{\$101}{(1.10)^5}$$

Which bond value will experience greater change in percentage terms if interest rates change?[16] To find out, we calculate the values of these bonds when interest rates are either 8 or 12 percent. The results are presented in Table 26.9. As we would expect, the 10 percent coupon bond always sells for more than the 1 percent coupon bond. Also, as we would expect, each bond is worth more when the interest rate is 8 percent than when the interest rate is 12 percent.

---

[16]The bonds are at different prices initially. Thus, we are concerned with percentage price changes, not absolute price changes.

TABLE 26.9
Value of Coupon Bonds at Different Interest Rates

Interest Rate	Five-Year, 10% Coupon Bond
8%	$107.99 = \dfrac{\$10}{1.08} + \dfrac{\$10}{(1.08)^2} + \dfrac{\$10}{(1.08)^3} + \dfrac{\$10}{(\$1.08)^4} + \dfrac{\$110}{(1.08)^5}$
10%	$100.00 = \dfrac{\$10}{1.10} + \dfrac{\$10}{(1.10)^2} + \dfrac{\$10}{(1.10)^3} + \dfrac{\$10}{(1.10)^4} + \dfrac{\$110}{(1.10)^5}$
12%	$\ 92.79 = \dfrac{\$10}{1.12} + \dfrac{\$10}{(1.12)^2} + \dfrac{\$10}{(1.12)^3} + \dfrac{\$10}{(1.12)^4} + \dfrac{\$110}{(1.12)^5}$

Interest Rate	Five-Year, 1% Coupon Bond
8%	$\$72.05 = \dfrac{\$1}{1.08} + \dfrac{\$1}{(1.08)^2} + \dfrac{\$1}{(1.08)^3} + \dfrac{\$1}{(1.08)^4} + \dfrac{\$101}{(1.08)^5}$
10%	$\$65.88 = \dfrac{\$1}{1.10} + \dfrac{\$1}{(1.10)^2} + \dfrac{\$1}{(1.10)^3} + \dfrac{\$1}{(1.10)^4} + \dfrac{\$101}{(1.10)^5}$
12%	$\$60.35 = \dfrac{\$1}{1.12} + \dfrac{\$1}{(1.12)^2} + \dfrac{\$1}{(1.12)^3} + \dfrac{\$1}{(1.12)^4} + \dfrac{\$101}{(1.12)^5}$

We calculate percentage price changes for both bonds as the interest rate changes from 10 to 8 percent and from 10 to 12 percent. These percentage price changes are

	10% Coupon Bond	1% Coupon Bond
Interest rate changes from 10% to 8%	$7.99\% = \dfrac{\$107.99}{\$100} - 1$	$9.37\% = \dfrac{\$72.05}{\$65.88} - 1$
Interest rate changes from 10% to 12%	$-7.21\% = \dfrac{\$92.79}{\$100} - 1$	$-8.39\% = \dfrac{\$60.35}{\$65.88} - 1$

As can be seen, the 1 percent coupon bond has a greater percentage price increase than does the 10 percent coupon bond when the interest rate falls. Similarly, the 1 percent coupon bond has a greater percentage price decrease than does the 10 percent coupon bond when the interest rate rises. Thus, we say that the percentage price changes on the 1 percent coupon bond are greater than are the percentage price changes on the 10 percent coupon bond.

Duration

The question, of course, is "Why?" We can answer this question only after we have explored a concept called **duration.** We begin by noticing that any coupon bond is actually a combination of pure discount bonds. For example, the five-year, 10 percent coupon bond is made up of five pure discount bonds:

1. A pure discount bond paying $10 at the end of year 1.
2. A pure discount bond paying $10 at the end of year 2.
3. A pure discount bond paying $10 at the end of year 3.
4. A pure discount bond paying $10 at the end of year 4.
5. A pure discount bond paying $110 at the end of year 5.

Similarly, the five-year, 1 percent coupon bond is made up of five pure discount bonds. Because the price volatility of a pure discount bond is determined by its maturity, we would like to determine the average maturity of the five pure discount bonds that make up a five-year coupon bond. This leads us to the concept of duration.

We calculate average maturity in three steps. For the 10 percent coupon bond, we

1. *Calculate present value of each payment.* We do this as

Year	Payment	Present Value of Payment by Discounting at 10%
1	$ 10	$ 9.091
2	10	8.264
3	10	7.513
4	10	6.830
5	110	68.302
		$100.00

2. *Express the present value of each payment in relative terms.* We calculate the relative value of a single payment as the ratio of the present value of the payment to the value of the bond. The value of the bond is $100. We have

Year	Payment	Present Value of Payment	Relative Value = $\dfrac{\text{Present Value of Payment}}{\text{Value of Bond}}$
1	$ 10	$ 9.091	$9.091/$100 = 0.09091
2	10	8.264	0.08264
3	10	7.513	0.07513
4	10	6.830	0.06830
5	110	68.302	0.68302
		$100.00	1.0

The bulk of the relative value, 68.302 percent, occurs at year 5 because the principal is paid back at that time.

3. *Weight the maturity of each payment by its relative value.* We have
   4.1699 years = 1 year × 0.09091 + 2 years × 0.08264 + 3 years ×
   0.07513 + 4 years × 0.06830 + 5 years × 0.68302

There are many ways to calculate the average maturity of a bond. We have calculated it by weighting the maturity of each payment by the percentage of total present value received at that maturity. We find that the *effective* maturity of the bond is 4.1699 years. *Duration* is a commonly used word for effective maturity. Thus, the bond's duration is 4.1699 years. Note that duration is expressed in units of time.[17]

---

[17]The mathematical formula for duration is

$$\text{Duration} = \frac{\text{PV}(C_1)1 + \text{PV}(C_2)2 + \ldots + \text{PV}(C_T)T}{\text{PV}}$$

and

$$\text{PV} = \text{PV}(C_1) + \text{PV}(C_2) + \ldots + \text{PV}(C_T)$$

$$\text{PV}(C_T) = \frac{C_T}{(1 + r)^T}$$

where C_T is the cash to be received at time T and r is the current discount rate.

Also note that in the above numerical example we discounted each payment by the interest rate of 10 percent. This was done because we wanted to calculate the duration of the bond before a change in the interest rate occurred. After a change in the rate to, say, 8 or 12 percent, all three of our steps would need to reflect the new interest rate. In other words, the duration of a bond is a function of the current interest rate.

Because the five-year, 10 percent coupon bond has a duration of 4.1699 years, its percentage price fluctuations should be the same as those of a zero-coupon bond with a duration of 4.1699 years.[18] It turns out that the five-year, 1 percent coupon bond has a duration of 4.8742 years. Because the 1 percent coupon bond has a higher duration than the 10 percent bond, the 1 percent coupon bond should be subject to greater price fluctuations. This is exactly what we found earlier. In general, we say

> The percentage price changes of a bond with high duration are greater than the percentage price changes of a bond with low duration.

A final question: Why does the 1 percent bond have a greater duration than the 10 percent bond, even though they have the same five-year maturity? As mentioned earlier, duration is an average of the maturity of the bond's cash flows, weighted by the present value of each cash flow. The 1 percent coupon bond receives only $1 in each of the first four years. Thus, the weights applied to years 1 through 4 in the duration formula will be low. Conversely, the 10 percent coupon bond receives $10 in each of the first four years. The weights applied to years 1 through 4 in the duration formula will be higher.

Matching Liabilities with Assets

Earlier in this chapter we argued that firms can hedge risk by trading in futures. Because some firms are subject to interest rate risk, we showed how they can hedge with interest rate futures contracts. Firms may also hedge interest rate risk by matching liabilities with assets. This approach follows from our discussion of duration.

EXAMPLE 26.5

The Colonist Bank of Canada has the following market value balance sheet:

THE COLONIST BANK OF CANADA
Market Value Balance Sheet

	Market Value	Duration
Assets		
Overnight money	$ 35 million	0
Accounts receivable–backed loans	500 million	3 months
Inventory loans	275 million	6 months
Industrial loans	40 million	2 years
Mortgages	150 million	14.8 years
	$1,000 million	
Liabilities and Owners' Equity		
Chequing and savings accounts	$ 400 million	0
Certificates of deposit	300 million	1 year
Long-term financing	200 million	10 years
Equity	100 million	
	$1,000 million	

The bank has $1,000 million of assets and $900 million of liabilities. Its equity is the difference between the two: $100 million (or $1,000 million − $900 million). Both the market value and the duration of each individual item are provided in the balance sheet. Both overnight

---

[18]Actually, this relationship only holds exactly in the case of a one-time shift in a flat yield curve, where the change in the spot rate is identical for all different maturities.

money and chequing and savings accounts have a duration of zero. This is because the interest paid on these instruments adjusts immediately to changing interest rates in the economy.

The bank's executives think that interest rates are likely to be volatile in the coming months. Because they do not know in which direction rates will move, they are worried that their bank's equity value is vulnerable to changing rates. They call in a consultant, Robert Charest, to determine hedging strategy.

Mr. Charest first calculates the duration of the assets and the duration of the liabilities.[19]

Duration of Assets:

$$2.56 \text{ years} = 0 \text{ years} \times \frac{\$35 \text{ million}}{\$1,000 \text{ million}} + \frac{1}{4} \text{ year} \times \frac{\$500 \text{ million}}{\$1,000 \text{ million}}$$

$$+ \frac{1}{2} \text{ year} \times \frac{\$275 \text{ million}}{\$1,000 \text{ million}} + 2 \text{ years} \times \frac{\$40 \text{ million}}{\$1,000 \text{ million}}$$

$$+ 14.8 \text{ years} \times \frac{\$150 \text{ million}}{\$1,000 \text{ million}} \tag{26.4}$$

Duration of Liabilities:

$$2.56 \text{ years} = 0 \text{ years} \times \frac{\$400 \text{ million}}{\$900 \text{ million}} + 1 \text{ year} \times \frac{\$300 \text{ million}}{\$900 \text{ million}} \tag{26.5}$$

$$+ 10 \text{ years} \times \frac{\$200 \text{ million}}{\$900 \text{ million}}$$

The duration of the assets, 2.56 years, equals the duration of the liabilities. Because of this, Mr. Charest argues that the firm is immune to interest rate risk.

Just to be on the safe side, the bank calls in a second consultant, Gail Ellert. Ms. Ellert argues that it is incorrect simply to match durations, because assets total $1,000 million and liabilities total only $900 million. If both assets and liabilities have the same duration, the price change on a dollar of assets should be equal to the price change on a dollar of liabilities. However, the total price change will be greater for assets than for liabilities, because there are more assets than liabilities. The firm will be immune from interest rate risk only when the duration of the liabilities is greater than the duration of the assets. Ms. Ellert states that the following relationship must hold if the bank is to be **immunized,** that is, immune to interest rate risk:

$$\begin{matrix} \text{Duration of} \\ \text{assets} \end{matrix} \times \begin{matrix} \text{Market value of} \\ \text{assets} \end{matrix} = \begin{matrix} \text{Duration of} \\ \text{liabilities} \end{matrix} \times \begin{matrix} \text{Market value} \\ \text{of liabilities} \end{matrix} \tag{26.6}$$

She says that the bank should not equate the duration of the liabilities with the duration of the assets. Rather, using Equation (26.6), the bank should match the duration of the liabilities to the duration of the assets. She suggests two ways to achieve this match.

1. *Increase the duration of the liabilities without changing the duration of the assets.* Ms. Ellert argues that the duration of the liabilities could be increased to

$$\text{Duration of assets} \times \frac{\text{Market value of assets}}{\text{Market value of liabilities}}$$

$$= 2.56 \text{ years} \times \frac{\$1,000 \text{ million}}{\$900 \text{ million}}$$

$$= 2.84 \text{ years}$$

---

[19]Note that the duration of a group of items is an average of the durations of the individual items, weighted by the market value of each item. This is a simplifying step that greatly increases duration's practicality.

Equation (26.5) then becomes

$$2.56 \times \$1 \text{ billion} = 2.84 \times \$900 \text{ million}$$

2. *Decrease the duration of the assets without changing the duration of the liabilities.* Alternatively, Ms. Ellert points out that the duration of the assets could be decreased to

$$\text{Duration of liabilities} \times \frac{\text{Market value of liabilities}}{\text{Market value of assets}}$$

$$= 2.56 \text{ years} \times \frac{\$900 \text{ million}}{\$1,000 \text{ million}}$$

$$= 2.30 \text{ years}$$

Equation (26.6) then becomes

$$2.30 \times \$1 \text{ billion} = 2.56 \times \$900 \text{ million}$$

Though we agree with Ms. Ellert's analysis, the bank's current mismatch was small anyway.

Duration in Practice

Huge mismatches have occurred between the durations of assets and liabilities of financial institutions. Probably the most famous example occurred in the United States savings and loan (S&L) industry. S&Ls invested large portions of their assets in mortgages. The durations of these mortgages were over 10 years. Many of the funds available for mortgage lending were financed by short-term credit, especially savings accounts. The duration of such instruments is quite small. A thrift institution in this situation faced major interest rate risk, because any increase in interest rates greatly reduced the value of the mortgages. Because an interest rate rise only reduced the value of the liabilities slightly, the equity of the firm fell. As interest rates rose over much of the 1960s and 1970s, many S&Ls found that the market value of their equity turned negative. Allowed to stay in business by regulators, these "zombie thrifts" increased the eventual clean-up costs by engaging in risky investments.[20]

Duration and the accompanying immunization strategies are useful in other areas of finance. For example, many firms establish pension funds to meet obligations to retirees. If the assets of a pension fund are invested in bonds and other fixed-income securities, the duration of the assets can be computed. Similarly, the firm views the obligations to retirees as analogous to interest payments on debt. The duration of these liabilities can be calculated as well. The manager of a pension fund could choose pension assets so that the duration of the assets is matched with the duration of the liabilities. In this way, changing interest rates would not affect the net worth of the pension fund.

Life insurance companies receiving premiums today are legally obligated to provide death benefits in the future. Actuaries view these future benefits as analogous to interest and principal payments of fixed-income securities. The duration of these expected benefits can be calculated. Insurance companies frequently invest in bonds where the duration of the bonds is matched to the duration of the future death benefits.

---

[20]This behaviour is a good example of a selfish investment strategy from Chapter 17. Firms near bankruptcy often take great chances, because they feel that they are playing with someone else's money. In this case, deposit insurance allowed S&Ls to play with taxpayers' money. The example also illustrates our discussion of deposit insurance as a put option in Chapter 23.

The business of a leasing company is quite simple. The firm issues debt to purchase assets, which are then leased. The lease payments have a duration, as does the debt. Leasing companies frequently structure debt financing so that the duration of the debt matches the duration of the lease. If the firm did not do this, the market value of its equity could be eliminated by a sudden change in interest rates.

Duration can also be used to speculate on interest rate movements. Bond managers for mutual funds and pension funds routinely calculate the duration of their portfolios. Applying the basic duration principle that bond price volatility is higher for bonds with high durations, fund managers lengthen duration when they predict that falling interest rates will boost bond prices. When they expect rates to rise, managers shorten duration to shield portfolios against losses. In contrast, other managers believe that forecasting interest rates accurately is impossible. These managers simply match the duration of their portfolio with the duration of their liabilities. Research on duration concludes that such duration strategies have been effective in controlling interest rate risk in Canadian bond portfolios.[21]

? Concept Questions
- **What is duration?**
- **How is the concept of duration used to reduce interest rate risk?**

26.6 Swap Contracts

A swap contract is an agreement between two parties to exchange, or swap, specified cash flows at specific intervals. **Swaps** were first introduced to the public in 1981 when IBM and the World Bank entered into a swap agreement. The growth in the use of this financing instrument clearly indicates its growing importance for today's corporations. By the middle of 2006, there was $250.8 trillion outstanding of interest rate swaps while cross-currency swaps and outstanding credit default swaps for the topped $26.0 trillion.[22]

Swaps are similar to forwards and futures contracts. A swap contract is essentially just a portfolio of forward contracts. With a swap, the only difference is that there are multiple exchanges instead of just one. In principle, a swap contract could be tailored to exchange anything. In practice, most swap contracts fall into one of three basic categories: currency swaps, interest rate swaps, and commodity swaps.

Interest-Rate Swaps

Like other derivatives, swaps are tools that firms can use easily to change their risk exposures and their balance sheets.[23] Consider a firm that has borrowed and carries on its books an obligation to repay a 10-year loan for $100 million of principal with a 9 percent coupon rate paid annually. Ignoring the possibility of calling the loan, the firm expects to have to pay coupons of $9 million every year for 10 years and a balloon payment of $100 million at the end of the 10 years. Suppose, though, that the firm is uncomfortable with having

[21]I. J. Fooladi and G. S. Roberts, "How Effective Are Duration-Based Bond Strategies in Canada?" *Canadian Investment Review* (Spring 1989), pp. 57–62; and "Duration Analysis and Its Applications," *FINECO* (1997); and by the same authors: "Bond Portfolio Immunization: Canadian Tests," *Journal of Economics and Business* 44 (1999), 3–17.

[22]For more information and statistics on swaps, visit the International Swaps and Derivatives Association at www.isda.org.

[23]Under current accounting rules, most derivatives do not usually show up on firms' balance sheets since they do not have a historical cost (i.e., the amount a bank would pay on the initial transaction day).

this large fixed obligation on its books. Perhaps the firm is in a cyclical business where its revenues vary and could, conceivably, fall to a point where it would be difficult to make the debt payment.

Suppose, too, that the firm earns a lot of its revenue from financing the purchase of its products. Typically, for example, a manufacturer might help its customers finance their purchase of its products through a leasing or credit subsidiary. Usually these loans are for relatively short time periods and are financed at some premium over the prevailing short rate of interest. This puts the firm in the position of having revenues that move up and down with interest rates while its costs are relatively fixed.

This is a classic situation where a swap can be used to offset the risk. When interest rates rise, it would have to pay more on the loan, but it would be making more on its product financing. What the firm would really prefer is to have a floating-rate loan rather than a fixed-rate loan. It can use a swap to accomplish this.

Of course, the firm could also just go into the capital markets and borrow $100 million at a variable interest rate and then use the proceeds to retire its outstanding fixed-rate loan. While this is possible, it is generally quite expensive, requiring underwriting a new loan and the repurchase of the existing loan. The ease of entering into a swap is its inherent advantage.

The particular swap would be one that exchanged its fixed obligation for an agreement to pay a floating rate. Every six months it would agree to pay a coupon based on whatever the prevailing interest rate was at that time in exchange for an agreement from a counter-party to pay the firm's fixed coupon.

A common reference point for floating-rate commitments is called LIBOR (London Interbank Offered Rate), and it is the rate that most international banks charge one another for dollar-denominated loans in the London market. LIBOR is commonly used as the reference rate for a floating-rate commitment, and, depending on the creditworthiness of the borrower, the rate can vary from LIBOR to LIBOR plus one percentage point or more over LIBOR.

If we assume that our firm has a credit rating that requires it to pay LIBOR plus 50 basis points, then in a swap it would be exchanging its fixed 9 percent obligation for the obligation to pay whatever the prevailing LIBOR rate is plus 50 basis points. Table 26.10 displays how the cash flows on this swap would work. In the table we have assumed that LIBOR starts at 8 percent and rises for four years to 11 percent and then drops to 7 percent. As the table illustrates, the firm would owe a coupon of 8.5% × $100 million = $8.5 million in year 1, $9.5 million in year 2, $10.5 million in year 3, and $11.5 million in year 4. The precipitous drop to 7 percent lowers the annual payments to $7.5 million thereafter. In return, the firm receives the fixed payment of $9 million each year. Actually, rather than

TABLE 26.10   Fixed-for-Floating Swap: Cash Flows ($ million)

	Coupons									
	Year 1	2	3	4	5	6	7	8	9	10
A. Swap										
Fixed obligation	9	9	9	9	9	9	9	9	9	9
LIBOR floating	−8.5	−9.5	−10.5	−11.5	−7.5	−7.5	−7.5	−7.5	−7.5	−7.5
B. Original loan										
Fixed obligation	−9	−9	−9	−9	−9	−9	−9	−9	−9	−9
Net effect	8.5	9.5	10.5	11.5	7.5	7.5	7.5	7.5	7.5	7.5

swapping the full payments, the cash flows would be netted. Since the firm is paying variable and receiving fixed—which it uses to pay its lender—in the first year, for example, the firm owes $8.5 million and is owed by its counterparty, who is paying fixed, $9 million. Hence, net, the firm would receive a payment of $0.5 million. Since the firm has to pay its lender $9 million, but gets a net payment from the swap of $0.5 million, it really only pays out the difference, or $8.5 million. In each year, then, the firm would effectively pay only LIBOR plus 50 basis points.

Notice, too, that the entire transaction can be carried out without any need to change the terms of the original loan. In effect, by swapping, the firm has found a counterparty who is willing to pay its fixed obligation in return for the firm paying a floating obligation.

Currency Swaps

FX stands for foreign exchange, and currency swaps are sometimes called FX swaps. Currency swaps are swaps of obligations to pay cash flows in one currency for obligations to pay in another currency.

Currency swaps arise as a natural vehicle for hedging the risks in international trade. For example, suppose a U.S. firm sells a broad range of its product line in the German market. Every year the firm can count on receiving revenue from Germany in euros. We will study international finance later in this book, but for now we can just observe that, because exchange rates fluctuate, this subjects the firm to considerable risk.

If the firm produces its products in the United States and exports them to Germany, then the firm has to pay its workers and its suppliers in dollars. But, it is receiving some of its revenues in euros. The exchange rate between dollars and euros changes over time. As the euro rises in value, the German revenues are worth more dollars, but as it falls they decline. Suppose that the firm can count on selling 100 million euros of goods each year in Germany. If the exchange rate is one euro for each dollar, then the firm will receive $100 million. But, if the exchange rate were to rise to two euros for each dollar, the firm would only receive $50 million for its 100 million euros. Naturally the firm would like to protect itself against these currency swings.

To do so the firm can enter into a currency swap. We will learn more about exactly what the terms of such a swap might be, but for now we can assume that the swap is for five years at a fixed term of 100 million euros for $100 million each year. Now, no matter what happens to the exchange rate between euros and dollars over the next five years, as long as the firm makes 100 million euros each year for the sale of its products, it will swap this for $100 million each year.

We have not addressed the question of how the market prices swaps, either interest-rate swaps or currency swaps. In the fixed-for-floating example and in the currency swap, we just quoted some terms. We won't go into great detail on exactly how it is done, but we can stress the most important points.

Swaps, like forwards and futures, are essentially zero-sum transactions, which is to say that in both cases the market sets prices at a fair level, and neither party has any substantial bargain or loss at the moment the deal is struck. For example, in the currency swap, the swap rate is some average of the market expectation of what the exchange rate will be over the life of the swap. In the interest-rate swap, the rates are set as the fair floating and fixed rates for the creditor, taking account of the creditworthiness of the counterparties. We can actually price swaps fairly once we know how to price forward contracts. In our interest-rate swap example, the firm swapped LIBOR plus 50 basis points for a 9 percent fixed rate, all on a principal amount of $100 million. This is equivalent to a series of forward contracts extending out the life of the swap. In year 1, for example, having made the swap, the firm is in the same position that it would be if it had sold a forward contract entitling the buyer to receive LIBOR plus 50 basis points on $100 million in return for a fixed payment of $9 million (9 percent on $100 million). Similarly, the currency swap can also be viewed as a series of forward contracts.

? Concept Questions

- **Show that a currency swap is equivalent to a series of forward contracts.**

Credit Default Swaps

Credit default swaps, along with other credit derivatives, make up one of the fastest growing markets in the financial world. A credit default swap (CDS) is a contract that pays off when a credit event occurs—default by a particular company, termed the reference entity. In this case, the buyer of the CDS has the right to sell corporate bonds issued by the reference entity to the CDS seller at their face value. Since bonds in default trade at a deep discount, the right to sell bonds at their face value becomes quite valuable when a default occurs.

Credit default swaps are an important risk management tool for financial institutions. By buying a CDS on a borrower, a bank sets up a payment in the event the borrower defaults on its loan. In effect, credit default swaps are a form of insurance against credit losses.[24]

Exotics

Up to now we have dealt with the meat and potatoes of the derivatives markets, swaps, options, forwards, and futures. **Exotics** are the complicated blends of these that often produce the surprising results for the buyers.

One of the more interesting types of exotics is called an *inverse floater.* In our fixed-for-floating swap, the floating payments fluctuated with LIBOR. An inverse floater is one that fluctuates inversely with some rate such as LIBOR. For example, the floater might pay an interest of 20 percent minus LIBOR. If LIBOR is 9 percent, then the inverse pays 11 percent, and if LIBOR rises to 12 percent, the payments on the inverse would fall to 8 percent. Clearly the purchaser of an inverse profits from the inverse if interest rates fall.

Both floaters and inverse floaters have a supercharged version called *superfloaters* and *superinverses* that fluctuate more than one for one with movements in interest rates. As an example of a superinverse floater, consider a floater that pays an interest rate of 30 percent minus *twice* LIBOR. When LIBOR is 10 percent, the inverse pays

$$30\% - 2 \times 10\% = 30\% - 20\% = 10\%$$

and if LIBOR falls by 3 percent to 7 percent, then the return on the inverse rises by 6 percent from 10 percent to 16 percent,

$$30\% - 2 \times 7\% = 30\% - 14\% = 16\%$$

Sometimes derivatives are combined with options to bound the impact of interest rates. The most important of these instruments are called *caps* and *floors.* A cap is so named because it puts an upper limit or a cap on the impact of a rise in interest rates. A floor, conversely, provides a floor below which the interest rate impact is insulated.

To illustrate the impact of these, consider a firm that is borrowing short-term and is concerned that interest rates might rise. For example, using LIBOR as the reference interest

---

[24]For more on credit default swaps, see John C. Hull, *Fundamentals of Futures and Options Markets,* 6th ed., Pearson Prentice Hall, NJ, 2006, Chapter 21.

rate, the firm might purchase a 7 percent cap. The cap pays the firm the difference between LIBOR and 7 percent on some principal amount, provided that LIBOR is greater than 7 percent. As long as LIBOR is below 7 percent, the holder of the cap receives no payments.

By purchasing the cap the firm has assured itself that even if interest rates rise above 7 percent, it will not have to pay more than a 7 percent rate. Suppose that interest rates rise to 9 percent. While the firm is borrowing short-term and paying 9 percent rates, this is offset by the cap, which is paying the firm the difference between 9 percent and the 7 percent limit. For any LIBOR rate above 7 percent, the firm receives the difference between LIBOR and 7 percent, and, as a consequence, it has capped its cost of borrowing at 7 percent.

On the other side, consider a financial firm that is in the business of lending short-term and is concerned that interest rates—and, consequently, its revenues—might fall. The firm could purchase a floor to protect itself from such declines. If the limit on the floor is 7 percent, then the floor pays the difference between 7 percent and LIBOR whenever LIBOR is below 7 percent, and nothing if LIBOR is above 7 percent. Thus, if interest rates were to fall to, say, 5 percent while the firm is only receiving 5 percent from its lending activities, the floor is paying it the difference between 7 percent and 5 percent, or an additional 2 percent. By purchasing the floor, the firm has assured itself of receiving no less than 7 percent from the combination of the floor and its lending activities.

We have only scratched the surface of what is available in the world of derivatives. Derivatives are designed to meet marketplace needs, and the only binding limitation is the human imagination. Nowhere should the buyer's warning *caveat emptor* be taken more seriously than in the derivatives markets, and this is especially true for the exotics. If swaps are the meat and potatoes of the derivatives markets, then caps and floors are the meat and potatoes of the exotics. As we have seen, they have obvious value as hedging instruments. But, much attention has been focused on truly exotic derivatives, some of which appear to have arisen more as the residuals that were left over from more straightforward deals. We won't examine these in any detail, but suffice it to say that some of these are so volatile and unpredictable that market participants have dubbed them "toxic waste."

26.7 Actual Use of Derivatives

Because derivatives do not usually appear in financial statements, it is much more difficult to observe the use of derivatives by firms when compared to, say, bank debt. Much of our knowledge of corporate derivative use comes from academic surveys. Most surveys report that the use of derivatives appears to be widespread among large publicly traded firms. It appears that over one-half of all publicly traded nonfinancial firms in the U.S. and Canada use derivatives of some kind.[25] Large firms are far more likely to use derivatives than small firms. For firms that use derivatives, foreign-currency and interest-rate derivatives are the most frequently used.[26]

Canadian multinational companies are far more likely (88 percent) to use derivatives than national firms (56 percent). Nonregulated companies are more likely to use derivatives

---

[25]G. M. Bodnar, G. S. Hayt, and Richard Marston, "1998 Wharton Survey of Finance Risk Management by U.S. Non-Financial Firms," *Financial Management* (Winter 1998); and A. Jalilvand, "Why Firms Use Derivatives: Evidence from Canada," *Canadian Journal of Administrative Sciences* (September 1999).

[26]Howton and Perfect report that interest rate derivatives are the most frequently used derivatives. Shawn D. Howton and Steven B. Perfect, "Currency and Interest-Rate Derivatives Use in U.S. Firms," *Financial Management* (Winter 1998). Jalilvand has similar findings for Canadian firms.

(83 percent) versus regulated companies (62 percent). All the gold and silver, paper and forest, pipelines, and agricultural companies that responded use derivatives. These companies have high exposure to commodity price risk. The lowest percentage of derivative users is in technology, health care, and distribution.

The prevailing view is that derivatives can be very helpful in reducing the variability of firm cash flows, which, in turn, reduces the various costs associated with financial distress. Therefore, it is somewhat puzzling that large firms use derivatives more often than small firms—because large firms tend to have less cash flow variability than small firms. Also some surveys report that firms occasionally use derivatives when they want to speculate about future prices and not just to hedge risks.[27]

However, most of the evidence is consistent with the theory that derivatives are most frequently used by firms where financial distress costs are high and access to the capital markets is constrained.[28]

26.8 SUMMARY AND CONCLUSIONS

1. Firms hedge to reduce risk. This chapter shows a number of hedging strategies.

2. A forward contract is an agreement by two parties to sell an item for cash at a later date. The price is set at the time the agreement is signed. However, cash changes hands on the date of delivery. Forward contracts are generally not traded on organized exchanges.

3. Futures contracts are also agreements for future delivery. They have certain advantages, such as liquidity, that forward contracts do not. An unusual feature of futures contracts is the mark-to-the-market convention. If the price of a futures contract falls on a particular day, every buyer of the contract must pay money to the clearinghouse. Every seller of the contract receives money from the clearinghouse. Everything is reversed if the price rises. The mark-to-the-market convention prevents defaults on futures contracts.

4. We divided hedges into two types: short hedges and long hedges. An individual or firm that sells a futures contract to reduce risk is instituting a short hedge. Short hedges are generally appropriate for holders of inventory. An individual or firm that buys a futures contract to reduce risk is instituting a long hedge. Long hedges are typically used by firms with contracts to sell finished goods at a fixed price.

5. An interest-rate futures contract employs a bond as the deliverable instrument. Because of their popularity, we worked with Government of Canada bond futures contracts. We showed that Government of Canada bond futures contracts can be priced using the same type of net present value analysis that is used to price Canada bonds themselves.

6. Many firms are faced with interest-rate risk. They can reduce this risk by hedging with interest-rate futures contracts. As with other commodities, a short hedge involves the sale of a futures contract. Firms that are committed to buying mortgages or other bonds are likely to institute short hedges. A long hedge involves the purchase of a futures contract. Firms that have agreed to sell mortgages or other bonds at a fixed price are likely to institute long hedges.

7. Duration measures the average maturity of all the cash flows in a bond. Bonds with high duration have high price variability. Firms frequently try to match the duration of their assets with the duration of their liabilities.

---

[27]Walter Dolde, "The Trajectory of Corporate Financial Risk Management," *Journal of Applied Corporate Finance* (Fall 1993).

[28]Shawn D. Howton and Steven B. Perfect, "Currency and Interest-Rate Derivatives Use in U.S. Firms," *Financial Management* (Winter 1998). See also H. Berkman and M. E. Bradbury, "Empirical Evidence on the Corporate Use of Derivatives," *Financial Management* (Summer 1996).

8. Swaps are agreements to exchange cash flows over time. The first major type is an interest-rate swap in which one pattern of coupon payments, say fixed payments, is exchanged for another, say, coupons that float with LIBOR. The second major type is a currency swap in which an agreement is struck to swap payments in one currency for payments in another currency over time.

KEY TERMS

Cash transaction 739	Futures contract 739	Marked to the market 740
Deliverable instrument 738	Hedging 737	Short hedge 745
Duration 756	Immunized 759	Swaps 761
Exotics 764	Long hedge 746	Taking delivery 738
Forward contract 738	Making delivery 738	

SUGGESTED READING

Several cases that illustrate the concepts, tools, and markets for hedging can be found in:
P. Tufano. "How Financial Engineering Can Advance Corporate Strategy." *Harvard Business Review* (January–February 1996).

A highly readable discussion of derivatives use in Canada is:
A. Jalilvand. "Why Firms Use Derivatives: Evidence from Canada." *Canadian Journal of Administrative Sciences* 16 (September 1999), pp. 213–228.

A clear discussion of the rationale for corporate risk management with derivatives is:
R. M. Stulz. "Rethinking Risk Management." in D. H. Chew, ed. *The New Corporate Finance; Where Theory Meets Practice.* 3rd Edition. McGraw-Hill Irwin, New York, 2001.

QUESTIONS & PROBLEMS

Forward and Futures Contracts

26.1   List and explain three ways in which futures contracts differ from forward contracts. Why do you think that futures contracts are much more common? Are there any circumstances under which you might prefer to use forwards instead of futures? Explain. If a firm is selling futures contracts on lumber as a hedging strategy, what must be true about the firm's exposure to lumber prices?

26.2   The following table lists the closing prices for wheat futures contracts (per bushel):

March 15	$3.06
March 16	$3.11
March 17	$3.16
March 18	$3.09
March 19	$3.07

Suppose you bought one futures contract for $3.00 as trading began on March 15.
a. Suppose you receive a notice of delivery from your broker at the end of trading on March 18.
  1. What is the delivery price per bushel?
  2. What price did you pay for the wheat (per bushel)?
  3. What are the daily cash flows associated with this contract?
  4. What is the net amount that you paid for one bushel of wheat?
b. Suppose you receive a notice of delivery from your broker at the end of trading on March 19.
  1. What is the delivery price per bushel?
  2. What price did you pay for the wheat (per bushel)?
  3. What are the daily cash flows associated with this contract?
  4. What is the net amount that you paid for one bushel of wheat?

26.3   You enter into a forward contract to buy a 15-year, zero coupon bond that will be issued in one year. The face value of the bond is $1,000, and the 1-year and 16-year spot interest rates are 4.2 percent and 8.5 percent, respectively.
a. What is the forward price of your contract?
b. Suppose both the 1-year and 16-year spot rates unexpectedly shift downward by 2 percent. What is the new price of the forward contract?

26.4   This morning you agreed to buy a one-year Canada bond in six months. The bond has a face value of $1,000. Use the semiannual spot interest rates listed below to answer the following questions.

Time Horizon	Semiannual Rate (%)
6 months	0.055
12 months	0.061
18 months	0.062
24 months	0.067
30 months	0.067
36 months	0.068
42 months	0.071

a. What is the forward price of this contract?

b. Suppose shortly after you purchased the forward contract, all rates decreased by 15 basis points. What is the price of a forward contract otherwise identical to yours given these changes?

26.5   Jonathon Simpleton is a speculator who believes that the futures price of zinc will decrease over the next month. What type of futures position Jonathon be interested in?

26.6   Leroy Hawkins is interested in entering the import/export business. During a recent visit with his financial advisers, he said, "If we play the game right, this is the safest business in the world. By hedging all of our transactions in the foreign exchange futures market, we can eliminate all of our risk." Do you agree with Mr. Hawkins' assessment of hedging? Why or why not?

26.7   Kevin Nomura is a Japanese student who is planning a one-year stay in the Vancouver. He expects to arrive in British Columbia in eight months. He is worried about depreciation in the yen relative to the dollar over the next eight months and wishes to take a position in foreign exchange futures to hedge this risk. What should Mr. Nomura's hedging position be? Assume the exchange rate between Japanese and Canadian currencies is quoted as yen/dollar.

26.8   You are long 10 gold futures contracts, established at an initial settle price of $680 per ounce, where each contract represents 100 ounces. Over the subsequent four trading days, gold settles at $673, $679, $682, and $686, respectively. Compute the cash flows at the end of each trading day, and compute your total profit or loss at the end of the trading period.

26.9   You are short 25 gasoline futures contracts, established at an initial settle price of $1.52 per gallon, where each contract represents 42,000 gallons. Over the subsequent four trading days, gasoline settles at $1.46, $1.55, $1.59, and $1.62, respectively. Compute the cash flows at the end of each trading day, and compute your total profit or loss at the end of the trading period.

26.10 Suppose there were call options and forward contracts available on coal, but no put options. Show how a financial engineer could synthesize a put option using the available contracts. What does your answer tell you about the general relationship between puts, calls, and forwards?

EXCEL

26.11 The forward price (f) of a contract on an asset with neither carrying costs nor conventional yield is the current spot price of the asset (S_0) multiplied by 1 plus the appropriate interest rate between the initiation of the contract and the delivery date of the asset. Derive this relationship by comparing the cash flows that result from the following two strategies:

   Strategy 1:   Buy silver on the spot market today and hold it for one year. Do not use any of your own money to purchase the silver.

   Strategy 2:   Take on a long position in a silver forward contract for delivery in one year.

Assume that silver is an asset with neither carrying costs nor convenience yield.

Duration

26.12 What is the duration of a bond with three years to maturity and a coupon of 10 percent paid annually if the bond sells at par?

26.13 Unchartered Bank has the following market value balance sheet:

Asset or Liability	Market Value (in millions)	Duration (in years)
Federal funds deposits	$ 28	0
Accounts receivable	580	0.20
Short-term loans	390	0.65
Long-term loans	84	5.25
Mortgages	315	14.25
Chequing and savings deposits	520	0
Certificates of deposit	340	1.60
Long-term financing	260	9.80
Equity	277	N/A

a. What is the duration of the assets?

b. What is the duration of the liabilities?

c. Is the bank immune from interest rate risk?

26.14 Ted and Alice Hansel have a son who will begin college three years from today. School expenses of $30,000 will need to be paid at the beginning of each of the four years that their son plans to attend college. What is the duration of this liability to the couple if they can borrow and lend at the market interest rate of 10 percent?

26.15 What is the duration of a bond with two years to maturity if the bond has a coupon rate of 8 percent paid semiannually, and the market interest rate is 7 percent?

EXCEL

26.16 Consider two four-year bonds. Each bond has a face value of $1,000. Bond A pays an annual coupon of 7 percent, and Bond B pays an annual of 10.7 percent.

a. Calculate the price and duration of each bond if the market interest rate is 10 percent per annum (effective annual yield)

b. Calculate the price of each bond if the market interest rate is 6 percent per annum (effective annual yield)

c. Which bond do you expect to experience the greatest percentage change in price? Explain.

d. What is the percentage change in the price of each bond?

EXCEL

26.17 Suppose that Hubcap Corporation is considering issuing one of three different bonds. Bond One is a seven-year bond and has a face value of $1,000. This bond pays an annual coupon of 5 percent. Bond Two is a six-year bond and has a face value of $1,000. This bond pays $35 coupons twice a year and Bond Three is a nine-year bond, has a face value of $1,000 and pays a 10 percent coupons annually.

a. Calculate the price and duration of each bond if the market interest rate is 4.56 percent per annum (effective annual yield)

b. Calculate the price of each bond if the market interest rate is 6 percent per annum (effective annual yield)

c. Which bond do you expect to experience the greatest percentage change in price? Explain.

d. What is the percentage change in the price of each bond?

e. If Hubcap is looking going to receive a large cash flow in six years with which it intends to pay back the bondholders, which bond should the company issue. Assume that all other factors are not being considered.

26.18 Consider Grandy Commercial Bank's market-value balance sheet:

	Market Value (in millions)	Duration (in years)
Assets		
Overnight money	$150	0
Loans	550	1
Mortgages	1,300	12.3
Liabilities		
Chequing and savings accounts	$300	0
Certifications of deposit	450	1.2
Long-term debt	600	19
Equity	650	—

a. What is the duration of Grandy's assets?

b. What is the duration of Grandy's liabilities?

c. Is the bank immune from interest-rate risk?

Swaps

26.19 In May 2007, Sysco Corporation, the distributor of food and food-related products (not to be confused with Cisco Systems), announced it had signed an interest rate swap. The interest rate swap effectively converted the company's $100 million, 4.6 percent interest rate bonds for a variable rate payment, which would be the six-month LIBOR minus 0.52 percent. Why would Sysco use a swap agreement? In other words, why didn't Sysco just go ahead and issue floating-rate bonds because the net effect of issuing fixed-rate bonds and then doing a swap is to create a variable rate bond?

26.20 Explain why a swap is effectively a series of forward contracts. Suppose a firm enters a swap agreement with a swap dealer. Describe the nature of the default risk faced by both parties.

26.21 Alternate Bridging Company and Staind Glass Corporation need to raise funds to pay for capital improvements at their manufacturing plants. Alternate Bridge is a well-established firm with an excellent credit rating in the debt market; it can borrow funds either at 11 percent fixed rate or at LIBOR + 1 percent floating rate. Staind Glass Corporation is a fledgling start-up firm without a strong credit history. It can borrow funds either at 10 percent fixed rate or at LIBOR + 3 percent floating rate.

a. Is there an opportunity here for ABC and XYZ to benefit by means of an interest rate swap?

b. Suppose you've just been hired at a bank that acts as a dealer in the swaps market, and your boss has shown you the borrowing rate information for your clients ABC and XYZ. Describe how you could bring these two companies together in an interest rate swap that would make both firms better off while netting your bank a 2.0 percent profit.

26.22 You are assigned to the risk management department of Swift Muffler Inc., a U.S. chain of auto service shops with outlets in North America and internationally. Your office is located in New Jersey, U.S.A., and the earnings of Swift are stated in U.S. dollars. Your responsibility is to manage the foreign exchange risk arising from operations in the European Community.

The current exchange rate is US$1.23 per euro. Currently Swift earns net profits from EC operations of €1 million per month, which are repatriated to the U.S. head office. The firm also has pension obligations to retired employees in the EC of €250,000 per month. Pension funds for the entire company are managed in the U.S. head office and invested in U.S. assets. While the pension obligations are quite stable, monthly profits are subject to fluctuation with economic conditions and seasonality.

The CFO has identified one month as the appropriate planning horizon, and foreign exchange forward contracts with a major bank, currency futures, currency swaps, and currency futures options (puts and calls) as possible hedging vehicles. To complete your engagement, you should do the following:

a. Assess Swift's exchange rate exposure.

b. Explain how Swift could hedge with each of the possible vehicles. For each, state the appropriate position (buy or sell) and state your reasons briefly.

c. Suppose the CFO is committed to hedging all the foreign exchange risk from European operations. In addition, the CFO is concerned about the variability in profits. How would these considerations affect your recommendation on the best choice of hedging vehicle?

d. Euro futures are traded on the CME in Chicago. Each contract is for €125,000 quoted in American dollars per euro. A movement of 0.0001 in the exchange rate translates to US$12.50 per contract. The June contract settled yesterday at 1.2280. How many futures contracts should Swift buy or sell, assuming the firm wishes to hedge all of its currency exposure? Explain briefly.

MINICASE: Williamson Mortgage Inc.

Jennifer Williamson recently quit her job as an investment banker and has decided to enter the mortgage brokerage business. Rather than work for someone else, she has decided to open her own shop. Her cousin Jerry has approached her about a mortgage for a house he is building. The house will be completed in three months, and he will need the mortgage at that time. Jerry wants a 25-year, fixed-rate mortgage in the amount of $500,000 with monthly payments.

Jennifer has agreed to lend Jerry the money in three months at the current market rate of 8.2 percent. Because Jennifer is just starting out, she does not have $500,000 available for the loan, so she approaches Max Cabell, the president of MC Insurance Corporation, about purchasing the mortgage from her in three months. Max has agreed to purchase the mortgage in three months, but he is unwilling to set a price on the mortgage. Instead, he has agreed in writing to purchase the mortgage at the market rate in three months. There are Canadian Government Bond (CGB) futures contracts available for delivery in three months. A CGB bond contract is for $100,000 in face value of bonds.

1. What is the monthly mortgage payment on Jerry's mortgage?
2. What is the most significant risk Jennifer faces in this deal?
3. How can Jennifer hedge this risk?
4. Suppose that in the next three months the market rate of interest rises to 9 percent.
   a. How much will Max be willing to pay for the mortgage?
   b. What will happen to the value of CGB futures contracts? Will the long or short position increase in value?
5. Suppose that in the next three months the market rate of interest falls to 7 percent.
   a. How much will Max be willing to pay for the mortgage?
   b. What will happen to the value of CGB futures contracts? Will the long or short position increase in value?
6. Are there any possible risks Jennifer faces in using CGB futures contracts to hedge her interest rate risk?

PART 7

Chapter 27

Short-Term Finance and Planning

EXECUTIVE SUMMARY

Up to now we have described many of the decisions of long-term finance: capital budgeting, dividend policy, and capital structure. This chapter introduces short-term finance. Short-term finance is an analysis of decisions that (1) affect current assets and current liabilities, and (2) will frequently have an impact on the firm within a year.

The term *net working capital* is often associated with short-term financial decision making. Net working capital is the difference between current assets and current liabilities. The focus of short-term finance on net working capital seems to suggest that it is an accounting subject. However, making net working capital decisions still relies on cash flow and net present value.

There is no universally accepted definition of short-term finance. The most important difference between short-term and long-term finance is the timing of cash flows. Short-term financial decisions involve cash inflows and outflows within a year or less. For example, a short-term financial decision is involved when a firm orders raw materials, pays in cash, and anticipates selling finished goods in one year for cash, as illustrated in Figure 27.1. A long-term financial decision is involved when a firm purchases a special machine that will reduce operating costs over the next five years, as illustrated in Figure 27.2.

Here are some questions of short-term finance:

1. What is a reasonable level of cash to keep on hand (in a bank) to pay bills?
2. How much raw material should be ordered?
3. How much credit should be extended to customers?

This chapter introduces the basic elements of short-term financial decisions. First, we describe the short-term operating activities of the firm, and then we identify alternative short-term financial policies. Finally, we outline the basic elements in a short-term financial plan and describe short-term financing instruments.

27.1 Tracing Cash and Net Working Capital

In this section we trace the components of cash and net working capital as they change from one year to the next. Our goal is to describe the short-term operating activities of the firm and their impact on cash and working capital.

Current assets are cash and other assets that are expected to be converted to cash within the year. Current assets are presented in the balance sheet in order of their **liquidity**—the ease with which they can be converted to cash at a fair price and the time it takes to do so. Table 27.1 on page 774 gives the balance sheet and income statement of the Tradewinds Manufacturing Corporation for 20X2 and 20X1. The four

FIGURE 27.1

Short-Term Financial Decision

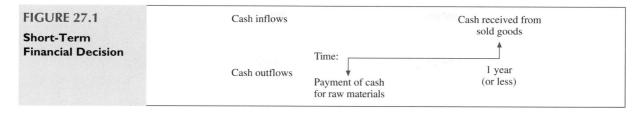

FIGURE 27.2

Long-Term Financial Decision

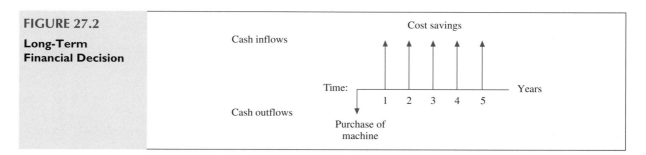

major items found in the current asset section of the Tradewinds balance sheet are cash, marketable securities, accounts receivable, and inventories.

As a counterpart to their investment in current assets, firms use several kinds of short-term debt called *current liabilities*. Current liabilities are obligations that are expected to require cash payment within one year or within the operating cycle, whichever is shorter.[1] The three major items found as current liabilities are accounts payable; accrued wages, taxes, and other expenses payable; and notes payable.

27.2 Defining Cash in Terms of Other Elements

Now we will define cash in terms of the other elements of the balance sheet. The balance sheet equation is

$$\frac{\text{Net working}}{\text{capital}} + \frac{\text{Fixed}}{\text{assets}} = \frac{\text{Long-term}}{\text{debt}} + \text{Equity} \qquad (27.1)$$

Net working capital is cash plus the other elements of net working capital; that is,

$$\frac{\text{Net working}}{\text{capital}} = \text{Cash} + \frac{\text{Other current}}{\text{assets}} - \frac{\text{Current}}{\text{liabilities}} \qquad (27.2)$$

Substituting Equation (27.2) into (27.1) yields

$$\text{Cash} + \frac{\text{Other current}}{\text{assets}} - \frac{\text{Current}}{\text{liabilities}} = \frac{\text{Long-term}}{\text{debt}} + \text{Equity} - \frac{\text{Fixed}}{\text{assets}} \qquad (27.3)$$

Rearranging, we find that

$$\text{Cash} = \frac{\text{Long-term}}{\text{debt}} + \text{Equity} - \frac{\text{Net working}}{\substack{\text{capital} \\ \text{(excluding cash)}}} - \frac{\text{Fixed}}{\text{assets}} \qquad (27.4)$$

---

[1]As we will learn in this chapter, the operating cycle begins when inventory is received and ends when cash is collected from the sale of the inventory.

TABLE 27.1
Financial Statements

TRADEWINDS MANUFACTURING CORPORATION December 31, 20X2, and December 31, 20X1		
Balance Sheet		
	20X2	**20X1**
Assets		
Current assets:		
Cash	$ 500,000	$ 500,000
Marketable securities (at cost)	500,000	450,000
Accounts receivable less allowance for bad debts	2,000,000	1,600,000
Inventories	3,000,000	2,000,000
Total current assets	6,000,000	4,550,000
Fixed assets (property, plant, and equipment):		
Land	450,000	450,000
Building	4,000,000	4,000,000
Machinery	1,500,000	800,000
Office equipment	50,000	50,000
Less: Accumulated depreciation	2,000,000	1,700,000
Net fixed assets	4,000,000	3,600,000
Prepayments and deferred charges	400,000	300,000
Intangibles	100,000	100,000
Total assets	$10,500,000	$ 8,550,000
Liabilities		
Current liabilities:		
Accounts payable	$ 1,000,000	$ 750,000
Notes payable	1,500,000	500,000
Accrued expenses payable	250,000	225,000
Taxes payable	250,000	225,000
Total current liabilities	3,000,000	1,700,000
Long-term liabilities:		
First mortgage bonds, 5% interest, due 20X5	3,000,000	3,000,000
Deferred taxes	600,000	600,000
Total liabilities	$ 6,600,000	$ 5,300,000
Shareholders' Equity		
Common stock: authorized, issued,		
and outstanding 300,000 shares	$ 1,500,000	$ 1,500,000
Capital surplus	500,000	500,000
Accumulated retained earnings	1,900,000	1,250,000
Total shareholders' equity	3,900,000	3,250,000
Total liabilities and shareholders' equity	$10,500,000	$ 8,550,000
Consolidated Income Statement		
Net sales	$11,500,000	$10,700,000
Cost of sales and operating expenses:		
Cost of goods sold	8,200,000	7,684,000
Depreciation	300,000	275,000
Selling and administration expenses	1,400,000	1,325,000
Operating profit	1,600,000	1,416,000
Other income:		
Dividends and interest	50,000	50,000
Total income from operations	1,650,000	1,466,000
Less: Interest on bonds and other liabilities	300,000	150,000
Income before provision for income tax	1,350,000	1,316,000
Provision for income tax	610,000	600,000
Net profit	$ 740,000	$ 716,000
Dividends paid out	$ 90,000	$ 132,000
Retained earnings	$ 650,000	$ 584,000

TABLE 27.2
**Sources and Uses
of Cash Statement**

TRADEWINDS MANUFACTURING CORPORATION Sources and Uses of Cash (in $ 000s)	
Source of cash:	
Cash flow from operations:	
Net income	$ 740
Depreciation	300
Total cash flow from operations	$1,040
Decrease in net working capital:	
Increase in accounts payable	250
Increase in notes payable	1,000
Increase in accrued expenses	25
Increase in taxes payable	25
Total sources of cash	$2,340
Uses of cash:	
Increase in fixed assets	700
Increase in prepayments	100
Dividends	90
Increase in net working capital:	
Investment in inventory	1,000
Increase in accounts receivable	400
Increase in marketable securities	50
Total uses of cash	$2,340
Change in cash balance	$ 0

The natural interpretation of Equation (27.4) is that increasing long-term debt and equity and decreasing fixed assets and net working capital (excluding cash) will increase cash to the firm.

The Sources and Uses of Cash Statement

We first introduced the cash flow statement in Chapter 2. This is the accounting statement that describes the sources and uses of cash. In this section we look at where cash comes from and how it is used. From the right-hand side of Equation (27.4), we can see that an increase in long-term debt or equity leads to an increase in cash. Moreover, an increase in net working capital or fixed assets leads to a decrease in cash. In addition, the sum of net income and depreciation increases cash, whereas dividend payments decrease cash.[2] This reasoning allows an accountant to create a sources and uses of cash statement, which shows all the transactions that affect a firm's cash position.

Let us trace the changes in cash for Tradewinds during the year. Notice that Tradewinds' cash balance remained constant during 20X2, even though cash flow from operations was $1.04 million (net income plus depreciation). Why did cash remain the same? The answer is simply that the sources of cash were equal to the uses of cash. From the firm's sources and uses of cash statement (Table 27.2), we find that Tradewinds generated cash as follows:

1. It generated cash flow from operations of $1.04 million.

2. It increased its accounts payable by $250,000. This is the same as increasing borrowing from suppliers.

_____
[2]Depreciation is really not a source of cash; it is added back as a correction because it was originally a noncash deduction from net income.

3. It increased its borrowing from banks by $1 million. This shows up as an increase in notes payable.

4. It increased accrued expenses by $25,000.

5. It increased taxes payable by $25,000, in effect borrowing from the Canada Revenue Agency.

Tradewinds used cash for the following purposes:

1. It invested $700,000 in fixed assets.

2. It increased prepayments by $100,000.

3. It paid a $90,000 dividend.

4. It invested in inventory worth $1 million.

5. It lent its customers additional money. Hence, accounts receivable increased by $400,000.

6. It purchased $50,000 worth of marketable securities.

This example illustrates the difference between a firm's cash position on the balance sheet and cash flows from operations.

? Concept Questions

- **What is the difference between net working capital and cash?**
- **Will net working capital always increase when cash increases?**
- **List the potential uses of cash.**
- **List the potential sources of cash.**

27.3 The Operating Cycle and the Cash Cycle

Short-term finance is concerned with the firm's **short-run operating activities.** A typical manufacturing firm's short-run operating activities consist of a sequence of events and decisions:

Events	Decisions
1. Buying raw materials	1. How much inventory to order?
2. Paying cash for purchases	2. To borrow, or draw down cash balance?
3. Manufacturing the product	3. What choice of production technology?
4. Selling the product	4. To offer cash terms or credit terms to customers?
5. Collecting cash	5. How to collect cash?

These activities create patterns of cash inflows and cash outflows that are both unsynchronized and uncertain. They are unsynchronized because the payment of cash for raw materials does not happen at the same time as the receipt of cash from selling the product. They are uncertain because future sales and costs are not known with certainty.

Figure 27.3 depicts the short-term operating activities and cash flows for a typical manufacturing firm along the **cash flow timeline.** The **operating cycle** is the time interval between the arrival of inventory stock and the date when cash is collected from receivables. The **cash cycle** begins when cash is paid for materials and ends when cash is collected from receivables. The cash flow timeline consists of an operating cycle and a cash cycle. The need for short-term financial decision making is suggested by the gap between the cash inflows and cash outflows. This is related to the lengths of the operating cycle and the accounts payable period. This gap can be filled either by borrowing or by holding

FIGURE 27.3

Cash Flow Timeline and the Short-Term Operating Activities of a Typical Manufacturing Firm

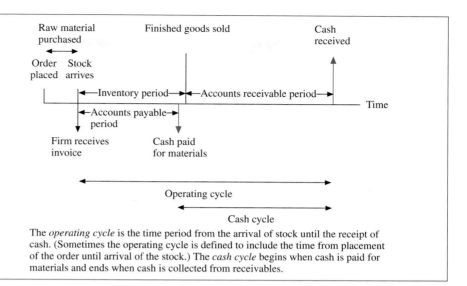

The *operating cycle* is the time period from the arrival of stock until the receipt of cash. (Sometimes the operating cycle is defined to include the time from placement of the order until arrival of the stock.) The *cash cycle* begins when cash is paid for materials and ends when cash is collected from receivables.

a liquidity reserve for marketable securities. The gap can be shortened by changing the inventory, receivable, and payable periods. Now we take a closer look at the operating cycle.

The length of the operating cycle is equal to the sum of the lengths of the inventory and accounts receivable periods. The *inventory period* is the length of time required to order, produce, and sell a product. The *accounts receivable period* is the length of time required to collect cash receipts.

The *cash cycle* is the time between cash disbursement and cash collection. It can be thought of as the operating cycle less the accounts payable period:

$$\text{Cash cycle} = \text{Operating cycle} - \text{Accounts payable period}$$

The *accounts payable period* is the length of time the firm is able to delay payment on the purchase of various resources, such as wages and raw materials.

In practice, the inventory period, the accounts receivable period, and the accounts payable period are measured by days in inventory, days in receivables, and days in payables, respectively. We illustrate how the operating cycle and the cash cycle can be measured in Example 27.1.

EXAMPLE 27.1

Tradewinds Manufacturing is a diversified manufacturing firm with the balance sheet and income statement shown in Table 27.1 for 20X1 and 20X2. The operating cycle and the cash cycle can be determined for Tradewinds after calculating the appropriate ratios for inventory, receivables, and payables. Consider inventory first:

$$\frac{\text{Average}}{\text{inventory}} = \frac{\$3 \text{ million} + \$2 \text{ million}}{2} = \$2.5 \text{ million}$$

The terms in the numerator are the ending inventory in the second and first years, respectively.
We next calculate the inventory turnover ratio:

$$\frac{\text{Inventory}}{\text{turnover ratio}} = \frac{\text{Cost of goods sold}}{\text{Average inventory}} = \frac{\$8.2 \text{ million}}{\$2.5 \text{ million}} = 3.3$$

This implies that the inventory cycle occurs 3.3 times a year. Finally, we calculate days in inventory:

$$\frac{\text{Days in}}{\text{inventory}} = \frac{365}{3.3} = 110.6 \text{ days}$$

Our calculation implies that the inventory cycle is slightly more than 110 days. We perform analogous calculations for receivables and payables:[3]

$$\frac{\text{Average}}{\substack{\text{accounts} \\ \text{receivable}}} = \frac{\$2.0 \text{ million} + \$1.6 \text{ million}}{2} = \$1.8 \text{ million}$$

$$\frac{\text{Average}}{\substack{\text{receivables} \\ \text{turnover}}} = \frac{\text{Credit sales}}{\text{Average accounts receivable}} = \frac{\$11.5 \text{ million}}{\$1.8 \text{ million}} = 6.4$$

$$\frac{\text{Days in}}{\text{receivables}} = \frac{365}{6.4} = 57 \text{ days}$$

$$\frac{\text{Average}}{\text{payables}} = \frac{\$1.0 \text{ million} + \$0.75 \text{ million}}{2} = \$0.875 \text{ million}$$

$$\frac{\text{Accounts payable}}{\text{deferral period}} = \frac{\text{Cost of goods sold}}{\text{Average payables}} = \frac{\$8.2 \text{ million}}{\$0.875 \text{ million}} = 9.4$$

$$\text{Days in payables} = \frac{365}{9.4} = 38.8 \text{ days}$$

These calculations allow us to determine both the operating cycle and the cash cycle:

$$\frac{\text{Operating}}{\text{cycle}} = \frac{\text{Days in}}{\text{inventory}} + \frac{\text{Days in}}{\text{receivables}}$$
$$= 110.6 \text{ days} + 57 \text{ days} = 167.6 \text{ days}$$

$$\frac{\text{Cash}}{\text{cycle}} = \frac{\text{Operating}}{\text{cycle}} - \frac{\text{Days in}}{\text{payables}}$$
$$= 167.6 \text{ days} - 38.8 \text{ days} = 128.8 \text{ days}.$$

Interpreting the Cash Cycle

Our examples show how the cash cycle depends on the inventory, receivables, and payables periods. Taken one at a time, the cash cycle increases as the inventory and receivables periods get longer. It decreases if the company is able to stall payment of payables, lengthening the payables period. Suppose a firm could purchase inventory, sell its product, collect receivables (perhaps selling for cash) and then pay suppliers all on the same day. This firm would have a cash cycle of zero days.

Some firms may meet this description but it is hard to think of many examples. Most firms have a positive cash cycle. Such firms require some additional financing for inventories and receivables. The longer the cash cycle, the more financing is required, other things being equal. Since bankers are conservative and dislike surprises, they monitor the firm's cash cycle. A lengthening cycle may indicate obsolete, unsaleable inventory or problems in collecting receivables. Unless these problems are detected and solved, the firm may require emergency financing or face insolvency.

---

[3]We assume that Tradewinds Manufacturing makes no cash sales.

Our calculations of the cash cycle used financial ratios introduced in Chapter 2. We can use some other ratio relationships from Chapter 2 to see how the cash cycle relates to profitability and sustainable growth. A good place to start is with the Du Pont equation for profitability as measured by return on assets (ROA):

$$\text{ROA} = \text{Profit margin} \times \text{Total asset turnover}$$
$$\text{Total asset turnover} = \text{Sales/Total assets}$$

Go back to the case of the firm with a lengthening cash cycle. Increased inventories and receivables that caused the cash cycle problem also reduce total asset turnover. The result is lower profitability. In other words, with more assets tied up over a longer cash cycle, the firm is less efficient and therefore less profitable. And, as if its troubles were not enough already, this firm suffers a drop in its sustainable growth rate.

Chapter 3 showed that total asset turnover is directly linked to sustainable growth. Reducing total asset turnover lowers sustainable growth. This makes sense because our troubled firm must divert its financial resources into financing excess inventory and receivables.

? Concept Questions
- **What does it mean to say that a firm has an inventory turnover ratio of 4?**
- **Describe the operating cycle and cash cycle. What are the differences between them?**

27.4 Some Aspects of Short-Term Financial Policy

The policy that a firm adopts for short-term finance will be composed of at least two elements:

1. *The size of the firm's investment in current assets.* This is usually measured relative to the firm's level of total operating revenues. A flexible or accommodative short-term financial policy would maintain a high ratio of current assets to sales. A restrictive short-term financial policy would entail a low ratio of current assets to sales.
2. *The financing of current assets.* This is measured as the proportion of short-term debt to long-term debt. A restrictive short-term financial policy means a high proportion of short-term debt relative to long-term financing, and a flexible policy means less short-term debt and more long-term debt.

The Size of the Firm's Investment in Current Assets

Flexible short-term financial policies include

1. Keeping large balances of cash and marketable securities.
2. Making large investments in inventory.
3. Granting liberal credit terms, which result in a high level of accounts receivable.

Restrictive short-term financial policies are

1. Keeping low cash balances and no investment in marketable securities.
2. Making small investments in inventory.
3. Allowing no credit sales and no accounts receivable.

Determining the optimal investment level in short-term assets requires an identification of the different costs of alternative short-term financing policies. The objective is to trade off the cost of restrictive policies against the cost of flexible policies to arrive at the best compromise.

Current asset holdings are highest with a flexible short-term financial policy and lowest with a restrictive policy. Thus, flexible short-term financial policies are costly in that they require higher cash outflows to finance cash and marketable securities, inventory, and accounts receivable. However, future cash inflows are highest with a flexible policy. Sales are stimulated by the use of a credit policy that provides liberal financing to customers. A large amount of inventory on hand ("on the shelf") provides a quick delivery service to customers and increases sales.[4] In addition, the firm can probably charge higher prices for the quick delivery service and the liberal credit terms of flexible policies. A flexible policy also may result in fewer production stoppages because of inventory shortages.[5]

Managing current assets can be thought of as involving a trade-off between costs that rise with the level of investment and costs that fall with the level of investment. Costs that rise with the level of investment in current assets are called **carrying costs.** Costs that fall with increases in the level of investment in current assets are called **shortage costs.**

Carrying costs are generally of two types. First, because the rate of return on current assets is low compared with that of other assets, there is an opportunity cost. Second, there is the cost of maintaining the economic value of the item. The cost of warehousing inventory is an example.

Shortage costs are incurred when the investment in current assets is low. If a firm runs out of cash, it will be forced to sell marketable securities. If a firm runs out of cash and cannot readily sell marketable securities, it may need to borrow or default on an obligation. (This general situation is called a *cash-out.*) If a firm has no inventory (a *stock-out*) or if it cannot extend credit to its customers, it will lose business.

There are two kinds of shortage costs:

1. *Trading or order costs.* Order costs are the costs of placing an order for more cash (*brokerage costs*) or more inventory (*production set-up costs*).

2. *Costs related to safety reserves.* These are costs of lost sales, lost customer goodwill, and disruption of production schedules.

Figure 27.4 illustrates the basic nature of carrying costs. The total costs of investing in current assets are determined by adding the carrying costs and the shortage costs. The minimum point on the total cost curve (CA*) reflects the optimal balance of current assets. The curve is generally quite flat at the optimum, and it is difficult, if not impossible, to find the precise optimal balance of shortage and carrying costs. Usually we are content with a choice near the optimum.

If carrying costs are low or shortage costs are high, the optimal policy calls for substantial current assets. In other words, the optimal policy is a flexible one. This is illustrated in the middle graph of Figure 27.4.

If carrying costs are high or shortage costs are low, the optimal policy is a restrictive one. That is, the optimal policy calls for modest current assets. This is illustrated in the bottom graph of the figure.

---

[4]This is true of some types of finished goods.

[5]This is true of inventory of raw material but not of finished goods.

FIGURE 27.4

Carrying Costs and Shortage Costs

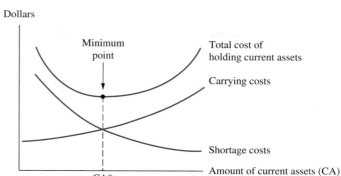

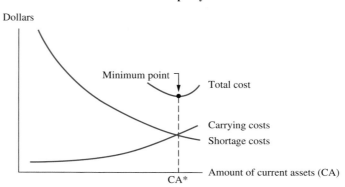

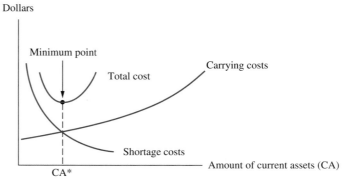

Carrying costs increase with the level of investment in current assets. They include both opportunity costs and the costs of maintaining the asset's economic value. *Shortage costs* decrease with increases in the level of investment in current assets. They include trading costs and the costs of running out of the current asset (for example, being short of cash).

*The optimal amount of current assets. This point minimizes costs.

Determinants of Corporate Liquid Asset Holdings

Firms with High Holdings of Liquid Assets Will Have	Firms with Low Holdings of Liquid Assets Will Have
High-growth opportunities	Low-growth opportunities
High-risk investments	Low-risk investments
Small firms	Large firms
Low-credit firms	High-credit firms

Firms will hold more liquid assets (i.e., cash and marketable securities) to ensure that they can continue investing when cash flow is low relative to positive NPV investment opportunities. Firms that have good access to capital markets will hold less-liquid assets.

Source: Tim Opler, Lee Pinkowitz, René Stulz, and Rohan Williamson, "The Determinants and Implication of Corporate Cash Holdings," *Journal of Financial Economics,* 52 (1999).

Opler, Pinkowitz, Stulz, and Williamson[6] examine the determinants of holdings of cash and marketable securities by publicly traded firms. They find evidence that firms behave according to the static trade-off model of short-term financial policy described earlier. Their study focuses only on liquid assets (i.e., cash and market securities), so that carrying costs are the opportunity costs of holding liquid assets and shortage costs are the risks of not having cash when investment opportunities are good.

Alternative Financing Policies for Current Assets

In the previous section we examined the level of investment in current assets. Now we turn to the level of current liabilities, assuming the investment in current assets is optimal.

An Ideal Model   In an ideal economy, short-term assets can always be financed with short-term debt, and long-term assets can be financed with long-term debt and equity. In this economy, net working capital is always zero.

Imagine the simple case of a grain elevator operator. Grain elevator operators buy crops after harvest, store them, and sell them during the year. They have high inventories of grain after the harvest and end with low inventories just before the next harvest.

Bank loans with maturities of less than one year are used to finance the purchase of grain. These loans are paid with the proceeds from the sale of grain.

The situation is shown in Figure 27.5. Long-term assets are assumed to grow over time, whereas current assets increase at the end of the harvest and then decline during the year. Short-term assets end at zero just before the next harvest. These assets are financed by short-term debt, and long-term assets are financed with long-term debt and equity. Net working capital—current assets minus current liabilities—is always zero.

Different Strategies in Financing Current Assets   Current assets cannot be expected to drop to zero in the real world because a long-term rising level of sales will result

---

[6]Tim Opler, Lee Pinkowitz, René Stulz, and Rohan Williamson, "The Determinants and Implication of Corporate Cash Holdings," *Journal of Financial Economics,* 52 (1999).

FIGURE 27.5

Financing Policy for an Idealized Economy

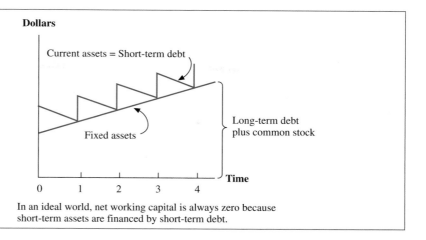

Dollars

Current assets = Short-term debt

Fixed assets

Long-term debt plus common stock

Time

0   1   2   3   4

In an ideal world, net working capital is always zero because short-term assets are financed by short-term debt.

in some permanent investment in current assets. A growing firm can be thought of as having both a permanent requirement for current assets and one for long-term assets. This total asset requirement will exhibit balances over time reflecting (1) a secular growth trend, (2) a seasonal variation around the trend, and (3) unpredictable day-to-day and month-to-month fluctuations. This is depicted in Figure 27.6. (We have not tried to show the unpredictable day-to-day and month-to-month variations in the total asset requirement.)

Now, let us look at how this asset requirement is financed. First, consider the strategy (strategy *F* in Figure 27.7) where long-term financing covers more than the total asset requirement, even at seasonal peaks. The firm will have excess cash available for investment in marketable securities when the total asset requirement falls from peaks. Because this approach implies chronic short-term cash surpluses and a large investment in net working capital, it is considered a flexible strategy.

When long-term financing does not cover the total asset requirement, the firm must borrow short-term to make up the deficit. This restrictive strategy is labelled strategy *R* in Figure 27.7.

Which Is Better?   Which is the more appropriate amount of short-term borrowing? There is no definitive answer. Several considerations must be included in a proper analysis:

1. *Cash reserves.* The flexible financing strategy implies surplus cash and little short-term borrowing. This strategy reduces the probability that a firm will experience financial

FIGURE 27.6

The Total Asset Requirement Over Time

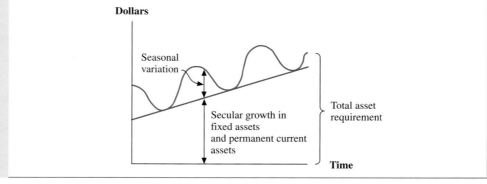

Dollars

Seasonal variation

Secular growth in fixed assets and permanent current assets

Total asset requirement

Time

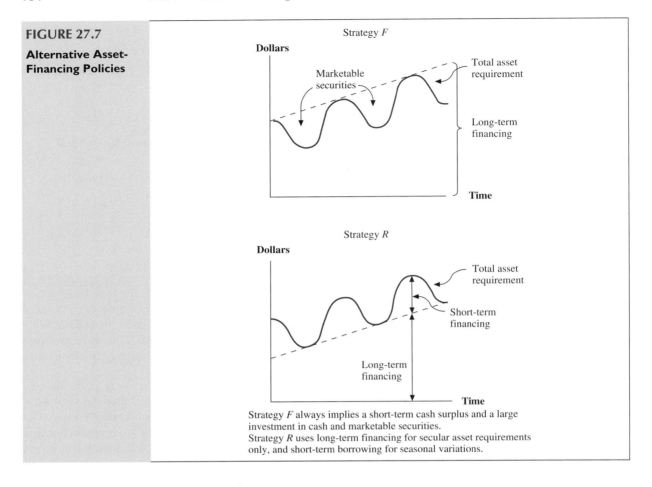

Strategy *F* always implies a short-term cash surplus and a large investment in cash and marketable securities.
Strategy *R* uses long-term financing for secular asset requirements only, and short-term borrowing for seasonal variations.

distress. Firms may not need to worry as much about meeting recurring, short-run obligations. However, investments in cash and marketable securities are zero net present value investments at best.

2. *Maturity hedging.* Most firms finance inventories with short-term bank loans, but pay for fixed assets with long-term financing. Firms tend to avoid financing long-lived assets with short-term borrowing. This type of maturity mismatching would necessitate frequent refinancing and is inherently risky because short-term interest rates are more volatile than longer rates.

3. *Term structure.* Short-term interest rates are normally lower than long-term interest rates. This implies that, on average, it is more costly to rely on long-term borrowing than on short-term borrowing.

Current Assets and Liabilities in Practice

Table 27.3 shows that current assets made up approximately 43.78 percent of all assets for Canadian Tire in 2006. For small firms, especially in the retailing and service sectors, current assets make up an even larger portion of total assets.

Over time, advances in technology will change the way Canadian firms manage current assets. With new techniques such as just-in-time inventory and business-to-business

TABLE 27.3
Current Assets and Current Liabilities as Percentages of Total Assets for Canadian Tire, 2005–2006

	2006	2005
Current assets:		
Cash and cash equivalents	12.77%	14.07%
Accounts receivable	5.87	10.96
Loans receivable	11.96	12.24
Inventories	11.50	11.34
Prepaid expenses and deposits	0.80	0.71
Future income taxes	0.89	0.73
	43.78%	50.05%
Current Liabilities		
Accounts payable and other	52.31%	49.15%
Income taxes payable	2.69	2.26
Current portion of long-term debt	0.10	6.50
	55.10%	57.91%

Source: Drawn from Canadian Tire *Annual Report,* 2006.

e-business (B2B) sales, industrial firms are moving away from flexible policies and toward a more restrictive approach to current assets.

Current liabilities are also declining as a percentage of total assets. Firms are practicing maturity hedging as they match lower current liabilities with decreased current assets. In addition to these differences over time, there are differences between industries in policies on current assets and liabilities.

The cash cycle is longer in some industries than in others, while various products and industry practices require different levels of inventory and receivables. For example, the drop in accounts receivable as a percentage of total assets for Canadian Tire can be attributed to a securitization program that Canadian Tire initiated for 2006. This is why we saw in Appendix 2A that industry average ratios are not the same. For example, the aircraft industry carries more than five times as much inventory as printing and publishing carries. Does this mean that aircraft manufacturers are less efficient? Most likely the higher inventory consists of airplanes under construction. Because building planes takes more time than most printing processes, it makes sense that aircraft manufacturers carry higher inventories than printing and publishing firms.

? Concept Questions

- **What keeps the real world from being an ideal one where net working capital can always be zero?**
- **What considerations determine the optimal compromise between flexible and restrictive net working capital policies?**

27.5 Cash Budgeting

The **cash budget** is a primary tool of short-run financial planning. It allows the financial manager to identify short-term financing needs (and opportunities). It will tell the manager the required borrowing in the short term. It is a way of identifying the cash flow gap on the cash flow time line. The idea of the cash budget is simple: It records estimates of cash receipts and disbursements. We illustrate cash budgeting in Example 27.2.

EXAMPLE 27.2

All of Fun Toys' cash inflows come from the sale of toys. Cash budgeting for Fun Toys starts with a sales forecast for the next year, by quarter:

	First Quarter	Second Quarter	Third Quarter	Fourth Quarter
Sales (in $ millions)	$100	$200	$150	$100

Fun Toys' fiscal year starts on July 1. Fun Toys' sales are seasonal and are usually very high in the second quarter, due to Christmas sales. But Fun Toys sells to department stores on credit, and sales do not generate cash immediately. Instead, cash comes later from collections on accounts receivable. Fun Toys has a 90-day collection period, and 100 percent of sales are collected the following quarter. In other words,

$$\text{Collections} = \text{Last quarter's sales}$$

This relationship implies that

$$\text{Accounts receivable at end of last quarter} = \text{Last quarter's sales} \qquad (27.5)$$

We assume that sales in the fourth quarter of the previous fiscal year were $100 million. From Equation (27.5), we know that accounts receivable at the end of the fourth quarter of the previous fiscal year were $100 million and collections in the first quarter of the current fiscal year are $100 million.

The first-quarter sales of the current fiscal year of $100 million are added to the accounts receivable, but $100 million of collections are subtracted. Therefore, Fun Toys ended the first quarter with accounts receivable of $100 million. The basic relation is

$$\text{Ending accounts receivable} = \text{Starting accounts receivable} + \text{Sales} - \text{Collections}$$

Table 27.4 shows cash collections for Fun Toys for the next four quarters. Though collections are the only source of cash here, this need not always be the case. Other sources of cash could include sales of assets, investment income, and long-term financing.

TABLE 27.4
Sources of Cash (in $ millions)

	First Quarter	Second Quarter	Third Quarter	Fourth Quarter
Sales	$100	$200	$150	$100
Cash collections	100	100	200	150
Starting receivables	100	100	200	150
Ending receivables	100	200	150	100

Cash Outflow

Next, we consider the cash disbursements. They can be put into four basic categories, as shown in Table 27.5.

1. *Payments of accounts payable.* These are payments for goods or services, such as raw materials. These payments will generally be made after purchases. Purchases will depend on the sales forecast. In the case of Fun Toys, assume that

$$\text{Payments} = \text{Last quarter's purchases}$$
$$\text{Purchases} = 1/2 \text{ of next quarter's sales forecast}$$

TABLE 27.5
Disbursement of Cash (in $ millions)

	First Quarter	Second Quarter	Third Quarter	Fourth Quarter
Sales	$100	$200	$150	$100
Purchases	100	75	50	50
Uses of cash				
Payments of accounts payable	50	100	75	50
Wages, taxes, and other expenses	20	40	30	20
Capital expenditures	0	0	0	100
Long-term financing expenses: interest and dividends	10	10	10	10
Total uses of cash	$ 80	$150	$115	$180

2. *Wages, taxes, and other expenses.* This category includes all other normal costs of doing business that require actual expenditures. Depreciation, for example, is often thought of as a normal cost of business, but it requires no cash outflow.

3. *Capital expenditures.* These are payments of cash for long-lived assets. Fun Toys plans a major capital expenditure in the fourth quarter.

4. *Long-term financing.* This category includes interest and principal payments on long-term outstanding debt and dividend payments to shareholders.

The total forecasted outflow appears in the last line of Table 27.5.

The Cash Balance

The net cash balance appears in Table 27.6, and a large net cash outflow is forecast in the second quarter. This large outflow is not caused by an inability to earn a profit. Rather, it results from delayed collections on sales. This results in a cumulative cash shortfall of $30 million in the second quarter.

Fun Toys had established a minimum operating cash balance equal to $5 million to facilitate transactions and to protect against unexpected contingencies. This means that it has a cash shortfall in the second quarter equal to $35 million.

? Concept Questions
- How would you conduct a sensitivity analysis for Fun Toys' net cash balance?
- What could you learn from such an analysis?

TABLE 27.6
The Cash Balance (in $ millions)

	First Quarter	Second Quarter	Third Quarter	Fourth Quarter
Total cash receipts	$100	$100	$200	$150
Total cash disbursements	80	150	115	180
Net cash flow	20	(50)	85	(30)
Cumulative excess cash balance	20	(30)	55	25
Minimum cash balance	5	5	5	5
Cumulative finance surplus (deficit) requirement	15	(35)	50	20

27.6 The Short-Term Financial Plan

Short-Term Planning and Risk

The short-term financial plan represents Fun Toys' "best guess" for the future. Large firms go beyond the "best guess" to ask "what if" questions using scenario analysis, sensitivity analysis, and simulation. We introduced these techniques in Chapter 9's discussion of project analysis. They are tools for assessing the degree of forecasting risk and identifying those components that are most critical to a financial plan's success or failure.

Recall that scenario analysis involves varying the base case plan to create several others: a best case, worst case, and so on. Each will produce different financing needs to give the financial manager a first look at risk.

Sensitivity analysis is a variation on scenario analysis that is useful in pinpointing areas where forecasting risk is especially severe. The basic idea of sensitivity analysis is to freeze all variables except one and then see how sensitive our estimate of financing needs is to changes in that one variable. If our projected financing turns out to be very sensitive to, say, sales, then we know that extra effort in refining the sales forecast will pay off.

Since the original financial plan was almost surely developed on a computer spreadsheet, scenario and sensitivity analysis are quite straightforward and widely used.

Simulation analysis combines features of scenario and sensitivity analysis, varying all variables over a range of outcomes simultaneously. Simulation analysis yields a probability distribution of financing needs.

Air Canada uses simulation analysis in forecasting its cash needs. The simulation is useful in capturing the variability of cash flow components in Canada's airline industry. Bad weather, for example, causes delays and cancelled flights with unpredictable dislocation payments to travellers and crew overtime. This and other risks are reflected in a probability distribution of cash needs, giving the treasurer better information for planning borrowing needs.

Short-Term Borrowing

Fun Toys has a short-term financing problem. It cannot meet the forecasted cash outflows in the second quarter from internal sources. In addition, much of the cash deficit comes from the large capital expenditure. Arguably, this is a candidate for long-term financing. If it chose equity financing through an initial public offering (IPO), Fun Toys would be following the example of Chapters Online. As the firm's Internet division, Chapters Online sold books, CD ROMs, DVDs, and videos through its website. In September 1999, Chapters Online went public, raising equity at an offering price of $13.50 per share. A little under a year later, in August 2000, analysts calculated Chapters Online's "burn rate," the rate at which the firm was using cash, to determine its cash position. Given that the stock price had fallen from the offering price of $13.50 to $2.80 per share, a further equity offering seemed unlikely and the discussion of the firm's financial health focused on the availability of short-term borrowing.

Here we concentrate on two short-term borrowing alternatives: (1) unsecured borrowing and (2) secured borrowing.

Operating Loans   The most common way to finance a temporary cash deficit is to arrange a short-term, **operating loan** from a chartered bank. This is an agreement under which a firm is authorized to borrow up to a specified amount for a given period, usually one year (much like a credit card).[7] Operating loans can be either unsecured or secured by collateral. Large corporations with excellent credit ratings usually structure the facility as an unsecured line of credit. Because unsecured credit lines are backed only by projections of future cash flows, bankers offer this "cash flow" lending only to top-drawer credits.

Short-term lines of credit are classified as either *committed* or *noncommitted*. The latter is an informal arrangement. Committed lines of credit are more formal, legal arrangements and usually involve a commitment fee paid by the firm to the bank. (Usually the fee is on the order of 0.25 percent of the total committed funds per year.) A firm that pays a commitment fee for a committed line of credit is essentially buying insurance to guarantee that the bank cannot back out of the arrangement (absent some material change in the borrower's status).

Compensating the Bank   The interest rate on an operating loan is typically set equal to the bank's prime lending rate plus an additional percentage, and the rate will usually float. For example, suppose that the prime rate is 3 percent when the loan is initiated and the loan is at prime plus 1.5 percent. The original rate charged the borrower is 4.5 percent. If after, say, 125 days, prime increases to 3.5 percent, the company's borrowing rate goes up to 5 percent and interest charges are adjusted accordingly.

The premium charged over prime will reflect the banker's assessment of the borrower's risk. Table 27.7 lists factors bankers use in assessing risk in loans to small business. Notice that risks related to management appear most often since poor management is considered the major risk with small business. There is a trend among bankers to look more closely at industry and economic risk factors. A similar set of risk factors applies to loans to large corporations.

Banks are in the business of lending mainly to low-risk borrowers. For this reason, bankers generally prefer to decline risky business loans that would require an interest rate above prime plus 3 percent. Many of the loan requests that banks turn down are from small businesses, especially start-ups. Around 60 percent of these "turn-downs" find financing elsewhere. Alternative sources include venture capital financing (discussed in Chapter 20) and federal and provincial government programs to assist small business.

In addition to charging interest, banks also levy fees for account activity and loan management. Small businesses may also pay application fees to cover the costs of processing loan applications. Fees are becoming increasingly important in bank compensation.[8] Fees and other details of any short-term business lending arrangements are highly negotiable. Banks will generally work with firms to design a package of fees and interest.

Letters of Credit   A **letter of credit** is a common arrangement in international finance. With a letter of credit, the bank issuing the letter promises to make a loan if certain conditions are met. Typically, the letter guarantees payment on a shipment of goods provided that the goods arrive as promised. A letter of credit can be revocable (subject to cancellation) or irrevocable (not subject to cancellation if the specified conditions are met).

---

[7]Descriptions of bank loans draw on L. Wynant and J. Hatch, *Banks and Small Business Borrowers* (London: University of Western Ontario, 1990).

[8]U.S. banks sometimes require that the firm keep some account of money on deposit. This is called a *compensating balance.* A compensating balance is some of the firm's money kept by the bank in low-interest or non–interest-bearing accounts. By leaving these funds with the bank and receiving no interest, the firm further increases the effective interest rate earned by the bank on the line of credit, thereby compensating the bank.

TABLE 27.7
Factors Mentioned in the Credit Files (1539 cases)

Factor	Percentage of Mentions
1. Economic environment	
Opportunities and risks	6.1%
2. Industry environment	
Competitive conditions, prospects, and risks	40.4
3. Client's marketing activities	
Strategies, strengths, and weaknesses	30.8
4. Firm's operations management	
Strengths and weaknesses	59.5
5. Client's financial resources, skills, and performance	
Financial management expertise	44.9
Historical or future profitability	84.8
Future cash flows	41.6
Future financing needs (beyond the current year)	20.5
6. Management capabilities and character	
Strengths and weaknesses	79.6
Length of ownership of the firm	95.1
Past management experience relevant to the business	57.1
7. Collateral security and the firm's net worth position	97.7
8. Borrower's past relationship with bank	65.3

Source: Larry Wynant and James Hatch, *Banks and Small Business Borrowers* (London: University of Western Ontario, 1990), p. 136.

Secured Loans   Banks and other financial institutions often require *security* for a loan. Security for short-term loans usually consists of accounts receivable or inventories. Table 27.7 shows that collateral security is a factor in virtually every small business loan. In addition, banks routinely limit risk through loan conditions called **covenants.** Table 27.8 lists common covenants in Canadian small business loans. You can see that bankers expect to have a detailed knowledge of their clients' businesses.

Under **accounts receivable financing,** receivables are either *assigned* or *factored.* Under assignment, the lender not only has a lien on the receivables but also has recourse to the borrower. Factoring involves the sale of accounts receivable. The purchaser, who

TABLE 27.8
Loan Conditions for Approved Bank Credits in the Credit File Sample (1382 cases)

Condition	Percentage of Cases*
Postponement of shareholder claims	39.8%
Life insurance on key principals	39.4
Fire insurance on company premises	35.7
Accounts receivable and inventory reporting	27.8
Limits on withdrawals and dividends	11.9
Limits on capital expenditures	10.5
Maintenance of minimum working capital levels	2.9
Restrictions on further debt	2.5
Restrictions on disposal of company assets	1.7
Maintenance of minimum cash balances	0.9
Other conditions	6.2

*Total is over 100 percent because of multiple responses.

Source: Larry Wynant and James Hatch, *Banks and Small Business Borrowers* (London: University of Western Ontario, 1990), p. 173.

is called a *factor,* must then collect on the receivables. The factor assumes the full risk of default on bad accounts.

Financial engineers have come up with a new approach to receivables financing. When a large corporation like Sears Canada Ltd. *securitized* receivables, it sold them to Sears Canada Receivables Trust (SCRT), a wholly owned subsidiary. SCRT issued debentures and commercial paper backed by a diversified portfolio of receivables. Since receivables are liquid, SCRT debt is less risky than lending to Sears Canada and the company benefits through interest savings.[9]

As the name implies, an **inventory loan** uses inventory as collateral. Some common types of inventory loans are

1. *Blanket inventory lien.* The blanket inventory lien gives the lender a lien against all the borrower's inventories.

2. *Trust receipt.* Under this arrangement, the borrower holds the inventory in trust for the lender. The document acknowledging the loan is called the *trust receipt.* Proceeds from the sale of inventory are remitted immediately to the lender.

3. *Field warehouse financing.* In field warehouse financing, a public warehouse company supervises the inventory for the lender.

When a firm purchases supplies on credit, the increase in accounts payable is a source of funds and automatic financing. As compared with bank financing, **trade credit** has the advantage of arising automatically from the firm's business. It does not require a formal financing agreement with covenants that may restrict the borrower's business activities. Suppliers offer credit to remain competitive; in many industries, the terms of credit include a cash discount for paying within a certain period.

Other Sources   There are a variety of other sources of short-term funds employed by corporations. The most important of these are the issuance of **commercial paper** and financing through **banker's acceptances.**

Commercial paper consists of short-term notes issued by large and highly rated firms. Firms issuing commercial paper in Canada generally have borrowing needs over $20 million. Rating agencies—the Dominion Bond Rating Service and Standard & Poor's (discussed in Chapter 21)—rate commercial paper similarly to bonds. Typically, these notes are of short maturity, ranging from 30 to 90 days with some maturities up to 365 days. Commercial paper is offered in denominations of $100,000 and up. Because the firm issues paper directly and because it usually backs the issue with a special bank line of credit, the interest rate the firm obtains is below the rate a bank would charge for a direct loan (usually by around 1 percent). Another advantage is that commercial paper offers the issuer flexibility in tailoring the maturity and size of the borrowing.

Banker's acceptances are a variant on commercial paper. When a bank "accepts" paper, it charges a stamping fee in return for a guarantee of the paper's principal and interest. Stamping fees vary from 0.20 percent to 0.75 percent. Banker's acceptances are more widely used than commercial paper in Canada because Canadian chartered banks enjoy stronger credit ratings than all but the largest corporations.[10] The main buyers of banker's acceptances and commercial paper are institutions including mutual funds, insurance companies, and banks.[11]

---

[9]M. Evans, "Sears Securitizes Some of Its Assets," *Financial Post* (November 19, 1991).

[10]The reverse situation prevails in the United States.

[11]Our discussion of commercial paper and banker's acceptances draws on "The Canadian Commercial Paper Market: Myth and Reality," *Canadian Treasury Management Review* (March–April 1991); and D. Hogarth, "Quick Money Peps Poor Balance Sheets," *Financial Post* (December 17, 1990).

A disadvantage of borrowing through banker's acceptances or commercial paper is the risk that the market might temporarily dry up when it comes time to "roll over" the paper.

? Concept Questions

- **What are the two basic forms of short-term financing?**
- **Describe two types of secured loans.**

27.7 SUMMARY AND CONCLUSIONS

1. This chapter introduces the management of short-term finance. Short-term finance involves short-lived assets and liabilities. We trace and examine the short-term sources and uses of cash as they appear on the firm's financial statements. We see how current assets and current liabilities arise in the short-term operating activities and the cash cycle of the firm. From an accounting perspective, short-term finance involves net working capital.

2. Managing short-term cash flows involves the minimization of costs. The two major costs are carrying costs (the interest and related costs incurred by overinvesting in short-term assets such as cash) and shortage costs (the cost of running out of short-term assets). The objective of managing short-term finance and of short-term financial planning is to find the optimal trade-off between these two costs.

3. In an ideal economy, the firm could perfectly predict its short-term uses and sources of cash, and net working capital could be kept at zero. In the real world, net working capital provides a buffer that lets the firm meet its ongoing obligations. The financial manager seeks the optimal level of each of the current assets.

4. The financial manager can use the cash budget to identify short-term financial needs. The cash budget tells the manager what borrowing is required or what lending will be possible in the short run. The firm has available to it a number of possible ways of acquiring funds to meet short-term shortfalls, including unsecured and secured loans.

KEY TERMS

Accounts receivable financing 790
Banker's acceptance 791
Carrying costs 780
Cash budget 785
Cash cycle 776
Cash flow timeline 776
Commercial paper 791
Covenant 790
Inventory loan 791
Letter of credit 789
Liquidity 772
Operating cycle 776
Operating loan 788
Shortage costs 780
Short-run operating activities 776
Trade credit 791

SUGGESTED READING

Books that describe working capital management include:
N. C. Hill and W. L. Sartoris. *Short-Term Financial Management.* New York: Macmillan, 1988.
J. C. Kallberg and K. Parkinson. *Corporate Liquidity: Management and Measurement.* Burr Ridge, IL: Irwin/McGraw-Hill, 1996.

QUESTIONS & PROBLEMS

Tracing Cash and Net Working Capital

27.1 Derive the cash equation from the basic balance sheet equation: Assets = Liabilities + Equity.

27.2 Indicate whether the following corporate actions increase, decrease, or cause no change to cash.
a. Cash is paid for raw materials purchased for inventory.
b. A dividend is paid.
c. Merchandise is sold on credit.
d. Common stock is issued.
e. Raw material is purchased for inventory on credit.

f. A piece of machinery is purchased and paid for with long-term debt.

g. Payments for previous sales are collected.

h. Accumulated depreciation is increased.

i. Merchandise is sold for cash.

j. Payment is made for a previous purchase.

k. A short-term bank loan is received.

l. A dividend is paid with funds received from a sale of common stock.

m. Allowance for bad debts is decreased.

n. A piece of office equipment is purchased and paid for with a short-term note.

o. Marketable securities are purchased with retained earnings.

p. Last year's taxes are paid.

q. This year's tax liability is increased.

r. Interest on long-term debt is paid.

Defining Cash In Terms of Other Elements

EXCEL

27.3 Below are the 20X9 balance sheet and income statement for Kountry Kettles Inc. Use this information to construct a sources and uses of cash statement.

Kountry Kettles Inc.
Balance Sheet
December 31, 20X9

	20X9	20X8
Assets		
Cash	$ 50,250	$ 42,000
Accounts receivable	103,675	94,250
Inventory	80,325	78,750
Property, plant, equipment	191,542	181,475
Less: Accumulated depreciation	67,327	61,475
Total assets	$358,465	$335,000
Liabilities and Equity		
Accounts payable	$ 23,243	$ 60,500
Accrued expenses	4,021	5,150
Long-term debt	15,000	15,000
Common stock	29,000	28,000
Retained earnings	287,201	226,350
Total liabilities and equity	$358,465	$335,000

Kountry Kettles Inc.
Income Statement
20X9

Net sales	$ 856,800
Cost of goods sold	514,080
Sales, general, and administrative costs	102,816
Advertising	29,988
Rent	50,400
Depreciation	5,852
Profit before taxes	153,664
Taxes	52,246
Net profit	$ 101,418
Dividends	$ 40,567
Retained earnings	$ 60,851

27.4   The following are the 20X2 balance sheet and income statement for the S/B Corporation. Use them to construct a sources and uses of cash statement.

S/B Corporation
Balance Sheet
December 31, 20X2
(in thousands)

	20X2	20X1
Assets		
Cash	$ 543	$ 388
Accounts receivable	2,058	1,470
Inventory	3,728	2,663
Net fixed assets	10,850	9,314
Total assets	$17,179	$13,835
Liabilities and Equity		
Accounts payable	$ 1,824	$ 282
Bank loan payable	1,820	1,300
Taxes payable	(25)	(33)
Accrued expenses payable	1,386	95
Mortgage	4,000	4,000
Common stock	4,000	4,000
Retained earnings	4,175	4,191
Total liabilities and equity	$17,180	$13,835

S/B Corporation
Income Statement 20X2
(in thousands)

Net sales	$1,121
Cost of goods sold:	
Materials	709
Overhead	70
Depreciation	54
Gross profit	287
Selling and administrative costs	107
Profit before taxes	181
Taxes	60
Net profit	$ 24
Dividends paid	$ 40

The Operating Cycle and Cost Cycle

27.5   On Eastern Printing Machines Co.'s income statement of 20X1, the cost of goods sold and the credit sales are $250 million and $297 million, respectively. The following data are from its balance sheets.

	($ millions)	
	Dec. 31, 20X1	Dec. 31, 20X2
Inventory	$42	$58
Accounts receivable	31	52
Accounts payable	11	30

a. How many days is Eastern Printing Machines' operating cycle?
b. How many days is Eastern Printing Machines' cash cycle?

27.6   Indicate the effect that the following will have on the operating cycle. Indicate whether there is an increase, a decrease, or no change.
  a.   Receivables average goes up.
  b.   Credit repayment times for customers are increased.
  c.   Inventory turnover goes from 3 times to 6 times.
  d.   Payables turnover goes from 6 times to 11 times.
  e.   Receivables turnover goes from 7 times to 9 times.
  f.   Payments to suppliers are accelerated.

27.7   Indicate the impact of the following on the cash and operating cycles, respectively. Indicate whether there is an increase, a decrease, or no change.
  a.   The terms of cash discounts offered to customers are made less favourable.
  b.   The cash discounts offered by suppliers are increased; thus, payments are made earlier.
  c.   An increased number of customers begin to pay in cash instead of with credit.
  d.   Fewer raw materials than usual are purchased.
  e.   A greater percentage of raw material purchases are paid for with credit.
  f.   More finished goods are produced for inventory instead of for order.

Some Aspects of Short-Term Financial Policy

27.8   Zeus and Mount Olympus are competing manufacturing firms. Their financial statements are printed below.
  a.   How are the current assets of each firm financed?
  b.   Which firm has the larger investment in current assets? Why?
  c.   Which firm is more likely to incur carrying costs, and which is more likely to incur shortage costs? Why?

ZEUS
Balance Sheet
December 31, 20X2

	20X2	20X1
Assets		
Cash	$ 18,021	$ 13,862
Net accounts receivable	27,100	23,887
Inventory	66,580	54,867
Total current assets	111,701	92,616
Fixed assets		
Property, plant, equipment	105,890	101,543
Less: Accumulated depreciation	37,287	34,331
Prepaid expenses	2,048	1,914
Other assets	14,975	13,052
Total assets	$197,327	$174,794
Liabilities and Equity		
Current liabilities:		
Accounts payable	$ 8,442	$ 6,494
Notes payable	13,628	10,483
Accrued expenses	9,649	7,422
Other taxes payable	12,901	9,924
Total current liabilities	44,620	34,323
Long-term debt	22,036	22,036
Total liabilities	$ 66,656	$ 56,359
Equity:		
Common stock	50,000	50,000
Retained earnings	80,670	68,435
Total equity	130,670	118,435
Total liabilities and equity	$197,326	$174,794

ZEUS
Income Statement
20X2

Income:	
Sales	$211,574
Other income	1,303
Total income	212,876
Operating expenses:	
Costs of goods sold	134,641
Selling and administrative expenses	37,044
Depreciation	2,956
Total expenses	174,641
Pretax earnings	38,236
Taxes	7,647
Net earnings	$ 30,588
Dividends	$ 18,353
Retained earnings	$ 12,235

Mount Olympus
Balance Sheet
December 31, 20X2

	20X2	20X1
Assets		
Cash	$ 11,741	$ 5,794
Net accounts receivable	27,100	26,177
Inventory	47,361	46,463
Total current assets	86,202	78,434
Fixed assets		
Property, plant, equipment	40,291	31,842
Less: Accumulated depreciation	20,220	19,297
Prepaid expenses	816	763
Other assets	3,420	1,601
Total assets	$110,509	$ 93,343
Liabilities and Equity		
Current liabilities:		
Accounts payable	$ 7,810	$ 6,008
Bank loans	1,520	3,722
Accrued expenses	5,530	4,254
Other taxes payable	6,870	5,688
Total current liabilities	21,731	19,672
Equity:		
Common stock	26,200	26,200
Retained earnings	62,578	47,471
Total equity	88,778	73,671
Total liabilities and equity	$110,509	$ 93,343

Mount Olympus
Income Statement
20X2

Income:	
Sales	$127,924
Other income	1,280
Total income	129,204
Operating expenses:	
Costs of goods sold	67,898
Selling and administrative expenses	28,909
Depreciation	923
Total expenses	97,730
Pretax earnings	31,474
Taxes	12,589
Net earnings	$ 18,884
Dividends	$ 3,777
Retained earnings	$ 15,107

27.9   In an ideal economy, net working capital is always zero. Why might net working capital be greater than zero in the real world?

Cash Budgeting

27.10 The following is the sales budget for the Smithe and Wreston Company for the first quarter of 20X1.

	January	February	March
Sales budget	$105,000	$100,000	$125,000

The aging of credit sales is
- 25 percent collected in the month of sale.
- 37 percent collected in the month after sale.

The accounts receivable balance at the end of the previous quarter is $36,000; $30,000 of that amount is uncollected December sales.
a. Compute the sales for December.
b. Compute the cash collections from sales for each month from January through March.

27.11 The sales budget for your company in the coming year is based on a 17 percent quarterly growth rate with the first-quarter projection at $100 million. In addition to this basic trend, the seasonal adjustments for the four quarters are 0, −10, −5, and 15 million dollars, respectively. Generally, 40 percent of the sales can be collected within the month and 40 percent in the following month; the rest of the sales are bad debt. All sales are credit sales. Compute the cash collections from sales for each quarter from the second to the fourth quarter.

27.12 Below are some important figures from the budget of Pine Mulch Company for the second quarter of 20X2.

	April	May	June
Credit sales	$175,000	$135,000	$205,000
Credit purchases	71,000	69,000	87,000
Cash disbursements:			
Wages, taxes, and expenses	8,000	7,000	8,400
Interest	4,000	4,000	4,000
Equipment purchases	52,000		2,500

The company predicts that 11 percent of its sales will never be collected; 45 percent of its sales will be collected in the month of the sale; and the rest of its sales will be collected in the following month. Purchases on trade accounts will be paid in the month following the purchase. In March 20X2 the sales were $250,000.

Use this information to complete the following cash budget:

	April	May	June
Beginning cash balance	$196,000		
Cash receipts:			
Cash collections from credit sales			
Total cash available			
Cash disbursements:			
Pay credit purchases	$ 71,520		
Wages, taxes, and expenses			
Interest			
Equipment purchases			
Total cash disbursed			
Ending cash balance			

27.13 What are the most important considerations in deciding the most appropriate amount of short-term borrowing?

The Short-Term Financial Plan

27.14 List several short-term external financing options.

27.15 Locate the annual balance sheets for Rogers Communications Inc. (RCI.A) and Barrick Gold Corporation (ABX). What is the cash amount as the percentage of assets for each company over the past two years? Why would these companies hold such different amounts of cash?

MINICASE: Keafer Manufacturing Working Capital Management

You have recently been hired by Keafer Manufacturing to work in its established treasury department. Keafer Manufacturing is a small company that produces highly customized cardboard boxes in a variety of sizes for different purchasers. Adam Keafer, the owner of the company, works primarily in the sales and production areas of the company. Currently, the company puts all receivables in one pile and all payables in another, and a part-time book keeper periodically comes in and attacks the piles. Because of this disorganized system, the finance area needs work, and that is what you have been brought in to do.

The company currently has a cash balance of $115,000, and it plans to purchase new machinery in the third quarter at a cost of $200,000. The purchase of the machinery will be made with cash because of the discount offered for a cash purchase. Adam wants to maintain a minimum cash balance of $90,000 to guard against unforeseen contingencies. All Keafer's sales to customers and purchases from suppliers are made with credit, and no discounts are offered or taken.

The company had the following sales each quarter of the year just ended:

	Q1	Q2	Q3	Q4
Gross Sales	$565,000	$585,000	$628,000	$545,000

After initial research and discussions with customers, you have projected that sales will be 8 percent higher in each quarter next year. Sales for the first quarter of the following year are also expected to grow at 8 percent. You calculate that Keafer currently has an accounts receivable period of 57 days and an accounts receivable balance of $426,000. However, 10 percent of the accounts receivable balance is from a company that has just entered bankruptcy, and it is likely that this portion will not be collected.

You have also calculated that Keafer typically orders supplies each quarter in the amount of 50 percent of the next quarter's projected gross sales, and suppliers are paid in 53 days on average. Wages, taxes, and other costs run about 25 percent of gross sales. The company has a quarterly interest payment of $120,000 on its long-term debt. Finally, the company uses a local bank for its short-term financial needs. It currently pays 1.2 percent per quarter on all short-term borrowing and maintains a money market account that pays .5 percent per quarter on all short-term deposits.

Adam has asked you to prepare a cash budget and short-term financial plan for the company under the current policies. He has also asked you to prepare additional plans based on changes in several inputs.

1. Use the numbers given to complete the cash budget and short-term financial plan.
2. Rework the cash budget and short-term financial plan assuming Keafer changes to a minimum cash balance of $70,000.
3. Rework the sales budget assuming an 11 percent growth rate in sales and a 5 percent growth rate in sales. Assume a $90,000 target cash balance.
4. Assuming the company maintains its target cash balance at $90,000, what sales growth rate would result in a zero need for short-term financing? To answer this question, you may need to set up a spreadsheet and use the "Solver" function.

Chapter 28

Cash Management

EXECUTIVE SUMMARY

Most large Canadian corporations hold some of their assets in highly liquid form—in cash and marketable securities. For example, in 2006, Magna International Inc., Canadian supplier of automotive components, held around 14.3 percent of its assets in cash and cash equivalents. Since cash earns no interest, why would a corporation hold cash? It would seem more sensible to put cash into marketable securities, such as Treasury bills, to earn some investment income. Of course, one reason Canadian companies hold cash is to pay for goods and services. They might prefer to pay their employees in Canada Treasury bills, but the minimum denomination of Treasury bills is $10,000! The firm must use cash because cash is more divisible than Treasury bills.[1]

This chapter is about how firms manage cash. The basic objective in cash management is to keep the investment in cash as low as possible while still operating the firm's activities efficiently and effectively. The chapter separates cash management into three steps:

1. Determining the appropriate target cash balance.
2. Collecting and disbursing cash efficiently.
3. Investing excess cash in marketable securities.

Determining the appropriate target cash balance involves an assessment of the trade-off between the benefit and cost of liquidity. The benefit of holding cash is the convenience in liquidity it gives the firm. The cost of holding cash is the interest income that the firm could have received from investing in Treasury bills and other marketable securities. If the firm has achieved its target cash balance, the value it gets from the liquidity provided by its cash will be exactly equal to the value forgone in interest on an equivalent holding of Treasury bills. In other words, a firm should increase its holding of cash until the net present value from doing so is zero. The incremental liquidity value of cash should decline as more of it is held.

After the optimal amount of liquidity is determined, the firm must establish procedures so that cash is collected and disbursed as efficiently as possible.

Firms must invest temporarily idle cash in short-term marketable securities. These securities can be bought and sold in the *money market*. Money market securities have very little risk of default and are highly marketable.

Cash management is not as complex and conceptually challenging as other topics such as capital budgeting and asset pricing. Still this is a very important activity and financial managers in many companies, especially in the retail and services industries, spend a significant portion of their time on cash management.

---

[1]Cash is liquid. One property of liquidity is divisibility, that is, how easily an asset can be divided into parts.

28.1 Reasons for Holding Cash

The term *cash* is a surprisingly imprecise concept. The economic definition of cash includes currency, demand deposits at commercial banks, and undeposited cheques. However, financial managers often use the term *cash* to include short-term marketable securities. Short-term marketable securities are frequently referred to as "cash equivalents" and include Treasury bills, certificates of deposit, and repurchase agreements. (Several different types of short-term marketable securities are described at the end of this chapter.) The balance sheet item "cash" usually includes cash equivalents.

The previous chapter discussed the management of net working capital. Net working capital includes both cash and cash equivalents. This chapter is concerned with cash, not net working capital, and it focuses on the narrow economic definition of cash.

The basic elements of net working capital management such as carrying costs, shortage costs, and opportunity costs are relevant for cash management. However, cash management is more concerned with how to minimize cash balances by collecting and disbursing cash effectively.

The primary reason for holding cash is to satisfy the **transactions motive.**[2] Transactions-related needs come from normal disbursement and collection activities of the firm. The disbursement of cash includes the payment of wages and salaries, trade debts, taxes, and dividends. Cash is collected from sales from operations, sales of assets, and new financing. The cash inflows (*collections*) and outflows (*disbursements*) are not perfectly synchronized, and some level of cash holdings is necessary to serve as a buffer. If the firm maintains too small a cash balance, it may run out of cash. If so, it must sell marketable securities or borrow. Selling marketable securities and borrowing involve *trading costs*. Perfect liquidity is the characteristic of cash that allows it to satisfy the transactions motive.

As electronic data interchange (EDI) and other high-speed, "paperless" payment mechanisms continue to develop, even the transactions demand for cash may all but disappear. Even if it does, however, there will still be a demand for liquidity and a need to manage it efficiently.

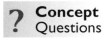

Concept Questions
- What is the transactions motive, and how does it lead firms to hold cash?
- What is the cost to firms of holding excess cash?

28.2 Determining the Target Cash Balance

The **target cash balance** involves a trade-off between the opportunity costs of holding too much cash (lost interest) and the trading costs of holding too little. Figure 28.1 presents the problem graphically. If a firm tries to keep its cash holdings too low, it will find itself selling marketable securities (and perhaps later buying marketable securities to replace those sold) more frequently than if the cash balance were higher. Thus, trading costs will tend to fall as the cash balance becomes larger. In contrast, the opportunity costs of holding cash

---

[2]John Maynard Keynes, in his great work, *The General Theory of Employment, Interest and Money,* identified three reasons why liquidity is important: the precautionary motive (to be able to react quickly to opportunities), the speculative motive (to benefit from deflation under which there is a positive return from holding cash), and the transactions motive. In the modern financial system, the speculative motive is met through credit cards and corporate credit lines and inflation is accepted as a permanent feature eliminating the speculative motive. As a result, our discussion focuses on the transactions motive.

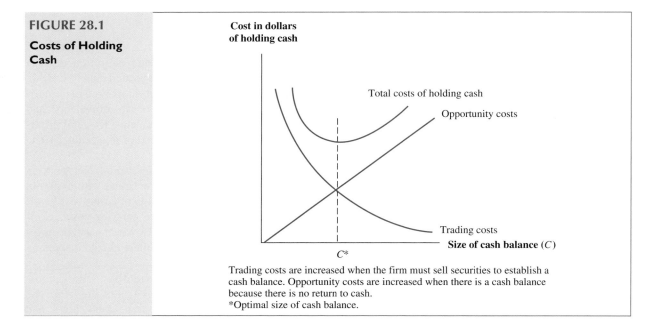

FIGURE 28.1

Costs of Holding Cash

Cost in dollars
of holding cash

Total costs of holding cash

Opportunity costs

Trading costs

Size of cash balance (C)

C^*

Trading costs are increased when the firm must sell securities to establish a cash balance. Opportunity costs are increased when there is a cash balance because there is no return to cash.
*Optimal size of cash balance.

rise as the cash holdings rise. At point C^* in Figure 28.1, the sum of both costs, depicted as the total cost curve, is at a minimum. This is the target or optimal cash balance.

The Baumol Model

William Baumol was the first to provide a formal model of cash management incorporating opportunity costs and trading costs.[3] His model can be used to establish the target cash balance.

Suppose the Golden Socks Corporation began week 0 with a cash balance of $C = \$1.2$ million, and outflows exceed inflows by \$600,000 per week. Its cash balance will drop to zero at the end of week 2, and its average cash balance will be $C/2 = \$1.2$ million/ $2 = \$600,000$ over the two-week period. At the end of week 2, Golden Socks must replace its cash either by selling marketable securities or by borrowing. Figure 28.2 shows this situation.

If C were set higher (say, at \$2.4 million), cash would last four weeks before the firm would need to sell marketable securities, but the firm's average cash balance would increase to \$1.2 million (from \$600,000). If C were set at \$600,000, cash would run out in one week and the firm would need to replenish cash more frequently, but its average cash balance would fall from \$600,000 to \$300,000.

Because transactions costs (for example, the brokerage costs of selling marketable securities) must be incurred whenever cash is replenished, establishing large initial cash balances will lower the trading costs connected with cash management. However, the larger the average cash balance, the greater the opportunity cost (the return that could have been earned on marketable securities).

---

[3]W. S. Baumol, "The Transactions Demand for Cash: An Inventory Theoretic Approach," *Quarterly Journal of Economics* 66 (November 1952).

FIGURE 28.2

**Cash Balances for
the Golden Socks
Corporation**

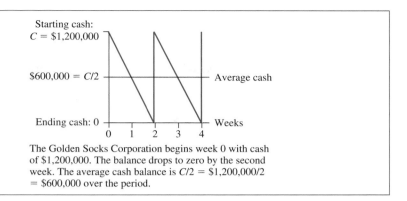

The Golden Socks Corporation begins week 0 with cash
of $1,200,000. The balance drops to zero by the second
week. The average cash balance is $C/2 = \$1,200,000/2
= \$600,000$ over the period.

To solve this problem, Golden Socks needs to know three things:

F = The fixed cost of selling securities to replenish cash

T = The total amount of new cash needed for transactions purposes over the
relevant planning period, say, one year

K = The opportunity cost of holding cash (the interest rate on marketable
securities)

With this information, Golden Socks can determine the total costs of any particular
cash balance policy. It can then determine the optimal cash balance policy.

The Opportunity Costs   The total opportunity costs of cash balances, in dollars, must
be equal to the average cash balance multiplied by the interest rate:

$$\text{Opportunity costs (\$)} = (C/2) \times K$$

The opportunity costs of various alternatives are given here:

Initial Cash Balance	Average Cash Balance	Opportunity Costs ($K = 0.10$)
C	$C/2$	$(C/2) \times K$
$4,800,000	$2,400,000	$240,000
2,400,000	1,200,000	120,000
1,200,000	600,000	60,000
600,000	300,000	30,000
300,000	150,000	15,000

The Trading Costs   Total trading costs can be determined by calculating the number of
times that Golden Socks must sell marketable securities during the year. The total amount
of cash disbursement during the year is $\$600,000 \times 52$ weeks = $31.2 million. If the initial cash balance is set at $1.2 million, Golden Socks will sell $1.2 million of marketable
securities every two weeks. Thus, trading costs are given by

$$\frac{\$31.2 \text{ million}}{\$1.2 \text{ million}} \times F = 26F$$

The general formula is

$$\text{Trading costs (\$)} = (T/C) \times F$$

A schedule of alternative trading costs follows:

Total Disbursements During Relevant Period	Initial Cash Balance	Trading Costs (F = $1,000)
T	C	(T/C) × F
$31,200,000	$4,800,000	$ 6,500
31,200,000	2,400,000	13,000
31,200,000	1,200,000	26,000
31,200,000	600,000	52,000
31,200,000	300,000	104,000

The Total Cost   The total cost of cash balances consists of the opportunity costs plus the trading costs:

$$\text{Total cost} = \text{Opportunity costs} + \text{Trading costs}$$

$$= (C/2) \times K + (T/C) \times F$$

Cash Balance	Total Cost	=	Opportunity Costs	+	Trading Costs
$4,800,000	$246,500		$240,000		$ 6,500
2,400,000	133,000		120,000		13,000
1,200,000	86,000		60,000		26,000
600,000	82,000		30,000		52,000
300,000	119,000		15,000		104,000

The Solution   We can see from the preceding schedule that a $600,000 cash balance results in the lowest total cost ($82,000) of the possibilities presented. But what about $700,000, $500,000, or other possibilities? To determine minimum total costs precisely, Golden Socks must equate the marginal reduction in trading costs as balances rise with the marginal increase in opportunity costs associated with cash balance increases. The target cash balance should be the point where the two are equal and offset each other. This can be calculated by using either numerical iteration or calculus.

Recall that the total cost equation is

$$\text{Total cost (TC)} = (C/2) \times K + (T/C) \times F$$

If we differentiate the TC equation with respect to cash balance and set the derivative equal to zero, we will find that

$$\frac{dTC}{dC} = \frac{K}{2} - \frac{TF}{C^2} = 0$$

$$\begin{matrix}\text{Marginal} & \text{Marginal} & \text{Marginal} \\ \text{total} & = \text{opportunity} + \text{trading} \\ \text{cost} & \text{costs} & \text{costs}^4\end{matrix}$$

The solution for the general cash balance, C^*, is obtained by solving this equation for C:

$$\frac{K}{2} = \frac{TF}{C^2}$$

$$C^* = \sqrt{2TF/K}$$

---

[4]Marginal trading costs are negative because trading costs are *reduced* when C is increased.

If $F = \$1,000$, $T = \$31,200,000$, and $K = 0.10$, then $C^* = \$789,936.71$. Given the value of C^*, opportunity costs are

$$(C^*/2) \times K = \frac{\$789,936.71}{2} \times 0.10 = \$39,496.84$$

Trading costs are

$$(T/C^*) \times F = \frac{\$31,200,000}{\$789,936.71} \times \$1,000 = \$39,496.84$$

Hence, total costs are

$$\$39,496.84 + \$39,496.84 = \$78,993.68$$

Limitations   The Baumol model represents an important contribution to cash management. The limitations of the model include the following:

1. *The model assumes the firm has a constant disbursement rate.* In practice, disbursements can be only partially managed, because due dates differ and costs cannot be predicted with certainty.
2. *The model assumes there are no cash receipts during the projected period.* In fact, most firms experience both cash inflows and outflows on a daily basis.
3. *No safety stock is allowed for.* Firms will probably want to hold a safety stock of cash designed to reduce the possibility of a cash shortage or *cash-out*. However, to the extent that firms can sell marketable securities or borrow in a few hours, the need for a safety stock is minimal.

The Baumol model is possibly the simplest and most stripped-down, sensible model for determining the optimal cash position. Its chief weakness is that it assumes discrete, certain cash flows. We next discuss a model designed to deal with uncertainty.

The Miller–Orr Model

Merton Miller and Daniel Orr developed a cash balance model to deal with cash inflows and outflows that fluctuate randomly from day to day.[5] In the Miller–Orr model, both cash inflows and cash outflows are included. The model assumes that the distribution of daily net cash inflows (cash inflow minus cash outflow) is normally distributed. On each day the net cash flow could be the expected value or some higher or lower value. We will assume that the expected net cash flow is zero.

Figure 28.3 shows how the Miller–Orr model works. The model operates in terms of upper (H) and lower (L) control limits, and a target cash balance (Z). The firm allows its cash balance to wander randomly within the lower and upper limits. As long as the cash balance is between H and L, the firm makes no transaction. When the cash balance reaches H, such as at point X, then the firm buys $H - Z$ units (or dollars) of marketable securities. This action will decrease the cash balance to Z. In the same way, when cash balances fall to L, such as at point Y (the lower limit), the firm should sell $Z - L$ securities and increase the cash balance to Z. In both situations, cash balances return to Z. Management sets the lower limit, L, depending on how much risk of a cash shortfall the firm is willing to tolerate.

Like the Baumol model, the Miller–Orr model depends on trading costs and opportunity costs. The cost per transaction of buying and selling marketable securities, F, is assumed to be fixed. The percentage opportunity cost per period of holding cash, K, is the

---

[5]M. H. Miller and D. Orr, "A Model of the Demand for Money by Firms," *Quarterly Journal of Economics* (August 1966).

FIGURE 28.3

The Miller–Orr Model

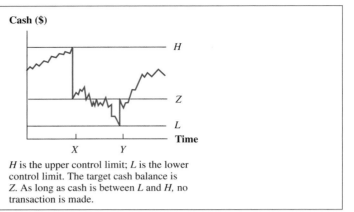

Cash ($)

H is the upper control limit; L is the lower control limit. The target cash balance is Z. As long as cash is between L and H, no transaction is made.

daily interest rate on marketable securities. Unlike the Baumol model, the number of transactions per period is a random variable that varies from period to period, depending on the pattern of cash inflows and outflows.

As a consequence, trading costs per period are dependent on the expected number of transactions in marketable securities during the period. Similarly, the opportunity costs of holding cash are a function of the expected cash balance per period.

Given L, which is set by the firm, the Miller–Orr model solves for the target cash balance (Z), and the upper limit (H). Expected total costs of the cash balance return policy (Z, H) are equal to the sum of expected transactions costs and expected opportunity costs. The values of Z (the return point) and H (the upper limit) that minimize the expected total cost have been determined by Miller and Orr:

$$Z^* = \sqrt[3]{3F\sigma^2/4K} + L$$

$$H^* = 3Z^* - 2L$$

where * denotes optimal values, and σ^2 is the variance of net daily cash flows.

The average cash balance in the Miller–Orr model is

$$\text{Average cash balance} = \frac{4Z - L}{3}$$

EXAMPLE 28.1

To clarify the Miller–Orr model, suppose that $F = \$1,000$, the interest rate is 10 percent annually, and the standard deviation of daily net cash flows is $2,000. The daily opportunity cost, K, is

$$(1 + K)^{365} - 1.0 = 0.10$$

$$1 + K = \sqrt[365]{1.10} = 1.000261$$

$$K = 0.000261$$

The variance of daily net cash flows is

$$\sigma^2 = (2,000)^2 = 4,000,000$$

Let us assume that $L = 0$:

$$Z^* = \sqrt[3]{(3 \times \$1{,}000 \times 4{,}000{,}000)/(4 \times 0.000261)} + 0$$

$$= \sqrt[3]{\$11{,}493{,}900{,}000{,}000} = \$22{,}568$$

$$H^* = 3 \times \$22{,}568 = \$67{,}704$$

$$\text{Average cash balance} = \frac{4 \times \$22{,}568}{3} = \$30{,}091$$

Implications of the Miller–Orr Model   To use the Miller–Orr model, the manager must do four things:

1. Set the lower control limit for the cash balance. This lower limit can be related to a minimum safety margin decided on by management.
2. Estimate the standard deviation of daily cash flows.
3. Determine the interest rate.
4. Estimate the trading costs of buying and selling marketable securities.

These four steps allow the upper limit and return point to be computed. Miller and Orr tested their model using nine months of data for cash balances for a large industrial firm. The model was able to produce average daily cash balances much lower than the averages actually obtained by the firm.[6]

The Miller–Orr model clarifies the issues of cash management. First, the model shows that the best return point, Z^*, is positively related to trading costs, F, and negatively related to K, the daily interest rate on marketable securities. These relationships are consistent with and analogous to the Baumol model. Second, the Miller–Orr model shows that the best return point and the average cash balance are positively related to the variability of cash flows. That is, firms whose cash flows are subject to greater uncertainty should maintain a larger average cash balance.

Other Factors Influencing the Target Cash Balance

Borrowing   In our previous examples, the firm obtains cash by selling marketable securities. Another alternative is to borrow cash. Borrowing introduces additional considerations to cash management.

1. Borrowing is likely to be more expensive than selling marketable securities because the interest rate on a loan is likely to be higher than the return on marketable securities.
2. The need to borrow will depend on management's desire to hold low cash balances. A firm is more likely to need to borrow to cover an unexpected cash outflow, the greater its cash flow variability and the lower its investment in marketable securities.

---

[6]D. Mullins and R. Homonoff discuss tests of the Miller–Orr model in "Applications of Inventory Cash Management Models," in *Modern Developments in Financial Management*, ed. S. C. Myers (New York: Praeger, 1976). They show that the model works very well when compared to the actual cash balances of several firms. However, simple rules of thumb do as good a job as the Miller–Orr model.

Relative Costs   For large firms, the trading costs of buying and selling securities are very small when compared to the opportunity costs of holding cash. For example, suppose a firm has $1 million in cash that won't be needed for 24 hours. Should the firm invest the money or leave it sitting?

Suppose the firm can invest the money overnight at the call money rate. To do this the treasurer arranges through a chartered bank to lend funds for 24 hours to an investment dealer. Suppose that the firm can do this at an annualized rate of 4 percent per year. The daily rate in this case is about one basis point (0.01 percent or 0.0001).

The daily return earned on $1 million is thus $0.0001 \times \$1$ million $= \$100$. In most cases, the order cost would be much less than this.

? Concept Questions

- **What is a target cash balance?**
- **What are the strengths and weaknesses of the Baumol model and the Miller–Orr model?**

28.3 Managing the Collection and Disbursement of Cash

A firm's cash balance as reported in its financial statements (*book cash* or *ledger cash*) is not the same thing as the balance shown in its bank account (*bank cash* or *collected bank cash*). The difference between bank cash and book cash is called **float** and represents the net effect of cheques in the process of collection.

EXAMPLE 28.2

Imagine that General Mechanics Inc. (GMI) currently has $100,000 on deposit with its bank. It purchases some raw materials, paying its vendors with a cheque written on July 8 for $100,000. The company's books (that is, ledger balances) are changed to show the $100,000 reduction in the cash balance. But the firm's bank will not find out about this cheque until it has been deposited at the vendor's bank and has been presented to the firm's bank for payment on, say, July 15. Until the cheque's presentation, the firm's bank cash is greater than its book cash, and it has *positive float*.

Position Prior to July 8:

$$\text{Float} = \text{Firm's bank cash} - \text{Firm's book cash}$$

$$= \$100,000 - \$100,000$$

$$= 0$$

Position from July 8 through July 14:

$$\text{Disbursement float} = \text{Firm's bank cash} - \text{Firm's book cash}$$

$$= \$100,000 - 0$$

$$= \$100,000$$

During the period of time that the cheque is *outstanding*, GMI has a balance with the bank of $100,000. Cheques written by the firm generate *disbursement float*, causing an immediate decrease in book cash but no immediate change in bank cash.

EXAMPLE 28.3

Imagine that GMI receives a cheque from a customer for $100,000. Assume, as before, that the company has $100,000 deposited at its bank and has a *neutral float position*. It processes the cheque through the bookkeeping department and increases its book balance by $100,000 to $200,000. However, the additional cash is not available to GMI until the cheque is deposited in the firm's bank. This will occur on, say, November 9, the next day. In the meantime, the cash position at GMI will reflect a collection float of $100,000.

Position Prior to November 8:

$$\text{Float} = \text{Firm's bank cash} - \text{Firm's book cash}$$

$$= \$100,000 - \$100,000$$

$$= 0$$

Position from November 8 to November 9:

$$\text{Collection float} = \text{Firm's bank cash} - \text{Firm's book cash}$$

$$= \$100,000 - \$200,000$$

$$= -\$100,000$$

Cheques received by the firm represent *collection float,* which increases book cash immediately but does not immediately change bank cash. The firm is helped by disbursement float and is hurt by collection float. The sum of disbursement float and collection float is *net float.*

A firm should be more concerned with net float and bank cash than with book cash. If a financial manager knows that a cheque will not clear for several days, he or she will be able to keep a lower cash balance at the bank. Good float management can generate a great deal of money. For example, the average daily sales of Exxon are about $248 million. If Exxon speeds up the collection process or slows down the disbursement process by one day, it frees up $248 million, which can be invested in marketable securities. With an interest rate compounded daily of 3 percent, this represents overnight interest of $20,384 [or ($248 million/365) $\times$ 0.03].

Float management involves controlling the collection and disbursement of cash. The objective in cash collection is to reduce the lag between the time customers pay their bills and the time the cheques are collected. The objective in cash disbursement is to slow down payments, thereby increasing the time between when cheques are written and when cheques are presented. Of course, to the extent that the firm succeeds in doing this, the customers and suppliers lose money, and the trade-off is the effect on the firm's relationship with them.

Collection float can be broken down into three parts: mail float, in-house processing float, and availability float:

1. *Mail float* is the time during which cheques are trapped in the postal system.
2. *In-house processing float* is the time it takes the receiver of a cheque to process the payment and deposit it in a bank for collection.
3. *Availability float* refers to the time required to clear a cheque through the banking system. In the Canadian banking system, availability float cannot exceed one day and is often zero, so this is the least important part.

EXAMPLE 28.4

A cheque for $1,000 is mailed by a customer on Monday, September 1. Because of mail, processing, and clearing delays, it is not credited as available cash in the firm's bank until the following Monday, seven days later. The float for this cheque is

$$\text{Float} = \$1,000 \times 7 \text{ days} = \$7,000$$

Another cheque for $7,000 is mailed on September 1. It is available on the next day. The float for this cheque is

$$\text{Float} = \$7,000 \times 1 \text{ day} = \$7,000$$

The measurement of float depends on the time lag and the dollars involved. The cost of float is an opportunity cost, because the cash is unavailable for use during the time cheques are tied up in the collection process. The cost of float can be determined by (1) estimating the average daily receipts, (2) calculating the average delay in obtaining the receipts, and (3) discounting the average daily receipts by the *delay-adjusted cost of capital.*

EXAMPLE 28.5

Suppose that Concepts Inc. received two items each month:

	Amount	Number of Days Delay	Float
Item 1	$5,000,000	× 3 =	$15,000,000
Item 2	3,000,000	× 5 =	15,000,000
Total	$8,000,000		$30,000,000

The average daily float over the month is equal to

Average Daily Float:

$$\frac{\text{Total float}}{\text{Total days}} = \frac{\$30,000,000}{30} = \$1,000,000$$

Another procedure that can be used to calculate average daily float is to determine average daily receipts and multiply by the average daily delay.

Average Daily Receipts:

$$\frac{\text{Total receipts}}{\text{Total days}} = \frac{\$8,000,000}{30} = \$266,666.67$$

$$\frac{\text{Weighted}}{\text{average delay}} = (5/8) \times 3 + (3/8) \times 5$$

$$= 1.875 + 1.875 = 3.75 \text{ days}$$

$$\frac{\text{Average}}{\text{daily float}} = \text{Average daily receipts} \times \text{Weighted average delay}$$

$$= \$266,666.67 \times 3.75 = \$1,000,000$$

EXAMPLE 28.6

Suppose Concepts Inc. has average daily receipts of $266,667. The float results in this amount being delayed 3.75 days. The present value of the delayed cash flow is

$$V = \frac{\$266,667}{1 + r_B}$$

where r_B is the cost of debt capital for Concepts, adjusted to the relevant time frame for daily compounding. Suppose the annual cost of debt capital is 6 percent. Then

$$r_B = 0.06 \times (3.75/365) = 0.0006$$

and

$$V = \frac{\$266,667}{1 + 0.0006} = \$266,507.10$$

Thus, the net present value of the delay float is $266,507.10 − $266,667 = −$159.90 per day. For a year, this is −$159.90 × 365 = −$58,363.50.

Electronic Data Interchange: The End of Float?

Electronic data interchange (EDI) is a general term that refers to the growing practice of direct electronic information exchange between all types of businesses. One important use of EDI, often called financial EDI, or FEDI, is to electronically transfer financial information and funds between parties, thereby eliminating paper invoices, paper cheques, mailing, and handling. It is even possible to arrange to have your chequeing account directly debited each month to pay many types of bills, and corporations now routinely directly deposit paycheques into employee accounts. More generally, EDI allows a seller to send a bill electronically to a buyer, thereby avoiding the mail. The buyer can then authorize payment, which also occurs electronically. Its bank then transfers the funds to the seller's account at a different bank. The net effect is that the length of time required to initiate and complete a business transaction is shortened considerably, and much of what we normally think of as float is reduced or eliminated. As the use of FEDI increases, float management will evolve to focus much more on issues surrounding computerized information exchange and fund transfers.

One of the drawbacks of EDI (and FEDI) is that it is expensive and complex to set up. For this reason, the use of extranet portals is gaining use over EDI especially in the electronics and high-tech industries.[7] Original equipment manufacturers (OEMs) are putting pressure on manufacturing suppliers to abandon EDI for Web-based business-to-business (B2B) extranets. One example of a B2B platform is RosettaNet, a non-profit consortium of 40 of the largest high-tech companies including Motorola, IBM, and Sony. Another of the drawbacks that firms face switching away from EDI (and FEDI) is that they would be losing efficiency in the switch because the extranets require more manual work compared to EDI. Because of security concerns and lack of standardization, don't look for e-commerce and extranets to completely eliminate the need for EDI anytime soon. In fact, it appears these complementary systems will most likely be used in tandem as the future unfolds.

---

[7]Extranet portals are private networks that use Internet protocol and public telecommunication systems to securely share information with certain stakeholders, while EDI implies direct computer-to-computer transactions into the vendors' databases and ordering systems.

FIGURE 28.4

The Cash Collection Process

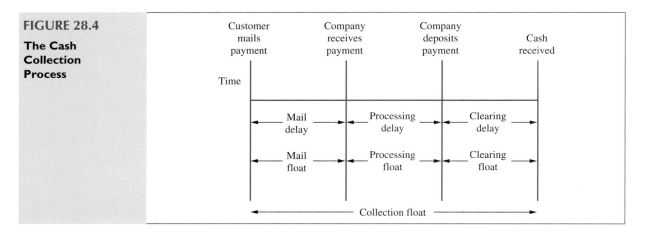

Accelerating Collections

Based on our discussion above, we depict the basic parts of the cash collection process in Figure 28.4. The total time in this process is made up of mailing time, cheque-processing time, and the bank's cheque-clearing time. The amount of time that cash spends in each part of the cash collection process depends on where the firm's customers are located and how efficient the firm is at collecting cash.

Coordinating the firm's efforts in all areas is its cash flow information system. Tracking payments through the system and providing the cash manager with up-to-date daily cash balances and investment rates are its key tasks. Linking the manager's computer with the bank's online, real-time system, the system gives the manager access to account balances and transactions plus information on money market rates.

Since it is the corporate equivalent of a bank machine, the cash management system has security features to prevent unauthorized use. Different passwords or smart cards allow access to each level of authority. For example, a receivables clerk could have access to deposit activity files but not to payroll.

We next discuss several techniques used to accelerate collections and reduce collection time: systems to expedite mailing and cheque processing as well as concentration banking.

Lockboxes   Lockboxes are special post office boxes set up to intercept accounts receivable payments. Figure 28.5 illustrates a lockbox system. The collection process is started by having business and retail customers mail their cheques to a post office box instead of sending them to the firm. The lockbox is maintained at a local bank branch. Large corporations may maintain a number of lockboxes, one in each significant market area. The location depends on a trade-off between bank fees and savings on mailing time.

In the typical lockbox system, the local bank branch collects the lockbox cheques from the post office daily. The bank deposits the cheques directly to the firm's account. Details of the operation are recorded (in some computer-usable form) and sent to the firm.

A lockbox system reduces mailing time because cheques are received at a nearby post office instead of at corporate headquarters. Lockboxes also reduce the processing time because the corporation does not have to open the envelopes and deposit cheques for collection. In all, a bank lockbox should enable a firm to get its receipts processed, deposited, and cleared faster than if it were to receive cheques at its headquarters and deliver them itself to the bank for deposit and clearing.[8]

---

[8]An example of lockbox services currently offered by one Canadian bank is at http://www.cibc.com/ca/lrg-corporate/cash-management/lockbox.html.

FIGURE 28.5

**Overview
of Lockbox
Processing**

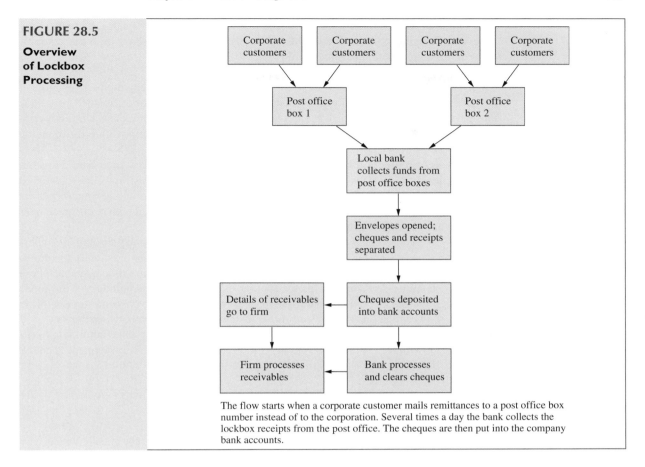

The flow starts when a corporate customer mails remittances to a post office box
number instead of to the corporation. Several times a day the bank collects the
lockbox receipts from the post office. The cheques are then put into the company
bank accounts.

Electronic Collection Systems   Lockbox systems are standard ways to reduce mail and
processing float time. They are used by almost all large firms in Canada that can benefit from them. Newer approaches focus on reducing float virtually to zero by replacing
cheques with electronic funds transfer. Examples used in Canada include preauthorized
payments, point-of-sale transfers, and electronic trade payables. We discuss the first two
here and the third later when we look at disbursement systems.

Pre-authorized payments are paperless transfers of contractual or installment payments from the customer's account directly to the firm's. Common applications are mortgage payments and installment payments for insurance, rent, and cable TV. This system
eliminates all paperwork in invoices as well as in deposit and reconciliation of cheques.
There is no mail or processing float. The system is presently limited mainly to annuity payments, but the technology could handle any payments.

Point-of-sale systems use **debit cards** to transfer funds directly from a customer's
bank account to a retailer's. Unlike with a credit card, the funds are transferred immediately. Point-of-sale systems are now widely used across Canada.

The next generation of cards for point-of-sale applications is the smart card mentioned
earlier in its role of security for corporate cash management systems. Smart cards differ
from debit cards in that they contain a chip that can hold a cash balance. Consumers can
download small amounts of money (usually under $300) directly on the card and then
spend it at point-of-sale terminals. The advantage of smart cards is that, with the balance
programmed on the card's chip, there is no need for the merchant to have technology that

goes online to the customer's bank. Canadian banks test marketed smart card technology in several Canadian communities in the late 1990s, but there has not yet been any commitment to broad application of smart card payment.

Cash Concentration   Using lockboxes or other collection systems helps firms collect cheques from customers and rapidly deposit them. But the job is not finished yet, since those systems give the firm cash at a number of widely dispersed branches. Until it is concentrated in a central account, the cash is of little use to the firm for paying bills, reducing loans, or investing.

With a **concentration banking** system, sales receipts are processed at bank branches providing lockbox services; they are then deposited locally. Surplus funds are transferred from the various local branches to a single, central concentration account. This process is illustrated in Figure 28.6, where concentration accounts are combined with over-the-counter collection and lockboxes in a total cash management system.

Large firms in Canada may manage collections across the country through one chartered bank. Chartered banks offer a concentrator account, which automatically electronically transfers deposits at any branch in Canada to the firm's concentration account. These funds receive **same-day value.** This means that the firm has immediate use of the funds even though it takes 24 hours for a cheque to clear in Canada. If the concentration involves branches of more than one bank, electronic transfers will take place between banks.

Once the funds are in the concentration account, the bank can make automatic transfers to pay down the firm's credit line or, if there is a surplus, to an investment account.

FIGURE 28.6

Lockboxes and Concentration Banks in a Cash Management System

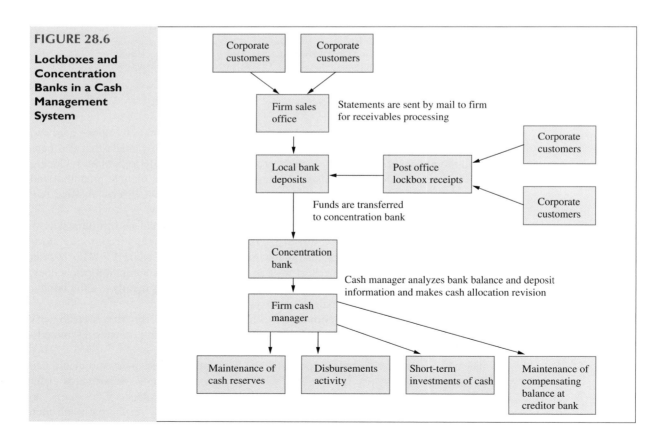

Transfers are made in units of minimum size agreed in advance; common practice is units of $5,000. Mid-sized firms lacking money-market expertise may invest in bank accounts at competitive interest rates. The largest firms are able to purchase money-market instruments electronically.

Controlling Disbursements

Accelerating collections is one method of cash management; slowing down disbursements is another. This can be a sensitive area—some practices exist that we do not recommend. For example, some small firms that are short of working capital make disbursements on the "squeaky wheel principle." Payables invoices are processed prior to their due dates and cheques printed. When the cheques are ready, the firm's controller puts them all in a desk drawer. As suppliers phone and ask for their money, the cheques come out of the drawer and go into the mail! We do not recommend the desk drawer method because it is bad for supplier relations and borders on being unethical.

Ethical and Legal Questions

The cash manager must work with collected bank cash balances and not the firm's book balance (which reflects cheques that have been deposited but not collected). If this is not done, a cash manager could be drawing on uncollected cash as a source for making short-term investments. Most banks charge a penalty rate for the use of uncollected funds. The issue is minor in Canada since there can be a maximum of only one day's deposit float. In the United States, however, smaller banks' accounting and control procedures may not be accurate enough to make them fully aware of the use of uncollected funds. This raises some ethical and legal questions for firms doing business across the border.

Controlling Disbursements in Practice   As we have seen, float in terms of slowing down payments comes from mail delivery, cheque-processing time, and collection of funds. As we just showed, in the United States, disbursement float can be increased by writing a cheque on a geographically distant bank. Because there are significant ethical (and legal) issues associated with deliberately delaying disbursements in these and similar ways, such strategies appear to be disappearing. In Canada, banks provide same-day availability so the temptation is easy to resist.

For these reasons, the goal is to control rather than simply to delay disbursements. A treasurer should try to pay payables on the last day appropriate for net terms or a discount.[9] The traditional way is to write a cheque and mail it timed to arrive on the due date. With the cash management system we described earlier, the payment can be programmed today for electronic transfer on the future due date. This eliminates paper along with guesswork about mail times.

The electronic payment is likely to come from a disbursement account, kept separate from the concentration account to ease accounting and control. Firms keep separate accounts for payroll, vendor disbursements, customer refunds, and so on. This makes it easy for the bank to provide each cost or profit centre with its own statement.

Firms use **zero-balance accounts** to avoid carrying extra balances in each disbursement account. With a zero-balance account, the firm, in cooperation with its bank, transfers in just enough funds to cover cheques presented that day. Figure 28.7 illustrates how such a system might work. In this case, the firm maintains two disbursement accounts: one for suppliers and one for payroll. As shown, if the firm does not use zero-balance accounts,

---

[9]We discuss credit terms in depth in Chapter 29.

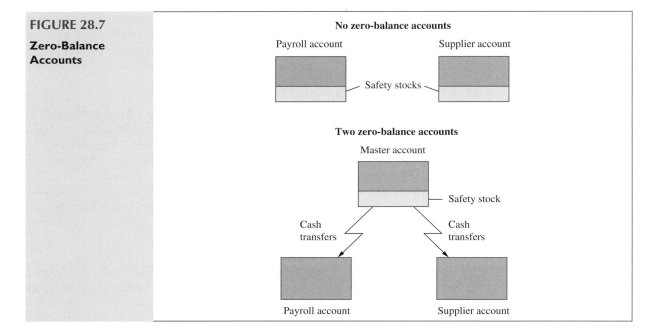

FIGURE 28.7

Zero-Balance Accounts

then each of these accounts must have a safety stock of cash to meet unanticipated demands. If the firm does use zero-balance accounts, then it can keep one safety stock in a master account and transfer in the funds to the two subsidiary accounts as needed. The key is that the total amount of cash held as a buffer is smaller under the zero-balance arrangement, thereby freeing up cash to be used elsewhere.

? **Concept** Questions
- **Describe collection and disbursement float.**
- **What are lockboxes? Concentration banking? Zero-balance accounts?**
- **How do computer and communications technologies aid in cash management by large corporations?**

28.4 Investing Idle Cash

If a firm has a temporary cash surplus, it can invest in short-term, or money market, securities. Short-term financial assets that trade in the money market have maturities of one year or less.

Most large firms manage their own short-term financial assets, transacting through banks and investment dealers. Some smaller firms use money market funds that invest in short-term financial assets for a management fee. The management fee is compensation for the professional expertise and diversification provided by the fund manager. Canadian chartered banks compete with money market funds offering arrangements in which the bank takes all excess available funds at the close of each business day and invests them for the firm.

Firms have temporary cash surpluses for these reasons: to help finance seasonal or cyclical activities of the firm, to help finance planned expenditures of the firm, and to provide for unanticipated contingencies.

Geoff Martin on Online Billing

Electronic bill payment and collection is finally starting to become the "killer app" that pundits have long predicted it would be, and the Government of Canada is leading the charge.

Worldwide, it has placed first in online services for four years running, according to a yearly study by global technology services firm, Accenture. And with the leadership of the federal Government On-Line (GOL) program (www.gol-ged.gc.ca), which aims to provide a majority of Canadian government services securely and efficiently by 2005, our lead over second-place countries, Singapore and the United States, continues to widen.

Since it deals with virtually every Canadian citizen and business, the Canada Revenue Agency (CRA) is leading the way with the GOL program. Last year, 10 million Canadians filed their taxes online, but CRA expects to significantly expand their services before the 2005 deadline to entice even greater numbers.

With their acquisition of webdoxs from BCE Emergis in July 2004, Canada Post's online payment service, called epost, is also poised to become a global trailblazer in e-billing. While epost currently offers services that allow its more than 400,000 registered users in major cities such as Calgary, Winnipeg, Toronto, and Ottawa to pay their municipal taxes and other bills online, the scheduled launch of merged services between epost and webdoxs in December will boast more than one million registered customers and the services of 97 companies. In Toronto, the service will enable electronic payment for seven of the 10 monthly bills received by an average household.

With numbers ramping upwards so sharply right across the country, it doesn't take a crystal ball to determine that e-billing is very quickly taking over in Canada. While the paperless society we've long been promised still seems a distant fairy tale, Canadian governments and businesses seem poised to achieve one of the world's first truly cashless societies in the very near future.

This discussion is excerpted from G. Martin, "No cash please," Summit Ottawa: Oct 2004. Vol. 7, Iss. 6, p. 11. Used with permission.

Seasonal or Cyclical Activities

Some firms have a predictable cash flow pattern. They have surplus cash flows during part of the year and deficit cash flows the rest of the year. For example, Toys "R" Us, a retail toy firm, has a seasonal cash flow pattern influenced by Christmas. Such a firm may buy marketable securities when surplus cash flows occur and sell marketable securities when deficits occur. Of course, bank loans are another short-term financing device. Figure 28.8 illustrates the use of bank loans and marketable securities to meet temporary financing needs.

FIGURE 28.8

Seasonal Cash Demands

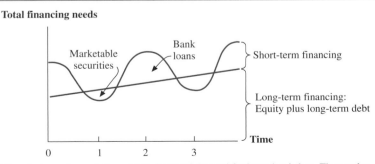

Time 1: A surplus cash flow exists. Seasonal demand for investing is low. The surplus cash flow is invested in short-term marketable securities. Time 2: A deficit cash flow exists. Seasonal demand for investing is high. The financial deficit is financed by selling marketable securities and by bank borrowing.

Planned Expenditures

Firms frequently accumulate temporary investments in marketable securities to provide the cash for a plant-construction program, dividend payment, and other large expenditures. Thus, firms may issue bonds and stocks before the cash is needed, investing the proceeds in short-term marketable securities, and then selling the securities to finance the expenditures.

Characteristics of Short-Term Securities

Given that a firm has some temporarily idle cash, there are a variety of short-term securities available for investing. Their most important characteristics are maturity, default risk, marketability, and taxability.

Maturity   *Maturity* refers to the time period over which interest and principal payments are made. For a given change in the level of interest rates, the prices of longer-maturity securities will change more than those for shorter-maturity securities. Our discussion of duration in Chapter 26 explored this relationship in detail. As a consequence, firms that invest in long-term securities are accepting greater risk than firms that invest in securities with short-term maturities. This type of risk is usually called *interest-rate risk.* Most firms limit their investments in marketable securities to those maturing in less than 90 days. Of course, the expected return on securities with short-term maturities is usually less than the expected return on securities with longer maturities.

EXAMPLE 28.7

Suppose you are the treasurer of a firm that needs $10 million to make a major capital investment after 90 days. You have decided to invest in Government of Canada obligations to eliminate all possible default risk. The newspaper (or your computer screen) lists securities and rates (Figure 28.9). The safest investment is three-month Treasury bills yielding 3.23 percent. Because this matches the maturity of the investment with the planned holding period, there is no interest rate risk. After three months, the Treasury bills will mature for a certain future cash flow of $10 million.[10]

If instead you invest in 10-year Canada bonds, the expected return will be higher, but so will the risk. If interest rates rise over the next three months, the bond will drop in price. The resulting capital loss will reduce the yield, possibly below the 3.23 percent on Treasury bills.

Default Risk   Default risk refers to the probability that interest and principal will not be paid in the promised amounts on the due dates. In Chapter 21, we observed that bond rating agencies, such as the Dominion Bond Rating Service (DBRS) and Standard & Poor's (S&P), compile and publish ratings of various corporate and public securities. These ratings are connected to default risk. Of course, some securities have negligible default risk, such as Canada Treasury bills. Given the purposes of investing idle corporate cash, firms typically avoid investing in marketable securities with significant default risk.

Small variations in default risk are reflected in the rates in Figure 28.9. For example, look at the rates on two alternative 90-day (three-month) Canadian investments. Since the maturities are the same, they differ only in default risk. In increasing order of default risk the securities are Treasury bills (4.14 percent yield), banker's acceptances (4.35 percent

---

[10]Treasury bills are sold on a discount basis so the future cash flow includes principal and interest.

FIGURE 28.9

Money Market Quotations

YIELDS & RATES

Supplied by Reuters. Indicative late afternoon rates.

CANADIAN YIELDS

	Latest	Prev day	Wk ago	4wks ago
T-Bills				
1-month	4.13	4.11	4.10	4.07
3-month	4.14	4.15	4.14	4.16
6-month	4.24	4.23	4.24	4.21
1-year	4.28	4.30	4.31	4.25
Bonds				
2-year	4.20	4.19	4.18	3.61
5-year	4.16	4.14	4.13	4.10
7-year	4.18	4.15	4.15	4.13
10-year	4.20	4.18	4.18	4.18
30-year	4.21	4.21	4.22	4.23
Banker's acceptances (ask price)				
1-month	4.34	4.34	4.32	4.32
3-month	4.35	4.35	4.35	4.34
6-month	4.40	4.40	4.38	4.35
3-mth forward rate agreement				
3-month	4.42	4.41	4.41	4.37
6-month	4.51	4.49	4.48	4.38
9-month	4.53	4.49	4.46	4.32

U.S. YIELDS

	Latest	Prev day	Wk ago	4wks ago
T-Bills				
1-month	4.70	4.72	4.68	4.99
3-month	4.84	4.92	4.86	5.02
6-month	4.98	5.00	5.01	5.08
Bonds				
2-year	4.72	4.67	4.63	4.71
5-year	4.58	4.54	4.54	4.64
10-year	4.66	4.63	4.64	4.73
30-year	4.83	4.80	4.81	4.91
Commercial paper				
1-month	5.19	5.22	5.20	5.21
3-month	5.18	5.17	5.22	5.19
6-month	5.12	5.17	5.11	5.13
3-mth forward rate agreement				
3-month	5.29	5.29	5.28	5.29
6-month	5.19	5.15	5.13	5.18
9-month	5.03	4.97	4.94	5.01

INTERNATIONAL

		Latest	Prev day	Wk ago	4wks ago
Euro-deposit rates (bid)					
US$	1-month	5.27	5.27	5.27	5.26
	3-month	5.28	5.24	5.26	5.28
	6-month	5.32	5.31	5.31	5.29
C$	3-month	4.17	4.17	4.17	4.17
euro	3-month	4.01	3.99	4.01	3.89
Yen	3-month	0.64	0.64	0.65	0.58
£	3-month	5.72	5.68	5.65	5.45
London interbank offer rate US$					
US$	1-month	5.32	5.32	5.32	5.32
	3-month	5.36	5.36	5.36	5.36
	6-month	5.36	5.36	5.36	5.36

BOND INDEXES

Supplied by Scotia Capital
(4 p.m. close, mid)

SC Bond Index	Index level	Total ret	Price ret	MTD tot.ret
Universe	638.62	−0.07	−0.08	−0.18
Short	495.39	−0.04	−0.06	−0.11
Mid	650.49	−0.06	−0.07	−0.23
Long	870.42	−0.10	−0.12	−0.24
Canada	146.32	−0.07	−0.08	−0.20
All Govt	630.33	−0.07	−0.08	−0.19
Federal	595.68	−0.06	−0.08	−0.19
Provincial	701.79	−0.08	−0.09	−0.20
Municipal	731.99	−0.07	−0.09	−0.22
All Corp	676.04	−0.06	−0.07	−0.15

BANK RATES

Canada		United States	
Bank of Canada	4.50	Discount	6.25
Overnight Money Market Financing	4.15	Prime	8.25
Prime	6.00	Federal Funds	5.19
Call Loan Average	4.25		

Source: *National Post*, May 10, 2007, FP13. Used with permission.

yield). Both are unsecured paper. Treasury bills (the less risky) are backed by the credit of the Government of Canada. Banker's acceptances are guaranteed by a chartered bank as well as by the issuing corporation.

Marketability   *Marketability* refers to how easy it is to convert an asset to cash. Sometimes marketability is referred to as *liquidity*. It has two characteristics:

1. *No price-pressure effect.* If an asset can be sold in large amounts without changing the market price, it is marketable. Price-pressure effects are those that come about when the price of an asset must be lowered to facilitate the sale.

2. *Time.* If an asset can be sold quickly at the existing market price, it is marketable. In contrast, a Renoir painting or antique desk appraised at $1 million will likely sell for much less if the owner must sell quickly on short notice.

In general, marketability is the ability to sell an asset for its face market value quickly and in large amounts. Perhaps the most marketable of all securities are Canada Treasury bills.

Taxability   Interest earned on money market securities is subject to federal and provincial corporate income taxes. Capital gains and dividends on common and preferred shares are taxed more lightly, but these long-term investments are subject to significant price fluctuations; most managers consider them too risky for the marketable securities portfolio.

One exception is the strategy of **dividend capture.** Under this strategy, portfolio managers purchase high-grade preferred stock or blue chip common stock just prior to a dividend payment. They hold the stock only long enough to receive the dividend. In this way, firms willing to tolerate price risk for a short period can benefit from the dividend exclusion allowing corporations to receive dividends tax-free from other Canadian corporations.

To mitigate price risk and to make their firms' preferred shares more attractive to managers seeking to capture dividends, financial engineers have invented various forms of floating-rate preferred shares. The idea is to make the dividends adjust to changes in market yields, keeping the price of the preferred share near par.[11]

Some Different Types of Money-Market Securities

The money-market securities listed in Figure 28.9 are generally highly marketable and short-term. They usually have low risk of default. These securities are issued by the federal government (for example, Treasury bills), domestic and foreign banks (for example, certificates of deposit), and business corporations (for example, commercial paper). There are many types in all, and we only illustrate a few of the most common here.

Treasury bills are obligations of the federal government that mature in three months, six months, or one year. They are sold at weekly auctions and traded actively over the counter by banks and investment dealers.

Commercial paper refers to short-term securities issued by finance companies, banks, and corporations. Typically, commercial paper is unsecured.[12] Maturities range from a few weeks to three months. There is no active secondary market in commercial paper. As a consequence, the marketability is low; however, firms that issue commercial paper will often repurchase it directly before maturity. The default risk of commercial paper depends on the financial strength of the issuer. DBRS and S&P publish quality ratings for commercial paper. These ratings are similar to the bond ratings we discussed in Chapter 21.

As explained earlier, *banker's acceptances* are a form of corporate paper stamped by a chartered bank that adds its guarantee of principal and interest.

Certificates of deposit (CDs) are short-term loans to chartered banks. Rates quoted are for CDs in excess of $100,000. There are active markets in CDs of three-month, six-month, nine-month, and twelve-month maturities, particularly in the United States.

Dollar swaps are foreign currency deposits that will be converted or swapped back into Canadian dollars at a predetermined rate by chartered banks. They allow the Canadian treasurer to place funds in major money markets outside Canada without incurring foreign exchange risk.

Our brief look at money markets illustrates the challenges and opportunities for treasurers today. Securitization has produced dramatic growth in banker's acceptances and commercial paper. Currency swaps are a financial engineering product driven by globalization of financial markets.

? Concept Questions
- **Why do firms find themselves with idle cash?**
- **What are some types of money-market securities?**

---

[11]The zero-growth formula of Chapter 6 values preferred shares: $P = $ Dividend rate $\times$ Par value/Discount rate. For floating rate preferreds, as the discount rate changes with market conditions, the dividend rate adjusts to remain equal to the discount rate. As a result, the price remains at par value. Since there is some lag in adjustment, the price can move away from the par value somewhat. Also, since all preferred shares bear some default risk, the floating rate does not protect investors from price declines arising from the downgrading of the issuer's credit rating.

[12]Commercial paper and banker's acceptances are sources of short-term financing for their issuers. We discussed them in more detail in Chapter 27.

28.5 SUMMARY AND CONCLUSIONS

1. A firm holds cash to conduct transactions and to compensate banks for the various services they render.

2. The optimal amount of cash for a firm to hold depends on the opportunity cost of holding cash and the uncertainty of future cash inflows and outflows. The Baumol model and the Miller–Orr model are two transactions models that provide rough guidelines for determining the optimal cash position.

3. The firm can make use of a variety of procedures to manage the collection and disbursement of cash in such a way as to speed up the collection of cash and slow down payments. Some methods to speed up collection are lockboxes, concentration banking, and electronic collection systems.

4. Because of seasonal and cyclical activities, to help finance planned expenditures, or as a reserve for unanticipated needs, firms temporarily find themselves with cash surpluses. The money market offers a variety of possible vehicles for parking this idle cash.

KEY TERMS

Concentration banking 814	Float 808	Target cash balance 801
Debit card 813	Lockbox 812	Transactions motive 801
Dividend capture 820	Same-day value 814	Zero-balance account 815

SUGGESTED READING

A good source on cash management practices is:
N. C. Hill, and W. L. Sartoris. *Short-Term Financial Management.* New York: Macmillan, 1992.

To keep up with Canadian practices, consult Canadian Treasurer, *published by the Treasury Management Association of Canada.*

QUESTIONS & PROBLEMS

Cash Management

28.1   Is it possible for a firm to have too much cash? Why would shareholders care if a firm accumulates large amounts of cash? What options are available to a firm if it believes it has too much cash? How about too little?

28.2   Some firms such as Microsoft maintain enormous amounts of cash positions. Why would firms like these hold such large quantities of cash?

The Cash Balance

28.3   Indicate the likely impact of each of the following on a company's target cash balance. Indicate whether there is an increase or a decrease. Briefly explain your reasoning in each case.
  a. Commissions charged by brokers decrease.
  b. Interest rates paid on money market securities rise.
  c. The compensating balance requirement of a bank is raised.
  d. The firm's credit rating improves.
  e. The cost of borrowing increases.
  f. Direct fees for banking services are established.

28.4   Explain how current trends in financial markets (discussed in Chapter 1) are changing the practice of cash management in Canada.

28.5   A company's weekly average cash balances are:

Week 1	$240,000
Week 2	$231,000
Week 3	$295,500
Week 4	$195,000

If the annual interest rate is 4.2 percent, what return can be earned on the average cash balances?

Cash Balance Models

28.6   The Joe Elvis Company is currently holding $700,000 in cash. It projects that over the next year its cash outflows will exceed cash inflows by $360,000 per month. How much of the current cash holding should be retained, and how much should be used to increase the company's holdings of marketable securities? Each time these securities are bought or sold through a broker, the company pays a fee of $500. The annual interest rate on money market securities is 6.5 percent. After the initial investment of excess cash, how many times during the next 12 months will securities be sold?

28.7   Lisa Tylor, CFO of Purple Rain Co., concluded from the Baumol model that the optimal cash balance for the firm is $10 million. The annual interest rate on marketable securities is 5.8 percent. The fixed cost of selling securities to replenish cash is $5,000. Purple Rain's cash flow pattern is well approximated by the Baumol model. What can you infer about Purple Rain's average weekly cash disbursement?

28.8   Gold Star Co. and Silver Star Co. both manage their cash flows according to the Miller–Orr model. Gold Star's daily cash flow is controlled between $95,000 and $205,000, whereas Silver Star's daily cash flow is controlled between $120,000 and $230,000. The annual interest rates Gold Star and Silver Star can get are 5.8 percent and 6.1 percent, respectively, and the costs per transaction of trading securities are $2,800 and $2,500, respectively.
a. What are their respective target cash balances?
b. Which firm's daily cash flow is more volatile?

28.9   The variance of the daily cash flows for the Pele Bicycle Shop is $960,000. The opportunity cost to the firm of holding cash is 7 percent per year. What should be the target cash level and the upper limit if the tolerable lower limit has been established as $150,000? The fixed cost of buying and selling securities is $500 per transaction.

28.10 Slap Shot Corporation has a fixed cost associated with buying and selling marketable securities of $100. The interest rate is currently .021 percent per day, and the firm has estimated that the standard deviation of its daily net cash flows is $75. Management has set a lower limit of $1,100 on cash holdings. Calculate the target cash balance and upper limit using the Miller–Orr model. Describe how the system will work.

Lockbox System

28.11 It takes Cookie Cutter Modular Homes Inc. about six days to receive and deposit cheques from customers. Cookie Cutter's management is considering a lockbox system to reduce the firm's collection times. It is expected that the lockbox system will reduce receipt and deposit times to three days total. Average daily collections are $140,000, and the required rate of return is 9 percent per year.
a. What is the reduction in outstanding cash balances as a result of implementing the lockbox system?
b. What dollar return could be earned on these savings?
c. What is the maximum monthly charge Cookie Cutter should pay for this lockbox system?

28.12 Bird's Eye Treehouses Inc., a Kootenay company, has determined that a majority of its customers are located in the Banff area. It therefore is considering using a lockbox system offered by a bank located in Calgary. The bank has estimated that use of the system will reduce collection time by two days. Based on the following information, should the lockbox system be adopted?

Average number of payments per day	600
Average value of payment	$1,100
Variable lockbox fee (per transaction)	$ 0.35
Annual interest rate on money market securities	6.0%

How would your answer change if there were a fixed charge of $1,000 per year in addition to the variable charge?

Float

28.13 Each business day, on average, a company writes cheque totalling $25,000 to pay its suppliers. The usual clearing time for the cheques is four days. Meanwhile, the company is receiving payments from its customers each day, in the form of cheques, totalling $40,000. The cash from the payments is available to the firm after two days.

a. Calculate the company's disbursement float, collection float, and net float.

b. How would your answer to part (a) change if the collected funds were available in one day instead of two?

28.14 Juve Wine receives an average of $9,000 in cheques per day. The delay in clearing is typically four days. The current interest rate is .025 percent per day.

a. What is the company's float?

b. What is the most Juve should be willing to pay today to eliminate its float entirely?

c. What is the highest daily fee the company should be willing to pay to eliminate its float entirely?

28.15 The Walter and Wayne Company disburses cheques every two weeks that average $250,000 in total and take four days to clear. How much can W&W save annually if it delays the transfer of funds from an interest-bearing account that pays 0.02 percent per day for four days?

28.16 Anthony Mariano, CFO of Thousand Yards, is evaluating two alternatives of float management: lockbox and concentration banking. The average number of daily payments to lockboxes is 300 with the average size of each payment at $11,000. The lockbox system can reduce the collection float by 1.5 days and concentration banking can reduce the collection float by half a day. However, the bank charges an annual fee of $32,500 and $0.15 per cheque processed for the lockbox service. Which method is more economical for Thousand Yards: the lockbox system or the concentration banking system? Assume daily interest on T-bills is 0.038 percent.

Investing Idle Cash

28.17 What are the important characteristics of short-term marketable securities?

MINICASE: Cash Management at Richmond Corporation

Richmond Corporation was founded 20 years ago by its president, Daniel Richmond. The company originally began as a mail-order company but has grown rapidly in recent years, in large part due to its website. Because of the wide geographical dispersion of the company's customers, it currently employs a lockbox system with collection centres in Vancouver, St. John's, Montreal, and Winnipeg.

Steve Dennis, the company's treasurer, has been examining the current cash collection policies. On average, each lockbox centre handles $130,000 in payments each day. The company's current policy is to invest these payments in short-term marketable securities daily at the collection centre banks. Every two weeks the investment accounts are swept, and the proceeds are wire-transferred to Richmond's headquarters in Regina to meet the company's payroll. The investment accounts each pay 0.015 percent per day, and the wire transfers cost 0.15 percent of the amount transferred.

Steve has been approached by SIBC Bank, located just outside Moose Jaw, about the possibility of setting up a concentration banking system for Richmond Corp. SIBC will accept the lockbox centres' daily payments via automated clearinghouse (ACH) transfers in lieu of wire transfers. The ACH-transferred funds will not be available for use for one day.

Once cleared, the funds will be deposited in a short-term account, which will also yield 0.015 percent per day. Each ACH transfer will cost $700. Daniel has asked Steve to determine which cash management system will be the best for the company. Steve has asked you, his assistant, to answer the following questions:

1. What is Richmond Corporation's total net cash flow from the current lockbox system available to meet payroll?
2. Under the terms outlined by SIBC should the company proceed with the concentration banking system?
3. What cost of ACH transfers would make the company indifferent between the two systems?

Chapter 29

Credit Management

EXECUTIVE SUMMARY

When a firm sells goods and services, it can (1) be paid in cash immediately or (2) wait for a time to be paid, that is, extend credit to customers. Granting credit is investing in a customer, an investment tied to the sale of a product or service. This chapter examines the firm's decision to grant credit.

An account receivable is created when credit is granted. These receivables include credit granted to other firms, called *trade credit,* and credit granted to consumers, called *consumer credit.* About 15 percent of all the assets of Canadian industrial firms are in the form of accounts receivable. For retail firms, the figure is much higher. Trade credit extended by a firm's supplier to the firm appears as an account payable. Figure 29.1 illustrates this aspect of trade credit.

The investment in accounts receivable for any firm depends on both the amount of credit sales and the average collection period. For example, if a firm's daily credit sales are $1,000 and its average collection period is 30 days, its accounts receivable will be $30,000. Thus, a firm's investment in accounts receivable depends on factors influencing credit sales and collection. A firm's credit policy affects these factors.

The following are the components of credit policy:

1. **Terms of the sale.** A firm must decide on certain conditions when selling its goods and services for credit. The terms of sale may specify the credit period, the cash discount, and the type of credit instrument.
2. **Credit analysis.** When granting credit, a firm tries to distinguish between customers who will pay and those who will not. Firms use a number of devices and procedures to determine the probability that customers will pay.
3. **Collection policy.** Firms that grant credit must establish a policy for collecting the cash when it becomes due.

This chapter discusses each of the components of credit policy that make up the decision to grant credit.

In some ways, the decision to grant credit is connected to the cash collection process described in the previous chapter. This is illustrated with a cash flow diagram in Figure 29.2.

The typical sequence of events when a firm grants credit is (1) the credit sale is made, (2) the customer sends a cheque to the firm, (3) the firm deposits the cheque, and (4) the firm's account is credited for the amount of the cheque.

29.1 Terms of the Sale

The terms of sale refer to the period for which credit is granted, the cash discount, and the type of credit instrument. Within a given industry, the terms of sale are usually fairly standard, but across industries these terms vary quite a bit. In many cases, the terms of

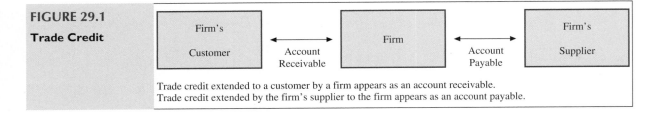

FIGURE 29.1

Trade Credit

Trade credit extended to a customer by a firm appears as an account receivable.
Trade credit extended by the firm's supplier to the firm appears as an account payable.

sale are remarkably archaic and literally date to previous centuries. Organized systems of trade credit that resemble current practice can be easily traced to the great fairs of medieval Europe, and they almost surely existed long before then.

Why Trade Credit Exists

Set aside the venerable history of trade credit for a moment and ask yourself why it should exist.[1] It is quite easy to imagine that all sales could be for cash and, from the firm's viewpoint, this would get rid of receivables' carrying costs and collection costs. Bad debts would be zero (assuming that the firm was careful to accept no counterfeit money).

Imagine this cash-only economy in the context of perfectly competitive product and financial markets. Competition would force companies to lower their prices to pass the savings from immediate collections on to customers. Any company that then chose to grant credit to its customers would have to raise its prices accordingly to survive. If a purchaser needed financing over the operating cycle, it could borrow from a bank or the money market. In this "perfect markets" environment, it would make no difference to the seller or the buyer whether credit were granted.

But, in practice, firms spend significant resources setting credit policy and managing its implementation. So deviations from perfect markets—market imperfections—must explain why trade credit exists. We look briefly at several imperfections and how trade credit helps to overcome them.

In practice, buyers and sellers have imperfect information. Buyers lack perfect information on the quality of the product. For this reason, the buyer may prefer credit terms that give time to return the product if it is defective or unsuitable. When the seller offers credit, it "signals" potential customers that the product is of high quality and likely to provide satisfaction.[2]

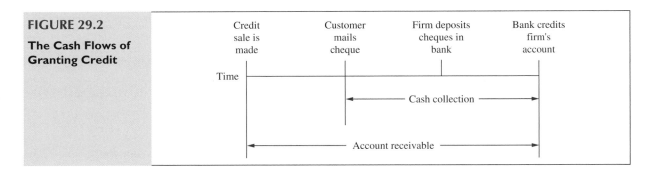

FIGURE 29.2

The Cash Flows of Granting Credit

---

[1]Our discussion of trade credit draws on N. C. Hill and W. S. Sartoris, *Short-Term Financial Management* (New York: Macmillan, 1988), Chapter 14.

[2]This use of signalling is very similar to dividend signalling discussed in Chapter 19. There, corporations signalled the quality of projected cash flows by maintaining dividends even when earnings were down.

In addition, in practice, any firm granting credit lacks perfect information on the credit-worthiness of the borrower. Although it is costly for a bank or other third-party lender to acquire this information, a seller that has been granting trade credit to a purchaser likely has it already. Further, the seller may have superior information on the resale value of the product serving as collateral. These information advantages may allow the seller to offer more attractive, more flexible credit terms and to be more liberal in authorizing credit.

Finally, perfect markets have zero transactions costs but, in reality, it is costly to set up a bank borrowing facility or to borrow in money markets. We discussed some of the costs in Chapter 27. It may be cheaper to utilize credit from the seller.

The Basic Form

Suppose a customer is granted credit with terms of 2/10, net 30. This means that the customer has 30 days from the invoice date within which to pay. (An **invoice** is a bill written by a seller of goods or services and submitted to the buyer. The invoice date is usually the same as the shipping date.) In addition, a cash discount of 2 percent from the stated sales price is to be given if payment is made in 10 days. If the stated terms are net 60, the customer has 60 days from the invoice date to pay and no discount is offered for early payment.

When sales are seasonal, a firm might use seasonal dating. O. M. Scott and Sons is a manufacturer of lawn and garden products with a seasonal dating policy that is tied to the growing season. Payments for winter shipments of fertilizer might be due in the spring or summer. A firm offering 3/10, net 60, May 1 dating, is making the effective invoice date May 1. The stated amount must be paid on June 30, regardless of when the sale is made. The cash discount of 3 percent can be taken until May 10.

Credit Period

Credit periods vary among different industries. For example, a jewellery store may sell diamond engagement rings for 5/30, net 4 months. A food wholesaler, selling fresh fruit and produce, might use net 7.[3] Generally a firm must consider three factors in setting a credit period:

1. *The probability that the customer will not pay.* A firm whose customers are in high-risk businesses may find itself offering restrictive credit terms.
2. *The size of the account.* If the account is small, the credit period will be shorter. Small accounts are more costly to manage, and customers are less important.
3. *The extent to which the goods are perishable.* If the collateral values of the goods are low and cannot be sustained for a long period, less credit will be granted.

Lengthening the credit period effectively reduces the price paid by the customer. Generally this increases sales.

Cash Discounts

Cash discounts are often part of the terms of sale. One reason they are offered is to speed up the collection of receivables. The firm must balance this against the cost of the discount.

---

[3]From T. Beckman and R. Bartels, *Credits and Collections: Management and Theory,* 8th ed. (New York: McGraw-Hill, 1969).

EXAMPLE 29.1

Edward Manalt, the chief financial officer of Charlottetown Grocers, is considering the request of the company's largest customer, who wants to take a 3 percent discount for payment within 20 days on a $10,000 purchase. In other words, the customer intends to pay $9,700 [or $10,000 × (1 − 0.03)]. Normally, this customer pays in 30 days with no discount. The after-tax cost of short-term debt capital for Charlottetown is 3 percent and represents the opportunity cost of investing in receivables. Edward has worked out the cash flow implications illustrated in Figure 29.3. He assumes that the time required to cash the cheque when the firm receives it is the same under both credit arrangements. He has calculated the present value of the two proposals:

Current Policy:

$$PV = \frac{\$10,000}{(1 + 0.03)^{30/365}} = \$9,975.73$$

Proposed Policy:

$$PV = \frac{\$9,700}{(1 + 0.03)^{20/365}} = \$9,684.30$$

His calculation shows that granting the discount would cost the Charlottetown firm $291.43 (or $9,975.73 − $9,684.30) in present value. Consequently, Charlottetown is better off with the current credit arrangement.[4]

FIGURE 29.3

Cash Flows for Different Credit Terms

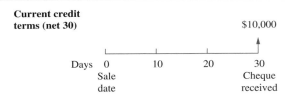

Current situation: Customers usually pay 30 days from the sale date and receive no discount.
Proposed situation: Customer will pay 20 days from the sale date at a 3 percent discount from the $10,000 purchase price.

---

[4]We can reinforce this division by calculating a *customer's* rate of return from taking the discount if it were offered. With the cash discount, a customer pays $9,700 instead of $10,000. By passing on the discount, the customer takes a loan for 20 days and pays 3/97 = 3.09% more for the order. By adopting the policy, the customer takes 365/20 = 18.25 loans per year. By investing, say, one dollar at 3.09 percent per period for 18.25 periods, the customer receives a future value at the end of one year of $(1.0309)^{18.25} = 1.7426$—a return of 74.26 percent annually.

In the previous example, we implicitly assumed that granting credit had no side effects. However, the decision to grant credit may generate higher sales and involve a different cost structure. Example 29.2 illustrates the impact of changes in the level of sales and costs in the credit decision.

EXAMPLE 29.2

Suppose that Charlottetown Grocers has variable costs of $0.50 per $1 of sales. If offered a discount of 3 percent, customers will increase the order size by 10 percent. This new information is shown in Figure 29.4. That is, the customer will increase the order size to $11,000 and, with the 3 percent discount, will remit $10,670 [or $11,000 × (1 − 0.03)] to Charlottetown in 20 days. It will cost more to fill the larger order because variable costs are $5,500. The net present values are worked out here:

Current Policy:

$$\text{NPV} = -\$5,000 + \frac{\$10,000}{(1.03)^{30/365}} = \$4,975.73$$

Proposed Policy:

$$\text{NPV} = -\$5,500 + \frac{\$10,670}{(1.03)^{20/365}} = \$5,152.73$$

Now it is clear that the firm is better off with the proposed credit policy. This increase is the net effect of several different factors, including the larger initial costs, the earlier receipt of the cash inflows, the increased sales level, and the discount.

FIGURE 29.4

Cash Flows for Different Credit Terms: The Impact of New Sales and Costs

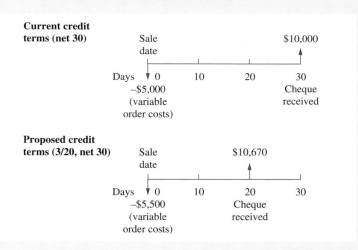

Credit Instruments

Most credit is offered on *open account*. This means that the only formal **credit instrument** is the invoice, which is sent with the shipment of goods, and which the customer signs as evidence that the goods have been received. Afterward, the firm and its customers record the exchange on their books.

When the order is large or the firm anticipates a problem in collections, it may require that the customer sign a *promissory note* or IOU. Promissory notes can prevent future controversies about the existence of a credit agreement.

However, promissory notes are signed after delivery of the goods. One way to obtain a credit commitment from a customer before the goods are delivered is through the use of a *commercial draft*. The selling firm typically writes a commercial draft calling for the customer to pay a specific amount by a specified date. The draft is then sent to the customer's bank with the shipping invoices. The bank has the buyer sign the draft before turning over the invoices. The goods can then be shipped to the buyer. If immediate payment is required, it is called a *sight draft*. Here, funds must be turned over to the bank before the goods are shipped.

Frequently, even the signed draft is not enough for the seller. In this case, the seller might demand that the banker pay for the goods and collect the money from the customer. When the banker agrees to do so in writing, the document is called a *banker's acceptance*. That is, the banker *accepts* responsibility for payment. Because banks generally are well-known and well-respected institutions, the banker's acceptance becomes a liquid instrument. In other words, the seller can then sell (*discount*) the banker's acceptance in the secondary market.

A firm can also use a *conditional sales contract* as a credit instrument. This is an arrangement where the firm retains legal ownership of the goods until the customer has completed payment. Conditional sales contracts usually are paid off in installments and have interest costs built into them.

? Concept Questions
- **What considerations enter into the determination of the terms of sale?**
- **Explain the design of common credit instruments.**

29.2 The Decision to Grant Credit: Risk and Information

Locust Industries has been in existence for two years. It is one of several successful firms that develop computer programs. The present financial managers have set out two alternative credit strategies: The firm can offer credit, or the firm can refuse credit.

Suppose Locust has determined that, if it offers no credit to its customers, it can sell its existing computer software for $50 per program. It estimates that the costs to produce a typical computer program are equal to $20 per unit.

The alternative is to offer credit. In this case, customers of Locust will pay one period later. With some probability, Locust has determined that if it offers credit, it can charge higher prices and expect higher sales.

Strategy 1: Refuse credit. If Locust refuses to grant credit, cash flows will not be delayed, and period 0 net cash flows, NCF, will be

$$P_0 Q_0 - C_0 Q_0 = \text{NCF}$$

The subscripts denote the time when the cash flows are incurred, where

$$P_0 = \text{Price per unit received at time } 0$$
$$C_0 = \text{Cost per unit incurred at time } 0$$
$$Q_0 = \text{Quantity sold at time } 0$$

The net cash flows at period 1 are zero, and the net present value to Locust of refusing credit will simply be the period 0 net cash flow:

$$\text{NPV} = \text{NCF}$$

For example, if credit is not granted and $Q_0 = 100$, the NPV can be calculated as

$$\$50 \times 100 - \$20 \times 100 = \$3,000$$

Strategy 2: Offer credit.   Alternatively, let us assume that Locust grants credit to all customers for one period. The factors that influence the decision are listed below.

	Strategy 1: Refuse Credit	Strategy 2: Offer Credit
Price per unit	$P_0 = \$50$	$P_0' = \$50$
Quantity sold	$Q_0 = 100$	$Q_0' = 200$
Cost per unit	$C_0 = \$20$	$C_0' = \$25$
Probability of payment	$h = 1$	$h = 0.90$
Credit period	0	1 period
Discount rate	0	$r_B = 0.01$

The prime (′) denotes the variables under the second strategy. If the firm offers credit and the new customers pay, the firm will receive revenues of $P_0'Q_0'$ one period hence, but its costs, $C_0'Q_0'$, are incurred in period 0. If new customers do not pay, the firm incurs costs $C_0'Q_0'$ and receives no revenues. The probability that customers will pay, h, is 0.90 in the example. Quantity sold is higher with credit, because new customers are attracted. The cost per unit is also higher with credit because of the costs of operating a credit policy.

The expected cash flows for each policy are set out as follows:

	Expected Cash Flows	
	Time 0	Time 1
Refuse credit	$P_0Q_0 - C_0Q_0$	0
Offer credit	$-C_0'Q_0'$	$h \times P_0'Q_0'$

Note that granting credit produces delayed expected cash inflows equal to $h \times P_0'Q_0'$. The costs are incurred immediately and require no discounting. The net present value if credit is offered is

$$\text{NPV(offer)} = \frac{h \times P_0'Q_0'}{1 + r_B} - C_0'Q_0'$$

$$= \frac{0.9 \times \$50 \times 200}{1.01} - \$5,000 = \$3,910.89$$

Locust Software's decision should be to adopt the proposed credit policy. The NPV of granting credit is higher than that of refusing credit. This decision is very sensitive to the probability of payment. If it turns out that the probability of payment is 81 percent, Locust Software is indifferent to whether it grants credit or not. In this case the NPV of granting credit is $3,000, which we previously found to be the NPV of not granting credit:

$$\$3,000 = h \times \frac{\$50 \times 200}{1.01} - \$5,000$$

$$\$8,000 = h \times \frac{\$50 \times 200}{1.01}$$

$$h = 80.8\%$$

The decision to grant credit depends on four factors:

1. The delayed revenues from granting credit, $P_0'Q_0'$.
2. The immediate costs of granting credit, $C_0'Q_0'$.

3. The probability of payment, h.

4. The appropriate required rate of return for delayed cash flows, r_B. This rate is the after-tax cost of debt, which represents the opportunity cost of investing in receivables.

The Value of New Information About Credit Risk

Obtaining a better estimate of the probability that a customer will default can lead to a better decision. How can a firm determine when to acquire new information about the creditworthiness of its customers?

It may be sensible for Locust Software to determine which of its customers are most likely not to pay. The overall probability of nonpayment is 10 percent. But credit checks by an independent firm show that 90 percent of Locust's customers (computer stores) have been profitable over the past five years and that these customers have never defaulted on payments. The less profitable customers are much more likely to default. In fact, 100 percent of the less profitable customers have defaulted on previous obligations.

Locust would like to avoid offering credit to the deadbeats. Consider its projected number of customers per year of $Q_0' = 200$ if credit is granted. Of these customers, 180 have been profitable over the past five years and have never defaulted on past obligations. The remaining 20 have not been profitable. Locust Software expects that all of these less profitable customers will default. This information is set out in a table:

Type of Customer	Number	Probability of Nonpayment	Expected Number of Defaults
Profitable	180	0	0
Less profitable	20	100%	20
Total customers	200	10%	20

The NPV of granting credit to the customers who default is

$$\frac{hP_0'Q_0'}{1 + r_B} - C_0'Q_0' = \frac{0 \times \$50 \times 20}{1.01} - \$25 \times 20 = -\$500$$

This is the cost of providing them with the software. If Locust can identify these customers without cost, it would certainly deny them credit.

In fact, it actually costs Locust $3 per customer to figure out whether a customer has been profitable over the past five years. The expected payoff of the credit check on its 200 customers is then

$$\begin{array}{ccccc} \text{Cost savings} \\ \text{from not} & & \text{Cost of} \\ \text{extending credit} & - & \text{credit checks} \\ \$500 & - & \$3 \times 200 & = & -\$100 \end{array}$$

For Locust, credit is not worth checking. It would need to pay $600 to avoid a $500 loss.

Future Sales

Up to this point, Locust has not considered the possibility that offering credit will permanently increase the level of sales in future periods (beyond next month). In addition, payment and nonpayment patterns in the current period will provide credit information that is useful for the next period. These two factors should be analyzed.

In the case of Locust, there is a 90 percent probability that the customer will pay in period 1. But, if payment is made, there will be another sale in period 2. The probability

FIGURE 29.5

Future Sales and the Credit Decision

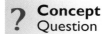

There is a 90 percent probability that a customer will pay in period 1. However, if payment is made, there will be another sale in period 2. The probability that the customer will pay in period 2 is 100 percent—if the customer has paid in period 1.

that the customer will pay in period 2, if the customer has paid in period 1, is 100 percent. Locust can refuse to offer credit in period 2 to customers that have refused to pay in period 1. This is diagrammed in Figure 29.5.

? Concept Question

- **List the factors that influence the decision to grant credit.**

29.3 Optimal Credit Policy

So far we have discussed how to compute net present value for two alternative credit policies. However, we have not discussed the optimal amount of credit. At the optimal amount of credit, the incremental cash flows from increased sales are exactly equal to the carrying costs from the increase in accounts receivable.

Consider a firm that does not currently grant credit. This firm has no bad debts, no credit department, and relatively few customers. Now consider another firm that grants credit. This firm has lots of customers, a credit department, and a bad-debt expense account.

It is useful to think of the decision to grant credit in terms of carrying costs and opportunity costs:

1. *Carrying costs* are the costs associated with granting credit and making an investment in receivables. Carrying costs include the delay in receiving cash, the losses from bad debts, and the costs of managing credit.

2. *Opportunity costs* are the lost sales from refusing to offer credit. These costs drop as credit is granted.

We represent these costs in Figure 29.6.

The sum of the carrying costs and the opportunity costs of a particular credit policy is called the *total credit cost curve*. A point is identified as the minimum of the total credit cost curve. If the firm extends more credit than the minimum, the additional net cash flow from new customers will not cover the carrying costs of the higher investment in receivables.

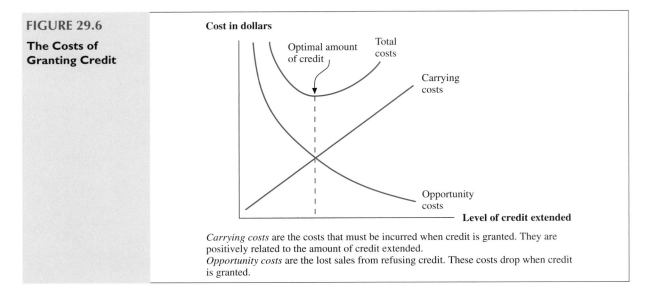

FIGURE 29.6

The Costs of Granting Credit

Carrying costs are the costs that must be incurred when credit is granted. They are positively related to the amount of credit extended.
Opportunity costs are the lost sales from refusing credit. These costs drop when credit is granted.

The concept of optimal credit policy in the context of modern principles of finance should be somewhat analogous to the concept of the optimal capital structure discussed earlier in the text. In perfect financial markets, there should be no optimal credit policy. Alternative amounts of credit for a firm should not affect the value of the firm. Thus, the decision to grant credit would be a matter of indifference to financial managers.

Just as with optimal capital structure, we could expect taxes, bankruptcy costs, and agency costs to be important in determining an optimal credit policy in a world of imperfect financial markets. For example, customers in high tax brackets would be better off borrowing and taking advantage of cash discounts offered by firms than would customers in low tax brackets. Corporations in low tax brackets would be less able to offer credit, because borrowing would be relatively more expensive than for firms in high tax brackets.

In general, a firm will extend trade credit if it has a comparative advantage in doing so. Trade credit is likely to be advantageous if the selling firm has a cost advantage over other potential lenders, if the selling firm has monopoly power it can exploit, if the selling firm can reduce taxes by extending credit, and if the product quality of the selling firm is difficult to determine. Firm size may be important if there are size economies in managing credit.

The optimal credit policy depends on characteristics of particular firms. Assuming that the firm has more flexibility in its credit policy than in the prices it charges, firms with excess capacity, low variable operating costs, high tax brackets, and repeat customers should extend credit more liberally than others.

Credit Insurance

Firms that run strictly internal credit operations are self-insured against default risk. An alternative is to buy credit insurance through an insurance company. The insurance company offers coverage up to a pre-set dollar limit for accounts. As you would expect, accounts with a higher credit rating merit higher insurance limits. Exporters may qualify for credit insurance through the Export Development Canada (EDC), a Crown corporation of the federal government. In 2005, EDC provided a total of $57.5 billion in financing for the sale of equipment and services by various Canadian suppliers. In 2004, EDC concluded

The Decision to Grant Credit

Trade credit is more likely to be granted by the selling firm if

1. The selling firm has a cost advantage over other lenders.
   Example: The Canadian Manufacturing Co. produces widgets. In a default, it is easier for the Canadian Manufacturing Co. to repossess widgets and resell than for a finance company with no experience in selling widgets to arrange for it.

2. The selling firm can engage in price discrimination.
   Example: National Motors can offer below-market interest rates to lower-income customers that must finance a large portion of the purchase price of cars. Higher-income customers pay the list price and do not generally finance a large part of the purchase.

3. The selling firm can obtain favourable tax treatment.
   Example: The A.B. Production Company offers long-term credit to its best customers. This form of financing may qualify as an installment plan and allow the A.B. Production Co. to book profits of the sale over the life of the loan. This may save taxes because the present value of the tax payments will be lower if spread over time.

4. The selling firm has no established reputation for quality products or services.
   Example: Advanced Micro Instruments (AMI) manufactures sophisticated measurement instruments for controlling electrical systems on commercial airplanes. The firm was founded by two engineering graduates from the University of Toronto in 1997. It became a public firm in 1998. To hedge their bets, aircraft manufacturers will ask for credit from AMI. It is very difficult for customers of AMI to assess the quality of its instruments until the instruments have been in place for some time.

5. The selling firm perceives a long-term strategic relationship.
   Example: Food.com is a fast-growing, cash-constrained Internet food distributor. It is currently not profitable. Acme Food will grant Food.com credit for food purchased, because Food.com will generate profits in the future.

Sources: Shezad I. Mian and Clifford W. Smith, "Extending Trade Credit and Financing Receivables," *Journal of Applied Corporate Finance* (Spring 1994); Marc Deloof and Marc Jegers; "Trade Credit, Product Quality and Intragroup Trade: Some European Evidence," *Financial Management* (Autumn 1996); and Michael Long, I. B. Malitz, and S. A. Ravid, "Trade Credit, Quality Guarantees, and Product Marketability," *Financial Management* (Winter 1993); Mitchell A. Petersen and Raghuram G. Rajan, "Trade Credit: Theories and Evidence," *The Review of Financial Studies* 10 (1997).

four financial agreements that facilitated an additional $133.9 million in export sales to Mexico. These four financial agreements included credit facilities to Mexican companies such as Nemak, Navistar, and Galvak, which work to benefit Canadian exporters in the automotive and industrial equipment sectors. In addition, the last agreement was a bonding guarantee for Q'Max Solutions that will facilitate the export of equipment and services from Alberta's oil and gas sector.

• **What are the advantages of credit insurance?**

29.4 Credit Analysis

When granting credit, a firm tries to distinguish between customers who will pay and those who will not pay. There are a number of sources of information for determining creditworthiness.

Credit Information

Information commonly used to assess creditworthiness includes the following:

1. *Financial statements.* A firm can ask a customer to supply financial information such as balance sheets and income statements. Minimum standards and rules of thumb based on financial ratios like the ones we discussed in Appendix 2A can then be used as a basis for extending or refusing credit.

2. *Credit reports on customer's payment history with other firms.* Several organizations sell information on the credit strength and credit history of business firms. D&B Canada and Creditel provide subscribers with credit references and credit reports on individual firms. Ratings and information are available for a huge number of firms, including very small ones.

3. *Banks.* Banks will generally provide some assistance to their business customers in providing information on the creditworthiness of other firms.

4. *The customer's payment history with the firm.* The most obvious way to obtain information about the likelihood of a customer's not paying is to examine whether the customer paid up in the past and how much trouble collecting turned out to be.

Credit Evaluation and Scoring

Once information has been gathered, the firm faces the hard choice of either granting or refusing credit. Many firms use the traditional and subjective guidelines referred to as the "five Cs of credit":

1. *Character.* The customer's willingness to meet credit obligations.
2. *Capacity.* The customer's ability to meet credit obligations out of operating cash flows.
3. *Capital.* The customer's financial reserves, or how much net worth the borrower has.
4. *Collateral.* A pledged asset in the case of default.
5. *Conditions.* General business conditions, which affect the customer's ability to repay.

   Credit scoring refers to the process of (1) calculating a numerical rating for a customer based on information collected, then (2) granting or refusing credit based on the result. For example, a firm might rate a customer on a scale of 1 (very poor) to 10 (very good) on each of the five Cs of credit using all the information available about the customer. A credit score could then be calculated based on the total. From experience, a firm might choose to grant credit only to customers with a score of more than, say, 30 out of a possible 50 points.

   Financial institutions have developed elaborate statistical models for credit scoring. This approach has the advantage of being objective as compared to scoring based on judgments on the five Cs. Usually, all legally relevant and observable characteristics of a large pool of customers are studied to find their historic relation to default rates. Based on the results, it is possible to determine the variables that best predict whether or not a customer will pay; then a credit score based on those variables is calculated.

Because credit-scoring models and procedures determine who is and who is not creditworthy, it is not surprising that they have been the subject of government regulation. In particular, the kinds of background and demographic information that can be used in the credit decision are limited. For example, suppose a consumer applicant was formerly bankrupt but had discharged all obligations. After a waiting period, which varies from province to province, this information cannot be used in the credit decision.

Credit scoring is used for business customers by Canadian chartered banks. Scoring for small business loans is a particularly attractive application because the technique offers the advantages of objective analysis without taking more of the lending officer's time than could be justified for a small account.

? Concept Questions
- **What is credit analysis?**
- **What are the five Cs of credit?**
- **What are credit scoring models and how are they used?**

29.5 Collection Policy

Collection refers to obtaining payment of past-due accounts. The credit manager keeps a record of payment experience with each customer.

Average Collection Period

Acme Compact Disc Players sells 100,000 compact disc players a year at $300 each. All sales are for credit with terms of 2/20, net 60.

Suppose that 80 percent of Acme customers take the discounts and pay on day 20; the rest pay on day 60. The **average collection period (ACP)** measures the average amount of time required to collect an account receivable. The ACP for Acme is 28 days:

$$0.8 \times 20 \text{ days} + 0.2 \times 60 \text{ days} = 28 \text{ days}$$

(The average collection period is frequently referred to as *days' sales outstanding* or *days in receivables*.)

Of course, this is an idealized example where customers pay on either one of two dates. In reality, payments arrive in a random fashion, so that the average collection period must be calculated differently.

To determine the ACP in the real world, firms first calculate average daily sales. The **average daily sales (ADS)** equal annual sales divided by 365. The ADS of Acme are

$$\text{Average daily sales} = \frac{\$300 \times 100,000}{365 \text{ days}} = \$82,192$$

If receivables today are $2,301,376, the average collection period is

$$\text{Average collection period} = \frac{\text{Accounts receivable}}{\text{Average daily sales}}$$

$$= \frac{\$2,301,376}{\$82,192}$$

$$= 28 \text{ days}$$

In practice, firms observe sales and receivables on a daily basis. Consequently, an average collection period can be computed and compared to the stated credit terms. For example, suppose Acme had computed its ACP at 40 days for several weeks, versus its credit terms of 2/20, net 60. With a 40-day ACP, some customers are paying later than usual. It may be that some accounts are overdue.

However, firms with seasonal sales will often find the *calculated* ACP changing during the year, making the ACP a somewhat flawed tool. This occurs because receivables are low before the selling season and high after the season. Thus, firms may keep track of seasonal movement in the ACP over past years. In this way, they can compare the ACP for today's date with the average ACP for that date in previous years. To supplement the information in the ACP, the credit manager may make up an accounts receivable aging schedule.

Aging Schedule

The **aging schedule** tabulates receivables by age of account. In the following schedule, 75 percent of the accounts are on time, but a significant number are more than 60 days past due. This signifies that some customers are in arrears.

Aging Schedule

Age of Account	Percentage of Total Value of Accounts Receivable
0–20 days	50
21–60 days	25
61–80 days	20
Over 80 days	5
	100

The aging schedule changes during the year. To avoid confusion, the aging schedule is often augmented by the payments pattern. The *payments pattern* describes the lagged collection pattern of receivables. Like a mortality table that describes the probability that a 23-year-old will live to be 24, the payments pattern describes the probability that a 67-day-old account will still be unpaid when it is 68 days old.

Collection Effort

The firm usually employs a sequence of procedures for customers that are overdue:

1. Sends a delinquency letter informing the customer of the past-due status of the account.
2. Makes a telephone call to the customer.
3. Employs a collection agency.
4. Takes legal action against the customer.

At times, a firm may refuse to grant additional credit to customers until arrearages are paid. This may antagonize a normally good customer, and it points to a potential conflict of interest between the collections department and the sales department.

One last point should be stressed. We have presented the elements of credit policy as though they were somewhat independent of each other. In fact, they are closely interrelated. For example, the optimal credit policy is not independent of collection and monitoring policies. A tighter collection policy can reduce the probability of default and this in turn can raise the NPV of a more liberal credit policy.

? **Concept** Question

• **What tools can a manager use to analyze a collection policy?**

29.6 Other Aspects of Credit Policy

Factoring

A *factor* is an independent company that acts as "an outside credit department" for the client. It checks the credit of new customers, authorizes credit, and handles collection and bookkeeping. As the accounts are collected, the factor pays the client the face amount of the invoice less a 1 or 2 percent discount.[5] If any accounts are late, the factor still pays the selling firm on an average maturity date determined in advance. The legal arrangement is that the factor purchases the accounts receivable from the firm. Thus, factoring provides insurance against bad debts since any bad accounts are the factor's problem.

Factoring in Canada is conducted by independent firms whose main customers are small businesses. Factoring is popular with manufacturers of retail goods—especially in the apparel business—because it allows outside professionals to handle the headaches of credit.

What we have described so far is *maturity factoring* and does not involve a formal financing arrangement. What factoring does is remove receivables from the balance sheet and so, indirectly, it reduces the need for financing. It may also reduce the costs associated with granting credit. Since factors do business with many firms, they may be able to achieve scale economies, reduce risks through diversification, and carry more clout in collection.

Firms financing their receivables through a chartered bank may also use the services of a factor to improve the receivables' collateral value. In this case, the factor buys the receivables and assigns them to the bank. This is called maturity factoring with assignment of equity. Or, the factor will provide an advance on the receivables and charge interest at prime plus 2.5 to 3 percent. In this case of advance factoring, the factor is providing financing as well as other services.

How to Finance Trade Credit

In addition to unsecured debt instruments described earlier in this chapter, there are three general ways of financing accounting receivables: secured debt, a captive finance company, and securitization.

Use of secured debt is usually referred to as asset-based receivables financing. This is the predominant form of receivables financing. Many lenders will not lend without security to firms with substantive uncertainty or little equity. With secured debt, if the borrower gets into financial difficulty, the lender can repossess the asset and sell it for its fair market value.

Many large firms with good credit ratings use captive finance companies. The captive finance companies are subsidiaries of the parent firm. This is similar to the use of secured debt because the creditors of the captive finance company have a claim on its assets and, as a consequence, the accounts receivable of the parent firm. A captive finance company is attractive if economies of scale are important and if an independent subsidiary with limited liability is warranted.[6]

---

[5]Our discussion of factoring draws on D. Reidy, "Factoring Smooths Banking Relationships," *Profit* (November 1991); and S. Horvitch, "Busy Days for Factoring Firms," *The Financial Post* (February 15, 1991).

[6]The trend toward securitization of receivables through wholly owned subsidiaries discussed in Chapter 28 is supporting evidence. For more on finance captives see G. S. Roberts and J. A. Viscione, "Captive Finance Subsidiaries and the M-Form Hypothesis," *Bell Journal of Economics* (Spring 1981), pp. 285–95; and S. Mian and C. Smith, "Extending Trade Credit and Financing Receivables," Journal of Applied Corporate Finance (Spring 1994), pp. 75–84.

Ken Hitzig on Keeping Business Liquid Through Factoring

Through subsidiaries in Canada and the United States, Accord Financial Corp. provides factoring services to small and medium-sized companies. Accord's customers are engaged in temporary staff placement, computer services, textiles, apparel, medical services, food distribution, sporting goods, leisure products, transportation, footwear, floor coverings, home furnishings, and industrial products.

Accord is engaged in the factoring business on both a recourse and non-recourse basis. Non-recourse factoring is a service provided to companies desiring to outsource their customer accounts receivable departments, including the risk of customer default. Almost all the work involving credit checking, recordkeeping, collections, and credit losses is effectively off-loaded on Accord for a predetermined fee. Financing is available, but few of Accord's clients avail themselves of this facility, preferring instead to fund their business through banks.

Accord's non-recourse service appeals to medium-sized companies (annual sales of $1–$10 million) which view the virtual elimination of customer credit risk as the single, most important benefit. Most of these clients

are privately owned and the owners are very aware of preserving capital and avoiding unnecessary risk. The failure of a large customer could cause the bank to reduce or cancel the operating line of credit and jeopardize the owner's life savings. Non-recourse factoring with Accord solves the problem. As one client described it: "Accord's credit is best described in three words— Ship and Sleep."

Recourse factoring is similar to non-recourse but the customer credit risk remains with the client company. Accord purchases the invoices from the client for cash; however, in the event of customer default, Accord has the right to resell the account back to the client. Recourse factoring is attractive to small and medium-sized companies needing liquidity but unable to borrow from banks on the strength of their financial statements. These companies are usually thinly capitalized, going through a turnaround phase, growing rapidly or a combination of some or all of these traits. They usually have better-than-average quality customers, and by factoring their sales, they effectively exchange paper for cash.

Ken Hitzig is a Commerce graduate of McGill University and a Chartered Accountant. After an 18-year career at Aetna Factors Corp. Ltd., he left to start Accord Business Credit Inc. in 1978. Along with Montcap Financial Corp. in Canada and J.T.A. Factors Inc. in South Carolina, Accord is now a subsidiary of Accord Financial Corp., a publicly-held company listed on the Toronto Stock Exchange. Mr. Hitzig is Chief Executive Officer of Accord Financial Corp.

? Concept Question

- **What services do factors provide?**

29.7 SUMMARY AND CONCLUSIONS

1. The three components of a firm's credit policy are the terms of sale, the credit analysis, and the collection policies.
2. The terms of sale describe the amount and period of time for which credit is granted and the type of credit instrument.
3. The decision to grant credit is a straightforward NPV decision, and can be improved by additional information about the payment characteristics of the customers. Additional information about the customers' probability of defaulting is valuable, but this value must be traded off against the expense of acquiring the information.
4. The optimal amount of credit the firm offers is a function of the competitive conditions in which it finds itself. These conditions will determine the carrying costs associated with granting credit and the opportunity costs of the lost sales from refusing to offer credit. The optimal credit policy minimizes the sum of these two costs.

5. We have seen that knowledge of the probability that customers will default is valuable. To enhance its ability to assess customers' default probability, a firm can score credit. This relates the default probability to observable characteristics of customers.

6. The collection policy is the method of dealing with past-due accounts. The first step is to analyze the average collection period and to prepare an aging schedule that relates the age of accounts to the proportion of the accounts receivable they represent. The next step is to decide on the collection method and to evaluate the possibility of factoring, that is, selling the overdue accounts.

KEY TERMS

Aging schedule 838
Average collection period
  (ACP) 837
Average daily sales
  (ADS) 837

Cash discount 827
Collection policy 825
Credit analysis 825
Credit instrument 829
Credit period 827

Credit scoring 836
Factoring 839
Invoice 827
Terms of the sale 825

SUGGESTED READING

An excellent textbook on short-term financial management is:
T. S. Maness and J. T. Zietlow. *Short-Term Financial Management.* Macon, Ohio: South-Western, 2005.

Current articles on credit management in Canada are in Canadian Treasurer.

Our treatment of the credit decision owes much to:
H. Bierman, Jr. and W. H. Hausman. "The Credit Granting Decision." *Management Science* 16 (April 1970); and Shezad I. Mian and Clifford W. Smith. "Extending Trade Credit and Financial Receivables." *Journal of Applied Corporate Finance* (Spring 1994).

Three articles that establish a theoretical framework and some empirical work on trade credit are:
S. I. Mian and C. Smith. "Extending Trade Credit and Financing Receivables." *Journal of Applied Corporate Finance* (Spring 1994).
M. S. Long, I. B. Malitz, and S. A. Ravid. "Trade Credit, Quality Guarantees, and Product Marketability." *Financial Management* (Winter 1993).
Y. W. Lee and J. D. Stowe. "Product Risk, Asymmetric Information and Trade Credit." *Journal of Financial and Quantitative Analysis* (June 1993).

An interesting normative article on how to establish trade credit limits is:
F. C. Scherr. "Optimal Trade Credit Limits." *Financial Management* (Spring 1996).

QUESTIONS & PROBLEMS

Credit Terms

29.1 A firm offer terms of 2/9, net 40. What effective annual interest rate does the firm earn when a customer does not take the discount? Without doing any calculations, explain what will happen to this effective rate if:
- The discount is changed to 3 percent.
- The credit period is increased to 60 days.
- The discount period is increased to 15 days.

29.2 Ronald places an order for 200 units of inventory at a unit price of $95. The supplier offers terms of 2/10, net 30.
a. How long does Ronald have to pay before the account is overdue? If he takes the full period, how much should he remit?
b. What is the discount being offered? How quickly must he pay to get the discount? If he takes the discount, how much should he remit?
c. If Ronald doesn't take the discount, how much interest is he paying implicitly? How many days' credit is he receiving?

29.3 The Prince Edward Potato Company has provided the following data:
- Annual credit sales: $14 million.
- Average collection period: 54 days.
- Terms: Net 20.
- Interest rate: 4.3%.

Prince Edward Potato proposes to offer a discount policy of 2/11, net 20. It anticipates that 54 percent of its customers will take advantage of this new policy. As a result, the collection period will be reduced to 32 days. Should the Prince Edward Potato Company offer the new credit terms?

29.4   Vitale, Baby! Inc. has weekly credit sales of $18,000, and the average collection period is 29 days. The cost of production is 80 percent of the selling price. What is Vitale's average accounts receivable figure?

29.5   Tick Tock Clocks sells on credit terms of net 30. Its accounts are on average 35 days past due. If annual credit sales are $6 million, what is the company's balance in accounts receivable?

29.6   The Tropeland Company has annual sales of $50 million, all of which are on credit. The current collection period is 45 days, and the credit terms are net 30. The company is considering offering terms of 2/10, net 30. It anticipates that 70 percent of its customers will take advantage of the discount. The new policy will reduce the collection period to 28 days. The appropriate interest rate is 6 percent. Should the new credit policy be adopted? How does the level of credit sales affect this decision?

The Decision to Grant Credit

29.7   Bismark Co. is in the process of considering a change in its terms of sale. The current policy is cash only; the new policy will involve one period's credit. Sales are 70,000 units per period at a price of $530 per unit. If credit is offered, the new price will be $552. Unit sales are not expected to change, and all customers are expected to take the credit. Bismark estimates that 2 percent of credit sales will be uncollectible. If the required return is 2 percent per period, is the change a good idea?

29.8   Silicon Wafers Inc. (SWI) is debating whether to extend credit to a particular customer. SWI's products, primarily used in the manufacture of semiconductors, currently sell for $1,850 per unit. The variable cost is $1,200 per unit. The order under consideration is for 12 units today; payment is promised in 30 days.

   a. If there is a 20 percent chance of default, should SWI fill the order? The required return is 2 percent per month. This is a one-time sale, and the customer will not buy if credit is not extended.

   b. What is the break-even probability in part (a)?

   c. This part is a little harder. In general terms, how do you think your answer to part (a) will be affected if the customer will purchase the merchandise for cash if the credit is refused? The cash price is $1,700 per unit.

29.9   The Silver Spokes Bicycle Shop has decided to offer credit to its customers during the spring selling season. Sales are expected to be 400 bicycles. The average cost to the shop of a bicycle is $280. The owner knows that only 97 percent of the customers will be able to make their payments. To identify the remaining 3 percent, she is considering subscribing to a credit agency. The initial charge for this service is $500, with an additional charge of $4 per individual report. Should she subscribe to the agency?

29.10   Berkshire Sports Inc. operates a mail-order running shoe business. Management is considering dropping its policy of no credit. The credit policy under consideration is this:

	No Credit	Credit
Price per unit	$45	$50
Cost per unit	$30	$37
Quantity sold	3000	4000
Probability of payment	99%	80%
Credit period	0	1
Discount rate	0	4.5%

     a. Should Berkshire offer credit to its customers?

     b. What must the probability of payment be before Berkshire would adopt the policy?

29.11 Champions Inc. is considering a change in its cash-only sales policy. The new terms of sale would be net one month. Based on the following information, determine if Champions should proceed. Describe the buildup of receivables in this case. The required return is 1.5 percent per month.

	Current Policy	New Policy
Price per unit	$900	$900
Cost per unit	$502	$503
Unit sales per month	1087	1295

29.12 The Fluffy Animals Corporation, a manufacturer of high-quality stuffed animals, does not extend credit to its customers. A study has shown that, by offering credit, the company could increase sales from the current 1750 units to 2100 units. The cost per unit, however, would increase from $44 to $47, reflecting the expense of managing accounts receivable. The current price of a toy is $50. The probability of a customer making a payment on a credit sale is 94 percent, and the appropriate discount rate is 3.7 percent. How much should Fluffy Animals increase the price to make offering credit an attractive strategy?

Investment in Receivables

29.13 The factoring department of Royal Imperial Dominion National Bank (RIDN) is processing 200,000 invoices per year with an average invoice value of $1,800. RIDN buys the accounts receivable at 3.5 percent off the invoice value. The average collection period is 45 days. Currently, 2.5 percent of the accounts receivable turns out to be bad debt. The annual interest rate is 10 percent. The annual operating expense of this department is $400,000. What are the gross profit before interest and tax for the factoring department of RIDN?

29.14 Blackjohn Inc. is in the business of manufacturing and selling hand-held multipurpose devices. It does not offer any credit sales currently. The per unit price and cost of each device is $900. Blackjohn is considering the possibility of credit sales. The market price of the device will stay the same with credit sales, but it is expected that the annual sales will increase from 50,000 units to 87,000 units and the per unit cost will go up by $76 due to the implementation cost of credit sales. The credit period will be two months and the appropriate discount rate for the credit period is 2.4 percent. What is the minimum probability of repayment that can make Blackjohn indifferent between whether or not to implement the new credit policy?

29.15 The Moose Factory Company has monthly credit sales of $1.7 million. The average collection period is 77 days. The cost of production is 77 percent of the selling price. What is Moose Factory's average investment in accounts receivable?

Optimal Credit Policy

29.16 In principle, how should we decide on the optimal credit policy?

Credit Analysis

29.17 What is the information commonly used to assess creditworthiness of a client?

MINICASE: Credit Policy at Braam Industries

Tricia Haltiwinger, the president of Braam Industries, has been exploring ways of improving the company's financial performance. Braam Industries manufactures and sells office equipment to retailers. The company's growth has been relatively slow in recent years, but with an expansion in the economy, it appears that sales may increase more quickly in the future. Tricia has asked Mats Eriksson, the company's treasurer, to evaluate Braam's current credit policy and compare it to different credit policies with the hopes of increasing profitability.

The company currently has a policy of net 30. As with any credit sales, default rates are always of concern. Because of Braam's screening and collection process, the default rate on credit is currently only 1.5 percent. Mats has examined the company's credit policy in relation to other vendors, and he has determined that three options are available.

The first option is to relax the company's decision when to grant credit. The second option is to increase the credit period to net 45, and the third option is a combination of the relaxed credit policy and the extension of the credit period to net 45. On the positive side, each of the three policies under consideration would increase sales. The three policies have the drawbacks that default rates would increase, the administrative costs of managing the firm's receivables would increase, and the receivables period would increase. The credit policy change would impact all four of these variables in different degrees. Mats has prepared the following table outlining the effect on each of these variables:

	Annual Sales (millions)	Default Rate (% of sales)	Administrative Costs (% of sales)	Receivables Period
Currency Policy	$120	1.5%	2.1%	38 days
Option 1	140	2.4	3.1	41 days
Option 2	137	1.7	2.3	51 days
Option 3	150	2.1	2.9	49 days

Braam's variable costs of production are 45 percent of sales, and the relevant interest rate is a 6 percent effective annual rate. Which credit policy should the company use? Notice that in option 3 the default rate and administrative costs are below those in option 2. Is this plausible? Why or why not?

PART 8

Chapter 30

Mergers and Acquisitions

EXECUTIVE SUMMARY

There is no more dramatic or controversial activity in corporate finance than the acquisition of one firm by another or the merger of two firms. This chapter addresses two basic questions: Why does a firm choose to merge with or acquire another firm, and how does it happen?

The acquisition of one firm by another is, of course, an investment made under uncertainty. The basic principle of valuation applies: A firm should be acquired if it generates a positive net present value to the shareholders of the acquiring firm. However, because the NPV of an acquisition candidate is very difficult to determine, mergers and acquisitions are interesting topics in their own right. Here are some of the special features of this area of finance:

1. The benefits from acquisitions are called *synergies*. It is hard to estimate synergies using discounted cash flow techniques.
2. There are complex accounting, tax, and legal effects when one firm is acquired by another.
3. Acquisitions are an important control device of shareholders. It appears that some acquisitions are a consequence of an underlying conflict between the interests of management and of shareholders. Agreeing to be acquired by another firm is one way that shareholders can remove managers with whom they are unhappy.
4. Acquisition analysis frequently focuses on the total value of the firms involved. But usually an acquisition will affect the relative values of stocks and bonds as well as their total value.
5. Mergers and acquisitions sometimes involve unfriendly transactions. Thus, when one firm attempts to acquire another, it does not always involve quiet negotiations. The sought-after firm may use defensive tactics, including poison pills, greenmail, and white knights.

This chapter starts by introducing the basic legal, accounting, and tax aspects of acquisitions. When one firm acquires another, it must choose the legal framework, the accounting method, and tax status. These choices will be explained throughout the chapter.

The chapter discusses how to determine the NPV of an acquisition candidate. The NPV of an acquisition candidate is the difference between the synergy from the merger and the premium to be paid. We consider the following types of synergy: (1) revenue enhancement, (2) cost reduction, (3) lower taxes, and (4) lower cost of capital. The premium paid for an acquisition is the price paid minus the market value of the acquisition prior to the merger. The premium depends on whether cash or securities are used to finance the offer price.

30.1 The Basic Forms of Acquisitions

There are three basic legal procedures that one firm can use to acquire another firm: (1) merger or consolidation, (2) acquisition of stock, and (3) acquisition of assets.

Merger or Consolidation

A **merger** refers to the absorption of one firm by another. The acquiring firm retains its name and identity, and acquires all of the assets and liabilities of the acquired firm. After a merger, the acquired firm ceases to exist as a separate business entity.

A **consolidation** is the same as a merger except that an entirely new firm is created. In a consolidation, both the acquiring firm and the acquired firm terminate their previous legal existence and become part of the new firm. In a consolidation, the distinction between the acquiring and the acquired firm is not important. However, the rules for mergers and consolidations are basically the same. Acquisitions by merger and consolidation result in combinations of the assets and liabilities of acquired and acquiring firms.

EXAMPLE 30.1

> Suppose firm *A* acquires firm *B* in a merger. Further, suppose firm *B* shareholders are given one share of firm *A*'s stock in exchange for two shares of firm *B*'s stock. From a legal standpoint, firm *A*'s shareholders are not directly affected by the merger. However, firm *B*'s shares cease to exist. In a consolidation, the shareholders of firm *A* and firm *B* exchange their shares for the shares of a new firm (firm *C*). Because the differences between mergers and consolidations are minor for our purposes, we shall refer to both types of reorganizations as *mergers*.

There are some advantages and some disadvantages to using a merger to acquire a firm:

1. A merger is legally straightforward and does not cost as much as other forms of acquisition. It avoids the necessity of transferring title of each individual asset of the acquired firm to the acquiring firm.

2. A primary disadvantage is that a merger must be approved by a vote of the shareholders of each firm.[1] Typically, two-thirds (or even more) of the share votes are required for approval. Obtaining the necessary votes can be time-consuming and difficult. Furthermore, as we discuss in greater detail below, the cooperation of the target firm's existing management is almost a necessity for a merger. This cooperation may not be easily or cheaply obtained.

Acquisition of Stock

A second way to acquire another firm is to purchase the firm's voting stock in exchange for cash, shares of stock, or other securities. This process will often start as a private offer from the management of one firm to another. At some point the offer is taken directly to the target firm's shareholders through a tender offer. A **tender offer** is a public offer to buy shares made by one firm directly to the shareholders of another firm.

If the shareholders choose to accept the offer, they tender their shares by exchanging them for cash or securities (or both), depending on the offer. A tender offer is frequently contingent on the bidder's obtaining some percentage of the total voting shares. If not enough shares are tendered, then the offer might be withdrawn or reformulated.

The takeover bid is communicated to the target firm's shareholders by public announcements such as newspaper advertisements. Takeover bids may be either by **circular bid** mailed directly to the target's shareholders or by **stock exchange bid** (through the facilities

---

[1] As we discuss later, obtaining majority assent is less of a problem in Canada than in the United States because fewer Canadian corporations are widely held.

of the TSX or other exchange). In either case, Ontario securities law requires that the bidder mail a notice of the proposed share purchase to shareholders. Furthermore, the management of the target firm must also respond to the bid, including its recommendation to accept or to reject the bid. In the case of a circular bid, the response must be mailed to shareholders. If the bid is made through a stock exchange, the response is through a press release.

The following are factors involved in choosing between an acquisition of stock and a merger:

- In an acquisition of stock, no shareholder meetings must be held and no vote is required. If the shareholders of the target firm do not like the offer, they are not required to accept it and they will not tender their shares.
- In an acquisition of stock, the bidding firm can deal directly with the shareholders of a target firm by using a tender offer. The target firm's management and board of directors can be bypassed.
- Acquisition of stock is often unfriendly and is used in an effort to circumvent the target firm's management, which is usually actively resisting acquisition. Resistance by the target firm's management often makes the cost of acquisition by stock higher than the cost by merger.
- Sometimes a minority of shareholders will hold out in a tender offer, and thus the target firm cannot be completely absorbed.
- Complete absorption of one firm by another requires a merger. Many acquisitions of stock end with a formal merger later.

Acquisition of Assets

One firm can acquire another by buying all of its assets. A formal vote of the shareholders of the selling firm is required. This approach to acquisition will avoid the potential problem of having holdout minority shareholders, which can occur in an acquisition of stock. But, acquisition of assets involves a costly legal process of transferring title.

A Classification Scheme

Financial analysts typically classify acquisitions into three types:

1. *Horizontal acquisition.* This is an acquisition of a firm in the same industry as the acquiring firm. The firms compete with each other in their product market.
2. *Vertical acquisition.* A vertical acquisition involves firms at different stages of the production process. The acquisition by an airline company of a travel agency would be a vertical acquisition.
3. *Conglomerate acquisition.* The acquiring firm and the acquired firm are not related to each other. The acquisition of Federated Department Stores by Campeau Corporation, a real estate company, was considered a conglomerate acquisition. We discuss this acquisition in detail in Appendix 30A, which can be accessed on the book's website at www.mcgrawhill.ca/olc/ross.

A Note on Takeovers

Takeover is a general and imprecise term referring to the transfer of control of a firm from one group of shareholders to another.[2] The bidder offers to pay cash or securities to obtain the stock or assets of another company. If the offer is accepted, the target firm will give

---

[2]*Control* may be defined as having a majority vote on the board of directors.

up control over its stock or assets to the bidder in exchange for the *consideration*—the bidder's stock, debt, or cash.

For example, when a bidding firm acquires a target firm, the right to control the operating activities of the target firm is transferred to a newly elected board of directors of the acquiring firm. This is a takeover by acquisition.

Takeovers can occur by acquisition, proxy contests, and going-private transactions. Thus, as shown in Figure 30.1, takeovers encompass a broader set of activities than acquisitions.

If a takeover is achieved by acquisition, it will be by merger, tender offer for shares of stock, or purchase of assets. In mergers and tender offers, the acquiring firm buys the voting common stock of the acquired firm.

Takeovers can occur with *proxy contests* in which a group of shareholders attempts to gain controlling seats on the board of directors by voting in new directors. A *proxy* authorizes the proxy holder to vote on all matters in a shareholders' meeting. In a proxy contest, proxies from the rest of the shareholders are solicited by an insurgent group of shareholders.

In **going-private transactions,** all of the equity shares of a public firm are purchased by a small group of investors. Usually, the group includes members of incumbent management and some outside investors. Such transactions have come to be known generically as **leveraged buyouts (LBOs)** because a large percentage of the money needed to buy up the stock is usually borrowed. Such transactions are also termed *management buyouts* (MBOs) when existing management is heavily involved. The shares of the firm are delisted from stock exchanges and no longer can be purchased in the open market.

There have been a large number of mergers and acquisitions in recent years, many of them involving very familiar companies. Table 30.1 lists some of the largest mergers in Canada in recent years.

EXAMPLE 30.2

In 2004, Rogers Wireless made a successful takeover bid for Microcell Communications, providers of the Fido cell phone service in Canada. Rogers Wireless planned to finance the $1.4 billion bid with cash on hand and a loan from its parent company, Rogers Communications. The two companies will have a combined 5.1 million customers, which would make the merged company the leader in the Canadian wireless market. At the time, the merger between Rogers and Fido made sense because both service providers used the popular global system for mobile (GSM) standard.

? Concept Questions
- **What is a merger? How does a merger differ from other forms of acquisition?**
- **What is a takeover?**

FIGURE 30.1

Varieties of Takeovers

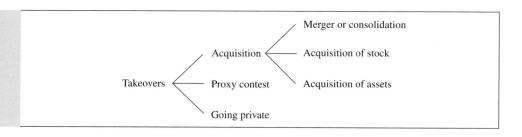

TABLE 30.1   25 Large Mergers and Acquisitions Involving Canadian Companies

Rank	Amount(in C$ billions)	Acquisition	Target Company	Acquiring Company
1	51.0	Nov '00	Seagram Co. Ltd.	Vivendi
2	19.8	Oct '06	Inco Ltd.	Compendia Vale do Rio Doce
3	19.2	Aug '06	Falconbridge Ltd.	Xstrata PLC
4	15.1	May '98	Polygram NV	Seagram Co. Ltd.
5	15.0	Sep '03	John Hancock Financial Services	Manulife Financial
6	12.2	Apr '95	E.I. du Pont de Nemours	Seagram Co. Ltd.
7	12.1	Dec '05	Placer Dome	Barrick Gold
8	11.0	Jan '98	*Nova Corp.	TransCanada Pipelines
9	10.7	Feb '00	Newbridge Networks Corp.	Alcatel
10	9.8	May '98	Bay Networks Inc.	Northern Telecom Ltd.
11	9.2	Jan '02	*PanCanadian Energy Corp.	Alberta Energy Co.
12	8.0	Jan '00	Canada Trust	TD Bank
13	7.8	Apr '95	MCA Inc.	Seagram Co. Ltd.
14	7.3	Dec '01	Clarica Life	Sun Life Financial
15	7.1	Feb '00	Donohue Inc.	Abitibi-Consolidated
16	7.0	Mar '99	*AT&T Canada Corp.	Metronet Communications
17	6.9	Aug '05	Terasen Inc.	Kinder Morgan Inc.
18	5.7	Oct '97	*HSN Inc.	Seagram Co. Ltd.
19	5.5	Mar '05	Telesystem International Wireless	Vodafone Group
20	5.2	Apr '97	Dome Petroleum Ltd.	Amoco Corp.
21	4.9	Jan '89	Texaco Canada Inc.	Imperial Oil Ltd.
22	4.9	Jul '98	Tropicana Products Ltd.	Pepsi Co. Inc.
23	4.6	Aug '00	Clearnet Communications	Telus Corp.
24	4.5	Sep '05	Acclaim Energy Trust*	Starpoint Energy Trust
25	4.5	Jul '04	Adolph Coors Co.	Molson Inc.

*No defined target or acquirer.
Source: *Mergers & Acquisitions in Canada*—various issues, and www.canoe.ca/MergerMania/home.html.

30.2 The Tax Forms of Acquisitions

If one firm buys another firm, the transaction may be taxable or tax-free. In a *taxable acquisition,* the shareholders of the target firm are considered to have sold their shares, and they may have realized capital gains or losses that will be taxed. In a *tax-free acquisition,* since the acquisition is considered an exchange instead of a sale, no realized capital gain or loss occurs.

Determinants of Tax Status

The general requirements for tax-free status are that (1) the acquisition involves two Canadian corporations subject to corporate income tax, and (2) there be a continuity of equity interest. In other words, the shareholders in the target firm must retain an equity interest in the bidder.

The specific requirements for a tax-free acquisition depend on the legal form of the acquisition, but, in general, if the buying firm offers the selling firm cash for its equity, it will be a taxable acquisition. If shares of stock are offered, it will be a tax-free acquisition.

In a tax-free acquisition, the selling shareholders are considered to have exchanged their old shares for new ones of equal value, and no realized capital gains or losses are experienced.

Taxable Versus Tax-Free Acquisitions

There are two factors to consider when comparing a tax-free acquisition and a taxable acquisition: the capital gains effect and the write-up effect. The *capital gains effect* refers to the fact that the target firm's shareholders may have to pay capital gains taxes in a taxable acquisition. They may demand a higher price as compensation, thereby increasing the cost of the merger. This is a cost of a taxable acquisition.

The bidder's shareholders may be willing to pay this cost because the bidder enjoys a *write-up effect* in a taxable acquisition. The tax status of an acquisition also affects the appraised value of the assets of the selling firm. In a taxable acquisition, the assets of the selling firm are revalued or "written up" from their historic book value to their estimated current market value. This is the write-up effect, and it is important because the depreciation expense on the acquired firm's assets can be increased in taxable acquisitions. Remember that an increase in depreciation is a non-cash expense, but it has the desirable effect of reducing taxes.

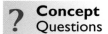

Concept Questions
- **What factors influence the choice between a taxable and a tax-free acquisition?**
- **What is the write-up effect in a taxable acquisition?**

30.3 Accounting for Acquisitions

Earlier in this text we mentioned that firms keep two distinct sets of books: the shareholders' books and the tax books. The previous section concerned the effect of acquisitions on the tax books. We now consider the shareholders' books. When one firm acquires another firm, the acquisition will be treated as a purchase on the shareholders' books.

The Purchase Method

The **purchase method** of reporting acquisitions requires that the assets of the acquired firm be reported at their fair market value on the books of the acquiring firm. This allows the acquiring firm to establish a new cost basis for the acquired assets.

In a purchase, an accounting entry called *goodwill* is created. **Goodwill** is the excess of the purchase price over the sum of the values of the individual assets acquired.

EXAMPLE 30.3

Suppose firm A acquires firm B, creating a new firm, AB. Firm A's and firm B's financial positions at the date of the acquisition are shown in Table 30.2. The book value of firm B on the date of the acquisition is $10 million. This is the sum of $8 million in buildings and $2 million in cash. However, an appraiser states that the sum of the fair market values of the individual buildings is $14 million. With $2 million in cash, the sum of the market values of the individual assets in firm B is $16 million. This represents the value to be received if the firm is liquidated by selling off the individual assets separately.

However, the whole is often worth more than the sum of the parts in business. Firm A pays $19 million in cash for firm B. This difference of $3 million (or $19 million − $16 million) is goodwill. It represents the increase in value by keeping the firm intact as an ongoing business. Firm

TABLE 30.2
Accounting for Acquisitions: Purchase (in $ millions)

Firm A				Firm B			
Cash	$ 4	Equity	$ 20	Cash	$ 2	Equity	$10
Land	16			Land	0		
Buildings	0			Buildings	8		
Total	$20		$20	Total	$10		$10

Firm AB			
Cash	$ 6	Debt	$19
Land	16	Equity	20
Buildings	14		
Goodwill	3		
Total	$39		$39

The assets of the acquired firm (firm B) appear in the combined firm's books at their fair market value.

A issued $19 million in new debt to finance the acquisition. The last balance sheet in Table 30.2 shows what happens under purchase accounting.

1. The total assets of firm AB increase to $39 million. The buildings of firm B appear in the new balance sheet at their current market value. That is, the market value of the assets of the acquired firm becomes part of the book value of the new firm. However, the assets of the acquiring firm (firm A) remain at their old book value. They are not revalued upward when the new firm is created.

2. The excess of the purchase price over the sum of the fair market values of the individual assets acquired is $3 million. This amount is reported as goodwill. Financial analysts generally ignore goodwill because it has no cash flow consequences. The current accounting practice says that each year firms must assess the value of goodwill on their balance sheets. If the value goes down (this is called *impairment* in accounting speak), the firm must deduct the decrease from earnings otherwise no amortization is required.

? Concept Question

• **What is the role of goodwill in purchase accounting for mergers?**

30.4 Determining the Synergy From an Acquisition

Suppose firm A is contemplating acquiring firm B. The value of firm A is V_A and the value of firm B is V_B. (It is reasonable to assume that, for public companies, V_A and V_B can be determined by observing the market prices of the outstanding securities.) The difference between the value of the combined firm (V_{AB}) and the sum of the values of the firms as separate entities is the *synergy* from the acquisition:

$$\text{Synergy} = V_{AB} - (V_A + V_B)$$

The acquiring firm must generally pay a premium for the acquired firm. For example, if stock of the target is selling for $50, the acquirer might need to pay $60 a share, implying a premium of $10 or 20 percent. Firm A will want to determine the synergy before entering into negotiations with firm B on the premium.

The synergy of an acquisition can be determined from the usual discounted cash flow model:

$$\text{Synergy} = \sum_{t=1}^{T} \frac{\Delta \text{CF}_t}{(1+r)^t}$$

where ΔCF_t is the difference between the cash flows at date t of the combined firm and the sum of the cash flows of the two separate firms. In other words, ΔCF_t is the incremental cash flow at date t from the merger. The term r is the risk-adjusted discount rate appropriate for the incremental cash flows. This is generally considered to be the required rate of return on the equity of the target reflecting the risk of the target's incremental cash flows.

From the chapters on capital budgeting we know that the incremental cash flows can be separated into four parts:

$$\Delta \text{CF}_t = \Delta \text{Rev}_t - \Delta \text{Costs}_t - \Delta \text{Taxes}_t - \Delta \text{Capital requirements}_t$$

where ΔRev_t is the incremental revenue of the acquisition, ΔCosts_t is the incremental costs of the acquisition, ΔTaxes_t is the incremental acquisition taxes, and $\Delta \text{Capital requirements}_t$ is the incremental new investment required in working capital and fixed assets.

30.5 Sources of Synergy From Acquisitions

It follows from our classification of incremental cash flows that the possible sources of synergy fall into four basic categories: revenue enhancement, cost reduction, lower taxes, and lower cost of capital.

Revenue Enhancement

One important reason for acquisitions is that a combined firm may generate greater revenues than two separate firms. Increased revenues may come from marketing gains, strategic benefits, and market power.

Marketing Gains   It is frequently claimed that mergers and acquisitions can produce greater operating revenues from improved marketing. Improvements can be made in:

1. Previously ineffective media programming and advertising efforts.
2. A weak existing distribution network.
3. An unbalanced product mix.

Strategic Benefits   Some acquisitions promise a *strategic* advantage.[3] This is an opportunity to take advantage of the competitive environment if certain situations materialize. In this regard, a strategic benefit is more like an option than like a standard investment opportunity. For example, imagine that a sewing machine company acquired a computer company. The firm would be well positioned if technological advances allowed computer-driven sewing machines in the future. Michael Porter has used the word *beachhead* in his description of the process of entering a new industry to exploit perceived opportunities.[4] The beachhead is used to spawn new opportunities based on *intangible* relationships. He views Procter & Gamble's initial acquisition of the Charmin Paper Company

---

[3]For a discussion of the financial side of strategic planning, see S. C. Myers, "Finance Theory and Finance Strategy," *Interfaces* 14 (January–February 1984), p. 1.

[4]M. Porter, *Competitive Advantage* (New York: Free Press, 1985).

as a beachhead that allowed Procter & Gamble to develop a highly interrelated cluster of paper products: disposable diapers, paper towels, feminine hygiene products, and bathroom tissue.

Market or Monopoly Power   One firm may acquire another to increase its market share and market power. Profits can be enhanced through higher prices and reduced competition for customers. In theory, such mergers are controlled by law. In practice, however, horizontal mergers are far more common in Canada than in the United States due to weaker legal restrictions against combinations of competitors that might limit market competition.[5]

Cost Reduction

One of the most basic reasons to merge is that a combined firm may operate more efficiently than two separate firms. A merger or acquisition can increase a firm's operating efficiency in several different ways: economies of scale, economies of vertical integration, complementary resources, and elimination of inefficient management.

Economies of Scale   If the average cost of production falls while the level of production increases, there is said to be an economy of scale. Figure 30.2 illustrates that economies of scale result while the firm grows to its optimal size. Beyond this size, diseconomies of scale occur. In other words, average cost increases with further firm growth. The phrase *spreading overhead* is frequently used in connection with economies of scale from horizontal mergers. This refers to the sharing of central facilities such as corporate headquarters, top management, and a large mainframe computer.

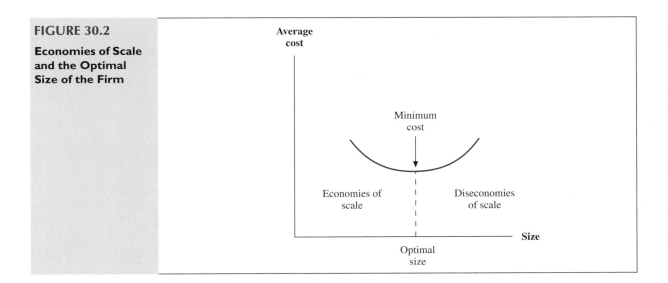

FIGURE 30.2

Economies of Scale and the Optimal Size of the Firm

[5]From the mid-1950s to the mid-1980s, only one merger in Canada was blocked under the *Combines Investigation Act.* Having been blocked by the finance minister on several occasions recently, bank mergers appear to be an exception to this statement. In the same period, U.S. antitrust laws "prevented several hundred horizontal mergers" according to B. E. Eckbo, "Mergers and the Market for Corporate Control: The Canadian Evidence," *Canadian Journal of Economics* (May 1986), pp. 236–60.

Economies of Vertical Integration   Operating economies can be gained from vertical as well as horizontal combinations. The main purpose of vertical acquisitions is to make coordination of closely related operating activities easier. This is probably the reason why most forest product firms that cut timber also own sawmills and hauling equipment. Economies from vertical integration probably explain why most airline companies own airplanes; it also may explain why some airline companies have purchased hotels and car rental companies.

Technology transfers are another reason for vertical integration. Consider the merger of General Motors and Hughes Aircraft in 1985. An automobile manufacturer might well acquire an advanced electronics firm if the special technology of the electronics firm can improve the quality of the automobile.

Complementary Resources   Some firms acquire others to make better use of existing resources or to provide the missing ingredient for success. Think of a ski equipment store that could merge with a tennis equipment store to produce more even sales over both the winter and summer seasons—and better use of store capacity.

Elimination of Inefficient Management   There are firms whose value could be increased with a change in management. For example, Jensen and Ruback argue that acquisitions can occur because of changing technology or market conditions that require a restructuring of the corporation.[6] Incumbent managers in some cases do not understand changing conditions. They have trouble abandoning strategies and styles they have spent years formulating.

The oil industry is an example of managerial inefficiency cited by Jensen. In the late 1970s, changes in the oil industry included reduced expectations of the future price of oil, increased exploration and development costs, and increased real interest rates. As a result of these changes, substantial reductions in exploration and development were called for. However, many oil company managers were unable to downsize their firms. For example, a study by McConnell and Muscarella reports that the stock prices of oil companies tended to drop upon announcements of increases in exploration and development expenditures in the period 1975–81.[7] By 1999, changes in the economic landscape resulted in the $81.38 billion acquisition of Mobil Corp. by Exxon Corp. One of the main forces propelling this merger forward was that throughout the 1990s the oil industry had been cutting costs to remain competitive, and analysts projected $2.8 billion annual cost savings.[8]

Acquiring companies sought out oil firms in order to reduce the investment levels of these oil companies.[9] For example, T. Boone Pickens of Mesa Petroleum perceived the changes taking place in the oil industry and attempted to buy several oil companies: Unocal, Phillips, and Getty. The results of these attempted acquisitions were reduced expenditures on exploration and development and huge gains to the shareholders of the affected firms.

---

[6]M. C. Jensen and R. S. Ruback, "The Market for Corporate Control: The Scientific Evidence," *Journal of Financial Economics* 11 (April 1983); and M. C. Jensen, "Agency Costs of Free Cash Flow, Corporate Finance and Takeovers," *American Economic Review* (May 1986).

[7]J. J. McConnell and C. J. Muscarella, "Corporate Capital Expenditure Decisions and the Market Value of the Firm," *Journal of Financial Economics* 14 (1985).

[8]A. Barrionuevo, S. Liesman, and J. R. Wilke, "Exxon-Mobil Merger Gets Approved; FTC May Be Tougher on Future Deals," *Wall Street Journal* (Dec. 1, 1999).

[9]More than 26 percent of the total valuation of all takeover transactions involved a selling firm in the oil and gas industry from 1981 to 1984 [W. T. Grimm, *Mergerstat Review* (1985), p. 41].

Mergers and acquisitions can be viewed as part of the labour market for top management. Jensen and Ruback have used the phrase *market for corporate control,* in which alternative management teams compete for the rights to manage corporate activities.

The Negative Side of Takeovers   While most financial analysts would likely agree that competition for corporate control can enhance efficiency, there is concern over whether the cost is too high. Critics of takeovers (and especially of LBOs) are concerned that social costs are not counted when the post-takeover search for efficiency gains leads to plant closures and layoffs. When plants close or move, workers and equipment can be turned to other uses only at some cost to society. For example, taxpayers may need to subsidize retraining and relocation programs for workers or tax incentives for investment. In an extreme case, suppose a mine is closed down in a rural area where there is no other large employer. All capital goods that cannot be moved may become worthless.

Critics of takeovers argue that they reduce trust between management and labour, thus reducing efficiency and increasing costs. They point to Japan, Germany, and Korea (where there are few takeovers) as examples of more efficient economies. They argue that, as an alternative to takeovers, a strong board of outside directors could maximize management's efficiency.[10]

Tax Gains

Tax gains often are a powerful incentive for acquisitions. Possible tax gains from an acquisition include

1. The use of tax losses.
2. The use of unused debt capacity.
3. The use of surplus funds.

Net Operating Losses   Firms that lose money on a pre-tax basis will not pay taxes. Such firms can end up with tax losses that they cannot use. These tax losses are referred to as *NOL* (an acronym for *net operating losses*).

A firm with net operating losses may be an attractive merger partner for a firm with significant tax liabilities. Barring any other effects, the combined firm will have a lower tax bill than the two firms considered separately. This is a good example of how a firm can be more valuable merged than standing alone. For example, tax savings made possible by Dome Petroleum's large losses were an important attraction to Amoco when it bought Dome in 1988.

There is an important qualification to our NOL discussion. Canadian tax laws permit firms that experience periods of profit and loss to even things out through loss carryback and carryforward provisions. A firm that has been profitable in the past but has a loss in the current year can obtain refunds of income taxes paid in the three previous years. After that, losses can be carried forward for up to seven years. Thus, a merger to exploit unused tax shields must offer tax savings over and above what can be accomplished by firms via carryovers.

---

[10]This section draws on C. Robinson's arguments in C. Robinson versus W. Block, "Are Corporate Takeovers Good or Bad? A Debate," *Canadian Investment Review* (Fall 1991), pp. 53–60; and on a piece by the late W. S. Allen, "Relegating Corporate Takeovers to the 'Campeaust' Heap: A Proposal," *Canadian Investment Review* (Spring 1990), pp. 71–76.

Unused Debt Capacity   We argued earlier in the text that the optimal debt–equity ratio is the one where the marginal tax benefit from additional debt is equal to the marginal increase in the financial distress costs from additional debt. Because some diversification occurs when firms merge, the cost of financial distress is likely to be less for the combined firm than is the sum of these present values for the two separate firms. Thus, the acquiring firm might be able to increase its debt–equity ratio after a merger, creating additional tax benefits—and additional value.[11,12]

Surplus Funds   Another quirk in the tax laws involves surplus funds. Consider a firm that has *free cash flow*—cash flow available after all taxes have been paid and after all positive net present value projects have been financed.

In this situation, aside from purchasing fixed income securities, the firm has several ways to spend the free cash flow, including

1. Pay dividends.
2. Buy back its own shares.
3. Acquire shares in another firm.

We discussed the first two options in Chapter 19 and showed that an extra dividend will increase the income tax paid by some investors. And, under Canada Revenue Agency regulations, share repurchase seldom reduces the taxes paid by shareholders when compared to paying dividends.

To avoid these problems, the firm can buy another firm. This avoids the tax problem associated with paying a dividend. Of course, if the purchase is a negative-NPV investment, this action exemplifies inefficient management and may make the bidder into a target.

The Cost of Capital

The cost of capital can often be reduced when two firms merge because the costs of issuing securities are subject to economies of scale. As we observed in earlier chapters, the costs of issuing both debt and equity are much lower for larger issues than for smaller issues.

? **Concept Question**   • **What are sources of possible synergy in acquisitions?**

30.6 Calculating the Value of the Firm After an Acquisition

Now that we have listed the possible sources of synergy from a merger, we examine how to value these sources. Consider two firms. Gamble Inc. manufactures and markets soaps and cosmetics. The firm has a reputation for its ability to attract, develop, and keep talented people and has successfully introduced several major products in the past two

---

[11]While unused debt capacity can be a valid reason for a merger, hindsight shows that many mergers in the 1980s overused debt financing. We discuss this in more detail later.

[12]Michael C. Jensen ["Agency Costs of Free Cash Flow, Corporate Finance and Takeovers," *American Economic Review* (May 1986)] offers another reason why debt is frequently used in mergers and acquisitions. He argues that using more debt provides incentives for the new management to create efficiencies so that debt can be repaid.

years. It would like to enter the over-the-counter drug market to round out its product line. Shapiro Inc. is a well-known maker of cold remedies. Al Shapiro, the great-grandson of the founder of Shapiro Inc., became chairman of the firm last year. Unfortunately, Al knows nothing about cold remedies, and as a consequence Shapiro Inc. has had lacklustre financial performance. For the most recent year, pre-tax cash flow fell by 15 percent. The firm's stock price is at an all-time low.

   The financial management of Gamble finds Shapiro an attractive candidate. It believes that the cash flows from the combined firms would be far greater than what each firm would have alone. The anticipated cash flows and present values from the acquisition are shown in Table 30.3. The increased cash flows (CF_t) come from three benefits.

1. *Tax gains.* If Gamble acquires Shapiro, Gamble will be able to use some tax-loss carryforwards to reduce its tax liability. The additional cash flows from tax gains should be discounted at the cost of debt capital because they can be determined with very little uncertainty. The financial management of Gamble estimates that the acquisition will reduce taxes by $1 million per year in perpetuity. The relevant discount rate is 5 percent, the after-tax cost of debt, and the present value of the tax reduction is $20 million.

2. *Operating efficiencies.* The financial management of Gamble has determined that Gamble can take advantage of some of the unused production capacity of Shapiro. At times, Gamble has been operating at full capacity with a large backlog of orders. Shapiro's manufacturing facilities, with a little reconfiguration, can be used to produce Gamble's soaps. Thus, more soaps and cold remedies can be produced without adding to the combined firm's capacity and cost. These operating efficiencies will increase after-tax cash flows by $1.5 million per year. Using Shapiro's discount rate and assuming perpetual gains, the PV of the unused capacity is determined to be $10 million.

3. *Strategic fit.* The financial management of Gamble has determined that the acquisition of Shapiro will give Gamble a strategic advantage. The management of Gamble believes that the addition of the Shapiro Bac-Rub ointment for sore backs to its existing product mix will give it a better chance to launch successful new skin care cosmetics if these markets develop in the future. Management of Gamble estimates that there is a 50 percent probability that $6 million in after-tax cash flow can be generated with the new skin care products. These opportunities are contingent on factors that cannot be easily quantified. Because of the lack of precision here, the managers decided to use a high discount rate. Gamble chooses a 20 percent rate, and it estimates that the present value of the strategic factors is $15 million (or 0.50 × $6 million/0.20).

TABLE 30.3
Acquisition of Shapiro Inc. by Gamble Inc.

	Net Cash Flow per Year (perpetual)	Discount Rate	Value
Gamble Inc.	$10.0 million	0.10	$100 million
Shapiro Inc.	4.5 million	0.15	30 million*
Benefits from acquisition:	5.5 million	0.122	45 million
Strategic fit	3.0 million	0.20	15 million
Tax shelters	1.0 million	0.05	20 million
Operating efficiencies	1.5 million	0.15	10 million
Gamble–Shapiro	20.0 million	0.114	175 million

*The market value of Shapiro's outstanding common stock is $30 million; 1 million shares are outstanding.

Avoiding Mistakes

The Gamble–Shapiro illustration is very simple and straightforward. It is deceptive because the incremental cash flows have already been determined. In practice, an analyst must estimate these cash flows and determine the proper discount rate. Valuing the benefits of a potential acquisition is harder than valuing benefits for standard capital budgeting projects. Many mistakes can be made. Here are some general rules:

1. *Do not ignore market values.* In many cases it is very difficult to estimate values using discounted cash flows. Because of this, an expert business appraiser should know the market prices of comparable opportunities. In an efficient market, prices should reflect value. Because the market value of Shapiro is $30 million, we use this estimate of Shapiro's current value.

2. *Estimate only incremental cash flows.* Only incremental cash flows from an acquisition will add value to the acquiring firm. Thus, it is important to estimate the cash flows that are incremental to the acquisition.

3. *Use the correct discount rate.* The discount rate should be the required rate of return for the incremental cash flows associated with the acquisition.[13] It should reflect the risk associated with the *use* of funds, not their *source.* It would be a mistake for Gamble to use its own cost of capital to value the cash flows from Shapiro.

4. *If Gamble and Shapiro combine, there will be transactions costs.* These will include fees to investment bankers, legal fees, and disclosure requirements.

30.7 A Cost to Shareholders from Reduction in Risk

The previous section discussed gains to the firm from a merger. In a firm with debt, these gains are likely to be shared by both bondholders and shareholders. We now consider how a merger could benefit the bondholders at the expense of the shareholders.

When two firms merge, the variability of their combined values is usually lower than if the firms remained separate entities. The variability of firm values can fall if the values of the two firms are less than perfectly correlated. The resulting reduction in the cost of borrowing will make the creditors better off than before because the probability of financial distress is reduced by the merger.

Unfortunately, the shareholders are likely to be worse off. The gains to creditors are at the expense of the shareholders if the total value of the firm does not change. The relationship among the value of the merged firm, debt capacity, and risk is very complicated. We now consider two examples.

The Base Case

Consider a base case where two all-equity firms merge. Table 30.4 gives the net present values of firm A and firm B in three possible states of the economy: prosperity, average, and depression. The market value of firm A is $60, and the market value of firm B is $40. The market value of each firm is the weighted average of the values in each of the three states. For example, the value of firm A is

$$\$60 = \$80 \times 0.5 + \$50 \times 0.3 + \$25 \times 0.2$$

---

[13]Recall that the required rate of return is sometimes referred to as the *cost of capital* or the opportunity cost of capital.

TABLE 30.4
Stock-Swap
Mergers

	NPV			Market Value
	State 1	State 2	State 3	
Base case: two all-equity firms before merger				
Firm *A*	$80	$50	$25	$60
Firm *B*	$50	$40	$15	$40
Probability	0.5	0.3	0.2	
After merger*				
Firm *AB*	$130	$90	$40	$100
Firm *A*, equity and risky debt before merger				
Firm *B*, all-equity before merger				
Firm *A*	$80	$50	$25	$60
Debt	$40	$40	$25	$37
Equity	$40	$10	$0	$23
Firm *B*	$50	$40	$15	$40
After merger†				
Firm *AB*	$130	$90	$40	$100
Debt	$40	$40	$40	$40
Equity	$90	$50	$0	$60

Value of debt rises after merger. Value of original stock in acquiring firm falls correspondingly.
*Shareholders in *B* receive stock value of $40. Therefore, shareholders of *A* have a value of $100 − $40 = $60 and are *indifferent to merger.*
†Because firm *B*'s shareholders receive stock in firm *A* worth $40, original shareholders in firm *A* have stock worth $20 (or $60 − $40). Gains and losses from merger are

$20 − $23 = −$3: Therefore, shareholders of *A* lose $3.
$40 − $37 = $3: Therefore, bondholders of *A* gain $3.

The values in each of the three states for firm *A* are $80, $50, and $25, respectively. The probabilities of each of the three states occurring are 0.5, 0.3, and 0.2, respectively.

When firm *A* merges with firm *B*, the combined firm *AB* will have a market value of $100. There is no synergy from this merger, and consequently the value of firm *AB* is the sum of the values of firm *A* and firm *B*. Shareholders of *B* receive stock with a value of $40, and therefore shareholders of *A* have a value of $100 − $40 = $60. Thus, shareholders of *A* and *B* are indifferent to the proposed merger.

The Case Where One Firm Has Debt

Alternatively, imagine firm *A* has some debt and some equity outstanding before the merger.[14] Firm *B* is an all-equity firm. Firm *A* will default on its debt in state 3 because the net present value of firm *A* in this state is $25, and the value of the debt claim is $40. As a consequence, the full value of the debt claim cannot be paid by firm *A*. The creditors take this into account, and the value of the debt is $37 (or $40 × 0.5 + $40 × 0.3 + $25 × 0.2).

Though default occurs without a merger, no default occurs with a merger. To see this, notice that, when the two firms are separate, firm *B* does not guarantee firm *A*'s debt. That is, if firm *A* defaults on its debt, firm *B* does not help the bondholders of firm *A*. However, after the merger, the bondholders can draw on the cash flows from both *A* and *B*. When one of the divisions of the combined firm fails, creditors can be paid from the profits of the other division. This mutual guarantee, which is called the *coinsurance effect,* makes the debt less risky and more valuable than before.

---

[14]This example was provided by David Babbel.

The bonds are worth $40 after the merger. Thus, the bondholders of *AB* gain $3 (or $40 − $37) from the merger.

The shareholders of firm *A* lose $3 (or $20 − $23) from the merger. That is, firm *A*'s stock is worth $23 prior to the merger. The stock is worth $60 after the merger. However, shareholders in firm *B* receive $40 of stock in firm *A*. Hence, those individuals who were shareholders in firm *A* prior to the merger have stock worth only $20 (or $60 − $40) after the merger.

There is no net benefit to the firm as a whole. The bondholders gain the coinsurance effect, and the shareholders lose the coinsurance effect. Some general conclusions emerge from the preceding analysis.

1. Bondholders in the aggregate will usually be helped by mergers and acquisitions. The size of the gain to bondholders depends on the reduction of bankruptcy risk after the combination. That is, the less risky the combined firm is, the greater are the gains to bondholders.

2. Shareholders of the acquiring firm will be hurt by the amount that bondholders gain.

3. The conclusions apply to mergers and acquisitions where no synergy is present. In the case of synergistic combinations, much depends on the size of the synergy.

How Can Shareholders Reduce Their Losses From the Coinsurance Effect?

The coinsurance effect allows some mergers to increase bondholder values by reducing shareholder values. However, there are at least two ways that shareholders can reduce or eliminate the coinsurance effect. First, the shareholders in firm *A* could retire its debt *before* the merger announcement date and reissue an equal amount of debt after the merger. Because debt is retired at the low, premerger price, this type of refinancing transaction can neutralize the coinsurance effect to the bondholders.

Also, note that the debt capacity of the combined firm is likely to increase because the acquisition reduces the probability of financial distress. Thus, the shareholders' second alternative is simply to issue more debt after the merger. An increase in debt following the merger will have two effects, even without the prior action of debt retirement. The interest deduction from new corporate debt raises firm value. In addition, an increase in debt after merger raises the probability of financial distress, thereby reducing or eliminating the bondholders' gain from the coinsurance effect.

? Concept Question

• **How is the distribution of merger gains complicated if one of the firms has debt outstanding?**

30.8 Two "Bad" Reasons for Mergers

Earnings Growth

An acquisition can create the appearance of earnings growth, which may fool investors into thinking that the firm is worth more than it really is. Suppose Global Resources Ltd. acquires Regional Enterprises. The financial positions of Global and Regional before the acquisition are shown in Table 30.5. Regional has had very poor earnings growth and sells at a price–earnings ratio much lower than that of Global. The merger creates no additional

TABLE 30.5
Financial Positions of Global Resources and Regional Enterprises

	Global Resources Before Merger	Regional Enterprises Before Merger	Global Resources After Merger	
			The Market Is "Smart"	The Market Is "Fooled"
Earnings per share	$ 1.00	$ 1.00	$ 1.43	$ 1.43
Price per share	$ 25.00	$ 10.00	$ 25.00	$ 35.71
Price–earnings ratio	25	10	17.5	25
Number of shares	100	100	140	140
Total earnings	$ 100.00	$ 100.00	$ 200.00	$ 200.00
Total value	$2,500.00	$1,000.00	$3,500.00	$5,000.00

Exchange ratio: 1 share in Global for 2.5 shares in Regional.

value. If the market is smart, it will realize that the combined firm is worth the sum of the values of the separate firms. In this case, the market value of the combined firm will be $3,500, which is equal to the sum of the values of the separate firms before the merger.

At these values, Global will acquire Regional by exchanging 40 of its shares for 100 Regional shares, so that Global will have 140 shares outstanding after the merger.[15] Because the stock price of Global is unchanged by the merger, the price–earnings ratio must fall. This is true because the market is smart and recognizes that the total market value has not been altered by the merger. This scenario is represented by the third column of Table 30.5.

Let us now consider the possibility that the market is fooled. One can see from Table 30.5 that the acquisition enables Global to increase its earnings per share from $1 to $1.43. If the market is fooled, it might mistake the 43 percent increase in earnings per share for true growth. In this case, the price–earnings ratio of Global may not fall after the merger. Suppose the price–earnings ratio of Global remains equal to 25. The total value of the combined firm will increase to $5,000 (or 25 × $200), and the stock price per share of Global will increase to $35.71 (or $5,000/140). This is reflected in the last column of Table 30.5.

This is earnings growth magic. Like all good magic, it is just illusion. For it to work, the shareholders of Global and Regional must receive something for nothing. This may work for a while, but in the long run the efficient market will work its wonders and the value will decline.

Diversification

Diversification often is mentioned as a benefit of one firm's acquiring another. For example, U.S. Steel included diversification as a benefit in its acquisition of Marathon Oil. In 1982 U.S. Steel was a cash-rich company. (Over 20 percent of its assets were in the form of cash and marketable securities.) It is not uncommon to see firms with surplus cash articulating a need for diversification.

However, we argue that diversification, by itself, cannot produce increases in value. To see why, recall that a business's variability of return can be separated into two parts: (1) what is specific to the business and called *unsystematic,* and (2) what is *systematic* because it is common to all businesses.

---

[15]This ratio implies a fair exchange because a share of Regional is selling for 40 percent ($10/$25) of the price of a share of Global.

Systematic variability cannot be eliminated by diversification, so mergers will not eliminate this risk at all. In contrast, unsystematic risk can be diversified away through mergers. However, the investor does not need widely diversified companies such as Onex and Brascan to eliminate unsystematic risk. Shareholders can diversify more easily than corporations by simply purchasing common stock in different corporations. For example, the shareholders of U.S. Steel could have purchased shares in Marathon if they believed there would be diversification gains in doing so. Thus, diversification through conglomerate merger may not benefit shareholders.[16]

Diversification can produce gains to the acquiring firm only if two things are true:

1. Diversification decreases the unsystematic variability at lower costs than investors could via adjustments to personal portfolios. This seems very unlikely.

2. Diversification reduces risk and thereby increases debt capacity. This possibility was mentioned earlier in the chapter.

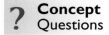

Concept Questions

• **Why can a merger create the appearance of earnings growth?**
• **Why is diversification generally a poor motive for a merger?**

30.9 The NPV of a Merger

Firms typically use NPV analysis when making acquisitions.[17] The analysis is relatively straightforward when the consideration is cash. The analysis becomes more complex when the consideration is stock.

Cash

Suppose firm *A* and firm *B* have values as separate entities of $500 and $100, respectively. They are both all-equity firms. If firm *A* acquires firm *B*, the merged firm *AB* will have a combined value of $700 due to synergies of $100. The board of firm *B* has indicated that it will sell firm *B* if it is offered $150 in cash.

---

[16]Evidence suggests that diversification can actually hurt shareholders. Randall Morck, Andrei Shleifer, and Robert W. Vishney, "Do Managerial Objectives Drive Bad Acquisitions," *Journal of Finance* 45 (1990), pp. 31–48, show that shareholders did poorly in firms that diversified by acquisition in the 1980s. There is also evidence that diversified firms trade at a discount relative to a portfolio of single-segment firms, most recently from Karl Lins and Henri Servaes, "The International Evidence on the Value of Corporate Diversification," *Journal of Finance* 54 (1999). On the other hand, Matsusaka and Hubbard and Palia find some benefits to diversification in internal capital allocation. See John Matsusaka, "Takeover Motives During the Conglomerate Merge Wave," *Rand Journal of Economics* 24 (1993). See also R. Glenn Hubbard and Darius Palia, "A Reexamination of the Conglomerate Merger Wave in the 1960s: An Internal Capital Markets View," *Journal of Finance* (June 1999).

One interesting recent study reports a positive relationship between focus and value for diversified firms. See P. G. Berger and E. Ofek, "Diversification's Effect on Firm Value," *Journal of Financial Economics,* 37 (1995). Also see P. G. Berger and E. Ofek, "Causes and Effects of Corporate Refocusing Program," *Review of Financial Studies* 12 (1999).

[17]The NPV framework for evaluating mergers can be found in S. C. Myers, "A Framework for Evaluating Mergers," in *Modern Developments in Financial Management,* S. C. Myers ed. (New York: Praeger, 1976).

Should firm A acquire firm B? Assuming that firm A finances the acquisition out of its own retained earnings, its value after the acquisition is[18]

$$
\begin{array}{ccc}
\text{Value of} & & \\
\text{firm } A \text{ after} & = & \text{Value of} & - & \text{Cash} \\
\text{the acquisition} & & \text{combined firm} & & \text{paid} \\
\end{array}
$$

$$
\begin{aligned}
&= \quad \$700 \quad - \$150 \\
&= \quad \$550
\end{aligned}
$$

Because firm A was worth \$500 prior to the acquisition, the NPV to firm A's shareholders is

$$\$50 = \$550 - \$500 \tag{30.1}$$

Assuming that there are 25 shares in firm A, each share of the firm is worth \$20 (or \$500/25) prior to the merger and \$22 (or \$550/25) after the merger. These calculations are displayed in the first and third columns of Table 30.6. Looking at the rise in stock price, we conclude that firm A should make the acquisition.

We spoke earlier of both the synergy and the premium of a merger. We can also value the NPV of a merger to the acquirer as

$$
\begin{array}{c}
\text{NPV of a merger} \\
\text{to acquirer}
\end{array} = \text{Synergy} - \text{Premium}
$$

Because the value of the combined firm is \$700 and the premerger values of A and B were \$500 and \$100, respectively, the synergy is \$100 [or \$700 − (\$500 + \$100)]. The premium is \$50 (or \$150 − \$100). Thus, the NPV of the merger to the acquirer is

$$
\begin{array}{c}
\text{NPV of merger} \\
\text{to firm } A
\end{array} = \$100 - \$50 = \$50
$$

One caveat is in order. This textbook has consistently argued that the market value of a firm is the best estimate of its true value. However, we must adjust our analysis when discussing mergers. If the true price of firm A *without the merger* is \$500, the market value of firm A may actually be above \$500 when merger negotiations take place. This occurs because the

TABLE 30.6
Cost of Acquisition: Cash Versus Common Stock

	Before Acquisition			After Acquisition: Firm A	
	(1)	(2)	(3)	(4) Common Stock: Exchange Ratio (0.75:1)	(5) Common Stock: Exchange Ratio (0.6819:1)
	Firm A	Firm B	Cash*		
Market value (V_A, V_B)	\$500	\$100	\$550	\$700	\$700
Number of shares	25	10	25	32.5	31.819
Price per share	\$ 20	\$ 10	\$ 22	\$ 21.54	\$ 22

*Value of firm A after acquisition—cash:
$$V_A = V_{AB} - \text{Cash}$$
$$\$550 = \$700 - \$150$$

*Value of firm A after acquisition—common stock:
$$V_A = V_{AB}$$
$$\$700 = \$700$$

---

[18]The analysis will be essentially the same if new stock is issued. However, it will differ if new debt is issued to fund the acquisition because of the tax shield to debt. An adjusted present value (APV) approach would be necessary here.

market price reflects the possibility that the merger will occur. For example, if the probability is 60 percent that the merger will take place, the market price of firm A will be

Market value of firm A with merger	×	Probability of merger	+	Market value of firm A without merger	×	Probability of no merger
$530 = 550	×	0.60	+	$500	×	0.40

The managers would underestimate the NPV from merger in Equation (30.1) if the market price of firm A is used. Thus, managers are faced with the difficult task of valuing their own firm without the acquisition.

Common Stock

Of course, firm A could purchase firm B with common stock instead of cash. Unfortunately, the analysis is not as straightforward here. In order to handle this scenario, we need to know how many shares are outstanding in firm B. We assume that there are 10 shares outstanding, as indicated in column 2 of Table 30.6.

Suppose firm A exchanges 7.5 of its shares for the entire 10 shares of firm B. We call this an exchange ratio of 0.75:1. The value of each share of firm A's stock before the acquisition is $20. Because 7.5 × $20 = $150, this exchange *appears* to be the equivalent of purchasing firm B in cash for $150.

This is incorrect: The true cost is greater than $150. To see this, note that firm A has 32.5 (or 25 + 7.5) shares outstanding after the merger. Firm B shareholders own 23 percent (7.5/32.5) of the combined firm. Their holdings are valued at $161 (or 23% × $700). Because these shareholders receive stock in firm A worth $161, the cost of the merger to firm A's shareholders must be $161, not $150.

This result is shown in column 4 of Table 30.6. The value of each share of firm A's stock after a stock-for-stock transaction is only $21.54 (or $700/32.5). We found out earlier that the value of each share is $22 after a cash-for-stock transaction. The difference is that the cost of the stock-for-stock transaction to firm A is higher.

This nonintuitive result occurs because the exchange ratio of 7.5 shares of firm A for 10 shares of firm B was based on the *premerger* prices of the two firms. However, since the stock of firm A rises after the merger, firm B shareholders receive more than $150 in firm A stock.

What should the exchange ratio be so that firm B shareholders receive only $150 of firm A's stock? We begin by defining α, the proportion of the shares in the combined firm that firm B's shareholders own. Because the combined firm's value is $700, the value of firm B shareholders after the merger is

Value of Firm B Shareholders after Merger:
$$\alpha \times \$700$$

Setting α × $700 = $150, we find that α = 21.43%. In other words, firm B's shareholders will receive stock worth $150 if they receive 21.43 percent of the firm after merger.

Now we determine the number of shares issued to firm B's shareholders. The proportion, α, that firm B's shareholders have in the combined firm can be expressed as

$$\alpha = \frac{\text{New shares issued}}{\text{Old shares + New shares issued}} = \frac{\text{New shares issued}}{25 + \text{New shares issued}}$$

Plugging our value of α into the equation yields

$$0.2143 = \frac{\text{New shares issued}}{25 + \text{New shares issued}}$$

Solving for the unknown, we have

$$\text{New shares} = 6.819 \text{ shares}$$

Total shares outstanding after the merger is 31.819 (or 25 + 6.819). Because 6.819 shares of firm *A* are exchanged for 10 shares of firm *B,* the exchange ratio is 0.6819:1.

Results at the exchange ratio of 0.6819:1 are displayed in column 5 of Table 30.6. Each share of common stock is worth $22, exactly what it is worth in the stock-for-cash transaction. Thus, given that the board of firm *B* will sell its firm for $150, this is the fair exchange ratio, not the ratio of 0.75:1 used earlier.

Cash versus Common Stock

In this section, we have examined both cash deals and stock-for-stock deals. Our analysis leads to the following question: When do bidders want to pay with cash and when do they want to pay with stock? There is no easy formula: The decision hinges on a few variables, with perhaps the most important being the price of the bidder's stock.

In the example of Table 30.6, firm *A*'s market price per share prior to the merger was $20. Let's now assume that at the time firm *A*'s managers believed the "true" price was $15. In other words, the managers believed that their stock was overvalued. Is it likely for managers to have a different view than that of the market? Yes—managers often have more information than does the market. After all, managers deal with customers, suppliers, and employees daily and are likely to obtain private information.

Now imagine that firm *A*'s managers are considering acquiring firm *B* with either cash or stock. The overvaluation would have no impact on the merger terms in a cash deal; firm *B* would still receive $150 in cash. However, the overvaluation would have a big impact on a stock-for-stock deal. Although firm *B* receives $150 worth of *A*'s stock as calculated at market prices, firm *A*'s managers know that the true value of the stock is less than $150.

How should firm *A* pay for the acquisition? Clearly, firm *A* has an incentive to pay with stock because it would end up giving away less than $150 of value. This conclusion might seem rather cynical because firm *A* is, in some sense, trying to cheat firm *B*'s shareholders. However, both theory and empirical evidence suggest that firms are more likely to acquire with stock when their own stocks are overvalued.[19]

The story is not quite this simple. Just as the managers of firm *A* think strategically, firm *B*'s managers will likely think this way as well. Suppose that in the merger negotiations, firm *A*'s managers push for a stock-for-stock deal. This might tip off firm *B*'s managers that firm *A* is overpriced. Perhaps firm *B*'s managers will ask for better terms than firm *A* is currently offering. Alternatively, firm *B* may resolve to accept cash or not to sell at all.

And just as firm *B* learns from the negotiations, the market learns also. Empirical evidence shows that the acquirer's stock price generally falls upon the announcement of a stock-for-stock deal.[20]

However, this discussion does not imply that mistakes are never made. For example, consider the stock-for-stock merger in January 2001 between AOL, an Internet service provider, and Time Warner (TW), a media firm. Although the deal was presented as a

---

[19]The basic theoretical ideas are presented in S. Myers and N. Majluf, "Corporate Financing and Investment Decisions When Firms Have Information That Investors Do Not Have," *Journal of Financial Economics* (1984).

[20]For example, see G. Andrade, M. Mitchell, and E. Stafford, "New Evidence and Perspectives on Mergers," *Journal of Economic Perspectives* (Spring 2001); and R. Heron and E. Lie, "Operating Performance and the Method of Payment in Takeovers," *Journal of Financial and Quantitative Analysis* (2002).

merger of equals and the combined company is now called Time Warner, AOL appears, in retrospect, to have been the acquirer. The merger was one of the biggest of all time, with a combined market capitalization between the two firms of about $350 billion at the time of the announcement in January 2000. (The delay of about a year between merger announcement and merger completion was due to regulatory review.) It is also considered one of the worst deals of all time, with Time Warner having a market value of about $70 billion in mid-2006.

AOL was in a precarious position at the time of the merger, providing narrow-band Internet service when consumers were hungering for broadband. Also, at least in retrospect, Internet stocks were greatly overpriced. The deal allowed AOL to offer its inflated stock as currency for a company not in the technology industry and, therefore, not nearly as overpriced, if overpriced at all. Had TW looked at the deal in this way, it might have simply called it off. (Alternatively, it could have demanded cash, though it is unlikely that AOL had the financial resources to pay in this way.)

Just as TW's managers did not understand all the implications of the merger right away, it appears that the market did not either. TW's stock price rose over 25 percent relative to the market in the week following the merger announcement.

? Concept Question

- **In an efficient market with no tax effects, should an acquiring firm use cash or stock?**

Defensive Tactics

Target firm managers frequently resist takeover attempts. Resistance usually starts with press releases and mailings to shareholders presenting management's viewpoint. It can eventually lead to legal action and solicitation of competing bids. Managerial action to defeat a takeover attempt may make target shareholders better off if it elicits a higher offer premium from the bidding firm or another firm. Of course, management resistance may simply reflect pursuit of self-interest at the expense of shareholders; the target firm's managers may resist a takeover in order to preserve their jobs. In this section, we describe various defensive tactics that have been used by target firm managements to resist unfriendly takeover attempts.

Divestitures

Target firm managers considering the prospect of a takeover may decide a narrowing of strategic focus can increase stock price, thereby making a takeover too expensive. If so, they will consider the pros and cons of four kinds of divestitures: a sale of assets, a spin-off, a carve-out, and the issuance of a tracking stock.

The most basic type of divestiture is the *sale* of a division, business unit, segment, or set of assets to another company. The buyer generally, but not always, pays in cash. A number of reasons are provided for sales. First, asset sales can act as a defence against hostile takeovers. Sales often improve corporate focus, leading to greater overall value for the seller. This same rationale applies when the selling company is not in play. Second, asset sales provide needed cash to liquidity-poor firms. Third, it is often argued that the paucity of data about individual business segments makes large, diversified firms hard to value. Investors may discount the firm's overall value because of this lack of transparency. Sell-offs streamline a firm, making it easier to value. However, this argument is inconsistent with market efficiency because it implies that large, diversified firms sell below their true value. Fourth, firms may simply want to sell unprofitable divisions. However, unprofitable divisions are likely to have low values to anyone. A division should be sold only if its value is greater to the buyer than to the seller.

There has been a fair amount of research on sell-offs, with academics reaching two conclusions. First, event studies show that returns on the seller's stock are positive around the time of the announcement of sale, suggesting that sell-offs create value to the seller. Second, acquisitions are often sold off down the road. For example, Kaplan and Weisbach[21] found that over 40 percent of acquisitions were later divested, a result that does not reflect well on mergers. The average time between acquisition and divestiture was about seven years.

In a spin-off a parent firm turns a division into a separate entity and distributes shares in this entity to the parent's stockholders. Spin-offs differ from sales in at least two ways. First, the parent firm receives no cash from a spin-off: Shares are sent for free to the shareholders. Second, the initial shareholders of the spun-off division are the same as the parent's shareholders. By contrast, the buyer in a sell-off is most likely another firm. However, because the shares of the division are publicly traded after the spin-off, the identities of the shareholders will change over time.

At least four reasons are generally given for a spin-off. First, as with a sell-off, the spin-off may increase corporate focus. Second, because the spun-off division is now publicly traded, the Ontario Securities Commission requires additional information to be disseminated—so investors may find it easier to value the parent and subsidiary after the spin-off. Third, corporations often compensate executives with shares of stock in addition to cash. The stock acts as an incentive: Good performance from managers leads to stock price increases. However, prior to the spin-off, executives can receive stock only in the parent company. If the division is small relative to the entire firm, price movement in the parent's stock will be less related to the performance of the manager's division than to the performance of the rest of the firm. Thus, divisional managers may see little relation between their effort and stock appreciation. However, after the spin-off, the manager can be given stock in the subsidiary. The manager's effort should directly impact price movement in the subsidiary's stock. Fourth, the tax consequences from a spin-off are generally better than from a sale because the parent receives no cash from a spin-off.

In a carve-out, the firm turns a division into a separate entity and then sells shares in the division to the public. Generally the parent retains a large interest in the division. This transaction is similar to a spin-off, and the first three benefits listed for a spin-off apply to a carve-out as well. However, the big difference is that the firm receives cash from a carve-out, but not from a spin-off. The receipt of cash can be both good and bad. On the one hand, many firms need cash. Michaely and Shaw[22] find that large, profitable firms are more likely to use carve-outs, whereas small, unprofitable firms are more likely to use spin-offs. One interpretation is that firms generally prefer the cash that comes with a carve-out. However, small and unprofitable firms have trouble issuing stock. They must resort to a spin-off, where stock in the subsidiary is merely given to their own stockholders.

Unfortunately, there is also a side to cash, as developed in the free cash flow hypothesis. That is, firms with cash exceeding that needed for profitable capital budgeting projects

---

[21]Steven Kaplan and Michael Weisbach, "The Success of Acquisitions: Evidence from Divestitures," *Journal of Finance* (March 1992).

[22]Roni Michaely and Wayne Shaw, "The Choice of Going Public: Spinoffs vs. Carveouts," *Financial Management* (Autumn 1995).

may spend it on unprofitable ones. Allen and McConnell[23] find that the stock market reacts positively to announcements of carve-outs if the cash is used to reduce debt. The market reacts neutrally if the cash is used for investment projects.

A parent corporation issues tracking stock to "track" the performance of a specific division of the corporation. For example, if the tracking stock pays dividends, the size of the dividend depends on the division's performance. However, although "trackers" trade separately from the parent's stock, the division stays with the parent. By contrast, the subsidiary separates from the parent in a spin-off.

The first tracking stock was tied to the performance of EDS, a subsidiary of General Motors. Later, large firms such as Walt Disney and Sony issued trackers. However, few companies have issued tracking stocks in recent years, and parents have pulled most of those issued in earlier times. Perhaps the biggest problem with tracking stocks is their lack of clearly defined property rights. An optimistic accountant can increase the earnings of a particular division, leading to a larger dividend. A pessimistic accountant will have the reverse effect. Although accountants affect the earnings of regular companies, a change in earnings will not directly impact dividends.

The Control Block and the Corporate Charter

If one individual or group owns 51 percent of a company's stock, this **control block** makes a hostile takeover virtually impossible. In the extreme, one interest may own all the stock. Examples are privately owned companies like Irving Oil and Crown corporations like Export Development Canada. Many Canadian companies are subsidiaries of foreign corporations that own control blocks. Many domestically owned companies have controlling shareholders.[24]

As a result, control blocks are typical in Canada, although they are the exception in the United States. Table 30.7 shows that only 15 percent of the top 100 corporations in Canada were widely held in 1989 versus 73 percent for the United States.[25] One important implication is that minority shareholders need protection in Canada. One key group of minority shareholders are pension funds and other institutional investors. They are becoming increasingly vocal in opposing defensive tactics that are seen to be entrenching management at the expense of shareholders. We will discuss several examples below.

TABLE 30.7
Ownership Makeup of the Top 100 Corporations

	Canada	United States
Widely held	15	73
Control block	50	25
Privately owned	28	2
Government-owned	7	0

Source: D. H. Thain and D. S. R. Leighton, "Ownership Structure and the Board," *Canadian Investment Review* (Fall 1991), pp. 61–66.

[23]Jeffrey Allen and John McConnell, "Equity Carve-outs and Managerial Discretion," *Journal of Finance* (February 1998).

[24]Important exceptions are chartered banks. As we stated in Chapter 1, the *Bank Act* prohibits any one interest from owning more than 10 percent of the shares.

[25]The list of top 100 corporations in Canada is from the *Financial Post* 500. The U.S. corporations list comes from *Fortune* 500. The table is from D. H. Thain and D. S. R. Leighton, "Ownership Structure and the Board," *Canadian Investment Review* (Fall 1991), pp. 61–66.

For widely held companies, the corporate charter establishes the conditions that allow for a takeover. The *corporate charter* refers to the articles of incorporation and corporate bylaws that establish the governance rules of the firm. Firms can amend corporate charters to make acquisitions more difficult. For example, usually two-thirds of the shareholders of record must approve a merger. Firms can make it more difficult to be acquired by changing this to a higher percentage. This is called a *supermajority amendment.* Many charters with supermajority provisions have what is known as a *board out* clause as well. Here, supermajority does not apply if the board of directors approves the merger. This clause makes sure that the provision hinders only hostile takeovers.

Another device is to stagger the election of the board members. This makes it more difficult to elect a new board of directors quickly. In examining samples of U.S. adopting firms, DeAngelo and Rice, and Linn and McConnell, found that antitakeover amendments to corporate charters had no adverse effect on stock prices.[26]

Standstill Agreements

Managers of target firms may simultaneously negotiate standstill agreements. *Standstill agreements* are contracts under which the bidding firm agrees to limit its holdings of another firm. These agreements usually lead to cessation of takeover attempts, and announcements of such agreements have had a negative effect on stock prices.

In the U.S., standstill agreements often occur at the same time that a targeted repurchase is arranged. In a targeted repurchase, a firm buys a certain amount of its own stock from an individual investor, usually at a substantial premium. These premiums can be thought of as payments to potential bidders to eliminate unfriendly takeover attempts. Critics of such payments view them as bribes and label them as greenmail. Paying greenmail may harm minority shareholders if it heads off a takeover that would also raise the stock price. Standstill agreements also occur in takeover attempts in Canada but without greenmail, which is ruled out by securities laws.

EXAMPLE 30.4

In March 2006, Wendy's International Inc. entered into a standstill agreement with the Nelson Peltz-led investor group that had a 5.5 percent stake in the fast-food empire. The investor group agreed to not acquire more than a 10 percent stake in Wendy's International before June 30, 2007. Also included in the agreement was that the investor group would not submit any shareholder proposals or solicit proxies during the 15-month standstill agreement period. In exchange for entering into the agreement, Wendy's promised to expand its board of directors from 12 to 15 members and nominate three candidates representing the Nelson Peltz-led investor group.

Exclusionary Offers and Nonvoting Stock

An *exclusionary offer* is a tender offer for a given amount of its own shares while excluding targeted shareholders.

A well-known example occurred in 1986 when the Canadian Tire Dealers Association offered to buy 49 percent of the company's voting shares from the founding Billes family.

---

[26]H. DeAngelo and E. M. Rice, "Antitakeover Charter Amendments and Stockholder Wealth," *Journal of Financial Economics* 11 (April 1983); and S. G. Linn and J. J. McConnell, "An Empirical Investigation of the Impact of Antitakeover Amendments on Common Stock Prices," *Journal of Financial Economics* 11 (April 1983).

The dealers' bid was at \$169 per share for voting shares trading at \$40 before the bid. The nonvoting shares were priced at \$14. Further, since the dealers were the principal buyers of Canadian Tire products, control of the company would have allowed them to adjust prices to benefit themselves over the nonvoting shareholders.

The offer was voided by the Ontario Securities Commission, and it appears that any future exclusionary offers are likely to be viewed as an illegal form of discrimination against one group of shareholders.

Going Private and Leveraged Buyouts

Going private transactions and leveraged buyouts have much in common with mergers, and it is worthwhile to discuss them in this chapter. A publicly traded firm *goes private* when a private group, usually composed of existing management, purchases its stock. As a consequence, the firm's stock is taken off the market (if it is an exchange-traded stock, it is delisted) and is no longer traded. Thus, in going-private transactions, shareholders of publicly held firms are forced to accept cash for their shares.

Going-private transactions are frequently *leveraged buyouts* (LBOs). In a leveraged buyout the cash offer price is financed with large amounts of debt. Part of the appeal of LBOs is that the arrangement calls for little equity capital. This equity capital is generally supplied by a small group of investors, some of whom are likely to be managers of the firm being purchased.

The selling shareholders are invariably paid a premium above market price in an LBO, just as in a merger. As with a merger, the acquirer profits only if the synergy created is greater than the premium. Synergy is quite plausible in a merger of *two* firms, and we delineated a number of types of synergy earlier in the chapter. However, it is more difficult to explain synergy in an LBO because only *one* firm is involved.

Two reasons are generally given for value creation in an LBO. First, the extra debt provides a tax deduction, which, as earlier chapters suggested, leads to an increase in firm value. Most LBOs are on firms with stable earnings and with low to moderate debt. The LBO may simply increase the firm's debt to its optimum level.

The second source of value comes from increased efficiency and is often explained in terms of "the carrot and the stick." Managers become owners under an LBO, giving them an incentive to work hard. This incentive is commonly referred to as the carrot, and the carrots in some LBOs have been huge. For example, consider the LBO of Gibson Greeting Cards (GGC), previously a division of RCA, for which the management buyout group paid about \$80 million. Because of the leveraged nature of the transaction, the group invested only about \$1 million of its own capital. The division was taken private in 1982, but only for a brief period; GGC went public as its own company in 1984. The value of the initial public offering (IPO) was almost \$300 million. One of the principals in the buyout group, William Simon, who was a former secretary of the U.S. Treasury, received \$66 million from the IPO on an investment of somewhat under \$350,000.

Interest payments from the high level of debt constitute the stick. Large interest payments can easily turn a profitable firm before an LBO into an unprofitable one after the LBO. Management must make changes, either through revenue increases or cost reductions, to keep the firm in the black. Agency theory, a topic mentioned earlier in this chapter, suggests that managers can be wasteful with a large free cash flow. Interest payments reduce this cash flow, forcing managers to curb the waste.

Though it is easy to measure the additional tax shields from an LBO, it is difficult to measure the gains from increased efficiency. Nevertheless, this increased efficiency is considered at least as important as the tax shield in explaining the LBO phenomenon.

Academic research suggests that LBOs have, on average, created value. First, premiums are positive, as they are with mergers, implying that selling shareholders benefit. Second, studies indicate that LBOs that eventually go public generate high returns for the management group. For example, Kohlberg Kravis Roberts and the Ontario Teachers' Pension Plan bought Yellow Pages from Bell Canada in a $3 billion LBO in 2002. In July 2003, they sold part of their holding for $1 billion in an income trust IPO. Finally, other studies show that operating performance increases after the LBO. However, we cannot be completely confident of value creation because researchers have difficulty obtaining data about LBOs that do not go public. If these LBOs generally destroy value, the sample of firms going public would be a biased one.

Regardless of the average performance of firms undertaking an LBO, we can be sure of one thing: Because of the great leverage involved, the risk is huge. On the one hand, LBOs have created many large fortunes, a prominent example being Gibson Greeting Cards. On the other hand, a number of bankruptcies and near-bankruptcies have occurred as well, perhaps the most infamous being Revco's LBO. Revco was taken private near the end of 1986, but it is still talked about extensively today. In retrospect, the management group overpaid (a premium almost 50 percent above market price) and overlevered (a debt-to-value ratio of 97 percent). Revco was also not an ideal LBO candidate, though it seemed to be at the time. As mentioned earlier, firms with stable cash flows can best handle the high leverage of LBOs. Revco, a chain of about 1400 drugstores, seemed to fit the bill here because sales in this retail industry are relatively unresponsive to the business cycle. However, Revco planned to add about 100 stores a year, a strategy necessitating large capital expenditures. The combination of high leverage and large capital commitments provided little margin for error. The firm went under about a year and a half after the LBO. Perhaps the depressed Christmas season of 1987 or the rise of the discounters pushed Revco over the edge. Because of the size of the transaction (total LBO financing over $1.4 billion) and the embarrassment to the LBO specialist (it was Salomon Brothers' first large LBO), pundits are still arguing about the cause of Revco's demise.

Other Defensive Devices

As corporate takeovers become more common, other colourful terms have become popular.

- **Golden parachutes.** Some target firms provide compensation to top-level management if a takeover occurs. This can be viewed as a payment to management to make it less concerned for its own welfare and more interested in shareholders when considering a takeover bid. Alternatively, the payment can be seen as an attempt to enrich management at the shareholders' expense.
- **Crown jewels.** Firms often sell major assets—crown jewels—when faced with a takeover threat. This is sometimes referred to as the *scorched earth strategy*.
- **White knight.** Target firms sometimes seek a competing bid from a friendly bidder—a white knight—who promises to maintain the jobs of existing management and to refrain from selling off the target's assets.

A recent Canadian example of a white knight coming to the rescue is when Future Shop placed a bid for Chapters, one of Canada's largest bookstore chains, in February of 2001. Before giving in to Trilogy Retail Enterprises' final takeover bid of $121 million, Chapters' board of directors and management explored takeover defences. Chapters had a poison pill in place to prevent a hostile takeover. When Trilogy made a partial bid which, if successful, would have given Trilogy 53 percent of Chapters, Chapters' shareholders (other than the hostile bidder) had a right to purchase additional Chapters' shares at half the market price. As well, 51 days after Trilogy's initial bid, Chapters announced an offer from white knight, Future Shop, which the Chapters' board recommended to the shareholders. Chapters entered into a support agreement with Future Shop, which provided that the poison pill would only be waived for competing bids upon the take-up of Chapters' shares by Future Shop, and remain in place to give Future Shop time to prepare and mail their offer. The poison pill was eventually removed because the OSC found that Future Shop had substantial time to prepare its bid. In the end, Future Shop's role as a white knight forced Trilogy to raise its bid to $121 million, finally resulting in the takeover after months of media-publicized drama.

- **Poison pill.** Poison pill is a term taken from the world of espionage. Agents are supposed to bite a pill of cyanide rather than permit capture. Presumably this prevents enemy interrogators from learning important secrets. In finance, poison pills are used to make a stock repellent to others. A poison pill is generally a right to buy shares in the merged firm at a bargain price. The right is granted to the target firm's shareholders, contingent on another firm acquiring control.[27] The right dilutes the stock so much that the bidding firm loses money on its shares. Thus, wealth is transferred from the bidder to the target.

EXAMPLE 30.5

In 1999, a takeover battle raged for Canadian Airlines. The bidders were Air Canada (the eventual victor) and Onex, a major Canadian firm specializing in acquiring and restructuring companies. The bidding war involved offers, counteroffers, and poison pill takeover defenses. Figure 30.3 gives a detailed timeline.

? Concept Question

- **What can a firm do to make a takeover less likely?**

30.10 Some Evidence on Acquisitions

One of the most controversial issues surrounding our subject is whether mergers and acquisitions benefit shareholders.

Do Acquisitions Benefit Shareholders?

Much research has attempted to estimate the effect of mergers and takeovers on stock prices of the bidding and target firms. These studies are called *event studies* because they estimate abnormal stock price changes on and around the offer announcement date (the event). Abnormal returns are usually defined as the difference between actual stock returns

---

[27]P. H. Malatesta and R. A. Walkling, "Poison Pill Securities: Stockholder Wealth, Profitability and Ownership Structure," *Journal of Financial Economics* (January/March 1988). The authors conclude that the poison pill reduces shareholder wealth. Also see R. A. Walkling and M. Long, "Agency Theory, Managerial Welfare and Takeover Bid Resistance," *Rand Journal of Economics* (Spring 1984). Detailed discussion of poison pills in Canada appears in P. Halpern, "Poison Pills: Whose Interest Do They Serve?" *Canadian Investment Review* (Spring 1990).

FIGURE 30.3 Timeline for Air Canada's Takeover of Canadian Airlines in 1999

- Aug. 13: Ottawa suspends *Competition Act* to let the airlines legally talk about restructuring.
- Aug. 20: Air Canada proposes to buy Canadian Airlines' international routes. It's rejected.
- Aug. 24: Onex announces plan. It involves Onex, backed by American Airlines parent AMR Corp., paying $1.8 million and assuming $3.9 billion in debt. Canadian said it would recommend the offer to its shareholders.
- Aug. 31: Air Canada adopts a poison pill aimed at thwarting a takeover. It schedules a shareholders' meeting for Jan. 7 to consider Onex's offer and others that might arise. Onex asks court to force Air Canada to hold shareholders' meeting by Nov. 8, one day before its offer expires.
- Sept. 2: 18,500 airlines employees say they'll strike Sept. 27 if the government doesn't guarantee there will be no forced job losses in airline restructuring.
- Sept. 13: Air Canada asks Federal Court to rule that Onex's bid isn't exempt from a review under *Competition Act.*
- Sept. 17: Air Canada reports early its strong financial results, to show shareholders before they make decisions on industry restructuring.
- Sept. 18: Schwartz accuses Air Canada of a smear campaign against his hostile bid for the carrier and calls on Ottawa to hold parliamentary hearings.
- Sept. 20: Air Canada board urges shareholders to reject Onex bid.
- Sept 23: Airline machinists call off threatened strike.
- Sept. 28: Onex wins court battle on shareholder vote, calls meeting for Nov. 8.
- Oct. 8: Onex makes "iron-clad" guarantees on jobs, regional service, fares.
- Oct. 19: Air Canada, backed by Lufthansa, United Airlines and CIBC, unveils a $930 million counterbid to the Onex offer. Air Canada offers $92 million for Canadian Airlines but says it would run its rival as separate company.
- Oct. 25: Canadian Airlines rejects the Air Canada counteroffer.
- Oct. 26: Onex CEO Gerry Schwartz denies American Airlines would dominate new merged airline.
- Oct. 28: Onex raises its offer for Air Canada to $13 a share.
- Nov. 1: Canadian Auto Workers union president Buzz Hargrove announces support for Onex bid after receiving job guarantees.
- Nov. 2: Air Canada raises the stakes, offering $16 a share to buy back 36.4 percent of the airline.
- Nov. 4: Air Canada unions say they won't support Onex bid.
- Nov. 5: Onex raises its offer to $17.50 a share.
- Nov. 5: Quebec judge says Onex offer illegal, breaking law that limits single shareholder in Air Canada to 10 per cent.
- Nov. 5: Onex withdraws its offer, Air Canada says it will press ahead with bid to take over Canadian Airlines.
- Nov. 8: Transport Minister David Collenette says he expects Air Canada to take over Canadian Airlines.
- Nov. 15: Air Canada mails $92 million takeover bid to Canadian shareholders.
- Nov. 22: Canadian CEO Kevin Benson meets privately with Oneworld alliance partners American Airlines, British Airways, Qantas and Cathay Pacific.
- Nov. 24: International Association of Machinists and Aerospace Workers signs deal with Air Canada to protect 6000 Canadian employees from lay-offs and relocations if the deal goes through.
- Nov. 25: Canadian Airlines sends a circular to shareholders, telling them to hold on to their shares while it takes more time to consider Air Canada's bid.
- Nov. 29: Board of Canadian Airlines responds to Air Canada bid, saying it is fair financially but because of certain conditions Canadian refrains from making a recommendation to shareholders.
- Dec. 4: Board of Canadian Airlines recommends Air Canada's $92 million bid to its shareholders, after failing to come up with a better alternative from its Oneworld partners.
- Dec. 7: The Air Canada offer expires at 5 p.m. ET. Air Canada extends the buyout until Dec. 23.
- Dec. 8: Air Canada takes control of Canadian Airlines with more than 50 percent of Canadian shares tendered.

    AMR Corp. agrees to sell its convertible preferred shares in Canadian Airlines to Air Canada for between $55 to $60 million. The two also reach an agreement on American Airlines' relationship with Canadian: allowing codesharing between the two airlines and maintaining a joint frequent flyer program.
- Dec. 21: The Federal Competition Bureau says it will allow Air Canada's takeover of Canadian if the airline meets certain conditions. Air Canada agreed to surrender some peak-hour runway slots at Toronto's Pearson Airport, sell Canadian Regional Airlines and maintain service to all current domestic routes.
- Dec. 23: Air Canada officially wins its bid for Canadian, after receiving more than half of Canadian's shares and striking a deal with American Airlines for its 25 percent stake in Canadian.

Source: CBC News Online, http://www.cbc.ca/news/indepth/airlines/timeline.html. Used with permission.

and a market index, to take account of the influence of marketwide effects on the returns of individual securities.

Table 30.8 summarizes the results of numerous studies that look at the effects of merger and tender offers on stock prices in the United States. Table 30.9 shows high points of studies on mergers in Canada. Both tables are relevant since firms from one country often purchase companies in the other.

The tables show that shareholders of target companies in successful takeovers gain substantially. Starting with U.S. takeovers in Table 30.8, the average abnormal percentage return across all mergers from 1980 to 2001 is 0.0135. This number combines the returns on both the acquiring company and the acquired company. Because 0.0135 is positive, the market believes that mergers on average create value. The other three returns in the first column are positive as well, implying value creation in the different subperiods. Many other academic studies have provided similar results. Thus, it appears from this column that the synergies we mentioned earlier show up in the real world.

However, the next column tells us something different. Across all U.S. mergers from 1980 to 2001, the aggregate dollar change around the day of merger announcement is −$79 billion. This means that the market is, on average, *reducing* the combined stock value of the acquiring and acquired companies around the merger announcement date.

TABLE 30.8   Percentage and Dollar Returns for U.S. Mergers

Time Period	Gain or Loss to Merger (Both Acquired and Acquiring Firms)		Gain or Loss to Acquiring Firms	
	Abnormal Percentage Return	Aggregate Dollar Gain or Loss	Abnormal Percentage Return	Aggregate Dollar Gain or Loss
1980–2001	0.0135	−$ 79 billion	0.0110	−$220 billion
1980–1990	0.0241	$ 12 billion	0.0064	−$ 4 billion
1991–2001	0.0104	−$ 90 billion	0.0120	−$216 billion
1998–2001	0.0029	−$134 billion	0.0069	−$240 billion

Source: Modified from Sara Moeller, Frederik Schlingemann, and Rene Stulz, "Wealth Destruction on a Massive Scale? A Study of Acquiring-Firm Returns in the Recent Merger Wave," *Journal of Finance* (April 2005), Table 1.

TABLE 30.9 Abnormal Returns in Successful Canadian Mergers

	Target	Bidder
1271 aquired, 242 targets, 1994–2000**	10%	1%
1930 mergers, 1964–1983*	9	3
119 mergers, 1963–1982†	23	11
173 going-private transactions, 1977–1989‡	25	NA
Minority buyouts	27	
Non-controlling bidder	24	

*From B. Espen Eckbo, "Mergers and the Market for Corporate Control: The Canadian Evidence," *Canadian Journal of Economics,* May 1986, pp. 236–60. The test for bidders excluded firms involved in multiple mergers.
†From A. L. Calvet and J. Lefoll, "Information Asymmetry and Wealth Effect of Canadian Corporate Acquisitions," *Financial Review,* November 1987, pp. 415–31.
‡Modified from B. Amoako-Adu and B. Smith, "How Do Shareholders Fare in Minority Buyouts?" *Canadian Investment Review,* Fall 1991, pp. 79–88.
**From A. Yuce and A. Ng, "Effects of Private and Public Canadian Mergers," *Canadian Journal of Administrative Sciences,* June 2005, pp. 111–124.

Though the difference between the two columns may seem confusing, there is an explanation. Although most mergers have created value, mergers involving the very largest U.S. firms have lost value. The abnormal percentage return is an unweighted average in which the returns on all mergers are treated equally. A positive return here reflects all those small mergers that created value. However, losses in a few large mergers cause the aggregate dollar change to be negative.

But there is more. The rest of the second column indicates that the aggregate dollar losses occurred only in the 1998 to 2001 period. While there were losses of $-\$134$ billion in this period, there were gains of \$12 billion from 1980 to 1990. And interpolation of the table indicates that there were gains of \$44 billion ($=\$134 - \$90$) from 1991 through 1997. Thus, it appears that some large U.S. mergers lost a great deal of value from 1998 to 2001.

The results in a table such as Table 30.8 are, unfortunately, ambiguous. On the one hand, you could focus on the first column, saying that mergers create value on average. Proponents of this view might argue that the great losses in the few large mergers were flukes, not likely to occur again. On the other hand, we cannot easily ignore the fact that over the entire period, mergers destroyed more value than they created.

The preceding results combined returns on both bidders and targets. Investors want to separate the bidders from the targets. Columns 3 and 4 of Table 30.8 provide returns for U.S. acquiring companies alone. The third column shows that abnormal percentage returns for bidders have been positive for the entire sample period and for each of the individual subperiods—a result similar to that for bidders and targets combined. The fourth column indicates aggregate dollar losses, suggesting that large mergers did worse than small ones.

Although the U.S. evidence just presented for both the combined entity and the bidder alone is ambiguous, the evidence for targets is crystal-clear. Acquisitions benefit the target's shareholders. Consider the following chart, which shows the median merger *premium* over different periods in the United States:[28]

Time Period	1973–1998	1973–1979	1980–1989	1990–1998
Premium	42.1%	47.2%	37.7%	34.5%

The premium is the difference between the acquisition price per share and the target's pre-acquisition share price, divided by the target's pre-acquisition share price. The average premium is quite high for the entire sample period and for the various subsamples. For example, a target stock selling at \$100 per share before the acquisition that is later acquired for \$142.1 per share generates a premium of 42.1 percent. Clearly, shareholders of any firm trading at \$100 would love to be able to sell their holdings for \$142.1 per share.

Turning to Canadian research in Table 30.9, we find that bidders experience modest returns here as well—on the order of 1 percent in the most recent study. As in the U.S., targets do much better than bidders with an average return on 10 percent for mergers between 1994 and 2000. The other studies found that target firm shareholders in going-private transactions enjoyed an abnormal return of 25 percent, a figure consistent with U.S. results in Table 30.8.

The Canadian study of going-private transactions also looked at whether minority shareholders suffer. You can see from Table 30.9 that the answer is no. Returns to minority

---

[28]Taken from Gregor Andrade, Mark Mitchell, and Erik Stafford, "New Evidence and Perspectives on Mergers," *Journal of Economic Perspectives* (Spring 2001), Table 1.

shareholders hardly differ from returns occurring when firms went private with no majority shareholder.[29]

For both countries, these gains are a reflection of the merger premium that is typically paid by the acquiring firm. These gains are excess returns, that is, returns over and above what the shareholders would normally have earned.

What conclusions can be drawn from Tables 30.8 and 30.9? First, the evidence strongly suggests that shareholders of successful target firms achieve substantial gains from takeovers.

The second conclusion we can draw is that shareholders of bidding firms earn significantly less from takeovers. The balance is more even for Canadian mergers than for U.S. ones. This may be because there is less competition among bidders in Canada. Two reasons for this are that the Canadian capital market is smaller, and there are federal government agencies to review foreign investments.[30]

The Managers versus the Shareholders

Managers of Bidding Firms   The preceding discussion was presented from the shareholders' point of view. Because, in theory, shareholders pay the salaries of managers, we might think that managers would look at things from the shareholders' point of view. However, it is important to realize that individual shareholders have little clout with managers. For example, the typical shareholder is simply not in a position to pick up the phone and give the managers a piece of her mind. It is true that the shareholders elect the board of directors, which monitors the managers. However, an elected director has little contact with individual shareholders.

Thus, it is fair to ask whether managers are held fully accountable for their actions. This question is at the heart of what economists call *agency theory.* Researchers in this area often argue that managers work less hard, get paid more, and make worse business decisions than they would if shareholders had more control over them. And there is a special place in agency theory for mergers. Managers frequently receive bonuses for acquiring other companies. In addition, their pay is often positively related to the size of their firm. Finally, managers' prestige is also tied to firm size. Because firm size increases with acquisitions, managers are disposed to look favourably on acquisitions, perhaps even ones with negative NPV.

A fascinating study[31] compared companies where managers received a lot of options on their own company's stock as part of their compensation package with companies where the managers did not. Because option values rise and fall in tandem with the firm's stock price, managers receiving options have an incentive to forgo mergers with negative NPVs. The paper reported that the acquisitions by firms where managers receive lots of options (termed *equity-based compensation* in the paper) create more value than the acquisitions by firms where managers receive few or no options.

Agency theory may also explain why the biggest merger failures have involved large firms. Managers owning a small fraction of their firm's stock have less incentive to behave responsibly because the great majority of any losses are borne by other shareholders. Managers of large firms likely have a smaller percentage interest in their firm's stock than do

---

[29]In contrast, in a later study of takeovers and dual class shares in Canada, Smith and Amoako-Adu find that shareholders with superior voting shares enjoy higher returns: B. F. Smith and B. Amoako-Adu, "A Comparative Analysis of Takeovers of Single and Dual Class Firms," *Financial Review* 29 (February 1994).

[30]Halpern, "Poison Pills," p. 66; and A. L. Calvet and J. Lefoll, "Information Asymmetry," p. 432.

[31]Sudip Datta, Mai Iskandar-Datta, and Kartil Raman, "Executive Compensation and Corporate Acquisition Decisions," *Journal of Finance* (December 2001).

managers of small firms (a large percentage of a large firm is too costly to acquire). Thus, the merger failures of large acquirers may be due to the small percentage ownership of the managers.

Earlier, in Chapter 17 of this text, we discussed the free cash flow hypothesis. The idea here is that managers can spend only what they have. Managers of firms with low cash flow are likely to run out of cash before they run out of good (positive NPV) investments. Conversely, managers of firms with high cash flow are likely to have cash on hand even after all the good investments are taken. Managers are rewarded for growth, so managers with cash flow above that needed for good projects have an incentive to spend the remainder on bad (negative NPV) projects. A paper tested this conjecture, finding that "cash-rich firms are more likely than other firms to attempt acquisitions. . . . cash-rich bidders destroy seven cents in value for every dollar of cash reserves held. . . . consistent with the stock return evidence, mergers in which the bidder is cash-rich are followed by abnormal declines in operating performance."[32]

The previous discussion has considered the possibility that some managers were knaves—more interested in their own welfare than in the welfare of their shareholders. However, a recent paper entertained the idea that other managers were more fools than knaves. Malmendier and Tate[33] classified certain CEOs as overconfident, either because they refused to exercise stock options on their own company's stock when it was rational to do so or because the press portrayed them as confident or optimistic. The authors find that these overconfident managers are more likely to make acquisitions than are other managers. In addition, the stock market reacts more negatively to announcements of acquisitions when the acquiring CEO is overconfident.

The divergence between shareholders' interests and management merger motivation became more extreme during the Internet bubble of 1997 to 2001. Using their firms' overvalued stock as currency, tech company management often could not resist going on a buying spree. For example, during this period Nortel Networks spent over $33 billion buying 19 companies. Later, Nortel's stock fell by 95 percent and most of the acquired companies were written off and their employees laid off. The result was large-scale destruction of shareholder value through mergers.[34]

However, that is only half of the story. Shareholders of target firms may have just as hard a time controlling their managers. While there are many ways that managers of target firms can put themselves ahead of their shareholders, two seem to stand out. First, we said earlier that because premiums are positive, takeovers are beneficial to the target's shareholders. However, if managers may be fired after their firms are acquired, they may resist these takeovers.[35] Tactics employed to resist takeover, generally called defensive tactics, were discussed in an earlier section of this chapter. Second, managers who cannot avoid takeover may bargain with the bidder, getting a good deal for themselves at the expense of their shareholders.

---

[32]From Jarrad Harford, "Corporate Cash Reserves and Acquisitions," *Journal of Finance* (December 1999), p. 1969.

[33]Ulrike Malmendier and Geoffrey Tate, "Who Makes Acquisitions? CEO Overconfidence and the Market's Reaction," unpublished paper, Stanford University (December 2003).

[34]For more on value destruction through mergers during the Internet bubble see: M. C. Jensen, "Agency Costs of Overvalued Equity," Finance Working Paper No. 39/2004, European Corporate Governance Institute, http://ssrn.com/abstract=480421 and S. B. Moeller, F. P. Schlingemann, and R. M. Stulz, "Wealth Destruction on a Massive Scale? A Study of Acquiring Firm Returns in the Recent Merger Wave," *Journal of Finance,* 2005.

[35]However, as stated earlier, managers may resist takeovers to raise the offer price, not to prevent the merger.

Claude Lamoureux on Corporate Governance

Governance matters to a company's performance. The point is well made in a study by Paul Gompers and Joy Ishii published in Harvard's Quarterly Journal of Economics entitled "Corporate Governance and Equity Prices." That study constructed an index of 24 governance rules and applied it to the performance of 1,500 firms during the 1990s. It found that companies with best governance practices had a higher stock return during this decade.

Yes, good governance matters. And more companies are paying attention. For instance, the Canadian banks are notable for their responsiveness to shareholder concerns. They and many of our large corporations are listening and have made changes to executive compensation and in some cases have even ended stock options for directors. But these are still the exceptions, not the rule.

Judging by the attitude of many companies during this year's proxy season and shareholder meetings, it is as if the recent spate of governance, accounting, and disclosure scandals never happened. There is no groundswell in the boardrooms of North America. Many directors and executives still do not accept that shareholders own the firms they govern and manage, and deserve to be treated as owners.

Ontario Teachers' has been advocating governance changes for more than a decade. It is clear to us that entrenched corporate reactionaries won't change unless change is forced upon them. First, by legislation. Second, through a strong and national securities regulator. Third, by informed and determined shareholders banding together to make things happen.

Let's look at how these forces might shape a better governance world. Do we really need more rules and regulations? I would like to say no, but unfortunately the answer is yes. Voluntary compliance by publicly traded companies does not work well enough to protect shareholder interests. The Toronto Stock Exchange has had voluntary guidelines since 1995. The majority of listed companies do not bother to report in their annual report or proxy circular whether or not they comply with the guidelines. Most who do state that they do not comply. Why should they? The TSX has no enforcement role. The TSX is the wrong body to impose governance compliance. Enforcement should be expressed in legislation and carried out by securities regulators.

Not surprisingly, the opinion in Canada's boardrooms is that we do not need more legislation and regulations. We heard that in the Canadian reaction to the Sarbanes-Oxley Act. We should not delude ourselves that there are deep differences between our corporate culture and capital markets compared with the U.S. The argument is often put forward that Canada is different from the U.S. because we have a greater number of small companies.

Consider Wulf's fascinating work on *mergers of equals* (MOEs).[36] Some deals are announced as MOEs, primarily because both firms have equal ownership in and equal representation on the board of directors of the merged entity. AOL and Time Warner, Daimler-Benz and Chrysler, Morgan Stanley and Dean Witter, and Fleet Financial Group and BankBoston are generally held out as examples of MOEs. Nevertheless, authorities point out that in any deal one firm is typically "more equal" than the other. That is, the target and the bidder can usually be distinguished in practice. For example, Daimler-Benz is commonly classified as the bidder and Chrysler as the target in their merger.

Wulf finds that targets get a lower percentage of the merger gains, as measured by abnormal returns around the announcement date, in MOEs than in other mergers. And the percentage of the gains going to the target is negatively related to the representation of the target's officers and directors on the postmerger board. These and other findings lead Wulf to conclude, "They [the findings of the paper] suggest that CEOs trade power for premium in merger of equals transactions."

---

[36]Julie Wulf, "Do CEOs in Mergers Trade Power for Premium? Evidence From 'Mergers of Equals,'" *Journal of Law, Economics, and Organization* (Spring 2004).

We also have many firms that are family owned or controlled by a single shareholder. They often assert control through multiple voting shares that are grossly out of proportion to their economic exposure as shareholders. Surely, if a company sells shares to the public it should be held to the same governance standards as any other public company—irrespective of size or controlling ownership.

This brings me to the second force that is needed to effectively shape corporate governance—a national securities regulator with the powers to act. Unlike other nations with sophisticated capital markets, Canada does not have a national securities regulator. We rank sixth in the world in terms of market capitalization. That is less than two percent of global market capitalization, and about five percent of North American market capitalization. Yet regulating this tiny market from the global perspective is carved up among thirteen jurisdictions. This balkanization is a disservice to Canadian investors, a burden on corporate issuers, and a discouragement to foreign investors.

Clear and enforceable legislation and an empowered national securities regulator would do a lot to move governance standards forward. But in our view the most vital force for change must be shareholders asserting their ownership rights. That means making management accountable to directors as the stewards for the shareholders.

Clearly the soft stuff is important. Good governance is about more than laws and regulations. It has to do with human nature and how individuals interact with each other.

Recently a group of institutional investors incorporated the Canadian Coalition for Good Governance as a non-profit corporation. In case you missed it, let me remind you of its mission. It is to represent institutional shareholders—as well as small shareholders—through the promotion of best corporate governance practices and align the interests of boards and management with those of shareholders. So how can we improve the situation? First, we should change the way directors are elected. The practice of voting for a slate of directors should be abolished. Second, more candidates should be nominated than there are board seats so that shareholders have choice. A third suggestion is a mandatory annual meeting of directors with major shareholders. Specifically, with shareholders who have owned shares for at least one year. Long-term shareholders are informed shareholders. They want the company to do well over the long term.

Speech entitled "In Their Own Words... Claude Lamoureux on Corporate Governance," excerpted with permission from a speech delivered in May 2003. For more information on corporate governance, see *www.otpp.com*.

Real Productivity

There are many potential synergies from mergers and acquisitions. Unfortunately, it is very hard to precisely measure synergy. In the previous section, we focused on stock market gains or losses to the shareholders of the acquiring and acquired firms. In very general terms, we found that target-firm shareholders experience stock market gains and acquiring-firm shareholders experience stock market losses. There appear to be net gains to stockholders. This would suggest that mergers can increase real productivity. In fact, several recent studies suggest that mergers can increase real productivity. Healey, Palepu, and Ruback report that merged companies' after-tax returns increased substantially after the mergers. They trace this gain to an increase in selling activity (turnover). They find no evidence that merged firms cut back on positive NPV capital expenditures.[37]

? Concept Question

- **What does the evidence say about the distribution of benefits of mergers and acquisitions?**

[37]P. Healey, K. Palepu, and R. Ruback, "Does Corporate Performance Improve After Mergers," *Journal of Financial Economics* 31 (1997).

30.11 SUMMARY AND CONCLUSIONS

1. One firm can acquire another in several different ways. The three legal forms of acquisition are merger and consolidation, acquisition of stock, and acquisition of assets. Mergers and consolidations are the least costly to arrange from a legal standpoint, but they require a vote of approval by the shareholders. Acquisition of stock does not require a shareholder vote and is usually done via a tender offer. However, it is difficult to obtain 100 percent control with a tender offer. Acquisition of assets is comparatively costly because it requires more difficult transfer of asset ownership.

2. Mergers and acquisitions require an understanding of complicated tax and accounting rules. Mergers and acquisitions can be taxable or tax-free transactions. In a taxable transaction, each selling shareholder must pay taxes on the stock's capital appreciation. Should the acquiring firm elect to write up the assets, additional tax implications arise. However, acquiring firms do not generally elect to write up the assets for tax purposes. The selling shareholders do not pay taxes at the time of a tax-free acquisition.

3. The synergy from an acquisition is defined as the value of the combined firm (V_{AB}) less the value of the two firms as separate entities (V_A and V_B):

$$\text{Synergy} = V_{AB} - (V_A + V_B)$$

The shareholders of the acquiring firm will gain if the synergy from the merger is greater than the premium.

4. The possible benefits of an acquisition come from
   a. Revenue enhancement.
   b. Cost reduction.
   c. Lower taxes.
   d. Lower cost of capital.
   In addition, the reduction in risk from a merger may actually help bondholders and hurt shareholders.

5. Some of the most colourful language of finance stems from defensive tactics in acquisition battles. *Poison pills, golden parachutes, crown jewels, white knights,* and *greenmail* are terms that describe various antitakeover tactics discussed in this chapter.

6. The empirical research on mergers and acquisitions is extensive. Its basic conclusions are that, on average, the shareholders of acquired firms fare very well, while the shareholders of acquiring firms do not gain much.

KEY TERMS

Circular bid 846	Golden parachute 871	Purchase method 850
Consolidation 846	Goodwill 850	Stock exchange bid 846
Control block 868	Leveraged buyout (LBO) 848	Tender offer 846
Crown jewels 871	Merger 846	White knight 871
Going-private transaction 848	Poison pill 872	

SUGGESTED READING

Several fun-to-read trade books on mergers and acquisitions have recently been published, including:
Bruce Wasserstein. *Big Deal: 2000 and Beyond.* Warner Books, 2000; and Regina M. Pitaro. *Deals, Deals and More Deals.* Gabelli University Press, 1998.

QUESTIONS & PROBLEMS

The Basic Forms of Acquisitions

30.1 The Blue Lager Brewery has acquired the Pickering Pickle Company in a vertical merger. Blue Lager has issued $546,000 to pay for its purchase. ($546,000 is the purchase price.) Construct the balance sheet for the new corporation. The balance sheets shown here represent assets of both firms at their true market values. Assume these market values are also the book values.

Blue Lager Brewery
Balance Sheet
(in $ thousands)

Current assets	$ 728	Current liabilities	$ 364
Other assets	182	Long-term debt	182
Net fixed assets	910	Equity	1,274
Total	$1,820	Total	$1,820

Pickering Pickle Company
Balance Sheet
(in $ thousands)

Current assets	$ 146	Current liabilities	$ 146
Other assets	73	Equity	218
Net fixed assets	146		
Total	$ 364	Total	$ 364

30.2 Suppose the balance sheet for Pickering Pickle in Problem 30.1 shows the assets at their book value and not their market value of $330,000. Construct a balance sheet for the new corporation.

Earnings Growth

30.3 Refer to the Global Resources example in Section 30.8 in the text.

Suppose that instead of 40 shares, Global exchanges 100 of its shares for 100 of Regional. The new Global Resources will now have 200 shares outstanding and earnings of $250. Assume the market is smart.
a. Calculate Global's value after the merger.
b. Calculate Global's earnings per share.
c. Calculate Global's price per share.
d. Redo your answers to (a), (b), and (c), if the market is fooled.

30.4 Skywalker Aviation has voted in favour of being bought out by Gardia Financial Corporation. Information about each company is presented below.

	Gardia Financial	Skywalker Aviation
Price–earnings ratio	18	11
Number of shares	160,000	84,000
Earnings	$423,000	$91,000

Shareholders in Skywalker will receive 0.525 of a share of Gardia for each share they hold.
a. How will the earnings per share (EPS) for these shareholders be changed?
b. How will EPS changes affect the original Gardia shareholders?

Valuation

30.5   Fly-by-Night Couriers is analyzing the possible acquisition of Flash-in-the-Pan Restaurants. Neither firm has debt. The forecasts of Fly-by-Night show that the purchases would increase its annual after-tax cash flow by $600,000 indefinitely. The current market value of Flash-in-the-Pan is $20 million. The current market value of Fly-by-Night is $35 million. The appropriate discount rate for the incremental cash flows is 8 percent. Fly-by-Night is trying to decide whether it would offer 25 percent of its stock or $25 million in cash to Flash-in-the-Pan.

 a. What is the synergy from the merger?
 b. What is the value of Flash-in-the-Pan to Fly-by-Night?
 c. What is the cost to Fly-by-Night of each alternative?
 d. What is the NPV to Fly-by-Night of each alternative?
 e. What alternative should Fly-by-Night use?

30.6   Sawchuk Inc. is considering making an offer to purchase Dryden Corp. Sawchuk's vice president of finance has collected the following information:

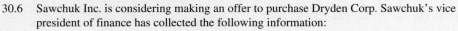

	Sawchuk	Dryden
Price–earnings ratio	18	12
Number of shares	1,000,000	250,000
Earnings	$1,000,000	$750,000

Sawchuk also knows that securities analysts expect the earnings and dividends of Dryden (currently $2 per share) to grow at a constant rate of 5 percent each year. Sawchuk management believes that the acquisition of Dryden will provide the firm with some economies of scale that will increase this growth rate to 7 percent per year.

 a. What is the value of Dryden to Sawchuk?
 b. What would Sawchuk's gain be from this acquisition?
 c. If Sawchuk were to offer $42 in cash for each share of Dryden, what would the NPV of the acquisition be?
 d. What is the most Sawchuk should be willing to pay in cash per share for the stock of Dryden?
 e. If Sawchuk were to offer 650,000 of its shares in exchange for the outstanding stock of Dryden, what would the NPV be?
 f. Should the acquisition be attempted? If so, should it be as in (c) or as in (e)?
 g. Sawchuk's outside financial consultants think that the 7 percent growth rate is too optimistic and a 6 percent rate is more realistic. How does this change your previous answers?

30.7   Pilate PLC has a market value of £600 million and 30 million shares outstanding. Bullseye Department Store has a market value of £250 million and 35 million shares outstanding. Pilate is contemplating acquiring Bullseye. Pilate's CFO concludes that the combined firm with synergy will be worth £1.2 billion and Bullseye can be acquired at a premium of £200 million.

 a. If Pilate offers 20 million shares to exchange for the 35 million shares of Bullseye, what will be the after-acquisition stock price?
 b. To make the value of the stock offer equivalent to a cash offer of £325 million, what would be the proper exchange ratio of the two stocks?

30.8   Company *A* is contemplating acquiring company *B*. Company *B*'s projected revenues, costs, and required investments appear in the accompanying table. The table also shows sources for financing company *B*'s investments if *B* is acquired by *A*. The table incorporates the following information:

 • Company *B* will immediately increase its leverage with a $110 million loan, which would be followed by a $150 million dividend to company *A*. (This operation will increase the debt-to-equity ratio of company *B* from 1/3 to 1/1.)

- Company A will use $50 million of tax-loss carryforwards available from the firm's other operations. The terminal, total value of company B is estimated to be $900 million in five years, and the projected level of debt then is $300 million.
- The risk-free rate and the expected rate of return on the market portfolio are 4 percent and 8 percent, respectively. Company A analysts estimate the weighted average cost of capital for their company to be 10 percent. The borrowing rate for both companies is 8 percent. The beta coefficient for the stock of company B (at its current capital structure) is estimated to be 1.30.
- The board of directors of company A is presented with an offer for $68.75 per share of company B, or a total of $550 million for the 8 million shares outstanding.

Evaluate this proposal. The accompanying table may help you.

Projections for Company B if Acquired by Company A (in $ millions)

	Year 1	Year 2	Year 3	Year 4	Year 5
Sales	800	900	1,000	1,125	1,250
Production costs	562	630	700	790	875
Depreciation	75	80	82	83	83
Other expenses	80	90	100	113	125
EBIT	83	100	118	139	167
Interest	19	22	24	25	27
EBT	64	78	94	114	140
Taxes	32	39	47	57	70
Net income	32	39	47	57	70
Investments:					
Net working capital	20	25	25	30	30
Net fixed assets	15	25	18	12	7
Total	35	50	43	42	37
Sources of financing:					
Net debt financing	35	16	16	15	12
Profit retention	0	34	27	27	25
Total	35	50	43	42	37

Cash Flows—Company A

	Year 0	Year 1	Year 2	Year 3	Year 4	Year 5
Acquisition of B	—					
Dividends from B	150	—	—	—	—	—
Tax loss carryforwards			25	25		—
Terminal value	—	—	—	—	—	—
Total	—	—	—	—	—	—

Calculating the Value of the Firm After an Acquisition

30.9   The following table shows the projected cash flows and their respective discount rates after the acquisition of Small Fry Co. by Whale Co. Fill in the blanks and calculate the stock price of the new firm if it has $128 million of debt and 6.7 million shares of stock outstanding.

	Net Cash Flow per Year (perpetual) (in $ millions)	Discount Rate (%)	Value (in $ millions)
Small Fry Co.	10	18%	?
Whale Co.	22	16	?
Benefits from acquisition	7	?	44.5
Revenue enhancement	4.5	?	14.5
Cost reduction	4	8	?
Tax shelters	2.5	7	?
Whale Co.	35	?	?

Risk Shifting

30.10 The Chocolate Ice Cream Company and the Vanilla Ice Cream Company have agreed to merge and form Fudge Swirl Consolidated. The two companies are exactly alike except for being located in different towns. The end-of-period value of each firm is determined by the weather, as shown.

Weather	Probability	Value
Rainy	0.20	$ 300,000
Warm	0.35	600,000
Hot	0.45	1,400,000

Because the towns are separated by a mountain range, their weather conditions are independent of each other. Furthermore, each company has an outstanding debt claim of $470,000. Assume that no premiums are paid in the merger.

a. What is the distribution of joint values?

b. What is the distribution of end-of-period debt values and stock values after the merger?

c. Show that the value of the combined firm is the sum of the individual values.

d. Show that the bondholders are better off and the shareholders are worse off in the combined firm than they would have been if the firms remained separate.

30.11 Red River Hydro, a public utility, provides electricity to the Prairies. Recent events at its Red Deer Nuclear Station have been discouraging. Several shareholders have expressed concern over last year's financial statements.

Income Statement Last Year (in $ millions)		Balance Sheet End of Year (in $ millions)	
Revenue	$327	Assets	$1,388
Fuel	149	Debt	1,090
Other expenses	89	Equity	297
Interest	89		
Net Income	$ 0		

Recently, a wealthy group of individuals has offered to purchase one-half of Red River's assets at fair market value. Management recommends that this offer be accepted because "We believe out expertise in the energy industry can be better exploited by Red River if we sell our electricity generating and transmission assets and enter the communications business. Although telecommunications is a riskier business than providing electricity as a public utility, it is also potentially very profitable." Should management approve this transaction? Why or why not?

Reasons for Mergers

30.12 Indicate whether you think the following claims regarding takeovers are true or false. In each case, provide a brief explanation for your answer.

  a. By merging competitors, takeovers have created monopolies that will raise product prices, reduce production, and harm consumers.

  b. Managers act in their own interests at times and in reality may not be answerable to shareholders. Takeovers may reflect runaway management.

  c. In an efficient market, takeovers would not occur because market price would reflect the true value of corporations. Thus, bidding firms would not be justified in paying premiums above market prices for target firms.

  d. Traders and institutional investors, having extremely short time horizons, are influenced by their perceptions of what other market traders will be thinking of stock prospects and do not value takeovers based on fundamental factors. Thus, they will sell shares in target firms despite the true value of the firms.

  e. Mergers are a way of avoiding taxes because they allow the acquiring firm to write up the value of the assets of the acquired firm.

  f. Acquisitions analysis frequently focuses on the total value of the firms involved. An acquisition, however, will usually affect relative values of stocks and bonds, as well as their total value.

30.13 Explain why diversification *per se* is probably not a good reason for merger.

30.14 In May 2005, high-end retailer Nieman Marcus announced plans to sell off its private label credit card business. Unlike other credit cards, private label credit cards can be used only in a particular merchant's store. Why might a company do this? Is there a possibility of reverse synergy?

 MINICASE: The Birdie Golf–Hybrid Golf Merger

Birdie Golf Inc. has been in merger talks with Hybrid Golf Company for the past six months. After several rounds of negotiations, the offer under discussion is a cash offer of $55 million for Hybrid Golf. Both companies have niche markets in the golf club industry, and the companies believe a merger will result in significant synergies due to economies of scale in manufacturing and marketing, as well as significant savings in general and administrative expenses.

Bryce Bichon, the financial officer for Birdie, has been instrumental in the merger negotiations. Bryce has prepared the following pro forma financial statements for Hybrid Golf assuming the merger takes place. The financial statements include all synergistic benefits from the merger:

	2008	2009	2010	2011	2012
Sales	$80,000,000	$90,000,000	$100,000,000	$112,500,000	$125,000,000
Production Costs	56,200,000	63,000,000	70,000,000	79,000,000	87,500,000
Depreciation	7,500,000	8,000,000	8,200,000	8,300,000	8,300,000
Other expenses	8,000,000	9,000,000	10,000,000	11,300,000	12,500,000
EBIT	$ 8,300,000	$10,000,000	$ 11,800,000	$ 13,900,000	$ 16,700,000
Interest	1,900,000	2,200,000	2,400,000	2,500,000	2,700,000
Taxable income	$ 6,400,000	$ 7,800,000	$ 9,400,000	$ 11,400,000	$ 14,000,000
Taxes (40%)	2,560,000	3,120,000	3,760,000	4,560,000	5,600,000
Net income	$ 3,840,000	$ 4,680,000	$ 5,640,000	$ 6,840,000	$ 8,400,000

Bryce is also aware that the Hybrid Golf division will require investments each year for continuing operations, along with sources of financing. The following table outlines the required investments and sources of financing:

	2008	2009	2010	2011	2012
Investments:					
Net working capital	$2,000,000	$2,500,000	$2,500,000	$3,000,000	$3,000,000
Fixed assets	1,500,000	2,500,000	1,800,000	1,200,000	700,000
Total	$3,500,000	$5,000,000	$4,300,000	$4,200,000	$3,700,000
Sources of financing:					
New debt	$3,500,000	$1,600,000	$1,600,000	$1,500,000	$1,200,000
Profit retention	0	3,400,000	2,700,000	2,700,000	2,500,000
Total	$3,500,000	$5,000,000	$4,300,000	$4,200,000	$3,700,000

The management of Birdie Golf feels that the capital structure at Hybrid Golf is not optimal. If the merger takes place, Hybrid Golf will immediately increase its leverage with a $11 million debt issue, which would be followed by a $15 million dividend payment to Birdie Golf. This will increase Hybrid's debt-to-equity ratio from .50 to 1.00. Birdie Golf will also to use a $2.5 million tax loss carryforward in 2009 and 2010 from Hybrid Golf's previous operations. The total value of Hybrid Golf is expected to be $90 million in five years, and the company will have $30 million in debt at that time.

Stock in Birdie Golf currently sells for $9.40 per share, and the company has 18 million shares of stock outstanding. Hybrid Golf has 8 million shares of stock outstanding. Both companies can borrow at an 8 percent interest rate. The risk-free rate is 6 percent, and the expected return on the market is 13 percent. Bryce believes the current cost of capital for Birdie Golf is 11 percent. The beta for Hybrid Golf stock at its current capital structure is 1.30.

Bryce has asked you to analyze the financial aspects of the potential merger. Specifically, he has asked you to answer the following questions:

1. Suppose Hybrid shareholders will agree to a merger price of $6.88 per share. Should Birdie proceed with the merger?
2. What is the highest price per share that Birdie should be willing to pay for Hybrid?
3. Suppose Birdie is unwilling to pay cash for the merger but will consider a stock exchange. What exchange ratio would make the merger terms equivalent to the original merger price of $6.88 per share?
4. What is the highest exchange ratio Birdie would be willing to pay and still undertake the merger?

Appendix 30A: Campeau Corp.'s Acquisition of Federated Department Stores

To access Appendix 30A, please go to the Online Learning Centre at **www.mcgrawhill.ca/olc/ross**.

Chapter **31**

Financial Distress

EXECUTIVE SUMMARY

This chapter discusses financial distress, private workouts, and bankruptcy. A firm that does not generate enough cash flow to pay interest or other contractually required payments will experience financial distress. If it defaults on a required payment, a firm may be forced to liquidate its assets. More often, a defaulting firm will reorganize its financial structure. Financial restructuring involves replacing old financial claims with new ones; it takes place with private workouts or legal bankruptcy. Private workouts are voluntary arrangements to restructure a company's debt, such as postponing a payment or reducing the size of the payment. Sometimes a private workout is not possible and formal bankruptcy is required. The Canadian retailer, Eaton's, went through most of these stages as shown in the chronology in Figure 31.1.

31.1 What Is Financial Distress?

Financial distress is surprisingly hard to define precisely—partly because of the variety of events befalling firms under financial distress. The list of events is almost endless. Examples include

- Dividend reductions.
- Plant closings.
- Losses.
- Layoffs.
- CEO resignations.
- Plummeting stock prices.

Financial distress occurs when a firm's operating cash flows are not sufficient to satisfy current obligations (such as trade credits or interest expenses) and the firm is forced to take corrective action.[1] Financial distress may lead a firm to default on a contract, and it may involve financial restructuring between the firm, its creditors, and its equity investors. Usually the firm is forced to take actions that it would not have taken if it had had sufficient cash flow. For example, Figure 31.1 shows that Eaton's had to close stores and business lines and move out of its head office when financial distress occurred.

Our definition of financial distress can be expanded somewhat by linking it to insolvency. *Insolvency* is defined in *Black's Law Dictionary* as

> Inability to pay one's debts; lack of means of paying one's debts. Such a condition of [one's] assets and liability that the former made immediately available would be insufficient to discharge the latter.[2]

---

[1] This definition is close to the one used by Karen Wruck, "Financial Distress: Reorganization and Organization Efficiency," *Journal of Financial Economics* 27 (1990), p. 425.

[2] *Black's Law Dictionary,* 5th ed. (St. Paul, Minn.: West, 1979), p. 716.

FIGURE 31.1   Eaton's: A Chronology

- **1854:** Timothy Eaton immigrated to Canada from Ireland.
- **1856:** Opened small store with his brother, later moved it to Stratford, Ont.
- **1869:** Opened his own store on Yonge Street in downtown Toronto.
- **1884:** Introduced the Eaton catalogue.
- **1907:** Eaton died at 72. His son John Craig Eaton took over the company.
- **1976:** Eaton's catalogue business was discontinued after 92 years in operation.
- **1977:** Eaton Centre shopping and office complex opened in downtown Toronto.
- **Early 1990s:** Rumours about Eaton's financial problems circulate. Company denies any troubles.
- **1991–1996:** Sales dropped by about $500 million a year.
- **1996:** Company records a pre-tax loss of $120 million.
- **February 1997:** Eaton's granted protection from creditors while it restructures.
- **June 5, 1997:** Former Hudson's Bay Co. president George Kosich becomes Eaton's new chief executive, replacing George Eaton.
- **July 1997:** Company negotiates deal to share pension surplus money with employees and makes other moves to conserve cash, including moving out of head office and ending home delivery service.
- **August 1997:** Company submits restructuring plan to Ontario court.
- **September 1997:** Creditors approve $419-million restructuring plan, saving Eaton's from bankruptcy.
- **Oct. 31, 1997:** Company emerges from court protection with a cash payment of $281 million to creditors and promises to pay most of the balance with interest by June 30, 1998.

- **Jan. 1, 1998:** Brent Ballantyne, an experienced turnaround executive, takes over as chairman from George Eaton.
- **June 10, 1998:** Eaton's goes public, issuing 11.7 million common shares at $15 each. Eaton family keeps control of the company with about 51 percent of its shares.
- **June 30, 1998:** Company cuts 600 jobs and plans to shut down its electronics and appliance business in favour of higher-profit fashion merchandise. Furniture and rug departments to close in 43 to 64 stores.
- **May 18, 1999:** Eaton's hires investment bank to "evaluate its strategic alternatives"—officially putting the company up for sale.
- **Aug. 23, 1999:** Eaton's granted protection from its creditors in Ontario Superior Court.
- **Aug. 24, 1999:** Eaton's lays off or gives termination notices to thousands of employees across the country. Eaton's shares suspended from trading on the Toronto Stock Exchange for failing to meet listing requirements.
- **Aug. 25, 1999:** Eaton's starts liquidation sales at its stores across the country.
- **Sept. 20, 1999:** Sears Canada announces a $50-million deal under which it will buy all of the shares of T. Eaton Co., eight of its stores, with option to buy five more. Sears Canada also purchased Eaton's name, trademarks, brands and Web site.
- **February 19, 2002:** After 133 years of operation, the Eaton name finally disappeared from Canada's retail landscape as Sears Canada decided to pull the plug on the retailer's seven remaining stores by midsummer of 2002.

Source: http://www.canoe.ca/MoneyGrowthNews/aug20_etntimeline.html. Used with permission.

This definition has two general themes: stocks and flows.[3] These two ways of thinking about insolvency are depicted in Figure 31.2. *Stock-based insolvency* occurs when a firm has negative net worth, so the value of its assets is less than the value of its debts. *Flow-based insolvency* occurs when operating cash flow is insufficient to meet current obligations. Flow-based insolvency refers to the inability to pay one's debts.

The two kinds of insolvency usually occur together, but this is not always the case. For example, a firm that had no current obligations could remain in business even if its debt exceeded its assets. Such a firm would be solvent according to the flow-based measure

---

[3] Edward Altman was one of the first to distinguish between stock-based insolvency and flow-based insolvency. See Edward Altman, *Corporate Financial Distress: A Complete Guide to Predicting, Avoiding and Dealing with Bankruptcy* (New York: John Wiley & Sons, 1983).

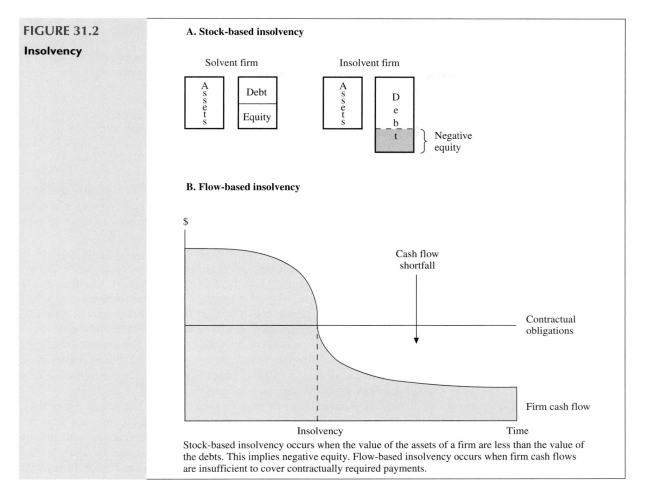

FIGURE 31.2

Insolvency

A. Stock-based insolvency

Solvent firm

Insolvent firm

B. Flow-based insolvency

Stock-based insolvency occurs when the value of the assets of a firm are less than the value of the debts. This implies negative equity. Flow-based insolvency occurs when firm cash flows are insufficient to cover contractually required payments.

but insolvent by the stock-based measure. When this occurs, firms often resort to creative accounting to hide their stock-based insolvency and increase their risk to try to increase the value of assets. This represents an agency cost of debt, as we discussed in Chapter 17.

? **Concept**
Questions

- **Describe financial distress.**
- **What are stock-based and flow-based insolvency?**

31.2 What Happens in Financial Distress?

In 1997, Eaton's, the venerable Canadian retailer founded in 1869, experienced financial distress brought on by five years of sales declines resulting in major losses. The firm restructured under court protection and, for the first time, appointed a non-family member as chairman. In 1998, Eaton's went public and restructured its business, shutting down unprofitable lines, such as appliances and furniture, and focusing on fashion merchandise. Despite these measures, losses continued and the firm had to declare bankruptcy in 1999. Later that year, after a liquidation sale of merchandise, Sears Canada bought all the shares along with the Eaton's name, trademarks, and brands.[4] Generalizing from the Eaton's example, firms deal with financial distress in many ways, such as

1. Selling major assets.
2. Merging with another firm.
3. Reducing capital spending as well as research and development.
4. Issuing new securities.
5. Negotiating with banks and other creditors.
6. Exchanging equity for debt.
7. Filing for bankruptcy.

Items (1), (2), and (3) concern the firm's assets. Items (4), (5), (6), and (7) involve the right-hand side of the firm's balance sheet and are examples of financial restructuring. Financial distress may involve both asset restructuring and financial restructuring—changes on both sides of the balance sheet.

Some firms may actually benefit from financial distress by restructuring their assets. In 1992, Olympia & York's decision to seek court protection allowed the company to restructure its assets and avoid formal bankruptcy liquidation. Olympia & York's cash flow was not sufficient to cover required payments, and it emerged from court protection as solely a property management company; previously, it was in many different lines of business. In another example, Air Canada sought bankruptcy protection in 2003 to allow time to cut expenses and wages and renegotiate arrangements with creditors. The company emerged from bankruptcy in October 2004 planning new strategic initiatives. These examples show that, for some firms, financial distress may bring about new organizational forms and new operating strategies. However, in this chapter we focus on financial restructuring.

Figure 31.3 shows how firms move through financial distress in Canada. Previously, most legal bankruptcies in this country ended with liquidation. However, new changes to the bankruptcy process are encouraging restructurings, reorganizations, and private workouts.

Financial distress can serve as a firm's "early warning" system for trouble. Firms with more debt will experience financial distress earlier than firms with less debt. However, firms that experience financial distress earlier will have more time for private workouts and reorganization. Firms with low leverage will experience financial distress later and, in many instances, be forced to liquidate.

? Concept Questions
- Why doesn't financial distress always cause firms to die?
- What is a benefit of financial distress?

31.3 Bankruptcy Liquidation and Reorganization

Firms that cannot or choose not to make contractually required payments to creditors have two basic options: liquidation or reorganization. **Liquidation** means termination of the firm as a going concern, and it involves selling off the assets of the firm. The proceeds, net of selling costs, are distributed to creditors in order of established priority. **Reorganization** is the option of keeping the firm a going concern; it often involves issuing new securities to replace old ones. Liquidation or reorganization is the result of a bankruptcy proceeding. Which occurs depends on whether the firm is worth more "dead" or "alive."

---

[4]Our discussion draws from the chronology in Figure 31.1.

FIGURE 31.3

What Happens in Financial Distress

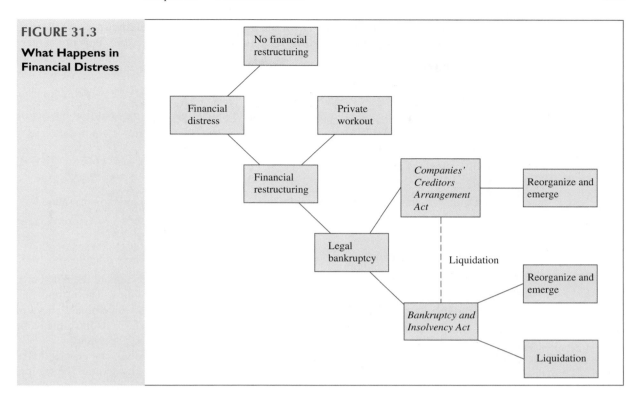

Liquidation and reorganization are covered under the *Bankruptcy and Insolvency Act* (1993); reorganization is also covered under the *Companies' Creditors Arrangement Act.* In late 1992, after intense criticism of the inherent difficulties of reorganization under the old law, the federal government introduced wide-ranging changes to the *Bankruptcy and Insolvency Act* to make it "debtor friendly." The changes have met with mixed reviews, but most industry experts agree that the changes facilitate corporate restructurings.[5]

Bankruptcy Liquidation

Liquidation occurs when the court directs sale of all assets of the firm. The following sequence of events is typical.

1. A petition is filed in a federal court. Corporations may file a voluntary petition, or involuntary petitions may be filed against the corporation by creditors. Creditors must give 10 days' notice before filing a petition.

2. A trustee-in-bankruptcy is elected by the creditors to take over the assets of the debtor corporation. The trustee will attempt to liquidate the assets.

3. When the assets are liquidated, after payment of the bankruptcy administration costs, the proceeds are distributed among the creditors.

4. If any assets remain, after expenses and payments to creditors, they are distributed to the shareholders.

[5]P. P. Farkas, "What's Really Wrong with Our Bankruptcy Act?" *CA Magazine* (June 1991), pp. 39–40.

The distribution of the proceeds of the liquidation occurs according to the following priority. (The higher a claim is on this list, the more likely it is to be paid. In many of these categories, there are various limitations and qualifications that we omit for the sake of brevity.[6])

1. Administrative expenses associated with the bankruptcy.
2. Other expenses arising after the filing of an involuntary bankruptcy petition but before the appointment of a trustee.
3. Wages, salaries, and commissions.
4. Municipal tax claims.
5. Rent.
6. Claims resulting from employee injuries that are not covered by workers' compensation.
7. Unsecured creditors.
8. Preferred shareholders.
9. Common shareholders.

Three qualifications to this list are in order. The first concerns unpaid federal source deductions such as income tax and employment insurance premiums. These funds are beyond the grasp of the bankruptcy trustee and must be paid to the government ahead of any payments to the claimants on our list. (Provincial source deductions have the same status only if the bankrupt company had kept them in a separate bank account.)

The second qualification concerns secured creditors. Such creditors are entitled to the proceeds from the sale of the security and are outside this ordering. However, if the secured property is liquidated and provides insufficient cash to cover the amount owed, the secured creditors join with unsecured creditors in dividing the remaining liquidated value. In contrast, if the secured property is liquidated for proceeds greater than the secured claim, the net proceeds are used to pay unsecured creditors and others.

EXAMPLE 31.1

The B. O. Drug Company is to be liquidated. Bonds worth $1.5 million are secured by a mortgage on the B. O. Drug Company corporate headquarters building, which is sold for $1 million; $200,000 is used to cover administrative costs and other claims (including unpaid wages, pension benefits, consumer claims, and taxes). This leaves an amount available to pay secured and unsecured creditors of $2.5 million. This is less than the amount of unpaid debt of $4 million. Following our list of priorities, all creditors must be paid before shareholders, and the mortgage bondholders have first claim on the $1 million obtained from the sale of the headquarters building.

The trustee has proposed the following distribution:

Type of Claim	Prior Claim	Cash Received Under Liquidation
Bonds (secured by mortgage)	$ 1,500,000	$1,500,000
Subordinated debentures	2,500,000	1,000,000
Common shareholders	10,000,000	0
Total	$14,000,000	$2,500,000

---

[6]Our discussion draws on R. Klapstein, *Legal Aspects of Financial Counselling* (Montreal: Institute of Canadian Bankers, 1994), Chapter 16.

Calculation of the Distribution

Cash received from sale of assets available for distribution	$2,500,000
Cash paid to secured bondholders on sale of mortgaged property	1,000,000
Available to bond and debenture holders	$1,500,000
Total claims remaining ($4,000,000 less payment of $1,000,000 on secured bonds)	$3,000,000
Distribution of remaining $1,500,000 to cover total remaining claims of $3,000,000	

Type of Claim Remaining	Claim on Liquidation Proceeds	Cash Received
Bonds	$ 500,000	$ 500,000
Debentures	2,500,000	1,000,000
Total	$3,000,000	$1,500,000

The third qualification is that, in reality, courts have a great deal of freedom in deciding what actually happens and who actually gets what in the event of bankruptcy. As a result, the priority set out above is not always followed.

The 1988 restructuring of Dome Petroleum is an example. Declining oil prices in 1986 left Dome in difficulties after a series of earlier debt reschedulings. Dome's board believed that if the company went into bankruptcy, secured creditors could force disposal of assets at fire-sale prices, producing losses for unsecured creditors and shareholders. One estimate obtained at the time projected that unsecured creditors would receive, at best, 15 cents per dollar of debt under liquidation. As a result, the board sought and received court and regulatory approval for sale of the company as a going concern to Amoco Canada. Unsecured creditors eventually received 45 cents on the dollar.

Bankruptcy Reorganization

The general objective of corporate reorganization is to plan to restructure the corporation with some provision for repayment of creditors. The new provisions introduced to the *Bankruptcy and Insolvency Act* in 1992 were intended to facilitate the corporate reorganization process. (Eaton's restructured in 1997 and 1998.) Here is a typical sequence of events:

1. A voluntary petition can be filed by the corporation, or an involuntary petition can be filed by creditors. Under the new legislation, creditors must provide the insolvent company with 10 days' notice before filing the petition.

2. A federal judge either approves or denies the petition. If the petition is approved, a time for filing proofs of claims is set. A debtor files a notice of intention to make a proposal (reorganization plan), and a stay of proceedings of 30 days is effected against all creditors. A further 21 days is added until the creditors meet to vote on the proposal. The court can add a maximum of five months to the stay period.

3. In almost all cases, the corporation (the "debtor in possession") continues to run the business. While the stay of proceedings is in effect, the new legislation has included several safeguards intended to prevent the collapse of the business.

4. The corporation is required to submit a proposal, which is the reorganization plan.

5. Creditors and shareholders are divided into classes. A class of creditors accepts the plan if a majority of the class (in dollars or in number) agrees. The secured creditors must vote before the unsecured creditors. The debtor decides on the classes of secured creditors, and can force proposals on uncooperative creditors.

6. After acceptance by creditors, the plan is confirmed by the court.

7. Payments in cash, property, and securities are made to creditors and shareholders. The plan may provide for the issuance of new securities.

EXAMPLE 31.2

Suppose B. O. Drug Co. decides to reorganize under the *Bankruptcy and Insolvency Act.* Generally, senior claims are honoured in full before various other claims receive anything. Assume that the "going concern" value of B. O. Drug Co. is $3 million and that its balance sheet is as shown:

Assets	$3,000,000
Liabilities	
Mortgage bonds	1,500,000
Subordinated debentures	2,500,000
Shareholders' equity	−1,000,000

The firm has proposed the following reorganization plan:

Old Security	Old Claim	New Claim with Reorganization Plan
Mortgage bonds	$1,500,000	$1,500,000
Subordinated debentures	2,500,000	1,500,000

and a distribution of new securities under new claim with reorganization plan:

Old Security	Receives Under Proposed Reorganization Plan
Mortgage bonds	$1,000,000 in 9% senior debentures
	$500,000 in 11% subordinated debentures
Debentures	$1,000,000 in 8% preferred stock
	$500,000 in common stock

The corporation may wish to allow the old shareholders to retain some participation in the firm. Needless to say, this may lead to protests by the holders of unsecured debt.

Companies' Creditors Arrangement Act   The *Companies' Creditors Arrangement Act* (CCAA)—federal legislation originally enacted during the 1930s—allows for the reorganization and continuation of insolvent businesses.[7] Some important differences between the CCAA and the *Bankruptcy and Insolvency Act* are

1. The *Bankruptcy and Insolvency Act* is primarily restricted to dealing with unsecured creditors, but the CCAA can deal with any or all creditors.

2. The CCAA is a brief statute that is silent on the framework for proceeding with an arrangement (reorganization plan). Therefore, a series of court orders must be used to develop an appropriate framework.

3. When a company applies for protection under the CCAA, there is no provision for the debtor to be placed in bankruptcy for failing to carry out the agreed-upon terms.

---

[7]An excellent description of the CCAA is provided in E. B. Leonard, *Guide to Commercial Insolvency in Canada* (Toronto: Butterworths Canada, 1988), pp. 20-1 to 20-6.

In the 1980s, the CCAA became a popular statute for major reorganizations. The advantage that it gives debtors in dealing with secured creditors makes this statute invaluable for certain corporate restructurings. In this regard, the CCAA is similar to Chapter 11 of the U.S. *Federal Bankruptcy Reform Act* of 1978, popularly referred to as just Chapter 11. Later in the chapter we will look at this statute's use in the reorganization of Olympia & York.

Agreements to Avoid Bankruptcy

When a firm defaults on an obligation, it may still be able to avoid bankruptcy. Because the legal process of bankruptcy can be lengthy and expensive, it is often in everyone's best interest to devise a *private workout* that avoids a bankruptcy filing. Much of the time, creditors can work with the management of a company that has defaulted on a loan contract. Voluntary arrangements to restructure the company's debt can be and often are made. This may involve *extension,* which postpones the date of payment, or *composition,* which involves a reduced payment.

? Concept Questions
- **What is bankruptcy?**
- **What is the difference between liquidation and reorganization?**
- **What is the *Companies' Creditors Arrangement Act?***

31.4 Current Issues in Financial Distress

In this section we examine two important tactics in financial distress: private workouts and prepackaged bankruptcies. It is expected that these responses to financial distress, prevalent in the United States, will grow in importance in Canada under the current legislation. For this reason, this section relates U.S. experience to the current Canadian law.

Private Workout or Bankruptcy: Which Is Best?

A firm that defaults on its debt payments will need to restructure its financial claims. The firm will have two choices: formal bankruptcy or **private workout.** The previous section described two types of formal bankruptcies: liquidation and reorganization. This section compares private workouts with bankruptcy reorganizations. Both types of financial restructuring involve exchanging new financial claims for old financial claims. Usually senior debt is replaced with junior debt, and debt is replaced with equity. Much academic research in the United States has described what happens in private workouts and formal bankruptcies.[8]

- Historically, one-half of financial restructurings have been private, but recently formal bankruptcy has dominated.
- Firms that emerge from private workouts experience stock price increases that are much greater than those for firms emerging from formal bankruptcies.
- The direct costs of private workouts are only about 10 percent of the costs of formal bankruptcies.
- Top management usually loses pay and sometimes jobs in both private workouts and formal bankruptcies.

---

[8]For example, see Stuart Gilson, "Managing Default: Some Evidence on How Firms Choose Between Workouts and Bankruptcy," *Journal of Applied Corporate Finance* (Summer 1991); and Stuart C. Gilson, Kose John, and Larry N. P. Lang, "Troubled Debt Restructuring: An Empirical Study of Private Reorganization of Firms in Defaults," *Journal of Financial Economics* 27 (1990).

These facts, when taken together, seem to suggest that a private workout is much better than a formal bankruptcy. In Canada, the new *Bankruptcy and Insolvency Act* has added increased costs and time commitments to the formal bankruptcy proceedings. Therefore, direct negotiations (private workouts) between creditors and debtors can be expected to increase. In some cases, however, formal bankruptcy is the better alternative.

Holdouts

Bankruptcy is usually better for equity investors than for creditors because equity investors can usually hold out for a better deal in bankruptcy. The priority of claims, which favours creditors over equity investors, is usually violated in formal bankruptcies. One study found that in 81 percent of recent U.S. bankruptcies, equity investors obtained some compensation.[9]

Complexity

A firm with a complicated capital structure will have more trouble putting together a private workout. Firms with secured creditors and trade creditors will usually use formal bankruptcy because it is too difficult to reach an agreement with many different types of creditors.

Lack of Information

There is an inherent conflict of interest between equity investors and creditors, and the conflict is accentuated when both have incomplete information about the circumstances of financial distress. When a firm initially experiences a cash flow shortfall, it may not know whether the shortfall is permanent or temporary. If the shortfall is permanent, creditors will push for a formal reorganization or liquidation. However, if the cash flow shortfall is temporary, formal reorganization or liquidation may not be necessary, and equity investors will take this viewpoint. This conflict of interest cannot easily be resolved.

These last two points are especially important. They suggest that financial distress will be more expensive if complexity is high and information is incomplete. Complexity and lack of information make cheap workouts less likely.

Prepackaged Bankruptcy

On October 1, 1986, the Crystal Oil Company filed for protection from its creditors under Chapter 11 of the U.S. Bankruptcy Code.[10] Given the firm's heavy indebtedness, perhaps the outcome was not very surprising. However, less than three months later, Crystal Oil came out of bankruptcy with a different capital structure. This surprised many people because, traditionally, bankruptcy has been very costly and often takes many years to emerge from. Crystal Oil avoided a lengthy bankruptcy by negotiating a reorganization plan with its creditors several months before the bankruptcy filing date.[11]

---

[9]Lawrence A. Weiss, "Bankruptcy Dissolution: Direct Costs and Violation of Priority and Claims," *Journal of Financial Economics 23* (1990). However, W. Beranek, R. Boehmer, and B. Smith, "Much Ado About Nothing: Absolute Priority Deviations in Chapter 11," *Financial Management* (Autumn 1996), find 33.8 percent of bankruptcy reorganizations leave the shareholders with nothing. They also point out that deviations from the absolute priority role are to be expected because the Bankruptcy Code allows creditors to waive their rights if they perceive a waiver to be in their best interest.

[10]Chapter 11 is the U.S. version of Canada's reorganization laws.

[11]John McConnell and Henri Servaes, "The Economics of Prepackaged Bankruptcy," *Journal of Applied Corporate Finance* (Summer 1991), describes prepackaged bankruptcy and the Crystal Oil Company.

This alternative reorganization arrangement has been called prepackaged bankruptcy. **Prepackaged bankruptcy** is a combination of private workout and legal bankruptcy. In prepackaged bankruptcy, the firm and most of its creditors agree to private reorganization outside formal bankruptcy. After the private reorganization is put together, the firm files a formal bankruptcy.

Prepackaged bankruptcy arrangements require that most creditors reach agreement privately. Prepackaged bankruptcy does not seem to work when there are thousands of reluctant trade creditors, such as in the case of retail trading firms.

The main benefit of prepackaged bankruptcy is that it forces holdouts to accept a bankruptcy reorganization. If a large fraction of a firm's creditors can agree privately to a reorganization plan, the holdout problem may be avoided. This makes a reorganization plan in formal bankruptcy easier to put together.[12]

A study by McConnell, Lease, and Tashjian reports that U.S. prepackaged bankruptcies offer many of the advantages of a formal bankruptcy, but they are also more efficient. Their results suggest that the time spent and the direct costs of resolving financial distress are less in a prepackaged bankruptcy than in a formal bankruptcy.[13]

? Concept Questions

- **What are two ways a firm can restructure its finances?**
- **Why do firms use formal bankruptcy?**
- **What is prepackaged bankruptcy?**
- **What is the main benefit of prepackaged bankruptcy?**

31.5 The Decision to Seek Court Protection: The Case of Olympia & York

Olympia & York (O&Y) was one of the largest companies in Canada. Privately held by the powerful Reichmann family, Olympia & York Developments was best known for its real estate development projects. The company was also involved in ownership of real estate, energy, natural resources, financial services, and beverage companies. Outside of Canada, O&Y was the largest landowner in Manhattan, New York, and owner of the Canary Wharf project in London, England.

On May 14, 1992, O&Y filed for court protection in Canada under the *Companies' Creditors Arrangement Act.* At the same time, several O&Y affiliates filed for Chapter 11 bankruptcy protection in the United States. Finally, on May 27, O&Y also filed for court protection in the U.K. due to an inability to meet payments on the Canary Wharf project.

The recession of the early 1990s led to a major decline in real estate prices and an increase in vacancy rates. O&Y (a highly leveraged company) could not service its debt because of a lack of cash flow. Here is a brief summary of the decision to file for protection and the events following.

---

[12]The original reorganization plan of Crystal Oil was accepted by the public creditors, but it was not accepted by the secured creditors. During bankruptcy a slightly revised plan was "crammed down" on the secured creditors. A bankruptcy court can force creditors to participate in a reorganization if it can be shown that the plan is "fair and equitable."

[13]John J. McConnell, Ronald Lease, and Elizabeth Tashjian, "Prepacks as a Mechanism for Resolving Financial Distress: The Evidence," *Journal of Applied Corporate Finance* 8 (1996).

1. In the late 1980s, O&Y embarked upon numerous real estate developments. As the largest landowner in the world, O&Y undertook large projects in North America and Europe.

2. The 1990s recession led to a liquidity crisis for O&Y, and the company could not service its debt.

3. In May 1992, O&Y filed for court protection in Canada, the United States, and the U.K.

4. Court protection allowed O&Y some breathing room, as its assets were not touchable by creditors until a formal restructuring plan had been presented.[14] In the United States and Canada, $8.6 billion of debt was immediately frozen from servicing. In the U.K., $7.7 billion of debt was frozen.

5. After numerous deadline extensions and a difficult eight months, O&Y presented a restructuring plan to creditors (over 100 in total) in Canada; it was approved on January 25, 1993. At that time, O&Y was still attempting to save some U.S. properties from Chapter 11. In the U.K., a buyer for the Canary Wharf project was being sought.

6. The acceptance of the Canadian restructuring plan resulted in O&Y's emerging as a small property management company, and the company was significantly downsized.

Costs of the O&Y restructuring include:

1. *Direct costs of restructuring.* Formal protection can be expensive and time consuming. O&Y was under court protection in Canada for eight months, and continued negotiating in the United States and the U.K. for some time. The first six months of restructuring were estimated to cost O&Y $20 million. Fees include

Legal fees	$5.75 million
Accounting fees	2.65 million
Costs of financial advisors	8.50 million

These fees are for O&Y alone and do not go beyond the first six months of restructuring. Creditors also paid huge legal fees; for example, one bank estimated its total legal bill to be $7 million.[15]

2. *Indirect costs of restructuring.* There are many indirect costs of financial distress, including management distraction, loss of customers, and loss of reputation. Indirect costs may occur whether or not formal bankruptcy is declared.

3. *Costs of a complicated financial structure.* Firms such as O&Y that have bank loans, senior subordinated debt, and junior subordinated debt with many different creditors will have a difficult time getting all claimholders to agree to an out-of-court settlement. It is axiomatic that the more complicated a firm's financial structure, the more difficult it will be to work out private arrangements to avoid bankruptcy. Conflicts between managers, shareholders, and creditors make reaching a private agreement difficult. There is a tendency for each group to try to gain value at the expense of the others.

? Concept Questions

- Was O&Y's insolvency stock-based or flow-based?
- What are some costs of the O&Y bankruptcy?

---

[14]As we stated in Section 31.3, the CCAA can apply to all creditors, which was important for O&Y.

[15]These fees were derived from "O&Y's Restructuring Bill to Reach $20M: Report," *The Globe and Mail* (June 20, 1992).

31.6 SUMMARY AND CONCLUSIONS

This chapter examines what happens when firms experience financial distress.

1. Financial distress occurs when a firm's operating cash flow is not sufficient to cover contractual obligations. Financially distressed firms are often forced to take corrective actions and to undergo financial restructuring. Financial restructuring involves exchanging new financial claims for old ones.

2. Financial restructuring can be accomplished with a private workout or formal bankruptcy. Financial restructuring can involve liquidation or reorganization. However, liquidation is becoming less common in Canada.

3. Two important tactics in restructuring are private workouts and prepackaged bankruptcies. Both are expected to increase in Canada with the advent of "debtor friendly" legislation.

4. In the example of Olympia & York's filing for court protection to avoid bankruptcy proceedings, we see how a complicated financial structure can make it hard to achieve agreement among creditors.

KEY TERMS

Financial distress 887   Prepackaged bankruptcy 897   Reorganization 890
Liquidation 890   Private workout 895

SUGGESTED READING

An excellent book on financial distress by a leading authority is:
E. A. Altman. *Corporate Financial Distress: A Complete Guide to Predicting, Avoiding and Dealing with Bankruptcy.* 2nd Edition. New York: John Wiley & Sons, 1993.

Many academic articles on financial distress appear in:
M. Jensen and R. Rubeck, eds. "Symposium on the Structure and Governance of Enterprise, Part II." *Journal of Financial Economics* 27 (1990). Articles by Lawrence Weiss, S. G. Gilson, K. John, L. N. P. Lang, S. Kaplan, D. Reishus, F. Easterbrook, and K. H. Wruck appear.
L. Senbet and James Seward. "Financial Distress, Bankruptcy and Reorganization." Chapter 28 in *Handbook in OR and MS,* Vol. 9, R. A. Jarrow, V. Maksimovic, and W. T. Ziemba, eds. (1995).

Canadian statutes regarding bankruptcy and insolvency are found in:
L. W. Houlden and C. H. Morawetz. *The Annotated Bankruptcy and Insolvency Act 1993.* Scarborough, Ontario: Carswell, 1992.

A highly readable history of Eaton's is:
R. McQueen. *The Eatons: The Rise and Fall of Canada's Royal Family.* Stoddart, 1998.

QUESTIONS & PROBLEMS

31.1 Define financial distress using the stock-based and flow-based approaches. Explain how a company could be insolvent under one measure but not under the other.

31.2 Why do so many firms file for legal bankruptcy when private workouts are so much less expensive?

31.3 What are some benefits of financial distress?

Visit us at www.mcgrawhill.ca/olc/ross

Bankruptcy

31.4 When the Beacon Computer Company (BCC) filed for bankruptcy liquidation under the Canadian *Bankruptcy and Insolvency Act,* it had the following balance sheet:

Liquidating Value		Claims	
Net realizable assets	$15,000	Trade credit	$ 3,000
		Secured notes (by a mortgage)	3,000
		Senior debenture	6,000
		Junior debenture	5,000
		Equity	(2,000)

As a trustee, what distribution of liquidating value do you propose?

31.5 When the Master Printing Company filed for bankruptcy reorganization under the Canadian *Bankruptcy and Insolvency Act,* it had the following balance sheet:

Assets		Claims	
Going concern value	$16,500	Mortgage bonds	$9,000
		Senior debenture	7,000
		Junior debenture	4,000
		Equity	(4,000)

As a trustee, what reorganization plan would you accept?

31.6 The A&Z Real Estate Company is to be liquidated. The book value of its assets is $60 billion. Bonds with a face value of $24 billion are secured by a mortgage on the company's Toronto and New York buildings. A&Z has subordinated debentures outstanding in the amount of $30 billion; shareholders' equity has a book value of $6 billion; $1.8 billion is used to cover administrative costs and other claims (including unpaid wages, pension benefits, legal fees, and taxes).

The company has a liquidating value of $28 billion. Of this amount, $15 billion represents the proceeds from the sale of the Toronto and New York buildings.

As the trustee in bankruptcy, you wish to follow the bankruptcy law strictly. What is your proposed distribution?

31.7 Now suppose that the A&Z Real Estate Company in Problem 31.6 wishes to reorganize instead of liquidating. In this case the company has a going concern value of $40 billion. What proposal would you recommend? How does this proposal differ from your solution in the case of liquidation? Explain briefly.

31.8 The Southeast Asia Corporation (SAC) is to be liquidated. The market value of its assets is $14.5 million. Bonds with a face value of $5.8 million are unsecured. SAC has no subordinated debentures outstanding; shareholders' equity has a market value of $1.8 million; $700,000 is used to cover administrative costs and other claims (including unpaid wages, pension benefits, legal fees, and taxes.

The company has a liquidating value of $12 million. Of this amount, $5 million represents the proceeds from the sale of their flagship Indonesian resort.

As a trustee in bankruptcy, you wish to follow the bankruptcy law strictly. What is your proposed distribution?

Appendix 31A: Predicting Corporate Bankruptcy: The Z-Score Model
To access Appendix 31A, please go to the Online Learning Centre at **www.mcgrawhill.ca/ olc/ross.**

Chapter 32

International Corporate Finance

EXECUTIVE SUMMARY

Canada has an open economy linked very closely by a free trade agreement to its largest trading partner, the United States. There are also important economic and financial ties to Mexico under NAFTA, to Europe, the Pacific Rim, and other major economies worldwide.

Corporations that have significant foreign operations are often referred to as *international corporations* or *multinationals*. International corporations must consider many financial factors that do not directly affect purely domestic firms. These include foreign exchange rates, different interest rates from country to country, complex accounting methods for foreign operations, foreign tax rates, and foreign government intervention. These topics are also of interest to many smaller Canadian businesses.

Smaller corporations do not qualify as multinationals in the league of Alcan or McCain, but their financial managers must know how to manage foreign exchange risk.

The basic principles of corporate finance apply to international corporations. Like domestic companies, international ones seek to (1) invest in projects that create more value for the shareholders than they cost and (2) arrange financing that raises cash at the lowest possible cost. That is, the net present value principle holds for both foreign and domestic operations. However, it is usually more complicated to apply the NPV principle to foreign operations.

Perhaps the most important complication of international finance is foreign exchange. The foreign exchange markets provide information and opportunities for an international corporation when it undertakes capital budgeting and financing decisions. The relationship among foreign exchange, interest rates, and inflation is defined by the basic theories of exchange rates: purchasing power parity, interest rate parity, and the expectations theory.

Typically, international financing decisions involve a choice of three basic approaches:

1. Export domestic cash to the foreign operations.
2. Borrow in the country where the investment is located.
3. Borrow in a third country.

We will discuss the merits of each approach.

32.1 Terminology

A common buzzword across all business school subjects is *globalization*. The first step in learning about the globalization of financial markets is to conquer the new vocabulary. Here are some of the most common terms used in international finance and in this chapter:

1. A **European currency unit (euro)** was a basket of 10 European currencies devised in 1979 and intended to serve as a monetary unit for the *European Monetary System* (*EMS*). Effective January 2002, the euro replaced the 10 domestic currencies.

2. The **cross rate** is the exchange rate between two foreign currencies, generally neither of which is the U.S. dollar. The U.S. dollar, however, is used as an interim step in determining the cross rate. For example, if an investor wants to sell Canadian dollars and buy Swiss francs, he would sell Canadian dollars against U.S. dollars and then buy francs with those U.S. dollars. So, although the transaction is designed to be Canadian dollars for francs, the U.S. dollar's exchange rate serves as a benchmark.

3. **Eurobonds** are bonds denominated in a particular currency and issued simultaneously in the bond markets of several European countries. For many international companies and governments, they have become an important way to raise capital. Eurobonds are issued outside the restrictions that apply to domestic offerings and are typically syndicated in London. Trading can and does take place anywhere there is a buyer and a seller.

4. **Eurocurrency** is money deposited in a financial centre outside of the country whose currency is involved. For instance, Eurodollars—the most widely used Eurocurrency—are U.S. dollars deposited in banks outside the United States.

5. **Foreign bonds,** unlike Eurobonds, are issued in a single country and are usually denominated in that country's currency. Often, the country in which these bonds are issued will draw distinctions between them and bonds issued by domestic issuers, including different tax laws, restrictions on the amount issued, or tougher disclosure rules.

   Foreign bonds often are nicknamed for the country where they are issued: Yankee bonds (United States), Samurai bonds (Japan), Rembrandt bonds (the Netherlands), and Bulldog bonds (Britain). Partly because of tougher regulations and disclosure requirements, the foreign bond market has not grown in past years with the vigour of the Eurobond market. A substantial portion of all foreign bonds are issued in Switzerland.

6. An **American Depository Receipt (ADR)** is a security issued in the United States to represent shares of a foreign stock, allowing that stock to be traded in the United States. Foreign companies use ADRs, which are issued in U.S. dollars, to expand the pool of potential U.S. investors. ADRs are available in two forms for about 690 foreign companies: company-sponsored, which are listed on an exchange, and unsponsored, which are usually held by the investment bank that makes a market in the ADR. Both forms are available to individual investors, but only company-sponsored issues are quoted daily in newspapers.

7. The **London Interbank Offered Rate (LIBOR)** is the rate that most international banks charge one another for loans of Eurodollars overnight in the London market. As discussed in Chapter 26, LIBOR is a cornerstone in the pricing of money-market issues and other short-term debt issues by both governments and corporate borrowers. Less creditworthy issuers will often borrow at a rate above LIBOR.

8. As discussed in Chapter 26, there are two basic kinds of **swaps:** interest rate and currency. An interest rate swap occurs when two parties exchange debt with a floating-rate payment for debt with a fixed-rate payment, or vice versa. Currency swaps are agreements to deliver one currency against another currency. Often both types of swaps are used in the same transaction when debt denominated in different currencies is swapped.

9. **Export Development Canada (EDC)** is a federal Crown corporation with a mandate to promote Canadian exports. EDC provides long-term financing for foreign companies that purchase Canadian exports. To qualify for EDC support, exporters must produce or market goods with a minimum Canadian content of 60 percent.

   Other government programs to support exports include the federal Programme for Export Market Development (PEMD), which reimburses part of the costs of developing export markets and a variety of provincial programs.

? Concept Question

- **What is the difference between a Eurobond and a foreign bond?**

32.2 Foreign Exchange Markets and Exchange Rates

The **foreign exchange market** is undoubtedly the world's largest financial market. It is the market where one country's currency is traded for another's. Most of the trading takes place in a few currencies: the U.S. dollar ($), euro (€), British pound sterling (£), Japanese yen (¥), and Swiss franc (SF).

The foreign exchange market is an over-the-counter market. There is no single location where traders get together. Instead, traders are located in the major banks around the world. They communicate using computer terminals, telephones, and other telecommunication devices.

The many different types of participants in the foreign exchange market include:

1. Importers who convert their domestic currency to foreign currency to pay for goods from foreign countries.

2. Exporters who receive foreign currency and may want to convert to the domestic currency.

3. Portfolio managers who buy and sell foreign stocks and bonds.

4. Foreign exchange brokers who match buy and sell orders.

5. Traders who make the market in foreign exchange.

Exchange Rates

An **exchange rate** is the price of one country's currency expressed in terms of another country's currency. In practice, almost all trading of currencies worldwide takes place in terms of the U.S. dollar.

Figure 32.1 reproduces exchange rate quotations. The first section represents major currencies. The first part of this section is labelled "per US$" and gives the amount of foreign currency it takes to buy one U.S. dollar. For example, the Canadian dollar spot rate is quoted at 1.0987, which means that you could buy one U.S. dollar today with 1.0987 Canadian dollars.[1] The second part under major currencies is labelled "per C$" and gives the amount of foreign currency it takes to buy one Canadian dollar. For example, the U.S. dollar spot rate is quoted here at 0.9102, so you could get 0.9102 U.S. dollars for one Canadian dollar. Naturally, this second exchange rate is just the reciprocal of the first one, $1/1.0987 = 0.9102$.

The last section of Figure 32.1 shows cross rates for major currencies. Notice that each of the cross rates *under* the diagonal has a counterpart *above* the diagonal that is symmetrical and equals the reciprocal. For example, in the first row it is shown that one U.K. pound equals $2.1802 Canadian. By looking at its counterpart in the fifth row, we realize that one Canadian dollar equals 0.4587 British pounds, which is the reciprocal of its counterpart, $1/2.1802 = 0.4587$.

There are two reasons for quoting all foreign currencies in terms of the U.S. dollar. First, it reduces the number of possible cross-currency quotes. For example, with seven major currencies, there would potentially be 14 exchange rates. Second, it makes **triangular arbitrage** more difficult. If all currencies were traded against each other, it would make inconsistencies more likely. That is, the exchange rate of the British pound against the Canadian dollar would be compared to the exchange rate between the U.S. dollar and

---

[1] The spot rate is for immediate trading. Forward rates are for future transactions and are discussed in detail later. When we write *today,* we refer to the date the rates were quoted in May 2007.

FIGURE 32.1   Exchange Rate Quotations

FOREIGN EXCHANGE

Supplied by Reuters. Listings indicative of late afternoon rates. Charts based on close.

Per US$	Latest	Prev day	4 wks ago	Day %ch	Wk %ch	4wk %ch	Per C$	Latest	Prev day	4 wks ago	Day %ch	Wk %ch	4wk %ch
Canada $	1.0987	1.1062	1.1309	−0.7	−0.6	−2.8	US$	0.9102	0.904	0.8843	+0.7	+0.6	+2.9
euro*	1.359	1.3549	1.3565	+0.3	+0.3	+0.2	euro*	1.4926	1.4984	1.5333	−0.4	−0.2	−2.7
Japan yen	120.22	120.38	118.92	−0.1	+0.2	+1.1	Japan yen	109.38	108.80	105.10	+0.5	+0.8	+4.1
UK pound*	1.9848	1.979	2.0059	+0.3	−0.2	−1.1	UK pound*	2.1802	2.1884	2.2674	−0.4	−0.8	−3.8
Swiss franc	1.2152	1.2192	1.2098	−0.3	−0.2	+0.4	Swiss franc	1.1057	1.1019	1.0692	+0.3	+0.3	+3.4
Australia $*	0.8331	0.8324	0.8367	+0.1	+0.5	−0.4	Australia $*	0.9149	0.9204	0.9457	−0.6	nil	−3.3
Mexico peso	10.807	10.7968	10.9795	+0.1	−0.3	−1.6	Mexico peso	9.8298	9.7549	9.703	+0.8	+0.2	+1.3
Hong Kong	7.8138	7.8122	7.8122	nil	−0.1	nil	Hong Kong	7.1102	7.0611	6.905	+0.7	+0.5	+3.0
Singapore $	1.5164	1.5156	1.5138	+0.1	−0.1	+0.2	Singapore $	1.3794	1.3695	1.3378	+0.7	+0.5	+3.1
China renminbi	7.681	7.68	7.733	nil	−0.2	−0.7	China renminbi	6.991	6.943	6.8379	+0.7	+0.4	+2.2
India rupee	40.65	40.61	41.71	+0.1	nil	−2.5	India rupee	37.00	36.71	36.88	+0.8	+0.6	+0.3
Russia rouble	25.7468	25.7919	25.7738	−0.2	−0.2	−0.1	Russia rouble	23.4348	23.3098	22.7868	+0.5	+0.4	+2.8
Brazil real	1.9809	2.0088	2.0385	−1.4	−2.2	−2.8	Brazil real	1.8031	1.8124	1.802	−0.5	−1.6	+0.1

*inverted

FORWARD EXCHANGE

Per US$	1 mo	3 mo	6 mo	1 yr	2 yr	3 yr	4 yr	5 yr
C$	1.0983	1.0975	1.0952	1.0898	1.0805	1.0730	1.0688	1.0693
euro	1.3595	1.3616	1.3658	1.3761	1.3963	1.4141	1.4298	1.4493
Yen	120.20	120.19	120.18	120.16	120.12	120.09	120.05	120.02
£	1.9814	1.9751	1.9674	1.9559	1.9417	1.9336	1.9231	1.9202
Per C$								
US$	0.9105	0.9112	0.9131	0.9176	0.9255	0.9320	0.9356	0.9352
euro	1.4931	1.4934	1.4938	1.4941	1.5088	1.5174	1.5282	1.5498
Yen	109.17	108.75	108.15	106.85	103.92	101.03	98.03	94.91
£	2.1762	2.1677	2.1548	2.1320	2.0990	2.0763	2.0572	2.0550

CURRENCY CROSS RATES

	C$	US$	euro	Yen	£	Sw.fr.	A$
C$	.....	1.0987	1.4926	0.0091	2.1802	0.9044	0.9157
US$	0.9102	.....	1.3590	0.0083	1.9848	0.8229	0.8331
euro	0.6700	0.7359	.....	0.6119	1.4603	0.6054	0.6128
Yen	109.38	120.22	163.33	.....	238.56	98.91	100.11
£	0.4587	0.5038	0.6846	0.4190	.....	0.4146	0.4196
Sw.fr.	1.1057	1.2152	1.6511	1.0106	2.4116	.....	1.0121
A$	1.0920	1.2003	1.6306	0.9980	2.3817	0.9875	.....
Gold	739.56	673.00	495.18	80922	339.06	817.90	807.63

Source: *National Post*, May 16, 2007, FP14. Used with permission.

the Canadian dollar. This implies a particular rate between the British pound and the U.S. dollar to prevent triangular arbitrage.

EXAMPLE 32.1

What if the pound traded for €4 in Frankfurt and US$1.60 in London? If the U.S. dollar traded for €2 in Frankfurt, there would be a triangular arbitrage opportunity. Starting with US$1.60, a trader could purchase £1 in London. This pound could then be used to buy €4 in Frankfurt. With the U.S. dollar trading at €2, the €4 could then be traded for US$2 in Frankfurt as illustrated in Figure 32.2. The net gain from going around this "triangle" would be (in U.S. dollars) $2.00 − $1.60 = $0.40. Imagine what the return would be on an initial US$1 billion purchase.

FIGURE 32.2

Triangular Arbitrage

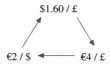

Types of Transactions

Three types of trades take place in the foreign exchange market: spot, forward, and swap. **Spot trades** involve an agreement on the exchange rate today for settlement in two days. The rate is called the **spot exchange rate. Forward trades** involve an agreement on exchange rates today for settlement in the future. The rate is the **forward exchange rate.** As seen in Figure 32.1, maturities for forward trades range from one month to five years. A swap is the sale (purchase) of a foreign currency with a simultaneous agreement to repurchase (resell) it sometime in the future. The difference between the sale price and the repurchase price is called the **swap rate.**

EXAMPLE 32.2

On October 11, bank *A* pays Canadian dollars to bank *B*'s account at a Toronto bank and *A* receives pounds sterling in its account at a bank in London. On November 11, as agreed on October 11, the transaction is reversed. *A* pays the sterling back to *B*, while *B* pays back the dollars to *A*. This is a swap. In effect, *A* has borrowed pounds sterling while giving up the use of Canadian dollars to *B*.

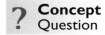 **Concept**
Question

• **What are the three kinds of foreign exchange transactions?**

32.3 The Law of One Price and Purchasing Power Parity

What determines the level of the spot exchange rate? One answer is the **law of one price (LOP).** The law of one price says that a commodity will cost the same regardless of the country in which it is purchased.[2] More formally, let $S_£(t)$ be the spot exchange rate, that is, the number of Canadian dollars needed to purchase a British pound at time t.[3] Let $P^{CDN}(t)$ and $P^{UK}(t)$ be the current Canadian and British prices of a particular commodity, say, apples. The law of one price says that

$$P^{CDN}(t) = S_£(t)\, P^{UK}(t)$$

for apples.

The rationale behind LOP is similar to that of triangular arbitrage. If LOP did not hold, arbitrage would be possible by moving apples from one country to another. For example, suppose that apples in Toronto are selling for $4 per bushel, while in London the price is £2 per bushel. Then the law of one price implies that

$$\$4 = S_£(t) \times £2$$

and

$$S_£(t) = \$2/£$$

That is, the spot exchange rate implied by the LOP is $2 per pound.

---

[2]In practice, the law of one price may not always be applicable. The main flaw is that it is not easy to move commodities from one country to another. In some cases, it is illegal to do so. Such restrictions on the movement of some commodities can have an impact on the price from one country or region to the next.

[3]Throughout this chapter, we quote foreign exchange in direct terms.

Figure 32.1 shows that the actual exchange rate is $2.1802 per pound. Starting with $4, a trader could buy a bushel of apples in Toronto, ship it to London, and sell it there for £2. The pounds sterling could then be converted into dollars at the exchange rate, $2.1802/£, yielding a total of $4.3604 for a gain of $0.3604 (or $4.3604 − $4).

The rationale of the LOP is that if the exchange rate is not $2/£ but is instead, $2.1802/£, then forces would be set in motion to change the rate and/or the price of apples. In our example, tonnes of apples would be flying from Toronto to London. Thus, demand for apples in Toronto would raise the dollar price for apples there, and the supply in London would lower the pound sterling price. The apple traders converting pounds sterling into dollars, that is, supplying pounds sterling and demanding Canadian dollars, would also put pressure on the exchange rate to drop from $2.1802/£.

As you can see, for the LOP to be strictly true, three assumptions are needed:

1. The transactions cost of trading apples—shipping, insurance, wastage, and so on—must be zero.

2. No barriers to trading apples, such as tariffs or taxes, can exist.

3. Finally, an apple in Toronto must be identical to an apple in London. It won't do for you to send red apples to London if the English eat only green apples.

Given the reality that transactions costs are not zero and that the other conditions are rarely exactly met, the LOP is really applicable only to traded goods, and then only to very uniform ones. The LOP does not imply that a Mercedes costs the same as a Ford or that a nuclear power plant in France costs the same as one in Ontario. In the case of the cars, they are not identical. In the case of the power plants, even if they were identical, they are expensive and very difficult to ship.

Because consumers purchase many goods, economists refer to **purchasing power parity (PPP),** the idea that the exchange rate adjusts so that a *market basket* of goods costs the same regardless of the country in which it is purchased. In addition, a relative version of purchasing power parity has evolved. **Relative purchasing power parity (RPPP)** says that the rate of change in the price level of commodities in one country relative to the rate of change in the price level in another determines the rate of change of the exchange rate between the two countries. Formally,

$$\frac{P^{CDN}(t+1)}{P^{CDN}(t)} = \frac{S_£(t+1)}{S_£(t)} \times \frac{P^{UK}(t+1)}{P^{UK}(t)}$$

$$1 + \begin{matrix} \text{CDN} \\ \text{inflation rate} \end{matrix} = \left(1 + \begin{matrix} \text{Change in foreign} \\ \text{exchange rate} \end{matrix}\right) \times \left(1 + \begin{matrix} \text{British} \\ \text{inflation rate} \end{matrix}\right)$$

This states that the rate of inflation in Canada relative to that in the U.K. determines the rate of change in the value of the dollar relative to that of the pound during the interval t to $t + 1$. It is common to write Π_{CDN} as the rate of inflation in Canada. $1 + \Pi_{CDN}$ is equal to $P^{CDN}(t+1)/P^{CDN}(t)$. Similarly, Π_{UK} is the rate of inflation in Great Britain. $1 + \Pi_{UK}$ is equal to $P^{UK}(t+1)/P^{UK}(t)$.

The above equation can be rearranged as

$$\frac{1 + \Pi_{CDN}}{1 + \Pi_{UK}} = \frac{S_£(t+1)}{S_£(t)} \tag{32.1}$$

We can rewrite this in an approximate form as

$$\Pi_{CDN} \approx \Pi_{UK} + \frac{\dot{S}_£}{S_£}$$

where $\dot{S}_£/S_£$ now stands for the rate of change in the dollars-per-pound exchange rate.

As an example, suppose that inflation in the European Union during the year is equal to 4 percent and inflation in Canada is equal to 10 percent. Then, according to RPPP, the price of the euro in terms of the Canadian dollar should rise; that is, the Canadian dollar declines in value in terms of the euro. Using our approximation, the dollars-per-euro exchange rate should rise by

$$\frac{\dot{S}_{\text{€}}}{S_{\text{€}}} \approx \Pi_{\text{CDN}} - \Pi_{\text{€}}$$
$$= 10\% - 4\%$$
$$= 6\%$$

where $\dot{S}_{\text{£}}/S_{\text{£}}$ stands for the rate of change in the dollars-per-euro exchange rate. That is, if the euro is worth \$0.70 at the beginning of the period, it should be worth approximately \$0.742 (or \$0.70 × 1.06) at the end of the period.

RPPP says that the change in the ratio of domestic commodity prices of two countries must be matched in the exchange rate. This version of the law of one price suggests that, to estimate changes in the spot rate of exchange, it is necessary to estimate the differences in relative inflation rates. In other words, we can express our formula in expectational terms as

$$E\left(\frac{\dot{S}_{\text{€}}}{S_{\text{€}}}\right) = E(\Pi_{\text{CDN}}) - E(\Pi_{\text{€}})$$

If we expect the Canadian inflation rate to exceed the EU inflation rate, we should expect the dollar price of euros to rise, which is the same as saying that the dollar is expected to fall against the euro.

The more exact relationship of Equation (32.1) can be expressed in expectational terms as

$$\frac{E(1 + \Pi_{\text{CDN}})}{E(1 + \Pi_{\text{UK}})} = \frac{E[S_{\text{£}}(t + 1)]}{S_{\text{£}}(t)} \tag{32.2}$$

? Concept Questions
- **What is the law of one price? What is purchasing power parity?**
- **What is the relationship between inflation and exchange rate movements?**

32.4 Interest Rates and Exchange Rates: Interest Rate Parity

The forward exchange rate and the spot exchange rate are tied together by the same sort of arbitrage that underlies the law of one price. To explain the link, we begin with some useful terminology. If forward exchange rates are greater than the spot exchange rate in a particular currency, the forward foreign currency is said to be at a *premium*. (This implies the domestic currency is at a discount.) If the values of forward exchange rates are less than the spot exchange rate, the forward rate on foreign currency is at a discount.

For example, in Figure 32.1, the spot U.S. dollar rate is US\$0.9102 = C\$1, and the one-month forward U.S. dollar is US\$0.9105 = C\$1. Because fewer U.S. dollars are needed to buy a Canadian dollar at the forward rate than are needed to buy at the spot rate, the U.S. dollar is more valuable in the forward market than in the spot market. This means that the one-month forward U.S. dollar is at a premium. Of course, the forward standing of the U.S. dollar must be opposite that of the Canadian dollar. In this example, the Canadian dollar is at a discount because its forward value is less than the spot value. Forward exchange is quoted in terms of the premium or discount that is to be added onto the spot rate.

Whether forward rates are at a premium or a discount when compared to a domestic currency depends on the relative interest rates in the foreign and domestic currency markets. The **interest rate parity theorem** states that, if interest rates are higher domestically than in a particular foreign country, the foreign country's currency will be selling at a premium in the forward market; and if interest rates are lower domestically, the foreign currency will be selling at a discount in the forward market.

We need some notation to develop the interest rate parity theorem. Let $S(0)$ be the current domestic currency price of spot foreign exchange (current time is denoted by 0). If the domestic currency is the Canadian dollar and the foreign currency is the euro, we might observe $S(0) = \$1.4926/€$ as shown in Figure 32.1. $S(0)$ is in direct terms. Let $F(0,1)$ be the current domestic currency price of forward exchange for a contract that matures in six months. Thus, the contract is for forward exchange six months hence. Let i and i^* be the yearly rates of interest paid on Eurocurrency deposits denominated in the domestic (i) and foreign (i^*) currencies, respectively. Of course, the maturity of the deposits can be chosen to coincide with the maturity of the forward contract.

Now consider a trader who has access to the interbank market in foreign exchange and Eurocurrency deposits. Suppose the trader has some dollars to invest for six months. The trader can make a dollar loan or a euro loan. The annual interest rate is 8 percent in euros and 7.5 percent in dollars. Which is better?

The Dollar Investment

Given an annual interest rate of 7.5 percent, the six-month rate of interest is 3.75 percent, assuming semiannual compounding. If the trader invests $1 million now, the trader will get $1 million $\times$ 1.0375 = $1,037,500 million at the end of six months. Here is an illustration:

Time 0	Time 1
Lend 1 unit of dollars	Obtain $1 + i \times (1/2)$ units of domestic currency
$1,000,000	$1,000,000 \times (1 + 0.0375) = \$1,037,500$

The Euro Investment

From Figure 32.1, the current spot rate is $1.4926/€. This means the trader can currently obtain $1 million/1.4926 = €669,971. The rate of interest on one-year euro loans is 8 percent. For six months, the interest rate is 0.08/2 = 0.04. Thus, at the end of six months the trader will obtain €669,971 $\times$ 1.04 = €696770. Of course, if the trader wants dollars at the end of the month, the trader must convert the euro back into dollars. The trader can fix the exchange rate for six-month conversion. Figure 32.1 shows that the six-month forward is $1.4938/euro. Then the trader can sell euros forward. This will ensure that the trader gets €696770 $\times$ 1.4938 = $1,040,835[4] at the end of the month. The general relationships are set forth here:

Time 0	Time 1
Purchase 1 unit [$1/S(0)$] of foreign exchange	Deposit matures and pays $[1/S(0)] \times [1 + i \times (1/2)]$ units of foreign exchange €669,971 $\times$ 1.04 = €696,770
Sell forward $[1/S(0)] \times [1 + i^* \times (1/2)]$ units of forward exchange at the forward rate $F(0,1)$	Deliver foreign exchange in fulfillment of forward contract, receiving $[1/S(0)] \times [1 + i^* \times (1/2)] \times [F(0,1)]$ $\times$ 1.04 $\times$ 1.6546 = $1,040,879 €669,971 $\times$ 1.04 $\times$ 1.4938 = $1,040,835

---

[4]Due to rounding, we are off by $100.

In our example, the investments earned exactly the same rate of return and $1 + i \times (1/2) = [1/S(0)] \times [1 + i^* \times (1/2)] \times [F(0,1)]$. In competitive financial markets, this must be true for risk-free investments. When the trader makes the euro loan, the interest rate is lower. But the return is the same because the euro must be sold forward at a higher price than it can be exchanged for initially. If the domestic interest rate were different from the covered foreign interest rate, the trader would have arbitrage opportunities.

To summarize, to prevent arbitrage possibilities from existing, we must have equality of the Canadian interest rate and covered foreign interest rates:

$$1 + i = \frac{1}{S(0)} \times (1 + i^*) \times F(0,1)$$

or

$$\frac{1 + i}{1 + i^*} = \frac{F(0,1)}{S(0)} \tag{32.3}$$

The last equation is the famous interest rate parity theorem. It relates the forward exchange rate and the spot exchange rate to interest rate differentials. Notice that, if $i > i^*$, the spot rate (expressed as dollars per unit of foreign currency) will be less than the forward rate.

EXAMPLE 32.3

Figure 32.1 shows the spot rate 1.4926/euro and the one-year forward rate $F(0,1) = 1.4941$/euro. Let the one-year rates on euro-Canadian dollar deposits and euro deposits be, respectively, $i = 6.00\%$ and $i^* = 5.89\%$. Then, comparing the return on domestic borrowing with the return on covered foreign lending,

$$\$(1 + 0.06) = \$1.06$$
$$\$[1/S(0)] \times (1 + i^*) \times F(0,1) = \$(1/1.4926 \times 1.0589) \times (1.4941) = \$1.06$$

For each dollar borrowed domestically, a trader must repay $1.06. The return from using the $1.00 to buy spot foreign exchange, placing the deposit at the foreign rate of interest, and selling the total return forward would be $1.055. These two amounts are equal, so it would not be worth anyone's time to try to exploit the difference. In this case, interest parity can be said to hold.

The Forward Discount and Expected Spot Rates

A close connection exists between forward exchange rates and expected spot rates. A trader's buy and sell decisions in today's forward market are based on the trader's market expectation of the future spot rate. In fact, if traders were completely indifferent to risk, the forward rate of exchange would depend solely on expectations about the future spot rate. For example, the one-year forward rate on the euro is $1.4941/euro [that is, $F(0,1) = \$1.4941$/euro]. This must mean that traders expect the spot rate to be $1.4941/euro in one year [$E(S(1)) = \$1.4941$/euro]. If they thought it would be higher, there would be an arbitrage opportunity. Traders would buy euros forward at the low price and sell euros one year later at the expected higher price. This implies that the forward rate of exchange is equal to the expected spot, or (in general terms)

$$F(0, 1) = E[S(1)]$$

and

$$\frac{F(0,1)}{S(0)} = \frac{E[S(1)]}{S(0)} \tag{32.4}$$

An equilibrium is achieved only when the forward discount (or premium) equals the expected change in the spot exchange rate.

Exchange Rate Risk

Exchange rate risk is the natural consequence of international operations in a world where foreign currency values move up and down. International firms usually enter into some contracts that require payments in different currencies. For example, suppose that the treasurer of an international firm knows that, one month from today, the firm must pay £2 million for goods it will receive in England. The current exchange rate is \$2.33/£, and if that rate prevails in one month, the dollar cost of the goods to the firm will be \$2.33/£ × £2 million = \$4.66 million. The treasurer in this case is obligated to pay pounds in one month. (Alternatively, we say that he is *short* in pounds.) A net short or long position of this type can be very risky. If, during the month, the pound rises to \$3/£, the treasurer must pay \$3/£ × £2 million = \$6 million, an extra \$1.34 million.

This is the essence of foreign exchange risk. The treasurer may want to hedge his position. When forward markets exist, the most convenient means of hedging is the purchase or sale of forward contracts. In this example, the treasurer may want to consider buying £2 million one month forward. If the one-month forward rate quoted today is also \$2.33/£, the treasurer will fulfill the contract by exchanging \$4.66 million for £2 million in one month. The £2 million he receives from the contract can then be used to pay for the goods. By hedging today, he fixes the outflow one month from now to exactly \$4.66 million.

Should the treasurer hedge or speculate? Building on our discussion in Chapter 26, we can identify two reasons why the treasurer usually should hedge:

1. In an efficient foreign exchange market, speculation is a zero-NPV activity. Unless the treasurer has special information, nothing will be gained from foreign exchange speculation.

2. The costs of hedging are not large. The treasurer can use forward contracts to hedge, and if the forward rate is equal to the expected spot, the costs of hedging are negligible. Of course, there are ways to hedge foreign exchange risk other than with forward contracts. For example, the treasurer can borrow dollars, buy pounds sterling in the spot market today, and lend them for one month in London. By the interest rate parity theorem, this will be the same as buying the pounds sterling forward.

Which Firms Hedge Exchange Rate Risk?   Not all firms with exchange rate risk exposure hedge. Géczy, Minton, and Schrand reported about 41 percent of *Fortune* 500 firms with foreign currency risk actually attempt to hedge these risks.[5] They find that larger firms with greater growth opportunities are more likely to use currency derivatives to hedge exchange rate risk than smaller firms with fewer investment opportunities. This suggests that some firms hedge to make sure that they have enough cash on hand to finance their growth opportunities. In addition, firms with greater growth opportunities will tend to have higher indirect bankruptcy costs. For these firms, hedging exchange rate risk will reduce indirect bankruptcy costs and increase the probability that they will not default on their debt obligations.

The fact that larger firms are more likely to use hedging techniques suggests that the costs of hedging are not insignificant. There may be fixed costs of establishing a hedging

---

[5]C. Géczy, B. Minton, and C. Schrand, "Why Firms Use Currency Derivatives," *Journal of Finance* (September 1997). See also D. R. Nance, C. Smith, Jr., and C. W. Smithson, "On The Determinants of Corporate Hedging," *Journal of Finance* (1993).

operation, in which case, economies of scale may explain why smaller firms hedge less than larger firms.

More Advanced Short-Term Hedges

Currency swaps, currency options, and other financially engineered products are taking considerable business away from the forward exchange market.[6] As introduced in Chapter 26, a **currency swap** is an arrangement among a borrower, a second borrower (called a *counterparty*), and a bank. The borrower and the counterparty each raise funds in a different currency and then swap liabilities. The bank guarantees the borrower's and counterparty's credit as in a banker's acceptance. The result is that the borrower obtains funds in the desired currency at a lower rate than for direct borrowing.

For example, in 1986, the federal government of Canada made an 80 billion-yen bond issue and swapped part of it into U.S. dollars. The interest rate was six-month LIBOR and the ending liability was in U.S. dollars, not yen. The interest cost turned out to be 54 basis points below the cost of direct borrowing in the United States.

Currency options are similar to options on stock (discussed in Chapter 23) except the exercise price is an exchange rate. They are exchange traded in the United States with exercise prices in various currencies, including the Canadian dollar. Currency options can be exercised at any time prior to maturity. In the jargon of options, they are **American options.** A call option on the Canadian dollar gives the holder the right, but not the obligation, to buy C$ at a fixed exercise price in US$. The call increases in value as the C$ exchange rate in US$ rises. A put option allows the holder to sell C$ at the exercise price. A put becomes more valuable when the C$ declines against the US$.

The basic idea behind hedging with options is to take an options position opposite to the cash position. For this reason, hedge analysis starts by looking at the unhedged position of the business. For example, suppose an exporter expects to collect receivables totalling US$1 million in 30 days. Suppose the present C$ exchange rate is US$0.75. If the rate remains at 75 cents, the exporter will receive US$1 million/0.75 = C$1,333,333 after 30 days. The exporter is at risk if the exchange rate rises so that the US$1 million will buy fewer Canadian dollars. For example, if the exchange rate rises to 0.77, the exporter will receive only US$1 million/0.77 = C$1,298,701. The loss of C$34,632 comes out of profits.

Since the exporter loses if the exchange rate rises, buying call options is an appropriate hedge. Calls on the C$ will increase in value if the exchange rate rises. The profit on the calls will help offset the loss on exchange. To implement this strategy, the exporter will likely seek expert advice on how many calls to buy.

The Hedging Decision in Practice

Hedging the exchange rate for the U.S. dollar is important for the Toronto Blue Jays.[7] When they won the World Series for the second consecutive year in 1993, the Blue Jays had the highest payroll in major league baseball—US$48.3 million. Players' contracts are negotiated in U.S. dollars and paid over the baseball season. The team receives some revenues in U.S. dollars from television contracts and gate receipts for games on the road, but the majority of its income—receipts at the Rogers Centre and Canadian television contracts—is in Canadian dollars. As a result, the team is exposed to currency losses if the

---

[6]Our discussion of currency swaps in practice draws on B. Critchley, "Explosion of New Products Cuts Foreign Currency Risk," *The Financial Post* (September 14, 1987).

[7]Our discussion is based on L. Millson, "Jays Fortunes Ride on Shaky Canuck Buck," *The Globe and Mail* (April 8, 1994), p. A12.

Canadian dollar falls. According to one estimate, the Jays lose $800,000 (Canadian) for every one-cent drop in the Canadian dollar.

Blue Jays management has used both forward contracts and currency options to hedge its exposure. At the start of the baseball season of 1994, management was tracking the results of its earlier decision not to hedge. As the Canadian dollar fell from around U.S. 80 cents in 1993 to under 73 cents, locking in the exchange rate looked more and more attractive. As the risk of a players' strike loomed large, the ideal hedge would have been with options, because options would have allowed the Jays to get out of the hedge when payroll obligations ceased.

? Concept Questions

- **What is the interest rate parity theorem?**
- **Why is the forward rate related to the expected future spot rate?**
- **How can one offset foreign exchange risk through a transaction in the forward markets?**
- **How can firms hedge using currency swaps or currency options?**

32.5 International Capital Budgeting

Kihlstrom Equipment, a Canadian-based international company, is evaluating an investment in France. Kihlstrom's exports of drill bits have increased to such an extent that it is considering operating a plant in France. The project will cost €2.8 million; it is expected to produce cash flows of €1.2 million a year for the next three years. The current spot exchange rate for euros is $S(0) = \$1.43/\text{euro}$. How should Kihlstrom calculate the net present value of the projects in Canadian dollars?

Although the investment is made abroad, this does not alter Kihlstrom's NPV criterion. The firm must identify incremental cash flows and discount them at the appropriate cost of capital. After making the required discounted cash flow calculations, Kihlstrom should undertake projects with positive NPVs. However, two major factors complicate such international NPV calculations: foreign exchange conversion and repatriation of funds.

Foreign Exchange Conversion

The simplest way for Kihlstrom to calculate the NPV of the investment is to convert all euro cash flows to Canadian dollars. This involves a three-step process:

Step 1. Estimate future cash flows in euros.

Step 2. Convert to Canadian dollars at the predicted exchange rate.

Step 3. Calculate NPV using the cost of capital in Canadian dollars.

In Table 32.1 we apply these three steps to Kihlstrom's French investment. Notice here that Kihlstrom's euro cash flows were converted to dollars by multiplying the foreign cash flows by the predicted foreign exchange rate.

How might Kihlstrom predict future exchange rates? Kihlstrom could calculate NPV using the foreign exchange market's implicit predictions—the forward rates. Finally, the NPV of the project is computed:

$$\text{NPV} = \sum_{t=0}^{3} \frac{\text{CF}_{\epsilon}(t) \times E[S_{\epsilon}(t)]}{(1 + r^*)^t}$$

where $\text{CF}_{\epsilon}(t)$ refers to the euros forecasted to be received in each of the next three years. The discount rate we use is Kihlstrom's Canadian cost of capital. We do not use the

TABLE 32.1
Net Present Value of Foreign Cash Flows: Kihlstrom Equipment

	End of Year			
	0	1	2	3
Incremental cash flows (CF_ϵ) (euro millions)	−2.8	1.2	1.2	1.2
Foreign exchange rate ($/euro)	1.43	1.42	1.40	1.35
Foreign exchange rate conversion	2.8 × 1.43	1.2 × 1.42	1.2 × 1.40	1.2 × 1.35
Incremental cash flows ($ millions)	−4.00	1.70	1.68	1.62

NPV at 15% = −$0.18 million.

Canadian risk-free rate because Kihlstrom's project is risky; a risk-adjusted discount rate must be used. Because the NPV at 15 percent is −$430,000, Kihlstrom should not invest in a subsidiary in France.

In this example, we used the foreign exchange market's implicit forecast as contained in forward exchange rates. Why not use management's own forecast of foreign exchange rates in the calculations? Suppose that the financial management of Kihlstrom feels optimistic about the euro. If its forecasts are sufficiently optimistic and they are used, Kihlstrom's investment in a French subsidiary will generate a positive NPV. But, in general, it is a good idea to separate the economic prospects of an investment from the foreign exchange prospects, and it is unwise to use the latter projections in the NPV calculation. If Kihlstrom wishes to speculate on an increase in the euro relative to the Canadian dollar, the best way to do this is to buy euros in the forward foreign exchange market. By using the forward exchange rates implicit in the domestic and foreign interest rates, the firm is using the actual dollar flows that it could, in principle, lock in today by borrowing in the foreign currency. This makes the foreign cash flows equivalent to domestic cash flows.

Unremitted Cash Flows

The previous example assumed that all after-tax cash flows from the foreign investment were remitted to the parent firm. The remittance decision is similar to the dividend decision for a purely domestic firm. Substantial differences can exist between the cash flows of a project and the amount that is actually remitted to the parent firm. Of course, the net present value of a project will not be changed by deferred remittance if the unremitted cash flows are reinvested at a rate of return equal (as adjusted for exchange rates) to the domestic cost of capital.

A foreign subsidiary can remit funds to a parent in many ways, including the following:

1. Dividends.
2. Management fees for central services.
3. Royalties on the use of trade names and patents.

International firms must pay special attention to remittance for two reasons. First, there may be present and future exchange controls. Many governments are sensitive to the charge of being exploited by foreign firms. Therefore, governments are tempted to limit the ability of international firms to remit cash flows. Funds that cannot be remitted are sometimes said to be blocked.

Another reason is taxes. It is always necessary to determine what taxes must be paid on profits generated in a foreign country. International firms must usually pay foreign taxes on their foreign profits. The total taxes paid by an international firm may be a function of the time of remittance. For example, Kihlstrom's French subsidiary would need to pay taxes in France on the profits it earns in France. Kihlstrom will also pay taxes on dividends it remits to Canada. In most cases, Kihlstrom can offset the payment of foreign taxes against the Canadian tax liability. Thus, if the French corporate income tax is 40 percent, Kihlstrom will not be liable for additional Canadian taxes.

The Cost of Capital for International Firms

An important question for firms with international investments is whether the required return for international projects should be different from that of similar domestic projects.

Lower Cost of Capital from International Firm Diversification   In the previous chapter, we expressed some skepticism concerning the benefits of diversification. We can make a stronger case for diversification in international firms than for purely domestic firms. Suppose barriers prevented shareholders in Canada from holding foreign securities; the financial markets of different countries would be segmented. Further suppose that Canadian firms were not subject to the same barriers. In such a case, a firm engaging in international investing could provide indirect diversification for Canadian shareholders that they could not achieve by investing within Canada. This could lead to the lowering of the risk premium on international projects. In general, if the costs of investing abroad are lower for a firm than for its shareholders, there is an advantage to international diversification by firms, and this advantage will be reflected in a lower risk adjusted discount rate.

Alternatively, if there were no barriers to international investing for shareholders, shareholders could obtain the benefit of international diversification for themselves by buying foreign securities. In this case the project cost of capital for a firm in Canada would not depend on whether the project was in Canada or in a foreign country. In practice, holding foreign securities involves substantial expenses. These expenses include taxes, the costs of obtaining information, and trading costs. This implies that although Canadian investors are free to hold foreign securities, they will not be perfectly internationally diversified.

Financial engineering is aiding investors in avoiding some of these costs. As a result, as investors diversify globally, the cost of capital advantage to firms will likely decline.

An *index participation* (*IP*) is a current example of a financially engineered vehicle for international diversification.[8] An IP on the Standard & Poor's 500 Index, for example, gives an investor an asset that will track this well-known U.S. market index. IPs are highly liquid, thus reducing trading costs. Information costs are also reduced since the holder need not research each of the 500 individual stocks that make up the index.

International diversification for Canadian investors was made easier by the lowering of an important barrier. In 2001, the maximum allowable foreign holding for pension funds and RRSPs was raised to 30 percent. Increased demand fuelled the development of global mutual funds and related new products to exploit this opportunity.

Lower Cost of Capital from International Shareholder Diversification   Recall our discussion of the CAPM and the market portfolio. Consider the Canadian stock market and a Canadian investor who is not internationally diversified but, instead, is invested only in Canadian stocks. From our previous discussion of diversification, we know this investor would be bearing more risk than if she were able to diversify in the stocks of different countries. Now imagine she can invest in many foreign stocks by diversifying

---

[8]G. Axford and Y. Lin, "Surprise! Currency Risk Improves International Investment," *Canadian Treasury Management Review,* Royal Bank of Canada (March–April 1990).

internationally. She should be able to reduce the variance (or standard deviation) of her portfolio significantly.

For this investor, the market risk premium will be lower than for investors who cannot diversify internationally. In internationally integrated markets, investors with internationally diversified portfolios will measure the risk of an individual stock in terms of a world-market portfolio and global betas. Therefore, the cost of capital of a particular firm will be in terms of a global CAPM, such as:

$$E(R_I) = r_F + B_G\ [E(R_G) - r_F]$$

where R_I is the required return on a stock when markets are global, r_F is the risk-free rate, B_G is the global beta, and R_G is the return on the world-market portfolio. A firm with internationally diversified investors will have a cost of capital with a lower market risk premium [i.e., $E(R_G) - r_F$] and a global beta when compared to a firm with investors that cannot diversify internationally.

Solnik has presented evidence that suggests that international diversification significantly reduces risk for shareholders.[9] He shows that the variance of an internationally diversified portfolio of common stocks is about 33 percent of the variance of individual securities. A diversified portfolio of U.S. stocks will reduce variance by only 50 percent. Table 32.2 shows that a world portfolio has lower risk than a portfolio of stocks within a single country. For example, a citizen of Hong Kong can reduce risk from 12.8 percent to 4.2 percent by investing in a world portfolio. This evidence is consistent with a lower global market-risk premium than is a purely domestic-risk premium. Global betas will be

TABLE 32.2
Risk Measures for Foreign Market Portfolios

	Beta	Monthly Standard Deviation (%)
Hong Kong	2.08	12.8%
Japan	1.42	6.1
Sweden	0.73	6.2
Norway	0.57	5.3
Belgium	1.06	6.0
Netherlands	1.01	5.6
United Kingdom	1.38	7.9
Denmark	0.49	5.5
France	0.69	7.4
Austria	0.19	5.4
Germany	0.70	6.0
Switzerland	0.83	5.7
Australia	1.39	8.2
Canada	1.04	5.9
United States	0.97	4.7
World	1.00	4.2

Source: Campbell R. Harvey,"The World Price of Covariance Risk," *Journal of Finance* (March 1991) from Table I, p. 122 and Table VI, p. 140.

[9]B. H. Solnik, "Why Not Diversify Internationally Rather than Domestically?" *Financial Analysts Journal* (July–August 1974). A recent estimate of the benefits of international diversification can be found in Georgio DeSantis and Bruno Gerard, "International Asset Pricing and Portfolio Diversification with Time-Varying Risk, *Journal of Finance* 52 (1997). They estimate that an internationally diversified portfolio will reduce standard deviation by 20 percent when compared to investing in U.S. stocks only.

different than purely domestic betas. Stulz has argued that the preceding claim for why internationalization reduces the cost of capital doesn't capture the complete picture. He agrees that the global market-risk premium is likely to be substantially lower than the risk premium for an isolated country. In addition, he argues that global investing is likely to improve corporate governance and reduce agency costs. The argument goes something like this: Firms in countries with less-developed financial markets will need to improve their governance so that they can raise capital in well-developed capital markets such as the U.S. or Canada. Foreign firms raising capital in the U.S. or Canada must appeal to more sophisticated investors and better market architectures with superior monitoring abilities.[10] Table 32.2 also shows that the systematic risk of foreign stock investment can be very low, as is the case of Austria, or very high, as is the case of Hong Kong. The U.S. and Canada have betas very close to unity because the U.S. is an economic colossus and Canada is closely integrated with it.[11]

? Concept
Questions

- **What problems do international projects pose for the use of net present value techniques?**
- **How is international capital budgeting affected by growing investor interest in international diversification?**

32.6 International Financing Decisions

An international firm can finance foreign projects in three basic ways:

1. It can raise cash in the home country and export it to finance the foreign project.
2. It can raise cash by borrowing in the foreign country where the project is located.
3. It can borrow in a third country where the cost of debt is lowest.

If a Canadian firm raises cash for its foreign projects by borrowing in Canada, it faces exchange rate risk. If the foreign currency depreciates, the Canadian parent firm will experience an exchange rate loss when the foreign cash flow is remitted to Canada. Of course, the Canadian firm may sell foreign exchange forward to hedge this risk. However, for many currencies, it is difficult to sell forward contracts beyond one year.

Firms may borrow in the country where the foreign project is located. This is the usual way of hedging long-term foreign exchange risk up to the amount borrowed. Any residual (equity) would not be hedged. Thus, if Kihlstrom Equipment wishes to invest €20 million in France, it may attempt to raise much of the cash in France. Toyota took this approach and financed assembly plants in the United States in U.S. dollars during the early 1970s. Volkswagen also built plants in the United States, but financed them in deutschemarks. During the late 1970s, the U.S. dollar dropped against both the yen and the deutschemark. Toyota was unaffected on the financing side, but Volkswagen faced increased costs, putting it at a disadvantage in selling low-end cars.

---

[10]René M. Stulz, "Globalization, Corporate Finance, and the Cost of Capital," *Journal of Applied Corporate Finance* 12 (1999). See also Ronald M. Schramm and Henry N. Wang, "Measuring the Cost of Capital in an International CAPM Framework," *Journal of Applied Corporate Finance* 12 (1999) and Thomas J. O'Brien, "The Global CAPM and a Firm's Cost of Capital in Different Currencies," *Journal of Applied Corporate Finance* 12 (1999).

[11]The betas in Table 32.2 are calculated using the Morgan Stanley value-weighted index as the world market portfolio.

Another alternative is to find a country where interest rates are low. However, foreign interest rates may be lower because of lower expected foreign inflation. Thus, financial managers must be careful to look beyond nominal interest rates to real interest rates.

EXAMPLE 32.4

> The two bridges spanning the Halifax Harbour are the responsibility of the Halifax–Dartmouth Bridge Commission.[12] In 1969, the commission, then chaired by A. Murray MacKay, decided to combine $3 million in outstanding debt from building the MacDonald Bridge in the mid-1950s with new borrowings for the MacKay Bridge built in 1970 for $39 million.
>
> Because Canadian interest rates were high in 1970, the commission decided to borrow in deutschemarks (DM). The exchange rate at the time was around DM 3.5 per Canadian dollar so the $42 million loan translated into approximately DM 150 million. Borrowing in deutschemarks left the commission exposed because its revenues (bridge tolls) were in Canadian dollars. In the 1970s and 1980s the deutschemark strengthened dramatically, reaching DM 1.47 per dollar by 1989. At this exchange rate the original DM 150 was worth $102 million—far more than the original cost of the loan. A refinancing in Swiss francs experienced the same problem. Only in 1991 was the debt converted to Canadian dollars and stabilized.

Short-Term and Medium-Term Financing

In raising short-term and medium-term cash, Canadian international firms have a choice between borrowing from a chartered bank at the Canadian rate or borrowing Euro-Canadian (or other Eurocurrency) from a bank outside Canada through the Eurocurrency market.

A **Eurodollar** is a dollar deposited in a bank outside the United States. For example, dollar deposits in Paris, France, are Eurodollars. The Eurocurrency markets are the banks (**Eurobanks**) that make loans and accept deposits in foreign currencies. Most Eurocurrency trading involves the borrowing and lending of time deposits at Eurobanks. For example, a Eurobank receives a Eurodollar deposit from a domestic U.S. bank. Afterward, the Eurobank will make a dollar-denominated loan to a borrowing party. This is the Eurocurrency market. It is not a retail bank market. The customers are corporations and governments.

One important characteristic of the Eurocurrency market is that loans are made on a floating-rate basis. The interest rates are set at a fixed margin above the London Interbank Offered Rate for the given period and currency involved. For example, if the margin is 0.5 percent for dollar loans and the current LIBOR is 8 percent for dollar loans, the dollar borrower will pay an interest rate of 8.5 percent. This rate is usually changed every six months. The dollar loans will have maturities ranging from 3 to 10 years.

It is obvious that in a perfectly competitive financial market the interest rate on a Eurodollar loan in a Eurocurrency market must be the same as the interest rate in the U.S. loan market. If the interest rate on a Eurodollar loan were higher than that on a domestic-dollar loan, arbitrageurs would borrow in the domestic-dollar market and lend in the Eurodollar market. This type of arbitrage trading would force interest rates to be the same in both dollar markets. However, from time to time there are differences between the Eurodollar loan rate and the domestic loan rate. Risk, government regulations, and taxes explain most of the differences.

---

[12]Our example is based on J. Myrden, "Bridges of Debt," *Halifax Chronicle Herald* (January 18, 1992), p. C1.

International Bond Markets

The worldwide bond market is made up of approximately US$31 trillion in bonds issued in many currencies. Table 32.3 shows that bonds issued by developing countries make up 93.0 percent of the total. The total worldwide bond market can be divided into domestic bonds and international bonds. Domestic bonds are those issued by a firm in its home country. International bonds are those issued by firms in another currency other than the currency of the home country.

Trading in international bonds is over-the-counter and takes place in loosely connected individual markets. These individual markets are closely tied to the corresponding domestic bond markets. International bonds can be divided into two main types: foreign bonds and Eurobonds.

TABLE 32.3
The World Bond Market

	(Billions of U.S. dollars)	(Percent in world bond market)
Developed countries	**28,985**	**89.6**
Euro area	6,861	21.2
Denmark	273	0.8
Iceland	11	0.0
Norway	86	0.3
Sweden	204	0.6
Switzerland	162	0.5
United Kingdom	1,313	4.1
Australia	206	0.6
Canada	640	2.0
Japan	4,825	14.9
New Zealand	19	0.1
United States	14,385	44.5
Emerging markets	**3,309**	**10.4**
Latin America	596	1.8
Asia	1,215	3.8
China	329	1.1
India	141	0.4
Indonesia	50	0.2
Korea	325	1.0
Malaysia	89	0.3
Pakistan	27	0.1
Philippines	32	0.1
Thailand	43	0.1
Taiwan	89	0.3
Emerging Europe	227	0.7
Other emerging	146	0.5
World	**32,294**	**100**

Notes: All data are as of end 2001. Data are from security-level data underlying *BIS Quarterly Review* Table 14B (International Bonds and Notes by Country of Residence) and the unpublished long-term debt component of *BIS Quarterly Review* Table 16A (Domestic Debt Securities). Local-currency-denominated debt is the sum of domestic long-term debt (from Table 16A) and the local currency portion of Table 14B. Domestic long-term debt for countries not available on Table 16A and data for Brady bonds are from Merrill Lynch (2002) Included in the total is $2.5 trillion in foreign currency bonds, denominated primarily in dollars, euros, and British pounds.

Source: John D. Burger and Francis E. Warnock, Local Currency and Bond Markets, International Monetary Fund, 2006.

Foreign Bonds   Foreign bonds are issued by foreign borrowers in a particular country's domestic bond market. They are often nicknamed for the country of issuance. They are denominated in the country's domestic currency. For example, suppose a Swiss watch company issues U.S. dollar–denominated bonds in the United States. These foreign bonds would be called *Yankee bonds*. Like all foreign bonds issued in the United States, Yankee bonds are usually rated by a bond-rating agency such as Standard & Poor's Corporation. Many Yankee bonds are listed on the New York Stock Exchange.

In Canada, bonds issued by foreign companies are termed maple bonds or Canuck bonds. Many foreign bonds are registered. This makes them less attractive to investors having a disdain for tax authorities. For obvious reasons, these traders like the Eurobond market better than the foreign bond market. Registered bonds have an ownership name assigned to the bond's serial number. Most Eurobonds are bearer bonds. Ownership is established by possession of the bond. The transfer of ownership of a registered bond can take place only via legal transfer of the registered name. Transfer agents (for example, banks) are required.

Eurobonds   Eurobonds are denominated in a particular currency and are issued simultaneously in the bond markets of several countries. The prefix *Euro* means that the bonds are issued outside the countries in whose currencies they are denominated.

Most issues of Eurobonds are arranged by underwriting. However, some Eurobonds are privately placed.[13] A public issue with underwriting is similar to the public debt sold in domestic bond markets. The borrower sells its bonds to a group of managing banks. Managing banks, in turn, sell the bonds to other banks. The other banks are divided into two groups: underwriters and sellers. The underwriters and sellers sell the bonds to dealers and fund investors. The managing banks also serve as underwriters and sellers. Underwriters usually sell Eurobonds on a firm commitment basis. That is, they are committed to buy the bonds at a prenegotiated price and attempt to sell them at a higher price in the market. Eurobonds appear as straight bonds, floating-rate notes, convertible bonds, zero-coupon bonds, mortgage-backed bonds, and dual-currency bonds.[14]

EXAMPLE 32.5

A Canadian firm makes an offering of $500 million of floating rate notes. The notes are offered in London. They mature in 2020 and have semiannual interest of 0.5 percent above the six-month London Interbank Offered Rate. When the bonds are issued, the six-month LIBOR is 10 percent. Thus, in the first six months the Canadian firm will pay interest (at the annual rate) of 10% + 0.5% = 10.5%.

 **Concept Questions**

• **What are the three ways firms can finance foreign projects?**
• **What sources of financing are available?**

---

[13]In general, the issue costs are lower in private placements, as compared to public issues, and the yields are higher.

[14]There is a small but growing international equity market. International equities are stock issues underwritten and distributed to a mix of investors without regard to national borders. Our definition of international equity encompasses two basic types: those issues that have been internationally syndicated and distributed outside all national exchanges (termed *Euroequities*) and those that are issued by underwriters in domestic markets other than their own.

32.7 Reporting Foreign Operations

When a Canadian company prepares consolidated financial statements, the firm translates the local currency accounts of foreign subsidiaries into the currency that is used for reporting purposes, usually the currency of the home country (that is, dollars). If exchange rates change during the accounting period, accounting gains or losses can occur.

Suppose a Canadian firm acquired a British company in 1982. At that time the exchange rate was £1 = $2. The British firm performed very well during the next few years (according to sterling measurements). During the same period, the value of the pound fell to $1.25. Did the corresponding increase in the value of the dollar make the Canadian company better off? Should the increase be reflected in the measurement of income?

These questions have been among the most controversial accounting questions in recent years. Two issues seem to arise:

1. What is the appropriate exchange rate to use for translating each balance-sheet account?

2. How should unrealized accounting gains and losses from foreign-currency translation be handled?

One obvious and consistent approach is simply to report the loss on the parent company's income statement. During periods of volatile exchange rates, this kind of treatment can dramatically impact an international company's reported EPS. This is purely an accounting phenomenon, but, even so, such fluctuations are disliked by financial managers.

The current, compromise approach to translation gains and losses is based on rules set out in the Canadian Institute of Chartered Accountants (CICA) *Handbook,* section 1650. The rules divide a firm's foreign subsidiaries into two categories: integrated and self-sustaining. For the most part, the rules require that all assets and liabilities be translated from the subsidiary's currency into the parent's currency using the exchange rate that currently prevails.[15] Since Canadian accountants consolidate the financial statements of subsidiaries owned over 50 percent by the parent firm, translation gains and losses are reflected on the income statement of the parent company.

For a self-sustaining subsidiary, any translation gains and losses that occur are accumulated in a special account within the shareholders' equity section of the parent company's balance sheet. This account might be labelled something like "unrealized foreign exchange gains (losses)." These gains and losses are not reported on the income statement. As a result, the impact of translation gains and losses will not be recognized explicitly in net income until the underlying assets and liabilities are sold or otherwise liquidated.

? **Concept**
Question

• **What issues arise when reporting foreign operations?**

---

[15]The rules also define the current exchange rate differently for the types of subsidiaries. An integrated subsidiary uses the exchange rate observed on the last day of its fiscal year. For a self-sustaining subsidiary, the exchange rate prescribed is the average rate over the year. For detailed discussion of CICA 1650, see A. Davis and G. Pinches, *Canadian Financial Management,* 4th ed. (New York: HarperCollins, 2000).

32.8 Political Risk

One final element of risk in international investing is **political risk**: changes in value that arise as a consequence of political actions. This is not a problem faced exclusively by international firms. For example, changes in Canadian tax laws and regulations may benefit some Canadian firms and hurt others, so political risk exists nationally as well as internationally.

Some countries have more political risk than others, however. When firms have operations in these riskier countries, the extra political risk may lead the firms to require higher returns on overseas investments to compensate for the possibility that funds may be blocked, critical operations interrupted, and contracts abrogated. In the most extreme case, the possibility of outright confiscation may be a concern in countries with relatively unstable political environments.

Political risk also depends on the nature of the business: Some businesses are less likely to be confiscated because they are not particularly valuable in the hands of a different owner. An assembly operation supplying subcomponents that only the parent company uses would not be an attractive takeover target, for example. Similarly, a manufacturing operation that requires the use of specialized components from the parent is of little value without the parent company's cooperation.

Natural resource developments, such as copper mining or oil drilling, are just the opposite. Once the operation is in place, much of the value is in the commodity. The political risk for such investments is much higher for this reason. Also, the issue of exploitation is more pronounced with such investments, again increasing the political risk.

Political risk can be hedged in several ways, particularly when confiscation or nationalization is a concern. The use of local financing, perhaps from the government of the foreign country in question, reduces the possible loss because the company can refuse to pay the debt in the event of unfavorable political activities. Based on our discussion in this section, structuring the operation in such a way that it requires significant parent company involvement to function is another way to reduce political risk.

32.9 SUMMARY AND CONCLUSIONS

The international firm has a more complicated life than the purely domestic firm. Management must understand the connection between interest rates, foreign currency exchange rates, and inflation, and it must become aware of a large number of different financial market regulations and tax systems.

1. This chapter describes some fundamental theories of international finance:
   - The purchasing power parity theorem (law of one price).
   - The expectations theory of exchange rates.
   - The interest rate parity theorem.

2. The purchasing power parity theorem states that $1 should have the same purchasing power in each country. This means that an apple costs the same whether you buy it in Toronto or in Tokyo. One version of the purchasing power parity theorem states that the change in exchange rates between the currencies of two countries is connected to the inflation rates in the countries' commodity prices.

3. The expectations theory of exchange rates states that the forward rate of exchange is equal to the expected spot rate.

4. The interest rate parity theorem states that the interest rate differential between two countries will be equal to the difference between the forward exchange rate and the spot exchange rate. This equality must prevail to prevent arbitrageurs from devising get-rich-quick strategies. The equality requires the rate of return on risk-free investments in Canada to be the same as that in other countries measured in Canadian dollars.

Of course, in practice the purchasing power parity theorem and the interest rate parity theorem cannot work perfectly. Government regulations and taxes prevent this. However, there is much empirical work and intuition that suggests that these theories describe international financial markets in an approximate way.

5. The chapter also describes some of the problems of international capital budgeting. The net present value rule is still the appropriate way to choose projects, but the main problem is to choose the correct cost of capital. We argue that it should be equal to the rate that shareholders can expect to earn on a portfolio of domestic and foreign securities. This rate should be about the same as for a portfolio of domestic securities. However, two adjustments may be necessary:

   a. The cost of capital of an international firm may be *lower* than that of a domestic counterpart because of the benefits of international diversification.

   b. The cost of capital of an international firm may be *higher* because of the extra risks of international investment.

6. We briefly describe international financial markets. International firms may want to consider borrowing in the local financial market or in the Eurocurrency and Eurobond markets. The interest rates are likely to appear different in these markets. Thus, international firms must be careful to consider differences in taxes and government regulations.

KEY TERMS

American Depository Receipt (ADR) 902
American options 911
Cross rate 902
Currency swap 911
Eurobanks 917
Eurobonds 902
Eurocurrency 902
Eurodollars 917
Euro (European currency unit) 901
Exchange rate 903

Export Development Canada (EDC) 902
Foreign bonds 902
Foreign exchange market 903
Forward exchange rate 905
Forward trades 905
Interest rate parity theorem 908
Law of one price (LOP) 905
London Interbank Offered Rate (LIBOR) 902

Political risk 921
Purchasing power parity (PPP) 906
Relative purchasing power parity (RPPP) 906
Spot exchange rate 905
Spot trades 905
Swap rate 905
Swaps 902
Triangular arbitrage 903

SUGGESTED READING

Interesting academic research in international finance appears in:
Journal of Applied Corporate Finance: "Global Finance" (Fall 1999); "Emerging Markets and the Asian Crisis" (Fall 1998); "Global Finance and Risk Management" (Fall 1997).

QUESTIONS & PROBLEMS

Some Basics

32.1   Use Figure 32.1 to answer the following questions:
   a. What is the quote in direct terms for the British pound sterling and the Canadian dollar on spot exchange? What is it in indirect terms for the euro and the Canadian dollar?
   b. Is the Japanese yen at a premium or a discount to the Canadian dollar in the forward markets?
   c. To which type of foreign exchange participants would the forward prices of the Japanese yen be important? Why? What types of transactions might these participants use to cover their exposed risk in the foreign exchange markets?
   d. Suppose you are a British exporter of watches. If you are to be paid in Canadian dollars three months from now for a shipment worth $100,000 made to Canada, how many British pounds would you receive if you locked in the price today with a forward contract? Would you buy or sell the dollar forward?
   e. Calculate the U.K. pound/euro cross rate for spot exchange in terms of the U.S. dollar. Do the same for the yen–Swiss franc cross rate.

  f. In the text a swap transaction is described. Why might both banks profit from the use of such a mutual agreement?

32.2 Determine whether arbitrage opportunities exist given the following foreign exchange rates.

  a. $1.6/£   €2.1/$ €3.8/£

  b. ¥100/$ €2/$ ¥50/€

  c. HKD9.1/$ ¥100/$ ¥13/HKD

The Law of One Price and Purchasing Power Parity

32.3 Are the following statements true or false? Explain why.

  a. If the general price index in Great Britain rises faster than that in Canada, we would expect the pound to appreciate relative to the dollar.

  b. Suppose you are a German machine tool exporter, and you invoice all of your sales in foreign currency. Further suppose that the euro monetary authorities begin to undertake an expansionary monetary policy. If it is certain that the easy money policy will result in higher inflation rates in Germany relative to those in other countries, then you should use the forward markets to protect yourself against future losses resulting from the deterioration in the value of the euro.

  c. If you could accurately estimate differences in the relative inflation rates of two countries over a long period while other market participants were unable to do so, you could successfully speculate in spot currency markets.

32.4 The treasurer of a major Canadian firm has $15 million to invest for six months. The annual interest rate is 6 percent. The interest rate in France is 7 percent. The spot rate of exchange is $1.40/€ and the six-month forward rate is $1.42/€. Barring transaction costs, in which country would the treasurer want to invest the company's capital if she can fix the exchange rate six months through a forward contract?

32.5 Suppose the spot and six-month forward rates on the Norwegian krone are Kr 6.43 and Kr 6.56, respectively. The annual risk-free rate in Italy is 5 percent, and the annual risk-free rate in Norway is 8 percent.

  a. Is there an arbitrage opportunity here? If so, how would you exploit it?

  b. What must the six-month forward rate be to prevent arbitrage?

32.6 The spot rate of foreign exchange between Canada and the United Kingdom at time *t* is $1.60/£. If the interest rate is 7 percent in Canada and 4 percent in the United Kingdom, what would you expect the one-year forward rate to be if no immediate arbitrage opportunities existed?

32.7 Suppose the rate of inflation in Mexico will run about 3 percent higher than the U.S. inflation rate over the next several years. All other things being the same, what will happen to the Mexican peso versus dollar exchange rate? What relationship are you relying on in answering?

32.8 If you are an exporter who must make payments in foreign currency one year after receiving each shipment and you predict that the domestic currency will appreciate in value over this period, is there any value in hedging your currency exposure?

32.9 The inflation rates for Australia and New Zealand are 6 percent and 8 percent respectively. At the beginning of the year, the spot rate between the two currencies is NZ$1.17 per AU$1.00. What is the approximate spot rate at year-end?

Interest Rates and Exchange Rates: Interest-Rate Parity

32.10 A Canadian drug company, Jagged Little Pill Inc., intended to import $53 million worth of pharmaceutical plants and will make payment in euros six months from now. The foreign exchange spot rate of the euro to the Canadian dollar is $1.78/€. Annual interest rates for the Canadian dollar and the euro are 3 percent and 9 percent respectively.

  a. What is the six-month forward rate for the euro if interest rate parity holds?

  b. How can Jagged Little Pill use currency trading to hedge against the foreign exchange risk associated with the purchase?

EXCEL

32.11 Use Figure 32.1 to answer the following questions. Suppose interest rate parity holds, and the current six-month risk-free rate in Canada is 3.8 percent. What must the six-month risk-free rate be in Great Britain? In Japan? In Germany?

International Capital Budgeting

32.12 Lakonishok Equipment has an investment opportunity in Europe. The project costs €12 million and is expected to produce cash flows of €2.7 million in year 1, €3.5 million in year 2, and €3.3 million in year 3. The current spot exchange rate is $1.22/€ and the current risk-free rate in the United States is 4.8 percent, compared to that in Europe of 4.1 percent. The appropriate discount rate for the project is estimated to be 13 percent, the U.S. cost of capital for the company. In addition, the subsidiary can be sold at the end of three years for an estimated €7.4 million. What is the NPV of the project?

EXCEL

32.13 You are evaluating a proposed expansion of an existing subsidiary located in Switzerland. The cost of the expansion would be SF 27.0 million. The cash flows from the project would be SF 7.5 million per year for the next five years. The dollar required return is 13 percent per year, and the current exchange rate is SF 1.72. The going rate on Eurodollars is 8 percent per year. It is 7 percent per year on Swiss francs.

    a. What do you project will happen to exchange rates over the next four years?
    b. Based on your answer in (a), convert the projected franc flows into dollar flows and calculate the NPV.
    c. What is the required return on franc flows? Based on your answer, calculate the NPV in francs and then convert to dollars.

32.14 An investment in a foreign subsidiary is estimated to have a positive NPV after the discount rate used in the calculations is adjusted for political risk and any advantages from diversification. Does this mean the project is acceptable? Why or why not?

32.15 Suppose it is your task to evaluate two different investments in new subsidiaries for your company, one in your own country and the other in a foreign country. You calculate the cash flows of both projects to be identical after exchange rate differences. Under what circumstances might you choose to invest in the foreign subsidiary? Give an example of a country where certain factors might influence you to alter this decision and invest at home.

32.16 If a Canadian firm raises funds for a foreign subsidiary, what are the disadvantages to borrowing in the United States? How would you overcome them?

International Capital Markets

32.17 What is a Euroyen?

32.18 If financial markets are perfectly competitive and the Euro-Canadian dollar rate is above that offered in the Canadian loan market, you would immediately want to borrow money in Canada and invest it in Eurodollars. True of false? Explain.

32.19 What distinguishes a Eurobond from a foreign bond? What particular feature makes the Eurobond more popular than the foreign bond?

32.20 How would you describe a bond issued by a Canadian firm in the United States with payments denominated in U.S. dollars?

Exchange Rate Risk

EXCEL

32.21 Suppose your company imports computer modems from China. The exchange rate is given in Figure 32.1. You have just placed an order for 60,000 modems at a cost to you of 530 renminbi each. You will pay for the shipment when it arrives in 90 days. You can sell the modems for $170 each. Calculate your profit if the exchange rate goes up or down by 10 percent over the next 90 days. What is the break-even exchange rate? What percentage rise or fall does this represent in terms of the Chinese renminbi versus the Canadian dollar?

32.22   Nokia stock trades as an American Depository Receipt on the New York Stock Exchange. Assume that one ADR is exchangeable for one share of Nokia stock on the Finnish stock market. Find today's closing price of the Nokia ADR. Assuming the exchange rate was $1.17/€ and Nokia shares traded for €19.48, explain how you could make an arbitrage profit. What was the profit per share? What exchange rate is necessary to eliminate the arbitrage opportunity?

MINICASE: Jackman Grills Goes International

Chaz Jackman, the owner of Jackman Grills, has been in discussions with a kitchen appliance dealer in Monaco about selling the company's grills in Europe. Jarek Jachowicz, the dealer, wants to add Jackman Grills to his current retail line. Jarek has told Chaz that he feels the retail sales will be approximately €5 million per month. All sales will be made in euros, and Jarek will retain 5 percent of the retail sales as commission, which will be paid in euros. Because the grills will be customized to order, the first sales will take place in one month. Jarek will pay Jackman Grills for the order 90 days after it is filled. This payment schedule will continue for the length of the contract between the two companies.

Chaz is confident the company can handle the extra volume with its existing facilities, but she is unsure about any potential financial risks of selling grills in Europe. In her discussion with Jarek she found that the current exchange rate is $1.20/€. At this exchange rate the company would spend 70 percent of the sales income on production costs.

This number does not reflect the sales commission to be paid to Jarek. Chaz has decided to ask Seamus O'Toole, the company's financial analyst, to prepare an analysis of the proposed international sales. Specifically she asks Seamus to answer the following questions:

1. What are the pros and cons of the international sales plan? What additional risks will the company face?
2. What will happen to the company's profits if the dollar strengthens? What if the dollar weakens?
3. Ignoring taxes, what are Jackman's projected gains or losses from this proposed arrangement at the current exchange rate of $1.20/€? What will happen to profits if the exchange rate changes to $1.30/€? At what exchange rate will the company break even?
4. How can the company hedge its exchange rate risk? What are the implications for this approach?
5. Taking all factors into account, should the company pursue international sales further? Why or why not?

Visit us at www.mcgrawhill.ca/olc/ross

Appendix A

Mathematical Tables

TABLE A.1	Present Value of $1 to Be Received after T Periods $= 1/(1 + r)^T$								
	Interest Rate								
Period	1%	2%	3%	4%	5%	6%	7%	8%	9%
1	0.9901	0.9804	0.9709	0.9615	0.9524	0.9434	0.9346	0.9259	0.9174
2	0.9803	0.9612	0.9426	0.9246	0.9070	0.8900	0.8734	0.8573	0.8417
3	0.9706	0.9423	0.9151	0.8890	0.8638	0.8396	0.8163	0.7938	0.7722
4	0.9610	0.9238	0.8885	0.8548	0.8227	0.7921	0.7629	0.7350	0.7084
5	0.9515	0.9057	0.8626	0.8219	0.7835	0.7473	0.7130	0.6806	0.6499
6	0.9420	0.8880	0.8375	0.7903	0.7462	0.7050	0.6663	0.6302	0.5963
7	0.9327	0.8706	0.8131	0.7599	0.7107	0.6651	0.6227	0.5835	0.5470
8	0.9235	0.8535	0.7894	0.7307	0.6768	0.6274	0.5820	0.5403	0.5019
9	0.9143	0.8368	0.7664	0.7026	0.6446	0.5919	0.5439	0.5002	0.4604
10	0.9053	0.8203	0.7441	0.6756	0.6139	0.5584	0.5083	0.4632	0.4224
11	0.8963	0.8043	0.7224	0.6496	0.5847	0.5268	0.4751	0.4289	0.3875
12	0.8874	0.7885	0.7014	0.6246	0.5568	0.4970	0.4440	0.3971	0.3555
13	0.8787	0.7730	0.6810	0.6006	0.5303	0.4688	0.4150	0.3677	0.3262
14	0.8700	0.7579	0.6611	0.5775	0.5051	0.4423	0.3878	0.3405	0.2992
15	0.8613	0.7430	0.6419	0.5553	0.4810	0.4173	0.3624	0.3152	0.2745
16	0.8528	0.7284	0.6232	0.5339	0.4581	0.3936	0.3387	0.2919	0.2519
17	0.8444	0.7142	0.6050	0.5134	0.4363	0.3714	0.3166	0.2703	0.2311
18	0.8360	0.7002	0.5874	0.4936	0.4155	0.3503	0.2959	0.2502	0.2120
19	0.8277	0.6864	0.5703	0.4746	0.3957	0.3305	0.2765	0.2317	0.1945
20	0.8195	0.6730	0.5537	0.4564	0.3769	0.3118	0.2584	0.2145	0.1784
21	0.8114	0.6598	0.5375	0.4388	0.3589	0.2942	0.2415	0.1987	0.1637
22	0.8034	0.6468	0.5219	0.4220	0.3418	0.2775	0.2257	0.1839	0.1502
23	0.7954	0.6342	0.5067	0.4057	0.3256	0.2618	0.2109	0.1703	0.1378
24	0.7876	0.6217	0.4919	0.3901	0.3101	0.2470	0.1971	0.1577	0.1264
25	0.7798	0.6095	0.4776	0.3751	0.2953	0.2330	0.1842	0.1460	0.1160
30	0.7419	0.5521	0.4120	0.3083	0.2314	0.1741	0.1314	0.0994	0.0754
40	0.6717	0.4529	0.3066	0.2083	0.1420	0.0972	0.0668	0.0460	0.0318
50	0.6080	0.3715	0.2281	0.1407	0.0872	0.0543	0.0339	0.0213	0.0134

*The factor is zero to four decimal places.

TABLE A.1 (concluded)

					Interest Rate					
10%	12%	14%	15%	16%	18%	20%	24%	28%	32%	36%
0.9091	0.8929	0.8772	0.8696	0.8621	0.8475	0.8333	0.8065	0.7813	0.7576	0.7353
0.8264	0.7972	0.7695	0.7561	0.7432	0.7182	0.6944	0.6504	0.6104	0.5739	0.5407
0.7513	0.7118	0.6750	0.6575	0.6407	0.6086	0.5787	0.5245	0.4768	0.4348	0.3975
0.6830	0.6355	0.5921	0.5718	0.5523	0.5158	0.4823	0.4230	0.3725	0.3294	0.2923
0.6209	0.5674	0.5194	0.4972	0.4761	0.4371	0.4019	0.3411	0.2910	0.2495	0.2149
0.5645	0.5066	0.4556	0.4323	0.4104	0.3704	0.3349	0.2751	0.2274	0.1890	0.1580
0.5132	0.4523	0.3996	0.3759	0.3538	0.3139	0.2791	0.2218	0.1776	0.1432	0.1162
0.4665	0.4039	0.3506	0.3269	0.3050	0.2660	0.2326	0.1789	0.1388	0.1085	0.0854
0.4241	0.3606	0.3075	0.2843	0.2630	0.2255	0.1938	0.1443	0.1084	0.0822	0.0628
0.3855	0.3220	0.2697	0.2472	0.2267	0.1911	0.1615	0.1164	0.0847	0.0623	0.0462
0.3505	0.2875	0.2366	0.2149	0.1954	0.1619	0.1346	0.0938	0.0662	0.0472	0.0340
0.3186	0.2567	0.2076	0.1869	0.1685	0.1372	0.1122	0.0757	0.0517	0.0357	0.0250
0.2897	0.2292	0.1821	0.1625	0.1452	0.1163	0.0935	0.0610	0.0404	0.0271	0.0184
0.2633	0.2046	0.1597	0.1413	0.1252	0.0985	0.0779	0.0492	0.0316	0.0205	0.0135
0.2394	0.1827	0.1401	0.1229	0.1079	0.0835	0.0649	0.0397	0.0247	0.0155	0.0099
0.2176	0.1631	0.1229	0.1069	0.0930	0.0708	0.0541	0.0320	0.0193	0.0118	0.0073
0.1978	0.1456	0.1078	0.0929	0.0802	0.0600	0.0451	0.0258	0.0150	0.0089	0.0054
0.1799	0.1300	0.0946	0.0808	0.0691	0.0508	0.0376	0.0208	0.0118	0.0068	0.0039
0.1635	0.1161	0.0829	0.0703	0.0596	0.0431	0.0313	0.0168	0.0092	0.0051	0.0029
0.1486	0.1037	0.0728	0.0611	0.0514	0.0365	0.0261	0.0135	0.0072	0.0039	0.0021
0.1351	0.0926	0.0638	0.0531	0.0443	0.0309	0.0217	0.0109	0.0056	0.0029	0.0016
0.1228	0.0826	0.0560	0.0462	0.0382	0.0262	0.0181	0.0088	0.0044	0.0022	0.0012
0.1117	0.0738	0.0491	0.0402	0.0329	0.0222	0.0151	0.0071	0.0034	0.0017	0.0008
0.1015	0.0659	0.0431	0.0349	0.0284	0.0188	0.0126	0.0057	0.0027	0.0013	0.0006
0.0923	0.0588	0.0378	0.0304	0.0245	0.0160	0.0105	0.0046	0.0021	0.0010	0.0005
0.0573	0.0334	0.0196	0.0151	0.0116	0.0070	0.0042	0.0016	0.0006	0.0002	0.0001
0.0221	0.0107	0.0053	0.0037	0.0026	0.0013	0.0007	0.0002	0.0001	*	*
0.0085	0.0035	0.0014	0.0009	0.0006	0.0003	0.0001	*	*	*	*

TABLE A.2	Present Value of an Annuity of $1 per Period for T Periods $= [1 - 1/(1 + r)^T]/r$								
	Interest Rate								
Number of Periods	1%	2%	3%	4%	5%	6%	7%	8%	9%
1	0.9901	0.9804	0.9709	0.9615	0.9524	0.9434	0.9346	0.9259	0.9174
2	1.9704	1.9416	1.9135	1.8861	1.8594	1.8334	1.8080	1.7833	1.7591
3	2.9410	2.8839	2.8286	2.7751	2.7232	2.6730	2.6243	2.5771	2.5313
4	3.9020	3.8077	3.7171	3.6299	3.5460	3.4651	3.3872	3.3121	3.2397
5	4.8534	4.7135	4.5797	4.4518	4.3295	4.2124	4.1002	3.9927	3.8897
6	5.7955	5.6014	5.4172	5.2421	5.0757	4.9173	4.7665	4.6229	4.4859
7	6.7282	6.4720	6.2303	6.0021	5.7864	5.5824	5.3893	5.2064	5.0330
8	7.6517	7.3255	7.0197	6.7327	6.4632	6.2098	5.9713	5.7466	5.5348
9	8.5660	8.1622	7.7861	7.4353	7.1078	6.8017	6.5152	6.2469	5.9952
10	9.4713	8.9826	8.5302	8.1109	7.7217	7.3601	7.0236	6.7101	6.4177
11	10.3676	9.7868	9.2526	8.7605	8.3064	7.8869	7.4987	7.1390	6.8052
12	11.2551	10.5753	9.9540	9.3851	8.8633	8.3838	7.9427	7.5361	7.1607
13	12.1337	11.3484	10.6350	9.9856	9.3936	8.8527	8.3577	7.9038	7.4869
14	13.0037	12.1062	11.2961	10.5631	9.8986	9.2950	8.7455	8.2442	7.7862
15	13.8651	12.8493	11.9379	11.1184	10.3797	9.7122	9.1079	8.5595	8.0607
16	14.7179	13.5777	12.5611	11.6523	10.8378	10.1059	9.4466	8.8514	8.3126
17	15.5623	14.2919	13.1661	12.1657	11.2741	10.4773	9.7632	9.1216	8.5436
18	16.3983	14.9920	13.7535	12.6593	11.6896	10.8276	10.0591	9.3719	8.7556
19	17.2260	15.6785	14.3238	13.1339	12.0853	11.1581	10.3356	9.6036	8.9501
20	18.0456	16.3514	14.8775	13.5903	12.4622	11.4699	10.5940	9.8181	9.1285
21	18.8570	17.0112	15.4150	14.0292	12.8212	11.7641	10.8355	10.0168	9.2922
22	19.6604	17.6580	15.9369	14.4511	13.1630	12.0416	11.0612	10.2007	9.4424
23	20.4558	18.2922	16.4436	14.8568	13.4886	12.3034	11.2722	10.3741	9.5802
24	21.2434	18.9139	16.9355	15.2470	13.7986	12.5504	11.4693	10.5288	9.7066
25	22.0232	19.5235	17.4131	15.6221	14.0939	12.7834	11.6536	10.6748	9.8226
30	25.8077	22.3965	19.6004	17.2920	15.3725	13.7648	12.4090	11.2578	10.2737
40	32.8347	27.3555	23.1148	19.7928	17.1591	15.0463	13.3317	11.9246	10.7574
50	39.1961	31.4236	25.7298	21.4822	18.2559	15.7619	13.8007	12.2335	10.9617

TABLE A.2		(concluded)							
					Interest Rate				
10%	12%	14%	15%	16%	18%	20%	24%	28%	32%
0.9091	0.8929	0.8772	0.8696	0.8621	0.8475	0.8333	0.8065	0.7813	0.7576
1.7355	1.6901	1.6467	1.6257	1.6052	1.5656	1.5278	1.4568	1.3916	1.3315
2.4869	2.4018	2.3216	2.2832	2.2459	2.1743	2.1065	1.9813	1.8684	1.7663
3.1699	3.0373	2.9137	2.8550	2.7982	2.6901	2.5887	2.4043	2.2410	2.0957
3.7908	3.6048	3.4331	3.3522	3.2743	3.1272	2.9906	2.7454	2.5320	2.3452
4.3553	4.1114	3.8887	3.7845	3.6847	3.4976	3.3255	3.0205	2.7594	2.5342
4.8684	4.5638	4.2883	4.1604	4.0386	3.8115	3.6046	3.2423	2.9370	2.6775
5.3349	4.9676	4.6389	4.4873	4.3436	4.0776	3.8372	3.4212	3.0758	2.7860
5.7590	5.3282	4.9464	4.7716	4.6065	4.3030	4.0310	3.5655	3.1842	2.8681
6.1446	5.6502	5.2161	5.0188	4.8332	4.4941	4.1925	3.6819	3.2689	2.9304
6.4951	5.9377	5.4527	5.2337	5.0286	4.6560	4.3271	3.7757	3.3351	2.9776
6.8137	6.1944	5.6603	5.4206	5.1971	4.7932	4.4392	3.8514	3.3868	3.0133
7.1034	6.4235	5.8424	5.5831	5.3423	4.9095	4.5327	3.9124	3.4272	3.0404
7.3667	6.6282	6.0021	5.7245	5.4675	5.0081	4.6106	3.9616	3.4587	3.0609
7.6061	6.8109	6.1422	5.8474	5.5755	5.0916	4.6755	4.0013	3.4834	3.0764
7.8237	6.9740	6.2651	5.9542	5.6685	5.1624	4.7296	4.0333	3.5026	3.0882
8.0216	7.1196	6.3729	6.0472	5.7487	5.2223	4.7746	4.0591	3.5177	3.0971
8.2014	7.2497	6.4674	6.1280	5.8178	5.2732	4.8122	4.0799	3.5294	3.1039
8.3649	7.3658	6.5504	6.1982	5.8775	5.3162	4.8435	4.0967	3.5386	3.1090
8.5136	7.4694	6.6231	6.2593	5.9288	5.3527	4.8696	4.1103	3.5458	3.1129
8.6487	7.5620	6.6870	6.3125	5.9731	5.3837	4.8913	4.1212	3.5514	3.1158
8.7715	7.6446	6.7429	6.3587	6.0113	5.4099	4.9094	4.1300	3.5558	3.1180
8.8832	7.7184	6.7921	6.3988	6.0442	5.4321	4.9245	4.1371	3.5592	3.1197
8.9847	7.7843	6.8351	6.4338	6.0726	5.4509	4.9371	4.1428	3.5619	3.1210
9.0770	7.8431	6.8729	6.4641	6.0971	5.4669	4.9476	4.1474	3.5640	3.1220
9.4269	8.0552	7.0027	6.5660	6.1772	5.5168	4.9789	4.1601	3.5693	3.1242
9.7791	8.2438	7.1050	6.6418	6.2335	5.5482	4.9966	4.1659	3.5712	3.1250
9.9148	8.3045	7.1327	6.6605	6.2463	5.5541	4.9995	4.1666	3.5714	3.1250

TABLE A.3		Future Value of $1 at the End of T Periods $= (1 + r)^T$							
				Interest Rate					
Period	1%	2%	3%	4%	5%	6%	7%	8%	9%
1	1.0100	1.0200	1.0300	1.0400	1.0500	1.0600	1.0700	1.0800	1.0900
2	1.0201	1.0404	1.0609	1.0816	1.1025	1.1236	1.1449	1.1664	1.1881
3	1.0303	1.0612	1.0927	1.1249	1.1576	1.1910	1.2250	1.2597	1.2950
4	1.0406	1.0824	1.1255	1.1699	1.2155	1.2625	1.3108	1.3605	1.4116
5	1.0510	1.1041	1.1593	1.2167	1.2763	1.3382	1.4026	1.4693	1.5386
6	1.0615	1.1262	1.1941	1.2653	1.3401	1.4185	1.5007	1.5869	1.6771
7	1.0721	1.1487	1.2299	1.3159	1.4071	1.5036	1.6058	1.7138	1.8280
8	1.0829	1.1717	1.2668	1.3686	1.4775	1.5938	1.7182	1.8509	1.9926
9	1.0937	1.1951	1.3048	1.4233	1.5513	1.6895	1.8385	1.9990	2.1719
10	1.1046	1.2190	1.3439	1.4802	1.6289	1.7908	1.9672	2.1589	2.3674
11	1.1157	1.2434	1.3842	1.5395	1.7103	1.8983	2.1049	2.3316	2.5804
12	1.1268	1.2682	1.4258	1.6010	1.7959	2.0122	2.2522	2.5182	2.8127
13	1.1381	1.2936	1.4685	1.6651	1.8856	2.1329	2.4098	2.7196	3.0658
14	1.1495	1.3195	1.5126	1.7317	1.9799	2.2609	2.5785	2.9372	3.3417
15	1.1610	1.3459	1.5580	1.8009	2.0789	2.3966	2.7590	3.1722	3.6425
16	1.1726	1.3728	1.6047	1.8730	2.1829	2.5404	2.9522	3.4259	3.9703
17	1.1843	1.4002	1.6528	1.9479	2.2920	2.6928	3.1588	3.7000	4.3276
18	1.1961	1.4282	1.7024	2.0258	2.4066	2.8543	3.3799	3.9960	4.7171
19	1.2081	1.4568	1.7535	2.1068	2.5270	3.0256	3.6165	4.3157	5.1417
20	1.2202	1.4859	1.8061	2.1911	2.6533	3.2071	3.8697	4.6610	5.6044
21	1.2324	1.5157	1.8603	2.2788	2.7860	3.3996	4.1406	5.0338	6.1088
22	1.2447	1.5460	1.9161	2.3699	2.9253	3.6035	4.4304	5.4365	6.6586
23	1.2572	1.5769	1.9736	2.4647	3.0715	3.8197	4.7405	5.8715	7.2579
24	1.2697	1.6084	2.0328	2.5633	3.2251	4.0489	5.0724	6.3412	7.9111
25	1.2824	1.6406	2.0938	2.6658	3.3864	4.2919	5.4274	6.8485	8.6231
30	1.3478	1.8114	2.4273	3.2434	4.3219	5.7435	7.6123	10.063	13.268
40	1.4889	2.2080	3.2620	4.8010	7.0400	10.286	14.974	21.725	31.409
50	1.6446	2.6916	4.3839	7.1067	11.467	18.420	29.457	46.902	74.358
60	1.8167	3.2810	5.8916	10.520	18.679	32.988	57.946	101.26	176.03

*FVIV > 99,999.

TABLE A.3   (concluded)

					Interest Rate					
10%	12%	14%	15%	16%	18%	20%	24%	28%	32%	36%
1.1000	1.1200	1.1400	1.1500	1.1600	1.1800	1.2000	1.2400	1.2800	1.3200	1.3600
1.2100	1.2544	1.2996	1.3225	1.3456	1.3924	1.4400	1.5376	1.6384	1.7424	1.8496
1.3310	1.4049	1.4815	1.5209	1.5609	1.6430	1.7280	1.9066	2.0972	2.3000	2.5155
1.4641	1.5735	1.6890	1.7490	1.8106	1.9388	2.0736	2.3642	2.6844	3.0360	3.4210
1.6105	1.7623	1.9254	2.0114	2.1003	2.2878	2.4883	2.9316	3.4360	4.0075	4.6526
1.7716	1.9738	2.1950	2.3131	2.4364	2.6996	2.9860	3.6352	4.3980	5.2899	6.3275
1.9487	2.2107	2.5023	2.6600	2.8262	3.1855	3.5832	4.5077	5.6295	6.9826	8.6054
2.1436	2.4760	2.8526	3.0590	3.2784	3.7589	4.2998	5.5895	7.2058	9.2170	11.703
2.3579	2.7731	3.2519	3.5179	3.8030	4.4355	5.1598	6.9310	9.2234	12.166	15.917
2.5937	3.1058	3.7072	4.0456	4.4114	5.2338	6.1917	8.5944	11.806	16.060	21.647
2.8531	3.4785	4.2262	4.6524	5.1173	6.1759	7.4301	10.657	15.112	21.199	29.439
3.1384	3.8960	4.8179	5.3503	5.9360	7.2876	8.9161	13.215	19.343	27.983	40.037
3.4523	4.3635	5.4924	6.1528	6.8858	8.5994	10.699	16.386	24.759	36.937	54.451
3.7975	4.8871	6.2613	7.0757	7.9875	10.147	12.839	20.319	31.691	48.757	74.053
4.1772	5.4736	7.1379	8.1371	9.2655	11.974	15.407	25.196	40.565	64.359	100.71
4.5950	6.1304	8.1372	9.3576	10.748	14.129	18.488	31.243	51.923	84.954	136.97
5.0545	6.8660	9.2765	10.761	12.468	16.672	22.186	38.741	66.461	112.14	186.28
5.5599	7.6900	10.575	12.375	14.463	19.673	26.623	48.039	86.071	148.02	253.34
6.1159	8.6128	12.056	14.232	16.777	23.214	31.948	59.568	108.89	195.39	344.54
6.7275	9.6463	13.743	16.367	19.461	27.393	38.338	73.864	139.38	257.92	468.57
7.4002	10.804	15.668	18.822	22.574	32.324	46.005	91.592	178.41	340.45	637.26
8.1403	12.100	17.861	21.645	26.186	38.142	55.206	113.57	228.36	449.39	866.67
8.9543	13.552	20.362	24.891	30.376	45.008	66.247	140.83	292.30	593.20	1178.7
9.8497	15.179	23.212	28.625	35.236	53.109	79.497	174.63	374.14	783.02	1603.0
10.835	17.000	26.462	32.919	40.874	62.669	95.396	216.54	478.90	1033.6	2180.1
17.449	29.960	50.950	66.212	85.850	143.37	237.38	634.82	1645.5	4142.1	10143.
45.259	93.051	188.88	267.86	378.72	750.38	1469.8	5455.9	19427.	66521.	*
117.39	289.00	700.23	1083.7	1670.7	3927.4	9100.4	46890.	*	*	*
304.48	897.60	2595.9	4384.0	7370.2	20555.	56348.	*	*	*	*

TABLE A.4	Sum of Annuity of $1 per Period for *T* Periods $= [(1 + r)^T - 1]/r$								
	Interest Rate								
Number of Periods	1%	2%	3%	4%	5%	6%	7%	8%	9%
1	1.0000	1.0000	1.0000	1.0000	1.0000	1.0000	1.0000	1.0000	1.0000
2	2.0100	2.0200	2.0300	2.0400	2.0500	2.0600	2.0700	2.0800	2.0900
3	3.0301	3.0604	3.0909	3.1216	3.1525	3.1836	3.2149	3.2464	3.2781
4	4.0604	4.1216	4.1836	4.2465	4.3101	4.3746	4.4399	4.5061	4.5731
5	5.1010	5.2040	5.3091	5.4163	5.5256	5.6371	5.7507	5.8666	5.9847
6	6.1520	6.3081	6.4684	6.6330	6.8019	6.9753	7.1533	7.3359	7.5233
7	7.2135	7.4343	7.6625	7.8983	8.1420	8.3938	8.6540	8.9228	9.2004
8	8.2857	8.5830	8.8932	9.2142	9.5491	9.8975	10.260	10.637	11.028
9	9.3685	9.7546	10.159	10.583	11.027	11.491	11.978	12.488	13.021
10	10.462	10.950	11.464	12.006	12.578	13.181	13.816	14.487	15.193
11	11.567	12.169	12.808	13.486	14.207	14.972	15.784	16.645	17.560
12	12.683	13.412	14.192	15.026	15.917	16.870	17.888	18.977	20.141
13	13.809	14.680	15.618	16.627	17.713	18.882	20.141	21.495	22.953
14	14.947	15.974	17.086	18.292	19.599	21.015	22.550	24.215	26.019
15	16.097	17.293	18.599	20.024	21.579	23.276	25.129	27.152	29.361
16	17.258	18.639	20.157	21.825	23.657	25.673	27.888	30.324	33.003
17	18.430	20.012	21.762	23.698	25.840	28.213	30.840	33.750	36.974
18	19.615	21.412	23.414	25.645	28.132	30.906	33.999	37.450	41.301
19	20.811	22.841	25.117	27.671	30.539	33.760	37.379	41.446	46.018
20	22.019	24.297	26.870	29.778	33.066	36.786	40.995	45.762	51.160
21	23.239	25.783	28.676	31.969	35.719	39.993	44.865	50.423	56.765
22	24.472	27.299	30.537	34.248	38.505	43.392	49.006	55.457	62.873
23	25.716	28.845	32.453	36.618	41.430	46.996	53.436	60.893	69.532
24	26.973	30.422	34.426	39.083	44.502	50.816	58.177	66.765	76.790
25	28.243	32.030	36.459	41.646	47.727	54.865	63.249	73.106	84.701
30	34.785	40.568	47.575	56.085	66.439	79.058	94.461	113.28	136.31
40	48.886	60.402	75.401	95.026	120.80	154.76	199.64	259.06	337.88
50	64.463	84.579	112.80	152.67	209.35	290.34	406.53	573.77	815.08
60	81.670	114.05	163.05	237.99	353.58	533.13	813.52	1253.2	1944.8

*FVIFA > 99,999.

TABLE A.4 (concluded)

10%	12%	14%	15%	16%	18%	20%	24%	28%	32%	36%
1.0000	1.0000	1.0000	1.0000	1.0000	1.0000	1.0000	1.0000	1.0000	1.0000	1.0000
2.1000	2.1200	2.1400	2.1500	2.1600	2.1800	2.2000	2.2400	2.2800	2.3200	2.3600
3.3100	3.3744	3.4396	3.4725	3.5056	3.5724	3.6400	3.7776	3.9184	4.0624	4.2096
3.6410	4.7793	4.9211	4.9934	5.0665	5.2154	5.3680	5.6842	6.0156	6.3624	6.7251
6.1051	6.3528	6.6101	6.7424	6.8771	7.1542	7.4416	8.0484	8.6999	9.3983	10.146
7.7156	8.1152	8.5355	8.7537	8.9775	9.4420	9.9299	10.980	12.136	13.406	14.799
9.4872	10.089	10.730	11.067	11.414	12.142	12.916	14.615	16.534	18.696	21.126
11.436	12.300	13.233	13.727	14.240	15.327	16.499	19.123	22.163	25.678	29.732
13.579	14.776	16.085	16.786	17.519	19.086	20.799	24.712	29.369	34.895	41.435
15.937	17.549	19.337	20.304	21.321	23.521	25.959	31.643	38.593	47.062	57.352
18.531	20.655	23.045	24.349	25.733	28.755	32.150	40.238	50.398	63.122	78.998
21.384	24.133	27.271	29.002	30.850	34.931	39.581	50.895	65.510	84.320	108.44
24.523	28.029	32.089	34.352	36.786	42.219	48.497	64.110	84.853	112.30	148.47
27.975	32.393	37.581	40.505	43.672	50.818	59.196	80.496	109.61	149.24	202.93
31.772	37.280	43.842	47.580	51.660	60.965	72.035	100.82	141.30	198.00	276.98
35.950	42.753	50.980	55.717	60.925	72.939	87.442	126.01	181.87	262.36	377.69
40.545	48.884	59.118	65.075	71.673	87.068	105.93	157.25	233.79	347.31	514.66
45.599	55.750	68.394	75.836	84.141	103.74	128.12	195.99	300.25	459.45	700.94
51.159	64.440	78.969	88.212	98.603	123.41	154.74	244.03	385.32	607.47	954.28
57.275	72.052	91.025	102.44	115.38	146.63	186.69	303.60	494.21	802.86	1298.8
64.002	81.699	104.77	118.81	134.84	174.02	225.03	377.46	633.59	1060.8	1767.4
71.403	92.503	120.44	137.63	157.41	206.34	271.03	469.06	812.00	1401.2	2404.7
79.543	104.60	138.30	159.28	183.60	244.49	326.24	582.63	1040.4	1850.6	3271.3
88.497	118.16	158.66	184.17	213.98	289.49	392.48	723.46	1332.7	2443.8	4450.0
98.347	133.33	181.87	212.79	249.21	342.60	471.98	898.09	1706.8	3226.8	6053.0
164.49	241.33	356.79	434.75	530.31	790.95	1181.9	2640.9	5873.2	12941.	28172.3
442.59	767.09	1342.0	1779.1	2360.8	4163.2	7343.9	22729.	69377.	*	*
1163.9	2400.0	4994.5	7217.7	10436.	21813.	45497.	*	*	*	*
3034.8	7471.6	18535.	29220.	46058.	*	*	*	*	*	*

TABLE A.5				Future Value of $1 with a Continuously Compounded Rate *r* for *T* Periods: Values of e^{rT}					
	Continuously Compounded Rate (*r*)									
Period (T)	1%	2%	3%	4%	5%	6%	7%	8%	9%	10%
1	1.0101	1.0202	1.0305	1.0408	1.0513	1.0618	1.0725	1.0833	1.0942	1.1052
2	1.0202	1.0408	1.0618	1.0833	1.1052	1.1275	1.1503	1.1735	1.1972	1.2214
3	1.0305	1.0618	1.0942	1.1275	1.1618	1.1972	1.2337	1.2712	1.3100	1.3499
4	1.0408	1.0833	1.1275	1.1735	1.2214	1.2712	1.3231	1.3771	1.4333	1.4918
5	1.0513	1.1052	1.1618	1.2214	1.2840	1.3499	1.4191	1.4918	1.5683	1.6487
6	1.0618	1.1275	1.1972	1.2712	1.3499	1.4333	1.5220	1.6161	1.7160	1.8221
7	1.0725	1.1503	1.2337	1.3231	1.4191	1.5220	1.6323	1.7507	1.8776	2.0138
8	1.0833	1.1735	1.2712	1.3771	1.4918	1.6161	1.7507	1.8965	2.0544	2.2255
9	1.0942	1.1972	1.3100	1.4333	1.5683	1.7160	1.8776	2.0544	2.2479	2.4596
10	1.1052	1.2214	1.3499	1.4918	1.6487	1.8221	2.0138	2.2255	2.4596	2.7183
11	1.1163	1.2461	1.3910	1.5527	1.7333	1.9348	2.1598	2.4109	2.6912	3.0042
12	1.1275	1.2712	1.4333	1.6161	1.8221	2.0544	2.3164	2.6117	2.9447	3.3201
13	1.1388	1.2969	1.4770	1.6820	1.9155	2.1815	2.4843	2.8292	3.2220	3.6693
14	1.1503	1.3231	1.5220	1.7507	2.0138	2.3164	2.6645	3.0649	3.5254	4.0552
15	1.1618	1.3499	1.5683	1.8221	2.1170	2.4596	2.8577	3.3201	3.8574	4.4817
16	1.1735	1.3771	1.6161	1.8965	2.2255	2.6117	3.0649	3.5966	4.2207	4.9530
17	1.1853	1.4049	1.6653	1.9739	2.3396	2.7732	3.2871	3.8962	4.6182	5.4739
18	1.1972	1.4333	1.7160	2.0544	2.4596	2.9447	3.5254	4.2207	5.0531	6.0496
19	1.2092	1.4623	1.7683	2.1383	2.5857	3.1268	3.7810	4.5722	5.5290	6.6859
20	1.2214	1.4918	1.8221	2.2255	2.7183	3.3201	4.0552	4.9530	6.0496	7.3891
21	1.2337	1.5220	1.8776	2.3164	2.8577	3.5254	4.3492	5.3656	6.6194	8.1662
22	1.2461	1.5527	1.9348	2.4109	3.0042	3.7434	4.6646	5.8124	7.2427	9.0250
23	1.2586	1.5841	1.9937	2.5093	3.1582	3.9749	5.0028	6.2965	7.9248	9.9742
24	1.2712	1.6161	2.0544	2.6117	3.3201	4.2207	5.3656	6.8210	8.6711	11.0232
25	1.2840	1.6487	2.1170	2.7183	3.4903	4.4817	5.7546	7.3891	9.4877	12.1825
30	1.3499	1.8221	2.4596	3.3204	4.4817	6.0496	8.1662	11.0232	14.8797	20.0855
35	1.4191	2.0138	2.8577	4.0552	5.7546	8.1662	11.5883	16.4446	23.3361	33.1155
40	1.4918	2.2255	3.3201	4.9530	7.3891	11.0232	16.4446	24.5235	36.5982	54.5982
45	1.5683	2.4596	3.8574	6.0496	9.4877	14.8797	23.3361	36.5982	57.3975	90.0171
50	1.6487	2.7183	4.4817	7.3891	12.1825	20.0855	33.1155	54.5982	90.0171	148.4132
55	1.7333	3.0042	5.2070	9.0250	15.6426	27.1126	46.9931	81.4509	141.1750	244.6919
60	1.8221	3.3201	6.0496	11.0232	20.0855	36.5982	66.6863	121.5104	221.4064	403.4288

TABLE A.5		(continued)								
				Continuously Compounded Rate (*r*)						
11%	12%	13%	14%	15%	16%	17%	18%	19%	20%	21%
1.1163	1.1275	1.1388	1.1503	1.1618	1.1735	1.1853	1.1972	1.2092	1.2214	1.2337
1.2461	1.2712	1.2969	1.3231	1.3499	1.3771	1.4049	1.4333	1.4623	1.4918	1.5220
1.3910	1.4333	1.4770	1.5220	1.5683	1.6161	1.6653	1.7160	1.7683	1.8221	1.8776
1.5527	1.6161	1.6820	1.7507	1.8221	1.8965	1.9739	2.0544	2.1383	2.2255	2.3164
1.7333	1.8221	1.9155	2.0138	2.1170	2.2255	2.3396	2.4596	2.5857	2.7183	2.8577
1.9348	2.0544	2.1815	2.3164	2.4596	2.6117	2.7732	2.9447	3.1268	3.3201	3.5254
2.1598	2.3164	2.4843	2.6645	2.8577	3.0649	3.2871	3.5254	3.7810	4.0552	4.3492
2.4109	2.6117	2.8292	3.0649	3.3201	3.5966	3.8962	4.2207	4.5722	4.9530	5.3656
2.6912	2.9447	3.2220	3.5254	3.8574	4.2207	4.6182	5.0531	5.5290	6.0496	6.6194
3.0042	3.3201	3.6693	4.0552	4.4817	4.9530	5.4739	6.0496	6.6859	7.3891	8.1662
3.3535	3.7434	4.1787	4.6646	5.2070	5.8124	6.4883	7.2427	8.0849	9.0250	10.0744
3.7434	4.2207	4.7588	5.3656	6.0496	6.8210	7.6906	8.6711	9.7767	11.0232	12.4286
4.1787	4.7588	5.4195	6.1719	7.0287	8.0045	9.1157	10.3812	11.8224	13.4637	15.3329
4.6646	5.3656	6.1719	7.0993	8.1662	9.3933	10.8049	12.4286	14.2963	16.4446	18.9158
5.2070	6.0496	7.0287	8.1662	9.4877	11.0232	12.0871	14.8797	17.2878	20.0855	23.3361
5.8124	6.8210	8.0045	9.3933	11.0232	12.9358	15.1803	17.8143	20.9052	24.5325	28.7892
6.4883	7.6906	9.1157	10.8049	12.8071	15.1803	17.9933	21.3276	25.2797	29.9641	35.5166
7.2427	8.6711	10.3812	12.4286	14.8797	17.8143	21.3276	25.5337	30.5694	36.5982	43.8160
8.0849	9.7767	11.8224	14.2963	17.2878	20.9052	25.2797	30.5694	36.9661	44.7012	54.0549
9.0250	11.0232	13.4637	16.4446	20.0855	24.5325	29.9641	36.5982	44.7012	54.5982	66.6863
10.0744	12.4286	15.3329	18.9158	23.3361	28.7892	35.5166	43.8160	54.0549	66.6863	82.2695
11.2459	14.0132	17.4615	21.7584	27.1126	33.7844	42.0980	52.4573	65.3659	81.4509	101.4940
12.5535	15.7998	19.8857	25.0281	31.5004	39.6464	49.8990	62.8028	79.0436	99.4843	125.2110
14.0132	17.8143	22.6464	28.7892	36.5982	46.5255	59.1455	75.1886	95.5835	121.5104	154.4700
15.6426	20.0855	25.7903	33.1155	42.5211	54.5982	70.1054	90.0171	115.5843	148.4132	190.5663
27.1126	36.5982	49.4024	66.6863	90.0171	121.5104	164.0219	221.4064	298.8674	403.4288	544.5719
46.9931	66.6863	94.6324	134.2898	190.5663	270.4264	383.7533	544.5719	772.7843	1096.633	1556.197
81.4509	121.5104	181.2722	270.4264	403.4288	601.8450	897.8473	1339.431	1998.196	2980.958	4447.067
141.1750	221.4064	347.2344	544.5719	854.0588	1339.431	2100.646	3294.468	5166.754	8103.084	12708.17
244.6919	403.4288	665.1416	1096.633	1808.042	2980.958	4914.769	8103.084	13359.73	22026.47	36315.50
424.1130	735.0952	1274.106	2208.348	3827.626	6634.244	11498.82	19930.37	34544.37	59874.14	103777.0
735.0952	1339.431	2440.602	4447.067	8103.084	14764.78	26903.19	49020.80	89321.72	162754.8	296558.6

TABLE A.5	(concluded)						
	Continuously Compounded Rate (r)						
Period (T)	22%	23%	24%	25%	26%	27%	28%
1	1.2461	1.2586	1.2712	1.2840	1.2969	1.3100	1.3231
2	1.5527	1.5841	1.6161	1.6487	1.6820	1.7160	1.7507
3	1.9348	1.9937	2.0544	2.1170	2.1815	2.2479	2.3164
4	2.4109	2.5093	2.6117	2.7183	2.8292	2.9447	3.0649
5	3.0042	3.1582	3.3201	3.4903	3.6693	3.8574	4.0552
6	3.7434	3.9749	4.2207	4.4817	4.7588	5.0351	5.3656
7	4.6646	5.0028	5.3656	5.7546	6.1719	6.6194	7.0993
8	5.8124	6.2965	6.8210	7.3891	8.0045	8.6711	9.3933
9	7.2427	7.9248	8.6711	9.4877	10.3812	11.3589	12.4286
10	9.0250	9.9742	11.0232	12.1825	13.4637	14.8797	16.4446
11	11.2459	12.5535	14.0132	15.6426	17.4615	19.4919	21.7584
12	14.0132	15.7998	17.8143	20.0855	22.6464	25.5337	28.7892
13	17.4615	19.8857	22.6464	25.7903	29.3708	33.4483	38.0918
14	21.7584	25.0281	28.7892	33.1155	38.0918	43.8160	50.4004
15	27.1126	31.5004	36.5982	42.5211	49.4024	57.3975	66.6863
16	33.7844	39.6464	46.5255	54.5982	64.0715	75.1886	88.2347
17	42.0980	49.8990	59.1455	70.1054	83.0963	98.4944	116.7459
18	52.4573	62.8028	75.1886	90.0171	107.7701	129.0242	154.4700
19	65.3659	79.0436	95.5835	115.5843	139.7702	169.0171	204.3839
20	81.4509	99.4843	121.5104	148.4132	181.2722	221.4064	270.4264
21	101.4940	125.2110	154.4700	190.5663	235.0974	290.0345	357.8092
22	126.4694	157.5905	196.3699	244.6919	304.9049	379.9349	473.4281
23	157.5905	198.3434	249.6350	314.1907	395.4404	497.7013	626.4068
24	196.3699	249.6350	317.3483	403.4288	512.8585	651.9709	828.8175
25	244.6919	314.1907	403.4288	518.0128	665.1416	854.0588	1096.633
30	735.0952	992.2747	1339.431	1808.042	2440.602	3294.468	4447.067
35	2208.348	3133.795	4447.067	6310.688	8955.293	12708.17	18033.74
40	6634.244	9897.129	14764.78	22026.47	32859.63	49020.80	73130.44
45	19930.37	31257.04	49020.80	76879.92	120571.7	189094.1	296558.6
50	59874.14	98715.77	162754.8	268337.3	442413.4	729416.4	1202604
55	179871.9	311763.4	540364.9	936589.2	1623346	2813669	4876801
60	540364.9	984609.1	1794075	3269017	5956538	10853520	19776403

TABLE A.6		Present Value of $1 with a Continuous Discount Rate r for T Periods: Values of e^{-rT}					
		Continuous Discount Rate (r)					
Period (T)	1%	2%	3%	4%	5%	6%	7%
1	0.9900	0.9802	0.9704	0.9608	0.9512	0.9418	0.9324
2	0.9802	0.9608	0.9418	0.9231	0.9048	0.8869	0.8694
3	0.9704	0.9418	0.9139	0.8869	0.8607	0.8353	0.8106
4	0.9608	0.9231	0.8869	0.8521	0.8187	0.7866	0.7558
5	0.9512	0.9048	0.8607	0.8187	0.7788	0.7408	0.7047
6	0.9418	0.8869	0.8353	0.7866	0.7408	0.6977	0.6570
7	0.9324	0.8694	0.8106	0.7558	0.7047	0.6570	0.6126
8	0.9231	0.8521	0.7866	0.7261	0.6703	0.6188	0.5712
9	0.9139	0.8353	0.7634	0.6977	0.6376	0.5827	0.5326
10	0.9048	0.8187	0.7408	0.6703	0.6065	0.5488	0.4966
11	0.8958	0.8025	0.7189	0.6440	0.5769	0.5169	0.4630
12	0.8869	0.7866	0.6977	0.6188	0.5488	0.4868	0.4317
13	0.8781	0.7711	0.6771	0.5945	0.5220	0.4584	0.4025
14	0.8694	0.7558	0.6570	0.5712	0.4966	0.4317	0.3753
15	0.8607	0.7408	0.6376	0.5488	0.4724	0.4066	0.3499
16	0.8521	0.7261	0.6188	0.5273	0.4493	0.3829	0.3263
17	0.8437	0.7118	0.6005	0.5066	0.4274	0.3606	0.3042
18	0.8353	0.6977	0.5827	0.4868	0.4066	0.3396	0.2837
19	0.8270	0.6839	0.5655	0.4677	0.3867	0.3198	0.2645
20	0.8187	0.6703	0.5488	0.4493	0.3679	0.3012	0.2466
21	0.8106	0.6570	0.5326	0.4317	0.3499	0.2837	0.2299
22	0.8025	0.6440	0.5169	0.4148	0.3329	0.2671	0.2144
23	0.7945	0.6313	0.5016	0.3985	0.3166	0.2516	0.1999
24	0.7866	0.6188	0.4868	0.3829	0.3012	0.2369	0.1864
25	0.7788	0.6065	0.4724	0.3679	0.2865	0.2231	0.1738
30	0.7408	0.5488	0.4066	0.3012	0.2231	0.1653	0.1225
35	0.7047	0.4966	0.3499	0.2466	0.1738	0.1225	0.0863
40	0.6703	0.4493	0.3012	0.2019	0.1353	0.0907	0.0608
45	0.6376	0.4066	0.2592	0.1653	0.1054	0.0672	0.0429
50	0.6065	0.3679	0.2231	0.1353	0.0821	0.0498	0.0302
55	0.5769	0.3329	0.1920	0.1108	0.0639	0.0369	0.0213
60	0.5488	0.3012	0.1653	0.0907	0.0498	0.0273	0.0150

TABLE A.6   (continued)

Period (T)	|||| Continuous Discount Rate (r) ||||									
	8%	9%	10%	11%	12%	13%	14%	15%	16%	17%
1	0.9231	0.9139	0.9048	0.8958	0.8869	0.8781	0.8694	0.8607	0.8521	0.8437
2	0.8521	0.8353	0.8187	0.8025	0.7866	0.7711	0.7558	0.7408	0.7261	0.7118
3	0.7866	0.7634	0.7408	0.7189	0.6977	0.6771	0.6570	0.6376	0.6188	0.6005
4	0.7261	0.6977	0.6703	0.6440	0.6188	0.5945	0.5712	0.5488	0.5273	0.5066
5	0.6703	0.6376	0.6065	0.5769	0.5488	0.5220	0.4966	0.4724	0.4493	0.4274
6	0.6188	0.5827	0.5488	0.5169	0.4868	0.4584	0.4317	0.4066	0.3829	0.3606
7	0.5712	0.5326	0.4966	0.4630	0.4317	0.4025	0.3753	0.3499	0.3263	0.3042
8	0.5273	0.4868	0.4493	0.4148	0.3829	0.3535	0.3263	0.3012	0.2780	0.2576
9	0.4868	0.4449	0.4066	0.3716	0.3396	0.3104	0.2837	0.2592	0.2369	0.2165
10	0.4493	0.4066	0.3679	0.3329	0.3012	0.2725	0.2466	0.2231	0.2019	0.1827
11	0.4148	0.3716	0.3329	0.2982	0.2671	0.2393	0.2144	0.1920	0.1720	0.1541
12	0.3829	0.3396	0.3012	0.2671	0.2369	0.2101	0.1864	0.1653	0.1466	0.1300
13	0.3535	0.3104	0.2725	0.2393	0.2101	0.1845	0.1620	0.1423	0.1249	0.1097
14	0.3263	0.2837	0.2466	0.2144	0.1864	0.1620	0.1409	0.1225	0.1065	0.0926
15	0.3012	0.2592	0.2231	0.1920	0.1653	0.1423	0.1225	0.1054	0.0907	0.0781
16	0.2780	0.2369	0.2019	0.1720	0.1466	0.1249	0.1065	0.0907	0.0773	0.0659
17	0.2567	0.2165	0.1827	0.1541	0.1300	0.1097	0.0926	0.0781	0.0659	0.0556
18	0.2369	0.1979	0.1653	0.1381	0.1153	0.0963	0.0805	0.0672	0.0561	0.0469
19	0.2187	0.1809	0.1496	0.1237	0.1023	0.0846	0.0699	0.0578	0.0478	0.0396
20	0.2019	0.1653	0.1353	0.1108	0.0907	0.0743	0.0608	0.0498	0.0408	0.0334
21	0.1864	0.1511	0.1225	0.0993	0.0805	0.0652	0.0529	0.0429	0.0347	0.0282
22	0.1720	0.1381	0.1108	0.0889	0.0714	0.0573	0.0460	0.0369	0.0296	0.0238
23	0.1588	0.1262	0.1003	0.0797	0.0633	0.0503	0.0400	0.0317	0.0252	0.0200
24	0.1466	0.1153	0.0907	0.0714	0.0561	0.0442	0.0347	0.0273	0.0215	0.0169
25	0.1353	0.1054	0.0821	0.0639	0.0498	0.0388	0.0302	0.0235	0.0183	0.0143
30	0.0907	0.0672	0.0498	0.0369	0.0273	0.0202	0.0150	0.0111	0.0082	0.0061
35	0.0608	0.0429	0.0302	0.0213	0.0150	0.0106	0.0074	0.0052	0.0037	0.0026
40	0.0408	0.0273	0.0183	0.0123	0.0082	0.0055	0.0037	0.0025	0.0017	0.0011
45	0.0273	0.0174	0.0111	0.0071	0.0045	0.0029	0.0018	0.0012	0.0007	0.0005
50	0.0183	0.0111	0.0067	0.0041	0.0025	0.0015	0.0009	0.0006	0.0003	0.0002
55	0.0123	0.0071	0.0041	0.0024	0.0014	0.0008	0.0005	0.0003	0.0002	0.0001
60	0.0082	0.0045	0.0025	0.0014	0.0007	0.0004	0.0002	0.0001	0.0001	0.0000

TABLE A.6		(continued)								
				Continuous Discount Rate (*r*)						
18%	19%	20%	21%	22%	23%	24%	25%	26%	27%	28%
0.8353	0.8270	0.8187	0.8106	0.8025	0.7945	0.7866	0.7788	0.7711	0.7634	0.7558
0.6977	0.6839	0.6703	0.6570	0.6440	0.6313	0.6188	0.6065	0.5945	0.5827	0.5712
0.5827	0.5655	0.5488	0.5326	0.5169	0.5016	0.4868	0.4724	0.4584	0.4449	0.4317
0.4868	0.4677	0.4493	0.4317	0.4148	0.3985	0.3829	0.3679	0.3535	0.3396	0.3263
0.4066	0.3867	0.3679	0.3499	0.3329	0.3166	0.3012	0.2865	0.2725	0.2592	0.2466
0.3396	0.3198	0.3012	0.2837	0.2671	0.2516	0.2369	0.2231	0.2101	0.1979	0.1864
0.2837	0.2645	0.2466	0.2299	0.2144	0.1999	0.1864	0.1738	0.1620	0.1511	0.1409
0.2369	0.2187	0.2019	0.1864	0.1720	0.1588	0.1466	0.1353	0.1249	0.1153	0.1065
0.1979	0.1809	0.1653	0.1511	0.1381	0.1262	0.1153	0.1054	0.0963	0.0880	0.0805
0.1653	0.1496	0.1353	0.1225	0.1108	0.1003	0.0907	0.0821	0.0743	0.0672	0.0608
0.1381	0.1237	0.1108	0.0993	0.0889	0.0797	0.0714	0.0639	0.0573	0.0513	0.0460
0.1154	0.1023	0.0907	0.0805	0.0714	0.0633	0.0561	0.0498	0.0442	0.0392	0.0347
0.0963	0.0846	0.0743	0.0652	0.0573	0.0503	0.0442	0.0388	0.0340	0.0299	0.0263
0.0805	0.0699	0.0608	0.0529	0.0460	0.0400	0.0347	0.0302	0.0263	0.0228	0.0198
0.0672	0.0578	0.0498	0.0429	0.0369	0.0317	0.0273	0.0235	0.0202	0.0174	0.0150
0.0561	0.0478	0.0408	0.0347	0.0296	0.0252	0.0215	0.0183	0.0156	0.0133	0.0113
0.0469	0.0396	0.0334	0.0282	0.0238	0.0200	0.0169	0.0143	0.0120	0.0102	0.0086
0.0392	0.0327	0.0273	0.0228	0.0191	0.0159	0.0133	0.0111	0.0093	0.0078	0.0065
0.0327	0.0271	0.0224	0.0185	0.0153	0.0127	0.0105	0.0087	0.0072	0.0059	0.0049
0.0273	0.0224	0.0183	0.0150	0.0123	0.0101	0.0082	0.0067	0.0055	0.0045	0.0037
0.0228	0.0185	0.0150	0.0122	0.0099	0.0080	0.0065	0.0052	0.0043	0.0034	0.0028
0.0191	0.0153	0.0123	0.0099	0.0079	0.0063	0.0051	0.0041	0.0033	0.0026	0.0021
0.0159	0.0127	0.0101	0.0080	0.0063	0.0050	0.0040	0.0032	0.0025	0.0020	0.0016
0.0133	0.0105	0.0082	0.0065	0.0051	0.0040	0.0032	0.0025	0.0019	0.0015	0.0012
0.0111	0.0087	0.0067	0.0052	0.0041	0.0032	0.0025	0.0019	0.0015	0.0012	0.0009
0.0045	0.0033	0.0025	0.0018	0.0014	0.0010	0.0007	0.0006	0.0004	0.0003	0.0002
0.0018	0.0013	0.0009	0.0006	0.0005	0.0003	0.0002	0.0002	0.0001	0.0001	0.0001
0.0007	0.0005	0.0003	0.0002	0.0002	0.0001	0.0001	0.0000	0.0000	0.0000	0.0000
0.0003	0.0002	0.0001	0.0001	0.0001	0.0000	0.0000	0.0000	0.0000	0.0000	0.0000
0.0001	0.0001	0.0000	0.0000	0.0000	0.0000	0.0000	0.0000	0.0000	0.0000	0.0000
0.0001	0.0000	0.0000	0.0000	0.0000	0.0000	0.0000	0.0000	0.0000	0.0000	0.0000
0.0000	0.0000	0.0000	0.0000	0.0000	0.0000	0.0000	0.0000	0.0000	0.0000	0.0000

TABLE A.6	(concluded)						
	Continuous Discount Rate (r)						
Period (T)	29%	30%	31%	32%	33%	34%	35%
1	0.7483	0.7408	0.7334	0.7261	0.7189	0.7118	0.7047
2	0.5599	0.5488	0.5379	0.5273	0.5169	0.5066	0.4966
3	0.4190	0.4066	0.3946	0.3829	0.3716	0.3606	0.3499
4	0.3135	0.3012	0.2894	0.2780	0.2671	0.2567	0.2466
5	0.2346	0.2231	0.2122	0.2019	0.1920	0.1827	0.1738
6	0.1755	0.1653	0.1557	0.1466	0.1381	0.1300	0.1225
7	0.1313	0.1225	0.1142	0.1065	0.0993	0.0926	0.0863
8	0.0983	0.0907	0.0837	0.0773	0.0714	0.0659	0.0608
9	0.0735	0.0672	0.0614	0.0561	0.0513	0.0469	0.0429
10	0.0550	0.0498	0.0450	0.0408	0.0369	0.0334	0.0302
11	0.0412	0.0369	0.0330	0.0296	0.0265	0.0238	0.0213
12	0.0308	0.0273	0.0242	0.0215	0.0191	0.0169	0.0150
13	0.0231	0.0202	0.0178	0.0156	0.0137	0.0120	0.0106
14	0.0172	0.0150	0.0130	0.0113	0.0099	0.0086	0.0074
15	0.0129	0.0111	0.0096	0.0082	0.0071	0.0061	0.0052
16	0.0097	0.0082	0.0070	0.0060	0.0051	0.0043	0.0037
17	0.0072	0.0061	0.0051	0.0043	0.0037	0.0031	0.0026
18	0.0054	0.0045	0.0038	0.0032	0.0026	0.0022	0.0018
19	0.0040	0.0033	0.0028	0.0023	0.0019	0.0016	0.0013
20	0.0030	0.0025	0.0020	0.0017	0.0014	0.0011	0.0009
21	0.0023	0.0018	0.0015	0.0012	0.0010	0.0008	0.0006
22	0.0017	0.0014	0.0011	0.0009	0.0007	0.0006	0.0005
23	0.0013	0.0010	0.0008	0.0006	0.0005	0.0004	0.0003
24	0.0009	0.0007	0.0006	0.0005	0.0004	0.0003	0.0002
25	0.0007	0.0006	0.0004	0.0003	0.0003	0.0002	0.0002
30	0.0002	0.0001	0.0001	0.0001	0.0001	0.0000	0.0000
35	0.0000	0.0000	0.0000	0.0000	0.0000	0.0000	0.0000
40	0.0000	0.0000	0.0000	0.0000	0.0000	0.0000	0.0000
45	0.0000	0.0000	0.0000	0.0000	0.0000	0.0000	0.0000
50	0.0000	0.0000	0.0000	0.0000	0.0000	0.0000	0.0000
55	0.0000	0.0000	0.0000	0.0000	0.0000	0.0000	0.0000
60	0.0000	0.0000	0.0000	0.0000	0.0000	0.0000	0.0000

Glossary

AAR Average accounting return.

Absolute priority rule (APR) Establishes priority of claims under liquidation.

Accounting insolvency Total liabilities exceed total assets. A firm with negative net worth is insolvent on the books.

Accounting liquidity The ease and quickness with which assets can be converted to cash.

Accounts payable Money the firm owes to suppliers.

Accounts receivable Money owed to the firm by customers.

Accounts receivable financing A secured short-term loan that involves either the assigning of receivables or the factoring of receivables. Under assignment, the lender has a lien on the receivables and recourse to the borrower. Factoring involves the sale of accounts receivable. Then the purchaser, called the factor, must collect on the receivables.

Accounts receivable turnover Credit sales divided by average accounts receivable.

ACRS Accelerated cost recovery system.

Additions to net working capital Component of cash flow of firm, along with operating cash flow and capital spending.

Adjusted present value (APV) Base case net present value of a project's operating cash flows plus present value of any financing benefits.

Advance commitment A promise to sell an asset before the seller has lined up purchase of the asset. This seller can offset risk by purchasing a futures contract to fix the sales price.

Agency costs Costs of conflicts of interest among shareholders, bondholders, and managers. Agency costs are the costs of resolving these conflicts. They include the costs of providing managers with an incentive to maximize shareholder wealth and then monitoring their behaviour, and the cost of protecting bondholders from shareholders. Agency costs are borne by shareholders.

Agency theory The theory of the relationship between principals and agents. It involves the nature of the costs of resolving conflicts of interest between principals and agents.

Aggregation Process in corporate financial planning whereby the smaller investment proposals of each of the firm's operational units are added up and in effect treated as a big picture.

Aging schedule A compilation of accounts receivable by the age of account.

Allocational efficiency When informational and operational efficiency are present, markets have allocational efficiency in allocating financing to companies with the best positive NPV projects.

American Depository Receipt (ADR) A security issued in the United States to represent shares of a foreign stock, enabling that stock to be traded in the United States.

American options Options contracts that may be exercised anytime up to the expiration date. A European option may be exercised only on the expiration date.

Amortization Repayment of a loan in installments.

Angels Individuals providing venture capital.

Annualized holding-period return The annual rate of return that, when compounded T times, would have given the same T-period holding return as actually occurred from period 1 to period T.

Annuity A level stream of equal dollar payments that lasts for a fixed time. An example of an annuity is the coupon part of a bond with level annual payments.

Annuity factor The term used to calculate the present value of the stream of level payments for a fixed period.

Annuity in advance An annuity with an immediate initial payment.

Annuity in arrears An annuity with a first payment one full period hence, rather than immediately. That is, the first payment occurs on date 1 rather than on date 0.

Appraisal rights Rights of shareholders of an acquired firm that allow them to demand that their shares be purchased at a fair value by the acquiring firm.

APT See *Arbitrage pricing theory*.

Arbitrage Buying an asset in one market at a lower price and simultaneously selling an identical asset in another market at a higher price. This is done with no cost or risk.

Arbitrage pricing theory (APT) An equilibrium asset pricing theory that is derived from a factor model by using diversification and arbitrage. It shows that the expected return on any risky asset is a linear combination of various factors.

Arithmetic average The sum of the values observed divided by the total number of observations—sometimes referred to as the mean.

Asset beta The beta of the assets of the firm.

Asset requirements A common element of a financial plan that describes projected capital spending and the proposed use of net working capital.

Assets Anything that a firm owns.

Auction market A market where all traders in a certain good meet at one place to buy or sell an asset. The NYSE is an example.

Autocorrelation The correlation of a variable with itself over successive time intervals.

Availability float Refers to the time required to clear a cheque through the banking system.

Average (mean) The average of the observations in a frequency distribution.

Average accounting return (AAR) The average project earnings after taxes and depreciation divided by the average book value of the investment during its life.

Average collection period Average amount of time required to collect an account receivable. Also referred to as *days sales outstanding*.

Average cost of capital A firm's required payout to the bondholders and the shareholders expressed as a percentage of capital contributed to the firm. Average cost of capital is computed by dividing the total required cost of capital by the total amount of contributed capital.

Average daily sales Annual sales divided by 365 days.

Balance sheet A statement showing a firm's accounting value on a particular date. It reflects the following equation: Assets = Liabilities + Shareholders' equity.

Balloon payment Large final payment, as when a loan is repaid in installments.

Banker's acceptance Agreement by a bank to pay a given sum of money at a future date.

Banking group See *Syndicate*.

Bankruptcy State of being unable to pay debts. Thus the ownership of the firm's assets is transferred from the shareholders to the bondholders.

Bankruptcy costs See *Financial distress costs*.

Bargain-purchase-price option Gives lessee the option to purchase the asset at a price below fair market value when the lease expires.

Basic IRR rule Accept the project if IRR is greater than the discount rate; reject the project if IRR is less than the discount rate.

Bearer bond A bond issued without record of the owner's name. Whoever holds the bond (the bearer) is the owner.

Best-efforts underwriting An offering in which an underwriter agrees to distribute as much of the offering as possible and to return any unsold shares to the issuer.

Beta A measure of the sensitivity of a security's return to movements in an underlying factor. It is a measured systematic risk.

Beta coefficient The response of the stock's return to a systematic risk.

Bidder A firm or person that has made an offer to take over another firm.

Binomial approach A basic method of valuing options where the Black–Scholes formula does not fit.

Binomial tree Illustration that captures all of the possible future development paths of an asset.

Black–Scholes call pricing equation An exact formula for the price of a call option. The formula requires five variables: the risk-free interest rate, the variance of the underlying stock, the exercise price, the price of the underlying stock, and the time to expiration.

Blanket inventory lien A secured loan that gives the lender a lien against all of the borrower's inventories.

Bond A long-term debt of a firm. In common usage, the term *bond* often refers to both secured and unsecured debt.

Book cash A firm's cash balance as reported in its financial statements. Also called ledger cash.

Book value of equity Per-share accounting equity value of a firm. Total accounting equity divided by the number of outstanding shares.

Borrow To obtain or receive money on loan with the promise or understanding of returning it or its equivalent.

Bought deal One underwriter buys securities from an issuing firm and sells them directly to a small number of investors.

Break-even analysis Analysis of the level of sales at which a project would make zero profit.

Bubble theory (of speculative markets) Security prices sometimes move wildly above their true values.

Business failure A business that has terminated with a loss to creditors.

Business risk The risk that the firm's shareholders bear if the firm is financed only with equity.

Buying the index Purchasing the stocks in the Standard & Poor's 500 in the same proportion as the index to achieve the same return.

Callable Refers to a bond that is subject to being repurchased at a stated call price before maturity.

Call option The right—but not the obligation—to buy a fixed number of shares of stock at a stated price within a specified time.

Call premium The price of a call option on common stock.

Call price of a bond Amount at which a firm has the right to repurchase its bonds or debentures before the stated maturity date. The call price is always set at equal to or more than the par value.

Call protected Describes a bond that is not allowed to be called, usually for a certain early period in the life of the bond.

Call provision A written agreement between an issuing corporation and its bondholders that gives the corporation the option to redeem the bond at a specified price before the maturity date.

Canada bond or note Debt obligations of the Government of Canada that make semiannual coupon payments and are sold at or near par value in denominations of $1,000 or more. They have original maturities of more than one year.

Canada plus call This new approach is designed to replace the traditional call feature by making it unattractive for the issuer ever to call the bonds. Unlike the standard call, with the Canada call the exact amount of the call premium is not set at the time of issuance. Instead, the Canada plus call stipulates that, in the event of a call, the issuer must provide a call premium that will compensate investors for the difference in interest between the original bond and new debt issued to replace it. This compensation cancels the borrower's benefit from calling the debt, and the result is that call will not occur.

Capital asset pricing model (CAPM) An equilibrium asset pricing theory that shows that equilibrium rates of expected return on all risky assets are a function of their covariance with the market portfolio.

Capital budgeting Planning and managing expenditures for long-lived assets.

Capital gain The positive change in the value of an asset. A negative capital gain is a capital loss.

Capital market line The efficient set of all assets, both risky and riskless, that provides the investor with the best possible opportunities.

Capital markets Financial markets for long-term debt and for equity shares.

Capital rationing The case where funds are limited to a fixed dollar amount and must be allocated among competing projects.

Capital structure The mix of the various debt and equity capital maintained by a firm. Also called financial structure. The composition of a corporation's securities used to finance its investment activities; the relative proportions of short-term debt, long-term debt, and owners' equity.

Capital surplus Amounts of directly contributed equity capital in excess of the par value.

CAPM See *Capital asset pricing model.*

CAR Cumulative abnormal return.

Carrying costs Costs that increase with increases in the level of investment in current assets.

Carrying value Book value.

Cash budget A forecast of cash receipts and disbursements expected by a firm in the coming year. It is a short-term financial planning tool.

Cash cow A company that pays out all earnings per share to shareholders as dividends.

Cash cycle In general, the time between cash disbursement and cash collection. In net working capital management, it can be thought of as the operating cycle less the accounts payable payment period.

Cash discount Discount given for a cash purchase. One reason a cash discount may be offered is to speed up the collection of receivables.

Cash flow Cash generated by the firm and paid to creditors and shareholders. It can be classified as (1) cash flow from operations, (2) cash flow from changes in fixed assets, and (3) cash flow from changes in net working capital.

Cash flow after interest and taxes Net income plus depreciation.

Cash flow from operations Earnings before interest and depreciation minus taxes that measure the cash generated from operations not counting capital spending or working capital requirements.

Cash flow timeline Line depicting the operating activities and cash flows for a firm over a particular period.

Cash offer A public equity issue that is sold to all interested investors.

Cashout Refers to a situation where a firm runs out of cash and cannot readily sell marketable securities.

Cash transaction A transaction where exchange is immediate, as contrasted to a forward contract, which calls for future delivery of an asset at an agreed-upon price.

Certificates of deposit Short-term loans to commercial banks.

Change in net working capital Difference in net working capital from one period to another.

Changes in fixed assets Component of cash flow that equals sales of fixed assets minus the acquisition of fixed assets.

Characteristic line The line relating the expected return on a security to different returns on the market.

CICA Canadian Institute of Chartered Accountants.

Circular bid Takeover bids may be either by circular bid mailed directly to the target's shareholders or by stock exchange bid (through the facilities of the TSX or other exchanges). In either case, Ontario securities law requires that the bidder mail a notice of the proposed share purchase to shareholders. In the case of a circular bid, the response must be mailed to shareholders.

Clean price The quoted price of a bond minus its accrued interest.

Clearing The exchanging of cheques and balancing of accounts between banks.

Clientele effect Argument that stocks attract clienteles based on dividend yield or taxes. For example, a tax clientele effect is induced by the difference in tax treatment of dividend income and capital gains income; high-tax-bracket individuals tend to prefer low-dividend yields.

Clienteles Groups of investors attracted to different payouts.

Coattail To protect the nonvoting shareholders, most companies have a coattail provision giving nonvoting shareholders the right either to vote or to convert their shares into voting shares that can be tendered to the takeover bid.

Coinsurance effect Refers to the fact that the merger of two firms decreases the probability of default on either's debt.

Collateral Assets that are pledged as security for payment of debt.

Collateral trust bond A bond secured by a pledge of common stock held by the corporation.

Collection float An increase in book cash with no immediate change in bank cash, generated by cheques deposited by the firm that have not cleared.

Collection policy Procedures followed by a firm in attempting to collect accounts receivable.

Commercial draft Demand for payment.

Commercial paper Short-term, unsecured promissory notes issued by corporations with a high credit standing. Their maturity ranges up to 270 days.

Common equity Book value.

Common stock Equity claims held by the "residual owners" of the firm, who are the last to receive any distribution of earnings or assets.

Compensating balance Deposit that the firm keeps with the bank in a low-interest or non-interest-bearing account to compensate banks for bank loans or services.

Competitive offer Method of selecting an investment banker for a new issue by offering the securities to the underwriter bidding highest.

Composition Voluntary arrangement to restructure a firm's debt, under which payment is reduced.

Compounding Process of reinvesting each interest payment to earn more interest. Compounding is based on the idea that interest itself becomes principal and therefore also earns interest in subsequent periods.

Compound interest Interest that is earned both on the initial principal and on interest earned on the initial principal in previous periods. The interest earned in one period becomes in effect part of the principal in a following period.

Compound value Value of a sum after investing it over one or more periods. Also called future value.

Concentration banking The use of geographically dispersed collection centres to speed up the collection of accounts receivable.

Conditional sales contract An arrangement whereby the firm retains legal ownership of the goods until the customer has completed payment.

Conflict between bondholders and shareholders These two groups may have interests in the corporation that conflict. Sources of conflict include dividends, dilution, distortion of investment, and underinvestment. Protective covenants work to resolve these conflicts.

Conglomerate acquisition Acquisition in which the acquired firm and the acquiring firm are not related, unlike a horizontal or vertical acquisition.

Consol A bond that carries a promise to pay a coupon forever; it has no final maturity date and therefore never matures.

Consolidation A merger in which an entirely new firm is created.

Consumer credit Credit granted to consumers. Trade credit is credit granted to other firms.

Contingent claim Claim whose value is directly dependent on, or is contingent on, the value of its underlying assets. For example, the debt and equity securities issued by a firm derive their value from the total value of the firm.

Continuous compounding Interest compounded continuously, every instant, rather than at fixed intervals.

Contributed surplus Refers to amounts of directly contributed equity capital in excess of par value.

Contribution margin Amount that each additional product, such as a jet engine, contributes to after-tax profit of the whole project: (Sale price − Variable cost) × $(1 − T_c)$, where T_c is the corporate tax rate.

Control block An interest controlling 50 percent of outstanding votes plus one; thereby it may decide the fate of the firm.

Conversion premium Difference between the conversion price and the current share price divided by the current share price.

Conversion price The amount of par value exchangeable for one share of common stock. This term really refers to the share price and means the dollar amount of the bond's par value that is exchangeable for one share of stock.

Conversion ratio The number of shares per $1,000 bond (or debenture) that a bondholder would receive if the bond were converted into shares of stock.

Conversion value What a convertible bond would be worth if it were immediately converted into the common stock at the current price.

Convertible bond A bond that may be converted into another form of security, typically common stock, at the option of the holder at a specified price for a specified period of time.

Corporation Form of business organization that is created as a distinct "legal person" composed of one or more actual individuals or legal entities. Primary advantages of a corporation include limited liability, ease of ownership transfer, and perpetual succession.

Correlation A standardized statistical measure of the dependence of two random variables. It is defined as the covariance divided by the standard deviations of two variables.

Cost of equity The required return on the company's common stock in capital markets. It is also called the equityholders' required rate of return because it is what equityholders can expect to obtain in a capital market. It is a cost from a firm's perspective.

Coupon The stated interest on a debt instrument.

Covariance A statistical measure of the degree to which random variables move together.

Covenant A written agreement or promise usually under seal between two or more parties especially for the performance of a particular action.

CRA Canada Revenue Agency.

Credit analysis The process of determining whether a credit applicant meets the firm's standards and what amount of credit the applicant should receive.

Credit instrument Device by which a firm offers credit, such as an invoice, a promissory note, or a conditional sales contract.

Creditor Person or institution that holds the debt issued by a firm or individual.

Credit periods Time allowed a credit purchaser to remit the full payment for credit purchases.

Credit scoring Determining the probability of default when granting customers credit.

Cross rate The exchange rate between two foreign currencies, neither of which is generally the Canadian dollar.

Crown jewels An anti-takeover tactic in which major assets—the crown jewels—are sold by a firm when faced with a takeover threat.

Cum dividend With dividend.

Cumulative abnormal return (CAR) Sum of differences between the expected return on a stock and the actual return that comes from the release of news to the market.

Cumulative dividend Dividend on preferred stock that takes priority over dividend payments on common stock. Dividends may not be paid on the common stock until all past dividends on the preferred stock have been paid.

Cumulative probability The probability that a drawing from the standardized normal distribution will be below a particular value.

Cumulative voting A procedure whereby a shareholder may cast all of his or her votes for one member of the board of directors.

Currency swaps These are sometimes called FX swaps; and are swaps of obligations to pay cash flows in one currency for obligations to pay in another currency.

Current asset Asset that is in the form of cash or that is expected to be converted into cash in the next 12 months, such as inventory.

Current liability Obligation that is expected to require cash payment within one year or the operating period.

Current ratio Total current assets divided by total current liabilities. Used to measure short-term solvency of a firm.

Date of payment Date that dividend cheques are mailed.

Date of record Date on which holders of record in a firm's stock ledger are designated as the recipients of either dividends or stock rights.

Dates convention Treating cash flows as being received on exact dates—date 0, date 1, and so forth—as opposed to the end-of-year convention.

Days in receivables Average collection period.

Days sales outstanding Average collection period.

Dealer market A market in which traders specializing in particular commodities buy and sell assets for their own account. The OTC market is an example.

Debenture An unsecured bond, usually with maturity of 15 years or more. A debt obligation backed by the general credit of the issuing corporation.

Debit card Point-of-sale systems use debit cards to transfer funds directly from a customer's bank account to a retailer's.

Debt Loan agreement that is a liability of the firm. An obligation to repay a specified amount at a particular time.

Debt capacity Ability to borrow. The amount a firm can borrow up to the point where the firm value no longer increases.

Debt displacement The amount of borrowing that leasing displaces. Firms that do a lot of leasing will be forced to cut back on borrowing.

Debt ratio Total debt divided by total assets.

Debt service Interest payments plus repayments of principal to creditors, that is, retirement of debt.

Decision tree A graphical representation of alternative sequential decisions and the possible outcomes of those decisions.

Declaration date Date on which the board of directors passes a resolution to pay a dividend of a specified amount to all qualified holders of record on a specified date.

Dedicated capital Total par value (number of shares issued multiplied by the par value of each share). Also called dedicated value.

Deed of trust See *Indenture.*

Deep-discount bond A bond issued with a very low coupon or no coupon and selling at a price far below par value. When the bond has no coupon, it is also called a pure-discount or original-issue-discount bond.

De facto Existing in actual fact although not by official recognition.

Default risk The chance that interest or principal will not be paid on the due date and in the promised amount.

Defeasance A debt-restructuring tool that enables a firm to remove debt from its balance sheet by establishing an irrevocable trust that will generate future cash flows sufficient to service the decreased debt.

Deferred call A provision that prohibits the company from calling the bond before a certain date. During this period the bond is said to be call protected.

Deferred nominal life annuity A monthly fixed-dollar payment beginning at retirement age. It is nominal because the payment is fixed in dollar amount at any particular time, up to and including retirement.

Deferred taxes Non-cash expense.

Deficit The amount by which a sum of money is less than the required amount; an excess of liabilities over assets, of losses over profits, or of expenditure over income.

Deliverable instrument The asset in a forward contract that will be delivered in the future at an agreed-upon price.

Denomination Face value or principal of a bond.

Depreciation A non-cash expense, such as the cost of plant or equipment, charged against earnings to write off the cost of an asset during its estimated useful life.

Depreciation tax shield The depreciation deduction multiplied by the tax rate.

Dilution Loss in existing shareholders' value. There are several kinds of dilution: (1) dilution of ownership, (2) dilution of market value, and (3) dilution of book value and earnings, as with warrants and convertible issues. Firms with significant amounts of warrants or convertible issues outstanding are required to report earnings on a "fully diluted" basis.

Direct lease Lease under which a lessor buys equipment from a manufacturer and leases it to a lessee.

Dirty Price The actual price paid for a bond, which includes accrued interest.

Disbursement float A decrease in book cash but no immediate change in bank cash, generated by cheques written by the firm.

Discount If a bond is selling below its face value, it is said to sell at a discount.

Discounted payback period rule An investment decision rule in which the cash flows are discounted at an interest rate and the payback rule is applied on these discounted cash flows.

Discounting Calculating the present value of a future amount. The process is the opposite of compounding.

Discount rate Rate used to calculate the present value of future cash flows.

Distribution A type of dividend paid by a firm to its owners from sources other than current or accumulated retained earnings.

Diversifiable (unique) (unsystematic) risk A risk that specifically affects a single asset or a small group of assets.

Diversification Process of combining assets so that the portfolio is always less risky than any one of the individual assets.

Dividend Payment made by a firm to its owners, either in cash or on stock. Also called the "income component" on the return of an investment in stock.

Dividend capture Under this strategy, portfolio managers purchase high-grade preferred stock or blue chip common stock just prior to a dividend payment. They hold the stock only long enough to receive the dividend.

Dividend growth model A model wherein dividends are assumed to be at a constant rate in perpetuity.

Dividend payout Amount of cash paid to shareholders expressed as a percentage of earnings per share.

Dividend payout ratio Cash dividends divided by net income.

Dividends per share Amount of cash paid to shareholders expressed as dollars per share.

Dividend yield Dividends per share of common stock divided by market price per share.

Double-declining balance depreciation Method of accelerated depreciation.

DuPont system of financial control Highlights the fact that return on assets (ROA) can be expressed in terms of the profit margin and asset turnover.

Duration The weighted average time of an asset's cash flows. The weights are determined by present value factors.

EAC See *Equivalent annual cost.*

EBIT Earnings before interest and taxes.

Economic assumptions Economic environment in which the firm expects to reside over the life of the financial plan.

Effective annual interest rate The interest rate as if it were compounded once per time period rather than several times per period.

Efficient market hypothesis (EMH) The prices of securities fully reflect available information. Investors buying bonds and stocks in an efficient market should expect to obtain an equilibrium rate of return. Firms should expect to receive the "fair" value (present value) for the securities they sell.

Efficient set Graph representing a set of portfolios that maximize expected return at each level of portfolio risk.

EMH See *Efficient market hypothesis.*

End-of-year convention Treating cash flows as if they occur at the end of a year (or, alternatively, at the end of a period), as opposed to the dates convention. Under the end-of-year convention, the end of year 0 is the present, the end of year 1 occurs one period hence, and so on.

Equilibrium rate of interest The interest rate that clears the market. Also called market-clearing interest rate.

Equity Ownership interest of common and preferred shareholders in a corporation. Also, total assets minus total liabilities, or net worth.

Equity beta Systematic risk of a firm's stock decomposed into contributions of risk from assets and financial leverage.

Equity kicker Used to refer to warrants because they usually are issued in combination with privately placed bonds.

Equity share Ownership interest.

Equivalent annual cost (EAC) The net present value of cost divided by an annuity factor that has the same life as the investment.

Equivalent loan The amount of the loan that makes leasing equivalent to buying with debt financing in terms of debt capacity reduction.

Erosion Cash flow amount transferred to a new project from customers and sales of other products of the firm.

Euro See *European currency unit.*

Eurobanks Banks that make loans and accept deposits in foreign currencies.

Eurobonds International bonds sold primarily in countries other than the country in whose currency the issue is denominated.

Eurocurrency Money deposited in a financial centre outside of the country whose currency is involved.

Eurodollar A dollar deposited in a bank outside Canada.

Eurodollar CD Deposit of dollars with foreign banks.

European currency unit (euro) An index of foreign exchange originally consisting of about 10 European currencies. Devised in 1979 and implemented in January 2002, it serves as a monetary unit for the European Monetary System (EMS). As of January 2008, the euro had replaced 13 domestic currencies, with Malta and Cyprus scheduled to convert.

European option An option contract that may be exercised only on the expiration date. An American option may be exercised anytime up to the expiration date.

Event study A statistical study that examines how the release of information affects prices at a particular time.

Exchange rate Price of one country's currency for another's.

Exchange traded funds (ETFs) Trusts that track a market index such as the Standard and Poor's 500, the S&P/TSX 60, or the Nekkei.

Exclusionary self-tender The firm makes a tender offer for a given amount of its own stock while excluding targeted shareholders.

Ex-dividend date Date four business days before the date of record for a security. An individual purchasing stock before its ex-dividend date will receive the current dividend.

Exercise price Price at which the holder of an option can buy (in the case of a call option) or sell (in the case of a put option) the underlying stock. Also called the strike price.

Exercising the option The act of buying or selling the underlying asset via the option contract.

Exotics The complicated blends of derivatives, swaps, options, forwards, and futures that often produce surprising results for their buyers.

Expectations hypothesis (of interest rates) Theory that forward interest rates are unbiased estimates of expected future interest rates.

Expected return Average of possible returns weighted by their probability.

Expiration date Maturity date of an option.

Export Development Canada (EDC) Federal crown corporation that promotes Canadian exports by making loans to foreign purchasers.

Ex-rights or ex-dividend Phrases used to indicate that a stock is selling without a recently declared right or dividend. The ex-rights or ex-dividend date is generally four business days before the date of record.

Extension Voluntary arrangements to restructure a firm's debt, under which the payment date is postponed.

Extinguish Retire or pay off debt.

Face value The value of a bond that appears on its face. Also referred to as par value or principal.

Factor A financial institution that buys a firm's accounts receivable and collects the debt.

Factoring Sale of a firm's accounts receivable to a financial institution known as a factor.

Factor model A model in which each stock's return is generated by common factors, called the systematic sources of risk.

Fair market value Amount at which common stock would change hands between a willing buyer and a willing seller, both having knowledge of the relevant facts. Also called market price.

Feasible set Opportunity set.

Field warehouse financing A form of inventory loan in which a public warehouse company acts as a control agent to supervise the inventory for the lender.

Financial distress Events preceding and including bankruptcy, such as violation of loan contracts.

Financial distress costs Legal and administrative costs of liquidation or reorganization (direct costs); an impaired ability to do business and an incentive toward selfish strategies such as taking large risks, underinvesting, and milking the property (indirect costs).

Financial intermediaries Institutions that provide the market function of matching borrowers and lenders or traders. Financial institutions may be categorized as depository, contractual savings, and investment-type.

Financial lease Long-term non-cancellable lease, generally requiring the lessee to pay all maintenance costs.

Financial leverage Extent to which a firm relies on debt. Financial leverage is measured by the ratio of long-term debt to long-term debt plus equity.

Financial markets Markets that deal with cash flows over time, where the savings of lenders are allocated to the financing needs of borrowers.

Financial requirements In the financial plan, financing arrangements that are necessary to meet the overall corporate objective.

Financial risk The additional risk that the firm's shareholders bear when the firm is financed with debt as well as equity.

Firm-commitment underwriting An underwriting in which an investment banking firm commits to buy the entire issue and assumes all financial responsibility for any unsold shares.

Firm's net value of debt Total firm value minus value of debt.

First principle of investment decision making An investment project is worth undertaking only if it increases the range of choices in the financial markets. To do this, it must be at least as desirable as what is available to shareholders in the financial markets.

Fixed asset Long-lived property owned by a firm that is used by a firm in the production of its income. Tangible fixed assets include real estate, plant, and equipment. Intangible fixed assets include patents, trademarks, and customer recognition.

Fixed cost A cost that is fixed in total for a given period of time and for given volume levels. It is not dependent on the amount of goods or services produced during the period.

Fixed-dollar obligations Conventional bonds for which the coupon rate is set as a fixed percentage of the par value.

Flat benefit formula Method used to determine a participant's benefits in a defined benefit plan by multiplying months of service by a flat monthly benefit.

Float The difference between bank cash and book cash. Float represents the net effect of cheques in the process of collection, or clearing. Positive float means the firm's bank cash is greater than its book cash until the cheques' presentation. Cheques written by the firm generate disbursement float, causing an immediate decrease in book cash but no change in bank cash. In neutral float position, bank cash equals book cash. Cheques written by the firm represent collection float, which increases book cash immediately but does not immediately change bank cash. The sum of disbursement float and collection float is net float.

Floaters Floating-rate bonds.

Floating-rate bond A debt obligation with an adjustable coupon payment.

Flow to equity (FTE) An alternative budgeting approach. A project's cash flow to equityholders (of the levered firm) is discounted at the cost of equity capital.

Force conversion If the conversion value of a convertible is greater than the call price, the call can be used to force conversion.

Foreign bond An international bond issued by foreign borrowers in another nation's capital market and traditionally denominated in that nation's currency.

Foreign exchange market Market in which arrangements are made today for future exchange of major currencies; used to hedge against major swings in foreign exchange rates.

Forward contract An arrangement calling for future delivery of an asset at an agreed-upon price.

Forward exchange rate A future day's exchange rate between two major currencies.

Forward trades Agreements to buy or sell based on exchange rates established today for settlement in the future.

Free cash flow Cash that the firm is free to distribute to creditors and shareholders because it is not needed for working capital or fixed asset investment.

Frequency distribution The organization of data to show how often certain values or ranges of values occur.

Fully diluted See *Dilution.*

Funded debt Long-term debt.

Futures contract Obliges traders to purchase or sell an asset at an agreed-upon price on a specified future date. The long position is held by the trader who commits to purchase. The short position is held by the trader who commits to sell. Futures differ from forward contracts in their standardization, exchange trading, margin requirements, and daily settling (marking to market).

Future value Value of a sum after investing it over one or more periods. Also called compound value.

GAAP See *Generally Accepted Accounting Principles.*

General cash offer A public issue of a security that is sold to all interested investors, rather than only to existing shareholders.

General partnership Form of business organization in which all partners agree to provide some portion of the work and cash and to share profits and losses. Each partner is liable for the debts of the partnership.

Generally Accepted Accounting Principles (GAAP) A common set of accounting concepts, standards, and procedures by which financial statements are prepared.

Geometric mean Annualized holding-period return.

Gilts British and Irish government securities.

Going-private transaction Publicly owned stock in a firm is replaced with complete equity ownership by a private group. The shares are delisted from stock exchanges and can no longer be purchased in the open market.

Golden parachute Compensation paid to top-level management by a target firm if a takeover occurs.

Goodwill The excess of the purchase price over the sum of the fair market values of the individual assets acquired.

Greenmail Payments to potential bidders to cease unfriendly takeover attempts.

Green shoe provision A contract provision that gives the underwriter the option to purchase additional shares at the offering price to cover overallotments.

Growing annuity A finite number of growing annual cash flows.

Growing perpetuity A constant stream of cash flows without end that is expected to rise indefinitely. For example, cash flows to the landlord of an apartment building might be expected to rise a certain percentage each year.

Growth opportunity Opportunity to invest in profitable projects.

Hedging Taking a position in two or more securities that are negatively correlated (taking opposite trading positions) to reduce risk.

High-yield bond Junk bond.

Holder-of-record date The date on which holders of record in a firm's stock ledger are designated as the recipients of either dividends or stock rights. Also called date of record.

Holding period Length of time that an individual holds a security.

Holding-period return The rate of return over a given period.

Homemade dividends An individual investor can undo corporate dividend policy by reinvesting excess dividends or selling off shares of stock to receive a desired cash flow.

Homemade leverage Idea that as long as individuals borrow (and lend) on the same terms as the firm, they can duplicate the effects of corporate leverage on their own. Thus, if levered firms are priced too high, rational investors will simply borrow on personal accounts to buy shares in unlevered firms.

Homogeneous expectations Idea that all individuals have the same beliefs concerning future investments, profits, and dividends.

Horizontal acquisition Merger between two companies producing similar goods or services.

Idiosyncratic risk An unsystematic risk.

Immunized Immune to interest-rate risk.

Income bonds Bonds on which the payment of income is contingent on sufficient earnings. Income bonds are commonly used during the reorganization of a failed or failing business.

Income statement Financial report that summarizes a firm's performance over a specified time period.

Incremental cash flow Difference between the firm's cash flow with and without a project.

Incremental IRR IRR on the incremental investment from choosing a large project instead of a smaller project.

Indenture Written agreement between the corporate debt issuer and the lender, setting forth maturity date, interest rate, and other terms.

Independent project A project whose acceptance or rejection is independent of the acceptance or rejection of other projects.

Inflation An increase in the amount of money in circulation, resulting in a fall in its value and rise in prices.

Inflation-escalator clause A clause in a contract providing for increases or decreases in inflation based on fluctuations in the cost of living, production costs, etc.

Informational efficiency An efficient capital market in which stock prices fully reflect available information.

Information-content effect The rise in the stock price following the dividend signal.

In-house processing float Refers to the time it takes the receiver of a cheque to process the payment and deposit it in a bank for collection.

Initial public offering (IPO) The original sale of a company's securities to the public. Also called an unseasoned new issue.

Inside information Nonpublic knowledge about a corporation possessed by people in special positions inside a firm.

Instruments Financial securities, such as money market instruments or capital market instruments.

Interest coverage ratio Earnings before interest and taxes divided by interest expense. Used to measure a firm's ability to pay interest.

Interest on interest Interest earned on reinvestment of each interest payment on money invested.

Interest rate The price paid for borrowing money. It is the rate of exchange of present consumption for future consumption, or the price of current dollars in terms of future dollars.

Interest rate on debt The firm's cost of debt capital. Also called return on the debt.

Interest rate parity theorem The interest rate differential between two countries will be equal to the difference between the forward exchange rate and the spot exchange rate.

Interest rate risk The chance that a change in the interest rate will result in a change in the value of a security.

Interest rate swap A swap that would exchange its fixed obligation for an agreement to pay a floating rate.

Interest subsidy A firm's deduction of the interest payments on its debt from its earnings before it calculates its tax bill under current tax law.

Internal financing Net income plus depreciation minus dividends. Internal financing comes from internally generated cash flow.

Internal rate of return (IRR) A discount rate at which the net present value of an investment is zero. The IRR is a method of evaluating capital expenditure proposals.

In the money Describes an option whose exercise would produce profits. Out of the money describes an option whose exercise would not be profitable.

Inventory A current asset, composed of raw materials to be used in production, work in process, and finished goods.

Inventory loan A secured short-term loan to purchase inventory. The three basic forms are a blanket inventory lien, a trust receipt, and field warehouse financing.

Inventory turnover ratio Ratio of annual sales to average inventory that measures how quickly inventory is produced and sold.

Investment bankers Financial intermediaries who perform a variety of services, including aiding in the sale of securities, facilitating mergers and other corporate reorganizations, acting as brokers to both individual and institutional clients, and trading for their own accounts.

Investment grade bond Debt that is rated BBB and above by Standard & Poor's or Baa and above by Moody's.

Invoice Bill written by a seller of goods or services and submitted to the purchaser.

IPO See *Initial public offering.*

IRR See *Internal rate of return.*

Irrelevance result The Modigliani–Miller theorem that a firm's capital structure is irrelevant to the firm's value.

Junk bond A speculative grade bond, rated Ba or lower by Moody's, or BB or lower by Standard & Poor's, or an unrated bond. Also called a high-yield or low-grade bond.

Law of one price (LOP) A commodity will cost the same regardless of what currency is used to purchase it.

LBO See *Leveraged buyout.*

Lease A contractual arrangement to grant the use of specific fixed assets for a specified time in exchange for payment, usually in the form of rent. An operating lease is generally a short-term cancellable arrangement, whereas a financial, or capital, lease is a long-term non-cancellable agreement.

Ledger cash A firm's cash balance as reported in its financial statements. Also called book cash.

Legal bankruptcy A legal proceeding for liquidating or reorganizing a business.

Lend To provide money temporarily on the condition that it or its equivalent will be returned, often with an interest fee.

Lessee One who receives the use of assets under a lease.

Lessor One who conveys the use of assets under a lease.

Letter of comment A communication to the firm from the U.S. Securities and Exchange Commission or the Ontario Securities Commission that suggests changes to a registration statement.

Letter of credit A common arrangement in international finance, where the bank issuing the letter promises to make a loan if certain conditions are met.

Level-coupon bond Bond with a stream of coupon payments that are the same throughout the life of the bond.

Leveraged buyout (LBO) Takeover of a company by using borrowed funds, usually by a group including some member of existing management.

Leveraged equity Stock in a firm that relies on financial leverage. Holders of leveraged equity face the benefits and costs of using debt.

Leveraged lease Tax-oriented leasing arrangement that involves one or more third-party lenders.

Liabilities Debts of the firm in the form of financial claims on a firm's assets.

LIBOR See *London Interbank Offered Rate.*

Limited-liability instrument A security, such as a call option, in which all the holder can lose is the initial amount put into it.

Limited partnership Form of business organization that permits the liability of some partners to be limited by the amount of cash contributed to the partnership.

Line of credit A non-committed line of credit is an informal agreement that allows firms to borrow up to a previously specified limit without going through the normal paperwork. A committed line of credit is a formal legal arrangement and usually involves a commitment fee paid by the firm to the bank.

Lintner's observations John Lintner's work (1956) suggested that dividend policy is related to a target level of dividends and the speed of adjustment of change in dividends.

Liquidating dividend Payment by a firm to its owners from capital rather than from earnings.

Liquidation Termination of the firm as a going concern. Liquidation involves selling the assets of the firm for salvage value. The proceeds, net of transaction costs, are distributed to creditors in order of established priority.

Liquidity Refers to the ease and quickness of converting assets to cash. Also called marketability.

Liquidity preference hypothesis Theory that the forward rate exceeds expected future interest rates.

Lockbox Post office box set up to intercept accounts receivable payments. Lockboxes are the most widely used device to speed up collection of cash.

London Interbank Offered Rate (LIBOR) Rate the most creditworthy banks charge one another for large loans of Eurodollars overnight in the London market.

Long hedge Protecting the future cost of a purchase by purchasing a futures contract to protect against changes in the price of an asset.

Long run A period of time in which all costs are variable.

Long-term debt An obligation having a maturity of more than one year from the date it was issued. Also called funded debt.

Low-grade bond Junk bond.

Mail float Refers to the part of the collection and disbursement process where cheques are trapped in the postal system.

Make a market The obligation of a specialist to offer to buy and sell shares of assigned stocks. It is assumed that this makes the market liquid because the specialist assumes the role of a buyer for investors if they wish to sell, and assumes the role of a seller if they wish to buy.

Making delivery Refers to the seller's actually turning over to the buyer the asset agreed upon in a forward contract.

Marked to the market The daily settlement of obligations on futures positions.

Marketability Refers to the ease and quickness of converting an asset to cash. Also called liquidity.

Market clearing Total demand for loans by borrowers equals total supply of loans from lenders. The market clears at the equilibrium rate of interest.

Marketed claims Claims that can be bought and sold in financial markets, such as those of shareholders and bondholders.

Market model A one-factor model for returns where the index that is used for the factor is an index of the returns on the whole market.

Market portfolio In concept, a value-weighted index of all securities. In practice, it is an index, such as the S&P 500, that describes the return of the entire value of the stock market, or at least the stocks that make up the index. A market portfolio represents the average investor's return.

Market price The current amount at which a security is trading in a market.

Market risk Systematic risk. This term emphasizes the fact that systematic risk influences to some extent all assets in the market.

Market-to-book (M/B) ratio Market price per share of common stock divided by book value per share.

Market value The price at which willing buyers and sellers trade a firm's assets.

Maturity date The date on which the last payment on a bond is due.

Mean The average of the observations in a frequency distribution.

Merger Combination of two or more companies.

Minimum variance portfolio The portfolio of risky assets with the lowest possible variance. By definition, this portfolio must also have the lowest possible standard deviation.

MM Proposition I A proposition of Modigliani and Miller (MM) stating that a firm cannot change the total value of its outstanding securities by changing its capital structure proportions. Also called an irrelevance result.

MM Proposition I (corporate taxes) A proposition of Modigliani and Miller (MM) stating that by raising the debt–equity ratio, a firm can lower its taxes and thereby increase its total value. Capital structure does matter.

MM Proposition II A proposition of Modigliani and Miller (MM) stating that the cost of equity is a linear function of the firm's debt-equity ratio.

Money markets Financial markets for debt securities that pay off in the short term (usually less than one year).

Money purchase plan A defined benefit contribution plan in which the participant contributes some part and the firm contributes at the same or a different rate. Also called an individual account plan.

Mortgage securities A debt obligation secured by a mortgage on the real property of the borrower.

Multiple rates of return More than one rate of return from the same project that make the net present value of the project equal to zero. This situation arises when the IRR method is used for a project in which negative cash flows follow positive ones.

Multiples Another name for price-earnings ratios.

Mutually exclusive investments Investment decisions in which the acceptance of a project precludes the acceptance of one or more alternative projects.

Negative covenant Part of the indenture or loan agreement that limits or prohibits actions that the company may take.

Negotiated offer The issuing firm negotiates a deal with one underwriter to offer a new issue rather than taking competitive bidding.

Net cash balance Beginning cash balance plus cash receipts minus cash disbursements.

Net float Sum of disbursement float and collection float.

Net investment Gross, or total, investment minus depreciation.

Net operating losses (NOL) Losses that a firm can take advantage of to reduce taxes.

Net present value (NPV) rule The present value of future cash returns, discounted at the appropriate market interest rate, minus the present value of the cost of the investment.

Netting out To get or bring in as a net; to clear as profit.

Net working capital Current assets minus current liabilities.

Neutral flat position See *Float*.

Nominal cash flow A cash flow expressed in nominal terms if the actual dollars to be received (or paid out) are given.

Nominal interest rate Interest rate unadjusted for inflation.

Non-cash items Expenses against revenue that do not directly affect cash flow, such as depreciation and deferred taxes.

Nonmarketed claims Claims that cannot be easily bought and sold in the financial markets, such as those of the government and litigants in lawsuits.

Normal annuity form The manner in which retirement benefits are paid out.

Normal distribution Symmetric bell-shaped frequency distribution that can be defined by its mean and standard deviation.

Note Unsecured debt, usually with maturity of less than 15 years.

NPV Net present value.

NPVGO model A model valuing the firm in which net present value of new investment opportunities is explicitly examined. NPVGO stands for net present value of growth opportunities.

Odd lot Stock trading unit of less than 100 shares.

Off-balance-sheet financing Financing that is not shown as a liability on a company's balance sheet.

One-factor APT A special case of the arbitrage pricing theory that is derived from the one-factor model by using diversification and arbitrage. It shows the expected return on any risky asset is a linear function of a single factor. The CAPM can be expressed as one-factor APT in which a single factor is the market portfolio.

Open account A credit account for which the only formal instrument of credit is the invoice.

Operating activities Sequence of events and decisions that create the firm's cash inflows and cash outflows. These activities include buying and paying for raw materials, manufacturing and selling a product, and collecting cash.

Operating cash flow Earnings before interest and depreciation minus taxes. It measures the cash generated from operations, not counting capital spending or working capital requirements.

Operating cycle The time interval between the arrival of inventory stock and the date when cash is collected from receivables.

Operating lease Type of lease in which the period of contract is less than the life of the equipment and the lessor pays all maintenance and servicing costs.

Operating leverage The degree to which a company's costs of operation are fixed as opposed to variable. A firm with high operating costs, when compared to a firm with a low operating leverage, has relatively larger changes in EBIT with respect to a change in the sales revenue.

Operating loan The most common way to finance a temporary cash deficit. This is an agreement under which a firm is authorized to borrow up to a specified amount for a given period, usually one year (much like a credit card).

Operational efficiency Measures the ease (or difficulty) with which capital markets operate.

Opportunity cost Most valuable alternative that is given up. The rate of return used in NPV computation is an opportunity interest rate.

Opportunity (feasible) set The possible expected return; standard deviation pairs of all portfolios that can be constructed from a given set of assets. Also called a feasible set.

Option A right—but not an obligation—to buy or sell underlying assets at a fixed price during a specified time period.

Original-issue-discount bond A bond issued with a discount from par value. Also called a deep-discount or pure-discount bond.

OSC Ontario Securities Commission.

Out of the money Describes an option whose exercise would not be profitable. In the money describes an option whose exercise would produce profits.

Oversubscribed issue Investors are not able to buy all the shares they want, so underwriters must allocate the shares among investors. This occurs when a new issue is underpriced.

Oversubscription privilege Allows shareholders to purchase unsubscribed shares in a rights offering at the subscription price.

Over-the-counter (OTC) market An informal network of brokers and dealers who negotiate sales of securities (not a formal exchange).

Partnership Form of business organization in which two or more co-owners form a business. In a general partnership each partner is liable for the debts of the partnership. Limited partnership permits some partners to have limited liability.

Par value The nominal or face value of stocks or bonds. For stock, it is a relatively unimportant value except for bookkeeping purposes.

Payback period rule An investment decision rule that states that all investment projects with payback periods equal to or less than a particular cutoff period are accepted, and all of those that pay off in more than the particular cutoff period are rejected. The payback period is the number of years required for a firm to recover its initial investment required by a project from the cash flow it generates.

Payments pattern Describes the lagged collection pattern of receivables (for instance the probability that a 72-day-old account will still be unpaid when it is 73 days old).

Payout ratio Proportion of net income paid out in cash dividends.

Pecking order Hierarchy of long-term financing strategies, in which using internally generated cash is at the top and issuing new equity is at the bottom.

Perfectly competitive financial markets Markets in which no trader has power to change the price of goods or services. Perfect markets are characterized by the following conditions: (1) Trading is costless, and access to the financial markets is free. (2) Information about borrowing and lending opportunities is freely available. (3) There are many traders, and no single trader can have a significant impact on market prices.

Perfect markets See *Perfectly competitive financial markets.*

Performance shares Shares of stock given to managers on the basis of performance as measured by earnings per share and similar criteria—a control device used by shareholders to tie management to the self-interest of shareholders.

Perpetuity A constant stream of cash flows without end. A British consol is an example.

Perquisites Management amenities such as a big office, a company car, or expense-account meals. "Perks" are agency costs of equity, because managers of the firm are agents of the shareholders.

Pie model A model of a firm's debt–equity ratio. It graphically depicts slices of "pie" that represent the value of the firm in the capital markets.

Plowback ratio Retained earnings divided by net income. Also called retention ratio.

Plug A variable that handles financial slack in the financial plan.

Poison pill Strategy by a takeover target company to make a stock less appealing to a company that wishes to acquire it. Political risk Changes in value that arise as a consequence to political actions.

Pooling of interests Accounting method of reporting acquisitions under which the balance sheets of the two companies are simply added together item by item.

Portfolio Combined holding of more than one stock, bond, real estate asset, or other asset by an investor.

Portfolio variance Weighted sum of the covariances and variances of the assets in a portfolio.

Positive covenant Part of the indenture or loan agreement that specifies an action that the company must abide by.

Positive float See *Float.*

Post Particular place on the floor of an exchange where transactions in stocks listed on the exchange occur.

Pre-emptive right The right to share proportionally in any new stock sold.

Preferred shares A type of stock whose holders are given certain priority over common shareholders in the payment of dividends. Usually the dividend rate is fixed at the time of issue. Preferred shareholders normally do not receive voting rights.

Premium If a bond is selling above its face value, it is said to sell at a premium.

Prepackaged bankruptcy A combination of private workout and legal bankruptcy. A private reorganization is prepackaged and then the firm files for formal bankruptcy.

Present value The value of a future cash stream discounted at the appropriate market interest rate.

Present value factor Factor used to calculate an estimate of the present value of an amount to be received in a future period.

Priced out Means the market has already incorporated information, such as a low dividend, into the price of a stock.

Price takers Individuals who respond to rates and prices by acting as if they have no influence on them.

Price-to-earnings (P/E) ratio Current market price of common stock divided by current annual earnings per share.

Primary market Where new issues of securities are offered to the public.

Principal The value of a bond that must be repaid at maturity. Also called the face value or par value.

Principle of diversification Highly diversified portfolios will have negligible unsystematic risk. In other words, unsystematic risks disappear in portfolios, and only systematic risks survive.

Private placement The sale of a bond or other security directly to a limited number of investors.

Private workout Financial restructuring agreement that does not involve formal, legal bankruptcy.

Profitability index (PI) A method used to evaluate projects. It is the ratio of the present value of the future expected cash flows after initial investment divided by the amount of the initial investment.

Profit margin Profits divided by total operating revenue. The net profit margin (net income divided by total operating revenue) and the gross profit margin (earnings before interest and taxes divided by the total operating revenue) reflect the firm's ability to produce a good or service at a high or low cost.

Pro forma statements Projected income statements, balance sheets, and sources-and-uses statements for future years.

Promissory note Written promise to pay.

Prospectus The legal document that must be given to every investor who contemplates purchasing registered securities in an offering. It describes the details of the company and the particular offering.

Protective covenants Parts of the indenture or loan agreement that limit certain actions a company takes during the term of the loan to protect the lender's interest.

Proxy A grant of authority by the shareholder to transfer his or her voting rights to someone else.

Proxy contest Attempt to gain control of a firm by soliciting a sufficient number of shareholder votes to replace the existing management.

Public issue Sale of securities to the public.

Purchase accounting Method of reporting acquisitions requiring that the assets of the acquired firm be reported at their fair market value on the books of the acquiring firm.

Purchase method A method of accounting for acquisitions in which the assets of the acquired firm are reported at their fair market value in the financial statements of the acquiring firm, allowing for the creation of goodwill.

Purchasing power parity (PPP) Idea that the exchange rate adjusts to keep purchasing power constant among currencies.

Pure discount bonds Bonds that pay no coupons and only pay back face value at maturity. Also referred to as bullets and zeros.

Put–call parity The value of a call equals the value of buying the stock plus buying the put plus borrowing at the risk-free rate.

Put option The right to sell a specified number of shares of stock at a stated price on or before a specified time.

Put provision Gives holder of a floating-rate bond the right to redeem his or her note at par on the coupon payment date.

Q **ratio or Tobin's** *Q* **ratio** Market value of firm's assets divided by replacement value of firm's assets.

Quick assets Current assets minus inventories.

Quick ratio Quick assets (current assets minus inventories) divided by total current liabilities. Used to measure short-term solvency of a firm.

Random walk Theory that stock price changes from day to day are at random; the changes are independent of each other and have the same probability distribution.

Real cash flow A cash flow is expressed in real terms if the current, or date 0, purchasing power of the cash flow is given.

Real interest rate Interest rate expressed in terms of real goods; that is, the nominal interest rate minus the expected inflation rate.

Receivables turnover ratio Total operating revenues divided by average receivables. Used to measure how effectively a firm is managing its accounts receivable.

Red herring First document released by an underwriter of a new issue to prospective investors.

Refunding The process of replacing outstanding bonds, typically to issue new securities at a lower interest rate than those replaced.

Registration statement The registration that discloses all the pertinent information concerning the corporation that wants to make the offering. The statement is filed with the Securities and Exchange Commission.

Regular cash dividends Cash payments by a firm to its shareholders, usually four times a year.

Regular underwriting The purchase of securities from the issuing company by an investment banker for resale to the public.

Regulation A The securities regulation that exempts small public offerings (those valued at less than $1.5 million) from most registration requirements.

Relative purchasing power parity (RPPP) Idea that the rate of change in the price level of commodities in one country relative to the price level in another determines the rate of change of the exchange rate between the two countries' currencies.

Reorganization Financial restructuring of a failed firm. Both the firm's asset structure and its financial structure are changed to reflect their true value, and claims are settled.

Replacement-chain problem Idea that future replacement decisions must be taken into account in selecting among projects.

Replacement value Current cost of replacing the firm's assets.

Repurchase agreement (repos) Short-term, often overnight, sales of government securities with an agreement to repurchase the securities at a slightly higher price.

Repurchase of stock Device to pay cash to firm's shareholders that provides more preferable tax treatment for shareholders than dividends. Treasury stock is the name given to previously issued stock that has been repurchased by the firm.

Residual dividend approach An approach that suggests that a firm pay dividends if and only if acceptable investment opportunities for those funds are currently unavailable.

Residual losses Lost wealth of the shareholders due to divergent behaviour of the managers.

Residual value Usually refers to the value of a lessor's property at the time the lease expires.

Restrictive covenants Provisions that place constraints on the operations of borrowers, such as restrictions on working capital, fixed assets, future borrowing, and payment of dividends.

Retained earnings Earnings not paid out as dividends.

Retention ratio Retained earnings divided by net income. Also called plowback ratio.

Return Profit on capital investment or securities.

Return on assets (ROA) Income divided by average total assets.

Return on equity (ROE) Net income after interest and taxes divided by average common shareholders' equity.

Reverse split The procedure whereby the number of outstanding stock shares is reduced; for example, two outstanding shares are combined to create only one.

Rights offer An offering that gives a current shareholder the opportunity to maintain a proportionate interest in the company before the shares are offered to the public.

Risk averse A risk-averse investor will consider risky portfolios only if they provide compensation for risk via a risk premium.

Risk class A partition of the universal set of risk measures so that projects that are in the same risk class can be comparable.

Risk premium The excess return on the risky asset that is the difference between expected return on risky assets and the return on risk-free assets.

Round lot Common stock trading unit of 100 shares or multiples of 100 shares.

R squared (R^2) Square of the correlation coefficient proportion of the variability explained by the linear model.

Safe harbour lease A lease to transfer tax benefits of ownership (depreciation and debt tax shield) from the lessee, if the lessee could not use them, to a lessor that could.

Sale and lease-back An arrangement whereby a firm sells its existing assets to a financial company, which then leases them back to the firm. This is often done to generate cash.

Sales forecast A key input to the firm's financial planning process. External sales forecasts are based on historical experience, statistical analysis, and consideration of various macroeconomic factors; internal sales forecasts are obtained from internal sources.

Sales-type lease An arrangement whereby a firm leases its own equipment, such as IBM leasing its own computers, thereby competing with an independent leasing company.

Same-day value On concentrator accounts, the firm has immediate use of the funds even though it takes 24 hours for a cheque to clear in Canada.

S&P 500 Standard & Poor's Composite Index.

Scale enhancing Describes a project that is in the same risk class as the whole firm.

Scenario analysis Analysis of the effect of different scenarios on the project, with each scenario involving a confluence of factors.

Seasoned new issue A new issue of stock after the company's securities have previously been issued. A seasoned new issue of common stock can be made by using a cash offer or a rights offer.

SEC U.S. Securities and Exchange Commission.

Secondary markets Already-existing securities are bought and sold on the exchanges or in the over-the-counter market.

Security market line (SML) A straight line that shows the equilibrium relationship between systematic risk and expected rates of return for individual securities. According to the SML, the excess return on a risky asset is equal to the excess return on the market portfolio multiplied by the beta coefficient.

Security market plane (SMP) A plane that shows the equilibrium relationship between expected return and the beta coefficient of more than one factor.

Semistrong-form efficiency Theory that the market is efficient with respect to all publicly available information.

Seniority The order of repayment. In the event of bankruptcy, senior debt must be repaid before subordinated debt receives any payment.

Sensitivity analysis Analysis of the effect on the project when there is some change in critical variables such as sales and costs.

Separation principle The principle that portfolio choice can be separated into two independent tasks: (1) determination of the optimal risky portfolio, which is a purely technical problem, and (2) the personal choice of the best mix of the risky portfolio and the risk-free asset.

Separation theorem The value of an investment to an individual is not dependent on consumption preferences. All investors will want to accept or reject the same investment projects by using the NPV rule, regardless of personal preference.

Serial correlation Correlation between the current return on a security and the return on the same security over a later period.

Serial covariance The covariance between a variable and the lagged value of the variable; the same as autocovariance.

Set-of-contracts viewpoint View of the corporation as a set of contracting relationships among individuals who have conflicting objectives, such as shareholders and managers. The corporation is a legal contrivance that serves as the nexus for the contracting relationships.

Shareholder Holder of equity shares. The terms *shareholders* and *stockholders* usually refer to owners of common stock in a corporation.

Shareholders' books Set of books kept by firm management for its annual report that follows Canadian Institute of Chartered Accountants rules. The tax books follow the Canada Revenue Agency rules.

Shareholders' equity The residual claims that shareholders have against a firm's assets, calculated by subtracting total liabilities from total assets; also called net worth.

Share rights plan (SRP) Provisions allowing existing shareholders to purchase stock at some fixed price if an outside takeover bid occurs, designed to discourage hostile takeover attempts.

Shelf life Number of days it takes to get goods purchased and sold, or days in inventory.

Shelf registration An SEC procedure that allows a firm to file a master registration statement summarizing planned financing for a two-year period, and then file short statements when the firm wishes to sell any of the approved master statement securities during the period.

Shirking The tendency to do less work when the return is smaller. Owners may have more incentive to shirk if they issue equity as opposed to debt, because they retain less ownership interest in the company and therefore may receive a smaller return. Thus, shirking is considered an agency cost of equity.

Shortage costs Costs that fall with increases in the level of investment in current assets.

Short hedge Protecting the value of an asset held by selling a futures contract.

Short run That period of time in which certain equipment, resources, and commitments of them are fixed.

Short-run operating activities Events and decisions concerning the short-term finance of a firm, such as how much inventory to order and whether to offer cash terms or credit terms to customers.

Short sale Sale of a security that an investor doesn't own but has instead borrowed.

Short-term debt An obligation having a maturity of one year or less from the date it was issued. Also called unfunded debt.

Short-term tax exempts Short-term securities issued by provinces, territories, municipalities, local housing agencies, and urban renewal agencies.

Side effects Effects of a proposed project on other parts of the firm.

Sight draft A commercial draft demanding immediate payment.

Signalling approach Approach to the determination of optimal capital structure asserting that insiders in a firm have information that the market does not; therefore the choice of capital structure by insiders can signal information to outsiders and change the value of the firm. This theory is also called the asymmetric information approach.

Simple interest Interest calculated by considering only the original principal amount.

Sinking fund An account managed by the bond trustee for the purpose of repaying the bonds.

Smart card Card with a built-in chip that carries a cash balance. A bank customer loads cash onto the card at a bank machine or by swiping it through a device connected to a home computer. When the customer goes shopping, funds are transferred to a merchant without having to go online to a central computer.

SML See *Security market line.*

SMP See *Security market plane.*

Socially responsible investing Funds that screen and select securities based on social or environmental criteria.

Sole proprietorship A business owned by a single individual. The sole proprietorship pays no corporate income tax but has unlimited liability for business debts and obligations.

Spot exchange rate Exchange rate between two currencies for immediate delivery.

Spot interest rate Interest rate fixed today on a loan that is made today.

Spot trades Agreements today on the exchange rates, for settlement in two days.

Spread The gap between the interest rate a bank pays on deposits and the interest rate it charges on loans.

Spreadsheet A computer program that organizes numerical data into rows and columns on a terminal screen, for calculating and making adjustments based on new data.

Spread underwriting Difference between the underwriter's buying price and the offering price. The spread is a fee for the service of the underwriting syndicate.

Stakeholders Both shareholders and bondholders.

Stand-alone principle Investment principle that states a firm should accept or reject a project by comparing it with securities in the same risk class.

Standard deviation The positive square root of the variance. This is the standard statistical measure of the spread of a sample.

Standardized normal distribution A normal distribution with an expected value of 0 and a standard deviation of 1.

Standby fee Amount paid to an underwriter who agrees to purchase any stock that is not subscribed to the public investor in a rights offering.

Standby underwriting An agreement whereby an underwriter agrees to purchase any stock that is not purchased by the public investor.

Standstill agreement Contract in which the bidding firm in a takeover attempt agrees to limit its holdings of another firm.

Stated annual interest rate The interest rate expressed as a percentage per annum, by which interest payment is determined.

Static theory of capital structure Theory that the firm's capital structure is determined by a tradeoff of the value of tax shields against the costs of bankruptcy.

Stock dividend Payment of a dividend in the form of stock rather than cash. A stock dividend comes from treasury stock, increasing the number of shares outstanding, and reduces the value of each share.

Stock exchange bid Takeover bids may be either by circular bid mailed directly to the target's shareholders or by stock exchange bid (through the facilities of the TSX or other exchanges). In either case, Ontario securities law requires that the bidder mail a notice of the proposed share purchase to shareholders. If the bid is made through a stock exchange, the response is through a press release.

Stockholder Holder of equity shares in a firm. The terms *stockholders* and *shareholders* usually refer to owners of common stock.

Stockout Running out of inventory.

Stock split The increase in the number of outstanding shares of stock while making no change in shareholders' equity.

Straight-line depreciation A method of depreciation whereby each year the firm depreciates a constant proportion of the initial investment less salvage value.

Straight voting A shareholder may cast all of his or her votes for each candidate for the board of directors.

Strike price Price at which the put option or call option can be exercised. Also called the exercise price.

Stripped common shares Entitle shareholders to receive either all the dividends from one or a group of well-known companies or an installment receipt that packages any capital gain in the form of a call option.

Strong-form efficiency Theory that the market is efficient with respect to all available information, public or private.

Subordinated debt Debt whose holders have a claim on the firm's assets only after senior debtholders' claims have been satisfied.

Subscription price Price that existing shareholders are allowed to pay for a share of stock in a rights offering.

Sum-of-the-year's-digits depreciation Method of accelerated depreciation.

Sunk cost A cost that has already occurred and cannot be removed. Because sunk costs are in the past, such costs should be ignored when deciding whether to accept or reject a project.

Super-majority amendment A defensive tactic that requires 80 percent of shareholders to approve a merger.

Surplus funds Cash flow available after payment of taxes in the project.

Sustainable growth rate The only growth rate possible with preset values for four variables: profit margin, payout ratio, debt-equity ratio, and asset utilization ratio, if the firm issues no new equity.

Swap Exchange between two securities or currencies. One type of swap involves the sale (or purchase) of a foreign currency with a simultaneous agreement to repurchase (or sell) it.

Swap rate The difference between the sale (purchase) price and the price to repurchase (resell) it in a swap.

Sweep account Account in which the bank takes all excess available funds at the close of each business day and invests them for the firm.

Syndicate A group of investment banking companies that agree to cooperate in a joint venture to underwrite an offering of securities for resale to the public.

Syndicated bank loan A corporate loan made by a group (or syndicate) of banks and other institutional investors. A syndicated bank loan may be publicly traded.

Systematic Common to all businesses.

Systematic (market) risk Any risk that affects a large number of assets, each to a greater or lesser degree.

Systematic risk principle Only the systematic portion of risk matters in large, well-diversified portfolios. Thus, the expected returns must be related only to systematic risks.

Takeover General term referring to transfer of control of a firm from one group of shareholders to another.

Taking delivery Refers to the buyer's actually assuming possession from the seller of the asset agreed upon in a forward contract.

Target cash balance Optimal amount of cash for a firm to hold, considering the trade-off between the opportunity costs of holding too much cash and the trading costs of holding too little.

Targeted repurchase The firm buys back its own stock from a potential bidder, usually at a substantial premium, to forestall a takeover attempt.

Target firm A firm that is the object of a takeover by another firm.

Target payout ratio A firm's long-run dividend-to-earnings ratio. The firm's policy is to attempt to pay out a certain percentage of earnings, but it pays a stated dollar dividend and adjusts it to the target as increases in earnings occur.

Taxable acquisition An acquisition in which shareholders of the acquired firm will realize capital gains or losses that will be taxed.

Taxable income Gross income less a set of deductions.

Tax books Set of books kept by firm management for Canada Revenue Agency that follows CRA rules. The shareholders' books follow Canadian Institute of Chartered Accountants rules.

Tax-free acquisition An acquisition in which the selling shareholders are considered to have exchanged their old shares for new ones of equal value, and in which they have experienced no capital gains or losses.

T-bill Treasury bill.

Technical insolvency Default on a legal obligation of the firm. For example, when a firm doesn't pay a bill.

Tender offer Public offer to buy shares of a target firm.

Term loan Direct business loan of, typically, one to five years.

Terms of sale Conditions on which a firm proposes to sell its goods and services for cash or credit.

Term structure Relationship between spot interest rates and maturities.

Time value of money Price or value put on time. Time value of money reflects the opportunity cost of investing at a risk-free rate. The certainty of having a given sum of money today is worth more than the certainty of having an equal sum at a later date because money can be put to profitable use during the intervening time.

Tobin's *Q* Market value of assets divided by replacement value of assets. A Tobin's *Q* ratio greater than 1 indicates the firm has done well with its investment decisions.

Tombstone An advertisement that announces a public offering of securities. It identifies the issuer, the type of security, the underwriters, and where additional information is available.

Total asset-turnover ratio Total operating revenue divided by average total assets. Used to measure how effectively a firm is managing its assets.

Total cash flow of the firm Total cash inflow minus total cash outflow.

T-period holding-period return The percentage return over the T-year period an investment lasts.

Trade acceptance Written demand that has been accepted by a firm to pay a given sum of money at a future date.

Trade credit Credit granted to other firms.

Trading costs Costs of selling marketable securities and borrowing.

Trading range Price range between highest and lowest prices at which a security is traded.

Transactions motive A reason for holding cash that arises from normal disbursement and collection activities of the firm.

Treasury bill Short-term discount debt maturing in less than one year. T-bills are issued weekly by the federal government and are virtually risk-free.

Treasury stock Shares of stock that have been issued and then repurchased by a firm.

Triangular arbitrage Striking offsetting deals among three markets simultaneously to obtain an arbitrage profit.

Trust receipt A device by which the borrower holds the inventory in "trust" for the lender.

Underpricing Issuing of securities below the fair market value.

Underwriter An investment firm that buys an issue of security from the firm and resells it to the investors.

Unfunded debt Short-term debt.

Unique risk See *Diversifiable risk.*

Unit benefit formula Method used to determine a participant's benefits in a defined benefit plan by multiplying years of service by the percentage of salary.

Unseasoned new issue Initial public offering (IPO).

Unsystematic What is specific to a firm.

Unsystematic risk See *Diversifiable risk.*

VA principle See *Value additivity principle.*

Value additivity (VA) principle In an efficient market the value of the sum of two cash flows is the sum of the values of the individual cash flows.

Variable cost A cost that varies directly with volume and is zero when production is zero.

Variance In a probability distribution, the expected value of squared deviation from the expected return.

Venture capital Early-stage financing of young companies seeking to grow rapidly.

Vertical acquisition Acquisition in which the acquired firm and the acquiring firm are at different steps in the production process.

WACC See *Weighted average cost of capital.*

Waiting period Time during which the U.S. Securities and Exchange Commission or the Ontario Securities Commission studies a firm's registration statement. During this time the firm may distribute a preliminary prospectus.

Warrant Security that gives the holder the right—but not the obligation—to buy shares of common stock directly from a company at a fixed price for a given time period.

Wash Gains equal losses.

Weak-form efficiency Theory that the market is efficient with respect to historical price information.

Weighted average cost of capital (WACC) The average cost of capital on the firm's existing projects and activities. The weighted average cost of capital for the firm is calculated by weighting the cost of each source of funds by its proportion of the total market value of the firm. It is calculated on a before- and after-tax basis.

Weighted average maturity A measure of the level of interest-rate risk calculated by weighting cash flows by the time to receipt and multiplying by the fraction of total present value represented by the cash flow at that time.

White knight A takeover defence in which the management seems to be a friendly bidder.

Winner's curse The average investor wins—that is, gets the desired allocation of a new issue—because those who knew better avoided the issue.

Wire transfer An electronic transfer of funds from one bank to another that eliminates the mailing and cheque-clearing times associated with other cash-transfer methods.

Yankee bonds Foreign bonds issued in the United States by foreign banks and corporations.

Yield to maturity The discount rate that equates the present value of interest payments and redemption value with the present price of the bond.

Zero-balance account (ZBA) A chequing account in which a zero balance is maintained by transfers of funds from a master account in an amount only large enough to cover cheques presented.

Zero-coupon bonds Bonds that make no coupon payments and thus are initially priced at a deep discount.

Index

All page numbers appearing in bold type refer to locations in the text where key terms are defined.

Some Useful Formulas

1   Present Value

The discounted value of T future cash flows

$$PV = \frac{C_1}{1 + r} + \frac{C_2}{(1 + r)^2} + \ldots + \frac{C_T}{(1 + r)^T} = \sum_{t=1}^{T} \frac{C_t}{(1 + r)^t}$$

2   Net Present Value

Present value minus initial costs

$$NPV = PV - \text{Cost}$$

$$C_0 = -\text{Cost}$$

$$NPV = C_0 + \sum_{t=1}^{T} \frac{C_t}{(1 + r)^t}$$

3   Perpetuity

The value of C received each year, forever

$$PV = \frac{C}{r}$$

4   Annuity

The value of C received each year for T years

$$PV = \frac{C}{r}\left[1 - 1/(1 + r)^t\right]$$

5   Growing Perpetuity

The value of a perpetuity that grows at rate g, where the first payment is C

$$PV = \frac{C}{r - g}$$

6   Growing Annuity

The value of a T-period annuity that grows at the rate g, where the first payment is C

$$PV = C\left[\frac{1}{r - g} - \frac{1}{r - g} \times \left(\frac{1 + g}{1 + r}\right)^T\right]$$

7   Measures of Risk for Individual Assets

$$\text{Var}(R_A) = \sigma_A^2 = \text{Expected value of } (R_A - \bar{R}_A)^2$$

$$\text{SD}(R_A) = \sigma_A = \sqrt{\text{Var}(R_A)}$$

$$\text{Cov}(R_A, R_B) = \sigma_{AB} = \text{Expected value of } [(R_A - \bar{R})_A)(R_B - \bar{R}_B)]$$

$$\text{Corr}(R_A, R_B) = \sigma_{AB} = \text{Cov}(R_A R_B)/\sigma_A \sigma_B$$

8   Expected Return on a Portfolio of Two Assets

$$\bar{R}_P = X_A \bar{R}_A + X_B \bar{R}_B$$